The
NEW GROVE
Book of
OPERAS

The
NEW GROVE
Book of
OPERAS

Edited by
STANLEY SADIE

MACMILLAN

First published 1996 by Macmillan

an imprint of Macmillan Publishers Limited
25 Eccleston Place, London SW1W 9NF
and Basingstoke

Associated companies throughout the world

ISBN 0 333 65107 3

1 3 5 7 9 8 6 4 2

A CIP catalogue record for this book is available from
the British Library.

Managing Editor: Elisabeth Ingles

Picture Research: Elisabeth Agate

Typeset by Spottiswoode and Ballantyne Ltd, Colchester, Essex.
Printed and bound in Great Britain by
BPC Hazell Books Ltd, a member of the British Printing Company Ltd.

Contents

OPERAS A–Z

1–687

Preface

The New Grove Book of Operas offers synopses of 264 of the most popular and most commonly performed operas. These are based on entries in The New Grove Dictionary of Operas (1992), written by leading authorities on the individual composers.

Like The New Grove Dictionary of Opera, and unlike other books of the kind, this volume is arranged in the simplest possible way: not by period and nationality, not by composer, but according to the alphabet. Thus if the reader wants to look up La traviata, she or he does not need to know that it is by Verdi, or that it was composed just after Rigoletto and Il trovatore and just before Les vêpres siciliennes and Simon Boccanegra; it is necessary only to know that the title begins with a T (not of course L). For the reader who wants to look up the Verdi opera whose name she or he can't quite remember, there is an index by composer (p. 756). For the reader who wants to look up the opera with Violetta in it, there is an index of character names (p. 700); and for one who wants to look up the opera with a song called 'Ah fors' è lui' or a cabaletta 'Sempre libera degg'io', there is an index of aria titles (p. 723). For anyone who is unsure what a cabaletta is, there is a Glossary (p. 688).

Most of the entries have been slightly modified as compared with those in The New Grove Dictionary of Opera, essentially to simplify any more complex discussion of a kind suited rather to an academic reference work as opposed to a book for the amateur and enthusiast. Further, information has been added about the singers who appeared in the premières of the operas. The form of entries has been made a little more consistent: after the opening statement about genre, première, librettist and cast, there is a cast list; then follows an outline of the background to the work's composition and the synopsis, and finally a note on the opera's salient musical features with a historical placing where appropriate.

As in the parent dictionary, character names are given, where there is an option, in the form most familiar to English-speaking readers. This applies principally to those drawn from mythology, the Bible, history (especially English) and English literature. Thus we refer to Orpheus and Hercules rather than Orfeo or Ercole, Julius Caesar rather than Giulio Cesare, Joan of Arc rather than Jeanne d'Arc or Giovanna d'Arco, Henry VIII rather than Enrico Otto, Philip II rather than Filippo II. Commonsense and established practice demand a number of exceptions, such as Verdi's Otello rather than Othello, Donizetti's Raimondo rather than Bide-the-Bent. The cast lists always show the name form in the language in which the opera was composed as well as the English form (in brackets), and all forms are shown in the Index of Role Names.

*

I am grateful to Elisabeth Ingles for her skilful and attentive editing, which has made a number of rough places plain in the prose and has valuably brought the experience of an exceptionally well-informed opera devotee to bear on the book; and to Elisabeth Agate, the picture editor, for her choice of illustrations, both intellectually enterprising and visually appealing.

Stanley Sadie
August 1996

List of Contributors

R.A.	Robert Anderson	D.L.	Dezső Legány
B.A.	Bruce Archibald	G.Le.	Geraint Lewis
W.A.	William Ashbrook	H.M.	Hugh Macdonald
A.B.	Antony Beaumont	S.M.	Simon Maguire
D.B.	David Bloch	B.M.	Barry Millington
P.B.	Peter Branscombe	R.M.	Rodney Milnes
C.B.	Clive Brown	D.M.	David Murray
J.B.	Julian Budden	O.W.N.	O. W. Neighbour
R.Ch.	Renato Chiesa	R.N.	Roger Nichols
C.C.	Caryl Clark	R.O.	Richard Osborne
A.C.	Andrew Clements	T.P.	Tim Page
M.N.C.	Martha Novak Clinkscale	A.D.P.	A. Dean Palmer
P.C.	Peter Cohen	R.P.	Roger Parker
R.Cd.	Richard Crawford	J.S.P.	John S. Powell
R.H.C.	Ronald Crichton	C.Pr.	Curtis Price
L.E.F.	Laurel E. Fay	C.Pu.	Charlotte Purkis
E.F.	Elizabeth Forbes	J.Ro.	John Rockwell
P.F.	Peter Franklin	E.R.	Ellen Rosand
M.G.	Michele Girardi	L.R.	Lois Rosow
A.G.	Amanda Glauert	J.Ru.	Julian Rushton
P.G.	Paul Griffiths	S.S.	Stanley Sadie
J.H.	Jeremy Hayes	G.Sa.	Graham Sadler
A.H.	Anthony Hicks	L.S.	Lionel Salter
S.Hn.	Stephen Hinton	J.Ss.	Jeremy Sams
D.K.H.	D. Kern Holoman	J.Sn.	Jim Samson
H.H.	Helmut Hucke	H.S.	Herbert Schneider
S.Hr.	Steven Huebner	A.Se.	Anthony Sellors
R.D.H.	Robert D. Hume	G.Sk.	Geoffrey Skelton
M.H.	Mary Hunter	J.Sy.	Jan Smaczny
D.J.	Douglas Johnson	A.St.	Andrew Stiller
M.Ky.	Michael Kennedy	R.T.	Richard Taruskin
A.K.	Allan Kozinn	J.T.	John Tyrrell
M.Ks.	Malena Kuss	J.W.	John Whenham
A.L.	Andrew Lamb	A.W.	Arnold Whittall
R.L.S.	Richard Langham Smith	S.C.W.	Stephen C. Willis
G.La.	Gordana Lazarevich	L.Z.	Luca Zoppelli

Illustration Acknowledgements

The publishers would like to thank the following individuals and institutions who have kindly provided the illustrations for this book.

Colour plate numbers are indicated in **bold**, black and white illustrations by page number.

AKG, London: 36, 162
Catherine Ashmore, London: **16, 66**
Les Arts Florissants, Paris/photo Michel Szabo: **50**; 49
Clive Barda (Performing Arts Library, London): **7, 12, 17, 24, 33, 42, 61, 82, 88, 91, 110, 111**; 558
Bayreuth, Nationalarchiv der Richard-Wagner-Stiftung/Richard-Wagner-Gedenkstätte: 232, 272, 486, 532, 584, 613, 658
Bayreuth, Universität, Forschungsinstitut für Musiktheater: 36
Bayreuther Festspiele/photo Jörg Schulze: 87
BBC Picture Library, London: 475
Berlin, Komische Oper/photo Arwid Lagenpusch: 34
Bettmann Archive, New York: 240
Bologna, Pinacoteca di Brera: 372
Boosey & Hawkes Music Publishers Ltd, London: 454
Emily Booth (Performing Arts Library, London): **73**
Bregenzer Festspiele: **116**
British Film Institute, London: 170
Brno, Moravské Museum: 65; 141
Budapest, Magyar Tudományos Akadémia (Bartók Archívum): 86
Budapest, Széchényi Nationalbibliothek (Theatersammlung): 43
Bulloz, Paris: 469
Byrd-Hoffman Foundation, New York: 176
Cologne, Universität, Theaterwissenschaftliche Sammlung: 41; 109, 127, 134 (© DACS, 1996), 154, 325, 594, 686
Donald Cooper, Milton Keynes: **29, 45, 84, 90, 96, 101**
Giancarlo Costa, Milan: **2, 6, 19, 30, 51, 59, 72, 74, 80, 95, 104**; 204, 397, 619, 641
Fritz Curzon (Performing Arts Library, London): **11**
Zoë Dominic, London: **85**
Dresden, Sächsische Landesbibliothek (Deutsches Fototek): 554
Drottningholms Slottsteater: **49**
Early Opera Project: **77**
English Bach Festival/photo Chris Davies: 115
Mary Evans Picture Library, London: 5, 260, 570

Elizabeth Forbes Collection, London: 57, 210, 436, 513, 539, 579
Anthony Gasson Collection, London: **39**
Nicholas Georgiadis/photo Richard Holltum: 129
M. I. Glinka, by A. Rozanov (Moscow: Muzïka, 1983) 353, 561
Guy Gravett: **52, 53, 58, 67, 83, 86, 112**
Hanover, Niedersächsische Staatstheater/photo Kurt Julius: 102
Houston Grand Opera/photo Jim Caldwell: **81**; 443
Hulton Getty Picture Collection Ltd, London: **99**; 14, 498, 529, 645
Illustrated London News: 640
Siegfried Lauterwasser, Überlingen: 57, **92, 98, 102, 103, 107**; 487, 630
London, © The British Library: 138, 180
London, © The British Museum: 77
London, The Royal Opera House, Covent Garden: 166
London, Trustees of the Victoria and Albert Museum: **32** (by permission of Lord Snowdon); 416, 424, 452, 521, 550, 577
Richard Macnutt, Withyham, Sussex: 214, 318
Mander and Mitchenson Theatre Collection, Beckenham: 356
Milan, Civica Raccolta delle Stampe Achille Bertarelli: 9
Milan, Museo Teatrale alla Scala: 31, 445, 597
Motley Books Ltd: 29, 120
Munich, Bayerisches Verwaltung der Staatlichen Schlösser, Gärten und Seen: **97**; 421, 626
Munich, Deutsches Theatermuseum/photo Klaus Broszat: **68**; 244, 481, 536, 612
M. P. Musorgsky by R. Shirinian (Moscow: Muzïka, 1987): 333
New York, Metropolitan Opera: **8, 115** (photos Winnie Klotz); 208, 254, 603, 606
Novosti, London: 346
Opera Rara, London: 107, 502
Paris, Archives Nationales: 412
Paris, Bibliothèque et Musée de l'Opéra/photo Bibliothèque Nationale: **46, 47, 75**; 18, 79, 111, 125, 132, 157, 168, 185, 248, 276, 293, 327, 394, 428, 449, 488, 496, 517, 637, 659, 616
Paris, Musée Carnavalet/Photothèque des Musées de la Ville de Paris/© DACS, 1996: **9**

Paris, Musée du Louvre/photo Réunion des Musées Nationaux: 16, 311, 504

Paris, Opéra National de Paris: 55 (photo Florian Kleinefenn), 63 (photo Jacques Moatti)

Myfanwy Piper/The Herbert Press, London: 25

Prague, Národní Muzeum (Muzeum České Hudby): 68

Sergey Prokofiev by M. Nest'yeva (Moscow: Muzïka, 1981): 365

Puccini nelle immagini by Leopold Marchetti (Garzanti, 1949): 89

Max-Reinhardt-Forschungs und Gedenkstätte, Salzburg/photo Madner: 71

N. A. Rimsky-Korsakov by A. Kruchinina and I. Obraztsova (Moscow: Muzïka, 1988): 350, 410, 564

Michael Rose Collection, London: 79; 472

Fondazione G. Rossini, Pesaro/photo Michele Alberto Seroni: 64

St Petersburg, All-Union Pushkin Museum: 44 (and jacket)

San Antonio,TX, McNay Art Museum (Tobin Collection): 26, 91

Lawrence A. Schoenberg, Pacific Palisades, CA/ © DACS, 1996: 193

B. Schott's Söhne, Mainz/photo Ilse Buhs: 342

Richard Smith (Dominic Photography, London): 26

Stockholm, Kungliga Biblioteket: 314

Stockholm, Kungliga Teatern: 76; 274 (photo Enar Rydberg)

Stuart-Liff Collection, Port Erin, Isle of Man: 98, 368, 386, 461, 473

P. I. Tchaikovsky by K. Yu. Davïdova, I. G. Sokolinskaya and P. E. Vaidman (Moscow: Muzïka, 1978): 678

Venice, Biblioteca e Museo Correr: 624

Venice, Fondazione Giorgio Cini (Fototeca del Istituto per le Lettere, il Teatro e il Melodramma): 263

Arena di Verona/photo Gianfranco Fainello: 3, 18, 71

Vienna, Museum der Stadt: 685

Vienna, Österreichisches Nationalbibliothek: 218 (© Dietrich Alfred Roller), 284, 400, 567, 670

Warsaw, Museum of the Wielki Theatre/photo Tadeusz Kazimierski: 280, 340

Weimar, Schloss Tiefurt/Stiftung Weimarar Klassik: 113

Reg Wilson, London: 1, 4, 5, 10, 13, 14, 15, 20, 21, 22, 23, 27, 28, 31, 35, 37, 38, 40, 43, 48, 54, 56, 60, 62, 64, 69, 70, 78, 89, 93, 94, 100, 105, 106, 108, 109

A

Acis and Galatea

Masque or serenata in one (later two) acts by George Frideric Handel to words by John Gay and others; Cannons, summer 1718 (revised version in three acts, incorporating Italian words by Nicola Giuvo, London, King's Theatre, 10 June 1732).

Acis *a shepherd*	tenor
Galatea *a sea-nymph*	soprano
Damon *a shepherd*	tenor
Polyphemus *a giant*	bass
Coridon *a shepherd*	tenor
Nymphs, shepherds	

During the period 1717–20 Handel spent much of his time at Cannons, the seat of James Brydges, Earl of Carnarvon (later Duke of Chandos), at Edgware, at that time a short distance north-west of London. As resident composer, he supplied his patron with church music, principally anthems, and two dramatic works, *Esther* (the first English oratorio) and *Acis and Galatea*, which has variously been described as a serenata, a masque, a pastoral or pastoral opera, a 'little opera' (in a letter while it was being written), an entertainment and even (incorrectly) an oratorio. Whether or not it was originally fully staged, given in some kind of stylized semi-dramatic form or simply performed as a concert work is uncertain; local tradition holds that it was given in the open air on the terraces overlooking the garden (the recent discovery of piping to supply an old fountain, suitable for the closing scene, might fancifully be invoked as support). It was performed on an unknown date, probably during the summer, in 1718.

Acis and Galatea, Handel's first dramatic work in English, had its models in the English pastoral operas by Pepusch (his colleague at Cannons), Galliard and others that had been given in 1715–18 at the Drury Lane theatre in rivalry to the Italian opera. The theme, drawn from Ovid's *Metamorphoses* (xiii. 750), had been the subject of a setting in 1701 by John Eccles, to a text by P. A. Motteux, but Pepusch's *Apollo and Daphne*, to a libretto by John Hughes, seems to have been a more specific inspiration for Handel's work. Gay's libretto – it is not certain how much he actually wrote himself – has features indicating that it was originally designed

for only three characters, and subsequently expanded, perhaps by Hughes and Pope (it includes lines by both, and also by Dryden), but there is no clear evidence that Handel considered setting it in that form. The Cannons version was almost certainly intended for just five singers – a soprano, three tenors and a bass – serving as 'chorus' as well as principals (Coridon, omitted from all modern editions, sings one air, added at a late stage to words by Hughes); the instrumental music could be supplied by seven players (strings, and oboes doubling recorders), though probably the violins were doubled, and some early copies indicate slightly fuller scoring including a bassoon.

Most of the music was published in 1722, and at least one early amateur performance is known of (in Wells, Somerset, in February 1719); but the work was not heard publicly until 1731, when it was given a single performance, without Handel's involvement, in London. The next year it was revived by an English opera company under Thomas Arne (father of the composer), performing at the Little Theatre in the Haymarket, immediately opposite the King's, where Handel gave Italian operas. It was claimed as 'with all the Grand Chorus's, Scenes, Machines, and other Decorations; being the first Time it ever was performed in a Theatrical Way'. Handel retaliated by converting it into a three-act serenata, performed by his Italian company, with substantial revisions and additions and 'a great Number of the best Voices and Instruments'. His revisions involved the incorporation of material from a cantata he had written in Italy on the same topic, *Aci, Galatea e Polifemo* (1708), and other music mainly from his Italian cantatas and operas; the result was an over-extended work, oddly shaped, mixed in style and language. He used this version, or revisions of it, up to 1741, but also gave English performances from 1739; it was at this point that the English version reached its two-act form, with a chorus added to conclude the first act. Handel never gave *Acis and Galatea* in the form in which it is generally heard today. It became very popular, however, in his own time and was easily the most widely performed of his dramatic works. In 1788 it was arranged by Mozart. It has remained popular and has been many times revived, on the stage and otherwise, during the 19th and 20th centuries.

The work, even if not staged by Handel, may be imagined in the kind of setting described in his advertisement for his 1732 performances: 'There will be no Action on the Stage, but the Scene will represent, in a Picturesque Manner, a rural Prospect, with Rocks, Groves, Fountains and Grotto's; amongst which will be disposed a Chorus of Nymphs and Shepherds, Habits, and every other Decoration suited to the Subject'.

*

Act 1 Nymphs and shepherds take delight in 'the pleasure of the plains'. Galatea, a part-divine sea-nymph, is in love with Acis, and attempts to silence the birds that inflame her desire ('Hush, ye pretty warbling quire!'). She and Acis seek each other, with occasional counsel from another shepherd, Damon; when at last they meet Acis sings a delectable siciliana-style serenade, 'Love in her eyes sits playing'. Their duet ('Happy we') is echoed by a chorus (not in the Cannons original).

Act 2 The amorous, pastoral mood now darkens at the threat to their love. The chorus, knowing of the approach of the 'monster Polypheme', warns the 'Wretched lovers', in sombre, fugal minor-key music, that 'no joy shall last'; the heavy steps of the hideous giant are heard in their music. The jealous Polyphemus enters in a part-comic *furioso* accompanied recitative, 'I rage, I melt, I burn', which is followed by his air 'O ruddier than the cherry', in which he is counterpointed by a small recorder ('a hundred reeds of decent growth', according to his recitative). He threatens force; another shepherd, Coridon, impartially counsels gentler wooing ('Would you gain the tender creature'). In militant tones, Acis determines to resist ('Love sounds th' alarm'), taking no heed of Damon's warning of the transience of amorous delight ('Consider, fond shepherd'). The lovers swear eternal devotion in what begins as a duet ('The flocks shall leave the mountains') but becomes a trio as the enraged Polyphemus intrudes and finally crushes Acis with a 'massy ruin'. The chorus mourn, joined by Galatea ('Must I my Acis still bemoan'); but they remind her of her divinity – she can transform him into a fountain. In a sublime climax, a *larghetto* air with the string tone softened by a pair of recorders, she exerts her powers ('Heart, the seat of soft delight'). The chorus celebrate his watery immortality.

*

Acis and Galatea represents the high point of the pastoral opera in England, indeed anywhere. Intended, typically of the genre, as a courtly entertainment about the simple, rural life, with many witty hints of self-parody in its words, it rises above itself through the elegance and the sensual force of Handel's music in the first act and the elegiac power of that in the second: and that in spite of the humour

maintained by the composer in his treatment of the secondary characters, Polyphemus and Damon, and their utterances, which in no way lessens the depth of the pathos with which the death of Acis and the grief of Galatea are depicted. The work is unique in Handel's output (though he tried to recapture elements of it in such works as *L'Allegro, il Penseroso ed il Moderato*, 1739, and *Semele*, 1744). The influence of Purcell has been claimed, and musical ideas indebted to Reinhard Keiser and others have been noted, but in approach it owes more to the Drury Lane pastoral operas than to any other source and in inspiration, conception and execution it remains wholly individual.   S.S.

Adriana Lecouvreur

Opera in four acts by Francesco Cilea to a libretto by Arturo Colautti after Eugène Scribe and Ernest Legouvé's play *Adrienne Lecouvreur*; Milan, Teatro Lirico, 6 November 1902.

The first cast included Enrico Caruso (Maurizio), Angelica Pandolfini (Adriana) and Giuseppe De Luca (Michonnet). The conductor was Cleofonte Campanini.

Adriana Lecouvreur *of the Comédie*		
Française		soprano
Maurizio *Count of Saxony*		tenor
Prince de Bouillon		bass
Princesse de Bouillon		mezzo-soprano
Michonnet *stage director of the Comédie*		
Française		baritone
Quinault		bass
Poisson	*members of the*	tenor
Mlle Jouvenot	*Comédie*	soprano
Mlle Dangeville		mezzo-soprano
Abbé de Chazeuil		tenor
Ladies, gentlemen, mute extras, stage hands, valets and dancers		
Setting Paris, March 1730		

Adriana Lecouvreur was commissioned by the publisher Edoardo Sonzogno following the success of Cilea's *L'arlesiana*. Cilea chose the subject for its mixture of comedy and tragedy, its 18th-century ambience, the loving intensity of its protagonist and the moving final act; three other operas use the story of Adrienne Lecouvreur (by Edoardo Vera, Tommaso Benvenuti and Ettore Perosio). Colautti reduced the intricate mechanism of Scribe's plot to a serviceable operatic framework, occasionally at the expense of clarity. The première, however, was outstandingly successful.

The first London performance took place at

Covent Garden in 1904 in the presence of the composer, with Rina Giachetti (Adriana), Giuseppe Anselmi (Maurizio) and Mario Sammarco (Michonnet), again under Campanini. Three years later the opera arrived at the Metropolitan Opera, New York, with Caruso (Maurizio), Lina Cavalieri (Adriana) and Antonio Scotti (Michonnet). Since then *Adriana Lecouvreur* has proved the only one of Cilea's three surviving operas to stay in the international repertory, mainly due to the opportunities it affords to an experienced prima donna who has already passed her prime. Famous among postwar exponents of the title role are Maria Caniglia, Renata Tebaldi, Magda Olivero, Renata Scotto and Joan Sutherland.

*

Act I *The foyer of the Comédie Française* The curtain is about to rise. Actors and actresses are snapping at one another and at Michonnet, who protests that he has only one pair of hands. The evening's tragedy is Corneille's *Bajazet*, featuring both Adriana and her rival Mlle Duclos (whom we never see). The Prince of Bouillon, La Duclos' lover, arrives with the Abbé of Chazeuil and pays affected compliments to the players. Adriana enters reading her lines; she tells her admiring hearers that she is merely the poet's handmaid ('Io son l'umile ancella'), to a melody which will serve as her theme throughout the opera. Alone with Adriana, Michonnet, who has recently come into an inheritance, is about to propose marriage to the actress, with whom he has been in love for years, when she gives him to understand that she herself loves an officer in the service of the Count of Saxony who will be in the theatre that night. But the man who now enters is Maurizio, the Count himself, who is wooing Adriana under a false identity. In a brief solo, 'La dolcissima effigie sorridente', he pours out his feelings for her. A love duet develops, after which Adriana leaves to go on stage, having given Maurizio a nosegay of violets and agreed to meet him after the performance. Meanwhile the Abbé has managed to intercept a letter addressed to Maurizio from, as he thinks, La Duclos arranging a tryst for that evening at the love-nest by the Seine in which the Prince has installed her. The Prince decides to surprise the guilty pair by organizing a party in the same house at the appointed hour. Receiving the letter, Maurizio is well aware that the writer is not La Duclos but the Princess of Bouillon, whose lover he has been in the past; and he decides for political reasons to keep the assignation. He therefore has a note conveyed to Adriana breaking their appointment. Adriana is duly upset; but on being invited to join the Prince's party, at which, she is told, the Count of Saxony himself will be one of the guests, she consents to come in order to have the opportunity of furthering her lover's career.

Act 2 *Mlle Duclos' villa by the Seine* The Princess is waiting anxiously for Maurizio ('Acerba voluttà, dolce tortura'). When he arrives she notices the nosegay and at once suspects another woman. With great presence of mind he offers it to her. She tells him that she has spoken on his behalf to the Queen of France, but finds his gratitude inadequate. Reluctantly he admits to another liaison. At the sound of a second carriage arriving he darts into the adjoining room. The Prince and the Abbé enter laughing and congratulate Maurizio on his latest conquest, whom they take to be La Duclos. Maurizio, grasping the situation, decides to keep up the deception. Adriana arrives, to be made aware for the first time of her lover's true identity. Their duet of happiness is interrupted by Michonnet, who has come with a message for La Duclos. He is told by the Abbé that she is somewhere in the villa, whereupon Adriana assumes that Maurizio has come for a secret rendezvous with her; but this he solemnly denies. There is indeed a woman in the next room, he says, with whom his relations are purely political. Adriana must see to it that no one enters that room and, once the guests have gone in to supper, must extinguish the lights and help the unknown visitor to escape in the dark. Adriana follows his instructions. However, the few words exchanged between the women in darkness make it apparent that both are in love with Maurizio. As lights are seen approaching Adriana determines to expose her rival. But the Princess has escaped, dropping a bracelet, which Michonnet picks up and hands to Adriana.

Act 3 *The Palais Bouillon* Preparations for a party are in train, under the supervision of the Abbé, who flirts discreetly with the Princess until her husband joins them. An amateur chemist, he has discovered a poisonous powder which, when inhaled, will induce delirium followed by death. (All this he describes to the Abbé and the Princess in a passage cut from certain editions of the opera.) Adriana arrives without her jewellery, which she has pawned in order to effect the release of Maurizio, imprisoned by order of the jealous Princess. Seeming to recognize her voice as that of her rival, the Princess lays a trap for Adriana. She tells her that Maurizio has been fatally wounded in a duel. The actress duly comes over faint; but she revives spectacularly when Maurizio himself enters and entertains the guests with tales of his military exploits ('Il russo Mencikoff'). A company of dancers perform *The Judgment of Paris*. In the general conversation that follows the Princess and Adriana fence with each other verbally. The Princess mentions a nosegay of violets. Adriana produces the compromising bracelet, which the Prince identifies as his wife's. To distract attention the Princess proposes that the great actress should recite from one of her famous roles. At the Prince's suggestion she chooses a passage from Racine's *Phèdre*, where the heroine denounces lustful women; and as she declaims the lines she looks straight at her rival. All applaud her performance except the Princess who, white with fury, determines on revenge.

Act 4 *Adriana's house* It is her birthday, but, convinced that Maurizio no longer loves her, Adriana has retired into solitude. Michonnet visits her in a vain attempt to bring her comfort. They are joined by four of her fellow artists, each with a present for her. Michonnet too offers a gift – Adriana's jewellery which he has redeemed with the inheritance from his uncle. Deeply touched, Adriana declares that she will return to the stage. Her colleagues entertain her with a gossipy madrigal. The maid comes in with a package labelled 'from Maurizio'. While the actors retire Adriana opens it and finds inside the nosegay of violets she had given him, now withered – a sign, she thinks, that their love is at an end. She pours out her grief in the aria 'Poveri fiori'; then she presses the flowers to her lips and throws them into the fire. But Michonnet has already summoned Maurizio, who now arrives, protests his undying devotion and offers her his hand in marriage. Adriana joyfully accepts, then suddenly turns pale. Her mind starts to wander. Clearly the nosegay was sprinkled with the poisonous powder, sent not by Maurizio but by the Princess. Adriana tries desperately to cling to life, but she is beyond help and dies in Maurizio's arms.

*

The texture of *Adriana Lecouvreur* is more richly woven and the style somewhat less emphatic than in most *verismo* operas of the time. The ensemble scenes, especially in Act 1, owe something to Verdi's *Falstaff*, though the orchestral figuration is often curiously pianistic. Use is made of recurring motifs, several of which anticipate the solos from which they derive. Some (e.g. that of the violets) are insufficiently theatrical for their associations to register. There are touches of period stylization in the dances of Act 3, but in the main Cilea is content to evoke a generalized elegance, varied by characteristic moments of lyrical effusion. Particularly effective is his recourse to unsung speech to point up Adriana's recitation at the end of the third act.   **J.B.**

Africaine, L' ('The African Maid')

Grand opera in five acts by Giacomo Meyerbeer to a libretto by Eugène Scribe; Paris, Opéra, 28 April 1865.

The cast at the première included Marie Sasse (Sélika), Marie Battu (Inès), Emilio Naudin (Vasco da Gama) and Jean-Baptiste Faure (Nélusko).

Sélika *a slave*	soprano
Vasco da Gama *a naval officer*	tenor
Inès *daughter of Don Diégo*	soprano
Nélusko *a slave*	baritone
Don Pédro *president of the Royal Council*	bass
Don Diégo *an admiral*	bass
Anna *Inès's confidante*	mezzo-soprano
Don Alvar *council member*	tenor
Grand Inquisitor of Lisbon	bass
High Priest of Brahma	bass/baritone

Councillors, naval officers, bishops, Brahmins, Indians, soldiers, sailors

Setting Lisbon and an island in the Indian Ocean, *c*1500

The genesis of *L'Africaine* is more complex than that of any other Meyerbeer opera. A first contract between Meyerbeer and Scribe for the production of the libretto was signed in May 1837; the point of departure for the plot seems to have been 'Le mancenillier', a poem by Millevoye about a young girl who sits under a tree that emits poisonous fragrances and is rescued by her lover. Doubts about the viability of the libretto, and the illness of Cornélie Falcon, for whom the title role was intended, caused Meyerbeer to abandon the project in favour of *Le prophète* in summer 1838. He returned to *L'Africaine* at the end of 1841, but it was set aside when he completed a draft in 1843, only to be taken up again eight years later when he decided to revise the work substantially. The original libretto was set in Spain during the reign of Philip III and features in the tenor role an obscure naval officer named Fernand, who purchases Sélika in a slave market; he sails for Mexico in Act 3, but a storm drives his ships to the coast of Africa and Sélika's realm on the Niger river. In the revision Portugal and India became the backdrop and the explorer Vasco da Gama was made the protagonist of the work; the working title was changed from *L'Africaine* to *Vasco da Gama*.

Meyerbeer dropped the project once more in 1853, briefly did some work on it in 1857, and settled down to *Vasco da Gama* in 1860. Since Scribe died in 1861, a number of other librettists had a hand in the final stages of preparation, including Charlotte Birch-Pfeiffer and Camille Du Locle. The work was fully orchestrated by November 1863 and the way cleared for a production at the Opéra when Meyerbeer died in May 1864. His widow placed the eminent Belgian musicologist and critic F.-J. Fétis in charge of the rehearsals. As Meyerbeer himself would have been compelled to do, Fétis made a large number of cuts to the long score. He also made changes to the libretto. The most striking of these concerns the title and the setting of the last two acts. Thinking *Vasco da Gama* too long and Sélika the most important character, Fétis reinstated *L'Africaine* as the title. The last two

'L'Africaine' (Meyerbeer), the storm scene in Act 3 as designed by Charles-Anton Cambon and Joseph Thierry for the original production at the Paris Opéra (Salle Le Peletier), 28 April 1865; engraving from 'L'illustration' (6 May 1865)

acts must therefore take place in Africa; though not explicit, the suggestion in the libretto, particularly in the Act 2 duet, is that Sélika's homeland is Madagascar. Nonetheless, confusion about the setting must inevitably arise in modern productions, since references to the Indian gods Brahma, Vishnu and Shiva were not expunged from the text.

*

Act I *The council room in the Admiralty of Lisbon* Inès has been called to attend a meeting of the council and tells her confidante, Anna, that she suspects news may be revealed about Vasco, who has been away at sea for two years. Inès is to marry Vasco upon his return; in a *romance* ('Adieu mon beau rivage') she recalls his final farewell beneath her balcony; thus, in a telescopic manner endemic to eventful grand opera librettos, Vasco's position as Inès's lover is established not in a long duet but rather through her recollection of his words in a more compact solo number. The piece exhibits the progression from minor to major characteristic of the genre, but an unusual effect evocative of Vasco's desolation before his departure is created in the minor section by alternating the voice with melodic fragments in the wind instruments. Don Diégo and Don Pédro appear to a pompous melody. The former insists that his daughter marry Don Pédro. The music projects complete nonchalance as they report to her that Vasco is among those who have perished on the ill-fated journey of the Portuguese fleet. In a brief trio

the two men express irritation at Inès's lyrical effusion about her lover's death. Inès is led off just before the Grand Inquisitor, bishops and members of the council enter with a march-like strain and an imposing unison prayer. Don Diégo asks whether a rescue party should be launched and the end of the first part of the finale is articulated by a reprise of the prayer.

Much to everyone's surprise, Vasco da Gama suddenly appears in the room, all impetuosity and hubris. He asks for support to explore uncharted regions beyond Africa. As evidence of his previous explorations he produces two slaves, Sélika and Nélusko, to a mildly exotic figure in the piccolo. Sélika, a queen in her native land, remains taciturn in the face of questions. Vasco attempts to coax her into responding and gives evidence of some attachment to her, since his words are accompanied by a melody in the cellos strongly reminiscent of a similarly scored passage before the *romance*, Inès's earlier recollection of his love for her. Nélusko seethes with anger and through manifold reiteration of the same musical figure staunchly refuses to reveal anything about himself. Vasco leaves and members of council deliberate, with the Inquisitor intoning the previously heard prayer and arguing that to speak of a land unmentioned in the Bible is heresy. The council does not support the request for a new fleet. When Vasco learns of the decision, he baldly accuses the tribunal of envy and jealousy. A prompt condemnation to life imprisonment by the Inquisitor brings the fulminations of a concluding *strette*, with Vasco's supporters outnumbered by his detractors.

Act 2 *An Inquisition prison in Lisbon* Sélika watches Vasco while he sleeps, racked by nightmares; much to her chagrin he expresses love for Inès. With the 'Air du sommeil', 'Sur mes genoux, fils du soleil', from her native land, Sélika attempts to calm him; the use of the triangle and short ornamental runs in muted strings and winds lend an exotic flavour to the piece, though the dialogue between voice and flute in one episode was a common operatic device. In another episode (with a verbal commonplace of the kind that is liberally distributed in Scribe's work) she beseeches the High Priest of Brahma to extinguish 'the flames of her heart'. Nélusko appears and moves to stab the sleeping man. Sélika restrains him and asks why his intentions are murderous. He responds in an *air* ('Fille des rois'), first by paying homage to Sélika's royal blood in stately double-dotted rhythms, and then, in the *cabalette*, by alluding with bravado to his love for her.

Vasco awakens, sends Nélusko away and ignores Sélika while he rages about his fate. On a map she shows him a way to reach her island in the Indian Ocean. Convinced that this is the route to his own glory, the explorer warms towards her and the two combine in cantabile parallel singing. Suddenly Inès, Anna, Don Pédro and Don Alvar burst in. In a vocal line punctuated by rests to suggest her sobbing, Inès informs Vasco that she has bought his freedom. He seeks to convince her that he feels no affection for Sélika by offering the African queen to Inès as a slave, and Inès leads an ensemble with a lyrical line expressing her realization that Vasco loves her after all. To a figure in the orchestra that brims with over-confidence, Don Pédro informs Vasco that he himself has been equipped with a fleet; the injury is magnified when Vasco learns that Inès has actually married Don Pédro. Following a conventional unison 'frozen moment' in which all give voice to conflicting emotions, musical interest is bestowed upon Inès (and not upon Vasco, as one might expect): to one of the most famous melodies of the opera ('Eh bien, sois libre par l'amour') she leads a concluding ensemble by advising him to place his own glory above his love for her.

Act 3 *Aboard Don Pédro's ship* It is dawn and, in a scene-setting chorus accompanied by gentle rocking motion in the low strings, Inès's attendants sing of the quick progress of the ship across the waves. The sailors are roused from sleep and anticipate the day's work ahead; Inès joins them in a prayer for safe passage. Nélusko has been made pilot of the boat by Don Pédro, who ignores Don Alvar's warnings that the slave is steering them towards danger. The suspicions are well founded, however: in a fiery

strophic *ballade*, 'Adamastor, roi des vagues profondes', Nélusko tells the sailors of the deadly sea monster, Adamastor. His macabre laughter and mock jovial music suggest that he expects the wrath of the monster will soon avenge him. Another Portuguese vessel is sighted and a small boat from it pulls beside Don Pédro's ship. Vasco disembarks and boldly informs Don Pédro that, out of concern for the safety of Inès, he has come to warn him that the course his ship has taken will lead to disaster. Don Pédro bristles at the impudence of Vasco and both hurl threats at each other; the *cabalette* of their duet is a static moment as, with swords drawn, both stand ready to duel. Suddenly a storm wells up. In the major scenic coup of the opera, the ship is driven against a reef; compatriots of Sélika and Nélusko stream on board the vessel and capture the Europeans.

Act 4 *Outside a Brahmin temple* Priestesses, priests, Amazons, jugglers and warriors enter in succession during a balletic *divertissement*. To a hymn-like strain the entire assembly expresses allegiance to its queen, Sélika. Nélusko gleefully informs her that all the Portuguese men who landed save one have been executed and that the women are being led to the manchineel tree, the poisonous fragrances of which will kill them. Vasco is the sole Portuguese male survivor; he appears, accompanied by a rapturous clarinet melody beneath flute tremolo, a musical translation of his bedazzlement by the lush surroundings. He takes up the clarinet tune in the slow section of a *grand air* ('O paradis sorti de l'onde'); his ecstatic music about the discovery of a new land is interrupted by shouts for his blood, and in the *cabalette* he begs the warriors for mercy. Just as he is to be beheaded, Sélika appears and orders her subjects to stop. She claims that Vasco must be spared since she is married to him and forces Nélusko reluctantly to confirm this. In a solemn ceremony Sélika and Vasco are united according to local custom and drink a philtre from the same cup. As the populace processes into the temple, Sélika tells Vasco that he may escape. Suddenly overcome with affection for the queen, Vasco refuses her offer. They both give voice to mutual love in a duet and, with a magical modulation from F♭ major to E♯ major, Vasco openly accepts Sélika as his wife. The procession returns from the temple and celebrates the union while the voices of the expiring Portuguese women are heard in the distance.

Act 5.i *The queen's gardens* Inès has escaped from the deadly perfume of the manchineel tree and has sought refuge in Sélika's gardens. Vasco sees her and declares that he must resist his rekindled love since he is married to another. Sélika's fury is aroused when she sees the two together. The ensuing duet for Sélika and Inès is too extended in its position at the denouement of the opera, especially since there are no developments in the drama across its various parts: both slow section and *cabalette* develop musically the distress of the women, Inès because she believes she can never have Vasco, and Sélika because Vasco's true love does not appear directed towards her. Sélika, who sees that her destiny is not with Vasco, instructs Nélusko to lead him and Inès to safety. She resolves to go to the manchineel tree.

5.ii *A promontory overlooking the sea, with the manchineel tree* Sélika arrives at her final place of rest ('D'ici je vois la mer'). She forgives Vasco and bids him farewell. She gathers the blossoms and presses them to her face. As a lyrical cello strain is heard she begins to hallucinate. To the accompaniment of harps and with light staccato singing, she envisages Vasco returning to her in a swan-drawn chariot. Nélusko, displaying musically a depth of emotion not associated with him before in the opera, joins her in death.

*

In *L'Africaine*, Meyerbeer and Scribe placed love relationships into greater relief than in their previous grand opera collaborations. Vasco is the common denominator in no fewer than three triangles: he challenges Don Pédro for Inès, causes Sélika anguish in continuing to love her rival and, in turn, arouses Nélusko's jealousy. Combined with the political backdrop and obligatory enactments of ritual, love is stretched rather thinly across the five-act frame of *L'Africaine*; as usual with Meyerbeer, intensity of emotion takes second place to manoeuvring of the characters into sensationalistic dramatic situations, especially in *finales*. The Vasco–Don Pédro–Inès and Vasco–Sélika–Inès triangles are played off against each other in the Act 2 *finale*, leaving Vasco (temporarily) with little more than his massive ego, and the Vasco–Nélusko–Sélika triangle generates suspense in the Act 4 *finale* as Nélusko ponders whether to reveal Sélika's ruse. Vasco's wavering between the women is not very admirable; however, the combination of the martial and the heroic supplies a truly memorable moment in his 'Je viens à vous' in Act 3. Nélusko is arguably the most interesting character in the opera, an echo of Marcel in *Les Huguenots* in combining musical grotesqueries with a more heartfelt core. Sélika, for her part, is an operatic forerunner to self-annihilating non-Europeans such as Delibes' Lakmé and Puccini's Madama Butterfly. The connection of female sexuality to the exotic, however, is less explicit in *L'Africaine* than in many later works, in part because of restrained use of musical *couleur locale* in Sélika's role (and in the opera as a whole) and also because Vasco's attraction to her occurs, in the first instance, as a result of his exploratory zeal and, later on, because of a philtre administered by the high priest.   S.Hr.

Agrippina

Drama per musica in three acts by George Frideric Handel to a libretto by Vincenzo Grimani; Venice, Teatro S Giovanni Gristostomo, 26 December 1709.

The original cast included Margherita Durastanti in the title role, Diamante Maria Scarabelli as Poppaea, Antonio Francesco Carli as Claudius, Francesca Vanini as Otho and her husband Giuseppe Maria Boschi as Pallas. Nero and Narcissus were sung by the castratos Valeriano Pellegrini and Giuliano Albertini.

Emperor Claudio [Claudius]	bass
Agrippina *his wife*	soprano
Nerone [Nero]	soprano
Pallante [Pallas]	bass
Narciso [Narcissus]	alto
Lesbo *Claudius's servant*	bass
Ottone [Otho]	alto
Poppea [Poppaea]	soprano
Giunone [Juno]	alto
Setting Rome in about AD 50	

The second and last opera Handel wrote during his stay in Italy (1706–10), *Agrippina* was a triumphant success. It effectively established his international reputation and provided him with influential contacts. According to John Mainwaring's *Memoirs of the Life of . . . Handel* (1760) it was performed 27 times (not an unusual run for the main opera of the Venetian carnival) and was enthusiastically received with cries of 'Viva il caro Sassone!' Durastanti was a former colleague of Handel's from Rome; Elena Croce (listed as the Agrippina in one MS source) may have replaced her in some performances. The opera was subjected to revision before performance and possibly during its initial run: there are significant differences between Handel's autograph and the printed wordbook of 1709 and between the autograph and most other MS sources, the latter generally conforming to the wordbook. A new scholarly edition is needed.

Handel did not himself revive *Agrippina* after leaving Italy, but he included two of its arias in *Rinaldo* (1711, London), and the overture and four vocal numbers (including 'Pensieri' and the popular 'Ho un non so che nel cor', originally written for *La resurrezione*) appeared in four other operas produced in London during the period 1710–14. There were independent revivals in Naples (1713, with additional music by Francesco Mancini), Hamburg (1718 and later, retaining the Italian text) and Vienna (1719 – a pasticcio with music also by Johann Joseph Fux and Antonio Caldara). The first modern revival was at Halle in 1943; it was given in Leipzig in 1959, at Abingdon in 1963 (its British première) and, among other revivals, in London in 1965, by Kent Opera in 1982, at Venice in 1983 and at Drottningholm in 1985.

The story is fictional, though it involves historical characters and touches on real events. In Act 1 the Emperor Claudius is away in Britain and his death is reported. His wife Agrippina uses the opportunity to secure the succession for Nero, her son by a previous marriage. She obtains help from her henchmen and putative lovers Pallas and Narcissus, but her plans are upset by the unexpected return of Claudius, announced by his servant Lesbo; his life has been saved by Otho, who has been granted the succession as reward. Agrippina hints to Poppaea that her lover Otho has relinquished her in return for the throne. In Act 2 Agrippina takes advantage of Claudius's passion for Poppaea – who is also wooed by Nero – and by various deceits uses her to turn Claudius against Otho. Otho is denounced as a traitor, but he manages to convince Poppaea that he is faithful to her, and she realizes tht she has been duped by Agrippina. Meanwhile Agrippina tries to trick Pallas and Narcissus into murdering Otho and each other, while encouraging Claudius to leave the throne to Nero. To help Otho (Act 3), Poppaea arranges for her three lovers to come to her house in quick succession, each hiding as the next arrives, and contrives to get Nero exposed to Claudius as an importunate rival. Pallas and Narcissus, joining forces, tell Claudius about Agrippina's double-dealing. Nevertheless Agrippina cunningly convinces her husband that she was acting throughout for his own good. Claudius finally attempts to satisfy everyone by awarding the succession to Otho, and Poppaea to Nero; but Nero protests that it would be double punishment to gain a wife and lose an empire, and so Claudius names Nero as his successor after all and Poppaea is given to Otho. The goddess Juno descends to bless their marriage.

*

Handel to some extent ensured the opera's success by drawing on the best music from works written earlier in Rome and Florence (the opera *Rodrigo*, the oratorio *La resurrezione* and cantatas), as well as making use of some memorable thematic fragments from Reinhard Keiser's *Der verführte Claudius* (1703, Hamburg). The effectiveness of the opera as a whole also owes much to Cardinal Grimani's witty and skilfully worked-out libretto – a typically Venetian anti-heroic comedy, in which all the main characters, apart from Otho, cheerfully and cynically intrigue for their own ends. They are nevertheless redeemed by certain underlying virtues – Agrippina's single-minded ambition is for her son rather than herself – and by the music, which always expresses genuine emotion. Otho is an entirely serious character – his F minor lament in Act 2 ('Voi che udite il mio lamento') is the most tragic

moment in the opera – but the dominant role is, rightly, that of Agrippina herself, always confident and occasionally menacing. A sense of triumph is present in her very first aria ('L'alma mia fra le tempeste', based on one of Handel's favourite tunes) and she is at her most formidable in the great scena 'Pensieri, voi mi tormentate' of Act 2, when in desperation she plans a triple murder.   A.H.

Aida

Opera in four acts by Giuseppe Verdi to a libretto by Antonio Ghislanzoni after a scenario by Auguste Mariette; Cairo, Opera House, 24 December 1871.

The first cast included Eleonora Grossi (Amneris), Antonietta Anastasi-Pozzoni (Aida), Pietro Mongini (Radames) and Francesco Steller (Amonasro).

The King of Egypt	bass
Amneris *his daughter*	mezzo-soprano
Aida *an Ethiopian slave*	soprano
Radames *Captain of the Guards*	tenor
Ramfis *Chief Priest*	bass
Amonasro *King of Ethiopia, Aida's father*	baritone
The High Priestess	soprano
A Messenger	tenor

Priests, priestesses, ministers, captains, soldiers, functionaries, Ethiopian slaves and prisoners, Egyptian populace
Setting Memphis and Thebes, during the reign of the Pharaohs

During the late 1860s the search for suitable librettos began to cause Verdi increasing problems. One of his most active helpers was the French librettist and impresario Camille Du Locle, with whom Verdi had collaborated in the making of *Don Carlos*. Du Locle sent Verdi a stream of possible subjects covering a wide variety of genres: from comic plots that might have continued the manner of *Un ballo in maschera* to large-scale topics suitable for conversion into grand opera. But Verdi became more and more difficult to please, finding the comic subjects structurally or temperamentally unsuitable, while often complaining of the 'patchwork' quality of grand opera, its inherent lack of coherence. The breakthrough came in the early months of 1870, when Du Locle sent Verdi a scenario by the archaeologist and Egyptologist Auguste Mariette, based on an invented story set in Egyptian antiquity. Verdi had the previous year refused to supply an inaugural hymn as part of the celebrations to open the Suez Canal; but he accepted this new Egyptian idea – which was to open the

'Aida' (Verdi), Act 2 scene ii (one of the city gates of Thebes): engraving showing the first production at the Paris Opéra (Salle Garnier), 22 March 1880

new Cairo Opera House – almost immediately, appointing as librettist Antonio Ghislanzoni, his collaborator in the revised *La forza del destino*. Work on the opera, whose scenario was adapted and enlarged by both Du Locle and Verdi, proceeded through 1870, Verdi as usual taking a considerable hand in the libretto's formation, even in minor details of line length and wording; the staging of the production was carried out in Paris under the eye of Mariette.

As the composer decided not to attend the Cairo première, he proceeded to complete the orchestration of his score in Italy; but by that stage it was clear that production of the opera would be delayed by the Franco-Prussian war, the siege of Paris having trapped the sets and costumes there. There were in addition a series of intense struggles over the première cast, in which as usual Verdi took a close interest. Eventually *Aida* was first performed in Cairo – with predictable success – in late 1871, directed by the famous double bass player Giovanni Bottesini. Verdi also devoted great attention to the Italian première at La Scala, making various slight changes to the score and minutely rehearsing a carefully chosen group of principals. This second perform-ance, conducted by Franco Faccio, took place on 8 February 1872, and included Maria Waldmann (Amneris), Teresa Stolz (Aida), Giuseppe Fancelli (Radames) and Francesco Pandolfini (Amonasro). It

was again hugely successful with the public, al-though some critics voiced reservations about passages they found conventional or old-fashioned. Verdi was reluctant to allow further performances in Italy without assurances of a sensitive staging, but by the mid-1870s the opera had entered the general repertory, where it has remained to the present day. Some time before the Milanese première, Verdi wrote a full-scale overture; but after hearing it rehearsed he decided to withdraw it and reinstate the prelude.

*

The prelude juxtaposes and combines two themes: the first, chromatic and presented on high strings, will be associated with Aida throughout the opera; the second, contrapuntally developed, will be associated with the priests.

Act I.i *A hall in the King's palace in Memphis* To the accompaniment of a restrained development of motifs from the prelude, Ramfis, the Chief Priest, and Radames are in conversation: Ramfis advises that the Ethiopian enemy is again on the attack, and that Isis has named the commander of the Egyptian troops. As Ramfis departs, Radames eagerly anticipates becoming that leader, and then muses on his beloved Aida in the *romanza* 'Celeste Aida', a ternary-form piece shot through with atmospheric instrumental effects. Radames is then joined by Amneris, who loves the young warrior, but whose sinuous string melody underlines her suspicions about the direction of his affections. Their agitated duet, 'Quale inchiesta!', is interrupted by the appearance of Aida (and her characteristic theme), and Radames's longing glances confirm Amneris's jealousy. The duet turns into a trio as Amneris relentlessly questions the confused lovers.

A series of fanfares heralds the King of Egypt, Ramfis and a large group of followers. A messenger announces that Amonasro, King of the Ethiopians, is leading an army against them; the King of Egypt reveals that Isis has named Radames as their commander. All join in the martial hymn, 'Su! del Nilo', Aida's syncopated line underlining her distress at the forthcoming battle. After a final unison cry of 'Ritorna vincitor!' ('Return victor!'), the crowd disperses, leaving Aida alone. Her long, multi-sectioned arioso, which begins with an anguished verbal echo of the chorus's 'Ritorna vincitor!', explores in depth her predicament: Amonasro is her father, but the victory of her family would see the defeat of her beloved Radames. The soliloquy ends with a delicate but intense prayer, 'Numi, pietà', in which she begs the gods to have pity on her suffering.

I.ii *Inside the temple of Vulcan in Memphis* The scene is an old-fashioned tableau, so beloved of French grand opera. An opening chorus, 'Possente Fthà', has many gestures to local colour, notably in its use of the melodic diminished 3rd. There follows a priestesses' dance during which Radames is conducted to the altar. In solemn tones, Ramfis bids Radames protect the homeland, and then leads off the concertato 'Nume, custode e vindice', which gradually gains in power, mingles with the opening strains of the scene, and culminates in a triumphant cry of 'Immenso Fthà!'

Act 2.i *A room in Amneris's apartments* A chorus of female slaves, singing of Radames's recent victories, is followed by a dance of Moorish slaves, Amneris punctuating the choral song with a languorous appeal for her warrior to return. Aida is seen approaching and Amneris dismisses her slaves, to begin one of the great confrontational duets of Verdi's later operas, a number that has echoes of the traditional four-movement form though with equally significant divergences. First comes a succession of contrasting episodes, 'Fu la sorte dell'armi', in which Amneris, with her characteristic sinuous chromaticism, attempts to trap Aida into admitting her love for Radames. Aida's confusion crystallizes into an anguished statement of her identifying theme, but Amneris continues the interrogation by announcing Radames's death, and then by contradicting the news. The intensity of Aida's reactions leaves no doubt of her feelings and, in an *adagio* second movement, 'Pietà ti prenda del mio dolore', she begs in vain for Amneris to show mercy. They are interrupted by fanfares, and an offstage chorus

singing the Act 1 'Su! del Nilo' (Verdi revised this final section after the first performance in Cairo). Over the choral musical background, Amneris and Aida sing a cabaletta substitute, 'Alla pompa che s'appresta', Amneris's line matching the martial atmosphere of the chorus, Aida's minor-mode answer – with syncopated accompaniment – in sharp contrast. Amneris storms out, to leave Aida alone for a last, desperate reprise of 'Numi, pietà'.

2.ii *One of the city gates of Thebes* In celebration of victory, the grand concertato finale – one of Verdi's most spacious – begins with a chorus, 'Gloria all'Egitto', which features interludes for a female group and for the priests, who have a version of their characteristic contrapuntal theme. The stage gradually fills to strains of the famous march for 'Egyptian' trumpets; then comes a ballet sequence, full of harmonic and instrumental local colour; then a reprise of 'Gloria all'Egitto' during which the victorious Radames finally appears. Amneris places a laurel wreath on Radames's head, and the King grants him any wish he may desire. Radames asks that the prisoners be brought forth and Aida sees among them Amonasro. She inadvertently reveals to all that he is her father, but Amonasro quickly stops her from disclosing his identity. The Ethiopian king now takes centre stage to lead off the central Andante, which begins with his account of the battle and then shades into the main lyrical passage, a prayer for clemency, 'Ma tu, Re, tu signore possente'. The prayer is taken up by Aida and the prisoners, is sharply rejected by the priests (who demand death for the defeated), and develops into a broad and lengthy tutti. The set-piece over, Radames asks the Egyptian king for clemency to be shown to the prisoners; Ramfis objects, but Radames carries the day. In a final gesture the King gives him a last reward: Amneris's hand in marriage. The scene concludes with a reprise of 'Gloria all'Egitto', varied and expanded to allow the principals to express their reactions to the new situation.

Act 3 *The banks of the Nile* A single note, G, is sustained by a complex blend of orchestral sonorities to invoke moonlight on the banks of the Nile. An offstage chorus adds to the effect by chanting a hymn to Isis, 'O tu che sei d'Osiride'. Amneris and Ramfis disembark from a boat and enter the temple to pray on the eve of Amneris's marriage. Aida's theme emerges as she cautiously enters for a clandestine meeting with Radames. In a *romanza* that Verdi added to the opera only at the last minute, 'Oh, patria mia', she invokes her long-lost homeland, the restless accompaniment and harmonies combining with a formal layout of remarkable freedom, even for the later Verdi.

Amonasro now appears; the ensuing duet is best seen as the first half of a conventional four-movement structure. After a brief scena in which Amonasro shows that he knows of her love for Radames, the first movement, 'Rivedrai le foreste imbalsamate', is the usual juxtaposition of contrasting lyrical sections: Amonasro invokes their beautiful homeland and reminds Aida of the cruelty of their enemies, but when she refuses to ask Radames about the route his troops will take, and so help the Ethiopians ambush the Egyptians, he angrily reproaches her in 'Su, dunque, sorgete'. Aida is by now broken down, and in the *andante* second movement, 'Padre! ... a costoro', painfully accepts her duty to the homeland: her fragmented line is 'healed' by Amonasro, and finally flowers into a lyrical acceptance of her fate. As Amonasro hides, Radames appears and a second, more conventional four-movement duet ensues. In a hectic first movement, Radames assures Aida of his love but warns that he must again lead his troops in battle. The *andantino* second movement, 'Fuggiam gli ardori inospiti', sees Aida recall the musical idiom of 'Oh, patria mia' in an effort to persuade Radames to run away with her. A brief transition movement, in which Aida accuses the still-reluctant Radames of not loving her, leads to the duet cabaletta, 'Sì: fuggiam da queste mura', in which Radames emphatically agrees to join her in flight. The cabaletta ceases abruptly before its final cadences as Aida asks Radames of the route his army will take. As soon as Radames discloses the information, Amonasro emerges from the shadows, triumphantly announcing that his troops will be there to meet the Egyptians. In a closing terzetto, 'Tu! ... Amonasro!', Radames rails at his lost honour. Aida and Amonasro try to comfort him, but they delay too long: Amneris and Ramfis emerge from the temple and discover Radames apparently in an act of treachery; Amonasro tries to kill Amneris but is prevented by Radames; and, as Aida and her father rush off, Radames gives himself up to justice at the hands of the priests.

Act 4.i *A hall in the King's palace* After an orchestral prelude based on the main theme of the terzetto in Act 1 scene i, Amneris sings an extended arioso in which she determines to save Radames. He is led on by the guards, and yet another multi-section duet ensues. In the first movement, 'Già i sacerdoti adunansi', Amneris begs Radames to defend himself and he refuses, having lost all interest in life. The central lyrical movement, 'Ah! tu dei vivere', allows Amneris to declare her love, but Radames still wishes only for death. The main melody of the opening movement returns in the third as Amneris reveals that Aida, whom Radames believed dead along with Amonasro, is still alive. This revelation eventually precipitates a brief cabaletta, 'Chi ti salva', in which Amneris explodes with renewed jealousy and Radames rejoices that he can now die to protect his beloved.

Radames is led back to the dungeon, and a restrained version of the priests' theme, punctuated by anguished cries from Amneris, sounds as the priests and Ramfis follow him in. They chant a solemn prayer, 'Spirto del Nume', before beginning Radames's trial. Radames is accused by Ramfis three times: each time he refuses to answer, the priests brand him traitor ('Traditor!') and Amneris begs the gods for mercy. The priests then pronounce the horrible sentence: he will be entombed alive below the altar of the god he has outraged. In an unrestrained arioso, Amneris begs for mercy; but the priests are inflexible. As they depart, she is left to hurl after them a bitter curse, 'Empia razza! Anatema su voi!'

4.ii *The scene is on two levels: the upper represents the interior of the temple of Vulcan, gleaming with gold and light; the lower is a vault* Priests close the stone over Radames's head as he sings his opening recitative, full of thoughts of Aida. But he hears a groan and quickly finds his beloved: she has previously stolen into the vault to die in his arms. Their duet has none of the usual contrasting movements, but is rather a sustained piece of delicate lyricism with three main ideas. First comes Radames's 'Morir! sì pura e bella!', in which he laments her death; Aida counters with 'Vedi? ... di morte l'angelo', whose scoring and vocal style suggest that the heroine is already speeding to a celestial haven. And finally, with the background addition of chanting from above, comes the most substantial lyrical idea, 'O terra addio', whose extreme simplicity of formal outline is matched, perhaps permitted, by the unusually angular melodic arch. In the final moments, with the lovers singing 'O terra addio' in unison, Amneris kneels above the vault and implores peace for the soul that lies beneath.

*

Although *Aida* is still one of Verdi's most popular operas, its reputation has perhaps declined slightly of late, overtaken for the first time by works such as *Don Carlos* and *Simon Boccanegra*. The reasons for this reverse are doubtless complex, but the comparative conservatism of *Aida* must surely have played a part. If any rough division of Verdi's mature output were made according to 'experimental' versus 'conservative' works (with, say, *Rigoletto*, *La traviata* and *La forza del destino* in the first category, and *Il trovatore* and *Un ballo in maschera* in the second), then *Aida* would undoubtedly figure with the latter group. In formal terms it concentrates on the conventional set-pieces of grand opera: the grand ceremonial scene and – most of all – the large-scale multi-sectional duet, of which there are several. True, there is a considerable array of variants within the recurring duet scheme, but both contemporary critics and more recent commentators have nevertheless seen certain elements of these formal structures as uncomfortable throwbacks to an earlier aesthetic. The level of musical characterization is also indicative of this conservative stance. In common with the characters of *Trovatore* and *Ballo*, the principal roles in *Aida* – with the partial exception of Amneris – hardly develop during the opera, tending to remain within their conventional vocal personalities as the plot moves their emotions hither and thither.

But to regard the restricted focus of *Aida* purely in these terms is to take a one-sided view of Verdi's capacities as a musical dramatist, and to emphasize unduly the radical aspect of his personality. Indeed, *Aida*'s greatest artistic successes are born of this 'conservatism': in magnificently controlled ceremonial scenes such as Act 2 scene ii – in which a kind of flexible variation technique allows episodes such as the opening chorus to reappear as the culmination of the scene; or in the telling effects gained when various multi-movement duets dovetail into each other, as in the sequence that closes Act 3.

There is, moreover, one important aspect in which *Aida* remains the most radical and 'modern' of Verdi's scores: its use of local colour. *Aida*, constantly alluding to its ambience in harmony and instrumentation, is the one Verdi opera that could not conceivably be transported to another geographical location. In this respect it was an important indication of the influence local colour would come to have over *fin-de-siècle* opera, and an object lesson on the delicacy and control with which this colour could be applied to the standard forms and expressive conventions of Italian opera.   R.P.

Akhnaten

Opera in three acts by Philip Glass to a libretto by the composer, Shalom Goldman, Robert Israel and Richard Riddell; Stuttgart, Staatsoper, 24 March 1984.

Paul Esswood sang Akhnaten and Milagro Vargas was Nefertiti at the première, which was conducted by Dennis Russell Davies; others in the cast included Maria Husmann, Helmut Holzapfel and Wolfgang Probst.

Akhnaten	countertenor
Nefertiti *his wife*	alto
Queen Tye *his mother*	soprano
Horemhab *army general*	baritone
Aye *Nefertiti's father*	bass
High Priest of Amon	tenor
Six Daughters of	
Akhnaten	sopranos and altos
Amenhotep	spoken
Tourist Guide	spoken

Male funeral party, mourners, priests,
    soldiers, people of Egypt, dancers, musicians,
    tourists
Setting Egypt in 1375 BC and in the present

Glass has called *Einstein on the Beach*, *Satyagraha* and *Akhnaten* a trilogy of 'portrait' operas. From a purely dramatic standpoint such a grouping makes sense, although all of the composer's later operas bear closer musical resemblance to *Satyagraha* (1980) than they do to *Einstein on the Beach* (1976), which stands on its own. In *Satyagraha* Glass developed his own distinctive mutation of 'traditional' opera and the works which have followed are cast in a related musical mould.

Akhnaten was inspired by the writings of Immanuel Velikovsky (*Worlds in Collision*, *Earth in Upheaval* and especially *Oedipus and Akhnaten*), in which he contends that events in the fictional life of Oedipus occurred hundreds of years earlier in the life of the Egyptian pharoah Akhnaten. Glass acknowledges that Velikovsky's cataclysmic theories are generally regarded as spurious and unscientific but considers him a 'lively, interesting and provocative writer'. Glass had hoped to work with Velikovsky himself on the opera but the writer died in November 1979. Looking to other collaborators, Glass began work on the libretto in 1982: Shalom Goldman excerpted the vocal text, in English, Hebrew and Egyptian, from sources ranging from the Egyptian Book of the Dead to the King James version of the Bible and James H. Breasted's *A History of Egypt*. 'Decrees, titles, letters, fragments of poems, etc., were all left to be sung in their original languages, thereby emphasizing the artifactual slant of our approach', Glass wrote. Only the 'Hymn' is always sung in the language of the audience.

The opera met with mixed reviews in Europe and America; an unsympathetic American première, presented in both New York and Houston, was blamed for the opera's unfavourable reception in the USA. However, David Freeman's revised version of the same production with Christopher Robson was immediately successful in London and the opera became part of the repertory of the English National Opera. For many, it was only with the release of the composer's supervised recording in 1987 that *Akhnaten* was recognized as one of Glass's major works.

The opera opens in 1375 BC. After a prelude, during which the narrator reads from ancient Egyptian texts, Act 1 begins with the funeral of the king, Amenhotep III, attended by his widow Queen Tye, his family and counsellors. His son is crowned as the new King Amenhotep IV, and immediately abolishes the Amon traditions of his father, taking the name Akhnaten. In Act 2 he deposes the Amon priests, destroying their temple, and proposes instead the monotheistic worship of Aten. The plans for his new city are drawn up, and he builds a temple, Akhetaten, in honour of Aten; he refuses to practise polygamy, preferring to remain true to his wife, Nefertiti, with whom he sings a love duet. Akhnaten's Hymn to the Sun uses the historical figure's own words. Akhnaten, his wife and his six daughters live harmoniously in his new city (Act 3). As he becomes increasingly isolated from his subjects by his preoccupations, the Amon priests, joined by Aye and Horemhab, incite the people to overthrow him. The city is razed and Akhnaten and his family are left roaming the ruined Akhetaten, mourning the passing of their epoch. In the present, tourists are guided round the ruins, while in an epilogue the spirits of the founder and his family still haunt the city and the temple.

*

Though *Akhnaten* is written for 12 solo voices, chorus and narrator, in general it is less determinedly 'operatic' than *Satyagraha*, with long orchestral interludes and much spoken text; moreover, the scoring is clarified, pared down (the large orchestra includes a range of percussion instruments but there are no violins), and almost neo-classical in its economy of means. One also finds a use of dissonance unprecedented in the composer's mature work; Akhnaten's 13-minute 'Hymn' in the second act is probably the most chromatic music Glass has written since his student days and has something of the spirit of the spare, chant-like late compositions of Stravinsky. (The exciting 'Funeral Music' in Act 1 was excerpted for use in the Jerome Robbins ballet *Glass Pieces*.)   T.P.

Albert Herring

Comic opera in three acts, op.39, by Benjamin Britten to a libretto by Eric Crozier, after Guy de Maupassant's short story *Le rosier de Madame Husson*; Glyndebourne, 20 June 1947.

The première had Peter Pears in the title role, Joan Cross as Lady Billows and a supporting cast including Frederick Sharp (Sid), Nancy Evans (Nancy) and Margaret Ritchie (Miss Wordsworth).

Lady Billows *an elderly autocrat*	soprano
Florence Pike *her housekeeper*	contralto
Miss Wordsworth *head teacher at the church school*	soprano
Mr Gedge *the vicar*	baritone
Mr Upfold *the mayor*	tenor
Superintendent Budd	bass
Sid *a butcher's shophand*	baritone
Albert Herring *from the greengrocer's*	tenor
Nancy *from the bakery*	mezzo-soprano
Mrs Herring *Albert's mother*	mezzo-soprano
Emmie	soprano
Cis *village children*	soprano
Harry	treble

Setting Loxford, a small market town in East Suffolk, during April and May of 1900

After the stormy inception of *Peter Grimes* at Sadler's Wells, Britten and Eric Crozier were among those who decided to launch a new, independent and progressive opera company. The English Opera Group was first associated with Glyndebourne, but this relationship gave rise to problems (connected with touring *The Rape of Lucretia*), and in the early days of 1947 the fully independent English Opera Group was finally established. Even so, Britten's second chamber opera was first performed, under his direction, at Glyndebourne, alongside a revival of *Lucretia*. Britten and his friends were now determined, however, to establish their own centre for performance. The Aldeburgh Festival was set up, and *Albert Herring* was the first opera performed there, in the Jubilee Hall in June 1948. Since then there have been many productions worldwide, the opera's strong local flavour proving no hindrance to its appeal. *Herring* returned to Glyndebourne in 1985 in an acclaimed production by Peter Hall, which was televised, and in 1989 the same production was presented at Covent Garden. A complete recording with Peter Pears as Albert and Britten conducting was made in 1964.

*

Act I.i *The breakfast room of Lady Billows's house* The fast-moving, often parodic style of this scene, with a mixture of piano-accompanied recitatives and through-composed solos and ensembles, sets the tone for the whole opera. The various dignitaries of Loxford assemble for their annual task of choosing a Queen of the May, but it soon becomes clear that none of the young women proposed meets the exacting moral standards of Lady Billows. It is the police superintendent who eventually proposes a radical solution: that they elect instead a King of the May. He has in mind one Albert Herring, and although Lady Billows is initially opposed to the idea, the only alternative seems to be to cancel the festival altogether. After further discussion she decisively announces her approval, and leads the committee in an exuberant contrapuntal ensemble. Scene ii follows after an orchestral interlude.

I.ii *Mrs Herring's shop* Sid is teasing Albert about his strait-laced subservience to his mother, and sings of the joys of poaching and courting; when Sid's sweetheart Nancy arrives and they start flirting, Albert grows increasingly agitated and embarrassed. Left alone he reflects on his lot, and shows the first

'Albert Herring' (Britten), Act 2 scene i (marquee in the vicarage garden) of the original production at Glyndebourne with Norman Lumsden (Superintendent Budd), Betsy de la Porte (Mrs Herring), Peter Pears (Albert Herring), and Joan Cross (Lady Billows)

signs of a desire to kick over the traces. Then Miss Pike, Lady Billows's housekeeper, arrives, followed by her ladyship and the rest of the festival committee. They give Albert and his mother their news. To Albert 'the whole thing's daft!', but his mother, excited at the prospect of the prize of £25, shouts down his dissent.

Act 2.i *Inside a marquee set up in the vicarage garden* It is the day of the ceremony, and tables are set out in the marquee for a festive tea. Sid tells Nancy about the special church service which has been taking place, with Albert on tenterhooks throughout. After Miss Wordsworth has rehearsed the schoolchildren in a song of welcome for the new May King, Sid adds a tot of rum to the glass of lemonade which has already been placed by Albert's plate, to 'loosen him up and make him feel bright'. Now Albert arrives, dressed in virginal white, with the local worthies in attendance. The children present Albert and his mother with flowers, Lady Billows embarks on a rambling homily; then the mayor, the schoolmistress and the police superintendent all offer the May King gifts or advice. Albert, called on to respond, is overcome by shyness and can only stammer out, after a painful silence, 'Thank you very much'. Then the entire company sing the anthem 'Albert the Good', at the end of which, to a short instrumental fantasia on the *Tristan* chord, the May King drains his rum-laced glass. As he is smitten with hiccups, the feast begins.

2.ii *Mrs Herring's shop, the same evening* Again an instrumental interlude links the new scene to its predecessor. Albert enters, thoroughly tipsy and rebellious, but still reluctant to take advantage of what he imagines to be Nancy's interest in him. Sid and Nancy pass by the shop and sing a lighthearted love duet after Sid has told Nancy that he thinks it's time for Albert to sow a few wild oats. As they leave, Albert, in increasing agitation, tosses one of the sovereigns that were his prize as May King. 'Heads for Yes and tails for No!' It comes down heads, and by the time Mrs Herring arrives home, worn out by the day's events, her son has set off in search of excitement and experience.

Act 3 *Mrs Herring's shop, the afternoon of the following day* Albert has not yet returned, and Nancy is miserable, Sid unrepentant at their part in encouraging his defection. Mrs Herring is convinced that he is dead, and the other characters assemble to offer condolences. When the orange-blossom crown presented to Albert as May King is brought in, 'found on the road to Campsey Ash, crushed by a cart', the evidence seems conclusive, and the nine principals join in an extended threnody, each in turn floating a solo line against the repeated refrain: 'In the midst of life is death, Death awaits us one and all, Death attends our smallest step, Swift and silent, merciful'. At the threnody's climax, Albert pokes his head round the shop door. With an instant change of atmosphere everyone turns on him and berates him for his lack of consideration in vanishing without warning. At first Albert responds reticently to their interrogation, but once he decides to offer an explanation he does so with increasing confidence. His revelations of drinking and fighting shock everyone except Nancy and Sid. Then Albert blames his mother for keeping him wrapped in cotton wool, so that the 'only way out was a wild explosion'. He then assures everyone that, grateful as he was for the prize-money that funded his adventure, he did not greatly enjoy the experience, and now wants to be left alone to get back to work. The worthies leave in disgust, Mrs Herring is put firmly in her place, and Sid and Nancy rejoice with Albert in his new-found self-possession.

*

Apart from Albert's extended scena in Act 2 scene ii, this is very much an ensemble opera. Other solos are relatively brief, and there is an emphasis on rapid dialogue, often with piano accompaniment played by the conductor. Even so, the 12-piece orchestra is used with the greatest skill, notably in the evocative night-music that frames Act 2 scene ii. Though the work may now seem rather dated in the treatment of its subject-matter, the energy and unaffected lyricism of Britten's music have not faded, reflecting his evident delight in the special possibilities of chamber opera. It also confirms that he was eminently capable of writing comic opera: in this respect *Albert Herring* fulfils the promise of *Paul Bunyan*, and many may regret that he made only one other contribution to the genre, *A Midsummer Night's Dream*.   **A.W.**

Alceste (i) [*Alceste, ou Le triomphe d'Alcide* ('Alcestis, or The Triumph of Alcides')]

Tragédie en musique in a prologue and five acts by Jean-Baptiste Lully to a libretto by Philippe Quinault after Euripides' *Alcestis*; Paris, Académie Royale de Musique (Opéra), 19 January 1674.

The casts at the Paris and court premières are uncertain. At Fontainebleau in 1677 the principal singers included Saint-Christophle (Alcestis and the Nymph of the Seine), La Garde (Céphise and Glory), Gaye (Hercules), Cledière (Admetus), Langeais (Lychas), Morel (Straton) and Godonesche (Charon, Lycomedes and Pluto); the principal dancers (all male) included Faure, Favier, Lestang and Magny.

Prologue

Nymph of the Seine	soprano
La Gloire [Glory]	soprano
Nymph of the Tuileries	soprano
Nymph of the Marne	soprano

Tragedy

Alceste [Alcestis] *Princess of Iolcos*	soprano
Admète [Admetus] *King of Thessaly*	haute-contre
Alcide [Alcides, or Hercules]	baritone
Licomède [Lycomedes] *brother of Thetis, King of Scyros*	bass
Lychas *confidant of Hercules*	haute-contre
Straton *confidant of Lycomedes*	bass
Céphise *confidante of Alcestis*	soprano
Cléante *knight of Admetus*	tenor
Pherès [Pheres] *father of Admetus*	tenor
Charon	baritone
Pluton [Pluto]	bass
Thétis [Thetis] *a sea-nymph*	soprano
Apollon [Apollo]	haute-contre
Proserpine [Proserpina]	soprano
The Ghost of Alcestis	silent role
Alecton [Alecto] *a Fury*	haute-contre
A Rebuffed Ghost	soprano
Eole [Aeolus] *King of the winds*	baritone
Diane [Diana]	soprano
Mercure [Mercury]	silent role

Followers of Glory, naiads, rustic divinities, river divinities, the Pleasures; Thessalians, pages and followers, sea divinities, sailors, four aquilons, four zephyrs; Lycomedes' soldiers, Thessalian soldiers, the Arts; afflicted women, sorrowful men; the shades, followers of Pluto; people of Greece, the nine Muses, the Games, shepherds and shepherdesses, herdsmen

Setting The city of Iolcos in Thessaly

This was Lully's second tragedy, performed at the recently constituted Académie, the royal monopoly of which had been transferred to him two years before. The king and courtiers saw a rehearsal at Versailles in November 1673 and were enthusiastic. However, poets and musicians jealous of Lully's growing power and of the success of *Cadmus et Hermione* organized a cabal to discredit *Alceste* after its première. Only Perrault defended the work at length, pointing out that everybody 'knows by heart' and sings everywhere the little songs that are said to be worthless, that the many scenes judged 'useless' by the critics (mainly scenes dominated by secondary characters) all have their dramatic purposes, and that the conventions of opera are different from those of spoken tragedy and comedy (*Critique de l'opéra*, 1674, attrib. Charles or Pierre Perrault).

Despite the cabal, *Alceste* succeeded. It had its court première at Versailles on 4 July 1674, as part of an extended celebration of the victory over Franche-Comté. Additional court productions were performed at Fontainebleau in 1677 and Saint-Germain-en-Laye in 1678. There were Paris Opéra revivals

'Alceste' (Lully): Jean Berain's design for the marine chariot of the sea-nymph Thetis for the original production at the Paris Opéra (Académie Royale de Musique) on 19 January 1674 (or possibly for the revivals of 1677–8)

regularly up to 1757. Between 1695 and 1730 *Alceste* was produced in Marseilles, Lyons, Brussels and other cities.

*

Prologue *Paris, on the banks of the Seine in the Tuileries garden* The Nymph of the Seine longs for Louis XIV to return from battle (extended rondeau, 'Le héros que j'attens ne reviendra-t'il pas?'). She is assured that he follows Glory (whose descent is announced by trumpets and timpani) but will return. The pastoral divinities celebrate. The *air* 'L'art accord avec la nature', sung by the Nymph of the Tuileries, was a favourite of early audiences.

Act I *A seaport* The tragedy begins at the wedding of Admetus and Alcestis. An undeclared suitor, Hercules, prepares to leave Iolcos. A jilted suitor, Lycomedes, abducts Alcestis under the guise of giving a party for the betrothed couple; his escape is aided by a storm at sea. The tempest scene, apparently inspired by an episode in Virgil's *Aeneid* (book 1), demonstrates well the flexible relationship between ballet and drama in the Lullian tragedy:

after a series of dances and dance-songs, Lycomedes' invitation to Alcestis to join him on his ship (marked by a change of key) seems to signal the end of the *divertissement* and the return to high drama; yet the presentation of that drama relies on the conventions of court ballet. Lycomedes' sister, the sea-nymph Thetis, rises from the sea on a marine chariot, and at her command four dancers representing storm winds stir up the water. The 'Entrée des Aquilons' is a dance in running semiquavers. In a soothing *air*, the wind god Aeolus calls on the gentle west winds to calm the sea. Four flying 'zephyrs' chase the four scurrying 'aquilons' into the sea, allowing Admetus's army (including Hercules) to pursue Lycomedes' ship.

A comic subplot, involving a love triangle among the confidants of the main characters, begins in Act 1; it continues in Acts 2 and 5. Céphise, a girl of 15 who makes a virtue of fickleness, is responsible for much of this opera's lyricism: she is frequently present and sings numerous charming little *airs*.

Act 2 *City on the island of Scyros* The *divertissement* is a spectacular battle: half the chorus and dancers represent the 'besieging soldiers' and the other half the 'besieged soldiers'. Hercules triumphs and delivers Alcestis, but Admetus is mortally wounded. Alcestis and the dying Admetus say a moving farewell: intertwined solo fragments grow progressively shorter and gradually give way to a duet. Apollo offers immortal glory to anyone who volunteers to die in Admetus's stead.

Act 3 *A monument raised by the Arts* A central altar will bear the image of the person who dies for Admetus. Only Alcestis will sacrifice herself. The *divertissement* is a monumental funeral scene including pantomime ballet; the introduction is organized around the choral refrain 'Alceste est morte!', and the conclusion is a choral chaconne during which the chorus and orchestra gradually fade. Hercules, who loves Alcestis, intends to try to bring her back from Hades and asks Admetus to relinquish her to him. In the hope of seeing Alcestis alive, Admetus agrees.

Act 4 *The River Acheron, then Pluto's palace* The act opens with one of Lully's best-known passages. In the *air* 'Il faut passer tôt ou tard', over a bass line representing the flowing River Acheron, a frankly comic Charon sings cheerfully of the inevitability of death. In the doubled continuo *air* 'Donne, passe', he collects a fare from the shades with bourgeois efficiency. Hercules simply jumps into the ferryboat and demands passage. Despite a majestic entrance *prélude* for Pluto and his retinue, this is not a solemn underworld: in a light and stylish *fête*, the shades welcome Alcestis to eternal peace. The *divertissement* is interrupted by Hercules' arrival, announced by the barking of Cerberus, cleverly represented by a male chorus. After hearing Hercules' entreaties, Proserpina persuades Pluto to allow him to take Alcestis.

Act 5 *A triumphal arch* In a *choeur en rondeau*, 'Alcide est vainqueur du trépas', different peoples of Greece, led by Admetus, cheer Hercules' triumph over death. Admetus and Alcestis sadly prepare to part. Hercules announces that, having conquered an army and conquered death, he will now conquer his own desires and allow Alcestis and Admetus to remain together. The final *divertissement* is a celebration of love and of Hercules' generosity.

*

Like most *tragédies en musique*, *Alceste* contains plenty of heroic action but no exploration of a tragic dilemma: the characters make their sacrifices without apparent second thoughts or consultation. In place of human dilemma and discussion, the genre offers human and supernatural spectacle, and these features were already fully developed in this early work. The ballet *divertissements* present a catalogue of stock topics, to which French librettists and composers would return many times: maritime celebration, tempest, battle scene, funeral, underworld scene and pastoral celebration. Compared with Lully's mature operas of the 1680s, *Alceste* makes sparing use of the full orchestra, and the recitative virtually never exploits subtle conflict between poetic and musical metre; yet the composer's general manner of structuring dialogues was well developed and successful by this time. From a modern point of view, the presence of comic scenes – criticized at the time – is a virtue rather than a vice, since Lully was a gifted musical comedian.   L.R.

Alceste (ii) ('Alcestis')

Italian version: *Tragedia* in three acts by Christoph Willibald Gluck to a libretto by Ranieri de' Calzabigi after Euripides; Vienna, Burgtheater, 26 December 1767.

French version: *Tragédie opéra* in three acts by Gluck to a libretto by Marie François Louis Gand Leblanc Roullet after Calzabigi; Paris, Académie Royale de Musique (Opéra), 23 April 1776.

The principals in the first performance of the Italian version included Antonia Bernasconi (Alcestis), Giuseppe Tibaldi (Admetus), Filippo Laschi (Apollo and the High Priest), Antonio Pilloni (Evander) and Teresa Eberardi (Ismene). Those in the première of the French version included Rosalie Levasseur (Alcestis), Joseph Legros (Admetus), Henri Larrivée (Hercules), Moreau (Apollo) and Nicolas Gélin (High Priest).

Italian Version

Alceste [Alcestis] *Queen of Pherae in Thessaly*	soprano
Admeto [Admetus] *her husband*	tenor
Eumelo [Eumelus] ⎫ *their children*	soprano
Aspasia ⎭	soprano
Evandro [Evander] *a confidant of Admetus*	tenor
Ismene *a confidante of Alcestis*	soprano
A Herald	bass
High Priest of Apollo	baritone
Apollo	baritone
Oracle	bass
Infernal Deity	bass
Courtiers, citizens, Alcestis's maids of honour, priests of Apollo, gods of the underworld	
Setting Classical Pherae, Thessaly	

French Version

Alceste [Alcestis] *Queen of Thessaly*	soprano
Admète [Admetus] *her husband*	tenor
Their two children	silent
Evandre [Evander] *leader of Pherae*	tenor
A Herald of Arms	bass

Design by François-Joseph Bélanger for Act 3 of the revised version of Gluck's 'Alceste', first performed at the Paris Opéra (Académie Royale de Musique), 23 April 1776

High Priest of Apollo	bass
Apollo *protector of the house of Admetus*	baritone
Hercule [Hercules]	bass
Oracle	bass
Thanatos *an infernal deity*	bass
Chorus Leaders	soprano, contralto, tenor, bass

Officers of the palace, Alcestis's attendants, citizens of Pherae, infernal deities, priests and priestesses in the temple of Apollo

Setting Classical Pherae, Thessaly

The Italian *Alceste* was the second of Gluck's three so-called reform operas written with Ranieri de' Calzabigi (the others were *Orfeo ed Euridice* and *Paride ed Elena*) in which a noble simplicity in the action and the music was intended to replace the complicated plots and florid musical style of *opera seria*. Although *Orfeo* was the first of these reform operas, it is *Alceste* that contains, in the first edition of the score, the famous preface in which Gluck and Calzabigi outlined their principles and ideals:

When I undertook to write the music for *Alceste*, I resolved to divest it entirely of all those abuses,

introduced into it either by the mistaken vanity of singers or by the too great complaisance of composers, which have so long disfigured Italian opera and made of the most splendid and most beautiful of spectacles the most ridiculous and wearisome. I have striven to restrict music to its true office of serving poetry by means of expression and by following the situation of the story, without interrupting the action or stifling it with a useless superfluity of ornaments; [. . .] Thus I did not wish to arrest an actor in the greatest heat of dialogue in order to wait for a tiresome ritornello, nor to hold him up in the middle of a word on a vowel favourable to his voice, not to make display of the agility of his fine voice in some long-drawn passage, nor to wait while the orchestra gives him time to recover his breath for a cadenza. I did not think it my duty to pass quickly over the second section of an aria of which the words are perhaps the most impassioned and important, in order to repeat regularly four times over those of the first part, and to finish the aria where its sense may perhaps not end for the convenience of the singer who wishes to show that he can capriciously vary a passage in a number of guises; in short, I have sought to abolish all the abuses against which good sense and reason have long cried out in vain.

I have felt that the overture ought to apprise the spectators of the nature of the action that is to be represented and to form, so to speak, its argument; that the concerted instruments should be introduced in proportion to the interest and the intensity of the words, and not leave that sharp contrast between the aria and the recitative in the dialogue, so as not to break a period unreasonably nor wantonly disturb the force and heat of the action.

Furthermore, I believed that my greatest labour should be devoted to seeking a beautiful simplicity, and I have avoided making displays of difficulty at the expense of clearness; nor did I judge it desirable to discover novelties if it was not naturally suggested by the situation and the expression; and there is no rule which I have not thought it right to set aside willingly for the sake of an intended effect. [trans. Eric Blom, 1936]

The opera was a great success; according to Calzabigi 60 performances were given in Vienna. It was choreographed not by Angiolini, the choreographer of *Orfeo* in 1762, but by his rival Jean-Georges Noverre, also an influential figure in the early *ballet d'action*. In 1770, for further performances in Vienna, Gluck rewrote the tenor role of Admetus for the soprano castrato Giuseppe Millico (just as he had the role of Orpheus for performances in Parma the previous year). *Alceste* was revived in Vienna in 1781 and 1786; there were 12 local premières elsewhere in Europe up to 1804.

Gluck's revision of *Alceste* for performance in Paris in 1776 amounts almost to a recomposition. His alterations were far more extensive than those he had made in his Paris adaptation of *Orfeo*. The French *Alceste* had a new text by Roullet, Gluck's librettist for *Iphigénie en Aulide*, based on Calzabigi's libretto but with alterations to the plot and the order of events.

At the first Paris performances of *Alceste* the Act 3 denouement was substantially different from the version familiar today, and closer to the Italian original. Gluck and Roullet, after much criticism, altered the act to incorporate a part for Hercules, who has no place in the Italian original. Just as Gluck was arranging more music to enlarge the final *divertissement*, again to please Parisian taste, he heard of the death of his adopted daughter Marianne in Vienna; he left Paris and assigned the completion of the *divertissement* to François-Joseph Gossec. This revised version, published in Paris in 1776, is the one that has nearly always been performed subsequently; the Italian version has rarely been revived since the 18th century, although it was recorded in 1956, with Kirsten Flagstad in the title role.

The French version has rarely been long out of the repertory, though as with so many of Gluck's operas (*Orfeo ed Euridice* apart) it has been performed far less often than the lip-service it receives might lead one to

imagine. Important productions have included one at the Paris Opéra in 1825 with Alexandrine Caroline Branchu as Alcestis; Berlioz saw it, and it may have influenced the edition he prepared for Pauline Viardot at the Opéra in 1861. Germaine Lubin was a notable Alcestis in Paris in the 1920s, 30s and 40s, and sang the role at Covent Garden in 1937. *Alceste* has received only sporadic performances in Britain in recent times, notably at Glyndebourne in the 1950s, at the Edinburgh Festival in 1974 and by Scottish Opera in 1996. Janet Baker chose it for her farewell performances at Covent Garden in 1981. Notable performances elsewhere include those by Wilhelmine Schröder-Devrient in Dresden in 1846; a production conducted by Liszt in Weimar in 1857; one at the Metropolitan Opera in New York in 1952 with Kirsten Flagstad; and one at La Scala in 1954 with Maria Callas, conducted by Carlo Maria Giulini (one of Callas's performances was recorded). Of the two recordings of the French *Alceste* to date (one with Jessye Norman, the other with Ethel Semser), neither is absolutely complete.

In the synopsis that follows, 'I' stands for the Italian version, 'F' for the French version (numerals in *italics* denote the French version).

*

Act I *The great square in the city of Pherae, with the façade of Admetus's palace on one side, filled by a crowd of distressed courtiers and citizens; also, in F, an entrance to the temple of Apollo at the back of the stage* The sombre overture is one of the earliest to set the mood for a tragic drama, according to Gluck's principles as outlined in the preface to the printed score of the opera. The Italian overture ends with an imperfect cadence before the herald's D major fanfare; the French has the first of many marvellous additions to the original as the chorus interrupts the overture with a short anguished plea to the gods to return Admetus to them beginning with an arresting diminished seventh chord.

I.i *(I, F)* The herald informs the crowd that Admetus is about to die and that nothing can save him. The people sing the first of the opera's choral laments ('Ah di questo afflitto regno'/'O dieux! qu'allons-nous devenir?'). This scene is more extended in the Italian version (no.4): the choral refrain returns twice, enclosing duet and solo sections for Evander and Ismene, and it includes too a sombre ballet movement, a recitative in which Evander suggests that they consult the Oracle in Apollo's temple, and a repeat of 'Ah di questo' with a solo for Evander before his announcement of Alcestis's approach (no.8). The French revision includes one statement of the choral lament (no.5), ending with a contrapuntal Allegro, immediately followed by Evander's briefer announcement of Alcestis's approach and a choral recitative (no.6).

I.ii (I, F) Another chorus of mourning ensues, 'Misero Admeto!'/'O malheureux Admète!', with chromatic harmony and antiphonal effects. Alcestis enters with a recitative and aria. In the Italian original she has one of the opera's few examples of conventional *recitativo secco* accompanied only by continuo. Her words, also conventional, would not be out of place in an *opera seria*: 'Popoli di Tessaglia' ('People of Thessaly, never were your tears more justified; to you no less than to these innocent children is Admetus a father': no.10). Her very different entry in the French revision (no.8) illustrates, in words and music, how far Gluck's dramatic powers had advanced. Not only is the French recitative orchestrally accompanied; in the middle of it seven bars from the chorus 'O malheureux Admète' heighten the pathos. Alcestis's aria, in which she beseeches the gods to delay their cruel decree ('Io non chiedo'/'Grands dieux!'), is in several sections of contrasting tempos, beginning with a long phrase for solo oboe (recalling 'Che puro ciel' in *Orfeo ed Euridice* and anticipating 'O malheureuse Iphigénie' in *Iphigénie en Tauride*). An agitated Allegro follows in which Alcestis sings of her suffering; in the Italian version this incorporates a short duet for Alcestis's children. In the French version the children were reduced to non-singing roles and the aria was substantially shortened. In both, its impassioned ending leads into a repeat of the chorus 'Misero Admeto!'/'O malheureux Admète!' (with the words changed to 'Miseri figli' in the Italian version).

Alcestis now urges the people, in a recitative (no.13/11), to join her in the temple of Apollo to beg the gods for mercy. In the French version this leads to a repeat of 'O dieux! qu'allons-nous devenir?'; the Italian has the chorus's cries in recitative of 'Al tempio', followed by a poignant two-and-a-half bars for two oboes linking the recitative to a repeat of the chorus 'Ah di questo afflitto regno', which this time ends with the contrapuntal section used in the French version.

I.iii (I, F) The temple of Apollo with a huge statue of the god in the middle A slow pantomime covers the change of scene; low divided flutes and first violins play one of Gluck's most sublime melodies as priests, priestesses and people process into the temple. The three trombones, whose solemn colours were prominent in the overture and in the choruses of the Italian version, are heard again as the High Priest begins his prayer (no.16/14). A chorus led by the High Priest restores the anguished mood of scene i, accompanied by trombones and with agitated rhythms in wind and strings. As in scene i, the repetition of choruses is an important part of the structure.

I.iv (I, F) Alcestis asks the god to accept her offerings and prayers. A repeat of the preceding chorus in the Italian version is replaced in the French by a chromatic pantomime to accompany the sacrifice (the dance from scene i of the Italian version, no.5). The High Priest, in a recitative (no.24/22) largely built from an arpeggio figure hammered out in octaves at the start, tells Alcestis that Apollo hears her prayers and receives her gifts favourably, and exhorts everyone to listen to the Oracle. The Oracle pronounces that Admetus will die that day unless another dies for him; the soft accompaniment of slow-moving trombones, woodwind and muted strings is, in the French version, a variation on the choral outburst at the end of the overture. The astonished people give vent to their terror; in the Italian version this chorus is animated by an offstage group of basses singing 'fuggiamo' ('let us flee') on a monotone, an effect Gluck removed when he adapted the opera for Paris. In the main Allegro Gluck gives a vivid impression of the frightened people fleeing in all directions, with disjointed musical fragments repeated again and again, gradually dying away to *pianissimo*.

I.v (I), v–vii (F) Alcestis, left alone (in the French version; with her two children in the Italian), resolves to die for Admetus so that the people can retain their king. Then comes the first of the major differences between the two versions. So far, the Italian has been the longer; but here the French version is expanded. Alcestis's resolution takes place in a lengthy recitative in the original; in the French, a much shorter recitative is followed by an air, 'Non, ce n'est point un sacrifice', where Alcestis declares that she could not live without Admetus: to die that he may live is no sacrifice. The refrain alternates with expressions of her sorrow at leaving her husband and children. After a short arioso ('Arbitres du sort des humains'), the High Priest reappears to tell Alcestis that her destiny is decided and that the spirits of the underworld are awaiting her (air, 'Déjà la mort s'apprête'). Alone, Alcestis sings an air of defiance ('Ombre, larve'/'Divinités du Styx'). The trombones, the deliberate arpeggios in the bass and the syncopated rhythms in the upper strings urge on this mighty rondo, which provides a powerful conclusion to Act 1 of the French revision.

I.vi (I) In the original, when the aria is over, Alcestis is joined by Evander and Ismene, who tell her to hurry to the palace if she wants to see her husband alive – he is close to death, and calling for her. The priests and people gather round Evander and Ismene and the ensemble and chorus reveal that all are afraid to die to save Admetus (Alcestis has not informed anyone of her resolve to take his place, as she has in the French version). The act ends with a lively, almost frivolous chorus in which the people sing that the gods ask too much but that rulers and subjects alike must endure suffering.

Act 2.i (I) A dense forest sacred to the gods of the

underworld; night Ismene asks Alcestis why she is leaving her dying husband to go to the forest and abandon herself to grief (this recitative begins with the restless chromatic figure for low violins which Gluck was to use in the underworld scene of the French version; compare no.32 with no.*64*). Alcestis tells Ismene to leave her, but first Ismene begs Alcestis to tell her what she is hiding (Gluck also used this music in the French version, for no.*29*, the High Priest's air).

2.ii *(I)* Alone, Alcestis is terrified by the darkness and silence and the hoarse cries of a night-bird (semiquaver triplets on the first violins, minor 3rd cries on chalumeaux and bassoons); calling to the Lord of the Underworld, she is answered by the slow, bass voice of the Infernal Deity. She gives vent to her agitation (aria, 'Chi mi parla?'), with her music echoed by the woodwind and obsessive triplets in the strings.

This leads into another choral tableau, of invisible infernal deities: 'E vuoi morire' (the basses sing on a monotone while the orchestra weaves chromatic lines above them). Rushing string scales and calls on horns and trombones (no.40) introduce a short aria for an infernal deity, calling her to the underworld. But Alcestis begs to return to the palace to bid her husband and children farewell. The tenderness of her aria, 'Non vi turbate, no', with its sighing phrases, muted strings and prominent english horns, surely reflects her words, 'I will die of love and happiness'. A solemn pantomime of gods of the underworld ends the scene.

2.iii *(I), i (F) A room in the palace of Admetus* In the Italian version, to the first truly joyful music of the opera, the people celebrate the miraculous recovery of their king (chorus, 'Dal lieto soggiorno', followed by a dance, an aria for Evander, another dance and a reprise of the chorus). The French version opens with a different chorus, 'Que les plus doux transports', telling how joy follows unhappiness and how the gods have changed the Thessalians' misfortunes, in a lively 6/8 with solos; then follows a celebratory *divertissement* on an expanded scale, with five dances and a reprise of the chorus.

2.iv *(I), ii (F)* Admetus expresses his astonishment at his recovery and elicits from Evander the news of the Oracle's pronouncement, supposing that some unknown subject has given up his life to save him. In the French version this is followed by another celebratory chorus, richly scored, rather like a minuet ('Vivez, aimez les jours dignes d'envie').

2.v *(I), iii (F)* Admetus and Alcestis are now reunited. In the Italian version, Admetus inquires why she is so sad. Most of their dialogue is in recitative, but there is a short, anguished duet ('Ah perchè con quelle lagrime'); eventually Alcestis reveals that it is she who is to die for him. The

recitative moves to a frenzied *presto* as the distraught Admetus tells Alcestis he will not accept her gift and will go to the temple to question the Oracle. Admetus proclaims his hatred of the heavens, the world and himself before plunging into an aria of despair, full of chromatic harmony and anguished leaps ('No, crudel, non posso vivere').

The equivalent scene in the French revision makes characteristic use of tragic irony as the dialogue for Admetus and Alcestis is punctuated by choruses and dances celebrating Admetus's return to health. These include the chorus which began the celebratory scene in the Italian original, 'Dal lieto soggiorno', as 'Livrons-nous à l'allégresse', and, with Alcestis's grief-stricken aside, the delightful chorus and dance 'Parez vos fronts de fleurs nouvelles' with its vocal solos and pizzicato accompaniment. Within this chorus Alcestis sings a moving lament ('O dieux! soutenez mon courage!'); it is akin to an instrumental piece with a subsidiary vocal part as flute and violas weave their desolate melody. Admetus, puzzled at her distress, tries to console her: 'Bannis la crainte et les alarmes' (the only da capo aria in the opera). This is more dramatic than the frenzied questioning in the corresponding scene in the Italian original, but when Admetus presses Alcestis for an answer (no.*15*) she sings a deceptively simple air in the manner of *Iphigénie en Aulide*: 'Je n'ai jamais chéri la vie', at once deceiving her husband by reassuring him that she lives only to love him, but also telling him the truth ('Je t'aimerai jusqu'au trépas, jusque dans la nuit éternelle': 'I will love you even to death, right up to eternal night' – an augmented sixth and a slower speed emphasize these words). Eventually Alcestis reveals that it is she who will die; the chorus breaks in with a cry of anguish on a repeated diminished seventh chord (as at the end of the overture); Admetus rages against the gods' cruelty, culminating in his air, 'Barbare! non, sans toi je ne puis vivre' (a revision of his aria at the corresponding point in the original). Before Admetus leaves, Alcestis interrupts briefly with a falling four-note scale figure, like a leitmotif for her in the French version.

2.vi *(I), iv (F)* Alcestis, growing weaker, asks Ismene to prepare her for making her final offerings to the gods. 'Oh come rapida nel suo bel fiore', Ismene sings, her lament taken up by the chorus (no.55), to begin another of Gluck's characteristic tableaux: this sombre F minor music with homophonic choral writing and falling orchestral figures alternates with another F minor chorus, led by Ismene ('Così bella! così giovane!'). In between come a recitative and two short arias, both for Alcestis, richly scored with pairs of chalumeaux, english horns, trombones and strings: in the first she prays to the goddess Vesta to look after her children, and in the second says that no new wife to Admetus could be more loving or faithful than her. After she has bidden her children farewell (they have a short duet), Alcestis sings an aria, 'Ah per questo', which again has an eloquent introduction for oboe before she gives expression to her emotions, especially (as the poignant final 6/8 section makes clear) her anguish at being parted from her children.

In the French revision, this scene is contracted to a single statement of the 'Così bella!' chorus (now 'Tant de graces') and two of the 'Oh come rapida' one ('Oh, que le songe de la vie'). The intervening material is cut too, except Alcestis's air 'Ah per questo' (now 'Ah, malgré moi', with solo flute rather than oboe). The fast part of this air is repeated after 'Oh, que le songe' and heard again to end the act with the same music that concluded Act 2 of the Italian original. The cuts reduce this final scene to seven musical numbers in the French version as opposed to the 13 of the original.

In Act 3 the differences are so extensive, with the order of events changed, that the two versions require separate discussion.

Act 3.i *(I) A large, open-air entrance hall of Admetus's palace, decorated with statues and trophies* Admetus has returned from the temple; in a recitative (first *secco*, later orchestral) he tells Evander of the Oracle's edict: Alcestis must die if Admetus is to live. He gives vent to his sorrow in an aria, 'Misero! E che farò!', his agitation expressed both in the semiquaver arpeggios in the second violins, the plangent oboes doubling the voice and the doleful bassoons imitating it. Finally it moves into passionate accompanied recitative: 'O Alceste, o figli, o divisione! O morte!'

3.ii *(I)* The music changes from anguished minor to radiant major as Alcestis enters with her children and Ismene to bid him a final farewell; her noble resignation and calmness contrast with Admetus's impatient dotted rhythms (duet, 'Cari figli, ah! non piangete'). The gods of the underworld come to claim Alcestis. An ensemble, for Ismene, Evander, Admetus, Aspasia and Eumelus, begins with a sinister octave G♭, like the sounding of a death-knell; tremolandos, falling chromatic figures and diminished seventh chords abound as they cry out in horror. The infernal deities remind Alcestis of her promise in a chorus in octaves reminiscent of those for the Furies in Act 2 of *Orfeo*; Admetus begs them to take him too, but in vain. An infernal deity orders Alcestis to follow them; she dies and is taken away by the gods of the underworld.

3.iii *(I)* A brief Lento, 'a sinfonia expressing terror and dismay', introduces a great scene of mourning. Ismene, Evander and the courtiers lament Alcestis's death in a massive tableau in which short duets and arias alternate with four statements of the chorus of lamentation, 'Piangi o patria, o Tessaglia'.

3.iv *(I)* Admetus bursts in, angry that the courtiers have disarmed him and prevented him from killing himself. He is reminded of his duty to his kingdom and his children, but can think of nothing but his dead wife.

3.v *(I)* String scales and flashes of lightning announce the arrival of Apollo. He and Alcestis appear on clouds, and in a simple, succinct scene Apollo restores Alcestis to life and to her husband: the gods have taken pity on them. The opera ends with a lively chorus of rejoicing in praise of Alcestis ('Regna a noi con lieta sorte').

Act 3.i *(F) A courtyard surrounded by colonnades in Admetus's palace* Evander and a female chorus leader sing a short lament for Alcestis ('Nous ne pouvons trop répandre des larmes'): this begins in F minor, with sighing phrases on oboes and violins, and a chromatically descending bass, continuing the mood and key of the end of the preceding act, as does the following chorus 'Pleure, ô patrie!' (a revision of no.79, 'Piangi o patria', in Act 3 of the original; much of this scene is based on the corresponding one in the Italian version). The translation of this chorus, 'Alcestis is going to die', points up an important difference between the two operas: in the original this scene of mourning takes place after she has actually died, but in the revision it precedes her confrontation with the spirits of the underworld.

3.ii *(F)* After this sombre C minor chorus, bustling wind and strings in E♭ major introduce a character new to the revision, Hercules. As in the Euripides original, Hercules happens to visit his friend Admetus to find the court in mourning for Alcestis. Hercules' recitative is interrupted by the astonished and delighted shout of the people at his arrival. Evander and the chorus-leader tell him what has happened; Hercules assures them he will bring back Alcestis from the underworld, expressing his strength and determination in a march-like air in A major with dotted rhythms, high horns and short, repeated melodic lines ('C'est en vain que l'enfer compte sur sa victime'). As in Euripides, Hercules is a grotesquely comic character, a foil lacking for the tragedy of the Italian original.

3.iii *(F) The entrance to the underworld; a ravaged scene with rocks, fallen trees and a gaping cavern, out of which smoke billows, with the altar of death visible on one side, adorned with a scythe; the light gradually dies* The first part of this scene is based on Act 2 scenes i and ii and Act 3 scene ii of the Italian original, beginning with the music that began Act 2 as Alcestis enters and is terrified by the place and what she has to do. The sinister night-bird of the original (Act 2 scene ii) is heard, Alcestis's fear and breathlessness here enhanced by a trembling rhythmic figure (three quavers and a quaver rest).

The voices of the gods of the underworld now call her, with their implacable repeated monotone

'Malheureuse, où vas-tu?' (no.*65*, based on no.35 of the original with the addition of parts for tenors and altos, and the more sombre clarinets replacing oboes; it is only heard once here, though twice in the original). It is followed by Alcestis's air 'Ah, divinités implacables!', an adaptation of 'Non vi turbate, no' of the original (Act 2 scene ii); Gluck changed it into a French air in two parts, each repeated, adding a G minor modulation in the second, making an even more poignant contrast, its F major following the bleak F minor of the chorus.

3.iv *(F)* Admetus appears (as in Act 2 scene v of the original, albeit in less congenial surroundings); he has followed Alcestis, determined to persuade her to live or else to die with her. Her response is one of the loveliest additions to the original, a short (13-bar) air, 'Vis pour garder le souvenir d'une épouse qui te fut chère', where pizzicato outer strings accompany the divided violas, the upper part doubling Alcestis's line. Admetus responds with the tormented air 'Alceste, au nom des dieux!' (an adaptation of his aria no.68, in Act 3 scene i of the original), making more dramatic effect as he addresses Alcestis rather than Evander. There Admetus interrupted the air; here it is Alcestis (as earlier, in 'Barbare! non sans toi'); again we hear her four-note descending scale at the beginning of the recitative, and tension increases in their duet, 'Aux cris de la douleur', emphasizing their mutual love and its betrayal rather than their children as in the original. This leads to the air for the infernal deity (no.73, reworked from no.40 in the original). A chorus of infernal deities follows (the ensemble for Ismene, Evander and Admetus in Act 3 scene ii of the original, no.72, with the vocal parts adjusted); it leads, via Alcestis's four-note falling figure ('Adieu, cher époux'), to Admetus's raging against the obdurate gods of the underworld who are taking away his wife ('Arrêtez! barbares déités!'), swearing he will follow them to Hades.

3.v *(F)* But that is not necessary, because Hercules appears, to universal astonishment, and charges off after the gods of the underworld. The music rushes on into the next number, where he fights the infernal deities (this is new material written for the French revision); rushing scales and repeated notes depict him setting about his victims with his club while Admetus provides an excited commentary including frequent exclamations of encouragement. Hercules' victory is announced as the infernal deities, reduced to a shocked *pianissimo*, in a sudden move to C major accompanied by pulsating strings, sing 'Notre fureur est vaine, cédons à sa valeur'; Hercules brings back Alcestis and presents her to Admetus.

3.vi *(F)* Apollo now appears; this is not essential to the drama in its revised form, but since Hercules' restoration of Alcestis would appear to go against the gods' decree, his appearance sanctions Hercules' action.

3.vii–ix *(F) A courtyard in Admetus's palace, thronging with people* The denouement is quite succinct, but it is expanded by Apollo's address to the Thessalian people, praising their devotion to their monarch, and a trio in praise of him for Alcestis, Admetus and Hercules, 'Reçois, dieu bienfaisant', which musically harks back to the mood of the celebratory numbers in Act 2. In a brief recitative Admetus, Alcestis and the chorus express their joy, Admetus singing similar words and identical music to that with which he made his first entry in this version of the opera (Act 2 scene ii). The final chorus comes from the end of Act 1 in the original; here it seems better placed.

The final *divertissement* is one of the largest in a Gluck opera. Of its six movements, three are known to be by Gluck: the Marche (no.*86*), the Andante with its flute solo reminiscent of the Dance of the Blessed Spirits from *Orphée et Eurydice* (no.*87*), and the lengthy concluding Chaconne (no.*90*). The others may be in whole or part by Gossec, bearing in mind Gluck's comment in a letter of 30 June 1776 concerning the work's publication: 'You can leave the opera as it stands; the little that Mr Gossec may have done for it can be of no consequence. This will make the opera no better and no worse, because it is the end of it'.

∗

The two versions of *Alceste*, it will be clear, are in effect distinct operas, with distinct merits; unlike Gluck's Orpheus operas they are so different as to preclude a 'best of both worlds' solution by incorporating music from one into the other. That is in any case unnecessary, because the French revision retains virtually all the best music of the Italian original and adds much more. The only music whose omission might give cause for regret is the marvellously expressive ensemble with chorus near the end of Act 1, 'E non s'offerse', Alcestis's richly scored arias in Act 2 (nos.58 and 60) and the almost Berliozian *introduzione* in Act 3 (no.77).

When he came to revise *Alceste* for Paris, Gluck took a different, more sophisticated and French-influenced view of the theatre. The original is to some extent hampered by its sheer size. The huge choral tableaux go a stage further than those in *Orfeo*; there the chorus comments on events rather in the manner of a Greek chorus, whereas in *Alceste* it assumes a character of its own – as the people of Thessaly, whose well-being depends on their king. Gluck's huge, monumental choral tableaux in the Italian version, although strikingly original as well as powerfully constructed, can with their sheer massiveness and their use of repeated sections seem static and unwieldy. There are far fewer repetitions of choruses in the French revision, and this greater concision leads to a more taut drama.

While due allowance has to be made for the different traditions – *opera seria* and *tragédie lyrique* – from which the works spring, the two principal characters emerge with greater humanity in the revised version. Arguably, Calzabigi went too far in his libretto in his quest for the 'beautiful simplicity' and 'strong passions' cited in his preface. The result is that the plot is basically reduced to a single incident – Alcestis's self-sacrifice – which is expressed in a language colder and more rhetorical than the passionate language of Calzabigi's two other reform operas. Further, the tension may flag after the dramatic climax of the opera in Act 2 scene ii; in his revision Roullet maintains it with his rearrangement of the order of events in Acts 2 and 3 and his postponement of the climax to Hercules' defeat of the infernal deities in Act 3 scene v. In tune with the changing times, and with French attitudes as opposed to Italian, Roullet's characters are today the more credible and sympathetic, and the relationship between Alcestis and Admetus (and their desire to die for each other rather than for their people) is expressed in more human terms. Admetus is more central, and Alcestis is transformed from a rather stiff and formal queen to a real wife, one of Gluck's greatest creations.

The revision focusses more strongly on the central drama by decreasing the role of the confidants; but it also introduces a new character, Hercules. The way in which he is introduced (not until Act 3, as a *homo ex machina*) and his music have been the subject of adverse criticism; but by restoring Hercules, so central and crucial in the Euripides original, Roullet and Gluck found an ideal foil for the predominant gloom of the rest of the tragedy.

The recitative in the French *Alceste* is orchestral throughout, like that in all French opera of the time and in *Orfeo ed Euridice*; why *secco* recitative occasionally appears in the Italian version – bearing in mind Gluck and Calzabigi's explicit renunciation of it in the preface – is a mystery. In spite of, or perhaps partially as a result of, the cuts, particularly in the choral scenes, the revised *Alceste* has a more continuous and fluid texture than the original; successive numbers often merge in structures more flexible than those of the more formal Italian original.

That is not to denigrate the boldness and power of what was in many ways Gluck's grandest conception. Had Gluck never revised his Italian *Alceste*, it would still be viewed as a great, if flawed, opera, but any comparisons with the French revision reflect favourably on the latter, which is a distillation of all that was best in the original, balanced by Gluck's increased musical and dramatic powers.   J.H.

Alcina

Opera in three acts by George Frideric Handel to an anonymous libretto after Cantos vi and vii of Ludovico Ariosto's *Orlando furioso*, adapted from the libretto for Riccardo Broschi's *L'isola di Alcina* (1728, Rome); London, Covent Garden Theatre, 16 April 1735.

The title role was sung at the première by Anna Maria Strada del Pò, Ruggiero by the celebrated castrato Giovanni Carestini; John Beard, at the start of a long career, sang Oronte, and the talented William Savage (then a boy treble, later a bass) Oberto.

Alcina *a sorceress*	soprano
Morgana *her sister*	soprano
Ruggiero *a knight*	alto castrato
Bradamante	contralto
Melisso *her governor*	bass
Oronte *Alcina's general*	tenor
Oberto	treble
Setting Alcina's magic island	

Handel composed *Alcina* in the early months of 1735 while presenting his first season at John Rich's newly built theatre at Covent Garden (the last page of the autograph score is dated 8 April 1735, eight days before the first performance). The rivalry which had developed in 1733 between Handel and a new company with powerful support, the 'Opera of the Nobility', was by now intense. The role of Oberto, which does not appear in the source libretto, seems to have been created specifically for Savage: the scenes involving him are all late additions. In common with Handel's other operatic productions in the same season (notably *Ariodante*) the opera contains dance sequences (originally performed by the French dancer Marie Sallé and her company, an added attraction on the operatic warfare under way) and choruses. Though these features show the influence of the French opera of the period, the customary predominance of da capo arias and the general structure of the opera place *Alcina* firmly in the Italian *opera seria* tradition.

In 1735 *Alcina* achieved a good run of 18 performances up to 2 July, the end of the season. Handel revived it in shortened form (without the dances) for three performances at the start of his 1736–7 season at Covent Garden (opening on 6 November 1736) and gave two further performances (when arias from *Arianna* and *Admeto* were added) on 10 and 21 June 1737. There were two revivals of *Alcina* in Brunswick in 1738. The first modern revival was in Leipzig on 14 June 1928. In Britain the work was revived by the Handel Opera Society at St Pancras Town Hall on 19 March 1957; Joan

Sutherland's singing of the title role in that and in Zeffirelli's production of 1960 for Venice (also given in Dallas and London) did much to establish the opera in the modern operatic repertory.

*

Act I The sorceress Alcina lures heroes to her enchanted island and, when she has tired of them, transforms them into rocks, streams, trees or wild beasts. Her latest captive is the knight Ruggiero, as yet untransformed. The opera begins with the arrival on the island of Ruggiero's betrothed, Bradamante, and her governor Melisso; Bradamante is disguised as her brother Ricciardo. The newcomers are met by Alcina's sister Morgana, who immediately begins to flirt with 'Ricciardo'. She brings them to Alcina's palace, where they find Ruggiero wholly captivated by Alcina and living a life of voluptuous luxury. He has no memory of his vows to Bradamante. Also on the island is the boy Oberto, searching for his father Astolfo. Bradamante and Melisso, realizing that Astolfo has been transformed by Alcina, evade the boy's questions. Alcina's general Oronte, who loves Morgana, is annoyed at Morgana's interest in 'Ricciardo'; Ruggiero is equally concerned that he may lose Alcina to 'Ricciardo'. Oronte warns him of the fate of Alcina's former lovers. Ruggiero, seeing no danger to himself, decides to persuade Alcina to transform 'Ricciardo'. Morgana warns 'Ricciardo' of this plan and openly declares her love for 'him'.

Act 2 Melisso appears to Ruggiero as his old tutor Atlante and by use of a magic ring displays Alcina's island as in reality a barren desert. On Melisso's instructions Ruggiero obtains leave from Alcina to go hunting. Oberto appears again, and is assured by Alcina that he will soon see his father. Oronte brings news that Ruggiero has fled, leaving Alcina distraught and vengeful. Ruggiero, restored to his senses, finally recognizes Bradamante and they resolve to defeat Alcina together. Morgana, overhearing them and now realizing the truth about 'Ricciardo', flies to warn her sister as Ruggiero bids a resigned farewell to the illusory beauty of the island. Alcina, alone in a subterranean cavern, calls on her spirits to prevent Ruggiero's flight, but because of the magic ring they refuse to obey her. She laments the loss of her powers. As she leaves spectres appear and dance.

Act 3 Oronte pretends to be indifferent to Morgana, thus prompting her to confess her love for him, now reawakened. Alcina confronts Ruggiero and finds him resolute in his love for Bradamante: she vows vengeance, but will forgive him if he returns to her. Oronte reports to Alcina that her warriors have been rendered powerless. Oberto's cheerful expectation of finding his father annoys the sorceress: she gives him a spear and orders

him to kill a lion with it, but Oberto recognizes the features of his father in the friendly beast and threatens Alcina instead. Ruggiero rejects Alcina's renewed pleas and obtains Oronte's support by offering him a sword and his freedom. Alcina and Morgana make a final appeal for mercy, but Ruggiero shatters the urn that holds the source of Alcina's magic powers and she vanishes with Morgana. The transformed heroes return to their true forms: among them is Astolfo, reunited with Oberto. All rejoice at their release.

*

Alcina is one of the greatest and most popular of Handel's operas, thanks to the rich and expansive invention of the music, the emotional range and power demanded from the singers of the two leading roles (especially Alcina herself) and the fantasy of the story (inviting a variety of allegorical interpretations). The title role includes three deeply felt minor-key arias, 'Ah! mio cor', 'Ombre pallide' and 'Mi restano le lagrime' – the second forming the climax of an extraordinary scene ('Ah! Ruggiero crudel') at the end of Act 2, in which Alcina's despair at the loss of her powers is conveyed by music of disturbing instability. Ruggiero's farewell to Alcina's island, 'Verdi prati', expresses yearning nostalgia with a melody of deceptive simplicity – according to Burney, Carestini at first refused to sing it and earned Handel's wrath – and his final resumption of true heroic status is aptly marked with the aria 'Sta nell'Ircana', a virtuoso piece in the fashionable 'Neapolitan' style with ringing high horns in the accompaniment. Bradamante's arias are also brilliant, portraying the doughty warrior maiden – except for her last, when she has abandoned her disguise and can sing with womanly warmth. Morgana's role includes the delectably seductive aria 'Tornami a vagghegiar', elaborated from an aria in Handel's early cantata *O come chiare e belle*; in 1736 Handel transferred it to Alcina – an unhappy translation, which some modern-day Alcinas have been too ready to adopt. All the minor roles are generously endowed with arias of high quality, and the dance music is delightful.   A.H.

Amahl and the Night Visitors

Opera for television in one act by Gian Carlo Menotti to his own libretto; NBC, New York, 24 December 1951.

The original cast featured Rosemary Kuhlmann (the Mother)and Chet Allen (Amahl), with Andrew McKinley (Kaspar), David Aiken (Melchior) and Leon Lishner (Balthazar). The conductor was Thomas Schippers.

Set design by Eugene Berman for Menotti's 'Amahl and the Night Visitors': ink and watercolour drawing dated 1952 and
dedicated to Thomas Schippers who conducted the original production

Amahl		boy soprano
His Mother		soprano
Kaspar		tenor
Melchior	*the Three Kings*	baritone
Balthazar		bass
Page		baritone
Shepherds, dancers, villagers		

Amahl was the first opera written expressly for
American television. The head of the NBC Opera
Company, Samuel Chotzinoff, suggested that NBC
commission Menotti, but at first he seemed not very
interested in the idea and it lay dormant for several
years. A visit to the Metropolitan Museum of Art
brought inspiration, when he was deeply impressed
by *The Adoration of the Magi* by the Flemish
Renaissance artist Hieronymus Bosch. He began the
opera only weeks before the scheduled broadcast on
Christmas Eve 1951, and rehearsals were begun
before the score was completed. A great success, it
was for years transmitted every Christmas Eve.

*

The stage is in two parts. One is the stark interior
of a shepherd's hut; surrounding it is the exterior
showing distant hills, a road winding off stage to the
left and reappearing among the hills, and a starry sky
with the star of Bethlehem shining brightly. After a
very short prelude of soft, tender music Amahl, a boy
of about 12 years old who is crippled, is seen and
heard playing his shepherd's pipe (oboe) in a
cheerful C major tune. He is seated outside the hut
wearing an oversized cloak. His Mother calls him to
go to bed. He delays as long as possible but finally
takes his crutch and hobbles into the hut. He tells her
of the large bright star; she replies that he is a chronic
liar and complains of their poverty. Amahl begins a
short duet in which he comforts his Mother; it closes
with 'Good night'. While they sleep, he on a bed of
straw and she on a bench, the voices of the Three
Kings are heard in the distance. Amahl wakes up and
hobbles to the window. He tells his Mother that he
sees three kings and, of course, she does not believe
him. Eventually, after he has tried three times to tell
her, the Kings and a page are allowed in by the
bewildered Mother. They settle in, the Kings seated
on the bench and the page on a stool, to a stately but
sprightly march from the orchestra. Amahl starts to
ask them as many questions as he can think of.
During the following conversation there is a humorous song by Kaspar, 'This is my box'. He shows off
the precious gems in his box, but most important is
the liquorice. He gives some to Amahl. In staged
performances this song is often sung with Kaspar
walking among the audience tossing out sweets.

Amahl goes to fetch the shepherds, while the Kings speak of the Child they seek, led by the star; Melchior begins a very moving quartet with the other two and the Mother. Immediately following the quiet close of the quartet the shepherds arrive to a joyful four-part chorus, bringing their simple gifts; they then perform a lively ballet. They depart on a quiet chorus of good night and farewell which fades into a return of the tender opening music of the opera. All sleep except the Mother, who is envying the Kings' riches. She thinks that they won't miss a little of it, and that her son's need is greater than the unknown Child's, but as she is about to take some she is caught by the page. The Kings are stunned and angry at first and Amahl reacts to seeing his Mother in the clutches of the page by beating him with his crutch. But Melchior forgives her in a beautiful aria accompanied by the tender opening music, and tells her to keep what she wants. She, repentant, refuses. As the Kings are about to leave Amahl offers them his crutch, that he made himself, to take to the Child: as he lifts it up a miracle occurs – he can walk! There is amazement and joy and Amahl dances around the room, then begins a lively quintet with the Kings and the page. They grant Amahl's request to go with them and take the crutch to the Child himself. The shepherds are heard in the distance singing of the dawn of peace. Amahl plays his shepherd's pipe as they leave, recapitulating his C major tune from the beginning which gradually fades to silence.

*

Amahl is scored for a small orchestra: two oboes and one each of flute, clarinet, bassoon, horn, trumpet, harp and piano, plus percussion and strings. This factor and the non-virtuoso vocal writing has allowed the work to be widely performed by non-professionals such as church, college and community opera groups. The music has tonal charm, is clearly diatonic and non-dissonant, and has many memorable melodies; choral sections form an important element. Menotti's sensitivity to his audience and his interest in the humanity of his characters contribute to the appeal of this most accessible of operas.

B.A.

Amore dei tre re, L' ('The Love of Three Kings')

Poema tragico in three acts by Italo Montemezzi to a libretto by Sem Benelli after his play; Milan, Teatro alla Scala, 10 April 1913.

The first cast included Nazzareno de Angelis (Archibaldo), Carlo Galeffi (Manfredo), Edoardo Ferrari-Fontana (Avito) and Luisa Villani (Fiora); the conductor was Tullio Serafin.

Baron Archibaldo	bass
Manfredo *his son*	baritone
Fiora *Manfredo's wife*	soprano
Avito *an Italian prince*	tenor
Flaminio *a guard*	tenor
People of the country	
Setting A remote castle in Italy in the Middle Ages	

The title refers to the love of the old chieftain for his son; of the son for his wife; and of the defeated prince, Avito, for the same woman. After the success of the first performance at La Scala, *L'amore dei tre re* was heard by Arturo Toscanini and Giulio Gatti-Casazza, who decided to stage it in New York; thus began the extraordinary worldwide rise of the opera, hailed on its appearance as one of the great masterpieces of the 20th century, equal to those of Debussy and Strauss.

*

The action takes place 40 years after a barbarian invasion. In the first act Baron Archibaldo, old and blind, is wandering restlessly around his castle at night, guided by Flaminio; he reflects on his heroic youth when he, a barbarian, had conquered Italy. His son Manfredo is away fighting, and Manfredo's young Italian wife Fiora has been left in the castle, where she meets her lover Avito, also an Italian, at night. Fiora and Avito were to have been married, but as part of the conquerors' policy of settlement she has been forced to marry Manfredo instead. Archibaldo guesses that Fiora and Avito have an adulterous relationship and interrogates her, but his blindness prevents him from discovering the truth and he has to repress his hatred of her. When Manfredo returns, innocently happy at seeing Fiora again, she receives him with cold courtesy.

In the second act Manfredo departs again, embittered and full of foreboding; he asks Fiora to climb to the top of the castle tower and send him on his way, waving a white scarf. Fiora, moved by her husband's goodness, promises to do so, but after he has left she is joined on the tower by Avito; she at first tries to repel his advances, but falls once more into his arms. Archibaldo arrives; Avito manages to avoid him, but the baron has heard his footsteps and insists that Fiora reveal the name of her lover. When she proudly refuses he strangles her just before Manfredo returns in haste, anxious that he can no longer see the scarf.

In the third act the people pay their respects to the dead Fiora in the castle crypt; when they leave, Avito enters and as he kisses his dead beloved he sways and falls. Manfredo appears and tells him that Archibaldo has sprinkled Fiora's lips with poison in order to discover the identity of her lover. Avito expires. But Manfredo does not wish for revenge; alone and in despair, he in turn kisses Fiora's lips. His old father gropes his way into the crypt and, hearing a groan, thinks he has caught the adulterer, but finds in his arms his dying son.

*

The story has clear echoes of *Tristan* in the lovers' rapturous desire for annihilation and in a structure centring on the great love duet of the second act, and of *Pelléas* in the presence of symbolist elements and the impersonality of three young people whose unwitting actions seem to be governed by a fatal destiny. Against them the powerful figure of the old blind baron stands out, struggling against his own physical impotence and providing the mainspring of the action (he is on stage at the end of each act). But there are also contrasting ethnic and moral elements, as the ferocity of the old barbarian is set against the nobility of the young Italians and the Italian-born Manfredo. The music is also affected by the two poles of Wagner and Debussy. The extraordinary density of the orchestral writing and the harmonic language suggest Wagner, notably when personalities and the relationships of the characters are depicted (for example the furious anger of Archibaldo and the inevitable chromatic writing of the love scenes), while Debussy is recalled in the enigmatic evocation of atmosphere and in the trance-like suspended sonorities (the text repeatedly refers to a dream state in which the characters move). The subtle orchestration is indebted to both composers.

The plot is advanced through dialogue: the 'hidden arias' typical of early 20th-century Italian opera occur only rarely (for Archibaldo at the beginning of the first act, for Manfredo at the beginning of the second), but the only relationships that are developed are those between the two lovers and between Fiora and Archibaldo. The character of Manfredo is hardly comprehensible, especially given the extreme brevity of the third act in which he might have been made the leading figure. There are leitmotifs of various kinds throughout the opera, some with a clear thematic outline such as those for the love between Fiora and Avito and for Archibaldo's ferocity, and others more allusive, such as the sequence of rhythmically irregular chords signalling the approach of the blind baron. The ostinato figures have an essential function. In some cases they have a precise meaning, such as the swift dactylic rhythm associated with barbarity, war and invasion; elsewhere they combine to form groups of suspended sonorities. The orchestration itself strongly underlines the meaning of the words and actions: a good example is provided by the sustained chords of pairs of woodwind linked to the cold courtesy with which Fiora addresses her husband.

Donald Grout described the work as 'without doubt the greatest Italian tragic opera since Verdi's *Otello*'. It was always more popular in the USA than in Europe, but like Montemezzi's other operas, it has in recent decades practically disappeared from the repertory, despite occasional revivals.   **L.Z.**

Andrea Chénier

Dramma istorico in four acts ('tableaux') by Umberto Giordano to a libretto by Luigi Illica; Milan, Teatro alla Scala, 28 March 1896.

The principals at the première were Giuseppe Borgatti (Chénier), then at the start of his career, Evelina Carrera (Maddalena) and Mario Sammarco (Gérard); the conductor was Rodolfo Ferrari.

Andrea Chénier *a poet*	tenor
Carlo Gérard *a servant, later a sans-culotte*	baritone
Maddalena de Coigny	soprano
Bersi *her maid, a mulatto*	mezzo-soprano
Madelon *an old woman*	mezzo-soprano
La Contessa de Coigny	mezzo-soprano
Roucher *a friend of Chénier*	bass/baritone
Pietro Fléville *a novelist*	bass/baritone
Fouquier Tinville *the Public Prosecutor*	bass/baritone
Mathieu *a sans-culotte*	baritone
An Incroyable	tenor
The Abbé *a poet*	tenor
Schmidt *a gaoler at St Lazare*	bass
Master of the Household	bass

Ladies, gentlemen, abbés, footmen, musicians, servants, pages, valets, shepherdesses, beggars, sans-culottes, the National Guard, soldiers of the Republic, gendarmes, shopkeepers

Setting In and around Paris, 1789–93

While still a student Giordano entered the competition held by the publisher Edoardo Sonzogno in 1889; his opera *Marina* was awarded sixth place (the winner was *Cavalleria rusticana*), but Sonzogno was sufficiently impressed to offer the young composer a commission, resulting in the successful *Mala vita* (1892), and a monthly retainer. On the failure of Giordano's next work Sonzogno decided to withdraw the stipend, but was persuaded otherwise by Alberto Franchetti. Illica's libretto, inspired by the life of the French poet André Chénier (1762–94), was ceded to Giordano in 1894 by Franchetti, for whom it was written. The opera was completed in mid-November the following year. After some hesitation it was accepted for performance at La Scala on the strong recommendation of Pietro Mascagni, and it proved the only success of a disastrous season given at that theatre under the management of Sonzogno, who excluded from the programme all works belonging to the rival firm of Ricordi. *Andrea Chénier* at once raised the composer to the front rank of the 'giovane scuola' ('young school'), along with Mascagni, Puccini and Leoncavallo. Today it remains the most widely performed of Giordano's operas, mainly as an effective vehicle for a star tenor. Borgatti owed to it the start of a notable Italian career. Outstanding exponents in recent times have included Franco Corelli and Placido Domingo.

*

Act I *A salon in the Château Coigny* Preparations are in hand for a party, viewed with disgust by Gérard. He inveighs against the idleness and cruelty of the aristocracy in whose service his aged father has slaved all his life as a gardener. The Countess enters and gives orders to the servants. With her are her daughter Maddalena and her maid, Bersi, who discuss clothes. Gérard, in spite of himself, nurses a hopeless passion for Maddalena. The guests begin to arrive; Fléville, the novelist, presents two friends, the Italian pianist Florinelli and the poet Andrea Chénier. They are joined by the Abbé; he brings the latest news from Paris, where revolution is in the air. The King has taken the advice of Necker and

summoned the Third Estate; the statue of Henri IV has been defaced by an unruly mob. To cheer the dejected company Fléville calls on the musicians to perform a madrigal to his own words, 'O pastorelle, addio'. Maddalena and her friends determine to tease Chénier out of his silence. Will he not recite a poem for them? He replies that poetry, like love, cannot be compelled; nonetheless he obliges with the Improvviso, 'Un dì all'azzurro spazio'. His love, he says, is the fair land of France, whose peasants are suffering while its clergy grows fat. The guests are offended; but the Countess begs their indulgence for a poet's wayward fancy. She commands a gavotte. But hardly has it begun when a lugubrious chant is heard from outside. Gérard comes in leading a crowd of beggars. Furious, the Countess orders them out of the house. Gérard's father goes on his knees to her; but his son raises him up, strips off his own livery and leads him and the beggars away. Recovering from a faint, the Countess declares herself totally bewildered – had she not always been generous to the poor? She bids the dance resume.

Act 2 *The Café Hottot, by the Pont de Peronnet* Three years have passed. Mathieu is present with a number of *sans-culottes* (republicans); Chénier sits at a table apart. Paper-boys announce the arrest of the King. Bersi arrives, followed by an Incroyable (dandy) whom she suspects of spying on her as an enemy of the Revolution. Accordingly she bursts out in its praise and joins in the cheers as a cartload of condemned prisoners passes by, to the strains of 'Ah, ça ira'. However, the Incroyable has seen her looking at Chénier and decides not to let her out of his sight. Roucher comes with a passport for Chénier, whom he advises to leave France with all speed. But Chénier has been intrigued by the receipt of letters written in a female hand and signed 'Hope'. A crowd gathers to watch the People's Representatives crossing the bridge. Among them the Incroyable notices Gérard, and draws him aside. From their conversation it appears that Gérard is in pursuit of Maddalena. The Incroyable promises to bring her to him that evening. Bersi now approaches Roucher; she has a message for Chénier: he must wait for 'Hope' at the nearby altar of Marat. She is overheard by the Incroyable. As Mathieu sings the *Carmagnole* a patrol passes by. Maddalena arrives, reveals her identity to Chénier and throws herself on his protection. The Incroyable goes off to summon Gérard. There follows a love duet between Maddalena and Chénier, 'Ecco l'altare', at the end of which Gérard appears. The two men, unaware of each other's identity, fight. Gérard, severely wounded, recognizes Chénier and tells him to save himself and protect Maddalena; when the *sans-culottes* return and ask him who his assailant was, Gérard professes ignorance.

Act 3 *The Hall of the Revolutionary Tribunal* To an

Gérard

Design for the costume of Gérard in an early (possibly the original) production of Giordano's 'Andrea Chénier' (1896)

assembled audience Mathieu declares that the country is in danger, threatened by rebellion from within and invasion from foreign powers. Gérard enters, to receive congratulations on his recovery. He calls on the women to give their sons and their jewelry to the nation. Old Madelon comes forward. Her son, she says, died fighting for his country; but she gladly offers her 15-year-old grandson to take his father's place. Much moved, the crowd disperse to the strains of the *Carmagnole*. Newspaper vendors proclaim the arrest of Andrea Chénier. The Incroyable assures Gérard that this will draw Maddalena into the trap. As he makes out the papers of accusation Gérard reflects in a famous monologue, 'Nemico della patria', that, once the slave of the aristocracy, he has now become a slave to his own passions. Maddalena is brought before him. To his ardent declaration of love she replies with an account of her miserable existence since her mother died and their castle was burnt, 'La mamma morta', until the voice of love bade her take heart and hope. Nonetheless she is prepared to yield to Gérard if she can thereby save Chénier's life. Deeply moved and remorseful, Gérard decides to defend his rival. The court assembles and the accused are led in, among them Chénier. Fouquier Tinville reads aloud the charges against him. Chénier stoutly defends himself as a patriot and a man of honour ('Sì, fui soldato'). Tinville calls for witnesses, whereupon Gérard springs up and insists that all his accusations were false. The court is astonished but resolved nonetheless on Chénier's execution.

Act 4 *The courtyard of the St Lazare prison* Chénier sits at a table, writing. Schmidt, the gaoler, admits Roucher, to whom Chénier reads his final poem, 'Come un bel dì di maggio', in which he compares the sunset of his life to that of a fine spring day. Roucher leaves; the distant voice of Mathieu can be heard singing the *Marseillaise*. Then Gérard is introduced together with Maddalena. She bribes the gaoler to allow her to take the place of one of the condemned. When Gérard has left, intending to intercede with Robespierre on the lovers' behalf, she and Chénier join in a heroic duet, 'Vicino a te s'acqueta', before being taken to the guillotine.

*

Like most *verismo* operas of the period *Andrea Chénier* has a loosely organized structure bound together by variegated orchestral figuration in which motifs, repeated at short range and in different keys, play a prominent part. Thematic recollection, however, is rare, being confined here to the final strain of Maddalena's 'La mamma morta'. The vocal delivery is naturalistic, freely mixing conversational, lyrical and declamatory elements. Solos and duets arise directly and without preparation from the dialogue and are rarely marked off by a full close. The

aristocratic ambience of Act 1 is conveyed by touches of period stylization such as the gavotte, while snatches of the *Carmagnole*, 'Ah, ça ira', and the *Marseillaise* evoke the atmosphere of the Revolution.   J.B.

Anna Bolena ('Anne Boleyn')

Tragedia lirica in two acts by Gaetano Donizetti to a libretto by Felice Romani after Ippolito Pindemonte's *Enrico VIII ossia Anna Bolena* and Alessandro Pepoli's *Anna Bolena*; Milan, Teatro Carcano, 26 December 1830.

Giuditta Pasta sang Anne and Giovanni Battista Rubini was Percy at the première; Jane was sung by Elisa Orlandi, King Henry by Filippo Galli.

Anna Bolena [Anne Boleyn]	soprano
Enrico [Henry] VIII	bass
Giovanna [Jane] Seymour *Anne's*	
lady-in-waiting	mezzo-soprano
Lord Rochefort *Anne's brother*	bass
Lord Percy	tenor
Smeton *musician*	mezzo-soprano
Hervey *court official*	tenor
Courtiers, soldiers, huntsmen	
Setting Windsor Castle and London in 1536	

This was Donizetti's first great international success, helped by the casting of Pasta and Rubini; it gave him his initial exposure to Paris and London audiences. With it he came into his own as a tragic composer. Immensely popular for almost half a century, the opera re-entered the modern repertory following a triumphant revival at La Scala with Callas in 1957. Since then the work has proved a favourite vehicle for such bel canto specialists as Joan Sutherland, Beverly Sills and Montserrat Caballé.

*

Anne is unhappy at the coolness of her husband King Henry towards her (cavatina, 'Come, innocente giovane'); indeed, his neglect of her also troubles Jane Seymour, who has yielded to the king's advances. In an interview with Henry, Jane is dismayed at his dark threats about Anne's future and upset at his talk of marriage to her while he is still Anne's husband. In their duet, 'Oh qual parlar', one of those powerful scenes of confrontation that are a Donizettian speciality, the composer modified the conventional structure inherited from Rossini in ways that underscore the conflict.

Rochefort, Anne's brother, is amazed to see Percy, her first love, returned from exile. Percy confides to Rochefort that he has heard rumours of Anne's distress, further admitting that his own life

*Giuditta Pasta in the title role of Donizetti's 'Anna Bolena'
(the mad scene in Act 2), which she created at the Teatro
Carcano, Milan, 26 December 1830: painting by Alexandre
Brülloff (1798–1877)*

has been a misery since he was separated from her.
Percy's entrance number takes the expected form of a
double aria, but the jagged melody of the cabaletta
with its daunting tessitura reveals at once his rash,
passionate nature. Henry appears with a hunting
party, having arranged Percy's return as a trap for
Anne, and is grimly amused at their emotion when
they meet again. The Larghetto of the quintet, 'Io
sentii sulla mia mano', with its canonic entrances, is
adapted from the *benedizione* in the opening scene of
Otto mesi in due ore of 1827.

Smeton, Anne's household musician and in love
with her, tries to return her miniature portrait, but he
is forced to hide when Rochefort persuades Anne
against her better judgment to admit Percy, who
pleads his love. Anne, distressed, begs him to find
another love. Their duet effectively mirrors the
shifting course of their feelings: hers, gradual loss of
composure; his, increasingly persuasive and desperate. Percy draws his sword to kill himself, whereupon Smeton rushes forward, just as Henry bursts in
and orders their arrest. Smeton, pleading Anne's
innocence, inadvertently drops the miniature at the
king's feet; Henry is enraged and Anne faints. The
sextet 'In quegli sguardi impresso', which develops
into a groundswell of emotion, shows Donizetti's
consummate skill at creating vocal ensembles that

expand in an apparently inevitable way the dramatic
tension of the moment. Protesting, Anne, Percy and
Smeton are led off.

In Act 2 Jane comes to Anne and tells her that the
king will spare her if she will confess to loving Percy.
When Jane allows that Henry loves another woman,
Anne demands to know her identity; unable to
restrain herself, Jane confesses. This powerful duet
moves ahead in a series of cogent solo passages, the
combination of voices being confined to the coda. At
Anne's trial Smeton lies and admits to being Anne's
lover, hoping to save her, but in fact he seals her fate.
Anne and Percy are summoned before the council.
Jane pleads with the king to spare Anne's life (aria,
'Per questa fiamma'). In the Tower, Percy urges
Rochefort to live (aria, 'Vivi tu'), but both refuse
clemency when they learn it does not extend to Anne.
In her cell, Anne's mind wanders as she recalls her
girlhood love for Percy (aria, 'Al dolce guidami castel
natio'). When cannons announce the king's new
marriage, Anne calls on heaven not to curse the royal
couple but to have mercy on them.

This final 20 minutes of *Anna Bolena* reveals for
the first time Donizetti's mature ability to flesh out an
aria-finale so that it provides the substance of a
gripping scene. After a fine F minor chorus ('Chi può
vederla'), Anne enters to a regal string prelude, with
which her appearance – clothes in disarray, her mind
unhinged – makes an ironic contrast. Her recitative
reflects her abruptly shifting moods, underpinning
them with short motivic ideas. Gradually she lapses
into nostalgia, thinking of Percy and the time they
first fell in love. An english horn introduces the
melody, later functioning as an obbligato to its
wistfully expansive measures. Unlike the slow
movements of Bellini's aria-finales, characteristically
ternary, Donizetti uses a binary form, each section
repeated and varied. After her fellow prisoners come
in, the transitional passage is expanded to include
what amounts to an extra little aria with *pertichini*,
scored for chamber orchestra, an exquisite variant of
the tune best known as 'Home, sweet home'. An
irruption of cannon and bells heralds the premature
marriage of Henry and Jane Seymour, producing a
shock that restores Anne's reason. Aware of her
desperate situation, she launches into her hard-
driving, wide-ranging cabaletta with its formidable
series of trills, granting her at the last a hysterical
apotheosis. Nothing Donizetti had done before
approaches the scope and multiform intensity of this
magnificent scene.

*

It was long a commonplace of criticism that with
Anna Bolena Donizetti at a single stroke emerged
from the shadow of Rossini into a more personal
style, yet one influenced by Bellini. Now, however,
thanks to our greater familiarity with the operas that

precede *Anna* in the Donizetti canon, this fallacious notion has been superseded by our understanding that it is, rather, a logical extension of directions that Donizetti had already explored. The part of the score that has been regarded as most 'Bellinian', Anne's Larghetto in the final scene, has on closer acquaintance turned out to be a reworking of an aria from Donizetti's first performed opera, *Enrico di Borgogna* of 1818 – seven years before the première of Bellini's first opera. The presence of other self-borrowings of material adapted from five of Donizetti's Neapolitan operas of the 1820s further strengthens the case that *Anna Bolena* is more a product of a self-motivated maturation than had been recognized.   **W.A.**

Arabella

Lyrische Komödie in three acts by Richard Strauss to a libretto by Hugo von Hofmannsthal; Dresden, Staatsoper, 1 July 1933.

The first Arabella was Viorica Ursuleac; Mandryka was sung by Alfred Jerger, with Margit Bokor as Zdenka and Friedrich Plaschke as Waldner (and Kurt Böhme, a future Waldner, as young Count Dominik).

Arabella	soprano
Zdenka *her sister*	soprano
Count Waldner *their father, a retired*	
cavalry officer	bass
Adelaide *their mother*	mezzo-soprano
Mandryka *a Croatian landowner*	baritone
Matteo *a young officer*	tenor
Count Elemer *one of Arabella's suitors*	tenor
Count Dominik *another*	baritone
Count Lamoral *a third*	bass
The Fiakermilli *belle of the*	
Coachmen's Ball	coloratura soprano
A Fortune-Teller	soprano
Welko, Djura, Jankel *Mandryka's*	
servants	spoken
Hotel Porter	spoken
A Chaperone, Three Card Players,	
a Doctor, a Waiter	silent
Coachmen, waiters, ball guests, hotel residents	
Setting Vienna in the 1860s, on Carnival Day	
(Shrove Tuesday)	

This opera was the last of the Hofmannsthal-Strauss collaborations: which fact is poignantly registered in the opera itself, not to its advantage. A few days after the writer had sent Strauss his final version of Act 1, his only son committed suicide, and within 36 hours Hofmannsthal himself suffered a fatal stroke. Out of respect, the grieving composer resolved to set both

the provisional draft of Act 2 and the still more tentative draft of Act 3 almost as they stood, though Act 1 – one of the best-made first acts in the repertory – had been the result of long and strenuous reworking by the partners. A certain diffuseness in the later acts is disguised by their best scenes (the betrothal duet and the final making-up) and sometimes also by performers who can make the most of their sympathetic characters even when the action limps. Despite a triumphal première, *Arabella* did not repeat the unassailable success of *Der Rosenkavalier*.

After their metaphysical excursions with *Die Frau ohne Schatten* and *Die ägyptische Helena*, they had agreed to try Viennese period-comedy again. Hofmannsthal proposed not one idea but two or three, to be woven together. The first was a 'psychological' sketch he had published in 1910 (subtitled 'Characters for an Unwritten Comedy') as *Lucidor* – the alias of Lucile, a 17-year-old tomboy in a youth's clothes, who befriends a rejected Slav suitor to her coquettish sister and falls in love with him, keeps him on hand by forging love-notes from 'Arabella', and at last impersonates her in bed with him. She would become our Zdenka/'Zdenko' in *Arabella*, bringing much of her doubtful family situation with her. The other, newer idea was to exploit a 19th-century Viennese institution, the annual *Fiakerball*, for picturesque effect. The *Fiaker* – coachmen, a robust Viennese clan – had been the colourful subjects of many an old play, including two by Mozart's librettist Emanuel Schikaneder. Though shy, anxious little Zdenka could not make a Strauss soprano lead, charming Arabella could, if sufficiently enhanced by a romantic-idealist dimension. Her transformation from seeming coquette to devout bride-to-be would become the heart of the drama; the original Slavonic swain would be split into two, the green-stick object of Zdenka's affection and a Croatian rough diamond who takes Arabella by surprise (though mysteriously foreseen). All the intrigues and misunderstandings could be arranged around the Coachmen's Ball, in a seedy, *déclassé* Vienna quite different from the imperial capital of *Rosenkavalier*.

As the opera grew, two flaws in the plan appeared. With the story newly adjusted – Arabella's betrothal above Zdenka's romantic deception – and elevated beyond mere operetta, the *Fiakerball* could add nothing but trivial colour, like the showy role of the 'Fiakermilli' herself. (Originally, Act 1 was to have introduced each of Arabella's vain suitors in his ludicrous ball-costume; in its final version only Elemer appears, and only to propose a sleigh-ride. Rather wildly, Strauss suggested inflating the ball itself with an expansive ballet on Balkan folk tunes, but Hofmannsthal was horrified.) Then the 'Lucidor' plot, *risqué* but touching, was not so easily relegated to the background. Strauss feared from the outset that the new Arabella-Mandryka 'drama' would make tame theatre, and though Zdenka's role dwindles after Act 1 to dramatic semaphoring the action still pivots upon her. The composer nurtured her so tenderly at the outset that he must surely have demanded more for her later had not fate abruptly withdrawn Hofmannsthal from further debate.

Scored for a normal Romantic-size orchestra (plus a fourth clarinet and Elemer's sleighbells), *Arabella* was dedicated to the conductor Fritz Busch and the première contracted to Dresden. When the time came, the Nazis had already had Busch sacked. The composer first insisted upon having him back, then threatened to withdraw the score; at last he agreed to fulfil the contract only with performers of his own choice, and so Clemens Krauss conducted his first Strauss première. Later Krauss would marry Ursuleac. In Vienna Lotte Lehmann had a greater success as the heroine. From the 1950s the fortunes of the opera waxed with a peerless central pair, Lisa Della Casa and Dietrich Fischer-Dieskau.

*

Act I *The drawing-room of the Waldners' smart hotel lodgings* While Zdenka, in her customary guise as a boy, 'Zdenko', fends off creditors at the door, her mother listens eagerly to the fortune-teller's obscure reading of Arabella's prospects from the cards. (As such prophecies go, this one proves remarkably accurate, and at suitable points Strauss insinuates some of the main themes to come.) We learn that only a rich marriage for Arabella can rescue the Waldner family from its straits, the chief cause of which is the Count's inveterate gambling, and that Zdenka's preferred boyish garb has been a lucky economy – dressing both of their daughters to a high social standard would have been ruinous. The ladies withdraw for further divination, and in a *prestissimo* monologue Zdenka worries that Arabella's rejected swain Matteo, her only friend, may become suicidal. Her fears are confirmed when he calls by (to a doleful little waltz): in the face of Arabella's rebuffs, he has begun to doubt 'her' precious letters and to despair. As he slips off, she swears to press his suit with her sister once more.

Arabella returns from a walk (the music, until now chromatic and volatile, settles into a warm, limpid F major) and is disappointed to learn that the fresh roses come merely from Matteo, not from the fur-coated stranger who watched her in the street with wide, serious eyes. Pleading vainly for her friend, Zdenka protests that she would rather be a 'boy' forever than an icy coquette like Arabella. Calmly and sweetly, Arabella explains ('Aber der Richtige') that she will recognize the Right One for her when he comes along – if there is one; but it is certainly not Matteo, nor perhaps any of the three

counts who are besieging her. Aside, Zdenka admits incomprehension, but is ready to do anything for her sister's happiness; their voices entwine in Strauss's most rapturous soprano duet (he adapted here one of the tunes he had found in a Balkan folksong collection).

Sleighbells herald Count Elemer, passionately overweening, who has won the toss to take Arabella for a ride today. She plays the tease, insists that 'Zdenko' must come along and sends Elemer downstairs to wait. As she goes to get ready, she espies the stranger again in the street below. The senior Waldners come in fantasizing about possible financial rescues; Waldner reveals that he has even sent Arabella's photograph to an old fellow-officer, rich, romantic Mandryka. No sooner has Adelaide drifted out than Count Mandryka himself is announced: not, however, the old Croatian friend, who has died, but his rustic-elegant nephew and heir (the stranger, of course – specified as 'no more than 35'). Bewitched by the photograph, he has sold a forest to make this trip and plead for Arabella's hand. He explains himself at length, with intense candour, and wins her father's heart by pressing a large loan upon him ('Teschek, bedien' dich!'). With an introduction promised for later, Mandryka leaves him alone and bedazzled.

Collecting himself, Waldner strolls grandly out to rejoin affluent society at the gambling tables. The worried 'Zdenko', still not dressed for the outing, promises Matteo that he will get another note from Arabella at the ball tonight. Her sister reappears to say that the horses are impatient. 'The horses – and your Elemer!' snaps Zdenka as she goes off. Arabella repeats 'Mein Elemer!' over a peculiar, deflating cadence: she resists the very idea, without knowing what she wants instead. Perhaps the stranger? – though surely he is a married man, and may never be seen again. In any case, she is about to be the carefree Queen of the *Fiakerball*; but then . . .? (Strauss demanded this rich closing soliloquy from Hofmannsthal; with a prominent solo viola the music draws earlier themes together, fluently and suggestively.) Zdenka returns, and they hurry off towards the sleighbells.

Act 2 *A public ballroom* Though the Coachmen's Ball is gaily under way, the curtain music is an elevated sigh of relief: with her mother, Arabella is descending the great staircase towards Mandryka and Waldner. For a moment she hesitates; then the introduction is briefly effected, and she and her exotic suitor feel their way towards their destined rapport. (Meanwhile counts Dominik and Lamoral, and later Elemer, in turn invite her to waltz, but are put off.) Cautiously coquettish, Arabella asks why he has come; Mandryka declares honestly what she already knows, and further that he is a widower with great possessions in his remote Austro-Hungarian province, where he hopes she will join him forever. He describes a village custom there in which a glass of water symbolizes a maiden's betrothal. They recognize each other as their longed-for partners, and unite in a rapt duet of mutual surrender (on another Balkan tune). Then Arabella begs liberty for the rest of the evening to say her maiden farewells – which she does, gracefully and irrevocably, to each of the disconcerted counts.

First the Fiakermilli, cued by Dominik, acclaims her as Queen of the Ball. During the subsequent chain of sub-*Rosenkavalier* waltzes not only does Arabella play out her tender goodbyes, but the desperate 'Zdenko' proffers secret hope to the amazed Matteo with the key to Arabella's bedroom, intending to be in there herself when he uses it. Their exchange is overheard by Mandryka, who is appalled by this unconventional 'farewell' and then frantic. Arabella has gone; he flirts drunkenly with the Fiakermilli, invites the whole company to be his guests, horrifies the Waldners with sarcastic gibes about their daughter's Viennese morals, and reels off home with them to ascertain the facts. The company toasts him cheerfully.

Act 3 *The main hall of the Waldners' hotel, late at night*
In Strauss's musical iconography, the long, unbridled orchestral prelude in E signifies Erotic Tumult, and the participants are identified by Zdenka's themes and an electrified version of Matteo's hesitation-waltz. (It carries no operatic conviction: nothing we have seen of those nervy adolescents fits the luxuriant passion represented in the music.) At curtain-rise Matteo, jacketless, is musing at the top of the hotel staircase, but retreats when the entry-bell rings. It is Arabella, reflecting (in folksong-style) upon her new life to come. Matteo reappears: he cannot understand why his bedded love of half an hour ago is 'returning' in cloak and ball-gown, and she is offended by his fond familiarity. As they dispute on the stairs Mandryka and the Waldners burst in, demanding explanations and heightening the confusion. Mandryka, bitterly disappointed, will not be taken for a fool; Arabella protests her innocence and requests corroboration from Matteo, who does the gentlemanly thing and lies – but after a tell-tale hesitation. Now everyone becomes furious, except some other hotel guests who arrive in their night-clothes to enjoy the show. Waldner challenges Mandryka to a duel.

Suddenly Zdenka rushes down in her negligée, ashamed and utterly distraught, on her way to drown herself in the Danube. While Arabella comforts her, all is revealed; Waldner is more relieved than shocked (unlike Adelaide), Matteo astounded but also excited, Mandryka overcome with guilt at doubting his beloved. The younger couple discover

themselves in love. Though Mandryka generously persuades Waldner to accept Matteo as a prospective son-in-law, Arabella retreats upstairs with tight-lipped dignity, merely asking for a glass of water to be brought to her. The onlookers go back to bed. Alone and abject, Mandryka curses his loutishness. – Then Arabella reappears above, and descends – to the staircase music that began Act 2, but brighter now in B major – bearing the glass of water. Pausing on the last step, she confesses her joy at finding him waiting ('Das war sehr gut, Mandryka'), for she knows still better now that he is the Right One. She ends her fervent testimony in E; Mandryka's full-hearted response comes in sturdy C major, and once he has drunk the water, smashed the glass and made a last plea ('Will you always remain what you are?' – 'I can't be anything else; you must take me as I am!') the opera flashes to a buoyant close in F.

*

The fact that Strauss broke off composing *Arabella* to re-write Mozart's *Idomeneo*, in 1930–31, may have betokened misgivings. Eventually he set the principals' heartfelt confessions searchingly and with grace, the provisional comic scenes in no better than routine style – Mandryka's drunken, stagy recoil, the Fiakermilli's yodelling, the farcical duel-of-honour – and did what he could with the meagre parts Hofmannsthal had sketched for Zdenka and her baffled Matteo. The story can seem over-stretched; many directors and conductors prefer some adaptation of the 'two-act version' which Strauss soon agreed to permit. The lusty closing chorus of Act 2 is cut to make an immediate transition to the Act 3 prelude. To save time some of the Fiakermilli's warblings may be stifled too, and usually the plot revelations of Act 3 are trimmed – often, sadly, at the cost of Zdenka's last intimate exchange with her sister. There is no 'right' solution. In abbreviated versions, however, the risk of romantic blandness that Strauss foresaw is real; and any principal pair engaging and subtle enough to scotch it could carry the fuller version just as well.

When *Arabella* makes its best overall impression, it is affectingly limpid. That is only in part because of the homely folktunes Strauss adapted for its central confessional scenes, reserving any chromatic turmoil for transient farce and melodrama (but for the overheated Act 3 prelude, the one place where the orchestra is given its head); and it would be tendentious to judge that he fell back on folk material because his own lyrical invention was drying up. Rather, he and Hofmannsthal had developed the structure of their opera – doubtless without intending it so – in the sentimental vein of late-Viennese operetta, quite distinct from Rossini or the younger Johann Strauss. Any repartee, suspense or strife in *Arabella* is relegated to mere by-play: it could have been shaped into musical numbers which advanced the action decisively, like almost every 'number' in their earlier operas, but there are none such here. Instead the musically expansive passages crystallize, make explicit, feelings which the action has already predicted, in line with the whimsically 'predestined' course of the story. They are serene apotheoses in which dramatic time is stretched or suspended, and they borrow their folksong-tinges to colour deeper instinctual motives than Viennese urbanity could capture. Arabella, too, like plucky little Zdenka, is a heroine to baffle and infuriate modern feminists: a spirited, confident mistress of her own fate, she chooses nevertheless to become an all-forgiving wife, in radiantly melting music. When faithfully sung in its dramatic context, the central submission-duet 'Und du wirst mein Gebieter sein' ('And you will be my master') commands sympathetic responses – tears of wishful recognition, for example – that transcend gender, political fashion and even common sense. **D.M.**

Ariadne auf Naxos ('Ariadne on Naxos')

Oper by Richard Strauss to a libretto by Hugo von Hofmannsthal, existing in two versions: '*Ariadne* I', in one act, to be played after a German version of Molière's *Le bourgeois gentilhomme*, and '*Ariadne* II', in a prologue and one act; I, Stuttgart, Hoftheater (Kleines Haus), 25 October 1912, and II, Vienna, Hofoper, 4 October 1916.

The singers at the première of the first version were Maria Jeritza (Ariadne), Margarethe Siems (Zerbinetta) and Hermann Jadlowker (Bacchus). Those in the première of the operatic two-act revision were Jeritza (once again), Selma Kurz (Zerbinetta), Béla von Környey (Bacchus), Lotte Lehmann (the Composer) and Hans Duhan (Harlequin and the Music-Master).

Prologue (II) and Opera (I, II)

The Prima Donna (later Ariadne)	soprano
The Tenor (later Bacchus)	tenor
Zerbinetta	coloratura soprano
Harlequin	baritone
Scaramuccio	tenor
Truffaldino	bass
Brighella	tenor

commedia dell'arte players

Prologue (II)

The Composer	mezzo-soprano
His Music-Master	baritone
The Dancing-Master	tenor
A Wigmaker	baritone
A Footman	bass
An Officer	tenor
The Major-Domo	spoken
Servants	

Opera (I, II)

Naiad	high soprano
Dryad	contralto
Echo	soprano

nymphs

Setting A large, under-furnished room in the house of a rich man (originally Molière's 'bourgeois gentilhomme' Monsieur Jourdain, but in the revised version an unseen, nameless Viennese *parvenu*), in which later the opera-within-the-opera will be performed

In early 1911, while *Der Rosenkavalier* – the first wholly purpose-built collaboration between Hofmannsthal and Strauss – enjoyed its triumphant first performances, ideas for three new projects came to them. One was to thank Max Reinhardt for his productions of Wilde's *Salomé* and Hofmannsthal's *Elektra* (which had inspired Strauss's third and fourth operas), and unofficially of *Der Rosenkavalier* itself, by turning a Molière comedy into a German words-and-music piece for his Berlin company. Another was for a half-hour chamber-opera on the Ariadne myth, in which *commedia dell'arte* characters would collide with 18th-century operatic stereotypes, and the third was for a 'sombre' but 'fantastic' opera *Das steinerne Herz*, after a fairy-tale by Wilhelm Hauff. This last would grow into *Die Frau ohne Schatten*; before that, however, the first two ideas coalesced into one project. The ironical-comical Ariadne miniature could serve as a closing *divertissement* for Molière's *Le bourgeois gentilhomme*, newly translated by Hofmannsthal, with room earlier in the play for scene music by Strauss. With Reinhardt's actors and with distinguished singers, it would make a gala performance.

As often during their partnership, the writer was more excited by his literary-dramatic idea than was Strauss by the prospect of composing it; but as usual, once the composer had warmed to his task the playing time stretched out far beyond their first intentions. For *Feuersnot* Strauss had already raided his 1900 sketches for *Die Insel Kythere*, a grand mock-Rococo ballet inspired (like Debussy's 1904 piano piece *L'isle joyeuse*, and later Poulenc) by Antoine Watteau's painting *L'embarquement pour Cythère*; now he drew upon it again, with better historical excuse, for two of the dances in the play and a main tune of Ariadne's aria (at 'Bald aber naht ein Bote'). Meanwhile Hofmannsthal became fascinated with his heroine, and rather against the grain of the original plan – *opera seria* pretensions subverted by down-to-earth comics – he elaborated her metaphysical plight to the point where Strauss begged to have her lines

Design by Ernst Stern for the original production of 'Ariadne auf Naxos' (Richard Strauss) which opened the Kleines Haus of the Hoftheater, Stuttgart, 25 October 1912

explained. Her climactic duologue with Bacchus swelled to Wagnerian scale, taxing Strauss's 36-strong band proportionately. In turn, the composer was adamant about giving their wryly pragmatic, promiscuous Zerbinetta a huge coloratura scena to vie with the *Lucia di Lammermoor* Mad Scene. Eventually the Molière play was compressed into two acts, each with a prelude and other musical numbers, and *Ariadne auf Naxos* became a long Act 3.

With the composer conducting, Reinhardt duly produced this Molière-Hofmannsthal-Strauss confabulation as *Der Bürger als Edelmann*, with his own Berlin troupe of actors. It had a mixed reception: respectful reviews, but discomfited factions in the audience wanting either less of the spoken acts or less of the expansive operatic one. Though the work was soon staged in several other cities, the cost of employing two different troupes discouraged revivals. The authors soon agreed upon a salvage operation.

A shortened *Ariadne* – with alterations notably to Zerbinetta's brilliant rondo and to the final scene (described below) – would now follow a new, operatic prologue-act. This would re-create the circumstances of the opera-within-the-opera as in *Der Bürger*, omitting Molière's 'bourgeois gentilhomme', Monsieur Jourdain, while of course retaining Hofmannsthal's new twist: the Master's

absurd command that the *commedia dell'arte* and the lofty *opera seria* be played simultaneously, so as to end in time for his firework display. Freshly developed characters would lend human interest to this Prologue – the young Composer of the opera-within-the-opera, falling victim to Zerbinetta's wily coquetry, and his protective Music-Master. Though Hofmannsthal, who imagined the Composer as a mature youth, was appalled at his becoming a mezzo breeches-role like the *Rosenkavalier* Octavian, Strauss retorted that any opera company could field an intelligent mezzo – and besides, there were already three tenors in the piece. The sympathy he felt for the beleaguered young artist may explain the intricate score he wrote for the prologue, where Hofmannsthal had expected (and doubtless wanted) little more than *recitativo secco*.

The 1916 two-act revision has been the established version of the opera ever since. In it Maria Ivogün, Adele Kern, Rita Streich, Erika Köth and Edita Gruberová have been famous Zerbinettas; Lotte Lehmann, Elisabeth Schumann and Sena Jurinac were much admired as the Composer (all sopranos, interestingly in the light of Strauss's comment above), and Ariadne has been memorably sung by Lehmann and by Elisabeth Schwarzkopf. It may still be argued that the original, longer *Ariadne* deserves reinstatement, with the new prologue or the old play-with-music. But Strauss wasted nothing: he licensed a revised *Bürger als Edelmann* theatre score without the *Ariadne* act (besides the Act 1 overture and the Act 2 prelude it includes pictorial dinner-music, songs and dances, some adapted from Lully), and also an orchestral suite extracted from it. All these alternatives count as belonging to his 'op.60'.

*

Prologue [*Ariadne II only*] The orchestral prelude in C, eager and volatile, shares only its key with the original *Bürger als Edelmann* overture. The latter had begun with sturdy mock-Baroque music for strings and continuo (i.e. pianoforte, prominent in all versions of op.60) – which returned with the smug *gentilhomme* himself to put an end to *Ariadne* I, thus setting wry quotation marks around the entire affair. But with Monsieur Jourdain expunged from the new libretto, *Ariadne* II needed a fresh start and a different conclusion: the new prelude is a candidly romantic potpourri of the best tunes, the Composer's new ones along with Bacchus-and-Ariadne's old ones and the Comedians' ditties – and the 'new' close would simply extend the D♭ raptures of the blessed pair, instead of putting them ironically in their place.

The stage and backstage area in the house of a rich Viennese The curtain rises to show the reverse side of a stage backcloth: anxious preparations for the rich man's post-prandial entertainment are under way. An overweening Major-Domo is telling the outraged Music-Master that immediately after *Ariadne*, his beloved pupil's *opera seria*, a vulgar *opera buffa* will be performed before the nine o'clock fireworks. As an officer thrusts his way into the dressing-room of Zerbinetta, star of the *commedia*, the young Composer arrives in hope of a last-moment rehearsal and hears the bad news. The Dancing-Master comments cynically, and the self-absorbed principals of both troupes preen and fret. The Major-Domo reappears with worse news still: to safeguard the timetable – and also to enliven the desert-isle *Ariadne* scene, which the Master thinks too mean for his status as grandee-host – he wants their shows played 'gleichzeitig', at the same time. That will involve severe cuts.

General horror soon gives way to canny professional reactions. Only the naive Composer tries to make a defiant stand. His guardian knows too well what the career cost of an angry withdrawal might be, and the Dancing-Master backs him up. The Ariadne-soprano and the Bacchus-tenor treacherously urge cuts in each other's roles. Zerbinetta sets out to extract the details of the *opera seria* from its author, charming him into compliance while calculating where her Comedians can best intervene. She is at least intrigued, though not remotely persuaded, by the impassioned metaphysical gloss he puts on

'*Ariadne auf Naxos*' (Richard Strauss): *final scene from the original production of the revised version (Hofoper, Vienna, 4 October 1916), with (left to right) Julius Betetto (Truffaldino), Georg Moisel (Brighella), Hermann Collos (Scaramuccio), Maria Jeritza (Ariadne), Bela von Környey (Bacchus), Charlotte Dahmen (Naiad), Hermine Kittel (Dryad), Selma Kurz (Zerbinetta) and Hans Duhan (Harlequin)*

the story. Ariadne, he explains, who gave Theseus the clue to the Labyrinth, is the archetype of a one-man woman. After Theseus abandons her on Naxos (never in fact a 'desert' island: it is the most fertile of the Cyclades) she gives herself up to Death, for whom later she happily mistakes the young god Bacchus, and is thereby 'transformed' and eternally fulfilled.

Until here, the music has been nervy, suggestive, bitty – unless in the hands of an *echt*-Straussian conductor who can make it seem a continuous web. As Zerbinetta teases the Composer tenderly, their duologue expands into a rapt E major idyll, if not quite a love duet. It is stopped abruptly by the order for curtain-rise. Still captivated and exalted, the Composer improvises a paean to the holy art of music ('Musik ist eine heilige Kunst'); then the clowns prance in, and he realizes too late the compromise he has been distracted into accepting. While he rushes away in despair, the prologue ends with his motif arrested by a stern C minor cadence – but the show goes on.

The Opera ('Ariadne auf Naxos') There is a winding, melancholy overture in G minor, with an Allegro of dismay and alarm just before the curtain of the stage-within-the-stage rises. Ariadne is prostrate before her rocky cave. Three Nymphs lament her inconsolable state, but their trio slips into light, flowing G major – Mozart's Three Ladies from *Zauberflöte* are not far off – as they admit that her ceaseless moaning has become as familiar to them as the lapping waves on the shore. Now she cries aloud, soullessly echoed by Echo, and tries to recapture a lost dream. (Until now Strauss's harmonium has been only a discreet sustaining instrument, but from here he entrusts specially plangent harmonies to its dusky tones.) From the wings the Comedians watch her with concern, doubting whether they can possibly cheer her up. Dimly she recalls something beautiful that used to be called Theseus-Ariadne ('Ein Schönes war'); she imagines herself a chaste maiden, calmly awaiting a pure death. The Comedians find her dementia deeply affecting. Zerbinetta urges Harlequin, the romantic baritone of the company, to try a philosophical little song, which he does ('Lieben, hassen') to salon-style piano. Like Pedrillo's serenade in Mozart's *Entführung* it has odd sideslips of harmony, and a touching gravity disproportionate to its span.

Ariadne ignores him, and returns to her visionary G♭ for her great monologue, 'Es gibt ein Reich': only in the realm of the Dead is everything pure, and soon Hermes will summon her there to self-forgetting freedom (lyric ecstasy in B♭). This is altogether too morbid for the Comedians, who burst in with a buoyant, rackety song-and-dance number, a *Bier-garten* quartet with descant by Zerbinetta. When it fails to have any therapeutic effect she sends them off, and addresses Ariadne ('Grossmächtige Prinzessin!') confidentially, woman-to-woman: do we not *all* want each lover to be once-and-forever? and surely we get over it in time for the irresistible next one to come along? She cites her own erotic adventures as confirmation. This is her monster coloratura showpiece – glittering recitatives, a pair of delectable ariettas and a spectacular rondo with variations and competing flute. In *Ariadne* I the central sections are in E, with top F♯; for *Ariadne* II not only did Strauss prudently lower their pitch by a whole tone, but he abbreviated the first arietta, erased the central cadenza and wrote an entirely new coda. In either version the showpiece is much more than a virtuoso exercise: besides the disarmingly winsome tunes, all the roulades and trills – as the best Zerbinettas know – can have the force of witty, self-mocking gestures.

During this performance Ariadne has withdrawn into her cave, refusing to hear. (Understandable, but damaging to the original plan: since the confronting sopranos simply deliver their lengthy main effusions one after the other, the intended comic friction between genres – and human types – dwindles to mere alternation.) Zerbinetta's monologue is followed and completed by the Comedians' principal scene, in which each privately seeks her favours but only Harlequin wins them. This stylized vaudeville builds to a lusty quick-waltz climax, whereupon they all disperse.

Suddenly, with fanfares, the excited Nymphs announce the arrival of 'Bacchus' – more correctly the 'Dionysus' of ancient Greek cults, not the merely bibulous Roman god – on a ship, and while awaiting him they recount the supernatural events of his young life. From afar his heroic tenor is heard, exulting over his escape from the witch-seductress Circe (it was his first affair). Ariadne, who expects a messenger of Death, is strangely stirred, and the Nymphs answer his defiant song with a melting lullaby. (In *Ariadne* I naughty Zerbinetta reappears here, bringing the music down to earth in C major as she rhapsodizes over the handsome intruder – 'What a man!' – for Ariadne's benefit; but Strauss chose to excise that passage, and also the following orchestral one which illustrated the hero's striding advent.)

In *Ariadne* II, just eight bars of ascending white-note chords bring him on. Startled, Ariadne takes him momentarily for Theseus, but then welcomes him more calmly as the ordained messenger. They are both bemused. Bacchus explains that he is a god; during a long duet of high-flown intensity, with intermittent support from the invisible trio of Nymphs, she gives herself up to the heaven-sent stranger. The rocky island disappears, a baldachin descends from a starry sky to enfold them, and (in this version) Zerbinetta appears briefly during an orchestral interlude to whisper again: 'When the new god comes, we surrender dumbly'. The lovers' entwined voices rise to an epiphany in D♭, with a fervent peroration by Bacchus, and the orchestra reiterates it in pompous *fortissimo* before shimmering away into silence. (*Ariadne* I was better ordered: Zerbinetta returned immediately *after* the duet, pulling the music cheerily back into D major, and the Comedians danced on to join her in a reprise of their chorus, 'That a heart should so fail to understand itself!' Upon their jocular exit, amid light scattershot chords, Monsieur Jourdain, the *gentil-homme*, reappeared blinking, puzzled to find that all his guests had slipped away. A quick coda recalled the *Bürger als Edelmann* overture, and concluded the whole piece in its original mischievous terms.)

*

First conceived as a little number opera, *Ariadne* offered Strauss no scope for the lyric interplay he had perfected in *Der Rosenkavalier*. Instead he relished composing the contrasted numbers, unlike almost everything in his previous operatic successes, and drawing brave effects from his unaccustomedly modest band (some of their calculated, off-colour appeal is lost when a large opera house deploys extra strings). If, as Stravinsky complained, the 'serious' music trades continually on the pathos of 6–4 chordal harmony, the Bavarian music-hall numbers set it in ironic focus – at least in *Ariadne* I. The inflated close of *Ariadne* II flatters neither the romantic element nor the original point of the piece. Though the *opera seria*, despite its meagre action and Hofmannsthal's over-wrought poesy, now seems meant to win, it does not persuade: not because of any intrinsic weakness, but because the very terms of the entertainment undermine it. Probably Strauss should bear the blame for the first fatal step. His insistence on an extravagant, period-pastiche tour de force for Zerbinetta incurred a matching solo scena for Ariadne, leaving too little room for comic dissonance between their troupes. Yet the divided spirit of the piece is beautifully captured in the score; the task of bringing it to theatrical life remains a challenge for a director. It would be an easier task if the *Ariadne* I conclusion could be adapted to the purpose, putting inverted commas around the *opera seria* apotheosis instead of succumbing to it.   D.M.

Ariane et Barbe-bleue ('Ariane and Bluebeard')

Tale in three acts by Paul Dukas to a libretto by Maurice Maeterlinck after Charles Perrault; Paris, Opéra-Comique (Salle Favart), 10 May 1907.

Ariane was first sung by Georgette Leblanc, Bluebeard by Félix Vieuille.

Barbe-bleue [Bluebeard]		bass
Ariane		mezzo-soprano
The Nurse		contralto
Sélysette	⎫	mezzo-soprano
Ygraine	⎪	soprano
Mélisande	*Bluebeard's former wives* soprano
Bellangère	⎪	soprano
Alladine	⎭	mime
An Old Peasant		bass
Second Peasant		tenor
Third Peasant		bass
Peasants		
Setting Bluebeard's castle		

Maeterlinck's many-sided, symbolic libretto (originally considered and rejected by Grieg) was written for his companion Georgette Leblanc, actress and singer. He claimed that it was based on actual experiences of hers. With typical Maeterlinckian ambiguity, questions are posed but not answered. We know by the end that the former wives are still attracted to their torturer and that they have refused Ariane's offer of liberty. Bluebeard's power is broken but uncertainty remains. In spite of her composure Ariane has achieved little except, as Dukas suggested, the possibility of liberating herself. *Ariane*, Dukas' only opera, completed in 1906 after seven years' work, won and has retained the high regard of musicians and particularly composers, including Schoenberg, Berg and Messiaen. Yet though it is one of the foremost examples of the abundantly productive post-Wagnerian phase in French opera it has never gained popular success. Even in Paris productions have been infrequent (one of them was brought to London for two performances at Covent Garden during the 1937 season). The complex principal role requires a singer of strong personality, vocal stamina and impeccable declamation (notable interpreters have included Suzanne Balguerie and Germaine Lubin).

*

Act I Through the windows of the great hall can be heard the cries of peasants attempting to rescue Ariane, whom Bluebeard is bringing home as his sixth wife. Accompanied by her Nurse, Ariane appears. She does not believe the rumours that her five predecessors are dead. Bluebeard has given her seven keys, six silver ones for the silver-locked doors beneath the six windows, and a golden one for the seventh, forbidden, and so far invisible door on which Ariane's curiosity is concentrated. She knows that the six doors conceal Bluebeard's hoard of jewels, and since these do not interest her she allows the Nurse to open them one by one. Out of the alcoves tumble successive cascades of amethysts, sapphires, pearls, emeralds and rubies, and finally a cataract of diamonds so overpoweringly brilliant that Ariane is momentarily distracted until, at the back of the alcove, she notices the golden lock of the forbidden seventh door. To the Nurse's alarm she turns the key. Out of the darkness come the voices, faint at first but gradually filling the hall, of the former wives, singing of the five daughters of Orlamonde searching for daylight and finding only a closed door which they fear to open. As the song reaches its climax, Bluebeard enters. 'You too?' he asks Ariane. 'I, above all', she answers. He tries to seize her. She cries out, and as they struggle, shouts are heard outside. The Nurse opens the central door to reveal the peasants massed on the threshold. Ariane calmly tells them: 'He has done me no harm'. They go. Bluebeard ruefully contemplates his drawn sword.

Act 2 Ariane and the unwilling Nurse have made their way past the seventh door, down to a vaulted subterranean chamber where there is no light except for Ariane's lamp. She discovers a group of motionless figures huddled together. The lamp reveals the five former wives, haggard, blinking, their clothes in rags. Shyly they begin to talk about their imprisonment. As she moves her hands over the wall at the back, Ariane feels huge shutters, bolted and barred. When she prises them open there is a faint glimmer, but when she breaks a pane of glass with a stone, a ray of bright light shines through. As she shatters more panes, the light becomes blinding. Urged on by Ariane, the women climb up to the broken window and gaze enraptured at countryside and sea. Midday strikes. Dancing with joy, they follow Ariane into the sunlight.

Act 3 In the great hall the alcove doors are still open. In Bluebeard's absence Ariane encourages her 'sisters' to prepare for their approaching freedom by adorning themselves with the jewels. The Nurse appears in distress to announce the return of Bluebeard. From the gallery beneath the open windows the wives describe how Bluebeard's coach is attacked by the peasants, armed with scythes and pitchforks. They haul him out, bind him and drag him towards the castle. Ariane opens the central door. Awed by her presence, the insurgents carry in their bound master. Ariane thanks them and closes the door. Bluebeard's wounds are bleeding. The wives gather round to tend him; one of them furtively kisses him. Ariane calls for a dagger to cut the cords. Bluebeard rises slowly, looks at each wife in turn and then fixes his gaze on Ariane, who holds out her hand in a gesture of farewell. Informing the wives that she is going far away where there is work for her to do, she asks if they will follow her. Not one accepts. Ariane and the Nurse leave the castle. The women look at one another, then at Bluebeard.

*

Formally *Ariane* is carefully considered. Act 1 has a sequence of appropriately brilliant variations for the discovery of the jewels and an unusual *coup de théâtre* in the swelling offstage song of the daughters of Orlamonde (a folktune also used by Vincent d'Indy in his Second Symphony), a theme much heard subsequently. The second act contains another, longer, more elaborate crescendo in the gradual progression, as Ariane discovers and then breaks the barred window, from darkness to light (C major against the prevailing tonalities of F♯ minor and major). Act 3, after a mournful prelude implying that the offer of liberation is a failure before it has been made, is a free recapitulation of the first, reflecting the jewel variations (which Dukas had left short enough – with the exception of the extended diamond section – to allow further development), the offstage revolt of the peasants and the return of Bluebeard, this time as a silent captive. The strong framework is matched with musical craftsmanship of outstanding excellence. The orchestration, polished to a luminosity surpassing Rimsky-Korsakov, has a sombre glow beneath the enamelled surface. Dukas was a man of wide culture and superior intelligence, intensely self-critical with a vein of scepticism and perhaps self-doubt. Nothing illustrates his independent position better than the contrast between *Ariane* and Debussy's *Pelléas et Mélisande* (also based on a Maeterlinck play). There is enough in common in the two musical styles, for instance in the use of the whole-tone scale, for brief quotations identifying Mélisande to sound perfectly natural, but the more deliberate dramatic pace, the less soloistic writing and generally richer, more solid sonorities are essentially different.   R.H.C.

Ariodante

Opera in three acts by George Frideric Handel to a libretto anonymously adapted from Antonio Salvi's *Ginevra, principessa di Scozia* (1708, Pratolino) after Ludovico Ariosto's poem *Orlando furioso*, cantos iv–vi; London, Covent Garden Theatre, 8 January 1735.

The original cast consisted of the castrato Giovanni Carestini (Ariodante), Anna Maria Strada del Pò (Ginevra), Maria Negri (Polinesso), John Beard (Lurcanio), Cecilia Young (Dalinda), Gustavus Waltz (King of Scotland) and Michael Stoppelaer (Odoardo).

The King of Scotland	bass
Ariodante *a vassal prince*	mezzo-soprano

Ginevra *daughter of the King of Scotland,*
    betrothed to Ariodante   soprano
Lurcanio *Ariodante's brother*   tenor
Polinesso *Duke of Albany*   alto
Dalinda *attendant on Ginevra, secretly in*
    love with Polinesso   soprano
Odoardo *favourite of the king*   tenor
Setting Edinburgh and its vicinity

Ariodante was the first new opera produced by Handel in his first season at Covent Garden Theatre. It was mostly written between 12 August and 24 October 1734, though some pre-performance revisions (such as the alteration of Dalinda's part from contralto to soprano) may have been made later. In common with the other operas of Handel's 1734–5 season, *Ariodante* contains dance sequences in each act, written for Marie Sallé and her company. (These originally included a ballet of Good and Bad Dreams at the end of Act 2, representing Ginevra's troubled thoughts and concluding with an accompanied recitative in which she wakes up; but the sequence seems to have been replaced before performance by a short 'Entrée de Mori' and transferred – without the recitative – to *Alcina*.) *Ariodante* received 11 performances before giving way to a series of oratorio concerts, all in competition with the opera season organized by the rival 'Opera of the Nobility' at the King's Theatre (*see Alcina*). It was revived (without the dances) for just two performances on 5 May 1736, apparently as a stopgap before the première of *Atalanta*. The soprano castrato Gioacchino Conti, who took over the title role, presumably did not have sufficient time to learn his part and was allowed to include several non-Handelian arias from his earlier continental repertory. There were no further performances until the revival at Stuttgart on 28 September 1928 in an arrangement by A. Rudolph. The first British revival was at the Barber Institute, Birmingham, on 7 May 1964.

*

Act 1 Although the action is set in Edinburgh there is no local colour in the music. The opening scene is Princess Ginevra's dressing room, where she confesses to Dalinda that she is in love, with her father's approval. Polinesso presumptuously enters and declares love for Ginevra, but she says he is odious to her and leaves. Dalinda tells Polinesso that Ariodante is his rival for Ginevra and coyly hints at her own love for Polinesso. He decides to use her to destroy Ariodante.

In the royal gardens, Ariodante and Ginevra pledge faith. The King gives them his blessing and tells Odoardo to prepare for their wedding the following day. Polinesso deceitfully convinces Dalinda that he loves her, and inveigles her into helping him take revenge on Ginevra for her insult,

although Dalinda is reluctant, and ignorant of Polinesso's destructive plotting: she is to dress that night in Ginevra's clothes and lead him into the royal apartments. Ariodante's brother Lurcanio tells Dalinda that he loves her, but she says she is not for him. In a beautiful valley, Ariodante and Ginevra are entertained by the singing and dancing of the local shepherds and shepherdesses.

Act 2 In a ruined place, from which a private door leads into the royal apartments, Polinesso meets Ariodante by moonlight and pretends to be amazed when Ariodante says that he will soon be married to Ginevra. Polinesso claims (overhead by Lurcanio, in hiding) that he already enjoys Ginevra's favours, as Ariodante will see for himself. The door to the apartments is opened by the disguised Dalinda, and Polinesso is admitted. Ariodante, horrified, and overwhelmed with grief, is about to kill himself but is prevented by Lurcanio, who urges him to avenge his betrayal. Unaware of what she has done, Dalinda leaves Polinesso to exult in his deceit.

In a gallery of the palace, Odoardo brings terrible news to the King: Ariodante has been seen to plunge from a high cliff into the sea and is presumed drowned. Ginevra is told and faints with grief. Lurcanio states that the cause of Ariodante's death is the wantonness of Ginevra: he presents the King with a signed account of what he believes was her assignation with Polinesso and is prepared to defend its truth with his sword. The King denounces Ginevra as a whore, leaving her in profound despair.

Act 3 Ariodante is in a wood; he has survived and curses the gods for letting him live. He meets and rescues Dalinda, fleeing from assassins employed by Polinesso to silence the truth; she now realizes Polinesso's treachery and explains to Ariodante how he was deceived.

Back at the palace Polinesso hypocritically presents himself to the King as Ginevra's champion against Lurcanio. Ginevra, under sentence of death for her alleged unchastity, is brought to her father. She begs to kiss his hand for the last time; moved, the King allows her to do so, and insists that Polinesso be her champion despite her protests.

On the tournament field, Lurcanio challenges Polinesso to a duel and mortally wounds him; he offers a further challenge, which the King himself is about to take up, when a new champion appears with the visor of his helmet down. The newcomer reveals himself to be Ariodante and promises to explain everything if Ginevra is granted a pardon. Odoardo announces that Polinesso has died after confessing his crimes. The King orders rejoicing. The chastened Dalinda yields to Lurcanio's assurance of his love.

Ginevra, in prison, resigns herself to death, but her despair is swiftly turned to joy with the appearance of Ariodante and the King, who renews his blessing on the lovers. In a royal hall the two couples are entertained with the dances of knights and ladies.

*

Ariodante is one of Handel's most appealing operas: the story is romantic and unusually straightforward, and the characters are portrayed with warm humanity. It is also one of the greatest: the music is of consistently high quality, making considerable technical demands on the singers, and covers a remarkable range of emotional expression. Despite the expansiveness there is always a sense of intimacy, partly suggested by the general modesty of the scoring (trumpets appear only in the public scenes of Act 3, horns being used for the King's aria 'Voli colla sua tromba la fama' and for pastoral scenes) and by minor deviations from the strict pattern of recitatives and da capo arias. Three scenes begin with short arioso songs – that for Ariodante in the garden scene of Act 1, with its oboe solo, is especially lovely – and the King's genial interruption of the Act 1 duet for Ariodante and Ginevra is a delightful moment. The formal arias for the main characters are among Handel's finest, with superb examples of optimism and joy expressed through vocal virtuosity (Ginevra's 'Volate amori', and Ariodante's 'Con l'ali di costanza' in Act 1, the latter's 'Dopo notte' in Act 3) contrasted with the bleak despair of Ariodante's 'Scherza infida' in Act 2 (coloured by a mournful obbligato for bassoons with muted upper strings and pizzicato bass) and Ginevra's moving farewell to her father in Act 3 ('Io ti bacio', significantly echoed by Iphis in Act 3 of *Jephtha*). Dramatic tension is compellingly maintained through the whole of Act 2, which begins with an evocative sinfonia suggesting the rising of the moon. The dances and choruses in the final scenes of Acts 1 and 3, though peripheral to the story, are essential to the structure and include a pair of pastoral dances touched by the melancholy yearning for a golden age often found in Handel's pastoral music. If *Ariodante* has not achieved the place in the modern repertory which its attractiveness would seem to justify, the reasons are largely practical: the length of the work, the presence of the dance episodes and the need for singers of special quality. If these demands are met, the opera reveals itself as an outstanding example of Baroque musical drama.   A.H.

Armida

Dramma eroico in three acts by Joseph Haydn to a libretto by Nunziato Porta, after Torquato Tasso's epic poem *Gerusalemme liberata*; Eszterháza, 26 February 1784.

The original cast featured Matilde Bologna (Armida), Prospero Braghetti (Rinaldo), Antonio Specioli (Ubaldo), Paolo Mandini (Idreno), Costanza Valdesturla (Zelmira) and Leopold Dichtler (Clotarco).

Armida *a sorceress*	soprano
Rinaldo *a Christian knight*	tenor
Ubaldo *a Frankish knight*	tenor
Idreno *King of Damascus*	bass
Zelmira *destined bride of Idreno*	soprano
Clotarco *a Danish knight*	tenor
Setting Damascus	

Armida, the most performed opera at Eszterháza and the last of Haydn's new operas to be performed there, received 54 performances between its première and 1788. It enjoyed modest success outside Eszterháza, where Haydn ran the court opera house; most later performances were in German. Haydn's work derives originally from an episode, extremely popular with composers and librettists, in Tasso's *Gerusalemme liberata* (published in 1581); but it relies more immediately on librettos on the same subject by Jacopo Durandi, Francesco de Rogatis, Giovanni Bertati and an unknown adapter (set by Antonio Tozzi, 1775). Today *Armida* is among the most admired of Haydn's operas. There is at least one recording (with Jessye Norman in the title role), and there were several staged performances in the 1980s, including one given at the 1981 Monadnock Festival in Keene, New Hampshire, directed by Peter Sellars and set in Vietnam.

*

The overture is in three parts. The *allegretto* middle section anticipates the music of the magic grove in Rinaldo's Act 3 scena; the outer *vivace* sections anticipate no themes exactly, but musical topics relevant to the characters and situations of the opera are explored.

Act I.i–iii *A council chamber in the royal palace of Damascus* Idreno announces the arrival of the Frankish crusaders in Damascus. Rinaldo, a Christian knight, who has been bewitched by the Saracen sorceress Armida and is loved by her, offers to help defend Damascus against his own former colleagues, singing 'Vado a pugnar contento', a heroic C major aria with military motifs and virtuoso coloratura. Armida fears for his safety, but Idreno promises that if Rinaldo defeats the enemy he will have the right to rule Damascus ('Se dal suo braccio oppresso'). Idreno's aria is another heroic piece, but with less vocal virtuosity and more orchestral bluster than Rinaldo's. Armida, left alone, worries that she might have encouraged Rinaldo to go to his death (accompanied recitative, 'Parti Rinaldo'). Her succeeding aria, 'Se pietade avete o Numi', is a

Design attributed to Pietro Travaglia for the costume of Armida, the title role of Haydn's opera, first performed at Eszterháza, 26 February 1784: pen and watercolour

hybrid two-tempo form in A major whose principal motif echoes the opening of the recitative. The piece ends with extensive coloratura and several opportunities for cadenzas. The intensity, variety and sustained virtuosity of this aria establish Armida as the emotional centre of the opera.

I.iv–v A steep mountain, on whose peak Armida's palace can be seen Scene iv begins with a short march for wind band, recalling the march theme in the overture. Ubaldo and Clotarco are seeking Rinaldo. Ubaldo's accompanied recitative ('Valorosi compagni') reveals that he is becoming bewitched. His *largo* aria, 'Dove son', includes particularly beautiful wind writing. The aria moves directly into a burst of accompanied recitative in which Ubaldo recovers his courage and decides to ascend Armida's enchanted mountain. Clotarco warns him that the mountain is swarming with monsters and enemy soldiers, but Ubaldo fights his way to the top. In scene v Zelmira explains to the audience that she has been co-opted by Armida and Idreno to entice the crusaders to their deaths. Seeing Clotarco, she is struck by his beauty, and sings a charming G major aria persuading him to follow her ('Se tu seguir mi vuoi').

I.vi–ix Armida's rooms Armida begs Rinaldo to

hide from the crusaders, but Ubaldo enters and tries to shame him into remembering his original obligations. Rinaldo starts to follow Ubaldo, but Armida restrains him in a passionate accompanied recitative, preceding their duet, 'Cara, sarò fedele', in which a tender opening gives way to a disturbed middle section, with a cheerful conclusion.

Act 2.i–vii A garden in Armida's palace Idreno reveals his plan to ambush the crusaders on their way back down the mountain and Zelmira tries unsuccessfully to dissuade him. In the following scenes Clotarco and Ubaldo plead for peace and try to persuade Rinaldo to return to his people; but (scene v) Rinaldo is torn between love and duty. His accompanied recitative and aria ('Armida ... oh affanno' and 'Cara, è vero', in which he bids Armida an agonized farewell, form the centrepiece of the opera. Armida moves from grief to rage in her accompanied recitative, 'Barbaro! e ardisci ancor', then sings the most celebrated aria in the opera, 'Odio, furor, dispetto, dolor'. This piece is justly famous for its concentration and its intensity; eschewing coloratura, the voice spits out brief syllabic motifs and howls long high notes over a turbulent accompaniment. It is the only minor-mode piece in the opera.

2.viii–x The crusaders' encampment Ubaldo welcomes the return of Rinaldo, singing 'Prence amato'. Armida arrives, and the act ends with a trio in which Rinaldo is torn between Armida and Ubaldo ('Partirò, ma pensa, ingrato').

The second act is notable for the through-composition of scenes v–vii. These scenes are also the first exploration of Rinaldo's divided loyalties, and the continuous music focusses attention on the emotions of the characters.

Act 3.i Part of the forest, near the enchanted grove Ubaldo reminds Rinaldo of his task.

3.ii–iii A fearsome grove, with a bushy myrtle tree in the middle Rinaldo is almost overcome by the enchantments of the grove. The orchestral accompaniment to his recitative 'Questa dunque è la selva?' conjures up streams, birds, monsters and sweet odours as he imagines and then describes them. Zelmira tries to persuade him to return to Armida ('Torna pure al caro bene'). Rinaldo resists bewitchment ('Qual tumulto d'idee'), and is about to strike the sacred myrtle when Armida appears out of the tree and stays his hand, singing a deeply felt *largo* aria, 'Ah, non ferir'. She departs, 'making gestures with her magic branch' and darkening the stage in the process, while the orchestral music depicts the infernal scene. Rinaldo's final aria, 'Dei pietosi', is a two-tempo piece which juxtaposes a tender and reflective first section with a valiant then panic-stricken second section. He strikes the myrtle, the furies and the grove disappear, and the crusaders' encampment reappears to a series of increasingly soft scales in the orchestra. The entire scene is through-composed. In the final scene, Armida curses Rinaldo and calls for her infernal carriage. The finale consists of two march-like choral sections in which all participants lament their cruel fates; these frame a brief central section in which Armida berates Rinaldo, who almost weakens again, after which Ubaldo reminds him of his duty once more.

*

Armida is probably Haydn's finest opera. The long through-composed scenes with accompanied recitatives at the ends of the second and third acts allowed him opportunities to exercise his formidable powers of orchestral illustration. They also project a remarkably natural dramatic rhythm; Armida's 'Ah, non ferir' in Act 3 scene ii is effective partly because she can begin it as an interruption of Rinaldo's recitative. The rather slow pace of dramatic action also suits Haydn's interest in extended explorations of character and situation. Armida is by far the most fully characterized role; like Amaranta in *La fedeltà premiata*, she portrays a wide and convincing emotional range. Rinaldo has a comparable variety of music. His aria 'Dei pietosi' is a powerful expression of incompatible sentiments; nevertheless, vacillation is a less operatically compelling condition than naked desire. In contrast to the central characters, the secondary figures seem flat and undifferentiated. They fade into the landscape, whose physical features and transformations are more vividly illustrated than the human qualities of its inhabitants.   M.H.

Armide

Drame héroïque in five acts by Christoph Willibald Gluck to a libretto by Philippe Quinault after Torquato Tasso's epic poem *Gerusalemme liberata*; Paris, Académie Royale de Musique (Opéra), 23 September 1777.

The principals in the first performance were Rosalie Levasseur (Armide), Joseph Legros (Renaud), Mlle Lebourgeois (Phénice), Mlle Châteauneuf (Sidonie), Nicolas Gélin (Hidraot), Mlle Durancy (Hatred), Etienne Lainé (The Danish Knight) and Henri Larrivée (Ubalde).

Armide *a sorceress, Princess of Damascus*	soprano
Renaud *one of the most famous crusaders*	tenor
Phénice ⎱ *confidantes of Armide*	soprano
Sidonie ⎰	soprano
Hidraot *magician, King of Damascus and Armide's uncle*	baritone
La Haine [Hatred]	contralto
The Danish Knight ⎱ *crusaders sent to*	tenor
Ubalde ⎰ *look for Renauld*	baritone
A demon *in the form of Lucinde, the Danish Knight's beloved*	soprano
A demon *in the form of Mélisse, Ubalde's beloved*	soprano
Artémidore *one of Armide's prisoners freed by Renaud*	tenor
Aronte *guard in charge of Armide's prisoners*	bass
A Naiad	soprano
A Shepherd	soprano
A Pleasure	soprano
People of Damascus, nymphs, shepherds and shepherdesses, attendants of Hatred, demons, pleasures	
Setting Damascus at the time of the First Crusade	

Armide was the fifth of the seven operas that Gluck wrote for the Académie Royale de Musique in Paris. In it, after the successes of *Iphigénie en Aulide*, *Orphée et Eurydice* and *Alceste*, Gluck paid homage to, and also confronted, the operatic traditions of Lully and Rameau by setting complete (except for the prologue) the libretto Quinault had written nearly 90 years earlier for Lully's last *tragédie lyrique*.

Performances of *Armide* since the 18th century have not been frequent. Among important revivals was one in Paris in 1825 when Alexandrine Caroline Branchu sang the title role and was much admired by Berlioz. Meyerbeer conducted it in Berlin in 1843, the year Wagner conducted it in Dresden with Wilhelmine Schröder-Devrient in the title role; and Berlioz conducted Act 3 the following year at the Paris Exhibition with 900 performers. Another extraordinary performance took place in Karlsruhe in 1853 when *Armide* was performed in German translation with new recitatives by Joseph Strauss. Toscanini conducted the opera at La Scala and at the Metropolitan Opera in New York. In 1905 Lucienne Bréval sang Armide in a Paris revival, and between 1906 and 1928 there were ten performances at Covent Garden with Frida Leider as Armide and Walter Widdop as Renaud.

In recent times *Armide* has had only occasional performances at festivals, in student productions and in concert performances. A controversial production by Wolf-Siegfried Wagner at the 1982 Spitalfields Festival in London was followed by a recording, the opera's only complete commercial recording to date. *Armide* was scheduled to open the 1996–7 season at La Scala, Milan.

*

Act I *A public square decorated by a triumphal arch in the city of Damascus* Armide's two confidantes Phénice and Sidonie are celebrating her recent victory over the crusaders and trying to distract her from her preoccupation with the idea of defeating Renaud, the most valiant crusader of them all. Armide describes how she has recently seen him in a dream in which she fell in love with him at the very moment he struck her a fatal blow. Gluck claimed that in *Armide* he managed to differentiate the expression of the characters to a degree that one can instantly tell whether Armide or another is singing. This is true from the opening scene of the opera where the lyrical, dance-like music for Phénice and Sidonie is sharply distinguished from the martial dotted rhythms and minor-key harmony of Armide's.

Hidraot and his retinue enter. He congratulates Armide on her victory over the crusaders but urges her to marry. His blustering music, almost from the world of *opera buffa*, contrasts vividly with Armide's: her *ariette* 'La chaîne de l'hymen m'étonne' is like an instrumental movement into which the vocal part has been fitted, its radiant major key and caressing phrases belying her words ironically. She confesses that, if she marries, it will only be to the man who defeats Renaud.

The people of Damascus celebrate Armide's victory with singing and dancing. Their rejoicing is interrupted by Aronte who staggers in, wounded, and tells them that all their prisoners have been rescued by one soldier, single-handed – Renaud. The act ends with the soloists and chorus swearing vengeance on him.

Act 2 *The countryside outside Damascus* Renaud tells Artémidore, one of the knights he has rescued, to return to the camp of the crusaders; he himself cannot do so because he has been banished by their leader, Godefroi. Artémidore warns him to beware of Armide, but in a short, martial air ('J'aime la liberté') Renaud declares his indifference to the danger she poses.

As they leave, Armide and Hidraot come in and invoke the spirits of the underworld to put a spell on Renaud (duet, 'Esprits de haine et de rage'). When Renaud appears, he is entranced by the beauty of the countryside, and sings an air ('Plus j'observe ces lieux') in which the solo flute represents birdsong and the constant quaver motion in the muted violins a gently flowing stream. Evil spirits transformed into naiads, nymphs, shepherds and shepherdesses lull him to sleep with songs and dances.

Armide suddenly appears, ready to stab the sleeping Renaud. But she cannot bring herself to do so, her indecision being expressed in a fine example of Gluck's suggestive orchestration as her avowals of hatred for Renaud are belied by warmer, more sensual music in the orchestra. She determines to make him love her, thereby avenging herself by seducing him from the field of battle. In shame and

desperation she calls on her spirits to take them both far away to the end of the universe ('Venez, venez, secondez mes désirs'). Their enchanted flight is vividly depicted by fleeting semiquaver triplets on the flute and violins, a syncopated accompaniment on divided violas and above them all a high, angular line for solo oboe which leads Armide's vocal part on ever higher.

Act 3 *A desert* Alone, Armide reflects that although, by means of her magic, she has made Renaud love her, she has failed to control her own amorous feelings for him (air, 'Ah! si la liberté me doit être ravie'). Phénice and Sidonie assure her that she has him completely in her power, but she knows she must choose between her love for Renaud and hatred and revenge on him (this scene includes Armide's air 'De mes plus doux regards Renaud sut se défendre'). Left alone, Armide summons Hatred to rescue her and exorcise love from her heart (air, 'Venez, venez, Haine implacable!').

Hatred and her demonic entourage appear from the underworld and, in a series of three airs with chorus, separated by two dances, they begin their incantations. But this is too much for Armide and, her mind made up, she joins in, rejecting Hatred's help. Armide's anguish is strikingly portrayed as her voice is suddenly left isolated, rising higher in a crescendo as she declares it impossible to take away her love for Renaud without breaking her heart.

Hatred scornfully predicts Armide's abandonment, saying that she could not punish her more harshly than by leaving her to the powers of Love. She then leads a mocking chorus ('Suis l'Amour, puisque tu le veux') before leaving Armide trembling with fear for her fate and putting her trust in Love. For this Gluck added four lines to Quinault's libretto; in them the persistent ostinato rhythms which have characterized Hatred continue to torment Armide in spite of the consoling phrases from the strings.

Act 4.i *A desert* The Danish Knight and Ubalde, sent to Armide's palace to find Renaud and bring him back to the war, find their way barred by Armide's monsters. They overcome these with the help of a talismanic diamond shield and a golden sceptre given them by a magician to counter Armide's magic powers.

4.ii The desert changes into beautiful countryside and the two knights are in turn tempted by demons who have been transformed by Armide to resemble their beloveds. They are not deceived for long; they dispel these visions with the golden sceptre and go on their way towards Armide's palace, singing a duet of heroic resolution ('Fuyons les douceurs dangereuses').

Act 5 *Armide's enchanted palace* Armide is now committed to loving Renaud but fears she will lose him (as Hatred predicted). His langorous sighing phrases at the opening are followed by an extended love duet containing some of the most passionate music Gluck ever wrote (as he must have realized when, in later years, he said that if he suffered damnation it would be for having written this duet).

Armide goes to consult her evil powers and leaves Renaud to be entertained by her retinue until she returns. They take the form of Pleasures who sing and dance for him in a lengthy *divertissement*. This begins and ends with a chaconne; in between there are airs with chorus and other dances. But Renaud cannot enjoy anything without Armide, and banishes the Pleasures with his lovesick air, 'Allez, éloignez-vous de moi'.

Ubalde and the Danish Knight enter and show Renaud the diamond shield; this breaks Armide's spell and awakens him to the fact of his desertion. As he is leaving with his companions, Armide returns: in an anguished recitative ('Renaud! Ciel! O mortelle peine!') with solo oboe she expresses her horror at seeing her fears of his betrayal confirmed. The chromatic, languishing phrases of Renaud's love music now give way to conventional, straightforward recitative as he bids Armide farewell; but there is a hint of his looking back at her longingly in the chromatic descending phrase 'Trop malheureuse Armide, Que ton destin est déplorable'.

After the knights have left, Armide alternates between despair and desire for vengeance. This final scene of the opera, an extended arioso whose opening grows from Renaud's parting words 'Que ton destin est déplorable', is one of Gluck's finest. At first Armide laments the departure of the perfidious Renaud; then the music becomes more violent and distraught as she regrets not having killed him when he was in her power (the orchestra vividly depicts her stabbing him in her imagination). Finally she orders the demons to destroy her enchanted palace, and she leaves on a flying chariot to seek revenge on Renaud.

*

Armide is the only one of Gluck's late operas to end tragically, with no *deus ex machina* appearing to put all to rights; instead its conclusion is the logical outcome of the events of the drama. Its shattering final scene – Armide's razing to the ground of her palace in lovetorn fury – provides what is arguably the most climactic close of any Gluck opera. The work is also unique as a setting of a libretto which was so much a part of an earlier French operatic tradition, with its five acts and abundance of spectacular effects and *divertissements*. That Gluck brought these to life with such success is a measure of his versatility, for the music is constantly on an inspired level. Gluck himself said that whereas *Alceste* 'must call forth tears', *Armide* must 'produce a

voluptuous sensation', and the opera contains some of the most sheerly beautiful and sensuous music that he ever wrote, notably Renaud's slumber scene in Act 2 and much of the fourth and fifth acts. But Gluck's evocation of evil and the supernatural in Act 3 is also as vivid as anything in *Orfeo ed Euridice* or *Alceste*.

There is more action *per se* in *Armide* than in any other of Gluck's major operas, and its structure is very fluid and continuous with comparatively few self-contained airs or set numbers of any length. Instead there are short airs, arioso and recitative; arguably *Armide* contains the most successful continuous arioso and recitative of any Gluck opera, for example in the last two scenes of Act 5. And it is in the recitative and arioso that Armide herself is most fully characterized. She dominates the opera, a combination of sorceress and seductress (like Kundry in *Parsifal* 100 years later), one of Gluck's great heroines and possibly his most rounded and fascinating female character. Posterity has undervalued this opera which Gluck regarded as 'perhaps the best of all my works'.   J.H.

Attila

Dramma lirico in a prologue and three acts by Giuseppe Verdi to a libretto by Temistocle Solera (with additional material by Francesco Maria Piave) after Zacharias Werner's play *Attila, König der Hunnen*; Venice, Teatro La Fenice, 17 March 1846.

The cast at the première included Ignazio Marini (Attila), Natale Costantini (Ezio), Sophie Loewe (Odabella) and Carlo Guasco (Foresto).

Attila *King of the Huns*	bass
Ezio *a Roman general*	baritone
Odabella *the Lord of Aquileia's daughter*	soprano
Foresto *a knight of Aquileia*	tenor
Uldino *a young Breton, Attila's slave*	tenor
Leone *an old Roman*	bass

Leaders, kings and soldiers, Huns, Gepids, Ostrogoths, Heruls, Thuringians, Quadi, Druids, priestesses, men and women of Aquileia, Aquileian maidens in warlike dress, Roman officers and soldiers, Roman virgins and children, hermits, slaves

Setting Aquileia, the Adriatic lagoons and near Rome, in the middle of the 5th century

Verdi had read Werner's ultra-Romantic play as early as 1844, and initially discussed the subject with Piave. However, for his second opera at La Fenice – a highly suitable subject, dealing with the founding of the city of Venice – the composer eventually fixed on

Solera, the librettist with whom – at least until then – he seems to have preferred working. Solera set about preparing the text according to his usual format, with plenty of opportunity for grand choral tableaux such as are found in *Nabucco* and *I Lombardi*; but the progress of the opera was beset with difficulties. First Verdi fell seriously ill, and then Solera went off to live permanently in Madrid, leaving the last act as only a sketch and necessitating the calling in of the faithful Piave after all. Verdi instructed Piave to ignore Solera's plans for a large-scale choral finale and to concentrate on the individuals, a change of direction that Solera strongly disapproved of. The première was coolly received, but *Attila* went on to become one of Verdi's most popular operas of the 1850s. After that it lost ground; however, it has recently been more than occasionally revived. Its first production at Covent Garden was mounted in 1990. In 1846 Verdi twice rewrote the *romanza* for Foresto in Act 3: the first time for Nicola Ivanoff, the second for Napoleone Moriani.

*

The prelude follows a pattern that later became common in Verdi's work: a restrained opening leads to a grand climax, then to the beginnings of melodic continuity that are quickly fragmented. It is the drama encapsulated.

Prologue i *The piazza of Aquileia* 'Huns, Heruls and Ostrogoths' celebrate bloody victories and greet their leader Attila who, in an impressive recitative, bids them sing a victory hymn. A group of captive female warriors is brought on, and their leader Odabella defiantly proclaims the valour and patriotic zeal of Italian women. Odabella's double aria is a forceful display of soprano power, its first movement, 'Allor che i forti corrono' showing an unusually extended form which allows Attila to insert admiring comments. Such is the force of this movement that the cabaletta, 'Da te questo', merely continues the musical tone, though with more elaborate ornamentation. Impressed by her bravery, Attila gives her his sword.

As Odabella leaves, the Roman general Ezio appears for a formal duet with Attila. In the Andante 'Tardo per gli anni, e tremulo', he offers Attila the entire Roman empire if Italy can be left unmolested and in Ezio's hands ('Avrai tu l'universo, resti l'Italia a me': 'For you the world, leave Italy to me' – a phrase with some resonance in the political struggles to come in the 1850s). Attila, angry at the whiff of treachery, rejects the proposal, and the warriors end with a cabaletta of mutual defiance, 'Vanitosi! che abbietti e dormenti'.

Prologue ii *The Rio-Alto in the Adriatic lagoons* The scene opens with a sustained passage of local colour (strongly suggesting that Verdi now had his eye on the fashions of the French stage). First comes a violent orchestral storm, then the gradual rising of dawn is portrayed with a passage of ever-increasing orchestral colours and sounds. Foresto leads on a group of survivors from Attila's attack on Aquileia; the settlement that they build there will eventually become Venice. In an Andantino which again shows unusual formal extension, 'Ella in poter del barbaro', his thoughts turn to his beloved Odabella, captured by Attila. In the subsequent cabaletta, 'Cara patria, già madre', the soloist is joined by the chorus for a rousing conclusion to the scene.

Act I.i *A wood near Attila's camp* A melancholy string solo introduces Odabella, who, refusing a chance to escape, and playing on Attila's obvious attraction to her, has remained in his camp in order to find an opportunity to murder him. In a delicately scored Andantino, 'Oh! nel fuggente nuvolo', Odabella sees in the clouds the images of her dead father and Foresto. Foresto himself appears: he has seen her with Attila and accuses her of betrayal. Their duet takes on the usual multi-movement pattern: Foresto's accusations remain through the minor–major Andante, 'Sì, quello io son, ravvisami', but Odabella convinces him of her desire to kill Attila, and they lovingly join in a unison cabaletta, 'Oh t'innebria nell'amplesso'.

I.ii *Attila's tent, later his camp* Attila tells his slave Uldino of a terrible dream in which an old man denied him access to Rome in the name of God ('Mentre gonfiarsi l'anima'). But he dismisses the vision with a warlike cabaletta, 'Oltre quel limite'.

A bellicose vocal blast from Attila's followers is interrupted by a procession of women and children led by Leone, the old man of Attila's dream (he is Pope Leo I, suitably disguised at the behest of the Italian censors). His injunction precipitates the Largo of the concertato finale, 'No! non è sogno', led off by a terrified Attila, whose stuttering declamation is answered by a passage of sustained lyricism from Foresto and Odabella. The concertato takes on such impressive proportions that Verdi saw fit to end the act there, without the traditional stretta.

Act 2.i *Ezio's camp* The scene is no more than a conventional double aria for Ezio. In the Andante, 'Dagl'immortali vertici', he muses on Rome's fallen state. Foresto appears and suggests a plan to destroy Attila by surprising him at his camp. In a brash cabaletta, 'E gettata la mia sorte', Ezio eagerly looks forward to his moment of glory.

2.ii *Attila's camp* Yet another warlike chorus begins the scene. Attila greets Ezio, the Druids mutter darkly of fatal portents, the priestesses dance and sing. A sudden gust of wind blows out all the candles, an event that precipitates yet another concertato finale, 'Lo spirto de' monti', a complex movement during which Foresto manages to tell Odabella that Attila's cup is poisoned. The formal slow movement concluded, Attila raises the cup to his lips, but is warned of the poison by Odabella (who wishes a more personal vengeance); Foresto admits to the crime, and Odabella claims the right to punish him herself. Attila approves, announces that he will marry Odabella the next day, and launches the concluding stretta, 'Oh miei prodi! un solo giorno'; its dynamism and rhythmic bite prefigure similar moments in *Il trovatore*.

Act 3 *A wood* Foresto is awaiting news of Odabella's marriage to Attila, and in a minor–major *romanza*, 'Che non avrebbe il misero', bemoans her apparent treachery. Ezio arrives, urging Foresto to speedy battle. A distant chorus heralds the wedding procession, but suddenly Odabella herself appears, unable to go through with the ceremony. Soon all is explained between her and Foresto, and they join Ezio in a lyrical Adagio.

Attila now enters, in search of his bride, and the stage is set for a Quartetto finale. In the Allegro, 'Tu, rea donna', Attila accuses the three conspirators in turn, but in turn they answer, each with a different melodic line. At the climax of the number, offstage cries inform us that the attack has begun. Odabella stabs Attila, embraces Foresto, and the curtain falls.

*

The final act is, as several have pointed out, more than faintly ridiculous in its stage action, and parts of Verdi's setting seem rather perfunctory; perhaps Solera's original plan for a grand choral finale would have been more apt. Perhaps indeed, the central problem with *Attila* is that it falls uncomfortably between being a drama of individuals (like *Ernani* or *I due Foscari*) and one that is essentially public (like *Nabucco* or *I Lombardi*). It is surely for this reason that two of the principals, Ezio and Foresto, are vague and undefined, never managing to emerge from the surrounding tableaux. On the other hand, Odabella and Attila, both of whom assume vocal prominence early in the opera, are more powerful dramatic presences. As with all of Verdi's early operas, there are impressive individual moments, particularly in those grand ensemble movements that constantly inspired the composer to redefine and hone his dramatic language.   R.P.

Atys ('Attis')

Tragédie en musique in a prologue and five acts by Jean-Baptiste Lully to a libretto by Philippe Quinault after Ovid's *Fasti*; St Germain-en-Laye, court, 10 January 1676.

Principal singers at the première included Baumavielle (Time), Verdier (Flora), Beaucreux (Melpomene), Cledière (Attis), Morel (Idas), Aubry (Sangaride), Brigogne (Doris), Saint Christophle (Cybele) and Gaye (Celaenus); principal dancers (all male) were Beauchamp, Dolivet, Faure, Favier, Lestang, Magny and Pécour.

Prologue

Le Temps [Time] *God of Time*		baritone
Flore [Flora] *a goddess*		soprano
Melpomène [Melpomene] *the tragic Muse*		soprano
Iris *a goddess*		soprano
A Zephyr		haute-contre
Hercule [Hercules], Antée [Antaeus], Etheocle [Eteocles], Polinice [Polynices], Castor, Pollux		dancers

Tragedy

Atys [Attis] *relative of Sangaride and favourite of Celaenus*		haute-contre
Sangaride *nymph, daughter of the River Sangarius*		soprano
Cybèle [Cybele] *a goddess*		soprano
Celenus [Celaenus] *King of Phrygia and son of Neptune, in love with Sangaride*		baritone
Idas *friend of Attis and brother of Doris*		bass
Doris *nymph, friend of Sangaride, sister of Idas*		soprano
Mélisse *confidante and priestess of Cybele*		soprano
Le Sommeil [Sleep] *God of Sleep*		haute-contre
Morphée [Morpheus]		haute-contre
Phobétor	*sons of sleep*	bass
Phantase		tenor
The God of the River Sangar [Sangarius] *father of Sangaride*		bass
Alecton [Alecto] *a Fury*		silent role

The Hours of the Day and Night, nymphs who follow Flora, four little zephyrs, heroes who follow Melpomene; Phrygians; followers of Celaenus, zephyrs, people attending the celebration of Cybele; Pleasant Dreams, Baleful Dreams; gods of the rivers and brooks, nymphs of the springs; gods of the woods and waters, Corybantes

Setting Ancient Phrygia

Lully's fourth tragedy was known as 'the king's opera'; it is not known why. Voltaire singled out *Atys*, along with *Armide*, to exemplify the librettist Quinault's mastery of the genre. 20th-century scholars have often cited *Atys* as marking the start of a style period, primarily for its avoidance of subplots and comic interludes in the Venetian manner, along with its 'Racinian serenity'.

Additional productions at St Germain took place in 1677, 1678 and 1682; Lully wrote supplementary dances for the 1682 production, and courtiers danced

'Atys' (Lully, 1676), scene from the 1986 production (shared between Opéra de Paris, Teatro Comunale Florence, and Opéra de Montpellier) given by Les Arts Florissants at the Teatro Metastasio-Prato, Florence (musical director William Christie; stage director Jean-Marie Villégier)

alongside the professional dancers. The public première was at the Paris Opéra in April (not August) 1676; there were seven Opéra revivals between 1689 and 1747 and a production (without the prologue) at Louis XV's court at Fontainebleau in 1753. In the Paris production of 1738 the final *divertissement* was suppressed; it 'had always seemed superfluous, after such a sad catastrophe' (C. and F. Parfaict, 1741). Between 1687 and 1749 *Atys* was produced in Amsterdam, Marseilles, Lyons, Rouen, Brussels, Metz, Lille and The Hague. A highly successful modern production was directed by William Christie in Paris and elsewhere from 1987 and recorded.

*

Prologue *Time's palace* Time and the chorus of Hours of the Day and Night praise a glorious 'hero' (Louis XIV). During a *menuet en rondeau* danced by flower-bearing nymphs, the goddess Flora enters, led by a dancing zephyr. Flora has come in winter to avoid missing her hero, for Glory will surely call him to war in the spring. Flora's celebrations are interrupted by the arrival of the tragic muse Melpomene, whose followers – Hercules, Antaeus and other heroes – enact their battles in a pantomime ballet. The goddess Iris, acting on Cybele's command, arrives to unite nature (Flora) and art (Melpomene) for the drama to follow. All celebrate.

Act I *A mountain consecrated to Cybele* The tragedy appears to begin with a brief monologue *air* for Attis, prefigured by its *ritournelle*, but as more characters gradually join him the *air* turns out to have been the first statement of a varied refrain: 'Allons, allons, accourez tous / Cybèle va descendre' . While they await the arrival of the goddess Cybele, Attis admits privately to Idas that he has been wounded by love, but tells Sangaride, whom he congratulates on her impending marriage, that he is indifferent to love. The modulatory phrase that announces the next segment of the act begins in the continuo alone but ends with a strong vocal cadence: 'Atys est trop heureux!' Alone with Doris, Sangaride confides that she loves Attis rather than her fiancé Celaenus and that she envies Attis his indifference. 'Atys est trop heureux!', the introductory remark, is later expanded into a brief lament. The next change of key marks Attis's return. In a much praised recitative scene he and Sangaride gradually reveal their love to each other. They hide their feelings as the Phrygians gather to honour Cybele's arrival (*divertissement*). The goddess's spectacular descent in her chariot, the climax of the act, is followed by the *air* and chorus 'Vous devez vous animer d'une ardeur nouvelle', over an intermittent ground bass. (This chorus became the basis for an English dance form of the period 1690 to 1710, called the 'Cibell'.)

Act 2 *Cybele's temple* Celaenus begs Attis for reassurances of Sangaride's love; Attis responds that, as Celaenus's wife, Sangaride will follow duty and glory. Their dialogue culminates in a pair of adjacent *airs*, contrasting the joy of indifference with the torment of love. Cybele tells Celaenus that she has chosen Attis to be her great Sacrificer. Alone with Mélisse, she admits that she loves Attis. Flying zephyrs appear in dazzling glory; zephyrs and people from different nations pay homage to the new Sacrificer (*divertissement*).

Act 3 *The palace of the great Sacrificer of Cybele* Attis, alone and troubled, is approached by Idas and Doris, who warn him that Sangaride intends to declare the truth to Cybele. Attis is torn between loyalty to Celaenus and his own desires. Left alone, he grows drowsy; Cybele has asked the god of Sleep to announce her love in a dream. This famous *divertissement*, the 'sommeil' scene, is an elaborate structure composed of a hypnotic passage for recorders and strings; solos and ensembles for Sleep and his sons ('Dormons tous'); dances for the Pleasant Dreams, who demonstrate Cybele's love to the sleeping Attis; and dances for the Baleful Dreams, who demonstrate, in jagged rhythms, the danger of resisting the goddess's love. An all-male chorus of Baleful Dreams hammers home a warning in insistent repeated chords. After a final dance, Attis awakes in fright; Cybele is there, asking for his love. When Sangaride enters and begs to be released from her engagement to Celaenus, Attis prevents her from announcing their love for each other. Cybele, however, senses a problem (monologue *air*, 'Espoir si cher et si doux').

Act 4 *The palace of the River Sangarius* Having misunderstood Attis's motives, Sangaride confides to Doris and Idas that Attis no longer loves her – the scene culminates in a painfully sweet trio – then promises herself to Celaenus. Sangaride and Attis then accuse each other of infidelity but eventually reaffirm their love. The god of the River Sangarius presents Celaenus to the water divinities, who approve the choice of husband for his daughter and celebrate with him; the *divertissement* is a series of exuberant dance-songs. However, the Sacrificer Attis – acting in Cybele's name – refuses to approve the marriage. The zephyrs carry Attis and Sangaride away as the chorus protests.

Act 5 *A pleasant garden* Cybele and Celaenus angrily confront Attis and Sangaride, their conversation consisting entirely of alternating duet fragments. Cybele calls on the Fury Alecto. During a brief *prélude* characterized by running semiquavers and dotted rhythms, Alecto arrives from the underworld and waves a torch over Attis's head, rendering him insane. As Phrygians and Cybele's priestesses watch in horror, Attis mistakes Sangaride for a monster; he

chases and kills her (the murder occurs off stage and is reported by Celaenus). Cybele ends Attis's insanity so that he might know what he has done. A choral refrain, 'Atys lui-même fait périr ce qu'il aime!', unifies the mad scene and its aftermath. As Cybele, alone with Mélisse, regrets the severity of the punishment, Attis enters: he has stabbed himself and is dying. Cybele transforms him into a pine tree that she will love for ever. The final *divertissement* is a scene of mourning; the gentle weeping of the nymphs is juxtaposed with the frenzy of the Corybantes.

*

Atys combines the brilliant use of spectacle and intricately structured *divertissements* in Lully's earlier operas with more subtly structured recitative dialogues and a new seriousness of dramatic content. Burlesque scenes and subplots are absent for the first time and do not return in subsequent operas. Inward conflict, a prominent feature of the late tragedies *Roland* and *Armide* but virtually absent from most of Quinault's other librettos, is present here. Although *Atys* is not Lully's only opera to end sorrowfully, it is the only one to conclude with unmitigated tragedy.   **L.R.**

Aufstieg und Fall der Stadt Mahagonny
('Rise and Fall of the City of Mahagonny')

Opera in three acts by Kurt Weill to a libretto by Bertolt Brecht; Leipzig, Neues Theater, 9 March 1930.

At the first performance Begbick was sung by Marga Dannenberg, Fatty by Hanns Fleischer, Moses by Walther Zimmer, Jenny by Mali Trummer and Jim by Paul Beinert; the producer was Walther Brügmann, the conductor Gustav Brecher, the stage designer Caspar Neher.

Leokadja Begbick	contralto/mezzo-soprano
Fatty [Willy] *the 'attorney'*	tenor
Trinity Moses [Dreieinigkeitsmoses]	baritone
Jenny Hill	soprano
Jim Mahoney [Johann Ackermann or Hans]	tenor
Jack O'Brien	tenor
Bill, alias Sparbüchsenbill [Heinz, alias Sparbüchsenheinrich]	baritone
Joe [Josef Lettner], alias Alaskawolfjo	bass
Tobby Higgins (can be doubled with the role of Jack)	tenor
Six girls from Mahagonny, the men of Mahagonny	

Weill's correspondence with his publishers, Universal Edition, records how his collaboration with

'Aufstieg und Fall der Stadt Mahagonny' (Weill), Act 1 scene xi in the original production at the Neues Theater, Leipzig, 9 March 1930

Brecht began in April 1927 with the idea of using the poet's 'Mahagonny-Gesänge' (from the collection *Hauspostille*) as the basis for the 'Songspiel' *Mahagonny*. This work resulted from a commission for a 'short opera' for the Deutsche Kammermusik Baden-Baden festival, 1927. The idea of the 'Songspiel' (a pun, of course, on 'Singspiel', the central ingredient being the American-influenced 'song' rather than operatic arias) was as an 'anti-opera', set in a boxing ring, with 'lowbrow' jazz music and intentional vulgarity. Later (1930) Weill described the Songspiel as 'a stylistic study by way of preparation for the operatic work, which was already begun and, the style having been tried out, was then continued', and it was effectively suppressed; it was not published until 1963.

That the composer wished retrospectively to relegate the Songspiel to the status of a mere stylistic study is understandable. But why he should also claim, by backdating the genesis of the full-scale opera, that this was his intention all along remains unclear. He obviously wished to stress the importance of the latter work to his theatrical output, partly no doubt because of Brecht's rather negative assessment, made public in his 'Notes' (1930).

Another factor may have been the charge of plagiarism levelled at Weill and Brecht by the playwright Walter Gilbricht: the earlier the inception of their work, the less likely it was that they could have known Gilbricht's *Die Gross-stadt mit einem Einwohner* ('The City with a Single Inhabitant'), completed in 1928. What is certain, however, is that the actual composition of the Songspiel preceded the full-length opera *Aufstieg und Fall der Stadt Mahagonny*. Moreover, although the Songspiel is related both thematically and stylistically to the later work, Weill's musical language evinces a change of attitude during the two-year genesis (1927–9) of the opera. Comparison of the music adapted from the Songspiel – especially the 'Alabama Song' – readily reveals those differences: the earlier harmonizations have been divested of their harsher dissonances.

As the composition of the opera progressed, Weill gradually distanced himself from the earlier acerbic 'song style' (though not from the song style as such, as *Happy End*, 1929, shows), cultivating 'a perfectly pure, thoroughly responsible style', as he himself described it in a letter to his publishers. The development culminates in the exquisite 'Cranes' Duet', added in October 1929 in response to strong criticism from the publishers, who urged that some of the work's more risqué material should be removed. It is indicative of the difficulties surrounding the opera that the question of where to place the love duet has never been satisfactorily solved, either dramatically or musically. It is also characteristic of the work's fate that Otto Klemperer, having been enthusiastic about the Songspiel, should reject the opera after the Kroll Oper, Berlin, had committed itself to giving the first performance under his direction. Like the publishers, Klemperer was perturbed by the depravity of the libretto. The work was therefore entrusted to the Neues Theater in Leipzig, where the first night provoked one of the greatest scandals in the history of 20th-century music. Further productions followed in Brunswick and Kassel, with both houses insisting on cuts for moral, religious and political reasons. Fuelled by Nazi sympathizers, protests nonetheless continued both in and out of the opera house. The work did not reach Berlin until December 1931, when, at the instigation of the impresario Ernst Josef Aufricht, it was given at the Theater am Kurfürstendamm in a radically reduced and shortened version by a team of singer-actors associated with *Die Dreigroschenoper*, with Zemlinsky as conductor. Members of the same ensemble, starring Lotte Lenya and conducted by Hans Sommer, contributed to the recording of highlights released in 1932. Lenya also starred (with her part rewritten) in the first complete recording (1956), conducted by Wilhelm Brückner-Rüggeberg.

The various cuts demanded by German opera houses in the early 1930s are indicated in the published vocal score, though their precise origin is not specified. The text published in Brecht's collected works (*Versuche*) in 1930 and in the new complete edition of his works (1988) represents a later version, in which – among other things – the ideological nature of divine authority is made less explicit. There are three authorized English translations: by Michael Feingold, by David Drew and Michael Geliot, and by Arnold Weinstein and Lys Symonette. The original published vocal score contains a note suggesting that because 'the pleasure city Mahagonny is in every sense international' the names of the characters may be replaced by names appropriate to the country of performance. Several alternatives for German performance are given, for example 'Willy' instead of 'Fatty', as used in the opera's première.

*

Act I.i Scene captions are projected on to a small white curtain which can be pulled aside. Inscriptions are also used for epic narration. As the music begins a 'wanted' poster appears, with photographs of Leokadja Begbick, Trinity Moses and Fatty; they are charged with procuring and fraudulent bankruptcy, and described as 'Fugitives from Justice'. Above the projection is an inscription: 'The Founding of the City of Mahagonny'. The backdrop depicts a desolate place. A large dilapidated truck arrives on stage. The engine stalls, and Trinity Moses climbs down from the driver's seat and crawls under the bonnet. Fatty gets out of the back of the vehicle and the dialogue begins. They are unable to continue on their way, so they found Mahagonny, 'the city of nets [Netzstadt]' – 'you get gold more easily from men than from rivers'. Begbick, Fatty and Moses sing together: 'Mahagonny only exists because everything is so bad, because there's no peace and no contentment and because there's nothing to hold on to'.

I.ii A city has quickly emerged. Jenny and the six girls sing the 'Alabama Song', in which they state their need for whisky and dollars.

I.iii The backdrop projection shows a huge city and photographs of large numbers of men. Fatty and Moses recruit the dissatisfied men to move to Mahagonny.

I.iv The caption reads: 'In the following years the malcontents from all continents descended on Mahagonny, city of gold'. Jim, Jack, Bill and Joe sing the praises of Mahagonny's whisky, women, horses and poker – and of the beautiful green moon of Alabama.

I.v The caption reads: 'Among those who came to the city of Mahagonny at that time was Jim Mahoney, and it is his story that we want to relate to you'. Jim, Jack, Bill and Joe stand next to a sign pointing to Mahagonny. Begbick introduces herself and tries to interest the men in 'fresh girls'. Jim gets to know Jenny.

I.vi The projection shows a map of Mahagonny. Jim and Jenny emerge, singing as they pass. Jenny asks Jim whether he likes her to wear underwear or not. He answers in the negative and inquires about her wishes. 'It's perhaps a little early to talk about that', she replies.

I.vii The caption reads: 'All great enterprises have their crises'; the backdrop displays statistics relating to crime and finance in Mahagonny. Inside the Hotel Rich Man, Fatty and Moses are sitting at a bar table. Begbick rushes in wearing white make-up. Business is bad. Fatty and Moses confront Begbick with the bitter truth: 'Cash breeds passion'.

I.viii The caption reads: 'Those who truly seek shall be disappointed'; the projection is of the wharf at Mahagonny. Jim arrives, coming away from the town; he is fed up, but his friends persuade him to stay and they all return to the city.

I.ix In front of the Hotel Rich Man the men of Mahagonny are smoking and drinking, listening to music and dreamily observing a white cloud moving across the sky. They are surrounded by placards: 'Treat my chairs with respect', 'Do not make any noise', 'Avoid offensive songs'. The onstage pianist plays Tekla Bądarzewska-Baranowska's *The Maiden's Prayer*. Jack declares, 'That's timeless art', but Jim is still dissatisfied: 'No one will ever be happy with this Mahagonny, because there's too much peace and too much harmony and because there's too much to hold on to'. The lights go out.

I.x On the backdrop, in gigantic letters, 'A typhoon' is followed by the inscription 'A hurricane moving towards Mahagonny'. The orchestra plays a fugue and the company bemoans the 'frightful phenomenon'. People flee and a wind blows leaves and scraps of paper across the stage. An inscription reads 'On this night of horror a simple lumberjack by the name of Jim Mahoney discovered the laws of human happiness'.

I.xi On the night of the hurricane, Jenny, Begbick, Jim, Jack, Bill and Joe sit on the ground, propped up against a wall. All are feeling desperate except for Jim, who is smiling. On the wall are placards inscribed 'It is forbidden'. The male chorus sings a chorale pleading for fearless acceptance of the hurricane's force, but Jim claims that people are just as destructive as hurricanes and challenges everyone to ignore what is forbidden and do whatever they please. The lights go out. In the background is a diagram with an arrow indicating the path of the hurricane.

Act 2.i In a pale light the girls and men are waiting on the road outside Mahagonny. The projection again shows the arrow moving towards Mahagonny. A loudspeaker makes intermittent announcements during the orchestral ritornello, plotting the hurricane's progress, until the danger is past. The chorus praises the 'miraculous resolution'.

2.ii The inscription reads: 'Business flourishes in Mahagonny after the great hurricane'. In silence, projections depict the transition from a simple goldmining town to a modern city. The male chorus intones the agenda: 'First, don't forget, comes grub; second the act of love; third don't forget boxing; fourth boozing, according to contract.' The men go on stage and take part in the proceedings. On the backdrop is the word 'Eating'. Men sit at individual tables, piled high with meat. Jack, now known as The Glutton, eats incessantly. After boasting that he has eaten two calves and would like to eat himself, he dies. The chorus laments him as 'a man without fear'.

2.iii On the backdrop is 'Love'. The men queue in front of the Mandalay brothel; erotic pictures appear on a screen. A small band is on stage, but no girls. Begbick admonishes the men to spit out their chewing gum, wash their hands, give her time and exchange a few words with her. Moses asks the men, who are being admitted in groups of three, to be patient. The male chorus expresses lyrical urgency.

2.iv In front of the backdrop, on which 'Boxing' is projected, a boxing ring is being set up under Fatty's

supervision. On a platform at the side a wind band is playing. Joe arrives with Jim and Bill. He bets all his money on himself but is slain by Moses.

2.v 'Boozing': the men sit down, put their feet on the table and drink. Jim, Bill and Jenny play pool. Jim orders a round but when Begbick asks for payment he realizes he has no money left. They have made a 'ship' using the pool table, a curtain rod and the like. Jim, Bill and Jenny get on it, and South Sea landscapes appear on the backdrop. The men indicate a storm by whistling and howling. Expecting to land elsewhere, they are disappointed to find themselves still at Mahagonny. Jim's friends leave him and, unable to pay, he is arrested. Jenny reaffirms the moral: 'You lie in the bed that you yourself make, no one else pulls up the covers, and if someone's going to do the kicking, it's me, if someone's going to be kicked, it's you'. Jim is removed. The chorus intones a new chorale: 'Don't be led on, there is no return. The end is nigh; you can already feel the nocturnal wind. There will be no more tomorrow'.

Act 3.i At night Jim lies with one foot chained to a lamp-post and sings a defiant aria against the coming day.

3.ii The inscription reads: 'The courts in Mahagonny were no worse than anywhere else'. A tent serves as a court room. Seated on the judge's chair is Begbick, on the defence's chair Fatty, on the prosecution bench, Tobby Higgins. Moses is selling tickets for the proceedings. Higgins is charged with premeditated murder but eventually offers a sufficiently large sum to be acquitted. Jim is charged with the indirect murder of a friend, disturbing the peace, the seduction of a girl named Jenny and failing to pay for Begbick's whisky and curtain rod, above all for lack of money. The 'Benares Song' is sung as the men read in their newspapers of an earthquake in Benares. There is nowhere left to go.

3.iii The inscription reads 'Execution and death of Jimmy Mahoney. Many people may prefer not to see the following execution of Jimmy Mahoney. But we believe that even you, ladies and gentlemen, would not wish to pay for him. Such is the respect for money in our time'. The projection is of Mahagonny, peacefully illuminated. Small groups of people stand around. Jim enters, accompanied by Moses, Jenny and Bill. Jim and Jenny are ordered to the front of the stage, where a duet is sung and leave is taken of Bill. All but Jim sing of God coming to Mahagonny.

3.iv On the backdrop, Mahagonny burns. Begbick, Fatty and Moses are standing and singing 'Aber dieses ganze Mahagonny . . .' ('But the whole of Mahagonny. . .'). A group of men arrive carrying placards: 'For money', 'For the battle against all'. A second group arrives with placards reading: 'For property', 'For love', 'For the saleability of love', 'For life without limits', 'For unlimited murder'. In another procession the placards read: 'For the unjust distribution of worldly goods', 'For the just distribution of unworldly goods'. A group of girls arrive with Jenny, carrying Jim's shirt and, on a cloth cushion, his ring, watch and revolver. They sing a reprise of the 'Alabama Song'. Bill, at the head of a procession of men bearing Jim's coffin, carries a placard: 'For justice'. The male chorus intones 'Can't help a dead man'. Moses, Begbick and Fatty enter with three more processions, each bearing different placards. They all move forward as if to march into the audience. The entire cast sings 'Can't help us and you and nobody!'

*

Weill's partnership with Brecht is surrounded by myth. The questions it throws up are not always easy to answer. What attracted them to each other in the first place? What were their individual contributions to the collaboration? Did Brecht, as he himself claimed, really dictate melodies? What caused the separation? The evidence for answers is flimsy. On a personal level, the relationship was cordial but never close. Politically they had a common sympathy for liberal causes, but Weill did not have Brecht's marked affinity for Marxist theory and practice. What brought them together professionally was an interest in writing a full-scale opera. *Aufstieg und Fall der Stadt Mahagonny* is on various levels an awkward work. Up to a point, that was the authors' purpose. But by the time Brecht came to write his *Anmerkungen* ('Notes') in 1930, he was all too willing to emphasize the more overtly destructive aspects, especially the generic ones. Weill's essays, written shortly before, convey more constructive ambitions and no doubt prompted Brecht's notes. The difficulty that any prospective director faces, notwithstanding the work's intentionally 'uncomfortable' aspects, stems in part from tensions in the Brecht-Weill partnership itself, 'the collision of two congenial yet incompatible minds' as the commentator David Drew sees it: 'The very nature of the work compels us to continue searching for ideal solutions long after we have recognized there are none to be found'.

For all its reliance on the 'song' idiom, musically the work aspires to be much more than the mere sum of its parts. Weill described it as a 'structure based on purely musical laws'. Just how incompatible his views were with Brecht's can be measured from the collaborators' divergent attitudes towards the use of the projected inscriptions. Weill was concerned with 'giving the links between the musical numbers a form that obstructs as little as possible the musical design of the whole'. For Brecht, on the other hand, the inscriptions constituted an important means of 'defamiliarization' (*Verfremdung*), something central to his theory of epic theatre. Just as the emergence of the opera out of the Songspiel reflects conflicts in the Weill-Brecht partnership, with Brecht's theorizing about the opera anticipating his later experiments in the genre of didactic theatre (the *Lehrstück*), so the opera itself invites directors and conductors to take sides in those conflicts.   S.Hn.

B

Ballad of Baby Doe, The

Opera in two acts by Douglas S. Moore to a libretto by John Latouche; Central City, Colorado, Opera House, 7 July 1956.

The cast at the première included Dolores Wilson (Baby Doe), Walter Cassel (Horace) and Frances Bible (Augusta).

Baby Doe	soprano
Horace Tabor	baritone
Augusta Tabor	mezzo-soprano
Miner	tenor
Mama McCourt	contralto
President Chester A. Arthur	tenor
Father Chapelle	tenor
William Jennings Bryan	bass-baritone
Miners, saloon girls, friends of Augusta and Tabor,	
hotel staff, politicians, wedding guests	

Moore had been attracted to the story of Elizabeth 'Baby Doe' Tabor as early as 1935, when he read accounts of her being found frozen to death near the abandoned mine where she had maintained a vigil since the death of her husband 36 years earlier. Nonetheless, no opera resulted until the Central City Opera Association suggested that subject in 1953. Following the première, projected revisions were halted by the death of Latouche (August 1956), after one new scene (Act 2 scene ii) and an additional aria for Baby Doe had been added. The revised version was first performed by the New York City Opera on 3 April 1958, with Beverly Sills as Baby Doe.

The complicated story is a true one, though some events have been compressed in time or space. Act 1 opens outside the Tabor Opera House, Leadville, Colorado, in 1880. A drunken Miner is thrown out of a neighbouring saloon. He has been rowdily celebrating the sale of his silver mine, the Matchless, to Horace Tabor for a large sum. Tabor, who built the new opera house and 'owns the whole dam[n] town', now appears with his rough cronies to take the air during the interval. He relishes the lively street life he finds there and dances with the saloon girls before being interrupted and upbraided by his dour wife, Augusta, who is obsessed with propriety and respectability. As he is going back into the opera house, Tabor is accosted by Baby Doe, newly arrived in town, who asks for directions to the Clarendon Hotel.

Outside the hotel later that evening (scene ii) Tabor overhears the saloon girls gossiping about Baby Doe. Apparently she has a husband in Central City and was given her nickname by the miners. Through her hotel-room window, she can be seen and heard singing her famous 'Willow Song' ('Willow, where we met together'); Tabor applauds and she responds with flirtatious flattery. Tabor is hopelessly smitten ('Warm as the autumn light').

In the Tabors' apartment several months later (scene iii) Augusta, while sorting through her husband's desk, finds a gift intended for Baby. She confronts him with it; he is unrepentant and Augusta threatens to create a scandal by publicizing their affair. In the lobby of the hotel (scene iv) Baby is preparing to leave. As she explains in a letter home ('Dearest Mama, I am writing'), the situation is impossible, and the affair with Tabor must end. She confirms this to Augusta, who has come to confront her, but when Augusta contemptuously ridicules Tabor, Baby tears up the letter and rushes into Tabor's arms as he arrives. Augusta's friends (scene v) are determined to create a scandal, but Augusta now resolves to maintain a dignified silence.

Augusta's reticence is in vain for by 1883 (scene vi) the two lovers have divorced their spouses and married each other, a marriage Tabor wishes to make respectable with a formal Catholic wedding in Washington, DC, where he has been appointed to a seat in the Senate. As the couple and the priest arrive for the reception at the Willard Hotel (boycotted by the other senators' wives), Mama McCourt, Baby's mother, vociferously supportive of her daughter, blackens the name of both Augusta and Baby's former husband Harvey Doe. The priest, unaware of the divorces, is scandalized, and a scene is avoided only by the arrival of President Arthur.

Back in Denver (Act 2 scene i), the couple are universally snubbed, but are so much in love that they are unconcerned. Augusta, who has mellowed, has heard from Washington that the USA is about to take its currency off the silver standard – which will ruin Tabor – and she warns Baby that the Matchless

Mine must be sold before it is too late. Tabor angrily rejects this advice and makes Baby promise that she will always keep the mine. Two years later (scene ii) Tabor, in serious financial trouble, throws in his lot with William Jennings Bryan and his 'free silver' platform. Bryan makes a rousing speech at the gate of the Matchless Mine (scene iii) but his campaign is doomed. Mama McCourt goes to Augusta (scene iv) to seek help for the now impoverished Tabors, but is gently rebuffed by Augusta, who knows that Tabor would never accept her money.

The final scene (scene v) abandons realism. In 1899 Tabor, dying and delirious, stumbles on to the darkened stage of his opera house in Leadville. There he relives his past and foresees the future: one of his daughters will disown him, the other will turn to prostitution. Baby arrives to comfort his dying moments and then is seen as an old woman. Slowly she crosses to the Matchless Mine (now visible on the stage) to take up her lonely vigil.

*

Immediately and resoundingly popular, *The Ballad of Baby Doe* was for a time thought of as 'the great American opera', and in 1976 (the bicentenary year) it was given at least five professional productions in the United States alone. The mixture of romance and frontier rowdiness in the tale ideally suited Moore's musical and dramatic strengths, allowing both for Broadway-like production numbers (the superb opening scene, Bryan's speech) and for set-piece songs in the early Tin Pan Alley style of the composer's youth (Baby Doe's 'Willow Song' and letter aria). Outside such high points the music relaxes into a bland arioso reminiscent of Moore's teacher D'Indy, and of Puccini. Nonetheless, with the right material Moore hits the target so squarely that dullness elsewhere is readily forgotten.   **A.St.**

Ballo in maschera, Un ('A Masked Ball')

Melodramma in three acts by Giuseppe Verdi to a libretto by Antonio Somma after Eugène Scribe's libretto *Gustave III, ou Le bal masqué*; Rome, Teatro Apollo, 17 February 1859.

The cast at the première included Gaetano Fraschini (Riccardo), Leone Giraldoni (Renato), Eugenia Julienne-Dejean (Amelia) and Zelina Sbriscia (Ulrica).

Riccardo *Count of Warwick, Governor of*		
Boston		tenor
Renato *a Creole, his secretary*		baritone
Amelia *Renato's wife*		soprano
Ulrica *a negro fortune-teller*		contralto
Oscar *a page*		soprano
Silvano *a sailor*		bass
Samuel		bass
Tom	*enemies of the Count*	bass
A Judge		tenor
Amelia's Servant		tenor
Deputies, officers, sailors, guards, men,		
women, children, gentlemen, associates of		
Samuel and Tom, servants, masks, dancing		
couples		
Setting In and around Boston, at the end of the		
17th century		

By February 1857 Verdi had agreed to write a new opera for the Teatro S Carlo in Naples, to be performed in the carnival season 1857–8. His first idea was to use *King Lear*, a setting of which he had planned with the playwright Antonio Somma, but (not for the first time) the S Carlo singers were not to his liking and the project was postponed. By September 1857 the composer was becoming anxious about his approaching deadline, and eventually proposed to Somma and the S Carlo – albeit with some reservations about the libretto's conventionality – that he set a remodelled and translated version of an old Scribe libretto entitled *Gustave III, ou Le bal masqué*, based on historical fact and written for Auber in 1833. Somma and the theatre agreed, and Verdi set to work advising his librettist, who had no experience of writing for the musical theatre, on the necessary poetic proportions of the subject.

As soon as a synopsis reached the Neapolitan censors, it became clear that the opera, which dealt with the assassination of the Swedish king Gustavus III, would have to be changed considerably if it was to be performed in Naples. Verdi agreed to change the king into a duke and to set the action back in time, and a new version of the story was patched together. However, soon after the composer arrived in Naples the censor rejected this version, making a series of new, more stringent demands, notably that Amelia become a sister rather than a wife, that there be no drawing of lots by the conspirators, and that the murder take place off stage. The authorities of the S Carlo attempted to answer these objections by cobbling together a new version entitled *Adelia degli Adimari*, but this Verdi angrily rejected. Eventually, negotiations broke down, the planned performances fell through, and Verdi undertook to fulfil his contract at a later date.

When it became clear that Naples would not stage the opera, Verdi decided to have it given at the Teatro Apollo, in Rome, even though it soon became clear that Roman censorship, while far less exigent than that at Naples, would require at least a change of locale and the demoting of the king to some lesser noble. Eventually Somma and Verdi established Riccardo, Conte di Warwick and a setting in the colonies of North America, although as a protest Somma did not allow his name to appear on the printed libretto. The première was a great success, and *Un ballo in maschera* became one of Verdi's most popular operas. Though not attaining the dissemination of *Rigoletto*, *Il trovatore* or *La traviata*, it has never lost its place in the international repertory. Many modern performances restore the opera to its original, 18th-century Swedish setting, even though such restoration seems not to have had Verdi's explicit approval. In the Swedish setting the names are as follows:

Riccardo	Gustavus III *King of Sweden*
Renato	Captain Anckarstroem
	Gustavus's secretary
Amelia	Amelia
Ulrica	Mam'zelle Arvidson
Oscar	Oscar
Silvano	Christian
Samuel	Count Ribbing
Tom	Count Horn
A Judge	Armfelt *Minister of Justice*

*

The brief prelude presents three of the main musical ideas of the opening scene, first a chorale-like opening chorus, then a fugato associated with the conspirators and finally Riccardo's first aria; the whole argument is punctuated by a tiny rhythmic figure first heard in the second bar.

Act I.i *A hall in the Governor's house* The opening chorus, 'Posa in pace, a' bei sogni ristora', continues the prelude's musical juxtaposition of Riccardo's loyal followers with the conspirators who are planning to overthrow him, led by Samuel and Tom. Riccardo appears and, in a style reminiscent of *opera buffa*, reviews with Oscar the guest list for the coming masked ball. At seeing the name of Amelia, however, he is visibly moved, and advances to the footlights to sing a brief aria privately expressing his guilty love for her, 'La rivedrà nell'estasi'. Its opening phrase will return later as a musical symbol of the love around which the story of the opera revolves. As the chorus disperses, the secretary Renato enters to warn Riccardo of plots against his life. His aria, 'Alla vita che t'arride', though formally more extended than Riccardo's, displays the same tendency towards condensation of traditional elements. Next to appear is a judge, requesting that Riccardo exile Ulrica, a fortune-teller suspected of supernatural practices. Oscar chooses to defend Ulrica in the ballata 'Volta la terrea', a French two-stanza form studded with the light coloratura which will typify the page throughout. Riccardo decides that he and his followers will disguise themselves and pay a personal call on Ulrica. He leads off the final stretta, 'Ogni cura si doni al diletto', a number that continues the

'Un ballo in maschera' (Verdi), Therese Tietjens as Amelia and Giuglini as Riccardo in a production at the Lyceum Theatre, London, in 1861: lithograph from a contemporary sheet music cover

Gallic atmosphere in its celebration of the pleasures of life, despite the continued mutterings of the conspirators in the musical background.

I.ii *The fortune-teller's dwelling* After an atmospheric orchestral introduction, full of low woodwind sonorities and sinister tritones, Ulrica sings the invocation 'Re dell'abisso', an aria that begins in the minor, is interrupted by Riccardo's entrance in disguise, and continues with a cabaletta substitute in the major. The atmosphere of foreboding is rudely interrupted by Silvano, a sailor who has seen no preferment and who – in the brief, sprightly solo 'Su, fatemi largo' – asks Ulrica to divine his future. Ulrica predicts wealth and a commission, something that Riccardo promptly brings to pass by secreting gold and the appropriate papers in Silvano's pocket. Silvano discovers his new-found wealth and all join in praise of Ulrica. They are interrupted by Amelia's servant, who requests for his mistress an interview with Ulrica. Ulrica dismisses the crowd; but Riccardo, who has recognized the servant, remains in his hiding place as Amelia comes in.

In an impassioned arioso, Amelia asks Ulrica to rid her of the love that torments her. Ulrica's reply is the sinuous, chromatic 'Della città all'occaso', which tells of a healing plant that grows in the gallows-field nearby. In the brief terzetto that ensues, 'Consentimi, o Signore', Amelia prays that she may be healed, while Ulrica tries to comfort her and Riccardo, still hidden, vows to follow her on her quest. As Amelia departs, the stage is filled with Riccardo's entourage. Riccardo, pretending to be a fisherman, sings the characteristic two-stanza canzone 'Di' tu se fedele', replete with the conventions of maritime musical language. He presents his hand to Ulrica who, in an imposing arioso, predicts that he will soon die by the hand of a friend. Riccardo attempts to disperse the tension by leading off the famous quintet 'È scherzo od è follia', in which his breathless, 'laughing' line is accompanied by sinister chattering from Samuel and Tom, and by a sustained, high-lying melody for Oscar. Riccardo asks the identity of his murderer: Ulrica says it will be the first person who shakes his hand, a prophecy seemingly made absurd by the faithful Renato, who hurries on soon after and immediately clasps his master's hand. The act closes with a martial hymn, 'O figlio d'Inghilterra', in which the principals emerge from the vocal mass to restate their differing positions.

Act 2 *A lonely field on the outskirts of Boston* Amelia's grand scene is preceded by a lengthy, impassioned orchestral prelude which features her melody from the Act 1 terzetto. Heavily veiled, she is frightened by her surroundings and in the aria 'Ma dall'arido stelo divulsa' prays for assistance in her ordeal. The aria, with the mournful english horn obbligato that is a traditional pointer of the isolated heroine, is interrupted by a terrifying vision at midnight sounds, but her final prayer re-establishes a kind of resigned calm. Riccardo appears, and so begins one of Verdi's greatest soprano-tenor duets, a number that, as was becoming common in middle-period Verdi, has a succession of contrasting 'dialogue' movements before its more conventional close with the cabaletta together. In the opening Allegro agitato the pace of exchange is rapid as Riccardo declares his love and Amelia begs him to leave; the musical continuity comes for the most part from a driving string melody. In a second movement, 'Non sai tu che se l'anima mia', their individual attitudes are explored at greater length, with a particularly impressive modulation as the discourse turns from Riccardo to Amelia; but eventually Riccardo's pleas win the day and, to a passionate, soaring melody, Amelia admits her love for him. A brief linking section leads to the cabaletta, 'Oh qual soave brivido', whose two stanzas and lively arpeggiated melody are separated by yet another impassioned declaration of mutual love.

The couple separate at the sound of footsteps. Riccardo recognizes Renato; Amelia, terrified, lowers her veil. In the first movement of the ensuing trio, 'Per salvarti da lor', Renato warns of the approaching conspirators, and lends his cloak to Riccardo in order to effect the latter's escape. Riccardo will leave only

after muffled pleas from Amelia, and he solemnly charges Renato to escort her, still veiled, to the gates of the city. Before Riccardo rushes off, the three principals pause for a furiously paced second trio movement, 'Odi tu come fremono cupi', in which the driving rhythm encloses a strictly patterned alternation of solo statements. Riccardo is safely away when the conspirators appear, singing the contrapuntal music first heard in the prelude to the opera. They are challenged by Renato and, finding their prey has disappeared, decide to amuse themselves by seeing the face of the mysterious woman. When it becomes clear that Renato, in his loyalty to the Count, will fight rather than permit this, Amelia herself raises her veil. Renato is astounded: the conspirators cannot contain their mirth at the notion of Renato's nocturnal assignation with his own wife, and break into the nonchalant 'laughing' chorus, 'Ve' se di notte qui colla sposa'. In between statements of the main idea, Renato accuses Amelia while she begs for mercy. As a parting gesture, Renato arranges a meeting with Samuel and Tom later that morning; the conspirators stroll off together, still vastly amused, their laughter echoing as the curtain comes down.

Act 3.i *A study in Renato's house* A stormy orchestral introduction ushers in Renato and Amelia. In an impassioned arioso, Renato insists that his wife must die. Although she admits her love for Riccardo, she insists that she has not betrayed her husband. Renato, however, is inflexible, and in the sorrowful aria 'Morrò, ma prima in grazia', Amelia begs to see her child before dying, a cello obbligato adding to the pathos of the scene. Renato agrees to her request and once she has departed hurls furious insults at the portrait of Riccardo, which has a prominent place in his study. His anger coalesces into the famous aria 'Eri tu', a minor–major *romanza* which in the second part turns from angry accusations to the pain of his lost love.

Yet again the contrapuntal theme introduces Samuel and Tom. Renato shows them that he knows of their conspiracy, but now offers to join in its execution though without telling them why, offering his son's life as proof of his good word. Samuel and Tom accept his word, and all three swear blood brotherhood in the martial hymn 'Dunque l'onta di tutti sol una'. They elect to draw lots to decide who will strike the fatal blow, and Renato takes advantage of Amelia's return to force her to draw the name from an urn. To dotted rhythms and tremolando strings, Amelia draws Renato's name, and the conspirators again join in the martial hymn, this time with a terror-stricken descant from Amelia.

In one of those abrupt changes of mood so characteristic of the opera, Oscar now appears, bringing with him once again the musical atmosphere of French comic opera. He has an invitation to tonight's masked ball, which Renato, Samuel and Tom all accept. To close the scene, they join in a stretta led off by Oscar, 'Di che fulgor', in which the terror and exultation of the principals are subsumed under Oscar's delicate musical idiom.

3.ii The Count's sumptuous study In an opening recitative, Riccardo decides to sign a paper sending Renato and Amelia back to England. He then muses on the loss of his love in the *romanza* 'Ma se m'è forza perderti', which moves from minor to major, but via an unusual intermediate section in which he feels a strange presentiment of death. Dance music is heard off stage, and Oscar brings an anonymous message warning Riccardo that he risks assassination at the ball. But Riccardo, as ever heedless of the danger, concludes the scene with a passionate recollection of his Act 1 aria of love for Amelia.

3.iii A vast, richly decorated ballroom The opening chorus, 'Fervono amori e danze', repeats the music heard off stage in scene ii. As Renato, Samuel, Tom and their followers appear, a new, minor-mode theme emerges over which the conspirators exchange passwords and search for the Count. A third theme is heard as Oscar recognizes Renato. However, in spite of Renato's anxious questions, Oscar refuses to reveal the Count's costume, singing instead a lively French *couplet* form, 'Saper vorreste'. The opening chorus is heard again, and Renato renews his questions, pleading important business. Oscar finally reveals that the Count is wearing a black cloak with red ribbon, after which he mingles with the crowd to yet more of the opening chorus. A new dance melody, this time a delicate mazurka, underpins a stifled conversation between Amelia and Riccardo: Amelia begs the Count to escape; he reiterates his love but tells her that she is to return to England with her husband. They are bidding a last, tender farewell when Renato flings himself between them and stabs Riccardo. In the subsequent confusion, Oscar rips off Renato's mask and the chorus expresses its fury in a wild Prestissimo. But then the gentle mazurka briefly returns (the offstage dance orchestra as yet unaware of the events) as Riccardo bids his people release Renato. Leading off the final concertato, 'Ella è pura', Riccardo assures Renato that Amelia's honour is intact. He bids his subjects farewell, and a brief stretta of universal horror brings down the curtain.

*

Un ballo in maschera, as many have remarked, is a masterpiece of variety, of the blending of stylistic elements. Verdi's experiment with a 'pure' version of French grand opera in the mid-1850s, *Les vêpres siciliennes*, was not entirely happy; here we see him instead gesturing to the lighter side of French opera, primarily with the character of Oscar, but also in aspects of Riccardo's musical personality. The

juxtaposition of this style with the intense, interior version of Italian serious opera that Verdi had preferred in the early 1850s is extremely bold, particularly in sections such as Act 1 scene ii (where Riccardo confronts Ulrica) or in the finale to Act 2 (the so-called laughing chorus), in both of which the two styles meet head on with little mediation. One of the reasons why the blend is so successful is that Verdi's treatment of the traditional forms at the backbone of his 'Italian' manner was itself changing, adapting towards the more elliptical manner of French models. *Ballo* is notable for the shortness and intensity of its principal arias, for the absence of grand design.

Another reason for the opera's success undoubtedly lies in its delicate balance of musical personalities. At the outer limits of the style, as it were, lie two musical extremes: Oscar, whose role throughout is cast in an unambiguously Gallic mould of light comedy; and Ulrica, whose musical personality is unrelievedly dark and austere. Within these two extremes lie Renato and Amelia, characters cast in the Italian style, fixed in their emotional range, but from time to time infected by 'French' influences. And at the centre comes Riccardo, who freely partakes of both worlds, and who mediates between them so movingly and persuasively.   R.P.

Bánk bán

Historical dramatic opera in three acts by Ferenc Erkel to a libretto by Béni Egressy after József Katona's play *Bánk bán*; Pest, National Theatre, 9 March 1861.

The cast at the première included József Ellinger as Bánk bán, Kornélia Hollósy as Melinda, Lajos Bignio as Endre II and Zsófia Hofbauer as Gertrud.

Bánk bán *Palatine of Hungary*	tenor
Melinda *his wife*	soprano
Endre II *King of Hungary*	baritone
Gertrud *his wife*	contralto
Otto *Duke of Meran, Gertrud's brother*	tenor
Petur bán *Lord Lieutenant of Bihar*	bass-baritone
Biberach *a knight-errant*	baritone
Tiborc *a peasant*	baritone
Courtiers, guests, insurgents, soldiers	
Setting The Hungarian royal palace and by the River Danube in the 13th century	

While King Endre II was at war over the Carpathian Mountains, which formed the frontier of Hungary, his power-drunk wife, Gertrud, from Meran in the Tyrol, filled the royal household with her foreign courtiers and lived with them in the greatest luxury.

Eventually she and her courtiers were killed in a revolt in 1213. Katona's fine drama (1815) based on this story of tragic conflict between strong historical characters is a mirror of Hungary's centuries-old struggle against foreign despotism. For that reason its performance was forbidden by the censor. The play was published in book form but was forgotten for two decades before being staged successfully. After the failure of the war of independence in 1848–9, it was again banned for many years.

It is impossible to tell when Erkel began to compose the opera; the only reliable information is that the librettist died in 1851. A newspaper mentioned in 1844 that Erkel intended to write an opera on the subject, but the libretto could not have been ready then. During 1850 and 1851 it was repeatedly stated in the newspapers that Erkel was working on the opera, though he could not at that time have hoped for permission to perform it. When the oppression began to decline in 1860, he must have been close to finishing the work: according to the dates on the score it was completed between August and October 1860.

Erkel's sons Gyula (1842–1909) and Sándor (1846–1900) contributed to the opera: Gyula helped with the orchestration, while Sándor copied some of the parts, both under their father's strict supervision. Erkel had earlier set a poem by Mihály Vörösmarty (1800–55); he decided to include this song as 'Keserű bordal' ('Drinking Song of Bitterness'). It became one of the most popular arias in the opera.

The première in the National Theatre, conducted by the composer, was enormously successful, performed by the theatre's best singers. Within Hungary it was not given as widely as Erkel's earlier *Hunyadi László* (1844) because it was more difficult to stage. Important premières took place however in nine cities over the next twenty years. By 1990 it had been performed 900 times in Budapest. The finest foreign performer to sing Melinda in the 19th century was Marie Wilt. In 1939 Nándor Rékai revised the music and Kálmán Nádasdy and Gusztáv Oláh wrote a new libretto, closer to Katona's play and in faultless verse. It is now performed in this revised version, with some small modifications to the music of Act 3 scene i made by Jenő Kenessey in 1953. Rékai made many deletions and rearranged the music to fit the rewritten libretto. He made two versions of the role of Bánk: tenor and baritone. The latter prevailed for a time but since 1959 the part has been sung by a tenor. Outside Hungary only the 1939 version was performed; it had premières in the USSR, Czechoslovakia, Germany, Finland and Belgium in translation. A Hungarian performance was given by the Budapest opera in the Nemirovich-Danchenko Music Theatre, Moscow, in 1958. The opera was first heard in London (in English) at University College in 1968. In

1990 only the 1939 version was available on record and in an edition. The discussion below therefore follows this version.

*

Act I.i *The ceremonial hall of the royal palace at Visegrád*
There is an overture and a short introduction including Melinda's principal melody; this is in a slow *verbunkos* (a Hungarian dance) style, similar in mood to the famous 'Death Song' in *Hunyadi László*. The curtain rises. The Queen's brother Otto tells the intriguer Biberach of his intention to seduce Melinda. Petur, the chief of the rebels, enters accompanied by the rebels' chorus and sings 'Keserű bordal' he protests against the carousing of Gertrud and her courtiers and voices the misery of the people. The rebels have sent a messenger to ask Bánk to come and help them and the country. A delegate from the King arrives, reporting that his army has gained a great victory, and a rejoicing chorus containing folklike tunes follows. There is a short ensemble for Otto, Gertrud and Melinda, whom Gertrud has summoned to her court in order to give Melinda as prey to Otto. After a repetition of the rejoicing chorus Bánk arrives. In a duet with Petur, he is made aware of the rebels' plans and of Melinda's danger (confirmed by Biberach). Bánk promises to be with the rebels that night and hurries away. The court returns, followed by the rebels' chorus and that of the courtiers and then by a dance in the form of a *csárdás* (a derivative of the *verbunkos*). The curtain falls, but the orchestra continues to play, linking the first scene to the next.

I.ii *The stairway of the royal palace* Otto lays siege to Melinda's heart, but she resists. Melinda's musical character, like that of the other main figures in the opera, undergoes constant development: first presented in the introduction as strongly nationalistic, it later – in the royal court full of foreign courtiers – begins to assume more general stylistic traits, but by the end of scene i Melinda is once again represented by the nationalistic theme of the introduction with its variants and closely related themes. Bánk witnesses the encounter between Otto and Melinda, having been set up by Biberach, who wants to take revenge on Gertrud, Otto, Melinda and everybody for not respecting his importance at court. Though Bánk is convinced of Melinda's devotion, he is tormented by jealousy. As with Melinda earlier, his character is not yet fully established, shown by a love aria typical of French or Italian opera. Biberach gives Otto a powder that will make Melinda lose consciousness, so that Otto can have his way with her. At the same time he is turning Bánk against Gertrud, who is the original instigator of Otto's plan. In a powerful finale Gertrud dismisses her guests, except for Melinda.

Act 2.i *The porch of the royal palace, facing the Danube* Bánk, in an impassioned aria 'Hazám, hazám, te mindenem!' ('Homeland, Homeland, my Everything'), worries about the fate of his country. Tiborc, an old peasant, enters and tells him of his family's misery. Biberach arrives with the news that Otto has now accomplished his evil plan. Melinda enters, staggering as though insane. In her despair she begs Bánk to kill her, only asking that he will be compassionate to their child. In this duet the tragedy of their situation is increasingly suggested by sharper rhythms and wider-ranging melodic patterns. Bánk places Melinda and the child in the care of Tiborc, who is to take them to Bánk's remote castle. The folklike chamber ensemble that accompanies them, including a cimbalom and a viola d'amore, brilliantly evokes their tragic situation.

2.ii *The Queen's room* Bánk enters. He and Gertrud confront one another in an increasingly violent exchange of accusations. Otto appears briefly, then vanishes. Both Bánk and Gertrud maintain their musical characters; Gertrud sings in a wilful, aristocratic manner, but gradually adopts Bánk's *verbunkos*-inspired style as she becomes more fearful for her own safety. This is in vain, however: it is she who has handed Melinda over, reduced the country to destitution and seized power for her courtiers, and her change of tone does not help her. She draws a dagger against Bánk, who stabs her with it.

Act 3.i *The banks of the River Tisza by moonlight, before a storm* In a short introduction inspired by folk music, two piccolos wonderfully evoke the landscape and the prevailing mood. Tiborc urges Melinda to cross the river without delay. The storm, the rough water and the lightning are only hinted at in the music, all attention being concentrated on Melinda, who has collapsed. She is mad and uncomprehending, and sings a rapid succession of arias, in which her characteristic motifs and intonation are merged with the *verbunkos* form, quickening towards a climax at which, clasping her infant, she throws herself into the river and dies. A solemn entr'acte follows.

3.ii *The state room of the royal palace* Endre II sits on one of the two thrones; the other is empty. A chamber beyond is hidden by curtains. The scene takes place in semi-darkness, lit only by torches. The King and court are in deep mourning. Endre accuses the lords of murder. The curtains are drawn back, revealing Gertrud's body on a catafalque; round it kneel their children and pages. The King persists in his violent accusations. The chorus of rebels denies the murder and reveals the misery that Gertrud has caused. Bánk then enters and throws down the emblem of his rank in front of the catafalque, claiming that he killed the Queen, that her crimes are widely known and that anyone else would have done

the same. The King commands him to be arrested. Bánk exclaims that only the nation may judge between the King and him. The King draws his sword to fight a duel with Bánk. A shepherd's pipe sounds in the distance, and Tiborc enters, followed by other peasants bearing the bodies of Melinda and the infant. Bánk, stricken with grief, asks to be buried with them. Everybody kneels. After a short funeral chorus the orchestra brings the opera to a close.

*

With its strongly national theme, its critical timing in relation to political events, and its readiness to draw on the world of folk melody and the formal principles of the Hungarian *verbunkos*, *Bánk bán* represents an important stage in the development of Hungarian opera. One striking device is the contrast in musical style for the opposing characters: Otto and Biberach, in common with all the 'negative' characters, are depicted in non-nationalistic idioms, and Otto always by richly sentimental music; while in his portrayal of Petur and the other 'positive' characters, Erkel succeeds in combining *verbunkos* dance rhythms with vocal melodies often reminiscent of actual folk music, and in developing them on an operatic level. Another feature is the use of the orchestra: throughout the opera it has an important role in its own right, not only delineating the principal characters with their motifs but also participating actively in the dramatic development and providing local colour where necessary, sometimes as a folklike chamber ensemble.

Bánk bán is widely regarded as the most significant Hungarian opera of its time, for although not as widely popular in Hungary as *Hunyadi László*, it shows a broader command of dramatic characterization and greater skill in accommodating a national idiom. The story of the 13th-century revolt against the Queen's hated foreign court seemed to have set free repressed passions in the composer. He filled his opera with broad, immediately striking melodies whose new flexibility was a direct result of the influence of folksong. Erkel also achieved a newly vivid dramatic characterization in the grand scenes (especially in the third act) through his handling of recitative and thematic transformation. He was particularly adept at evoking a pastoral nostalgia in instrumental passages composed in folk style; the cimbalom was used here for the first time in composed music. As the fruit of many years of idiomatic development, *Bánk bán* represents a high point in Erkel's output; his development thereafter took different directions and he never again succeeded in writing with such naturalness and vitality.

D.L.

Barbiere di Siviglia, II ('The Barber of Seville')
[*Almaviva, ossia L'inutile precauzione* ('Almaviva, or The Useless Precaution')]

Commedia in two acts by Gioachino Rossini to a libretto by Cesare Sterbini after Pierre-Augustin Beaumarchais' *Le barbier de Séville* and the libretto often attributed to Giuseppe Petrosellini for Giovanni Paisiello's *Il barbiere di Siviglia* (1782, St Petersburg); Rome, Teatro Argentina, 20 February 1816.

The singers at the first performance included Geltrude Righetti-Giorgi as Rosina, Manuel García as Almaviva (his singer's fee higher than Rossini's commissioning fee), Luigi Zamboni as Figaro, Zenobio Vitarelli as Don Basilio and Bartolomeo Botticelli as Dr Bartolo.

Count Almaviva	tenor
Bartolo *a doctor in Seville*	baritone
Rosina *well-to-do ward of Dr Bartolo*	contralto
Figaro *a barber*	baritone
Don Basilio *music teacher, hypocrite*	bass
Fiorello *Count Almaviva's servant*	bass
Ambrogio *Bartolo's servant*	bass
Berta *Bartolo's old housekeeper*	mezzo-soprano
Officer	baritone
Notary	silent

Musicians, soldiers, police officers
Setting Seville, in the 18th century

Beaumarchais' play *Le barbier de Séville* had been used as a subject for opera by a number of composers before Rossini. Of these, by far the most successful was Giovanni Paisiello; indeed, the continuing popularity of that composer's *Il barbiere di Siviglia* (1782) obliged Rossini to issue a number of public and private disclaimers in which he extolled the virtues of Paisiello's art and affirmed the newness of his own treatment of the Beaumarchais play. This was further underlined by Rossini's choice of an alternative title for his opera, *Almaviva*. The present title was not used until the Bologna revival of August 1816, two months after Paisiello's death. Rossini had signed the contract for the opera on 15 December 1815, just over two months before the first night. Legend has it that he wrote the work in 13 days (nine days, in some versions). However, conceiving a work and writing it are two very different matters and there can be little doubt that Beaumarchais' play (and Paisiello's decorative and conservative treatment of it) had long been in Rossini's sights.

The initial launch of the opera was a fiasco. The commissioning impresario Duke Sforza-Cesarini died on 6 February, and the opening night a fortnight later was marred by stage 'accidents' and persistent disruption by followers of Paisiello. Rossini, who directed the first performance, was considerably upset by the furore. Despite contractual obligations, he declined to direct any subsequent performances. He did, however, sanction the introduction into the opera of the now famous overture, originally written for his *Aureliano in Palmira* (1813). One must also assume that he was agreeable to having Righetti-Giorgi take over Almaviva's lengthy Act 2 bravura aria 'Cessa di più resistere' for the Bologna revival in August 1816. This proved to be a temporary expedient; the following year, Rossini adapted the music for Righetti-Giorgi as part of the finale of *La Cenerentola*.

Though the opera was by no means the most popular of Rossini's works with contemporary audiences, its fame rapidly spread. In London in

'Il barbiere de Siviglia' (Rossini), costume for Figaro (as sung by Vincenzo-Felice Santini) in an early production at the Théâtre Italien, Paris: engraving from A. Martinet, 'La petite galerie dramatique'

March and April 1818 it played 22 times at the King's Theatre, Haymarket; it quickly reached Paris, Berlin and St Petersburg (where Paisiello's version had first been heard in 1782); and it became the first opera to be sung in Italian in New York when Manuel García's family troupe visited the Park Theatre in November 1825. To name a selection of the vast numbers of interpreters of the main roles in the course of the opera's subsequent stage history would be invidious. However, it is important to record the degree to which singers have sometimes distorted Rossini's intentions. The most serious distortion has been the upward transposition of the role of Rosina, turning her from a lustrous alto into a pert soprano. Parallel to this was a longstanding tradition, now happily largely redundant, of turning the Act 2 'music lesson' into a show-stopping cabaret. Adelina Patti's repertory in this scene included Arditi's 'Il bacio', followed by the Bolero from Verdi's *I vespri siciliani*, the Shadow Song from Meyerbeer's *Dinorah* and 'Home Sweet Home'. Melba provided a similar programme, accompanying herself on the piano in the final number. Patti should have known better; as a young girl she gave an unusually florid rendering of 'Una voce poco fa' during one of Rossini's Saturday soirées, only to be met by the composer's polite inquiry, 'Very nice, my dear, and who wrote the piece you have just performed?' The difficulty of Bartolo's 'A un dottor della mia sorte' led *buffo* basses of the period to opt for a substitute aria by Pietro Romani, 'Manca un foglio', an aria that replaced Rossini's own in many printed editions. Rossini's carefully written recitatives were also replaced by simple *parlato*.

The result of all these changes was to simplify and schematize the opera, turning Rossini's shrewdly drawn realizations of Beaumarchais' characters into stage marionettes. Vittorio Gui's detailed work on original source materials for his 1942 revival of the opera at the Teatro Comunale, Florence, did much to root out the worst mistreatments and adaptations that tradition had imposed on the opera; and since the publication of Alberto Zedda's critical edition (Ricordi) Rossini's original text has been restored to general circulation, while soprano Rosinas are now few and far between. But the tradition of treating *Il barbiere* as a vulgar romp or an impersonal farce rather than a comedy of character has not entirely vanished.

*

Act I.i *A square in Seville* Dr Bartolo lives in a secluded square in a household that contains two servants and his wealthy young ward, Rosina. Determined to marry her himself, Bartolo keeps her very much under lock and key. Unfortunately for him, the independent-minded young woman has already attracted the attention of a young Spanish nobleman, Count Almaviva. He has followed her from Madrid, disguised as the student Lindoro, for if Rosina is ever to be the Countess Almaviva, it must be for himself and not for his land and money. As the curtain rises, it is shortly before dawn and the Count is preparing to serenade Rosina, aided by his servant Fiorello and a band of musicians. The serenade 'Ecco, ridente in cielo' is musically eloquent but strategically ineffective. Frustrated by Rosina's lack of response, Almaviva pays off the musicians – even their noisy gratitude fails to rouse the household – and determines to keep vigil alone.

Suddenly, the voice of a rumbustious, roistering sort of fellow is heard in the distance. It is Figaro, barber and general factotum to the city of Seville. As he explains in his famous cavatina 'Largo al factotum della città', he is in demand everywhere. And we can believe it. The explosive vigour of the music establishes Figaro as a typically Rossinian creation full of impulse and concentrated energy. Figaro and Almaviva, it now turns out, have met before. Almaviva explains why he is in Seville incognito and is overjoyed to discover that Figaro is barber, wigmaker, surgeon, gardener, apothecary, vet – in short, Jack-of-all-trades – to the Bartolo household. Figaro is also able to tell him that Rosina is Bartolo's ward, not his daughter. While they are talking, Rosina appears on the balcony with a note she has written to the handsome young stranger who has been visiting the square. Unfortunately, her guardian is just behind her; but amid much kerfuffle and a good deal of excited coming and going by Dr Bartolo, the note floats safely down to the waiting Almaviva. Alarmed by his ward's furtive behaviour, Bartolo determines to expedite his marriage plans, leaving instructions that while he is away no one, not even the music teacher Don Basilio, should be admitted to the house.

With Rosina still hovering behind the shutters, Figaro persuades Almaviva to answer her note in another serenade. In Beaumarchais' play, Almaviva makes clear how nervous he is about his guitar-playing. This is omitted in Sterbini's libretto but the number he and Rossini concocted brilliantly captures Almaviva's unease. Though the minor-key 'Se il mio nome' can be sung as a piece of fine bel canto (Fernando De Lucia made some famous recordings of it), it is also a telling portrait of a man sick with nerves. Sterbini's verse lines are irregular and deliberately awkward, and Rossini's music is also awkward in key and in the lie of the phrasing and the vocal line. The number is almost a parody of the conventional aubade, and as such is precisely the kind of effect we look for in vain in Paisiello's much blander setting. Rosina is about to respond to the serenade when she is interrupted, making it obvious to Figaro and Almaviva that some kind of entry to the house must be effected. Stimulated by the promise of gold from Almaviva (duet, 'All'idea di quel metallo'), Figaro helps formulate a plot. A regiment is due in town that day and, posing as a soldier, the Count will ask at the house for a billet. To help the ploy further, he will also act drunk. As they are about to part, Almaviva calls Figaro back: 'Where can I find you? Where's your shop?' In Paisiello's setting this is the only section of the scene to be given extended musical treatment. With Rossini it comes as a dazzling and increasingly exciting cabaletta-like Allegro that rounds off a multisection movement which began with Figaro's contemplation of his reward and develops with a particularly fine interweaving of rapid patter and accompanied recitatives.

I.ii A room in Dr Bartolo's house Thrilled by the sound of her admirer's voice, Rosina launches into her cavatina 'Una voce poco fa', in which she portrays herself as a placid creature until crossed – but then, she tells us, she becomes a viper. Verdi once referred to Rossini's 'accuracy of declamation', a point that is well illustrated in this cavatina, which Rossini adapted from a smooth-running aria for Queen Elizabeth in his *Elisabetta, regina d'Inghilterra* (1815). In its new context, it is a keenly pointed, sharply observed portrait in words and music of a beguiling, vixenish creature. Rosina's minatory pointing of the word 'ma' – 'but' – is enough to send a shiver down any man's spine.

Figaro has meanwhile inveigled his way into the house and had a brief meeting with Rosina. Bartolo, angry with Figaro's busybodying and disrespect, quizzes Rosina about the meeting; he also quizzes his servants – Berta who is always sneezing and Ambrogio who is forever yawning, a delightful scene in Paisiello that Rossini does not even attempt to challenge. When the musician-cum-marriage-broker Don Basilio arrives, Bartolo informs him of the new urgency in the situation. Basilio agrees; the Count Almaviva is said to be in Seville and it may be prudent to run him out of town on a tide of slander. Dr Bartolo is not so sure about this, but Basilio insists in his aria 'La calunnia è un venticello': 'calumny is a little breeze, a gentle zephyr which insensibly, subtly, lightly and sweetly begins to whisper . . . to gather force . . . and finally explodes like a cannon'. Here Rossini gratefully deploys Beaumarchais' original list of dynamic extremes – *piano, pianissimo, rinforzando*, the famous *crescendo* itself – and also revels in musical onomatopoeia as the buzzing sound of scandal makes its poisonous progress through the community. Figaro, having overheard the conversation, now seeks out Rosina to tease her a little and prepare the ground for the entrance of her mystery lover, the penniless Lindoro. But Figaro soon discovers, in their duet 'Dunque io son', that Rosina is already several moves into

the game. 'Donne, donne, eterni Dei' he exclaims – 'Women, women, eternal gods, who can attempt to make you out?'

Dr Bartolo is equally maddened and intoxicated by Rosina's wiles, but his dignity is offended when her protestations of innocence fail to square with inky fingers, sharpened quills and missing sheets of paper. In his aria 'A un dottor della mia sorte', he advises Rosina to dream up better excuses when dealing with a man of his intellect. The aria is in two parts: a grandiloquent Andante maestoso and a lightning Allegro vivace which, as befits the doctor's academic status, is in full sonata form. Stage directors underestimate Rossini's Dr Bartolo at their peril. The first act ends with Almaviva's appearance in Bartolo's house disguised as the drunken officer. This is one of the most powerful and amusing of all Rossini's first-act finales, Beethovenian in the sheer disruptiveness of its comic energies. This is particularly evident in Almaviva's initial appearance and in the violence of his response when Bartolo unearths his exemption from the military billet. Equally, there are some surprising interludes amid the mayhem, such as the sly pathos of Rosina's 'sempre un'istoria' as she bewails her sad fate. The arrival of Basilio and Figaro adds to the confusion and with the appearance of the local militia there is a crazed Vivace: a dazzling canonic passage in which the characters, locked by the music into febrile acts of imitation, vehemently protest to the officers about each other's behaviour. An attempt to arrest Almaviva is aborted when he passes a document to the officer in charge, leaving everyone, and not least Dr Bartolo, totally confused about the day's events.

Act 2 *A music room in Dr Bartolo's house with a window and balcony nearby* Almaviva presents himself to Dr Bartolo in a new disguise: as 'Don Alonso', music-teacher, and pupil of the 'indisposed' Don Basilio. Like Paisiello, Rossini gives Don Alonso a solemn nasal whine for his aria of greeting 'Pace e gioia sia con voi!', but Rossini's setting is funnier, with excruciating violin colours and lightning-quick parlando outbursts from the double-dealing Count. Further to gain Bartolo's confidence, Don Alonso reveals that he has intercepted a note from Count Almaviva to Rosina. With this note as evidence, he hopes to use his 'music lesson' to convince Rosina of the Count's duplicity. Bartolo falls for the story and hurries off to fetch Rosina to her lesson. She performs a rondo from *L'inutile precauzione* ('The Useless Precaution') and while Bartolo dozes she and 'Lindoro' express their mutual affection. Bartolo awakes and, bored by contemporary music, performs an example of the music of his youth, 'Quando mi sei vicina'.

Figaro now arrives to shave Bartolo. When Bartolo sends him out to fetch shaving materials,

Figaro takes the opportunity to steal the key to the balcony. He then smashes a pile of glass and crockery to lure the fretful Bartolo away from the music-room. All is going to plan when Don Basilio appears. But he is offered money and in a wittily crafted quintet, 'Buona sera, mio signore', he accepts the conspirators' story that he is suffering from scarlet fever, and makes a lugubrious withdrawal. The shaving of Bartolo now resumes to the accompaniment of one of Rossini's frothiest allegros while Rosina is alerted to Figaro's plot to spirit the lovers away at midnight. But Bartolo is not entirely off his guard. Creeping over to the piano, he overhears Almaviva talk of disguise. 'Il suo travestimento!' exclaims Bartolo, and once more the game is temporarily up for the lovers.

Berta is left to comment on the foolishness of old men wanting to marry young wives, 'Il vecchiotto cerca moglie'. When Dr Bartolo discovers that Don Basilio has never heard of Don Alonso he determines to marry Rosina straight away. To help advance his case, he presents Rosina with her letter to Lindoro, claiming that he obtained it from a certain Count Almaviva on whose behalf Lindoro is clearly acting. A storm rages. As it settles, Figaro and Almaviva make their entrance over the balcony only to be confronted by Rosina, furious at being 'used' by Lindoro to further the Count's wicked plans. Almaviva is forced to reveal his true identity which Rosina accepts without demur. Time now being of the essence, Figaro becomes increasingly frustrated (trio, 'Ah! qual colpo') as the lovers bill and coo together. Figaro's mockery is conveyed by a simple echo effect at the end of their simpering phrases. Here Rossini redeploys ideas originally used in his early cantata Egle ed Irene to ingenious comic effect. There is also another of Rossini's sophisticated musical jokes as the lovers' delay is prolonged by the duet's need to end with a fully worked-out cabaletta. When they finally try to leave, the ladder has been removed from the balcony. But the situation is saved by Basilio arriving with the notary Dr Bartolo has hastily engaged. Bribed with a valuable ring and threatened with a couple of bullets through the head, Basilio agrees to stand witness to the marriage of Rosina and Almaviva. Bartolo arrives with soldiers, but it is too late. It is vain to resist, Almaviva tells him, in the lengthy and expendable aria 'Cessa di più resistere'. Bartolo accepts that he has been beaten and the opera ends with a jaunty vaudeville in which Figaro, Rosina and the Count celebrate their good fortune with the company at large.

*

In earlier years, the comic radicalism of Rossini's setting daunted some contemporary audiences who had been brought up, not on works like Falstaff, Gianni Schicchi and Albert Herring, but on the more genteel offerings of Cimarosa, Paisiello and others. Rossini's Il barbiere came, in Lord Derwent's phrase, as 'a nervous outburst of vitality', a quality that clearly commended the work to Beethoven (who allegedly said to Rossini 'Be sure to write more Barbers!') and to Verdi. Beyond the physical impact of a piece like Figaro's 'Largo al factotum' there is Rossini's ear for vocal and instrumental timbres of a peculiar astringency and brilliance, his quick-witted word-setting, and his mastery of large musical forms with their often brilliant and explosive internal variations. Add to that what Verdi called the opera's 'abundance of true musical ideas', and the reasons for the work's longer-term emergence as Rossini's most popular opera buffa are not hard to find.   R.O.

Barbier von Bagdad, Der
('The Barber of Baghdad')

Komische Oper in two acts by Peter Cornelius to his own libretto after a story from The Thousand and One Nights; Weimar, Hoftheater, 15 December 1858.

At the première, conducted by Liszt, Roth appeared as the Barber, Caspari as Nureddin and Rosa von Milde-Agthe as Margiana.

The Caliph	baritone
Baba Mustapha a Cadi	tenor
Margiana his daughter	soprano
Bostana a relative of the Cadi	mezzo-soprano
Nureddin	tenor
Abul Hassan Ali Ebn Bekar a barber	bass
First Muezzin	bass
Second Muezzin	tenor
Third Muezzin	tenor

Servants of Nureddin, friends of the Cadi, wailing women, followers of the Caliph, people of Baghdad

Setting Baghdad in ancient times

Cornelius began writing the text of Der Barbier von Bagdad in September 1855. His friend and patron Liszt initially disapproved of the subject matter, but later became intimately involved with the work's evolution. The text was finished in November 1856 and the music in February 1858. The première in Weimar succeeded musically, but the occasion was marred by a demonstration against the conductor by the supporters of the theatre's manager, with whom Liszt was engaged in a feud. As a result Liszt left his position at Weimar and the opera was never performed again in Cornelius's lifetime.

Der Barbier remained closely associated with Liszt. It was he who orchestrated the new overture that Cornelius wrote shortly before his death in 1874, and who subsequently interested Felix Mottl in the work. Mottl first conducted his shortened and revised form of the opera in Karlsruhe on 1 February 1881. Hermann Levi restored some of the cut material for the Munich première, on 15 October 1885, and it was this version that was published in Leipzig in 1886. Despite these efforts to ensure the opera's popularity, it never really gained an audience until Max Hasse successfully reintroduced the original version at the Weimar Hoftheater on 10 June 1904. Since then it has retained a place, if only a minor one, in German opera houses. It opened the Munich opera festival in 1984, with Kurt Moll as the Barber, Lucia Popp as Margiana and Peter Seiffert as Nureddin. The first recording was made by Erich Leinsdorf in 1956, with Oscar Czerwenka, Elisabeth Schwarzkopf and Nicola Gedda.

*

Act I *Nureddin's house* Cornelius's second overture introduces many of the opera's themes, whereas the original one restricts itself to setting the mood, mingling lyrical and burlesque elements. As the curtain rises, Nureddin reclines in bed while his servants serenade him ('Sanfter Schlummer'); lingering chromaticism underlines their fear that his death from unrequited love is near. He responds with an incongruously healthy outpouring to his Margiana ('Komm deine Blumen'). As the servants imagine him in paradise ('In Strahlen ew'gen Lichts'), their song's tripping rhythms also suggest earthly rather than heavenly joys, joining Nureddin's love song in reassuring harmony.

Left alone, the young man indulges his feelings in one of the opera's few uninterrupted aria sections ('Vor deinem Fenster'). The mood changes abruptly at the entrance of Bostana, her speech punctuated by garrulous wind figures as she reveals that Margiana has agreed to a meeting. In his excitement Nureddin joins in with her comically exaggerated expressions, calling Bostana a dove and his heart a writhing snake, all with appropriate illustrations from the orchestra. Their unanimity of mood is perfectly expressed in a swiftly moving canonic duet ('Wenn zum Gebet') as they rehearse the details of the lovers' rendezvous. There is only one moment of solemnity, when Bostana recommends a barber to restore Nureddin's looks. As Nureddin awaits the barber, scurrying strings show his impatience. His flow of feelings is checked somewhat by the imposing figure of Abul Hassan, and the scene is set for a humorous conflict between Nureddin's youthful ardour and the barber's ponderousness. The latter repeats his formal greeting so often that the sequence appears to be never-ending ('Mein Sohn, sei Allah's Frieden hier'). Nureddin interrupts while the barber discusses whether the stars are auspicious for such a shaving. The wind section joins Nureddin in urging the music

forward, while the strings mimic the old man's exaggerated gestures.

Yet the barber has more resources at his command than at first appear. When Nureddin tries to dismiss him, he recites all his attributes in a virtuoso patter song rich in textual as well as musical invention ('Bin Akademiker'). Nureddin is left speechless, unable to prevent Abul Hassan from embarking on the story of his six brothers, with comic asides from the wind and percussion as he invents oriental-style epithets. Nureddin tries to throw the old man out. The servants bustle in, but faced with the mock-heroic resistance of the barber, razor in hand, they bustle out again.

Nureddin appeases the barber and the shaving finally begins. Abul Hassan accompanies himself with a love song to a past loved one also named Margiana; interesting rhythmic and harmonic twists give his melody an irresistibly haunting quality ('Lass dir zu Füssen wonnesam mich liegen'). Nureddin joins in, forgetting his impatience, until Abul Hassan embarks on italianate cadenzas. Breaking in, Nureddin seeks to hurry the barber by telling him of his assignation. This provokes more witty exchanges, for Margiana's father, the Cadi, is an enemy of Abul Hassan's (because he shaves himself). The barber thus proposes to escort Nureddin to his meeting, despite the young man's objections.

While Nureddin leaves to adorn himself, Abul muses on the dangers of love ('So schwärmet Jugend'), the bassoon echoing his solemn refrain, 'Liebe'. Nureddin's final recourse on finding the barber still there is to convince his servants that Abul is ill, with a comic recitation of symptoms worthy of the barber himself. The servants respond with an equally fast list of remedies. For once the musical pace wrests the initiative from Abul Hassan; he is smothered with blankets, leaving Nureddin free to meet Margiana alone.

Act 2 *The Cadi's house* A prelude establishes a mood of exotic languor; this music, the most oriental of the opera, later serves to call the faithful to prayer. The focus changes to more immediate emotions as Margiana awaits Nureddin, joined sympathetically by Bostana ('Er kommt! Er kommt!'). The entry of the Cadi unexpectedly changes the duet into a trio, adding tension because he is awaiting not Nureddin, but his old friend Selim as Margiana's suitor. Margiana echoes her father's praises of Selim's trunk of gifts. Yet while she and Bostana answer the Cadi's flowing phrases and join him in three-part harmony, they whisper to each other that a young lover is the only true treasure.

As the Muezzin's distant call draws the Cadi to the mosque, its dream-like quality sets the scene for Nureddin's appearance, and with an accompaniment of solo cellos his love song ('O, holdes Bild in Engelschöne') sustains the delicate mood. The lovers' passion emerges only gradually as their voices rise in unison ('So mag kein anders Wort erklingen'). Their restraint is offset by an expansive phrase from Abul Hassan, escaped to come to Nureddin's aid after all and now encouraging the lovemaking from beneath the window. Although this causes some comic disruption, Abul's singing adds much to the musical momentum of the scene once the lovers decide to ignore him.

A slave's warning cry represents a far more serious disruption, the arrival of the Cadi. A light and continuous rhythmic patter conveys the confusion as Abul thinks Nureddin is being attacked, while Margiana and Bostana hide the young man in Selim's trunk. The action reaches a crisis when Abul begins to remove the trunk (to funereal brass chords), thinking it contains Nureddin's dead body. His way is barred by the Cadi, who calls him a thief for removing his treasures. In the manner of a large-scale passacaglia, the same phrase is repeated many times over, with one side calling out theft and the other murder, the ensemble swollen by a growing crowd of servants, wailing women and townspeople.

This musical continuity is broken by the entry of the Caliph, cutting through the barber's wordy explanations and offering the simple solution of opening the trunk. As Nureddin's apparently lifeless body is revealed, the Cadi, Caliph and barber seem themselves to fall into a trance, repeating the same unaccompanied phrases. Margiana and Bostana try to recall Nureddin to life, but it is the barber's love song, aided by the scent of Margiana's flowers, which achieves the miracle, dissolving all barriers to the lovers' union, including her father's opposition. Although the Caliph then arrests the barber, this is only so that he can take him to the palace to hear the old man's stories. Abul sings the Caliph's praises in a final display of invention, and the chorus repeats his ceremonial greeting, 'Salamaleikum'.

*

The freedom and originality of Cornelius's style are best appreciated in *Der Barbier von Bagdad*, and the virtuosity with which he spins out musical details to follow the twists and turns of this plot has gained the opera a high reputation despite its chequered performance history. With the libretto, he created a sophisticated comedy out of mimicking the exaggerated inflections of oriental speech and gesture, a sophistication matched throughout by the opera's orchestral, harmonic and melodic features. Some of this subtle characterization is lost in theatrical performance, for Cornelius lacked the ability to project details as large-scale dramatic gestures. However, the refined nature of the humour of *Der Barbier* and the integrity of the relationship between libretto and music succeeded in creating a new ideal

for German comic opera. Cornelius may not have fully realized this ideal himself, but his influence upon operas such as Hugo Wolf's *Der Corregidor* and Wagner's *Die Meistersinger* is unmistakable.

A.G.

Bartered Bride, The [Prodaná nevěsta]

Comic opera in three acts by Bedřich Smetana to a libretto by Karel Sabina; Prague, Provisional Theatre, 30 May 1866 (definitive version, Prague, Provisional Theatre, 25 September 1870).

The original cast included Eleanora z Ehrenbergů as Mařenka; the celebrated actor Jindřich Mošna as the Circus Master; Jindřich Polák (Jeník), František Hynek (Kecal), Josef Paleček (Krušina) and Vojtěch Šebesta (Micha).

Krušina *a farmer*	baritone
Ludmila *his wife*	soprano
Mařenka *their daughter*	soprano
Mícha *a smallholder*	bass
Háta *his wife*	mezzo-soprano
Vašek *their son*	tenor
Jeník *Mícha's son from his first marriage*	tenor
Kecal *a village marriage-broker*	bass
Circus Master	tenor
Esmeralda ⎫ *circus artists*	soprano
Indian ⎭	bass

Villagers, circus artists, boys

Setting A village at festival time in the afternoon and early evening

The first permanent Czech opera house, the Provisional Theatre, had opened in 1862. Smetana's first opera, *The Brandenburgers in Bohemia*, won the competition for a Czech opera organized by Count Harrach (it was completed in 1863); it was presented at the theatre in January 1866. Smetana commissioned a libretto for a comic opera from the same librettist, Sabina, and, according to his diary entry on 5 July 1863, received it apparently in the form of a one-act piece. On 1 September 1864 the periodical *Slavoj* announced that Smetana had completed the overture to a two-act opera of which he had now received the first act. As yet it had no name. Smetana seems to have finished the piano sketch during the first months of 1865 (only then did he give a name to the opera); orchestration was completed on 15 March 1866, simultaneously with sketching his next opera, *Dalibor*. Two duets for the Circus Master and Esmeralda, not in the libretto, were added after this date. Smetana himself rehearsed and conducted the first performances; the producer was Josef Jiří Kolár, the designer Josef Macourek.

Terezie Rückaufová as Mařenka at a performance of Smetana's 'The Bartered Bride' at the Provisional Theatre, Prague, in 1867

At first the opera was far less successful than *The Brandenburgers*, and its popularity with the Czech public grew only gradually. Its worldwide popularity – for many years it was the only Czech opera in general repertory – dates from the performances given by the Prague National Theatre at the Vienna Music and Theatre Exhibition in 1892.

Its original version was much shorter, in two acts (the first act ended where the present second act ends), without dances and other numbers, and with spoken dialogue. Over the next four years many changes were made. In October 1866 a duet for the Circus Master and Esmeralda was replaced by the Act 1 ballet from *The Brandenburgers*. In January 1869 Act 1 was divided into two scenes (the second set in the inn, beginning with a new drinking chorus). A new polka opened Act 2 (before Vašek's aria) and Mařenka's final solo was extended. In June of that year the opera was divided into three acts, corresponding to the final division except that the new *furiant* is at the end of Act 1 after the polka (now

transferred to this position). Act 3 included a new *skočná* (to replace the *Brandenburgers* ballet) and an introductory march for the circus troupe. Finally, in September 1870, at its 30th performance, new recitatives replaced spoken dialogue and the *furiant* was transferred to Act 2, after the drinking chorus. It is this definitive version that is described below.

*

Act I *The village green beside a tavern* The long, separate overture is a tour de force of the genre. It is followed by a leisurely prelude, providing a genre description of the village at church festival time. The prelude (based on an earlier piano piece) includes one of the first of many bagpipe imitations in Czech opera: open 5th drones, and perky, decorated wind parts. The chorus that it prepares for, 'Proč bychom se netěšili?' ('Why shouldn't we be glad?'), was noted down untexted as a 'Chorus for a comedy' in Smetana's 'Notebook of Motifs' in October 1862; Sabina was presumably instructed to fit his words to it. The solo middle section introduces the lovers Jeník and Mařenka, with the chorus motif now inflected into the minor to suggest Mařenka's low spirits.

In the following recitative, originally of course prose dialogue, Mařenka explains her unhappiness. Mícha is due to arrive in the village to negotiate a marriage between her and his son Vašek. She fears that her parents will try to force her into it. Of course she will remain faithful to Jeník, but she knows so little of his past, as she explains in her aria; why did he leave his native village? Jeník responds (in recitative) that he was the son of a wealthy father, but his mother died young, his father married again and his stepmother drove him from home. Their charming duet 'Jako matka' ('Like a mother') is followed by a brief recitative link that leads into the well-loved section about constancy ('Věrné milování'), with its lilting clarinet accompaniment. They go off singly.

Another celebrated number follows: Kecal the marriage-broker, accompanied by Mařenka's parents Ludmila and Krušina, announces that everything is ready, 'Jak vám pravím, pane kmotře' ('As I said to you'). Kecal's verbose and self-important character (his name means 'babbler') is immediately established by his music – at first limited to two pitches and then to rapid patter. Ludmila thinks they are moving too fast – there might be some obstacles. In his most portentous vein, Kecal declares that their wills and his cleverness will overcome all obstacles.

In the following recitative Krušina says that he knows Mícha, the father of the proposed bridegroom, but has never met his two sons – which one is being proposed? Kecal replies that it is the second, Vašek, for the first is a good-for-nothing vagabond, and in a terzetto he provides a flattering character reference for Vašek. Mařenka enters. In the conversational quartet that follows, Kecal tells Mařenka that he has a husband for her, and Mařenka declares that there may be a problem: with the return of the lilting clarinet theme she explains that she already has a lover. In his typical staccato patter Kecal orders that the lover be sent packing; Mařenka responds expressively, in long notes, that she has already given her heart. Little is resolved in the following recitative, especially when Kecal lets drop that the prospective bridegroom is shy and not used to talking to women. He decides to talk to Jeník himself to sort things out. The discussions are cut short by the polka that now breaks out as young people surge on to the stage and dance. The act concludes with choral voices added to the polka.

Act 2 *A room in the tavern* The act opens with a strophic drinking song for the male chorus celebrating beer ('To pivečko'). Between the second and third verses Jeník and Kecal are heard, championing (respectively) love and money above alcohol. This chorus scene ends with another dance, a *furiant*, and paves the way for the chief business of the act: the separate attempts by Mařenka and Jeník to overcome the obstacles placed in their marital path. The fact that these are uncoordinated and unknown to each other leads almost to tragedy in Act 3. First Mařenka seeks out Vašek, charms him and, painting her in the blackest colours, attempts to put him off his promised bride. Vašek does not of course realize that this gruesome creature is Mařenka herself and readily swears devotion to the engaging young woman he has just met. Vašek is introduced with a short solo, 'Má ma-ma-ma-tič-ka po-po-povídala' ('My m-m-mother s-s-said' – his stutter is a notable feature). Mařenka conducts her campaign first in recitative and then in a duet (Andante amoroso, 3/4), 'Známť já jednu dívčinu' ('I know a girl who burns for you'), in which her lyrical lines and Vašek's stuttering responses are brilliantly contrasted. The music flows into a brisker 2/4 as Mařenka extracts from him a promise to abandon the proposed match: its stretto ending leads to a triumphant *fortissimo* version of the opening 3/4 Andante.

Kecal and Jeník follow them on to the stage. Their duet 'Nuže, milý chasníku' ('Now, dear young fellow') is one of the longer musical structures of the opera. In the first section (2/4, Allegro comodo) Kecal learns that Jeník is from 'far away'; he recommends that he return home since the local girls aren't up to much. Maybe, Jeník responds, but Mařenka is a 'real diamond'. The next section (3/4, Moderato) is mostly a solo for Kecal in which he argues that all the beauties of the world will fade. In the final section (2/4, Allegro comodo), Kecal offers Jeník a rich bride and money, 'Znám jednu dívku' ('I know a girl who has ducats'), with Jeník happily repeating after Kecal all the wonders offered him.

The real bargaining, however, happens in the final recitative, as Jeník pushes up to 300 florins Kecal's original offer for renouncing his bride. Jeník makes a decent show of unwillingness, but eventually agrees to 'sell' his bride (as the Czech title has it – 'bartered' is less accurate if more euphonious). But he makes his own conditions: Mařenka must marry no one but Mícha's son, and as soon as Mařenka and Mícha's son are married Mícha's debt to Mařenka's father must be cancelled. Kecal agrees and runs off triumphantly for witnesses to the contract.

'How can he believe that I would sell my Mařenka?' ('Jak možná věřit') Jeník asks in a short aria when left alone. The finale begins with a return to the opening of the overture as Kecal's witnesses (the entire chorus) flood on to the stage. Kecal dictates the terms and Jeník confirms them. Krušina is impressed by Jeník's 'good heart' in giving up Mařenka voluntarily, until he hears about the money that Jeník will receive. The chorus is similarly shocked at such callous behaviour and the growing groundswell of disapproval brings Act 2 to an end.

Act 3 *The village green beside a tavern* Vašek is confused by the turn of events. As before, he is seen alone; an orchestral prelude recalls the opening of his Act 2 aria and the duet music with which he was seduced. The music is dark (a rare minor key) and in its intensity he virtually loses his stutter. Once again he is the victim of others' machinations. The arrival of a small circus is announced with a brief, colourfully orchestrated march (trumpet, piccolo, percussion). In his opening patter the Circus Master describes his troupe: the dancer Esmeralda, an 'Indian' and, their greatest attraction, an American bear who will perform a can-can with Esmeralda. Their wares are further displayed in the brilliant *skočná* (a fast 2/4 folkdance). But there is a crisis: the Indian announces to the Circus Master that the 'bear' has got too drunk to appear. They need a substitute and come upon Vašek, seen admiring Esmeralda's legs. Esmeralda begins chatting him up, describing the life of 'artists' in glowing terms. The recitative leads into a sparkling strophic duettino between the Circus Master and Esmeralda, 'Milostné zvířátko uděláme z vás' ('We'll make a nice little animal of you').

The circus people go off, and Vašek is joined by his parents and Kecal. All are amazed (in the following quartet) when he is unwilling to sign the agreement, and ask what he has against his prospective bride. She will poison him, he declares: he has been told so by an unknown girl. Vašek withdraws, his place taken by Mařenka and her parents. Mařenka has just heard about Jeník's renunciation of her but refuses to believe it. A further complication occurs when Kecal calls back Vašek, who announces that the girl with his parents is the one who spoke to him, and whom he is perfectly willing to marry. He goes off. One obstacle is thus removed, but Mařenka says she needs time. In a sextet Kecal and the parents encourage her to think it over ('Rozmysli si, Mařenko!') and then leave her.

Her aria 'Och, jaký žal' ('Oh, what pain') was extended in the first of the 1869 revisions with a much more substantial section, 'Ten lásky sen' ('That dream of love'). Here, as Mařenka sings of her disappointment, the librettist abandoned his usual trochees in favour of a more formal iambic verse and Smetana responded with more passionate and darker music than anywhere else in the opera. By the time Jeník appears she is able to dismiss him as heroically as a prima donna, refusing even to listen to his explanations. She will marry Vašek, she declares. She is further provoked when Jeník cannot hide his amusement: both vent their frustration in a spirited polka-like duet. Kecal joins them and in the following trio Jeník attempts to pacify Mařenka, who simply wants to get the whole affair over. Then Jeník steps aside.

The finale begins with the entry of the chorus and two sets of parents wishing to know Mařenka's decision. She says she will go ahead with her marriage to Vašek, calling Jeník's bluff, as she thinks. But when Jeník steps out, addressing Mícha as 'father', Vašek's parents are astonished to see the long-lost elder son. Although seemingly unwelcome, as he observes, he can at least claim the right to marry Mařenka, being the son of Mícha – as the contract specifies. At last Mařenka understands Jeník's behaviour, and falls into his arms. Kecal acknowledges himself beaten and fears for his reputation. All this business has been conducted in solo dialogue; now, however, the ensemble grows, with the chorus providing a continuous background, the parents expressing their frustration, Kecal his shame and indignation, and the young couple their triumph. The ensemble builds up to a climax, interrupted by cries of terror off stage: boys from the village run on to say that the 'bear' has broken loose and is heading that way. And indeed it appears, only to take off its headdress and reveal itself to be Vašek. His mother is mortified and marches him off, but Krušina takes the opportunity of suggesting to Mícha that Vašek is not ready for marriage, and, as recitative gives way to sustained orchestral background, Mícha is persuaded to consent to the marriage of Mařenka and Jeník. He blesses the young couple. The music of the opening chorus returns slowly in the orchestra and, as it quickens in tempo and grows in volume, chorus and soloists join to acknowledge that all has turned out well.

*

Czechs consider *The Bartered Bride* as quintessentially Czech; but while the characteristic dances (polka, *skočná* and *furiant*) support this claim, as do individual details such as the bagpipe imitation in the opening prelude, there is little else that is concretely 'Czech'. Czech productions usually lavish attention on the authenticity of the setting and costumes, but this is merely a matter of staging which anyway dates back only to the production made for Vienna in 1892. A better claim for the opera's intrinsic 'Czechness' derives from the fact that the somewhat casually concocted text was one of the few Czech librettos of its time to be written mostly in trochees or even prose (rather than high-style iambs), thus matching the natural first-syllable stress of the language (but even this was occasionally sabotaged by Smetana's clumsy and inexperienced handling of Czech word-stress). Another claim may be made from the closeness to Czech dance metres of many individual numbers. Smetana's settings fall mostly into two main types: fast duple and slow triple, thus corresponding to the polka (and related dances) and the slow, triple-time *sousedská* (a Ländler-type waltz). The simplicity of the music must also have encouraged audiences to see a stronger folk base in it than contemporary, more declamatory and complicated works and indeed more than in Smetana's next opera, *Dalibor*.   J.T.

Bassarids, The

Opera seria with intermezzo in one act (four movements) by Hans Werner Henze to a libretto by W. H. Auden and Chester Kallman after Euripides' *The Bacchae*; Salzburg, Grosses Festspielhaus, 6 August 1966.

The first performance (in German) was conducted by Christoph von Dohnányi with a cast led by Ingeborg Hallstein (Autonoe), Kerstin Meyer (Agave), Vera Little (Beroe), Loren Driscoll (Dionysus), Helmut Melchert (Tiresias), Kostas Paskalis (Pentheus), William Dooley (Captain of the Guard) and Peter Lagger (Cadmus); the première of the original English-language version took place at Santa Fe in 1967, conducted by the composer.

Dionysus *who also sings:*	
A Voice, A Stranger	tenor
Pentheus *King of Thebes*	baritone
Cadmus *his grandfather, founder of Thebes*	bass
Tiresias *an old blind prophet*	tenor
Captain of the Royal Guard	baritone
Agave *Cadmus's daughter and*	
mother of Pentheus	mezzo-soprano
Autonoe *her sister*	soprano
Beroe *an old slave, once nurse to*	
the deceased Semele	mezzo-soprano
Young woman *slave in Agave's household*	silent

'The Bassarids' (Henze): scene from the original production at the Grosses Festspielhaus, Salzburg, 6 August 1966, designed by Filippo Sanjust

Child *her daughter*   silent
Bassarids, Theban citizens, guards and servants
Setting The Royal Palace, Thebes, and Mount
    Cytheron, in antiquity

Henze's second collaboration with Auden and
Kallman, after the successful première of *Elegy for
Young Lovers*, was commissioned by the Salzburg
Festival. The libretto was prepared in 1963, but
Henze did not begin work on the score until more
than a year later, after he had completed *Der junge
Lord*. In 1974 *The Bassarids* was staged by the English
National Opera at the London Coliseum, with a cast
that included Josephine Barstow, Katherine Pring,
Anne Collins, Gregory Dempsey, Kenneth Woollam,
Norman Welsby and Tom McDonnell; Henze conducted and directed the performances. A concert
performance at the Deutsche Oper in Berlin in 1986,
conducted by Gerd Albrecht, formed the basis of a
subsequent commercial recording (1991), in which
the intermezzo in the third movement was omitted
(a cut approved by the composer).

                          *

First movement *The courtyard of the Royal Palace*
Cadmus, founder of Thebes, has abdicated in favour
of his grandson Pentheus. The citizens of Thebes
gather to sing a hymn in praise of their new king,
but Pentheus is in retreat, praying and fasting; he
plans to convert his people gradually to a rational
monotheism. Next to the palace is the grave of
Semele, a daughter of Cadmus, who, according to
legend, had borne a son by Zeus: Dionysus. An
offstage Voice interrupts the hymn, proclaiming
'Ayayalya, the God Dionysus has entered Boeotia!',
and the brass fanfares that underpinned the choral
celebration give way to lyrical lines of flute and
strings, while the chorus takes up the melismatic
chant as, transformed into Bassarids (Bacchae), they
follow the Voice to Mount Cytheron. Cadmus, Beroe,
Agave and Tiresias discuss the Dionysian cult.
Cadmus is fearful, Tiresias suspicious, Beroe clings to
the old religion; only Agave welcomes the new faith.

    The Bassarids' hymn continues in the back-
ground. Autonoe arrives as Agave praises the handsome Captain of the Guard, who reads a proclamation from Pentheus forbidding his people to believe
that Dionysus is the son of Semele and Zeus.
Pentheus himself reinforces his command by
extinguishing the flame on Semele's grave, threatening death to anyone who relights it. Cadmus is
horrified. Agave and Autonoe pledge their loyalty
to Pentheus, but the offstage voice of Dionysus
interrupts them with a seductive serenade, urging
them to Mount Cytheron, to the land of eternal
happiness. The sisters follow, as if hypnotized.

    Second movement Despite Cadmus's warnings,
Pentheus sends his guards to imprison all those who
celebrated the festival of the Bassarids. As the
Bassarids' chorus is heard again, Pentheus confesses
in a long aria to Beroe his fear of the Dionysian cult,
and swears to abstain 'from wine, from meats, and
from woman's bed'; she prays that the new king
will be protected. Entranced detainees from Mount
Cytheron are brought before Pentheus; they include

his mother Agave, her sister Autonoe, Tiresias and a stranger suspected of being a Dionysian priest. Pentheus attempts to wake his mother, but she can only sing an aria describing the delights of Cytheron. He places her and Autonoe under house arrest, and orders the destruction of Tiresias's house. Beroe has recognized the stranger as Dionysus; when Pentheus threatens him with torture, Dionysus responds with an aria describing his voyage to Naxos.

Third movement The Bassarids' hymn continues. As the stranger is tortured Thebes is struck by an earthquake; the prisoners escape and rush off to Mount Cytheron. The stranger offers Pentheus a vision in a mirror of the feast of the Bassarids.

In an intermezzo Pentheus is shown a rococo enactment of the Judgment of Calliope, in effect his own repressed sexual fantasies: Agave and Autonoe appear as Aphrodite and Persephone in erotic play with the Captain of the Guard as Adonis. The scene is accompanied by onstage mandolins and guitar, and the music itself is neo-classical, with recitative, arias, duets and a final quartet.

Pentheus is appalled by what has been brought from his own subconscious; the stranger suggests he disguise himself as a woman and follow him to Mount Cytheron. Beroe and Cadmus await Pentheus's return. On the mountain Pentheus hides to watch his people, who are transformed into Bassarids and Maenads. The voice of Dionysus tells them there is a spy among them; led by Agave, who fails to recognize her son's pleas, the Bassarids kill Pentheus.

Fourth movement While Cadmus and Beroe keep watch at dawn, a triumphant procession returns to Thebes. Agave displays the head of her son; still entranced, she believes she has killed a lion. Questioned by Cadmus, she comes gradually to her senses, and identifies the stranger as perpetrator of the murder. He admits he is Dionysus; he exiles the remainder of the Theban royal family and orders the burning of their palace. Among the flames he summons his mother Semele from her grave and commits her to Mount Olympus as the goddess Thyone. When the flames subside Semele's grave is bedecked in vines, and adorned with statues of Dionysus and Thyone. In the morning sunshine, the people kneel to worship their new gods.

*

When Auden and Kallman took on the commission they specified that Henze listen to *Götterdämmerung* before composing the music. Henze in turn requested a libretto shaped into the four-movement plan of a symphony, and the music of *The Bassarids* represents a conscious attempt to come to terms with the post-Wagnerian tradition, continued through Mahler and Schoenberg. Though traditional operatic forms, arias and ensembles are embedded in the structure, each of the four movements is derived from a symphonic archetype: the first is a sonata form in which the hard-edged Pentheus material and the more sensuous music for the Bassarids provide the two subject groups; the second is a scherzo made from a sequence of dances; the third a slow movement interrupted by the intermezzo and culminating in the music of the hunt for Pentheus; the fourth is founded on a 43-note theme that flows into a final passacaglia.   A.C.

Beatrice di Tenda

Tragedia lirica in two acts by Vincenzo Bellini to a libretto by Felice Romani after Carlo Tedaldi-Fores's play *Beatrice di Tenda*; Venice, Teatro La Fenice, 16 March 1833.

Giuditta Pasta, for whom the work was expressly written, sang Beatrice at the first performance; Orazio Cartagenova sang Filippo. The other singers (disliked by Bellini) included Alberico Curioni as Orombello and Anna del Serre as Agnese.

Filippo Maria Visconti *Duke of Milan,*	
in love with Agnese	baritone
Agnese del Maino *secretly in love*	soprano or
with Orombello	mezzo-soprano
Orombello *Signore of Ventimiglia*	tenor
Beatrice di Tenda *Filippo's wife,*	
widow of Facino Cane	soprano
Rizzardo del Maino *Agnese's brother,*	
confidant to Filippo	tenor
Anichino *former minister of Facino, friend to*	
Orombello	tenor
Courtiers, judges, guards, ladies-in-waiting	
Setting The castle of Binasco, Milan, in 1418	

By 24 May 1832 Bellini had agreed to write another opera for La Fenice, for which he had composed *I Capuleti e i Montecchi* in 1830. Romani had chosen the subject of *Cristina di Svezia* (after Dumas), but in October Bellini, for the first time in their collaboration, forced a new subject on Romani, *Beatrice di Tenda*, prompted by Pasta's enthusiasm for Monticini's ballet which she had recently seen in Milan. He hoped that Romani would play down the similarities to his libretto for Donizetti's *Anna Bolena* and would draw instead on Schiller's *Maria Stuart* for the ending.

Bellini reached Venice on 8 December 1832 in order to stage *Norma* with Pasta, but Romani was simultaneously at work on five other librettos and did not arrive until 1 January 1833. By mid-February Bellini still had the 'entire second act to do', and predicted a fiasco. At a late stage the role of Filippo was reassigned to the young Cartagenova, causing alterations to at least three pieces. At the end of his preface to the original libretto Romani included an apology for his 'fragment' of melodrama, 'because inevitable circumstances have affected the plot, the colours, the characters. It requires the full indulgence of readers'. The unfortunate outcome was mutual recrimination and the eventual breach of their partnership.

The six performances were largely unsuccessful. In the years following Bellini's death, however, the opera achieved a respectable circulation. In 1837 it was performed in Trieste as *Il castello d'Ursino*; the same year Romani's libretto was set by Rinaldo Ticci for Siena. Bellini's Beatrice was a particular favourite of Erminia Frezzolini. *Beatrice di Tenda* was the first opera by Bellini to be published in full score, in an edition by Pittarelli (Rome, *c*1840) that contains material not in the Ricordi scores, particularly some relevant to the problematical Act 2 finale.

*

Beatrice, the widow of Facino Cane, is now married to the avaricious and dissolute Duke Filippo. Having acquired Beatrice's lands, Filippo is more interested in her young lady-in-waiting, Agnese. The short prelude uses themes from the opera, notably that from Beatrice's arioso in the Act 1 finale.

Act I.i The entrance hall to the castle of Binasco A grand celebration is taking place. Meeting Filippo, a group of courtiers ask why he is leaving. Filippo, continuing their choral melody, replies that he can no longer bear his wife, and the courtiers sympathize. Agnese is heard off stage singing a romanza, 'Ah! non pensar che pieno sia nel poter diletto'. Filippo vows that he will find a way to free himself and expresses his feelings in 'Divina Agnese . . . Come t'adoro, e quanto'.

I.ii Agnese's quarters Agnese, who loves Orombello, has sent him a letter, inviting him to a rendezvous. Orombello arrives, expecting to find Beatrice, and in his confusion, inadvertently discloses that he loves the Duchess. (Furious, Agnese hints at revenge.)

I.iii A grove in the gardens of the ducal palace In the cavatina 'Ma la sola, ohimè! son io' Beatrice laments to her ladies-in-waiting the suffering she has brought on everyone by marrying Filippo, who mistreats her subjects (the autograph of the cabaletta contains a less decorated vocal line than do the Ricordi scores). Filippo enters with Rizzardo, Agnese's brother, whom he instructs to watch Orombello. After wondering why his wife's unfaithfulness should annoy him, Filippo accuses Beatrice of infidelity and of treason. In the duet 'Odio e livore! – ingrato!' (part of whose accompaniment derives from Bellini's unsuccessful early work *Zaira*), Beatrice rejects both accusations, but Filippo produces incriminating documents provided by Agnese. Beatrice demands justice and a fair trial.

I.iv A remote part of the castle In a chorus, 'Lo vedeste? Sì; fremente', the men-at-arms predict Orombello's downfall. Beatrice, kneeling before a statue of her late husband, Facino Cane, prays to his spirit for assistance in 'Deh! se mi amasti un giorno'. Orombello enters, swearing to protect her, and confessing that he loves her. Beatrice orders him to leave but he refuses. Filippo and the entire court crowd in to find the apparently guilty couple together. Both Beatrice and Orombello proclaim their innocence, but Filippo orders their arrest and they are surrounded by guards.

Act 2.i A hall in the castle The courtiers and Beatrice's ladies discuss her forthcoming trial and the sufferings of Orombello under torture, which have led to an admission of his own and Beatrice's guilt. Filippo enters and, in spite of Anichino's warnings that popular sympathy for Beatrice may lead to an uprising, orders the trial to begin. Beatrice denies the judges' accusations and has an angry altercation with Filippo. Orombello is brought in and Agnese is mortified by the suffering that her jealousy has caused him. Upbraided by Beatrice for his disloyalty, Orombello recounts his tortures and retracts his confession. Their duet leads into the quintet with chorus 'Al tuo fallo ammenda festi' for Beatrice, Agnese, Orombello, Anichino, Filippo and the judges, the finest number in the score. Filippo suggests that the passing of sentence be postponed, but the judges demand further interrogation of both prisoners. Beatrice pleads with Filippo, until he orders that she and Orombello be taken away. The remorseful Agnese comes to beg forgiveness for Beatrice. Filippo refuses, then relents, acknowledging in 'Qui m'accolse oppresso, errante' the honour and power that Beatrice has brought him; but when news is brought of a popular uprising in support of Beatrice, Filippo signs her death warrant.

2.ii A vestibule above the castle prison Beatrice's maids lament her fate. She is brought in, proudly proclaiming that she said nothing under torture. Agnese confesses that she is the cause of Beatrice's downfall and asks for pardon. At first Beatrice is outraged, but the voice of Orombello, heard from his cell, urges her to forgive Agnese in 'Angiol di pace' (the melody of which comes from Orosmane's aria in *Zaira*, Act 2), and in the ensuing trio Beatrice's anger is transformed into forgiveness. A funeral bell announces the arrival of the death procession. Beatrice bids a moving farewell in the aria 'Ah! se un'urna è a me concessa', asking that flowers be laid on her grave. In the cabaletta (from *Bianca e Fernando*) she asserts that her death brings victory, not sorrow or pain.

*

Beatrice di Tenda marks a stage in the progress of Bellini's art both in the elaboration of its forms and in the variety of its harmonies. The design of the *introduzione* is something new: a dialogue between chorus and soloist followed by an offstage canzone for the comprimaria, and a cantabile for the principal baritone in two strophes punctuated by a rapid choral ritornello which also functions as a concluding stretta. The Act 1 finale impressed the young Verdi sufficiently for him to recommend it to Piave as a model of effective theatre. The judgment scene contains darker colours than have appeared in Bellini so far. Unfortunately the recourse to earlier material in the opera's final scenes betrays Bellini's haste. Beatrice deserves a less generic final cabaletta than the one borrowed from *Bianca e Fernando*. It is a pity, too, that Bellini had no time to set the duet for Beatrice and Agnese leading to their terzetto with Orombello, for which Romani had provided the text. Sketches for the music exist; and it is clear from a letter to Ricordi that Bellini intended to complete them. Another weakness lies in the portrayal of Filippo Visconti, an exceptionally odious villain (as Bellini himself recognized) who emerges as just another baritone antagonist, far more convincing in his moments of remorse than in his anger. All this doubtless explains why *Beatrice di Tenda*, despite many excellent qualities, has failed to establish itself in the repertory.   S.M., E.F., J.B.

Béatrice et Bénédict ('Beatrice and Benedick')

Opéra in two acts by Hector Berlioz to his own libretto after William Shakespeare's *Much Ado about Nothing*; Baden-Baden, Theater der Stadt, 9 August 1862.

Béatrice [Beatrice]	soprano
Bénédict [Benedick]	tenor
Héro [Hero] *Beatrice's cousin*	soprano
Claudio *Hero's lover*	baritone
Léonato [Leonato] *governor of Messina*	spoken
Don Pedro *military commander*	bass
Somarone *maestro di cappella*	bass
Ursula *Hero's attendant*	mezzo-soprano
Townspeople, soldiers	
Setting Messina in Sicily	

The celebrated overture, though not a pot-pourri in the usual sense, characterizes the substance of the opera by alluding to quite a number of passages to follow. The first act takes place in the garden of Leonato, the governor. The townspeople rejoice that the invading Moors have fled from Don Pedro and his force. Soon the victors will be home, and Hero will be reunited with her intended, Claudio. Less pleased is Beatrice, her cousin, to contemplate the return of Benedick, with whom she has long enjoyed 'a kind of merry war'. Those so far assembled dance a *sicilienne* based on Berlioz's first published song, *Le dépit de la bergère* (*c*1819) – an acknowledgment, perhaps, that he expected *Béatrice et Bénédict* to be his last work. Hero's aria is one of ecstasy at the thought of seeing Claudio again.

Don Pedro and his retinue arrive; at once Beatrice and Benedick, in their duet, begin to taunt each other. The wedding of Hero and Claudio will take place that evening – an example, it is noted, that should tempt Benedick. In his trio with Claudio and Don Pedro, Benedick insists he would much prefer the cloistered life to marriage: if ever he consents to that yoke, they can put a sign on his roof, 'Here you see Benedick, the married man'. Following his exit, his companions determine to trick Beatrice and Benedick into acknowledging their love.

Somarone, the *maestro di cappella*, whose gifts of composition are questionable, arrives with his choristers and oboists to rehearse the nuptial song, an absurd double fugue; a reprise with comic oboe ornamentation is offered before Don Pedro. Benedick, hidden behind a hedge, overhears an arranged conversation to the effect that Beatrice is indeed in love with him; suddenly he begins to consider some of the advantages of marriage. Hero and Ursula, having arranged a similar ruse as regards Beatrice, come to the garden to escape the festive commotion within. During their famous Duo-Nocturne, 'Nuit paisible et sereine!', Hero's access of melancholy is calmed by the play of moonlight and shadows, the breeze's caress, the murmur of nightingale and crickets, the aroma of spring blossoms. The effect is much the same as in 'Nuit d'ivresse' from *Les Troyens*.

The entr'acte is a reprise of the *sicilienne*. Act 2 takes place in a great hall in the governor's palace, with the wedding banquet in an adjoining room off stage. The guests, drinking heavily, prevail on Somarone to improvise a song on the merits of the local wines, accompanied by a rustic band and the pounding of wine-glasses on the tables; with effort, on stage, he finishes a second verse. Beatrice, in her aria, acknowledges that she, too, has fallen victim to love. Hero and Ursula, recognizing the change, join her in a trio of promised joys and happiness; Beatrice is lost in thought as an offstage chorus summons the bride. In a chance encounter Beatrice and Benedick, each safe in the knowledge that the other has been uncontrollably smitten, continue mercilessly to bait each other. The bridal procession enters. After the bride and groom have signed their contract, the scribe produces a second, asking who else wishes to be married. Beatrice and Benedick take each other out of pity, and banners bearing the words 'Ici on voit

Bénédict, l'homme marié' are duly proffered. A truce has been signed; the warring will recur on the morrow.

*

Béatrice et Bénédict represented for Berlioz a lighthearted turn away from the rigours of *Les Troyens*. Whereas the Virgilian tragedy summarizes the epic tendencies of his imagination, *Béatrice et Bénédict* affirms both his mordant wit and his overall good humour. He was pleased to return to Italian subject matter and to music of triple metres, street dances, tambourines and guitars. Somarone is Berlioz's invention; his line 'The piece which you are about to have the honour to perform is a masterpiece! Let us begin!' is said to have been uttered by Spontini at a rehearsal of *Olimpie* in Berlin. Elsewhere the text often follows Shakespeare closely.   D.K.H.

Beggar's Opera, The

Ballad opera in three acts arranged by Johann Christoph Pepusch to a libretto by John Gay; London, Lincoln's Inn Fields, 29 January 1728.

The first cast included Thomas Walker as Macheath and Lavinia Fenton (later the Duchess of Bolton) as Polly.

Macheath *celebrated highwayman*	
and womanizer	tenor/baritone
Peachum *a seller of stolen goods*	bass
Mrs Peachum *his wife*	soprano
Polly Peachum *his daughter and*	
Macheath's wife	soprano
Lockit *a corrupt gaoler*	baritone/bass
Lucy Lockit *his daughter and*	
Macheath's mistress	soprano
Filch *a thief in Peachum's employment*	tenor
Diana Trapes	soprano
Beggar	speaking role
Player	speaking role

Macheath's Gang (Matt of the Mint, Jemmy
    Twitcher, Crook-Finger'd Jack, Wat Dreary,
    Robin of Bagshot, Nimming Ned, Harry
    Padington, Ben Budge), Women of the Town
    (Jenny Diver, Mrs Coaxer, Dolly Trull, Mrs
    Vixen, Betty Doxy, Mrs Slammekin, Suky
    Tawdry, Molly Brazen), constables, Drawer,
    Turnkey
Setting London in 1727

The Beggar's Opera took London by storm, and it remains one of the most frequently performed operatic works in English. There was no precedent or model for the work. Gay was a disappointed seeker of court patronage at the time of the première. A friend of Pope and Swift, he had written seven mostly undistinguished plays and a fair quantity of verse. The genre he invented was to prove enormously successful and long influential.

The ballad opera form consists of spoken dialogue interspersed with thematically relevant songs, taken from a variety of mostly popular sources. Of the 69 songs, 28 have been traced to English ballads and 23 to popular Irish, Scottish and French tunes. The remaining 18 are drawn from Purcell (3), John Barrett (2), Jeremiah Clarke (2), Handel (2), Henry Carey (2), Bononcini, John Eccles, possibly Geminiani, John Wilford, Pepusch, Frescobaldi and Lewis Ramondon. The overture is based on 'One evening, having lost my way', an air in Act 3. The musical arrangement is usually credited to Pepusch, but there is no definite evidence to support this attribution. Most of the tunes were extremely familiar to the original audience, and Gay was clever at creating ironic overtones and interplay between the music and his new lyrics. For example, the heroic overtones of the original words for Purcell's melody clang oddly against the very ugly sexual realities of Polly's 'Virgins are like the fair Flower'.

Gay offered the work to Drury Lane, where it was refused by Colley Cibber, perhaps because of its genuine oddity or because of its unflattering allusions to the Whig Prime Minister, Sir Robert Walpole, in the characters of Macheath and Peachum. John Rich agreed to mount it at Lincoln's Inn Fields, where its success was unprecedented in the history of the London theatre. It received 62 performances during its first, partial season (leading to the aphorism that it made 'Gay rich, and Rich gay') and was immediately pirated. The first production created a popular craze for *Beggar's Opera* fans, playing cards, porcelain figures and illustrations (Hogarth's are the best known). The piece was performed in London every season for the rest of the century and productions were mounted throughout the English-speaking world, including Dublin, Dover, Norwich, Bath, Newcastle, Canterbury, Bristol, Glasgow, Edinburgh, Jamaica, New York, Boston, Philadelphia, Providence, Newport, Baltimore, Richmond, Williamsburg, Norfolk and Charleston. It was less often performed during the 19th century but returned to hit status in the famous Frederic Austin arrangement given at the Lyric Theatre, Hammersmith, on 5 June 1920 – a production that ran a startling 1463 nights and was frequently revived.

In 1928 Bertolt Brecht created a German adaptation with music by Kurt Weill, *Die Dreigroschenoper* ('The Threepenny Opera'). Despite that work's enormous international popularity, *The Beggar's Opera* continues to hold the stage. The annalist Alfred Loewenberg reported numerous productions before 1940, and since then they have, if anything, multiplied. The work has been revived regularly in the commercial theatre in London and New York, as well as in the National Theatre, London. It has also been made into a film by Sir Laurence Olivier (1953). Most late 20th-century productions have been executed with little comprehension of the musical and dramatic style of the original, which was designed for performance by actors rather than singers.

The first edition of *The Beggar's Opera* (1728) gave the tunes of the songs, the second (also 1728) added the overture on four staves, and the third (1729) included the basses of the songs, and also the text and songs from Gay's sequel, *Polly*. No MS orchestral parts of *The Beggar's Opera* survive, but parts for other ballad operas suggest that the songs were performed with short orchestral preludes and postludes derived from the tunes themselves; these were never published. Thus the third edition of *The Beggar's Opera* is almost a full score, for such songs were normally accompanied by strings alone with only the harpsichord to fill in between tune and bass. More elaborate accompaniments have been provided by Thomas Linley the elder, John Addison, John Hatton, Austin, E. J. Dent, Arthur Bliss and Benjamin Britten, among others.

*

Introduction (followed by the overture). The Beggar explains his 'Opera' to the Player: 'I have introduc'd the Similes that are in all your celebrated *Operas* . . . Besides, I have a Prison Scene which the Ladies always reckon charmingly pathetick. As to the Parts, I have observ'd such a nice Impartiality to our two Ladies [i.e. Polly and Lucy – a jibe at the bitter rivalry between the prima donnas Faustina Bordoni and Francesca Cuzzoni, which had culminated in a scuffle on stage six months before], that it is impossible for either of them to take Offence. I hope I may be forgiven, that I have not made my Opera throughout unnatural, like those in vogue; for I have no Recitative'.

Act I *Peachum's house* Peachum is going over his accounts and gives us his view of the world: 'Through all the Employments of Life / Each Neighbour abuses his Brother . . . All Professions berogue one another . . . And the Statesman, because he's so great, / Thinks his Trade as honest as mine'; doctors, priests, lawyers and statesmen live by 'Cheats', just as he does. Filch enters with questions about various thieves in Peachum's employment who have been arrested. Peachum says Black Moll may plead her belly (i.e. pregnancy); that he will collect the £40 reward when Tom Gagg is hanged, etc. Peachum returns to his review of his affairs, going over a list of thieves with whom he deals, including '*Robin* of *Bagshot*, alias *Gorgon*, alias *Bluff Bob*, alias *Carbuncle*, alias *Bob Booty* . . . he spends his

Life among Women' – and hence should be impeached for the reward (this is a manifest allusion to Walpole). Mrs Peachum enters, and the two of them discuss the dashing Captain Macheath. She regrets that 'the Captain hath not more Discretion. What business hath he to keep Company with Lords and Gentlemen? He should leave them to prey upon one another'.

Peachum expresses horror at the idea of his daughter's marrying and putting her husband in possession of the family secrets, and goes off to berate Polly and warn her against matrimony. Filch enters and gives Mrs Peachum the seven handkerchiefs he has just stolen at the opera. He admits that he has promised Polly he will not tattle on her, and Mrs Peachum takes him off for a drink while she worms the truth out of him. Polly and her father enter, with Polly insisting that 'A Woman knows how to be mercenary, though she hath never been in a Court or at an Assembly. . . . If I allow Captain *Macheath* some trifling Liberties, I have this Watch and other visible Marks of his Favour to show for it'. In an air she tells us that 'Virgins are like the fair Flower in its Lustre . . . when once pluck'd, 'tis no longer alluring,/To Covent-Garden 'tis sent, (as yet sweet,)/There fades, and shrinks, and grows past all enduring,/Rots, stinks, and dies, and is trod under feet'. As Polly comments, 'A Girl who cannot grant some Things, and refuse what is most material, will make but a poor hand of her Beauty, and soon be thrown upon the Common'. Mrs Peachum, however, enters 'in a very great Passion' singing 'Our Polly is a sad Slut!', having discovered the horrible truth: Polly has secretly married Macheath. Her parents abuse her ('Do you think your Mother and I should have liv'd comfortably so long together, if ever we had been married? Baggage! . . . thou foolish Jade, thou wilt be as ill-us'd, and as much neglected, as if thou hadst married a Lord!'). Polly defends herself. 'I did not marry him (as 'tis the Fashion) coolly and deliberately for Honour and Money. But, I love him'. Mrs Peachum is horrified: 'Love him! worse and worse! I thought the Girl had been better bred', and has to be revived with two stiff drinks. Peachum realizes that they 'must all endeavour to make the best of it', and proposes that Polly 'Secure what he hath got, have him peach'd the next Sessions, and then at once you are made a rich Widow'. Polly protests that her duty to her husband forbids this; her mother says her duty to her parents requires obedience: 'Away, Hussy. Hang your Husband, and be dutiful'. Alone for an exaggeratedly 'pathetic' scene, Polly imagines the execution at Tyburn ('I see him at the Tree! . . . even Butchers weep!'). She has hidden Macheath in her room, and they take romantic leave of each other in a series of five songs, including 'Pretty Polly, say' and 'O what Pain it is to

'The Stage Medley', satirical engraving aimed at the taste of the town and its admiration for John Gay's 'The Beggar's Opera' (music arranged by J. C. Pepusch), first performed at Lincoln's Inn Fields theatre, 29 January 1728 (top left are portraits of Lavinia Fenton and Thomas Walker, the first Polly Peachum and Macheath)

part!' Macheath swears fidelity, and Polly assures him 'I have no Reason to doubt you, for I find in the Romance you lent me, none of the great Heroes were ever false in Love'.

Act 2 *A Tavern near Newgate* Macheath's gang are discovered congratulating themselves upon their 'try'd Courage, and indefatigable Industry' and saying that all of them would die for the sake of a friend ('Show me a Gang of Courtiers that can say as much'). Macheath enters and explains that he will have to go into hiding. To the strains of the 'March in [Handel's] *Rinaldo*' they sing 'Let us take the Road' and disperse. Macheath remains chatting with the Drawer (the tapster of the tavern), singing 'If the Heart of a Man is deprest with Cares,/The Mist is dispell'd when a Woman appears', while women are fetched. Macheath frolics, sings and dances with the whores. Jenny sings 'Before the Barn-door crowing,/The Cock by Hens attended'. The women signal to Peachum, who enters with constables and arrests Macheath.

Macheath arrives at the prison in Newgate, where Lockit demands 'Garnish' in return for lighter fetters. Macheath laments his condition, especially when Lucy Lockit enters and berates him. He promises to marry her at the first opportunity and denies his marriage to Polly. In another part of the prison Peachum and Lockit try to settle their joint accounts, proclaiming that 'Business is at an end – if once we act dishonourably', – piety quickly degenerating into a quarrel in which they 'collar' one another and threaten impeachment and hanging. Just as Macheath is trying to persuade Lucy to help him raise money to escape ('Money well tim'd, and properly apply'd, will do any thing'), Polly enters and proclaims herself his wife – to Lucy's fury. Macheath sings 'How happy could I be with either,/Were t'other dear Charmer away!'; Polly and Lucy sing 'I'm bubbled', and Peachum enters and hauls Polly off. Macheath tries to explain himself to Lucy, who agrees to help him escape and concludes the act with 'I like the Fox shall grieve,/Whose Mate hath left her side'.

Act 3 *Newgate* Lockit abuses Lucy – not for letting Macheath escape, but for failing to get paid for it. While Macheath is in a gaming house, Peachum and Lockit plot his recapture in Peachum's Lock. Diana Trapes enters and tells them how to find him. Back in Newgate, Lucy has 'the Rats-bane ready' for Polly. They exchange insincere commiserations; Polly drops the poisoned glass when Macheath is hauled in again; Lucy concludes grumpily that 'she was not happy enough to deserve to be poison'd'. The two women squabble furiously over the unhappy Macheath (though Peachum says 'Away Hussies! This is not a time for a Man to be hamper'd with his Wives'). 'A Dance of Prisoners in Chains'

covers the trial, off stage. Macheath, in the 'Condemn'd Hold', seeks consolation in drink and sings ten rousing songs in quick succession to bolster his spirits, concluding with 'Since Laws were made for ev'ry Degree ... I wonder we han't better Company, / Upon Tyburn Tree!' (to the tune of 'Green Sleeves'). Macheath expresses distress that Jemmy Twitcher should testify against him, saying glumly 'Tis a plain Proof that the World is all alike, and that even our Gang can no more trust one another than other People'. Polly and Lucy enter to take leave of their husband, but when 'Four Women more ... with a Child a-piece' are announced Macheath says 'This is too much'; he is ready to be hanged.

At this point we return to the frame with the entry of the Player and the Beggar. The Beggar says he intends to have Macheath hanged for the sake of 'doing strict poetical Justice'. The Player objects that this would make 'a down-right deep Tragedy. The Catastrophe is manifestly wrong, for an Opera must end happily'. The Beggar accepts the objection and orders a reprieve, saying that 'in this kind of Drama, 'tis no matter how absurdly things are brought about ... All this we must do, to comply with the Taste of the Town'. The work concludes with a dance and an air, 'Thus I stand like the Turk, with his Doxies around' (to the tune 'Lumps of Pudding').

*

The Beggar's Opera has been called everything from 'a sentimental lollipop' to 'a terse social fable'. Most critics have been anxious to find as much significance and serious satire as possible in the work. It is witty at the expense of a number of obvious targets, notably Sir Robert Walpole, the conventions of Italian opera at the Royal Academy of Music in the 1720s, the generic customs of both tragedy and comedy of sentiment, and society's structure and conventional assumptions. The radical inversions of high and low life are startling and amusing, and the many comparisons of humans with animals ('Of all Animals of Prey, Man is the only sociable one', 3.ii) must have disconcerted the original audience. In elementary ways, however, the work fails to function effectively as a satire on its obvious targets. Gay offers no genuine alternatives: he demeans high life, but without suggesting that low life is better. Macheath's revelation that 'the World is all alike' seems to reflect Gay's own view of things – and if all the world is irremediably corrupt, then there is little point to satire, which attacks evil in support of the good. The tone is lighthearted, but the ultimate ideological implications are exceedingly bleak – far more so than in *Die Dreigroschenoper*, where evils are angrily attacked on the assumption that the world can be changed. Nevertheless the work is one of the most genuinely original in the history of the theatre, and was Gay's one stupendous and virtually inexplicable success – how he got the idea for it no one has ever been able satisfactorily to explain.

The Beggar's Opera may fairly be called 'frivolously nihilistic'. Ironically, it is almost always now staged as a period romp, and appears to have been given in an equally superficial way during the 18th century. Other kinds of production are possible, as David Freeman demonstrated in his Opera Factory production of 1982, replete with punk rock additions but giving the text the ugliness and despair that are almost always masked in performance by surface jollity.   R.D.H.

See also Dreigroschenoper, die

Belle Hélène, La ('Fair Helen')

Opéra bouffe in three acts by Jacques Offenbach to a libretto by Henri Meilhac and Ludovic Halévy, after classical mythology; Paris, Théâtre des Variétés, 17 December 1864.

The first Helen was Hortense Schneider; Paris was first sung by José Dupuis, with Eugène Grenier (Calchas), Henri Couder (Agamemnon), Jean Kopp (Menelaus) and Léa Silly (Oreste).

Hortense Schneider as Helen in Offenbach's 'La belle Hélène', the role she created in the original production at the Théâtre des Variétés, Paris, 17 December 1864

Hélène [Helen] *Queen of Sparta*	soprano
Oreste [Orestes] *son of*	
Agamemnon	mezzo-soprano
Pâris [Paris] *son of King Priam of Troy*	tenor
Ménélas [Menelaus] *King of Sparta*	tenor *buffo*
Agamemnon *King of Kings*	baritone
Calchas *grand soothsayer to Jupiter*	baritone
Achille [Achilles] *King of*	
Phthiotis	tenor or baritone
Ajax I *King of Salamis*	tenor or baritone
Ajax II *King of the Locrians*	tenor or baritone
Bacchis *Helen's maid*	soprano

Guards, slaves, people, princes, princesses, mourners of Adonis, Helen's handmaidens

Setting Sparta and Nauplia, just before the Trojan War

La belle Hélène followed *Orphée aux enfers* of six years earlier as a satirical treatment of the classics, and as a very thinly disguised comment on many aspects of Second Empire society life. It was one of Offenbach's greatest successes, epitomized, above all others of his works, in the music he composed for Schneider and Dupuis. Other roles were filled by members of the Théâtre des Variétés company. Later famous Helens have included Maria Jeritza in 1911 at Salzburg, Jarmila Novotna in 1931 in Berlin (both productions by Max Reinhardt) and, in recent years, Jane Rhodes, while Jussi Björling's recording of Paris's outstandingly lyrical 'Au mont Ida' has set the standard by which other versions are judged.

*

Act I *A public square in Sparta, before the temple of Jupiter* Calchas, High Priest of Jupiter, is bemoaning the meagre sacrifices at his temple and the increase in popularity of Venus since she won the golden apple from the shepherd Paris and promised him the most beautiful maiden on earth. This is generally recognized to be Helen, wife of the somewhat dull King Menelaus, and she is excitedly contemplating what fate has in store for her ('Amours divins! Ardentes flammes!'). Orestes now comes in, singing a chirpy song ('Au cabaret du Labyrinthe'). The shepherd Paris arrives to claim his prize, describing how he judged the beauty contest ('Au mont Ida'), and Calchas promises to help him. Helen is immediately drawn to the shepherd, but the Greek kings Achilles, Agamemnon and the two Ajaxes are busy assembling for a ceremonial contest ('Voici les rois de la Grèce!'). This takes the form of a game of charades which, to the kings' chagrin, Paris duly wins. He now reveals his identity as the son of King Priam – much to Helen's consternation ('L'homme à la pomme'). He is crowned winner by Helen, and in order to facilitate Venus's scheme Calchas declares that the gods have banned the reluctant Menelaus to Crete for a month ('Pars pour la Crète!').

Act 2 *In Queen Helen's apartments* A month later Helen gazes at the wall painting of Leda and the Swan (her father and mother) and, contemplating her destiny, asks Venus what pleasure she finds in destroying her virtue ('On me nomme Hélène la blonde'). Paris arrives and insists that, after a month of indecision, she really must give herself to him as promised by Venus. She continues to prevaricate, and Paris vows to resort to subterfuge, as the four kings settle down to a board game, which Calchas wins by the use of loaded dice. Helen retires to her bed, asking Calchas to arrange that she at least dream of her shepherd. Seeing Paris hiding in the room dressed as a slave, Calchas decides to let matters take their course. Paris proceeds to make love to Helen, who is convinced that it is merely her dream ('Oui, c'est un rêve') until the illusion is shattered by the return of Menelaus and the hasty departure of Paris. The husband summons his fellow kings, as Helen seeks to put the blame on to him for returning from Crete without warning ('Un mari sage est en voyage'). The kings denounce Paris in incongruously seductive waltz tempo ('Un vile séducteur!').

Act 3 *The beach at Nauplia* The whole court has come to Nauplia for the bathing season. Menelaus presses Helen to explain her action, but she is adamant that she is blameless ('Là! Vrai, je ne suis pas coupable'). Menelaus continues to express his indignation, but his fellow kings declare that it is the fault of Venus who, they claim, has turned Greece into one gigantic orgy ('Lorsque la Grèce est un champ de carnage'). Menelaus has demanded a visit from the High Priest of Venus, who now arrives yodelling a message from the goddess ('Je suis gai, soyez gais!'). He explains that he will take Helen to Cythera to sacrifice 100 white heifers to Venus. Only after the High Priest whispers in her ear is Helen finally persuaded to go, and after the boat has set sail the Priest throws off his disguise and reveals himself as Paris. He tells the people that he is taking Helen to Troy, and the kings vow they will go to war against Troy to avenge the affront to Menelaus.

*

As with most of Offenbach's greatest works, the creation of *La belle Hélène* seems to have been largely untroubled. With some of the composer's most shapely and expressive vocal writing in the music for Helen and Paris, some of his most beguiling waltz tunes, and such outstanding numbers as the March of the Kings and the rousing patriotic chorus which brilliantly parodies that in Rossini's *Guillaume Tell*, the work's popularity was established from the first. There is a twinkle in the eye throughout, not least in bewitching parodies such as the mock-operatic ensemble 'L'homme à la pomme'. Offenbach composed alternative numbers for the Viennese production with Marie Geistinger, and the original

German score, published by Bote & Bock in 1865, also contains the subsequently celebrated overture.

A.L.

Benvenuto Cellini

Opera semiseria in two acts by Hector Berlioz to a libretto by Léon de Wailly and Auguste Barbier, assisted by Alfred de Vigny, after the memoirs of Benvenuto Cellini; Paris, Opéra, 10 September 1838. Revised version, Weimar, Grossherzogliches Hoftheater, 20 March 1852; with further revision in three acts, 17 November 1852.

The first cast included Julie Dorus-Gras as Teresa, Gilbert Duprez in the title role, and Prosper Dérivis as Balducci.

Benvenuto Cellini *a goldsmith*	tenor
Giacomo Balducci *papal treasurer*	bass
Teresa *his daughter*	soprano
Ascanio *his apprentice*	soprano
	(mezzo-soprano in 1838)
Fieramosca *a sculptor*	baritone
	(tenor in 1838)
Francesco ⎱ *Cellini's artisans*	tenor
Bernardino ⎰	bass
Pompeo *a swordsman*	baritone
Innkeeper	tenor
Cardinal Salviati	bass

Setting 16th-century Rome during the papacy of Clement VII

Cellini was composed with comparative ease, even abandon, though opportunities to concentrate on it were limited by Berlioz's increasing activities as journalist and promoter of his own symphonic concerts. Censorship in Paris did not allow a pope to be represented on stage, so the part became that of Cardinal Salviati at the première and in all subsequent versions. The overture, a triumph of rhythmic imagination, portends the general vivacity to follow; among the themes are allusions to the cardinal's arioso and to the lovely 'Ariette d'Arlequin' of the dumb show.

*

Act 1 tableau i opens on Shrove Monday in the home of the papal treasurer, Giacomo Balducci. He is vexed that Clement VII has commissioned a bronze statue of Perseus from the libertine genius Cellini instead of Fieramosca, the papal sculptor and suitor of Balducci's daughter Teresa. Passing maskers sing of the carnival and toss Teresa flowers, along with a billet-doux from Cellini. To be torn between love and duty, she complains in her cavatina 'Entre l'amour et le devoir', is no laughing matter; but at the age of 17 it would be a pity to behave. (This replaced an earlier cavatina, 'Ah, que l'amour une fois dans le coeur'.) Cellini comes to pay Teresa court, but their duet becomes a trio when Fieramosca tiptoes into the room and takes cover behind a door. (Berlioz re-used the melody of the duet 'O Teresa, vous que j'aime plus que ma vie' as the english horn solo in the overture *Le carnaval romain*; the other theme in the concert overture is the saltarello from the carnival scene.) Fieramosca overhears the lovers planning to elope to Florence (the trio 'Demain soir mardi gras'): the following evening, at the carnival, Cellini and his apprentice Ascanio will come disguised as monks to the Piazza Colonna, there to effect a rendezvous with Teresa. Balducci enters, surprised to find his daughter still awake; Cellini slips out of the open door. Teresa, stammering an explanation, says she has heard a prowler, and to her great surprise it is Fieramosca who is found in her room. Servants and neighbours are summoned to capture the seducer, but in the confusion he manages to get away. They chase him towards the public fountain.

Tableau ii begins at nightfall in the Piazza Colonna, with a tavern on one side and Cassandro's theatre, a place of lampoons, on the other. Cellini reflects that while glory was once his only goal, now Teresa alone rules his heart. The two ensemble scenes that follow – the goldsmiths' chorus ('Honneur aux maîtres ciseleurs') and the Roman carnival – are the musical high points of the opera, summarizing in orchestration, rhythm and organizational device the growth of Berlioz's style since his Italian sojourn. There is revealed, moreover, a bright sense of humour that until then had only been heard in the Abruzzi serenade from *Harold en Italie*. The smiths' apostrophe to their noble art, for example, is interrupted by the cross old innkeeper, who tallies a list of wine consumed and will deliver no more until the account is paid. Ascanio appears with money from the papal treasury, surrendering it only after Cellini's oath that the statue will be cast the next day. But the amount tendered by the parsimonious Balducci is scarcely enough to pay the innkeeper.

Cellini goes off to arrange an appropriate evening's entertainment with Cassandro, impresario of the adjoining theatre, as the goldsmiths' chorus is reprised. Fieramosca, beaten and bruised, has engaged a henchman, the swordsman Pompeo; they plan to appear at the carnival in habits identical to those of Cellini and Ascanio, in which dress they hope to succeed in abducting Teresa. Fieramosca practises his swordsmanship.

Trumpet fanfares summon the public to Cassandro's theatre, and the piazza begins to fill with revellers. Balducci and Teresa enter, then Cellini and Ascanio, in white and brown habits respectively; the conversation of the four intermingles in a *réunion des thèmes*. In the famous saltarello Cassandro's players attract the crowd ('Venez voir! venez voir!') as the women and children dance. The pantomime of King Midas, or The Donkey's Ears, begins: a papal treasurer unmistakably resembling Balducci remunerates Harlequin's lovely arietta and the buffoonery, including ophicleide and bass drum, of the donkey-eared Pasquarello (Polichinelle in 1838). A single coin goes to Harlequin, much as the pittance had gone to Cellini for the wine account; the rest is paid to the ass. Balducci, recognizing himself, assaults the players; the rival friars converge on Teresa. During the confusion Cellini stabs Pompeo. Just as the crowd sees that a monk has been killed, the cannon of the fortress of Sant'Angelo sounds the end of the carnival and the beginning of Lent. The revellers extinguish their candles, and in the ensuing darkness Cellini escapes and Ascanio spirits Teresa away. Fieramosca, mistaken for Cellini, is arrested for murder.

The foreboding entr'acte is a sinister version of the 'Chant des ciseleurs' from the previous act. Act 2 tableau iii opens in Cellini's studio at dawn on Ash Wednesday. A model of the statue of Perseus dominates the stage. Ascanio and Teresa pray for Cellini's safety as White Friars pass in the street chanting a litany to the Virgin. Cellini, still in his white habit, has been of their number. Reunited with Teresa, he describes his escape; the statue, they resolve, will be abandoned as they elope together. Ascanio tries to warn of the arrival of Balducci and Fieramosca, but it is too late. The principals encounter each other in a sextet, the centrepiece of the tableau; just as Balducci gives Teresa's hand to Fieramosca, the cardinal enters with his retinue. Finding the statue unfinished and Cellini accused of murder and kidnapping, the cardinal orders the casting to be done by someone else. Cellini, in audacious defiance, threatens to smash the plaster model. The gesture is impudent but effective: the cardinal has no choice but to return that evening. If by that time the Perseus is not cast, Cellini will hang.

Tableau iv opens later that afternoon, in Cellini's foundry in the Colosseum. Ascanio feigns optimism at the situation ('Tra-la-la . . . mais qu'ai-je donc?'); Cellini pauses to long for a pastoral life far from the city's din ('Sur les monts les plus sauvages'). Off stage, the foundry workers sing symbolically of sailors at large on the sea. (Here there followed a 'scène et choeurs' including further reverses, excised by Berlioz before the first performance. The later Weimar version, sanctioned by the composer, conflates and reorders tableaux iii and iv for Act 3.) Balducci and the cardinal return to observe the casting, but metal is in short supply and the meld begins to congeal. Cellini, on the verge of losing everything, orders his assistants to fetch all his artworks – gold, silver, copper, bronze – and throw them into the furnace. The crucible explodes and the molten metal flows through the trenches and into the mould. The statue is done, Cellini pardoned, Teresa's hand earned, and the reward of the *maîtres ciseleurs* is immortal glory.

*

The clumsy second act was the primary cause of the vicissitudes that befell *Benvenuto Cellini*. Not even the Weimar revisions could fully correct the confusions of the denouement. Moreover, the work was of surpassing technical difficulty. Berlioz behaved gracefully after each failure of *Benvenuto Cellini*, but 'I cannot help recognizing', he wrote in 1850 or so, 'that it contains a variety of ideas, an energy and exuberance and a brilliance of colour such as I may perhaps never find again, and which deserved a better fate'.   D.K.H.

Billy Budd

Opera in two acts, op.50, by Benjamin Britten to a libretto by E. M. Forster and Eric Crozier, after Herman Melville's story; in four acts, London, Covent Garden, 1 December 1951 (revised in two acts, Covent Garden, 9 January 1964; previously broadcast, BBC, 13 November 1961).

The cast at the first performance included Theodor Uppman in the title role, Peter Pears (Vere), Frederick Dalberg (Claggart), Hervey Alan (Redburn), Geraint Evans (Flint), Michael Langdon (Ratcliffe), Inia Te Wiata (Dansker); it was conducted by the composer.

Billy Budd *able seaman*	baritone
Edward Fairfax Vere *Captain of HMS Indomitable*	tenor
John Claggart *Master-at-arms*	bass
Mr Redburn *First Lieutenant*	baritone
Mr Flint *Sailing Master*	bass-baritone
Lieutenant Ratcliffe	bass
Red Whiskers *an impressed man*	tenor
Donald *a sailor*	baritone
Dansker *an old seaman*	bass
Novice	tenor
Squeak *a ship's corporal*	tenor
Bosun	baritone
First Mate	baritone
Second Mate	baritone
Maintop	tenor
Novice's friend	baritone
Arthur Jones *an impressed man*	baritone
Four Midshipmen	boys' voices
Cabin Boy	spoken

Officers, sailors, powder-monkeys, drummers, marines
Setting On board the *Indomitable*, a seventy-four, during the French wars of 1797, as she sails near enemy waters

Billy Budd was commissioned by the Arts Council of Great Britain for the Festival of Britain, 1951. Britten had discussed a possible opera on Melville's story with Crozier and Forster in late 1948 and early 1949, before the work was actually commissioned. The libretto evolved through four versions during 1949, and composition was begun in earnest during the summer of 1950. Originally planned in two acts, it was first performed in a four-act version. In 1960 Britten produced a two-act revision, in which the main change was the excision of the original Act 1 finale where Captain Vere appears to general acclaim and addresses the crew. The revised version was first heard the next year under the composer's baton and has since remained the accepted one. The opera has not achieved the extensive international success of *Peter Grimes*, although the scenes televised in New York in 1952 were apparently the first operatic music by Britten to be so broadcast. The fact that the cast is all-male is unlikely to be a contributing factor. Productions of *Billy Budd* by the WNO (1972), the Royal Opera (1979) and the ENO (1988) all featured Thomas Allen in the title role, and a video recording of the ENO production was issued in 1989. A complete gramophone recording, with Peter Glossop as Budd, Peter Pears as Vere and Michael Langdon as Claggart, conducted by Britten, was issued in 1968.

*

Prologue *Captain Vere in old age* To music whose quiet oscillating motion and persistent harmonic clashes embody conflict and indecision, Captain Vere, long since retired, muses on the inseparability of good and evil. Neither, his experience tells him, is absolute. The conflict of 3rds (B♭/D♮, B♮/D♮) generates the opera's most pervasive melodic idea (the *Rights o' Man* motif), which is used for Vere's climactic self-questioning ('Oh what have I done?'), growing naturally out of the eloquent arioso which is the opera's principal formal feature. In old age Vere still cannot explain exactly what happened all those years ago, or why. The main action of the opera is therefore like a gigantic flashback in which Vere relives the decisive events of 1797 in the hope of finding illumination and peace, and it gives his character a dimension not found in Melville, where he dies on active service.

Act I.i *The main deck and quarterdeck of HMS Indomitable* Two parties of sailors are holy-stoning the main deck under the harsh instructions of their officers. They sing a shanty-like refrain, 'O heave, O heave away, heave!' to the opera's principal motif. In the mêlée a Novice accidentally bumps into the Bosun and is dragged away to be flogged. Meanwhile a guard-boat approaches, having been sent out to a passing merchant ship to pressgang the most likely-looking sailors for war service. The officers complain that the results of such forays are rarely satisfactory but in time of war they must take what they can get. As the three impressed men are brought forward the Master-at-arms, John Claggart, questions them in turn. The first, Red Whiskers, objects to being pressganged, and Claggart reveals his menacing side. Neither Red Whiskers nor Arthur Jones pleases the officers, but the third man is very different. He gives his name cheerfully as Billy Budd. He is an able, willing seaman and, although he reveals a stammer when trying to explain that he was a foundling child, he satisfies the officers and the Master-at-arms, who describes him as 'a find in a thousand'. Billy is overjoyed to be assigned to the foretop, and sings ecstatically of the joys of 'working aloft'. Then he cries out an eloquent farewell to his former ship, *Rights o' Man* (the main motif reappears with emphasis here), and the officers, misunderstanding the innocent, even childlike Billy and fearing the response of the other sailors, quickly call for the decks to be cleared. Left alone, Claggart reveals his bitterness at existence on this 'accursed ship' and his disdain for the officers. He instructs the ship's corporal Squeak to put Budd to the test by taking every opportunity to annoy him. As Squeak runs off the Novice, who is barely able to walk, is helped in by a group of sailors. Claggart, moving away, regards him with contempt but, after a short ensemble in which the Novice sings of his despair and his comrades echo his lament ('We're all of us lost on the sea'), Billy appears and expresses his sympathy. Budd has been befriended by an old seaman, Dansker, and they join Red Whiskers and Donald in an ensemble expressing their reactions to the Novice's punishment. As the watch changes, Claggart returns. He is brusque with Billy, ordering him to remove a 'fancy neckerchief: this is a Man-o'-War'. Then, with sinister emphasis, he tells Billy to 'take a pride in yourself, Beauty, and you'll come to no harm'. Dansker warns Billy to avoid Claggart, and when the sailors begin to sing with enthusiasm of the captain, 'Starry Vere', Billy jubilantly expresses his desire to serve him.

I.ii Captain Vere's cabin, a week later Vere, who is reading Plutarch and finds parallels between present-day troubles and those of the Greeks and Romans, summons his senior officers for a glass of wine. They drink a toast to the king, and the officers, looking forward to action as they near enemy waters, express dislike of all things French – especially ideas of the kind that promoted the Revolution and which were held responsible for the recent naval mutinies,

at Spithead and the Nore ('the floating republic', sung to the *Rights o' Man* motif). In his own reactions to these events, Vere reveals his fear of sedition, 'the infamous spirit of France'. The officers mention Budd as a potential source of trouble, but Vere disagrees: all Budd is guilty of is 'youthful high spirits'. As if to confirm the captain's optimism, the sound of the sailors singing a shanty becomes audible. As the officers leave, and Vere resumes his reading, an orchestral interlude based on the shanty culminates in a massive choral ensemble, simple yet powerful, in Britten's finest vein.

I.iii The berth-deck Billy, with Donald and Red Whiskers, sings another lively shanty. Dansker refuses to join in and when Billy, to cheer him up, goes to his kitbag for some tobacco, he finds Squeak rifling his belongings. Anger brings on his stammer and the two men fight. In the uproar, Claggart appears, and after silencing Squeak, who is trying to explain that he was only obeying Claggart's orders, he turns to Billy with a smile and words of praise. Left alone, Claggart reveals that it is Billy's very 'handsomeness' and 'goodness' that attract his sadistic desire to destroy him. He instructs the Novice, willing to do anything to avoid further flogging, to carry out his plan; and the Novice, with great reluctance, agrees. Waking Billy, the Novice tries to tempt him with money (provided by Claggart) into leading a gang of dissidents who are plotting mutiny. Billy is initially attracted by the gold, but when he realizes what it is for he grows angry, his stammer starts up, and the Novice runs off. Dansker appears and helps Billy calm down. Billy tells him of the mutiny plan and his resistance to it. Dansker warns him that Claggart is hostile to him, but Billy refuses to believe it. The two men sing together: Billy is enraptured at the prospect of promotion – he may even become captain of the mizzen top. But Dansker, to Claggart's own baleful motif, continues to warn him.

Act 2.i Main deck and quarterdeck, some days later Vere and the officers are on deck, while mist swirls round the ship. As Claggart approaches Vere and begins to tell him about the danger of mutiny, the mist lifts and a French ship is sighted. The whole crew swings rapidly into action. The *Indomitable* prepares her sails for pursuit and her guns for the assault in a complex and exciting ensemble for all the various groups of officers and seamen, including the treble powder-monkeys. Soon all is ready, but there is still only a light breeze. Despite the lack of progress, Vere orders a shot. To great excitement a cannon is fired, but the shot falls far short. The French ship is out of range, the wind dies and the mist closes in once more. Depressed, the crew disperses. Now Claggart approaches the captain again and this time he tells the full story, claiming that Budd offered gold to the Novice if he would join the mutineers. Vere reacts with anger and disbelief, but he agrees to interview Budd in Claggart's presence.

2.ii *The captain's cabin* In a state of great agitation, Vere asserts that 'Claggart is evil, Billy good. Claggart, he claims, will fail. But the florid music of this brief, hectic soliloquy has more of hysteria than confidence. Billy arrives, expecting news of his promotion, and sings fluently of his longing for action and his wish to be Vere's coxswain. But he makes no complaint when Vere explains that promotion is not the reason for this interview. Claggart is admitted and (to a variant of the *Rights o' Man* motif) accuses Billy of mutiny. As Vere urges him to defend himself, the stammer takes hold; unable to speak, Billy strikes Claggart down with a single blow. When Vere discovers that Claggart is dead he sends Billy into a side cabin and summons the officers. In a short, tormented monologue he blames his own lack of foresight for the catastrophe.

The officers hastily convene a drumhead court. Confronted with the charge of murder, Billy can only explain that he was unable to answer Claggart's false accusation with words: 'I had to say it with a blow'. He cannot explain why Claggart should have wrongfully accused him, and when he and the officers turn to Vere for an explanation the captain refuses to respond. With Billy sent back to the side cabin, the death sentence is pronounced. After the officers have left, Vere is at first resolute in his acceptance of the sentence and the circumstances that make it just. Then, in a more turbulent phase, he sees himself doomed as well: he it is who must destroy handsomeness and goodness. As he enters the side cabin to tell Billy his fate the scene's orchestral coda unfolds a sequence of common chords, all harmonizing notes of the F major triad and expressing a mixture of resolution, compassion and resignation in a startlingly direct yet subtle manner.

2.iii *A bay of the gundeck, shortly before dawn the next day* Billy, only half awake, calmly contemplates his imminent death. Dansker brings him food and drink, and the news that the ship is now indeed close to mutiny, the sailors determined to prevent Billy's execution. Billy tells Dansker to stop them: fate decrees his death, just as it decreed Claggart's, and determined Vere's inability to save Billy. After Dansker has left, Billy sings an expansive farewell ('Billy in the Darbies'), affirming his acceptance of his fate to a reminiscence of the chord-sequence from the end of the previous scene.

2.iv *Main deck and quarterdeck, dawn* The ship's company assemble to martial music. Billy is brought in and the First Lieutenant reads from the Articles of War, ending with the sentence of death. In a last salutation, Billy sings out 'Starry Vere, God bless you!' and the entire ship's company, including the

officers, echo his cry. Then he is marched off. At the moment of his death a wordless rumble of revolt begins among the sailors and wells up to a fierce climax. Vere remains motionless and silent; under the officers' orders the marines force the men to disperse.

Epilogue *Vere in old age* To the prologue's uneasily tranquil opening music, Vere describes how, after Billy's execution and burial at sea, the ship sailed on. He acknowledges that he could have saved Billy, but no longer seeks to explain why he did not do so. Instead, he explains that it is Billy, rather, who has saved him. To music echoing Billy's own farewell in Act 2 scene iii Vere claims that he too has found contentment, and the piled-up dissonances resolve into a radiant, powerfully reiterated B♮ major triad. As this chord dies away, Vere sings again the words that ended the prologue, to a vocal line whose descending pitches cast a shadow over the serenity of the harmonic resolution. Whether he has truly found peace, or whether he is doomed endlessly to relive the most powerful and traumatic event of his life, unable to find release even in death, is a question the opera leaves open.

*

Billy Budd, like *Peter Grimes* and *Gloriana*, demonstrates Britten's ability to create an opera in a distinctively 'grand manner' through the use of elaborate ensembles and unrestrained outpourings of emotion, often with richly orchestrated accompaniments. Its departures from Melville's original story, with Billy (in his song of farewell) achieving an unprecedented articulateness, and Vere, whose emotions are evidently intended to carry an element of sexual attraction, are fully justified by the power of the resulting music. In the way motivic and harmonic processes integrate the evolving drama into a flexible yet coherent form, *Billy Budd* is Britten's most richly worked operatic score, even though it lacks the purely technical progressiveness, with respect to 12-note features, of *The Turn of the Screw* and its successors. Of all Britten's operas, *Billy Budd* is the one in which the composer's instinct for tellingly simple musical ideas, and his sense of how far such ideas could be extended and enriched to serve an ambivalent but never obscure dramatic theme, is most impressively displayed.   A.W.

Bluebeard's Castle [*A Kékszakállú herceg vára* ('Duke Bluebeard's Castle')]

Opera in one act, op.11, by Béla Bartók to a libretto by Béla Balázs after a fairy-tale by Charles Perrault; Budapest, Opera, 24 May 1918.

At the première the singers were Oszkár Kálmán

and Olga Haselbeck; it was conducted by Egisto Tango and produced by Dezsó Zádor.

Duke Bluebeard [A Kékszakállú
   herceg]   baritone
Judith [Judit] *his wife*   (mezzo-)soprano
Prologue   spoken
Bluebeard's three former wives   silent
Setting A hall in Bluebeard's castle in
   legendary times

Balázs belonged to the same generation as Bartók, and shared his determination to create an opera which was both Hungarian and modern. Thus where Bartók was influenced by the modality and rhythmic irregularity he found both in Transylvanian music and in Debussy, Balázs looked at once to folk ballads and to Maeterlinck. His immediate source was Maeterlinck's *Ariane et Barbe-bleue*, already set by Dukas; but he changed the story significantly. Where Ariane's quest is for independence and escape from the castle/prison, Judith wants a relationship with Bluebeard which will make the castle a prison no longer. And where Ariane is by far the most important character, with Bluebeard present for only two brief, if critical, moments, Balázs's libretto is cast throughout for Judith and Bluebeard together, and alone.

Balázs wrote the text for either Bartók or Kodály to set; Bartók wrote his version in 1911 and entered it in a national competition for one-act operas. It failed to win a prize, and the Budapest Opera was reluctant to produce it until after the success of the Bartók-Balázs ballet *The Wooden Prince* in 1917. It was in a double-bill with the ballet that the work had its first performance.

The libretto is cast almost exclusively in trochaic tetrameters, a constant reminder that this is the world of ballad, though Bartók's setting fluctuates around the basic model of quaver beats in 2/4 and 4/4. Bluebeard's part is centred on this plainest sort of declamation, while Judith's hazards more triple time and more rhythmic variety, seeming to want to loosen the rigidity in which she is contained; there is a parallel in the modal construction of the opera, Bluebeard preferring pentatonic expressions whereas Judith sings in richer modes. No doubt Bartók's word-setting, in what was his first important vocal work, owed much to what he had heard of folk music, but Debussy showed the way too, through the example of his own Maeterlinck opera. As in *Pelléas et Mélisande*, the setting is syllabic, the vocal lines follow speech patterns, and there are few occasions where they rise to self-contained melody or high register. The differences in vocal style in the two operas, which include a preponderance of falling phrases in *Bluebeard's Castle*, can be ascribed to differences

between the languages: in this regard, as with the use of trochaic metre, the opera is locked into Magyar as securely as Bluebeard is locked into the castle which is his self.

*

After the prologue, the stage reveals a circular Gothic hall with seven great doors and, to the left, a smaller door through which Bluebeard and Judith enter. Their opening dialogue has Bluebeard introducing his new wife to his home, but also inviting her to reconsider her decision to live with him (it seems a poignant and almost cruel admonitory gesture that Bartók should have dedicated the work to his own new wife, Márta, whom he had married two years earlier). Judith proclaims firmly that she has made up her mind, and there is then a passionate embrace, which brings forward for the first time nearly the whole of the large orchestra Bartók uses here, a larger ensemble than in anything else he wrote. Bluebeard calls for the door to be bolted, and the music returns to the austere pentatony with which it had begun. This is the castle reasserting itself, and Judith notices that its walls are 'weeping' (symbolically, of course, they are the walls of Bluebeard's skull). Again she is offered the opportunity to go back; again she declines.

Next Bluebeard turns his attention to her motivation and suddenly asks her why she came, a question which she answers only indirectly, declaring that she will warm and dry his castle for him. But this is not what he wants. Nor does he want her to open the seven doors which she now notices, and when she violently insists the castle itself answers for him in a sound effect described as 'a cavernous sighing, as when the night wind sighs down endless, gloomy labyrinths'. Perhaps in hope (his feelings are very often ambiguous) Bluebeard asks if she is frightened, but she is not, and recovers to repeat her request for the keys. Now, however, she does not demand but uses the argument of her love for him, and this he cannot resist. He gives her a key, and as she opens the first door the sigh is heard again. Xylophone and high woodwind, harshly rushing up and down scales through a tritone, present an image of the torture chamber that stands revealed: here, as when the other doors are unlocked, the graphic musical illustration recalls that, before Debussy, Strauss had been one of Bartók's chief enthusiasms. At the same time (and at very much the same time as Skryabin in *Prometheus* or Schoenberg in *Die glückliche Hand*) he uses lighting effects to intensify his harmonic resources. From within the torture chamber a beam of red light is thrown across the floor; the next three openings complete the spectrum in rays of yellowish-red, gold and bluish-green, and then the fifth doorway brings a flood of radiance, which the sixth withdraws, 'as though a shadow

'Bluebeard's Castle' (Bartók): set design for the original production at the Budapest Opera, 24 May 1918

were passing over'. Gradually Judith assembles an image of Bluebeard's inner life, and when that image is complete it is taken from her.

The warnings, though, are present from the start. Not only is Judith first mesmerized and then horrified by the instruments of torture, she also sees blood on the castle walls: the motif of a minor second, here played shrilly by trumpets and oboes, recurs as a symbol of blood at each doorway. However, Judith reinterprets the redness as that of dawn, and confidently asks for the remaining keys. When she again gives love as her reason, Bluebeard capitulates and hands her the second key, which opens the door on his armoury (the music includes trumpet fanfares in E♭). Once more there is blood, and once again, even more resolutely, Judith turns to demand the rest of the keys. Bluebeard gently tries to warn her off, and when that does not work he rises to a rare lyricism, in warm C♯ major with solo horn. But she is adamant that she must know his secrets because she loves him, and he gives her three more keys.

If the first two doors had shown the force sustaining Bluebeard's power, the next three reveal the pleasures of that power. First there is the jewel house, glittering with harps and celesta in D major; then the gardens, evoked in a spacious E♭ major. In both cases Bluebeard offers everything to Judith, and in both cases she notices the blood as she had before. Now, though, she does not turn from anguished awareness to firm demand: instead it is Bluebeard who moves her on swiftly from one door to the next,

so that they come with a rush to the fifth door; there is a burst of C major throughout the orchestra, with organ, as it opens on the vista of Bluebeard's domain. Judith sees the blood again, but Bluebeard is concerned rather to praise the light she has brought to his castle: her work is now done, he suggests. But she cannot stop at this point. She has become obsessed with knowing Bluebeard's secrets, and obsessed too, the music suggests, with the blood she has seen everywhere: she gains the accompaniment of a *moto perpetuo* circling through minor seconds. Bluebeard gives in and hands her another key, which she turns, and as at the start there is a sigh, only this time it has come nearer and invaded the orchestra (a *glissando* in lower strings with bassoons).

As the light fades, a lake of tears is revealed, and there is a harmonic darkening at A minor. Hope is now gone. The first half of the work has brought the music round from the F♯ of Bluebeard's gloomy castle to the bright light of C major: now at the A tonality the music returns cyclically in minor 3rds to the original F♯. The awesome prospect holds Judith in thrall. She is even for a moment compliant when Bluebeard says the last door must remain shut, and she joins him in a second passionate embrace. But her inquisitiveness only grows. She asks if Bluebeard really loves her; she asks whom he loved before, she asks how and how much he loved her predecessor. He tries to stop her questioning, but inevitably she arrives at the demand to know what lies behind the last door, and when he remains silent she leaps to the conclusion that the rumours were right: he has murdered all his former wives, hence the blood and the tears. There is now no point in holding back. Numbly Bluebeard hands over the final key.

As Judith opens the seventh door the fifth and sixth swing shut and it becomes much darker, with only the coloured beams from the first four doors and a silver ray of moonlight from the last. Three ex-wives silently step out, and in a second passage of elevated arioso Bluebeard addresses them as the loves of his dawns, noons and evenings. Through all this Judith can only give voice to her comparative unworthiness (it is perhaps some feeling of insecurity that has brought her thus far), but Bluebeard turns to her as the most beautiful of them all, destined to reign over his nights once she has taken her place, as she must, with the rest. The wives, all four, go back behind the seventh door, and Bluebeard is left alone, in the pentatonic F♯ of his solitary castle, with an addition only to his memories.

*

The opening of the doors, which in Maeterlinck occupied only about a half of the first of the three acts, with Bartók becomes the main dramatic business. The two characters are on stage from the first, and all that happens, until the very end, is that doors are successively opened. As a result, *Bluebeard's Castle* is unusually successful as an opera for the ears alone, whether in concert performance or on record, and one might wonder whether Bartók the folksong-collector's familiarity with recording, with listening to disembodied voices, had some effect on the nature of the work. Even in a stage production the spoken prologue, if it is not omitted, alerts the audience to the fact that what they are to see is an interior drama, a mirror of a real action taking place inside the head of each spectator.

Bartók never attempted opera again: like *Fidelio*, that other work of marriage, *Bluebeard's Castle* is the unique operatic expression of a musical mentality that was essentially concerned with large-scale process and abstract form. Bartók's natural reticence also seems to have disinclined him from works speaking their meanings in words. Nor has the work gained any notable successors from other composers, remaining, like its central character, in its own world, alone.   P.G.

Bohème, La ('Bohemian Life')

Opera in four acts by Giacomo Puccini to a libretto by Giuseppe Giacosa and Luigi Illica after Henry Murger's novel *Scènes de la vie de bohème*; Turin, Teatro Regio, 1 February 1896.

The principals at the première were Cesira

Ferrani (Mimì), Camilla Pasini (Musetta), Evan Gorga (Rodolfo), Michele Mazzini (Colline) and Antonio Pini-Corsi (Schaunard); the conductor was Arturo Toscanini.

Rodolfo *a poet*	tenor
Mimì *a seamstress*	soprano
Marcello *a painter*	baritone
Schaunard *a musician*	baritone
Colline *a philosopher*	bass
Musetta *a singer*	soprano
Benoit *their landlord*	bass
Alcindoro *a state councillor*	bass
Parpignol *a toy vendor*	tenor
A customs official	bass
Students, working girls, townsfolk,	
* shopkeepers, street-vendors, soldiers,*	
* waiters and children*	
Setting Paris, about 1830	

Puccini's intention to base an opera on Murger's picaresque novel appears to date from the winter of 1892–3, shortly before the première of *Manon Lescaut*. Almost at once it involved him in a controversy in print with Ruggero Leoncavallo, who in the columns of his publisher's periodical *Il secolo* (20 March 1893) claimed precedence in the subject, maintaining that he had already approached the artists whom he had in mind and that Puccini knew this perfectly well. Puccini rebutted the accusation in a letter to *Il corriere della sera* (drafted by Illica, but signed by the composer) and at the same time welcomed the prospect of competing with his rival and allowing the public to judge the winner.

Scènes de la vie de bohème existed both as a novel, originally published in serial form, and as a play written in collaboration with Théodore Barrière. There were good reasons why neither Puccini nor Leoncavallo should have availed themselves of the latter, whose plot in places runs uncomfortably close to that of *La traviata* (Mimì is persuaded to leave Rodolfo by her lover's wealthy uncle, who uses the same arguments as Verdi's Germont). As the novel was in the public domain the publisher Giulio Ricordi's attempt to secure exclusive rights to it on Puccini's behalf were unsuccessful. Work proceeded slowly, partly because Puccini had not yet definitely renounced his idea of an opera based on Giovanni Verga's *La lupa* and partly because he spent much of the next two years travelling abroad to supervise performances of *Manon Lescaut* in various European cities. By June 1893 Illica had already completed a prose scenario of which Giacosa, who was given the task of putting it into verse, entirely approved. Here the drama was articulated in four acts and five scenes: the Bohemians' garret and the Café Momus (Act 1), the Barrière d'Enfer (Act 2), the courtyard of

Musetta's house (Act 3) and Mimì's death in the garret (Act 4).

Giacosa completed the versification by the end of June and submitted it to Puccini and Ricordi, who felt sufficiently confident to announce in the columns of the *Gazzetta musicale di Milano* that the libretto was ready for setting to music. He was premature. Giacosa was required to revise the courtyard and Barrière scenes, a labour which he found so uncongenial that in October he offered – not for the last time – to withdraw from the project; however, he was persuaded by Ricordi to remain.

At a conference with his publisher and the librettists during the winter of 1893–4, Puccini insisted on jettisoning the courtyard scene, and with it Mimì's desertion of Rodolfo for a rich 'Viscontino' only to return to the poet in the final act. The librettists strongly objected, but Illica finally proposed a solution whereby the last act, instead of opening with Mimì already on her deathbed as originally planned, would begin with a scene for the four Bohemians similar to that of Act 1, while Mimì's absence would be the subject of an aria by Rodolfo. The aria became a duet, but otherwise Illica's scheme was adopted in all essentials. At the time the Café Momus scene was still envisaged as a 'concertato finale' to Act 1; nor is it clear precisely when it was made into a separate act. At one point Illica wished to eliminate it altogether, but Puccini stoutly defended the Latin quarter 'the way I described it . . . with Musetta's scene which *I* invented'. His own doubts, curiously, concerned the Barrière d'Enfer, a scene that owes nothing to Murger and which the composer felt gave insufficient scope for musical development. His suggestion that they replace it with another episode from the novel was curtly refused by Illica.

Having finally decided to abandon *La lupa* in the summer of 1894 Puccini began the composition of *La bohème*. From then on the librettists' work consisted mostly of elimination, extending even to details on whose inclusion Puccini had originally insisted, such as a drinking song and a diatribe against women, both allocated to Schaunard. The score was finished on 10 December 1895.

Since La Scala was now under the management of the rival publisher Edoardo Sonzogno, who made a point of excluding all Ricordi scores from the repertory, the première was fixed for the Teatro Regio, Turin (where *Manon Lescaut* had received its première in 1893). The public response was mixed: favourable to Acts 1 and 4, less so to the others. Most of the critics saw in the opera a falling-off from the level attained by *Manon Lescaut* in the direction of triviality. But nothing could stop its rapid circulation. A performance at the Teatro Argentina, Rome, under Edoardo Mascheroni (23 February) introduced Rosina Storchio as Musetta, a role in which she later

excelled. A revival at the Politeama Garibaldi, Palermo (24 April) under Leopoldo Mugnone included for the first time the Act 2 episode where Mimì shows off her bonnet. On this occasion Rodolfo and Mimì were played by Edoardo Garbin and Adelina Stehle (the original young lovers of Verdi's *Falstaff*), who did much to make *La bohème* popular in southern Italy in the years that followed. Outside Italy most premières of *La bohème* were given in smaller theatres and in the vernacular of the country. In Paris it was first given in 1898 by the Opéra-Comique, as *La vie de bohème*, and achieved its 1000th performance there in 1951. After a performance at Covent Garden by the visiting Carl Rosa company in 1897 *La bohème* first established itself in the repertory of the Royal Italian Opera on 1 July 1899 with a cast that included Nellie Melba (Mimì), Zélie de Lussan (Musetta), Alessandro Bonci (Rodolfo), Mario Ancona (Marcello) and Marcel Journet (Colline). From then on its fortunes in Britain and America were largely associated with Melba, who was partnered, among others, by Fernando de Lucia, John McCormack, Giovanni Martinelli and, most memorably of all, Enrico Caruso. Today *La bohème* remains, with *Tosca* and *Madama Butterfly*, one of the central pillars of the Italian repertory; its centenary performances in February 1996 confirmed its perennial appeal.

*

***Act I** A garret overlooking the snow-covered roofs of Paris; Christmas eve* The act opens in a conversational style based on two motifs, one instrumental, the other vocal. The first, taken from the central section of Puccini's *Capriccio sinfonico* (1883), is associated with Marcello and the Bohemians generally; the second, to the words 'Nei cieli bigi', derives from sketches for the abandoned *La lupa* and belongs to Rodolfo. Both men are chafing at the cold. Marcello suggests chopping up a chair for firewood; but Rodolfo prefers to burn the five-act drama on which he has been working. Colline enters to find the hearth ablaze. Just as the fire is about to die a brisk orchestral theme heralds the arrival of Schaunard accompanied by two boys carrying logs and victuals. While his three friends take charge of their disposal Schaunard explains his sudden wealth. He had been employed by a rich milord to play to a neighbour's noisy parrot until it dropped dead. He charmed the chambermaid into giving him some parsley which he fed to the parrot, who promptly died; hence his own reward. The Bohemians decide to celebrate by dining out in the Latin Quarter (and here the orchestra adumbrates a motif of parallel triads which will connote the Café Momus), when there is a knock at the door. It is their landlord, Benoit, come to demand the rent. They receive him cordially and ply him with wine together with much flattery regarding his amorous exploits; when he waxes indiscreet over his wife's ugliness and ill-nature they pretend to be shocked and throw him out. They depart for the Café Momus, leaving Rodolfo to finish writing an article before joining them. Soon there is another, more timid knock on the door. It is Mimì, their neighbour, whose candle has gone out. Rodolfo ushers her into a chair as she is clearly ailing and revives her with a glass of wine. She is about to leave when she discovers that she has dropped her key. Together they look for it. Rodolfo finds it and slips it into his pocket; then his hand touches Mimì's, prompting his aria 'Che gelida manina' ('Your tiny hand is frozen'), which incorporates a reminiscence of his own motif. Mimì replies with a modest story of her life, 'Mi chiamano Mimì', whose opening strain will serve as her own identifying motif. The voices of the Bohemians are heard below urging Rodolfo to make haste. He replies that he is not alone. He then turns to see Mimì bathed in a shaft of moonlight and the act concludes with their duet 'O soave fanciulla', which is partly a reprise of 'Che gelida manina'.

Act 2 *A crossroads with the Café Momus to one side* Tables are set out on the pavement, between which waiters hurry to and fro. To the 'Momus' motif, resplendent on brass, vendors from nearby shops hawk their wares. Schaunard disputes with a shopkeeper, Rodolfo takes Mimì to buy a bonnet, Colline exults over the purchase of a book and Marcello ogles the passing girls. He, Colline and Schaunard carry out a table from the café and sit down at it, to the annoyance of other clients, and Rodolfo presents Mimì to his friends. Mimì expresses delight in her new bonnet. To a vigorous theme in 9/8, one of whose phrases will be associated with her throughout the opera, Musetta makes a spectacular entrance, followed by her latest 'protector', the state councillor Alcindoro. Seeing Marcello, the lover to whom she always returns, she stages a scene for his benefit. She torments Alcindoro by complaining about the service, smashing a plate and then bursting • into song ('Quando me'n vo'), a shameless piece of exhibitionism which forms the musical basis of an ensemble. Finally, she gets rid of her escort by pretending that her shoes are hurting and sending him off to buy another pair. Then she falls into Marcello's arms, to the delight of the bystanders. The waiter arrives to settle accounts. As a military tattoo passes by Musetta tells the Bohemians to add their bill to hers. They leave as Alcindoro returns with the shoes and is presented with the bill.

Act 3 *The Barrière d'Enfer* A descending motif on flute and harp evokes a cold winter's dawn. From the nearby tavern come the sounds of revelry. The toll-gate keepers admit street cleaners and then milkmaids. Mimì enters to a reminiscence of her motif, broken off by a fit of coughing. She inquires for Marcello and when he appears pours out her heart to

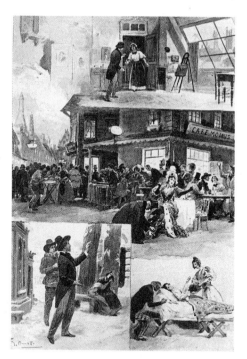

'La bohème' (Puccini), illustrations by Giuseppe d'Amato showing scenes from the first Paris production, at the Opéra-Comique, on 13 June 1898: from 'L'illustration' (18 June 1898)

him. Rodolfo has ruined their life together with his unreasonable jealousy. As Marcello attempts to comfort her Rodolfo comes out of the inn. Mimì hides and overhears him telling Marcello that he intends to leave her because she is a flirt; then under pressure from Marcello he admits the real reason for their separation; she is dying of consumption and he is unable to provide for her. This revelation is couched in an elegiac terzettino which forms the dramatic crux of the act. Here Puccini uses for the first time a device that served him in the future to depict painful situations: an insistent alternation of minor chords and dissonances over which the voice declaims in monotones. Mimì reveals her presence. Marcello, hearing Musetta's brazen laugh, hurries into the tavern, and Mimì takes a sad farewell of her lover in an arietta interwoven with musical reminiscences ('Donde lieta uscì'). In a final quartet, whose melody is taken directly from Puccini's song 'Sole e amore' (1888), Mimì and Rodolfo decide after all to remain together until the spring, and Musetta and Marcello quarrel furiously.

Act 4 *The garret, several weeks later* Rodolfo and Marcello are once more at their work, but their thoughts stray to their absent sweethearts ('Ah, Mimì, tu più non torni'). They are joined by

Schaunard and Colline bearing meagre provisions. There follows a scene of forced high spirits and horseplay, interrupted by the arrival of Musetta with the dying Mimì. Rodolfo assists her to the bed; Musetta gives her earrings to Marcello, telling him to buy medicine and to send for a doctor; she herself will buy a muff for Mimì's cold hands. Colline bids a mournful farewell to his overcoat which he intends to pawn so as to help the dying girl, in an arietta ('Vecchia zimarra'); he then leaves with Schaunard. During their final duet ('Son partiti? Fingero di dormire') the lovers recall their first meeting, to appropriate musical quotations. The others return, Musetta with the muff, pretending that Rodolfo has paid for it; Mimì sinks silently into her death, of which Rodolfo becomes aware only after a burst of agonized questioning (spoken, not sung), answered by the orchestra with a thunderous peroration that combines the opening of 'Son partiti' with the closing bars of 'Vecchia Zimarra' – one of the most tear-jerking of operatic endings.

*

In their preface to the printed libretto Giacosa and Illica claimed to have made their heroine a composite of Murger's Mimì and Francine. In fact she is based almost entirely on Francine, a marginal character in the novel who appears with her lover, the sculptor Jacques, in one chapter only ('Francine's muff') in total isolation from the other Bohemians. Unlike his pert, wilful Mimì, Murger conceived Francine in purely romantic terms – all innocence and fragility. By taking Francine as a model for their Mimì the librettists allowed Puccini not only to distinguish her musically from Musetta, as Leoncavallo was never able to do, but also to achieve that perfect balance of realism and romanticism, of comedy and pathos which makes La bohème, on its own level, one of the most satisfying works in the operatic repertory.

There is a retreat here both from the 'symphonism' that marked Act 1 of Manon Lescaut as well as from the unrestrained emotionalism of its last two acts. Mimì, an archetypally fragile Puccinian heroine, tugs at the heart-strings mostly by a subdued pathos; only once in Act 3 does she burst out in an agony of soul ('O buon Marcello, aiuto!'). La bohème establishes a first-act design, already outlined in Manon Lescaut, which served Puccini for all the operas of his middle period, namely a lively opening with much variety of incident that eventually broadens out into a calm love-duet. Throughout, the harmonic idiom is bolder yet more subtle than in his previous operas (the triads of the Café Momus theme would not disgrace the Stravinsky of 15 years later). His ability to conjure up a particular ambience is nowhere shown to better advantage than at the start of Act 3, with its suggestion of falling snowflakes conveyed by a succession of open 5ths on flutes and harp over a

cello line. Debussy, who disliked the works of the Giovane Scuola ('young school'), is reported to have said to Falla that he knew of no one who had described the Paris of that time better than Puccini.   J.B.

Bomarzo

Opera in two acts, op.34, by Alberto Ginastera to a libretto by Manuel Mujica Láinez after his own novel Bomarzo; Washington, DC, Lisner Auditorium, 19 May 1967.

The original cast included Salvador Novoa (Pier Francesco Orsini), Isabel Penagos (Julia), Claramae Turner (Diana Orsini), Richard Torigi (Silvio de Narni) and Joanna Simon (Pantasilea). The première was conducted by Julius Rudel and directed by Tito Capobianco.

Pier Francesco Orsini, Duke of Bomarzo	tenor
Gian Conrado Orsini *his father*	bass
Diana Orsini *his grandmother*	contralto
Girolamo *his elder brother*	baritone
Maerbale *his younger brother*	baritone
Julia Farnese *his wife*	soprano
Abul *his slave*	mime
Nicolas *his nephew, Maerbale's son*	contralto or tenor
Silvio de Narni *an astrologer*	baritone
Pantasilea *a Florentine courtesan*	mezzo-soprano
A Shepherd Boy	treble
Boys, prelates, courtiers, pages and servants	
Setting Bomarzo, Florence and Rome in the 16th century	

The central character of the work is Pier Francesco, a member of the great Orsini family, who created not far from his palace (near Viterbo) a garden of bizarre and nightmarish grotesques (*grotteschi*) carved from the volcanic rock. This stirred the imagination of the Argentine writer Mujica Láinez, who interpreted the place as the extension of a tormented Renaissance figure, twisted in body and mind, in the form of timeless monuments through which he sought his own immortality and the reflection of himself. The result was the novel Bomarzo (1962), which became a best-seller and won several prizes. In 1964 Mujica Láinez provided the text for the Cantata Bomarzo, and when a year later Hobart Spalding commissioned a stage work for the Opera Society of Washington, Ginastera returned to the same subject. At its première, the opera caused a sensation and was hailed as a triumph, but its explicit eroticism caused it to be banned in Buenos Aires by the repressive regime of President Onganía; it was not given there until 1972. An instrumental suite, with substitutions

Ming Cho Lee's design for the 'Mouth of Hell' (modelled on one of Pier Francesco Orsini's grotteschi) for the original production of Ginastera's 'Bomarzo' by the Opera Society of Washington in 1967

for the vocal parts, received its first performance in 1970.

*

The two acts of the opera are divided into 15 scenes (each consisting of the classic Greek infrastructure of exposition, crisis and resolution) linked by orchestral interludes. The action takes place as a series of recollections of Pier Francesco's inner life, re-enacted at overlapping levels of reality, dream and fantasy in the mind of the dying Duke, seen in the first and last scenes. The orchestra includes harpsichord, mandolin, viola d'amore and a huge array of 68 percussion instruments, and the chorus (employing techniques including hissing, humming, cries and choral speaking) operates from the orchestra pit: in the Prelude it sings on isolated consonants to suggest the ghostly whispering of the stone statues.

Act I.i A shepherd boy is heard singing (to the melody of the 14th-century 'Lamento di Tristano') that, poor as he is, he would not change places with the Duke, who is carrying in his hump the burden of his sins. Standing by one of his stone carvings, which represents the 'Mouth of Hell', the Duke is persuaded to drink a magic potion that he has been promised will bring him immortality. Instead, he finds that he has been poisoned; and the flashbacks begin.

I.ii As a child, Pier Francesco is bedevilled by his brothers, who torment him by dressing him up as a girl. His stern father, mocking his weakness, shows him a secret panel where he sees the reclining figure of a skeleton; in his fantasy the skeleton dances, filling him with an abject terror that is to haunt him all his life.

I.iii Now a young man, he is fearful that his father will put him to death. But his astrologer predicts immortality for him and by black magic invokes demons to protect him; as peacocks foretelling tragedy are heard in the garden, a messenger announces that the old Duke has been mortally wounded in the siege of Florence.

I.iv To deride his virility, the wounded Duke has sent him to Pantasilea; her sensuality and voluptuous beauty stand in contrast with his impotence and deformity, reflected in mirrors all about him. 'Break the mirror you are carrying within yourself', says Pantasilea as she taunts him with aphrodisiacs.

I.v The Duke's impending death brings Pier Francesco no comfort, for his brother Girolamo, heir to the title, hates him too. As Girolamo, about to bathe in the Tiber, boasts about his strength he loses his foothold, hitting his head on a rock. Pier Francesco tries to save him but Diana Orsini holds him back protectively: 'Come with me . . . Now you are Duke of Bomarzo, forever'.

I.vi In a magnificent ceremony Pier Francesco is proclaimed Duke (to the sound of the Gregorian melody *O rex gloriae*). His grandmother introduces him to the lovely Julia Farnese, pointing out the advantages of alliance with her powerful family; but Maerbale leads Julia away, and Pier Francesco is haunted by his father's ghost.

I.vii At the celebratory ball Maerbale dances with Julia. In a soliloquy Pier Francesco identifies with the yet uncarved and enigmatic stones, his dream of possessing Bomarzo fulfilled. His fancy conjures up a ballet in which an idealized form of himself dances with Julia, Pantasilea and his slave Abul while they struggle to possess him.

l.viii Returning from fighting against Charles V in Picardy, he admires the portrait of an anonymous nobleman by Lorenzo Lotto, the idealized image of himself. When he uncovers an adjacent mirror the reflection becomes an image of the 'Mouth of Hell'; in a frenzy he smashes the mirror.

Act 2.ix Pier Francesco becomes insanely jealous watching Maerbale at Julia's feet as she sings a madrigal. He bursts in on them and spills red wine on her dress; the stains are seen as an omen.

2.x He has married Julia, but in the bridal chamber he sees demonic faces invisible to her.

2.xi Unable to possess Julia, he has visions of the still uncarved *grotteschi*. In the erotic ballet that follows, disembodied figures of himself and Julia lose themselves in a forest of intertwined couples, the chorus murmuring the word 'love' in more than 30 languages. In his dream he possesses her.

2.xii In the gallery of the palace he embraces a statue of the Minotaur. As his ambiguous sexuality has alienated him from his ancestors, he identifies with the fate and alienation of the mythical creature.

2.xiii Crazed by jealousy and frustration, he orders the astrologer to entice Maerbale into Julia's bedchamber; Abul is then to stab him.

2.xiv Now carved, each of the *grotteschi* in Bomarzo's garden symbolizes an episode in his puzzling existence. The astrologer mixes the potion that carries the promise of immortality made to Pier Francesco in his horoscope, as figures of alchemists of the past dance like furies around him warning him that Pier Francesco has challenged the supreme powers. Nicolas, Maerbale's son, poisons the potion to avenge his father's murder.

2.xv As in Act 1 scene i, he lies dying below the 'Mouth of Hell', his promised immortality transferred to the permanence of the carvings. The shepherd boy approaches the lifeless Duke and kisses his face. The final quote from the 'Lamento di Tristano' restores innocence and timeless peace to Bomarzo.

*

Ginastera's musical language here is based on 12-note systems and also makes use of microtones, aleatory procedures and chord clusters. The idea of permanence is associated with the basic 12-note series, which, when presented as a static cluster, provides a musical analogue for the timelessness of the rocks. (This cluster also closes Ginastera's *Don Rodrigo*, intentionally beginning the second opera where the first ends.) Reproducing the circular direction of the tableaux, the opera begins and ends with this cluster on C. Just as permanence contains a set of opposite modalities – innocence and guilt, dream and reality, love and rejection, beauty and deformity – so the basic 12-note series contains subordinate and derived 12-note rows associated

with dream (Act 1.vii) and death (the Villanella of Interlude xii). The circle closes when permanence subsumes dream and death in the Elegy that forms Interlude xiv. The dramaturgy of *Bomarzo* might be defined in terms that have been applied to the place of Antonio Gaudí in architecture: 'A chance encounter of genius with medieval revival, art nouveau, savagely erotic shapes and Spanish religiosity' (R. McCullen, *Horizon*, 1968).   M.Ks., L.S.

Boris Godunov

Opera in seven scenes, or a prologue and four acts, by Modest Petrovich Musorgsky to his own libretto, adapted from the historical tragedy by Alexander Sergeyevich Pushkin, and supplemented (in the revised version) by material partly derived from historical works by Nikolay Mikhaylovich Karamzin and others; St Petersburg, Mariinsky Theatre, 27 January/8 February 1874 (revised version; original version, Leningrad, State Academic Theatre of Opera and Ballet, 16 February 1928; first Rimsky-Korsakov version, concert performance, St Petersburg, Great Hall of the Conservatory, 28 November/10 December 1896, staged Moscow, Solodovnikov Theatre, Savva Mamontov's Private Russian Opera, 7/19 December 1898; 'standard' version, with additional music by Rimsky-Korsakov, Paris, Opéra, 19 May 1908).

The 1874 première, the first version to be heard, was conducted by Eduard Nápravník, with Ivan Mel'nikov in the title role, Yuliya Platonova as Marina, Fyodor Komissarzhevsky as the Pretender, Osip Petrov as Varlaam, Antonina Abarinova as the Innkeeper and Pavel Bulakhov as the Holy Fool. Rimsky's 1896 version was conducted by him, with Fyodor Stravinsky as Varlaam. The Paris première of the 'standard' version was produced by Sergey Dyagilev and directed by Alexander Sanin, with Felix Blumenfeld conducting, Fyodor Shalyapin as Boris and Dmitry Smirnov as the Pretender.

Boris Godunov	baritone or bass
Xenia *his daughter*	soprano
Fyodor *his son*	mezzo-soprano
Pretender *known as* Grigory (*under Pimen's tutelage*) ['False Dmitry']	tenor
Marina Mniszek* *daughter of the Sandomierz commander*	mezzo- or dramatic soprano
Pimen† *hermit chronicler*	bass
Prince Vasily Ivanovich Shuysky	tenor
Andrey Shchelkalov *secretary to the Boyars' Council*	baritone
Varlaam† } *tramps*	bass
Missail† }	tenor

Rangoni* *covert Jesuit*	bass
Innkeeper	mezzo-soprano
Yurodivïy ('Fool-in-God') [Holy Fool]	tenor
Xenia's [former]	
wet-nurse	low mezzo-soprano
Nikitich *police officer*	bass
Mityukha *a peasant*	bass
Boyar-in-attendance	tenor
Boyar* Khrushchyov	tenor
Lewicki* } *Jesuits*	bass
Czernikowski*	bass
	tenor
	soprano
Voices from the crowd *peasants*	mezzo-
	soprano

*Boyars, their children, musketeers, royal
bodyguards, police officers, Polish lords and
ladies*, maidens of Sandomierz*, blind pilgrims
(and the boys who guide them), inhabitants of
Moscow*

Setting Russia (Moscow and its environs, an
inn near the Lithuanian border, Sokol'niki-
on-the-Dnepr) and Sandomierz, Poland;
1598–1605

* role only in the revised version
† Pimen, Varlaam and Missail are monks in the
Pushkin play and in Musorgsky's adaptation; but
owing to a censorship regulation that forbade the
portrayal of Orthodox clergy on the stage, their
identity had to be concealed in the original published
score and libretto

The original version of *Boris Godunov*, composed
between October 1868 and 15/27 December 1869,
consists of seven scenes grouped into four 'parts'
(acts). The revised version, accomplished between
February 1871 and 23 June/5 July 1872, consists of
nine scenes (six of the original, more or less radically
altered, plus three newly composed) grouped into a
prologue and four acts. A vocal score of the revised
version was published in 1874; both versions are in
the complete edition of Musorgsky's works, edited
by Pavel Lamm (1928).

The opera was composed at a time when historical
drama was the dominant Russian theatrical genre,
musical or otherwise, reflecting the widespread conviction that art had a civic obligation – an attitude that
tends to flourish in states where open discussion of
public policy is not permitted. In 19th-century Russia,
such discussion took place mainly in the 'Aesopian'
guise of historiography and literary criticism – and on
the stage itself, where dramatists strove to invest their
work with content 'worthy of the attention of a
thinking man', to quote Nikolay Chernïshevsky, the
most influential radical critic of the 1860s.

Musorgsky, influenced in this by a number of
friends and mentors, including the historian Vladi-

mir Nikol'sky and the arts publicist Vladimir Stasov,
took these principles more seriously than any other
Russian musician. He was also much preoccupied
with the actual mechanics of musical representation.
At first his model was Dargomïzhsky's opera *The
Stone Guest*, a direct setting of a short verse play by
Pushkin that sought in the name of realism to bypass
the artificialities of the conventional libretto. Later
Musorgsky adopted (from Aristotle by way of the
German literary historian Georg Gervinus) a radically positivistic theory of emotional expression
and character portrayal in music by means of meticu-
lously objective imitation of 'natural' conversational
speech. During the late 1860s Musorgsky systematically applied this technique in a series of avowedly
experimental vocal works culminating in *Marriage*, a
recitative opera based on the unaltered prose text
of a comedy by Gogol, on which he worked during
summer 1868, producing one act in vocal score.

So when in the autumn of that year Nikol'sky
suggested as an operatic subject Pushkin's famous
drama of Boris Godunov and his troubled reign (the
acknowledged prototype for the historical spectacles
that were lately so fashionable), the composer
immediately recognized it as the natural and necessary field for the full deployment of his talents. The
play, which had been finally cleared by the censor
for stage performances in 1866, had everything: an
important historical theme; a 'Shakespearean' mixture of poetry and prose, tragedy and comedy, which
would vouchsafe the opportunity to combine the
approaches of *The Stone Guest* and *Marriage* and so
evade the monotony of style that had plagued both
works; a wide range of character types from boyar
to beggar, to be portrayed naturalistically through
declamation; and a large role for the crowd that
would enable the composer to project his ideas of
formal realism and naturalistic declamation on a
large canvas. Perhaps not least, owing to the
'predominance of politics' in it and the absence of
romance, *Boris Godunov* had been pronounced unfit
for (conventional) operatic treatment by Alexander
Serov, the chief musical pundit of the day, to whom
The Five or 'mighty kuchka' – Musorgsky and his
group – felt particularly hostile. Selecting Pushkin's
play as a subject was thus an act of typical 'kuchkist'-
cum-realist bravado.

As to actual text, the libretto of the original
version of the opera was almost entirely drawn
from Pushkin. With the sole exception of Boris's
hallucination in scene 5 (suggested, ironically
enough, by Holofernes' hallucination in *Judith*, an
opera by Serov) there is nothing in the action of
Musorgsky's drama that was not in Pushkin. The
scene in Pimen's cell and the scene at the Lithuanian
border were verbatim settings of scenes from the
original play (the former in verse à la *Stone Guest* and

the latter in prose à la *Marriage*). Musorgsky boiled the rest of Pushkin's play down to a length suitable for musical setting by a very simple expedient: he threw out every scene in which the title character failed to appear, leaving a total of six scenes (out of 23) from which to fashion the five remaining scenes of his libretto (two of Pushkin's scenes being conflated to provide the text for the long one in which Musorgsky's Boris sings his big soliloquies). The result was a characteristic canvas for what Musorgsky called *opéra dialogué* – i.e. a 'sung play' in recitative dialogue (the genre to which *Pelléas*, *Salome* and *Wozzeck* also belong).

For many years, beginning in 1896, the opera was performed exclusively in a re-orchestrated revision by Rimsky-Korsakov; this itself exists in two versions (published in 1896 and 1908) of which the more complete second ('standard' version in list of premières above) is the one that first achieved international repertory status. Of other performing versions two should be mentioned: by Shostakovich (1939–40, an orchestration of the vocal score in the complete edition), used mainly at the Kirov Theatre since 1960; and by Karol Rathaus, commissioned by the Metropolitan Opera, New York, and used there for two decades from 1952. Since the mid-1970s Musorgsky's own versions have gradually been displacing those of Rimsky-Korsakov and others on the world's stages. A critical edition by David Lloyd-Jones, published in 1975, has been used increasingly since that date. The title role has been a great vehicle for Russian and Russian-style basses: Mark Reyzen sang in the première of the 1869 version, and other noted interpreters have included, besides Shalyapin, Vanni-Marcoux, Alexander Kipnis, Nicola Rossi-Lemeni, Boris Christoff, George London, Nicolai Ghiaurov and Martti Talvela. In recordings, some singers have taken both Boris's role and that of Pimen or Varlaam; both Reyzen and Christoff made recordings in which they sang all three.

RÉSUMÉ
(incorporating the events of both versions)

The Tsarevich Dmitry, the nine-year-old son of Ivan the Terrible, and next in line (after his feeble-minded half-brother Fyodor) to the Russian throne, is murdered in the town of Uglich in 1591, at the instigation of the boyar Boris Godunov, Ivan's brother-in-law and regent under Fyodor (modern historians do not subscribe to the theory of Boris's guilt, but Ivan Karamzin, the official Russian historian of the early 19th century, asserted it, and Pushkin and Musorgsky accepted it as the basis for their dramas). On Fyodor's death in 1598, Boris is elected tsar and, after a show of reluctance, accepts and is crowned. He reigns wisely and in peace for several years and is portrayed by the dramatists as a loving father, devoted in particular to grooming his son Fyodor to succeed him and establish a dynasty.

In spite of his good intentions and wise policies, Russia is visited by famines, which those who know of Boris's crime attribute to divine judgment. Among his enemies is an old soldier who witnessed the murder. He has become a monk and taken the name Pimen. He records Boris's crime in a chronicle, which he shows to his ward, the novice Grigory Otrep'yev, who is exactly the same age as the slain tsarevich. Grigory vows to pose as the tsarevich risen from death and claim the throne. With two vagabond monks, Varlaam and Missail, who do not know his plan, he sets out for Poland/Lithuania, Russia's hostile Roman Catholic neighbour to the west, to enlist support. In an inn near the border he is recognized by a patrol and narrowly escapes capture. Reaching Sandomierz, he falls in love with Marina, the daughter of the local governor, who is induced by the Jesuit Rangoni to feign love in return, so to co-opt the Pretender's campaign on behalf of the Church.

Boris is informed of the Pretender's rise, and his formidable Polish support, by Prince Vasily Shuysky, a powerful but treacherous courtier. The news sends Boris into a paroxysm of fear, accompanied by hallucinations. He orders a church service so as to pronounce an anathema on the Pretender. On his way out he is accosted by a Holy Fool, who complains to Boris that some boys have stolen a penny from him, and that the tsar should have them killed, the way he had had the tsarevich killed. Boris asks the holy man to pray for him but is rebuffed. Shuysky now conspires with Pimen. The latter visits the court and frightens Boris with a false tale of the slain tsarevich, now a miracle-working saint, who, Pimen says, has cured him of blindness. At this Boris has a seizure and, after a last farewell to his son, whom he points out to the assembled boyars as their new tsar, expires. The Pretender, meanwhile, makes his way through the countryside, accompanied by a retinue of Jesuits and mercenaries (including Varlaam and Missail), plus an ever-increasing mob of peasants and local gentry who believe him to be the risen tsarevich. The Holy Fool, witnessing the credulous procession, laments the fate of unhappy Russia.

Original version, 1869
(matter in **bold italics** exclusive to this version)

Revised version, 1872
(matter set in **bold italics** exclusive to this version)

I   **Part 1.i** *Courtyard of the Novodevichiy Monastery, Moscow*

I   **Prologue** *i   Courtyard of the Novodevichiy Monastery, Moscow*

a   After an orchestral introduction, a policeman is seen ordering the crowd on its knees to beg Boris to accept the throne; chorus of supplication; the policeman returns; the crowd banter with him; ordered to beg again they uncomprehendingly comply; Shchelkalov, secretary of the Boyars' Council, exhorts the crowd with a gloomy arioso about Boris's feigned implacability and its consequences; a group of blind pilgrims arrives to add their voices to the crowd entreating Boris.

a   as *a* opposite

b   *The crowd again express their incomprehension, particularly of the pilgrims. They agree to come the next day to resume their entreaties, but cynically.*

2   **Part 1.ii** *Square in the Moscow Kremlin*
Boris is crowned. Processions before and after. The new tsar expresses humility and invites all to a feast. The forced praises of the crowd are sung to the words and tune of an old Russian fortune-telling song from the L'viv-Pratsch anthology (2/1806) chosen because it happens to include the word 'Glory!' as a refrain.

2   **Prologue** *ii   as opposite*

3   **Part 2.i** *Cell in the Chudov Monastery*

3   **Act 1.i** *Cell in the Chudov Monastery*

a   Pimen's monologue, on finishing his chronicle but for one last tale.

a   as *a* opposite

b   *Chorus of monks behind the scenes.*

b   Grigory wakes.

c   Grigory wakes (different music).
d   *Second chorus of monks behind the scenes.*

c   Grigory recounts a dream of being exalted, then dashed.

e   as *c* opposite

d   Pimen recalls Ivan the Terrible's visit to the monastery and the saintliness of the late Tsar Fyodor.

f   as *d* opposite

e   *Pimen's narrative of the murder of the Tsarevich Dmitry.*

f   Grigory's question about the tsarevich's age; chorus of monks behind the scenes; Grigory's vow.

g   as *f* opposite

4   **Part 2.ii** *Inn on the Lithuanian Border*

4   **Act 1.ii** *Inn on the Lithuanian Border*

a   Orchestral introduction.

a   as *a* opposite
b   *Innkeeper sings a song about a drake as she darns an old padded jacket.*

b   Arrival of Grigory, Varlaam, Missail.

c   as *b* opposite

c   Varlaam's first song ('Song about Kazan') [Pushkin quotes the first line of the song ('Oh, 'twas in Kazan town') in his play; it is a *khorovod* song, about a monk who renounces the cowl for a gayer life with women.

d   as *c* opposite

   After his little by-play with Grigory, Pushkin's Varlaam resumes his song with the second line, also supplied by the poet. Not knowing the original reference, Musorgsky assumed Varlaam was now singing a different song, and adapted a tune he had learnt from Rimsky-Korsakov to his own words.]

d   Varlaam waves Grigory aside and strikes up another song; while he sings, Grigory learns the way to Lithuania from the innkeeper; the police come; Grigory tries to convince them that Varlaam is the Pretender, but Varlaam, laboriously making out the warrant, exposes him; he makes a fenestral exit.

e   as *d* opposite, but for the music that accompanies Grigory's escape at the very end.

5   **Part 3** The Tsar's Quarters (Terem) in the Kremlin

a   Xenia laments her lost bridegroom.
b   *Fyodor sings at his map.*
c   Nurse comforts Xenia.

5   **Act 2** The Tsar's Quarters (Terem) in the Kremlin
    [both words and music of this scene were rewritten in 1871–2; even items that conform to the old scenario are in fact new].
a   as *a* opposite
b   *The children with the chiming clock.*
c   as *c* opposite
d   *Song of the Gnat.*
e   *Handclapping game (text conflated from eight different children's songs in P. V. Sheyn's anthology of Russian folklore, 1870; music original).*

d   Boris's entrance; he comforts Xenia and sends her away.
e   Boris and Fyodor at the map.
f   The opening portion of the title character's great soliloquy on kingship and conscience, 'Dostig ya vïsshey vlasti' ('I have attained the highest power'), set almost verbatim from Pushkin in the form of a lengthy scena in melodic recitative over an orchestral tissue of leitmotifs, most of them derived from music written earlier for *Salammbô*.
g   The boyar-in-attendance announces Shuysky's arrival and denounces his treachery.

f   as *d* opposite

g   as *e* opposite

h   Boris's monologue, recast as an aria to a heavily adapted text that refers much more openly than Pushkin's had done to Boris's crime and the popular discontent it has brought about. The main lyric theme, broadly developed in the vocal part as well as the orchestra, is also a derivation from *Salammbô*.
i   *Tumult of nurses' voices off stage.*
j   as *g* opposite

k   *Fyodor explains the disturbance off stage with his 'Song of the Parrot'; Boris praises his narrative and encourages him to continue improving his mind.*
l   as *h* opposite

h   Boris curses Shuysky; Shuysky delivers the news of the False Dmitry; Boris obtains Shuysky's assurance that the tsarevich was truly dead in Uglich.
i   Boris's hallucination, preceded by the concluding portion of the soliloquy begun in section *f* above.

m   Boris's soliloquy concluded, culminating in

n   *The hallucination with the chiming clock.*

6   **Act 3.i** Marina's Boudoir in Sandomierz Castle
a   *Chorus of Polish maidens serenade Marina as she dresses.*
b   *Marina's aria (in mazurka style), expressing her haughtiness, her boredom, her ambition and her determination to use the Pretender as her path to queenhood.*
c   *Rangoni overpowers Marina and obtains her vow to help him convert the Pretender and, through him, all of Russia.*

7   **Act 3.ii** Garden by the Fountain
a   *Dmitry awaits Marina; Rangoni appears and fans his passion.*
b   *Polonaise for the 'Pans and Pannas' (Polish nobles).*
c   *Marina appears; love duet.*

6   **Part 4.i** *Square before St Basil's*
a   *Crowd uncomprehendingly discuss the anathema service.*
b   Boys steal a penny from a Holy Fool.
c   *Boris and his retinue leave the church; the crowd beseech him for bread.*
d   *The Holy Fool confronts Boris with his crime and refuses to pray for him.*
e   The Holy Fool laments the fate of Russia.

7   **Part 4.ii** *Granovitaya Palace, the Kremlin*
a   Orchestral introduction (adapted from *Salammbô* music).
b   *Shchelkalov reads Boris's ukase convening the meeting of the Boyars' Council to consider means of halting the Pretender's advance.*
c   The boyars discuss the matter, sense futility, express annoyance at Shuysky's absence.
d   Shuysky arrives and describes Boris's hallucination.
e   Boris enters in grip of hallucination.
f   Pimen's narrative about the wonder-working Dmitry.
g   Boris's farewell to his son.
h   Death of Boris.

8   **Act 4.i** *Granovitaya Palace, the Kremlin*
a   as *a* opposite

b   as *c* opposite

c   as *d* opposite, with some small cuts (28 bars)
d   as *e* opposite
e   as *f* opposite, less six bars

f   as *g* opposite, with some small cuts (13 bars)
g   as *h* opposite

9   **Act 4.ii** *A forest glade near Kromï*
a   *Orchestral introduction, entrance of the crowd with the captive boyar Khrushchyov.*
b   *Mocking 'glorification' of Khrushchyov (based on a folk-song Musorgsky learnt from Balakirev).*
c   Boys steal a penny from a Holy Fool (transferred from *Part 4.i, 6b* opposite).
d   *Entrance of Varlaam and Missail: their song is based on an old epic song Musorgsky had transcribed from the singing of the famous bard Trofim Ryabinin.*
e   *'Revolutionary' chorus in da capo form: the middle section based on a song from Balakirev's anthology of 1866.*
f   *The False Dmitry's (Pretender's) procession, including Jesuit hymns; Dmitry's proclamation and the crowd's glorification of him (procession music adapted from* **Salammbô***).*
g   The Holy Fool laments the fate of Russia (from the end of *Part 4.i, 6e* opposite).

Boris Godunov is the pre-eminent representative of the historical genre in Russian opera and the sole survivor of its type in the permanent international repertory (the increasingly standard *Khovanshchina* by the same composer being its only possible rival). It owes its position primarily, if not exclusively, to the extraordinary portrayal of the title character – one of the great bass/baritone roles, offering tremendous scope to a charismatic singing actor (it was the chief vehicle for Shalyapin's world acclaim), clearly the creation of a musical psychologist of genius.

Musorgsky's radical condensation of Pushkin's play had the effect of casting the title character into much greater prominence than the poet had accorded him. This, of course, worked very much to the opera's advantage, since it provided a heroic role at the centre of the drama. It was an advantage the composer was uniquely equipped to exploit, though the role achieved its full stature only in the revised version of 1872.

The concomitant disadvantage of the original libretto was the elimination of the 'Polish' scenes

Boris Christoff in the title role of Musorgsky's 'Boris Godunov'

view of the nature of musical drama. The revision of *Boris Godunov* was motivated by considerations of historiographical ideology, dramatic tone, and consistency in the deployment of leitmotifs. The résumé and parallel synopsis of the two versions, above, give a basis from which an interpretation of their differences may be essayed.

The revised *Boris* was no longer an *opéra dialogué*. In part this change was dictated by practical necessity, since Pushkin's Polish scenes did not include the ingredients from which Musorgsky fashioned his Act 3. Musorgsky had to write the text for Marina's aria, for the big love duet and for the scenes with Rangoni, a character absent in Pushkin, who embodied a xenophobic anti-Catholicism that was entirely the composer's. He now freely paraphrased Pushkin even where it was possible to quote him directly. His melodies became rounder, more lyrically self-sufficient, and underwent a more conventional sort of development.

But if this conventionalizing turn could be indirectly attributed to the demands of the Imperial Theatres Directorate, Musorgsky bears sole responsibility for the decision he made, on completing the 'Polish Act', to go back and refashion the central Terem scene (the old Part 3, now Act 2) as well. He happily de-Pushkinized its text, and, as he put it in a letter to Stasov, 'perpetrated an arioso' for the title character, very much along the more thematically generalized, lyrical lines of the love duet. At the same time he removed from the opera a great deal that was especially characteristic of his earlier manner. This applies particularly to the St Basil's scene and the closing section of the very first scene, which in its original conception had been the boldest dramaturgical stroke: a scene of naturalistic prose recitative for the chorus. Clearly we are dealing with a retrenchment.

Its motivation may be located in a letter from Musorgsky to Rimsky-Korsakov, written during the year in which the original version was in limbo between completion and rejection (23 July/4 August 1870), following a party at which the composer had run through his opera before a handpicked audience. 'As regards the peasants in *Boris*', he wrote with bemusement, 'some found them to be *bouffe* (!), while others saw tragedy'. In other words, it became evident to the composer that his naturalistic methods carried ineluctable associations with comedy, their traditional medium. From this experience, perhaps, rather than the subsequent rejection, dated Musorgsky's first impulse to revise his opera, born of a wish to clarify its genre – that is, to elevate its tone unambiguously to the level of tragedy.

Accordingly, to restore the title character to full tragic dimension, it was necessary not only to 'perpetrate an arioso' for him but to surround the

and, with them, of the only major feminine role in Pushkin's play, that of Marina Mniszek. This deficiency, subsequent legends notwithstanding, was the sole reason for the opera's rejection by the selection committee of the Imperial Theatres Directorate in February 1871, which (theatre being at the time a state monopoly in Russia) precluded its performance. The composer was forced to revise the opera, a task he undertook almost immediately upon receiving news of the rejection and completed at the beginning of the summer of 1872.

To meet the directorate's demands all Musorgsky would have had to do was reinstate the love scene for Marina and the Pretender, a scene which (according to Vladimir Stasov) he had originally intended to include, and even sketched, when he first embarked on the opera. In fact, he went so much further than that in revising the opera that it is impossible to regard the second version as anything less than a total reconception, now very much at variance with Pushkin, implying not only an entirely different reading of Russian history, but an entirely different

arioso with a profusion of trivial genre pieces. (The new Terem scene was modelled, in fact, on the second act of Cui's *William Ratcliff*: in both, a lengthy *divertissement* full of songs and games is suddenly interrupted by the entrance of the stern baritone protagonist, who, having dispersed the revellers, proceeds to sing a crucial and self-revealing monologue.) The formally petty methods of naturalism are replaced by larger structural entities, and the subtle expressive vagaries of recitative are replaced by sustained moods, their succession calculated for maximum contrast. As a result, to quote Abram Gozenpud, the foremost Soviet historian of the Russian operatic stage, 'though much of poetic enjoyment and beauty was lost, [Musorgsky] undeniably achieved a rough and gaudy theatricality that had been lacking in Pushkin'. It seems clear, moreover, that the composer took the formerly despised Verdi – and particularly *Don Carlos*, which had its Russian première during the gestation of *Boris Godunov* – as an important model in achieving the dramatic scale he needed.

The new historiographical conception embodied in the revised *Boris* can best be viewed by comparing the Kromï Forest scene with the scene it replaced (St Basil's). That Musorgsky never meant the two of them to be performed side by side (as has become a 20th-century tradition, originally fostered by the Moscow Bol'shoy Theatre, which in 1925 commissioned Mikhail Ippolitov-Ivanov to make an orchestration of the scene suitable for insertion into the standard Rimsky-Korsakov edition) is clear from the fact that Musorgsky transferred two sections from the one to the other – physically ripped them out of the earlier score, in fact. The earlier scene portrayed the crowd (following Pushkin) as cowed and submissive to the tsar. The Holy Fool, who challenges and insults Boris, is the embodiment of nemesis, which in the first version of the opera took the form of the 'Tsar-Herod's' conscience.

In the revised opera, that overriding theme was replaced by another, timelier one: that of Tsar *v.* People, the latter viewed as the real driving force in history. It was a view that accorded with the social outlook of the 1860s and 70s. In Kromï, the crowd is viewed in active revolt against the criminal tsar. At the same time, and almost paradoxically, their music is far less 'radical' than the crowd music in the earlier version. Instead of mass recitative, it is now a series of vast choral numbers in strophic, or (especially telling) da capo form. In making the crowd a tragic protagonist (literally so, in Aristotelian terms: though powerful and just in their righteous condemnation of Boris, they have a tragic flaw, namely the credulousness that causes them to accept the claims of the Pretender), Musorgsky subjected their music to the same kind of formal

'elevation' as he had the music of their antagonist in Act 2.

A similar concern for formal unity (expressed through symmetry) governs the whole of the revised *Boris*, quite belying the frequent complaint (true enough if applied to the radically 'realist' first version) that the opera is an 'inorganic' assemblage of disconnected scenes. The three focal characters in the revised scenario – Tsar, Pretender, Crowd – are balanced in a palindromic equilibrium, with the people, seen from two radically differing points of view, at beginning and end:

Prologue	1. Novodevichiy	Crowd
	2. Coronation	Boris
Act 1	3. Monastery cell ⎫	
	4. Inn ⎭	Pretender
Act 2	5. Terem	Boris
Act 3	6. Marina's boudoir ⎫	
	7. Fountain ⎭	Pretender
Act 4	8. Death of Boris	Boris
	9. Kromï Forest	Crowd

The final perspective from which to view the revised *Boris Godunov* as a total musico-dramatic conception pertains to the use of leitmotifs. On the face of it, their importance is much diminished. The earlier version of the opera was saturated with identifying and recalling themes, with every character, however insignificant, so equipped. In the three newly composed scenes of the revised version, the role of leitmotifs (except for the Pretender's) is minimal. In the revised Terem scene, they are much attenuated, particularly with reference to the title character and his central monologue. The role of the Pretender's leitmotif, however, is both expanded and refined, in a way that affects not only his portrayal, but Boris's as well. Where in the earlier version the leitmotif could refer either to the 'real' or the False Dmitry, their confusion (especially in Boris's mind) being the whole point of its deployment, in the new version its treatment is stricter, to magnificently ironic effect. It now refers only to the Pretender – except in Boris's deranged mind, where just as unwaveringly it refers to the slain infant heir. The consistency with which otherwise inexplicable alterations (particularly deletions) realize this change leaves no doubt as to Musorgsky's intention.

Rimsky-Korsakov's version still has its adherents. Its virtues, besides the surefire orchestration that made such an overwhelming impression in Paris, can be gauged from a trio of comparative examples drawn from the title role. In ex.1, the beginning of the central Act 2 aria, Rimsky expertly inserted a single chord to effect a polished modulation. In ex.2, from the climax of the aria, Rimsky transposed the second half of the melody to

Ex.1
(a) Musorgsky

['Learn, my child! . . . I have attained the highest power.']

(b) Rimsky-Korsakov

Ex.2
(a) Musorgsky

['And in cruel sorrow, sent down by God as punishment for our grievous sin']

(b) Rimsky-Korsakov

Ex.3
(a) Musorgsky

['Stand guard, a soldier for the true faith, revere the holy servants of God']

(b) Rimsky-Korsakov

give the singer (now definitely a baritone) a more felicitous tessitura. In ex.3, from the Act 4 farewell, Musorgsky's organum-like archaisms were replaced by a more grateful, Balakirevesque 'modality' that skirts forbidden parallels. Stravinsky may have been unfair to accuse his former teacher of having perpetrated a 'Meyerbeerization' of Musorgsky's work; the original, too, owed a heavy debt to Meyerbeer (as what 19th-century historical opera did not?). But Rimsky did conventionalize it in ways that may have facilitated its early acceptance, but now seem gratuitously to soften the harsh and hopeless impression Musorgsky calculated his opera to produce. The composer's revised version, it now seems clear, is a work not of raw genius alone but of a fastidious dramatist in sure command of his materials. It possesses an integrity of structure, of style and of purport – in short, of sullen historical vision – no other version, least of all the *ad hoc* conflations that have increasingly become the rule, can match.

R.T.

Boulevard Solitude

Lyrisches Drama in seven scenes by Hans Werner Henze to a libretto by Grete Weil after Walter Jockisch's *Boulevard Solitude*, itself based on Antoine-François Prévost's *Manon Lescaut*; Hanover, Landestheater, 17 February 1952.

The first cast was led by Sigrid Klaus and Walter Buckow.

Manon Lescaut	high soprano
Armand des Grieux *a student*	lyric tenor
Lescaut *Manon's brother*	baritone
Francis *Armand's friend*	baritone
Lilaque *père, a rich old*	
gentleman	high buffo tenor
Lilaque *fils*	baritone
A Prostitute	dancer
Servant to Lilaque *fils*	mime
Two Drug Addicts	dancers
A Cigarette Boy	dancer
Newspaper sellers, beggars, whores, police, students,	
travellers	

Setting Paris, after the end of World War II

Henze's first fully fledged opera (after the 1949 'opera for actors' *Das Wundertheater*, and the radio opera after Kafka, *Ein Landarzt*, 1951) was composed in 1950 and 1951. Its updating of the Manon Lescaut story, transferring the focus of attention from Manon to Armand des Grieux, as well as its carefully regulated mixture of idioms, ensured immediate and considerable success. The first performance was conducted by Johannes Schüler; it was staged twice in Italy in 1954 (in Naples, conducted by Ionel Perlea, and Rome, conducted by Nino Sanzogno). The British première took place in London (at Sadler's Wells) in 1962 where the cast included April Cantelo, John Carolan and Peter Glossop.

*

Scene i *A railway-station waiting-room in a large French town* After a brief introduction built up from percussion ostinatos, Francis is seen bidding farewell to his friend Armand. Manon enters with her brother Lescaut, and they sit at Armand's table. While Lescaut goes to get a drink, Manon and Armand begin to talk; she is going to finishing school in Lausanne, he is returning to life as a student in Paris. His self-pitying account of his loneliness there is interrupted by Manon who provides it with a happier ending; the couple leave the waiting-room together.

Scene ii *An attic room in Paris* Armand and Manon are together. Lying in bed they sing a bittersweet duet. Armand has stopped his studies, and his father has withdrawn his allowance; they have no money. When Armand leaves, Lescaut appears, to tell Manon that he has found her a new admirer, an old man but very rich. After Armand has returned briefly, Lescaut comments sarcastically in an extravagant aria that the more cruelly Manon treats her lovers the more successful she will become; he gives her five minutes to decide where her future lies.

Scene iii *An elegant boudoir in the house of Lilaque père* Manon writes to Armand assuring him that she is happy and well treated. Her only disappointment is that she cannot see him, and she suggests a subterfuge. Lescaut interrupts her, furious that she should be writing to Armand rather than paying attention to her sugar-daddy. He tears up the letter; when Manon protests that he is killing the one thing she values, his response is brutal: she is his source of income and he needs more money. He steals money from a strong-box and the two are joined by Lilaque. In a highly expressive trio Lilaque's initial warmth (couched in tenor lines of very high tessitura) turns to rage when he discovers the robbery; he throws out both of them.

Scene iv *A university library* The students, Armand and Francis among them, are studying Catullus. While their choral murmurings form a backdrop to the scene, Armand confesses that still he can think only of Manon. He does not believe Francis when he is told that she has robbed Lilaque, and when Francis leaves, indignant, Manon appears. The couple read a love poem that mirrors their own predicament and builds into a passionate duet.

Scene v *A dive* Manon and Armand have parted again, and he has resorted to drugs. Against a background of dance music, he sings of his attempts

'Boulevard Solitude' (Henze): set by Jean-Pierre Ponnelle for scene iv (a university library) of the original production at the Landestheater, Hanover, 17 February 1952

to forget the past. Lescaut arrives with Lilaque's son, his new client for Manon. He demands to know where she is, but Armand wants only more cocaine which Lescaut supplies. When Manon arrives to join her brother and Lilaque *fils*, Armand is enraged, threatening Lilaque. Manon tries to calm him, and they leave. A girl enters with a letter for Armand. As he reads it he hears Manon's voice asking him to meet her the following night, and in the meantime she will arrange for him to spend the night with one of the most beautiful girls in Paris (the bearer of the letter). Armand is too drugged to absorb it all.

Scene vi *The apartment of Lilaque fils* Manon and Armand are together at dawn. Though Manon is pleased with her upward mobility, Armand reminds her that once they were always together. Lescaut has kept a lookout, and arrives to warn Armand to leave before the servants see him; he notices a modern painting on the wall and takes it from its frame. They hear the voice of Lilaque *père* and Manon hides both men. For all her efforts the old man, who in spite of the past is glad to see her, insists on entering the room to look at the painting and discovers the theft. All the old suspicions return, and he calls to the servant to fetch the police. Lescaut shoots him, forces the revolver into Manon's hand and escapes; Manon and Armand are discovered, by Lilaque *fils*, standing over the body.

Scene vii *Outside a prison* In the depths of winter Armand waits to catch a final sight of Manon before she goes off to prison. His pathetic aria ends when Manon and the prisoners are taken away without any chance for the lovers to talk, and the action dissolves into a fast-moving 'revue' over a rumba rhythm in which images from their life together flood back, and a children's choir sings 'Jubilate exultate'.

*

In his first full-scale opera Henze was able to combine a heterogeneous collection of idioms – from jazz through neo-classical pastiche to serialism – in a dramatic scheme combining dance, drama, cinematic and older operatic conventions which demonstrated how an eclectic stylistic palette could be derived from a single 12-note series. Several aspects of the opera recall Berg, not only in the use of dance music as an image of degradation (in scene v) which evokes the Tavern scene in *Wozzeck*, but in the surreal exits and entrances throughout the opera, which recall the similar farcical elements of *Lulu*. Yet Henze casts his net wider still; the seven scenes and the orchestral intermezzos between them move between tonality and atonality with total freedom, while the closed vocal forms, recitative, aria and ensemble, hark back to 18th- and 19th-century usages.   **A.C.**

C

Calisto ('Callisto')

Drama per musica in a prologue and three acts by Francesco Cavalli to a libretto by Giovanni Faustini after Ovid's *Metamorphoses* (book 2); Venice, Teatro S Apollinare, 28 November 1651.

Giove [Jupiter]	bass
Calisto [Callisto]	soprano
Diana	soprano
Mercurio [Mercury]	tenor
Endimione [Endymion]	contralto
Giunone [Juno]	soprano
Pan	bass
3 Furies	sopranos
Linfea	soprano
Sylvan	alto
Satyr	alto

In Act 1 Jupiter has descended from Olympus to re-establish the world after the devastation of recent war. He quickly forgets his noble mission when he sees the nymph Callisto and falls in love with her. But Callisto, a follower of the goddess Diana, has taken a vow of chastity. She is determined to resist Jupiter's advances. Mercury persuades Jupiter to transform himself into Diana. Thus Jupiter succeeds in luring the naive and foolish Callisto into his arms instead of those of her adored goddess. Meanwhile, the virtuous Diana, in the aria 'Ardo, sospiro e piango', expresses her longing for the shepherd Endymion. Callisto approaches and implores Diana for more kisses. The goddess becomes incensed at this betrayal of her chaste ideals and expels Callisto from her charmed circle. With self-righteous nonchalance, Diana resumes her intensive dalliance with Endymion.

Juno has learnt (Act 2) that her husband is pursuing a new conquest. Always suspicious of Jupiter and wearied by his amorous adventures, Juno realizes that she must again rectify the mistakes caused by his excessive ardour. As she undertakes her mission, the first earthly soul she encounters is Callisto, weeping at her rejection by Diana. Juno recognizes that Jupiter is to blame for Callisto's plight. Meanwhile Pan, who is in love with Diana, captures Endymion; he and his satyrs treat him

roughly. In Act 3 Juno takes her revenge at her husband's duplicity by invoking the Furies, who turn Callisto into a bear. Jupiter is swift to overcome Juno's mischievous magic. He changes Callisto back to her human form and, by doing so, at last attains her loving and compliant surrender. He places her among the stars of the constellation Ursa Minor, where she will revel in the joys of 'celestial harmony' and eternal life.

Calisto is the ninth of 11 operas that Cavalli composed during the 1640s and early 1650s with the librettist Giovanni Faustini; its initial run was from 28 November to 31 December 1651. As experienced and skilful collaborators, they understood that short and incisive *mezz'arie* quicken and tighten the action. The brevity of the concerted arias as well as the swift tempos cogently set off the personalities of both serious and comic characters. Composer and librettist sympathetically illustrate the myth of Callisto and Jupiter, a tale of human frailty injured by the arrogant insensitivity of the gods. Two gentle humans, Callisto and Endymion, earn our respect through their unwavering loyalty to the goddess Diana. On the other hand, the quarrelling Jupiter and Juno deserve the ridicule hurled at them by two comic figures, the ancient nymph Linfea and a young satyr. Despite such scorn, Juno and Jupiter emerge individually successful: she at the mid-point of the opera and he at the triumphant finale.

M.N.C.

Capriccio

Konversationsstück für Musik in one act by Richard Strauss to a libretto by the composer and Clemens Krauss; Munich, Staatsoper, 28 October 1942.

The Countess at the première was sung by Viorica Ursuleac; Hans Hotter sang Olivier and Horst Taubmann Flamand, with Georg Hann as the director La Roche (a loving caricature of the great Max Reinhardt).

Countess Madeleine *a young widow*	soprano
The Count *her brother*	baritone
Flamand *a composer*	tenor

Olivier *a poet*	baritone
La Roche *a theatre director*	bass
Clairon *an actress*	contralto
Monsieur Taupe *a prompter*	tenor
Two Italian Singers	soprano and tenor
The Major-Domo	bass
Eight Servants	four tenors, four basses

A young ballerina, three onstage musicians

Setting A drawing-room in the Countess's
château near Paris; May 1777

The conception of *Capriccio*, Strauss's 15th and last
opera, arose from Stefan Zweig's research in the
British Museum, where in 1934 he came upon a short
comedy by Giovanni Battista Casti, a rival of
Mozart's librettist Da Ponte. *Prima la musica e poi le
parole* ('First the music, then the words') had in fact
been set to music by Mozart's own rival Antonio
Salieri, and shared its première at Schönbrunn with
Mozart's *Der Schauspieldirektor*. Mozart's little comedy was about opera as a practical business, but Casti
and Salieri also represented the words-versus-music
tension built into opera itself by including as
characters a composer and his poet. The idea, though
not the trivial plot, seized Zweig's imagination, and
Strauss liked it too; even before the première of their
Die schweigsame Frau, the writer had enlisted Joseph
Gregor's collaboration on a libretto. The Jewish
Zweig knew that his days in Nazi Germany were
numbered and hoped that his 'Aryan' friend might
take his literary place at the composer's side.
So Gregor did, for Strauss's next three operas
(*Friedenstag, Daphne, Die Liebe der Danae*) – but his
1935 draft for a neo-Casti piece found no favour, nor
did his later attempt when Strauss's interest was
rekindled in 1939.

What the composer really wanted was nothing
much like a story, but a 'theoretical comedy' or
'theatrical discussion': a wry, self-illustrating debate
about the nature of Opera. That was beyond Gregor's
range. Eventually it was the conductor Clemens
Krauss (who had prompted substantial changes in
Gregor's *Daphne* scenario) and Strauss himself who
devised the 'conversation-piece' he needed, with the
eventual label *Capriccio* to mark its status as a *jeu
d'esprit*. At one time he imagined it as a curtain-raiser
for *Daphne*, which would then count as the opera
created by the personnel of *Capriccio* – or rather of
'Prima le parole, dopo la musica', an interim title.
Soon it outgrew that modest scale, and Strauss
allowed himself a generous orchestra. Yet he took
unprecedented care to make (nearly) all the words
audible, for the dramatic contest would otherwise
have been a fake from the start. Knowing that the
opera was unlikely to work in a 'big house', he hoped
for a small-house Salzburg Festival première; instead,
Krauss arranged a grand Strauss Festival in Munich,

with *Capriccio* as its centrepiece in the Staatsoper and
his wife Viorica Ursuleac as the Countess.

The prologue-sextet had already had its first
performance at the home of the Nazi Gauleiter and
arts-lover Baldur von Schirach, who helped Strauss
to secure his Belvedere home in Vienna at a difficult
time. In 1943 the Staatsoper was bombed out, but
while the war continued *Capriccio* was performed in
Darmstadt, Dresden and Vienna, and in Zürich
under Karl Böhm. The opera has made its way slowly
but steadily into the international repertory – chiefly
because of its marvellous soprano-finale, and then
the charms of the sextet and the 'moonlight
interlude'; but much else is regularly lost. For full
appreciation, the veteran Strauss's subtle even-
handedness with words-versus-music throughout
requires not only an intimate performing scale, but
delivery in the language of the audience.

                              *

Before the curtain rises on *Capriccio* we hear a sextet,
played by first-desk strings in the pit. It is the
composer Flamand's latest piece, sweetly serene in F
at start and finish – with a theatrical eruption of
passion in the middle, soon mollified (it fixes
perfectly the urbane, nothing-too-serious manner of
the whole opera). In a garden salon in early afternoon
Flamand watches the Countess Madeleine's reaction
to his sextet, continuing now in the next room – and
so do Olivier, his rival for her affections, and the
dozing theatre director La Roche. They exchange
banter about words, music and modern productions,
and slip off to prepare the private theatre as the
Countess-Muse enters with her talented amateur
brother. La Roche has come to direct the poet's new
play, with the Count and the famous actress Clairon,
once the poet's mistress, as hero and heroine. Count
and Countess tease each other about their 'artistic'
partialities (this becomes a lively duet); then the
others return, still arguing, and Clairon makes a
dashing entrance. She and the Count read through a
fraught scene from the play, culminating in his
passionate sonnet ('Kein Andres, das mir so im
Herzen loht': Ronsard's 'Je ne sçaurois aimer autre
que vous', freely and elegantly translated by the
conductor Hans Swarowsky). When La Roche leads
them away to rehearse, Olivier recites the sonnet
again as an intimate declaration to Madeleine –
inspiring Flamand to rush off and compose it. The
poet seizes the chance to press his ardent suit, in E♭,
but the Countess still hesitates to choose between
poetry and music.

Flamand returns triumphantly (wrenching the
key up to F♯); he has set the sonnet, and forthwith sings the result to his own harpsichord
accompaniment. Muted divided strings shadow his
voice. Strauss rose superbly to the occasion with this
song, which is of course to haunt the rest of the score.

At 'Leben ... oder Tod', the close of the 'octave' verses, it drops theatrically and briefly into D minor; but its subtle life lies in continual rhythmic displacements, such as only a master of lied prosody could devise. (In an earlier, higher-lying draft of the sonnet, which has been published, there are fascinating variants.) Without missing a beat, the song is now recycled as a glowing trio: Flamand strums the chords and repeats the phrases that please him most, the Countess effuses over this higher synthesis of words and notes, Olivier – like Mozart's Guglielmo in the *Così* wedding-quartet – emits cross-grained complaints (he has been moved, but thinks the composer has wrecked his scansion). Now La Roche comes to demand a cut in Olivier's script, and as they go off to discuss it Flamand seizes the chance to bare his own heart to Madeleine (in E, more shyly and sweetly than the lusty poet, with thematic echoes of *Ariadne*'s young Composer). Having extracted her promise to make a final choice by 11 o'clock next morning, he flees in rapt confusion. Rehearsal noises are heard again, and the Countess orders chocolate in the salon for everybody. (In the two-act version often used now, her spoken line ends Act 1.)

Her brother returns first, professing his entrancement by Clairon, while Madeleine reports her suitors' protestations and her inability to decide between them. They mock each other's plights. The others join them for the refreshments, with a *divertissement* arranged by La Roche – an Italian soprano-and-tenor duo, preceded by a young *danseuse*. For her three dances Strauss wrote pastiches of Rameau and Couperin. During her Passepied the director regales the Count with predictions of a golden future for her, in royal beds as well as the ballet; her Gigue accompanies Olivier's peace overtures to Clairon (smartly rebuffed); only her Gavotte earns courteous general attention. Ever susceptible, the Count exclaims that music is after all only an adjunct to dance, thus cueing the 'theatrical fugue' which Strauss had always imagined as his centrepiece (surely with Verdi's final *Falstaff* fugue in mind). Starting in plain C, the subject – 'Tanz und Musik/steh'n im Bann des Rhythmus' ('Dance and music stem from rhythm') – generates a long and lively debate over what the fundamental, instinctive art must be: rhythmic movement, or human speech, or the ordering of tones? In midstream the Count reflects that 'Eine Oper ist ein absurdes Ding' ('an opera is an absurd thing'), to an expansive tune borrowed from Strauss's old *Krämerspiegel* song cycle.

The preening Italians' operatic duet makes a diversion, but also shows that the debate has been too narrow. What about the direct *Affekt* of the singing voice? – even in banal words, and the crudest musical routine? (Easy parody here: Strauss caricatures the vocal gestures of Italian opera over a stolid *Biergarten* pulse, and the singers invariably make a contest of upstaging each other.) Now La Roche announces the grand spectacle he plans for Madeleine's birthday: fake-mythological, hugely epic. Unable to contain themselves, his junior colleagues begin an elaborate 'Laughing Ensemble'; as tempers rise it becomes a 'Strife Ensemble', topped by the tipsy Italian soprano. Deeply wounded, the theatre director mounts a towering defence – 'Hola! ihr Streiter in Apoll!' – of his own art, devoted to rescuing the thin-blooded efforts of modern composers and librettists. Everyone relents graciously, and La Roche joins his fellow artists in a rhetorical 'Homage Quartet' to himself. But a new birthday plan has emerged: what he must direct is a new opera by Olivier and Flamand. Possible subjects are discussed, including those of earlier Strauss operas, which the orchestra duly quotes; but the outcome is that the competing swains will write an opera, *Intermezzo*-like, on the events of this day, the very opera that we are hearing. The ending has yet to be decided by Madeleine.

Twilight falls as the guests depart for Paris, escorted by the Count. Coming to tidy the salon, a servants' octet assesses the situation: everyone is playing Theatre, and 'the Countess is in love but doesn't know with whom'. In the darkness Monsieur Taupe emerges like a mole, having fallen asleep in his prompt box, and the patient Major-Domo hears out his dreamy claim that the show really depends upon *him*, before arranging his transport home. The moon rises; a solo horn begins an ecstatic interlude (on the *Krämerspiegel* song) while the Countess reappears, pensive in a new evening-gown. The Major-Domo reminds her that a decision is expected by 11 tomorrow morning. Crying 'Morgen mittag um elf!', she interrogates her own heart, and then her mirror-image – with no clearer result. This rich operatic epiphany (in D♭, of course) is Strauss's last, and Madeleine concludes her soliloquy with a wry question: 'Is there any ending that isn't trivial?' 'Supper is served', says the Major-Domo; both Flamand's and Olivier's themes peep in before the silvery, uncommitted closing cadences.

*

The musical idiom of *Capriccio* lies close to Strauss's 1946 Oboe Concerto: artfully serene and warmly tonal, with the merest chromatic squalls *en passant*. The Countess is a gift to seasoned Strauss sopranos (tactfully, we are not told which birthday it is that she will be celebrating); Flamand is one of Strauss's rarely gentle, lyrical tenors. Clever singer-actors can make even the seemingly under-composed roles of the Count, Olivier and Clairon blossom, and the quarrel-ensembles are brilliantly transparent. Though the action is selfconsciously contrived to the point of frank 'deconstruction', Strauss manages, like his 'Italian' duo, to command gut reactions from his audience, with the ironic blessing of Krauss's arch, know-all text.   D.M.

Capuleti e i Montecchi, I
('The Capuleti and the Montecchi')

Tragedia lirica in two acts by Vincenzo Bellini to a libretto by Felice Romani; Venice, Teatro La Fenice, 11 March 1830.

At the première Romeo was sung by Giuditta Grisi, Giulietta by Maria Carradori-Allan, Tebaldo by Lorenzo Bonfigli and Lorenzo by Ranieri Pocchini Cavalieri.

Tebaldo *betrothed to Giulietta*	tenor
Capellio *chief of the Capuleti, father of*	
Giulietta	bass
Lorenzo *doctor and retainer of the*	
Capuleti	tenor or bass
Romeo *head of the*	
Montecchi	soprano or mezzo-soprano
Giulietta *in love with Romeo*	soprano
Capuleti, Montecchi, maidens, soldiers, guards	
Setting Verona in the 13th century	

Behind the libretto stand many Italian, ultimately Renaissance, sources rather than Shakespeare's *Romeo and Juliet*: the theme was very popular in Italy. Romani rewrote for Bellini the *Giulietta e Romeo* he had written originally for Nicola Vaccai (1825, Milan), which drew on a play *Giulietta e Romeo* of 1818 by Luigi Scevola, and which had also been set by E. Torriani (1828, Vicenza). The first Italian libretto explicitly based on Shakespeare's play was by M. M. Marcello, for Marchetti's *Romeo e Giulietta* (1865, Trieste).

In Venice to prepare the local première of *Il pirata* with Giuditta Grisi as Imogene, Bellini wrote *I Capuleti* in a month and a half (starting about 20 January) after the Teatro La Fenice had been let down by Giovanni Pacini. He wrote the part of Romeo for Grisi (whose presence, together with a relatively weak male company, may have conditioned the choice of subject); it rarely descends below *c'*. Bellini had intended the part of Lorenzo for a bass, but in Act 1 of the autograph score he transposed it for tenor, and in Act 2 the part is written in the tenor clef throughout. Although these changes were possibly for Senigallia (summer 1830), Cavalieri, the singer at the première, appears to have been a tenor. (Published scores and most subsequent performances have assigned the role to a bass.)

Bellini thoroughly reworked ten melodies from his unsuccessful *Zaira* (1829, Parma) and one from

Adelson e Salvini (1825, Naples) into *I Capuleti e i Montecchi*. He prepared a version for La Scala (26 December 1830), lowering Giulietta's part for the mezzo-soprano Amalia Schütz-Oldosi. Early librettos divide the opera into four parts; at Bologna in 1832 Maria Malibran replaced the last part with the tomb scene from Vaccai's final act, a tradition followed by contralto Romeos such as Marietta Alboni. This version was performed at Paris and London with Giuditta Pasta as Romeo in 1833, but in Florence the following year Giuseppina Ronzi De Begnis restored Bellini's ending. Wilhelmine Schröder-Devrient's singing as Romeo in Leipzig (1834) and Magdeburg (1835) created a profound impression on the young Wagner. *I Capuleti* was revived in 1935, the centenary of Bellini's death, at Catania and in 1954 at Palermo, with Giulietta Simionato as Romeo and Rosanna Carteri as Giulietta. In 1966 Claudio Abbado prepared a version for La Scala in which Romeo was sung by a tenor, Giacomo Aragall; the cast included Renata Scotto as Giulietta and Luciano Pavarotti as Tebaldo. This version was also performed in Amsterdam, Rome and Philadelphia and at the 1967 Edinburgh Festival but is no longer used.

*

The opening sinfonia uses themes from the following *introduzione* and Giulietta's 'Ah! non poss'io partire'.

Act I.i ('*Parte prima*') *A gallery in the Capuleti palace* The Guelph followers of Capellio gather, fearing an attack from their Ghibelline rivals, the Montecchi. Capellio and Tebaldo warn them that the Ghibelline chief, Romeo, whom they have never seen and who has recently killed Capellio's son, is sending an envoy urging peace. Tebaldo swears to take vengeance on Romeo himself to mark his forthcoming marriage to Giulietta. His military cavatina, 'È serbata a questo acciaro', uses a thoroughly reworked version of Corasmino's opening cavatina in *Zaira*, while the Allegro 'L'amo tanto, e m'è si cara' is new. Romeo enters unrecognized, posing as his own envoy, and expresses regret for the accidental death of Capellio's son in the cavatina 'Se Romeo t'uccise un figlio' (adapted from Nerestano's rondò from *Zaira*, Act 2). He offers to seal peace through the union of Romeo and Giulietta but is told that she is betrothed to Tebaldo. The Capuleti reject Romeo's offer of peace and he warns of future bloodshed in 'La tremenda ultrice spada' (from Zaira's aria in Act 2).

I.ii *A room in Giulietta's apartment* A horn solo introduces Giulietta's *romanza* 'Oh! quante volte, oh! quante' (adapted from *Adelson e Salvini*); there is a contrast between her festive raiment and her unfulfilled longing for Romeo. Lorenzo then leads in Romeo, who urges Giulietta to flee with him in the

'I Capuleti e i Montecchi' (Bellini), scene from a German production (1835) with Wilhelmine Schröder-Devrient as Romeo: engraving

duet 'Sì, fuggire: a noi non resta' (derived in part from the duet in *Zaira*, finale to Act 1). Giulietta resists all his pleading and begs him to cause her no more torment.

1.iii ('Parte seconda') A courtyard in Capellio's palace The Capuleti prepare for Giulietta's wedding to Tebaldo. Lorenzo finds Romeo disguised as a Guelph and awaiting the help of his friends to abduct Giulietta. The Montecchi launch their attack on the Capuleti and during the commotion Giulietta meets Romeo who again urges her to flee with him, but they are discovered by Capellio and Tebaldo, who recognize Romeo as the enemy ambassador. He reveals his true identity, introducing the finale, 'Soccorso, sostegno'. The Montecchi arrive and the act ends with Romeo and Giulietta separated by their respective factions. Bellini contrasts their high voices, in unison, with those of their antagonists in 'Se ogni speme è a noi rapita' (taken from the trio 'Non si pianga, si nasconda' in *Zaira*, Act 1).

Act 2.i ('Parte terza') An apartment in Capellio's palace An arioso for cello introduces Giulietta, who wonders what has happened to Romeo. Lorenzo enters offering her a sleeping potion that will counterfeit death and assuring her that Romeo will be with her when she wakes. Her aria 'Morte io non temo, il sai' (revised from Zaira's Act 2 aria) expresses her fear that she will never wake, despite Lorenzo's interpolated protestations. Probably for the production in Milan, Bellini added an unpublished ensemble passage, 'Morir dovessi ancora', as Giulietta takes the potion. Capellio enters and she begs his forgiveness as she feels herself growing weaker ('Ah! non poss'io partire', taken directly from Nerestano's aria in *Zaira*, Act 2). Capellio is left anxious and suspicious, and has Lorenzo watched.

2.ii A deserted place near Capellio's palace Alone, Romeo complains that Lorenzo has not made contact with him. He comes face to face with Tebaldo and their furious duet, 'Stolto! a un sol mio grido', is about to lead to a duel when they hear an offstage chorus of lament ('Pace alla tua bell'anima', taken directly from *Zaira*, Act 2). When they learn that it is Giulietta's cortège the two antagonists end the scene, united in their grief.

2.iii ('Parte quarta') At the tombs of the Capuleti The Montecchi have come to mourn Giulietta. Romeo appears and approaches her tomb, which his followers force open for him. Romeo makes his farewell to Giulietta in 'Deh! tu, bell'anima' (the melody is from Zaira's Act 1 aria celebrating her forthcoming marriage), after which he takes poison himself. A phrase for clarinet and flute in octaves marks Giulietta's revival and she tells an incredulous Romeo about Lorenzo's potion. Their increasingly agitated exchanges are mirrored in the accompaniment as Romeo admits that he has taken poison. His strength quickly ebbs. When he expires, Giulietta falls dead upon his body, to the horror of the Capuleti and Montecchi who rush in. This entire scene, a continuous alternation of chorus, recitative, arioso and ensemble, is, emotionally and dramatically, the most powerfully effective yet written by Bellini.

In *I Capuleti e i Montecchi* (particularly the final scene) Bellini establishes something of the formal unconventionality found in the works of his maturity. The concentration of the action on the two principal characters is notably successful. The opera is primarily a work of reclamation, in which previously written material is skilfully adapted to its new context. Admittedly the haste with which it was put together is reflected in a certain schematicism and lack of rhythmic variety in the closed numbers. On the other hand the subject of star-crossed lovers enabled Bellini to play from strength as a purveyor of tender, elegiac melody. Here, as in *Zaira*, he infused the simple, syllabic vocal writing of *La straniera* with melismatic bravura, preparing the way for that perfect synthesis of expression and virtuosity attained in *La sonnambula*. *I Capuleti* survived throughout the century as a favourite warhorse for star sopranos such as Wilhelmine Schröder-Devrient and Johanna Wagner, despite the hostility of progressives such as Liszt, who dismissed it as intolerably old-fashioned, and the ambivalence of Wagner, who loved its melodies while deploring its dramatic conception. Berlioz was no less contemptuous, though he singled out the unison cantilena for the lovers in the Act 1 finale for special praise.   S.M., E.F., J.B.

Cardillac

Opera in three acts, op.39, by Paul Hindemith to a libretto by Ferdinand Lion after E. T. A. Hoffmann's story *Das Fräulein von Scuderi*, Dresden, Staatsoper, 9 November 1926; revised in four acts to a libretto by Hindemith after Lion, Zürich, Stadttheater, 20 June 1952.

The original cast included Robert Burg (Cardillac), Grete Merrem-Nikisch (the Lady), Ludwig Eybisch (the Cavalier), Claire Born (the Daughter) and Max Hirzel (the Officer).

Cardillac *a goldsmith*	baritone
His Daughter	soprano
An Officer	tenor
A Cavalier	tenor
A Lady	soprano
A Gold Dealer	bass
The King	silent role

Setting Paris in the 17th century

In Act 1 the streets are in uproar, murderers are at large and the crowd call for action. Cardillac appears and the people respectfully make way for him, in awe of his legendary craftsmanship. A Cavalier explains to a Lady that whoever buys a trinket from the goldsmith is immediately robbed of it and stabbed to death. The Lady bids the Cavalier, if he wishes her favour, to bring her 'the finest object Cardillac ever made'. Accepting the challenge, the Cavalier brings to her bedroom a golden belt (scene ii). While he is receiving his reward, a masked figure breaks in, kills him and escapes with the belt.

Act 2 reveals Cardillac in his workroom, discussing a purchase with the Gold Dealer, who suspects him. So possessive is Cardillac of his work that he resents even a visit by the King and refuses to sell him anything: he would have had to kill him, he admits to himself. Cardillac's Daughter, torn between her father and her lover, an Officer, is indifferently told to marry him if she wants; as Cardillac informs the Officer, his work is more important to him than his daughter. The Officer, perceiving Cardillac's weak point and anxious to break his power over his daughter, insists on buying a gold chain, despite the risk to himself. Cardillac, who has tried to dissuade him, is unable to bear its loss and follows him in disguise.

Act 3 takes place outside a tavern, where Cardillac overtakes the Officer and stabs him. The Gold Dealer witnesses the deed and recognizes the attacker, denouncing him to the crowd. However, the wounded Officer protects him out of pity for his daughter, accusing the Gold Dealer of being the unknown murderer's accomplice. Cardillac, unwilling to be indebted to anyone, at first claims to know the identity of the murderer; when the crowd threaten to destroy his work unless he reveals the name, he admits that he is guilty and the enraged crowd kill him.

Despite the romantic nature of the subject, Hindemith chose a demonstratively anti-romantic line for the music of his first full-length opera, modelling it on Handelian opera, which was then enjoying a revival in Germany. The music begins and ends with extended polyphonic choral numbers (depicting the crowd's unrest over the murders and their determination to find and punish the murderer);

'Cardillac' (Hindemith), Act 1: scene from the original production at the Staatsoper, Dresden, 9 November 1926, with (from left to right) Grete Merrem-Nikisch as the Lady, Eybisch as the Cavalier and Robert Burg as Cardillac

between these are 15 musical sections, each identified by name (aria, arioso and duet, scena and quartet, etc.). The action, however, is continuous, moving forward with a minimum of recitative. A tight control of length, combined with rhythmic variety, ensures that there is no sense of the drama being held up by the demands of musical form. Hindemith nevertheless finds room for dramatic devices of a distinctly Verdian hue, as in the accompaniment to the Cavalier's Act 1 aria, where he is torn between temptation and the fear of death, and the Lady's aria, full of restless erotic desire. The anticipated love duet is replaced by a 'pantomime' for two flutes in which, to a minuet rhythm, Cavalier and Lady silently admire the belt the Cavalier has brought. Traces of Verdi are also apparent in the innocent Daughter's vacillation between father and lover in the second act, and in Cardillac's aria as he wrestles with his conscience before setting out to murder his daughter's lover.

In the revised version, Hindemith's main object was to humanize his hero in order to shed further light on the question of the artist's responsibility to society, the subject of both his later works *Mathis der Maler* and *Die Harmonie der Welt*. In bringing the story closer to Hoffmann's original, he rewrote the text but fitted his words to the existing music, altering the order of some numbers and at times changing the vocal line. The Lady becomes the Opera Singer (soprano) and the Daughter's lover is Cardillac's Journeyman (tenor). In Act 1 a new duet between Cardillac and the Cavalier replaces the Cavalier's solo: here Cardillac behaves in a kindly way until the Cavalier insists on buying a diadem for the Opera Singer, when his mood darkens. The Opera Singer is seen bidding farewell to a Marquis (silent role) before the Cavalier arrives, and her intervening solo (to the same music) tells of her disillusionment with, rather than her desire for, men. However, the outcome is the same. In Act 2 the King's visit is replaced with a visit by the Marquis and the opera company who have come, in Cardillac's absence, to buy a crown for the Opera Singer to wear on stage. She recognizes the diadem stolen from her, but accepts it without revealing her suspicions. The naive Journeyman is arrested by a Police Officer (bass-baritone) on suspicion of being the murderer, but he escapes and begs Cardillac to allow his daughter to flee with him. Cardillac refuses, and the Journeyman, though hinting that he knows Cardillac to be the murderer, is thrown out. Cardillac sets off in pursuit of the missing diadem. The new third act consists of three numbers, the first being a stage performance of scenes from Lully's opera *Phaëton*. Against this, in a juxtaposition of music and action, the Journeyman comes to warn the Opera Singer (wearing the diadem as Theo in Lully's opera), followed by the Police Officer and Cardillac. After the opera has ended, the Opera Singer dismisses the other singers and returns the diadem to Cardillac. A duet hints at his redemption through her understanding and sympathy, but, finding the diadem gone yet again (the Police Officer has surreptitiously taken it), Cardillac relapses and goes off in pursuit. In Act 4 it is the Police Officer whom Cardillac wounds and the Journeyman, attempting to intervene, whom the crowd accuse of being the murderer. The Police Officer protects him, and the opera ends as before, with Cardillac revealing and defending his own murderous deeds, whereupon the enraged crowd kill him.

Hindemith's revised text is stronger in motivation than the original, but its argumentative tone is less suited to the form of the music, and the interpolated third act, however ingenious, lessens the dramatic tension. It has not proved as popular as its forerunner.   G.Sk.

Carmen

Opéra comique in four acts by Georges Bizet to a libretto by Henri Meilhac and Ludovic Halévy after Prosper Mérimée's novel; Paris, Opéra-Comique (Salle Favart), 3 March 1875.

The original cast included Célestine Galli-Marié as Carmen, Paul Lhérie as Don José and Jacques Bouhy as Escamillo.

Carmen *a gypsy*	mezzo-soprano
Don José *a corporal*	tenor
Escamillo *a bullfighter*	bass/baritone
Micaëla *a country girl*	soprano
Zuniga *a lieutenant*	bass
Moralès *a corporal*	baritone
Frasquita ⎱ *gypsies*	soprano
Mercédès ⎰	soprano
Lillas Pastia *an innkeeper*	spoken
Andrès *a lieutenant*	tenor
Le Dancaïre ⎱ *smugglers*	tenor/baritone
Le Remendado ⎰	tenor
A Gypsy	bass
A Guide	spoken
An Orange-Seller	contralto
A Soldier	spoken
The Alcalde *[mayor]*	silent

Soldiers, young men, cigarette factory girls, Escamillo's supporters, gypsies, merchants and orange-sellers, police, bullfighters, people, urchins

Setting Seville around 1830

Despite the failure of *Djamileh* in 1872, the Opéra-Comique directors, Du Locle and De Leuven, invited Bizet to compose an opera in three acts. Meilhac and Halévy were named as librettists and various subjects suggested. It was Bizet himself who put forward Mérimée's novel *Carmen* as a subject. The librettists were enthusiastic, but De Leuven was alarmed at the thought of Carmen being killed on stage and other elements unsuitable in what he regarded as a family opera house. He soon resigned, while the project went ahead. Bizet worked on the score in 1873, interrupted by the never completed *Don Rodrigue*, and at the end of that year Galli-Marié was engaged to sing the role of Carmen. The opera was orchestrated in the summer of 1874, and rehearsals began in September. During the unusually long rehearsal period Bizet had to contend with objections from both the orchestra, who found the forthright style of scoring beyond their reach, and the chorus, who were expected to act convincingly as individuals rather than respond in unison as a group. He also encountered the ill-will of Du Locle, who publicly expressed his incomprehension, calling the score 'Cochin-Chinese' music, and urged Bizet to tone down the realistic force of the opera. Fortunately Bizet was firmly supported by Galli-Marié and Lhérie, so that few compromises had to be made. The most shocking features of the opera were Carmen's blatant sexuality and her readiness to discard men like picked flowers; also the rowdy women's chorus who both fight and smoke on stage. To have Carmen murdered on stage at the final curtain was too strong for many tastes.

The opera eventually opened on 3 March 1875, and a vocal score was issued by Choudens at the same time. Despite the notorious response of the press and the evident outrage of many in the audience, *Carmen* was not truly a failure, although its uncomprehending reception angered Bizet and may have contributed to his final illness. It ran for 45 performances in 1875 with three more in 1876, sustained partly by its reputation as a shocker and by the appalling misfortune of Bizet's death on the night of the 33rd performance, 3 June 1875. Discerning musicians, such as Saint-Saëns and Tchaikovsky, recognized its force and originality from the first; it displayed on every page Bizet's immense talent for penetratingly original music in a highly coloured setting and his wonderfully sure feeling for the human voice. Parisian managements, however, kept clear of the work until 1883, by which time it already enjoyed world success. This grew from a production in Vienna in October 1875 in a version for which Guiraud adapted the dialogue as recitative. The opera was soon heard in many cities all over Europe and beyond, often with Galli-Marié in the title role. Both Brahms and Wagner expressed admiration, and

Nietzsche issued his famous assertion that it was the perfect antidote to Wagnerian neurosis. Its posthumous fame raised Bizet to a pinnacle of glory far higher than anything he ever experienced in his lifetime.

Carmen has remained one of the most frequently performed operas in the entire repertory. Many great singers have been associated with its leading roles. The orchestral suite drawn from the opera is often played and in 1954 it extended its currency in a freely adapted film version, *Carmen Jones*, with a contemporary libretto and setting and an all-black cast. For three-quarters of a century it was regularly played not as an *opéra comique* with dialogue, as Bizet wrote it, but with the Guiraud recitatives. It is now played almost everywhere in *opéra comique* format, although the edition on which modern performances rely, that of Fritz Oeser published in 1964, has aroused bitter controversy since it includes a quantity of music that Bizet himself rejected in his own edition of the vocal score published in 1875. That first edition, published by Choudens, is exceedingly rare, for it was replaced at an early stage by the first of many corrupt editions from the same house.

*

The prelude to Act 1 introduces three themes from the opera: the energetic *corrida* from Act 4 makes a noisy, vigorous opening in A major. This switches directly to the famous Toreador Song, from Act 2, in F. A fuller reprise of this melody has an ingenious modulation back to A for a return of the opening music. The prelude has a separate second part which introduces a strong note of tragedy with the chromatic motif associated both with fate and with Carmen throughout the opera. This links directly to the first scene.

Act I *A public square in Seville; a tobacco factory on the right faces a guardroom on the left with a covered gallery in front* Some soldiers watch people coming and going in the square ('Sur la place, Chacun passe'). Micaëla shyly enters, looking for a corporal by the name of Don José. Moralès, a sergeant, tells her that he belongs to a different company but begs her to wait with them, with the assurance that she will be in safe hands. She evades their entreaties and runs away. This introductory scene begins and ends according to convention with the same music, a picturesque chorus. In between, Bizet moves swiftly through many keys and with many nuggets of melody, including the playful military tune for 'Il y sera', a tune which Micaëla shares with the soldiers. Moralès then sings some *couplets*, 'Attention! Chut! Taisons-nous!', which were retained for 30 performances in 1875, then dropped. They serve to fill the space between Micaëla's exit and Don José's arrival, for a trumpet-call is heard, announcing the changing of the guard. Two piccolos and a chorus of urchins

CARMEN
Opéra-Comique en quatre actes.

H. MEILHAC et L. HALÉVY.   MUSIQUE de GEORGES BIZET

Poster by Prudent Leray for Bizet's 'Carmen' (showing the final scene in Act 4) printed for Choudens at the time of the original production at the Opéra-Comique (Salle Favart), Paris, in 1875

('Avec la garde montante') provide accompaniment. A solo violin and solo cello in canon provide background for the *mélodrame* in which Moralès tells José that a girl was asking after him. The guard moves off, leaving José with Zuniga, the lieutenant.

In dialogue José tells Zuniga about the cigarette girls who will shortly return to the factory after lunch; he also explains that he is from Navarre and that Micaëla, a 17-year-old orphan, has been brought up by his widowed mother. The factory bell rings and a crowd gathers to watch the girls go by ('La cloche a sonné'). José shows no interest. The girls' chorus is placid and seductive. But when La Carmencita (Carmen) arrives with a flower in her mouth and a following of admirers the music takes a more angular turn, echoing the theme of fate already heard at the end of the prelude. In the famous Habanera, 'L'amour est un oiseau rebelle', Carmen expounds her view of love as something to be seized when it passes: 'If I love you, take care!' Bizet borrowed the melody from a song by Iradier but transformed it with his inimitable harmonic style and the haunting habanera rhythm. The fate theme is forcefully heard as Carmen breaks out of the throng and approaches José, who has remained apart from the others, busy with his rifle primer. She throws a flower at his feet. He is transfixed by this provocative gesture. The girls go into the factory and the crowd disperses, leaving José alone. He picks up the flower but hides it hurriedly when Micaëla comes up. She has brought a letter and some money from his mother and, as she shows in a deeply affecting duet, a kiss. José asks her to return the kiss. The duet's enchanting stream of melody is interrupted in the middle by his sudden fear of a 'demon' whose meaning Micaëla does not grasp. His mother's letter urges him to marry Micaëla, who leaves while he is reading it to run some errands for his mother.

Suddenly there is an uproar in the factory. The girls rush out to tell Zuniga of a fight between Carmen and another girl. Zuniga sends José into the factory to restore order; with two soldiers he brings her out (this very lively scene was somewhat shortened by Bizet, removing a contrapuntal combination of José's theme with Carmen's fate theme). In dialogue José reports the fight to Zuniga, who challenges Carmen to respond. She does so by nonchalantly humming a few tra-la-las. Zuniga gives orders for her to be led off to prison and instructs José to conduct her. Left alone with José she attempts to suborn him, assuring him that he will do what she wants 'because you love me'. She knows he has kept the flower she threw him. In the seguidilla which follows ('Près des remparts de Séville') she sings of her friend Lillas Pastia's tavern and of her taste for free living and loving. The music and Carmen's behaviour are so seductive that José quickly yields to temptation, especially since she has said that if he loves her, she will love him. In the brief finale which follows at once, Zuniga arrives with the order for her arrest, so José and the soldiers lead her off. She whispers to José to fall when she pushes him. He does so, and in the noisy confusion Carmen escapes.

Act 2 *Lillas Pastia's tavern* The entr'acte, based on Don José's offstage song in the coming act, is a perfectly crafted *divertissement* alternating minor and major. The curtain rises on Carmen, Frasquita and Mercédès who are sitting with some officers, including Zuniga and Moralès. Gypsy girls are dancing and Carmen suddenly rises to sing 'Les tringles des sistres tintaient' to tambourine accompaniment. The others girls join in and the piece works up to a frenzy of noise and movement. The landlord is preparing to close, so the officers invite the girls to the theatre. They refuse. Carmen learns from Zuniga that José was reduced to the ranks and sent to prison for a month for allowing her to escape. He was released the day before.

Outside, voices are heard applauding the famous toreador Escamillo. Zuniga invites them in and persuades Pastia to keep serving drinks. To the sound of triumphant C major fanfares Escamillo appears and immediately launches into his *couplets*,

the famous Toreador Song 'Votre toast, je peux vous le rendre', the main melody of which has already been heard in the prelude. Everyone joins in the refrains. Escamillo finds himself next to Carmen, but she rebuffs him, saying that for the moment she is not available. The soldiers leave, although Zuniga tells Carmen that he will be back in an hour. The three gypsy girls are left with Pastia, who reveals that the smugglers Le Dancaïre and Le Remendado have arrived. Pastia calls them in and they unveil their plan in a brisk quintet ('Nous avons en tête une affaire'), whose pace and lightness are breathtaking, especially since the two smugglers are stock comic figures from *opéra comique* in a scene of intrinsic comedy. But Carmen tells the others that she cannot join them on their smuggling expedition since she is in love. She has no sooner told them that she is awaiting the soldier who went to prison for setting her free than José's voice is heard.

They leave Carmen, urging her to bring José to join them the next day. Before their duet begins, Carmen orders food and drink, and even tests José's jealousy by telling him that she was dancing with Zuniga not long before. José quickly declares his love, while Carmen promises to repay her indebtedness to him. The duet begins with Carmen taking her castanets (in the first text she breaks a plate and simulates castanets with the pieces) and singing another of her seductive Spanish songs, dancing now to make up to José. The song, entirely diatonic, also serves as foreground to offstage bugles sounding the retreat, a compelling dramatic moment since José is torn between Carmen's alluring humming and his military duties. When he says he has to go, Carmen taunts him, saying he does not love her. To prove her wrong he draws the crumpled flower from his uniform and sings the Flower Song ('La fleur que tu m'avais jetée'), an ecstatic, beautifully scored outpouring of love. But instead of the duet ending conventionally as a climax of shared passion, Carmen continues to doubt and test José's love by urging him to join her and her friends in the mountains. José refuses, and bids her a final farewell. Suddenly there is a knock; Zuniga bursts in. He taunts José and orders him to leave. José stands firm and a clash of swords is only avoided by Carmen's summons to the smugglers, who suddenly appear and disarm Zuniga. He is led away by some of the gypsies while Carmen turns to José to ask if he is now prepared to join them. José has no choice, and as they pick up Carmen's earlier song about the thrills of mountain life and the lure of liberty, he joins in with gusto. There is no turning back.

Act 3 *A rocky place near Seville at night* The entr'acte is an exquisite solo for flute and harp, with other wind and strings joining in. It suggests a Grecian pastoral or perhaps a virginal idyll, quite remote from the hot tempers and fiery passions of Carmen's Spain. There is no evidence to support the widely repeated supposition that it was originally intended for *L'arlésienne*, yet its purpose at this point is far from clear.

The curtain rises. To a stealthy march there appear a number of smugglers, heavily laden. Among them are Carmen, Frasquita, Mercédès, Le Remendado, Le Dancaïre and Don José. In comic-opera style (almost entirely homophonic) they sing about the perils of the smuggler's trade: the rewards are fabulous when nothing goes wrong. Bizet offers a breathtaking series of descending chromatic chords on 'Prends garde de faire un faux pas!' Le Remendado and Le Dancaïre go off to reconnoitre, while Carmen and José resume what has evidently been a quarrel. She admits her love is already fading, and when José mentions his mother she suggests he would be better off if he left them now. Carmen says the cards have been telling her that they would 'end up together'. José seems to be threatening her if she were to betray him. There follows a trio in which Frasquita and Mercédès rather frivolously hope to read their fortunes in the cards.

When Carmen joins them the tone of the music darkens and the fate theme is heard. She immediately turns up cards that foretell the deaths of herself and then Don José, and sings a tragic cantilena ('En vain pour éviter les réponses amères') asserting that the cards never lie. Somewhat artificially the other girls resume their lighthearted song, with doomladen interjections from Carmen. The smugglers decide to proceed into the city since the three girls can take care of the three guards on duty (José smarts with jealousy at this suggestion). José is posted nearby to guard their things. To a rousing ensemble in jaunty style, with some effective and very characteristic harmonic twists, the smugglers set off for the city.

Micaëla now arrives at the deserted encampment, led by a guide who seems more frightened than she is. She sings an air ('Je dis que rien ne m'épouvante') with prominent parts for four horns which is in essence a prayer for strength. Its sweet sentiment in the outer sections encloses a more dramatic middle section. She espies José and calls out to him, at which he fires his rifle, thinking she is an intruder. She dives for cover, and at that very moment, against all probability, Escamillo enters, hat in hand. The bullet has narrowly missed him.

José appears and challenges him. In the duet that follows, Escamillo at once reveals that he has come to find Carmen, with whom he is in love. José, enraged, draws his knife. A fight ensues in which at first Escamillo has José on the ground but spares his life. They resume, and this time Escamillo is floored by José, who is about to strike when Carmen and Le Dancaïre appear on the scene. (Bizet shortened the

fight considerably in 1875.) Carmen thus saves Escamillo's life. The toreador invites them all to his next bullfight in Seville, while José can barely restrain himself. Escamillo leaves to a ravishing version of the Toreador Song in D♭ major scored for four cellos. The smugglers are about to set off when Le Remendado discovers Micaëla hiding. She immediately resumes her great melody from Act l, imploring José to return to his mother. Carmen too suggests he should go, whereupon in a thrilling burst of defiance José, insane with jealousy, declares he will stay with Carmen, even if it costs him his life. Micaëla then reveals that his mother is in fact dying. This changes his mind. As Escamillo's voice is again heard in the distance, José and Micaëla rush off.

Act 4 *Outside the bullring in Seville* The entr'acte, based on some Spanish songs compiled by Manuel García, is a lively Spanish dance which sets the tone for the final scene. Street sellers are busy calling their wares to the crowd. In the dialogue, Frasquita learns from Zuniga that an order for José's arrest has been issued but that he has not been found. Frasquita is alarmed for Carmen's safety. To the lively music that began the prelude a procession begins, culminating in the arrival of Escamillo, acclaimed by all. He and Carmen exchange a brief sentimental duet in which she declares her love for him. The Alcalde takes his place at the head of the procession. Frasquita warns Carmen that José is there in the crowd, but Carmen affects not to be afraid and even waits outside while everyone else enters the bullring. She confronts José boldly, and although he implores her, gently at first, to make a new life with him, she insists that she cannot be untrue to herself and that all is over between them. Although she knows her life is in danger, she never wavers. José's passionate pleas are in vain. Cries of victory are heard from the bullring. As Carmen moves towards the entrance, José bars her way, and even in the face of such danger she affirms her love for Escamillo. The fate theme is heard ever more menacingly. She throws down the ring José had given her, triggering José's rage. He stabs her and she falls dead. The Toreador Song is heard off stage. As the screen opens and a triumphant Escamillo appears with the crowd, José stands over Carmen's body and gives himself up.

*

Carmen's success may be attributed to its felicitous inclusion of conventionally comic and sentimental scenes alongside stark realism and a tale of risqué morality. Its exoticism is due to more than just the Spanish setting, for if a tavern and a smugglers' hide-out were familiar operatic settings, the atmosphere of the bullring and the outrageous behaviour of the cigarette girls brought a new dimension to the operatic stage. Yet much of the opera is not Spanish at all. It belongs to the tradition of French *opéra comique*, as we can tell both from the dialogue and from the two-verse songs which give the singer an opportunity to present himself to his listeners on both sides of the footlights. Carmen's Habanera in Act 1 and Escamillo's *couplets*, the Toreador Song, are of this kind, both crowned by rousing choral refrains (although the latter is a famous example of Bizet's often less than fastidious word-setting). The depiction of the two smugglers Le Dancaïre and Le Remendado as comic figures belongs to the same tradition. There is also a strong strain of French lyricism derived from Gounod, Bizet's devoted mentor; Gounod jokingly said that Micaëla's Air in Act 3, 'Je dis que rien ne m'épouvante', was stolen from him. It faithfully echoes his style in such works as *Roméo et Juliette* (on which Bizet had worked as pianist and assistant). So too does José's Flower Song, which is miraculously touched by Bizet's genius; Gounod would never have incorporated so fine a solo within an extended duet, as Bizet does. Also derived from Gounod is the character of Escamillo, a first cousin of Ourrias, the braggart cowherd from the Camargue in *Mireille*, which Bizet also knew well.

Neither Micaëla nor Escamillo is of any importance in Mérimée's novel. They were introduced by the librettists as balancing characters to make the story convincingly operatic. Micaëla's devotion to Don José, her purity and her attachment to his dying mother make Carmen's personality all the more brazen, although the contrast is not simply one of goodness and badness. Escamillo is the irresistible lure that entices Carmen from Don José, although the bullfighter, unlike the soldier, would never shed a tear over her infidelity.

Above all, Bizet had reached the peak of his inventive powers, bestowing on this score such melodic, harmonic and orchestral richness that every number seems to be shaped to perfection. He had never before had such a strong libretto, and never before did he have such a consistent stream of inspiration at his command. The memorability of Bizet's tunes will keep the music of *Carmen* alive in perpetuity, and the title role will always be a challenge for great singing actresses. No other French opera has ever achieved the same status as a popular classic.   H.M.

Castor et Pollux ('Castor and Pollux')

Tragédie en musique in a prologue and five acts by Jean-Philippe Rameau to a libretto by Pierre-Joseph Bernard; Paris, Académie Royale de Musique (Opéra), 24 October 1737.

The first cast included Denis-François Tribou (Castor), Claude Chassé de Chinais (Pollux), Marie

Pélissier (Telaira) and the dancers Marie Sallé and Louis Dupré.

Minèrve [Minerva]	soprano
L'Amour [Cupid]	haute-contre (or soprano)
Mars	baritone
Vénus [Venus]	soprano
Phébé [Phoebe] *a Spartan princess*	soprano
Télaïre [Telaira] *daughter of the Sun*	soprano
Pollux *son of Jupiter and Leda*	bass
Two Athletes	haute-contre, bass
The High Priest of Jupiter	tenor
A Follower of Hébé [Hebe]	soprano
Castor *son of Tyndareus and Leda*	haute-contre
A Blessed Spirit	soprano
Jupiter	bass
Mercure [Mercury]	dancer
	[haute-contre in revised version]
A Planet	soprano
Cléone *Phoebe's confidante* [revised version only]	soprano

Arts and Pleasures, Spartans, athletes, priests of Jupiter, Celestial Pleasures, Hebe's attendants, demons, Blessed Spirits, stars

Setting Sparta; the Elysian Fields

At its first appearance, Rameau's third opera was only moderately successful. Audiences compared it unfavourably with *Hippolyte et Aricie* and *Les Indes galantes* which, though initially controversial, had by now gained support among open-minded opera-goers. This cool reception explains the brevity of *Castor*'s first run – 21 performances compared with about 40 for *Hippolyte* and 64 for *Les Indes* – despite a distinguished cast.

Exceptionally, *Castor* had to wait 18 years for a revival: it reappeared in June 1754, at the height of the Querelle des Bouffons (the dispute over the respective merits of French and Italian opera). This time the opera was ecstatically received: it was widely seen (with *Platée*, revived earlier that year) as a more effective counterblast to the Bouffonistes than any of the pro-French pamphlets. By the time it was revived again in 1764, equally triumphantly, *Castor* had come to be seen as Rameau's crowning achievement. Among the cast was the young Sophie Arnould as Telaira, a role eventually regarded as one of her finest. The work, increasingly disfigured by cuts and additions, remained in the repertory until 1785 – longer than any of Rameau's others; some of the music was still performed at the Opéra as late as 1817. The first modern revival, organized by Charles Bordes, took place at Montpellier on 23 January 1908 and the work was presented in a concert performance at the Schola Cantorum, Paris, six days later.

*

Revival of Rameau's 'Castor et Pollux' (1754 version) by the English Bach Festival in 1981

Prologue *Ruined buildings and mutilated statues; in the distance, military camps* Minerva implores Venus and Cupid to subdue Mars with the power of love. During a *symphonie* contrasting trumpet and flute, Mars and Venus descend: the symbols of war disappear and those of the Arts and Pleasures are restored. Mars, his heart softened, announces the return of peace. The ensuing *divertissement* is rich in graceful and varied airs and dances, among them a tambourin, later reused in the *Pièces de clavecin en concerts* (1741), and a menuet from the *Nouvelles suites de pièces de clavecin* (c1729–30).

Act I *The Spartan kings' burial place* Castor, mortal twin of the immortal Pollux, has been slain by Lyncaeus. As they prepare for Castor's funeral, the Spartans mourn. Their chorus 'Que tout gémisse', from which the opening chorus of Gluck's *Orfeo* is descended, is notable for its chromatic ritornellos and quasi-religious character. (At Rameau's own memorial services it was indeed adapted as a Kyrie.) Alone with Phoebe, who is in love with Pollux, Telaira is disconsolate: what compensation is vengeance for the loss of one's dearest love? She renounces the light of day now that Castor can no longer experience it; in her monologue 'Tristes apprêts' Rameau eschews chromatic extremes and the minor mode, capturing the dignity of Telaira's sorrow by means of simple but telling harmony and a sombre bassoon obbligato. Pollux enters with athletes and soldiers bearing Lyncaeus's body. Their victory chorus 'Que l'Enfer applaudisse' is interspersed with recollections of Castor's fate. The

athletes' dances re-enact the battle. After they have left, Pollux offers Telaira his love as a substitute for Castor's. Telaira is taken aback but exploits this revelation, persuading Pollux to ask his father Jupiter to restore Castor to life.

Act 2 *The vestibule of Jupiter's temple, prepared for a sacrifice* In 'Nature, Amour, qui partage mon coeur', an elegiac soliloquy characterized by drooping scales of paired quavers, Pollux resignedly debates the implications of Telaira's request. When she arrives, Pollux compares his fate unfavourably with his brother's: Castor's life was short, but at least he had the satisfaction of pleasing Telaira. Jupiter descends. At first he refuses Pollux's request, but eventually he reveals the price his son must pay: if Castor is restored to life, Pollux must take his place. Pollux selflessly agrees. Jupiter commands Hebe, goddess of eternal youth, to remind Pollux of what he would sacrifice by renouncing immortality. Hebe sends her Celestial Pleasures to reveal, in a series of exquisitely sensual airs and dances, a vision of eternal bliss. Pollux is unmoved: breaking the garlands which bind him, he departs.

Act 3 *The fiery cavern at the entrance to Hades, guarded by monsters* The spurned Phoebe exhorts the Spartans to bar their king from hell. When Pollux brushes her aside, she resolves to end her life by following him to the underworld. Phoebe's despair increases when she learns of his love for Telaira. As Pollux prepares to enter the cavern he, Telaira and Phoebe sing a short trio in which each reflects on the outcome of the mission. Demons emerge from hell. In the tersely contrapuntal trio 'Sortez de l'esclavage', Pollux and Telaira fend them off while Phoebe encourages them. The demons threaten Pollux, their chorus 'Brisons tous nos fers' menacingly unmelodic. Mercury descends, strikes the demons with his caduceus and disappears with Pollux into Hades.

Act 4 *The Elysian Fields* Castor has found no happiness in Elysium. His nostalgic soliloquy 'Séjour de l'éternelle paix', dominated by plaintive dotted rhythms for flutes and strings, captures the heartache of separation. In a sequence of ethereal choruses and airs, the Blessed Spirits vainly try to divert him. When Pollux appears, the brothers greet each other ecstatically. Castor is overjoyed that he will again see the light of day but disconcerted by Pollux's confession of love for Telaira. When he learns the price of freedom – Pollux's own life – Castor refuses. He eventually agrees to return to Telaira, but for a single day: afterwards he will go back to Elysium and let Pollux regain his life and love. Mercury appears as Castor's escort, while the Blessed Spirits implore him to return.

Act 5 *A pleasant prospect in Sparta* Having seen the lovers reunited, Phoebe expresses impotent rage ('Soulevons tous les Dieux'). When Telaira, alone with Castor, realizes that his return is temporary she is incredulous; but Castor holds to his promise, despite her pleas and taunts. Thunder is heard and Jupiter descends. Declaring Destiny satisfied, he absolves Castor of his oath and grants him immortality. As the twins are reunited, Pollux renounces his love for Telaira: he has been so moved by Castor's selflessness that he can let nothing cloud his happiness. The only victim, he reveals, is Phoebe, who is now in Hades. Jupiter commands the skies to open, revealing the Zodiac with the Sun crossing it and gods assembled around Olympia's temple. During a Festival of the Universe, the Heavenly Twins take their places in the Zodiac, while Telaira is granted a place in the firmament. A Planet sings an *ariette*, 'Brillez, astres nouveaux', the orchestral parts characteristically more elaborate than the vocal line. Of the dances, the finest is the chaconne. Another, the 'Entrée des Astres', reworks part of the overture, a device Rameau was to develop extensively.

*

For the 1754 revival, Bernard and Rameau made substantial changes. The dramatically irrelevant prologue was omitted: in commemorating the Peace of Vienna (1736) it was no longer topical. (Besides, most French operas after 1749 were given without prologues.) A new expository act was inserted before Act 1. Here, Telaira is to marry Pollux although she loves Castor. As she prepares for the wedding, Castor discloses his own feelings but, to her distress, plans self-imposed exile rather than be forever reminded of his hopeless love. Pollux, overhearing

this conversation, vetoes his brother's plan. To their astonishment, he encourages Castor to marry Telaira, since he cannot bear to see the unhappiness of the two he values most. The Spartans congratulate the lovers and praise Pollux's magnanimity. Their *divertissement* is curtailed by news that Lyncaeus is attacking the palace in an attempt to abduct Telaira. The brothers take up arms. Sounds of battle are interrupted by sudden silence, whereupon an offstage voice announces Castor's death. The Spartans call for vengeance. During the entr'acte (an adaptation of a *bruit de guerre* from the 1744 *Dardanus*) the noise of battle continues.

To compensate for this new material, the original Acts 1 and 2 now became 2 and 3 respectively while the former Acts 3 and 4 were combined. In the process, many details were changed. Mercury was now played by a singer rather than a dancer. The role of Phoebe was expanded, though not improved, by the assignment to her of magic powers, and she now has a confidante, Cléone. Moreover, the libretto was pruned by well over a quarter, a compression achieved largely by cutting recitative.

As with most of Rameau's revisions, dramatic gains involved musical pruning. In the case of *Castor* this is comparatively slight. True, the outstandingly beautiful but irrelevant prologue was omitted, but several of the best pieces were moved to the Act 4 *divertissement*. Almost all the most memorable movements remain, including the *tombeau* 'Que tout gémisse', Telaira's 'Tristes apprêts' and Castor's 'Séjour de l'éternelle paix'. One exception is Pollux's soliloquy 'Nature, Amour'; yet his new air, 'Présent des dieux', is a hymn to friendship as affecting as the piece it replaces. Of three fine new *ariettes*, 'Tendre Amour, qu'il est doux' (Act 5 scene v) must be one of the most purely beautiful of its kind. Rameau here resists the temptation to end with brilliant display; instead he provides Castor with an air of exquisite tenderness, enriched in the final section by the unexpected but beguiling entry of the semi-chorus. Among the ballet movements there are many substitutions, seldom for the worse. Much of the new music is orchestrated in the more varied style which Rameau had developed by the 1750s. Even so, the 1754 orchestra is less colourful than that in several of the operas prior to the revision.

In its emphasis on brotherly love *Castor* was unusual, since French opera of the period reserved a central role for the romantic kind. Bernard's libretto has many virtues: not only does it provide convincing pretexts for ballet and spectacle, but it develops logically; especially in the revised version, it is arguably the tautest, best constructed and most elegant of any that Rameau set. *Castor* may lack the elements of pure tragedy that make *Hippolyte et Aricie* such a powerful if flawed masterpiece, but it compensates for this with an abundance of conflicts of sentiment: the struggle between Pollux's inclination and duty, the complication of his love for Telaira, Phoebe's jealousy, the conflict provoked by the twins' mutual affection where neither can bear to benefit at the other's expense. Despite this, the opera has an evenness of tone unique among Rameau's *tragédies*. Much of the music is characterized by an ethereal, nostalgic beauty, while the lean, athletic style adopted in the more energetic episodes seems a deliberate evocation of the conventional image of Lycurgus's Sparta, anachronistic though that is to the Castor myth.   G.Sa.

Cavalleria rusticana ('Rustic Chivalry')

Melodramma in one act by Pietro Mascagni to a libretto by Giovanni Targioni-Tozzetti and Guido Menasci after Giovanni Verga's play based on his story; Rome, Teatro Costanzi, 17 May 1890.

The singers in the first performance included Gemma Bellincioni (Santuzza) and Roberto Stagno (Turiddu), later husband and wife; the conductor was Leopoldo Mugnone.

Santuzza *a young peasant woman*	soprano
Turiddu *a young peasant*	tenor
Lucia *his mother, an innkeeper*	contralto
Alfio *a carrier*	baritone
Lola *Alfio's wife*	mezzo-soprano
Villagers	

Setting A village in Sicily on Easter Sunday 1880

Verga's play *Cavalleria rusticana* received its first performance in the Teatro Carignano, Turin, on 14 January 1884 with Eleanora Duse as Santuzza. Mascagni saw it less than a month later in Milan but did not think of making it into an opera until June 1888, when he read in *Il secolo* that the publisher Edoardo Sonzogno had announced the second competition for a one-act opera (Puccini had unsuccessfully submitted *Le villi* for the first). Mascagni commissioned the libretto from his fellow-citizen Targioni-Tozzetti who, worried about his ability to satisfy the precise terms of the competition, enlisted the help of another Livornese writer, Menasci. The libretto was ready in December 1888, the opera in May 1889; part of it was sent to Puccini and he in turn sent it to the publisher Giulio Ricordi, who failed to realize its worth, thus losing a golden opportunity. Needless to say, the opera, Mascagni's first apart from a rarely performed operetta, won the competition and made a fortune for Sonzogno, who had arranged that the short season at the Teatro Costanzi

in Rome would include the operas of the three finalists. Mascagni's masterpiece was a resounding success and within a few months had been rapturously received in all the principal cities of Europe and America. For over a century it has found a place in the repertory of leading singers and conductors, from Mahler, who conducted it in Budapest and included it in the programmes of the Vienna Staatsoper, through Hermann Levi and Felix Weingartner to Herbert von Karajan, among more recent performers. Today *Cavalleria* is usually paired with Ruggero Leoncavallo's *Pagliacci*, a work of similar concision from which it has become virtually inseparable.

*

During the prelude, before the curtain rises, Turiddu is heard singing of his love for Lola (siciliana, 'O Lola ch'hai di latti la cammisa'); his voice, accompanied by offstage harps, at once places Sicily at the core of the action. As the curtain rises many of the villagers are going into church. Santuzza is in distress; she has been seduced by Turiddu, whom she loves, and is pregnant, but he has returned to his earlier love who, tired of waiting for him to return from army duty, has married Alfio.

Mascagni's instinct was primarily to create, through a series of continuous scenes, a fluid background to the individual passions. In the first scene, devoted to the Sicilian peasants, the atmosphere of an important religious feast is conveyed by an attractive orchestral waltz, a barrel-organ piece above which the chorus is heard and which reappears when the church service is over. Turiddu's entrance is delayed until interest in him has been aroused by the siciliana. In a dramatic dialogue Santuzza starts to tell Mamma Lucia about her sorry situation, but they are interrupted by the arrival of Alfio. He asks for Turiddu, and is told that he is away fetching wine supplies for the tavern; but Alfio says that he saw Turiddu only that morning near his house. Alfio makes his entrance with a character-piece ('Il cavallo scalpita') in which, like Bizet's toreador, he boasts about his occupation, accompanied by the chorus; but there is in his song an element of ambiguity arising from the syncopation and the sinister nature of the melody and harmony in the middle section, which give the lie without a trace of irony to Alfio's words ('Mi aspetta a casa Lola, che m'ama e mi consola').

As he leaves, Santuzza leads the chorus of peasants in the Easter hymn, the powerful prayer ('Inneggiamo, il Signor non è morto') that follows the *Regina coeli* of the offstage chorus. The tripartite Romanza e Scena rounds out her portrait in a generous and sensuous but elegant vocal line that remains within the traditional stylized limits: the middle section is skilfully crafted from variants of the tragedy motif, and the number ends with a final reference to the prelude.

Santuzza now tells Lucia everything: Turiddu has abandoned her and visits Lola secretly in Alfio's frequent absences. Santuzza feels she cannot enter the church because of her sin. On Turiddu's entrance she berates him for lying: the beginning of his duet with her ('Tu qui, Santuzza?'), the first of four sections, takes the form of a recitative interspersed with brief arioso passages. The tension approaches a climax but is frozen for a few moments by the simple *stornello*, 'Fior di gaggiolo', which Lola begins to sing off stage. It is clear that Lola is a heartless, shallow flirt; she upsets Santuzza, and the tension explodes with renewed force in the continuation of the duet after Lola has gone into the church and her melody is recalled on the flute.

Turiddu makes to follow her but Santuzza tries to hold him back; he scorns her and goes after Lola. Alfio returns looking for his wife, and in her anger and distress Santuzza blurts out what is going on. Alfio gives vent to his rage. The tension between Santuzza and Turiddu is resolved in the melodic impulse of the vocal line, with high *appassionato* phrases in the first violins doubled at various octaves by the orchestra, and in the contrast between sonorities and dynamics: the marking *quasi parlato* is placed only on Santuzza's 'Mala Pasqua', though it is often disregarded by the singer. The ensuing duet for Alfio and Santuzza ends with a fiery cabaletta in F minor ('Ad essi non perdono') .

All the tension that has accumulated up to this point is channelled into the Intermezzo, a hymn in F based on the melody of the *Regina coeli* with which the service began, metrically varied and doubled by the violins with a simple chorale-like harmonization. Played with the curtain up, it marks the end of the Easter ceremony, but the story continues to unfold, the serenity of village life being contrasted with the passions devouring the main characters.

Everyone emerges from church, Turiddu and Lola together. He invites his friends to go to his mother's inn. Alfio joins them, but refuses a drink. After the orchestral reprise of the waltz heard at the beginning, mingling with the sound of bells and followed by the chorus, the tonality is raised to G for Turiddu's brindisi, 'Viva il vino spumeggiante', one of the most brilliant drinking-songs in all opera. It conveys well the atmosphere of nervous excitement surrounding Turiddu and Alfio at the moment of the challenge and prepares the tragic ending. As the women nervously withdraw, Alfio challenges his rival. Turiddu bids farewell to his mother, asking her to take care of Santuzza; he goes off and the fight takes place off stage. The anxious whispering of divided violins accompanies the fragmented recitative in which Turiddu addresses his mother; he takes his leave of her ('Mamma, quel vino è generoso') in an impassioned progression towards

the top note, a last *cri de coeur* before the cries of the women off stage announce that he has been killed and the tragedy motif brings the opera to an end.

*

All the tragic elements of the story are concentrated in a musical framework calculated to convey maximum immediacy. In this Mascagni followed a line of logical adherence to the traditional plan of 19th-century opera, returning to the closed numbers already abandoned by Verdi: although the prelude appears at first to be typical in its exposition of the principal melodies of the work, the way in which they are later recalled re-evokes its entire structure in the listener's memory, with the orchestral crescendo interrupted by the siciliana and resumed more strongly when the voice behind the curtain ceases. In the continuation of the duet between Santuzza and Turiddu, the central point of the drama, the reprise of the prelude is in the orchestra only, intensifying the emotion of the concluding *appassionato* section.

Mascagni attained his aim of creating an opera realistically dominated by sentiment by using formal means, more effective in their subtlety than openly veristic and impassioned ones, of which there are indeed few. Conscious of the need to write an 'Italian' work, he made use above all of the special qualities of the closed number and its interaction with recitative. The melody on the lower strings that accompanies Santuzza's entrance is in effect a leitmotif, reminiscent of the theme that concludes the overture to *Carmen*. In using it in proximity to the song of Alfio, Turiddu's executioner, which immediately follows, Mascagni links him with Santuzza as different facets of a common destiny, the motif itself being linked not so much to Santuzza as to the deadly destiny she brings. It reappears at all the high points of the drama, from the *romanza* to the 'Mala Pasqua' she tragically hurls at Turiddu, before concluding the opera and so revealing itself as the musical symbol of the tragic ending. This sense of conclusion is reinforced by the use of the key of F at crucial moments, from the prelude (in the major) to the central series of numbers and the Intermezzo, and to the final statement, in the minor, of the 'tragedy' motif.

It has often been said that Verga's *Cavalleria* inaugurated the *verismo* period in Italian theatre. Mascagni stressed his adherence to the play as his source, insisting that it was Verga's treatment of the subject which had spurred him to set it and rejecting the idea of a close affinity between his opera and Bizet's *Carmen*. But *Cavalleria* is as closely linked to the French opera, which, as the box-office hit of the day, was widely admired and imitated, as it is to Verga's text, which was performed everywhere and so available to any composer in need of a good subject.

1. 'Acis and Galatea' (Handel, 1718), the 1966 English Opera Group production with Elizabeth Harwood as Galatea

2. 'Adriana Lecouvreur' (Cilea, 1902), poster printed for the publisher Edoardo Sonzogno at the time of the first production at the Teatro Lirico, Milan

Above: 3. *'Aida' (Verdi, 1871), scene from the production by Gianfranco De Bosio at the Arena di Verona, 1982*

Left: 4. *'Akhnaten' (Glass, 1984), scene from the 1985 English National Opera production by David Freeman (designed by David Roger) at the London Coliseum, with Christopher Robson in the title role*

5. 'Andrea Chénier' (Giordano, 1896), scene from the production (in association with Cologne Opera) directed by Michael Hampe (sets William Orlandi, costumes Franca Squarciapino) at the Royal Opera House, Covent Garden, 1984, with José Carreras, Rosalind Plowright and Bernd Weikl

6. 'Anna Bolena' (Donizetti), set design by Alessandro Sanquirico for Windsor Castle in the original production at the Teatro Carcano, Milan, in 1830

7. 'Arabella' (Richard Strauss, 1933), scene from Act 2 of the English National Opera production by Jonathan Miller (sets Patrick Robertson, costumes Rosemary Vercoe) at the London Coliseum, 1980, with Josephine Barstow (Arabella), Peter Glossop (Mandryka) and Marilyn Hill Smith (the Fiakermilli)

8. 'Ariadne auf Naxos' (Richard Strauss, 1912), scene from the production by Elijah Moshinsky (sets and costumes Michael Yeargan) at the Metropolitan Opera, New York, 1993, with Jessye Norman (Ariadne), Ruth Ann Swenson (Zerbinetta) and Mark Oswald (Harlequin)

Above: 9. 'Atys' (Lully, 1676), anonymous set design for the Prologue in a Paris revival, probably of 1708

Below: 10. 'Un ballo in maschera' (Verdi, 1859), Act 1 scene ii in the production directed by Götz Friedrich (designed by Gottfried Pilz and Isabel Ines Glathar) at the Deutsche Oper, Berlin, in 1993

11. 'Il Barbiere di Siviglia' (Rossini), scene from the English National Opera production directed by Jonathan Miller (designed by Tanya McCallin) at the London Coliseum, 1993, with Alan Opie (Figaro), Louise Winter (Rosina), Paul Nilon (Count Almaviva), Richard Van Allan (Don Basilio) and Andrew Shore (Bartolo)

12. 'The Bartered Bride' (Smetana, 1866), scene from the production by Rudolf Noelte (sets Jan Schlubach, costumes Elisabeth Urbancic) for the Welsh National Opera, 1989

Right: *13. 'Benvenuto Cellini' (Berlioz, 1838), scene from the production (designed by Beni Montresor) at the Royal Opera House, Covent Garden, 1976, with Nicolai Gedda in the title role*

Below: *14. 'Billy Budd' (Britten, 1951), scene from the production by Francesca Zambello (designer Alison Chitty) at the Royal Opera House, Covent Garden, 1995, with Rodney Gilfry in the title role*

15. 'La Bohème' (Puccini, 1896),
scene from Act 1 of the 1974 John
Copley production (designed by Julia
Trevelyan-Oman), at the Royal Opera
House, Covent Garden, with Katia
Ricciarelli as Mimi and Placido
Domingo as Rodolfo

Carmen was in reality a decisive model for the dramatic composition of *Cavalleria*, not only because jealousy is in both cases the driving force of the action and its bloody outcome (presented more realistically on stage in the French work), but above all because Bizet had chosen a subject set not in the remote East as was then fashionable but under more familiar Mediterranean skies, clearly indicating a shift in stylistic influence. Mascagni sketched in the local background from the beginning, including an example of the dialect siciliana within the prelude, so providing a true prologue to the action in his use of a formal element that breaks with tradition but is consonant with the rustic code of honour of the melodrama. Sicily is several times evoked in the course of the opera, with a descriptive capacity arguably even greater than Bizet's prelude and the *chanson bohémienne*.

The entire structure of *Cavalleria*, in which almost all the action occurs while the Easter Mass is taking place in the church, mirrors Act 4 of *Carmen*, where the enthusiasm of the spectators at the bullfight serves as background to the murder of the Spanish gypsy. But here too Mascagni outdoes his model, in which collective pleasure is contrasted with individual tragedy and the new lover with the old, because the church that dominates the square, and the popular devotion expressed in the Easter hymn, symbolize the violated innocence of Santuzza, more dishonoured by Alfio's insult to Turiddu.

Cavalleria rusticana achieved a perfect balance between all its components, the dominant feature still being stylization in the 19th-century sense. Even such possible defects as the conventional orchestration and academic harmony have their place in the dramatic characterization, combined with felicitous melodic invention and an original way of handling the standard formal operatic situations so as to please both the traditional Italian opera-going public and that of foreign theatres in a nostalgic frame of mind. Mascagni's masterpiece hastened the end of an epoch by exhausting its possibilities, leaving to Puccini the task of representing Italy in the context of international opera and the *fin-de-siècle* crisis. It was soon evident that this national path led nowhere, and the spirit of his unrepeatable masterpiece haunted its composer for the rest of his life.   M.G.

Cendrillon ('Cinderella')

Conte de fées in four acts by Jules Massenet to a libretto by Henri Cain after Charles Perrault's fairy-tale of the same title (published in *Contes de ma mère l'oye*, 1698); Paris, Opéra-Comique (Salle Favart), 24 May 1899.

The title role at the first performance was sung by Julia Guiraudon, an Opéra-Comique Micaëla and Mimì who later married Cain; the Fairy Godmother by Georgette Bréjean-Gravière (later Bréjean-Silver), Madame de la Haltière by Blanche Deschamps-Jehin, Prince Charming by Mlle Emelan and Pandolfe by Lucien Fugère. The conductor was Alexandre Luigini, composer of the infamous *Ballet égyptien*.

Cendrillon	soprano
Madame de la Haltière	
her stepmother	mezzo-soprano
Le Prince Charmant [Prince	
Charming]	soprano ('Falcon')
La Fée [Fairy Godmother]	coloratura soprano
Noémie ⎱ *Cendrillon's*	soprano
Dorothée ⎰ *stepsisters*	mezzo-soprano
Pandolfe *her father*	bass
Le Roi [The King]	baritone
Le Doyen de la Faculté	tenor
Le Surintendant des plaisirs	baritone
Le Premier Ministre	bass
Fairies, servants, courtiers, doctors, ministers	

Preliminary plans for *Cendrillon* were apparently laid at the Cavendish Hotel, Jermyn Street (later made famous by its flamboyant proprietress Rosa Lewis), when Massenet and Cain were in London for the world première of their *épisode lyrique La Navarraise* in 1894. The score was completed in 1896, the year in which Massenet first declined the directorship of the Conservatoire and resigned from the chair of composition to devote himself full-time to the theatre. The première planned for the following year was postponed until 1899; it was one of the first important premières in the regime of Albert Carré, who was appointed director of the Opéra-Comique after the death of Léon Carvalho in December 1897. (Before the dress rehearsal Carré persuaded Massenet to cut a Prologue in which the characters introduce themselves to the audience, but a brief epilogue in which they step out of character survives.)

The lavish production as well as the quality of the music ensured an immediate success for *Cendrillon*: there were 50 performances before the end of 1899. The charm of the work conquered even the habitual sarcasm – when writing about Massenet – of 'Willy' (Henri Gauthier Villars, the publisher and Colette's first husband). *Cendrillon* was staged frequently on both sides of the Atlantic in the first 15 years of its existence; there was a notable production in Chicago in 1911 with Maggie Teyte in the title role and Mary Garden as the Prince. Lord Berners was responsible for the British stage première in Swindon in 1939. The work has never entirely lapsed from the repertory, and has enjoyed frequent revivals in recent years. There is a complete recording with Frederica von

'Cendrillon' (Massenet), Act 3 (a magic landscape around a great oak tree) in the original production at the Opéra-Comique (Salle Favart), Paris, 24 May 1899, with Julia Guiraudon (Cendrillon, left), Georgette Bréjean-Gravière (Fairy Godmother, in the oak tree) and Mlle Emelan (Prince Charming): photograph from 'Le théâtre' (July 1899)

Stade, alas with a tenor in the travesty role of the Prince: there is neither authority nor tradition for this reprehensible practice.

*

Act I *A state room in Madame de la Haltière's town house, with a large chimney-piece* Servants bustle to prepare for the ball. The henpecked Pandolfe wonders why he ever left his country estate to take as his second wife an overbearing countess with two daughters ('Ai-je quitté ma ferme et nos grands bois!'), and pities the lot of his own child Lucette (Cendrillon). He leaves as his wife enters to instruct her daughters on strategy ('Le bal est un champ de bataille') and supervise a troupe of milliners, tailors and hairdressers. Pandolfe, late for departure, is not allowed to say goodnight to his daughter. Cendrillon enters and, in a quasi-folksong not dissimilar to Rossini's in the parallel situation (see *Cenerentola, la*), sits by the fire to regret her lot ('Reste au foyer, petit grillon') before falling asleep. Her Fairy Godmother appears in a flurry of coloratura and to a graceful waltz orders her attendants to dress Cendrillon for the ball ('Pour en faire un tissu'). She warns her charge to leave before midnight, and tells her that the glass slippers are a talisman to prevent her being recognized by her family.

Act 2 *The royal palace* A gaggle of courtiers and a stage band of glass flute, lute and viola d'amore fail to alleviate the melancholy that the Prince shares with his counterpart in Gozzi's (and Prokofiev's) *L'amore delle tre melarance* ('Coeur sans amour, printemps sans roses'). The King orders him to marry. Eligible princesses arrive in five danced entrées. The unknown beauty appears to a Rossinian unaccompanied concertato of general amazement, and the Prince launches a rapturous love-at-first-sight duet ('Toi qui m'es apparue'). She responds with a phrase of characteristic Massenetian simplicity, repeated in later acts, 'Vous êtes mon Prince Charmant'. As midnight strikes she hurries away, losing a slipper.

Act 3.i *As in Act I* Cendrillon relives the glamour of the ball and the terror of her precipitate nocturnal flight before singing once more of the *petit grillon*. The family returns. Madame de la Haltière reminds Pandolfe of her greatly superior ancestry (including a Doge, a dozen bishops, six abbesses and 'two or three royal mistresses') before disputing his account of the ball. According to her, the Prince and the courtiers decisively rejected the bold intruder. Pandolfe notices that Cendrillon is about to faint, finally loses his temper and brusquely orders the women from the room. In a duet of great tenderness he promises that he and Cendrillon will return to his country seat ('Viens, nous quitterons cette ville'). When he exits to prepare for the journey, Cendrillon gives way to despair: rather than allow her father to share her pain, she decides to run away and die on her own ('Adieu, mes souvenirs de joie').

3.ii *A magic landscape around a great oak tree* Fairies and will-o'-the-wisps interrupt their dance as Cendrillon and the Prince approach separately, and the Fairy Godmother conjures up a magic arbour so that they may hear but not see each other. After praying to be released from their misery, they recognize each other's voices and reaffirm their love in a mystical ceremony. The Prince hangs his bleeding heart on the oak, and both fall into an enchanted sleep.

Act 4.i *A terrace* Pandolfe watches over his sleeping daughter. Months have passed since she was found by a stream half dead with cold. In her delirium she has been singing about the ball, the mysterious oak, the bleeding heart and the missing slipper. None of this ever happened, her father assures her, and she resigns herself to having dreamt it all. They celebrate her recovery by greeting the spring ('Printemps revient'). Madame de la Haltière enters with the news of a grand assembly of princesses (from as far away as Japan, Norway and the banks of the Thames) to try on the glass slipper that was found, and Cendrillon joyfully realizes that her dream was true. To the glittering 'Marche des Princesses' (a favourite concert item) the scene changes.

4.ii *The palace* Cendrillon steps forward ('Vous êtes mon Prince Charmant'), and the opera ends amid general rejoicing.

*

Cendrillon is the Massenet opera most readily approachable by those with reservations about his idiom. His musical sense of humour, all too seldom given full rein, is here at its frothiest, and liberally spiced with dry Gallic wit. Variety is assured by the four distinct soundworlds conjured up to tell the fairy-tale: the vigour and pomp of the court music, with Massenet's best dance numbers apart from *Le Cid* and affectionate pastiche of classical forms from the ages of Lully and Rameau; the shimmering music for the fairy world, which has the airiness and harmonic savour of Mendelssohn crossed with Richard Strauss; the writing for Cendrillon and Pandolfe, showing Massenet at his most artlessly economical to match the simple virtues they represent; and the love music, which in its heavily perfumed chromaticism reminds one constantly how well Massenet knew his Wagner (as a student he may have played percussion in the Opéra orchestra at the famous *Tannhäuser* fiasco of 1861, and there are

distinct echoes of its Bacchanale in Act 2 of *Cendrillon*). The mystical marriage of Act 3 is one of the composer's most succulent love scenes.

The characteristic motifs – 'Vous êtes mon Prince Charmant', or the phrase associated with Cendrillon's dream – are recalled with more discretion than is often the case with this composer; indeed, *Cendrillon* could almost be subtitled 'the art of reminiscence'. All these elements serve to present through music a wide range of characters, with the broad comedy of the termagant Madame de la Haltière in neat counterpoint to the tender-hearted, downtrodden Pandolfe, whose humour is tinged with overwhelming melancholy. The way the latter role is written helps one to imagine the appeal of Fugère, for whom it was written. The treatment of Cendrillon and the Prince as lost, desperate children reinforces the musical reasons for never countenancing the casting of a tenor as the Prince. The whole character of the relationship is changed thereby from innocence to mere operatic sentiment.

R.M.

Cenerentola, La [*La Cenerentola, ossia La bontà in trionfo* ('Cinderella, or Goodness Triumphant')]

Dramma giocoso in two acts by Gioachino Rossini to a libretto by Jacopo Ferretti after Charles Perrault's *Cendrillon* and librettos by Charles-Guillaume Etienne for Nicolas Isouard's *Cendrillon* (1810, Paris) and Francesco Fiorini for Stefano Pavesi's *Agatina, o La virtù premiata* (1814, Milan); Rome, Teatro Valle, 25 January 1817.

Rossini's first Rosina, Geltrude Righetti Giorgi, sang Cenerentola in the first production, Giacomo Guglielmi sang Don Ramiro and Giuseppe de Begnis, Dandini. The Don Magnifico, Andrea Verni, had sung the same role at La Scala on 10 April 1814 in the first performance of Pavesi's Cinderella opera.

Cenerentola (Angelina) *Don Magnifico's step-daughter*	contralto
Don Ramiro *Prince of Salerno*	tenor
Dandini *valet to Don Ramiro*	bass
Don Magnifico *Baron of Monte Fiascone*	baritone
Clorinda } *his daughters*	soprano
Tisbe }	mezzo-soprano
Alidoro *a philosopher, tutor to Don Ramiro*	bass
Ladies and gentlemen of the Prince's court	
Setting Don Magnifico's mansion and the court of Don Ramiro	

Rossini was in Naples for six years (1816–22) under contract to the Teatro S Carlo, but he was able to undertake commissions for other theatres. He wrote

La Cenerentola in a little over three weeks in January 1817. As with two earlier comic masterpieces, *L'italiana in Algeri* and *Il barbiere di Siviglia*, Rossini and his librettist had important precedents with which to work, enabling a text to be assembled and musical and dramatic perspectives to be calculated in the shortest possible time. The première was noisily received by the Roman audience but the fiasco of the first night of *Il barbiere di Siviglia* was not repeated.

Rossini's opera quickly proved to be enormously popular in Italy and abroad. It was performed in Barcelona in April 1818, in London at the King's Theatre, Haymarket, in January 1820, and in Vienna, in German, the following August. In New York in 1826 it was given by Manuel García's company. In February 1844 it became the first opera to be performed in Australia. Distinguished interpreters of the title role in Rossini's time included Laure Cinti-Damoreau, Henriette Sontag, Maria Malibran, Pauline Viardot and Marietta Alboni, who appeared with the Royal Italian Opera at Covent Garden in 1848; Antonio Tamburini sang Dandini and Michael Costa conducted. Like many Rossini operas, *La Cenerentola* was performed only intermittently in the years following the composer's death in 1868, but it began to return to the repertory in the 1920s and early 1930s. In June 1934, Covent Garden staged the opera for the first time since 1848 with Conchita Supervia, the outstanding Cenerentola of the time, and a cast that included Dino Borgioli as Don Ramiro and Ezio Pinza as Don Magnifico; for this production ballet was added, choreographed by Ninette de Valois. The opera has received a number of distinguished revivals at the Glyndebourne Festival beginning in 1950 with Carl Ebert's production, to designs by Oliver Messel, conducted by the incomparable Vittorio Gui. Marina de Gabarain sang Cenerentola, Juan Oncina, Don Ramiro, and Sesto Bruscantini, Dandini. The EMI recording of the production remains one of the most charmingly idiomatic accounts of the opera on record. However, the 1973 La Scala revival, conducted by Claudio Abbado and also recorded, had the advantage of a new performing edition by Alberto Zedda; the production was by Jean-Pierre Ponnelle and the Cenerentola was Lucia Valentini-Terrani. On record, and at some later revivals, the role was sung by Teresa Berganza, one of the leading Rossini interpreters of her generation.

The recitatives and three of the 16 numbers performed at the première are not by Rossini and were not subsequently replaced by him. They are Alidoro's aria 'Vasto teatro è il mondo', the chorus 'Ah, della bella incognita', and Clorinda's aria 'Sventurata! Me credea'; according to Ferretti, these and the recitatives are the work of the Roman composer Luca Agolini. When the opera was revived at the Teatro Apollo, Rome, in December 1820

Rossini composed a new grand aria for Alidoro, 'Là del ciel nell'arcano profondo'; the text is also Ferretti's. The rondo that concludes the opera is an adaptation of Almaviva's final aria from *Il barbiere di Siviglia*. No overture was composed for *La Cenerentola*; instead Rossini used the overture to *La gazzetta*, the *opera buffa* which had first been performed in Naples in September 1816.

*

Act I.i *A room in the tumbledown castle of the Baron, Don Magnifico* Clorinda and Tisbe, the two ugly sisters, are locked in one of their habitual disputes while Cenerentola quietly goes about her household chores. As she works, she sings her favourite song 'Una volta c'era un re': the tale of a king who, bored by being alone, chooses a bride not for her ostentation or her wealth but for her innocence and her goodness. Rossini's sad, minor-key 'folk tune', which crops up several times during the opera, paints to perfection Cenerentola's solitary and expiatory mood. He also keeps sentimentality at bay as the song is cruelly mocked by the ugly sisters at its first reprise, the obsessive, birdlike tones of the two sopranos set, here and elsewhere, in stark contrast to Cenerentola's velvety contralto. A knock is heard at the door and Don Ramiro's tutor, Alidoro, appears disguised as a beggar. The sisters spurn him with disgust but Cenerentola manages surreptitiously to give him bread and a mug of coffee. The sisters' mood changes when courtiers announce the imminent arrival of Prince Ramiro, who proposes to escort Don Magnifico's two daughters to his palace; there festivities are to be held during which the Prince will choose a bride. The sisters immediately goad the servants into action, remorselessly chivvying the endlessly harassed Cenerentola in a brilliant stretta during which Alidoro and the courtiers look wryly on.

The hubbub arouses Don Magnifico who proceeds, in his cavatina 'Miei rampolli femminini', to relate the contents of a bizarre dream he has just had; the dream, he suggests somewhat improbably, presages royal connections for Clorinda, Tisbe and himself. When the prince, Don Ramiro, arrives disguised as his valet Dandini, the room is deserted. Alidoro has alerted him to the presence in the household of a woman worthy of his hand and he is determined to pursue the matter further. Cenerentola is so shocked to see the stranger that she drops a cup and saucer. The duet 'Un soave non so che', full of tenderness and shy, hesitant affection, reveals the mature Rossini's ability to point psychological detail within a long, evolving dramatic movement. For Cenerentola's gabbled and nonsensical 'Quel ch'è padre, non è padre' ('My father's not my father'), Rossini uses comic patter and a sinking tonality to convey to us Cenerentola's pathetically confused state of mind; he further heightens the tension by the brilliant use of minatory offstage calls from the ugly sisters.

The 'Prince', actually Dandini, finally makes his entrance with an absurdly grandiloquent cavatina in which he is joined by the chorus and Magnifico's sycophantic household (the 'beggar' is still there). The sisters leave for the ball but Ramiro and Dandini overhear Cenerentola's request that she may go too (quintet, 'Signor, una parola'). Magnifico refuses, gratuitously insulting the girl while at the same time trying to ingratiate himself with Ramiro and Dandini. Unhappily for him, Alidoro now chooses to re-enter, as himself, with information about a third daughter in the household. Magnifico blusters briefly and then, with Cenerentola standing beside him, he announces that the third daughter is in fact dead. In a naive aside, Cenerentola denies the story but Magnifico, warming to his morbid lie, repeats it with a chilling assumption of sincerity as the orchestra judders to one of opera's most shocked silences. Having reduced the audience to numbed disbelief, Rossini launches into one of those ensembles in which the characters attempt to work out with dispassionate concern who is duping whom. Alidoro, disguised once more as the beggar, returns to take Cenerentola to the ball. In the scena and aria added by Rossini for the 1820 Rome revival, 'Là del ciel nell'arcano profondo', Alidoro tells her of the Lord of Creation who will not allow innocence to be crushed.

I.ii *A room in Don Ramiro's country house* 'Prince' Dandini offers Don Magnifico the position of court vintner on the strength of his having sampled 30 barrels without signs of undue staggering. Newly installed, Magnifico passes a decree forbidding the adulteration of wine. The Act 1 finale begins with one of Rossini's finest conspiratorial duets, 'Zitto, zitto, piano, piano', as the Prince and Dandini briefly compare notes on their impressions so far of the Magnifico family. They are mystified by Alidoro's idea of one of the daughters' suitability. When Clorinda and Tisbe track the 'Prince' down he offers his servant Dandini as a possible husband. They are predictably outraged, but outrage turns to bemusement when a girl strangely resembling Cenerentola appears at the ball in the company of Alidoro. Confusion reigns but Dandini, in his role as enterprising puppet-master, announces a feast and the entire company takes off to dinner in a whirlwind stretta in which, not for the first time in a Rossini finale, the characters rue the fact that they no longer appear to be in touch with reality.

Act 2.i *A room in Don Ramiro's country house* The banquet is over but Don Magnifico harbours doubts about the progress he and his daughters are making. In the aria 'Sia qualunque delle figlie' he reassures

himself that he will eventually be the Prince's father-in-law. Tired of being pursued by 'Prince' Dandini, Cenerentola tells him that she prefers his servant. This is overheard by the Prince and Alidoro; overjoyed, the Prince reveals himself, but Cenerentola forbids him to follow her: if he truly loves her, she insists, he must search her out once she has left the court. She gives him a bracelet that matches one she always wears. In the bravura aria 'Sì, ritrovarla io giuro', the Prince resolves to find and win the mysterious girl. Meanwhile, Dandini is confronted by Magnifico demanding a decision on whom he is going to marry. Dandini launches a superb comic duet, 'Un segreto d'importanza', by counselling patience; then, choosing his moment carefully, he reveals to Magnifico that he is in fact the servant, which throws Magnifico into bewilderment and fury.

2.ii *A room in Don Magnifico's castle* Cenerentola, once more dressed in rags, is singing 'Una volta c'era un re'. Magnifico and his daughters return, remarking again on the similarity between Cenerentola and the guest at the ball. A splendid Rossinian storm breaks, during which Alidoro so arranges events that the Prince's carriage comes to grief right outside Don Magnifico's castle. Safely inside, the Prince soon recognizes Cenerentola, to the mingled joy and consternation of the various parties. They gradually unpick 'the snarled knot, the tangled web' in the great sextet 'Siete voi?' The magnificent 357-bar movement has its apogee in Cenerentola's great plea to the Prince that Magnifico and his daughters be forgiven, 'Ah, signor, s'è ver che in petto'. It is a moment that marks the final transformation of Cenerentola from mouse-like skivvy to a mature woman capable of real passion.

2.iii *The throne room in Don Ramiro's palace* The fairy-tale transformation of Cenerentola is completed in the final scene into which she enters in triumph to sing the showpiece scena and rondo finale 'Nacqui all'affanno e al pianto'. Here music originally drafted for Almaviva in the final scene of *Il barbiere di Siviglia* finds its proper voice and dramatic resting-place. In particular, a note of pathos and longing is struck amid the vocal triumphalism, making it a worthy conclusion to a score that is less purely comic than is sometimes supposed. Brilliantly entertaining as much of *La Cenerentola* is, it also reveals Rossini's unnervingly dispassionate gaze and, at times, his almost morbid sensitivity to the crueller and more venal aspects of human affairs.   R.O.

Christmas Eve [*Noch' pered rozhdestvom*]

'Carol come-to-life' (*bïl'-kolyadka*) in four acts by Nikolay Andreyevich Rimsky-Korsakov to his own libretto after the eponymous story in Nikolay Vasil'yevich Gogol's collection *Evenings on a Farm near Dikanka* (ii, 1832); St Petersburg, Mariinsky Theatre, 28 November/10 December 1895.

At the first performance the opera was conducted by Eduard Nápravník, with Ivan Yershov as Vakula, Yevgenia Mravina as Oxana and Fyodor Stravinsky as Panas (alternating with Fyodor Shalyapin in the first production).

Vakula *a blacksmith*	tenor
Solokha *his mother, a witch*	mezzo-soprano
The Devil	tenor
Chub	bass
Oxana *his daughter*	soprano
Panas	bass
The Mayor	baritone
The Priest	tenor
Woman with Purple Nose	mezzo-soprano
Woman with Ordinary Nose	soprano
Patsyuk *a medicine man*	bass
Tsaritsa	mezzo-soprano
Cossacks, witches, wizards, dancers, imps,	
fairies	

Composed in 1894–5, almost immediately after Tchaikovsky's sudden death, *Christmas Eve* was at least the fourth opera on Gogol's tale to be performed, the others being *Vakula kuznets* ('Vakula the Smith') by Tchaikovsky, its reincarnation as *Cherevichki* ('The Slippers'), and *Vakula kuznets* by Nikolay Solov'yov, written to the same libretto as Tchaikovsky's and for the same contest. 'Please note', Rimsky-Korsakov wrote sententiously to Alexander Glazunov, 'my opera is called *Christmas Eve*, not *Cherevichki* and not *Vakula kuznets*'. But in fact he used the Gogol tale as little more than a springboard for another essay in pantheistic primeval Slavonic mythology in the manner of *The Snow Maiden* – at the other end, so to speak, of the solar calendar.

*

Act I *Ist tableau* Solokha, a widow and the local witch, expresses her hopes for a new lover. The Devil, taking her up on this, conspires with her to steal the moon and whip up a blizzard; this makes difficulties for Solokha's son Vakula, who, in love with Oxana, Chub's daughter, comes out to serenade her. Chub and his friend Panas also have trouble finding their way in the darkness; they are intent on visiting the Priest in the hope of a drink or two, but get lost in the blizzard and Chub attempts to go home. Vakula, thinking Chub is a rival for Oxana's affections, gives him a beating.

2nd tableau Oxana, admiring herself in her mirror, feels that her beauty is unparalleled. When Vakula proposes, she responds, to his dismay, that she will accept only if he can bring her the ultimate Christmas present, a pair of the Tsaritsa's boots.

Act 2 *3rd tableau* Solokha and the Devil are getting cosily amorous when they are interrupted by the Mayor. The Devil hides in a sack. The next to seek Solokha's favours is the Priest, at whose entry the Mayor hides in a sack . . . this goes on until four sacks (the last containing Chub) are found by Vakula on his return. Grumbling at the weight, the blacksmith carries them out to the smithy.

4th tableau The villagers emerge to celebrate Christmas Eve, singing carols and collecting delicacies to take home. Vakula, in despair at Oxana's impossible request, goes miserably off with the smallest sack; the villagers eagerly open the others, to find three somewhat sheepish worthies trying to laugh off their curious circumstances.

Act 3 *5th tableau* Vakula goes to see Patsyuk, the medicine man or shaman, believing that he will be able to help. Patsyuk points out that the Devil, who can solve Vakula's problem for him, is in fact being carried on the smith's back. Vakula releases the Devil and keeps him in order by brandishing a cross.

6th tableau The Devil is forced to agree to transport him to St Petersburg. The two fly through the air, although swarms of devils try to stop their progress.

7th tableau The Tsaritsa's court. The Empress, amused by the request, gives Vakula her boots. He sets off home, with the Devil's help.

8th tableau Vakula arrives back in the village at dawn, with the bells ringing for Christmas.

Act 4 *9th tableau* Oxana is remorseful, worried that Vakula might have killed himself. He suddenly appears with the boots, only to find that Oxana loves him anyway and the present is unnecessary; everyone greets him and all ends happily.

*

Rimsky-Korsakov's contemporaries were on the whole unsympathetic to this heavily mythologized treatment of Gogol's rather innocent tale, and the opera did not hold the stage. In his autobiography Rimsky conceded that he had been carried away, 'but this mistake gave me the chance to write a lot of interesting music'. It is indeed the fantastic music that lives in *Christmas Eve*, carrying to a new power the extravagant if schematic harmonic and colouristic invention that was Rimsky's special genius. The orchestration is also full of new and ingenious artifices (and a new instrument, the celesta, henceforth Rimsky's magic colour *par excellence*).

The opera's stage career was especially frustrating to Rimsky-Korsakov because a pair of grand dukes, attending the dress rehearsal, took offence at the inclusion in the cast of Empress Catherine II (as in Gogol's tale – Yakov Polonsky, Tchaikovsky and Solov'yov's librettist, had prudently replaced her with an unnamed 'Highness'). They demanded that her part be hastily written out of the opera, and in consequence the offended composer boycotted the première. (One of the noblemen, the Grand Duke Vladimir Alexandrovich, was the employer of Modest Solov'yov, brother of the composer of one of the competing operas.)   R.T.

Cid, Le ('The Cid')

Opéra in four acts and ten scenes by Jules Massenet to a libretto by Adolphe d'Ennery, Edouard Blau and Louis Gallet after Pierre Corneille's drama (1637); Paris, Opéra, 30 November 1885.

At the première the cast included Jean de Reszke (Rodrigue) and his brother Edouard (Don Diègue), Fidès Devriès (Chimène) and Pol Plançon (Count of Gormas).

Edouard de Reszke (left) as Don Diègue and Jean de Reszke as Rodrigue in the original production of Massenet's 'Le Cid' at the Paris Opéra in 1885

Rodrigue, 'The Cid'	tenor
Chimène	soprano
Count of Gormas *her father*	bass
Infanta of Spain	soprano
Don Diègue *Rodrigue's father*	bass
King of Spain	baritone
St Jacques [St James]	baritone
Moorish Envoy	bass

Lords and ladies, bishops and priests, soldiers, people, dancers

Setting Spain in the 11th century

The first performance of *Le Cid* confirmed Massenet's reputation as a successful opera composer, marking as it did his return to the Opéra for the first time since *Le roi de Lahore* eight years previously and coming a year after the double triumph of *Manon* by the Opéra-Comique and the first performances in Paris of *Hérodiade* (Théâtre Italien). The De Reszke brothers had sung in *Hérodiade* and both were engaged for *Le Cid*.

After a conventional sonata-form overture, rare in French opera, the action follows the outlines of Corneille's play. In the first act preparations are in hand for the investiture of Rodrigue as a knight of St James of Compostella. Chimène tells her father, the Count of Gormas, of her love for Rodrigue and receives his blessing. She is joined by the Infanta, also in love with Rodrigue but barred by rank from marrying him, and they sing a tender duet ('Laissez le doute dans mon âme'). Rodrigue is duly invested ('O noble lame étincelante'). The Count, confident of

being appointed guardian of the king's son, learns that Rodrigue's father Don Diègue has been preferred and insults him in public. Don Diègue incites his son to avenge his honour before revealing the identity of the proposed victim.

In the second act Rodrigue provokes the Count to a duel and kills him. Chimène interrupts a ballet-fiesta with her public accusation of Rodrigue and demands justice. A Moorish envoy declares war, and Rodrigue begs to be allowed to lead the Spanish forces, promising to return to whatever punishment the king sees fit. The third act is launched with the most famous number in the score, Chimène's 'Pleurez, pleurez mes yeux', and she voices her operatically conflicting emotions in an extended duet of farewell with Rodrigue. On the battlefield Rodrigue prays for victory ('O souverain, ô juge, ô père') and is reassured by a vision of St James. In the fourth act news is brought of his death in battle, but after Chimène and Don Diègue have reacted at some length this proves to be false: he returns in triumph and Chimène forgives him.

*

Le Cid was Massenet's last attempt at a conventional Meyerbeerian *grand opéra*. While he catches the scale of the work efficiently enough – his ease when writing in 9/8 or 12/8 time comes in useful when setting the lines by Corneille that survive in the libretto – he is patently less at home with stage fanfares, triple choruses and the whole paraphernalia of the form than with more intimate subjects. Comparison between Rodrigue's investiture and Radames's (*Aida*) is instructive. The successful numbers (much recorded) are good – the energetic 'O noble lame' (reprised before the third-act battle), the Prayer with its humming-chorus background, Chimène's 'Pleurez' – and the justly famous second-act ballet is one of Massenet's best. But having to write for the comparatively heroic voices of Jean de Reszke and Devriès finds Massenet oddly inflexible in his response, and the role of Don Diègue is longer than it needs to be dramaturgically simply because Edouard de Reszke was available. The reminiscence motifs are short-breathed, and applied rather than integrated, very much after the manner of Debussy's 'visiting-card' jibe at the leitmotifs in *Das Rheingold*.

The loyalty of the De Reszke brothers and Plançon ensured considerable success for *Le Cid* both in France and America, and it achieved 150 performances at the Opéra by 1919. It has since lapsed from the repertory, not least because of difficulties of casting. There is an incomplete live recording (1976) with Placido Domingo in the title role.

R.M.

Clemenza di Tito, La ('The Clemency of Titus')

Opera seria in two acts, K621, by Wolfgang Amadeus Mozart to a libretto by Pietro Metastasio adapted by Caterino Mazzolà; Prague, National Theatre, 6 September 1791.

The first cast was Antonio Baglioni (Titus), Maria Marchetti-Fantozzi (Vitellia), Domenico Bedini (Sextus), Carolina Perini (Annius, the travesty role), Gaetano Campi, a well-known *buffo* singer (Publius); with one Signora Antonini singing Servilia.

Tito [Titus Flavius Vespasianus] *Roman*	
Emperor	tenor
Vitellia *daughter of the deposed Emperor*	
Vitellius	soprano
Servilia *sister of Sextus, in love with*	
Annius	soprano
Sesto [Sextus] *friend of Titus,*	
in love with Vitellia	soprano castrato
Annio [Annius] *friend of Sextus,*	
in love with Servilia	soprano
Publio [Publius] *prefect of the praetorian*	
guard	bass
Senators, ambassadors, praetorian guards, lictors,	
people of Rome	
Setting Rome, in about AD 80	

Although mostly composed after *Die Zauberflöte*, *La clemenza di Tito* was performed first. Its gestation has been dated back to 1789, when Mozart was in contact with the impresario Domenico Guardasoni, but the subject cannot have been chosen then. Guardasoni obtained an open commission from the Bohemian Estates only in July, for an opera designed to celebrate Emperor Leopold II's coronation as King of Bohemia, and to some degree adapted to his particular taste. Contrary to an opinion often expressed, the commission was far from unwelcome to Mozart; he wanted to show his strength in *opera seria*.

Metastasio's libretto, already set by more than 40 composers, was 'ridotta a vera opera' ('reduced to a proper opera'), as Mozart wrote in his catalogue. Only seven arias and one chorus (designated 'Metastasio' below) were unchanged; Metastasio's aria and recitative texts were manipulated in the ensembles and finales devised by Mazzolà. Reduced by a third, the libretto gains clarity and the musical numbers pertinence, at the expense of dramatic weight.

Mozart probably composed all of *La clemenza* between late July and September 1791. He arrived in Prague on 28 August and despite illness finished work on the eve of the performance. The chief artistic drawback of the short time available was that he sub-contracted the simple recitatives, possibly to Süssmayr. The choruses and ensembles were worked out with Mazzolà in Vienna and written there, as were some arias. The singer Mozart knew best was Baglioni, two of whose arias were written in Vienna; the only ensemble composed in Prague (the trio early in Act 2) probably replaced intended arias for Vitellia and Sextus. Problems in these roles are apparent from surviving sketch and autograph material. Mozart began by assuming that Sextus would be a tenor, and Vitellia's 'Non più di fiori', the Act 2 rondò, is distinctly lower in tessitura than the rest of the role.

The reception was modest until a triumphant last night was reported to Mozart (who had left Prague on 15 September) on the day of the première of *Die Zauberflöte* (30 September). Concert performances of extracts and of the whole opera were arranged by Constanze Mozart for her own benefit. In Vienna on 29 December 1791 and in later performances Aloysia Lange sang Sextus. After a further performance in Vienna in 1795 Constanze took the work to Graz, Leipzig and Berlin, herself singing Vitellia. In 1796 a German translation by Rochlitz was performed in Dresden and used in most German centres (including Vienna) within the next 15 years. The first performance outside Germany and Austria was also the first of any Mozart opera in London, on 27 March 1806, for the benefit of Mrs Billington. Performances followed in all the main European centres, usually in Italian

(1809, Naples; 1816, Paris and Milan; 1817, in Russian, St Petersburg). Until about 1830 *La clemenza di Tito* was one of Mozart's most popular operas; it then went into eclipse. It has never fully entered the modern repertory and is often described as unworthy of Mozart, hastily assembled for a commission he could not refuse. Critical estimates have risen since World War II, and it is now seen as a positive step in the further reform of *opera seria*.

*

Despite its lack of overt thematic connection with the rest of the opera the overture has been described as a dramatic argument according to Gluck's principles.

Act I *Vitellia's apartments* Titus is in love with the Jewish queen Berenice; Vitellia denies being jealous, but believes she, an emperor's daughter, should be his consort. Overtly motivated by the need to avenge her father, she induces Sextus to lead an assassination plot. A loyal friend of Titus, he adores her blindly and cannot resist her commands. He begs her to say how he can please her, for she is his destiny (duet, 'Come ti piace, imponi'). She asks why he is delaying; he requests only a tender glance. In the Allegro, both admit to the confusion of their feelings. Annius reports that Titus has dismissed Berenice for

reasons of state. Vitellia allows herself to hope, and tells Sextus to suspend the plot. In measured tones (a slow minuet) she declares that to win her he must not exhaust her with suspicions (Metastasio: 'Deh se piacer me vuoi'). The following Allegro returns to the opening words; its principal message, conveyed in a capricious mixture of sturdy rhythms and decorative flourishes, is that doubt encourages deception. Annius asks Sextus for his sister's hand, which he gladly grants in the duettino ('Deh prendi un dolce amplesso'), a winning expression of brotherly affection.

Before the Roman forum Senators and delegates from the provinces gather at the heart of the Imperial city. Titus enters in state, with lictors, guards and citizens. A march leads directly to a chorus in praise of Titus (Metastasio: 'Serbate, o dei custodi'). After formal expressions of homage from Publius and Annius, Titus replies that his sole aim is to be a good father to his people. The chorus is repeated; Titus calls for Sextus, and the stage is cleared during a repeat of the march. Private conversation (with Annius present) reveals the intimacy of Sextus and Titus. The emperor must publicly deny his love for Berenice by taking a Roman wife; who better than his friend's sister? Annius bravely eulogizes the

'La clemenza di Tito' (Mozart), final scene of Act 2: design by Giorgio Fuentes for the 1799 production at the Nationaltheater, Frankfurt

emperor's choice. In a mellow Andante (Metastasio: 'Del più sublime soglio') Titus declares that the only happiness afforded by supreme power is to reward virtue. Annius reveals the emperor's decision to Servilia; the exquisite melody of their farewell (duet, 'Ah perdona al primo affetto') touches a nerve of painful tenderness within this severely political opera.

A garden in the Imperial palace on the Palatine To Publius Titus expounds his philosophy of disarming enmity by forgiveness. Servilia dares to confess that she and Annius are in love; he thanks heaven for her frankness, and releases her (Metastasio: 'Ah, se fosse intorno al trono'). The sweep of the melody in this short Allegro conveys his open-hearted nature; if the throne were flanked by such honesty, the cares of office would turn to joy. Vitellia bitterly compliments Servilia on her good fortune; Servilia, piqued, does not reveal her refusal. Deaf to reason, and unimpressed by his devotion to Titus, Vitellia upbraids Sextus for dilatoriness: the emperor must die. Before embarking on his fatal mission he asks again for the loving glance which destroys his loyalty and assures his happiness (Metastasio: 'Parto, parto'). This aria with basset clarinet obbligato is in three sections, accelerating, as sentiment yields to determination, from a nobly extended Adagio through an impassioned Allegro ('Guardami, e tutto obblio') to a brilliant conclusion. Publius and Annius announce to Vitellia that she is the emperor's chosen consort (trio, 'Vengo! aspettate!'); the others mistake her confusion for excess of joy and comment sympathetically, but she is terrified that it is too late to stop the plot (her frantic message recalling Sextus ended Metastasio's first act). This gripping number is dominated by Vitellia's agitation, expressed in gasping phrases and, when the musical line is more sustained, cruelly high tessitura (touching d''').

A portico before the Capitol Sextus has launched the conspiracy, but is wracked by guilt (obbligato recitative); his weakness has made him a traitor. He cannot turn back; the Capitol is already in flames. The bulk of the finale is an action ensemble. Sextus, in words Metastasio intended as recitative, seems to begin an aria (a prayer for Titus's safety), but to Annius he babbles of his shame and rushes away; Annius is prevented from following by the need to keep Servilia out of danger. Cries of horror are heard from the offstage chorus; Publius appears, fearing for Titus, then Vitellia, frantically searching for Sextus. He returns, looking for a place to hide; all believe Titus dead. Sextus is about to confess when Vitellia silences him. In a concluding Andante all the characters and the distant chorus join in lamenting the murderous treachery.

Act 2 *Palace gardens* Annius tells Sextus that Titus is alive. Sextus admits that he instigated the plot, refusing to give any reason. Annius gently urges him to throw himself on the emperor's mercy ('Torna di Tito a lato'), his concern enhanced by his repetition, to the end, of 'torna' ('return'). Vitellia warns Sextus too late; Publius comes with guards to arrest him (trio, 'Se a volto mai ti senti'). Sextus bids Vitellia a lingering farewell; the music darkens suddenly as her admiration for his devotion conflicts with her fear that he will implicate her. In the Allegretto, Sextus asks Vitellia to remember his love; she is gripped with remorse; Publius, though touched, remains firm (Metastasio's second act ends here).

A large room, with a writing-table The chorus (patricians, praetorian guards and people) thank Fate for sparing Titus ('Ah grazie si rendano'). In the middle section of this ironically serene Andante, Titus thanks them for their loyalty. He tries to understand the conspirators; Lentulus (who led the attack) is clearly guilty; perhaps he has accused Sextus to protect himself. In a short aria (Metastasio: 'Tardi, s'avvede') Publius bluffly comments that the good-natured find it hard to believe others capable of betrayal. A moment later he returns with Sextus's confession and news of his condemnation by the Senate. Annius pleads for mercy ('Tu fosti tradito'): Titus has been betrayed, but hope remains if he consults his heart (an episode in Metastasio in which Annius is accused is omitted). Bitterly hurt, Titus condemns his own hesitation in signing the death warrant, but the word 'death' stops him short (obbligato recitative, 'Che orror! che tradimento!'). He sends for Sextus; incisive orchestral gestures yield to sustained harmonies as he persuades himself that he cannot refuse the hearing which justice offers the meanest citizen. Publius brings in Sextus. The first speeches are sung aside (trio, 'Quello di Tito è il volto'). Sextus's fear is mirrored in his music: can this be the face of Titus? Titus can barely recognize his guilt-ridden friend; Publius witnesses the emperor's tangled emotions. Titus commands Sextus to approach, but he is rooted to the spot. The ensemble freezes in the Allegro, Sextus's angular line again dominating while the others comment on his evident terror. Titus reduces Sextus to tears of contrition by addressing him kindly. But Sextus, protecting Vitellia, cannot justify his treachery. Titus dismisses him coldly. Gathering his feelings into a nobly arching melody, Sextus asks Titus to remember their earlier friendship (rondò, 'Deh, per questo istante solo'). In the Allegro the boundaries of the tonic (A major) are twice burst by cries of despair; its gentler principal melody ('Tanto affanno soffre un core') becomes hectic in the faster coda. Titus signs the fatal paper, then tears it up; he is no Brutus, and cannot begin a career of tyranny by executing a friend. He tells Publius only that Sextus's fate is settled

Set by Nicholas Georgiadis for Mozart's 'La clemenza di Tito' (Aix-en-Provence, 1988)

(Metastasio: 'Se all' impero, amici dei'); if the noble gods require an emperor to be cruel, they must deprive him of empire or give him another heart. This is the only aria in the modern equivalent of da capo form; its weight, balanced by considerable floridity, prepares fully for Titus's renunciation of revenge, while underlining his strength of purpose in a march-like coda.

Publius tells Vitellia he has heard nothing of the emperor's conversation with Sextus. Annius and Servilia, still unaware of her complicity, ask the empress-designate to help. Servilia's lightly-scored minuet (Metastasio: 'S'altro che lagrime') is a gentle but penetrating plea; weeping is not enough to save Sextus. At last moved by Sextus's constancy, Vitellia is at the point of decision (obbligato recitative, 'Ecco il punto, o Vitellia'); can she betray him to die alone? No chains of flowers will accompany the descent of Hymen (rondò, 'Non più di fiori'); the music, with basset-horn obbligato, paints the serene image which she must renounce. Her despair breaks out in the Allegro ('Infelice! qual orrore!'); she cannot live knowing the horror of what she has done. The aria merges into a transition with the character of a slow march.

A public place, before a temple The chorus acclaims the god-like emperor ('Che del ciel'). Annius and Servilia ask for mercy, but Titus addresses Sextus with severity. Before he can pronounce sentence (which all assume will be death) Vitellia intervenes, claiming sole responsibility for the conspiracy. Titus is bewildered; he was about to absolve one criminal, and another appears (obbligato recitative, 'Ma, che giorno'). But he defies the stars to deter him; all must be forgiven. In the finale they praise him and he rewards them with his confidence; may he die when

Rome's good is not his chief concern. Chorus and principals together ask the gods to grant him long life.

*

La clemenza di Tito, like several of its predecessors, ends in forgiveness, here predicated in the title. The goodness of Titus is so strongly presented in his arias that the outcome of his struggle in Act 2 is predictable; his role is close to Metastasio's conception and his music has a correspondingly old-fashioned cut. Vitellia is capricious in the opening scenes, selfish and hard but perplexed about her own motivation in the Act 1 trio, yet capable of noble renunciation ('Non più di fiori'). Sextus is an equally rewarding role, with two large arias and the dominant part in several ensembles.

As in *Così fan tutte*, several of the musical numbers are very brief, allowing the expansion of crucial arias and the first-act finale within a short opera. The use of accompanied recitative is traditional, but the arias range from *buffo* simplicity for Servilia and Publius, through the more developed but still direct style of Annius, to the fully elaborated arias of the three main characters: of these two are rondòs, and two were given obbligatos for the clarinettist and basset-horn player Anton Stadler. In the context of *opera seria*, however, the highest originality lies in the ensembles. There is a strong predilection for movements with two tempos (the usual slow–fast reversed in the first finale). While the folklike duets of the first act approach the style of *Die Zauberflöte*, the trios show that *buffo* textures are equally suited to tragic situations. The first finale is unique in Mozart's output, bridging the gap between Gluck and the 19th century in the realism of its opening, its stark modulation from E♭ to G♭, and its offstage chorus and tremolando; compared to *Idomeneo*, the sparing use of such effects corresponds to the absence of a supernatural dimension to the plot.

Had he lived to prepare further performances, Mozart would surely have replaced the simple recitatives (which do not always end in an appropriate key). He might have increased the orchestrated recitative to a quantity approaching that in *Così* and, as he had planned for *Idomeneo*, rearranged the vocal forces, with a tenor Sextus. Now that performances and recordings, and a general revival of 18th-century repertory, encourage reassessment of its virtues, *La clemenza di Tito* clearly appears a conception not fully realized, but still masterly and amply rewarding study and performance.

J.Ru.

Comte Ory, Le ('Count Ory')

Opéra in two acts by Gioachino Rossini to a libretto by Eugène Scribe and Charles-Gaspard Delestre-Poirson after their own play; Paris, Opéra, 20 August 1828.

In the original production Ory was sung by Adolphe Nourrit, Countess Adèle by Laure Cinti-Damoreau and Isolier by Constance Jawureck; Henri-Bernard Dabadie sang Raimbaud and Nicolas Levasseur was the Tutor.

Count Ory	tenor
Countess Adèle	soprano
Raimbaud	baritone
Ragonde *the Countess's*	
stewardess	mezzo-soprano
Tutor	baritone
Isolier *page to Ory*	mezzo-soprano
Alice *a peasant girl*	soprano
Young Nobleman *friend of Ory*	tenor
Setting The castle of Formoutiers in about 1200	

In 1817 Scribe and Delestre-Poirson wrote a one-act vaudeville on the exploits of the libidinous Count Ory, a real-life Don Juan who became the subject of a popular late 18th-century ballad. Shortly after settling in Paris Rossini, in his turn, had written a coronation entertainment in 1825 for the French king Charles X, *Il viaggio a Reims*, one of the supreme masterpieces of occasional music but a piece too closely tied to the circumstances of its composition to survive as an opera-house repertory work. For *Le comte Ory*, the music was adapted and extended and the one-act vaudeville turned into a two-act drama to make a work that is not only astonishingly cogent in its own right but also one of the

wittiest, most stylish and most urbane of all comic operas.

*

The Count of Formoutiers and his men have left on crusade to the Holy Land, leaving his sister, the Countess Adèle, exposed to the wiles of young Count Ory and his henchmen, led by the trusty Raimbaud. Ory establishes himself outside the castle as a hermit; and although the villagers, among them the Countess's stewardess Ragonde, are taken in by this, Ory's Tutor is more than a little suspicious. Isolier, Ory's page (an obvious forerunner of Oscar in Verdi's *Un ballo in maschera*), has himself been smitten by the Countess's beauty and, failing to recognize his master through the hermit's outfit, confides in him his plan to enter the castle disguised as a pilgrim. Ory approves the idea, but once inside the castle, on the pretext of advising in matters of love, he solemnly warns the Countess to be wary of young Isolier. Ory's own advances are progressing very satisfactorily when he is unmasked by his Tutor. But, with a day to go before the return of the crusaders, Ory determines to make a further assault.

At the start of Act 2, the women angrily discuss Ory's dissimulation. A storm breaks and cries are heard from a band of 'pilgrims' – in reality, Ory and his men disguised as nuns – outside the castle. The pilgrims are given shelter and, on Raimbaud's initiative, soon discover the castle's wine cellars, a discovery leading to an uproarious scene in which spirited carousings alternate with solemn prayer whenever strangers approach. This time, though, Isolier has his wits about him and recognizes Ory. To ingratiate himself with the Countess he tells her the truth and with her help lays a trap, luring Ory into a secret assignation. In the darkness of the bedchamber, misled by the Countess's own voice, Ory mistakenly addresses his amorous overtures to his page. Trumpet calls announce the arrival of the crusaders, leaving Ory and his men no alternative but to make good their escape.

*

Though sometimes designated an *opéra comique*, *Le comte Ory* is a uniquely Rossinian creation with skilfully structured ensembles and a sophistication in the orchestral and vocal writing that transcends anything to be found in the works of such composers as Auber or Hérold. It is a wry and witty piece that appropriates and develops the gentle guying of the romantic sensibility of *Il viaggio a Reims* while developing in the famous Act 2 trio, newly written, a degree of vocal and instrumental sensibility and sophistication that even Berlioz was bound to marvel at. The critic Henry Chorley noted that 'there is not a bad melody, there is not an ugly bar in *Le comte Ory*', adding that there is in the piece 'a felicitous curiousness in the modulations . . . a crispness of finish, a resolution to make effects by disappointing the ear, which not only bespeaks the master's familiarity with the greatest classical writers, but also a wondrous tact in conforming to the taste of the new public whom he was to fascinate'.   R.O.

Consul, The

Musical drama in three acts by Gian Carlo Menotti to his own libretto; Philadelphia, Shubert Theatre, 1 March 1950.

The original cast featured Patricia Neway as Magda, Cornell MacNeil as John, Marie Powers as the Mother, Gloria Lane as the Secretary and Leon Lishner as the Police Agent.

John Sorel	baritone
Magda Sorel *his wife*	soprano
John's Mother	contralto
The Consul's Secretary	mezzo-soprano
Nika Magadoff (The Magician)	tenor
Assan *a glass-cutter*	baritone
Secret Police Agent	bass
Vera Boronel	contralto
Mr Kofner	bass-baritone
Foreign Woman	soprano
Anna Gomez	soprano

Setting An anonymous European city in 1950

The Philadelphia première was a try-out for a Broadway run that began on 15 March 1950 at the Ethel Barrymore Theatre with Thomas Schippers conducting. It was enormously successful and that year won the New York Drama Critics' Circle Award for the best musical play and the Pulitzer Prize for Music. It enjoyed a run of 269 performances in New York and the following year was produced at La Scala, Milan, and in London, Zürich, Berlin and Vienna. It has been translated into 12 languages and performed in over 20 countries.

The action takes place in Magda Sorel's shabby apartment and in the waiting-room of a consulate in a large European city. The opera begins in the dark and empty apartment with the sound of a gramophone recording of a French popular song drifting through the open windows from a café below. Suddenly the orchestra plays, loud and dissonant and at a much faster tempo as John Sorel, wounded, runs in and falls to the floor; his meeting of freedom fighters has been raided by the secret police. Magda, his wife, and his Mother rush in from the other side of the apartment. John hides as the police, trailing him, arrive and question the two women, who have hastily removed any betraying evidence. After the men have left he says he must flee to a neighbouring

country and that Magda must obtain a visa to get there and join him. They bid each other a sad farewell. He tells them that if one of the windows is broken by a stone it will be a message from him via the glass-cutter, Assan.

In scene ii Magda, at the consulate, encounters bureaucratic delays. She pleads with the Secretary but the Consul does not appear. Other people in the same predicament as herself try to cope with the impervious Secretary and the endless red tape; most notable among them is the Magician, Nika Magadoff, who performs a few tricks to prove his calling. The act closes with a despairing quintet.

Act 2 also opens with the offstage recording of the French song. It is a few weeks later. The Mother sings a lullaby to Magda's dying baby while Magda sleeps and has a hallucinatory nightmare in which her husband and the Secretary appear. A stone crashes through a window, the prearranged signal for them to send for Assan, who will bring news of John. The Secret Police Agent comes to question Magda again, hinting that she could have her visa if she would give him details of the freedom fighters' identities. Enraged, Magda orders him to leave. Assan arrives and tells them that John is hiding out in the mountains and will not cross the border until he is sure she can come. Fearful for John's safety, Magda tells Assan to convey the message that the precious visa has come through. Meanwhile, the Mother notices that the baby has died. The major part of scene ii (in the waiting-room, a short time later) is dominated by the Magician, who performs more tricks, hypnotizes the waiting people and leads them into a waltz. After a bitter argument with the Secretary Magda has a grand climactic aria, 'To this we've come'. Finally, the Secretary says that Magda can see the Consul as soon as an important visitor leaves. When she discovers that the visitor is the Secret Police Agent Magda faints.

Act 3 begins with Magda again attempting to see the Consul. While the waiting continues, just one person, Vera Boronel, is delighted to obtain her papers. In counterpoint to this Assan arrives to tell Magda that John wants to come back to fetch her. This frightens them both, but Magda gives Assan a note for John that will effectively stop him – she will not say how she has solved the problem, however. She then rushes off, forgetting her handbag. John appears, looking for her, and is arrested by the police who have followed him. The Secretary promises him that she will telephone his wife. A funeral march in quintuple time leads into the final scene, in which Magda commits suicide by gas: she experiences a hallucinatory visitation of all the characters and a dance of death led by the Magician. At the moment of death the telephone rings.

*

The Consul is a grim, intense drama, replete with powerful theatrical effects and some of Menotti's strongest and most dissonant music. While much of the music is traditionally tonal, often with a modal flavour, several passages could be classified as atonal. There is a considerable increase over earlier works in the amount and the level of dissonance, as at the orchestral opening. Considered by many to be his greatest work, *The Consul* uses the *verismo* of Puccini's day to treat a contemporary situation. Music and stage techniques combine to communicate strongly and directly.   **B.A.**

Contes d'Hoffmann, Les ('The Tales of Hoffmann')

Opéra fantastique in five acts by Jacques Offenbach to a libretto by Jules Barbier after the play by Barbier and Michel Carré based on the stories of E. T. A. Hoffmann; Paris, Opéra-Comique (Salle Favart), 10 February 1881.

At the première Hoffmann was sung by Jean-Alexandre Talazac, with Adèle Isaac as his lovers, the baritone Alexandre Taskin as the villains and Pierre Grivot as the servants; Nicklausse was sung by the young soprano Marguerite Ugalde.

Hoffmann *a poet*	tenor
Olympia *a doll*	
Antonia *Crespel's daughter*	
Giulietta *a courtesan*	soprano
Stella *a prima donna*	
Nicklausse *a friend of Hoffmann*	
The Muse	mezzo-soprano
A Ghost *Antonia's mother*	mezzo-soprano
Counsellor Lindorf	
Coppélius *a maker of eyes*	bass or baritone
Dr Miracle	
Captain Dapertutto *a magician*	
Spalanzani *a physician*	tenor
Crespel *a violin maker, Antonia's father*	bass or baritone
Andrès *Stella's servant*	
Cochenille *Spalanzani's servant*	
Frantz *Crespel's servant*	tenor
Pitichinaccio *Giulietta's servant*	
Luther *innkeeper*	baritone
Nathanaël	tenor
Wolframm	baritone
Hermann *students*	baritone
Wilhelm	baritone
Peter Schlemil	baritone

Students, tavern waiters, guests of Spalanzani, gamblers, valets, spirits of beer and wine
Setting Nuremberg, Paris, Munich, Venice in the early 19th century

Alexandre Taskin (Dr Miracle) and Adèle Isaac (Antonia) in the roles they created in the original production of Offenbach's 'Les contes d'Hoffmann' at the Opéra-Comique, Paris, in 1881

The opera is based upon an 1851 play in which the poet E. T. A. Hoffmann is portrayed as a participant in various of his own stories. His spiritual and moral decline is depicted through successive loves – a frivolous infatuation with a mechanical doll, Olympia, genuine but thwarted love with the singer Antonia, and idle tarrying with the courtesan Giulietta. The three acts depicting these episodes are framed by a prologue and epilogue. In them Hoffmann is depicted telling these stories while awaiting his latest love, the prima donna Stella, who is finally recognized as a combination of the three earlier loves. Similarly, his constant companion Nicklausse is revealed as a personification of his poetic muse. To emphasize these unities, his various loves are properly sung by a single singer, as are Nicklausse and the Muse and also Hoffmann's four adversaries Lindorf, Coppélius, Dr Miracle and Dapertutto.

Offenbach seemingly regarded *Les contes d'Hoffmann* as a last chance for recognition as a composer of serious opera rather than of the frivolous and apparently ephemeral *opéras bouffes* for which he was best known. While coping with other pressing commissions, he devoted to it a considerable part of his energies during what were to prove the last few years of his life. Along the way the plan for the opera underwent some fundamental changes. Offenbach designed it first for the Théâtre de la Gaîté-Lyrique, with recitatives, a baritone Hoffmann and a lyric soprano. Then he was forced to rework it for the Opéra-Comique with spoken dialogue, a tenor Hoffmann and a coloratura soprano.

When Offenbach died the opera was in rehearsal and the music apparently conceived in its entirety, including the orchestration, although some detailed working out of the fourth act (Giulietta) and the final act (epilogue) remained to be done. The composer and teacher Ernest Guiraud was brought in to produce a finished version, but before the opera reached production crucial changes were made. First, the mezzo-soprano Alice Ducasse was replaced and her combined role of Nicklausse and the Muse divided between two young singers. Then dissatisfaction with the Giulietta act caused its deletion at the première, with some of its numbers dispersed to other acts. Even when the Giulietta act was finally performed and published, it was placed before the Antonia act, perhaps to mask its less wholly satisfactory state. Successive editions of the score have provided varying texts, some with recitatives by Guiraud.

Some of the original material may possibly have been destroyed in the fire at the Salle Favart on 25 May 1887. Certainly the opera's association with the horrific fire at the Ringtheater in Vienna on 8 December 1881, when it was about to receive its second Viennese performance, gave it a reputation for bad luck that slowed its international acceptance. Only after a spectacular production in Berlin in 1905 did it really establish its international popularity. By then it had been subjected to further rewriting for a production at Monte Carlo in 1904. At the instance of the director, Raoul Gunsbourg, the Giulietta act was built up by inserting two new passages with music fashioned by André Bloch to words by the original librettist's son, Pierre Barbier.

Using music from Le voyage dans la lune (1875), they fashioned a new aria 'Scintille, diamant' for the baritone Maurice Renaud in the role of Dapertutto, and also added a 'septet' (actually for six solo voices and chorus), 'Hélas, mon coeur s'égare encore', built on the theme of the barcarolle, to provide a brilliant climax. These changes were perpetuated in the 1907 Choudens score, which also transferred Dapertutto's original aria 'Tourne, tourne, miroir' to Coppélius with different words as 'J'ai des yeux, de vrais yeux' and added a further passage to the Giulietta act in which Hoffmann discovers the loss of his reflection. In this form the opera has retained widespread popularity for its spectacular staging and for individual numbers such as Hoffmann's 'Legend of Kleinzach', Olympia's 'Doll's Song' and, above all,

the 'Barcarolle' – one of the world's most popular melodies, which Offenbach had taken from an earlier work, Die Rheinnixen. During the 20th century the work has been produced repeatedly at opera houses throughout the world, often with the leading soprano roles assigned to different singers – a fundamental denial of the opera's dramatic unity, but a rare opportunity to parade multiple leading ladies in a single opera.

Since World War II numerous attempts have been made to restore Offenbach's original conception. Thanks especially to the conductor and Offenbach scholar Antonio de Almeida, important manuscript sources continued to be uncovered into the 1980s. These have been used for new performing editions by Fritz Oeser (Vienna, 1976) and Michael Kaye (Los Angeles, 1988). Oeser published important material for the first time, notably numbers for Nicklausse and the Muse, but added accretions of his own to those of Guiraud, whereas Kaye confined himself to authentic Offenbach. It remains to be seen to what extent these versions will replace the traditional text; but it is anyway impossible to produce a 'definitive' text for an opera which lacked the final finish and pruning. However, key elements of the restorations – the original order of acts, a single soprano heroine and single baritone villain, the identification of Nicklausse with the Muse, the restoration of deleted music for the latter, and the dropping of the alterations by Pierre Barbier and Bloch – must be observed to give a faithful representation of Offenbach's conception.

*

Act 1 (Prologue) *Luther's tavern close to the opera house in Nuremberg* In the moonlight an invisible chorus of spirits of beer and wine sets the scene ('Glou, glou, glou'). Hoffmann's Muse bemoans the poet's dissolute life ('La vérité, dit-on, sortit d'un puits') and assumes the identity of his student friend Nicklausse. Counsellor Lindorf, a powerful local politician with designs on Hoffmann's current lover, Stella ('Dans les rôles d'amoureux langoureux'), succeeds in obtaining the key to her dressing-room from her servant Andrès. A rowdy bunch of students arrive ('Jusqu'au matin remplis mon verre'), followed by Hoffmann, who is in an agitated state. They persuade him to tell his story of the dwarf Kleinzach ('Il était une fois à la cour d'Eisenach'), but his mind (and the song) wanders to his dreams of a beautiful woman before he is persuaded to resume the story. Seeing Lindorf, Hoffmann recognizes him as his perpetual adversary in his love affairs and foresees another disaster. Prevailing upon Hoffmann to tell the stories of his loves, the students recharge their glasses and settle down for the evening.

Act 2 (Olympia) *The laboratory of the physicist Spalanzani* The eccentric inventor Spalanzani is

Design by László Moholy-Nagy for Act 1 of Offenbach's 'Les contes d'Hoffmann' (Berlin, Kroll Opera, 1929): blueprint with pen, ink and gouache

hoping that his latest invention, a mechanical doll, will earn enough money to recoup the losses sustained from the bankruptcy of his banker. He is worried, though, that his former partner Coppélius may claim part of the proceeds. Hoffmann arrives as a pupil of Spalanzani, who talks of his 'daughter' Olympia. Spalanzani leaves to prepare for the arrival of his guests, and Hoffmann's heart leaps when, behind a curtain, he sees what he takes to be the sleeping figure of the daughter. Nicklausse vainly attempts to make light of his infatuation ('Une poupée aux yeux d'émail'). Coppélius enters with a collection of optical instruments, including a pair of magic spectacles which make anything seen through them beautiful ('Je me nomme Coppélius'). When Spalanzani returns, Coppélius demands a share of the profits from the mechanical doll, whose eyes he has supplied. To get rid of him, Spalanzani gives him a worthless cheque as the guests enter to a stately minuet ('Non aucun hôte vraiment'). Spalanzani presents his 'daughter', who attracts admiration with a coloratura aria ('Les oiseaux dans la charmille'), punctuated from time to time by pauses for her to be recharged. Hoffmann, deceived by his magic spectacles into believing her human, is completely bewitched and sings a rapturous romance ('Ah! vivre deux'). The guests return from dinner and begin waltzing ('Oui, pauvres fous'), but a furious Coppélius enters; he has discovered the cheque to be worthless and vows vengeance. Hoffmann is left breathless by his animated dance with Olympia, who then retires to her room. From it comes the sound of breaking machinery as Coppélius destroys Spalanzani's invention and the object of Hoffmann's infatuation. The guests gather around Hoffmann, mocking his foolishness.

Act 3 (Antonia) *A room in Crespel's house in Munich* The walls of the room are decorated with Crespel's musical instruments and a portrait of his dead wife. Seated at the piano, his daughter Antonia sings a nostalgic song about a lost love ('Elle a fui, la tourterelle') but afterwards collapses exhausted. Her father rushes in to remind her that she has inherited her mother's fatal chest complaint and that to continue singing will mean an early death. Crespel has hurried to Munich to protect Antonia from the influence of her lover Hoffmann, and he instructs his old servant Frantz not to open the door. However, Frantz is deaf and befuddled ('Jour et nuit je me mets en quatre'), and soon Hoffmann and Nicklausse gain admission. Nicklausse tries out a violin ('Vois sous l'archet frémissant') and Hoffmann sits at the piano and sings a snatch of a love song ('C'est une chanson d'amour'). Antonia appears and, despite Nicklausse's efforts, she joins Hoffmann in the song. She tells him she has been forbidden to sing and, when her father returns, flees to her room. Hoffmann hides and overhears an exchange with the mysterious Dr Miracle, whom Crespel accuses of being responsible for his wife's death and seeking to bring about his daughter's. However, Miracle claims that he alone can cure her ('Pour conjurer le danger'). After their departure, Hoffmann persuades Antonia to agree to give up singing, but no sooner has he left than Miracle reappears and urges her to sing, conjuring up the voice of her dead mother ('Chère enfant!'). Seizing a violin, Miracle leads the girl and her mother's ghost in a frantic trio, which leaves Antonia exhausted. Crespel and Hoffmann rush in, but both despair as Miracle declares Antonia dead; Crespel turns on Hoffmann, blaming him, as Miracle vanishes.

Act 4 (Giulietta) *A palace overlooking the Grand Canal in Venice* To the strains of a barcarolle ('Belle nuit, ô nuit d'amour') a gondola carrying Nicklausse and the courtesan Giulietta draws up outside the palace. A wild party is in progress, and Hoffmann sings a vigorous drinking song ('Amis, l'amour tendre et rêveur, erreur!'). Giulietta provocatively introduces Hoffmann to her current lover, Schlemil. Despite Nicklausse's warnings against her charms, Hoffmann rises to the bait. The magician Dapertutto enters and tempts Giulietta in a sinister aria ('Tourne, tourne, miroir'). He promises her a diamond ring if, as she has already done with Schlemil, she will obtain for him Hoffmann's other self – in the form of his reflection. Left alone with Giulietta, Hoffmann expresses his passion for her ('O Dieu! de quelle ivresse') and a rapturous duet follows. When she asks for his reflection to remember him by, he agrees, finding that he is indeed no longer visible in the mirror. Schlemil arrives and finds them together, and Giulietta flees to her boudoir. Schlemil challenges Hoffmann to a duel, and is killed. Hoffmann takes the key to Giulietta's boudoir from around Schlemil's neck, only to find her throwing her arms around her servant Pitichinaccio. Nicklausse drags Hoffmann away as Dapertutto adds to the mocking laughter.

Act 5 (Epilogue) *Luther's tavern in Nuremberg* At the end of his melancholy tale Hoffmann seeks solace in wine, until the revelries are interrupted by the entrance of Stella, fresh from her triumph in the opera house. Hoffmann, however, merely sees in her

his three lost loves and rejects her. She leaves on Lindorf's arm as the poet sinks into a drunken stupor. Nicklausse remains and, metamorphosing afresh into Hoffmann's Muse, tells him to rekindle the fire of his creative genius ('Des cendres de ton coeur'). A final chorus ('On est grand par l'amour') points the moral that one is enriched by love and sadness.

*

On the face of it, *Les contes d'Hoffmann* represents a stark contrast to the frivolous *opéras bouffes* that represent Offenbach's other claims to enduring fame. He was, though, thoroughly at home in opera composition, and throughout his career he had occasionally composed more serious works for productions at opera houses. In the Antonia act especially, he showed that he could write music of real passion, and that his musical style, serving humorous ends when matched with incongruous words, could appeal no less when presented entirely seriously. Elsewhere *Hoffmann* has plentiful moments when the music of *Orphée aux enfers, La belle Hélène* and *La Périchole* is close at hand, and the fact that the music for 'Scintille, diamant' could be lifted straight from an operetta for one of the more sinister moments shows how much the effect created by Offenbach's music depended on its lyrics and context. *Les contes d'Hoffmann* cannot rival the dramatic power of Bizet's *Carmen*, but Offenbach's thorough technique, his popular touch, and the particular appeal of the Hoffmann creation have combined to provide a work of endless fascination to audiences. A.L.

Corsaro, II ('The Corsair')

Opera in three acts by Giuseppe Verdi to a libretto by Francesco Maria Piave after Byron's poem *The Corsair*; Trieste, Teatro Grande, 25 October 1848.

The first cast included Gaetano Fraschini (Corrado), Achille De Bassini (Seid) and Marianna Barbieri-Nini (Gulnara).

Corrado *Captain of the corsairs*	tenor
Giovanni *a corsair*	bass
Medora *Corrado's young beloved*	soprano
Seid *Pasha of Coron*	baritone
Gulnara *Seid's favourite slave*	soprano
Selimo *an Aga*	tenor
A Black Eunuch	tenor
A Slave	tenor

Corsairs, guards, Turks, slaves, odalisques, Medora's maids, Anselmo (a corsair)

Setting An island in the Aegean and the city of Coron, at the beginning of the 19th century

Verdi had toyed with setting Byron's poem as early as 1844 and kept the subject in mind during the years immediately following. In 1845 he considered using it to fulfil a commission from Her Majesty's Theatre in London: Piave wrote the libretto, but the London trip was postponed. A year later Verdi showed his continuing enthusiasm for the topic by asking Piave not to give the libretto to any other composer. Eventually, however, this keenness faded and Verdi wrote the opera simply to fulfil the final part of a long-standing contract with Giovanni Ricordi's rival publisher Francesco Lucca, a man with whom Verdi had had unfortunate dealings ever since Lucca and Ricordi had come to legal blows over the rights to *Nabucco* in 1842. Anxious above all to be rid of his obligation, Verdi set Piave's libretto in the winter of 1847–8, giving the opera to Lucca without any idea of where or when it would first be performed. For a composer who in all previous operas had taken an enormous, often fanatical interest in the details of his creations' first staging, such indifference is suspicious: many have seen it as an indication that Verdi had little faith in his new opera. Lucca eventually placed the opera at the Teatro Grande in Trieste, but Verdi did not even trouble to attend the first performances. The première was poorly received and the work managed only a few revivals before it disappeared from the repertory. It has occasionally been revived in modern times.

*

The prelude, based on material from the opera, is one of extreme contrasts, with the opening orchestral storm music followed by a lyrical subject of great simplicity.

Act I.i *The corsairs' island in the Aegean* A boisterous offstage chorus of corsairs introduces Corrado, who bemoans his life of exile and crime in 'Tutto parea sorridere', an aria that delicately hovers between Italian formal convention and the French two-verse variety. A letter containing military intelligence is presented to Corrado, who resolves to set sail, rallying his troops with the cabaletta 'Sì: de' Corsari il fulmine'; in the manner of Verdi's earliest successes, the chorus joins the soloist for the final lines.

I.ii *Medora's apartments in the old tower* Medora, awaiting Corrado's arrival, takes up her harp and sings a two-verse *romanza*, 'Non so le tetre immagini', full of vague forebodings though not without elaborate vocal ornament. Corrado enters and a conventionally structured duet finale closes the act. The first lyrical movement, 'No, tu non sai', a dissimilar type in which Medora's disturbed chromatic line is settled by Corrado's reassuring melodic stability, is unusual in its progressive deceleration of tempo; the cabaletta, 'Tornerai, ma forse spenta', which sees Corrado about to depart yet again, is more traditionally paced, with a final faster section

in which the lovers sing an extended passage in 3rds and 6ths.

Act 2.i *Luxurious apartments in Seid's harem* A chorus of odalisques, graced with high woodwind local colour, introduces Gulnara, who hates Seid and seeks to escape from the harem. Her cavatina, 'Vola talor dal carcere', is conventionally scored but has much of that harmonic and orchestral density we expect from post-*Macbeth* Verdi. She agrees to attend a banquet of Seid's and in the cabaletta 'Ah conforto è sol la speme' prays that Heaven will take pity on her.

2.ii *A magnificent pavilion on the shores of the harbour of Coron* After a brief chorus of greeting, Seid salutes his followers and joins them in a solemn hymn to Allah, 'Salve Allah!', a number whose rhythmic cut is more than a little reminiscent of the famous choruses in *I Lombardi* and *Ernani*. A Dervish appears, asking for protection from the corsairs. He and Seid have time for the brief first movement of a duet, 'Di': que' ribaldi tremano', before flames are seen and offstage cries signal an attack. The Dervish throws off his disguise to reveal himself as Corrado, who calls for his followers. In an extended battle sequence, Corrado and his troops attempt to save the women of the harem, a delay in the attack that causes their defeat and his wounding. In the ensuing Andante of the concertato finale, 'Audace cotanto mostrati pur sai?', Seid derides the fallen hero, Corrado is defiant and Gulnara and the odalisques find their amorous feelings aroused by these handsome would-be saviours. More prisoners are brought on, but Seid is above all happy to have Corrado in his power and leads off the stretta 'Sì, morrai di morte atroce', promising his prisoner an agonizing death.

Act 3.i *Seid's apartments* The baritone has so far seen little of the vocal limelight, and room is now made for a full-scale double aria. In the Andantino, 'Cento leggiadre vergini', Seid regrets that of all the women available to him, the one whom he loves has spurned him. As in Corrado's Act 1 aria, though even more economically, the aria is notable for its orchestral reprise of the main melody. In the cabaletta 'S'avvicina il tuo momento', a movement more reminiscent of Verdi's first opera *Oberto* than of the post-*Macbeth* style, Seid looks forward to Corrado's grisly death.

Gulnara enters to plead for Corrado's life. The first movement of the ensuing duet, 'Vieni, Gulnara!', is a free dialogue over a complex orchestral melody of a kind later to be made famous in the Rigoletto-Sparafucile duet. But Seid will not be persuaded and eventually concludes that Gulnara must love Corrado. His anger bursts forth in the duet cabaletta, 'Sia l'istante maledetto'.

3.ii *Inside a prison tower* A sombre prelude featuring solo cello and viola introduces Corrado, alone and in chains. He laments his fate in a spare but expressive recitative before falling asleep. Gulnara steals in and awakens him. In the long, expressive and unusually free first movement of their duet, 'Seid la vuole', Gulnara offers Corrado a means of escape, saying that she herself will kill Seid. Corrado's personal honour obliges him to refuse her help, and he further distresses her by admitting his love for Medora. Gulnara departs, and the orchestra sounds a reprise of the stormy music first heard in the prelude to Act 1. As the storm subsides Gulnara returns to announce that Seid is dead. Corrado now assures her of his protection and in the cabaletta 'La terra, il ciel m'abborrino' they prepare to escape together.

3.iii The corsairs' island (as I.i) An orchestral prelude featuring fragments of Medora's Act 1 *romanza* introduces Corrado's beloved, near death and without hope of seeing him again. But suddenly a ship is sighted, Corrado and Gulnara arrive, and the lovers are in each other's arms. Corrado and Gulnara relate something of their adventures before Medora leads off the Andante concertato, 'O mio Corrado, appressati', whose opening melody appeared in the prelude to the opera. Corrado and Gulnara heighten the emotional temperature by protesting at fate, but Medora's strength fails. In an agony of despair, Corrado flings himself from the cliffs.

*

It is important to recall that the libretto to *Il corsaro* (and therefore its essential dramatic structure) was fixed as early as 1846, some time before Verdi worked on *Macbeth*: much of the opera seems rather old-fashioned in relation to the works that surround it in the Verdian canon. It is also – perhaps for this reason, perhaps (as mentioned earlier) because of Verdi's feud with the publisher Lucca – an uneven work, with an element of the routine in certain passages. On the other hand, there are many moments, particularly in the final act, that stand comparison with the best operas of this period, and some formal experiments – strange and elliptical as they may be in their dramatic context – that were to bear much fruit in the years to come.   R.P.

Così fan tutte [*Così fan tutte, ossia La scuola degli amanti* ('All Women do the Same, or The School for Lovers')]

Opera buffa in two acts, κ588, by Wolfgang Amadeus Mozart to a libretto by Lorenzo da Ponte; Vienna, Burgtheater, 26 January 1790.

The first cast consisted of Da Ponte's mistress, Adriana Ferrarese del Bene (Fiordiligi), Susanna in the 1789 *Figaro*; Louise Villeneuve (Dorabella); Vincenzo Calvesi (Ferrando); and three stalwarts from the 1786 *Figaro*, Dorotea Bussani (Despina), Francesco Benucci (Guglielmo) and Francesco Bussani (Alfonso).

Fiordiligi ⎫	*ladies from Ferrara, sisters,*	soprano
Dorabella ⎭	*living in Naples*	soprano
Guglielmo	*an officer, Fiordiligi's lover*	bass
Ferrando	*an officer, Dorabella's lover*	tenor
Despina	*maidservant to the sisters*	soprano
Don Alfonso	*an old philosopher*	bass
Soldiers, servants, sailors, wedding guests		
Setting Naples, in the 18th century		

Così fan tutte was commissioned following the successful revival of *Le nozze di Figaro* in August 1789. The libretto is original; there is no hard evidence for the theory that it was based on a recent Viennese scandal. It has a mythological and literary ancestry in the Procris story, and in Boccaccio, Shakespeare (*Cymbeline*) and Cervantes, all of whom anticipate elements of the plot: the trial of female constancy and the wager.

Così fan tutte was rehearsed at Mozart's apartment on 31 December, and in January with Haydn present. It received five performances before the death of Joseph II on 20 February closed the theatres; five more followed from June to August. There is little information about its genesis or reception.

Performances followed in 1791 in Prague, Leipzig and Dresden, and in German in Frankfurt (as *Liebe und Versuchung*), Mainz and Amsterdam. At Leipzig in 1794 and in other centres it appeared as *Weibertreue, oder Die Mädchen sind von Flandern*, translated by C. F. Bretzner, author of the source of *Die Entführung aus dem Serail*. No Mozart opera received such frequent 'improvement' or so many alternative titles besides the standard German *So machen es alle*. The alleged immorality of the libretto encouraged such treatment; some adaptations had the ladies learn of the plot and avenge themselves by turning the tables on their lovers. Critical opinion suggested that it was one of Mozart's weaker pieces, and the music appeared in pasticcios or with a completely different story. Today the opera is given in its original form, even with the restoration of Mozart's own cuts. *Così* was the second opera performed at Glyndebourne (1934) and productions since World War II are too numerous to mention; it is by now as much a repertory piece as the other Mozart-Da Ponte operas.

*

The short introduction to the overture concludes with a motto, a double cadence of striking simplicity (*piano*, interrupted, then *forte*, perfect), later sung to the words of the title. The sonata-form Presto mockingly tosses a figure among the woodwind, its cadence taken from Basilio's line 'Così fan tutte le

belle' (*Figaro*, the Act 1 trio, 'Cosa sento!'). The motto reappears just before the end.

Act I *A coffee-house* Ferrando and Guglielmo proclaim the virtues of the sisters Dorabella and Fiordiligi, to whom they are betrothed; Alfonso is sceptical (trio, 'La mia Dorabella'). The young men prepare to defend the ladies' honour with swords, but the diatonic brilliance of music shared by all three argues no great discord. Alfonso declines to fight, but calls them simpletons to trust female constancy: a faithful woman is like a phoenix; all believe in it but none has seen it (his mocking *pianissimo* unison cadence resembles the motto). The others insist that the phoenix is personified in Dorabella/Fiordiligi (trio, 'È la fede delle femmine'). Alfonso wagers 100 zecchini that the girls' fidelity will not endure a day of the lovers' absence; he will prove it if they promise to obey him while wooing each other's betrothed in disguise. Ferrando plans to spend his winnings on a serenade, Guglielmo (the first division between them) on a meal; Alfonso listens politely (trio, 'Una bella serenata'). An extended orchestral coda closes a scene of purely *buffo* electricity.

A garden by the sea [morning] The girls sing rapturously of their lovers (duet, 'Ah guarda sorella'); Dorabella (surprisingly, in view of the sequel) touches a note of melancholy before they launch into voluptuous coloratura in 3rds, united in loving the idea of loving. Alfonso appears, the prolonged F minor cadences of his tiny aria ('Vorrei dir') choking back the awful news: their lovers are to leave for active service. The men take solemn leave with only hints at lyricism (quintet, 'Sento, o Dio'). The girls' agitation is touching; Alfonso quells any premature delight on the men's part at this evidence of love. Ferrando's lyricism (to a motif from the trio, 'Una bella serenata') now matches the girls'; Guglielmo sings with Alfonso (this inevitable consequence of differences in tessitura continually invites

differentiation of character). The girls declare they will die; in a prepared speech (duettino, 'Al fato dan legge') the men promise to return. A march is heard (chorus, 'Bella vita militar'). They embrace, promising a daily letter, their rapturous indulgence in misery (particularly intense in the melodic line, taken by Fiordiligi) counterpointed by Alfonso's efforts not to laugh (quintet, 'Di scrivermi ogni giorno'). The men embark (reprise of the chorus), and Alfonso joins the girls in a moving prayer for their safety (trio, 'Soave sia il vento'), the orchestra evocative yet sensuous. Alfonso in an arioso prepares for action: 'He ploughs the waves, sows in sand, traps the wind in a net, who trusts the heart of a woman'.

A furnished room Despina has prepared the ladies' chocolate and is sampling it when they burst in. Dorabella explains their despair, but her extravagant grief leaves her barely coherent (obbligato recitative and the first real aria, 'Smanie implacabili'). Despina cannot take them seriously; surely they can find other lovers. In the teeth of their protests she inverts Alfonso's creed (aria, 'In uomini'): men, especially soldiers, are not expected to be faithful; women should also use love to enjoy themselves. Alfonso bribes Despina to assist him, without revealing the ramifications of the plot. The men enter as lovelorn 'Albanians', their bizarre disguise impenetrable even to the sharp-witted Despina (sextet, 'Alla bella Despinetta'). Recovering from laughter, she helps them to plead for a moment's kindness from the ladies; they are rejected in a furious Allegro. Alfonso, emerging, claims them as his friends, but after the men's voices unite, turning recitative towards arioso, Fiordiligi articulates her constancy in a powerful recitative and aria ('Come scoglio'); she stands firm as a rock in tempestuous seas. The three sections grow in brilliance and versatility; near the start, after leaps of a 10th and 12th, she ascends majestically over two octaves (the total range is a–c'''); near the end she takes the bass line. Guglielmo's patter-song in praise of his own appearance (especially the moustaches) finds no favour ('Non siate ritrosi'; there is a longer, rejected alternative, 'Rivolgete a lui lo sguardo'). As the outraged girls depart, the men bubble with delight (trio, 'E voi ridete?'), brilliantly covering Alfonso's insistence that the more the girls protest, the more sure is their fall. Guglielmo wonders when they can get lunch; Ferrando enjoys the atmosphere of love ('Un' aura amorosa'), muted violins and clarinets supporting his ardently extended line.

The garden [afternoon] At the beginning of the finale, the girls unwittingly share Ferrando's mood of longing, spinning a tender D major melody to a gently ironic rococo decoration of flutes and bassoons. How their fate has changed! Their sighs are displaced by fear when the men rush in drinking poison, to music (in G minor) suddenly suggestive of tragic violence. Alfonso and Despina go for help, instructing the ladies to nurse the men, who are thoroughly enjoying themselves; yet minor modes prevail as never before in Mozart's finales. Despina, to a pompous G major minuet, appears disguised as the doctor, invoking Mesmer as she magnetizes out the poison. The key abruptly changes to B♭: the men profess to believe they are in paradise. In the final Allegro the men request a kiss and are again rebuffed.

Act 2 *A room* Despina tries to persuade her shocked employers that there is no harm in a little flirtation. In Mozart's slyest *buffo* soprano aria ('Una donna a quindici anni'), she explains that a young girl who knows the arts of attracting men can have them at her mercy. The girls agree that there can be nothing wrong in enjoying the men's company, and they select partners (duet, 'Prenderò quel brunettino'). Dorabella will take the brown-haired one (Guglielmo), Fiordiligi the blond (Ferrando; thus they fall in with the men's plan, for which they have been subtly primed); and they prepare to amuse themselves.

Furnished garden by the sea [early evening] The serenade on wind instruments, repeated by the lovers and chorus ('Secondate, aurette amiche'), is a prayer for success in love. The four meet but are tongue-tied; Alfonso and Despina give a lesson in etiquette (quartet, the ladies silent, 'La mano a me date'), and join their hands. The couples prepare to walk round the garden. Guglielmo is all too successful in winning Dorabella's heart and a mark of her favour, replacing Ferrando's portrait by his own gift, a pendant heart (duet, 'Il core vi dono'). The gently bantering 3/8, in F major, matches Dorabella's innocent flirtatiousness; Guglielmo can hardly believe his success, but falls comfortably in with her mood. Fiordiligi rushes in, pursued by Ferrando: she has seen in him temptation, a serpent, a basilisk; he is stealing her peace. He protests that he wants only her happiness and asks for a kindly glance, noting that she looks at him and sighs. Her lovely soul will not long resist his pleading; otherwise her cruelty will kill him ('Ah lo veggio quell'anima bella'). In this lightly flowing rondo, as in 'Un'aura amorosa', woodwind are added only at the reprise; the ending achieves an unexpected intensity. This aria is traditionally omitted, but without it Ferrando's exit is inexplicable. Fiordiligi wrestles with her conscience, her obbligato recitative ('Ei parte') running a gamut of feeling while traversing tonal space from B♭ to E. In her deeply expressive aria ('Per pietà, ben mio') the elaborate wind parts (notably the horns) have an *opera seria* formality; sheer musical beauty articulates her cry of despair, as she asks her absent lover's forgiveness. There has been no simple recitative since

before the duet for Guglielmo and Dorabella; the symmetry of the couplings breaks down in over 400 bars of continuous music.

The men compare notes: when he learns of Dorabella's fickleness Ferrando is roused to fury (obbligato recitative, 'Il mio ritratto! Ah perfida!'). Guglielmo tries to console him by adopting Alfonso's philosophy (aria, 'Donne mie la fate a tanti'); he is fond of women and defends their honour, but their little habit of deceiving men is reprehensible. The restless perpetual motion conveys Guglielmo's smug confidence that the tragedy will not befall him. Ferrando's feelings are in turmoil (obbligato recitative, 'In qual fiero contrasto'). An obsessive orchestral figure projects shame ('Alfonso! how you will laugh!') and anger ('I will cut the wretch out of my heart') beyond the decorum of comedy. In a cavatina ('Tradito, schernito') he denounces Dorabella's treachery but admits (clarinets entering as C minor turns to E♭ major) that he still loves her. Alfonso and Guglielmo overhear the reprise in which the E♭ melody recurs in C, oboes replacing clarinets: this new instrumental colour (his previous arias used no oboes) may be prophetic. His pride piqued, he agrees to a further attack on Fiordiligi.

A room, with several doors, a mirror, and a table Despina praises Dorabella's good sense; Dorabella answers Fiordiligi's protests in a graceful 6/8 aria ('È amore un ladroncello') which, despite its sophisticated instrumentation, shows her conversion to Despina's recommendation of easy virtue; love is a thief, a serpent, but if you let him have his way, he brings delight. Alone, Fiordiligi resolves to repel her new suitor; sadistically observed by the men, she prepares to join her lover at the front, and orders Despina to bring his uniform. She launches an aria ('Fra gli amplessi'), but as she quickens the tempo from Adagio Ferrando joins in. Her anguished plea (Allegro) holds a striking allusion to Ferrando's first phrase in the Act 1 trio, 'Una bella serenata'. Ferrando's lyricism outdoes hers. The note of true ardour is intensified when the acceleration of tempo is halted by a Larghetto; it is hard not to believe that Ferrando is genuine. Despite a high *a″* on 'crudel', Fiordiligi's responses are tremulous; the solo oboe rises above her, speaks for her, as she admits defeat ('hai vinto'). The fourth (Andante) section of this greatest of Mozart's duets combines their voices in an intimacy never vouchsafed to Dorabella and Guglielmo. Guglielmo is enraged; Ferrando is ironic; Alfonso tells them their only revenge is to marry their 'plucked crows'. Women are always accused of fickleness, but he forgives them; they are not responsible for their own nature ('Tutti accusan le donne'). All three sing the motto from the overture: 'Così fan tutte'.

A reception room prepared for a wedding An Allegro,

resembling the opera's opening number, begins the finale, as Despina orders the servants to prepare a feast (brief choral response) and Alfonso applauds their work. The chorus greets the couples; in their carefree response the accident of casting matches the composer's dramatic insight by bringing Fiordiligi and Ferrando together in expansive coloratura. With Dorabella they sing the toast, a ravishing canon; Guglielmo, whose range prevents him from following on, mutters curses. Alfonso enters with Despina disguised as a notary. Coughing formally, she reads the marriage contract; the ladies sign it. But then the Act 1 march in D, associated with the officers' departure, is heard. Consternation: their lovers are returning. The Albanians are bundled into hiding, and the men reappear jauntily as their old selves, pretend puzzlement at their reception, drag out the notary, revealed as Despina, and find the marriage contract: indignation, confession, blame (on Alfonso), threats of revenge. They return half-changed into Albanians: Ferrando greets Fiordiligi, Guglielmo greets Dorabella (quoting their love duet), and both address the flabbergasted Despina as the doctor (a reference to the first finale). Alfonso calms them down; the ladies beg pardon; the men condescend to forgive, and all agree to follow Alfonso's idea of reason: to laugh when there is cause to weep, and so find equilibrium.

*

Only in the 20th century has a serious interest been taken in *Così fan tutte*. At first it was considered a heartless farce clothed in miraculous music, a view supported by its obvious artificiality (the lovers' disguises, the 24-hour time-scale). A number of cuts, particularly of Act 2 arias, became customary. Recently directors and critics have sought deeper meanings, and even questioned the restoration of the original pairing of lovers, which it seems legitimate to assume from the conventionality of the conclusion but which is not specified in the libretto or clarified by the music.

Così has been seen as revealing a dark side to the Enlightenment, an anti-feminist sadism. Yet by any showing the most admirable character is Fiordiligi. The girls develop more than the men. Dorabella at least learns to understand her own lightness; and 'Fra gli amplessi' suggests that Fiordiligi has matured through learning the power of sexuality. There is little sign that Guglielmo learns anything in the school for lovers, even that those who set traps deserve to get caught, although his vanity is wounded as deeply as his purse. Ferrando, however, comes to live as intensely as Fiordiligi, and may appear to have fallen in love with her. To suggest that they should marry (leaving Guglielmo for Dorabella) is, however, still less satisfactory than reversion to the original pairings. The conclusion represents not a solution, but a way of bringing the action to a close with an artificiality so evident that no happy outcome can be predicted. The music creates this enigma, but cannot solve it.

By standards other than Mozart's, the instrumentation in *Così* would be of novel richness. The invention of B♭ trumpets allows their substitution for horns in 'Come scoglio' and 'Ah lo veggio', divorced from the timpani; three other numbers also use trumpets without horns. The resourceful use of woodwind, application of string mutes, and exploration of a wider than usual range of keys and key relations, creates an unprecedentedly voluptuous colouring (E major and A♭ major are juxtaposed in the second finale, the former used in three other numbers, a concentration unusual in Mozart).

Much of the style of *Così* has been attributed to parody, but a stylistic mixture had long been a feature of *opera buffa*. Guglielmo sings pure *buffo* arias, but all Ferrando's strike serious notes reflected in their variety of form. The girls' first arias overplay feelings which will not endure: Dorabella's prolonged cadences in 'Smanie implacabili' recall Alfonso's mock-seriousness in 'Vorrei dir'. 'Come scoglio' is sometimes considered pure parody, Fiordiligi's second aria 'Per pietà' essentially serious; yet the latter has equally wide leaps and even more florid instrumentation, the differences in perception of them explained by the fact that one administers a rebuff to the 'Albanian' strangers and the other, following a disturbing attack on her loyalty to Guglielmo, is an internal monologue.

There are fewer arias in *Così* than in the other Da Ponte operas, but they are correspondingly more important in unfolding the inner drama. The increased number of ensembles is balanced by the brevity of several of them, not only the sparkling *buffo* trios for the men but also 'Soave sia il vento', a gem in which even Alfonso appears moved; it bids farewell to innocence as well as to the lovers. There is a marked increase in the amount of obbligato recitative, which with the tone of some of the arias (notably Fiordiligi's) brings *Così* closer to *opera seria* than the other Da Ponte operas.

Così fan tutte is likely to remain a disturbing experience because of, not despite, its aesthetic attractions. The libretto was originally destined for Salieri; its superb pacing does not mask its potential triviality. Mozart found in it ways to seek out hitherto unplumbed depths in the human psyche, making the uncut whole, for an increasing number of commentators, the profoundest of his Italian comedies.   J.Ru.

Cunning Little Vixen, The [*Příhody Lišky Bystroušky* ('The Adventures of the Vixen Bystrouška')]

Opera in three acts by Leoš Janáček to his own libretto after Rudolf Těsnohlídek's novel *Liška Bystrouška*; Brno, National Theatre, 6 November 1924.

The original Vixen was Hana Hrdličková; Arnold Flögl sang the Gamekeeper, with Božena Snopková as the Fox.

Bystrouška ('Little Sharp Ears')	
[the Vixen]	soprano
(as a cub)	child soprano
(as a young woman)	dancer
Fox [*Zlatohřbítek*, 'Golden-mane']	soprano
Gamekeeper	baritone
Schoolmaster ⎫	tenor
Mosquito ⎭	
Badger ⎫	bass
Priest ⎭	
Blue Dragonfly	dancer
Cricket	child soprano
Grasshopper	child soprano
Frog	child soprano
Gamekeeper's Wife ⎫	contralto
Owl ⎭	
Lapák *the dog*	mezzo-soprano
Frantík *a boy*	soprano
Pepík *a boy*	soprano
Cock ⎫	soprano
Jay ⎭	
Chocholka *the hen*	soprano
Pásek *an innkeeper*	tenor
Woodpecker	contralto
Harašta *a poultry dealer and poacher*	bass
Mrs Pásková *the innkeeper's wife*	soprano

Hens, creatures of the forest, offstage chorus, fox cubs (children)

Ballet: midges, squirrels, hedgehog

Setting A forest near Brno, a farmyard at the Gamekeeper's lodge and Pásek's inn; about 1920

(The cast-list specifies that four pairs of characters should be sung by the same singers: Schoolmaster/ Mosquito; Priest/Badger; Gamekeeper's Wife/Owl; Cock/Jay.)

Těsnohlídek's novel came about as a text which the Brno newspaper *Lidové noviny* commissioned to go with a collection of drawings made many years earlier by the painter Stanislav Lolek. These told the story of a clever vixen reared from a cub by a gamekeeper but who escapes and raises a family. Těsnohlídek's *Liška Bystrouška* was serialized in *Lidové noviny* between 7 April and 23 June 1920, though it was not until 1921 (when the novel was published in book form) that Janáček began to

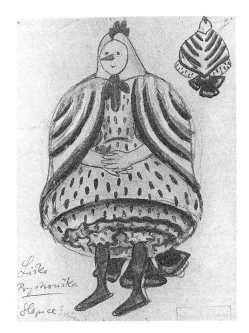

'The Cunning Little Vixen' (Janáček): costume design for a hen by Josef Čapek for the first Prague production, 18 May 1925

consider making an opera out of it. He began work on 22 January 1922 and after completing an early draft of Act 1 (26 March) he contacted Těsnohlídek for his permission. Janáček made his own libretto: Acts 1 and 2 correspond roughly to the novel; Act 3 is a free amalgam of passages from the novel and other elements. Janáček completed the opera on 10 October 1923 and Universal Edition published a vocal score (made by Janáček's pupil Břetislav Bakala) in July 1924, some months ahead of the Brno première on 6 November under František Neumann. The Prague première followed on 18 May 1925 under Otakar Ostrčil.

Max Brod's German version took considerable liberties in attempting to clarify and unify the plot, with a much more tangible relationship between the Vixen and Terynka, a young girl talked about by the humans but never seen. The German première (Mainz, 13 February 1927) was not particularly successful and the opera had to wait until Walter Felsenstein's celebrated production at the Komische Oper in Berlin in 1956 to enjoy international acclaim.

*

Act I *A wooded glen, a sunny summer afternoon* During the orchestral prelude the Badger emerges from his sett, smoking a pipe. Flies swirl round and dance, followed by the Blue Dragonfly. They disperse as the Gamekeeper approaches. Tired from the heat, he lies down and dozes off. The Cricket and Grasshopper make music (a delicately scored waltz) and are joined by the tipsy Mosquito. The Frog tries to catch the Mosquito but has himself attracted the attention of the young Vixen; in his efforts to escape her, he lands on the Gamekeeper's nose. The Gamekeeper wakes up, seizes the Vixen and takes her home 'for the children'. The music of the opening prelude returns as the Blue Dragonfly searches vainly for the Vixen.

The yard of the Gamekeeper's lodge; autumn, in afternoon sun After a short prelude the Vixen and Lapák the dog discuss their lack of experience in love. When Lapák makes advances to the Vixen she knocks him over. The children Pepík and Frantík run out and torment the Vixen. She attacks Pepík and attempts to escape but is tied up by the Gamekeeper. In a substantial interlude, night falls and the Vixen dreams she is a young girl. The dawn breaks; whole-tone harmonies give way to a radiant B♭ major and a soaring new theme.

Lapák and the Cock advise the Vixen to submit to captivity, while the Hens (a two-part chorus) industriously lay eggs. The Vixen rebukes the Hens for their slavish devotion to the Cock, and in disgust at their reactionary attitudes feigns suicide. Intrigued, the Cock approaches, is seized by the Vixen and is killed. In the commotion which follows (an energetic finale) the Gamekeeper tries to beat the Vixen but she bites through her leash and escapes into the woods.

Act 2 *The Badger's sett in the wood, late afternoon* The music of the prelude provides material for the subsequent scene in which the Vixen disturbs the Badger and then mockingly criticizes him, encouraged by the chorus of forest animals. Physically beaten by the enraged Badger, the Vixen retaliates by fouling his sett. This forces the Badger to leave and the Vixen promptly occupies it. An interlude leads into the next scene.

A room inside the inn 'U Pásků' ['At the Páseks'] The Schoolmaster and Gamekeeper are playing cards. The Priest joins them as the Gamekeeper, teasing the Schoolmaster about rumours of his impending marriage, sings a song about Veronika, a woman loved and lost, 'Bývalo' ('It used to be'). To get his own back the Schoolmaster taunts the Gamekeeper with the Vixen's escape. Hearing the cock crow, the Schoolmaster and then the Priest leave. The Gamekeeper reflects drily on the Schoolmaster's infatuation but leaves abruptly when Pásek reminds him of the Vixen's escape. An interlude leads into a scene in the forest.

The forest, a path leading uphill with sunflowers growing against the fence; a moonlit night The Schoolmaster drunkenly makes his way home, regretting his unsteady gait. The Vixen, who has watched his antics, hides behind a sunflower which the Schoolmaster mistakes for Terynka, the young

woman he admires from afar. He declares his love for her and, in attempting to embrace the sunflower, falls over the fence. The Vixen escapes and now observes the approaching Priest, who remembers bitterly his deception by a young girl when he was a student. The Gamekeeper is heard searching for the Vixen. She runs off; the Schoolmaster and Priest take fright (singing together briefly) and make their separate ways home as two shots ring out. The Gamekeeper comes out from the trees, convinced that he saw the Vixen.

The Vixen's burrow in the moonlight A gentle vocalise for offstage chorus opens the scene. The Vixen approvingly observes the Fox, who approaches and strikes up a conversation. The Vixen boasts of her home and her past exploits at the Gamekeeper's (a set-piece narrative condensing many chapters of the novel and establishing her fearless and assertive personality). Impressed, the Fox introduces himself and then dashes off while the Vixen, in a lyrical interlude, muses on her 'beauty'. The Fox returns with a freshly killed rabbit. In further conversation they admit to each other their sexual inexperience. When the Fox makes advances the Vixen at first rejects them but this prompts him to a passionate declaration of his love. She is won over: her 'Chcu!' ('I want!') is heard over languorously sensuous music and they go into her burrow. Time passes (a repeat of the Blue Dragonfly music from Act 1) and the Owl and the Jay comment censoriously on the turn of events. The Vixen comes out again crying; she whispers something to the Fox and he decides they must be married at once. The opening offstage chorus (now designated 'the voice of the forest') returns to provide a background to the ceremony, which is celebrated by a Woodpecker. Then the chorus music accelerates into an exuberant and substantial dance to close the act.

Act 3 *A clearing in the forest; autumn, noon, a clear sky* An assertive, mostly minor-key, prelude announces the approach of Harašta, who sings a three-stanza song 'Déž sem vandroval' ('When I went a-wandering'). He notices a dead hare on the path but is surprised by the Gamekeeper, whom he tells of his impending marriage to Terynka. The Gamekeeper warns him about poaching and examines the dead hare. He notices a fox-trail and, convinced that it is the Vixen's, sets a trap for her. The Gamekeeper and Harašta leave the clearing separately.

Immediately the Fox Cubs run on. Their song – a two-stanza folk-text 'Běží liška k Táboru' ('A vixen runs to Tábor'), in a delightful modal setting – develops into a suspicious investigation of the baited hare. With the help of the Vixen and the Fox they contemptuously recognize it as a trap. Surrounded by their many children, the Vixen and Fox look forward to breeding again in May. Over their lyrical duet the voice of Harašta is heard again singing another folk-text, 'Když jsem já šel okolo' ('When I went round the green grove'). He enters with a pannier full of poultry. The Vixen lies down in his path and feigns injury. Harašta reaches for his gun but the Vixen lures him away until he stumbles, and bloodies his nose. Meanwhile the Vixen and her family devour the contents of the pannier. Angered, Harašta fires wildly; the foxes scatter but the Vixen lies dying.

A bowling alley in the garden at 'U Pásků'; unaccustomed quiet The prelude develops into a nostalgic Adagio (marked both 'espressivo' and 'dolcissimo'). Time has passed. Only the Gamekeeper and the School-master are left at Pásek's inn. The Gamekeeper teases the Schoolmaster about his encounter with the sunflower, but is immediately sympathetic when he sees his friend grieving over Terynka's wedding. The Priest has moved to a new parish and has written that he is lonely (the nostalgic music of the prelude flowers into a new variant). The Gamekeeper complains of getting old like his dog, Lapák. He leaves, and a brief interlude follows based on the new nostalgic variant. Soon it gives way to vigorous music chiefly for horn quartet (a post-première addition to help with the scene change).

A wooded glen as in the opening scene, the sun shining after a shower The Gamekeeper is walking home. He notices a fungus growing and is reminded of happily picking mushrooms with his wife on their honey-moon. He contemplates the scene in one of the most lyrical outpourings of Janáček's late operas, 'Je to pohádka či pravda?' ('Is it a fairy-tale or true?'), expressing his love for the sunlit evenings in the forest and imagining the seasonal return of the fairy spirits and the unearthly joy which they bring to mankind. He falls asleep and the animals from the opening scene return. In his dream the Gamekeeper sees a vixen-cub, looking exactly like the Vixen Bystrouška herself. As he reaches out towards her he catches hold of a frog instead – the grandson (it explains) of the one which landed on his face in Act 1. In silent reverie the Gamekeeper lets his gun slip to the ground.

*

Janáček wrote *The Vixen*, the second of his four major late operas, on the eve of his 70th birthday and in this, his sunniest work, he came to terms with his years and his inevitable death. Thus he boldly introduced the death of the Vixen into the opera, but without fuss or pathos, and ended the opera with an evocation of its beginning and a strong message of renewal into which death is subsumed. The images emphasized in his libretto and in his music are cyclical; the seasons come and go, and though the humans get older, they are juxtaposed against images of youth. The children's voices that Janáček carefully specified help to underline this point. Their enlargement of the vocal spectrum, together with the inventive use of mime and ballet, also serves to portray the animal world.   J.T.

D

Dalibor

Opera in three acts by Bedřich Smetana to a libretto by Josef Wenzig; Prague, New Town Theatre, 16 May 1868.

The first cast included Jan Ludvík Lukes (Dalibor), Emilia Benevicová-Miková (Milada), Eleanora z Ehrenbergů (Jitka) and Josef Paleček (Beneš).

Vladislav *Czech King*	baritone
Dalibor *a knight*	tenor
Budivoj *commander of the king's castle guard*	baritone
Beneš *a gaoler*	bass
Vítek *Dalibor's messenger*	tenor
Milada *sister of the Burgrave of Ploškovice*	soprano
Jitka *a country girl on Dalibor's estates*	soprano
Zdeněk *a musician (vision)*	silent
Judges, the King's soldiers, Dalibor's messengers and servants, the people, priests	
Setting 15th-century Prague, partly in the castle and its environs, partly in the lower town	

Dalibor was one of Josef Wenzig's six plays and opera librettos based on Czech history. As a Czech sympathizer but German-speaker he wrote in German and his *Dalibor* and *Libuše* texts had to be translated into Czech. This was undertaken by his pupil Ervín Špindler, who preserved the line lengths and metres of the original so that, it is claimed, the operas could be performed in either Czech or German (an odd concept for such nationalist works). It seems more likely that Špindler had little option as far as *Dalibor* is concerned, since Smetana began composition on his third opera on 15 April 1865, even before Wenzig finalized his text (Wenzig's completed German text is dated 16 June 1865). According to references in his letters, Smetana completed Act 1 in sketch by 12 October 1865 and on 3 April 1866 he was working on Act 2. The full score was completed by 29 December 1867.

Dalibor was first performed on the day of the ceremonial laying of the foundation stone of the National Theatre, by which time Smetana had become chief conductor at the Provisional Theatre; he conducted the opera's première. By the next performance it was clear that the work was not popular with audiences and it was attacked in the press for not sounding sufficiently 'Czech'. The permanent members of the theatre company were lacking in dramatic sopranos and heroic tenors, which may also have had something to do with it. Its lack of success encouraged Smetana to make revisions. He made two cuts, amounting to over 70 bars, in the Act 2 scene between Dalibor and Milada and revised and extended the end of Act 3. These changes, made in 1870, had no effect on the opera's fortunes; it was given a few times and then disappeared from the repertory. Its later popularity with Czech audiences dates from 5 December 1886 when it was performed for the first time at the Prague National Theatre.

*

Act I The castle courtyard There is no overture. A 22-bar prelude, introducing the motto theme (ex.1) of

Ex.1 Largo maestoso

this predominantly monothematic opera, leads into a sombre chorus of the people, waiting to hear the fate of Dalibor, who is arrested and in prison. Individual sentiments are voiced by Jitka, an orphan whom Dalibor has cared for. The brief recapitulation of the choral-orchestral opening brings Jitka to a decision: Dalibor will be freed, and her new sentiments are conveyed by the joyous Allegro variant of ex.1, 'Ze žaláře' ('A glow beckons from jail').

Four offstage trumpets announce the arrival of King Vladislav. His entry music, based on a descending variant of ex.1, is slow-paced, finely crafted and surprisingly long: 57 bars. Although about to judge Dalibor and thus placed in opposition to the opera's hero, Vladislav is depicted sympathetically and in the round. As he describes Dalibor's crime (disturbing the peace of the land, attacking the castle of Ploškovice and killing the Burgrave there), his solo goes through eight tempo changes, but the dominant manner is expressive and stately.

Before sentencing Dalibor, the court invites Milada, sister of the murdered Burgrave, to speak. She is introduced by a solo harp cadenza, soon joined by a pair of clarinets. One of the glories of the Czech repertory, her speech is a substantial, multi-section declamation, its tempos and expression reflecting the different moods of the words as she pleads for vengeance and describes in vivid language the battle in which her brother fell. The part is written for a dramatic soprano with a strong lower register but capable of a thrilling climactic cry of 'Dalibor' to a top B. At the end her voice combines with that of Jitka in a new variant of ex.1 expressing the two women's different reactions. This duet provides a link to the third important entrance: that of Dalibor himself to a brief, stately transformation of ex.1. All, including Milada, comment on his calm and noble bearing.

In recitative, Vladislav describes Dalibor's crime and invites his response. Far from denying the crime, Dalibor describes his friendship with the musician Zdeněk (a gentle variant of ex.1 with throbbing triplet accompaniment) and then, in a martial passage, how Zdeněk fell in battle in Dalibor's longstanding feud with the Burgrave. In a strongly declamatory passage Dalibor declares how, even had the King stood in his way, he would have avenged his friend's death. The judges (a unison bass chorus) pronounce that Dalibor has condemned himself to death, and confer with the King.

A slow, lyrical episode follows in which Dalibor reveals himself untroubled by his probable fate, since his life has been empty since the death of Zdeněk. Milada, whose voice occasionally mingles with his, is appalled. Then Dalibor's sentence is confirmed by one of the judges; he is to languish in gaol until he dies. His response is ecstatic: over the 'Zdeněk' variant he sings 'quasi in exaltazione' that he looks forward to seeing his friend again. Twice the chorus punctuate his solo with their astonishment at his noble bearing.

Milada is quite overcome. In a violent change of mood (Presto) she begs Vladislav to pardon him but, as the judges explain, Dalibor has threatened the King and must die. Vladislav himself, in a quiet passage with solemn brass accompaniment, declares that the law must be upheld. To a repeat of his entrance music, he withdraws with his retinue. The people disperse, leaving Milada and Jitka.

In a passionate 6/8 Presto Milada describes her feelings, 'Jaká, jaká to bouře ňadra mi plní' ('What a storm fills my breast!'). On her last word her voice combines with that of Jitka, who has observed her

growing love for Dalibor and suggests action. This is agreed in an extended duet (repeating her earlier Allegro theme) as Jitka describes her plan for rescuing Dalibor from prison. Milada takes up her part; the two voices combine in what is in effect a vigorous cabaletta, a joyful pendant to the duet they sang before Dalibor's entrance.

Act 2.i *A road in the lower town, with an inn* A new atmosphere is suggested by a brief prelude and by the strophic offstage chorus for soldiers – one of the few parts of the opera whose 'Czechness' appealed to its early audiences. Jitka meets her lover Vítek, their unanimity reflected in the intertwining 3rds and 6ths of their duet. Jitka then describes how Milada has dressed as a boy and with harp in hand has charmed her way into the castle in search of Dalibor. The soldiers come out of the tavern; their chorus is heard again with added parts for the two soloists. As they go off a long orchestral interlude covers the scene change and introduces the subdued mood of the next scene; a chromatic figure leads into a Largo with ostinato quavers in the bass.

2.ii *An inner room in the castle* Budivoj questions Beneš the gaoler about his new assistant, a 'poor musician', then, warning him to be vigilant over Dalibor, he departs. The chromatic figure and ostinato quavers of the interlude return to preface Beneš's aria about the hard life of a gaoler ('Ach, jak těžký žalářníka život jest'), a simple *ABA* structure against the quaver ostinato.

To exuberant music Milada, now dressed as a boy, runs in with food for her new employer. Before he eats, Beneš goes to fetch his old violin (Dalibor has asked for a violin to relieve his boredom). Left alone, Milada expresses her agitation at the thought of seeing Dalibor) and, to a surging orchestral accompaniment, her feelings of 'unbounded joy' ('Radostí nesmírnou') in her aria. Beneš returns with a lamp and a violin for Milada to take to the prisoner, and, after a brief duet passage, both go off. An extended interlude includes Milada's harp cadenza from Act 1 and a new version of the Zdeněk variant.

2.iii *A dark prison* Dalibor has woken from a dream about Zdeněk; in a broad Andante amoroso he expresses his thoughts about embracing him. His reverie is interrupted by the arrival of Milada. Dalibor is thrilled with the violin and cries out to Zdeněk; only then does he notice the 'boy' and asks who he is. To the passionate theme from her first solo in Act 1 Milada reveals herself; regretting her earlier pleas for vengeance, she has come to try and rescue him. Then in an Andante (a slow, major-key variant of ex.1) she begs forgiveness. They vow faithfulness to one another and the act concludes with their Largo duet 'O ně výslovné štěstí lásky' ('O the unutterable happiness of love'), in which their voices intertwine as artlessly as those of the younger lovers at the beginning of the act. An orchestral postlude concludes with the Zdeněk variant of the motto theme.

Act 3.i *The royal chamber, brightly lit* The prelude includes Vladislav's march, Beneš's quaver ostinato and a new, stately theme. Budivoj warns King Vladislav of a rebellion by Dalibor's people and Beneš describes how his harp-playing assistant has disappeared, leaving instead a purse and a note telling him to keep silent. They withdraw. While his advisers confer, Vladislav sings a lyrical aria about the burdens of office. His advisers decree that Dalibor must die that day and Vladislav reluctantly gives instruction to Budivoj. The interlude begins with the motto theme in its original form and key (ex.1), passing on to Vladislav's march, the concluding duet of Act 2, and Jitka's 'freedom' motif.

3.ii *Dalibor's prison* Dalibor, now unfettered, sings a vigorous aria contemplating his impending freedom, 'Ha, kým to kouzlem' ('What magic is this'). His exultation is shortlived; just as he is about to give a signal on his violin to his supporters, Budivoj appears with his soldiers and takes him off, to the strains of a march.

3.iii *In front of the prison; night, faint moonlight* Milada, Jitka, Vítek and their company are waiting for Dalibor's signal. When instead they hear an offstage chorus of monks, Milada realizes that they have been betrayed and, sword in hand, she leads her soldiers into the castle. All return, with Dalibor now bearing the mortally wounded Milada. They bid farewell to one another, and Milada dies. Budivoj and his soldiers emerge and celebrate their victory. Dalibor throws himself into battle with them and dies joyfully with the thought that Zdeněk and Milada await him.

*

With Milada's Leonore-like bid to rescue Dalibor from his prison, this opera, Smetana's most advanced, has been criticized for being a Czech *Fidelio*. There are, however, striking differences. This is not an opera about marital fidelity or the brotherhood of man. Dalibor shows more interest in his dead friend Zdeněk than in his would-be rescuer Milada. With its continuous scene-change music and thematic metamorphosis, the opera's aesthetic is that of Liszt and early Wagner, not of Beethoven. And in supplying Dalibor with a violin, the opera reinforces a favourite myth about the Czechs being good musicians. As Beneš, the music-loving gaoler who supplies the instrument for his charge, declares: 'What Czech does not love music?'   J.T.

Death in Venice

Opera in two acts (17 scenes), op.88, by Benjamin Britten to a libretto by Myfanwy Piper based on Thomas Mann's novella *Der Tod in Venedig*; Snape, the Maltings, 16 June 1973.

The original cast included Peter Pears (Aschenbach), John Shirley-Quirk (Traveller) and James Bowman (Apollo).

Gustav von Aschenbach *a novelist*	tenor
The Traveller *who also sings:*	
The Elderly Fop	
The Old Gondolier	
The Hotel Manager	
The Hotel Barber	bass-baritone
The Leader of the Players	
The Voice of Dionysus	
The Voice of Apollo	countertenor
The Polish Mother	
Tadzio *her son*	choreographed
Jaschiu *his friend*	

Youths and girls, hotel guests and waiters, gondoliers and boatmen, street vendors, touts and beggars, citizens of Venice, choir in St Mark's, tourists, followers of Dionysus
Choreographed roles: Tadzio's two sisters, his governess, other boys and girls, strolling players, beach attendants
Setting Munich and Venice

Britten had *Death in Venice* in mind as an operatic subject for many years, and in September 1970, very soon after the completion of *Owen Wingrave*, he invited Myfanwy Piper to write the libretto. She had finished a draft of Act 1 by September 1971, and it seems probable that Britten began the music that December, using preliminary sketches made during an autumn visit to Venice. The opera was complete by the end of 1972, although some quite significant changes were still to come, and additional modifications were made between the première and the publication of the vocal score in 1975.

Of all Britten's operas, *Death in Venice* is the most dependent on the particular vocal qualities of his lifelong partner Peter Pears, to whom it is dedicated. The intimate, intense character of the music reflects the refinement and delicacy of the Pears sound at that relatively late stage of his career, and the musical idiom – an economical blend of Britten's personal adaptation of 12-note features in association with those fundamental elements of tonal harmony that he never abandoned – is the fullest demonstration of the flexibility and focus of Britten's own late style. Not surprisingly, Pears was an indispensable asset to early revivals of the work after the première, as was John Shirley-Quirk in the bass-baritone roles. The opera was first given at Covent Garden in October 1973 and at the Metropolitan in October 1974. A recording, conducted by Steuart Bedford, was made at Snape in April 1974.

*

Act I.i *Munich* The 'master writer' Aschenbach is weary and unable to work, but affirms his belief in order rather than passion. A traveller appears, whose account of the mysterious marvels of distant places stirs Aschenbach's desire to 'travel to the south'. In the first of the 'quasi parlando' recitatives with piano that are a special feature of the work (the pitches moulded to the inflections of Pears's speaking voice), Aschenbach persuades himself that such a journey may restore his 'flagging inspiration'.

I.ii *On the boat to Venice* This scene is punctuated by a haunting refrain on the word 'Serenissima' (adapting the 'magic' motif of the traveller's music from scene i). Among the predominantly young and lighthearted passengers is an elderly fop, rouged and dressed in a forlorn attempt to belie his age. Aschenbach is apprehensive that Venice will not provide its usual welcome. The scene ends with an interlude in barcarolle style, called 'overture', evoking the waters and bells of the city.

I.iii *The journey to the Lido* Aschenbach's belief in the healing powers of Venice is restored, despite the sinister refusal of his gondolier to obey orders, or wait to be paid. In a lyrical arioso Aschenbach muses on the fact that a black gondola is 'a vision of death itself'.

I.iv *The first evening at the hotel* The manager sings the praises of his establishment. To an expansive, consonant yet tonally unstable motif he obsequiously shows the writer the view of the beach from his room, then leaves Aschenbach to reflect in recitative on his aims and ambitions as a creative artist. After a while he is drawn back to the view before him. Among the hotel guests from various countries who pass he notices a Polish family, including a boy of great physical beauty (characterized by a sinuous modal motif on the vibraphone) whose name, he learns, is Tadzio. Aschenbach meditates on the irresolvably ambiguous relation between the artist's sense of beauty and his desire to achieve a purely formal perfection.

I.v *On the beach* Aschenbach finds the atmosphere oppressive and cannot work, but nevertheless wishes to remain in Venice. As he watches, Tadzio arrives on the beach with his family and plays with other children, who accept him as their leader. Aschenbach reflects that he feels 'a father's warmth' for a beauty 'I might have created'.

I.vi *The foiled departure* Crossing from the Lido to Venice proper, which is crowded and stifling, Aschenbach resolves to leave. Back at the hotel he informs the manager of his decision, but after

crossing to the city once more to take the train back to Germany, he learns that his baggage has been sent to Como. He returns to the hotel, both angry and delighted that his departure has been prevented. Seeing Tadzio on the beach, he makes a firm decision to stay on.

I.vii *The games of Apollo* Aschenbach witnesses beach sports in which Tadzio takes part: the games are presented in choreographed form with a choral commentary and interpolations from the voice of Apollo. At the end Tadzio's victory is celebrated, and Aschenbach exclaims ecstatically that 'the boy . . . shall inspire me . . . The power of beauty sets me free'. He develops this theme in an extended lyrical outpouring, and is forced to recognize the truth. As Tadzio passes him on his way into the hotel and smiles at him, Aschenbach confesses – though the boy cannot hear him – 'I love you!'

Act 2 In a recitative, Aschenbach attempts to come to terms with his love, and regrets his inability even to speak to Tadzio.

2.viii *The hotel barber's shop* He hears the first rumours of a sickness that is causing people to leave Venice, but the barber becomes evasive when questioned.

2.ix *The pursuit* Aschenbach crosses to the city and learns that 'citizens are advised to take precautions against infection', but that 'rumours of cholera' are being denied. His only concern is that the Polish family should not hear such rumours; he begins to follow them about the city and, finally, back to the hotel, still without making any direct contact with Tadzio.

2.x *The strolling players* Aschenbach is with other hotel guests on the terrace after dinner. A troupe of actor-singers presents a parody of courtship, with its leader adding a mock lament, 'So I shall never be able to marry'. Aschenbach accosts the leader, seeking the truth about the possible plague. Once again, the answers are worryingly evasive, and the leader's final song, with its chorus of mocking laughter, turns into a sinister attack on the hotel guests.

2.xi *The travel bureau* Aschenbach arrives as a crowd of visitors seeks information and an early escape from Venice. At first the English clerk offers the usual evasive responses, but in the end he admits to Aschenbach that 'death is at work. The plague is with us'. He advises him to leave before the city is blockaded.

2.xii *The lady of the pearls* Aschenbach rehearses how he might warn Tadzio's mother of the danger, but when she appears in the hotel he cannot speak to her. In despair and joy he realizes that all he cares about is his love for Tadzio.

2.xiii *The dream* In a feverish sleep, Aschenbach seems to hear a debate between Apollo and Dionysus: with the victory of Dionysus his followers sing and dance in triumph. Waking, he recognizes that he can 'fall no further'.

2.xiv The empty beach Aschenbach watches as Tadzio and a few friends begin to play their beach games, only to abandon them and run off.

2.xv The hotel barber's shop He submits to the kind of rouging and hair-colouring that marked the elderly fop in scene ii.

2.xvi The last visit to Venice Aschenbach is almost hysterically exuberant in his new guise, although the effects of illness are beginning to become apparent. Once again he follows the Polish family through the city, ever more strongly convinced that Tadzio understands his feelings and is encouraging him. He buys some strawberries, but they are musty and overripe. Bitterly he recalls his proclamation of his own creative beliefs from scene i, and in an understated yet supremely eloquent arioso summarizes the celebrated Platonic exchange between Socrates and Phaedrus which traces the path from the sensual discovery of beauty to the abyss of passion.

2.xvii The departure This begins with a richly orchestrated fantasia on the 'view' motif from scene iv. The hotel manager and a porter discuss the departure of the guests. Aschenbach learns that the Polish family is about to leave, and the manager assumes that Aschenbach himself will soon follow them. Tadzio and a few other children play on the beach, and this time the game turns rough, with Tadzio being knocked down, his face pressed into the sand by Jaschiu. As Aschenbach cries out the boy gets up, unharmed. Aschenbach calls Tadzio's name, and, when the boy beckons him, collapses and dies in his chair. To a short postlude combining Tadzio's unearthly theme and the melody from scene vii for Aschenbach's phrase about the indissoluble fusion of feeling and thought, 'Tadzio continues his walk far out to sea'.

*

Music and plot work together most effectively in Britten's operas at the level of psychological motivation, and nowhere is this more evident than in *Death in Venice*, his final opera. The work is concerned less with pederasty, or even weakened creativity, than with their causes and consequences: guilt, self-doubt, masochistic resignation. The work will always seem disconcerting to those who believe that Mann's claustrophobically intense story demands a music of Bergian expressionistic force – or Mahlerian nostalgia, as in Visconti's film – to do it justice. Yet Britten's relatively narrow range of tone colours, with the dry piano of Aschenbach's recitatives at one extreme and the gamelan-style tuned percussion for Tadzio and the beach games at the other, together with his unfailingly concise musical forms, bring Aschenbach's inhibitedness and obsession with the structures of art unerringly into the dramatic foreground. It is clear that

we are seeing Venice solely through Aschenbach's eyes, and the simplicity with which the enticing Tadzio and Aschenbach's own fumbling attempts to express love are represented demonstrate how justified Britten was in trusting his own aesthetic principle and in 'tear[ing] all the waste away'. Aschenbach's death is as much resolution as dissolution, hence the extraordinarily ambivalent mixture of fulfilment and loss we experience in the opera's final moments. The ultimate distillation of Britten's highly personal eloquence is the brief 'Phaedrus' monologue in scene xvi, a passage of surpassing poignancy which only the most disciplined and sensitive artist could have conceived, while the opera's hushed ending is an inspired synthesis of the work's most memorable qualities – intensity and restraint.   A.W.

Dialogues des Carmélites
('Dialogues of the Carmelites')

Opera in three acts by Francis Poulenc to his own libretto after Georges Bernanos' play; Milan, Teatro alla Scala, 26 January 1957.

The cast at the première included Virginia Zeani (Blanche), Leyla Gencer (the new Prioress), Eugenia Ratti (Constance) and Fiorenza Cossotto (in the small part of Mathilde); the conductor was Nino Sanzogno. At the Paris première the singers were Denise Duval (Blanche), Régine Crespin (the new Prioress), Rita Gorr (Mother Marie) and Liliane Berton (Constance); Pierre Dervaux was the conductor.

The Marquis de la Force	baritone
Blanche de la Force *his daughter*	soprano
The Chevalier de la Force *his son*	tenor
Madame de Croissy *Prioress*	contralto
Madame Lidoine *the new Prioress*	soprano
Mother Marie of the Incarnation	
assistant Prioress	mezzo-soprano
Sister Constance of St Denis *a young*	
nun	soprano
Mother Jeanne of the Child Jesus	
dean of the community	contralto
Sister Mathilde	mezzo-soprano
Mother Gerald	
Sister Claire	*old nuns*
Sister Antoine (Portress)	
Sister Catherine	sopranos,
Sister Felicity	mezzo-
Sister Gertrude	sopranos,
Sister Alice	contraltos
Sister Valentine	
Sister Anne of the Cross	
Sister Martha	
Sister St Charles	

Father Confessor of the Convent	high baritone
First Officer	tenor
Second Officer	baritone
Gaoler	baritone
Thierry *a valet*	baritone
M. Javelinot *a physician*	baritone

Officials of the municipality, officers, police, prisoners, guards

Setting Chiefly the Carmelite convent at Compiègne, later Paris during the French Revolution and subsequent Terror, 1789–94

The story of the Compiègne Carmelites was first told by one of their number, Mother Marie of the Incarnation of God, who survived the Terror and lived until 1836. The publication of her *Relation* led to the beatification of the nuns in 1906. In 1931 their story was turned into a novel by the German Catholic convert Gertrude von Le Fort; the heroine Blanche was her invention. In 1947 the Austrian priest and French resistance fighter Father Brückberger devised a cinematic scenario on the subject and engaged the French novelist Georges Bernanos to write the dialogue. Just as Gertrude von Le Fort had written herself into her heroine (she named her 'de la Force'), so Bernanos, then suffering from terminal cancer, concentrated on the crisis of faith of the dying Prioress (even giving her his precise age, 59) as well as exploring his own religious obsessions. His work was deemed uncinematic but it eventually surfaced as a stage play, in which form Poulenc saw it in the early 1950s. When the Ricordi publishing house suggested it as an opera Poulenc seized the chance enthusiastically; but despite rapid composition (1953–6) the première was postponed because of legal wrangles over the rights to the piece.

The opera was first performed (in Italian) at La Scala in a production by Margherita Wallmann. The Paris première was given a few months later (June 1957) with Poulenc's intended cast; the producer was again Wallmann, and for reasons of staging, extra orchestral interludes were composed for this production. Performances at Cologne, San Francisco and on American television followed in the same year. The first Covent Garden cast (1958) included Elsie Morison, Joan Sutherland and Jeannette Sinclair with Rafael Kubelík conducting. Notable recent productions include that of John Dexter, seen in America and Paris, often with Crespin as the old Prioress, a role which she recreated in Wallmann's 1983 production at Covent Garden with Felicity Lott (Blanche), Pauline Tinsley (Mother Marie), Valerie Masterson (the new Prioress) and Lillian Watson (Sister Constance).

*

Act 1.i *The library of the Marquis de la Force* The opera opens in a mood of anxiety. The Chevalier de la Force voices his fears for his sister Blanche, whom he knows to be nervous and easily frightened, for her carriage has been held up by a protesting crowd. In a breathless Allegro, the Chevalier's father, the Marquis, recalls the Royal Fireworks Panic he and his wife were caught up in 19 years earlier, when his wife died giving birth to Blanche. Blanche appears, seemingly composed: only the shifting unrelated harmonies of her music betray her inner uncertainty. On her way to bed she is terrified by a shadow on the wall; she returns and with a mixture of resignation and resolution expresses her resolve to take the veil and join the Carmelite order.

1.ii *The parlour of the Carmelite convent* Some weeks later the Prioress, seated because of her age and infirmity, is interviewing Blanche. In a long flowing arioso (underpinned by the anxious rising interval of a minor 3rd which permeates the whole opera) she reminds her of the nature of their order. As the scene continues the tone changes into rapid recitative (more violent minor 3rds in the orchestra) as the interview becomes more like an interrogation to discover Blanche's true motivation. The order can protect nobody; it is a house of prayer which must be protected by its own members. The Prioress's music switches rapidly from brusque accusatory outburst to lyrical and loving lines when prayer is discussed. Blanche's resolve survives this ordeal and touches the Prioress, who gives her her blessing.

1.iii *Inside the convent* An austere plainsong ritornello leads to a surprising scherzo as we meet young Sister Constance, Blanche's complete opposite. She is a peasant girl, fun-loving and frothy, who can speak of life and death with the same levity with which she treats the convent chores. She shocks and disarms Blanche by admitting her premonition, her happy premonition, that she and Blanche will both die young, and on the same day.

1.iv *The infirmary* A plangent clamour of bells introduces the Prioress's death scene, one of the most protracted, and realistic, in all opera. Over a steady ostinato rhythm she veers from visionary calm to delirium and agony-induced profanity: 'who am I to concern myself with God – let him first concern himself with me'. The loyal and stolid Mother Marie is in attendance, chiefly concerned with avoiding a scandal. The Prioress consigns Blanche, her youngest and thus most beloved daughter, to Marie's particular care. Blanche appears twice – firstly to receive a blessing, then, mysteriously unbidden, at the end of the tortuous scene to witness the Prioress's last undignified agony.

Act 2.i *The chapel* A simple and moving requiem sung for the dead Prioress is interrupted by the jagged music of terror. Blanche has been left alone to watch over the body and runs away in panic. She is admonished and forgiven by the ever-watchful

Marie. In an interlude the music regains its calm as Constance voices her thought, central to Bernanos' theology, that perhaps we die not for ourselves but for others. Perhaps we even die each other's deaths, so the Prioress's agony might afford a poor sinner an easy passing: 'Perhaps the Lord God gave her the wrong death, as a cloakroom attendant might give you the wrong coat'.

2.ii *The chapter room* In the opera's most extended arioso the new Prioress warns the convent of the adversity ahead. The simple harmonies and rhythmic implacability underline her strength and humility. The scene closes with a moving *Ave Maria*. Panic intrudes in a brief interlude in which a stranger is announced – Blanche's brother. Mother Marie allows the interview on the condition that she can be present.

2.iii *The parlour* In an extended duet, the nearest thing to a traditional love duet in the opera, the Chevalier begs his sister to leave with him. As an aristocrat and a nun she is doubly in danger from the encroaching Terror. Poulenc's harmonic restraint is loosened to produce music of Puccinian intensity as Blanche, by turns aloof, agitated and affectionate, restates her desire to stay, to die if need be.

2.iv *The sacristy* The act ends with a finale of Verdian dimensions. It opens with the Father Confessor leading the sisters in the opera's third prayer, an intense and sensual *Ave verum corpus*. He then bids them farewell; he has been forced to go into hiding. The Prioress warns the sisters against easy pride, the temptation of martyrdom. These are timely words as an angry crowd is heard followed by knocks at the door. Commissars enter and read a decree of expulsion from the convent. Their grotesquerie is compounded when one of their number admits that he is secretly sympathetic but in these dangerous times is forced to 'howl with the pack' (collaboration was still a recent memory when this work was written). Amid the general stupefaction Blanche is given a statue of the Infant Jesus. However a second wave of terrifying noise from the street causes her to drop the statue, smashing it on the stone floor.

Act 3.i *The chapel* A stately sarabande (Mother Marie's motif) bears witness to the sisters' strength in adversity. The convent is devastated, desecrated. In the absence of the Prioress, Mother Marie proposes that the sisters take the vow of martyrdom. To ensure complete assent she suggests a secret vote. There is one dissenting vote, Blanche's, thus rendering the decision invalid. Constance rushes forward claiming the vote was hers, and that she has now reconsidered. The vote is allowed to stand and Blanche, without the courage either to live or to die, runs away. An interlude shows the nuns in numb disbelief as they hear their community declared illegal in any form. In

a lyrical codetta the Prioress agrees to endorse the vow made in her absence. It was, after all, made to God.

3.ii *The library of the Marquis* We see and hear Blanche at her most tortured and traumatized. Her father has been guillotined, his house ransacked. She is living there as a servant. Mother Marie arrives; her music is a rock in Blanche's sea of troubles. She tells Blanche that she may have saved her life but not her soul. In a spoken interlude with ad libitum percussion set near the Bastille, Blanche hears that the Compiègne Carmelites have been arrested.

3.iii *The conciergerie* In an arioso of ineffable calm the Prioress tries to fill her imprisoned charges with strength and courage. The music is interrupted, becomes frenzied and chattery as a gaoler enters and delivers their death sentence. The Prioress concludes her interrupted aria with a loving, maternal blessing. An interlude reveals Mother Marie at the height of anguish because she is not with her condemned sisters. The Father Confessor calms her. If God has another destiny for her, that is His will.

3.iv *Place de la Révolution* The final prayer of the opera, the *Salve regina*, is sung to music of great lyrical beauty. Over a rhythmic ostinato (again based on minor 3rds) the nuns' voices rise and fuse as they sing their way to the scaffold. A crowd looks on, murmuring and gasping as, one by one, the voices are silenced as the nuns are guillotined. Blanche appears, now transfigured and fearless. Constance sees her and walks to the scaffold, her face irradiated with joy. Blanche sings alone until she too is guillotined. Dumbfounded, the crowd disperses.

*

This opera among others of his late works consolidates the religious and musical discoveries Poulenc made in the years 1936–40, when the untimely death of a friend triggered a new maturity and he rediscovered his Catholic faith. Although it displayed both technical and formal mastery, Poulenc used to apologize for the unashamedly old-fashioned musical language of his opera. 'It seems,' he wrote, 'that my Carmelites can only sing tonal music. You must forgive them.' He acknowledged his debt to the past in the work's dedication: to Musorgsky, Monteverdi, Debussy and Verdi. He could have added Stravinsky, but in a sense such a debt is reflected in most of his output. The carefully placed and prosodically precise recitatives are redolent of *Pelléas et Mélisande* and *Poppea*; the epic sweep echoes that of *Boris Godunov* and *Don Carlos*. The orchestration is extravagant (triple wind, two harps, piano – and guillotine) but sparingly deployed, often in sections. The tessituras are equally carefully planned: Poulenc's grand operatic models are Amneris (Mother Marie), Kundry (old Prioress), Desdemona (new Prioress), Thaïs (Blanche) and

Zerlina (Sister Constance). The opera's musical language is further enriched by a series of motifs which stand not only for various characters but also for the qualities those characters embody, even when perceived in other people. Thus, when the first Prioress tells Blanche to be steadfast, the orchestra seems to say, 'be just like Mother Marie'. When the second Prioress sings of her love for the sisters we hear music used by Blanche when singing to her brother. This sharing of musical material runs throughout the work and seems a felicitous musical analogue for Bernanos' view of martyrdom: the transference of grace, the universality of suffering. As Sister Constance says in the opera, 'Perhaps we do not die for ourselves, but for each other, or even instead of each other. Who knows?'   J.Ss.

Dido and Aeneas

Tragic opera in three acts by Henry Purcell to a libretto by Nahum Tate after the same poet's play *Brutus of Alba* and Virgil's *Aeneid*; first known performance at a girls' boarding school at Chelsea, before December 1689.

Dido *Queen of Carthage*	soprano
Belinda *her confidante*	soprano
Aeneas *a Trojan prince*	baritone
Sorceress	baritone/mezzo-soprano
Spirit *in form of Mercury*	alto
Sailor	soprano
Choruses of courtiers, witches, sailors and cupids	
Setting Dido's palace at Carthage; a nearby cave; a grove; the quayside	

The only known performance during Purcell's lifetime was at Chelsea, in a boarding school run by Josias Priest, a famous dancer and choreographer. This happened some time before December 1689, when Thomas D'Urfey's spoken epilogue was published in his collection of *New Poems*. Allusions in both the prologue and epilogue suggest that the première probably took place in springtime, but the year is uncertain. On stylistic grounds, the opera could have been composed by 1685 or perhaps even earlier.

Nahum Tate based the libretto on his five-act tragedy *Brutus of Alba, or The Enchanted Lovers* (1678), which he had originally called 'Dido and Aeneas', and various translations of the fourth book of Virgil's *Aeneid*. The libretto is highly condensed and elliptical; certain key events, such as the manner of Dido's death, are unspecified or (as in the case of the lovers' night of passion in the cave) discreetly glossed over.

The opera was obviously written in response to John Blow's *Venus and Adonis* (c1683). Tate and Purcell relied on this for broad structure (three-act tragedy with allegorical prologue, in imitation of *tragédie lyrique*) and details of dramatic form: both works use dance to articulate the story; in each the chorus plays several different roles (courtiers, huntsmen, cupids, witches, sailors and so on); and Purcell largely adopted Blow's style of arioso recitative and even alluded to his teacher's opera in Act 2 scene ii (the grove) where Aeneas displays a boar's head trophy impaled upon his spear (Adonis was killed by the Aedalian boar).

The early performance history of the two operas may have similar parallels. *Venus and Adonis* was composed for the private entertainment of Charles II and then adapted for the girls of Priest's school in April 1684, with the part of Adonis (originally a baritone) being transposed up an octave and sung by Priest's daughter. Following this pattern, *Dido and Aeneas* too may have been written for a court performance and later arranged for schoolgirls. This hypothesis would help explain several discrepancies between the libretto printed for the Chelsea amateur production ('perform'd by young gentlewomen') and the earliest surviving score: this includes a baritone Aeneas as well as countertenor, tenor and bass chorus parts, which could hardly have been executed by Priest's young pupils. Furthermore, the fairly elaborate stage directions in the Chelsea libretto ('*Phoebus* Rises in the Chariot'; '*Venus* Descends in her Chariot'; '*Cupids* appear in the Clouds o'er [Dido's] Tomb') would probably have been unrealizable by a boarding school and are therefore more likely to relate to an earlier professional or court performance.

Allusions in the libretto itself offer several hints at the occasion for which *Dido and Aeneas* may have been composed, but none is sufficiently topical to be taken as hard evidence of one date or another. The prologue (the music of which is lost) seems to refer to the Glorious Revolution of 1688, with Phoebus and Venus representing William and Mary, the new political order; the Act 1 chorus 'When monarchs unite, how happy their state, / They triumph at once o'er their foes and their fate' would also appear to compliment the new king and queen. But the opera itself, in which the prince deserts his queen with tragic consequence, would have been offensive during any part of the reign of William and Mary. In a poem of about 1686 Tate himself alluded to James II as Aeneas, who is misled by the evil machinations of the Sorceress and her witches (representing Roman Catholicism, a common metaphor at the time) into abandoning Dido, who symbolizes the British people. The same symbolism may apply to the opera, but the poem brings us no closer to the date of the première.

The style of the music suggests a date closer to 1685 than to 1689; it is generally simpler than that of the music Purcell is known to have composed around 1690. (Of course, that could be taken as evidence that *Dido* was written for a school performance.) But, because *Dido* is Purcell's only true opera, it is difficult to find suitable pieces with which to compare it, so the stylistic evidence too is inevitably inconclusive.

There is no other recorded performance of the opera during Purcell's lifetime (he died in 1695) and it seems to have attracted no contemporaneous comment, unless Dryden's remark of about that year – that the story of Aeneas at Carthage is too big a subject even for an opera – is a veiled criticism. The first piece from the opera to be published was Dido's aria 'Ah! Belinda' (in *Orpheus britannicus*, 1698), transposed up a tone. In 1700 the opera was incorporated into an adaptation of *Measure for Measure* given by Thomas Betterton's troupe at the theatre in Lincoln's Inn Fields. It was apparently arranged by John Eccles (who wrote the act music for the play); the prologue was transformed into the finale and the second scene of Act 2 was enlarged. On this occasion, the Sorceress was sung by a Mr Wiltshire, a bass-baritone, who also impersonated the sailor at the beginning of Act 3. This casting may reflect Purcell's conception of the role of the Sorceress as a baritone, since on the Restoration stage witches and sorceresses were almost always acted by men. *Dido and Aeneas* was revived in 1704 in conjunction with other plays and then disappeared; it was rediscovered in the late 18th century and adapted as a concert piece.

The earliest score (in the Bodleian Library) dates from after 1777 and differs from the Chelsea and 1700 *Measure for Measure* librettos in several important ways: the score lacks the prologue and the end of the second act; the acts and scenes are somewhat differently disposed, though the running order is the same as in the Chelsea libretto (as described below); the Sorceress is a mezzo-soprano; several dances, including the final Cupids' Dance, are omitted. This manuscript may have been copied from a score used for a performance after 1700 and is likely to be several stages removed from Purcell's lost autograph. Though unquestionably a masterpiece and one of the greatest of all musical tragedies, *Dido and Aeneas*, as it has come down to us, is a mutilated fragment of Purcell's original. There is no reason to believe, however, that the basic musical text lacks authority; the complex and subtle rhythms of the vocal lines, the frequent dissonances and meticulous setting of words are all perfectly characteristic. Even the notation of the manuscript is unmodernized and typical of late 17th-century practice.

*

Act I *The palace* Dido, the widowed Queen of Carthage, has been entertaining Prince Aeneas after his escape from the sack of Troy. Though encouraged by her confidante Belinda and other courtiers, she is reluctant to express her love for Aeneas, but whether she hesitates out of respect for her late husband or duty to the State is not made clear by the libretto. Aeneas presses his suit and, after token resistance, Dido gives in, as her courtiers celebrate the prospect of a royal union. After the exceptionally severe C minor overture the act opens with Belinda's arietta 'Shake the cloud from off your brow', which is joined to the chorus 'Banish sorrow, banish care', in the same style but to different music. This pairing of air and chorus is the basic dramatic unit of the opera. The first substantial piece is Dido's aria, 'Ah! Belinda, I are press'd'. Built over a three-bar ground bass, it is actually a miniature da capo aria, with an opening declamatory passage: the aria proper begins at the third line 'Peace and I are strangers grown'. The act continues swiftly in arioso with frequent choral interjections. The recitative is modelled on the declamatory airs of Henry Lawes, Matthew Locke and especially the very similar passages in Blow's *Venus and Adonis*; it is characterized by plastic vocal lines invariably set in duple metre over bass lines which begin in long notes and then move on in measured crotchets and quavers. Significant words are highly decorated, but never so artificially that one loses sight of the human drama that the recitatives convey. With an unerring sense of pace and the need for contrast, Purcell punctuates the emotional exchanges with formal set pieces, such as 'Fear no danger to ensue', a carefree triple-metre duet and chorus in the French style. Aeneas's first appearance (in recitative) is brusque and perfunctory, the real conquest being conveyed by the exquisitely dissonant E minor chorus 'Cupid only throws the dart', the only piece in the first act which is not in the key of C minor or major. Dido's submission is unvoiced but, as Belinda remarks, 'her eyes confess the flame her tongue denies'. The act concludes with a rejoicing chorus, 'To the hills and the vales', and the Triumphing Dance, also on a ground bass.

Act 2.i *The cave* In sharpest contrast to the formal, courtly rejoicing at the end of the first act, the second finds the Sorceress with her coven of witches (or 'enchantresses', as Tate called them), plotting Dido's death. Their hatred is without motive and unexplained, the Sorceress's malevolence replacing Aeneas's destiny as the engine of the impending tragedy. She is nevertheless an imposing character, who sings only in recitative accompanied by four-part strings, her evil utterances being answered by cackling acolytes in 'Ho, ho, ho!' choruses. When the Sorceress imagines the royal couple on the hunt which is now in progress, the strings flourish D major arpeggios which are both vivid and eerie. The

Sorceress unfolds a plot: she will conjure a storm to ruin the hunt and drive the royal party back to Carthage; one of her witches will then appear to Aeneas in the shape of Mercury and order him to sail away; he will not disobey the divine command. The scene continues with the noble (and therefore slightly incongruous) chorus 'In our deep vaulted cell', cast in the then popular form of a series of echoes; Purcell's original touch is to contrive false echoes which are altered in subtle and weird detail. The same is true of the much more boisterous Echo Dance of Furies which concludes the scene.

2.ii The grove In the only moment of repose in the taut drama, Dido and Aeneas are entertained after the hunt (and their first night together, in the cave) by Belinda and the chorus in the languid 'Thanks to these lonesome vales', then by the Second Woman who sings another piece on a ground bass, 'Oft she visits this lone mountain'. The latter recounts the tale of Actaeon, who was killed by his own hounds – an ominous foreshadowing. The moment of tranquillity is shattered when Aeneas displays the head of the wild boar he has just killed and the Sorceress's storm breaks out. The courtiers are sent running for cover, singing the difficult contrapuntal chorus 'Haste, haste to town'. Left behind, Aeneas is confronted by the false Mercury, who orders him to sail that night. He responds in a recitative, 'Jove's commands shall be obey'd', his only substantial solo, in which he dreads having to break the news to Dido. While the recitative expresses true anguish, Aeneas remains the least developed of the main characters, a gullible, perfidious weakling, though Purcell manages to find some sympathy for his predicament. In the libretto the second scene of Act 2 concludes with a chorus and dance of witches gloating over their deception, though no music survives. The act thus ends abruptly and in a different key from that in which it began, which is unusual for Purcell.

Act 3.i The ships In an ironic juxtaposition, Aeneas's men are preparing to set sail, having heard of his decision to leave even before Dido has been told. They will 'take a boozy short leave' of their nymphs as Aeneas has resolved to abandon his queen. Though the air and chorus 'Come away, fellow sailors' is a jolly sea shanty, it cynically presages the descending chromatic tetrachord through which Dido will later die. The Sorceress and the witches demonically celebrate the success of their plot in a series of ariettas, duets and a chorus ('Destruction's our delight, delight our greatest sorrow') in the same vein as before. The scene concludes with a freakish Witches' Dance, of piecemeal construction and with rapid changes of mood: 'Jack of the Lanthorn leads the Spaniards out of their way among the Inchantresses'. The exact meaning of this choreography is unclear, but one should

appreciate the balletic aspect of the opera, in which dance is used both to entertain and to advance the plot.

3.ii The palace The final meeting of Dido and Aeneas takes place in a remarkable recitative, 'Your counsel all is urg'd in vain', in which Dido mocks Aeneas's hollow protestations of fidelity, spurns his offer to disobey the gods and stay, and then dismisses him after the two have joined in a brief, bitter duet. But she realizes that 'death must come when he is gone', and time seems to ebb away during the deceptively brief chorus 'Great minds against themselves conspire'. The most famous piece in the opera, the lament 'When I am laid in earth', is built on a five-bar ground bass, a descending chromatic tetrachord, a cliché Purcell borrowed from contemporary Venetian opera. But with the soft, four-part string accompaniment, the miraculous avoidance of cadences in expected places, Dido's impassioned yet plaintive cries of 'Remember me' and the final ritornello during which she dies, Purcell achieved one of the great moments in opera, a tragic love-death, pathos without sentimentality. During the final chorus, 'With drooping wings', cupids appear in the clouds and scatter roses on Dido's tomb.

*

Tate's libretto has been criticized for extreme compression of the story, under-development of the character of Aeneas and poor poetry ('Our plot has took/The queen's forsook'). But the pace and concision of the drama are manifest and the short, irregular and sometimes unscanning lines (which Dryden advocated as being ideal for opera) obviously appealed to Purcell, whose flexible phrases always capture the meaning of the words and touch the passions. The reliance on Blow's *Venus and Adonis* should not be underestimated, for in that brilliantly original work Tate and Purcell found a model which they followed faithfully. But what distinguishes *Dido* from its predecessor is that *Venus and Adonis* has practically no arias, whereas in *Dido* the drama gravitates towards them – quite apart, that is, from the quality of the music and the human scale of the tragedy it conveys.   C.Pr.

Doktor Faust

Opera by Ferruccio Busoni to his own libretto based on the 16th-century puppet plays; Dresden, Sächsisches Staatstheater, 21 May 1925.

At the première Robert Burg sang the title role and Theo Strack was Mephistopheles; Fritz Busch conducted an ensemble which also included Meta Seinemeyer (Duchess of Parma), Paul Schöffler and Erna Berger.

Doktor Faust	baritone
Wagner *his famulus*	bass
Mephistopheles	tenor
The Duke of Parma	tenor
The Duchess of Parma	soprano
Master of Ceremonies	bass
Gretchen's Brother	baritone
A Lieutenant	tenor
A Theologian	baritone
A Law Student	baritone
A Scientist	baritone
Prologue	speaker
Helena [Helen of Troy]	dance or mime
Three Students from Cracow	male voices
Five Spirit Voices *servants of Lucifer*	male voices
Four Students in Wittenberg	male voices
Three Voices from On High	female voices

Churchgoers, spirit voices, soldiers, courtiers,
  Catholic and Protestant students, huntsmen,
  peasants
Setting Wittenberg and Parma in the 16th
  century

Busoni considered several subjects, including the Wandering Jew, Leonardo da Vinci and Don Juan, before finally deciding on Faust. He wrote the libretto between 1910 and 1915, the most significant portion coming to him impulsively at Christmas 1914. Although he knew Goethe's work well, he preferred to base his opera on the original sources, which more clearly reflected his own Faustian vision. The first draft was published in 1917 (in *Die weissen Blätter*) and a revised version in 1920 (by Kiepenheuer, Berlin). Work on the score was begun in 1916, although the first musical studies for the opera date from 1912. Ill-health began to impede Busoni's progress from 1921, and when he died in 1924 two substantial passages were still incomplete, the apparition of Helen to Faust in scene ii and the closing scene. For the première, in Dresden, the missing music was provided by Philipp Jarnach.

An abridged recording with Dietrich Fischer-Dieskau in the title role, conducted by Ferdinand Leitner, was issued in 1969. In 1974, hitherto unknown sketches for the missing scenes were acquired by the Staatsbibliothek Preussischer Kulturbesitz, Berlin, from Philipp Jarnach. Antony Beaumont's new completion, based on this material, was first performed at the Teatro Comunale in Bologna on 2 April 1985.

The opera begins with a Symphonia in which distant bell sounds are followed by music which

'Doktor Faust' (Busoni), Main Play, scene ii (a tavern in Wittenberg): design by Karl Dannemann for the original production at the Sächsisches Staatstheater, Dresden, 21 May 1925

vacillates between darkness (the *Nocturne symphonique*) and light (an Easter chorale). Invisible voices chime out the word 'Pax' as if they are bells.

*

Prologue *('Der Dichter an die Zuschauer')* In ten verses of *ottava rima*, the poet outlines the genesis of the libretto and stresses its puppet origins.

Prelude I *Faust's study in Wittenberg, at Easter* Wagner admits the three students from Cracow, who present Faust with a magic book. When Wagner returns but cannot see the students, Faust begins to realize who they are. The music is largely adapted from Busoni's *Sonatina seconda* for piano, composed in 1912, the work in which he made his closest approach to atonality.

Prelude 2 *The same scene at midnight* With the aid of the book, Faust summons the servants of Lucifer. Mephistopheles, the highest of six spirit voices, claims to be 'swifter than the thoughts of mankind'. Faust seeks unconditional freedom, but has to settle for freedom at a price – that of serving the spirit for eternity. Mephistopheles draws up the traditional pact, which Faust signs with his own blood, while a distant chorus of worshippers sings the creed. Faust collapses.

The opening adagio in C♯ minor returns at the central point of the scene and again, in C major, at the close. Mephistopheles' first utterances, rising to a bloodcurdling high C, are followed by a brilliant scherzo. The adagio music encircles two sets of variations: orchestral variations to depict the increasing swiftness of the servants of Lucifer, and choral variations for the Easter music, which builds from a distant trio of solo voices to a clamorous setting of 'Et iterum venturus est' for double chorus, offstage brass, bells and organ.

Scenic Intermezzo *A Romanesque chapel* The brother of Gretchen, whom Faust has seduced, vows to avenge her; Mephistopheles engineers his brutal murder. A sombre D minor prelude for organ and orchestra in expanded rondo form is interrupted by a military march, which accompanies the six soldiers conjured up by Mephistopheles.

Main Play Scene i *The ducal park in Parma* At the climax of the Duke's wedding celebrations, the Master of Ceremonies presents Faust to the court as a celebrated magician. In three visions (Samson and Delilah, Solomon and the Queen of Sheba, Salome and John the Baptist), Faust expresses his love for the Duchess whom, with the aid of Mephistopheles, he soon succeeds in winning. The Duchess sings of her infatuation with Faust, then flees with him. Disguised as court chaplain, Mephistopheles advises the Duke to remarry, raising his clawed hand in ghastly benediction.

The scene opens with a *cortège* and continues with a brilliant ballet sequence. Busoni's Divertimento for flute op.52 provided the substance for the Duchess's solo scene, while the dialogue between the Duke and Mephistopheles is adapted from the Toccata for piano. A sombre symphonic intermezzo (a shortened version of the Sarabande from op.51) marks the turning-point in the drama.

Scene ii *A tavern in Wittenberg* Faust mediates in an argument between Catholic and Protestant students, but his words only lead to further uproar. Mephistopheles, disguised as a courier, brings the dead body of the Duchess's child. He sets it alight and out of the flames emerges Helen of Troy. Faust, unable to grasp the visionary figure, is confronted by the students from Cracow, who tell him that he is to die at midnight. He welcomes his final hour.

Busoni considered the students' dispute to be his most perfect operatic composition technically. Faust's monologue 'Traum der Jugend', in which he muses ecstatically on the achievements of generations not yet born, is a visionary episode, dating from the spring of 1923. This was the last music for the opera that Busoni lived to complete.

Scene iii *A street in Wittenberg* The nightwatchman (Mephistopheles) calls the hour. Students skittishly serenade Wagner, who has succeeded Faust as rector. Faust gives alms to a beggar woman carrying a child: she is the Duchess, who urges him to 'finish the work before midnight'. He transfers his soul to the dead child and, as the nightwatchman calls the midnight hour, he falls dead. The child arises in his place and strides out into the night.

The first part of the scene is an extended scherzo. Faust's entry is followed by a succession of musical reprises. Busoni's score breaks off shortly before the reappearance of Helen, at bar 490.

*

Busoni considered this work to be the culmination of all his artistic endeavours. The score is assembled from numerous musical studies ranging from unfinished fragments (lieder, piano pieces etc.) to published works including the *Nocturne symphonique* op.43, the Sarabande and Cortège op.51, the *Tanzwalzer* op.53 for orchestra, the *Sonatina seconda* and Toccata for piano and several Goethe settings. Diverse as these sources are, they are unified by what Busoni described as his 'Faustian' musical vocabulary: tonal music of extreme harmonic subtlety, with predominantly polyphonic textures and clear but sophisticated orchestral sonorities.

Busoni distinguished between Wagnerian music drama and his own (epic) theatre, in which words and music are intended to fulfil their own, separate functions. In 1922 he published his essay 'Über die Partitur des "Doktor Faust"', in which he stressed that each section of his score is shaped into an organic if unorthodox symphonic form: the festivities at Parma (scene i) are cast in the form of a dance suite, while the tavern scene at Wittenberg (scene ii) features a scherzo, chorale and fugue. The introspective Faustian element is counteracted in each main scene by lighter, extrovert episodes. Hence the work can be understood as a modern mystery play, part folk festival, part Passion. **A.B.**

Don Carlos

Opéra in five acts by Giuseppe Verdi to a libretto by Joseph Méry and Camille Du Locle after Friedrich von Schiller's dramatic poem *Don Carlos, Infant von Spanien*; Paris, Opéra, 11 March 1867. Revised version in four acts (French text revised by Du Locle, Italian translation by Achille de Lauzières and Angelo Zanardini), Milan, Teatro alla Scala, 10 January 1884.

The cast at the première included Louis-Henri Obin (Philip), Paul Morère (Don Carlos), Jean-Baptiste Faure (Posa), Marie Sasse (Elisabeth) and Pauline Guéymard-Lauters (Eboli). The cast for the revised version included Alessandro Silvestri (Filippo), Francesco Tamagno (Don Carlo), Paul Lhérie (Rodrigo), Abigaille Bruschi-Chiatti (Elisabetta) and Giuseppina Pasqua (Eboli).

Philip II *King of Spain*	bass
Don Carlos *Infante of Spain*	tenor
Rodrigue *Marquis of Posa*	baritone
The Grand Inquisitor	bass
Elisabeth de Valois *Philip's queen*	soprano
Princess Eboli *Elisabeth's*	
lady-in-waiting	mezzo-soprano
Thibault *Elisabeth's page*	soprano
The Countess of Aremberg	silent
The Count of Lerma	tenor
An Old Monk	bass
A Voice from Heaven	soprano
A Royal Herald	tenor
Flemish Deputies	basses
Inquisitors	basses

Lords and ladies of the French and Spanish court,
woodcutters, populace, pages, guards of Henry
II and Philip II, monks, officers of the
Inquisition, soldiers

Setting France and Spain, about 1560

Schiller's *Don Carlos* had been suggested to Verdi – and rejected by him – as a possible subject for the Paris Opéra in the early 1850s, when negotiations were beginning for the work that would become *Les vêpres siciliennes*. In 1865, with another full-scale Verdi grand opera being planned for Paris's foremost theatre, the composer clearly saw new potential in the subject. Emile Perrin, the new director of the Opéra, had discussed various topics with Verdi, for the most part via the composer's French publisher and friend Léon Escudier. Verdi pronounced *King Lear*, ever near to his heart at this period, too lacking in spectacle for the Opéra; *Cleopatra* was better, but the lovers would not arouse sufficient sympathy. *Don Carlos*, however, was now 'a magnificent drama', even though Verdi immediately saw the need to add two new scenes to the scenario offered him: one between the Inquisitor and Philip, the other between Philip and Posa. As the libretto took shape, the composer took his usual active part in advising on everything from large structural matters to minute details of phrasing and vocabulary.

Verdi worked steadily on the opera during the first half of 1866 and arrived in Paris in July of that year with most of the score completed. Then came the notoriously long, arduous rehearsal period at the Opéra, during which Verdi made several important changes, including the addition of a scene for Elisabeth at the start of Act 5. As the rehearsals neared completion in February 1867 it became clear that the opera was far too long, and Verdi made substantial cuts, among which were the lengthy and impressive Prelude and Introduction to Act 1, part of the Philip-Posa duet in Act 2, and both the Elisabeth-Eboli and the Carlos-Philip duets in Act 4. The première was not a great success, and *Don Carlos* disappeared from the Opéra repertory after 1869.

Early Italian revivals, in a translation by Achille de Lauzières, were sometimes successful; but the opera's length continued to present problems, and it was frequently given in severely cut versions. In 1872 Verdi himself made further revisions, restoring and rewriting passages of the Philip-Posa duet and cutting a portion of the final duet between Carlos and Elisabeth. Then, in 1882–3, he made a thoroughgoing revision, in part to reduce the opera to more manageable proportions, in part to replace pieces he now found unsatisfactory. The most important cuts were the whole of Act 1 (though Carlos's aria was inserted into the following act), the ballet and its preceding scene in Act 3 and the Act 5 Chorus of the Inquisitors. Many other passages were revised, recomposed or reordered. The La Scala première of this new, four-act version was given in Italian translation. Some two years later a further version which restored the original Act 1 began to be performed and was published (we must assume with Verdi's approval).

It is important to bear in mind that, although the 1884 version was first given in Italian, the revisions Verdi made were to a French text: in other words, there is no 'Italian version' of *Don Carlos*, merely an 'Italian translation'. The following outline will move through the opera by act, marking in italic the version to which various passages belong: *1867* means the version eventually performed at the Parisian

Design by Alfred Albert for one of the costumes for Philip II of Spain in the original production of Verdi's 'Don Carlos' at the Paris Opéra, 11 March 1867

première, *1884* the substantially revised four-act version. Where appropriate, French titles or incipits are followed by their Italian equivalents.

*

Act I *The forest at Fontainebleau 1867* An impressive introductory chorus was cut during rehearsals, leaving the opera to start with a brief Allegro brillante; offstage fanfares and huntsmen's calls introduce the princess Elisabeth, who (observed by Carlos) gives alms to the woodcutters and then departs.

Carlos, who has come incognito from Spain, has now seen for the first time his betrothed, Elisabeth, and in the brief, italianate aria 'Je l'ai vue' ('Io la vidi') he announces love at first sight. He is about to follow Elisabeth when a horn call tells him that night is falling. Thibault and Elisabeth, lost in the wood, appear, and Carlos offers help, introducing himself simply as 'a Spaniard'. Thibault goes off for assistance, so making way for the duet that will dominate this brief act. The opening movement, 'Que faites-vous donc?' ('Che mai fate voi?'), is formed from a series of contrasting episodes, the tension rising as Elisabeth eagerly questions this stranger about the Infante Carlos whom she is to marry. Carlos presents her with a portrait of her betrothed, which she immediately recognizes as the man before

her. This precipitates the second movement, 'De quels transports' ('Di qual amor'), a cabaletta-like celebration of their good fortune, based on a melody that recurs through the opera as a symbol of their first love.

The joy is short-lived. Thibault returns to announce that Henry II has decided to give Elisabeth to the widowed Philip instead of to his son, so decisively putting an end to the war between Spain and France. The couple express their horror in the restrained, minor-mode 'L'heure fatale est sonnée!' ('L'ora fatale è suonata!'), which is immediately juxtaposed with the major-mode offstage chorus of celebration, 'O chants de fête' ('Inni di festa'). The Count of Lerma arrives to request Elisabeth's formal approval of the match, a female chorus adding their pleas for peace. Elisabeth reluctantly accepts, and the stage clears to a triumphant reprise of 'O chants de fête'. Carlos is left alone to bemoan his fate.

Act 2/I.i *The cloister of the St Yuste monastery Both versions* A solemn introduction for four horns precedes the offstage chorus 'Charles-Quint, l'auguste Empereur' ('Carlo, il sommo Imperatore'), a funeral dirge for the Emperor Charles V. A solitary old Monk adds his prayer to theirs, but admits that Charles was guilty of folly and pride.

1867 Carlos enters: he has come to the monastery to forget the past. In a solemnly intoned, sequential passage, 'Mon fils, les douleurs de la terre', the Monk tells him that the sorrows of the world also invade this holy place. The Monk's voice reminds a terrified Carlos of the late emperor himself.

1884 Carlos's extended scena explores his anguish at losing Elisabeth and culminates in a revised version of 'Je l'ai vue' ('Io la vidi') from the original Act 1 (the act entirely omitted from this version). There follows a curtailed conversation with the Monk.

1867 Rodrigue, Marquis of Posa, appears and is greeted by Carlos. Posa launches into a description of the battles in Flanders (a first portion of this part of the duet, beginning 'J'étais en Flandre', was cut from the 1867 version during rehearsals), and Carlos responds with a lyrical declaration of friendship, 'Mon compagnon, mon ami'. Carlos then admits his secret love for Elisabeth, now the wife of his father Philip. Posa reiterates his friendship in a reprise of 'Mon compagnon', advising Carlos to forget his sorrows in the battle for Flanders.

1884 The above-described portion of the duet was further condensed and enriched, with a skilful link from the scene with the Monk, and with 'Mon compagnon' becoming 'Mon sauveur, mon ami' ('Mio salvator, mio fratel') .

Both The final section of the duet, the cabaletta 'Dieu tu semas dans nos âmes' ('Dio, che nell'alma

infondere'), is a 'shoulder-to-shoulder' number reminiscent of Verdi's earliest manner, the tenor and
baritone vowing eternal friendship in parallel 3rds.
In an impressively scored coda, Philip, Elisabeth and
a procession of monks cross the stage and enter the
monastery. Carlos and Posa join the chanting monks
before a thrilling reprise of their cabaletta brings the
scene to a close.

*2/1.ii A pleasant spot outside the St Yuste monastery
gates* Eboli and the other ladies-in-waiting are not
allowed in the monastery, so they amuse themselves
outside. The female chorus sets the scene with 'Sous
ces bois au feuillage immense' ('Sotto ai folti,
immensi abeti'), and then Eboli sings her famous
'Chanson du voile' (Veil Song), 'Au palais des fées'
('Nel giardin del bello'): the two-stanza song with
refrain, packed with both harmonic and instrumental
local colour, tells the story of Achmet, a Moorish king
who one evening mistakenly wooed his own wife in
the garden. A disconsolate Elisabeth appears, soon
followed by Posa, who hands the Queen a letter from
her mother in which is hidden a note from Carlos. As
Elisabeth reads, Posa makes courtly conversation
with Eboli; but in the background of their dalliance
we hear from Elisabeth that Carlos's letter asks her to
trust Posa. At a word from Elisabeth, Posa begins his
two-stanza cantabile *romance*, 'L'Infant Carlos, notre
espérance' ('Carlo, ch'è sol il nostro amore'), in which
he tells how Carlos, whose requests have been
rejected by his father, requests an interview with his
new 'mother'. In between stanzas, Eboli wonders
whether Carlos's dejection has been caused by love
for her, while Elisabeth trembles with confusion.
With the completion of the second stanza, however,
Elisabeth agrees to the interview; Posa and Eboli
walk off together, and the ladies-in-waiting leave.

The ensuing duet between Carlos and Elisabeth,
'Je viens solliciter' ('Io vengo a domandar'), is one of
Verdi's boldest attempts to match musical progress
to the rapid alternations of spoken dialogue: there is
little sense of a conventional four-movement form
(except perhaps for a cabaletta-style ending), the
duet instead passing through a rapid series of
contrasting episodes, some sense of strictly musical
connection coming from shared motifs. In a
controlled opening, Carlos asks Elisabeth to intercede on his behalf with Philip, who will not allow
him to leave for the Spanish possession of Flanders:
there is trouble there stemming from religious
persecution, and Carlos, who is in sympathy with the
dissidents, feels strongly that he can calm the
situation. Elisabeth agrees to help, but Carlos can
restrain himself no further and pours out his love.
Elisabeth at first attempts to deflect him, but
eventually admits her feelings; Carlos falls into a
swoon, and Elisabeth fears he is dying. As he
awakens he begins a final, passionate declaration,

'Que sous mes pieds' ('Sotto al mio pie''), but when
he attempts to embrace his beloved, she recovers
herself and angrily rejects him, telling him
sarcastically that to claim her he must kill his father.
Carlos rushes off in despair, just as Philip himself
appears, angry that Elisabeth has been left alone. He
orders the guilty lady-in-waiting, the Countess of
Aremberg, back to France; Elisabeth bids the Countess a tender farewell in the two-stanza, minor–major
romance, 'O ma chère compagne' ('Non pianger, mia
compagna'). Philip, left alone, gestures for Posa to
remain with him.

1867 After a brief recitative, Posa begins the first
movement of a duet by describing his soldierly life
('Pour mon pays') and narrating his journeys in war-
torn Flanders ('O Roi! j'arrive de Flandre'). Philip
stresses the need for political control, and sternly
curbs Posa's idealism. The impasse produces a lyrical
second movement, 'Un souffle ardent', in which the
two voices are placed in patterned opposition before
joining in a final section. Posa throws himself at
Philip's feet: Philip forgives his rashness, but bids
him beware the Inquisitor. The King then confides in
Posa, beginning the closing cabaletta, 'Enfant! à mon
coeur éperdu', with an admission of his troubled
personal feelings.

1884 In this radical revision, virtually all trace of
the conventional four-movement form disappears
from the duet, being replaced by the kind of fluid
dialogue we find in *Otello*. Posa's 'O Roi! j'arrive de
Flandre' ('O signor, di Fiandra arrivo') is retained,
but most of the remaining music is new. Particularly
impressive is Philip's advice to beware the Inquisitor,
in which solemn chords serve momentarily to halt
the musical flow. Philip is more explicit about his
fears, going so far as to mention Carlos and Elisabeth;
but he closes the duet with yet another sinister
reference to the power of the Inquisitor.

Act 3/2.i *The Queen's gardens*
1867 Festivities are in progress; Philip is to be
crowned the next day. In a further essay in local
colour, the offstage chorus sings 'Que de fleurs et
que d'étoiles' to the accompaniment of castanets.
Elisabeth appears with Eboli: the Queen is already
weary of the celebrations and changes masks with
Eboli so that she can retire to seek religious
consolation. When Elisabeth leaves, Eboli has a brief
solo, 'Me voilà reine pour une nuit', which recalls the
central section of the Veil Song. She writes a letter of
assignation to Carlos, hoping to entice him.

The ensuing ballet, entitled 'La Pérégrina', tells of
a fisherman who happens on a magic cave containing
the most marvellous pearls in the ocean. He dances
with the White Pearl; gradually the other pearls join
in. Philip's page enters to the strains of a Spanish
hymn played by the brass; he has come to find for his
master the most beautiful pearl in the world. At the

climax of the ballet, Eboli (posing as Elisabeth) appears as La Pérégrina: the page's search is at an end. Verdi's music for the ballet, some 15 minutes long, is the traditional mixture of orchestral sophistication and extreme musical simplicity.

1884 A short, understated prelude is based on the first phrase of Carlos's 'Je l'ai vue' ('Io la vidi'); it clearly belongs to Verdi's late manner, particularly in the overt use of thematic transformation and the ease with which it moves between distantly related keys.

Both Carlos enters, reading the letter of assignation; this briefly sets the scene for the ensuing ensemble, which follows the common Italian four-movement pattern, led off by a condensed series of contrasting lyrical episodes, each punctuated by some dramatic revelation. As Eboli appears, Carlos breaks into a passionate declaration of love, thinking she is Elisabeth. Eboli responds with matching phrases, but the lyrical development abruptly breaks down as she removes her mask. Eboli at first misconstrues Carlos's confusion, and attempts to reassure him: but she soon guesses the truth, and accuses him of loving the Queen. At this point Posa arrives, and a brief transitional passage leads to the second main movement, 'Redoubtez tout de ma furie!' ('Al mio furor sfuggite invano'), in which the baritone's and mezzo's agitated rhythms are set against the tenor's long, impassioned melody. A brief transition movement, during which Carlos restrains Posa from killing Eboli, leads to the final stretta, 'Malheur sur toi, fils adultère' ('Trema per te, falso figliuolo'), in which Eboli brings down furious curses on the man who has rejected her and threatens to denounce him. She rushes off, leaving Carlos and Posa; they act out a brief coda in which Carlos – after some hesitation – is persuaded to entrust his friend with some secret papers relating to Flanders, in case Eboli carries out her threat. The scene concludes with a brash orchestral reprise of their earlier cabaletta, 'Dieu tu semas dans nos âmes' ('Dio, che nell'alma infondere').

3/2.ii A large square in front of Valladolid Cathedral This central finale, the grand sonic and scenic climax of *Don Carlos*, is formally laid out along traditional Italian lines but, in response to the added resources of the Opéra, is on a scale Verdi had never before attempted. The opening chorus, 'Ce jour heureux' ('Spuntato ecco il dì'), is a kind of rondo: the main theme alternates with a funereal theme to which monks escort heretics to the stake, and with a more lyrical idea in which the monks promise salvation to those who repent. A solemn procession fills the stage, after which a herald announces Philip, who appears on the steps of the cathedral. He is confronted by six Flemish deputies, escorted by Carlos. They kneel before him and, with a solemn prayer for their country, 'Sire, la dernière heure' ('Sire, no, l'ora

estrema'), lead off a grand concertato movement in which all the principals join, Elisabeth, Carlos and Posa adding their pleas, while Philip and the monks stubbornly resist. A transitional movement begins as Carlos steps forward, asking to be sent to Flanders (to undergo some training for kingship as much as to remove himself from the presence of Elisabeth). When Philip, wary of Carlos's sympathy for the Protestant Flemish, refuses, Carlos threateningly draws his sword. No one dares intervene until Posa steps forward and demands Carlos's surrender. To a soft, veiled reprise of their friendship cabaletta, Carlos relinquishes his weapon, upon which Philip pronounces Posa promoted to a dukedom. The scene closes with a grand reprise of the opening choral sequence. As the heretics go to their death, a Voice from heaven assures them of future bliss.

Act 4/3.i The King's study The King, alone with his official papers, sings the famous 'Elle ne m'aime pas!' ('Ella giammai m'amò!'). As a complex psychological portrait, the aria has few rivals in Verdi. The King's mood swings from self-pity at his emotional isolation (an arioso accompanied by obsessive string figures and culminating in the passionate outburst of 'Elle ne m'aime pas!'), to a sombre meditation on his mortality (mock-medieval horns accompany his picture of the stone vault in which he will lie), to a recognition of his power (a triplet bass melody hinting at the musical grandeur of the preceding concertato finale). But the aria closes with a reprise of its opening outburst: Philip's tragedy, at this point in the drama, is primarily a personal one.

The subsequent duet with the old and blind Grand Inquisitor, 'Suis-je devant le Roi?' ('Sono io dinanzi al Re?'), continues the aria's relative formal freedom, its sense that the music reacts immediately and flexibly to the shifting emotions of the dialogue. The opening orchestral idea, with its concentration on low strings, ostinato rhythms and restricted pitches, sets the scene for this power struggle between two basses. Philip seems in command as he asks the Inquisitor how to deal with Carlos and his support for the religious reforms in Flanders; but, as the controlled opening gives way to freer declamation, the Inquisitor takes over, stating that Posa, with his liberal idealism, is the more serious threat and demanding that he be turned over to the Inquisition. Philip resists, but in an imposing declamatory climax the Inquisitor warns him that even kings can be brought before the tribunal. As the opening orchestral idea returns, Philip attempts to restore peace; but the Inquisitor is indifferent and leaves Philip in no doubt as to how the struggle will be resolved.

The *scène* and quartet that follows (much revised for the 1884 version) is more conventionally structured. To the kind of lyrically enriched recitative that was by now the Verdian norm, Elisabeth rushes in to announce the theft of her jewel case. Philip produces it – Eboli had purloined it –and invites her to reveal its contents; when she refuses he breaks the lock and finds inside a picture of Carlos. In spite of her protestations, he accuses her of adultery; the Queen faints, and Philip summons Posa and Eboli, who arrive to precipitate the formal quartet, 'Maudit soit le soupçon infâme' ('Ah! sii maledetto, sospetto fatale'). The ensemble is at first dominated by Philip, whose opening statements – fragmentary expressions of regret – gradually form into a lyrical melody that interweaves with Posa's decision to take action and Eboli's cries of remorse. But towards the end Elisabeth's sorrowful lament takes on increasing urgency and focus.

Philip and Posa leave. Originally the scene continued with a duet for Elisabeth and Eboli, but this was cut during rehearsals for the 1867 première, when the cut extended some way into Eboli's confession; however, Verdi recomposed and expanded this for the 1884 version, in which Eboli first admits her love for Carlos and then, to a bare, almost motif-less rhythmic idea in the strings, reveals that she has been the King's mistress. Elisabeth orders Eboli to quit the court, and then departs. Eboli's ensuing aria, 'O don fatal' ('O don fatale'), in which she laments her fatal beauty, is cast in a conventional minor–major form, with the major section (in which she bids farewell to the Queen) strongly reminiscent in its chromaticism and wide-spaced orchestral sonority of Verdi's late style. In a cabaletta-like coda, Eboli resolves to spend her final hours at court in an attempt to save Carlos.

4/3.ii Carlos's prison A string introduction of unusual depth and density introduces Posa to the waiting Carlos. Posa bids farewell to his friend in a rather old-fashioned *romance*, 'C'est mon jour suprême' ('Per me giunto è il dì supremo'), and then explains that Carlos's secret papers have been discovered on him. A shot rings out; Posa falls mortally wounded. After telling Carlos that Elisabeth awaits him at the monastery of St Yuste, he delivers a second *romance*, 'Ah! je meurs' ('Io morrò'), happy that he can die for the sake of his dear friend. A duet for Philip and Carlos that followed this episode (cut before the 1867 première, though Verdi drew on its material for the 'Lacrymosa' of the Requiem) was replaced with a riot scene (subsequently pruned for the 1884 version) in which Eboli appears at the head of a group intent on liberating Carlos. Philip also appears, but the crowd is silenced by the entry of the Inquisitor, who orders all to their knees before the King.

Act 5/4 *The monastery at St Yuste* An impressive and extended orchestral prelude introduces Elisabeth at the tomb of Charles V. Her aria, 'Toi qui

sus le néant' ('Tu, che le vanità'), is in French ternary form: the outer sections are a powerful invocation of the dead emperor, and their firm structure stabilizes the number, allowing for remarkable variety and musical contrast during the long central section in which the Queen's thoughts stray to memories of the past. Carlos appears for their final duet (from here to the end of the opera, Verdi made a number of important revisions in 1884). The set-piece begins with the conventional series of contrasting sections, in the most prominent of which, 'J'avais fait un beau rêve' ('Sogno dorato io feci!'), Carlos announces that he has done with dreaming and will now try to save Flanders. The final movement, 'Au revoir dans un monde' ('Ma lassù ci vedremo'), a kind of ethereal cabaletta in which the couple bid each other a tender farewell, is similar to the closing duet of *Aida* in its restraint and delicate orchestral fabric. As they say 'Adieu! et pour toujours' for the last time, Philip bursts in accompanied by the Inquisitor and various officials. The King tries to deliver his son to the priests, but Carlos retreats towards the tomb of Charles V. The tomb opens and the old Monk appears, wearing the emperor's crown and mantle. He gathers Carlos to him and, with a few sententious words, draws him into the cloister.

*

Soon after the first Paris performances of *Don Carlos*, Verdi voiced his doubts about the Parisian tradition of grand opera. While he was always ready to praise the care with which productions were mounted – particularly in comparison with much of Italy, where he often judged standards to be unbearably low – he was also aware that the sheer size of the undertaking, the number of different demands that had to be catered for, could take their toll on a work's balance and coherence of effect. He might well have had *Don Carlos* in mind. As we have seen, the opera in rehearsal proved impracticably long; the subsequent cuts were made for practical rather than dramatic reasons, leaving the 1867 version with many inconsistencies and imbalances. Clearly some of the outstanding problems were put straight by the composer's revisions of the 1870s and 1880s; but even the final versions of the opera pose uncomfortable dramatic questions.

Possibly the most serious difficulty comes in the comparative weight assumed by various characters. Philip and Eboli are the most successful and well-rounded portraits, though arguably Elisabeth achieves her proper sense of importance by means of her magnificent fifth-act aria and duet. Posa's musical physiognomy is strangely old-fashioned: his music almost all dates from the earliest layers of the score, and even then recalls the Verdi of the early 1850s (or even 1840s). On the other hand, it can be argued that this sense of anachronism is in keeping with Posa's dramatic position – as a nostalgic look at youthful days of action within the context of sterner political realities. With Carlos, however, few would deny an unsolved problem: his musical portrait never seems to find a centre, a true nexus of expression such as each of the other principals eventually achieves.

It is perhaps an indication of our changing views and tastes that, in spite of these difficulties, *Don Carlos* has of late become one of the best-loved and most respected of Verdi's operas. The simple fact is, of course, that Verdi dedicated to the work some of his greatest dramatic music. One need think only of the magnificent series of confrontational duets that form such a great part of the drama. As has been noted briefly above, several of these break decisively with traditional models, forging for themselves a vital new relationship between musical and dramatic progress. It is for such moments that *Don Carlos* will be remembered and treasured, and they will surely continue to prove more powerful than any large-scale dramatic obstacles the work might present.   R.P.

Don Giovanni [*Il dissoluto punito, ossia Il Don Giovanni* ('The Libertine Punished, or Don Giovanni')]

Opera buffa in two acts, K527, by Wolfgang Amadeus Mozart to a libretto by Lorenzo da Ponte; Prague, National Theatre, 29 October 1787.

Don Giovanni *a young and extremely licentious nobleman*	baritone
Commendatore	bass
Donna Anna *his daughter*	soprano
Don Ottavio *her betrothed*	tenor
Donna Elvira *a lady from Burgos*	soprano
Leporello *Giovanni's servant*	bass
Masetto *a peasant, betrothed to Zerlina*	bass
Zerlina *a peasant girl*	soprano
Peasants, servants, demons	

Setting A Spanish town (traditionally Seville), in the 16th century

Although commissioned by the Prague theatre, Mozart surely had in mind production in Vienna with the personnel of the original *Figaro*. The original and Vienna casts are listed together:

	Prague 1787	*Vienna 1788*
Leporello	Felice Ponziani	Francesco Benucci
Anna	Teresa Saporiti	Aloysia Lange
Giovanni	Luigi Bassi	Francesco Albertarelli
Commendatore/		
Masetto	Giuseppe Lolli	Francesco Bussani
Ottavio	Antonio Baglioni	Francesco Morella
Elvira	Caterina Micelli	Caterina Cavalieri
Zerlina	Caterina Bondini	Luisa Mombelli/ Therese Teyber

The commission for *Don Giovanni* followed the triumphant production of *Le nozze di Figaro* in Prague (December 1786). The impresario Domenico Guardasoni probably asked Mozart to expand Bertati's one-act *Don Giovanni*, set by Gazzaniga for Venice in February 1787. Da Ponte's memoirs suppressed his indebtedness, but he improved Bertati in every respect and drew on other sources, notably Molière's *Dom Juan* and versions from popular theatre. About half the libretto, between the Act 1 quartet and the graveyard scene, is original.

Mozart began work during the summer, leaving for Prague on 1 October. This season in the Bohemian capital has the flavour of legend; but there is no reason to suppose that Mozart's compositional processes were abnormal, even in the late composition of the overture (on the eve of the performance, already twice postponed, or of the final rehearsal). He may have had to resist Bassi's demand for a big aria, and possibly did not know Baglioni when he composed 'Il mio tesoro'.

The new triumph in Prague was not repeated in Vienna, although *Don Giovanni* received more performances than *Figaro* had done in 1786. Mozart wrote a replacement aria for Ottavio, an additional *scena* for Elvira, so that her role became approximately equal to Anna's, and a *buffo* duet for Mombelli and Benucci. The final scene, after Giovanni's disappearance, may have been omitted.

Don Giovanni soon acquired a reputation for exceptional difficulty, derived from the superimposed dance metres of the first finale and the unprecedented harmonic richness of the second. Guardasoni gave it in Warsaw in 1789; and it made rapid progress in Germany as a Singspiel, becoming after *Die Entführung* the Mozart opera most performed in his lifetime. At least three translations were made. German was used in Prague in 1791, Vienna in 1792, and outside Germany in Amsterdam (1793) and St Petersburg (1797). *Don Giovanni* became popular in France, often in adapted versions in French or Italian. The Italian première was at Bergamo in 1811, followed that year by Rome. In England there is some doubt over the earliest performances, which may have been partly amateur affairs. In 1817 it appeared at rival theatres in Italian and in English; it remained popular in both languages. The first American performances, in 1826, were by García's company in association with Da Ponte. Nearly every opera singer of note has been associated with one of the main roles.

*

Set design by Giulio Quaglio for the Graveyard scene (Act 2) in a 1789 production of Mozart's 'Don Giovanni'

The overture begins with the imposing music for the entrance of the 'stone guest'. Its emergence into the D major Allegro establishes the ambivalence of the opera, its perilous balance of humour and tragedy. The full sonata form has been interpreted as a portrait of Giovanni, or as justice (the heavy five-note figure) pursuing the mercurial seducer. There is no final cadence; the coda modulates to a new key (F major) for the opening scene.

Act I *Courtyard of the Commendatore's house; night* Leporello is always on guard (*Introduzione*, 'Notte e giorno faticar'), but indulges in fantasy tinged with resentment ('Voglio far il gentiluomo'). He hides at the approach of Anna, pursuing Giovanni (who conceals his face); the music is still formal despite its growing intensity (as often hereafter, Leporello comments in the background). Anna's father confronts Giovanni; musical formality yields to disordered gesture as they fight and Anna flies for help. The old man dies at a rare moment of stillness, even Giovanni being moved (in the short trio in F minor, he has a melody formerly sung by Anna in a faster tempo). Giovanni and Leporello escape. Anna returns with Ottavio and faints over the body (obbligato recitative and duet, 'Fuggi, crudele'); reviving, she responds to Ottavio's tender invitation to take him as husband and father by demanding an oath of vengeance. Their voices unite in powerful D minor cadences which form the first decisive closure of the opera.

A street; dawn Elvira, in travelling clothes, is pursuing her seducer (aria, 'Ah, chi mi dice mai'); her sincere, slightly ridiculous pose is conveyed by a sweeping melodic line and formal orchestral gestures. Giovanni scents adventure; mutual recognition comes too late to prevent his unctuous advance, which covers the cadence of the aria. He escapes her reproaches, leaving Leporello to show her the catalogue (aria, 'Madamina, il catalogo è questo'). Giovanni's conquests total 640 in Italy, 230 in Germany, 100 in France, 91 in Turkey, but in Spain, 1003. Bubbling patter is succeeded by a luscious minuet as Leporello details the types of women who have yielded; although willing to take anybody, Giovanni prefers the young beginner (an orchestral and tonal shiver underlines this depravity).

[Mid-morning] Peasants invade the stage (a bucolic G major chorus): a wedding is in the offing. Attracted to the bride, Zerlina, Giovanni invites them all to his house. He dismisses the groom, the jealous Masetto, who, recognizing the nobleman for what he is, upbraids Zerlina in an action aria ('Ho capito, signor, sì') before being dragged away. Giovanni flatters Zerlina with an offer of marriage in the duettino 'Là ci darem la mano'. 'Vorrei, e non vorrei', she wavers: held by the hand, and following his melodic lead, Zerlina still worries about Masetto, but her impending submission is not in doubt, as the music proclaims while their voices join in a pastorale

('Andiam mio bene'). Elvira intervenes with a homily to Zerlina ('Ah fuggi il traditor'), a very short aria of Baroque vigour and formality, ending with strident coloratura. Anna and Ottavio greet Giovanni as a friend who will help in their quest for vengeance; the devil is frustrating his every plan, but he offers his assistance with exaggerated courtesy. Elvira interrupts again; recognizing a social equal, she tells Anna in measured tones not to trust Giovanni (quartet, 'Non ti fidar, o misera'). Anna and Ottavio are puzzled; Giovanni tries to hush Elvira and explains that the poor girl is mad. In the course of a finely wrought ensemble her denunciation grows more vehement, even shameless. Something about Giovanni's farewell tells Anna, as she explains to Ottavio, that Giovanni was the man who tried to seduce her the previous night. Her harrowing description (obbligato recitative) revives the orchestral turbulence of the music after her father's death; her aria in D major ('Or sai chi l'onore') bespeaks her valiant determination to avenge her father. Ottavio can hardly believe Giovanni's villainy, but his role is to support Anna. (His exquisite aria, 'Dalla sua pace', was added for Vienna.) Giovanni congratulates Leporello on disposing of Elvira and prepares for a brilliant afternoon's work (aria, 'Fin ch'han dal vino'); wine will warm up the guests, they will mix the minuet, follia and allemande, and ten more names will enter the catalogue.

Giovanni's garden [afternoon] In Mozart's most enchanting melodic vein, with cello obbligato, Zerlina wins Masetto back in her aria, 'Batti, batti' (like 'Là ci darem' it begins in 2/4 and ends in a honeyed 6/8). When she hears Giovanni's voice, though, she is too obviously disturbed. The finale begins as Giovanni gives orders to his servants; then, espying Zerlina as she tries to hide, he resumes his blandishments. Masetto pops out of hiding; to the sound of a contredanse they go inside. Elvira leads Anna and Ottavio, masked, towards Giovanni's lair. Leporello sees them (the minuet is heard from the window), and they are invited in. Their short prayer for vengeance ('Protegga il giusto ciel') is a moment of stillness at the heart of one of Mozart's most active finales.

The ballroom To music resembling the earlier bucolic chorus, Giovanni and Leporello entertain the peasants. Masetto urges prudence on his bride. The central key-change from E♭ to C, resplendent with trumpets, greets the masked trio with the acclamation 'Viva la libertà!' Now in G major, in a *tour de force* using three small stage bands, the ball resumes. The minuet is danced by Anna and Ottavio; on it is superimposed the contredanse in 2/4 with the same pulse (the 'follia' of Giovanni's aria) danced by Giovanni and Zerlina, and the 'teitsch' (Allemande)

with a bar of 3/8 to the prevailing beat, which Leporello forces Masetto to dance. Giovanni drags Zerlina out. She screams; Masetto rushes after them; and as the violently interrupted tonalities return via F to the tonic C, Giovanni complacently blames Leporello and offers to kill him on the spot. The trio, unmasking, and Zerlina denounce him and he is momentarily nonplussed, but in a whirlwind ensemble he outfaces them all.

Act 2 *A street* Giovanni scorns Leporello's furious attempts to leave his service (duet, 'Eh via buffone'). A purse changes hands, but when Leporello tells his master to give up women he claims to need them 'as much as the food I eat and the air I breathe'. His love is universal; faithfulness to one woman betrays all the rest. Leporello is forced to exchange clothes with him for the seduction of Elvira's maid. It is twilight; Elvira, on a balcony, tries to repress her desire for Giovanni but her fluttering heart betrays her (trio, 'Ah taci, ingiusto core'). Giovanni adopts her melody, but in the more intense dominant (sonata form perfectly matches Mozart's dramatic requirements). In the middle section his ardour is extreme, as he anticipates the melody of his serenade. She denounces him; he presses her; she weakens; though he pities her, Leporello, watching, is in danger of laughing aloud. She comes down to the disguised servant, who, told to keep her occupied, begins to enjoy the act. Giovanni chases them away and to a mandolin accompaniment serenades the maid with his canzonetta, 'Deh vieni alla finestra'. But Masetto and a group of peasants, bearing crude weapons, are after Giovanni's blood. The false Leporello sympathizes and in an action aria ('Metà di voi quà vadano') gives instructions on how to search the streets and recognize the villain. He keeps Masetto with him and gives him a beating before disappearing. Hearing groans, Zerlina offers the balm only she can provide; a heart-easing melody in a gentle 3/8 invites Masetto to lay his hand on her bosom (aria, 'Vedrai, carino').

A courtyard at Anna's house Leporello, seeing lights, retreats with Elvira into the dark yard, intent on desertion. She begs him not to leave her; he gropes for the exit (sextet, 'Sola in buio loco'; in E♭). A moment of magic – soft trumpets and drums mark a key-change from the dominant (B♭) to D – brings Anna and Ottavio with servants and lights. His renewed plea for marriage, and her prevarication, unfold in long melodic spans which draw the tonality to C minor. Elvira's search for 'Giovanni', and Leporello's for the gate, are interrupted by Zerlina and Masetto. All denounce the betrayer, in a scene of unreality (for the true villain is absent) made pathetic by Elvira's plea for mercy on him, and comic by Leporello's terror and abject submission when he identifies himself. This movement resembles a short finale, for it ends with a huge ensemble of consternation. Then everybody turns on Leporello, who babbles excuses as he escapes (aria, 'Ah pietà, Signori miei'). Ottavio decides to go to the authorities; he asks the others to watch over Anna while he avenges her. His aria, 'Il mio tesoro', is a full-length virtuoso piece accompanied by muted strings and clarinets.

(In the Vienna version, Leporello escapes in a recitative, using only a motif from the Prague aria; Ottavio decides to go to the authorities. Then Zerlina drags Leporello back and ties him up, threatening dire punishments (duet, 'Per queste tue manine'); Leporello again escapes. Masetto claims to have prevented another of Giovanni's crimes. Elvira vents her mixed feelings: obbligato recitative, 'In quali eccessi', and aria, 'Mi tradì', a piece of vertiginous emotion embodied in perpetual-motion quavers.)

A graveyard [night] Giovanni escapes an adventure by leaping the wall. Leporello joins him, complaining that once again he has nearly been killed. Giovanni arrogantly narrates the conquest of Leporello's girl; his heartless laughter is rebuked by the dead Commendatore (an oracular utterance, with trombones). They find his statue and Leporello, terrified, is forced to read the inscription: 'I await vengeance on the villain who slew me'. Giovanni forces Leporello to invite the statue to supper. This most sinister situation is handled as a *buffo* duet ('O statua gentilissima') mainly reflecting the fear of Leporello as he approaches and retreats. The statue nods, then sings its acceptance; even Giovanni is puzzled and subdued, but he leads Leporello off to prepare the meal.

A darkened room in Anna's house Ottavio is again pressing his suit; he calls Anna cruel. She protests at the word (obbligato recitative, 'Crudele! Ah nò, mio bene'); society would frown on an immediate wedding. The recitative anticipates the Larghetto of the aria ('Non mi dir'), an undulating melody of great sweetness. In the Allegro she hopes that heaven will take pity on her; the blossoming coloratura corresponds to the strength of her resolve. Ottavio is determined to share her martyrdom.

A dining-room in Giovanni's house (finale) Giovanni enjoys a meal without waiting for his guest; Leporello is envious, while astonished at his appetite. A sequence of popular tunes (from Martín y Soler's *Una cosa rara*, Sarti's *Fra i due litiganti* and Mozart's *Figaro*) played by onstage wind band accompanies the farce of Leporello stealing food and being caught with his mouth full. Elvira bursts in, making a last appeal to Giovanni to reform. He laughs at her, invites her to join him, and to a newly minted melody drinks a toast to wine and women, 'Sostegno e gloria d'umanità'. Recognizing that she will not change him, Elvira runs despairingly off; then, from outside,

utters a piercing scream. Leporello investigates and returns in terror, babbling of a white stone man with earth-shaking strides. When knocking is heard he hides under the table and Giovanni opens the door. The overture music is reinforced by trombones as the statue enters to a crushing diminished 7th. His solemn grandeur, Giovanni's polite, then impatient responses, and Leporello's terrified asides are musically characterized but subsumed to a harmonic development of unparalleled richness. The statue cannot take mortal food, but he invites Giovanni to sup with him. With admirable fearlessness, in a phrase of marked dignity, Giovanni accepts; but on grasping the statue's chilling hand he is overcome by his impending fate. Offered a chance to repent, he proudly refuses and is dragged into the engulfing flames. The chorus of demons exactly reflects the cadences of the vengeance duet, at the beginning of Act 1. The others rush on with the police, to find only Leporello, who stammers out enough for them to understand. In an extended Larghetto, Ottavio again pleads with Anna; she tells him to wait a year for their wedding. Elvira will enter a convent, Zerlina and Masetto will marry, Leporello will find a better master. All join to point the moral in a bright fugato: 'This is the end of the evil-doer: his death is as bad as his life'.

*

There are two authentic versions of *Don Giovanni*, the differences mainly in the distribution of arias. Each has only one for Ottavio, since when including a new aria for Elvira (Cavalieri) in Act 2, Mozart omitted 'Il mio tesoro' as well as a short aria for Leporello. The concentration of arias in Act 2 which results from the common practice of including in succession those for Leporello, Ottavio and Elvira was never the authors' intention. The additional duet for Zerlina and Leporello, its coarseness perhaps designed to humour the Viennese, is generally omitted, but Elvira's 'In quali eccessi . . . Mi tradì' is too good to lose; some 19th-century performances, including one that may have had Da Ponte's approval, removed it to Act 1.

In musical form and dramatic technique, particularly the proportion and design of arias and ensembles, *Don Giovanni* is largely modelled on *Figaro*. Exceptions include the 'Catalogue' aria, with its fast–slow tempo pattern; the first finale which besides the unique dance sequence covers a change of location; and the extended introduction, embedded in a vast structure extending from the overture to the end of the duet 'Fuggi, crudele'. The harmonic language associated with Don Giovanni's fall, including that duet and the second finale, marks a decisive departure from *buffo* norms (certainly not anticipated by Gazzaniga, whose setting may have influenced Anna's first entry). The designation 'dramma giocoso' used by Da Ponte (though not by Mozart) has no particular significance; the serious characters are as much embroiled in the intrigue as they are in *Figaro*.

The tragic elements nevertheless form a new synthesis of *buffo* and serious styles, and explain why *Don Giovanni* has gripped the imagination of writers and philosophers. In particular they have been attracted by the daemonic in Giovanni, and by the impossibility of penetrating a character so mercurial, whose music says so little about his motivation; even 'Fin ch'han dal vino' is a set of instructions to Leporello, though also an explosion from his joyous daemon. Whereas the other characters are remarkably three-dimensional, Giovanni adapts the style of each of his victims, including the Commendatore who brings out the heroic in him and Leporello whom he chaffs in pure *buffo* style. He woos Anna by courtly flattery, Zerlina by condescension, Elvira's maid by disguise; Elvira herself he evades or mocks, but he can also woo her with false ardour (in the trio at the beginning of Act 2).

Elvira, ignored in the 19th century, now seems the most interesting because psychologically the most complex of the women. Though the greatest singers, such as Patti, sometimes sang Zerlina, Anna attracted most interest; E. T. A. Hoffmann suggested that she had been seduced by Giovanni and was in love with him rather than Ottavio, a fantasy which received comic treatment in Shaw's *Man and Superman*. Stendhal and Kierkegaard used Giovanni to illustrate aspects of love and the erotic. Significantly, Kierkegaard was aware of earlier dramatic treatments but derived his views from the music, not the libretto or the historical evolution of the character.

Don Giovanni is governed by a single idea, Giovanni's flouting of society's norms in pursuit of sexual pleasure, which binds together a disparate set of ambivalent or comic incidents. The libretto has been unfairly criticized; its episodic nature is a condition of the subject, in which respect it differs from *Figaro* and *Così*. Divine retribution appears like an act of God, or a different kind of life-force personified in the statue; what in previous treatments had been comic, perfunctory or merely gruesome, is raised to sublimity by Mozart's music.　　J.Ru.

Don Pasquale

Dramma buffo in three acts by Gaetano Donizetti to a libretto by Giovanni Ruffini and the composer after Angelo Anelli's libretto for Stefano Pavesi's *Ser Marcantonio* (1810); Paris, Théâtre Italien, 3 January 1843.

The cast at the première consisted of Giulia Grisi (Norina), Luigi Lablache (Don Pasquale), Giovanni Matteo Mario (Ernesto) and Antonio Tamburini (Malatesta), with Federico Lablache, the great bass's son, as the Notary.

Don Pasquale *an elderly bachelor*	bass
Dr Malatesta *his physician*	baritone
Ernesto *his nephew*	tenor
Norina *a youthful widow, Ernesto's beloved*	soprano
A Notary *Malatesta's cousin Carlino*	bass
Servants	
Setting Don Pasquale's bourgeois villa in Rome and the adjacent garden, as well as Norina's house, in the mid-19th century	

Don Pasquale, Donizetti's comic masterpiece, was an instant success as introduced by the quartet of stars at the 'Italiens'. The Italian première took place at La Scala, Milan, on 17 April 1843, with Ottavia Malvani (Norina), Napoleone Rossi (Pasquale), Leone Corelli (Ernesto) and Achille De Bassini (Malatesta). For its Viennese première, at the Kärntnertortheater on 14 May 1843 in Italian (a production prepared by Donizetti), he added to the score the baritone-*buffo* duet 'Cheti, cheti, immantinente', borrowing it from a discarded section of the unperformed *L'ange de Nisida*. Its London première, at Her Majesty's on 19 June 1843, used the same cast as the Paris première, with one exception (Luciano Fornasari as Malatesta). It was first given in New York, in English, on 9 May 1846. As can be seen, *Don Pasquale* travelled across Europe at a remarkably rapid pace. Its popularity has continued undiminished, and it can truly be said never to have left the international repertory, being a particular favourite in German-language theatres.

Some memorable 20th-century revivals include those at the Metropolitan, 24 December 1904, with Marcella Sembrich, Arcangelo Rossi, Enrico Caruso and Antonio Scotti, and on 23 February 1935 with Lucrezia Bori, Ezio Pinza, Tito Schipa and Giuseppe De Luca, conducted by Héctor Panizza. There was a notable revival at La Scala on 21 December 1904 with Rosina Storchio, Antonio Pini-Corsi, Leonid Sobinov and De Luca. It was revived in 1905 at Covent Garden, but was not heard there again until the coronation season of 1937. It was a feature in the repertory at the Cambridge Theatre in London between 1946 and 1948, evenings made unforgettable by Alda Noni's Norina, Italo Tajo's Pasquale and Mariano Stabile's incomparable Malatesta. It had been introduced at Glyndebourne in 1938 by Fritz Busch, with Audrey Mildmay (Norina), Salvatore Baccaloni (Pasquale), Dino Borgioli (Ernesto) and Stabile (Malatesta). More recent exponents of the title role include Geraint Evans, Fernando Corena,

Gabriel Bacquier, Renato Capecchi and Sesto Bruscantini.

*

Act I.i *A room in Pasquale's house* The action is preceded by a brilliant overture which gives prominence to two melodies heard later, Ernesto's serenade and Norina's self-characterizing aria, 'So anch'io la virtù magica'. The elderly Don Pasquale is determined to marry and sire an heir more direct than his nephew Ernesto, whom he plans to disinherit because of that young man's unreasonable infatuation with a youthful widow, Norina. (Don Pasquale has not met her.) To reassure himself about his generative powers, Pasquale consults Dr Malatesta, who gives a favourable prognosis, but as he is a devoted friend to both Ernesto and Norina he starts to tell Pasquale about a young woman, a certain 'Sofronia', his own sister, he says, who would be perfect for such a marriage – and she is beautiful besides (Larghetto cantabile, 'Bella siccome un angelo'). The old bachelor is delighted with what he takes to be the symptoms of a regained youth (Vivace, 'Un fuoco insolito'). Ernesto enters and is surprised at his uncle's exuberance, and disconcerted when he hears that he plans to take a wife. Their duet,

'Don Pasquale' (Donizetti): Act 3 scene ii from the London première at Her Majesty's Theatre, 19 June 1843, with (left to right) Giovanni Mario (Ernesto), Giulia Grisi (Norina), Luciano Fornasari (Malatesta) and Luigi Lablache (Don Pasquale); the same cast (with the exception of Fornasari) had sung in the original Paris production earlier that year, when the part of Malatesta was sung by Antonio Tamburini

'Prender moglie!', contrasts an elegiac melody for Ernesto, 'Sogno soave casto', with Pasquale's patter, half-rancorous, half-gleeful.

I.ii *A room in Norina's house* Norina, reading, laughs over a silly romantic tale; she knows her own ability to exert charm. The contrast in style between the slightly exaggerated, bel canto tale of chivalry (Andante, 'Quel guardo il cavaliere') and the good-humoured dance tune (Allegretto, 'So anch'io la virtù magica'), is not only a capital piece of musical characterization but also an implied musical criticism, vintage 1843, as this work was first played in contemporary dress rather than period costume. Malatesta calls on her and together they plot just how she should enact the supposed bride, a part she is ready and eager to play if it will help her ultimately to win Ernesto (duet, 'Pronta io son').

Act 2 *A living-room in Pasquale's house* Ernesto is feeling sorry for himself, imagining his future as an exile and lamenting his lost love. His Larghetto, 'Cercherò lontana terra', is preceded by an eloquent introduction with a trumpet solo, and is a classic example of Donizetti's ability to write melodies grateful to the lyric tenor voice. Ernesto leaves just before Pasquale enters, afire with impatience to meet his bride. Malatesta leads in a veiled lady, Norina of course, who feigns terror but is actually so amused at Pasquale's antique gallantry that she can hardly keep herself from collapsing in laughter. Malatesta pretends to encourage her (trio, 'Via, da brava'). Later, he introduces a supposed notary, in reality his cousin Carlino, who takes down the marriage agreement Pasquale dictates, assuring 'Sofronia' that she will be the absolute mistress of all his possessions. Just as the document is signed and the notary asks where the second witness might be, Ernesto storms in to take leave of Pasquale. He is enraged at the spectacle of Norina apparently in the act of marrying his testy uncle; Malatesta whispers an explanation and the young man remains to watch the fun (quartet, 'Ah, figliuol, non mi far scene'). As soon as the notary declares them man and wife, Sofronia turns into a shrew, reproving Pasquale's manners, demanding a *cavalier servente* and carrying on so outrageously that the old man seems turned to stone (quartet, 'È rimasto là impietrato'). This second act, with its economy and unflagging comic inspiration, everywhere given tongue by melodic wit and allusiveness, stands as one of Donizetti's greatest achievements.

Act 3.i *A living-room in Pasquale's house* Sofronia has continued her high-handed ways, ordering jewels and clothes, hiring more servants. When she appears dressed to go out, Pasquale stops her (Allegro, 'Signorina, in tanta fretta'). She orders him to bed and, when he protests more urgently, slaps his cheek (Larghetto, 'È finita Don Pasquale'). He threatens her with divorce, and in an aside she expresses sympathy for the old fellow's pain; then as she blithely leaves she drops a note implying that she has a rendezvous in the garden that night. The stunned Pasquale summons Malatesta. The servants comment on the constant comings and goings in this unpredictable household ('Che interminabile andirivieni!'). Malatesta arrives and snatches a hasty word with Ernesto, stressing that Pasquale should not recognize him when he plays his part in the apparent assignation. Pasquale enters and recounts all his problems with his bride: her extravagance, her blow on his cheek and now infidelity. Malatesta struggles to keep a straight face. Then they plot how they will catch the lovers redhanded, the verve of their patter duet, 'Cheti, cheti, immantinente', catching the very spirit of the situation.

3.ii Don Pasquale's garden In the garden Ernesto sings a tender serenade, praising the balmy April night and longing for his beloved to appear ('Com'è gentil'). Norina steals in and they sing a rapturous duet (Notturno, 'Tornami a dir che m'ami'). Don Pasquale and Malatesta have observed this scene from behind a bush. The outraged 'husband' now storms out of hiding to confront Norina and order her to leave his house at once. When she adamantly refuses, Malatesta takes charge of the scene, with Pasquale's consent, and informs Sofronia that tomorrow Ernesto's bride Norina will be installed as mistress of the house. Sofronia says she would rather leave than live under the same roof as Norina. Malatesta then tells Pasquale that he can get rid of Sofronia only by marrying Norina to Ernesto that very evening. Pasquale agrees, and Ernesto is summoned and told to fetch Norina. When the supposed Sofronia turns out to be Norina herself, and the whole plot is explained to Pasquale, he accepts the situation with good grace. All comment on the fact that a man who marries in old age is asking for trouble (rondo, 'La morale in tutto questo').

*

Don Pasquale has been described as 'Mozartian', and clearly it shares certain characteristics with Mozart's approach: the characters are humanized, not mere farcical stereotypes, and the melodies mirror the emotions they express. This comparison is often made in apparent astonishment that a Donizetti could achieve such an irresistibly heartfelt comedy. Rather, it is more appropriate to describe the opera as supremely 'Donizettian', for it stands as a summation of all his most valuable qualities.

It is a 'romantic' comedy with 19th- rather than 18th-century values. The difference comes out in Norina's opening aria. To an irresistible dance tune she laughs at sentimental tales and asserts her own ability to stimulate love. She does not rely on someone else to provide 'qualche ristoro', the relief that Mozart's Countess longs for; Norina, with a 'testa bizzarra' that goes along with her 'core eccellente', depends on her own very persuasive charm. The humour of the piece is compounded of high spirits, captivatingly revealed in the Norina-Malatesta duet and the Act 2 trio 'Sta a vedere', and of sympathy, as Norina feels sorry for the slap she gave Pasquale, 'È duretta la lezione' ('The lesson is a little bitter'), her words set to a melody of expansive tenderness. It is precisely Norina's capacity for tenderness that keeps her sense of humour within the bounds of good taste. And that good taste is found everywhere in the music, which contains not the faintest hint of vulgarity.

It used to be a matter of comment that Donizetti composed the opera in a remarkably short time, about two weeks. ('Composition', of course, did not include the orchestration, a chore to be accomplished during the rehearsal period.) That rapidity was possible because of several typically Donizettian attributes. Not only was he trained as a boy to think in terms of complete musical structures, but he also had the advantage of long experience in the theatre – *Don Pasquale* is after all his 64th opera. A further consideration helps explain his celerity. In the score he adapted a good deal of music that originally had been written for other contexts: duets from scores he had abandoned, salon songs, and (for the chorus of servants in the last act) a waltz he had written in an aristocratic lady's album. It is mistaken, however, to regard such heterogeneity of sources as something reprehensible; Donizetti worked with extraordinary concentration and was able to endow the mixture of new and adapted music with a freshness and piquancy that remain unimpaired to this day.

This concentration is also clear in the bounds of the work itself. With one exception, the whole action is carried by four principals, and in the organic growth of the extraordinary second act, expanding only so far as a quartet, the inventiveness is such that it produces the effect of a more complex ensemble. The chorus has one moment of prominence in the last act, and then appears as background for Ernesto's serenade and the rondò-finale; everything else is for the four principals.

A particular feature of *Don Pasquale* is the natural melodiousness of the recitative, here accompanied by strings rather than employing the traditional harpsichord heretofore associated with *opera buffa*. There are other unusual aspects to the score. The Norina-Malatesta duet, although in two tempos, is in effect a continuously increasing outpouring of comic brio, effected by melodic reminiscence from the first section in the second, and by the harmonic echoes from one to the other (both being in F major). The natural sequence of one movement on the heels of another in the second act, from Pasquale's entrance to the conclusion, gives no sense of separate 'numbers' but achieves an effortless musical continuity. This spontaneity animates the encounter between Norina and Pasquale at the beginning of Act 3. Here, her waltz tune 'Via, caro sposino' has a simplicity that makes it seem the inevitable mode of utterance for her character at that moment, and can be said to represent the distillation of Donizetti's comic style at its purest amalgam of humour and wry tenderness.   W.A.

Don Quichotte ('Don Quixote')

Comédie-héroïque in five acts by Jules Massenet to a libretto by Henri Cain after Jacques Le Lorrain's verse play *Le chevalier de la longue figure* (1904, after Miguel de Cervantes' *Don Quixote*); Monte Carlo, Opéra, 19 February 1910.

Fyodor Shalyapin was the first Don Quichotte and Lucy Arbell the first Dulcinée; Sancho Panza was sung by André Gresse.

Don Quichotte		bass
Sancho Panza		bass-baritone
La Belle Dulcinée		mezzo-soprano
Pedro	⎫	soprano
Garcias		soprano
Rodriguez	*Dulcinée's admirers*	tenor
Juan	⎭	tenor
Chef des Bandits		baritone
Townspeople, bandits		
Setting Spain		

Don Quichotte is the most successful of the six operas commissioned from Massenet by Raoul Gunsbourg for the Opéra de Monte Carlo. The title role was necessarily written for Shalyapin, a regular guest artist in Monaco, about whom Massenet was distinctly cool in his memoirs; the composer much preferred Vanni-Marcoux, who sang the role in Paris at the Gaîté Lyrique later the same year, with Lucien Fugère, another of his favourite singers, as Sancho. In the Paris production Dulcinée was again sung by Lucy Arbell, the young mezzo (40 years his junior) with whom Massenet was deeply infatuated. Both Shalyapin and Vanni-Marcoux left substantial recorded extracts. The opera maintained a precarious hold on the repertory after World War II, mainly as a star vehicle for Slavonic basses in the Shalyapin tradition (Boris Christoff, Miroslav Čangalović), and has since seen an upsurge in popularity both with audiences and with such basses as Ruggero Raimondi and Samuel Ramey. There is a good complete recording with Nicolai

Ghiaurov, Gabriel Bacquier and Régine Crespin (1978).

*

Act 1 *A square outside the house of La Belle Dulcinée* To the background of conventional pastiche-Spanish dance music Dulcinée, a capricious small-town tart, is serenaded by her four admirers. She replies with the first of two meditations on what life holds for women as the years pass by ('Quand la femme a vingt ans'). Don Quichotte and Sancho Panza are greeted with affection by the townspeople and scorn by the four admirers. Quichotte, who imagines Dulcinée to be his ideal of womanhood, serenades her with 'Quand apparaissent les étoiles', a typically self-generating Massenet melody, much reprised. It is interrupted by Juan, who challenges the old man to a duel. This is in turn interrupted by Dulcinée, who dismisses Juan and archly teases Quichotte for his adoration, eventually ordering him to prove his devotion by retrieving a pearl necklace stolen from her bedroom by the local bandit chief. The act ends with a rapt reprise of the Serenade.

Act 2 *Open countryside, dawn* During his quest for the necklace, Quichotte composes a new serenade. Sancho, fearing the expedition to be a wild goose chase, launches into a comic tirade against womankind ('Comment peut-on penser du bien'), the text of which (though not the music) is a conscious echo of

Vanni-Marcoux in the title role of Massenet's 'Don Quichotte'

the Catalogue Aria in *Don Giovanni*. At its conclusion the mists rise and a line of windmills is revealed. Quichotte duly does battle with them.

Act 3 *In the mountains, twilight* Still on the trail of the bandits, Quichotte falls asleep. Sancho flees when the bandits surround them, and Quichotte is quickly overcome. As they prepare to murder him, Quichotte consigns his soul to God in a prayer of sombre simplicity ('Seigneur, reçois mon âme'); shamed, the bandit chief asks the old man who he is, and is so moved by his reply ('Je suis le chevalier errant') that he returns the necklace. Quichotte, recalling how the oppressed and the criminal have always understood him, blesses the bandits as he leaves. This short act, lasting some 17 minutes, is one of Massenet's most perfectly crafted dramatic paragraphs, its control of mood from broad farce to religiosity to pure sentiment quite faultless.

Act 4 *Dulcinée's garden* Surrounded by her admirers, Dulcinée sings the second and more sombre of her meditations ('Lorsque le temps d'amour a fui') and longs for some new sensation to satisfy her hungry flesh. She then chases away her melancholy mood with a flamboyant song to her own guitar accompaniment ('Ne pensons qu'au plaisir d'aimer') and the company retires. Quichotte and Sancho enter. Imagining that marriage beckons and his days of knight-errantry are over, Quichotte promises Sancho a carefree retirement on his own island. Dulcinée returns. Quichotte produces the necklace in triumph and solemnly proposes marriage, much to the amusement of her entourage. Dulcinée dismisses them and in a tender duet ('Oui, je souffre votre tendresse') gently disabuses Quichotte of his folly. In her rejection of him lies proof of her affection: her function is to give love freely, and she could not bear to deceive him. The crestfallen Quichotte thanks her at least for her frankness. She leaves, but the guests return to mock the old man. Sancho rounds on them in a broad C major melody ('Riez, allez, riez du pauvre idéologue') and rebukes them for their cruelty before leading his dazed master away.

Act 5 *A mountain pass, night* Propped up against a tree, Quichotte recognizes that he has long outlived his proper function and prepares to die. He reminds Sancho of his promise of an island ('Prends cette île'), the only island it is in his power to give – the island of dreams. In the planet Jupiter shining brightly in the heavens he seems to see a vision of Dulcinée as he dies.

*

Just as there was a strong element of autobiography in the verse play loosely based on Cervantes by the studiedly eccentric Jacques Le Lorrain, so there is in Massenet's setting. The 67-year-old composer, in poor health, portrayed himself (flatter-

ingly) as the courtly, vague, otherworldly knight, and the ambitious Lucy Arbell (less flatteringly) as the tough but ultimately sensitive gold-digger. Of the four styles of music in the score, the pastiche-Spanish so beloved of French composers is the least interesting; like Meyerbeer before him, Massenet tended not to waste time on music he knew would serve as background to stage action. Dulcinée is drawn with that flirtatiousness and regret at lost youth that male composers flatter themselves to think appropriate to ladies of easy virtue: she is Thaïs's little sister. But Sancho's rumbustious, *opera buffa* idiom and the quirky, mock-academic musical language devised for Quichotte himself are perfectly judged. The opera starts weakly, but for a score of just two hours of music this is not too serious. The windmill scene, the prayer, the duet in which two utterly different worlds meet briefly before going their separate ways and, above all, the death scene show Massenet at his most sensitive and unobtrusively skilful. R.M.

Dreigroschenoper, Die ('The Threepenny Opera')

Play with music in a prologue and three acts by Kurt Weill (music), Bertolt Brecht (book) and Elisabeth Hauptmann (translation) after John Gay's THE BEGGAR'S OPERA; Berlin, Theater am Schiffbauerdamm, 31 August 1928.

Macheath was first sung by the operetta singer Harald Paulsen; the other principal roles were created by singing actors from the spoken theatre (Lotte Lenya as Jenny, Erich Ponto) and cabaret (Rosa Valetti, Roma Bahn, Kurt Gerron).

Jonathan Jeremiah Peachum *head of a band of beggars*	baritone
Frau Peachum	contralto
Polly *her daughter*	soprano
Macheath [Mac the Knife] *head of a band of street robbers*	tenor
Brown *London's chief of police*	baritone
Lucy *his daughter*	soprano
Jenny *a whore*	soprano
Trauerweidenwalter Hakenfingerjakob Münzmatthias Sägerobert Ede Jimmy } *Macheath's men*	tenors and basses
Filch *one of Peachum's beggars*	spoken
Smith *first constable*	spoken
Moritatensänger *(ballad singer)*	baritone
Beggars, whores, constables	
Setting Soho, London	

Still from G. W. Pabst's film of Weill's 'Die Dreigroschenoper' (1931) with Ernst Busch as the ballad singer

First came the idea of adaptation. Having been alerted to the huge success of Nigel Playfair's revival of John Gay's *The Beggar's Opera* at the Lyric Theatre, Hammersmith, which had opened on 5 June 1920, Brecht had his collaborator Elisabeth Hauptmann prepare a working translation of the piece in the winter months of 1927–8. Shortly afterwards he was approached by the young impresario Ernst Josef Aufricht, who was looking for a play with which to launch his new company at the Theater am Schiffbauerdamm in Berlin. Brecht offered Aufricht *The Beggar's Opera*, even though work on it had scarcely begun. Between its inception early in 1928 and its first performance on 31 August eight or so months later, the 'play with music' underwent numerous and substantial reworkings, especially during the chaotic final month of rehearsal under the direction of Erich Engel. Apart from the Gay text, Brecht also used poems by François Villon (for which he was later charged with plagiarism, having failed to credit the German translator, K. L. Ammer) and Rudyard Kipling. Announced in May as *The Beggar's Opera*, the work initially bore the subtitle *Die Luden-Oper* ('The Pimps' Opera'). The title *Die Dreigroschenoper* did not emerge until a week or so before the première. There were also last-minute cast changes. Radical cuts were necessary. Most of the Kipling

material, for example, was removed (only 'Pollys Lied', a translation of 'Mary, Pity Women!', remained). The ballad ('Moritat') of Mac the Knife (Mackie Messer) was the last interpolation of all, created to satisfy the vanity of Paulsen as Macheath, but performed in the end by the ballad singer. The work was not expected to succeed. In the event, however, it proved to be the biggest theatrical success of the Weimar Republic, running for more than 350 performances over the next two years. The Lewis Ruth Band, a seven-man outfit of versatile jazz studio musicians, named after the band's flautist and saxophonist, Ludwig Rüth, provided the instrumental accompaniment. Theo Mackeben directed from the piano. In its final form, revised by the composer immediately after the première, the full score requires a total of 23 instruments.

The *Dreigroschen*-fever which gripped Germany from 1928 to 1930 soon spread to other countries. By 1933 Weill's publisher, Universal Edition, had licensed a total of 133 new productions worldwide. The work has been translated into most of the major languages, into English no less than eight times. 2611 consecutive performances were given at the Theatre de Lys, New York, in the mid-1950s, in the acclaimed production of Marc Blitzstein's translation and arrangement, making *The Threepenny Opera* for a while the longest-running musical show in history. The same production also marked the comeback of Lotte Lenya, Weill's widow, the original Jenny.

Weill's score, his second collaboration with Brecht, retains only one of the original airs arranged by Pepusch for *The Beggar's Opera* ('Peachum's Morning Hymn', Act 1.i); the rest is a completely new composition. There are several versions of the book. The original 1928 libretto, which already departs significantly from Gay, was published in that year as loan material to theatres. It contains a certain amount of stage business deleted from all later editions of the text. The 'literary' version which Brecht prepared for the collected edition of his works (the *Versuche*) in 1931 is the one commonly used today, even though it was produced independently of the composer. The changes, some of them substantial, document an attempt to bring the piece into line with the author's latest theories of epic theatre; they also suggest a desire to appease Marxist critics, who had originally missed any 'modern social or political satire' and described Brecht as a 'bohemian'. In the postwar period Brecht presented yet another version entitled *Die Dreigroschen-Oper* (with the all-important hyphen) for copyright reasons, including revised song texts with references to the atrocities of National Socialism. Of the numerous recordings, the album of highlights made in December 1930 with members of the Schiffbauerdamm cast holds particular interest for the evidence it offers of 'authentic' performance practice.

Brecht devised captions for the stage version as part of the work's epic structure (displayed on screens in the theatre) and a narration for a concert version. The titles of the separate numbers were also originally displayed on screens.

*

Prologue After the overture the first caption reads: 'A fair in Soho. The beggars are begging, the thieves thieving, the whores whoring. A ballad singer sings the "Ballad of Mac the Knife"' ('Die Moritat von Mackie Messer').

Act I.i The caption reads: 'To combat the increasing callousness of mankind Jonathan Jeremiah Peachum, a man of business, has opened a shop where the poorest of the poor can acquire the sort of appearance that can still touch the hardest of hearts' ('Morgenchoral des Peachum': 'Peachum's Morning Hymn'). Jonathan Peachum learns from his wife that his daughter Polly is having a relationship with a certain young man. He tells her that his daughter's beloved, Macheath, is the notorious gang leader Mac the Knife ('Anstatt dass-Song': 'Instead of Song').

I.ii At five o'clock the next afternoon, Mac the Knife is celebrating his marriage to Polly Peachum, in a stable fitted out with exclusive furnishings which

his gang have stolen ('Hochzeitslied': 'Wedding Song'). But he is not happy with the work of his gang. It is the work of apprentices, not of grown men. To clear the air and liven things up a little, Polly volunteers to sing a song ('Seeräuberjenny': 'Pirate Jenny'). London's chief of police, Brown, arrives. The bandits call him Tiger Brown. He is a good friend of Mac the Knife, whose evil deeds he neither sees nor hears. Brown has come to congratulate Mac on his wedding ('Kanonen-Song': 'Cannon Song') and then quickly takes his leave. He still has preparations to make for the coronation celebrations the following day. Once the bandits have also left, the wedding night begins, and Polly and Mac sing their 'Liebeslied'.

I.iii In his outfitting shop for beggars, Peachum realizes that the loss of his daughter spells utter ruin. Polly is received by her parents ('Barbara Song') and the act ends with the 'Erstes Dreigroschenfinale' ('First Threepenny Finale') .

Act 2.i On Thursday afternoon, Mac takes leave of his wife in order to flee from his father-in-law to Highgate moor. Jonathan Peachum wants to hand Mac over to the law. Mrs Peachum suspects that Mac is hiding out in Turnbridge with his whores and wants to bribe the girls to give him away. Polly, however, springs to his defence and points out that the chief of police is his best friend. She informs Mac of the danger, and advises him to flee. During his absence she will continue to run the business as captain of the gang. They take leave of each other in 'Melodram' and in 'Pollys Lied' ('Polly's Song'). (The next number, 'Die Ballade von der sexuellen Hörigkeit': 'The Ballad of Sexual Dependency', was cut from the 1928 version.)

2.ii The caption reads: 'The coronation bells had not yet died down and Mac the Knife was still sitting with the whores of Turnbridge. The whores betray him. It is Thursday evening.' Mac and the whore Jenny remember in a song the pleasant hours they have spent together ('Zuhälterballade': 'Pimps' Ballad'). While Mac is singing, Jenny stands at the window and gives a signal to the constable.

2.iii Although betrayed by the whores, Macheath will be freed from prison through the love of another woman. Brown is unhappy; he could have spared his friend the trouble he is in ('Die Ballade vom angenehmen Leben': 'The Ballad of the Easy Life'). Lucy and Polly meet in front of Mac's prison. Lucy, Brown's daughter, is secretly married to Mac. She and Polly sing the 'Eifersuchtsduett' ('Jealousy Duet'). (Lucy's aria, 'Eifersucht! Wut, Liebe und Furcht zugleich', was omitted on the first night but is usually included in modern performances and recordings and is the most overtly operatic number in the work.) The quarrel comes to an abrupt conclusion: Mrs Peachum appears and drags Polly off. Lucy stands her ground. Mac succeeds (with Lucy's help) in escaping from prison. He makes a beeline for the whores. When Peachum wishes to pay Mac a visit he finds only the police chief Brown. In order to frighten him about the consequences of his carelessness in letting Mac escape, Peachum tells him a story with an obvious reference to the coronation celebrations taking place the next day. Mac sings (with Mrs Peachum) the parable about what keeps man alive ('Zweites Dreigroschenfinale': 'Second Threepenny Finale').

Act 3.i That same night Peachum prepares to set off. His intention is to disturb the coronation procession with a demonstration of misery and squalor. He delivers a speech to his beggars but is arrested by Brown. Peachum, however, warns him about being too hasty ('Das Lied von der Unzulänglichkeit menschlichen Strebens': 'The Song of the Insufficiency of Human Endeavour' and 'Salomon-Song': 'Solomon Song'). He has the police chief in the palm of his hand and blackmails him, thus forcing his own release. Moreover, he again puts Brown on the trail of Mac.

3.ii On Friday morning at six o'clock Macheath, who has gone again to the whores, is once again betrayed by them. He is to be hanged. Once more he tries, by means of bribery, to escape ('Ruf aus der Gruft': 'Call from the Grave'). The bells of Westminster are ringing. All Mac the Knife's acquaintances have appeared in the prison to bid him farewell as he is taken to the gallows. He begs everyone for forgiveness ('Grabschrift': 'Epitaph'). Unlike real life, however, *The Threepenny Opera* has a happy end. After 'Gang zum Galgen' ('Walk to the Gallows'), the king's mounted messenger saves Mac from execution. The gratification of all concerned is expressed by Peachum:

> Now, ladies and gentlemen, in our show
> We should witness Mac's hanging
> For in the Christian world, as well you know,
> Nothing comes from nothing.
> But lest you might be tempted
> To accuse us of some crass collusion
> Mac will now be exempted
> We offer instead an alternative conclusion.
> Mercy, it's said, tempers justice
> In opera, that's par for the course
> So let's have the theory in practice
> And behold the King's envoy – on a horse.

The opera ends with the 'Drittes Dreigroschenfinale' ('Third Threepenny Finale') and 'Schlussgesang' ('Chorale').

*

Die Dreigroschenoper has been described (by Hans Keller) as 'the weightiest possible lowbrow opera for highbrows and the most full-blooded highbrow musical for lowbrows'. For Weill it was not just 'the most consistent reaction to Wagner'; it also marked a positive step towards an operatic reform. By explicitly and implicitly shunning the more earnest traditions of the opera house, Weill and Brecht created a mixed form which incorporated spoken theatre and popular musical idioms. Parody of operatic convention – of Romantic lyricism and happy endings – constitutes a central device. The through-composed music drama is replaced by the 'prototype' of the number principle: rather than carry the drama forward, the music stops the action in its tracks in a way comparable to *opera seria*. Nor does it contribute to dramatic characterization in any general or substantial way. Often the protagonists merely 'adopt attitudes', to use Brecht's expression. The piece is a montage rather than an organic construction. The music even undermines the sense of the words. Writing to his publisher about the 'Zuhälterballade', for instance, Weill observed: 'The charm of the piece rests precisely in the fact that a rather risqué text … is set to music in a gentle, pleasant way.' The pervading tone is thoroughly ironic, a deliberately unsettling mixture of sentimentality with cynicism and caustic social criticism.

If generic ambiguity is a key to the work's enduring success, it has also encouraged a performing tradition at odds with the composer's original intentions. Weill wrote for musically gifted all-round performers. Yet the work has more often than not been performed by actors who, of necessity, bellow and bark their songs rather than sing them. Any parodic and comic effects should result from an abundance – not a paucity – of musical talent.

S.Hn.

Due Foscari, I ('The Two Foscari')

Tragedia lirica in three acts by Giuseppe Verdi to a libretto by Francesco Maria Piave after Byron's play *The Two Foscari*; Rome, Teatro Argentina, 3 November 1844.

The première cast included Achille De Bassini (Francesco Foscari), Giacomo Roppa (Jacopo) and Marianna Barbieri-Nini (Lucrezia).

Francesco Foscari *Doge of Venice*	baritone
Jacopo Foscari *his son*	tenor
Lucrezia Contarini *Jacopo's wife*	soprano
Jacopo Loredano *member of the Council of Ten*	bass
Barbarigo *senator, member of the Giunta*	tenor
Pisana *Lucrezia's friend and confidante*	soprano
Officer of the Council of Ten	tenor
Servant of the Doge	bass

Members of the Council of Ten and the Giunta,
   Lucrezia's maids, Venetian women, populace
   and masked figures of both sexes
Walk-on parts: Il Messer Grande, Jacopo Foscari's
   two small children, naval commanders, prison
   guards, gondoliers, sailors, populace, masked
   figures, pages of the Doge
Setting Venice in 1457

Soon after the première of Ernani in Venice, Verdi agreed to write a new opera with Piave for the Teatro Argentina in Rome. The first choice was Lorenzino de' Medici, but this proved unacceptable to the Roman censors, and a setting of Byron's The Two Foscari was agreed upon. It is clear from Verdi's early descriptions that he conceived of the opera as in the Ernani vein (relatively small-scale, concentrating on personal confrontations rather than grand scenic effects), although he did urge Piave to attempt something grandiose for the first-act finale. The correspondence between composer and librettist reveals the extent to which Verdi intervened in the making of the libretto, a good deal of the large-scale structure of the opera being dictated by his increasingly exacting theatrical instincts. The composer was also concerned with matters of ambience and anxious to introduce certain moments in which scenic effects could be exploited.

Composing I due Foscari occupied Verdi for about four months (a long time by the standards of most of its predecessors). Its first performance was not a great success, possibly because the expectations of the audience had been driven too high by the enormous and widespread success of Ernani. In 1846 Verdi supplied the famous tenor Mario with a replacement cabaletta for Jacopo in Act 1 (first performed at the Théâtre Italien, Paris).

                                        *

The prelude depicts an atmosphere of stormy conflict before introducing two themes from the opera, the first a mournful clarinet melody to be associated with Jacopo, the second an ethereal flute and string passage from Lucrezia's cavatina.

Act 1.i *A hall in the Doge's Palace in Venice* The curtain rises as the Council of Ten and the Giunta are gathering. Their opening chorus ('Silenzio ... Mistero') immediately casts over the opera a subdued yet menacing atmosphere, suggested musically by dark instrumental and vocal sonorities and by tortuous chromatic progressions. The prelude's clarinet melody is heard as Jacopo, the Doge's son, falsely accused of murder and exiled from Venice, appears from the prisons to await an audience with the Council. In a delicately scored arioso he salutes his beloved Venice and begins the first section of a two-part cavatina. The first movement, 'Dal più remoto esilio', evokes local colour in its 6/8 rhythm,

prominent woodwind sonorities and unusual chromatic excursions. The cabaletta, 'Odio solo, ed odio atroce', is routinely energetic, although it defies convention in allowing the tenor to linger over a high A♭ as the orchestra undertakes a reprise of the main theme.

1.ii *A hall in the Foscari Palace* Lucrezia, Jacopo's wife, enters to a rising string theme, associated with her at intervals through the opera. She is determined to confront the Doge in an attempt to save her husband, but first offers a prayer, 'Tu al cui sguardo onnipossente'. This preghiera exhibits a more highly ornamental vocal style than is usual in early Verdi, although the decoration is – typically for the composer – strictly controlled within fixed phrase lengths. The ensuing cabaletta, 'O patrizi, tremate l'Eterno', is novel in formal design, beginning with an arioso-like passage in the minor and dissolving into open-structured ornamental writing at the end.

1.iii *A hall in the Doge's Palace (as 1.i)* The Council has concluded its meeting and, in part with a return to the music of the opening chorus, confirms that Jacopo's 'crime' must be punished with exile.

1.iv *The Doge's private rooms* The Doge's 'Scena e Romanza' opens with yet another theme that is to recur through the course of the opera, this time a richly harmonized melody for viola and divided cellos. The romanza 'O vecchio cor, che batti', in which the Doge apostrophizes his son, is clearly a companion piece to Jacopo's earlier 'Dal più remoto esilio' (notice, for example, the identical opening accompaniment figures), although the baritone father sings with far more direct emotional appeal than his tenor son. The ensuing finale of Act 1 is a lengthy scene between Lucrezia and the Doge, in which Jacopo's wife begs the Doge to show mercy. One of Verdi's finest early soprano-baritone duets, the number falls into the conventional four-movement pattern, but individual sections boast considerable inner contrast, responding closely to the differing emotional attitudes of the principals.

Act 2.i *The state prisons* A fragmentary, highly chromatic prelude for solo viola and cello introduces Jacopo, alone in prison. He has a terrifying vision of Carmagnola, a past victim of Venetian law, and in the romanza 'Non maledirmi, o prode' begs the vision for mercy. 'Non maledirmi' is conventional in its move from minor to major, but has an unusual return to the minor as the vision of Carmagnola reappears to haunt the prisoner and eventually render him unconscious. Lucrezia, accompanied by her rising string theme, enters and, after reviving Jacopo, announces his sentence of exile. There follows one of Verdi's very rare love duets, this one laid out in the usual multi-movement form though without an opening 'action' sequence. The closing portions of the duet see an injection of local colour: gondoliers singing in praise of Venice interrupt husband and wife, giving them fresh hope for the future. The Doge, powerless to affect the decision of the Council, whose ruling he must put into effect, now enters to bid a sad farewell to his son. The first lyrical movement of the ensuing trio, 'Nel tuo paterno amplesso', makes much of the contrast in vocal personalities – declamatory tenor, sustained, controlled baritone, breathless, distraught soprano – while the final stretta (in which the principals are joined by a gloating Loredano, their enemy) simplifies matters by uniting Jacopo and Lucrezia in syncopated unison.

2.ii *The hall of the Council of Ten* An opening chorus, again partly built on material from Act 1 scene i, explains that Jacopo's crimes are murder and treason against the state. The Doge appears, soon followed by his son, who continues to protest his innocence. The Doge will not listen, but all are dumbfounded by the sudden appearance of Lucrezia, who has brought her children with her in a final plea for mercy. The stage is set for the concertato finale, 'Queste innocenti lagrime', led off by Jacopo, who is seconded by Lucrezia. This grandiose movement develops impressive momentum up to the final peroration (the passage sometimes termed 'groundswell'), but its last cadence is interrupted: Jacopo returns to the minor mode and intimate musical language of his opening phrases, and is in turn interrupted by a further tutti repetition of the 'groundswell' idea. The extreme juxtaposition creates sufficient dramatic charge to close the act without a traditional fast stretta.

Act 3.i *The old piazzetta di S Marco* Local colour in the form of an 'Introduzione e Barcarola' begins the act, with gondoliers offering a more developed reprise of the music that had earlier interrupted the Jacopo-Lucrezia duet. Jacopo is brought forth for the final parting. His 'All'infelice veglio' is *romanza*-like in its progress from minor to major but is enriched by contributions from Lucrezia and, eventually, from the chorus, making the scene a fitting grand climax to the tenor's role.

3.ii *The Doge's private rooms (as 1.iv)* First comes a scena for the Doge in which he is presented with a deathbed confession that reveals Jacopo's innocence. But the message is too late: Lucrezia rushes on to announce that Jacopo died suddenly on leaving Venice. Lucrezia's aria 'Più non vive!' is, as befits this late stage of the drama, highly condensed, and is perhaps best considered a kind of bipartite cabaletta, allowing (as did her first-act aria) more room than is usual in early Verdi for ornamental flourishes. As she leaves, the Council of Ten appear, led by Loredano, and ask the Doge to relinquish his power on account of his great age. He answers in an impassioned aria, 'Questa dunque è l'iniqua mercede'. In many ways the most powerful section of the opera, this 'aria' is really a duet between the Doge and the male chorus: he in declamatory triplets demanding the return of his son; they in inflexible unison. The great bell of St Mark's sounds to mark the election of a new Doge – not Loredano, in spite of his ambitions – and, after a final apostrophe to Jacopo, the Doge falls lifeless to the ground.

*

I due Foscari, as Verdi himself was later to admit, suffers somewhat from being too gloomy in its general tone, in spite of periodic evocations of the Venetian lagoon. But the opera nevertheless offers several interesting experiments. Perhaps most striking is the use of recurring themes to identify the principals. These proto-'leitmotifs' are here perhaps applied too rigidly, serving ultimately to deny any sense of development or progression in the characters; but the experiment itself is significant, suggesting that Verdi was anxious to explore new means of musical and dramatic articulation. The increased importance of local colour is also notable in the light of Verdi's future development. Although in *I due Foscari* the sense of a precise ambience seems imposed on the score rather than emerging from it, Verdi's awareness of the potential of this added dimension in musical drama was decisive; from this time onwards he would rarely employ local colour in quite the mechanical way he had in his earliest operas.   **R.P.**

E

Einstein on the Beach

Opera in four acts and five 'knee plays' (intermezzos) by Philip Glass and Robert Wilson to a libretto by Christopher Knowles, Lucinda Childs and Samuel M. Johnson; Avignon Festival, 25 July 1976.

Einstein is scored for a 16-strong chamber choir, including soprano and tenor soloists, the Philip Glass Ensemble (two keyboards, three wind players, one soprano), and a solo violinist. In the original production the violinist was dressed as Albert Einstein and placed between the stage and orchestra pit.

Created between 1974 and 1976, it is the longest and most famous of Glass's music-theatre works, the first of three operas each concerning a man who changed the world. It is, however, in many ways unrepresentative, being much more than the usual collaboration between librettist and composer. Glass first became aware of Robert Wilson's stage work in 1973 when he attended a 12-hour production by the latter based on the life and times of Joseph Stalin. He was immediately attracted to what he called Wilson's sense of 'theatrical time, space and movement', and the two promptly determined to collaborate on a theatrical work based on the life of a historic figure. Discarding Chaplin, Hitler and Gandhi, they agreed upon Albert Einstein, naming the piece *Einstein on the Beach on Wall Street*. The title was later shortened; neither creator now remembers when or why. The opera is intended as a metaphorical look at Einstein: scientist, humanist, amateur musician – and the man whose theories, for better and for worse, led to the splitting of the atom. The composer has described it as 'an opera about a great mathematician who loved music, [. . .] for amplified ensemble and small chorus singing a text comprised of numbers (actually the beats of the music) and solfege syllables'. Although it is difficult to discern a 'plot' in *Einstein*, the final scene may be interpreted as nuclear holocaust: with its renaissance-pure vocal lines, the blast of amplified instruments, a steady pulse and the hysterical chorus chanting numerals as quickly and frantically as possible, it seemed to many a musical reflection of the anxious, almost *fin-de-siècle* mood of the late 1970s.

The opera runs for four hours and 40 minutes without an interval (the audience is invited to wander in and out at liberty during performances), and is in four interconnected acts. These are alternated with what Glass and Wilson called 'knee plays' – brief interludes that also provide time for scenery changes. In Wilson's original videotaped production, the first knee play is already in progress when the audience is admitted to the auditorium. After about 15 minutes the chorus enters very slowly and takes its place in the orchestra pit. Thus the audience's perception of time is challenged from the outset, and an allusion is made to one aspect of Einstein's theories. The 'story' of *Einstein* comprises visual images and aural references relating to Albert Einstein, his life and his work. Glass and Wilson used as a 'libretto' a sketchbook of visual themes, before developing a spoken and sung text during the rehearsal period. As well as numbers and solfege syllables the text consists of some cryptic poems by Christopher Knowles, a young, neurologically-impaired man with whom Wilson had worked (as an instructor of disturbed children). To this were added short texts by the choreographer Lucinda Childs and Samuel M. Johnson, an actor who played the Judge in the 'Trial' scenes and the Bus Driver in the finale. References are made to Patricia Hearst, who was on trial for bank robbery during the creation of the opera, to the radio line-up on New York's WABC, to the popular song 'Mr Bojangles', to the teen idol David Cassidy and to the Beatles.

The music is based on two techniques Glass worked with from the mid-1960s: additive process and cyclic structures. Additive process involves the expansion and contraction of tiny musical modules; a grouping of five notes might be played several times, followed by a group of six notes, similarly repeated, then by seven notes, and so on. Thus a simple figure can maintain the same general melodic configuration while taking on a very different rhythmic shape. Glass defines rhythmic cycles as the simultaneous repetition of two or more different rhythmic patterns, which, depending on the length of the pattern, will eventually arrive together back at the starting points, making for one complete cycle. With these two techniques as the basis of his individual style, Glass had already begun to build a music of increasing richness and appeal. *Einstein* added a new functional

Drawings from Robert Wilson's sketchbook of visual themes (the train) for 'Einstein on the Beach' (Glass)

harmony that set it aside from the early conceptual works.

Einstein was revived in 1984 at the Brooklyn Academy of Music. In 1989 Achim Fryer attempted a new visual interpretation of Glass's music for the opera at the Stuttgart State Opera, which was generally judged unsuccessful. It is, however, the Glass/Wilson *Einstein* that has become one of the more famous operatic collaborations of the century, creating something unique and powerful. The sound recording of *Einstein* (recorded in 1977 and released in 1979) won considerable attention, though it necessarily lacked Wilson's visual complement and Glass abridged the music to fit on to four LP discs. The opening scene was cut from 40 minutes to a little more than 20 minutes by reducing the number of repeats.

Einstein on the Beach may be said to represent the apogee of Glass's modernism. As the composer observed in *Music by Philip Glass*:

In its own way, the pre-*Einstein* music, rigorous and highly reductive, was more 'radical' in its departure from the received tradition of Western music than what I have written since. But as I had been preoccupied at the point with that more radical-sounding music for over ten years, I felt I could add little more to what I had already done. Again, it is surely no coincidence that it was at the moment that I was embarking upon a major shift in my music to large-scale theater works that I began to develop a new, more expressive language for myself.

T.P.

Elegy for Young Lovers

Opera in three acts by Hans Werner Henze to a libretto by W. H. Auden and Chester Kallman; Schwetzingen, 20 May 1961 (in a German translation by Ludwig Landgraf).

The first cast included Eva-Marie Rogner (Hilda Mack) and Dietrich Fischer-Dieskau (Mittenhofer), with Ingeborg Bremert, Lilian Benningsen, Friedrich Lenz, and Karl Christian Kohn.

Gregor Mittenhofer *a poet*	baritone
Dr Wilhelm Reischmann *a physician*	bass
Toni Reischmann *his son*	tenor
Carolina Gräfin von Kirchstetten	
Mittenhofer's secretary	contralto
Elisabeth Zimmer *his young mistress*	soprano
Hilda Mack *a widow*	soprano
Josef Mauer *an alpine guide*	speaker
Servants at 'Der schwarze Adler'	

Setting 'Der schwarze Adler', an inn in the
    Austrian Alps, 1910

Henze asked Auden and Kallman for an opera libretto in 1958, specifying a scenario that would require 'tender, beautiful noises'. The première at the Schwetzingen Festival was conducted by Heinrich Bender and produced by Henze himself. The text was heard in its original English at Glyndebourne in 1963, although Act 3 scenes vii and viii were omitted. The cast included Dorothy Dorow, Elisabeth Söderström, Kerstin Meyer and Thomas Hemsley; John Pritchard was the conductor.

        *

Act I: *'The Emergence of the Bridegroom'* The parlour *and terrace of 'Der schwarze Adler'*

    I.i *('Forty years past')* In a highly expressive, wide-ranging aria, whose mixture of coloratura and Sprechgesang will define her vocal character throughout the opera, Hilda Mack remembers the day in the 1870s when her husband went off to climb the Hammerhorn.

    I.ii *('The order of the day')* Dr Reischmann watches Mittenhofer's aristocratic but down-trodden secretary Carolina as she sorts press cuttings. In a duet they comment on their various obligations to the poet, for which they receive little thanks though he could hardly do without them.

    I.iii *('A scheduled arrival')* Reischmann waits for his son Toni, who is difficult and has no enthusiasm for anything.

    I.iv *('Appearances and visions')* Carolina invites Hilda Mack into the inn, just as Mittenhofer is leaving arm in arm with Elisabeth Zimmer. As Mittenhofer begins the introductions Hilda goes into an extravagant coloratura fantasy; it fascinates the poet, appals Toni and contains a foreshadowing of the death of two young people.

1.v (*'Worldly business'*) Mittenhofer is delighted with his 'research', and then rails at Carolina for mistakes in her typing until she faints. Reischmann rushes in to minister to her.

1.vi (*'Help'*) Mittenhofer searches the inn for money, finds what he wants – carefully placed by Carolina – and disappears to his own quarters.

1.vii (*'Unworldly weakness'*) Carolina remains distraught.

1.viii (*'Beauty in death'*) Josef Mauer reports that a body has been found on the Hammerhorn – a young man, almost certainly Frau Mack's husband.

1.ix (*'Who is to tell her?'*) Carolina and Dr Reischmann agree that Elisabeth must tell Hilda of the discovery.

1.x (*'Today's weather'*) Elisabeth breaks the news to Hilda as carefully as possible. She eventually gets through to the widow in a canonic duet; Toni is impressed by her tact.

1.xi (*'A visionary interlude'*) Toni sings a highly expressive aria in which he remembers his mother, long dead; he remains staring at the spot where Elisabeth had been standing.

1.xii (*'Tomorrow: two follies cross'*) Hilda's emotions suddenly erupt. She joins Toni in a rapturous duet, while he pours out his emerging love for Elisabeth.

Act 2: 'The Emergence of the Bride'

2.i (*'A passion'*) Elisabeth and Toni express their love in a duet: Toni urges her to leave Mittenhofer. Carolina discovers them, and summons the doctor to help her end their dalliance.

2.ii (*'Sensible talk'*) Reischmann tries to talk Toni round, while Carolina attempts the same with Elisabeth.

2.iii (*'Each in his place'*) In two separate monologues interwoven as a duet, the lovers express their anger at the interference in their affairs.

2.iv (*'The Master's time'*) While Elisabeth asks Toni to take her away, Carolina tells Mittenhofer of the burgeoning affair: he asks Carolina to invite Elisabeth to join him for tea.

2.v (*'Personal questions'*) In an extended monologue Mittenhofer tries to play on Elisabeth's feelings of guilt, while feigning self-pity; she cannot get a word in.

2.vi (*'The troubles of others'*) Elisabeth expresses her distress in a slow aria that flows into an orchestral meditation.

2.vii (*'What must be told'*) Elisabeth tells Toni that she has said nothing to the poet; he says that he will instead.

2.viii (*'The wrong time'*) Toni tells Mittenhofer of his love for Elisabeth: his declaration expands into a large-scale quartet as they are joined by Elisabeth (later replaced by Carolina) and the doctor.

2.ix (*'The bird'*) Frau Mack interrupts with an extrovert aria that spirals ever upwards, and then comforts Elisabeth. Mittenhofer asks Reischmann to give his blessing to the lovers.

2.x (*'The young lovers'*) Surrounded by the protagonists, Mittenhofer introduces his new poem *The Young Lovers* which seems to crystallize all their dilemmas.

2.xi (*'The flower'*) The doctor gives his blessing and Mittenhofer asks the couple to stay a few days until his 60th birthday. He asks them to find an Edelweiss flower for him on the Hammerhorn.

2.xii (*'The vision of tomorrow'*) After a brief ensemble, Mauer tells the poet that the following day will be fair enough for the lovers to find the Edelweiss.

2.xiii (*'The end of the day'*) Mittenhofer's rage, previously suppressed, erupts in a fierce declamation in which he attacks all those around him, wishing the lovers dead. It ends only when Hilda Mack confronts him with her hysterical laughter.

Act 3: 'Man and Wife'

3.i (*'Echoes'*) Hilda is preparing to leave. Toni and Elisabeth set off up the mountain singing a folksong as Hilda bids them goodbye. They are joined in an ensemble by Mittenhofer practising his verse.

3.ii (*'Farewells'*) Frau Mack leaves, giving Carolina the scarf she has been knitting for 40 years.

3.iii (*'Scheduled departures'*) Hilda and Carolina, Mittenhofer and Dr Reischmann join in an elaborate quartet.

3.iv (*'Two to go'*) Carolina attempts unsuccessfully to calm Mittenhofer. Mauer warns that a blizzard is threatened on the Hammerhorn, but the poet denies that he knows of anyone who is on the mountain.

3.v (*'Mad happenings'*) In a confrontation between Mittenhofer and Carolina her sanity finally cracks: he suggests she go away for a rest.

3.vi (*'A change of scene'*) The action moves outside the inn; the blizzard is portrayed in an extended orchestral interlude of increasing violence. Toni and Elisabeth are seen through the snow, unable to continue.

3.vii (*'Man and wife'*) In a long duet over fragile instrumental lines Toni and Elisabeth imagine themselves married for many years. They reflect on their lives together, their children, their infidelities.

3.viii (*'Toni and Elisabeth'*) The lovers prepare for death, fortified by the truth they have discovered in each other.

3.ix (*'Elegy for young lovers'*) Mittenhofer is preparing to give a public reading of his poetry in Vienna. He dedicates his new poem to 'the memory of a brave and beautiful young couple, Toni and Elisabeth'. The wordless offstage voices of Hilda,

Elisabeth, Carolina, Toni and the doctor are heard as he finishes the poem.

*

The 'tender, beautiful noises' that Henze wished to draw from Auden and Kallman's libretto are supplied by a chamber orchestra of single wind and strings with a wide range of tuned and untuned percussion. They are used to create textures of great transparency, while a specific instrumental colour is assigned to each of the protagonists: a flute accompanies Hilda Mack, brass the poet, violin and viola signify the young lovers, an english horn Carolina, a bassoon (later an alto saxophone) Dr Reischmann. The highly structured text is matched in Henze's musical setting by an intricate network of set pieces – arias, recitatives and ensembles – though the boundaries between them are sometimes blurred.

A.C.

Elektra ('Electra')

Tragödie in one act by Richard Strauss to a libretto by Hugo von Hofmannsthal after Sophocles' *Electra*; Dresden, Hofoper, 25 January 1909.

Annie Krull, Strauss's first Diemut in *Feuersnot*, sang the first Electra; Chrysothemis and Orestes were Margarethe Siems and Karl Perron, and Clytemnestra was the redoubtable Ernestine Schumann-Heink.

Electra *Agamemnon's daughter*	soprano
Chrysothemis *her sister*	soprano
Klytemnästra [Clytemnestra] *their mother, Agamemnon's widow*	mezzo-soprano
Her Confidante and her Trainbearer	sopranos
A Young and an Old Servant	tenor, bass
Orest [Orestes] *son of Agamemnon*	baritone
Orestes' Tutor	bass
Aegisth [Aegisthus] *Clytemnestra's paramour*	tenor
An Overseer	soprano
Five maidservants	contralto, two mezzo-sopranos, two sopranos

Men and women of the household

Setting Ancient Mycenae: the inner courtyard of Agamemnon's palace

At the age of 17 Strauss had set a chorus from Sophocles' *Electra* for male voices and orchestra, but it was probably not until November 1903, when he saw Max Reinhardt's Berlin production of the tragedy as 'rewritten for the German stage by Hugo von Hofmannsthal', that the notion of a full operatic setting entered his head. Earlier that year, the Reinhardt staging of Oscar Wilde's *Salomé* (with the same leading actress, Gertrud Eysoldt) had similarly fired his imagination, and the composer was already hard at work on what was to be his first great operatic success. Only in 1906, with *Salome* safely launched, did Strauss ask Hofmannsthal for permission to set his *Elektra*. The writer was not only amenable, but excited about the prospective partnership; he accepted that the text would need shortening, and also agreed to write new passages as required. It was upon receiving one of those, in July 1908 – some extra lines for the Recognition scene, which Hofmannsthal supplied exactly as Strauss had prescribed – that the composer declared his new collaborator to be 'the born librettist'.

Yet Strauss had undertaken the piece hesitantly. He feared lest it seem too similar in cut to *Salome* and wondered whether he ought not instead, for canny commercial contrast, to look for a romantic comedy. (Throughout the composing of *Elektra* he and his writer played with ideas for such a project – something about Casanova's exploits, perhaps, or a mythological fantasy after Calderón – until at last the concept of *Der Rosenkavalier* germinated.) On the question of the awkward similarity, Hofmannsthal's reassurances to Strauss make piquant reading. The only parallels he admitted were the single-act form, the eponymous classical heroines and the fact that Fräulein Eysoldt played them both in Berlin; but anybody else might also remark that each heroine is in the grip of an obsession which fuels the main drama, that after their early arrivals each dominates the action until the end (with climactic solo dances unprecedented in opera), and that both texts trade in morbid psychology and strenuous decadence.

There is good reason to think that Hofmannsthal's *Elektra*, hastily written in mid-1903 to Reinhardt's commission, had taken its inspiration directly from the Reinhardt-Eysoldt *Salome*. The writer protested that the 'blend of colour in the two subjects' was 'quite different in all essentials' – certainly his fervid penetration into his characters was far removed from Wilde's decadent cartoons (he had been reading Freud and Breuer on hysteria, and Rohde's *Psyche*), and he preferred Shakespearean pentameter to Wilde's poetical prose. Yet the broad theatrical form was much the same; it was ultimately the composer who had to establish the difference in musico-dramatic terms. That he did, so persuasively that the two operas do not seem variations on a single form but fiercely individual tales with some points of abstract resemblance. For the monumental effects of *Elektra* Strauss prescribed a still larger orchestra: eight clarinets, for example, and besides his eight horns a sonorous quartet of Wagner tubas, also three groups each of violins and violas – with the first six violists required twice to switch instruments and become a fourth violin section. He completed the score on 22 September 1908, at his new villa in Garmisch.

Four months later *Elektra* was presented in Dresden by the conductor Ernst von Schuch and the director Willi Wirk, who had been responsible for the première of *Salome*. Productions in all the usual countries followed swiftly (though *Elektra* was initially banned at the New York Metropolitan, and had to be performed elsewhere in Manhattan – in French). As conductor, Strauss shared the first British performances in 1910 with Sir Thomas Beecham.

The opera made a forceful mark everywhere, by no means always favourable. Many hearers found it rebarbative, gross and brutal, and a Vienna newspaper commented sourly, 'How beautiful was the Princess Salome . . .'. It was a sign of Strauss's commitment to the through-composed music drama that his *Elektra* offered no feasible excerpts for concerts or recording (until the advent of LPs), but as a result we can hear scarcely anything now of his earlier interpreters. He judged Salomea Kruszelnicka 'perfect' as both Electra and Salome; a famous Clytemnestra was Anna Bahr-Mildenburg, whose husband Hermann Bahr advised Strauss on *Intermezzo* – but the role is a gift to intelligent dramatic mezzos past their vocal prime, and there have been too many of them to mention. In recent years the Electras of Astrid Varnay, Christel Goltz, the young Gerda Lammers and Birgit Nilsson have left powerful impressions.

In literary fact Electra is neither a figure of Greek mythology nor of pre-classical epic, but an invention of later poets and dramatists. Like her fabled brother Orestes and (in this version) a younger sister Chrysothemis, she is a child of the Mycenaean king Agamemnon, who went off to the Trojan war and stayed away for ten years. Meanwhile his queen Clytemnestra, sister of Helen, took a lover, Aegisthus; when the king returned they netted and slew him on the way to his homecoming bath – and prudently sent young Orestes into obscure exile. The guilty pair now rule, and the daughters have become young women, barely tolerated in the royal household: Chrysothemis timorous and self-effacing, Electra recalcitrant and implacably vengeful. The stern heroine of Sophocles' *Electra* grew from an austere silhouette in the *Choephoroe* of Aeschylus, but it is uncertain whether Euripides' more 'modern', psychologically fraught portrait came before or after that of Sophocles. It is often remarked that the Euripides version would seem more apt for Hofmannsthal; perhaps he chose the plainer, less subjective Sophocles as basis so that he could do his own psychological freighting.

*

Elektra has no prelude, but the opening scene for Clytemnestra's servants is a prologue in effect. As the curtain rises, the orchestra bellows 'Agamemnon!' – or more exactly 'A-ga-MEMMMMM!-(non)' – in unison and very loudly, on the notes of the D minor triad. Though we might not have known what it was saying, had we not read our programme notes, Electra herself will shortly invoke her father to that leitmotif. In Hofmannsthal's original text, nobody uttered the name until much later. Strauss had good Wagnerian reasons for introducing it sooner (the motif is to haunt the score, much as the unspoken name hung over the play text); but his treatment of names is always significant. Here it is striking that whereas 'Elektra' and 'Orest' are voiced again and again as passionate pleas, the names of Clytemnestra and Aegisthus are mentioned only in passing, and poor Chrysothemis is never once named aloud: even in Electra's mouth she is merely 'daughter of my mother', or just 'girl'.

Five maids, watched by overseers, are drawing water from a well at twilight, and wondering aloud whether Electra will arrive as usual to wail for the dead king. She does, wildly, almost before the orchestral 'Agamemnon!' has ceased to reverberate, but on seeing the other women she flings an arm over her face and 'darts back like an animal to its lair'. Four of the maids gossip and gloat over Electra's self-willed bestial condition, and her lofty contempt for them; the fifth and youngest protests that she is uniquely noble and scandalously maltreated – she would love to see the other maids hanged in reparation for the wrongs done to her Princess. (Like Mozart's Barbarina in *Figaro*, Strauss's Fifth Maid has long been a role in which promising young sopranos are tried out.) An outraged Overseer thrusts her off to the servants' quarters for a beating. Electra re-emerges to find herself alone.

Since the initial pronouncement of 'Agamemnon!' the music has been tonally frantic – either harmonized in no clear key at all, or slipping into some friendly key (as with the Fifth Maid) only to veer off again into no-man's-land. Yet after the graphic offstage beating, it subsides firmly upon the original D, as if concluding a first paragraph; and now Electra is properly introduced (like Salome) by a restatement of her opening music, as if a symphonic 'development' were under way. The key declines to a curdled B♭ minor, however, and the tempo to a dim, sluggish pulse, as she calls upon her father. She relives his grisly death (the music veers again into wild chromatics), and imagines him returning as a spectre to approve a bloody vengeance on his murderers; then, with her siblings, she will slay the royal horses and hounds to honour him, and will dance gloriously at last over the corpses to show the world that this was a king. Studded with pictorial detail, the music of this extraordinary soliloquy is also a fast-forward preview of the rest of the opera,

*'Elektra' (Richard Strauss): Annie Krull as Electra (right)
and Ernestine Schumann-Heink as Clytemnestra (centre) in
the original production at the Hofoper, Dresden, 25 January
1909; drawing by W. Gause from the 'Illustrirte Zeitung'
(Leipzig, 28 January 1909)*

ported by a pair of servile intimates, Clytemnestra staggers in. Sleepless nights have driven her to breaking-point (Strauss abandons any key signature while he illustrates her nightmares with monstrous, unheard-of effects), and she is in desperate search of the sacrifice that will give her release. She has long suspected that Electra enjoys clairvoyant powers; now, finding her docile, she sues humbly for advice. Electra agrees that a sacrifice is justly required – at once the music pulls itself together in stark C minor, ready to go into bloodthirsty hunt mode – and she spells it out at length with feral excitement: the unclean woman and her paramour must be tracked through the palace corridors by Orestes with the sacred axe. Clytemnestra reels back speechless. But secret news is suddenly brought to her; crowing with hysterical relief, she sweeps out. Her other daughter hurries in with the report that Orestes is dead. A young servant calls for a horse: he must bear an urgent message to Aegisthus.

With her long-nurtured hopes facing ruin, Electra tries to enlist Chrysothemis in matricide. She croons over her sister's nubile body, ripe for marriage and motherhood, and promises to be her selfless handmaiden forever if she will collaborate in the murder. (If not quite a love duet, this is certainly a seduction scene.) At the last moment Chrysothemis takes fright and bolts. Electra curses her, and begins digging alone for the buried axe.

While she scrabbles in the earth an apparent stranger arrives with his companion, to strange, sombre chorale chords. At first he takes her for a wretched servant, but as she bewails her familial lot (the agonized theme echoes the wailing wind of the Inferno in Liszt's *Dante Sonata*) Orestes realizes who she must be. Aged retainers come to kiss their young master's feet. Finally recognition dawns for Electra too, and there is a seismic crash from the orchestra, like a great house falling down. Brother and sister embrace speechless; the music churns for a long time before reaching haven in soft, glowing A♭. Electra pours out her joy and relief, and her shame at her abject condition. Orestes assures her that he knows what duty he has come to fulfil – but his tutor interrupts them to enjoin prudent silence, and no more delay.

The two men enter the palace. In the long, shuddering suspense, Electra remembers the forgotten axe too late. Clytemnestra's death-cry is heard, and Electra screams to her brother to strike again. Her frightened sister and the first four maids gather anxiously in the forecourt with other servants. The return of Aegisthus is heralded; all but Electra flee in dismay, leaving her to enact an ironical welcome. To light his way she dances around him with a torch, which unnerves him (he shares a querulous, petulant vein with Strauss's Herod – and Electra's mocking

which will prove to echo the sequence of Electra's imaginings (in fact this is the 'symphonic exposition' proper). With the visionary dance it stamps into C major, as the opera itself will do at the end – but now the anxious arrival of Chrysothemis breaks it off.

This is the first of the four confrontations with Electra which supply the greater part of the opera. (Then come the murders, and the fatal triumph-dance: like Salome, Electra never leaves the stage.) Chrysothemis has come to warn her that their mother and Aegisthus mean to imprison her in a dark tower. Against Electra's stoic defiance her sister pleads her own tearful, mellifluous despair; all she wants is a quiet, normal life with a decent husband and children. Though the waltz music Strauss gives her is often described as bland and regressive, his intention was surely to present her as a simple, warmhearted, conventional soul – the better to set off the intemperate extremes of everyone else. She gets no comfort from Electra, and the next confrontation is imminent; chromatic heavings and churnings in the orchestra herald Clytemnestra's latest parade of sacrificial victims. Chrysothemis flees in terror, but her sister awaits her mother with baleful purpose.

Raddled, bedecked with luck-charms and sup-

waltz presages *Der Rosenkavalier*), but he proceeds into the palace. A moment later he is seen at a window, shrieking in the clutches of his murderers.

Until this moment of grim triumph, a signal omission from Hofmannsthal and Strauss's ersatz-classical tragedy has been the antique Chorus. Now, while Chrysothemis and her women return to rejoice, massed voices off stage hail 'Orest!' some 27 times. As the music flings itself into raw, brazen tonality (abrupt modulations screwing the excitement ever higher), the sisters exult together, the younger pleading repeatedly 'Who has ever loved us?' Electra declares that nothing but silence and dance should celebrate their release, and herself begins to tread rapturous maenadic steps. The sister shrinks away in terror from the wild display, but reappears at the height of the dance to witness Electra collapsing dead to the earth. The orchestra thunders 'Agamemnon!' in C minor, and gets only a deathly-soft E♭ minor chord for reply. Crying vainly for Orestes, Chrysothemis pounds at the locked palace door. (We may guess why no answer comes: he is already pursued by the Furies.)

*

The music of *Elektra* is often diagnosed as marking an 'advanced' point – i.e. on the way to modernist atonality – from which the composer then staged a prudent, inglorious retreat. That bespeaks a prejudice which he never espoused. Though passages in the opera share the queasy harmonic climate of Schoenberg's op.11 no.2 piano piece (1909), Strauss felt no natural urge towards atonality as the Music of the Future. The sporadic 'atonalisms' in *Elektra*, as in his Ophelia songs, were meant to convey the exacerbated spiritual condition of his characters, not to promote some more radical cause. Had Hofmannsthal hit upon the idea for *Der Rosenkavalier* a year or two sooner, Strauss would instead have addressed himself to that just as happily. In fact his anti-tonal devices here are few and simple, though hugely effective; often they undermine, rather than underpin, the Romantic harmonies that float over them. The apparent similarities between *Electra* and, say, Schoenberg's atonal *Erwartung* (also 1909) lie in their violent extremes – of vocal line and histrionic moods, of dynamics and post-Romantic orchestration. Strauss's score, however, absolutely presupposes a secure tonal norm against which to measure its harsh, disorientating dramatic effects for an audience with late Romantic ears.   **D.M.**

Elisir d'amore, L' ('The Elixir of Love')

Melodramma giocoso in two acts by Gaetano Donizetti to a libretto by Felice Romani after Eugène Scribe's text for Daniel-François-Esprit Auber's *Le philtre* (1831); Milan, Teatro Cannobiana, 12 May 1832.

The singers at the première were Sabine Heinefetter (Adina), Giambattista Genero (Nemorino), Henri-Bernard Dabadie (Belcore) and Giuseppe Frezzolini (Dr Dulcamara).

Nemorino *a simple peasant, in love with*	
Adina	tenor
Adina *a wealthy landowner*	soprano
Belcore *a sergeant*	baritone
Dr Dulcamara *an itinerant medicine man*	bass
Giannetta *a peasant girl*	soprano
Peasants, soldiers of Belcore's platoon	
Setting An Italian village in the early 19th century	

Donizetti's greatest popular success, *L'elisir* was composed in the six-week period between the premiere of *Ugo, conte di Parigi* (13 March 1832) and the time the opera went into rehearsal (about 1 May). That the work was evolving up to the last minute we know, as the censors came to the dress rehearsal to give their final approval (which normally was given before the rehearsal period began). The first run was a huge success at the Cannobiana. Its vogue in southern Italy was launched by its production at the Teatro del Fondo, Naples, in the spring of 1834, when it was given with Fanny Tacchinardi-Persiani (Adina), Lorenzo Salvi (Nemorino), Antonio Ambrogi (Belcore) and Luigi Lablache (Dulcamara). On 27 September 1835, it was first given at La Scala with Maria Malibran (Adina), Antonio Poggi (Nemorino) and Celestino Salvatori (Belcore), with Frezzolini repeating his famous impersonation of Dulcamara. *L'elisir* continued its rapid triumphal progress across Italy where, as the musical press of the period shows, it was the most frequently performed opera between 1838 and 1848, a time when one out of every four productions in the country was of a work by Donizetti. It went to Berlin as *Der Liebestrank* in June 1834 and to Vienna, in Italian, on 9 April 1835, with a cast headed by Eugenia Tadolini, and Genero and Frezzolini in the parts they had created, and proved a hardy staple on German-language stages for a number of years.

L'elisir was put on at the Lyceum Theatre in London on 10 December 1836 and the following year it entered the repertory at Her Majesty's. It was given in New York in English in June 1838, but not in its original language until 1844. It was received with delight when introduced to Paris at the 'Italiens' on 17 January 1839, with Persiani, Nicola Ivanoff (Nemorino – that role later becoming the property of Giovanni Mario), Antonio Tamburini (Belcore) and Lablache.

A notable revival at La Scala was that of 17 March

1900, when, under the baton of Arturo Toscanini, L'elisir was sung by Regina Pinkert (Adina), Enrico Caruso, Antonio Magini-Coletti and Federico Carbonetti (Dulcamara). Caruso's great days began with the frantic applause that greeted 'Una furtiva lagrima' that night. The work was never given at Covent Garden during the seasons he appeared there, but it formed a central part of his repertory in New York – he appeared in it during ten of his 17 seasons as a member of the Metropolitan company. There Nemorino was later assumed by Beniamino Gigli, Tito Schipa, Ferruccio Tagliavini, Nicolai Gedda, Luciano Pavarotti and Placido Domingo. The opera was relatively late in entering the Glyndebourne repertory, first being given there on 24 May 1961 in a production by Franco Zeffirelli with a cast that included Eugenia Ratti, Luigi Alva, Enzo Sordello and Carlo Badioli.

Adina's music following 'Una furtiva lagrima' has undergone some changes over the years. Malibran sang a setting of 'Prendi, per me sei libero' by her husband Charles de Bériot designed to fit her mezzo-soprano range and agile voice. For Tadolini Donizetti wrote an air for this point that he subsequently re-used as part of Norina's duet with Don Pasquale. More recently a manuscript was found in a Paris library of another air that Donizetti intended to use here; this discovery was performed in Bergamo in 1987.

*

Act I.i *Outside Adina's farmhouse* There is a prelude, consisting of variations on a theme which is not heard again. While the peasants rest from their labours one of them, Nemorino, watches the owner of the farm, the beautiful Adina, engrossed in a book. He loves her, but he is able only to sigh (cavatina, 'Quanto è bella!'). When Adina laughs aloud at the absurd story she is reading, the others crowd round to discover why. It is the story of Iseult and of the magician who gave Tristan such a powerful love potion that 'Iseult never left him again', adding that she wished she knew the recipe for such an elixir; her cavatina, 'Della crudele Isotta', consists of *couplets* with a choral refrain. A drum-roll announces Sergeant Belcore and his platoon. Belcore glances at the girls and then without hesitation takes a nosegay from the barrel of his musket and presents it to Adina. He likens himself to Paris when he awarded the golden apple to Aphrodite, and has given flowers to Adina in hopes of a favourable response. His cavatina, 'Come Paride vezzoso', is in two stanzas, the second embellished; instead of a cabaletta Donizetti supplies a well-wrought ensemble. Nemorino is upset by the sergeant's self-assurance. Belcore reminds Adina that later Aphrodite yielded to Ares, a warrior like himself. When Adina declares that she is in no hurry to make up her mind, Belcore

observes that time flies; Adina retorts that some soldiers claim a victory before the battle has even begun.

Nemorino wishes he had the courage to declare his feelings for Adina as openly as Belcore did. When they are left alone he wants to talk, but she is tired of his sighing and tells him to go to look after his ailing uncle. Nemorino assures her he is the worse off; love makes him indifferent to the prospect that his uncle might die and leave his fortune to another heir. Adina tells him that although he is kind and modest, she is capricious and feels nothing for him; ask the gentle breezes why they are always in motion, she tells him – it is the nature of things, and like them she is fickle and inconstant (duet, 'Chiedi all'aura lusinghiera'). He swears he cannot leave her and, when she wonders why, he suggests she ask the river why it goes down to the sea – it is irresistibly drawn. As she insists on her capriciousness, and he on his constancy, she mocks the obstinacy of one who would die of love. This two-movement duet is one of the parts of Romani's libretto that has no counterpart in its French source, and it contributes through the purling melody of the first movement and the spirited rhythm of the second to the aura of pastoral romanticism that colours this beguiling score.

I.ii *The village square* A trumpet call summons the curious villagers. Dr Dulcamara, the travelling quack, arrives in his gaudy carriage (or, in some productions, descends by balloon) and stands to address the crowd, describing the powers of his medicines that can cure anything from impotence to the infirmities of old age. His 'Udite, udite, o rustici' is one of the great *buffo* arias, a torrent of patter set to a series of unctuous melodies that characterize this irresistible fraud. When he has finished his spiel, Nemorino shyly comes to ask if he sells the elixir of Queen Iseult. Needless to say, Dulcamara has just what Nemorino wants. While he is being profusely thanked, the doctor observes that of all the blockheads he has met none can equal this fellow (duet, 'Obbligato, ah, sì! obbligato!'). After drinking the elixir, Dulcamara explains, the 'patient' must wait until the next day for results (by which time the doctor will be gone and Nemorino – as Dulcamara tells the audience – will have drunk a bottle of harmless Bordeaux). Dulcamara enters the inn, leaving Nemorino alone to sample his purchase. He is starting to feel its effects when Adina appears, wondering how he can be so cheerful. His gauche nonchalance puzzles and annoys her; but he can think only of what tomorrow will bring. Adina asks if he has followed her advice to find another, wondering if that explains his coldness; he assures her that tomorrow his heart will be cured.

Belcore marches in and Adina informs him that she has considered his offer and will marry him in six

16. 'Boris Godunov' (Musorgsky, 1874), scene from the production by Irina Morozova (designed by Fyodor Federovsky) at the Bolshoi Theatre, Moscow, in 1987

17. 'Capriccio' (Richard Strauss, 1942), scene from the 1991 production (shared with San Francisco Opera) by John Cox (sets Mauro Pagano, costumes Gianni Versace) at the Royal Opera House, Covent Garden, with Kiri Te Kanawa (Countess Madeleine), Anne Howells (Clairon), David Rendall (Flamand), William Shimell (Olivier) and Lillian Watson and Bonaventura Bottone (the Italian Singers)

18. 'Carmen' (Bizet, 1875), the 1995 production by Franco Zeffirelli at the Arena di Verona

19. 'Cavalleria rusticana' (Mascagni, 1890), chromolithograph (1891) by Luigi Morgari showing the moment when
Alfio challenges Turiddu to a duel by biting his rival's earlobe

20. 'La clemenza di Tito' (Mozart, 1791), scene from the 1974 production by Anthony Besch (designed by John Stoddart) at the Royal Opera House, Covent Garden, with Eric Tappy (Titus), Janet Baker, Yvonne Minton and Anne Howells

21. 'La Cenerentola' (Rossini, 1817), scene from the 1973 La Scala production by Jean-Pierre Ponnelle (brought to the Royal Opera House, Covent Garden, in 1976), with Teresa Berganza as Angelina

22. 'Les contes d'Hoffmann' (Offenbach, 1881), scene from the production by John Schlesinger (sets William Dudley, costumes Maria Björnson) at the Royal Opera House, Covent Garden, 1980, with Placido Domingo (Hoffmann), Luciana Serra (Olympia), Robert Lloyd (Lindorf), Geraint Evans (Coppélius) and Robert Tear (Spalanzani)

23. 'Così fan tutte' (Mozart, 1790), scene from the finale of Act 1 in the 1968 production by John Copley (sets Henry Bardon, costumes David Walker) at the Royal Opera House, Covent Garden, with Josephine Veasey (Dorabella), Pilar Lorengar (Fiordiligi), Luigi Alva (Ferrando), Wladimiro Ganzarolli (Guglielmo), Lucia Popp (Despina) and Keith Engen (Don Alfonso)

24. 'The Cunning Little Vixen' (Janáček, 1924), some of the animals and insects from the 1990 production by Bill Bryden (designer William Dudley) at the Royal Opera House, Covent Garden

25. 'Death in Venice' (Britten, 1973), study by John Piper for the sets of the original production at the Snape Maltings

26. 'Don Giovanni' (Mozart, 1787), Thomas Allen (Don Giovanni) and Gwynne Howell (Commendatore) in the production
by Peter Wood (costumes David Walker) at the Royal Opera House, Covent Garden, 1988

27. 'Don Carlos' (Verdi, 1867), scene from the 1957/58 production designed and directed by Luchino Visconti at the Royal Opera House, Covent Garden (1968), with David Ward (Philip II), Gwyneth Jones (Elisabeth de Valois) and Carlo Cossutta (Don Carlos)

28. 'Don Pasquale' (Donizetti, 1843), scene from the Opéra-Comique, Paris, production, 1994, with Gabriel Bacquier in the title role and Leontina Vaduva as Norina

29. 'Elektra' (Richard Strauss, 1909), Marjana Lipovšek as Klytemnestra in the production by Götz Friedrich at the Royal Opera House, Covent Garden, in 1990 (sets Hans Schavernoch, costumes Lore Haas)

days' time. While Belcore exults, Nemorino cannot help laughing because he is confident that he will be irresistible to Adina the very next day. Giannetta enters, followed by the soldiers, who tell Belcore that new orders have arrived which require their departure tomorrow morning. Adina agrees to advance the wedding to that very evening. Nemorino is appalled (concertato, 'Adina, credimi'). As persuasively as he can, he begs her to wait just one more day, but Belcore, angered by the intrusion, orders Nemorino away; Adina defends him as a maladroit youth who has a fixation about her. When Adina offers to fetch the notary, Nemorino calls for Dulcamara's help. Everyone except Nemorino looks forward to the celebration. The first finale, launched by Nemorino's 'Adina, credimi', is a minor–major sequence of great tenderness; when Adina takes up this melody it is clear that she is not impervious to Nemorino's plight. The giddy stretta shows Donizetti's fondness for dance-like tunes in triple metre.

Act 2.i *The interior of Adina's farmhouse* Music is provided by the military band among Belcore's troops. To cap everyone's enjoyment Dulcamara proposes that he and Adina sing a 'barcarolle for two voices' (a musical joke: it is in 2/4 metre rather than the characteristic 6/8). As a senator he urges his love on a lady gondolier ('Io son ricco e tu sei bella'), while she refuses him, preferring someone of her own station; their efforts are cheered. When the notary arrives, Adina does not want the ceremony to take place without Nemorino as she is still offended by his indifference. Soon he appears, downcast, and tells Dulcamara that he needs more elixir in a hurry. Dulcamara prescribes repeating the dosage until the desired results are obtained; he agrees to wait in the inn for one more hour, as Nemorino has no money. Belcore is annoyed at Adina's delaying tactics; when Nemorino tells him he needs money right away, Belcore informs him that an enlistment pays a bounty of 20 scudi (duet, 'Venti scudi'). Belcore describes the manly delights of a soldier's life, which Nemorino will endure to win Adina. Handed the enlistment papers, Nemorino duly affixes his 'X'.

2.ii *A rustic courtyard* Giannetta and the village girls gossip about the news that Nemorino's immensely wealthy uncle has died and left him his only heir. Nemorino comes in somewhat unsteadily, having spent all the bounty on elixir. The girls express their interest in him, a response which Nemorino attributes to the power of the potion. Dulcamara is amazed at the spectacle of Nemorino surrounded by attentive young females. Adina comes to inquire about his enlistment, for which she feels responsible. Nemorino is sure that Adina is about to declare her feelings, but his sudden popularity with the girls (which Dulcamara now proudly attributes to his elixir) has aroused her

jealousy. This scene evolves into a quartet with female chorus, 'Dell'elisir mirabile', the situation being a bit like a comic equivalent of Parsifal amid the flowermaidens; it vividly sets off the varied responses of the characters, yet fuses them into a propulsive ensemble. Nemorino goes off, the girls tagging after. Dulcamara boasts to Adina about the efficacy of his decoction, and when he mentions Iseult she asks if he has sold the elixir to Nemorino. The doctor describes the pitiable state of hopeless love that reduced Nemorino to enlist to pay for the elixir. Adina now realizes the depth of Nemorino's feelings. As Dulcamara offers to concoct a potion for her (duet, 'Quanto amore!'), she tells him she has a better one of her own – a glance, a smile, a tender gesture; his slick patter is set against her gentle musing, which turns sprightly and coquettish in the final Allegro.

Nemorino, reflecting on the tell-tale tear he espied in Adina's eye when the village girls were crowding around him, has realized that she loves him, and he could himself die of love: this is expressed in his *romanza*, 'Una furtiva lagrima', with its haunting bassoon obbligato and its beautifully inflected minor–major melody. When Adina enters, she tells him that she has bought back his enlistment papers and hands them to him; her cantabile, 'Prendi, per me sei libero' with its melody at once suave and highly figured, contrasts markedly with her more brittle earlier music. She is happy that he can remain among his own people. As she turns to go, he asks if she wants to say something more, but she does not: whereupon he gives her back the enlistment papers – if the doctor has duped him, he would prefer to die a soldier. Finally Adina confesses her love for him, and Nemorino swears that Dulcamara has not deceived him. Belcore, surprised to see the lovers arm in arm, takes his dismissal in good spirit. Dulcamara reveals to the crowd the news of Nemorino's inheritance, which neither Adina nor Nemorino had yet heard; he boasts how his wondrous remedy can make people fall in love and even turn paupers into millionaires. Dulcamara drives off, leaving the lovers grateful for his elixir.

*

The score of *L'elisir* forms a good example of Donizetti's skill at presenting the conventional forms in fresh ways. For instance, the first three vocal numbers follow each other with a minimum of recitative. Nemorino's introductory cavatina, 'Quanto è bella!', is the middle section of a choral introduction, thereby defining the existing relationship between social group and individual. The transition to Adina's cavatina is accomplished by means of her burst of laughter over the tale she is reading and a few interchanges with the peasants (*recitativo stromentato*) before she launches into a *couplet*-style aria set to contrasting dance-rhythms. The transition to Belcore's aria is the march (borrowed from Donizetti's *Alahor in Granata*, 1826) that brings on his platoon. His cavatina is concluded not by a solo cabaletta but by what develops into a sizeable ensemble. Although in the strictest sense the opening number consists of just the introductory chorus with Nemorino's 'Quanto è bella!' in the middle of it, the cumulative impression of the first three numbers is of a series of contrasting musical episodes that form a single compound structure, creating a balance with the three successive episodes of the Act 1 finale.

Donizetti's score is a study in shrewd contrasts: from the fairly florid lines of the duet 'Chiedi all'aura' – florid yet always rhetorically tidy – to the bumptious 3/8 stretta of the Act 1 finale, or from the sharply differentiated tones of Nemorino and Belcore in the 'Venti scudi' duet, to the comic irony in the duet for Adina and Dulcamara, 'Quanto amore!', which sets off the potion as charm against the charm of Adina herself. The wonderful, apparently effortless outpouring of melody is never melodiousness for its own sake but always describes some aspect of character; moreover, there are those moments of genuine pathos ('Adina, credimi' and 'Una furtiva lagrima', for instance) that keep this comedy from seeming merely heartless or cruel. Ultimately, the continuing appeal of *L'elisir* lies in the appropriateness of Donizetti's music to this bucolic variant of the 'male Cinderella' myth. Nemorino's goodheartedness and his singleness of purpose win out in spite of potions and unforeseen inheritances.

W.A.

Enfant et les sortilèges, L'
('The Child and the Spells')

Fantaisie lyrique in one act by Maurice Ravel to a libretto by Colette; Monte Carlo, 21 March 1925.

At the first performance the Child was sung by Marie-Thérèse Gauley.

The Child	mezzo-soprano
Mother	contralto
The Louis XV Chair [*La Bergère*]	soprano
The Chinese Cup	mezzo-contralto
The Fire/The Princess/ The Nightingale	soprano
The Tomcat	baritone
The Dragonfly	mezzo-soprano
The Bat	soprano
The Owl	soprano
The Squirrel	mezzo-soprano
A Shepherdess	soprano
A Shepherd	contralto
The Armchair	bass
The Grandfather Clock	baritone
The Teapot (Black Wedgwood)	tenor
The Little Old Man (Arithmetic)/ The Frog	tenor†
The Female Cat	mezzo-soprano
A Tree	bass

Settle, Sofa, Ottoman, Wicker Chair, Numbers, Shepherds, Shepherdesses, Frogs, Animals, Trees

Setting An old-fashioned country house and its garden

† The libretto asks for a 'Trial' tenor, that is, a thin nasal tone like that of Antoine Trial (1737–95)

During World War I Jacques Rouché, the newly appointed director of the Paris Opéra, asked Colette to write the scenario for a fairy ballet, and she accepted with enthusiasm his suggestion of Ravel as collaborator. A copy of her libretto finally reached Ravel in 1918; the following year he wrote to her, touching on one or two details of what he now envisaged as an opera, but progress was held up by his poor health and by work on the Sonata for violin and cello. At some point the initiative passed from the Paris Opéra to that of Monte Carlo, where Raoul Gunsbourg had mounted a highly successful production of Ravel's 1911 opera *L'heure espagnole* and was keen to have a sequel. Ravel worked unremittingly on *L'enfant* throughout 1924 and the early months of 1925, and it was ready just in time for the première (five days beforehand he was writing to Colette, asking her for words to fit a few recently composed bars). The work was conducted by Victor de Sabata, with ballet sequences by the young Balanchine.

After an enthusiastic reception in Monte Carlo, the opera was first given in Paris by the Opéra-Comique on 1 February 1926. Colette wrote that it was 'playing twice a week before a packed but turbulent house ... The modernists applaud, and shout down the others, and during the "meeowed" duet there's a fearful uproar'. Performances were given in Brussels ten days later, in Prague, Leipzig, Vienna and San Francisco over the next four years and at the Paris Opéra in 1939. It reached London in a production at Sadler's Wells in 1965–6, although a series of amateur performances had been given by the Oxford University Opera Club in 1958. It was not seen at the Metropolitan until 1981, when it was conducted by Ravel's friend and pupil Manuel Rosenthal, with sets by David Hockney.

*

Scene I *A low-ceilinged room in the house giving on to the garden; midday* Before the curtain rises, two oboes are heard playing a succession of perfect 4ths and 5ths

(ph. H. Manuel)

« Opéra-Comique » : L'Enfant et les Sortilèges.
L'Enfant (Mlle GAULEY) n'est pas sage et Maman (Mme CALVET) le gronde....Et les sortilèges
vont bientôt effrayer l'enfant taquin !

(ph. H. Manuel)
La Princesse aux cheveux d'or

'L'enfant et les sortilèges' (Ravel), scenes from the first Paris production at the Opéra-Comique, in 1926: from 'Minerva'
(28 February 1926)

with apparent aimlessness. As the curtain rises, the audience discerns the relevance of this aimlessness to the predicament of the Child, stricken with laziness ('en pleine crise de paresse') in front of his home-work. But as might be expected from Ravel, the aimlessness is carefully structured, with the same paragraph returning first at the rise of the curtain, then at the first words of the Child and at the entrance of the Mother. However, Ravel deliberately with-holds any firm tonal basis at this juncture.

The Child resists motherly encouragement to apply himself and finally sticks his tongue out at her. She responds by giving him tea with no sugar, bread with no butter and a long period until dinner-time in which to reflect on his behaviour. Alone, the Child indulges in an orgy of destruction and cruelty, smashing cups and torturing his pet Squirrel and Tomcat, to bitonal sounds from the piano. Exhausted, he is about to sink into an Armchair when it moves away from him, 'hobbling like an enormous toad', and launches into a duet in minuet rhythm with the Louis XV Chair. Other objects follow suit and sing of the sufferings they have endured at the hands of the little monster, who has kicked holes in the Armchair, pulled the pendulum out of the Grandfather Clock, spilt the kettle on the Fire and reduced both wallpaper and storybook to tatters. All this allows free rein to Ravel's unparalleled gift for parody, culminating in the ragtime duet of the Teapot and the Chinese Cup; at the same time his increase in dramatic control since *L'heure espagnole* may be seen in the gradual efflorescence of emotion, beginning with the song of the Shepherds and Shepherdesses on the wallpaper, growing through the aria of the storybook Princess (a duet with solo flute in which the previous uneasy bitonality resolves into a modal C minor) and culminating in the Child's brief but heart-stopping monologue ('Toi, le coeur de la rose'). Ravel based these 20 bars, according to Manuel Rosenthal, on the 'Air de la table' from Massenet's *Manon*.

In his desolation, the Child gives a kick to his mathematics primer on the floor. Out of it springs a host of Numbers, marshalled by the Little Old Man, who proceeds to spout the traditional problems posed by taps running into reservoirs, even if his grasp of arithmetic ('four and four make eighteen') is not beyond question. The ensemble reaches a dizzying climax before the tormentors finally retire, leaving the Child once more exhausted. The moon now comes out, and by its light the black Tomcat in the room and his white mate in the garden sing a duet, not in human language (both Colette and Ravel, as cat-lovers, knew that no cat would thus demean itself) but in a variety of 'miinhous', 'môrnâous' and 'moâous' on the linguistic accuracy of which Ravel lavished the greatest care. As the Tomcat jumps out of the window to join his beloved, the careful pastiche begins to take on a new depth, with threateningly irrational glissandos in the brass; and as the bitonality yet again resolves, this time on to bare, widely spaced 5ths on the strings, the scene moves outside into the garden.

Scene 2 *The garden* In the second half of the opera the denizens of the garden pursue their complaints against the Child: first the Trees whose bark he has cut into with a knife, then the Dragonfly and the Bat whose mates he has killed. The distinction between the normally inanimate trees and their animate successors is simply made by a change of time signature, and the new waltz rhythm takes the music on into the only extended orchestral passage in the opera, the Frogs' Dance. Here, to strains reminiscent of his *Valses nobles et sentimentales* and *La Valse*, Ravel cleverly offers the audience a respite from wordplay, as well as setting apart the crucial entry of the Squirrel, whom the Child released during his first fit of temper. The Squirrel is physically unharmed, but now he mourns the lost years of imprisonment in yet another preparation for the true emotional climax of the work. The Child, realizing suddenly the wealth of love between the animals from which he is excluded, utters the talismanic word 'Maman!' to Ravel's favourite descending 4th.

At once, sensing his fear and loneliness, the animals turn on him, but in the mêlée the Squirrel is wounded. The Child for the first time in the opera is able to find a point of entry into the 'paradis de tendresse', and ties up the Squirrel's wounded paw with a ribbon. Overcome with amazement at this loving act, the animals gently lead the Child back to the house as they try to imitate the strange human noise that had been the signal for their fury. Mostly they fail to get the interval right, and it is the full orchestra that sets them straight, resolving the bitonal pressures for the last time and grounding the music in its final tonality for the opera's emotional climax. As the animals begin a fugal hymn to the Child's kindness, a light comes on in the house. The oboes of the opening return, now comfortingly supported by G major harmonies, and with his final cry of 'Maman!' the Child's spiritual journey is at an end.

*

Ravel told his friend Hélène Jourdan-Morhange that *L'enfant* contained everything: Massenet, Puccini, Monteverdi and American musical comedy. This, together with his earlier admission that he was 'transported by the idea of having two negroes singing ragtime at the Paris Opéra', has sometimes led critics to miss the profoundly serious feeling at the heart of this vivid and entertaining work. In answer to those who complained that his music was artificial, Ravel said: 'Does it not occur to these people that I may be artificial by nature?' In *L'enfant et les sortilèges* Ravel summons up all the artifices of

his transcendent technique to reach both Nature and what is most natural in our childhood selves.
R.N.

Entführung aus dem Serail, Die
('The Abduction from the Seraglio')

Singspiel in three acts, κ384, by Wolfgang Amadeus Mozart to a libretto by Christoph Friedrich Bretzner (*Belmont und Constanze, oder Die Entführung aus dem Serail*), adapted and enlarged by Gottlieb Stephanie the Younger; Vienna, Burgtheater, 16 July 1782.

Caterina Cavalieri was Konstanze at the first performance, Valentin Adamberger was Belmonte; Osmin was sung by Ludwig Fischer, Blonde by Therese Teyber, Pedrillo by Johann Ernst Dauer.

Selim *Pasha*	spoken
Konstanze *a Spanish lady, Belmonte's betrothed*	soprano
Blonde *Konstanze's English maid*	soprano
Belmonte *a Spanish nobleman*	tenor
Pedrillo *servant of Belmonte, now supervisor of the Pasha's gardens*	tenor
Osmin *overseer of the Pasha's country house*	bass
Klaas *a sailor*	spoken
Mute *in Osmin's service*	silent
Chorus of Janissaries, guards	
Setting The country palace of Pasha Selim, on the Mediterranean coast in an unidentified part of the Turkish Empire	

Dismissed from service with the Archbishop of Salzburg, Mozart must have felt satisfaction in writing to his father on 1 August 1781: 'the day before yesterday Stephanie junior gave me a libretto to compose'. Gottlieb Stephanie, director of the National Singspiel, wanted Bretzner's *Belmont und Constanze* set quickly for the visit in September of the Russian Grand Duke Paul Petrovich. Bretzner was a popular librettist, whose name assured interest (*Belmont und Constanze* had been set in Berlin by Johann André). Yet with the postponement of the royal visit (it eventually took place in November, when Gluck's operas were played), *Die Entführung* might have suffered the fate of the Singspiel *Zaide* (1779), which remained unperformed in Mozart's lifetime, had not Stephanie and, no doubt, the singers maintained support for him. Mozart had already composed much of Act 1, and he wrote in detail to his father on 26 September about the arias for Belmonte, Osmin and Konstanze.

Since time was available, he urged Stephanie to enlarge Act 1. By adding an aria at the beginning for Belmonte and making Osmin's opening number a duet, Mozart virtually turned Bretzner's opening dialogue, with Osmin's song originally its only music, into a continuous introduction. He established Osmin as a major force with 'Solche hergelauf'ne Laffen' (Mozart sent Stephanie the music for words to be added), and wrote the overture, musically linked with the opening aria. His comments to his father concerning Osmin's and Belmonte's arias, 'Solche hergelauf'ne Laffen' and 'O wie ängstlich', contain some of his most important recorded views on operatic aesthetics. The Janissary chorus is 'short, lively and written to please the Viennese'; he also admitted that he had 'sacrificed Konstanze's aria ('Ach ich liebte') a little to the flexible throat of Mlle Cavalieri'.

Mozart and Stephanie recast the remaining two acts more extensively. The women and Osmin received one additional aria each ('Martern aller Arten', 'Welche Wonne' and 'O, wie will ich triumphieren'), while Belmonte received two (the second, opening Act 3, often cut in modern performances or nonsensically replaced by the first). They devised a new situation for a long ensemble (finale to Act 2) and a new denouement: the libretto thus remains essentially Bretzner's (he alone was credited on the original playbill and libretto), but with significant differences. Mozart began setting a quintet which, in Bretzner, covers the whole elopement scene. The loss of such an extended action ensemble is tantalizing; doubtless it was rejected because it could not form a finale. Instead the elopement is in dialogue and reaches a musical climax only after its failure, with Osmin's aria. The enhanced importance of Osmin sharpens the oriental setting and makes him a tangible menace; whether this change resulted from, or merely took advantage of, Fischer's immense range and full deep notes, is impossible to determine.

Mozart finished the score in April 1782. Rehearsals began in June and, despite some delays, an alleged cabal and the difficulty of the music, the first performance was a success. Performances continued until the closure of the National Singspiel early in 1783; the German company at the Kärntnertor revived it (1784–5) with Mozart's sister-in-law Aloysia Lange as Konstanze.

The fame of the new opera spread rapidly. The second production, also in 1782, was in Prague, which at once took Mozart to its heart. *Die Entführung* was the foundation of Mozart's reputation outside Austria. In 1783 there were productions in Warsaw, Bonn (under Neefe, Beethoven possibly assisting), Frankfurt and Leipzig.

The first translation (Polish) followed in November, again at Warsaw. In 1784 there were productions in Mannheim, Carlsruhe, Cologne and Salzburg; Dresden, Munich and other German cities followed

in 1785. It was given in some 40 centres in Germany and the Austrian Empire, and reached Amsterdam in Mozart's lifetime. It was performed in French (1798, Paris), in a version by Gluck's librettist Moline; it was also the first opera ever heard in German in Paris (1801).

The first London performance, in English, was at Covent Garden in 1827, the score arranged by C. Kramer with an altered plot; the setting was moved by the translator, W. Dimond, to a Greek island. Such alterations were standard in 19th-century revivals. In Paris the 1859 revival to a translation by Prosper Pascal reordered several numbers and gave 'Martern aller Arten' to Blonde (no less a Mozartian than Beecham placed this aria in Act 3). Later in the century London also saw it in German and Italian (the title *Il Seraglio* is still often used in English). The American première was in New York in 1860, probably in German. The Italian première was not until 1935, in Florence, by which time the 20th-century revival of Mozart was under way; it had already appeared at Glyndebourne.

The background is the territorial and cultural intersection of the Islamic lands and the older Christian civilization of Europe, especially Spain; Belmonte's father is Governor of Oran on the coast of North Africa. A major stimulus for artistic interest in things Turkish was the menacing but in the end unsuccessful siege of Vienna in 1683, but the action evokes an earlier period when piracy was rife and crossing between religions not uncommon; Pasha Selim is a renegade Christian.

*

The overture is a bubbling Allegro in C major, its 'Turkish' style martial and colourful yet, in Mozart's hands, subject to abrupt changes of mood; a promising crescendo lurches into the dominant minor, anticipating the confusion of the action to come. A slow middle section in C minor brings a foretaste of sentiment, its melody by turns hesitant and passionate, richly clothed in woodwind sound. The Allegro resumes, ending on the dominant and leading straight into the opening aria.

Act I *A plaza before Selim's palace, near the sea* A major-key version of the middle section of the overture ('Hier soll ich dich denn sehen') forms a short aria by the standards of this opera, but after a hesitating start its lyrical cadences convey Belmonte's ardent desire for reunion with Konstanze. Osmin enters with a ladder, and begins picking figs; he sings a moral Volkslied (lied and duet, 'Wer ein Liebchen hat gefunden': 'Whoever finds a lover, let him beware'). When Belmonte speaks Osmin refuses to answer, directing the later verses at him instead: plausible strangers bring danger to lovers. Belmonte now enquires for Pedrillo, wrenching the tempo to Allegro, but the wrath of the Turk, enraged by mention of the name, dominates the ensemble. In a furious Presto he drives Belmonte away.

Pedrillo asks Osmin whether Selim has returned. Still not answering, Osmin fumes about vagabond fops fit only to be hanged ('Solche hergelauf'ne Laffen'). This exit aria, portentous and often contrapuntal, flies off the handle in the coda to which Mozart added 'Turkish' music for comic effect. Belmonte reveals himself. Pedrillo assures him that Selim will not force love on Konstanze, but they are in great danger and Osmin watches everything. Belmonte's heart is beating with anxiety and ardour ('O wie ängstlich, o wie feurig'); both melody and orchestra are suffused with feeling as well as detailed imitation of a lover's symptoms.

A march (possibly cut by Mozart, but restored by the Neue Mozart-Ausgabe) announces the arrival of the Pasha in a boat with Konstanze; the Janissaries greet them with a vigorous chorus in 'Turkish' style. Selim asks why Konstanze remains sad and promises that her answer will not anger him. In the Adagio of her aria Konstanze relives her past love ('Ach ich liebte, war so glücklich!'); the Allegro compresses the Adagio's melodic outline into a vehement protest; all happiness has fled (the Adagio text and mood return in the middle of the Allegro). Mozart's sacrifice for Cavalieri brings coloratura to an inappropriate text ('Kummer ruht in meinem Schoss': 'sorrow dwells in my heart'), but this emphatic utterance tells us that Konstanze is a considerable character. Selim is angry, but when she leaves he admits that he loves her all the more for her resistance. Pedrillo introduces Belmonte as an Italian-trained architect; Selim approves his entry into the household. But Osmin has other ideas. A vivacious trio in C minor ('Marsch, marsch, marsch! trollt euch fort!'), ending with a faster major section, forms a comic finale; eventually the Europeans force an entry.

Act 2 *The palace garden, with Osmin's house to one side* Osmin is pursuing Blonde, whom the Pasha has given him as a slave; but she will have none of his Turkish ways; tenderness, not force, wins hearts ('Durch Zärtlichkeit und Schmeicheln'). Her Andante aria is the epitome of Mozartean elegance. Osmin indignantly orders her to love him, but she merely laughs, and wards off an assault by threatening his eyes with her nails and reminding him that her mistress is the Pasha's favourite (duet, 'Ich gehe, doch rate ich dir'). Osmin warns her not to flirt with Pedrillo; she mocks his low notes with her own. In a lugubrious Andante Osmin declares that the English are mad to allow their women such liberties; Blonde rejoices in her freedom.

At the nadir of her fortunes, Konstanze turns to the most intense style of *opera seria*, obbligato recitative ('Welcher Wechsel herrscht in meiner Seele', and aria, 'Traurigkeit ward mir zum Lose'). In an exquisite Adagio Mozart paints her sighing breaths, her halting steps. The aria, its orchestra enriched by basset-horns, is a sustained lament in G minor, like Ilia's (*Idomeneo*, Act 1) but attaining a new poignancy through its higher tessitura.

Blonde tries to comfort her mistress. Selim threatens not death, which Konstanze welcomes, but every kind of torture. Her aria ('Marten aller Arten': 'Every kind of torture awaits me; I laugh at pain; death will come in the end') picks up Selim's threat, but not before a 60-bar ritornello with obbligato flute, oboe, violin and cello has unfolded a rich motivic tapestry founded on a march rhythm (with trumpets and timpani). The closing words are given more emphasis by a faster tempo. This magnificent piece, coming immediately after another long aria for Konstanze, presents a challenge to the actors and the director; but as the expression of stubborn resistance to coercion from a woman with no hope of deliverance, it is of immense dramatic power. Selim is baffled; affection and force having failed, he wonders if he can use cunning. (This exit line perhaps prefigured a new intrigue intended for Act 3 but not included.)

Pedrillo tells Blonde of Belmonte's arrival. Blonde's reaction, a rondo with a melody from the flute concerto κ314 ('Welche Wonne, welche Lust'), sparkles with unalloyed delight. Pedrillo musters his courage in a martial D major ('Frisch zum Kampfe!'), but a nagging phrase ('Nur ein feiger Tropf verzagt': 'Only a cowardly fool despairs') shows his underlying lack of confidence. He succeeds in getting Osmin drunk (duet, 'Vivat Bacchus'), and sends him to sleep it off so that the lovers can meet. Belmonte's aria of *galanterie* ('Wenn der Freude Tränen fliessen': tears of joy are love's sweetest reward) is a slow gavotte and then a serenade-like minuet announced by the wind and embellished with wide-ranging passage-work.

The escape is planned before the finale (quartet, 'Ach Belmonte!'). The first mature Mozart ensemble to incorporate dramatic development begins with a lively D major Allegro. Joy gives way to anxiety (Andante, G minor); have the women yielded to blandishment? In a faster tempo, Konstanze expresses hurt, Blonde slaps Pedrillo's face, and the voices come together in mingled relief and regret. The men ask forgiveness (Allegretto); Blonde withholds it, singing in compound time against the simple time of the others (a device Mozart might have picked up from *opéra comique*). But eventually misunderstanding is cleared away and the four join in praise of love.

Act 3 *The scene of Act 1; Osmin's house to one side. Midnight* Pedrillo and Klaas bring two ladders. Belmonte is assured that all is ready, but they must wait for the guards to finish their rounds. Pedrillo advises him to sing; he himself often sings at night and no one will notice the difference. In a long Andante, featuring clarinets and extended coloratura, Belmonte builds his hopes on the power of love ('Ich baue ganz auf deine Stärke').

Pedrillo gives the agreed signal, a romance ('In Mohrenland gefangen war ein Mädchen'). The opera's second lied, this too refers to the dramatic situation. Its haunting melody, to a plucked accompaniment, rests upon harmonic ambiguity and ends unresolved after four verses when Pedrillo sees a light. Belmonte fetches Konstanze; they hurry off as Pedrillo climbs up for Blonde. But the mute has seen them. Suspecting thieves and murderers, the bleary-eyed Osmin sends for the guard and dozes. Blonde and Pedrillo spot him too late; all four Europeans are arrested. In a brilliant rondo ('O, wie will ich triumphieren'), with piccolo but without trumpets or Turkish music, which Mozart keeps in reserve, Osmin anticipates the delight of torturing and killing his enemies, his lowest bass notes (to D) filled with ghoulish relish.

The interior of the palace Osmin claims credit for the arrest. Selim confronts the lovers. Konstanze admits guilt in his eyes, but pleads loyalty to her first lover. She begs to die if only his life can be spared. Belmonte humbles himself; he is worth a fine ransom; his name is Lostados. Selim recognizes the son of the enemy who chased him from his homeland. He bids them prepare for the punishment Belmonte's father would certainly have meted out, and leaves them under guard. Belmonte movingly laments his folly in bringing Konstanze to her doom; she blames herself for his destruction, but death is the path to an eternal union, symbolized by serenely extended arabesques (recitative and duet, 'Welch ein Geschick! O Qual der Seele!').

Selim asks if they are prepared for judgment. Belmonte says they will die calmly, absolving him from blame. Selim, however, bids him take Konstanze and go. He despises Belmonte's father too much to imitate him; clemency will be his revenge. As he takes dignified leave of them, Pedrillo begs freedom for himself and Blonde. Osmin is overruled; does he not value his eyes? In a vaudeville finale, each sings a verse of suitable sentiment, with a moral sung by the ensemble: those who forget kindness are to be despised. Blonde is interrupted by Osmin whose rage boils over into the litany of torture from his Act 1 aria, complete with 'Turkish' percussion. He rushes off; the others draw the further moral that nothing is so hateful as revenge. A brief chorus in praise of the Pasha, in the principal key, C major, brings back the merry 'Turkish' style of the overture.

The viewpoint of *Die Entführung* is decidedly European. Muslim life-style is crudely represented as luxurious but immoral; the Enlightenment, through Blonde, makes tart observations about the social position of women. Selim himself, raised to eminence by ability rather than rank, reflects Enlightenment values; he is not moved to clemency by religion, but contrasts his action with the cruelty of Belmonte's Christian father. This ending adds a new dimension to Bretzner's drama in which, implausibly, Belmonte proves to be Selim's son. It is a pity that, unlike the denouement of *Die Zauberflöte*, this scene was not set to music.

The lavish musical invention of *Die Entführung* perhaps exceeds what the dramatic structure is fit to bear; nor is its design immaculate. Apart from the cluster of arias for Konstanze in Act 2, there is surely one aria too many for Belmonte, and the length of the individual numbers (if not their forms) suggests *opera seria* and contrasts starkly with the speed of the dialogue. Was it length or plenitude of instrumentation which induced Joseph II's famous (but probably apocryphal) comment: 'Too many notes, my dear Mozart'? Such problems cannot be overcome by making alterations, still less by cutting the dialogue, for Mozart carefully controlled the flow between speech and music, running some numbers closely together but separating others. His prodigality of invention, however, is also a cause of the opera's enduring fascination. Even as it endangers the dramatic whole, the music, paradoxically through its creation for a specific group of remarkable singers, turns the actors in this serious comedy into humans a little larger than life but of universal appeal.   J.Ru.

Ernani

Dramma lirico in four acts by Giuseppe Verdi to a libretto by Francesco Maria Piave after Victor Hugo's play *Hernani*; Venice, Teatro La Fenice, 9 March 1844.

The cast at the première included Carlo Guasco (Ernani), Antonio Superchi (Don Carlo), Antonio Selva (Silva) and Sophie Loewe (Elvira).

Ernani *the bandit*	tenor
Don Carlo *King of Spain*	baritone
Don Ruy Gomez de Silva *a Spanish grandee*	bass
Elvira *his niece and betrothed*	soprano
Giovanna *her nurse*	soprano
Don Riccardo *the King's equerry*	tenor
Jago *Silva's equerry*	bass
Rebel mountaineers and bandits, knights and members of Silva's household, Elvira's	

maids-in-waiting, the King's knights, members
of the Lega, Spanish and German nobles,
Spanish and German ladies
Walk-on parts: Mountaineers and bandits, electors
and nobles of the imperial court, pages of the
imperial court, German soldiers, ladies and
male and female followers
Setting The Pyrenees, at Aix-la-Chapelle and at
Saragossa, in 1519

Verdi's fifth opera was commissioned by the Teatro
La Fenice, Venice, and was the first he wrote for a
theatre other than La Scala. The Venetian authorities,
impressed by the recent reception of Nabucco at La
Fenice and of I Lombardi at La Scala, allowed the
young composer to negotiate a sizeable fee, and to
make various unusual conditions, notably that he
would have the right to choose from that season's
company the singers for his new opera. A contract
was signed in June 1843, and various subjects and
librettists were mulled over; Verdi made it clear that
he intended to break with the format of his previous
two Milanese successes. A subject attributed to Sir
Walter Scott and entitled Cromvello (or, sometimes,
Allan Cameron) was initially decided upon, the
librettist to be an unknown poet called Francesco
Maria Piave; but Verdi became enthusiastic about
Victor Hugo's Hernani and, in spite of worries that its
political plot would create difficulties with the
censor, persuaded Piave to switch course.

During autumn 1843 the correspondence between Verdi, Piave and the theatre management
makes it clear that the composer took an unusually
active interest in shaping the libretto; he intervened
on several important points, insisting for example
that the role of Ernani be sung by a tenor (rather than
by a contralto, as had originally been planned). At
least in part, this new concern for the poetic text was
necessitated by his working with Piave, who was
inexperienced in theatrical matters and occasionally
made what Verdi deemed errors in broad dramatic
planning. Last-minute alterations to the cast caused
Verdi to make various late changes to his score,
notably in adding a cantabile for Silva to the Act 1
finale. The première run of performances was an
enormous success.

Ernani quickly became immensely popular, and
was revived countless times during its early years. In
general, Verdi was adamant that no changes be made
to the score; but he did allow at least one exception.
At the request of Rossini, who was acting on behalf of
the tenor Nicola Ivanoff, he supplied an aria with
chorus for Ernani as an alternative ending to the Act 2
finale. The piece was first performed in Parma on 26
December 1844. Although there is no direct evidence,
it is possible that Verdi also sanctioned the addition
of a cabaletta for Silva in Act 1. This piece, originally

written for the bass Ignazio Marini as part of an
additional aria in Oberto (1841–2, Barcelona), was
inserted by Marini into performances of Ernani at La
Scala in the autumn of 1844.

*

The prelude economically sets forth musical ideas
connected with the two main dramatic issues of the
opera: first, intoned on solo trumpet and trombone,
the theme associated with Ernani's fatal oath to Silva;
and then a lyrical theme whose initial rising 6th
might plausibly be thought to suggest the love
between Ernani and Elvira in its purest state.

Act I: 'The Bandit'

I.i The Pyrenees; Silva's castle is seen in the distance A
simple opening chorus ('Evviva! beviam!') sets the
scene by introducing the boisterous, carefree world
of 'mountaineers and bandits'. Their leader Ernani
(in reality Don Giovanni of Aragon) has been
proscribed by the King, his enemy. He enters to tell of
his love for Elvira; all agree to help him steal her
away from Don Ruy Gomez de Silva, her uncle,
guardian and fiancé. Ernani's cavatina is in the
conventional double-aria format, but the first movement, 'Come rugiada al cespite', shows an expansion
of the usual lyrical section as Ernani dwells on his
hatred of his rival Silva. The cabaletta, 'O tu, che
l'alma adora', makes prominent use of syncopation
to suggest Ernani's impatience for action.

I.ii Elvira's richly furnished apartments in Silva's castle
Elvira's cavatina, during which she meditates on her
beloved Ernani, repeats the double-aria formal
outline of Ernani's, though the entire scene is more
expansively developed musically. The Andantino,
'Ernani! . . . Ernani involami', has the expanded but
still highly schematic form that was becoming
common in Verdi's early works and, again characteristically, shows a rigorous control of the soprano's
ornamental gestures. A jaunty, Spanish-sounding
middle section, during which Elvira's entourage
compliment her on her forthcoming marriage to
Silva, leads to a forceful cabaletta, 'Tutto sprezzo che
d'Ernani', in which the opening phrase's vocal and
expressive range gives some indication of the new
demands that Verdi was placing on his principal
interpreters. Elvira and her women sweep out and
the stage is taken by a disguised Don Carlo, King of
Spain. Carlo, also in love with Elvira and outraged
that he has been passed over, sends Giovanna,
Elvira's nurse, to fetch his beloved. Elvira enters to
express outrage at his audacity and they settle into
one of Verdi's most successful formal vehicles, the
so-called 'dissimilar' duet between baritone and
soprano. The first movement, as usual, is rapid-fire
dialogue with continuity preserved by the orchestra,
but this soon gives way to a first statement of fixed
positions: Carlo leads off with a lyrical outpouring,
'Da quel dì che t'ho veduta'; Elvira counters in the

parallel minor with spiky dotted rhythms. The third movement offers a thoroughly Romantic *coup de scène*: Carlo impatiently tries to drag Elvira away, she grabs his knife to defend her honour, and at the peak of the action Ernani himself appears through a secret door. There is a shocked *declamato* from Carlo before Elvira and Ernani launch into the furious stretta of the duet-turned-trio, one that is full (perhaps too full) of syncopations to emphasize the young lovers' defiant energy.

The extended cadences of the stretta are immediately followed by the appearance of Elvira's third suitor, the aged Silva, and the start of the first finale. Silva is of course dismayed at the scene that greets him and, after angrily summoning his followers, engages in a sorrowful, chromatically inflected Andante, 'Infelice! e tu credevi'. (This is sometimes followed by the cabaletta 'Infin che un brando vindice'; see above.) But there are more surprises to come and, soon after Silva has finished, emissaries reveal the true identity of the King. The revelation precipitates the central Adagio of the finale, which begins in utter confusion but gradually finds lyrical voice, notably through the repetition and development of a small cadential motif. As the Adagio ends, Silva kneels to ask the King's forgiveness, which the latter grants, explaining that he is there to canvass support for the forthcoming election of an emperor. In an aside the King offers to help Ernani – wishing to exact revenge himself later rather than leaving it to Silva – and, openly announcing that the bandit is under royal protection, orders him to leave. Ernani's angry aside, in which he threatens to follow Carlo merely to take his own revenge, leads off the stretta of the finale, which begins in hushed but pointed minor and progresses to the major mode with a simple but highly effective crescendo.

Act 2: 'The Guest'
A magnificent hall in Silva's castle After a routine, scene-setting chorus praising Silva and Elvira, there occurs an example of the kind of complex articulated scene Verdi often favoured in the middle of an opera. The number is entitled 'Recitativo e Terzetto', but enfolds within its trio a prolonged duet. As the crowd disperses, Silva grants entry to a 'pilgrim' who has asked for shelter. Elvira appears and Silva introduces her as his future bride, at which the 'pilgrim' (who is of course Ernani) throws off his disguise and offers his own head as a wedding present. The ensuing Andante, 'Oro, quant'oro ogn'avido' – Ernani angry at Elvira's apparent betrayal, Elvira miserable, Silva (who has not recognized Ernani) simply confused – is dominated by Ernani, and makes dynamic use of triplet figures. Silva assures his 'guest' of protection and speeds off to arm his castle. As soon as the lovers are alone, Elvira assures Ernani that she had intended to kill herself on the wedding night, and their reconciliation is sealed by a brief Andantino with prominent harp and woodwind. When Silva returns he is horrified to find them in each other's arms. He learns that Don Carlo is waiting for Ernani outside the castle, with hostile intent; but he will not give up the bandit, wishing in his turn for a more personal revenge, and in an angry stretta ushers Ernani into a secret hiding place as the lovers voice their despair.

Carlo's entry heralds a long passage of accompanied recitative. The King asks Silva to reveal Ernani's whereabouts and, on being denied, disarms the old man and orders a search of the castle. During the search Carlo sings 'Lo vedremo, o veglio audace', the first movement of what is formally entitled an 'aria', but in which Silva joins freely. The King's anger manifests itself in a wide-ranging, highly declamatory line while Silva denies him with obsessively restricted rhythms and pitches. The middle movement, though often lyrical, is packed with stage action: Carlo's followers return, having found nothing in the castle; the King threatens Silva; Elvira 'enters precipitously' and begs for mercy; Carlo takes her as a hostage. The closing cabaletta, 'Vieni meco, sol di rose', is a magnificent dramatic stroke: after all the action and conflict, Verdi ends with a passage of pure baritone lyricism, full of gentle ornaments as the King invites Elvira to join him. The stage clears to leave Silva alone. He releases Ernani from hiding and immediately challenges him to a duel. Ernani refuses, and reveals that the King himself is pursuing Elvira. In order to join forces with Silva in taking revenge on Carlo, Ernani offers the old man a hunting-horn – as honour demands, his life is forfeit – and proposes a deadly pact, suitably emphasized with solemn brass chords: when Silva wishes Ernani to kill himself, he must simply sound the horn. The deal is struck; Ernani joins Silva and his followers in an explosive Prestissimo, 'In arcione, in arcion', to close the act.

Act 3: 'Clemency'
Subterranean vaults containing the tomb of Charlemagne at Aix-la-Chapelle Dark instrumental colours suitable to the setting begin the act. Carlo enters with Riccardo, his equerry. It is the day of the election of the Holy Roman Emperor, and Carlo has heard that conspiracy is afoot. He instructs Riccardo to fire three cannon shots if the election goes in his favour. Left alone 'to converse with the dead', the King bitterly reviews his misspent youth and resolves to rise in stature if he is elected. The aria that illustrates this most important turning point in the drama, 'O de' verd'anni miei', is notable for its extreme change in atmosphere halfway through: from sombre musical recollections of the florid baritone that has characterized the previous acts to a new-found strength and broadness of expression at the words 'e vincitor de' secoli'. Carlo conceals himself in

Charlemagne's tomb as the conspirators enter: sombre orchestral colours reassert themselves as the plotters exchange the password and draw lots for the task of assassinating the King. Ernani wins and, with the triplet figures that have been sprinkled through the scene gradually gaining ascendency in the orchestra, all join in a grand chorus, 'Si ridesti il Leon di Castiglia'. In rhythmic stamp, this piece bears a certain relationship to 'Va pensiero' (*Nabucco*) and 'O Signore, dal tetto natio' (*I Lombardi*), but here the rhythmic vitality and consequent spur to action is far more immediate. The three cannon shots sound, and Carlo emerges triumphantly from the tomb as the stage fills with his followers. In a magnificent finale to the act, Carlo forgives the conspirators and even consents to the marriage of Ernani and Elvira; his closing peroration to Charlemagne, 'Oh sommo Carlo', eventually draws everyone into his musical orbit.

Act 4: 'The Mask'
A terrace in the palace of Don Giovanni of Aragon [Ernani] in Saragossa As is common with Verdi and his contemporaries, the final act is by far the shortest. A chorus and a group of dancers tell us that wedding preparations for Ernani and Elvira are under way. The two lovers emerge for a brief but intense affirmation of their happiness, but are cut short by the sound of a distant horn. Ernani attempts to hide the truth from Elvira by complaining of an old wound and sending her for help. Left alone, he momentarily convinces even himself that the horn was an illusion. But Silva appears to demand the life that is owed him. Elvira returns as Ernani takes the proffered dagger; and so begins the final trio, 'Ferma, crudel, estinguere', justly one of the most celebrated pieces in the score, notable above all for its profusion of melodic ideas. The close of the trio is followed immediately by Silva's repetition of the pact music. In spite of Elvira's protests, Ernani takes the dagger and stabs himself. The lovers have time only for a last, desperate affirmation of love before the hero dies, leaving his bride to faint away as the curtain falls.

*

As Verdi himself stated more than once, *Ernani* represents an important change of direction in his early career. His two earlier successes, *Nabucco* and *I Lombardi*, had both been written for La Scala, one of the largest stages in Italy and well suited to the grandiose choral effects of those works. For the more intimate atmosphere of La Fenice, he created an opera that instead concentrated on personal conflict, carefully controlling the complex sequence of actions necessary to bring characters into intense confrontation. This new format brought about a fresh consideration of the fixed forms of Italian opera, in particular an expansion and enrichment of the solo

aria and duet, together with a more flexible approach to the musical sequences that bind together lyrical pieces. Most important, however, was Verdi's gathering sense of a musical drama's larger rhetoric, his increasing control over the dynamics of entire acts rather than merely of entire numbers. In this respect, the third act of *Ernani* sets an imposing standard of coherence, one that is rarely equalled until the operas of the early 1850s.   R.P.

Erwartung ('Expectation')

Monodrama in one act, op.17, by Arnold Schoenberg to a libretto by Marie Pappenheim; Prague, Neues Deutsches Theater, 6 June 1924.

The first performance was given by Marie Gutheil-Schoder; the conductor was Alexander von Zemlinsky.

The Woman	soprano

In August 1909, shortly before starting work on *Erwartung*, his first opera, Schoenberg described in letters to Ferruccio Busoni the ideal towards which he was then striving in his music. He wanted to leave behind him the traditional concentration on separate feelings in unreal isolation, along with the associated musical structures controlled by conscious logic, and find a means of expressing the multiplicity of contradictory feelings that can arise simultaneously from the unconscious. He had just asked a young doctor of his acquaintance, Marie Pappenheim, to write an opera libretto for him on a subject of her own choosing. It is clear from the resulting drama that she was familiar with recent psychological and psychoanalytical thought, and that she must have known about Schoenberg's current preoccupations; it may not be irrelevant that her relative Bertha Pappenheim was the 'Anna O.' whose illness had been successfully treated by Josef Breuer and described in his and Freud's *Studien über Hysterie* (1895). She was, however, surprised at Schoenberg's request because, although she had published verse pseudonymously, she had never written for the stage. Doubting her ability to cope with a more conventional libretto, she hit on the solution offered by a monologue for a single character.

The work consists of three brief scenes taking only a quarter of the total playing time of nearly half an hour, followed by a long final scene. The first shows a moonlit landscape with a road disappearing into a dark wood. A Woman enters in search of her lover. She is full of apprehension at the solitude and the darkness that confronts her. A scene change finds her groping her way through the darkest part of the

Sketch by Schoenberg for the setting of his monodrama 'Erwartung', first performed at the Neues Deutsches Theater, Prague, 6 June 1924

wood, starting with terror at every unaccustomed sound and, where a clearing opens up in the next scene, at every movement in the shadows. In the fourth scene she emerges in a state of exhaustion into more open countryside, her dress torn, her hair dishevelled, and her face and hands scratched. In the distance a shuttered house is visible where, apparently, her lover may have been visiting another woman. She stumbles against something which proves to be his still bleeding, murdered body. From here on the action is purely psychological. After disbelief has given way to horrified certainty her reaction passes through three main phases: an initial outburst of love and grief, paroxysms of jealousy and rage, and finally contemplation of an empty future ending in a dreamlike resumption of her search.

A dreamlike quality is, however, present throughout the piece, because the woman is constantly obsessed with erotic reminiscence and the longing experienced during her fruitless wait for her lover earlier in the evening, so that she scarcely distinguishes between present and past, or between her dead lover and her living memories of him. Schoenberg once remarked that the whole work could be interpreted as a nightmare, and on another occasion that it represented in slow motion everything that occurs in a single second of the greatest psychological stress. His score marks the extreme point in his cultivation of what later came to be known as expressionism, which he preferred to call the art of representing inner processes. Having in the previous year abandoned tonality as a central

controlling factor, he succeeded in juxtaposing and sometimes superimposing in his piano and orchestral pieces of 1909 remoter contrasts than music had hitherto known. Pappenheim's drama required him to pursue this line even further, and in an attempt to capture the uncensored spontaneity appropriate to it he set himself the prodigious task of composing it in a fortnight (in the event it took him 17 days, from 27 August to 12 September, but with a short break when he had to consult Pappenheim by post).

It is perhaps understandable that a work of this nature should be heard more often in the concert hall than in the opera house, but like most stage works it loses by the practice. Schoenberg was anxious that it should not fall into the hands of a director whose only interest would be to turn it into something entirely different from what he had intended. He had had every scenic effect precisely before his eyes while composing and was particularly concerned that the forest should be represented naturalistically; it was essential to make the woman's fear of it evident, and while one might shudder at a stylized forest one could not be afraid of it. He always remembered with gratitude the acting as well as the singing of Gutheil-Schoder, who gave the belated first performance.

O.W.N.

Etoile, L' ('The Star')

Opéra bouffe in three acts by Emmanuel Chabrier to a libretto by Eugène Leterrier and Albert Vanloo; Paris, Bouffes-Parisiens, 28 November 1877.

The cast at the première included Daubray (Michel-René Thibaut) as King Ouf, Paola Marié as Lazuli, Berthe Stuart as Laoula, Alfred Joly as Hérisson and Scipion as Sirocco.

King Ouf I	tenor
Lazuli	mezzo-soprano
Sirocco *astrologer*	bass
Princess Laoula	soprano
Hérisson de Porc-Epic *ambassador*	baritone
Aloès *his wife*	mezzo-soprano
Tapioca *his secretary*	baritone
Chief of Police	spoken
Mayor	spoken
Courtiers, guards, people	

Act 1 opens with King Ouf, in disguise, trying to provoke seditious remarks from the populace, so that he may continue the tradition of entertaining his subjects annually with a public execution. He is having little luck, as he tells Sirocco the Astrologer, who, he adds, is bound by a clause in the king's will to die a quarter of an hour after the king's own death. Ambassador Hérisson de Porc-Epic, his wife Aloès, his secretary Tapioca, and the Princess Laoula, King Ouf's betrothed, enter, also in disguise. Lazuli, a pedlar, has fallen in love with Laoula, but is told, untruthfully, that she is Hérisson's wife. In his disappointment he argues with the king, who is still hoping for a victim, and strikes him, unaware of his identity. The king, delighted, has him arrested. However, when Sirocco the Astrologer tells Ouf that his star and that of Lazuli are so intimately bound up that they will both die on the same day, Ouf hastily cancels the execution and sets up Lazuli in the palace.

In Act 2 Lazuli is waited on hand and foot, the subject of anxious concern by the king and Sirocco. Hérisson now comes to present his credentials, but the interview does not go well and the situation is saved only when Hérisson brings in Princess Laoula. To give Lazuli a clear path, Sirocco packs Hérisson off to prison. The lovers are joined by Aloès and Tapioca, who are also romantically involved. The king sends Lazuli and Laoula off together just as Hérisson returns, enraged. He has escaped and discovered what is going on between his wife and his secretary, and, angry at Laoula's defection, has sent guards to capture the lovers. To the king's utter consternation a shot is heard, and Laoula returns alone.

The king and Sirocco wait for their end, which seems inevitable (Act 3). Lazuli, however, has survived, and witnesses the two trying to keep their spirits up with the help of a glass or two of cordial. He is reunited with Laoula, but the king decides he wants to marry her. The clock now strikes the hour of death, but when nothing happens the king's relief is such that he pardons the lovers and all ends happily.

*

Chabrier's score, light as thistle-down, is composed in the best tradition of Offenbachian *opéra bouffe*, with each singer perfectly characterized in his or her music. Princess Laoula has a charming Rose Air, while Lazuli sings gratefully to his star, 'Oh ma petite étoile'. There is a splendid sentimental quartet and a comic duet for Ouf and Sirocco, which was always encored at the Bouffes-Parisiens.   E.F.

Euryanthe

Grosse heroisch-romantische Oper in three acts, J291, by Carl Maria von Weber to a libretto by Helmina von Chezy after the early French romance *L'histoire du très-noble et chevalereux prince Gérard, conte de Nevers, et de la très-virtueuse et très chaste princesse Euriant de Savoye, sa mye*; Vienna, Kärntnertortheater, 25 October 1823.

Henriette Sontag sang the title role at the première; Adolar was sung by Anton Haizinger, Eglantine by Therese Grünbaum and Lysiart by Anton Forti (who it seems was also capable of singing tenor parts).

King Louis VI of France	bass
Adolar *Count of Nevers and Rethel*	tenor
Lysiart *Count of Forest and Beaujolais*	bass
Euryanthe of Savoy	soprano
Eglantine of Puiset	soprano
Rudolf	tenor
Bertha	soprano
Ladies, noblemen, knights and countryfolk	
Setting Préméry and Nevers in 1110	

On 11 November 1821, as a direct result of the success of *Der Freischütz* some five months earlier, Weber received a letter from the impresario Domenico Barbaia in Vienna, asking him to compose 'an opera in the style of *Der Freischütz*' for the 1822–3 season at the Kärntnertortheater. From the start, though, Weber intended to write a very different kind of opera. He was not alone in thinking that the next stage in the development of German opera should be the replacement of spoken dialogue with continuous music. Some composers with whom Weber was in direct contact had already taken this step; Johann Nepomuk Poissl and Ignaz von Mosel had produced examples of through-composed German operas that

achieved a measure of success. But these, with their Classical orientation, were far from the ideal for which Weber was striving. Two other composers who were thinking along lines much closer to Weber's were Louis Spohr and Schubert, who each produced a through-composed German opera (*Jessonda* and *Alfonso und Estrella*) at about the same time as *Euryanthe*. Schubert's efforts were unknown to the other two, but it seems probable that there was even an element of personal rivalry between Weber and Spohr. Weber was certainly determined to show those (including Spohr) who were critical of his 'pandering to popular taste' in *Der Freischutz* that he could successfully conquer the realm of high art.

Weber's first problem was to find a suitable libretto, and it was his failure to do this that marred a potential masterpiece. Having rejected a number of possibilities, he made the mistake of persuading a fellow member of the Dresden literary circle known as the 'Liederkreis', Helmina von Chezy, to provide him with a libretto, despite her protestations that she lacked experience. From a number of suggestions he accepted *Euryanthe* and, after much modification and rewriting of Chezy's drafts, set to work on the music in May 1822; by August 1823 the whole opera, except for the overture, was complete. Its reception in Vienna, with Weber conducting, was initially enthusiastic, but this was probably a tribute more to the composer than to the work. Some voices were raised against the opera even before its première; it was seen as fatally flawed, labouring as it did under the weight of its impossible libretto. Schubert, who admired *Der Freischütz*, complained about *Euryanthe*'s 'formlessness' and 'lack of melody' and commented: 'whenever a scrap of tune appears, it is crushed like a mouse in a trap by the weighty orchestration'. Many found the plot confusing and felt that the whole opera was too long. Weber himself sanctioned cuts totalling 172 bars, and after his departure from Vienna the conductor Conradin Kreutzer removed a further 352 bars. Despite these efforts to make the opera more effective, audiences quickly fell off, and it was withdrawn after the 20th performance. Nevertheless, *Euryanthe* was subsequently staged in many theatres and has retained a tenuous place in the operatic repertory in spite of its irredeemable shortcomings.

The excellence of much of the music in *Euryanthe*, and the many individual moments at which Weber's vivid dramatic gift shines through, banishing all thought of the feeble libretto, have led to various attempts to make new performing versions, but none of these has succeeded.

*

Act I *King Louis' castle at Prémery* At a celebration of peace the King asks Adolar to sing. Accompanying himself on a 'zither', he sings the romance 'Unter blüh'nden Mandelbäumen' in praise of his bride, Euryanthe; pizzicato strings suggest his accompaniment. Everyone joins in Euryanthe's praise in the chorus 'Heil Euryanth' except Lysiart, who in the ensuing recitative wagers his lands against Adolar's that he can prove Euryanthe unfaithful. In a trio with chorus Adolar accepts the wager, asserting 'Ich bau' auf Gott und meine Euryanth' ('I rely on God and my Euryanthe') to a melody which has already been heard in the overture and which recurs later in the opera.

The castle at Nevers Euryanthe sings of her longing for Adolar in the cavatina 'Glöcklein im Thale'. This leads straight into a recitative as Eglantine, who covertly hates Euryanthe, enters. She attempts to discover the secret of Euryanthe's strange nocturnal behaviour; the orchestral accompaniment is dominated by a chromatic motif representing her deceitfulness, which plays an important part in later numbers. In the aria 'O mein Leid' Eglantine asserts that banishment would be preferable to being barred from Euryanthe's confidence; while the orchestra plays the 'ghost' music heard in the overture, Euryanthe reluctantly reveals that the ghost of Adolar's sister Emma appeared to her and told her that, out of grief at her lover Udo's death in battle, she committed suicide with poison contained in her ring and cannot find rest until the ring has been washed by the tears of an innocent girl in despair. Euryanthe has been nightly praying at Emma's tomb for the repose of her soul and is horrified at having betrayed the secret, but in the duet 'Unter ist mein Stern gegangen' Eglantine assures her of her trustworthiness. After Euryanthe has departed, Eglantine, again accompanied by the Deceit motif, vents her rage in the scena and aria 'Bethörte!'; she plans to denounce Euryanthe to Adolar, whom she secretly loves. She is interrupted by the sound of Lysiart's arrival. Country folk greet him, and Euryanthe bids him welcome. A passion for her is awakened in him. Eglantine plans to ask him for help with her plot.

Act 2 *The castle at Nevers* Night has fallen and Lysiart, alone, wavers between guilt and desire in the scena and aria 'Wo berg' ich mich?'; as he resolves to pursue his evil scheme ('So weih' ich mich den Rach' gewalten') his inner turbulence is reflected by rushing strings. (Weber's portrayal of Lysiart here, as a man divided against himself, strongly recalls Spohr's treatment of Faust in his 1813 opera.) Eglantine, having removed the poison ring from Emma's corpse, comes out of the tomb and, unaware of Lysiart's presence, once more gives way to her jealousy of Euryanthe. She is interrupted by Lysiart, who proposes an alliance and marriage. In the duet 'Komm denn' they cement their pact.

The King's hall at Prémery Adolar stills his anxiety and expresses his longing for Euryanthe in the aria

'Wehen mir Lüfte Ruh!'; the section beginning 'O Seligkeit, dich fass' ich kaum' is set to a melody already heard as the second subject of the overture. Euryanthe hurries in. They express their love for one another in the duet 'Hin nimm die Seele mein'. After the court has welcomed Euryanthe, Lysiart advances to claim victory in the wager. At first Adolar expresses his confidence in Euryanthe by singing the melody of 'Ich bau' auf Gott' to the words 'Komm an mein Herz'; but when Lysiart produces Emma's ring and reveals that he knows the secret of the tomb, all are reluctantly convinced of Euryanthe's guilt. Adolar's estates are forfeit and he leads away the distraught Euryanthe to wander in the wilderness.

Act 3 *A rocky mountain gorge* Adolar plans to kill Euryanthe. Rising 6ths, which form an important melodic feature in the scene, recall the prominent rising 6ths in 'O Seligkeit' and the love duet 'Hin nimm die Seele mein', but here the harmonic context gives them a forlorn quality, underlining Adolar's disillusionment. In the recitative 'Hier weilest du?' Euryanthe protests her innocence. Their duet 'Wie liebt' ich dich' is interrupted by the approach of a serpent; Euryanthe interposes herself between it and Adolar to protect him, but he rushes after it to attack it. Euryanthe waits anxiously ('Schirmende Engelshaar') until, having slain the serpent, Adolar returns and tells Euryanthe that he will abandon her, not kill her. In the scena and cavatina 'So bin ich nun verlassen' Euryanthe longs for death, hoping that the flowers by her grave will tell Adolar that 'she did not betray you', but her musing is cut short by the sound of hunting horns. The Huntsmen's Chorus 'Die Thale dampfen', in the 'courtly' key of E♭, contrasts effectively with the preceding gloomy scene. The King and his hunting party are astonished to discover Euryanthe. In the duet with chorus 'Lasst mich hier' Euryanthe, explaining Eglantine's deceit, easily convinces the King of her innocence. At the thought of being reunited with Adolar, Euryanthe gives expression to her joy in the aria with chorus 'Zu ihm! zu ihm!', but as they are about to lead her away she collapses.

An open space in front of the castle at Nevers Country folk are singing a May song as Adolar approaches. When they recognize him they tell him of Euryanthe's innocence and the treachery of Lysiart and Eglantine. In the solo with chorus 'Vernichte kühn das Werk' they pledge their support and implore him to overthrow the traitors. To the sound of a wedding march, Lysiart and Eglantine approach. The ghost music haunts Eglantine and she falters. Adolar steps forward. In a duet with chorus, 'Trotze nicht!', the people curse Lysiart, while he and Adolar confront one another. The King arrives in time to prevent armed conflict. In the finale he tells Adolar

that Euryanthe's heart is broken. In the ensuing confrontation Eglantine pours scorn on Lysiart, who stabs her to death. Lysiart is led away. To the sound of hunting horns, Euryanthe, now recovered from her collapse, is brought in. A final fragment of the ghost music indicates that, innocent tears having washed the ring, Emma is at rest. A chorus of rejoicing concludes the opera.

*

From the purely musical point of view, *Euryanthe* is in many ways Weber's masterpiece. The way in which he manages the transitions between set-pieces and more fluid sections of recitative and arioso is highly effective. Weber's use of chromaticism, particularly to characterize the evil pair, is masterly, and his employment of musical motif is more subtle than in *Der Freischütz*. The orchestration is vivid and imaginative, contributing much to the overall atmosphere of the opera. Despite the obvious dramatic deficiencies of the work as a whole, its influence on later composers, notably Marschner, Schumann, Liszt and Wagner, was considerable.

C.B.

Excursions of Mr Brouček, The
[Výlety páně Broučkovy]

Opera in two parts by Leoš Janáček; Prague, National Theatre, 23 April 1920. Part 1, 'Výlet pana Broučka do měsíce' ('The Excursion of Mr Brouček to the Moon') to a libretto by Janáček with František Gellner, Viktor Dyk, F. S. Procházka and others after Svatopluk Čech's novel *Pravý výlet pana Broučka do měsíce* ('The True Excursion of Mr Brouček to the Moon'); Part 2, 'Výlet pana Broučka do XV. století' ('The Excursion of Mr Brouček to the 15th Century') to a libretto by F. S. Procházka after Čech's novel *Nový epochální výlet pana Broučka, tentokráte do XV. století* ('The Epoch-making Excursion of Mr Brouček, this time to the 15th Century').

The cast at the première included Mirko Štork as Brouček, Miloslav Jeník (Mazal), Vilém Zítek (Sacristan), Václav Novák (Würfl), Ema Miřiovská (Málinka) and Věra Pivoňková (Kedruta).

Note Characters appear on earth/on the moon/and [Part 2] in the 15th century. Mr Brouček's Housekeeper, listed in the vocal score, appeared in Part 1, Act 3, which was subsequently suppressed by Janáček.

Brouček ('Mr Beetle') *a landlord*   tenor
Sacristan *of St Vít's Cathedral*/Lunobor/
   Jan, known as Domšík od zvonu
   ('from the sign of the bell') *a citizen of*
   15th-century Prague   bass-baritone

Málinka *the Sacristan's daughter*/Etherea
    Lunobor's daughter/Kunka *Domšík's*
    daughter   soprano
Mazal ('Dauber') *a painter*/Blankytný
    ('Sky blue') *a moon poet*/Petřík   tenor
Artist at the Vikárka/Oblačný
    ('Cloudy')/Vacek Bradatý ('Bearded
    Vacek')   baritone
Artist at the Vikárka/Duhoslav/Vojta od
    pávů ('Vojta from the Peacocks')   tenor
Artist at the Vikárka/Harfoboj/Miroslav
    the goldsmith   tenor
Artist at the Vikárka/Větroboj/Voice of
    the Professor   tenor
Würfl *publican at the Vikárka*/Čaroskvoucí
    ('Magically-shining') *a*
    patron/Alderman   bass
Young Waiter *at the Vikárka*/Child
    Prodigy/Student   soprano
The Apparition of the Poet (Part 2)
    (Svatopluk Čech)   tenor
[Mr Brouček's Housekeeper]/Kedruta
    (Part 2)   contralto
First Taborite (Part 2)   baritone
Second Taborite (Part 2)   tenor
Jan Žižka *the Hussite commander*
    (Part 2)   silent role
Chorus in Part 1: *artists at the Vikárka, Etherea's*
    companions, moon artists
Chorus in Part 2: *armed men, children, Hussite*
    people, Prague and Taborite soldiers,
    priests
Setting Part 1: the Vikárka pub in the castle
    precincts of Prague towards the end of the
    19th century; on the moon. Part 2: the
    Vikárka pub; Prague, Old Town Square in
    1420, and in Domšík's house

Janáček's interest in Svatopluk Čech's first Brouček novel became evident in 1888, the year of its publication, when he reprinted an extract from it in his musical periodical, *Hudební listy*, but it was not until after Čech's death in 1908 that the composer seems to have contemplated it as a possible opera subject. He secured the rights to it on 21 March 1908 and immediately began drafting a scenario. Then followed a long and frustrating period in which he failed to find a librettist. Karel Mašek agreed to help, wrote a scene (17 May 1908), but dropped out by the autumn of 1908. Dr Zikmund Janke's primitive Act 1 libretto (16 December 1908) yielded only a couple of suitable lines of a drinking song and he gave up when in January 1909 Janáček proposed far-reaching changes, basically the addition of earth characters to parallel those on the moon (taken by the same singers). Janáček tried many other possible librettists, but in the end had to do most of the work himself.

This was a feasible approach for the moon scenes, where Čech's dialogue could be adapted; much less so in the earth scenes, which hardly exist in Čech. Janáček also needed several strophic songs for Act 2. These eventually came from František Gellner in the second half of 1912. Janáček completed two acts by 12 February 1913 and then put the opera aside until the acceptance of *Jenůfa* by Karel Kovařovic at Prague in the autumn of 1915 encouraged him to continue. He then had help from both Viktor Dyk and F. S. Procházka, enabling him to revise the opera, to fill in the gaps and to compose the third act, an epilogue showing Mr Brouček back at home. He wrote several versions of this, the final one completed in March 1917, by which time Janáček thought of adding a second 'Excursion'.

Čech's first novel (1888) satirically places a philistine Prague landlord 'on the moon', which turns out to be inhabited by over-precious artistic people of the art-for-art's-sake movement; the humour arises from the comic confrontation of these two alien worlds. In Čech's second Brouček novel (1889) Mr Brouček is confronted with the more patriotic circumstances of the Hussite wars of the early 15th century. This was a heroic time in Czech history when the Czechs, defending their own distinctive brand of early Protestantism, beat off Crusader armies drawn from all of Europe. The subject became increasingly relevant as Czech independence (1918) drew nearer: the final dedicatee of the score was T. G. Masaryk, the first president of the new Czechoslovak Republic. For the second part F. S. Procházka provided a complete libretto, written between 30 April and 28 October 1917. Janáček began composition as soon as he received Act 1 (early May 1917), and completed his work by the end of that year. His epilogue to the first excursion was now redundant and he dropped it in January 1918. Publication and performance, both initiated while the opera was a single 'excursion', were protracted. Universal Edition published a vocal score only in September 1919. A production under Otakar Ostrčil took place in Prague the next spring, an embittered affair with considerable hostility from the singers despite the simplification of the voice parts. It was Janáček's only original Prague première and the production survived just nine further performances before being taken off in 1921. The only other production in Janáček's lifetime was of the *Moon Excursion* (Part 1) alone, given in Brno in 1926 under František Neumann.

*

Part I 'The Excursion of Mr Brouček to the Moon'

Act I *The Vikárka street in Hradčany, Prague; a moonlit night* The prelude is made of a jaunty pentatonic theme in 2/4 which gives way to and then combines with a broadly lyrical theme in 3/2. One of

Janáček's objectives was to lighten the satire with 'a whiff of Bohemian love'. He did this by introducing a pair of lovers, Málinka and Mazal, seen after the prelude in the middle of a tiff; she will marry Mr Brouček, she declares, as Mr Brouček, after a heavy evening's beer-drinking, staggers on and is teased by his tenant, Mazal. The atmosphere is filled out by the sounds of songs from the nearby Vikárka pub. The first brief drinking song is Dr Janke's single contribution to the libretto; the second is an attractive waltz, 'Lásko, lásko, čarovný květ' ('Love, love, magical flower'), to words by Viktor Dyk. There are more Vikárka sounds: the Young Waiter chasing after Brouček with a string of sausages for him, the publican Würfl wishing his guests a prompt return. After another scene between the lovers (they end by singing above the lyrical theme from the overture), Brouček contemplates the moon and, over the pentatonic theme of the overture, imagines life to be much happier there. He is mysteriously drawn to the moon – physically, too – and is borne aloft to the fading sounds of earth revels.

A moonscape The ethereal atmosphere in which Brouček is now discovered is depicted by a theme for solo violin. Blankytný approaches leading his winged horse and Brouček takes him for an elaborately dressed version of his earthly counterpart, Mazal. Brouček's claim of owning a three-storey house cuts no ice with his companion, while Blankytný's boast that his name as a poet is known 'throughout the moon' is Brouček's first indication of his new location. This suspicion is confirmed by the arrival of Etherea who, it turns out, needs to be worshipped, like all moonwomen, from a kneeling position. Accompanied by her companions, she sings a robust waltz-song, 'Své písně přináším vám' ('I bear my songs to you'). Etherea is immediately attracted to Brouček, and a lively ensemble-finale is woven out of elements of her song, Brouček's protests and Blankytný's horrified cries at the turn of events. Lunobor, Etherea's father, proposes reading the earth-guest some chapters of his book on moon aesthetics, but his guest has escaped – flying away with Etherea on Blankytný's winged horse Pegasus, to Blankytný's hollow laughs of despair.

Act 2 *The Cathedral of All Arts* This is the hub of artistic activity on the moon – a central hall with wings going off towards the poets, the painters and the musicians. It is presided over by the patron, Čaroskvoucí, who sings a strophic song about the difficulties of a patron's calling, 'Také prochodil jsem školu' ('I also went through school'), to the adulation of the poets. Etherea and Brouček arrive, pursued by Blankytný and Lunobor, and seek Čaroskvoucí's protection as 'lovers' (as Etherea puts it, to Brouček's dismay). Čaroskvoucí wishes to show his earth-guest the artistic delights of the moon. These include a banquet of flower scents which Brouček is encouraged to sniff to the accompaniment of the moon anthem (a spoof of the Czech national song, including its opening words, 'Domov můj': 'My homeland') sung by the Child Prodigy. Etherea serenades Brouček with another passionate song, 'Již prchám jako vánkem vůně května' ('I'm already vanishing, like the scent of May in the breeze'). There is a recitation by a moon poet, Oblačný – two verses as melodrama over an orchestral waltz, the third sung. When Brouček falls asleep and is urged once again to 'sniff', he testily declares that his *nose* has had quite enough already. This turns out to be a lapse in etiquette: noses are unmentionable on the moon. He is immediately ostracized by all but Duhoslav, who shows Brouček his latest painting. Brouček remembers his sausages from the Vikárka and eats them, delicately covering his face with his handkerchief. This behaviour Duhoslav takes to be weeping: at last the earth-guest has been affected by some form of art and he calls back the company to witness this miracle. They are quickly disillusioned: Brouček announces that he is eating and proceeds to list the contents of his sausages, which upsets even further the vegetarian moon-beings (a cue for a shocked 'meat' chorus). A finale builds up: love songs from Etherea, cries of anguish from Blankytný, aesthetics from Lunobor, and as Brouček decides to make a getaway on Pegasus, musicians led by Harfoboj eulogize Čaroskvoucí with an exuberant chorus, 'Požehnáni tvoji rtové' ('Blessed be thy lips'). Brouček flies back to earth in an orchestral interlude, a sumptuous development of the lyrical theme from the overture. The musicians' chorus turns into the chorus of artists on earth celebrating Würfl's beer. Würfl's voice is heard, bidding his guests come again soon; the Young Waiter laughs as Brouček is carried home in a barrel. Finally Málinka and Mazal enter and make up their quarrel, ending the first part of the opera in radiant Puccinian octaves.

Part 2 'The Excursion of Mr Brouček to the 15th Century'

Act 1 *The jewel-chamber of Václav IV; darkness* The tense opening of the prelude with its suggestions of war (off-beat cymbal clashes) gives way to a more expansive section with prominent harp chords as the curtain goes up on the deserted jewel-chamber. The voices of Brouček and his drinking companions at the Vikárka are heard offstage. Würfl bids them goodnight. Brouček loses his way and tumbles into the jewel-chamber; he is amazed by the sight, but manages to find his way out. His place is taken immediately by Svatopluk Čech, who apostrophizes the great day of the Hussite victory.

The Prague Old Town Square; early morning Brouček makes his way through the town, now unfamiliar to him since he has travelled back to 1420. He is outraged by the absence of police and of street lighting. When he calls for help, he is confronted by the Alderman (in 'fancy dress,' Brouček decides), who finds Brouček's strange (19th-century) dress and speech suspicious and, with the enthusiastic support of the chorus, arrests him as a spy of the German emperor Sigismund. Offstage strains of the Hussite chorale 'Slyšte rytieři boží' ('Hear, warriors of God') are heard, sung by armed men. Realizing his danger, Brouček gives himself out as a Czech who has returned after many years abroad. He is welcomed by the kind-hearted Domšík, who offers him accommodation in his nearby house. The sound of the Hussite chorale grows, and the armed men enter and go into the Týn Church on the Old Town Square, to a triumphant C major peroration of the chorale.

Act 2 *An inside room in Domšík's house; a late spring morning* After a short prelude, Brouček is discovered, rubbing his eyes in disbelief at his time-travelling. Domšík enters and insists that Brouček get into suitable clothes, and Brouček reluctantly dons bicoloured tights and other oddities. While he completes dressing, the chorale 'Slyšte rytieři' is heard again, indicating the return from church of Domšík's daughter Kunka and her friends. Kunka gives a glowing account of the service and of the sermon by Jan Rokycana, one of the leading Hussite preachers of the day. Brouček is introduced to the other guests, who soon get embroiled in religious arguments. Their doctrinal quarrels, however, pall into insignificance at Brouček's seeming indifference to the present national peril. An ugly scene is forestalled only by the sudden arrival of Petřík, announcing that the Crusaders have forded the Vltava, and most of the men rush off. Brouček reluctantly takes a halberd as Domšík bids his daughter farewell. The war cries of the fighting men and the clash of arms are heard off stage while Kunka recites the Lord's Prayer. Unable to stand the tension she rushes out with a weapon; Domšík's servant Kedruta continues the prayer, now combining with the sound of the most famous Hussite chorale of all, 'Kdož jste boží bojovníci' ('You, who are warriors of God'), the only chorale Janáček used with its original tune.

Brouček slinks back and gets into his 19th-century clothes, pulling on a hood over the ensemble. He lights up a cigar to the consternation of Kedruta, who sees it as a sign of the devil, and then goes off pursued by her hostile cries of 'Antichrist!' against a final offstage chorale. Kunka returns dejectedly as the curtain falls (Act 3 was to have begun at this point), though the continuous interlude soon gives way to triumphant sounds: offstage trumpet fanfares, a march and cries of triumph first from children and then from the whole chorus.

The Old Town Square; sunset The curtain goes up on a scene of triumph as the armies and people return from their famous victory over Sigismund's forces.

Petřík leads the people in a victory chorale ('Dítky, v hromadu se sendĕme'). The victory procession that goes into the Týn church to give thanks includes the figure of the Hussite general Jan Žižka and his captains. (Janáček later added voice parts welcoming Žižka over the orchestral interlude.)

Attempting to make his escape, Brouček hides from the crowd going into the Týn church, but is discovered by two Taborites (members of an extreme Hussite sect) looking for wounded people. Brouček is treated sympathetically at first and spins an elaborate story of his heroism in the battle. Petřík, coming out of the church and overhearing Brouček in full flood, declares him a liar. The scene is interrupted by the arrival of Kunka, mourning the death of Domšík ('Umřel mi tatíček'). Then the real circumstances of Brouček's 'heroism' are revealed: Petřík describes how he surrendered, in German, to the Crusaders. In his defence, Brouček can only say that he is not a fighter, that he is 'a son of the future'. For his cowardice he is condemned to death and is forced into a beer-barrel to the cries of the hostile crowd and Kedruta's 'Antichrist!'

An orchestral interlude dissolves this scene (the curtain briefly falls), and Brouček is discovered in the courtyard of the Vikárka. He is stuck in a beer-barrel and his cries have attracted Würfl. Brouček is much relieved to be home. When Würfl asks where he has been, he gives a discreetly edited account of his latest adventure: 'But not a word to anyone!' The orchestra ends the opera with a brief reminiscence of the victory music, capped by a peal of satirical, scherzando flourishes.

*

The Excursions of Mr Brouček will always remain a problematic opera. The distinctly patchwork moon excursion comes across with much more theatrical verve than the 15th-century excursion, which has a more unified libretto, but also longueurs quite uncharacteristic of this energetic composer. It is the only one of Janáček's mature operas which needs some local knowledge to understand the intricacies of its plot. It is unique in several other respects. If one discounts the early and unrepresentative *The Beginning of a Romance* it was his only comic opera, and it was the last opera in which he employed a librettist. Difficulties with the libretto stretched out its period of composition to a decade, the longest time he spent on any work, and during this time his style and his fortunes changed. Halfway through he gave up thoughts of continuing to write operas and abandoned the score; when he took it up again and finished it he stood on the threshold of the great period of his four late operas. An understanding of *Brouček* is crucial to an understanding of Janáček's development as an opera composer.   J.T.

F

Fair at Sorochintsï, The
[*Sorochinskaya yarmarka* ('Sorochintsy Fair')]

Opera, left incomplete, in three acts by Modest
Petrovich Musorgsky to his own libretto (with
Arseny Golenishchev-Kutuzov) after the story in
Nikolay Vasil'yevich Gogol's collection *Evenings on a
Farm near Dikanka* (i, 1831); Moscow, Free Theatre,
8/21 October 1913.

Solopy Cherevik	bass
Khivrya *Cherevik's wife*	mezzo-soprano
Parasya *Cherevik's daughter, Khivrya's*	
stepdaughter	soprano
Kum *Cherevik's 'buddy'*	baritone
Grits'ko *a peasant lad*	tenor
Afanasy Ivanovich *son of a village priest*	tenor
A Gypsy	bass
Chernobog *master of the Demons*	bass

Tradespeople, peasants, drivers, gypsies, Jews,
    Cossacks, lads and lasses; in 'The Peasant Lad's
    Dream Vision': Kashchey, Cherv, Topolets,
    Chuma, Death; demons, witches, gnomes
Setting Village of Velikiye Sorochintsï, near
    Poltava in 'Little Russia' (Ukraine)

Musorgsky conceived the opera in 1874; it remained
incomplete on his death in 1881. Three numbers
appeared in vocal score in 1886, and three were
orchestrated by Anatoly Lyadov and published in
1904. Various fragments, edited by Vyacheslav
Karatïgin, were performed in concert form with
piano and spoken continuity at St Petersburg on
16/29 March 1911 (to commemorate the 30th anniversary of Musorgsky's death); Act 2, completed by
Karatïgin, with the Introduction and Fair from Act 1,
orchestrated by Lyadov, were given at the Comedia
Theatre, St Petersburg, on 17/30 December 1911.

There have been four stage versions. (1): with
Musorgsky's completed numbers revised and or-
chestrated by Lyadov and Karatïgin, incorporating
Rimsky-Korsakov's version of *A Night on Bald
Mountain* with a little supplementary music by
Yury Sergeyevich Sakhnovsky (1866–1930) and the
musical numbers connected by dialogue drawn from
Gogol's text; this was the version first performed in
Moscow in 1913, under Konstantin Saradzhev. Later,

Sakhnovsky completed the work in continuous
music, in which form it was given at the Bol'shoy
Theatre, Moscow, under Nikolay Golovanov on 10
January 1925. (2): completed and orchestrated by
César Cui, 1915–16, using Golenishchev-Kutuzov's
supplementary text; it was published in 1916 and
given under Grzegorz Fitelberg at the Theatre of
Musical Drama, St Petersburg, on 13/26 October
1917. (3): as a pastiche, by Nikolay Tcherepnin,
incorporating items from (1) and (2) with other music
by Musorgsky; it was given at the Monte Carlo
Opera House on 27 March 1923 and published the
same year. (4): edited by Pavel Lamm, completed
and orchestrated by Vissarion Shebalin; it was
first performed under Grigory Stolyarov at the
Nemirovich-Danchenko Musical Theatre, Moscow,
on 12 January 1932 (this was a revision of a version
prepared by Shebalin in 1930 and given at the Malïy
Opera Theatre, Leningrad, 21 December 1931). This,
published in Lamm's critical edition of Musorgsky's
works (1933), has become the standard performing
version and the only one to have been recorded.

The Fair at Sorochintsï is generally regarded as the
third and last of the Musorgsky operas in repertory
today. Although it was composed alongside
Khovanshchina, it was started later and was much
further from completion at the composer's death. The
idea for the opera – originally intended as a vehicle
for the great bass Osip Petrov and his wife, the
contralto Anna Vorob'yova (as Cherevik and
Khivrya) – came to Musorgsky in 1874. After a period
of doubt as to a Russian composer's ability to manage
Ukrainian speech patterns in recitative, he began
composing in July 1876. As was his occasional habit,
he worked at the initial stage without a libretto or
even a scenario. The first music to be written was the
little chorus for girls in Act 1 (fig.26 in the Lamm–
Shebalin score), but Musorgsky probably already
intended to link that chorus up with one he had
written four years earlier for an abandoned group
project, *Mlada*: a market scene, it is now the opera's
opening number. Also recycled from *Mlada* was the
choral ballet in Act 3, itself a recycling of the tone
poem *St John's Eve on Bald Mountain* (1867), arbitrarily
inserted into the action of the new opera in the guise
of a dream vision. (The familiar concert number *A
Night on Bald Mountain* is Rimsky-Korsakov's free

adaptation, without voices, of the version in *The Fair at Sorochintsï*, the last of its several incarnations in Musorgsky's work.)

A scenario was finally written down (at the Petrovs') in 1877, a year wholly devoted to *The Fair*. Osip Petrov's death in 1878 dashed the composer's original hopes for the piece and slowed work considerably. He left it in fragments. Those for Act 3, to pick the worst case, were decorative 'inserts' only; the whole denouement and resolution were lacking both in music and in text. Nor do the surviving fragments entirely conform to the scenario, so that even their placement within a reconstruction must remain speculative to some degree (this is undoubtedly why Rimsky-Korsakov never attempted one). The synopsis that follows is based on the Lamm–Shebalin version; the items completed by Musorgsky in vocal score are, besides the Prelude, in Act 1, *a*, *b* and *d*; in Act 2, only *a*; and in Act 3, *b*, *c* and *e*. (Their dates, where known, are given in 'Old Style'.)

*

Prelude: 'A Warm Day in Little Russia' (orchestrated by Musorgsky).

Act I *a* Market scene with a merry din of traders and the crowd (chorus adapted from *Mlada*); Grits'ko arrives with his companions and Cherevik with Parasya. She happily looks round while he is preoccupied with the sale of his mare and his wheat. The Gypsy attracts the crowd's attention and tells a mysterious story of a red jacket the Devil himself is seeking (the first sketches for the Gypsy were composed by 31 August 1876). Grits'ko flirts with Parasya; Cherevik objects but is mollified when he finds that Grits'ko is the son of an old friend. They go to the tavern to celebrate their meeting.

b Evening. Cherevik and Kum leave the tavern, reeling. They strike up an old song ('Dudu, rududu, rududu', based on a Ukrainian folksong from the Rubets collection of 1872).

c Khivrya enters, scolds Cherevik and forbids Parasya's marriage to Grits'ko; Grits'ko overhears the exchange.

d Grits'ko is disconsolate; he sings 'The Peasant Lad's Dumka', in the style of a melismatic folksong, accompanied by solo wind. (According to the 1877 scenario, this number was meant for Act 3, but all revisers have agreed it fits in best with the existing manuscripts at this point.)

e The Gypsy appears and promises to solve Grits'ko's problem in return for the latter's bullocks.

Act 2 *a* Khivrya picks a quarrel with Cherevik to get him out of the house (that is, Kum's house, where they are staying) so that she can keep her date with Afanasy Ivanovich, the priest's son. She bustles around the stove preparing food and sings 'Otkoli zh ya Brudeusa vstretila?' ('How in the world did I meet Brudeus?', based on a Ukrainian song taken down

from a friend's singing in November 1876; MS dated 16 July 1877). Afanasy Ivanovich arrives; Khivrya plies him with goodies and he makes amorous advances. Their farcical tryst is interrupted by the tumultuous arrival of Kum and Cherevik, with other guests. They are in a panic: the red jacket has been spied, and so has the Devil with a pig's snout. After drinking, courage is restored; Cherevik brazenly invites the red jacket to the house. Kum recounts the tale of the red jacket in all its details (Musorgsky's MS breaks off after a few bars of this narrative).

b Kum finishes the tale; suddenly the window is flung open and a great pig's snout is thrust in. All disperse in great commotion, including the priest's son who runs from his hiding place.

Act 3.i *a* Cherevik and Kum are running wild and bumping into each other. The Gypsy and peasant lads enter and accuse them of theft. Grits'ko appears and persuades the others to let Kum and Cherevik go if the latter will agree to his marrying Parasya; Cherevik having promised, he and Kum are released. All go home except Grits'ko, who falls asleep under a tree and has a fantastic dream.

b 'The Peasant Lad's Dream Vision' is an elaborate ballet with chorus depicting a Witches' Sabbath ('St John's Eve on Bald Mountain'), presided over by Chernobog (the Devil, in old Slav religion). The chimes of the morning bell and church singing put the demons and witches to flight. Grits'ko awakens and ponders his dream. (The autograph vocal score of this number, adapted from the *Mlada* music, is dated 10 May 1880.)

3.ii *c* Parasya comes out of Kum's house, missing Grits'ko. The warm sun dispels her melancholy: she sings a merry song and breaks into a hopak. Cherevik spies her and joins in ('Parasya's Dumka': MS dated 3 July 1879; an orchestral score exists, begun by Musorgsky and finished by Rimsky-Korsakov).

d Kum and Grits'ko enter with a group of peasant lads and lasses. Taking advantage of Khivrya's absence, Cherevik blesses his daughter's marriage. When the furious Khivrya returns, the Gypsy suddenly materializes, seizes her, and with the help of the peasant lads carries her off.

e General merriment, ending in a gradual exit (finale, 'Hopak of the merry lads'); whether this general dance (with choral song, indicated with staves and clefs in Musorgsky's piano score but actually written by Shebalin, to a Ukrainian folk text) was intended for this finale, or for that to Act 1, is unclear.

*

Unlike Musorgsky's serious operas, *The Fair at Sorochintsï* is frankly a number opera, possibly modelled to some degree on Gulak-Artemovsky's popular 'Little Russian' Singspiel *Zaporozhets za Dunayem*. As traditionally befits a peasant comedy, even the dialogue scenes are modelled not on speech but on folktunes. Nevertheless, Musorgsky's uncanny gift for musical characterization remains as sharply honed as ever: especially droll is the portrayal in Act 2 of Afanasy Ivanovich, the priest's son, through a patchwork of hackneyed ecclesiastical cadences. Presumably in an effort to be discreet, Shebalin supplied the missing scenes in a modest recitative that skilfully parodies Musorgsky's earlier speechsong manner (as in *Marriage*, or the Inn Scene from *Boris Godunov*). That style having been largely superseded in *The Fair*, Shebalin's contribution to the opera came out sounding in an odd way more like Musorgsky than Musorgsky's.   R.T.

Falstaff

Commedia lirica in three acts by Giuseppe Verdi to a libretto by Arrigo Boito after William Shakespeare's plays *The Merry Wives of Windsor* and *King Henry IV*; Milan, Teatro alla Scala, 9 February 1893.

At the première, conducted by Edoardo Mascheroni, the cast included Victor Maurel (Falstaff), Antonio Pini-Corsi (Ford), Emma Zilli (Alice), Edoardo Garbin (Fenton), Adelina Stehle (Nannetta) and Giuseppina Pasqua (Mistress Quickly).

Sir John Falstaff	baritone
Fenton	tenor
Dr Caius	tenor
Bardolfo [Bardolph] } *followers of*	tenor
Pistola [Pistol] } *Falstaff*	bass
Mrs Alice Ford	soprano
Ford *Alice's husband*	baritone
Nannetta *their daughter*	soprano
Mistress Quickly	mezzo-soprano
Mrs Meg Page	mezzo-soprano
Mine Host at the Garter	silent
Robin *Falstaff's page*	silent
Ford's Page	silent

Bourgeoisie and populace, Ford's servants,
  masquerade of imps, fairies, witches
Setting Windsor, during the reign of Henry IV
  of England

Verdi, who by the time he wrote his last operas had become a national monument, talked intermittently of writing a comic opera during the latter part of his career, but never found a libretto to his taste until, some two years after the success of *Otello* in 1887, his librettist for that opera, Arrigo Boito, suggested a work largely based on Shakespeare's *The Merry Wives of Windsor*. Verdi was immediately enthusiastic about the draft scenario Boito concocted, made relatively few large structural suggestions, and by August 1889

even announced that he was writing a fugue (quite possibly the comic fugue that ends the opera). Composer and librettist worked closely together during the winter of 1889–90, and by the spring of 1890 the libretto was complete.

The composing of the opera took a considerable time, or rather was carried out in short bursts of activity interspersed with long fallow periods. Act 1 was completed – at least in short score – shortly after the libretto was finished, but then Verdi fell into a depression, the deaths of various close friends making him fear he would not live to finish the project, and the remaining two acts were only gradually completed. It seems that, unusually for Verdi, certain scenes were finished out of chronological order (perhaps an indication of the relative independence of individual scenes). By September 1891 the opera was largely complete in short score, and a year later Verdi had finished the orchestration. The première at La Scala took place six years almost to the day after that of *Otello*. It was, perhaps inevitably at this stage of Verdi's career, a huge triumph, and was soon seen in the major international opera houses. Verdi made various minor changes to the score (notably recomposing and shortening the final minutes of Act 3 scene i) during these early revivals. *Falstaff* has always retained its place in the international repertory, though it is far less frequently heard than many of the middle-period works.

                                        *

Act I.i *Inside the Garter Inn* An offbeat C major chord and descending arpeggio set in immediate motion a scene (indeed an opera) that is remarkable above all for its sense of rapid change and relentless forward movement. Falstaff, who is busy sealing two letters as the curtain rises, is upbraided by Dr Caius, who accuses him of causing drunken confusion in Caius's house. Falstaff calmly accepts the charge, at which Caius accuses Pistol and Bardolph of getting him drunk and stealing his money. Pistol challenges the doctor to a mock duel and exchanges a furious round of insults with him. But Caius has had enough, and storms out after making a solemn promise never to get drunk with such scoundrels again. This hectic first episode is dominated by two main themes: the arpeggiated idea that opened the opera and a contrasting second theme of more regular tread, appearing as Falstaff replies to Caius's first accusation. The two themes are played out in an overtly developmental manner, with various comic allusions to sonata form, not least in the ineptly contrapuntal 'Amen' intoned by Pistol and Bardolph as Caius leaves and the 'sonata' comes to a close.

After some vain searching for funds, Falstaff lambasts his companions before celebrating his enormous belly in a suitably grandiose climax. Then, in a relatively stable musical episode, the central thread of the drama is first put forth: Falstaff reveals that he has amorous designs on both Alice Ford and Meg Page, the wives of rich townsfolk. But Pistol and Bardolph refuse to deliver his love letters, saying it is beneath their 'honour' to do so. Falstaff sends off his page with the letters and then, in the famous 'Onore' monologue, excoriates the traitors and their high-flown ideals. The solo is typical of the opera as a whole, rapidly shifting in mood, full of ironic references, a veritable index of startling orchestral combinations and textures. As C major makes a late, triumphant return, Falstaff takes up a broom and drives his followers from the room.

I.ii The garden outside Ford's house A scherzo-like introduction leads in Meg and Mistress Quickly, who meet Alice and her daughter Nannetta on the threshold of Alice's house. Meg and Alice discover that Falstaff has sent them identical letters, extracts from which they quote, first to the mournful accompaniment of an english horn, later to a passionately lyrical phrase, undermined at the final cadence by mocking vocal trills. In an elaborate unaccompanied quartet, they pour scorn on the amorous knight and vow to revenge themselves on him. From the other side of the stage appears a male quintet (Fenton, Caius, Bardolph, Pistol and Ford) who, unaware of the ladies, superimpose their own ensemble. As the ladies fade into the background, Bardolph and Pistol warn Ford of Falstaff's designs; Ford vows to keep a close watch. The ladies return and the two groups, at the sight of each other, disperse, leaving Fenton and Nannetta together for the first of their brief love duets, 'Labbra di foco'. One of Boito's early ideas for the drama was to present the young lovers 'as one sprinkles sugar on a tart, to sprinkle the whole comedy with [their] love', and Verdi responded by weaving round them a musical world quite separate from the main body of the score: relaxed and lyrical, shot through with delicate chromaticism and soft orchestral textures. But the spell is soon broken: the ladies return and resolve to send Quickly to Falstaff as their go-between. Nannetta and Fenton snatch a further few moments; then the men reappear, Ford announcing that he will visit Falstaff in disguise to ascertain his intentions. The finale of the scene involves a masterly super-imposition of the women's and men's ensembles. The ladies have the last word: a triumphantly derisive reprise of Falstaff's most impassioned epistolary style.

Act 2.i The Garter Inn The opening of the act is extraordinary – even in the context of *Falstaff* – for the extravagant manner in which musical ideas match verbal tags: first as Pistol and Bardolph make elaborate, chest-beating penance before Falstaff; then as Mistress Quickly introduces herself with a low

'Reverenza!'; then as she expresses the amorous states of Alice and Meg with the phrase 'Povera donna!'; and finally as she makes an appointment for Falstaff with the former, 'dalle due alle tre' ('between two and three'). Quickly leaves, and Falstaff has time for a gleeful episode of self-congratulation, 'Va, vecchio John', before 'Mastro Fontana' (Ford in disguise) is shown in. In the ensuing duet, Fontana offers Falstaff money to seduce one Alice Ford (who will thus be made easier for Fontana to conquer); and Falstaff gleefully agrees, saying that he has already arranged an appointment 'between two and three'. The passage carries vague echoes of earlier 19th-century formal practice – perhaps particularly in the cabaletta-like close – but is more usefully seen as a kind of musical prose, in constant flux as the moods of the principals swing to and fro. Highlights include the magnificent orchestral depiction of the money Ford offers Falstaff; Ford's passionate declaration of his feelings for Alice (a hint of the deeply serious tone that will soon break through); and Falstaff's rousing conclusion in 'Te lo cornifico' ('I'll cuckold him for you'). As the knight goes off to pretty himself, Ford is left alone to brood on what he has heard (the impassioned arioso 'È sogno?'). For the first and only time, the opera swings for an extended period into the language of serious opera: to horn-calls (a pun on cuckoldry) and with tortured fragments of the preceding duet (in particular 'dalle due alle tre'), Ford contemplates what he believes is his wife's deception. However, no sooner has Verdi sealed the monologue with a stunning orchestral climax than there is yet another stylistic volte-face: to a delicate, trilling violin melody, Falstaff appears, tricked out in his finest clothes; the two men show exaggerated politeness before leaving the scene together to an orchestral reprise of 'Va, vecchio John'. Our knight, the orchestra seems to tell us, is winning the day.

2.ii A room in Ford's house A bustling string introduction ushers in Alice and Meg. They are soon joined by Quickly, who gives a detailed narrative of her interview with Falstaff, replete with mocking repetitions of 'dalle due alle tre'. Realizing that the hour of assignation is almost upon them, the women hurry about their preparations, ushering in a large laundry basket; but the busy mood is interrupted by Nannetta, who tearfully reveals that Ford has ordered her to marry old Dr Caius. Alice will have none of this, and assures Nannetta of her support. Preparations then continue, with Alice directing operations and briefly coming to the fore with 'Gaie comari di Windsor!', one of the few, brief moments (at least before the final scene) in which Verdi even hints at a conventional solo aria. Alice then settles down to strum her lute, and is soon joined by Falstaff, who offers elaborate courtship with an ornamented song of Beckmesser-like awkwardness before cele-

'Falstaff' (Verdi): Act 2 scene ii (a room in Ford's house) in the original production at La Scala, Milan (9 February 1893), with sets and costumes by Adolf Hohenstein: engraving from 'L'illustrazione italiana', 19 February 1893

brating his younger, nimbler self in the delightful vignette, 'Quand'ero paggio del Duca di Norfolk'.

However, just as the courtship reaches an intimate stage, Quickly rushes in to announce the imminent arrival of Meg Page. The music dives into a furious Allegro agitato, so beginning the first movement of a conventionally structured but highly complex concertato finale. This first section is in a near-constant state of manic energy: Falstaff hides behind a screen as Meg enters to announce the arrival of an insanely jealous Ford; Ford appears at the head of a band of followers, searches the laundry basket, then rushes off to seek his wife's lover elsewhere; Falstaff is then wedged painfully into the basket and covered with dirty clothes. A brief moment of calm ensues as Nannetta and Fenton meet and slip behind the screen for a few moments together, but very soon the energy is again released as the men reappear to continue their search. The music grinds to a halt as a loud kiss is heard behind the screen: the men are sure they have trapped their quarry, and the realization precipitates the second movement of the concertato, the Andante 'Se t'agguanto!' In the traditional way, this movement forms a still centre during which all can reflect on their contrasting positions: the men cautiously prepare to pounce; the women vow to keep the game alive; Falstaff emits muffled cries from his suffocating confinement; and Nannetta and

Fenton, oblivious to all, rise above the ensemble in lyrically expansive phrases. Eventually the spell is broken. The men overturn the screen, only to find Nannetta and Fenton, the latter angrily rebuked by Ford. But Bardolph seems to see Falstaff outside, and the men rush off again, allowing the women to summon their pages who – with a huge effort – hoist the basket up to the window. The men return just in time to see Falstaff tipped into the river below, and the act closes with a riotous fanfare of triumph.

Act 3.i *Outside the Garter Inn* As Boito remarked in a letter to Verdi, the problem in finding dramatic form for comic subjects was one of predictability: how to convince the audience that they should stay for the third act when the unravelling of the plot is already clear. In the case of *Falstaff* this problem is acute, as the protagonist's most clamorous punishment has already been inflicted by the close of Act 2. The startlingly original solution Boito and Verdi chose to this problem will be revealed in the second half of this act: but perhaps this first scene suffers slightly, the tempo of the opera winding down, its direction wavering. Falstaff's opening monologue is certainly the most fragmented passage in the opera, occasional reminiscences jostling with a series of violent changes as the knight bemoans his disgrace, calls for wine, and finally revives as the liquor tingles through his body to the accompaniment of a magnificent orchestral trill. The ensuing duet with Quickly repeats some of the motifs of their earlier encounter as Falstaff is again convinced, at first with some difficulty, of Alice's affection. A new assignation is made: Falstaff is to await his intended paramour at midnight under Herne's Oak in the Royal Park, disguised as the Black Huntsman. Quickly paints an evocative picture of the super-natural ambience and, as she leads Falstaff into the inn, the evocation is taken up by Alice, who has been observing the scene with Ford, Meg, Nannetta, Fenton and Caius. The scene then plays itself out in a relaxed, French-influenced musical setting, as the plotters decide on their disguises. Quickly overhears Ford and Caius, who are planning Caius's marriage to Nannetta that very night, and privately vows to stop them.

3.ii *Windsor forest* Distant horn-calls introduce Fenton, whose extended solo immediately marks the departure taken in this final scene, which for the most part is structured in discrete units, without the rapid changes that characterize the remainder of the opera. And the delicate, nocturnal ambience serves further to make this final scene self-contained, separate in both formal and timbral terms from the main drama, thus sidestepping the danger of anticlimax that Boito had feared. That the scene begins with Fenton's extended sonnet, 'Dal labbro il canto', is also significant, because the delicate atmosphere estab-lished in intervals by the young lovers through the opera now becomes the dominant strain in the music.

Fenton is rudely interrupted by Alice, who provides him with a disguise before they rush off to take their positions. Falstaff appears and solemnly counts the 12 bells of midnight. He is joined by Alice, and a fleeting repetition of their earlier meeting ensues before Meg enters to warn of an approaching pack of witches. As Falstaff throws himself to the ground, fearing death if he sets eyes on these supernatural beings, Nannetta begins a delicate invocation that eventually flowers into 'Sul fil d'un soffio etesio', yet another aria suffused with the soft orchestral colours that characterize this scene. A sudden Prestissimo ushers in the rest of the cast, who begin tormenting Falstaff in earnest. Their gleeful chorus, 'Pizzica, pizzica', later adorned with mock religious chanting, is halted only when Bardolph gets carried away and allows his hood to slip. Falstaff immediately recognizes him and bestows on him a generous torrent of abuse. Soon the entire deception is revealed, Falstaff assuming new stature in his philosophical acceptance of what has befallen him.

A gentle minuet introduces Caius and 'The Queen of the Fairies' (whom Caius believes to be Nannetta). They are joined by another couple and both pairs receive Ford's blessing. But with Ford's final words, the deception is revealed: 'The Queen of the Fairies' turns out to be Bardolph in disguise, and the other couple are – of course – Fenton and Nannetta. This time it is Ford's turn to admit defeat and (the minuet returning) he agrees to accept his daughter's marriage. Falstaff leads off the final ensemble, a comic fugue to the words 'Tutto nel mondo è burla' ('Everything in the world is a joke'). The ironic reference to an academic form, the polyphony and confusion of voices and, most of all, the constant, driving energy of the piece form a fitting end to Verdi's final opera.

*

Perhaps the most immediately obvious level of difference between *Falstaff* and all Verdi's previous operas lies in the music's tendency to respond in unprecedented detail to the verbal element of the drama. In much of the score, but especially in the great duets and monologues, the listener is bombarded by a stunning diversity of rhythms, orchestral textures, melodic motifs and harmonic devices. Passages that in earlier times would have furnished material for an entire number here crowd in on each other, shouldering themselves uncere-moniously to the fore in bewildering succession. And a large number of these fresh ideas spring in a direct and literal way from the words. Such exaggerated literalism would be obtrusive in a tragic opera, in which the need for underlying emotional communication often overrides responses to individual words. But here, in the comic context, it furnishes an important means of filling the musical space with an endless variety of colours. And this is by no means the only level of diversification in the score, for it is clear that Verdi was fully aware of the opera's 'polyphonic' texture and was – on occasion – even prepared to interrupt the drama in order to enhance it. As he said in a letter to Boito discussing Fenton's sonnet in Act 3, 'as far as the drama goes we could do without it; but . . . the whole piece provides me with a new colour for the musical palette'.

These new aspects, possible only through the medium of comedy, served to stimulate Verdi's creative imagination to new levels of fecundity. In the midst of an increasingly fragmented aesthetic world, he was able to follow the whim of the moment, to gaze back serenely on past achievements and, as he said so many times in letters to Boito, simply to enjoy himself. Few would deny how richly Verdi deserved this final triumph, or how heartening a message *Falstaff* offers. The opera leaves us with a musical image that exactly reflects those famous photographs of Verdi in his last years: an old man, in black hat, with eyes that have lived through a lifetime of struggle, smiling out wisely at the world.

R.P.

Fanciulla del West, La ('The Girl of the West' [The Girl of the Golden West])

Opera in three acts by Giacomo Puccini to a libretto by Guelfo Civinini and Carlo Zangarini after David Belasco's play *The Girl of the Golden West*; New York, Metropolitan Opera House, 10 December 1910.

The cast at the première included Emmy Destinn (Minnie), Enrico Caruso (Dick Johnson), and Pasquale Amato (Jack Rance), with Antonio Pini-Corsi, creator of Schaunard in *La bohème*, in the minute role of Happy. The conductor was Arturo Toscanini.

Minnie	soprano
Jack Rance *sheriff*	baritone
Dick Johnson/Ramerrez *bandit*	tenor
Nick *bartender at the Polka saloon*	tenor
Ashby *Wells Fargo agent*	bass
Sonora	baritone
Trin	tenor
Sid	baritone
Bello *miners*	baritone
Harry	tenor
Joe	tenor
Happy	baritone
Larkens	bass
Billy Jackrabbit *a Red Indian*	bass
Wowkle *his squaw*	mezzo-soprano
Jake Wallace *a travelling camp minstrel*	baritone
José Castro (*mestizo*) *one of Ramerrez's band*	bass
The Pony Express Rider	tenor
Men of the camp and boys of the ridge	

Setting A miners' camp at the foot of the Cloudy Mountains, California, during the gold rush, 1849–50

Early in 1907, during his first visit to New York for the Metropolitan premières of *Manon Lescaut* and *Madama Butterfly* (the latter based on a play by Belasco), Puccini saw three more of Belasco's plays performed on Broadway, among them *The Girl of the Golden West*. He was not enthusiastic. 'I like the ambience of the West', he wrote to Tito Ricordi (son of Giulio), 'but in all the "pièces" I've seen I've found only a few scenes here and there. Never a simple thread, all muddle and at times bad taste and old hat'. However, a seed had been sown; and when at the end of May Puccini went to London, his friend Sybil Seligman urged him to consider Belasco's drama, an Italian translation of which she procured for him.

By July Puccini was firmly decided. He wrote to his publisher asking him to obtain the rights as well as the author's permission to make certain changes to the action (these would amount to transferring the 'schoolmarm' episode from the third act to the first and writing a new final act set in the Californian forest, the action of which derives mostly from Octave Mirbeau's play *Les mauvais bergers*, a subject which Puccini had proposed in 1905, but which Illica had vetoed as too left-wing).

Of his previous librettists, Giuseppe Giacosa had died in 1906 and Luigi Illica was fully engaged on a libretto about Marie Antoinette (for which Puccini had contracted but which he never set). Tito Ricordi indicated Carlo Zangarini as the ideal collaborator, especially since his mother was American. In August the contracts were signed for what Puccini foretold would prove 'a second *Bohème*, only stronger, bolder and more spacious'.

Zangarini completed the libretto in January 1908. Puccini was satisfied with his general scheme but insisted that he take on a partner to polish the details. Zangarini threatened to go to law, but eventually agreed to collaborate with the Livornese poet Guelfo Civinini. By May the first two acts had been re-worked to Puccini's satisfaction and he was able to begin composition, but in October a domestic tragedy occurred. Their maidservant Doria Manfredi was suspected by Puccini's wife of having an affair with him; she persecuted Doria to such an extent that the girl committed suicide. An autopsy proved her to be a virgin, whereupon her family sued Elvira Puccini for defamation, and it was only after some time that a settlement was reached, Elvira escaped a prison sentence and the episode was closed. Resuming in August 1909, after a hiatus of nine months, Puccini completed the score a year later. To Sybil Seligman goes the credit for settling on the exact title. The opera was dedicated to the British queen, Alexandra, a keen admirer of Puccini's music, which often figured in private concerts at Buckingham Palace organized by Sir Paolo Tosti, music master to the royal family and himself a close friend of the composer.

In November 1910 Puccini set sail for America for what would be the first world première ever held at the Metropolitan. Belasco himself assisted Tito Ricordi with the production, on which no expense had been spared. To all appearances the opera was a triumphant success, the composer receiving 55 curtain calls, but the critics were guarded; many of his admirers were alienated by the work's new harmonic elaboration, combined with a curbing of the lyrical impulse that had marked his earlier scores. The Covent Garden première followed on 29 May 1911, again in Puccini's presence, conducted by Cleofonte Campanini with Emmy Destinn (Minnie), Amadeo Bassi (Johnson) and the Metropolitan's Sonora, Dinh Gilly, as Jack Rance. There the reception was less encouraging. *La fanciulla del West* was finally introduced to Italy at the Teatro Costanzi, Rome, on 12 June that year under Toscanini, with Eugenia Burzio (Minnie), Amadeo Bassi (Johnson) and Pasquale Amato (Rance), but it achieved no more than a *succès d'estime*. Although Puccini declared it his best opera to date it failed to enter the general repertory; nor until late in the century was it estimated at its true worth. However, the tenor solo from Act 3, 'Ch'ella mi creda libero e lontano', is said to have been sung by Italian troops during World War I as an equivalent to the English song 'It's a long way to Tipperary'.

*

Act I *The Polka saloon, at sunset* A prelude, intended by Puccini to evoke the vast Californian forest, presents two important ideas: the lyrical theme associated with the hero and heroine's first embrace (ex.1) and a modified version of the cake-walk motif which on its later appearance connotes the bandit

Ex.1 Allegro non troppo

Ramerrez. Then the distant voices of the approaching miners are heard. They enter in twos and threes to a hoedown theme, to be welcomed by Nick. Happy, Harry, Bello and Joe sit down to a game of faro with Sid as banker. Jake Wallace regales the company with the nostalgic song 'Che faranno i vecchi miei' (ex.2,

Ex.2 JAKE WALLACE
Andante tranquillo

Che fa – ran-noi vec-chi miei là lon – ta – no, là lon-

– ta – no? che fa – ran – no

['What will my old folks be doing there, far away?']

one of the most frequently repeated motifs in the opera, derived not, as generally stated, from the song 'Old Dog Tray', but from the 'Festive Sun Dance of the Zuni Indians' as arranged by Carlos Troyer), which causes Larkens to break down in tears. All present contribute money for his passage home. Sid is caught cheating and the miners threaten to hang him, but Rance pins a two of spades to his lapel as a mark of shame and has him thrown out of the saloon. Ashby arrives with news of the imminent capture of the bandit Ramerrez. A quarrel breaks out between Rance and Sonora, both in love with Minnie, and Sonora draws a revolver. Trin grabs his arm and diverts the shot. The appearance of Minnie herself to a broad, wide-intervalled theme (ex. 3, a fine example

of Puccini's newly enriched harmonic style) calms the atmosphere. The miners offer her their modest gifts and settle down to a bible-class, which she takes.

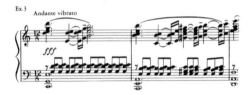

Ex.3 Andante vibrato

The Pony Express Rider arrives with the mail and Ashby interrogates him about one Nina Micheltorena, the bandit's mistress, who is expected to reveal his whereabouts. The men go into the adjoining dance hall leaving Rance alone with Minnie. He declares his love for her and talks of his unhappy background ('Minnie, dalla mia casa'). She, knowing him to be already married, imagines a different picture of domestic bliss based on memories of her own happy childhood ('Laggiù nel Soledad, ero piccina'). Nick returns with a stranger, whose identity is betrayed to the audience by the 'Ramerrez' motif (ex.2). He gives his name as Johnson. Rance takes an instant dislike to him and orders the men to force him to account for his presence. But Minnie, who remembers once meeting him on the road, vouches for him. A waltz is struck up in the hall, where Minnie and Johnson dance together. Ashby and a group of men enter from outside dragging in José Castro. Pretending to have deserted Ramerrez's band, Castro promises to lead them to the chief. His real purpose is to draw the miners away from the Polka so that Ramerrez may rob the saloon. When Johnson re-enters Castro manages to whisper his plan to him – a whistle outside will be the signal for him to proceed. The miners prepare to ride away with Castro, leaving Minnie to guard their earnings. She and Johnson express their dawning sympathy for one another in a duet based mainly on a reprise of the waltz melody. The whistle is heard but Johnson takes no action. He accepts Minnie's invitation to visit her later at her mountain hut, then leaves. Nick returns to find Minnie absorbed in the recollection of Johnson's last words to her – that she has the face of an angel. To echoes of ex. 3 the curtain falls.

Act 2 *Minnie's cabin, later that evening* Wowkle sings to her child a lullaby that develops into a duet with Billy Jackrabbit as both think vaguely of getting married. Minnie enters, orders supper for two and with subdued excitement prepares to receive her visitor. Johnson arrives; Minnie fends off his attempt to embrace her and to a recall of the waltz they begin a decorous conversation, during which Minnie describes her life at the camp ('Oh, se sapeste'). As Wowkle brings the food the orchestra outlines a

Emmy Destinn as Minnie and Pasquale Amato as Jack Rance (Caruso, as Dick Johnson, has collapsed at the table) in Act 2 of the original production of Puccini's 'La fanciulla del West' at the Metropolitan Opera House, New York, 10 December 1910

pentatonic theme loosely related to the waltz that will frame the love duet, whose central movement is evolved from ex.1, initially twisted into a whole-tone scale. Johnson offers to leave, but a blizzard makes it necessary for him to stay the night.

The posse headed by Rance knock at the door. After concealing Johnson behind the bed-curtain Minnie admits them. They are concerned for her safety, Rance tells her, having discovered that Johnson is in fact Ramerrez and is still in the neighbourhood. Minnie sends them away, then rounds angrily on her guest. Remorsefully he makes excuses for his past life, which he now intends to abandon for ever. Minnie can forgive the bandit, but not the man who stole her first kiss under false pretences, and she orders him out of the house. A shot rings out, and he staggers back against the door wounded. Minnie helps him into the attic before Rance arrives, certain that he has found his man. Minnie defies him to search the premises. Thwarted, Rance is about to leave when a drop of blood falls from the ceiling onto his hand. Ignoring Minnie's protests he orders Johnson to come down. Johnson does so and collapses in a faint. Minnie plays her last card. Knowing Rance to be a gambler she challenges him to a game of poker. If he wins, he may take her as

his 'wife'; if he loses then Johnson belongs to her. Rance accepts, and is on the point of winning when she pretends to feel faint; as he goes to fetch her a glass of water she takes a new pack of cards from her stocking and lays out a winning hand. He accepts her victory with a bad grace.

Act 3 *A clearing in the Californian forest at dawn, some time later* Rance and Nick are brooding before a fire; Ashby, Billy Jackrabbit and several miners are sleeping nearby. Nick attempts to console Rance, commending his gallant behaviour in dealing with Minnie. At the sound of distant voices Ashby and the men wake up and joyfully predict the bandit's capture. Rance exults in the prospect of revenge, while Ashby hurries away to join the man-hunt. As the orchestra builds up an impressive action scene recalling previous themes, various miners posted on the look-out describe Johnson's attempts to elude his pursuers. He is brought in tethered to his horse to face an accusing mob. Billy Jackrabbit is ordered to prepare a noose for the lynching, but is secretly bribed by Nick to take his time. Johnson proudly defends himself against the charge of murder. In the few minutes remaining to him he asks only that Minnie never be told of his fate. In the aria 'Ch'ella mi creda libero e lontano', the one self-contained piece in the entire score, he expresses the wish that she may believe him to have gone free to lead a better life in some distant land. Enraged, Rance punches him in the face; but Johnson's words have already caused the men to hesitate. Minnie rides in on horseback to a harmonically distorted version of ex. 3. When her pleas for mercy prove vain she rushes to Johnson's side, draws a pistol and threatens to shoot both him and herself. During the ensemble that follows opinion among the miners is divided. In the end it is Sonora who sways the balance. Johnson is released, and as he and Minnie ride away to a future of happiness the men bid their beloved 'sister' a sorrowful farewell to the strains of ex.3.

*

La fanciulla del West is a remarkable instance of self-renewal on the part of a composer who would seem to have exhausted a vein of predominantly feminine softness. The opera's atmosphere is unyieldingly masculine, at times brutal, the harmonies more astringent than ever before with plentiful use of whole-tone chords and unresolved dissonances, the rhythms vigorous, sometimes syncopated and the lyrical moments comparatively few. The influence of Debussy is clear, though, as always, perfectly integrated within the composer's personal style. The Californian ambience is evoked with the aid of American folktunes and folkdances, either authentic or imitated, with a Red Indian chant to characterize Billy Jackrabbit and his squaw. Minnie is unique among Puccini's heroines – cheerfully authoritative with a touch of the Puritan schoolmistress yet susceptible to tender passion and ready to compromise her strict principles for the sake of the man she loves.

Orchestrally La fanciulla del West is Puccini's most ambitious undertaking before Turandot, his forces including quadruple woodwind, two harps and an assortment of percussion, from all of which he distilled a vast range of instrumental colour from the delicate to the barbaric. Though it has never attained the easy popularity of its three predecessors, the opera has always won the respect of musicians, among them Webern and Ravel.   J.B.

Faust

Opéra in five acts by Charles-François Gounod to a libretto by Jules Barbier and Michel Carré after Carré's Faust et Marguerite and Johann Wolfgang von Goethe's Faust, Part I (in the French translation by Gérard de Nerval); Paris, Théâtre Lyrique, 19 March 1859.

At the première Marie Caroline Carvalho, wife of the theatre's director, sang the role of Marguerite,

Emile Balanqué sang Méphistophélès, and Joseph-Théodore-Désiré Barbot took the role of Faust, having learnt it in only three weeks.

Le docteur Faust a philosopher	tenor
Méphistophélès	bass
Marguerite	soprano
Valentin a soldier, Marguerite's brother	baritone
Wagner friend of Valentin	baritone
Siébel student of Faust	soprano
Marthe Marguerite's guardian	soprano
Young girls, labourers, students, soldiers, burghers, matrons, invisible demons, church choir, witches, queens and courtesans of antiquity, celestial voices	
Setting Germany, 16th century	

During his tenure of the Prix de Rome, 1839–2, Gounod's interest in Faust Part I as an operatic subject was aroused by Nerval's translation of Goethe's play. He attempted a setting of the church scene as early as 1849, but plans for an opera did not materialize until he met the libretto-writing team of Barbier and Carré in 1855. Carré himself had already written Faust et Marguerite, a three-act play loosely fashioned after Goethe that was moderately successful at the Gymnase-Dramatique in 1850. It provided the basic scaffolding for Gounod's work, including the idea of enlarged roles for Valentin and Siébel (a minor player in Goethe's Auerbachs Keller episode). Some elements from Goethe not included by Carré were also brought into the opera, most notably the death of Valentin, the Walpurgisnacht, the prison scene and the apotheosis; Goethe's play, however, is best not taken into account in critical assessments of Gounod's opera as a piece of music theatre.

Gounod finished composing Faust in autumn 1858 and it was immediately put into rehearsal at the Théâtre Lyrique. In the course of dress rehearsals at the end of February 1859 Hector Gruyer's inability to cope with the part of Faust became painfully clear, and he was replaced at that late stage by Barbot, a veteran from the Opéra-Comique roster.

The score that Gounod brought to rehearsals was much longer than the one eventually performed. Several entire numbers were cut before the première: a trio in Act 1 for Siébel, Faust and Wagner; a duet in Act 2 for Marguerite and Valentin; three sets of couplets for one of Marguerite's girlfriends (Lise), Valentin and Siébel, as well as a chorus of young girls in Act 4; and a large strophic piece for Marguerite in the last act. The couplets for Valentin ('Chaque jour nouvelle affaire') were replaced before the première by the Soldiers' Chorus, 'Gloire immortelle de nos aïeux', the music of which was taken from Gounod's aborted operatic project Ivan le terrible. During the

*'Faust' (Gounod), Act 1 (Faust's study): Jean-Baptiste Faure (left) as Méphistophélès and Giovanni Mario as Faust, with the
vision of Marguerite in the background (Covent Garden, 1864); lithograph from a contemporary sheet music cover*

first rehearsal period the church scene was also
transferred from its initial spot after Valentin's
couplets to the end of the fourth act, possibly at the
insistence of Carvalho. Gounod tore the cut sections
out of his autograph full score, and none of this music
was published in his lifetime, save for Siébel's Act 4
couplets 'Versez vos chagrins', which appeared as an
extract from the opera shortly after the première. The
autographs of the trio, duet and Valentin's *couplets*,
however, surfaced in public collections during the
1970s.

Faust was a considerable success during its first
run at the Théâtre Lyrique in 1859. It was published
in June of that year by Antoine Choudens, who
helped arrange productions of the work in
Strasbourg, Rouen and Bordeaux in 1860. Gounod
supplied recitatives to replace the original spoken
dialogue for these performances. Productions on
many major German stages followed in the next two
years; at the Dresden première in August 1861 the
work was called *Margarethe* for the first time, a
symbolic distancing from Goethe's play that has
endured in Germany. In the second edition of the

vocal score (1860), as well as in several early
productions, the church scene was moved from the
end of the fourth act to before the Soldiers' Chorus;
the composer himself was non-committal on the
placement of the church scene and there is a long
record for both solutions. *Faust* had its Italian
première at La Scala in November 1862 and was first
produced in England (in Italian) at Her Majesty's
Theatre in June 1863. At the first English-language
production in January 1864 (also at Her Majesty's)
Gounod arranged music from the opera's prelude to
create a new solo number in Act 2 for Valentin (sung
by Charles Santley), 'Even the bravest heart may
swell', to a text by his friend Henry Chorley (the poet
Onésime Pradère later supplied the French verse
'Avant de quitter ces lieux'); the composer made
this famous addition reluctantly, however, and the
number never appeared in a French vocal score in his
lifetime. Following the bankruptcy of the Théâtre
Lyrique, *Faust* had a lavish production at the Opéra
in March 1869 with a ballet and a new set of *couplets*
for Méphistophélès supplied by the composer;
Christine Nilsson sang Marguerite, Jean-Baptiste

Faure was Méphistophélès. It became the most frequently performed opera at that house (six new productions over 100 years) and one of the staples of the international repertory, though since World War II its popularity has waned somewhat.

*

Act 1 *Faust's study* Rather than foreshadow later melodies and situations or the opera's principal dramatic argument, the instrumental prelude illustrates Faust's dilemma at the beginning of the work: it alludes both to his erudition, by means of chromatic contrapuntal texture, and to the simple joys of nature, through music tinged with pastoral *couleur locale*. At the outset Faust is deeply depressed by his inability to attain fulfilment through knowledge. In an opening number dominated by measured declamation and rapidly changing textures (an unusual first scene for French opera of the period) he contemplates suicide, but is twice stopped short of drinking poison by the sound of an offstage pastoral chorus. He condemns happiness, science and faith, and calls upon Satan for deliverance: Méphistophélès duly appears (duet, 'Me voici'). Faust confesses that he covets youth above all and launches into an energetic *cabalette* ('A moi les plaisirs'). Méphistophélès agrees to indulge the philosopher in return for eventual service in the nether regions. When Faust hesitates to accept that condition, Méphistophélès conjures up a vision of Marguerite, while love music from the later garden scene is anticipated in the orchestra. Immediately enamoured, Faust signs the parchment and is transformed into a young nobleman. Both sing an ensemble reprise of 'A moi les plaisirs', a semitone higher than at its first appearance, to bring down the curtain.

Act 2 *Fairgrounds at the town gates; a tavern is seen on the left* The curtain opens to a festive chorus of students, soldiers, burghers, young girls and matrons who sing individually at first and are then contrapuntally combined in Meyerbeerian style in a rousing conclusion. The soldier Valentin appears, clutching a medallion given to him by his sister Marguerite; he is about to leave for battle and instructs his friends, including Wagner and Siébel, to look after her. They sit down for a final drink. Méphistophélès suddenly materializes and entertains them with a strophic song about the golden calf (*ronde*, 'Le veau d'or'), the blasphemy rendered more trenchant by a musical parody of hymn style just before the refrain is heard each time. Valentin is incited to violence when Méphistophélès takes the name of his sister lightly, but his sword breaks in mid-air before reaching its target. Realizing that they are confronted with a sinister supernatural power, Valentin and his companions brandish the crossed pommels of their swords before the Devil (chorale, 'De l'enfer qui vient émousser') – a visual echo of the Benediction of the Swords in Meyerbeer's *Les Huguenots*. Méphistophélès, left alone on the stage, is soon joined by Faust and a group of waltzing villagers (waltz and chorus, 'Ainsi que la brise légère'). When Marguerite appears among the villagers, Faust offers her his arm. She modestly rejects his advance and quickly departs, a first appearance for the tragic heroine that is effective because it is understated, brief and set against a background of nonchalant *divertissement*.

Act 3 *Marguerite's garden* Siébel is in love with Marguerite and leaves a bouquet for her (*couplets*, 'Faites-lui mes aveux'). Faust and Méphistophélès enter; while the latter procures a gift for Marguerite, Faust apostrophizes her home and the protective embrace of nature (*cavatine*, 'Salut! demeure chaste et pure'). Méphistophélès returns and places a jewel box for the young girl to find. Marguerite appears, wondering about Faust in a recitative that is confined to a single pitch low in the tessitura, a restrained musical utterance for unaccustomed thoughts. She goes on to sing a large three-part *air*. The initial slow section of this composite set piece is a ballade about the King of Thulé (Il était un roi de Thulé') with an archaic flavour rendered by modal inflections in the music. In the ensuing section Marguerite comes across the offerings of both suitors; mesmerized by the jewels, she sings a *cabalette* (the 'Jewel Song') that exudes breathless excitement through effective distribution of the text ('Ah! je ris de me voir'). Dame Marthe, Marguerite's guardian, tells her that the jewels must be a gift from an admirer. Méphistophélès and Faust join the two women. The former attempts to seduce Marthe, accompanied by music bustling with comic verve, while Faust and Marguerite converse in a more sentimental vein and with more naturalistic declamation (quartet, 'Prenez mon bras'). After both temporarily disappear from view, Méphistophélès casts a spell over the flowers in the garden; the sound of horns beneath shimmering strings evokes an aura of the supernatural. When the lovers return, Faust woos her directly (duet, 'Laisse-moi, laisse-moi contempler ton visage'), and Marguerite coyly responds by plucking petals of a daisy in the game of 'He loves me, he loves me not'; a rising sequence in 3rds carries the music from F major to B major, a far-reaching modulation that underlines her final 'He loves me'. The music veers to an incandescent D♭ major for the central section of the duet ('O nuit d'amour'), containing Marguerite's confession of love. She suddenly breaks away from Faust's embrace and in an agitated *cabalette* ('Partez, partez') begs him to leave. The *cabalette* does not, however, bring the number to a close: Faust continues with a reminiscence of his *cavatine*, and, before running off, Marguerite promises to see him the next day. Faust resolves to abandon his pursuit but is suddenly prevented from doing so by Méphistophélès, who sardonically suggests to the philosopher that he remain to witness Marguerite's soliloquy at her window. She yearns for Faust's quick return, her line running above the fragmentation and development (with continually changing instrumental colours) of the melody that will burst forth in complete form and *fortissimo* at the moment Faust emerges from the shadows to take her into his arms.

Act 4.i *Marguerite's room* Marguerite has given birth to Faust's child; she is ignored by young girls in the street. Saddened that Faust seems to have abandoned her, she sits down to spin. Her *air*, 'Il ne revient pas', compares favourably with the more famous spinning songs for the same character by Schubert and Berlioz; particularly evocative is the setting for the refrain 'Il ne revient pas', an apt illustration of her desolation. Siébel, ever faithful, attempts to revive her spirits.

4.ii *A public square* The return of Valentin is heralded by a Soldiers' Chorus ('Gloire immortelle de nos aïeux'), including a noisy stage band. After receiving evasive replies from Siébel to enquiries about his sister, Valentin furiously charges into the house. While he is inside, Méphistophélès and Faust appear. The former satirically plays a lover delivering a strophic serenade beneath Marguerite's window ('Vous qui faites l'endormie'); the effect is made particularly grotesque by the faulty declamation and incisive chromatic turns in the orchestra – in stark contrast with the suave and heartfelt delivery of Faust beneath her window in the previous act. Valentin re-emerges and demands to know who is responsible for Marguerite's fall from innocence. Faust draws his sword while Valentin and Méphistophélès exchange threats (trio, 'Que voulez-vous, messieurs?'); the orchestra unleashes a juggernaut of dotted rhythms that culminate in the duel between Valentin and Faust. Valentin is mortally wounded. As he dies, he lays the blame upon Marguerite and damns her for eternity; the assembled townspeople urge him to display Christian compassion.

4.iii *A church* Marguerite attempts to pray but organ music, imprecations from Méphistophélès and a liturgical chorus (originally set to the Latin text of the 'Dies irae') combine to oppress her. Formal coherence is achieved largely by two extended periodic solos for each of the principals: Marguerite's 'Seigneur accueillez ma prière' in C major is a counterpoise to Méphistophélès' previous 'Souviens-toi du passé' in C minor. She succeeds in completing her prayer but faints when Méphistophélès unleashes a final curse.

Act 5.i *The Harz Mountains: Walpurgis Night* A chorus of will-o'-the wisps is heard as Méphistophélès and Faust appear. They are soon surrounded by a group of witches (chorus, 'Un, deux, et trois'; only

in the first edition). Faust wishes to flee but Méphistophélès hastens to carry him off.

5.ii *A decorated cavern peopled with queens and courtesans of antiquity* Faust is surrounded by the most beautiful women in history and momentarily loses his presence of mind in a strophic drinking song ('Doux nectar', only in the first edition; the ballet may be inserted in place of the song). Suddenly Faust sees an image of Marguerite and demands to be taken to her. As Méphistophélès and Faust depart, the mountain closes and the witches return.

5.iii *The interior of a prison* Marguerite has been incarcerated for infanticide, but through the offices of Méphistophélès Faust has obtained the keys to her cell. Marguerite awakens ecstatically to the sound of Faust's voice. They sing a love duet ('Oui c'est toi je t'aime') in which past moments of bliss are recalled (the latter section, 'Viens! viens! quittons ces lieux!', appeared for the first time in Italian-language editions in 1864 and is absent from most French editions). Faust begs her to flee with him. Méphistophélès suddenly appears and urges Faust and Marguerite to follow him. Marguerite resists and calls for divine protection, singing the wide-spanning heroic melody 'Anges purs, anges radieux' in an ascending stepwise sequence. The goal of the sequence is the C major of the concluding apotheosis 'Christ est ressuscité!' (recalling the tonality of Marguerite's supplication in the church scene), at which she dies. Faust falls to his knees in prayer as Marguerite's soul rises to heaven.

*

The case against *Faust* has been made often and vociferously. Buttressed by views of Marguerite as part society débutante, Méphistophélès as tinged with shades of Leporello, and Faust as little more than lovesick, many have not detected the sort of universality in the characters often admired in other 19th-century masterpieces. As a corollary, the transcendental significance apparently demanded by Goethe's play has been considered as sacrificed to bathetic sentimentality, while the musical style has been criticized as wanting in dramatic chiaroscuro, merely elegant and sometimes even saccharine.

Standing prominently on the other side of the critical ledger is the sheer effectiveness of many scenes on the stage. In a highly personal adaptation of Goethe's episode of Valentin's death, Gounod draws a clear and theatrically vivid line between the intolerance of Valentin and the Christian morality of the majority. The church tableau brilliantly captures Marguerite's isolation against an impersonal background of archaic organ preludes, chant-like choral writing and a gothic set. The ringing down of the Act 3 curtain with Méphistophélès' laughter and a *fortissimo* orchestral statement of a melody heard earlier only softly, and in a fragmented form, was so impressive that the procedure was taken up by composers such as Ponchielli and Cilea. The concluding apotheosis works well as a spectacular culmination to the musically uplifting 'Anges purs, anges radieux'. Gounod is also successful with the more intimate episodes for Marguerite in Act 3. For example, there is a touching spontaneity in her declaimed interruptions in her ballade to wonder about Faust that was new to the French stage in its day and a harbinger of the naturalistic characterization of later figures in French opera such as Massenet's Manon. The ensuing quartet features a wealth of finely wrought detail, both in orchestration (too often overlooked in critiques of the work) and shaping of the melodic line.

Faust became particularly important to the French musical establishment at the end of the century. A work by a winner of the Prix de Rome that could claim to be thoroughly modern and personal in style at its première, and go on to international stages, was a significant enhancement to the musical prestige of a French operatic culture previously dominated by Meyerbeer and the none-too-easily exportable genre of opéra comique. Its national value was enhanced because, after some initial assessments as 'Wagnerian', Gounod's compositional voice in Faust was heard as important in the definition of a 'French' musical aesthetic.   S.Hr.

Favorite, La [*La favorita* ('The Favoured One')]

Opéra in four acts by Gaetano Donizetti to a libretto by Alphonse Royer and Gustave Vaëz, with additions by Eugène Scribe, partly based on the plot of *L'ange de Nisida* (derived in some measure from Baculard d'Arnaud: *Le comte de Comminges*), on which the story of Eleonora di Guzman is grafted; Paris, Opéra, 2 December 1840.

The original cast was headed by Rosine Stoltz (Léonor), Gilbert Duprez (Fernand), Paul Barroilhet (Alphonse) and Nicholas Levasseur (Balthazar).

Alphonse XI (Alfonso XI) *King of Castile*	baritone
Léonor de Guzman (Leonora di Gusmann) *his mistress*	mezzo-soprano
Inès (Inez) *her confidante*	soprano
Fernand (Fernando) *a novice*	tenor
Don Gaspar *a king's officer*	tenor
Balthazar (Baldassare) *Superior of a monastery*	bass
Monks, ladies-in-waiting, courtiers	
Setting The Monastery of St James of Compostela, the island of León, and the gardens and halls of the Alcázar, about 1340	

Donizetti had moved to Paris in 1838, engaged to write three works for the Opéra. The following year he also completed *L'ange de Nisida* for the Théâtre de la Renaissance, but this was never performed as the management went bankrupt. Donizetti salvaged much of its score for *La favorite*, which contains some of his finest music. It derives from a tangle of sources: the oldest discernible strand goes back to an incomplete Italian *opera semiseria*, *Adelaide*, a good deal of which went into *L'ange de Nisida*. Much of the first three acts and all of Act 4 of *La favorite*, except for two solo passages, derive from *L'ange de Nisida*, as the dated autograph testifies. The chief new music is found in the *airs*, which in Donizetti's usual fashion were tailored to the particular vocal aptitudes of his first cast.

The work was last performed at the Opéra, its 692nd outing, in 1918, and although it disappeared from this repertory, it continued to be given by French provincial theatres. In 1912 *La favorite* was recorded, nearly complete, with a French-language cast, including Ketty Lapeyrette (Léonor) and Henri Albers (Alphonse).

Outside France, the work is best known in its corrupt Italian version. It was first given in Italy at Padua in June 1842, as *Leonora di Guzman*, and at La Scala, in a different translation, in August 1843, as *Elda*, with Marietta Alboni in the title role. Donizetti had nothing to do with either of these productions. The opera had already come out in a German translation, first at Kassel, on 31 May 1841, and in December of that year in Vienna, as *Richard und Mathilde*. It was also a feature of the Italian seasons in Berlin and Vienna in the 1840s.

In London, it was first given in an English translation by Edward Fitzball on 18 October 1843. Its first Italian production there was on 16 February 1847; however, its great popularity, lasting nearly half a century, began in 1848 when the leading roles were first assumed by Giulia Grisi and Giovanni Mario. At Covent Garden, Pauline Lucca, Zélia Trebelli, Medea Mei[-Figner] and Sofia Scalchi were popular Leonoras.

The opera was introduced to the USA at New Orleans in its original French guise (9 February 1843), and it was in French that the work was first given in New York two years later; it was not sung there in Italian until 1855. Its first Metropolitan production, featuring Eugenia Mantelli, Giuseppe Cremonini, Mario Ancona and Pol Plançon, was in 1895; ten years later it was revived with Edyth Walker, Enrico Caruso and Antonio Scotti, after which it had to wait 73 years for another run, when Shirley Verrett and Luciano Pavarotti took the leading roles. The opera survives most hardily in Italy, where it has been particularly associated in the last half-century with Ebe Stignani, Giulietta Simionato and Fiorenza

Cossotto. Gianni Poggi and Gianni Raimondi were well received as Fernando, as was Ettore Bastianini's Alfonso. There have been a number of recordings in Italian, including one with a cast headed by Cossotto and Pavarotti.

*

Act I.i *The courtyard of the Monastery of St James of Compostela* There is a restless, brooding overture. As the monks enter the chapel, singing a chorus based on a C major scale, Balthazar asks Fernand why he holds back. The novice confesses that he is obsessed by an unknown woman whom he had seen praying in the chapel; his *air* ('Un ange, une femme inconnue'/'Una vergine, un angiol di Dio') conveys his ardent nature in the subtly varied rhythm of his phrases. Balthazar tries to restore Fernand's thoughts to piety (duo, 'Sais-tu que devant la tiare'/'Non sai tu che un giusto'), but the young novice remains obdurate and the Superior orders him away.

I.ii *A bosky retreat on the Island of León* Inès and the chorus of ladies enjoy their surroundings (*air* and chorus, 'Rayons dorés'/'Bei raggi lucenti' – borrowed from *Pia de' Tolomei*). Fernand, blindfold at Léonor's instigation, arrives in a small boat and is warmly greeted (*air* and chorus, 'Doux zéphyr, sois-lui fidèle'/'Dolce zeffiro il seconda'). He asks for information, but they teasingly remain silent and

Rosine Stoltz as Léonor and Gilbert Duprez as Fernand in Act 4 (the courtyard of the Monastery of St James of Compostela) of Donizetti's 'La favorite' in the original production at the Paris Opéra (Salle Le Peletier), 2 December 1840: lithograph by Desmaisons after Lépaulle, frontispiece to the first edition of the vocal score (Paris: Schlesinger, 1840)

then go off as the beautiful Léonor enters (duo, 'Mon idole'/'Ah, mio bene'). Unaware of her status as *maîtresse en titre* to the king, Fernand seeks to learn her identity, but she knows she cannot love the young cavalier without dishonouring him and she hands him a military commission, hoping to assure his future. She leaves him convinced that she loves him, however, even though she is evasive. Alone, he considers the prospects of glorious achievement in battle as a means of winning her favour (*air*, 'Oui, ta voix m'inspire'/'Sì, che un tuo solo accento').

Act 2 *The gardens of the recently conquered Alcázar* King Alphonse meditates on the beauty of the palace so recently conquered from the Moors, won for him by a certain Fernand. Don Gaspar informs him that a papal messenger demands an audience, but the king's thoughts are only of Léonor, as his *air* ('Léonor, viens'/'Vien, Leonora'), at once sensuous and impulsive, shows. She appears, sad and withdrawn (duo, 'Quand j'ai quitté le château de mon père'/'Quando le soglie paterne vareai'), but does not reveal that her affections have changed; instead of concluding with a rapid section, this episode ends with an Andante duet ('O mon amour'/'Ah! l'alto ardor'), in which the irony of the situation is reflected in the parallel writing for the voices. The court enters to behold the ballet the king has ordered for the victory celebrations. Don Gaspar reveals to the king that a letter to Léonor from an unknown suitor has been intercepted. She confesses that she loves another, but they are interrupted by the entrance of the furious Balthazar, papal bull of excommunication in hand. He begins the finale, where his denunciation ('Redoutez la fureur d'un Dieu'/'Ah paventa d'un Dio vendicatore') shows that Donizetti remembered the outraged cardinal in Halévy's *La Juive* (which he had heard in Paris in 1835); Balthazar demands that the king renounce his mistress and reinstate his legal consort. When Alphonse angrily refuses, Balthazar delivers an anathema, while the courtiers and Léonor recoil in horror at the inescapable threat of excommunication. This extensive finale, largely built on predictable sequences, is unusual in that it makes do without the principal tenor; Fernand does not appear in Act 2.

Act 3 *The interior of the Alcázar* Fernand has been summoned to court to be ennobled. Don Gaspar enters with the king, discussing what is to be done about Léonor. Alphonse greets Fernand as his benefactor and urges him to ask whatever favour he pleases; Fernand confesses his love for a noblewoman whom he would make his wife. Léonor enters and, when Fernand indicates that she is the lady, the king is cynically amused at this solution to an embarrassing problem. Alphonse's suave aria with *pertichini* ('Pour tant d'amour'/'A tanto amor') is a gem of ironic courtliness. Léonor is left alone to confront her shame and weigh the chances of Fernand's forgiving her when he learns the truth, as she does in a double aria ('O mon Fernand'/'O, mio Fernando'). Léonor entrusts Inès with the delicate task of revealing her situation to Fernand before the ceremony; but her messenger is detained by Don Gaspar and other spiteful courtiers (chorus, 'Déjà dans la chapelle'/'Di già nella cappella').

At the ceremony Fernand shows his usual gallantry; but while the marriage is being solemnized, the contemptuous courtiers denounce him as an opportunist (chorus, 'Quel marché de bassesse'/'Questo è troppo in mia fè!'). Emerging from the chapel, Fernand is outraged when the courtiers, declaring that honour means more than love, refuse his hand. He threatens to fight them, when Balthazar, learning of Fernand's marriage, reveals that his bride is the king's mistress. Léonor discovers that her message went undelivered; before she can explain, Fernand confronts the king, tears off his orders and breaks his sword, which he casts at the king's feet. Alphonse recognizes Fernand's innate nobility (finale, 'O ciel! de son âme la noble fierté'/'O ciel, di quell'alma il puro candor'); Léonor is beside herself, but at the end Balthazar takes his disillusioned novice back to the monastery.

Act 4 *The courtyard of the Monastery of St James of Compostela* Balthazar, in an *air* of noble simplicity ('Les cieux s'emplissent d'étincelles'/'Splendon più belle in ciel le stelle'), leads the monks and novices in evening prayer. Fernand is about to take his final vows when Balthazar is summoned to a novice, just arrived. Fernand's thoughts return to Léonor, whom he loves in spite of her past. His *romance* ('Ange si pur'/'Spirto gentil') is a fine example of Donizetti's gift for making long structures from simple melodic germs. Balthazar returns and leads Fernand into the chapel for the long-awaited service. The new novice is Léonor, stricken with a fatal illness but impelled to see Fernand once more. When she understands that he is pronouncing his vows, she makes to leave, but her strength fails. Coming from the chapel, Fernand assists his 'brother' but is outraged when he discovers it is Léonor; he orders her away, but she begs for mercy (Larghetto, 'Fernand, imite la clémence du ciel'/'Pietoso al par del nume'). He is so moved when he understands that she is desperately ill that, in an impassioned duet ('Viens, viens, je cède éperdu'/'Vieni, ah! vieni') he resolves to go away with her. Hearing his forgiveness, she dies in his arms while the monks pray for her soul; Fernand is convinced that tomorrow they will repeat their prayer for him.

*

This grand but sober work proved the most substantial success of Donizetti's serious French operas. Its fourth act has long been regarded, not least by

Toscanini, as one of Donizetti's supreme accomplishments. Léonor's 'O mon Fernand' stands as one of the great monologues of French opera. A critical edition of the original French *La favorite* was used for a production in Bergamo in 1991, but a new Italian version is badly needed to restore to international audiences this noble work in a form consistent with Donizetti's intentions.   **W.A.**

Fedeltà premiata, La ('Fidelity Rewarded')

Dramma giocoso in three acts by Joseph Haydn to a libretto by Giambattista Lorenzi; Eszterháza, 25 February 1781.

The singers at the first performance were Maria Jermoli (Fillide/Celia), her husband Guglielmo Jermoli (Fileno), Teresa Taveggia (Amaranta), Benedetto Bianchi (Count Perrucchetto), Costanza Valdesturla (Nerina and Diana), Leopold Dichtler (Lindoro) and Antonio Pesci (Melibeo).

Fillide/Celia *lover of Fileno*	mezzo-soprano
Fileno *lover of Fillide*	tenor
Amaranta *a vain and arrogant*	
woman	mezzo-soprano
Count Perrucchetto	baritone
Nerina *a nymph, inconstant in love*	soprano
Lindoro *brother of Amaranta, a temple*	
assistant	tenor
Melibeo *high priest at the temple, in love*	
with Amaranta	bass
Diana *Roman goddess of the hunt*	soprano
Choruses of nymphs, shepherds, hunters and	
followers of Diana	
Setting Countryside in the land of Cumae, near	
Naples	

In Haydn's opera the nine characters of Lorenzi's original libretto, *L'infedeltà fedele* (set by Cimarosa in 1779), are reduced to eight: the role of Viola, a peasant girl in love with Vuzzachio, is conflated with that of Nerina; Nerina is no longer the daughter of Melibeo; and Vuzzachio's name is changed to the loftier-sounding Lindoro. The serious roles, Fileno and Fillide, and the comic parts, Count Perrucchetto and Amaranta, remain unchanged. All traces of Neapolitan dialect are removed and the crude jokes of Viola and Vuzzachio are excised. Also omitted are Amaranta's haughty French phrases; she is a more refined character in Haydn's setting. Even the Count and Lindoro are less silly than in the earlier version, in part because several aria texts are entirely new. Despite these changes the basic structure of the original drama remains unchanged; *serio* and *giocoso* still unite to create, in Lorenzi's words, 'a mixed entertainment, discreetly containing elements of both, so that everyone ... [might] find a theatrical event corresponding to his taste'.

La fedeltà premiata, written for the inauguration of the new opera house built to replace the one destroyed by fire on 19 November 1779, was Haydn's most successful comic opera, remaining in the repertory until 1785. It was completed in the autumn of 1780, but delays in the construction of the new theatre pushed the opening date into the new year. Haydn's pride in the work is recorded in a letter to the publisher Artaria dated 27 May 1781: 'I assure you that no such work has been heard in Paris up to now, nor perhaps in Vienna either'. A second, shorter version, as a 'dramma pastorale giocoso', was first performed on 29 September 1782, with only two of the original seven cast members. The opera subsequently received highly acclaimed German language productions at the Kärntnertortheater, Vienna, in 1784, seen by Joseph II and perhaps also Mozart, and at the Erdödy Theatre, Pressburg (Bratislava), 1785–7. The fantastic elements, including the festive hunt for the feast of Diana and her appearance as 'dea ex machina', were spectacularly rendered by Jean-Pierre Ponnelle at the Holland Festival (1970) and again in Zürich (1975). Bernard Haitink conducted the opera at Glyndebourne in 1979, and a condensed (two-act) version was presented at the Stadttheater, Basle, in 1986.

*

Act 1.i *Pastoral setting outside the Temple of Diana* After the opening chorus, Amaranta reads an inscription on an altar, giving an outline of the plot: every year two faithful lovers must be sacrificed to the local sea monster until a hero offers his own life. Only then will peace return to the land of Cumae. The time for the sacrifice is near. Thus begins the hunt – vividly presented in the overture, subsequently used as the last movement of Symphony no.73, 'La chasse' – for sacrificial victims to be offered to Diana. The characters have ample justification for their circumspect actions, since to be in love without the consent of the devious high priest, Melibeo, means certain disaster. Under Melibeo's protection, Lindoro switches his allegiance from Nerina to the noble Celia. Amaranta is in the process of accepting Melibeo's favour when Count Perrucchetto (literally 'wig-maker') arrives (shouting 'Salva, salva, aiuto'), claiming to have been pursued by thieves. His fright, cowardice and slightly deranged state are readily portrayed in this breathless G minor aria reminiscent of Haydn's *Sturm und Drang* style. Viewing the Count as her entrée to the nobility, Amaranta soon curries his favour, arousing Melibeo's jealousy.

1.ii *A garden* Fileno, heartbroken, laments Fillide, his beloved, who, so he believes, died several years ago. Nerina, attracted to him, listens to his tale of woe

and consoles him with her own love problems. Neither yet realizes that Celia and Fillide are one and the same person.

1.iii *A pleasant grove* Celia, guarding her sheep, mourns her lost love in a short cavatina, 'Placidi ruscelletti'; the babbling brook and idyllic setting are depicted in the lyrical melody of the flute and a rippling accompaniment pattern. Having been lulled to sleep, Celia awakens to find Fileno at her side, but is forced to hide her love since they are observed by Lindoro and Melibeo. Fileno vents his torment. The Count is attracted briefly to Nerina, causing Amaranta to fly into a rage in the B minor 'Vanne, fuggi, traditore', her changes of mood explicit in the oscillation between contrasting themes.

1.iv *An atrium* Melibeo informs Celia, whose dissembling did not work, that she must either marry Lindoro or go to the sea monster with Fileno. Celia, in soliciting Nerina's aid, expresses her intense suffering in an aria, 'Deh soccorri un infelice'. The difficult, muted horn solo in this piece, probably written for Anton Eckhardt, was later given to the bassoon, perhaps when the music was transposed upwards for soprano. In the finale Celia is nearly forced to accept Lindoro's marriage proposal, when Nerina rushes in unexpectedly, pursued by angry satyrs. Celia is carried away by one of the satyrs, bringing the action to an abrupt end.

Act 2.i *A lovely country field* Melibeo devises a plan to pair Celia with the Count, thereby gaining Amaranta for himself. He persuades Nerina to seek Fileno's favour, which she easily wins since Fileno wishes to provoke Celia, who has been unable to show her true feelings.

2.ii *Mountainous countryside with laurels and cypresses* Heralded by a spirited hunting chorus, all search for a sacrificial offering to Diana. Amaranta is chased by a wild boar which Fileno kills, but Count Perrucchetto claims victory. The Count addresses the not-quite-inert beast in the delightfully comic piece, 'Di questo audace ferro'.

2.iii *A cave* Two back-to-back solo scenes for the serious characters form the dramatic climax of Act 2. Fileno's attempt at suicide ('Bastano i pianti') is thwarted when, after carving an account of his fate in a nearby tree trunk, his arrow breaks. Upon finding the message and broken arrow, Celia contemplates her own death in 'Ah come il core', a musically adventurous section. Both scenes are sectional, the wide-ranging emotional states of the characters amply served by the flexibility of the music.

2.iv *Outside the cave* Nerina and Melibeo enter, followed by shepherds carrying two white robes and two floral crowns. Jealous of the love vows exchanged by Amaranta and Count Perrucchetto, Melibeo sends him into the cave where Celia has sought refuge. The Count and Celia are then brought forth as the sacrificial couple in the second-act finale.

Act 3.i *A hall* Celia, in a white robe and flanked by shepherds, tries to convince Fileno of her innocence, but throughout their duet he remains indignant and remorseless. They depart in opposite directions as Count Perrucchetto, also clad in white, enters with Melibeo while preparations for the sacrifice continue.

3.ii *Landscape with lake* Fileno has realized that Celia speaks the truth. In a noble deed, worthy of a Metastasian hero, he announces that, rather than see Celia devoured by the sea monster, he will offer himself as the single sacrificial victim. Moved by his devotion, Diana appears amid thunder and lightning to save him. She unites Celia and Fileno, Nerina and Lindoro, and Amaranta and Count Perrucchetto. Melibeo is taken as her victim, for having manipulated events for his own benefit.

*

Despite its convoluted plot and disjointed structure, *La fedeltà premiata* contains some of Haydn's best operatic music and efforts at character definition. The virtues of honesty and fidelity are timeless; their relevance to Haydn, whose affair with the singer Luigia Polzelli was well under way by late 1780, may explain the high level of musical sensitivity shown throughout the score. Haydn derived compositional impetus from Cimarosa's *L'infedeltà fedele*; he owned a copy of this opera and sometimes used it as a springboard for his own invention, especially in the Act 1 finale. Similarities in opening melodic gestures, however, probably reflect common practice of the period. In the Act 2 finale Haydn's parody of Gluck's 'Coro di furie' from *Orfeo ed Euridice*, performed at Eszterháza in 1776, was probably meant to please his musically astute patron.   **C.C.**

Ferne Klang, Der ('The Distant Sound')

Opera in three acts by Franz Schreker to his own libretto; Frankfurt, Oper, 18 August 1912.

At the première Fritz was sung by Karl Gentner and Grete by Lisbeth Sellin.

Old Graumann *a retired minor official*		bass
His Wife		mezzo-soprano
Grete Graumann *their daughter/*Greta *a 'dancer'* [Act 2]/Grete ('Tini') [Act 3]		soprano
Fritz *a young artist*		tenor
Innkeeper of the Tavern 'Zum Schwan'		bass
A Strolling Player		baritone
Dr Vigelius *a shady lawyer*		high bass
An Old Woman		mezzo-soprano/ high contralto
Mizi	}	soprano
Milli	} *dancers*	mezzo-soprano
Mary	}	soprano
A Spanish Girl	}	contralto
The Count *aged 24*	}	baritone
The Baron *aged 50*	} *bons viveurs*	bass
The Chevalier *aged 30–35*	}	tenor
Rudolf *Fritz's close friend and doctor*		high bass/baritone
The Actor		baritone
First Chorus-member		tenor
Second Chorus-member		bass
The Waitress		mezzo-soprano
An Unsavoury Character		tenor
A Policeman		bass
A Servant		spoken

Guests, male and female staff and servants from the tavern 'Zum Schwan'; girls, dancers of all nationalities, men and women (some masked); theatre personnel, members of the audience, serving girls, cab attendants etc.

In the course of a somewhat dissolute lifestyle as a young man, Schreker gathered experiences that were to bear fruit in the conception of his first staged opera. Although he completed the libretto in 1903, when he was 25, he did not finish the composition until after a performance of the third-act interlude (as *Nachtstück*) in Vienna under Oskar Nedbal in 1909. The première eventually took place in Frankfurt under Ludwig Rottenberg. Its remarkable success established Schreker as a leading opera composer of the modern school. While difficult to stage, the work has been revived with considerable effect (1984, Venice; 1988, Brussels; 1992, Leeds, for example). Until the Hagen Opera recording, under Michael Halasz, in 1989, only extracts were available on commercial recordings. These included the 'Waldszene und nächtlicher Reigen' (1.ii), recorded by the composer in 1927, with his wife, Maria Schreker, as Grete.

*

Act I.i *The modest living-room of the Graumanns' family home in a small town; the present* A mysterious prelude introduces music associated with the image of 'the distant sound'. Grete Graumann is talking through the window to her boyfriend Fritz outside. He has told her that he must leave in search of his goal – the 'distant sound' that he hears in his heart, whose source and nature he associates with artistic achievement, fame and fortune. Only when these are his will he return to marry her. Sadly, she resigns herself to his decision and lets him go. A strange old woman engages her in conversation and promises to return, as Grete's mother now enters. The reality of the family's situation becomes clear: old Graumann has

'Der ferne Klang' (Schreker), Act 3 scene i (a street tavern): design by Alfred Roller for the original production at the Frankfurt Oper, 18 August 1912

taken to drink and run up serious debts. Noises from the nearby inn prove to come from a skittle-game in which he has consistently lost; finally he has wagered his daughter away. Grete is horrified when the news is brought by Dr Vigelius, accompanied by staff and customers of the inn in coarsely jocular mood. Apparently promising her mother that she will agree to marry the victor (the Innkeeper), she grasps a momentary opportunity and escapes in search of Fritz.

I.ii A woodland clearing, with a lake, close to the edge of town Grete is lost and distraught. She contemplates drowning herself, but experiences involuntary ecstasy as the lake shimmers in the light of the moon and deer come to drink. She drifts into sleep. The strange old woman reappears (accompanied by musical material that will be developed in Act 2) and leads the weary Grete away in search of a 'beautiful young sweetheart'. Grete promises to do anything, if she will only promise not to take her back home. They disappear into the darkness.

Act 2 *A lavish dance hall and bordello on an island in the Gulf of Venice, ten years later* The Venetian act, with lamp-lit gondolas arriving in the background of a scene depicting the lavish and brilliant Casa di Maschere, opens with a prelude in which are shortly heard the siren-like calls of the 'dancers', greeting the arriving male revellers. To these are added an offstage Venetian band, a dreamy love song

(women's chorus) and, once the curtain has risen, an onstage Hungarian gypsy orchestra with elaborately notated 'improvised' cimbalom and fiddle music. Schreker indicated that the strands of sung and spoken conversation should emerge indistinctly from the complex textural polyphony. Only gradually does the action come to focus clearly on Grete, now 'Greta', the most beautiful and sought-after hostess of the Casa di Maschere. She is courted by the Count and the Chevalier in a miniature song contest. The Count's gloomy ballad, 'Die glühende Krone' (beginning 'There lived a pale king with a strange crown'), pleases Grete less, however, than the Chevalier's humorous 'Das Blumenmädchen von Sorrent' ('Who doesn't know the sweet little flowergirl of Sorrento?'). The Count's jealousy grows threatening as a boat arrives, bearing the now bearded Fritz, who is pale and distractedly nervous.

He is astonished to encounter Grete and confesses that in his bitter recent life, brightened only by partial and hard-won artistic achievement, his thoughts had begun to turn back to her. Grete finds herself torn between the easy seductive manner of her profession and recollection of her old love for him. Fritz, however, is horrified to discover what she has really been doing and storms away, bitterly denouncing her as a whore. Wounded, Grete turns back to the jealous Count, commands the gypsy band to strike up a *csárdás*, and falls into his arms as the wild dance, accompanied by general confusion, concludes the act.

Act 3.i *Late evening; the open-air seating of a street tavern in a large city, with the 'Court Theatre' visible across the street; five years later* There is no overture; the first sounds emanate from the theatre in the background (offstage ensemble), where Fritz's opera is being performed. Applause and motifs from *Der ferne Klang* itself (including the opera's actual closing bars) drift towards the tables where Dr Vigelius and the Actor are drinking and reminiscing. Grete is helped to a seat by a policeman; deeply moved, she had become ill in the theatre. Now a street prostitute, known as 'Tini', she is accosted by an unsavoury character who claims to have been with her the day before. Dr Vigelius, remembering her, comes to Grete's rescue as the theatre audience streams out, many criticizing the opera's weak ending. Grete sinks into a faint. She comes round, sobbing, recalling her woodland vision that has been revived by Fritz's 'wild music'. As the curtain falls, the implied memory of that music turns into an extended orchestral interlude in which the motivic material of the entire opera is reviewed in a passionate stream of consciousness leading directly into the final scene.

3.ii *Fritz's study, through a window of which is seen a garden in the first light of a spring morning* Fritz, grey-haired and ill, sits at his desk, gazing into the garden. The dawn chorus (realistically notated) has over-whelmed him. All too late he has realized that the secret of the 'distant sound' lay in Nature itself. The sun rises and Rudolf comes to persuade him to rewrite the last act of his opera. He also has news of the woman who had collapsed in the theatre. Fritz begins to suspect who she was and sends Rudolf to find her as he hears the 'distant sound' itself (a series of mysterious arpeggiated chords for offstage celesta and piano), apparently emanating from the garden, and growing in intensity. Dr Vigelius then arrives, but is unable to penetrate Fritz's distracted mood until it becomes clear that he has brought Grete. She enters and they are reconciled, the 'distant sound' now at the peak of its intensity. Ecstatic, Fritz decides that he will rewrite the last act, but he dies in Grete's arms. She cries out as the curtain falls to the E♭ minor chords of the 'distant sound'.

*

Der ferne Klang remained in the German operatic repertory until the 1930s. Its mixture of romantic fantasy with petty bourgeois realism and its richly subtle orchestral and harmonic language initially excited Schreker's contemporaries. It has been suggested that Berg (who prepared the first piano score) was influenced by formal and scenic features of the work in *Wozzeck*, and by the powerful central role of Grete in *Lulu*. **P.F.**

Fidelio [*Leonore, oder Der Triumph der ehelichen Liebe* ('Leonore, or The Triumph of Married Love')]

Opera in two (originally three) acts by Ludwig van Beethoven to a libretto by Joseph von Sonnleithner (1805), with revisions by Stephan von Breuning (1806) and George Friedrich Treitschke (1814), after Jean-Nicolas Bouilly's French libretto *Léonore, ou L'amour conjugal*; Vienna, Theater an der Wien, 20 November 1805 (first version); Theater an der Wien, 29 March 1806 (second version); Kärntnertortheater, 23 May 1814 (final version).

The principal singers at the 1805 première were Anna Milder as Leonore and Friedrich Christian Demmer as Florestan. At the 1806 performances Joseph Röckel replaced Demmer. In 1814 Anna Milder again took the role of Leonore and an Italian tenor named Radichi that of Florestan; Pizarro was sung by the baritone Johann Michael Vogl, later a friend and champion of Schubert.

Florestan *a prisoner*	tenor
Leonore *his wife and assistant to Rocco*	
under the name of Fidelio	soprano
Rocco *gaoler*	bass
Marzelline *his daughter*	soprano
Jaquino *assistant to Rocco*	tenor
Don Pizarro *governor of the prison*	bass-baritone
Don Fernando *minister and Spanish*	
nobleman	bass
Soldiers, prisoners, townspeople	
Setting A Spanish state prison not far from Seville	

At some time in the early part of 1803 Beethoven moved into an apartment in the Theater an der Wien and began work on his first opera; the libretto was *Vestas Feuer*, by the theatre's director Emanuel Schikaneder. By January 1804 he had abandoned this project and taken up a new libretto, *Léonore, ou L'amour conjugal*. This drama by J.-N. Bouilly had been set by Pierre Gaveaux in 1798 and was also set in Italian by Ferdinando Paer in 1804 and Simon Mayr in 1805. Beethoven worked from a German version translated and enlarged by the Viennese court secretary Joseph von Sonnleithner. The choice was probably influenced both by the recent success in Vienna of another, very similar drama by Bouilly, *Les deux journées*, in a setting by Cherubini, and by the attractiveness of the subject matter, whose themes of undeserved suffering and heroic resolve were very much in Beethoven's mind at about this time.

Composition of the opera continued through much of 1804 and 1805, and last-minute difficulties with the censors delayed the première until 20 November 1805. There were only three performances. Vienna was under occupation by French

*Wilhelmine Schröder-Devrient as Leonore in Beethoven's
'Fidelio': lithograph by W. Santer*

troops, and many of Beethoven's supporters had left the city. The opera was also felt to be too long, and Beethoven was persuaded to abridge and alter it slightly. A revised version in two rather than three acts, with Rocco's aria omitted and other sections shortened and rearranged, was performed on 29 March and 10 April 1806. To avoid confusion with the operas of Gaveaux and Paer, the theatre had insisted on the title *Fidelio* in the 1805 and 1806 productions; Beethoven himself preferred *Leonore*, and that title appears in the 1806 libretto (which was printed at his own expense) and the vocal score published in 1810. The title *Leonore* is now commonly used to designate the first two versions of the opera. The overtures written for the 1805 and 1806 performances are now known as the *Leonore* no.2 and no.3 respectively. The *Leonore* no.1 overture, earlier thought to have been played in 1805, has recently been shown to date from 1807, when a performance of the opera was planned in Prague.

Although a vocal score of the 1806 version of *Fidelio*, minus the overture and the two finales, appeared in 1810, the opera was not performed again until 1814. By this time Beethoven's deafness had progressed to the point where his performing career was effectively at an end. This, combined with his general irascibility, meant that he would have found it difficult to accept the compromises and manage the personal relationships that are required in the production of opera, and he never composed another in spite of his attraction to the genre. When, however, he was approached about a revival of *Fidelio*, following some very successful concerts of his orchestral music, he himself insisted on further revisions. These were undertaken with the help of the poet Georg Friedrich Treitschke. More cuts were made, and nearly every number was changed in some way. This final version was performed on 23

May 1814; it is this that is described below. There was also a new overture, the fourth, now identified as the *Fidelio* overture, which however was not ready until the second performance. A vocal score prepared by Ignaz Moscheles appeared in 1814; no full score was published until 1826.

The most famous of 19th-century singers to achieve success with *Fidelio* was Wilhelmine Schröder-Devrient, whose performances as Leonore starting in 1822 exerted a powerful effect on a younger generation of musicians. A revival of the first version was not attempted until 1905, on the centenary of the première. There have been many modern recordings of the final version, perhaps most famously with Jon Vickers in the role of Florestan. The first version has also been recorded.

*

Act I.i *A courtyard of the prison* Marzelline is ironing; Jaquino presses her on the subject of marriage in their duet, 'Jetzt, Schätzchen'. She rejects his pleas, for she has fallen in love with Fidelio, her father's new assistant ('O wär ich schon mit dir vereint'). Rocco enters, followed by Leonore, who has disguised herself as a young man, Fidelio, in her efforts to find her missing husband; she is laden with chains and supplies. Rocco takes Fidelio's hard work as a sign of interest in Marzelline; in the quartet in canon, led by Marzelline, 'Mir ist so wunderbar!', Fidelio and Jaquino express anxious thoughts of very different kinds. Rocco encourages the romance, but cautions that a successful marriage requires money ('Hat man nicht auch Gold beineben'). Fidelio tests Rocco's trust by asking to accompany him to the subterranean cell where a prisoner is kept who she suspects may be her husband, Florestan ('Gut, Söhnchen, gut').

I.ii *[Act 2, 1805 version] A courtyard of the prison* To the sound of a march, the soldiers enter. Pizarro follows. He reads the dispatches, which include a letter warning of a surprise visit by the minister to question him about prisoners being held without cause. Having imprisoned Florestan for political reasons (only vaguely specified), Pizarro is forced to act. He stations a trumpeter in the tower and resolves to take his revenge at once (aria with chorus, 'Ha! welch ein Augenblick!'). Pizarro calls Rocco aside and attempts, unsuccessfully, to enlist his aid in the proposed murder (duet, 'Jetzt, Alter, jetzt hat es Eile!'). The men leave. Leonore, who has observed them plotting, curses Pizarro and reaffirms her hope and her own resolve (accompanied recitative, 'Abscheulicher! Wo eilst du hin?'; aria in two sections, 'Komm, Hoffnung'; 'Ich folg' dem innern Triebe'). Rocco and Marzelline enter, and Leonore (now in her role as Fidelio again) persuades Rocco to allow some of the prisoners out into the open air. They emerge and sing in praise of freedom ('O welche Lust!'); this begins the finale to Act 1. Rocco tells Fidelio that he has obtained permission for the marriage to Marzelline. He will also be able to take Fidelio to the cell of the mysterious prisoner, whose grave they must prepare. Jaquino and Marzelline rush in and warn of Pizarro's arrival. Pizarro is enraged by Rocco's presumption in letting the prisoners out, but Rocco deflects his anger by citing the king's name-day and noting that one prisoner has remained inside. The prisoners return to their cells ('Leb wohl, du warmes Sonnenlicht').

Act 2.i *[Act 3, 1805 version] A subterranean cell* An orchestral introduction depicts the bleakness of the scene. In an accompanied recitative Florestan curses the darkness but accepts God's will ('Gott! welch' dunkel hier!'). His two-part aria laments the loss of his happiness as the price of having spoken the truth ('In des Lebens Frühlingstagen') and ends with a vision of rescue by Leonore ('Und spür' ich nicht linde, sanftsäuselnde Luft?'). Leonore enters, but with Rocco; she has to help him uncover an abandoned cistern that is to serve as the prisoner's grave (melodrama and duet, 'Nur hurtig fort, nur frisch gegraben'). She is still not certain of his identity, but is determined to save him whoever he is. When the grave is ready, Florestan stirs and she recognizes him. He asks for help and for water. Fidelio comes forward with wine and bread, which Rocco allows Florestan to receive in a communion-like trio ('Euch werde Lohn in bessern Welten'). Rocco gives a signal, and Pizarro enters. The ensuing action takes place in a quartet ('Er sterbe!'): Pizarro reveals his identity to Florestan, who stands defiant; when Pizarro draws his dagger, Leonore steps forward and reveals her own identity at last: 'Töt' erst sein Weib!' ('First kill his wife!'); as she halts Pizarro with a pistol, the trumpet from the tower signals the arrival of the minister. After Rocco and Pizarro have hurriedly left the cell, Florestan and Leonore celebrate their reunion in a duet, 'O namenlose Freude!'

2.ii *The parade grounds of the prison* This entire scene is set musically as the finale of the act. The townspeople and the prisoners are assembled to greet Don Fernando, who enters accompanied by Pizarro ('Heil sei dem Tag'). Rocco brings in Florestan and Leonore. Don Fernando recognizes his friend, believed dead, and orders Pizarro's arrest. The privilege of unlocking Florestan's chains is given to Leonore ('O Gott! O welch ein Augenblick!'). The opera ends with a chorus in praise of Leonore's bravery ('Wer ein holdes Weib errungen, stimm' in unsern Jubel ein').

*

Most of the important differences between the 1805 and 1814 versions of *Fidelio* can be accounted for by reference to Bouilly's original libretto, which Sonnleithner followed closely. Dramatically, the only

important difference in Act 2 (Act 1 scene ii of the 1814 version) is that Pizarro, who has only a speaking role, tells Rocco merely that a masked man will kill Florestan once the grave is prepared. The dramatic action of Act 3 (Act 2 in 1814) is similar up to the point of the trumpet signal, though the confrontation that Beethoven was to set as a quartet is done here in spoken dialogue. When Pizarro and Rocco leave the cell Rocco takes the pistol from Leonore, so that she and Florestan are still in doubt about their rescue as they sing their duet. The concluding scene takes place in the cell itself, starting with an offstage chorus demanding vengeance and concluding with the minister's discovery of the truth, all spoken, and a chorus in praise of Leonore.

The only important dramatic change that Sonnleithner introduced was to make Pizarro's intentions clear to Rocco in their first scene together, in the duet 'Jetzt, Alter'. As in Bouilly, the last act ends in the cell. But Sonnleithner did extend the text at many points to accommodate more musical numbers. In some cases, such as the trio 'Gut, Söhnchen, gut' and Pizarro's aria, he worked from spoken lines in Bouilly. In others he expanded scenes with new material; this is most apparent in the trio 'Ein Mann ist bald genommen', the quartet 'Mir ist so wunderbar', the duet 'Jetzt, Alter' and the finale of Act 2 (Act 1 in 1814), which is expanded to include a second aria for Pizarro. Most of these changes create opportunities for ensemble numbers, which were not a priority in the *opéra comique* conceived by Bouilly and Gaveaux, but which Beethoven no doubt requested.

In its 1806 revision, *Fidelio* was presented in two acts rather than three (the first two being combined). There were many small changes in the music, but the important dramatic changes were few. Rocco's aria was omitted, and both the duet 'Um in der Ehe froh zu leben' and the trio 'Ein Mann ist bald genommen' were shifted to a position after Leonore's aria, which now followed the Pizarro-Rocco duet directly. The changes had the positive effect of moving the action more quickly through the opening scene, but the two ensembles that now fell between Leonore's aria and the Act 1 finale slowed the drama again at that point.

The revisions of 1814 went much further. Rocco's aria was restored, but the two offending ensembles before the Act 1 finale were cut. The finale itself was rewritten, eliminating Pizarro's second aria in favour of a second chorus as the prisoners return to their cells. In Act 2 the quartet is interrupted by Jaquino with the news of the minister's arrival. Leonore and Florestan sing their duet knowing they are safe, and the final scene is moved from the darkness of the cell into the light of day. Beethoven also exchanged the position of the first two numbers; the new overture in E major now precedes the duet in A major, whereas

Design by Ewald Dülberg for Act 2 of 'Fidelio' (Berlin, Kroll Opera, 1927): gouache

the overtures of 1805 and 1806, both in C, had been followed by Marzelline's aria in C minor. Of the many changes in the text, the most important were a new introduction to Leonore's aria (the accompanied recitative 'Abscheulicher! wo eilst du hin?') and a new concluding section to Florestan's aria, replacing a memory of past happiness with a vision of deliverance by Leonore in the form of an angel. At least in the case of Leonore's recitative, the new text may have been inspired by the German translation of Paer's *Leonora* ('Abscheulicher Pizarro! wo gehst du hin?').

Fidelio has two interlocking plots. Leonore, in her real and disguised roles, and Rocco, as father and gaoler, participate in both. The domestic plot involves them in the emotional world of Jaquino and Marzelline. The heroic plot involves them in the deadly confrontation of Pizarro and Florestan. The music of the first scenes, before Pizarro's entrance, is simpler in form and expression than what follows. Marzelline and Rocco sing strophic arias (Jaquino has none). Marzelline and Jaquino have a comic duet, interrupted by a knocking at the gate – a dramatic device foreshadowing the trumpet signal that interrupts the Act 2 quartet. When Fidelio sings, the mood darkens, but the canonic quartet is mysterious rather than complex and the closing trio of scene i (Act 1 in 1805) reaches furthest emotionally when Pizarro is mentioned. After this scene Marzelline and Jaquino effectively disappear from the action, and there is no more music as light as that of the first few

numbers (this is not true of the 1805 and 1806 versions).

Pizarro's aria, in a growling D minor and set in sonata form with a coda accompanied by the shocked troops, raises the level of the musical argument. Equally ambitious in its unusual shape, its contrasts and its chromaticism is the following duet, which draws Rocco into the world of Pizarro's conspiracy. Leonore now enters a second time, alone and therefore unconstrained by her disguise. Her scene is distinguished musically from all that has come before: we hear accompanied recitative for the first time, and the aria falls into two large sections in contrasting tempo, with three obbligato horns supporting her heroic resolve. Beethoven duplicates this format in Florestan's solo scene at the beginning of Act 2: accompanied recitative and an aria in two sections in contrasting tempo, this time with a long orchestral introduction to establish the mood. Thus the characters of *Fidelio* are identified and related by the style of their music, with Leonore and Florestan paired at one extreme, Rocco and Marzelline paired at the other, and Pizarro in the middle. Similar hierarchies are present in Mozart's operas, most obviously in *Die Zauberflöte*.

Beethoven planned the tonal structure of the opera with equal care: a great circle-of-5ths progression leads to the C major of the final scene. It appears there may also be some symbolic significance to his choice of keys for the individual characters. Leonore (E major) and Florestan (F minor/A♭ major) are presented as the extreme poles, four sharps and four flats removed from the key of resolution, as if to emphasize the distance that separates them. Pizarro (aria in D minor/major) and the prisoners (chorus in B♭ major) are placed symmetrically within these extremes.

Some of the musical gestures of *Fidelio* have been ascribed directly to the influence of the earlier setting by Gaveaux. Similarities with Paer's setting have also been noted, but there is no firm evidence that Beethoven saw or heard Paer's work before its first Viennese performance in 1809. He seems not to have known Mayr's opera.

Less ambiguous is Beethoven's use of his own earlier music. The duet for Leonore and Florestan, 'O namenlose Freude!', is taken from a trio that he had written for the abandoned opera *Vestas Feuer* in 1803. And for the moment in the Act 2 finale when Leonore unlocks Florestan's chains, 'O Gott! O welch ein Augenblick!', Beethoven reached back to the cantata on the death of Joseph II (WoO 87) that he had composed in Bonn. Less obviously, the introduction to the opening chorus of the cantata is recalled in the gloomy orchestral introduction to Florestan's aria. The symbolic triumph of light over darkness, explicit in the text of the cantata, is implicit in the second act of *Fidelio* in its final form, reflecting the triumph of reason over hysteria, good over evil, ultimately life over death.

Of the many other influences on *Fidelio* that have been proposed, those of Mozart and of post-revolutionary French opera are the most widely acknowledged. The latter repertory is no longer well known, but beginning in 1802 much of it was performed in Vienna. Echoes of Cherubini's *Lodoïska* and *Les deux journées* are easy to hear in *Fidelio,* and the idea of the trumpet signal, anticipated in the overture, may have come from Méhul's *Héléna* (also to a libretto by Bouilly). The musical rhetoric of Cherubini and his French contemporaries, which is quite distinct from Mozart's, is evident throughout *Fidelio* and the other great works of Beethoven's middle period.

It is tempting to associate the influence of Mozart particularly with the power of Beethoven's large-scale forms, an area in which he clearly surpasses Cherubini. Indeed Beethoven's musical logic is sometimes so compelling that it transcends even the particulars of the drama that prompted it. This seems true of a movement like 'Mir ist so wunderbar', where the dramatic motivation is much less obvious than in its probable model, the canonic quartet in *Così fan tutte*. More important, however, and more inherently dramatic, are the many movements in sonata form. Beethoven had used sonata form to very powerful effect in his instrumental works, and in Mozart he saw how effectively its essential

procedures could be adapted in setting ensemble texts. In the duet 'Jetzt, Alter', and elsewhere Beethoven created structures of such musical power that they take on a dramatic life of their own. In this respect he may have missed something in his Mozartian models.

Fidelio has been criticized as two-dimensional in its portrayal of character and as melodramatic in its action. Leonore and Florestan reveal little beyond their primary traits; Pizarro never vacillates. And Rocco, the one character who must choose between his duty and his dignity, is given little musical opportunity to consider his dilemma. Beethoven lacked Mozart's tolerance for human frailty and ambivalence. He formulated the choices in his own life in similarly unambiguous terms.

Let me tell you that my most prized possession, my hearing, has greatly deteriorated. . . I must withdraw from everything, and my best years will pass away without my being able to achieve all that my talent and strength have commanded me to do! Sad resignation, to which I am forced to have recourse; needless to say, I am resolved to overcome all this, but how will it be possible?

Thus he wrote to a friend in 1801. 'In the springtime of my life my happiness has flown from me' and 'I follow my inner drive; nothing can deter me' – these words of Florestan and Leonore, which echoed his own, are fixed as the divided emotional centres of his opera. And so the reunion, Florestan's loss restored and Leonore's bravery rewarded, must have reconciled symbolically the conflicting emotions in Beethoven himself. Whatever its limitations may be, *Fidelio* endures as a hymn of praise to those virtues of patience and determination that saw Beethoven through his own darkest days.   D.J.

Fiery Angel, The

[*Ognenniy angel* ('The Flaming Angel')]

Opera in five acts, op.37, by Sergey Prokofiev to his own libretto after the novel (1907) by Valery Bryusov; Venice, Teatro La Fenice, 14 September 1955 (Act 2, abridged, Paris, Opéra, 14 June 1928; concert performance, Paris, Théâtre des Champs-Elysées, 25 November 1954, as *L'ange de feu*).

At the Venice première Dorothy Dow sang Renata and Rolando Panerai was Ruprecht; the conductor was Nino Sanzogno.

Ruprecht *a knight*	baritone
Renata	dramatic soprano
Hostess	contralto
Jakob Glock	tenor
Agrippa von Nettesheim	tenor altino

Count Heinrich	silent
Mephistopheles	tenor
Faust	bass
Porter	bass
Fortune Teller	mezzo-soprano
Mathias	tenor
Doctor	tenor
Host	baritone
Mother Superior	contralto
Inquisitor	bass

Neighbours, nuns

Setting The Rhineland in 1543

The full title of Bryusov's erudite novel, which purports to be a translation of a 16th-century manuscript containing a mercenary's confessions, gives a fair idea both of its content and that of Prokofiev's opera: 'The Fiery Angel; or, a True Story in which is related of the Devil, not once but often appearing in the Image of a Spirit of Light to a Maiden and seducing her to Various and Many Sinful Deeds, of Ungodly Practices of Magic, Alchymy, Astrology, the Cabalistical Sciences and Necromancy, of the Trial of the Said Maiden under the Presidency of His Eminence the Archbishop of Trier, as well as of Encounters and Discourses with the Knight and thrice Doctor Agrippa of Nettesheim, and with Doctor Faustus, composed by an Eye-witness'. As one might expect from a leader of the Russian symbolists, Bryusov's purpose, to quote the penultimate sentence of the novel, was 'to cross that sacred edge that divides our world from the dark sphere in which float spirits and demons' so as metaphorically to explore the ambiguities of reality and experience – and, ultimately, of morals. On another level the book is an autobiographical *roman à clef* motivated by, and describing, a love triangle in which the author was involved at the time of its writing, along with the poet and translator Nina Petrovskaya, and Bryusov's rival for the latter's affections, the great writer Andrey Bely (known for, among other things, his brilliant red hair).

Prokofiev came across Bryusov's novel in America, shortly after finishing *The Love for Three Oranges*. He began sketching a scenario – originally in three acts (11 scenes) that hewed far closer than the final version to the novel's plot – late in 1919. At first composition proceeded slowly owing to the composer's heavy concert schedule, but in March 1922 he retreated to Ettal, in the Bavarian Alps, to devote his full time to the opera in a location congruent with its setting. A piano score was completed before the end of the next year. The work is cast in the same declamatory idiom as Prokofiev's earlier opera, *The Gambler*, except that far greater reliance is placed on a conventional network of orchestral leitmotifs. In addition, there are several

extended monologues for the main character – the possessed maiden, Renata – which make an effect comparable with that of a traditional operatic scena, if not an aria. Thus *The Fiery Angel* is not quite so extreme an anti-opera as its predecessor.

Prokofiev revised the work, and orchestrated it with the help of an assistant named Georgy Nikolayevich Gorchakov, pursuant to its acceptance by Bruno Walter for production at the Städtische Oper, Berlin. Delays in the copying of parts prevented performance in the 1927–8 season, and the production was cancelled. When in 1930 the Metropolitan Opera expressed interest in the score, Prokofiev began another revision, for which two additional scenes were planned, but that production too fell through. As Charles Bruck, who conducted the 1954 concert performance, put it, the opera was then 'carefully packed up and consigned to oblivion' in the basement of the Editions Russes de Musique (Koussevitzky's firm) when Prokofiev returned to his Soviet homeland, then the least hospitable venue imaginable for an opera having to do with religious mysticism.

That Prokofiev never saw staged the work he considered the magnum opus of his period in emigration was surely his greatest artistic disappointment. (He salvaged some of the music by basing his Third Symphony on the opera's themes, many of which had been originally conceived for various instrumental projects, including a 'white [i.e. diatonic] quartet'; thus the symphony should not be regarded as merely an operatic pastiche.) After the war the score was unearthed by Hans Swarsenski of Boosey & Hawkes, which firm had acquired the Koussevitzky catalogue. Despite periodic revivals following its much publicized Venice première, under Nino Sanzogno, the opera has had difficulty holding the stage. The first Russian production was in the provincial city of Perm in 1987; the Mariinsky Theatre finally staged it in St Petersburg in December 1991, in a joint production with the Royal Opera that opened in London in April 1992. A vocal score with the original Russian text was not available until 1985.

*

Act I The knight Ruprecht seeks shelter for the night in a wayside inn. During the night he is awakened by shrieks from a room nearby, and bursts in to find another traveller, Renata, in a state of abject terror. He calms her and leads her back to her bed. She relates how she has had a guiding spirit, a Fiery Angel, since she was a child. As she grew up her desire for purity was transmuted into erotic longing and she pleaded with the angel, Madiel, for sexual intimacy. He refused angrily, but before he vanished he promised to return as a man. She met Count Heinrich and believed him to be Madiel; she lived with him for a year, but then he too disappeared and now she is searching for him, despairing and disturbed by nightmare visions.

Ruprecht does not know what to make of all this; he is attracted to Renata but wonders if she is perhaps possessed by the devil. The inn's hostess and the porter come to throw her out, calling her a witch and a whore. Ruprecht agrees to go with her to Cologne to seek Heinrich. A Fortune Teller predicts Renata's future, seeing blood on both of them.

Act 2.i Renata consults a book of magic in an effort to find Heinrich. She is obsessed with her quest for her angel, while Ruprecht thinks only of her. He is willing to help even though he knows the dangers of black magic. Jakob Glock, a magician, brings more learned tomes; Renata mixes a potion. In answer a knocking is heard, and she realizes it is the demons whom she sees so often in her nightmares. They tell her Heinrich is coming, but no one appears. Glock refers them to Agrippa of Nettesheim, who is famous for the power of his magic art, and Ruprecht leaves to seek him.

2.ii Agrippa is in his study with three dogs and three skeletons. He tells Ruprecht that he is not a mere practitioner of the black arts, but is wise and can foretell the future. The skeletons deny the truth of this, but Ruprecht is oblivious. Agrippa can do nothing to help.

Act 3.i Renata has tracked Heinrich down, but he refuses to have anything to do with her. When Ruprecht arrives, Renata tells him she was wrong about Heinrich: he is merely mortal, and she tries to persuade Ruprecht to kill him. He accuses Heinrich of besmirching Renata's honour; Heinrich, rushing to a window to escape, is bathed in light and appears to Renata to be her Fiery Angel after all. Ruprecht challenges him to a duel, and she is horrified that 'Madiel' might be hurt.

3.ii It is Ruprecht who has been wounded; his friend Mathias looks after him. Renata is remorseful, as she now reciprocates his love. A doctor is summoned.

Act 4 Ruprecht has recovered, and he and Renata have been living together. Renata now feels this is sinful and wishes to enter a convent. Ruprecht pleads that he loves her, but she sees only the Devil in him. At this Faust and Mephistopheles appear; they order a meal in a tavern, and when it does not come quickly Mephistopheles eats the serving boy. The Host begs him to restore the boy, his only helper, and Mephistopheles does so. He and Faust arrange to meet Ruprecht the following day.

Act 5 Renata has entered a convent, but finds no peace; she is tormented by her demons and her presence is upsetting to the other nuns. The Inquisitor comes to perform an exorcism. During his questioning of Renata devilish knockings are heard. Hysteria gradually takes over: two young nuns are the first to be overcome, but all of them realize they are in the presence of evil. Renata and six nuns try to prevail against the demons but the other nuns recognize that she is the focus of the evil. Ruprecht with his companions, Faust and Mephistopheles, appear and watch as Renata and the six nuns accuse the Inquisitor of being sent by the Devil. They are repulsed, and the Inquisitor orders Renata to be put to a fiery death at the stake.

*

One of the reasons for the opera's continued neglect is its unusual fixation on a single very difficult – and dramatically static – role. Whereas the novel, as a first-person narrative, inevitably centred around Ruprecht, the author's surrogate, Prokofiev's libretto overwhelmingly emphasizes Renata, the possessed maiden. Her perpetual hysterics dominate every scene but two, making her role one of the longest and (in terms of range and volume) most demanding in opera. The concentration on Renata entailed the sacrifice of a great deal of colourful action (Ruprecht's attendance, real or imagined, at a black mass, his duel with Count Heinrich etc.), resulting in a stagnant quality the composer himself recognized (and which his aborted 1930 revision would have addressed). The two scenes in which Renata does not appear – Ruprecht's visit to Agrippa (Act 2 scene ii, based on Bryusov's chapter 6) and his encounter with Faust and Mephistopheles (Act 4 scene ii, based on chapter 11) – are poorly integrated into the libretto and lend the action an episodic quality difficult to overlook in a work the literary source of which is not widely familiar. Finally, Prokofiev's garish music, while often strikingly evocative of Renata's obsessions – e.g. the scene of conjuration (Act 2 scene i, best known from the scherzo of the Third Symphony), or the last act, in which a whole stageful of nuns are infected with her madness – undeniably overworks the device of ostinato. Though its difficult stage career and its reputation as the composer's most modernistic work have lent *The Fiery Angel* the aura of a *cause célèbre*, familiarity has not always worked to its advantage.   R.T.

Fille du régiment, La [*La figlia del reggimento* ('The Daughter of the Regiment')]

Opéra comique in two acts by Gaetano Donizetti to a libretto by Jules-Henri Vernoy de Saint-Georges and Jean-François-Alfred Bayard, later revised to an Italian translation by Calisto Bassi; Opéra-Comique (Salle de la Bourse), 11 February 1840 (revised version, Milan, Teatro alla Scala, 3 October 1840).

The cast of the première consisted of Juliette Bourgeois (who sang in Italy under the name Borghese) as Marie, Marie-Julie Boulanger (the

Marchioness), Luigi Henry (Sulpice) and Mécène
Marié de L'Isle (Tonio).

Marie (Maria) *a vivandière*	soprano
Tonio *a young Tyrolean*	tenor
La Marquise (La Marchesa) de Berkenfeld [The Marchioness]	mezzo-soprano
Sulpice Pingot (Sulpizio) *a sergeant of the 21st regiment*	bass
Hortensius (Ortensio) *major-domo of the Marchioness*	bass
A Corporal	bass
A Notary	spoken
La Duchesse (La Duchessa) de Crackentorp [The Duchess]	spoken
A Valet	spoken

French soldiers, Tyrolean peasants, wedding guests, servants

Setting The Tyrolean countryside and the château of the Marchioness, not long after the battle of Marengo, 1800

While in Paris at the behest of the Opéra management, Donizetti also wrote several works for other theatres. When *La fille du régiment* was produced for the Opéra-Comique, Berlioz quipped: 'One can no longer speak of the opera houses of Paris but only of the opera houses of M. Donizetti'. The work soon established itself at the Opéra-Comique, where it had been given more than 1000 times by 1914. Donizetti prepared an Italian *opera buffa* version, cutting some numbers and adding others, and substituting recitatives for the French spoken dialogue. This version was first performed at La Scala in 1840, with Luigia Abbadia (Maria), Lorenzo Salvi (Tonio) and Raffaele Scalese (Sulpizio). During the 19th century the Italian version proved more popular than the French in England and the USA (except in New Orleans) and many famous singers, including Henriette Sontag, Jenny Lind and Adelina Patti made their mark as the vivandière. At Covent Garden the work disappeared about 1875, but it was resuscitated happily more than 80 years later with Joan Sutherland as Marie. In Italy during the 1920s Toti dal Monte was an admired Maria.

La fille first appeared at the Metropolitan, in its original French form, on 6 January 1902 with Marcella Sembrich and Charles Gilibert (Sulpice). Later revivals starred Frieda Hempel with Antonio Scotti in 1918 and Lily Pons with Salvatore Baccaloni in 1940, and on 17 February 1972 it returned with Sutherland, Luciano Pavarotti and Fernando Corena. The Italian version *La figlia del reggimento* served at Hammerstein's Manhattan Opera as a showcase for Luisa Tetrazzini, John McCormack and Gilibert, introduced on 22 November 1910. In the late 20th century, however, and not just in the USA, *La fille*

began to enjoy increased popularity and can surely be said to have re-entered the repertory after being on its fringes for nearly a century.

*

Act I *A field in the Tyrolean Alps* The opera is preceded by a sparkling overture which makes prominent use of the melody of the song of the 21st regiment of the French Army ('Chacun le sait'/'Ciascun lo dice'). Women kneel before a wayside shrine, praying for protection from the enemy, whose cannon sound in the distance. The Marchioness is terrified, but her overseer Hortensius tries to calm her. A peasant, Tonio, announces that the French troops have departed, news that is greeted with great relief. The Marchioness comments on the lack of respect for rank and position of the unruly French (*couplets*, 'Pour une femme de mon nom'; not in the Italian version). She retires to wait for Hortensius, whose intent – to find out if they may safely continue their journey– is interrupted by the formidable figure of Sergeant Sulpice of the 21st regiment. Sulpice assures the trembling villagers that his troops have come to restore peace and order. Marie, the pride and joy of the regiment, arrives and is affectionately greeted by Sulpice (duo, 'Au bruit de la guerre'/'Apparvi alla luce'); in this duet the military flavour of the score is established, with brilliant orchestration and a vocal line that imitates bugle calls and drum-rolls ('rataplan'). Sulpice reminds her how she was found as an infant on the battlefield and raised by the regiment as their 'daughter'. When he remarks on her recent curious behaviour she explains that she was picking flowers near a precipice when she slipped and fell into the stalwart arms of Tonio, who has lost his heart to her. Sulpice reminds her that she may marry only a member of the regiment.

Troops enter with Tonio as their prisoner, having taken him for a spy. When Marie tells them that Tonio saved her life, they release him, and he explains that he approached the troops only to see the girl he loves. The soldiers decide to toast their daughter's saviour rather than shoot him, and the festivities include Marie's rendition of the 21st's regimental song (*couplets*, 'Chacun le sait'); this infectious tune with its dance-rhythm refrain is, perhaps surprisingly, a self-borrowing from one of Noah's utterances from *Il diluvio universale* (1830). A drum signals a formation, and the soldiers go off, leaving Tonio as Marie's 'prisoner'. He confesses that he loves her; her response, in a solo passage during their charming duo ('De cet aveu si tendre'/'A voti così ardente'), after one of Donizetti's characteristic modulations up a semitone, convinces us of her tender heart. He explains that she has come to occupy his every thought, and she admits that she is not impervious to his presence. Sulpice returns to see Tonio kissing Marie, and reminds her of her promise to marry only within the ranks of the 21st. Tonio departs, determined to win from her other 'fathers' the permission that Sulpice gruffly refuses to grant. Marie, rebellious at his opposition, threatens to join another regiment; Sulpice charges her with ingratitude.

The Marchioness asks permission to return home to her château of Berkenfeld. Hearing that name, Sulpice inquires if she had known a certain 'Robert', by whom, it seems, her sister had a child – who turns out to be none other than Marie. The Marchioness is determined to rescue the girl from her unfortunate environment, especially after hearing her command of soldierly oaths. Marie insists on bidding farewell to her comrades before she goes off with her aunt. The soldiers reassemble (chorus, 'Rataplan, rataplan, rataplan!'); with them is Tonio, now in uniform, having joined in order to marry Marie (aria, 'Ah, mes amis, quel jour de fête'/'Amici miei, che allegro giorno'). When the troops consent to give their daughter to Tonio, his joy is unbounded (air, 'Pour mon âme'/'Qual destino, qual favor': the passage is famous for its nine c''s). Marie returns to say goodbye (couplets, 'Il faut partir'/'Convien partir') and is even more moved when she understands the significance of Tonio's enlistment. Her air, with its english horn obbligato and affecting F minor melody, modulates to the major for the refrain, creating a memorable intensification of feeling. The drums roll, the soldiers in formation salute Marie as, in tears, she departs with her aunt. Marie's air is in effect the slow movement of the finale, which ends in a stretta with a fugato-style interlude.

Act 2 *A salon in the château of Berkenfeld* Several months have elapsed. The Marchioness and the Duchess of Crackentorp discuss the terms of a wedding contract between Marie and the Duchess's son, the Duke Scipion, to be signed that evening. Sulpice appears; wounded three months previously, he has been recuperating at the château. The Marchioness tells him of her intentions for Marie, who arrives for a singing lesson (trio, 'Le jour naissait dans la bocage'/'Sorgeva il dì del bosco'); Sulpice induces her to sing the regimental ditty, to the Marchioness's irritation, rather than her 'period' *romance* (adapted from a salon song by Garat). This lesson scene is a moment of high comedy, a musical joke in excellent taste, and one that permits the soprano to indulge herself, legitimately, in a lather of *fioritura*. Alone with him, Marie confesses to Sulpice that she dreads this marriage as she remembers Tonio fondly; as he leaves he reminds her of her duty.

Marie thinks sadly of the meaninglessness of position and money without warm human affection (air, 'Par le rang et par l'opulence'/'Le ricchezze ed il grado fastoso'). She hears a march and is filled with patriotic fervour (cabaletta, 'Salut à la France'/

'Salvezza alla Francia'; this at one time served as an unofficial patriotic anthem, and its place in Donizetti's first opera written for a French-language theatre suggests that it is also a personal statement). Her friends of the 21st crowd into the room; among them is Tonio, now an officer. When Hortensius protests at their intrusion, the soldiers carry him off. Marie, Tonio and Sulpice celebrate their reunion (trio, 'Tous les trois réunis'/'Stretti insiem tutti tre'). Tonio tells them that his uncle, the mayor of Laèstrichk, has revealed a secret that assures everyone's happiness and tells the Marchioness that he loves Marie more than life itself; his *romance* ('Pour me rapprocher de Marie'; not in the Italian version), in modified *couplets*, injects once more a needed touch of sincerity into the artificialities of the plot. She remains adamant in her plan for Marie's aristocratic marriage, so Tonio reveals that the Marchioness had no sister and Marie cannot be her niece; she therefore is free to marry whom she pleases. The Marchioness, alone with Sulpice, reveals that in fact she is Marie's mother.

The guests start to arrive. The Marchioness identifies herself to Marie as her mother, and the girl offers to sign the contract. But now Tonio and the regiment burst in, declaring that Marie was a vivandière and the daughter of this regiment; the guests recoil in horror. Marie tells the assembled company that she can never repay her debt to the loyal soldiers; the Marchioness is so moved at the goodness of heart that she impulsively gives her permission to marry Tonio. Everyone bursts into a reprise of 'Salut à la France'.

The score of *La fille du régiment* is notable for its deft mixture of military tunes, moments of pathos and straightforward sentiment. The plot may be banal, but it is carried out with a good taste everywhere matched by Donizetti's aristocratic elegance of melody and structure; this charming comedy of manners should not be treated as though it were a vulgar farce. Marie's F minor–F major air in the finale to Act 1 stands as one of Donizetti's greatest accomplishments in communicating genuine, deeply felt emotion. Tonio's air to the Marchioness, 'Pour me rapprocher de Marie', shows an equal refinement of sentiment and distinction of melody. The ease and naturalness of Donizetti's setting of the French text is admirable. The exuberance of the regimental song 'Chacun le sait', as surely as the ennui of the singing lesson in Act 2, provide justifiable occasions for coloratura expansiveness. Everywhere in *La fille* Donizetti's grateful writing for the voice is in evidence. If there is one part of the score that shows some diminishing of effect, it is the finale to Act 2, a shortcoming often remedied by the insertion of an aria. For that purpose, Hempel favoured the Adam variations on Mozart, 'Ah! vous dirai-je, maman', and Tetrazzini the waltz from Gounod's *Mireille*; in the context of World War II, however, Lily Pons opted for the *Marseillaise* and carried a flag with the cross of Lorraine.   W.A.

Finta giardiniera, La ('The Pretended Garden-Girl')

Opera buffa in three acts, κ196, by Wolfgang Amadeus Mozart; Munich, Salvatortheater, 13 January 1775.

The casting of the first production remains largely unknown. Rosa Manservisi sang Sandrina and the soprano castrato Tommaso Consoli, Ramiro, although the range suits the modern (female) mezzo. Other likely singers include Teresa Manservisi (Arminda or Serpetta), Johann Walleshauser (Belfiore), Augustin Sutor (the Mayor) and Giovanni Rossi (Nardo).

Ramiro *a knight*	soprano castrato
Don Anchise *Mayor (Podestà) of Lagonero*	tenor
Marchioness Violante Onesti *disguised as*	
Sandrina, working in the Mayor's	
garden	soprano
Roberto *her servant, disguised as Nardo,*	
a gardener	baritone
Serpetta *the Mayor's housekeeper*	soprano
Arminda *a Milanese lady, the Mayor's*	
niece	soprano
Count (Contino) Belfiore	tenor
Setting The Mayor's estate at Lagonero near	
Milan	

No published libretto of *La finta giardiniera* acknowledges its authorship. The first setting, by Anfossi, was given at Rome during Carnival 1774; Mozart's followed within a year.

The Mozarts left Salzburg three weeks before the planned first performance (29 December), which was postponed, Leopold wrote (28 December), to allow more time to learn the music and actions. Three performances took place, the first and third with great success in the old court theatre; the second, in the Redoutensaal, was truncated because one singer was ill.

The first revival was as a Singspiel, *Die verstellte Gärtnerin*. Mozart probably helped with the adaptation, which was performed by Johann Böhm's company in Augsburg (1 May 1780). Böhm took it to other German centres including Frankfurt (1782; the first Mozart opera given in North Germany). After 1797 it was not heard until 1891, in Vienna. Until recently, 20th-century revivals necessarily used the German form since no source survived of the Italian first act. Its rediscovery (in time for the Neue Mozart-Ausgabe, 1978) permits revival of the original version (Munich and Salzburg, 1979; several subsequent productions). English performances have been given under the title *Sandrina's Secret*.

*

Act I   The Mayor's garden   In an *Introduzione* the characters introduce themselves and their situations, and develop their initial feelings in their first arias. Ramiro, spurned by Arminda, finds love a snare; the Mayor compares his love for the garden-maid to a series of musical instruments ('Dentro il mio petto', an aria which had some currency outside the opera). Sandrina (Violante) reminds Nardo (Roberto, pretending to be her cousin) of the background to the story; she is seeking her lover Belfiore who a year ago stabbed her in a lovers' tiff and fled, leaving her for dead. Her pastoral aria maintains her disguise in front of Ramiro. Nardo is in love with Serpetta, but she intends to marry her master. Arminda clamours for attention until the arrival of her betrothed, who proves to be Belfiore, singing the praises of female beauty. Arminda threatens punishment for any unfaithfulness. Belfiore traces his pedigree to the heroes of Greece and Rome. Serpetta engages in banter with Nardo (each sing a verse of an aria); she adds a sprightly aria of her own.

Hanging Gardens   Sandrina bewails her fate in an eloquent cavatina. She still hopes to find, and forgive, her lover. On learning the name of Arminda's betrothed she faints. In the finale Belfiore recognizes her, but she denies her identity. In a brilliantly varied multi-movement 'ensemble of perplexity', Ramiro is pleased, Nardo concerned, Serpetta and Arminda jealous, Sandrina upset, Belfiore bemused and the Mayor vexed by the turmoil in his household.

Act 2   Hall of the Mayor's house   Having dismissed Ramiro, Arminda turns on Belfiore for his faithlessness (an aria in a vibrantly emotional G minor). Nardo woos Serpetta in Italian, French and English, but she is too jealous of his 'cousin' to admit to liking him. Sandrina muddles Belfiore still more by giving an eyewitness account of her own death; in his amorous aria in response he accidentally pays court to the Mayor, from whom Sandrina has to repel a further advance. Ramiro appears with a warrant for Belfiore's arrest for killing Violante; the Mayor cannot allow a murderer to marry his niece. Ramiro pleads his cause in the warmest melody of the opera ('Dolce d'amor compagna').

Another room   Belfiore is confronted with the accusation. Sandrina defends him: there was no murder, for she is Violante. The others only half-believe her and to Belfiore she denies it again, saying she spoke only to save him. This finally unhinges him (obbligato recitative and aria). Meanwhile we learn that Arminda has had Sandrina abandoned in the wild woods; everyone hastens to the rescue. Serpetta's roguish aria leads without a break into the new scene; the music is now continuous to the end of the act.

A dark wood, with rocks and caves Sandrina cries out in fear (Agitato in C minor; 'Crudeli, fermate'; cavatina and recitative); she hides in a cave. In the finale the others appear one by one and pair off in a comedy of mistaken identity revealed when the practical Ramiro brings a light. But Sandrina and Belfiore find harmony in madness, acting the part of mythological characters amid general consternation.

Act 3 A room The lunatics mistake Nardo for each other. He makes his escape, leaving them prey to imaginary disasters (aria and duet). The Mayor complains that he cannot understand what is going on. Arminda is still determined to marry Belfiore; Ramiro gives vent to his feelings in a powerful C minor aria ('Va pure ad altri').

The garden Sandrina and Belfiore are sleeping. They awake restored and take leave of one another in a long recitative and duet, then decide, with ecstatic finality, that they must never part. This news reconciles Arminda with Ramiro; Serpetta, seeing that the Mayor will always sigh for Sandrina, marries Nardo. In a short finale all sing Sandrina's praises.

*

La finta giardiniera is Mozart's first mature *opera buffa*, but it is a far cry from the swiftly unfolding, ensemble-driven plots of the Da Ponte operas. Its ancestry lies in Goldoni's librettos, mingling serious emotions with comedy; apart from the finales it consists almost entirely of arias. The *Serva padrona* tradition remains in the Serpetta–Nardo–Mayor intrigue, and the disguised noblewoman, victim of jealousy, descends from Piccinni's *La buona figliuola*. Whereas the Count, who seems decidedly weak in the head, is both comic and pathetic, Ramiro is entirely serious, while Arminda appears to caricature *opera seria*.

The music is almost too elaborate, but it is an astounding achievement for an 18-year-old: richly coloured, distinctive in characterization, alternately good-humoured and searchingly expressive in the arias, and brilliantly inventive in the finales. Characterization includes class distinction. The nobles employ a more developed musical idiom, including obbligato recitative and a greater degree of coloratura, than Ramiro and Arminda (despite the vehemence of their minor-mode arias) and the Mayor. The servants bring a simpler melodic style, largely syllabic word-setting, and lighter orchestration.

The opera contains an almost wilful variety of emotional entanglements but its resolution remains obstinately symmetrical, like that of *Così fan tutte*. Love-ties across class barriers (Arminda–Belfiore; Serpetta or Violante/Sandrina–Mayor) do not work out. The restoration of the aristocrats' wits, and the union of social equals in three couples, symbolize restoration of the order threatened by the aftermath of Belfiore's rash attack on Violante.   J.Ru.

Fledermaus, Die ('The Bat')

Komische Operette in three acts by Johann Strauss to a libretto by Carl Haffner and Richard Genée, after Henri Meilhac and Ludovic Halévy's *Le réveillon*; Vienna, Theater an der Wien, 5 April 1874.

The original cast included Marie Geistinger as Rosalinde, Jani Szika as Eisenstein, Ferdinand Lebrecht as Falke, Caroline Charles-Hirsch as Adele and Irma Nittinger as Orlofsky.

Gabriel von Eisenstein *a man of*	
private means	tenor buffo
Rosalinde *his wife*	soprano
Frank *a prison governor*	baritone
Prince Orlofsky	mezzo-soprano
Alfred *his singing teacher*	tenor
Dr Falke *a notary*	light baritone
Dr Blind *a lawyer*	tenor buffo
Adele *Rosalinde's maid*	soprano
Ida *her sister*	soprano
Yvan *the Prince's valet*	speaking role
Frosch *a jailer*	speaking role
Guests and servants of the Prince	
Setting A spa town, near a big city	

Meilhac and Halévy's vaudeville was first translated for Vienna by Carl Haffner as a straight play. However, the peculiarly French custom of the *réveillon* (a midnight supper party) caused problems, which were solved by the decision to adapt the play as a libretto for Johann Strauss, with the *réveillon* replaced by a Viennese ball. At this point Haffner's translation was handed over for adaptation to Richard Genée, who subsequently claimed not only that he had made a fresh translation from scratch but that he had never even met Haffner.

Two anecdotes attached to the early history of *Die Fledermaus* require comment: the first that the work was composed in 42 days, and the second that it was such a failure that it had to be taken off after 16 nights. The work was indeed sketched out in six weeks, but six months elapsed from start of composition to production. Moreover, Rosalinde's *csárdás* had already been performed by Geistinger at a charity performance, and her disguise as a Hungarian at Orlofsky's party was a means of enabling it to be taken over into the operetta. The work was indeed taken off after 16 performances, but only because of a pre-booked visiting operatic company season, after which it returned. It was Lebrecht's death of a heart attack on stage at the Theater an der Wien that gave Alexander Girardi, later Strauss's principal stage interpreter, his first Strauss role as Falke in September 1874.

The libretto's French origins originally prevented its production in Paris, and the music was first adapted for France (with interpolations from Strauss's 1875 work *Cagliostro in Wien*) to a new libretto as *La tzigane* in 1877, finally being performed in Paris as *La Chauve-Souris* (with Meilhac and Halévy's original character names retained) in 1904. Operatic productions began in Hamburg in March 1894 with Katharina Klafsky as Rosalinde, Heinrich Bötel as Alfred and Ernestine Schumann-Heink as Orlofsky, conducted by Gustav Mahler, and continued at the Hofoper, Vienna, that same year under the composer's direction; subsequent revivals there included one in 1920 with Maria Jeritza (Rosalinde), conducted by Richard Strauss. Other celebrated productions include that at Covent Garden on 14 May 1930 with Willi Wörle (Eisenstein), Lotte Lehmann (Rosalinde), Gerhard Hüsch (Falke), Elisabeth Schumann (Adele) and Maria Olszewska (Orlofsky), conducted by Bruno Walter, and at the Vienna Staatsoper on 31 December 1960, with Eberhard Wächter (Eisenstein), Hilde Güden (Rosalinde), Rita Streich (Adele), Erich Kunz (Frank) and Walter Berry (Orlofsky), conducted by Herbert von Karajan. (It was fairly customary after World War I for Orlofsky to be sung by a baritone.)

*

Act I   *A room in Eisenstein's house*   Following the potpourri overture, a voice off stage is heard serenading Rosalinde, the lady of the house ('Täubchen, das entflattert ist'). She recognizes the voice as that of her lover, the singing teacher Alfred, whose ringing tenor she finds irresistible. Adele, Rosalinde's maid, has received a letter from her sister Ida, with an invitation to a ball that evening at the villa of the young Russian Prince Orlofsky. She asks her mistress for the evening off 'to visit a sick aunt'. Rosalinde refuses, as her husband is due to start a short prison sentence that evening for assault. When Adele has left the room, Alfred appears and is persuaded to leave only on condition that he can return that evening when Eisenstein has gone to jail.

Eisenstein enters, arguing with his stuttering lawyer Blind ('Nein, mit solchen Advokaten'), his sentence having been increased on appeal; a spirited trio ensues. After Blind has left, Eisenstein's friend Falke arrives and sets about persuading Eisenstein to delay starting his prison sentence in order to accompany him to Orlofsky's party. At the prospect of all the attractive young ladies who promise to be at the party, Eisenstein is soon enough persuaded ('Komm mit mir zum Souper').

When Adele and Rosalinde reappear, Rosalinde, now looking forward to an evening alone with Alfred, tells Adele that she may have the evening off after all. At the prospect of Rosalinde now supposedly being left alone for the evening, she, Eisenstein and Adele, in a delectable trio, each feign a sadness that none of them feels ('So muss allein ich bleiben?'). Eisenstein and Adele leave for their evening commitments, whereupon Alfred reappears. He settles down for an intimate supper with Rosalinde, donning Eisenstein's smoking cap and dressing gown ('Trinke, Liebchen, trinke schnell').

They are interrupted by the arrival of the prison governor, Frank, who has come to collect Eisenstein to start his prison sentence. Discovered alone with a man wearing her husband's smoking cap and dressing gown, Rosalinde protests at the notion that he could be anyone but her husband ('Mein Herr, was dächten Sie von mir?'), and Alfred is forced to go along with the pretence. He reluctantly allows himself to be led off, fortified by a lingering farewell kiss from Rosalinde.

Act 2   *At Prince Orlofsky's villa*   Orlofsky's guests are all thoroughly enjoying the party ('Ein Souper heut' uns winkt'). Adele, posing as an actress named Olga, is there with her sister Ida, while Falke is talking to the Prince. From their conversation it soon emerges that an elaborate charade is in progress, set up by Falke to amuse the young Prince. 'The bat's revenge', he calls it, and he picks out the characters in it for the Prince. Adele is apparently one of them; but then she spots the leading character arriving – Eisenstein, who is introduced as the 'Marquis Renard'. Orlofsky commands his guests to drink. His wealth has left him permanently bored, but he insists that his guests enjoy themselves ('Ich lade gern mir Gäste ein').

Eisenstein soon spots Adele in her mistress's dress, but when he comments on her likeness to his maid she dismisses the suggestion in her famous 'laughing song' ('Mein Herr Marquis'). Next Falke introduces Eisenstein to a guest who has arrived somewhat late. It is Frank, the prison governor, posing as the 'Chevalier Chagrin', and the two struggle to hold a conversation in schoolboy French. Then a masked Hungarian countess arrives, who turns out to be none other than Rosalinde in disguise. Eisenstein has been flirting outrageously with the young ladies at the party, demonstrating his unusual repeater watch, but when he tries the same technique on the supposed Hungarian countess in a charming duet ('Dieser Anstand, so manierlich'), she ends up by pocketing the watch.

The guests press the Hungarian countess to remove her mask, but Orlofsky defends her, and she proceeds to convince everyone of her credentials by singing a brilliant and fiery Hungarian *csárdás* ('Klänge der Heimat'). Enchanted by her performance, the guests now turn to Falke to urge him to tell them the story of the bat, but it is Eisenstein who triumphantly relates the story of how some years ago, after a fancy-dress ball, he had left Falke to walk home in broad daylight dressed as a bat.

The guests sit down to supper, and Orlofsky proposes a toast to champagne, the king of all wines ('Im Feuerstrom der Reben'). As the wine flows, Falke leads the guests in a declaration of everlasting brotherhood in a slow, gently sentimental waltz ('Brüderlein und Schwesterlein'). All then embark on a fast, swirling waltz, already heard in the overture ('Ha, welch' ein Fest!'); but, as the clock strikes six in the morning, Eisenstein and Frank both seize their hats and cloaks and rush off.

Act 3 *The prison governor's office* The voice of Alfred singing in his cell can be heard off stage, despite the efforts of the drunken jailer Frosch to silence him. Frank enters unsteadily, recalling the delights of Orlofsky's party. Then Adele and Ida arrive, asking for the 'Chevalier Chagrin'. She confesses that she is not really an actress, but she believes that the 'Chevalier', as a man of obvious influence, will be able to help her get on the stage, and she proceeds to give him a demonstration of her versatile acting talents ('Spiel' ich die Unschuld vom Lande').

Eisenstein now arrives to start his prison sentence and is surprised to encounter the 'Chevalier Chagrin'. When Eisenstein gives his real identity, Frank points out that he had personally arrested Eisenstein the previous evening and now has him safely under lock and key. Frosch is sent to fetch him. Then Dr Blind arrives, claiming that Eisenstein has summoned him. Anxious to discover who it might be who had been found in his smoking cap and dressing gown in his wife's company, Eisenstein borrows Blind's wig, gown and spectacles. Frosch returns with Alfred, and they are joined shortly afterwards by Rosalinde. Eisenstein, affecting Blind's stutter, questions them about the events of the previous evening, finding it difficult to remain impassive as the details emerge ('Ich stehe voll Zagen'). Eventually, unable to control his moral indignation any longer, Eisenstein reveals his identity, to the dramatic music heard at the beginning of the overture.

Rosalinde shows herself equal to the challenge by producing the repeater watch with which the Marquis Renard had the previous evening sought to seduce the Hungarian countess. Now all the other principal characters arrive, and Falke reveals to Eisenstein that the whole affair had been set up by him as the bat's revenge. Eisenstein can do nothing but take it in good heart, and the whole company agree that the blame for any misdemeanours can be laid firmly at the door of King Champagne ('O Fledermaus, O Fledermaus').

*

Just as the wit and originality of Meilhac and Halévy had provided Offenbach with his most enduring successes, so also, in translation, the same writers inspired Johann Strauss to a vitality and sparkle that he achieved in no other of his operettas. The resultant work has, more than any other operetta, transcended its origins to become an acknowledged cornerstone of the operatic repertory.   A.L.

Fliegende Holländer, Der ('The Flying Dutchman')

Romantische Oper in three acts by Richard Wagner to his own libretto after Heinrich Heine's *Aus den Memoiren des Herren von Schnabelewopski*; Dresden, Königliches Sächsisches Hoftheater, 2 January 1843.

The première was conducted by Wagner, with Wilhelmine Schröder-Devrient as Senta and Johann Michael Wächter as the Dutchman.

Daland *a Norwegian sailor*	bass
Senta *his daughter*	soprano
Erik *a huntsman*	tenor
Mary *Senta's nurse*	contralto
Daland's Steersman	tenor
The Dutchman	bass-baritone
Norwegian sailors, the Dutchman's crew, young women	
Setting The Norwegian coast	

The supposedly autobiographical inspiration of the *Holländer* vividly described in *Mein Leben* – according to which the work took shape during the Wagners' stormy sea crossing in July and August 1839 – is in part a fantasy. If any musical sketches were made in the months following the voyage on the *Thetis*, they have not survived. The first numbers to be composed were Senta's Ballad, and the choruses of the Norwegian sailors and Dutchman's crew, some time between 3 May and 26 July 1840. The poem was written in May 1841 and the remainder of the music during the summer, the overture being completed last, in November 1841.

Heine's retelling of the nautical legend provided Wagner with his chief source, but the composer, who identified himself with the persecuted, uprooted, sexually unfulfilled protagonist, introduced what was to become the characteristic theme of redemption by a woman. The purchase of Wagner's original prose scenario in July 1841 by Léon Pillet, the director of the Paris Opéra, led ultimately to a commission not for Wagner (as he had hoped) but for Pierre-Louis Dietsch. Contrary to what is frequently stated, Dietsch's librettists, Paul Foucher and Bénédict-Henry Révoil, based their opera *Le vaisseau fantôme* not primarily on Wagner's scenario but on

'Der fliegende Holländer'
(Wagner), drawing by
Michael Echier of the
final scene in Act 3 in the
1864 Munich revival, with
sets by Heinrich Döll

Captain Marryat's novel *The Phantom Ship*, as well as on Sir Walter Scott's *The Pirate* and tales by Heine, Fenimore Cooper and Wilhelm Hauff. However, the appearance of *Le vaisseau fantôme* on the stage at the Opéra in the same month (November 1842) as rehearsals for the *Holländer* began in Dresden was undoubtedly one reason for the 11th-hour changes in Wagner's score. Until just a few weeks before the première, Wagner's opera was set off the Scottish coast, with Daland and Erik named Donald and Georg respectively. Other factors in the change may have been Wagner's desire to reinforce the autobiographical element and to distance himself at the same time from the Scottish setting of Heine.

Wagner originally conceived his work in a single act, the better to ensure its acceptance as a curtain-raiser before a ballet at the Opéra; his later claim that it was in order to focus on the dramatic essentials rather than on 'tiresome operatic accessories' may be retrospective rationalization. By the time he came to write the music, the first consideration no longer applied, his proposal having been rejected by the Opéra. He therefore elaborated the scheme in three acts, but at this stage to be played without a break. Then, some time after the end of October 1842, when he retrieved his score from the Berlin Opera (and possibly acting on advice from that quarter), he recast it in three separate acts – the form in which it was given in Dresden and subsequently published. Following Cosima Wagner's example when she introduced it at Bayreuth in 1901, the work is now often given, both there and elsewhere, in the single-act version. There is, however, an ideological element in Bayreuth's preference for the version that presents the work most convincingly

as an incipient music drama (as Wagner himself viewed it in retrospect), and both versions have some claim to authenticity.

Wagner made revisions to the score, largely in the orchestration, in 1846 and again in 1852. In 1860 (not, as sometimes stated, in 1852) the coda of the overture was remodelled (and accordingly the ending of the whole work), introducing a motif of redemption; the textures of the 1860 revision also reflect Wagner's recent preoccupation with *Tristan*.

The first performance in London was in 1870 (in Italian); it was given there in English in 1876 and in German in 1882. The American première (1876, Philadelphia) was also in Italian; it was first given in New York the following year and at the Metropolitan in 1889. Notable interpreters of the title role have included Anton van Rooy, Friedrich Schorr, Hans Hotter, Hermann Uhde, George London, Robert Hale and James Morris. Senta has been sung by Emmy Destinn, Maria Müller, Astrid Varnay, Anja Silja, Gwyneth Jones, and Hildegard Behrens.

*

Act I *A steep, rocky shore* The curtain rises to a continuation of the stormy music of the overture, but now in B♭ minor, in contrast to the overture's D minor/major. Daland's ship has just cast anchor. The cries of the Norwegian sailors ('Johohe! Hallojo!') as they furl the sails allude to their chorus first heard in its entirety in Act 3. The crew is sent to rest and the steersman left on watch. His song, 'Mit Gewitter und Sturm aus fernem Meer', begins confidently, but the phrases of its second stanza are repeatedly interrupted by orchestral comments as he succumbs to slumber. Immediately the storm begins to rage again, and open-5th 'horn calls', string tremolos and a shift of tonality (from B♭ major to B minor) signify the appearance of the Flying Dutchman's ship with its blood-red sails.

The Dutchman's monologue that follows begins with a recitative, 'Die Frist ist um', in which he tells how he is permitted to come on land once every seven years to seek redemption from an as yet unnamed curse. A section in 6/8 marked 'Allegro molto agitato', 'Wie oft in Meeres tiefsten Schlund', projects a powerfully declaimed vocal line against a storm-tossed accompaniment. An earnest entreaty for deliverance is then sung over relentlessly tremolo strings, in a manner criticized by Berlioz, and the monologue ends with a broadly phrased section, 'Nur eine Hoffnung', in which the Dutchman looks forward to Judgment Day. From their ship's hold, his crew distantly echo his last words.

Daland comes on deck, sees the strange ship, and hails its captain, whom he sees on land. The captain introduces himself simply as 'a Dutchman', going on to give a diplomatically compressed account of his voyaging, 'Durch Sturm und bösen Wind verschlagen'. The regular four-bar phrasing of the latter section, contrasted with the freer phrase structures of 'Die Frist ist um', signify what is to become a characteristic of the score: the 'exterior', public world of Daland, Erik and the Norwegian sailors and maidens is represented by traditional forms and harmonies, while the 'interior', self-absorbed world of the Dutchman and Senta frequently breaks out of the straitjacket of conventionality.

The Dutchman offers Daland vast wealth in exchange for a night's hospitality. Daland, who cannot believe his ears, is no less delighted by the wealthy stranger's interest when he tells him he has a daughter, and in the ensuing duet, 'Wie? Hört' ich recht?', the Dutchman's rugged individuality is entirely submerged by Daland's triteness. Daland's greedy, meretricious character is perfectly conveyed both here and in the duet's continuation, with its jaunty rhythms and elementary harmonic scheme. With the Dutchman preparing to follow Daland to his house, the Norwegian sailors steer the tonality back to B♭ major for a full-chorus reprise of the Steersman's Song.

Act 2 *A large room in Daland's house* To cover the scene change in the original continuous version, Wagner wrote a passage in which the virile double-dotted rhythms of the sailors are transformed into the humming of the spinning wheels in the opening chorus of the second act, 'Summ und brumm'. The full dramatic effect of that transition is lost when the work is given in three separate acts, though the repetition of music from the end of Act 1 at the beginning of Act 2 has a deleterious effect only when the opera is heard on recordings, not in the theatre

with an intervening interval. (A similar situation arises between Acts 2 and 3.)

The repetitive figures (both melodic and accompanimental) of the Spinning Chorus evoke not only the ceaseless turning of the wheels, but also the humdrum (if contented) existence of the young women. Urged on by Mary, Daland's housekeeper and Senta's nurse, the women spin in order to please their lovers who are away at sea. Senta is meanwhile reclining reflectively in an armchair, gazing at a picture hanging on the wall of a pale man with a dark beard in black, Spanish dress. She is reproached for her idleness by Mary and mocked in onomatopoeic cascades of laughter by the other women. Senta retaliates by ridiculing the tediousness of the Spinning Chorus, asking Mary to sing instead the ballad of the Flying Dutchman. Mary declines and continues spinning as the other women gather round to hear Senta sing it herself.

Senta's Ballad, 'Johohoe! Johohohoe!', begins with the same bracing open 5ths on tremolo strings that began the overture, and with the 'horn-call' figure of the Dutchman heard first as a pounding bass and then in the vocal line itself. The startling effect of these opening gestures is enhanced, in the version familiar today, by the unprepared drop in tonality from A major to G minor; however, the Ballad was originally in A minor, and Wagner transposed it down at a late date (the end of 1842) for Schröder-Devrient. The strophic structure of Senta's Ballad sets it firmly in the early 19th-century operatic tradition of interpolated narrative songs; indeed, there is a direct link with the song sung by Emmy in Marschner's *Der Vampyr*, which Wagner had prepared for performance in Würzburg in 1833. Each of Senta's three turbulent stanzas (in which we learn that the Flying Dutchman's curse was laid on him for a blasphemous oath) is followed by a consolatory refrain featuring the motif associated with redemption; the final refrain is taken by the chorus, but in an abrupt breach of precedent, Senta, 'carried away by a sudden inspiration', bursts into an ecstatic coda expressing her determination to be the instrument of the Flying Dutchman's salvation. Wagner's retrospective account of the genesis of the *Holländer*, representing Senta's Ballad as the 'thematic seed' or conceptual nucleus of the whole work, was designed to depict the opera as an incipient music drama. But although some elements of the Ballad appear elsewhere in the work, and even in some of its central numbers, the use of the various motifs bears little relation to the closely integrated structural organization of the later works such as the *Ring*.

Erik, who is in love with Senta, is horrified to hear her outburst as he enters. He announces that Daland's ship has returned, and the young women busily prepare to welcome their menfolk. Erik

detains Senta and launches into a passionate protestation of love, 'Mein Herz voll Treue bis zum
Sterben', whose conventionality of utterance and
regularity of period scarcely commend themselves to
Senta in her present mood. She struggles to get away
but is forced to endure another stanza. After an
exchange in which Senta alarms Erik by telling of her
empathy with the strange seafarer in the picture, the
huntsman recounts a dream whose ominous significance he now dimly discerns: 'Auf hohem Felsen'.
From several points of view, Erik's Dream Narration
represents the most advanced writing in the work.
Where in his previous song the regular phrases had
frequently forced normally unaccented syllables on
to strong beats, in the Dream Narration the length of
phrases is determined by the rhythms of the lines.
The lack of melodic interest is an indication of how
far Wagner had yet to go to achieve the subtle
musico-poetic synthesis of his mature works; nevertheless it is a worthy precursor of the narrations of
Tannhäuser and Lohengrin. As Erik recounts how he
dreamt that Senta's father brought home a stranger
resembling the seafarer in the picture, Senta, in a
mesmeric trance, relives the fantasy, her excited
interjections latterly adopting the rising 4th of the
Dutchman's motif.

Erik rushes away in despair and Senta muses on
the picture. As she croons the 'redemption' refrain of
the Ballad, the door opens and her father appears
with the Dutchman. Recognizing him as the seafarer
in the picture, Senta is spellbound and fails to greet
her father. Daland approaches her and introduces the
Dutchman in a characteristically breezy, four-square
aria, 'Mögst du, mein Kind'.

Daland retires and, after a coda based on themes
associated with Daland, the Dutchman and Senta, the
long duet that occupies most of the rest of the act
begins. Its unconventionality is signified by the
opening statements of both characters in turn, each
absorbed in his and her own thoughts. The voices
eventually come together and there is even a quasi-
traditional cadenza. A new plane of reality is
signalled by a slight increase in tempo and a shift
from E major to E minor. The pair now address each
other, and in response to the Dutchman's inquiry,
Senta promises obedience to her father's wishes. She
goes on to express her desire to bring him
redemption, and in an *agitato* section he warns of the
fate that would befall her if she failed to keep her vow
of constancy. Against an accompaniment of repeated
wind chords redolent of a celestial chorus, Senta
pledges faithfulness unto death, and the final
exultant section of the duet is launched with the
singers heard first separately and then together.
Although not free of the constraints of traditional
opera, the duet is the musical and emotional high
point of the work.

Daland re-enters to ask whether the feast of
homecoming can be combined with that of a
betrothal. Senta reaffirms her vow and the three join
in a rapturous trio to bring the act to an end.

Act 3 *A bay with a rocky shore* Daland's house
stands in the foreground, to one side. In the
background the Norwegian ship is lit up and the
sailors are making merry on the deck, while the
Dutch ship nearby is unnaturally dark and silent.
According to Wagner's account in *Mein Leben*, the
theme of the Norwegian Sailors' Chorus, 'Steuer-
mann! Lass die Wacht!', was suggested to him by the
call of the sailors as it echoed round the granite walls
of the Norwegian harbour of Sandviken, as the *Thetis*
took refuge there on 29 July 1839. After the first
strains of the chorus, the men dance on deck,
stamping their feet in time with the music. The
women bring out baskets of food and drink and call
out to the Dutch ship, inviting the crew to participate.
Men and women cry out in turn, but a deathly silence
is the only response. The lighthearted appeals of
sailors and womenfolk, again in alternation, become
more earnest, and tension is accumulated in the
orchestral texture too. A *forte* and then a *fortissimo* cry
are both unanswered, and the Norwegians only half-
jestingly recall the legend of the Flying Dutchman
and his ghostly crew. Their carousing becomes more
manic, and the Dutchman's motif in the orchestra,
accompanied by sinister chromatic rumblings, builds
to a climax. A storm rises in the vicinity of the Dutch
ship, and the crew finally burst into unearthly song,
the wind whistling through the rigging. The Norwegian sailors attempt to compete, in a powerful piece
of writing for double chorus, but they are eventually
subdued.

Senta comes out of the house, followed by Erik,
who demands to know why she has changed her
allegiance. In a cavatina of conventional cut, 'Willst
jenes Tags du nicht dich mehr entsinnen', he reminds
her that she had once pledged to be true to him. The
Dutchman, who has overheard, makes to return to
his ship and releases Senta from her vow to him. She
protests her fidelity and the Dutchman, Erik and
Senta all voice their emotions in a trio (often
needlessly cut).

In a recitative, the Dutchman tells of his terrible
fate and how he is saving Senta from the same by
releasing her. He boards his ship, and Senta,
proclaiming her redeeming fidelity in a final ecstatic
outcry, casts herself into the sea. The Dutchman's
ship, with all its crew, sinks immediately. The sea
rises and falls again, revealing the Dutchman and
Senta, transfigured and locked in embrace.

*

The first work of Wagner's maturity, *Der fliegende
Holländer* brings together several ingredients characteristic of the later works, notably the single-minded

attention given to the mood and colour of the drama, and the themes of suffering by a Romantic outsider and of redemption by a faithful woman. The initial stages of a tendency towards dissolution of numbers and towards a synthesis of text and music also endorse Wagner's assertion that with the *Holländer* he began his career as a true poet. **B.M.**

Forza del destino, La ('The Power of Fate' [*The Force of Destiny*])

Opera in four acts by Giuseppe Verdi to a libretto by Francesco Maria Piave after Angel de Saavedra, Duke of Rivas's play *Don Alvaro, o La fuerza del sino*, with a scene from Friedrich von Schiller's play *Wallensteins Lager*, translated by Andrea Maffei; St Petersburg, Imperial Theatre, 29 October/10 November 1862 (revised version, with additional text by Antonio Ghislanzoni, Milan, Teatro alla Scala, 27 February 1869).

The première starred Caroline Barbot (Leonora), Francesco Graziani (Carlo), Enrico Tamberlik (Alvaro) and Constance Nantier-Didiée (Preziosilla). The cast for the revised version included Teresa Stolz (Leonora), Luigi Colonnese (Carlo), Mario Tiberini (Alvaro) and Ida Benza (Preziosilla).

The Marquis of Calatrava	bass
Donna Leonora *his daughter*	soprano
Don Carlo di Vargas *his son*	baritone
Don Alvaro	tenor
Preziosilla *a young gypsy*	mezzo-soprano
The Padre Guardiano	bass
Fra Melitone *a Franciscan*	baritone
Curra *Leonora's maid*	mezzo-soprano
An Alcalde	bass
Mastro Trabuco *a muleteer, then pedlar*	tenor
A Surgeon *(in the Spanish army)*	bass

Muleteers, Spanish and Italian peasants,
    Spanish and Italian soldiers of various
    rank, their orderlies, Italian recruits,
    Franciscan friars, poor mendicants,
    vivandières
Dancers: Peasants, Spanish and Italian vivandières,
    Spanish and Italian soldiers
Walk-on parts: Innkeeper, innkeeper's wife, servants
    at the inn, muleteers, Spanish and Italian
    soldiers, drummers, buglers, peasants
    and children of both nations, a tumbler,
    pedlars
Setting Spain and Italy, around the middle of
    the 18th century

After *Un ballo in maschera* (finished in early 1858), Verdi experienced his most serious compositional hiatus to date, repeatedly telling friends that he had ceased to be a composer and that his farmlands at S Agata now took up all his time. In fact he had now become a national figure beyond the operatic world; in 1859 his name was apparently taken up as an acrostic message of nationalistic aspirations ('Viva VERDI' standing for Viva Vittorio Emanuele Re D'Italia); in 1861, during the first shaky months of Italian statehood, he agreed, at the personal insistence of Cavour, to serve as a member of the newly formed Italian parliament. And in 1859 he and Strepponi had finally been married after more than ten years together.

The breakthrough to fresh creativity came in late 1860 when the famous tenor Enrico Tamberlik wrote to Verdi offering him a commission from the Imperial Theatre at St Petersburg. Verdi first suggested Victor Hugo's *Ruy Blas*, which initially met with censorship problems and then apparently failed to hold the composer's interest. By the middle of 1861 he had decided on Rivas's *Don Alvaro*, a Spanish romantic melodrama, written under the influence of Hugo. The librettist was again to be Piave, although Verdi approached his friend and former collaborator Andrea Maffei about including material from Schiller's *Wallensteins Lager* – a move that immediately indicated his intention of writing an opera of wide-ranging dramatic ambience. Serious work began on the opera in August 1861 and by November it was more or less complete (except, as usual, for the orchestration, which Verdi still preferred to complete nearer the time of performance, when he had experienced the singers and the theatrical acoustics at first hand). Verdi left for Russia in late 1861, but the première was postponed owing to the illness of the prima donna. He undertook several lengthy European trips during the first half of 1862 and returned to supervise rehearsals at St Petersburg in September of that year. The first performance was praised in some journals, but was at best only a moderate success.

It is clear that Verdi was not entirely happy with this or subsequent performances, and by 1863 he was talking of making alterations to the score, notably to the endings of Acts 3 and 4. Various large-scale structural alterations were discussed during the next few years with a view to a Parisian première in the mid-1860s, but pressure of other work caused plans to be shelved. Then in 1868 – after the première of *Don Carlos* at the Opéra – Verdi agreed to a new production of *La forza* at La Scala the following year. The librettist Antonio Ghislanzoni was drafted to help with modifications (the devoted Piave had in 1867 succumbed to a stroke which incapacitated him for the rest of his life); Verdi eventually elected to replace the *preludio* with a full-scale overture, to revise portions of Act 3, to make various minor

Set design by Carlo Ferrario for the première of Verdi's revised 'La forza del destino', La Scala, Milan, 27 February 1869, showing the village of Hornachuelos in Act 2 scene i

alterations to other passages and, perhaps most important, to replace the bitter catastrophe of the final scene (in which all three principals die) with a scene of religious consolation. The performance, ably conducted by Angelo Mariani, was a considerable success and *La forza* remained a popular element of the repertory during the later years of the 19th century. There is some evidence that Verdi was actively involved in a cut-down French version of the score, first heard in Antwerp in 1882; but this version seems to have survived only in vocal score and was never sanctioned by Verdi's publisher Ricordi.

*

The overture (which, as mentioned above, belongs to the 1869 version, though deriving from the shorter *preludio* of 1862) is a potpourri of the score's most memorable tunes. It begins with a solemn three-note unison (usually called the 'fate' motif) and then a driving string theme that proves to be the dominant idea. Subsequent melodies are taken, in order of appearance, from the final-act duet between Alvaro and Carlo, from Leonora's Act 2 aria, 'Madre, pietosa Vergine', and from Leonora's Act 2 duet with Padre Guardiano (two themes, one associated with Leonora, one with the priest). The overture makes few concessions to classical ideas of balance, though it is given at least a surface impression of greater coherence by continual 'motivic' references to the main theme.

Act I *The Marquis of Calatrava's house in Seville*
After twice sounding the three-note unison that began the overture, the scene begins with a restrained string theme, though one whose syncopations and minor inflections hint at troubled undercurrents. The Marquis of Calatrava bids goodnight to his daughter, concerned by her sadness. Leonora can offer only anguished asides. As the Marquis retires, Curra begins preparations for Leonora's elopement. Leonora's indecision is intense, but Curra outlines the bloody consequences for her lover Alvaro, who is thought racially inferior, if he is now deserted. In the aria 'Me pellegrina ed orfana', which is in two contrasting sections and – as befits its dramatic position – involves no large-scale internal repetitions, Leonora bids a tender farewell to her homeland. The sound of approaching horses heralds Alvaro, who climbs in through a window. He immediately launches a duet, in four movements, conventionally patterned though economical. The first movement, 'Ah, per sempre', is dominated by Alvaro's impetuosity, but when Leonora shows signs of reluctance he settles into a more lyrical second movement ('Pronti destrieri'), which begins as a typical 3/8 wooing piece for romantic tenor but develops unusual vocal power as Alvaro recalls the gods of his native land (he is South American). The third movement (somewhat revised for 1869) as usual injects new action: Leonora begs that the elopement be postponed another day, protesting her love amid weeping that makes Alvaro suspicious; he accuses her of not loving him; she passionately affirms her feelings – and so to the cabaletta, 'Seguirti fino agl'ultimi', in which the lovers prepare to depart, and which is skilfully structured so that the final, curtailed reprise is preceded and precipitated

by the sound of approaching footsteps. A brief recitative, in which Alvaro draws his pistol, is followed by the 'scena-finale', an action movement dominated by the pulsating main theme of the overture, modulating rapidly and purposefully to match events on stage. The Marquis of Calatrava enters. He insults Alvaro, goading him to a duel; Alvaro refuses and throws down his pistol. But the weapon accidentally discharges, fatally wounding the old man, who with his dying breath curses his daughter. Alvaro and Leonora make their escape, thus closing one of the most tightly constructed, economical acts in all Verdi.

Act 2.i *The village of Hornachuelos and its surroundings* This scene is as expansive and repetitious as the previous one was tight and economical. 18 months have passed. The sprightly opening chorus, 'Holà! Ben giungi, o mulattier', gives way to a peasant dance, both pieces richly imbued with Spanish local colour (the first more than a little reminiscent of passages in *Il trovatore*). Supper is announced at the inn and a 'student' (in fact Don Carlo, in search of his sister and 'her seducer') says grace. The dance music continues. Leonora enters dressed as a young man, recognizes her brother and immediately retreats. The stage is now taken by Preziosilla, who encourages the young men to leave for Italy to join battle against the invading Germans and sings a rousing canzone, 'Al suon del tamburo', a French-influenced strophic song with refrain which recalls Oscar's music in *Un ballo in maschera*. During the final stages of the song Preziosilla consents to read Carlo's fortune and predicts a miserable future.

A chorus of pilgrims is heard in the distance; their chant forms the basis of a large-scale concertato movement, 'Padre Eterno Signor', which is punctuated by Leonora's desperate cries for divine mercy. As the pilgrims depart, Carlo takes centre stage and treats the company to a narrative ballata, 'Son Pereda, son ricco d'onore': his name is Pereda and he has been helping a friend track down the friend's sister and her lover. The predictable form and simple rhythm retain something of the comic opera atmosphere, although contrasting internal episodes give hints of tragic undercurrents. But Preziosilla and the others are happy enough, and the scene ends with some elaborate exchanges of 'goodnight' and a lively reprise of the opening chorus and dance tune.

2.ii *A small clearing on the slopes of a steep mountain* Leonora struggles towards the door of a monastery, and in a turbulent recitative recalls her horror on hearing her brother's story at the inn, especially his news that Alvaro, from whom she was separated in flight, has returned to his homeland. She falls on her knees to beg divine forgiveness in the famous 'Madre, pietosa Vergine', which is cast as a minor–major *romanza*, the first part underpinned by an obsessive string motif, the second based on the aspiring melody that had served as climax to the overture.

Leonora rings the monastery bell and, as Melitone (a comic character) departs to find the Padre Guardiano (Father Superior), she sings a further arioso in which the overture's main theme is once again juxtaposed with the aspiring melody. The Padre appears and dismisses Melitone, so beginning one of the opera's grand duets. After a brief scena, the number falls into the conventional four movements, although with the basic difference that Leonora and the Padre have comparatively little interaction: both remain enclosed within their very different views of the world. The first movement, 'Infelice, delusa', is as usual a series of sharply contrasted episodes, as Leonora tells her story and begs for a refuge from life. The second movement, 'Chi può legger nel futuro', offers a brief respite as the two voices come together, but in the third contrast returns. Eventually the Padre agrees to help her, and they join in a final cabaletta, 'Sull'alba il piede all'eremo'.

The great door of the church opens and a long procession of monks files down the sides of the choir. In a solemn ritual, the Padre tells the monks that a hermit is to live in the holy cave, and that no one must invade his seclusion. All join in a curse on any violator, 'Il Cielo fulmini, incenerisca'. The act closes with a quiet, simple hymn, 'La Vergine degli Angeli', before Leonora sets off to her hermitage.

Act 3.i *In Italy, near Velletri: a wood, at dead of night* Both Alvaro and Carlo have become involved in the war that is raging. A robust orchestral introduction and offstage chorus are hushed as Alvaro comes forward to the strains of a long clarinet solo, which elaborates a theme first heard in the Act 1 love duet. In an arioso punctuated by wisps of clarinet sound, Alvaro explains his noble birth and unhappy childhood. Then, in 'Oh, tu che in seno agli angeli', he asks Leonora (whom he believes dead) to look down on him from heaven. The aria begins in conventionally patterned phrases but soon takes on the 'progressive' form so typical of Verdi's later style.

Offstage noises disrupt Alvaro's pensive mood and he departs to investigate. Moments later he returns with Carlo, having saved him from assassins. The two hurriedly exchange false names and then swear eternal allegiance in a brief, sparsely accompanied duet. Further offstage cries alert them to a renewed enemy attack, and they rush off together.

3.ii *Morning: the quarters of a senior officer of the Spanish army* As the scene changes, the orchestra depicts a battle and a surgeon describes its progress. Although victory is announced, Alvaro is carried on severely wounded. Carlo tries to rally him, promising the Order of Calatrava; but Alvaro reacts violently to the name. The wounded man requests a private interview with Carlo, and in the famous duet 'Solenne in quest'ora' entrusts his new friend with the key to a case wherein lies a packet, to be burnt if Alvaro dies. The 'duet', dominated by Alvaro, is reminiscent of a traditional minor–major *romanza*: the opening minor section as the tenor issues his solemn commands, the major emerging as he rejoices that he can now die in peace.

Left alone, Carlo recalls Alvaro's reaction at the name of Calatrava and begins to suspect that he may be Leonora's seducer. He is tempted to break open the packet, but in 'Urna fatale', a cantabile within whose early 19th-century conventionality is buried powerful progressive elements, he tells how his honour forbids him from finding the truth. He looks elsewhere in the case and soon finds a portrait of Leonora. Just then the surgeon announces that Alvaro will live and Carlo, knowing he will now be able to wreak his vengeance, breaks into a cabaletta of savage joy, 'Egli è salvo!'

3.iii *A military encampment near Velletri* In the 1862 version the scene progresses from a long choral episode to the quarrel between Alvaro and Carlo, an offstage duel, and then a double aria for Alvaro; the 1869 version – which defers the choral episode to the end of the act, has the duel on stage and omits Alvaro's aria – has much to commend it, not least that it clarifies the action and shortens one of Verdi's most demanding tenor roles.

The scene opens with a comic-opera-style chorus, 'Compagni, sostiamo' (new for 1869), in which a patrol makes a tour of inspection. Alvaro enters, accompanied by the minor-mode version of the clarinet theme that introduced him earlier in the act. Carlo joins him and, after innocently inquiring whether his wounds are healed (we must assume that several days have passed), calls Alvaro by his true name, so precipitating a grand duet. The first movement is the traditional series of contrasting sections: Carlo reveals his own identity, Alvaro protests his innocence and finally Carlo informs Alvaro that Leonora is still alive. The second movement, 'No, d'un imene il vincolo', is a powerfully 'dissimilar' Andantino, in which Alvaro celebrates the news of his beloved's survival only to be confounded by Carlo's insistence on revenge. This leads swiftly to a closing cabaletta, 'Morte! Ov'io non cada', in which the two swear mutual defiance and begin to fight. But they are separated by a passing patrol; Carlo is dragged off, and Alvaro casts aside his sword, swearing that he will seek refuge in the cloister.

Rolls on the side drum introduce the sequence of choruses and brief solos that will close the act. First comes 'Lorchè pifferi e tamburi', a brief, lively chorus that leads directly into Preziosilla's two-strophe

French-influenced song 'Venite all'indovina', in which she offers to tell the soldiers' fortunes. A further brief round of choral celebrations precedes Trabuco's 'A buon mercato', a Jewish pedlar song in which the chorus again joins. The mood darkens with the next episode, in which a group of beggars, their lands destroyed by the war, are followed by a group of miserable conscripts. But some vivandières and Preziosilla soon brighten the atmosphere, leading the conscripts in a tarantella. Melitone enters as the dance is at full tilt and treats the company to an elaborate comic sermon (the passage is taken almost word for word from Maffei's translation of Schiller's *Wallensteins Lager*). The soldiers eventually tire of Melitone and chase him away, leaving Preziosilla to round off the act with the famous 'Rataplan' (military) chorus.

Act 4.i *Inside the monastery of Our Lady of the Angels, near Hornachuelos* Five years have passed. A crowd of beggars appears, quickly followed by Melitone carrying a cauldron of soup. In a comic-opera *parlante*, Melitone chides the beggars for asking too much, continuing even when the Padre Guardiano advises kindness to the suffering poor. Eventually Melitone's patience runs out: he kicks the pot over and orders the beggars away in the comic cabaletta 'Il resto, a voi prendetevi'. In the subsequent recitative, Melitone mentions to the Padre the strange behaviour of 'Father Raffaele' (who, we soon guess, is none other than Alvaro). The Padre counsels patience in a brief closing duet, 'Del mondo i disinganni', which contrasts his solemn ecclesiastical style with Melitone's frankly comic idiom.

The monastery bell rings loudly; Melitone answers, to find Carlo, who dispatches him to seek 'Father Raffaele'. In the ensuing recitative Carlo reiterates his desire to avenge the family honour. Alvaro enters, thus starting a grand duet in which the traditional four movements are still present though radically altered in the light of the dramatic situation. The first movement, 'Col sangue sol cancellasi', offers the usual stark contrasts: Carlo's calls for a duel are underpinned by a martial theme in the orchestra, while Alvaro's offers of peace are more lyrical and subdued. The central Andante, 'Le minaccie, i fieri accenti', based on the second theme of the overture, is of the 'dissimilar' type – each having different musical material – with Alvaro's opening melody repeated by Carlo with agitated orchestral accompaniment. The movement breaks down as Carlo taunts Alvaro as a half-breed: this is too much, and Alvaro takes up the challenge. Before rushing off to fight, the two offer mutual defiance in a very brief, coda-like cabaletta, 'Ah, segnasti la tua sorte!'

4.ii *A valley amid inaccessible rocks* Strains of the overture's main theme introduce Leonora, pale, worn and in great agitation. Her famous aria, 'Pace, pace, mio Dio!', in which she restates her love for Alvaro and begs God for peace, is like a distant homage to Bellini, whose 'long, long, long melodies' Verdi had so admired. Length indeed is here, as is the simple arpeggiated accompaniment typical of Bellini, but Verdi's line is injected with declamatory asides and harmonic shifts, a perfect expression of the new aesthetic that had overtaken Italian opera. As the aria comes to a close, she takes up food left by Padre Guardiano, but retreats hurriedly as others approach.

In the 1862 version, the opera's final scene reached a bloody conclusion. Alvaro and Carlo enter duelling; Carlo falls mortally wounded; Alvaro summons Leonora. On recognizing each other they sing a brief duet before Carlo calls Leonora to him as he dies, and, vengeful to the last, stabs her fatally. The heroine has a final, intense arioso, 'Vedi destino! io muoio!', before dying in Alvaro's arms. Sounds are heard below, and the monks appear. Padre Guardiano calls Alvaro, but he retreats to the highest point of the mountain and hurls himself into the abyss. For 1869 Verdi decided on a radical change. The opening arioso, which includes the offstage duel up to Alvaro and Leonora's meeting, is largely the same, but there is no duettino for the lovers, merely a continuation of the declamation until Leonora departs to help her brother. Alvaro has time for a brief soliloquy before an offstage scream interrupts him. Leonora, mortally wounded, is led on by Padre Guardiano: furious, dissonant 'death figures' in the orchestra cause a breakdown in the musical flow. But from this arises the final, lyrical trio, 'Non imprecare, umiliati', led off in the minor by Padre Guardiano. At first the two lovers can offer only fragmentary comments, but then the music turns to major, and a new, transfiguring melody arises from the orchestra, over which Alvaro declaims that he is 'redeemed'. Leonora in her death throes leads off the final section, which concludes the opera with a sense of resolution and lyrical space.

*

La forza del destino reached something of a low point in the early years of this century, its sprawling action and mixture of comic, tragic and picturesque finding no resonance in a climate dominated by the Wagnerian model. But times have changed, and since the 1930s the opera has become one of the most popular of Verdi's works after the three middle-period masterpieces. This swing of fortune suggests an important shift in our expectations of what constitutes satisfying musical drama, because La forza is undoubtedly Verdi's most daring attempt at creating a 'patchwork' drama – or, as he once called it, an 'opera of ideas'. We look in vain for the kind of unifying colours found in Rigoletto or Il trovatore, and

it is surely no accident that Verdi's 1869 revision could so radically change certain sequences in the action, even – as in Act 3 – transferring passages from one part of a scene to another. The opera is, in other words, only loosely linear: a significant precursor of 'native' Russian operas such as Prince Igor and Boris Godunov.

The presence of certain recurring themes, in particular the main theme of the overture (frequently dubbed a 'destiny' or 'fate' motif) has often been mentioned by commentators and is sometimes advanced as exemplifying the score's 'musical unity'. Perhaps that is so, but one could equally well see these recurring elements as an attempt to give some semblance of musical connectedness to a score that conspicuously lacks the cohesion Verdi so effortlessly achieved in his middle-period works. Nor, of course, are the themes used in anything like a consistent manner. An opera such as this, whose time gaps and scope make necessary a steady sequence of narratives (all the major characters are obliged to explain their past actions to each other), might easily have used a system of recurring motifs on a large scale. Nothing like that is attempted; indeed, in one sense the recurring motifs by their very literalness alert us to the extravagant gaps that are constantly and excitingly thrown up by this most challenging of works.   R.P.

Four Saints in Three Acts

'An opera to be sung' in a prologue and four acts by Virgil Thomson to a libretto by Gertrude Stein with scenario by Maurice Grosser; Wadsworth Atheneum, Hartford, Connecticut, 8 February 1934.

The first cast included Edward Matthews, Embry Wayne, Beatrice Robinson Howard, Bruce Bonner and Bertha Fitzhugh Baker.

St Settlement	lyric soprano
Commère	mezzo-soprano
Compère	bass
St Teresa I	soprano
St Teresa II	contralto
St Ignatius	baritone
St Chavez	tenor

Choral roles: St Plan, St Stephen, St Sara, St Cecilia, St Celestine, St Lawrence, St Jan, St Placide, St Absalon, St Eustace, St Genevieve, St Anne, St Answers

Setting Spain, in the 16th century

Thomson met Stein, a poet and playwright older and more famous than he, in 1926, when they were both living in Paris. By early the following year they were

'Four Saints in Three Acts' (Thomson): Prologue from the original production at Wadsworth Atheneum, Hartford, Connecticut, 8 February 1934

planning an opera. Thomson, whose musical idiom was born of the Baptist hymns of his Kansas City youth by way of Erik Satie, was drawn to Stein, who 'liked rhymes and jingles and . . . had no fear of the commonplace'. Her love for artfully constructed verbal edifices using the simplest of means, her contrapuntal interweaving of repeated words and phrases, as well as her childlike abstraction, all defined an inherently musical sensibility. 'She wrote poetry . . . very much as a composer works', Thomson recalled. 'She chose a theme and developed it, or rather, she let the words of it develop themselves through the free expansion of sound and sense . . . I took my musical freedom, following her poetic freedom, and what came out was a virtually total recall of my Southern Baptist childhood in Missouri.'

The theme Stein and Thomson chose for their first opera was the lives of 16th-century Spanish saints. 'We saw among the religious a parallel to the life we were leading', Thomson wrote, 'in which consecrated artists were practising their art surrounded by younger artists who were no less consecrated, and who were trying to learn and needing to learn the terrible disciplines of truth and spontaneity, of channeling their skills without loss of inspiration.'

The music was composed between June 1927 and July 1928, but not orchestrated until 1933. Its style was direct and accessible, in the manner of Kurt Weill and other exponents of a folksy leftism in the 1930s but purged of any political subtext. For the première Thomson's friend, the painter Maurice Grosser, provided a scenario sympathetic to Stein's dreamy poetic abstraction, yet offering some clues as to the significance of this enigmatic work.

The first performance was presented not by an established opera company but by an organization called the Friends and Enemies of Modern Music. There was an all-black cast, stage direction and movement by Frederick Ashton and John Houseman and cellophane décor by Florine Stettheimer. The same production was presented that year on Broadway and in Chicago, for a run of more than 60 performances. Despite this success, which established Thomson as an intellectuals' darling, and which vastly augmented Stein's notoriety ('Pigeons on the grass alas', from the third act, became a humorist's watchword for vanguard silliness), the opera has never entered the repertory of major opera houses. This is partly because Stein's poetry is something of an acquired taste, and partly because Thomson's *faux-naïf* music now seems prescient of minimalism. Its chamber scoring (for an orchestra of about 25, using modest strings, although the string complement can be expanded for larger theatres) has, however, made it a feasible work for smaller companies. Thomson insisted that the precedent of an all-black cast need not be considered binding, but major productions with white or mixed casts have remained rare, and most companies find it difficult to assemble all-black casts of this size. (A Robert Wilson production in 1996, seen in big opera houses in Houston, New York and Edinburgh, used a mixed cast to fine effect.) This synopsis is drawn from Grosser's scenario; it could not be deduced from Stein's words alone. The music throughout is an American patchwork of marches, waltzes, hymns and singsong recitative.

*

Prologue A choral introduction to all the saints, some 30 counting the chorus, but concentrating on the four principals (with St Teresa sung by two singers) and including the Commère and Compère.

Act I ('A Pageant, or Sunday School Entertainment') *On the steps of Avila Cathedral* This consists of seven tableaux focussed on St Teresa II and revealed through a portal by the drawing of a small curtain. The first tableau shows St Teresa II in an early-spring garden, painting Easter eggs and conversing with St Teresa I. In the second scene St Teresa II, holding a dove, is photographed by St Settlement. St Ignatius serenades the seated St Teresa II in the third scene, at the end of which she rises and asks, 'Can women have wishes?' (Stein was an early feminist). St Ignatius offers St Teresa II flowers in the fourth tableau, and in the fifth the two saints admire a model house, a Heavenly Mansion. In the sixth, St Teresa II is shown in 'an attitude of ecstasy'. Finally, she rocks an imaginary child in her arms: 'The act ends with comments, congratulations, and general sociability.'

Act 2 *A garden party in the country near Barcelona* The Compère and Commère, dressed in formal attire, observe the action from the side. A Dance of Angels is performed, St Chavez organizes a game and the Compère and Commère share 'a tender scene', observed by the two St Teresas. Everyone peers through a telescope at a vision of the Heavenly Mansion. As all pack to leave, St Ignatius refuses to give back St Teresa I's telescope; St Chavez consoles her, and remains alone on stage after the others depart.

Act 3 *A monastery garden on the coast near Barcelona* St Ignatius and his Jesuits mend fishing nets. The two St Teresas and St Settlement discuss monastic life with St Ignatius and see a vision of the Holy Ghost ('Pigeons on the grass alas', etc.). After a military drill St Chavez lectures the men, the women saints enter, doubt the vision, and are reproved by St Ignatius, who predicts the Last Judgment. After a storm passes, the saints file out, chanting and singing hymns about their future heavenly life.

Act 4 The Compère and Commère argue before the curtain as to whether there should be a fourth act. The curtain rises to reveal the saints in heaven. They remember with pleasure their earthly existence and sing a communion hymn ('When this you see remember me'). The opera ends when the Compère sings, 'Last act', and everyone else shouts, 'Which is a fact'.

*

Despite its infrequency of performance, *Four Saints* and Thomson's music in general have risen steadily in prestige, especially since the waning of total serialism among American academic composers after the 1970s. Thomson's style, which knits short phrases with rich indigenous influences, is seen now as an anticipation not just of minimalism, but of the entire movement towards simplicity, accessibility and vernacular inspiration that has defined composition in the 1980s and 90s.   J.Ro.

Francesca da Rimini ('Francesca of Rimini')

Tragic opera in four acts by Riccardo Zandonai to a libretto by Tito Ricordi the younger from the play by Gabriele D'Annunzio, after Dante Alighieri's *Inferno*, v:97–142; Turin, Teatro Regio, 19 February 1914.

The cast at the première included Linda Cannetti (Francesca), Giulio Crimi (Paolo) and Francesco Cigada (Gianciotto).

Ostasio	baritone
Francesca *his sister*	soprano
Giovanni Malatesta (Gianciotto)	baritone
Paolo *his brother*	tenor
Samaritana *Francesca's sister*	soprano
Smaragdi *a slave*	contralto
Malatestino *brother of Gianciotto and Paolo*	tenor
Biancofiore ⎫	soprano
Garsenda ⎪ *Francesca's ladies*	soprano
Altichiara ⎬	mezzo-soprano
Donella ⎭	mezzo-soprano

Ladies, archers, musicians

Setting Ravenna and Rimini in the early 14th century

D'Annunzio's tragedy, written in 1901 for Eleonora Duse and defined by the poet as 'an epic of blood and lust', needed few basic changes to become a libretto, and to some extent he himself assisted with the adaptation. Sections that, although justifiable in the decadent atmosphere of the play, were not essential to the action and would have presented serious musical difficulties were eliminated. What remains is the essence of the story of Francesca, basically as outlined by Dante but with increased sensuality and darker, more amoral overtones.

Act 1 is set in the house of Francesca's family, the Polentani, in Ravenna. Ostasio arranges a political marriage for his sister Francesca with Giovanni Malatesta, 'lo Sciancato' (the Cripple), known as Gianciotto. Surrounded by her maids, Francesca is comforted by her sister Samaritana, and believes her intended husband to be Paolo il Bello, whom she sees passing and to whom she offers a rose; she falls in love with him, though they exchange not a word, but Paolo is only representing his ungainly and cruel brother in a proxy marriage. Their wordless 'love duet' (with offstage voices) concludes Act 1. In Act 2 Francesca, now Gianciotto's wife, is living in the Malatesta house at Rimini; wounded during a battle, Paolo reveals his love to Francesca, to her distress.

Act 3 takes place in Francesca's apartments, where her ladies are singing a spring song when the slave Smaragdi announces Paolo's arrival; the two are left alone and fall passionately in love, with the encouragement of the love story of Lancelot and Guinevere which they read together (as narrated in Canto v of Dante's *Inferno*). Act 4 is in two parts, the first containing the most dramatic moments of the opera: Francesca is spied on by Malatestino, Paolo and Gianciotto's degenerate brother, who has also fallen under her spell; he discovers her adulterous liaison with Paolo and crudely attempts to blackmail her, and when she rejects him he denounces the lovers to Gianciotto. In the second part the lovers are together, confident that Gianciotto has departed; but he has in fact set a trap for them, and discovers and kills them.

*

Francesca da Rimini, considered Zandonai's masterpiece, and certainly his most popular work in Italy, is not only the most successful of the operas based on the plays of D'Annunzio (others are by Alberto Franchetti, Ildebrando Pizzetti, Gian Francesco Malipiero, Pietro Mascagni, Italo Montemezzi): it is also one of the most original and polished Italian melodramas of the 20th century. Zandonai combines a powerful gift for Italian melody, more nervous and fragmentary than Puccini's, with an exceptional command of orchestration, to some extent influenced by Strauss. *Verismo*-style vocal writing, in the tradition of Mascagni, is on the whole confined to the male voices, especially in Act 2 and the first part of Act 4, the most dramatic points of the opera, which have a degree of rhetorical inflation. The most inspired music, often with a magical effect not to be found in other contemporary composers, is in the evocation of atmosphere (with some careful use of ancient instruments), in the delicate treatment of the female choruses and, in general, in the close fidelity to the natural rise and fall of the words themselves. Particularly effective are the Act 1 finale, where the Paolo theme is developed in a context of great sweetness, and especially Act 3, the finest in the opera, which includes the charming spring song and the ardent love duet between Paolo and Francesca. There are other strongly expressive sections in the music for Francesca and Samaritana in the first and fourth acts. The dominant feeling conveyed by the score, whose harmonic world has some Debussian colouring, is melancholy and oppressed, somewhat distant from the heavy and erotic atmosphere of D'Annunzio's tragedy. Among the most impressive arias are those of Francesca ('Chi ho veduto?' and 'Paolo, datemi pace!') and of Paolo ('Inghirlandata di violette'). But some of the most striking music comes in numbers of a less traditional kind, such as the duets between Francesca and Samaritana and

between Paolo and Francesca, and the whole of the first part of Act 4 with Francesca, Gianciotto and Malatestino.   R.Ch.

Frau ohne Schatten, Die
('The Woman Without a Shadow')

Oper in three acts by Richard Strauss to a libretto by Hugo von Hofmannsthal; Vienna, Staatsoper, 10 October 1919.

Maria Jeritza and Karl Aagaard Oestvig sang the first imperial couple. The Barak pair were Richard Mayr and Lotte Lehmann, with Lucie Weidt as the Nurse and Franz Schalk conducting.

The Emperor	tenor
The Empress *Keikobad's daughter*	high dramatic soprano
The Nurse *her guardian*	dramatic mezzo-soprano
Barak *a dyer*	bass-baritone
Barak's Wife	high dramatic soprano
The One-Eyed ⎫	high bass
The One-Armed ⎬ *Barak's brothers*	bass
The Hunchback ⎭	high tenor
A Spirit Messenger	high baritone
The Voice of the Falcon	soprano
The Apparition of a Youth	high tenor
The Guardian of the Threshold	soprano/countertenor
A Voice from Above	contralto
Voices of Unborn Children	three sopranos, three contraltos
Voices of Three Nightwatchmen	baritones
Servants of the Empress, other children and beggar-children, Spirit-servants and Spirit-voices	
Setting The Emperor's palace, Barak's hut, fantastic caves and landscapes	

Soon after the première of their *Rosenkavalier* in 1911, Hofmannsthal suggested to Strauss that they might make an opera out of a fairy-tale by Wilhelm Hauff, to be called *Das steinerne Herz* ('The Heart Turning to Stone'). In the event they first created *Ariadne auf Naxos*, in both its 1912 and 1916 versions; so the fairy-tale piece – now entitled *Die Frau ohne Schatten*, and retaining only threads from Hauff – became their third full operatic collaboration. (*Elektra* had been an independent play before Strauss set it as an opera.) By then much was expected of them, as they knew too well. Hofmannsthal liked to think of *Die Frau ohne Schatten* as 'their' *Zauberflöte*, against *Der Rosenkavalier* as 'their' *Figaro*. The work proceeded slowly, for his mind teemed with so many ideas for it that he had to write a separate prose tale to accommodate them all. What with their collaboration on the ballet *Josephslegende*, Strauss's new *Alpine Symphony*, the outbreak of war and the reworking of *Ariadne*, it was 1917 before the new opera was completed.

Its philanthropic, regenerative message is 'Make children!' (a message echoed by Poulenc's *opéra-bouffe Les mamelles de Tirésias* 27 years later). Hofmannsthal's young fairy-Empress is barren, 'casts no shadow', because her immature huntsman-Emperor does nothing but self-absorbedly pursue his game. The librettist chose to give them no scene together until Act 3, when the Emperor is already freezing into stone. Understandably, the composer complained that he found this pair cold and uninspiring. The other childless couple were another matter: the librettist had confessed at the start that he was imagining the Dyer's Wife after Strauss's own formidable Pauline, and Strauss could comfortably identify himself with the decent, much-put-upon Barak.

At almost no time has the opera been staged regularly enough for any singer to establish a famous claim to a role – though Barak's music has been a gift to many mellifluous bass-baritones, and the musico-dramatic rewards of all three soprano roles have been well explored. One exception: though Strauss must have had his Emperor and the Menelaus of his *Ägyptische Helena* in mind when he used later to regret never having learnt to write for tenor, around the start of the 1960s the young American Jess Thomas was in great and justifiable demand as an Emperor *sans pareil*.

*

Act 1.i *A roof above the imperial gardens* As in *Elektra*, there is no prelude but the orchestral pronouncement of a sacred name, whose bearer – there Agamemnon, here the Empress's celestial father ('KEIK!-o'Bad', growled thrice in A♭ minor) – will never appear. At daybreak on an imperial terrace where the Nurse skulks, the Spirit Messenger (akin to the Speaker in *Die Zauberflöte*) arrives on a minatory errand. Though 12 moons have passed since the young Emperor with his Falcon brought down the Peri (fairy or spirit), wandering in the form of a gazelle, and took her to wife, she is all light still; if after three days more she casts no shadow, she must return to Keikobad, King of the Spirits, and the Emperor will turn to stone. The Nurse gloats. Now the Emperor himself passes through, eulogizing his bride-prize 'to the end of time' – for he goes off to hunt every day, and makes love to her every night. Dawn brightens into shimmering F♯ as the Empress enters, still half-dreaming about her husband; then she sees the long-lost Falcon return, weeping and bleeding, to recite the Messenger's warning. Aghast, she pleads for advice from her Nurse, who admits reluctantly that

she has often bartered the souls of men, whom she despises, and can help her find a human shadow. As they descend towards the human world an orchestral interlude boils up: much like that in *Rheingold* for Wotan's descent into Nibelheim, down to the raw percussion (here, wooden switch and castanets) that signal their arrivals in the midst of the workaday world.

1.ii *Barak's hut* In the poor dyer Barak's one-room workshop-home, his disabled, dependent brothers are quarrelling again, and his grim young Wife loses patience. Gently, Barak restores temporary peace, and promises her that he could also manage to support the children he longs for. Given no reassuring word, he goes wearily off with his dyed skins to market. Amid insidious chromatics Empress and Nurse, disguised, appear as if from nowhere. The Nurse flatters the Wife's beauty, deplores her waste of it on a lowly, aging man, and illustrates the price her shadow could fetch by conjuring up an erotic idyll with slave-girls and an unseen lover (in extreme sharp keys, like the analogous music in *Salome*). The Wife is dazzled and tempted, but then remembers that she has done nothing about dinner, nor the chaste new sleeping arrangements she wants. At a clap of the Nurse's hands the marital bed splits apart, and five fishes spring into the frying-pan – but they wail in childish voices, pleading to be born. When Barak comes home he has to be content with dry bread and a single bed. Outside, nightwatchmen (recalling *Die Meistersinger*) hymn the praises of fruitful married love in a grave coda.

Act 2.i *Barak's hut* Nurse and Empress are now installed as servants in the dyer's house. As soon as he has gone with his brothers to market, the Nurse calls up the seductive idyll again for his Wife, with the lover now in the remembered form of a Youth she secretly fancied. Just in time Barak returns, bringing a rich feast for the family, neighbours and beggars. Amid the long, gluttonous ensemble which ensues, the Wife's bitter frustration sounds a dissonant note. An orchestral interlude carries the hearty scene some way further, then declines slowly into G minor ponderings.

2.ii *The Emperor's falconer's cottage, in a forest* High woodwinds repeat the plangent cry of the Falcon, which has led the Emperor to his falconer's cottage: the Empress sent the bird with a message that she and her Nurse would retreat here for three days. Full of premonitions, he waits now in the shadows. (This is his heroic solo scena.) Soon the women return furtively and slip into the house. He scents the stench of mankind upon them, and is seized by jealousy and grief: must he not kill his gazelle? But he cannot bring himself to that, and the music descends into E♭ minor as he beseeches the Falcon to lead him away to lonely despair.

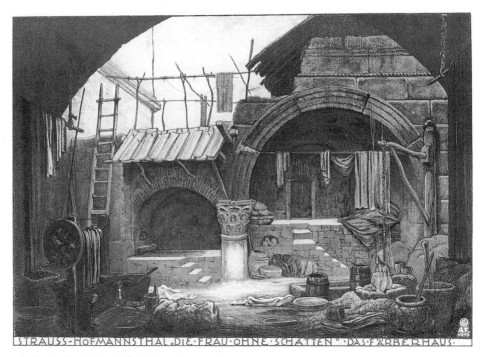

Design by Alfred Roller for Barak's hut in the original production of Richard Strauss's 'Die Frau ohne Schatten' at the Staatsoper, Vienna, 10 October 1919

2.iii *Barak's hut* A short interlude leads back to the dyer's home. In sultry heat Barak works doggedly, while his Wife prods him to get off to market and out of the house. The Nurse resolves the impasse by drugging his wine; he slumps, and immediately she revives the apparition of the Youth, now in impassioned voice. At the point of succumbing the Wife abruptly takes fright, rouses her dazed husband ('There's a man in the house!'), rails at him for his lack of understanding, announces that his home is no longer hers and stalks out with the Nurse. Picking up his tools, poor Barak finds someone helping him: 'I, master, your servant!', says the Empress.

2.iv *The falconer's cottage* Asleep in the cottage with the Nurse, the Empress is restless and troubled. She cries out that she has wronged Barak by causing his Wife to repulse him. In a lucid dream she sees the Emperor finding his way into a cavern and towards a bronze door, while invisible men's voices dare him on and the Falcon caws its warning; the door opens, and closes behind him. Keikobad's motto is repeated, and the motif that says 'He turns to stone!' The Empress wakes with a shriek, and bewails her guilt in a monologue that twists painfully from B minor to E♭ minor.

2.v *Barak's hut* At midday an uncanny darkness is closing upon Barak's house. Barak feels weighed down and his Wife yearns for escape, while Empress

and Nurse voice their contrary sentiments. Then the Wife musters the courage for her declaration of independence. She claims to have betrayed Barak during his absences, though she could not expunge his face from her mind, and now she has found the means of freeing herself: she has sold her shadow, and there will be no children. General horror; as the fire flares up, she seems indeed to cast no shadow. (Urged by the Nurse to seize it, the Empress refuses.) The Nurse conjures a sword into Barak's angry hand – but before he can strike, the unfamiliar vision of him as righteous husband and stern judge stirs his Wife to the core. Ready to die, she confesses that she lied, the bargain was not yet sealed. Over his brothers' protests Barak raises the sword, and suddenly the whole house founders. The brothers flee, the Baraks sink into the earth and the Nurse sweeps her Empress away, crowing that higher powers are in play.

Act 3.i *A subterranean vault, divided by a wall* The orchestra suggests cries and whimpers, almost atonal. In a pair of subterranean chambers, unaware of each other, Barak broods and his Wife weeps. She laments her false confession and her failure to see her husband for what he truly was ('Schweigt doch, ihr Stimmen'); Barak reproaches himself for threatening the young creature given into his trust ('Mir anvertraut'), and then their voices combine in a grand duet in Strauss's maturely ardent vein. Now a voice from above exhorts each in turn to come up: 'The way is free!' The orchestra exults, while clouds cover the scene.

3.ii *A rocky landscape outside a temple* In a setting like that of the Empress's dream, a boat with Nurse and Empress glides towards a rocky terrace, with a bronze portal high above. The fearful Nurse pleads with the Empress to fly with her – she will get her a better shadow; but the Empress hears the trombone summons from beyond the great door, where she expects to find Keikobad and throw herself upon his mercy. Their long, urgent duologue runs on triplet quavers like a frantic scherzo, ever faster until the Empress cuts it off; she has come to love self-rescuing, self-renewing mankind, and rejects the Nurse's contempt for that weak race. She strides up to the door and enters. Abandoned, the Nurse curses men, and when Barak and then his Wife appear seeking each other she cruelly misdirects them. While their unhappy voices continue from different places, the Messenger announces that Keikobad has cast the Nurse out; she let her charge escape her, and must now wander among men forever. The boat carries her swiftly away.

3.iii *Within the temple* Spirits light the Empress's way into the temple. The Guardian of the Threshold urges her to drink from a golden fountain which will assure her of the Wife's shadow; she refuses, though the ghastly stone form of the Emperor becomes visible in an alcove, only his eyes still alive and desperate. In anguish, she still finds the will to refuse again – whereupon her own shadow stretches cleanly across the floor, and her husband advances to greet her. Their raptures call up the chorus of Unborn Children once more, heard through a silvery orchestral haze.

3.iv *A fairy-tale landscape* The Baraks are reunited and the Wife again casts a shadow. The imperial couple join them, and the childish voices too. The rest is rejoicing, lustily led by Barak ('Now will I rejoice, like nobody before!') in a key which Strauss has reserved until now: honest, down-to-earth C major.

*

Unlike *Zauberflöte* or *Tirésias*, *Die Frau ohne Schatten* has no social dimension whatever. As with *Ariadne*, Hofmannsthal's imagination was gripped by 'Two Womanly Types' – one a spirit maid, ethereal to the point of suffocation, the other all-too-human. Beyond their baffled husbands and the ambiguous Nurse, the rest of the numerous cast supply only local colour and celestial commentary; the ethical fable is really concerned with inner, psychic malaises, and the visible 'action' is sketchy. Hofmannsthal aimed nevertheless at an epic-operatic dimension, and to that purpose Strauss enlisted a huge performing apparatus – violas and cellos in double sections like the violins, mostly quadruple winds, extensive percussion (including glass harmonica), an offstage woodwind septet and a dozen extra brass, organ, wind-machine and thunder-machine. Yet he saw that there was no dramatic licence for any communal outcry: even at the triumphal close, the exulting principals are supported only by their invisible Unborn Children, before a rapt diminuendo coda for Spirit-voices. Despite the scale of his forces, Strauss set much of the score in chamber-orchestral terms of pleading delicacy. (Originally, he meant to reserve an *Ariadne*-size band to the Spirit world.) Directors are often led astray by the grandiose scenic descriptions; in fact the life of *Die Frau ohne Schatten* consists in intimate vignettes strung upon a rich orchestral chain, not so unlike Debussy's *Pelléas et Mélisande*.

As usual, Strauss projected his score from a full quiver of leitmotifs. They are more easily labelled and 'heraldic', perhaps, than before – tonally fractured or curdled when he wanted a memorable nickname or motto, but unashamedly 19th-century-Romantic for positive emotions. On the other hand he developed them with high authority, especially in the interludes, revelling in advanced polytonal polyphony. That may have been compensation for the constraint he evidently felt when setting Hofmannsthal's newly elevated stage-poetry, which embodied neither a fraught interpersonal drama like *Elektra* nor the conversational fluency of *Rosenkavalier*. The result was a hugely expressive orchestral canvas (including scenic pictures), which carries a few lyrical set-pieces and a great deal of glorified recitative – like the Nurse's florid, crucial role, which boasts scarcely one memorable phrase. Though *Die Frau* suggests a noble new conception of opera, it is never easy to bring it into persuasive theatrical focus.   D.M.

Freischütz, Der ('The Freeshooter')

Romantische Oper in three acts, j277, by Carl Maria von Weber to a libretto by Johann Friedrich Kind after Johann August Apel and Friedrich Laun's *Gespensterbuch*; Berlin, Schauspielhaus, 18 June 1821.

At the première Max was sung by Heinrich Stümer, Agathe by Karoline Seidler, Caspar by Heinrich Blume and Aennchen by Johanna Eunicke.

Max *an assistant forester*	tenor
Kilian *a wealthy peasant*	baritone
Cuno *a hereditary forester*	bass
Caspar *an assistant forester*	bass
Aennchen *Agathe's relative*	mezzo-soprano
Agathe *Cuno's daughter*	soprano
Samiel *the 'Black Huntsman'*	speaking role

Four bridesmaids	sopranos
Ottokar *a sovereign prince*	baritone
Hermit	bass

Hunters, peasants, spirits, bridesmaids,
  attendants
Setting Bohemia at the end of the Thirty Years
  War

Shortly after taking up the post of Kapellmeister of
the German opera in Dresden in 1817, Weber revived
the idea of writing an opera on the *Freischütz* story,
which he had first considered seven years earlier
after reading the tale in Apel and Laun's newly
published *Gespensterbuch*. He discussed the project
with Johann Friedrich Kind, a fellow member of the
Dresden literary 'Liederkreis', who rapidly produced
the draft of a libretto provisionally entitled *Der
Probeschuss* ('The Test Shot'). Between the publication
of the *Gespensterbuch* and Kind's libretto, the story
had been used as the basis for a number of other
theatrical pieces. The first treatment of it, by Franz
Xaver von Caspar with music by Carl Neuner (1812,
Munich), may have provided certain elements for
Kind's libretto. Another two versions were produced
in Vienna in 1816. In 1818 Louis Spohr, with the
collaboration of Georg Döring, also began to
compose an opera on Apel's tale, but hearing that
Weber was working on the same subject he
abandoned it in favour of *Zemire und Azor*.

During the composition of *Der Freischütz* Weber
made a number of changes to the libretto, the most
important of which was the deletion, against Kind's
wishes, of the scenes between the Hermit and Agathe
which were to have opened the first act. In these the
Hermit sees a horrifying vision which he interprets as
a warning of danger to Agathe. When Agathe brings
him food and tells him of Max's nervousness over the
Probeschuss, he gives her, for her protection, roses
from a tree brought from Palestine.

Weber's work on *Der Freischütz* progressed
slowly. His duties in Dresden and his efforts to
promote German opera there were burdensome and
often frustrating. He was also distracted by other
commissions, and his health was increasingly weakened by the progress of tuberculosis. During 1819,
however, after he had arranged with the Intendant
of the Berlin opera, Count Brühl, for the opera (at
that stage known as *Die Jägersbraut*, 'The Hunter's
Bride') to have its première in the newly rebuilt
Schauspielhaus, he worked more intensively. By 30
November he had completed the first act and was
able to promise Brühl that he would finish the opera
by March 1820. (In the event it was not finished until
13 May.) On 18 June the following year *Der Freischütz*
became the first musical piece to be staged in the
Schauspielhaus. Its success was immediate and
long-lasting. It was by far the most widely popular

German opera of its generation, and within a few
years it conquered all the major stages of Europe. By
1830 it had been given in nine languages, and before
1850 it was staged as far afield as Cape Town, Rio de
Janeiro and Sydney. It has long been regarded as one
of the seminal works of German Romantic opera.

*

The C major–minor overture sets the scene for the
opera, its two principal tonalities representing the
healthy aspects of life as opposed to evil and the dark
powers. Horns conjure up a vision of forests and
hunting; low clarinets, timpani and especially the
sound of the diminished 7th chord, associated with
the evil Samiel, presage the dark side of the drama.
The Molto vivace is based on Max's 'Doch mich
umgarnen finstre Mächte' in Act 1, full of foreboding,
and Agathe's exultant 'Süss entzückt entgegen ihm'
in Act 2.

Act I *In front of an inn in the Bohemian forest* In a
bright, rustic D major chorus the peasants congratu-
late one of their fellows, Kilian, for his victory in a
shooting competition. They make fun of the forester
Max's failure and accompany Kilian's mocking solo
('Schau der Herr') with laughter. A fight between
Max and Kilian is prevented only by the arrival of
Cuno and some of his foresters, among whom is
Caspar. Kilian explains that they were teasing Max
because he had missed all his shots. Caspar (who,
jealous of Max, has made a compact with the Black
Huntsman), after giving thanks in an aside to Samiel
for his own accuracy, suggests that Max's gun must
be bewitched; he mockingly proposes to call on the
dark powers for assistance. Cuno intervenes, rebuking Caspar, but warns Max that if he fails in the
shooting trial the next day he will not be allowed to
marry his beloved Agathe, Cuno's daughter. Cuno
explains the origins of the shooting trial for whoever
is to inherit the chief forester's position. In the trio
with chorus 'O! diese Sonne' Max remains despondent, while Cuno admonishes him and Caspar
tempts him to rash measures. The trio opens in A
minor, and its use of a diminished 7th chord in the
third bar hints at the imminence of the dark powers.
The ensuing hunting chorus ('Lasst lustig die Hörner
erschallen!') turns to a wholesome F major. In the
dialogue Kilian wishes Max luck and invites him to
join the dance. The peasants exit, dancing to a waltz
which gradually fades and disintegrates, giving way
in a highly effective manner to a dramatic scena
('Nein! länger trag' ich nicht die Qualen') as Max is
left alone, pondering the abrupt alteration in his
success. At one point, as he wonders if Heaven has
forsaken him, the diminished 7th is heard and Samiel
is seen in the distance. As the music finishes, Caspar
comes out of the inn. He orders wine and insists on
Max's drinking several toasts with him; he then sings
a coarse drinking song which enrages Max ('Hier im

30. 'L'elisir d'amore' (Donizetti, 1832), set design for Act 2 scene i (interior of Adina's farmhouse) by Alessandro Sanquirico, probably for the original production at the Teatro Cannobiana, Milan

31. 'L'elisir d'amore' (Donizetti, 1832), scene from the John Copley production (designed by Beni Montresor) at the Royal Opera House, Covent Garden, in 1975, with Yasuko Hayashi (Adina), Geraint Evans (Dulcamara), Thomas Allen (Belcore) and José Carreras (Nemorino)

Above: 32. 'Die Entführung aus dem Serail' (Mozart, 1782), model of Oliver Messel's design for Act 1 (a plaza before Selim's palace, near the sea) of the 1956 Glyndebourne production

Below: 33. 'The Excursions of Mr Brouček' (Janáček, 1920), scene from the production by David Pountney (sets Stefanos Lazaridis, costumes Marie-Jeanne Lecca) for the English National Opera, London Coliseum, 1992, with Graham Clark as Mr Brouček

34. 'Falstaff' (Verdi, 1893), scene from the production by Andreas Homoki (sets by Frank Philipp Schlössmann, costumes Mechthild Seipel) at the Komische Oper, Berlin, in 1996

35. 'Faust' (Gounod, 1859), scene from Act 3 of the production by John Copley (designer Desmond Heeley) at the Royal Opera House, Covent Garden, 1974, with Stuart Burrows (Faust), Norman Treigle (Méphistophélès), Kiri Te Kanawa (Marguerite) and Heather Begg (Marthe)

36. 'Fidelio' (Beethoven, 1805 rev. 1814), set design (a courtyard of the prison) by Ludwig Sievert for the 1935 production at the Staatsoper, Berlin

Facing page: 37. 'Fidelio' (Beethoven, 1805 rev. 1814), the same scene, the prisoners' chorus from the production by Stéphane Braunschweig for the Deutsche Staatsoper, Berlin (sets Giorgio Barberio Corsetti, costumes Bettina Juliane Walter), seen at the Théâtre du Châtelet, Paris, in 1996, with Nadine Secunde (Leonore)

Above: 38. 'The Fiery Angel' (Prokofiev, 1955), final scene from the production (with the Kirov Opera) by David Freeman (staged by Robert Chevara, designer David Roger) at the Royal Opera House, Covent Garden, in 1992, with Paata Burchuladze as the Inquisitor

Left: 39. 'La fille du régiment' (Donizetti, 1840), Jenny Lind as Marie in a London production

40. 'Die Fledermaus' (Johann Strauss, 1874), scene from the production by Harry Kupfer (sets Hans Schavernoch, costumes Reinhard Heinrich) for the Komische Oper, Berlin, 1995, with Günter Neumann (Gabriel von Eisenstein) and Dagmar Schellenberger (Rosalinde)

41. 'Der fliegende Holländer' (Wagner, 1843), set design by Ewald Dülberg for the 1929 production at the Kroll Oper, Berlin

Left: 42. 'Die Frau ohne Schatten'
(Richard Strauss, 1919), the Dyer's
Hut in the production by John Cox
(designed by David Hockney) at the
Royal Opera House, Covent Garden,
in 1992, with Franz Grundheber
(Barak), Gwyneth Jones (Barak's
Wife) and Jane Henschel (the Nurse)

Main picture: 43. 'Der Freischütz'
(Weber, 1821), the Wolf's Glen scene
from the Götz Friedrich production
(sets by Gunther Schneider-
Siemssen, costumes Aliute Meczies)
at the Royal Opera House, Covent
Garden, in 1978, with Donald
McIntyre as Caspar and Peter
Hofmann as Max

ird'schen Jammerthal'); from its initial B minor tonality it modulates to D major, a key which Weber associates with the rustic life, but is wrenched back to B minor to the accompaniment of a shrill piccolo. When Max is about to leave Caspar tells him that he can help him succeed in the trial, and proves the point by giving him his gun to shoot at a distant bird. Max shoots and brings down a massive eagle. Caspar explains that the gun was loaded with a *Freikügel*, a magic bullet that always hits its mark; but it was his last. However, seven more can be cast if Max will meet him in the Wolf's Glen at midnight. After Max has departed, Caspar, who plans to offer him as a victim to Samiel in place of himself, exults in Max's impending damnation and his own triumph in the aria 'Schweig, schweig'.

Act 2 *A room in Cuno's house* Aennchen is fixing a portrait of Cuno's ancestor, which had fallen down and slightly injured Agathe. In the duet 'Schelm, halt' fest!' the characters of the two young women are nicely established; Aennchen's sprightly phrases show her carefree disposition, while Agathe's slower-moving ones indicate her more serious nature and her concern for Max. Aennchen cheers Agathe in a lively arietta in polonaise rhythm, 'Kommt ein schlanker Bursch gegangen', and Agathe explains that her brooding was caused by the outcome of her morning visit to the Hermit. Left alone, Agathe sings a recitative and aria in E major, 'Wie nahte mir der Schlummer . . . Leise, leise', not altogether free from the Italian influence about which Weber was so frequently critical, but highly effective in painting her character. During this number her uneasiness gives way to joy at the thought of her coming wedding day, when she hears Max's footsteps approaching. Max enters and explains that he must hurry away again to collect a stag which he has shot in the forest near the Wolf's Glen. At the mention of this dreadful place Agathe, in a C minor beginning to the E♭ trio 'Wie? was? Entsetzen!', and Aennchen express their horror, while Max explains that a hunter cannot be afraid of the forest at night when he has his duty to perform. Samiel's diminished 7th chord is heard as Max exclaims that the bright moonlight will soon be gone. By the end of the trio Aennchen has recovered her usual light-heartedness, oblivious to the anxieties of the others.

The Wolf's Glen The music of the finale begins in F♯ minor with pianissimo string tremolandos and low sustained clarinets and trombones. The subsequent tonalities of the scene are those of the individual notes of the diminished 7th chord which accompanies each of Samiel's appearances. Caspar intones a spell and a chorus of invisible spirits, accompanied by shrieks on the woodwind, answers him with owl-like calls. As a distant clock strikes

twelve, Caspar, in a short section of melodrama, calls up Samiel. As the music moves to C minor, Samiel appears and agrees to allow him three more years of life in return for another victim; Caspar suggests that Samiel direct the seventh bullet at Agathe. The music modulates to E♭ as Max arrives; he is horrified by visions of his dead mother and Agathe, but nevertheless descends into the glen. The music returns to C minor and the two men begin casting the bullets. As they are cast, the music alternates between C minor and A minor with copious use of diminished 7ths. Between each of the seven castings there are supernatural manifestations of mounting horror: flapping nightbirds; a black boar; a hurricane; cracking whips, trampling horses and wheels of fire; a wild hunt; thunder, lightning, hail, meteors and fire; and finally Samiel himself. Caspar and Max fall unconscious and the tonality returns to F♯ minor. As the clock strikes one, calm returns.

Act 3 *A forest* After an entr'acte with horn-calls, the curtain rises on a hunting party in the forest. Max has made three magnificent shots and has only one magic bullet left; he asks Caspar for more, but is refused. Caspar uses up his last magic bullet so that Max has the only one remaining, the one that belongs to Samiel.

Agathe's room Wearing her wedding dress, Agathe affirms her trust in God in the cavatina 'Und ob die Wolke'. She has had a bad dream in which she saw herself as a white dove: when Max fired his gun she fell; the dove vanished and she was Agathe again, but a bleeding black bird lay at her feet. Aennchen enters and tries to dispel Agathe's anxiety. In a *romanza* and aria, 'Einst träumte', which Weber added to the opera for his first Aennchen, she tells a tale of a cousin who had fearful nightmares which resulted from the sound of the dog rattling its chain. The bridesmaids arrive and sing a folksong about the bridal wreath, 'Wir winden dir den Jungfernkranz'. Aennchen returns with a box; the picture of Cuno's ancestor has again fallen, and the box is found to contain a funeral wreath. Both women are thoroughly shaken, but decide to make a new wreath from roses which the Hermit had given Agathe. To the final chorus of the bridesmaids' song they all depart, but the music modulates disturbingly through D minor to A minor, ending with sinister tremolos in the bass. These are answered by a sudden explosion of D major as the orchestral introduction to the rousing Huntsmen's Chorus, 'Was gleicht wohl auf Erden', begins.

A 'romantic landscape' Prince Ottokar and his retainers wait for the shooting contest to begin. Cuno requests that it take place before Agathe arrives. The Prince chooses a white dove on a branch as target. As Max takes aim Agathe enters and cries to him to hold fire, since she is the dove. The Hermit touches the

'Der Freischütz' (Weber), the Wolf's Glen scene in Act 2: engraving showing an early production

bough and the dove flies off to another tree behind which Caspar is hiding. Max shoots; both Agathe and Caspar fall to the ground and the finale begins, in C minor, the key of the dark powers. The people think Max has shot Agathe, but she is unhurt. Caspar has been fatally wounded and as Samiel, accompanied by his diminished 7th, appears to him he dies, cursing Heaven and Hell. At this point C major begins to reassert itself. Max makes a full confession, after which, despite the pleas of Cuno, Agathe and the people, the Prince banishes him. However, on the intervention of the Hermit, the Prince agrees that Max be given a year to prove himself, at the end of which the Prince will himself officiate at Max's wedding to Agathe. The opera ends with a hymn of praise for God's mercy in which the triumphant theme from Agathe's Act 2 aria, which had also crowned the overture, plays a prominent part.

*

Der Freischütz was the culmination of an important phase in Weber's struggle to realize a new, more rounded conception of German opera, a progression from the uneasy compromise between drama and music in which both elements were trivialized. His idea of combining the resources of these two

elements with the visual aspect of theatre in a unified art work was only partly realized in Der Freischütz; but, owing much to the example of French opera, he moved far beyond the limitations of Singspiel as it was practised by the majority of his German contemporaries. Along with Spohr (Faust, 1813) and Hoffmann (Undine, 1816), who had similar aims, he attempted, with considerable success, to express the essential elements of the drama in his music. Like them, Weber used tonality, musical motif, orchestral colour and various formal and structural devices. Spohr's Faust in particular, which Weber had introduced in 1816 during his term as opera director in Prague, may have exerted a considerable influence on his own use of motif. Weber himself had recognized the effectiveness of Spohr's employment of 'a few melodies, felicitously and aptly devised, [which] weave like delicate threads through the whole, and hold it together artistically', as a Prague newspaper described it. His use of motif in Der Freischütz is less subtle and pervasive than Spohr's, but for precisely that reason, perhaps, it is more effective; while even the alert listener may fail to observe the transformations of Spohr's Hell motif, Samiel's diminished 7th, with its sinister orchestration, is unmistakable. Another point of similarity between all three composers was the use of librettos that explored the relationship of the natural and supernatural worlds, a theme which continued to find favour with the German Romantic school. However, while Hoffmann's *Undine* failed to enter the repertory, and the operas of Spohr (and later those of Marschner) enjoyed only limited success in the long term, *Der Freischütz*, despite the limitations of its libretto, has held the stage uninterruptedly. This may be attributed largely to Weber's extraordinary ability to judge the effectiveness of his music in the theatre, honed by his years of work in revitalizing the opera companies in Prague and Dresden, and to his gift for combining musical substance with accessibility. Almost every number of the opera still speaks to its audiences with refreshing vigour and directness.   **C.B.**

From the House of the Dead [*Z mrtvého domu*]

Opera in three acts by Leoš Janáček to his own libretto after Fyodor Mikhaylovich Dostoyevsky's novel *Zapiski iz myortvogo doma* ('Memoirs from the House of the Dead'); Brno, National Theatre, 12 April 1930 (in Osvald Chlubna and Břetislav Bakala's arrangement).

The following singers took part in the première: Emil Olšovský (Filka), Antonín Pelc (Skuratov), Géza Fischer (Šiškov), Vlastimil Šíma (Gorjančĭkov), Božena Žlábková (Aljeja), Leonid Pribytkov (Prison Governor).

Alexandr Petrovič Gorjančikov	baritone
Aljeja *a young Tartar*	mezzo-soprano
Luka Kuzmič (Filka Morozov)	tenor
Skuratov	tenor
Šiškov	baritone
Prison Governor	bass
Tall Prisoner	tenor
Short, fat Prisoner	baritone
First Guard	tenor
Second Guard	bass
Elderly Prisoner	tenor
Voice *(off stage)*	tenor
Prisoner-cook	bass
Priest	baritone
Čekunov	bass
Drunk Prisoner	tenor
Šapkin	tenor
Prisoner-blacksmith	baritone
Prisoner/Kedril	tenor
Prisoner/Don Juan/The Brahmin/Devil	bass
Young Prisoner	tenor
Prostitute	mezzo-soprano
Čerevin	tenor

Male chorus: prisoners (taking silent parts in the Act 2 plays); guests, prison guards (silent)

Setting A Russian prison on the River Irtysh, about 1860

Janáček began sketching his final opera in February 1927. He worked directly from his Russian edition of Dostoyevsky's novel, translating into Czech as he went along. He used no libretto, simply brief notes with lists of characters, incidents and page numbers. A first version was complete by 16 or 17 October 1927, a second by 4 January 1928. From March until 20 June 1928, he worked closely with his two copyists (Václav Sedláček and Jaroslav Kulhánek), who together made a fair copy of his autograph which incorporated many changes. By the end of July 1928 Janáček had checked through Acts 1 and 2; Act 3 was on his desk when he died. Apart from any further corrections, doublings and adjustments to the orchestration that Janáček might have made at rehearsals, there is no reason to consider the opera as anything but complete. However, its sometimes chamber-like orchestration persuaded his pupils Brětislav Bakala and Osvald Chlubna to revise the opera before its first performance in Brno in 1930. Their work consisted mostly of filling out the orchestration and adding an 'optimistic' ending (an apotheosis of the freedom chorus) to replace Janáček's grim march. The later history of the opera has consisted largely of shedding these accretions. In 1961 Rafael Kubelík conducted a version in Munich based mostly on Janáček's original autograph; in 1964 Universal Edition added the original ending as an appendix to their vocal score; and in 1980 Decca released a recording by Charles Mackerras, prepared by Charles Mackerras and John Tyrrell on the basis of the copyists' score.

*

The overture was originally conceived as a violin concerto titled in successive versions 'Duše' ('Soul') and 'Putování dušičky' ('The Wandering of a Little Soul'). Its affinity with the opera is suggested by the inclusion of 'chains' in its instrumentation. Janáček's final revision placed it firmly as the separate 'úvod' ('introduction') to the opera, and some of its musical material, for instance the opening motif, is employed in the opera. In form it is a rondo; its final *maestoso* episode is a heroic fanfare which suggests the optimistic dimension of Janáček's motto for the opera, 'In every creature a spark of God'.

Act I *A courtyard in a Siberian prison; early morning* The opening motif of the opera (ex.1), with its painful dissonances, is a motto theme that runs through the whole of this act. Prisoners come in from the barracks and wash and argue. They talk of a new prisoner, a gentleman (Alexandr Petrovic Gorjančikov), whose arrival soon follows. His fear and vulnerability are suggested by a high solo violin, heard above ex.1. The

Ex.1   Moderato

Prison Governor interrogates him and on learning that he is a 'political prisoner' orders him to be flogged. Soon ex.1 combines with a new motif and cries of pain off stage.

This music merges into the next episode. The Tall Prisoner brings out a captured eagle; the prisoners torment it but admire its defiance in captivity, proclaiming it an 'orel lesů' ('eagle of the forests'). Suddenly the Governor returns with his guards and orders the prisoners off to work. Half of them depart to outdoor work, singing a 'mournful song' to words quoted by Dostoyevsky, 'Neuvidí oko již' ('My eye will never again see the land of my birth'), punctuated by ex.1.

Skuratov is among those who remain. He sings snatches of a 'cheerful song' (words from Dostoyevsky) and annoys Luka, who picks a quarrel with him. Skuratov recalls his life in Moscow and his previous trade as a cobbler. He breaks into a wild dance, then collapses (a harsh version of ex.1).

Luka, as he sews, recalls his previous imprisonment for vagrancy. He tells how he incited the other prisoners to rebellion and how he killed the officer who came to quell the disturbance. This is a substantial monologue which grows in intensity to the point where Luka describes plunging his knife into the officer (a *fortissimo* version of ex.1). Then follows a dreamy version on two solo violins of the opening motif from the overture. A march-like variant of this theme builds up to an exciting climax, again dominated by ex.1, as Luka describes how he was flogged. Tension is dissolved by a naive question from the Elderly Prisoner. Alexandr Petrovič, who has meanwhile been punished in a similar way, is brought back by the guards, half dead. The long orchestral postlude is built up by a hypnotic peroration on the theme from Skuratov and Luka's quarrel, silenced by a *fortissimo* timpani solo.

Act 2 *The bank of the river Irtysh with a view of the steppe; a year after Act 1, towards sunset* The prelude, with an offstage vocalise, evokes the openness of the wide steppe – a contrast to the enclosed prison yard of Act 1. Prisoners are working on a ship – the sounds of metal implements and a saw are specified in the instrumentation.

Alexandr Petrovič asks the Tartar boy Aljeja about his family and offers to teach him to read and write, an offer warmly accepted. With the day's work over (the ship's mast is heard falling), the prisoners throw down their tools. Bells sound from afar, then from the settlement. A colourful march accompanies the arrival of the Governor and Guests, and of the Priest, who blesses the food and the river before going off with the Governor. The prisoners sit down to eat. Skuratov, with the occasional interruption from the Drunk Prisoner, tells how he killed the man his sweetheart Luiza was forced to marry. This is the gentlest and most lyrical of the three major narratives of the opera, a rondo based on a charming, modally inflected motif. Its end is overwhelmed by the prisoners' excitement at the thought of the 'theatre'.

On an improvised stage the prisoners perform two plays, mostly in mime: 'Kedril [i.e. Leporello] and Don Juan' (who is taken off by devils at the end) and 'The Miller's Beautiful Wife', based on Gogol's tale of a wife hiding various lovers around the room while her husband is absent. The last lover is a 'Brahmin' who turns out to be Don Juan in disguise and who dances off with the Miller's Wife before being consumed by flames.

It grows dark. The Young Prisoner goes off with a Prostitute. A mood of quiet contentment is evoked by offstage folksongs (Luka and chorus). While Alexandr Petrovič and Aljeja are drinking tea the belligerent Short Prisoner, resenting Alexandr Petrovič's 'gentleman-like behaviour', picks a quarrel. He breaks a jug over Aljeja, who falls to the ground. Guards rush in to keep order: the act dies on a sustained side-drum roll.

Act 3.i *The prison hospital, towards evening* The gentle prelude ends with a triumphant theme in C major. Aljeja, delirious with fever, is watched over by Alexandr Petrovič. Čekunov waits on both of them, to the rage of Luka, who is dying on an adjacent bed. Šapkin describes how a police officer interrogated him and almost pulled his ears off. Skuratov, now mad, cries for Luiza.

Night falls, suggested by chamber textures and duet-like writing in the orchestra as the prisoners go to sleep. The silence is broken by the Elderly Prisoner's lament that he will never see his children again. Egged on by Čerevin, Šiškov tells the story of Akulka (Akulina), Filka Morozov's sweetheart. Filka refused to marry her, declaring that he had already slept with her. Šiškov has to marry her instead. On his wedding night he beats her and then discovers she is pure. He attempts to take revenge on Filka, who alleges that Šiškov was too drunk to notice her state. Šiškov beats her again, and discovering that she still loves Filka, kills her. This brutal tale, Janáček's longest monologue, is sustained by the virtuoso vignettes (usually in direct speech) of its many characters, and by the tension between the wrongs done to Akulka and the music of utmost tenderness with which she is depicted. It is punctuated both by Čerevin's questions and by the strange choral sighs of the sleeping prisoners. Luka dies as the story ends. An irony added by Janáček is that only now does Šiškov recognize Luka as Filka. Šiškov is almost speechless with rage, but the comment of the Elderly Prisoner that a mother gave birth even to Filka is more true to the humanitarian message of the opera. A Guard calls for Alexandr Petrovič. An automaton-like march leads to scene ii.

3.ii As Act I The Governor, drunk, apologizes to Alexandr Petrovič before the other prisoners and tells him that he is to be released. To a warm-sounding version of ex.1 Alexandr Petrovič's chains are knocked off and he bids farewell to Aljeja, who has run in from the hospital. As Alexandr Petrovič leaves the prisoners release the eagle and celebrate its freedom in a brief chorus; it flies away to the triumphant theme from the prelude to the act. The guards order the prisoners off to work. The automaton-like march that led into this scene ends the opera.

*

This is Janáček's most extraordinary and arguably his greatest opera, fuelled by music of an intense driving force, startling even for him. There is virtually no plot (the arrival and departure of Alexandr Petrovič provides its slender narrative frame), and except for the tiny part of the Prostitute and the trouser role of Aljeja, there are no women in this opera. There are also no main characters: instead it is a 'collective' opera in which soloists emerge from the chorus and then blend back into anonymity. For all this, it is a compelling stage work, the most powerfully charged of all Janáček's operas, and yet the most tender and compassionate.   J.T.

G

Gazza ladra, La ('The Thieving Magpie')

Melodramma in two acts by Gioachino Rossini to a libretto by Giovanni Gherardini after *La pie voleuse* (1815) by J. M. T. Badouin d'Aubigny and Louis-Charles Caigniez; Milan, Teatro alla Scala, 31 May 1817.

The first cast included Teresa Belloc-Giorgi (Ninetta), Savino Monelli (Giannetto), Filippo Galli (Fernando) and Antonio Ambrosi (the Mayor).

Ninetta	soprano
Fabrizio Vingradito	bass
Lucia *his wife*	mezzo-soprano
Giannetto *their son*	tenor
Pippo	contralto
Isacco *a pedlar*	tenor
Fernando Villabella *Ninetta's*	
father	bass-baritone
Gottardo *the Mayor*	bass-baritone
Giorgio *town clerk*	bass
Antonio *warder*	tenor
Ernesto *Fernando's friend*	bass
Magpie	dancer
Setting A French village	

Musically, *La gazza ladra* is the finest of Rossini's several essays in the *semiseria* genre – comedy mixed melodramatically with potential tragedy – that stretch from *L'equivoco stravagante* (1811) to *Matilde di Shabran* (1821). In this instance, the work can be seen to derive in part from the French drama *larmoyant* or sentimental comedy, in part from the so-called 'rescue' opera such as Beethoven's *Fidelio*. The opera deals with a wide range of social groupings, and conforms to the tradition of the happy ending, the heroine saved from execution at the eleventh hour, even though in the original French play (said to be based on a true story) she dies on the gallows.

The score of the opera underwent extensive alterations and cutting in subsequent years. Rossini himself pointed the way with revised performing editions, supervised by himself, in Pesaro in 1818 and in Naples, at the Teatro del Fondo in 1819 and the S Carlo in 1820. Of these the 1818 Pesaro revival is perhaps the most significant, with the addition of a cavatina for Fernando, 'Dunque invano i perigli e la morte'. In Paris in 1866 Rossini wrote embellishments and variations for Ninetta's cavatina for use by Giuseppina Vitali and it would appear that in the following year he wrote embellishments and cadenzas for Adelina Patti. In 1941 the opera was revived in Pesaro in an edition by the composer Riccardo Zandonai, which makes substantial changes to the narrative and to the music, including the orchestration; though used for a distinguished revival at the 1959 Wexford Festival, it is a largely spurious version. A definitive critical edition, edited by Alberto Zedda, was published by the Fondazione Rossini, Pesaro, in 1979.

*

The overture is thematically linked with the action of the opera. The story centres on the serving girl Ninetta, who works in the house of the wealthy tenant farmer Fabrizio Vingradito and his wife Lucia. Their son Giannetto is about to return from the wars and it is Fabrizio's intention that he should be allowed to marry Ninetta. They have been in love for some time, but it is a match of which Lucia disapproves. She thinks Ninetta unreliable and casual with family possessions – a fork has recently gone missing. Ninetta sings of her love for Giannetto in her cavatina 'Di piacer mi balza il cor', and Giannetto is duly welcomed and feasted, with one of Fabrizio's young workers, the gamesome Pippo, proposing the toast. A pedlar, Isacco, visits the farm. (His whiningly nasal music makes him an obvious forebear of Verdi's Trabuco in *La forza del destino*.) A vagrant also appears whom Ninetta instantly recognizes as her father, the soldier Fernando Villabella. He has quarrelled with his commanding officer and has deserted to avoid summary execution. Ninetta's attempt to hide him is compromised by the arrival of an unwanted admirer, the mayor of the village (*podestà*), Gottardo. Outwardly this is a *buffo* role but in reality he is a vindictive philanderer well used to manipulating the course of justice: a rural forerunner of Puccini's Scarpia. Ninetta urges her father to leave. To raise the necessary money for him to survive in hiding he asks her to sell a piece of valuable cutlery (it is his own and bears the initials F. V.) and deposit the money in an old chestnut tree nearby. Before either the Mayor or Fernando can be got off the premises, the town clerk, Giorgio, brings news of a deserter on the run. The Mayor has mislaid his glasses, and asks Ninetta to read the description, which she does, altering the details to make it as unlike her father as possible. While the Mayor is weighing the evidence and contemplating the old tramp, a magpie alights in the room and, unobserved, steals a spoon from the table. In due course the spoon is missed by Lucia; Pippo unwittingly lets on that Ninetta has sold something to the pedlar, and Isacco's testimony that he bought a spoon from her initialled F. V. is one of several pieces of circumstantial evidence that lead to her arrest for theft. Giannetto is devastated, but the turn of events delights the Mayor, whose advances Ninetta has continued to repulse.

The first scene of Act 2 takes place in the courtyard of the prison where Ninetta is awaiting trial. Thanks to the leniency of the kindly warder Antonio she is visited by Giannetto, to whom she protests her innocence (although she does not mention her father's inadvertent part in her troubles). The Mayor appears but is again repulsed. Ninetta, desperate to help her father, decides to enlist the aid of Pippo: she takes the gold cross she wears and asks him to sell it and put the money in the old chestnut tree. The deeply affecting recitative and duet for Ninetta and Pippo, 'Deh pensa che domani ... E ben, per mia memoria', is one of the opera's highlights. Meanwhile, Ninetta's father, filled with anxiety at not knowing where she is, presents himself at the farmhouse; when he learns of her arrest he resolves to attend the trial. Lucia is now also beginning to have doubts about Ninetta's guilt (her aria 'A questo seno', which can come either side of the Trial Scene, was usually cut in Rossini's time). In the magnificent Trial Scene Ninetta is found guilty. Fernando intervenes, but to no avail, and what is more he is recognized by the Mayor and arrested as a deserter. The final scene takes place in the village square. The action is resolved partly by an act of clemency granted Fernando by the King, partly by Pippo's discovery of the magpie's activities: it has been stealing cutlery and coins and storing them in its nest in the church tower, as Pippo and Antonio confirm by climbing up to it. The discovery is made, though, only after we have witnessed Ninetta's grim march to the scaffold, eerily scored by Rossini in a manner that anticipates Berlioz's orchestrations. However, Ninetta is reprieved in the nick of time, the villagers celebrate, and only the Mayor is left angry and discomfited.

*

As with the character of Cenerentola in his immediately preceding opera, so with the falsely accused Ninetta Rossini achieves a telling naturalness of musical characterization. A simple force of human emotion also permeates the portrayal of Ninetta's father Fernando. Relations between fathers and children in Rossini's operas can be almost as charged with emotion as they were later to be in Verdi's.

R.O.

Gianni Schicchi

Opera in one act by Giacomo Puccini to a libretto by Giovacchino Forzano after a passage from Dante Alighieri's narrative poem *Commedia*, part 1: 'Inferno'; New York, Metropolitan Opera House, 14 December 1918 (as no.3 of *Il trittico*).

The cast at the première included Giuseppe De Luca (Schicchi), Florence Easton (Lauretta), Giulio Crimi (Rinuccio), Kathleen Howard (Zita) and Adam Didur (Simone); the conductor was Roberto Moranzoni.

Gianni Schicchi *(aged 50)*	baritone
Lauretta *his daughter (aged 21)*	soprano
Zita *cousin of Buoso Donati (aged 60)*	contralto
Rinuccio *Zita's nephew (aged 24)*	tenor
Gherardo *Buoso's nephew (aged 40)*	tenor
Nella *Gherardo's wife (aged 34)*	soprano
Gherardino *their son (aged 7)*	contralto
Betto di Signa *Buoso's brother-in-law (of uncertain age)*	bass
Simone *cousin of Buoso (aged 70)*	bass
Marco *Simone's son (aged 45)*	baritone
La Ciesca *Marco's wife (aged 38)*	mezzo-soprano
Maestro Spinelloccio *a doctor*	bass
Ser Amantio di Nicolao *a notary*	baritone
Pinellino *a cobbler*	bass
Guccio *a dyer*	bass
Setting Florence, 1299	

Authorities disagree as to whether Puccini or Forzano first had the idea of basing a comedy on a brief passage in Canto 30 of Dante's *Inferno* concerning a sly rogue who cheated the poet's own relatives by marriage out of a substantial inheritance. Forzano submitted his scheme in March 1917 and completed the libretto in June. Puccini began work on it immediately, before laying it aside to finish the second part of *Il trittico, Suor Angelica*. The autograph is dated 3 February 1918. The Italian première took place on 11 January 1919 (Rome, Teatro Costanzi), conducted by Gino Marinuzzi; Carlo Galeffi took the title role with Edoardo Di Giovanni (Edward Johnson) as Rinuccio and Gilda dalla Rizza as Lauretta. Of the three operas that make up *Il trittico*, *Gianni Schicchi* won the readiest acceptance both at home and abroad though it was later to be rivalled by

'Gianni Schicchi' (Puccini): scene from the original production at the Metropolitan Opera House, New York,
14 December 1918

Il tabarro. It remains nonetheless among the acknowledged masterpieces of Italian comedy.

*

A bedroom in the house of Buoso Donati Before a large
four-poster bed, whose curtains conceal the body of
Buoso Donati, recently defunct, Donati's relatives are
kneeling in a state of well-simulated grief. The air is
filled with their sobs and groans, which give way to
anxious whisperings when Betto mentions a rumour
that the deceased has left all his property to the
Monastery of S Reparata. They turn for guidance to
Simone, as he is the oldest family member present
and a former mayor of Fucecchio. He suggests that
they search for the will immediately. All begin
frantically emptying drawers and cabinets. The
parchment is found by Rinuccio, but before handing
it over to his aunt Zita as head of the family he makes
her promise, should the terms prove satisfactory, to
allow his marriage with Lauretta, daughter of Gianni
Schicchi. A broad theme, evolving in lyrical sequences, indicates the warmth of Rinuccio's feelings

Ex.1 Allegro

(ex.1). Rinuccio bribes Gherardino to fetch Schicchi
and the girl. Meanwhile the relatives gather round
Zita to read the will, their expressions slowly
changing from eager anticipation to dismay and

finally to fury, as they discover that the rumour was
all too well founded. They launch into a tirade
against the monks, picturing them pointing the
finger of scorn at the impoverished Donati family. If
only the will could be changed! But this time Simone
cannot help.

Rinuccio suggests that they seek advice from
Gianni Schicchi, but by now Zita will not even hear
his name mentioned. Gherardino returns to tell them
that Schicchi is on his way. Annoyance all round:
the man is a mere parvenu, a peasant from the
backwoods. Rinuccio springs to his defence in an aria
('Avete torto') which introduces a motif to be
associated with Schicchi's cunning, and whose concluding section ('Firenze è come un albero fiorito'),
marked 'to be sung in the manner of a Tuscan
stornello [folksong]', compares Florence to a tree that
draws its sustenance from the surrounding countryside. Schicchi arrives with his daughter, astonished
to find the family plunged in genuine grief, until he
learns that they have been disinherited. A quarrel
breaks out between him and Zita, to the chagrin of
Lauretta and Rinuccio, who see their hopes of
marriage fading (the theme of ex.1 recurs in elegiac
vein). Rinuccio begs Schicchi to help them, but in
vain, and it is Lauretta who carries the day with her
desperate plea, 'O mio babbino caro' ('Oh my
beloved daddy') – the score's one detachable number, whose opening strain has been anticipated by the
orchestra during Rinuccio's *stornello* as symbolizing
the glories of Florence.

After sending his daughter out to the terrace
Schicchi proceeds to give his instructions. Buoso's
body must be removed and the bed remade. There is
a knock at the door and Schicchi slips behind the

curtains as Spinelloccio, the doctor, enters and asks after his patient. Imitating Buoso's voice Schicchi declares that he is much recovered and asks him to call again that evening. The doctor leaves, well pleased with the effect of his past ministrations. After a crow of triumph (the 'cunning' motif) Schicchi unfolds his plan in an aria ('Si corre dal notaio'). Rinuccio must summon a lawyer and two witnesses; he himself will dress up in Buoso's nightgown and bonnet and dictate a new will leaving everything to the family. Delighted, they discuss the division of the property. There is perfect agreement until they reach the most valuable part of the legacy: the villa, the mule and the mills at Signa. Before the issue can be settled there is a brief alarm as a funeral bell tolls from nearby. They wonder whether news of Buoso's death can have broken, but the tolling turns out to have been for the butler of a wealthy neighbour. Amid general relief they decide to leave the allocation of the coveted items to Schicchi himself, but as they file past him, each handing him an article of clothing, they offer him bribes, all of which he pretends to accept. In a lyrical trio ('Spogliati, bambolino') Zita, Nella and La Ciesca assist him to change clothes. Before retiring behind the curtains he makes them repeat after him the penalty meted out to all who are party to the falsification of a will: namely to have their hands cut off and to be banished from the city. Obediently they chant a mock lament ('Addio, Firenze, addio, cielo divino').

Rinuccio arrives with the lawyer, Ser Amantio, and two witnesses, Guccio and Pinellino. The formalities are gone through, amid universal praise for 'Buoso's' generosity. All hold their breath as he reaches the villa, the mule and the mills. These, in succession, are left to 'my dear, devoted and much loved friend, Gianni Schicchi'. The family react with smouldering rage, but, as Schicchi's intermittent chanting of 'Addio, Firenze' reminds them, they are hardly in a position to protest. Only when the lawyer and witnesses have departed do they burst out, rampaging through the house and seizing everything they can lay their hands on, until Schicchi drives them away. The lovers, on the other hand, are perfectly happy, for now that Lauretta is assured of a dowry there can be no obstacle to their marriage – the theme of ex.1 is heard in radiant mood. And Gianni Schicchi feels justified in asking the audience's indulgence, to a recurrence of the motif associated with his cunning.

*

As early as *La bohème* (1896) Puccini had shown a gift for robust comedy, with which he never failed to leaven his most pathetic plots. In *Gianni Schicchi* this style appears refined and concentrated. Verbal inflection here is as pointed as in Verdi's *Falstaff;* but the organization remains based on recurrent

orchestral motifs, mostly sharp and piquant, often lacking precise associations but always sure in their theatrical effect. The harmonic idiom comprises rows of parallel unresolved dissonances, as in the scene with Spinelloccio, together with bland, schoolroom procedures, as in the reading of the will, as well as chattering reminiscences of *opera buffa*. Lauretta's aria, by far the best-known number in the entire *Trittico*, is sometimes condemned as a concession to popular taste, but its position at the turning point of the action is precisely calculated so as to provide a welcome moment of lyrical repose.   J.B.

Giasone ('Jason')

Drama musicale in a prologue and three acts by Francesco Cavalli to a libretto by Giacinto Andrea Cicognini loosely based on Apollonius's *Argonautica*; Venice, Teatro S Cassiano, 5 January 1648 [=1649].

Apollo	soprano
Amore [Cupid]	soprano
Ercole [Hercules] *an Argonaut*	bass
Besso *Captain of Jason's Guard*	bass
Giasone [Jason] *leader of the Argonauts*	alto
Rosmina *a gardener*	soprano
Medea *Queen of Colchis*	soprano
Egeo [Aegeus] *King of Athens*	tenor
Oreste [Orestes] *Hypsipyle's confidant*	bass
Demo *Aegeus's servant*	tenor
Delfa *Medea's nurse*	alto
Isifile [Hypsipyle] *Queen of Lemnos*	soprano
Alinda *Hypsipyle's lady-in-waiting*	soprano
Volàno *a spirit*	tenor

Gods, winds, spirits, Argonauts, soldiers, sailors

Setting The island of Colchis and the mouth of the River Danube on the Black Sea in mythological times

The only collaboration between Cicognini and Cavalli, *Giasone* became the most frequently performed opera of the entire 17th century. In addition to possible performances in Milan in 1649 and 1650 and Lucca in 1650, published librettos document 21 revivals in various Italian cities between 1650 and 1690 (sometimes with a different title). An unusually large number of these performances are documented by scores. It was also one of the few operas to inspire a play that led an independent existence.

*

Prologue *A beach with a view of the island of Colchis* In a celestial debate over the outcome of the impending drama, Apollo champions Medea and Cupid supports Hypsipyle as Jason's future wife.

Act I.i–ii *A delicious garden with a palace, adjoining*

the kingdom of Colchis Hercules and Besso fear that Jason's amorous nightly activities with an unknown princess may make him incapable of stealing the Golden Fleece, an event planned for this very day. Jason shares their concern but nevertheless hopes for a successful outcome.

I.iii Rosmina, a gardener, sings a flirtatious love song ('Per sanar quest'appetito').

I.iv–v The throne room of Colchis Medea, who is the unknown princess, expresses her love for Jason. When her former suitor Aegeus arrives, she rejects him, leaving him to bewail his unhappiness.

I.vi–vii [The nearby countryside] Orestes, sent by Hypsipyle to search for Jason, meets the stuttering hunchback Demo, from whom he vainly attempts to extract information; the two then retire for liquid refreshment. (Demo's halting delivery of his identifying song 'Son gobbo, son Demo', which culminates in a hilarious duet with Orestes, is one of the opera's high spots.)

I.viii–xiii [Medea's apartments] In a two-strophe aria, Delfa discourses on the problems of fleeting youth and the frustrations of old age ('Voli il tempo, se sà'). She sees Jason approaching and rushes off to warn Medea. Jason, who does not recognize Medea, since he has never seen her face, asks her help in capturing the Golden Fleece. She scolds him for having violated her hospitality by seducing (and fathering twins on) a noblewoman of Colchis (in fact herself), and makes him promise to marry her. He agrees because he is anxious to know his beloved's identity. She teasingly attempts to pass off Delfa as the lady in question but finally identifies herself, to Jason's great joy. The two depart, leaving Delfa to philosophize in a recitative and strophic aria ('Troppo soavi i gusti') on the mores of a society in which girls first prove their capacity as mothers and then get married.

I.xiv Landscape with tents at the mouth of the Danube, with a view of the Black Sea Hypsipyle dreams of her betrothed, Jason, father of her twin sons. On awakening, she remembers that she has left her homeland, Lemnos, with Orestes and Alinda to search for him, and wonders when Orestes will return with news.

I.xv Medea's magic chamber Medea's incantation, 'Dell'antro magico', invokes the spirits of the underworld to aid Jason in his quest and they assure her that he will be successful.

Act 2.i–ii Landscape with tents at the mouth of the Danube, with a view of the Black Sea Still awaiting Orestes' return with news of Jason, Hypsipyle confides her desperation to Alinda, who, in a three-strophe aria ('Per prova sè'), advises her to find another lover. Hypsipyle rejects her advice and falls asleep, whereupon Orestes, who meanwhile has returned, serenades his sleeping mistress with an aria

('Vaghi labri scoloriti') as prelude to an attempted rape. She awakens just in time, and learns that Jason has fallen in love with another woman; she resolves to travel to Colchis to kill her rival.

2.iii–vi Courtyard of the castle that houses the Golden Fleece Encouraged by Medea, who provides him with a magic ring, and accompanied by Besso, Jason enters the castle, overcomes the monsters on guard and captures the Golden Fleece. Hercules reports that the populace is up in arms over its loss and urges Jason to flee to Corinth. Medea insists on joining him, and they set sail on Jason's ship, the *Argo.*

2.vii Demo has overheard their plans and informs Aegeus, who follows them, with Demo, in a small boat, which, however, sinks in a storm.

[*2.viii The caves of Aeolus* Jove, Aeolus, Cupid and a chorus of winds are angered by Jason's success and join forces to sabotage it with a storm. (This scene is not set.)]

2.ix–x A ruined port at the mouth of the Danube, with a view of the Black Sea During a love scene of their own, Orestes and Alinda comment on their mistress's unhappy state. They are interrupted by Demo, who has been washed up on the shore and manages to stutter his way through an explanation of what has happened. Orestes departs to inform Hypsipyle of the latest developments.

2.xi–xiv More fortunate than Aegeus's small boat, the *Argo* sails into the port and Jason and Medea disembark with their entourage and set up a temporary camp. Alinda observes them and meets Besso, with whom she immediately falls in love. Their scene, with its multiple puns on music, war and castratos, is one of the most amusing in the opera. Orestes returns to report Hypsipyle's imminent arrival. When she appears and reminds Jason of his vows, he pretends she is a madwoman he met in Lemnos who thinks that events in other people's lives have happened to her. He goes off with Medea, leaving Hypsipyle to vow revenge.

Act 3.i–v A verdant wood Orestes and Delfa compare notes on their respective employers and find that both love Jason and both are the mothers of twins. Jason and Medea, meanwhile, sing a beautiful lullaby duet before falling asleep ('Dormi, dormi'). This is overheard by Orestes, who comments lasciviously in an aria ('Non è più bel piacer') on what will happen next. Hypsipyle comes upon the sleeping couple and awakens Jason, who promises to return to her if she will leave without disturbing Medea. But Medea overhears the conversation and extracts Jason's promise that he will have Hypsipyle murdered. Accordingly, Jason instructs Hypsipyle to meet Besso at the nearby valley of Orseno during the night and to ask him whether Jason's orders have been carried out. He tells her that this question is the password that will entitle her to an audience with him. Besso, on the other hand, is ordered to respond to the question by throwing the questioner into the sea.

3.vi Aegeus arrives at the port and meets Demo, who thinks at first that he is seeing his master's ghost; the two go off together.

3.vii–viii Hypsipyle, rejoicing in the prospect of reunion with Jason, prepares to go to meet Besso but is delayed by Orestes, who urges her to nurse her children first and goes off to collect them.

3.ix–xii *Valley of Orseno* Medea, wishing to ascertain that her rival has been killed, asks Besso if Jason's orders have been carried out; following his instructions he throws her into the sea. When Hypsipyle arrives and asks the same question, Besso responds angrily 'Torna a Giason e di/Ch'io solo uccido una persona al dì' ('Tell Jason that I kill only one person a day'), a line that Cavalli enhances by setting it in a jaunty aria style.

3.xiii–xv Aegeus arrives just in time to rescue the drowning Medea, whom he promises to avenge by killing Jason.

3.xvi–xxi *An uninhabited, ruined palace* Jason, meanwhile, having learnt from Besso that his orders were carried out, and overcome with remorse at the presumed death of Hypsipyle, falls asleep. He is about to be stabbed by Aegeus when Hypsipyle grabs the knife and is arrested as a murderer. Seeing that Hypsipyle is alive, Jason accuses Besso of failing to carry out his orders but then is told that Medea died instead. But then Medea appears, explaining that since she was saved by Aegeus she now owes him her affection. She urges Jason to return to Hypsipyle. He protests but is won over after a moving lament by Hypsipyle ('Infelice, che ascolto'). With all the tensions resolved and the proper lovers united, the opera ends with a succession of duets and a final quartet.

[**3.xxii** Jove, Cupid, a chorus of gods and Zephyr all rejoice in Cupid's – and Hypsipyle's – victory. (This scene is not set.)]

*

Although it was called 'the first and most perfect drama in existence', the opera was blamed for having opened the floodgates to all kinds of abuses: the mixing of genres, the abandonment of linguistic elegance and purity and, through the introduction of arias, the destruction of verisimilitude in drama. Its success in its own time was justified, however. As an opera, *Giasone* represents an ideal meeting of music and drama. In it the definitive separation of aria and recitative was finally achieved; formal distinctions were clarified by dramatic function, with recitative reserved primarily for action and commentary and arias for formal songs or moments of intense, reflective feeling. Hypsipyle's lament in Act 3 ('Infelice, che ascolto') fuses the two with its affective recitative and aria based on the descending tetrachord ostinato; Delfa's aria at the end of Act 1 illustrates Cavalli's comic style, with its narrow range and strictly syllabic text-setting alternating with exaggerated melismas – the frequent pauses between phrases were presumably for brief dance interpolations. Most of the operatic conventions of the period are represented, with great musico-dramatic effectiveness: as well as Hypsipyle's lament, a sleep scene (Act 2) and the powerful incantation scene (1.xv), containing Medea's 'Dell'antro magico', with its stark, chordal motion and repetitive *sdrucciolo* rhythm. The libretto, too, is more varied, more individualized and poetically more sophisticated than any other of the period. It stands out for its mixture of comic and serious characters and for the dramatic impact of the poetry itself.   E.R.

Gioconda, La

Dramma lirico in four acts by Amilcare Ponchielli to a libretto by Tobia Gorrio (Arrigo Boito) after Victor Hugo's play *Angélo, tyran de Padoue*; Milan, Teatro alla Scala, 8 April 1876.

The singers at the première were Maddalena Mariani-Masi (La Gioconda), Maria Biancolini-Rodriguez (Laura), Ormondo Maini (Alvise), Eufemia Barlani-Dini (La Cieca), Julián Gayarre (Enzo) and Gottardo Aldighieri (Barnaba); the conductor was Franco Faccio.

La Gioconda *a singer*	soprano
Laura Adorno *a Genoese lady*	mezzo-soprano
Alvise Badoero *a chief of the State Inquisition,*	
husband of Laura	bass
La Cieca *Gioconda's mother*	contralto
Enzo Grimaldi *a Genoese prince, disguised*	
as a sea captain	tenor
Barnaba *a ballad singer and spy of the*	
Inquisition	baritone
Zuàne *a competitor in the Regatta*	bass
A Singer	bass
Isèpo *a public scrivener*	tenor
A Pilot	bass

Regatta spectators, senators, noblemen and women,
   masks (harlequins, pantaloons, dominoes),
   populace, sailors, midshipmen, monks, knights,
   singers
Mute extras: mace-bearers, squires, cut-throats,
   trumpeters, Dalmatians, Moors, the Grand
   Chancellor, the Council of Ten, six trainbearers,
   a boatswain, the victor of the Regatta, a ship's
   captain, the Doge
Setting Venice in the 17th century

In response to the growing interest shown towards Ponchielli's operas during the early 1870s the publisher Giulio Ricordi commissioned *La Gioconda* in 1874. He entrusted the libretto to Boito, who modelled it strictly on the 'grand opera' style of Eugène Scribe (then enjoying a belated vogue in Italy), with massed choral scenes, spectacular historical framework, abundance of contrasts and a central ballet. Taking as his basis a drama that had already served Mercadante (*Il giuramento*, 1837), he diminished the importance of Hugo's title role, idealized the heroine and elevated the Venetian spy into a satanic figure conceived in his most lurid vein. Boito presented the resulting confection under an anagram of his own name which deceived no one.

The reception was generally cordial. Milan's leading critic, Filippo Filippi, declared that, Verdi apart, only Ponchielli among contemporary Italian composers was capable of producing a work of such importance. Successive revivals, however, were to bring important modifications. For the Venetian première, at the Teatro Rossini on 18 October the same year, Ponchielli added the Furlana to Act 1 and wrote a new cabaletta ('O grido di quest' anima') for the duet between Enzo and Barnaba as well as a prayer for Laura in Act 2 and a new aria for Alvise in Act 3 (later discarded) that included the lines 'La Morte è il nulla / E vecchia fola il Ciel', which Boito subsequently transferred to Iago's Credo in Verdi's *Otello*. For the Teatro Apollo, Rome (23 January 1877), Ponchielli wrote a new finale to Act 1, suppressing the reprise of the Furlana, and ended the second act with a duet for Enzo and Gioconda in place of the original naval battle. The definitive version of *La Gioconda* was first given at Genoa on 27 November 1879, although it received critical attention only when it returned to La Scala on 12 February 1880; Ponchielli had recomposed Alvise's aria a second time and made an important alteration to the finale of Act 3, replacing the original stretta with an orchestral peroration of the principal theme of the preceding *pezzo concertato* (ensemble) – a procedure that was considered entirely novel at the time and which was not lost on the composer's best pupil, Puccini. Thereafter the opera entered the Italian repertory, where it has remained ever since. Abroad, it has tended to be confined to theatres such as the New York Metropolitan which can afford the resources that it requires. The 'Danza delle ore' (Dance of the Hours), however, has established itself in the concert hall as an international classic of light music ever since its performance at the Paris Exhibition of 1878.

*

Act I: 'The Lion's Mouth'

The courtyard of the Doge's Palace A reflective prelude establishes two of the opera's motifs: a broad cantilena that will connote the rosary that saves the life of Laura Adorno, and a fidgeting figure portraying the villainy of Barnaba. The curtain rises with the Venetians *en fête*, watched cynically by Barnaba. Bells and trumpets announce the Regatta. As the people hurry away to watch it, Barnaba compares the strings of his guitar to the threads of a spider's web, designed to entrap his victims, one of whom now approaches – La Cieca, supporting her blind mother, La Cieca. A terzettino ('Figlia che reggi il tremulo piè') introduces a sinuous phrase sung by La Cieca ('Tu canti agli uomini le tue canzoni') which will recur as a symbol of Gioconda's filial devotion; beneath the upper voices can be heard the Barnaba 'fidget'. Gioconda leaves her mother to her devotions and goes in search of her betrothed, Enzo; Barnaba comes forward and makes advances to her, only to be repulsed with scorn. The crowd returns with the winner of the Regatta. Barnaba persuades the loser, Zuàne, that his craft was bewitched by La Cieca. The prayers which she seems to be uttering, he says, are evil spells, and he rouses the people to murderous fury against her. Enzo appears; he is posing as a sea-captain, since the Venetians have put a price on his head. Failing to quell the tumult, he goes to rally his sailors in La Cieca's defence.

At that moment Alvise comes out of the palace with Laura, and the crowd falls silent. Ignoring Gioconda's pleas he orders the old woman's arrest and torture. But his wife, noticing La Cieca's rosary, successfully intercedes for her. In her aria 'Voce di donna o d'angelo', La Cieca expresses her gratitude, in token of which she presents Laura with her rosary. Meanwhile Laura and Enzo, who were once betrothed, have recognized one another. Alone with Enzo, Barnaba tells him that he knows his true identity, and that while Enzo loves Gioconda like a brother, the real object of his passion is Laura, for whose sake he has risked his life in coming to Venice. As a state informer he could have Enzo arrested; but instead he has arranged for Laura to meet Enzo that night on his brigantine while Alvise is occupied with his official duties. He thus hopes to further his own cause with Gioconda by demonstrating her idol's treachery. Enzo curses him for his villainy but is overjoyed nonetheless. When he has left, Barnaba calls for the scribe Isèpo and, overheard by Gioconda, dictates a denunciation of Enzo, revealing the plan of elopement. In a monologue after the style of *Rigoletto* ('O monumento'), Barnaba muses on the two faces of Venice – the city of perpetual carnival and the squalid police state. He then deposits the missive in the mouth of the great stone lion, the Inquisition's traditional receptacle for such denunciations, and departs. The courtyard fills once more with masqueraders, who dance a Furlana. As the organ sounds from the nearby church, signalling the Angelus, all fall on their knees in prayer, among them

Gioconda, heartbroken at Enzo's betrayal, and La Cieca, who tries vainly to comfort her.

Act 2: 'The Rosary'

A brigantine It is night. Sailors and midshipmen are making ready to sail. Barnaba arrives in the guise of a fisherman and jokes with the crew, who echo the refrain of his barcarolle ('Pescator, affonda l'esca'). He orders Isèpo to prepare an assault on the brigantine and leaves to fetch Laura. As he waits for her, Enzo apostrophizes the nocturnal scene in the aria 'Cielo e mar', one of the gems of the tenor repertoire. Laura arrives, somewhat unnerved by her escort's sinister appearance. In their love duet ('Deh, non turbare') Enzo calms her fears. He goes below to give his orders, and Laura offers up a prayer to the Virgin ('Stella del marinar'). Meanwhile Gioconda has entered unobserved. The two women confront one another in a duet ('L'amo come il fulgor del creato'), each claiming precedence in their love for Enzo. Gioconda is about to stab her rival, when she catches sight of the rosary that Laura is clutching. Recognizing the woman who saved her mother's life, she gives Laura her own mask and thrusts her into a boat which will carry her to safety. Enzo, returning, is dismayed to find Gioconda. Triumphantly she points to where Laura is making her escape, then to a craft on which Alvise can be seen approaching. Barnaba, she says, has betrayed his plan. Enzo sets fire to the brigantine to prevent it falling into his enemy's hands and dives into the sea.

Act 3: 'The Ca' d'oro'

3.i A room in Alvise's palace In a *scena ed aria* ('Sì, morir ella de'!'), Alvise resolves to avenge his family's honour by having his wife die by poison. When she enters he ironically compliments her on her beauty and then passes to accusations, which she tries vainly to rebut. He leads her into an adjoining room, where a catafalque is laid out. As a serenade sounds in the distance he gives her a phial of poison, instructing her to drain it before the music has ceased. He leaves and Gioconda enters, suspecting that Laura may need her help. She exchanges the poison for a sleeping-draught which will give the appearance of death.

3.ii A large hall Alvise is receiving guests, among whom are Enzo and Gioconda. He has devised for their entertainment a spectacular ballet, The Dance of the Hours. At its conclusion Barnaba enters, dragging La Cieca, whom he claims to have discovered casting spells. She protests that she was offering up prayers for the dead; and indeed a distant funeral bell is heard. Barnaba tells Enzo that it tolls for Laura. At this, Enzo flings aside his disguise and reveals himself to Alvise, who orders his arrest. During the huge *pezzo concertato* or ensemble piece which forms the architectural pinnacle of the score, Gioconda promises Barnaba her favours if he will obtain Enzo's

release. At the climax of the ensemble Alvise discloses the catafalque on which lies the body of his apparently dead wife.

Act 4: 'The Orfano Canal'

The inner court of a ruined palace on the Isola della Giudecca Gioconda is alone, absorbed in melancholy thoughts. Her friends carry in the sleeping Laura and lay her on a bed. Gioconda begs them to help find her mother, who has disappeared. When they have gone she expresses a longing for death in her grand aria ('Suicidio!'). Enzo arrives, unable to understand why he has been set free. All he wants is to mourn on Laura's tomb. When Gioconda tells him that it is empty, he accuses her of preying on the dead like a hyena. He is about to stab her when Laura's voice is heard. Gioconda explains her deception and indicates the boat which she has got ready for the lovers' escape. Deeply moved, Enzo and Laura bid her farewell in a terzetto ('E così sia! quest'ultimo'). She is about to go in search of La Cieca when Barnaba enters and reminds her of their bargain. Pretending to adorn herself for his delight, she seizes a dagger and kills herself. Barnaba tries to make her understand that he has drowned her mother out of spite; but she no longer hears him.

*

Ponchielli, by nature conservative, lacked self-confidence and had a retiring temperament which put him at a disadvantage in the competitive world of the theatre. Though possessed of a genuine dramatic instinct combined with a lyrical flair, he never took charge of an operatic structure as Verdi always did. La Gioconda, his masterpiece, inevitably suffers by comparison with those of his great contemporary. However, apart from Verdi's *Aida*, *La Gioconda* is the only Italian 'grand opera', or 'opera-ballo', to have stayed the course. Its style, in places almost Donizettian, is old-fashioned for the 1870s, but it is fully assured. The score, like that of *Aida*, is articulated in closed numbers embedded in a musical continuum in which conversational, as distinct from arioso, recitative is kept to a minimum and much of the dialogue is carried on to orchestral 'parlanti'. Of the three recurring motifs only the insistent 'fidget' that connotes the sinister Barnaba is purely instrumental. The theme of the rosary is formed from the culminating period of La Cieca's aria; while the undulating strain associated with Gioconda's filial love is taken from her Act 1 terzetto with her mother and the concealed Barnaba. La Cieca is clearly modelled on Meyerbeer's Fidès (*Le prophète*); otherwise there is little attempt at characterization throughout the opera. Unlike those of Rigoletto, Barnaba's monologue tells us nothing about the man himself. Gioconda herself is less a personality than a succession of moods and attitudes – wilting and forlorn in Act 1, the avenging tigress in Act 2, an

'La Gioconda' (Ponchielli), scenes from the original production at La Scala, Milan, 8 April 1876: engraving from 'L'illustrazione italiana' (28 May 1876)

almost 'veristic' victim in her great aria in Act 4, from which her descent – in the final scene – to the coquettish language of Violetta in Act 1 of *La traviata* verges on the bathetic.

The opera is sensational rather than truly dramatic, abounding in 'effects without causes' (to borrow Wagner's phrase about Meyerbeer); but it contains some fine descriptive touches. Night on the lagoon is evoked in Act 2 by an atmospheric prelude and offstage chorus in which one can sense the lapping of water against the hold of the brigantine, and also by the diaphanous scoring that introduces Enzo's aria 'Cielo e mar', notable for its original use of strophic variation. Above all *La Gioconda* demonstrates Ponchielli's skill as a ballet composer. Not only does the Dance of the Hours form, alone among opera ballets, a complete, self-sufficient musical statement; much of the entire score is permeated by dance rhythms which lend extra vitality to the opera's wealth of spontaneous, if not invariably distinguished, lyricism.   J.B.

Giovanna d'Arco ('Joan of Arc')

Dramma lirico in a prologue and three acts by Giuseppe Verdi to a libretto by Temistocle Solera in part after Friedrich von Schiller's play *Die Jungfrau von Orleans*; Milan, Teatro alla Scala, 15 February 1845.

The cast at the première included Antonio Poggi (King Charles), Filippo Colini (Giacomo) and Erminia Frezzolini in the title role.

Carlo VII [Charles VII] *King of France*	tenor
Giacomo *a shepherd in Dom-Rémy*	baritone
Giovanna [Joan of Arc] *his daughter*	soprano
Delil *an officer of the King*	tenor
Talbot *supreme commander of the English army*	bass

King's officers, villagers, people of Reims, French soldiers, English soldiers, blessed spirits, evil spirits, nobles of the realm, heralds, pages, young girls, marshals, deputies, knights and ladies, magistrates, halberdiers, guards of honour

Setting Dom-Rémy, Reims and near Rouen in 1429

There is virtually no evidence, but it seems that Verdi had arranged to write an opera for the 1844–5 Carnival season at La Scala as early as December 1843, and that soon afterwards he suggested to the impresario Bartolomeo Merelli that Solera be engaged as the librettist. Solera was duly hired, and – with typical exaggeration – made much of the fact that his libretto on the life of Joan of Arc was 'original', owing nothing either to Shakespeare or to Schiller. Verdi's correspondence makes no mention of any changes to the libretto, and we must assume that, as with Solera's earlier *Nabucco* and *I Lombardi*, the composer was willing to set the text more or less as it stood. The score was written during the autumn and winter of 1844–5. Its first performance at La Scala (preceded by a revival of *I Lombardi*) was a great public success, but the standards of production were far below Verdi's expectations and caused a rift between him and Merelli that resulted in Verdi's avoiding premières at La Scala for many years.

*

The overture is in three movements. The first is stormy and uncertain; the second is an Andante pastorale featuring solo flute, oboe and clarinet (with more than shades of Rossini's *Guillaume Tell* overture); the last returns to the stormy minor but concludes in a triumphant and bellicose major. It is hardly a masterpiece but is worth its occasional concert-hall revival.

Prologue i *A great hall in Dom-Rémy* The opening scene is a conventional cavatina for the tenor, though with unusually important choral interventions (Verdi and Solera no doubt wished to sustain their image with the Milanese after *Nabucco* and *I Lombardi*). Even before the tenor enters, the unison chorus decries the sad fate of France in 'Maledetti cui spinge rea voglia', and choral forces are again prominent in the soloist's lyrical movements, particularly in an unusually long *tempo di mezzo*. King Charles, after admitting defeat by the English forces, narrates a dream ('Sotto una quercia'): as he was lying beneath an oak tree, the Madonna told him to place before her his helmet and sword. On hearing that such an oak exists nearby, he decides to visit it, though insisting that he can no longer remain as king.

ii *A forest* The shepherd Giacomo appears for a brief scena, voicing fears that his daughter Joan may be in league with the devil. He retires, to be replaced by Joan. In a highly ornamented, Bellinian Andante ('Sempre all'alba ed alla sera'), she prays for weapons in the coming battle. As she falls asleep, a chorus of devils (jauntily recommending sins of the flesh) and of angels (promising her glory as the saviour of her country) jostle for her attention. She awakes to find Charles before her, and immediately declares herself ready for battle. They join in a lively, syncopated cabaletta, during which Giacomo sees them together and concludes that his daughter has in some way bewitched the King.

Act I.i *A remote place scattered with rocks* The English soldiers have been routed and feel that supernatural forces are against them. Talbot tries unsuccessfully to allay their fears. Giacomo, still convinced that his daughter is in the grip of evil forces, comes on to announce that the woman inspiring the French forces can be their prisoner that evening. In an Andante sostenuto, 'Franco son io', he tells them of his dishonour, as he thinks, at the hands of Charles; the ensuing cabaletta, 'So che per via di triboli', explores a father's tender feelings. The usual progression from lachrymose Andante to energetic cabaletta is thus reversed, which allows for a moderate-paced, unusually touching Donizettian cabaletta, quite lacking in characteristic Verdian rhythmic drive.

I.ii *A garden in the court of Reims* Joan of Arc has fulfilled her mission but is unwilling to leave Charles and the court: the demon voices still torment her. She sings of her simple forest home in 'O fatidica foresta', another delightful example of Verdian pastoral, before Charles arrives to initiate an impressive four-movement duet-finale in which he and Joan admit their love for each other. Particularly notable is the Adagio ('T'arretri e palpiti!'), which includes a remarkable range of emotional attitudes as Joan struggles with her conflicting voices and as Charles swings between unease at her behaviour and attempts to calm her with expressions of love.

Act 2 *A square in Reims* A somewhat routine 'Grand triumphal march' introduces the victorious troops, prominent among whom are Charles and Joan. Giacomo looks on, giving vent to his religious zeal in a minor–major *romanza*, 'Speme al vecchio era una figlia', which never seems to find its true point of climax. Then comes the grand central finale of the opera, in which Giacomo denounces his daughter. The most interesting movement is the Andante, 'No! forme d'angelo': unaccompanied duet fragments from Charles and Giacomo are juxtaposed with an extended cantabile for Joan; and even in the grand cadential close Verdi finds room to give rein to her fragile musical persona. The remainder of the number offers high drama as Joan refuses three times to deny Giacomo's accusations of sacrilege; she is turned on by the crowd in the stretta, 'Fuggi, o donna maledetta'.

Act 3 *Inside a fort in the English camp* Joan of Arc, imprisoned, looks on as the English and French do battle, noting with dismay that Charles has been surrounded. Her ardent prayers alert Giacomo to his mistake in accusing her of immorality, and they join in a duet of explanation and reconciliation, the most impressive section of which is the slow lyrical movement, 'Amai, ma un solo istante', in which a moving succession of melodic ideas underpins the father's gradual acceptance of his daughter's purity.

Joan is released by her father and rushes to aid the French; now it is Giacomo's turn to comment on the battle, which with his daughter's help swings decisively against the English. Charles enters victorious, forgives Giacomo, but learns that Joan has been mortally wounded. In the *romanza* 'Quale più fido amico', delicately scored for solo english horn and cello, he bemoans his loss. Joan is brought in to the strains of a funeral march, and has enough strength left to salute her father and king and to look forward to a welcome in heaven. She leads off the final ensemble with an elaborately ornamented solo accompanied by obbligato cello before a long-breathed theme for the onlookers carries all before it as she expires.

*

Giovanna d'Arco is unlikely ever to be a mainstream repertory work, but there is nevertheless much to admire. Although the opera was probably intended as a sequel to the grand choral tableau works Verdi and Solera had previously created together, in the end it is dominated by the role of Joan of Arc – Verdi probably being encouraged in this change by the extraordinary skills of his leading soprano, Erminia Frezzolini. And Joan is by no means the typical early Verdian soprano, being entrusted with the kind of delicate ornamentation the youthful composer so rarely saw fit to linger over. The other principals are perhaps less successfully projected, but they are involved in powerfully original ensembles, numbers which again and again make clear that the young Verdi was constantly experimenting with the formal vehicles through which his drama was projected.

R.P.

Giulio Cesare in Egitto [*Giulio Cesare*]
('Julius Caesar in Egypt')

Opera in three acts by George Frideric Handel to a libretto by Nicola Francesco Haym adapted from Giacomo Francesco Bussani's *Giulio Cesare in Egitto* (1677, Venice) and a later version of the same libretto (1685, Milan); London, King's Theatre, 20 February 1724.

The cast at the first performance consisted of the castratos Senesino (Caesar), Gaetano Berenstadt (Ptolemy) and Giuseppe Bigonzi (Nirenus), with Francesca Cuzzoni (Cleopatra), Margherita Durastanti (Sextus), Anastasia Robinson (Cornelia), Giuseppe Boschi (Achillas) and John Lagarde or Laguerre (Curius).

	Romans	
Giulio Cesare [Julius Caesar]		alto castrato
Curio [Curius] *tribune*		bass
Cornelia *widow of Pompey*		contralto
Sesto [Sextus] *son of Pompey*		soprano

	Egyptians	
Cleopatra *Queen of Egypt*		soprano
Tolomeo [Ptolemy] *her brother,*		
King of Egypt		alto castrato
Achilla [Achillas] *general, Ptolemy's*		
adviser		bass
Nireno [Nirenus] *confidant of*		
Ptolemy and Cleopatra		alto castrato

Caesar's soldiers, Egyptians

Setting Egypt, 48–47 BC

Giulio Cesare was Handel's fifth full-length opera for the Royal Academy of Music and received 13 performances on its first run, for which he assembled an unusually splendid cast. It made a sensational effect with its sumptuous scoring and melodic richness, and gave Senesino and Cuzzoni roles that fully stretched their vocal and dramatic talents. Handel revived it three times at the King's Theatre: on 2 January 1725, 17 January 1730 and 1 February 1732. There were revisions for all of these performances, notably in 1725 when Sextus was recast as a tenor and received three new arias; there was also a new aria for Ptolemy. Two further arias were added during the 1725 run for the soprano Benedetta Sorosina as Nerina – the role of Nirenus converted

into Cleopatra's lady-in-waiting. On 21 March 1730 two new arias were added for the benefit performance of Anna Maria Strada del Pò, who took over the role of Cleopatra that season. The popularity of *Giulio Cesare* was also reflected in numerous productions at Hamburg and Brunswick over the period 1725–37, and a concert version was given in Paris in the summer of 1724.

Oskar Hagen's production at Göttingen in 1922 was the first in the 20th century, though using a heavily transformed version of the score which was also followed in the many subsequent revivals. In various versions – though hardly ever any of Handel's own – *Giulio Cesare* has found a place in the repertory of several modern opera houses; it was given at the New York City Opera in 1966 and by the English National Opera in 1980. Handel's complete score of 1724, with all voices at their correct pitch, was given its first modern revival at the Barber Institute, Birmingham, on 20 January 1977, a precedent that has rarely been followed. The role of Cleopatra has attracted such singers as Lisa Della Casa, Joan Sutherland, Evelyn Lear, Beverly Sills and Montserrat Caballé.

*

The action is founded on Julius Caesar's visit to Egypt in 48–47 BC; most of the characters are historical, but the details of plot are largely fictional and the character of Caesar seems to be much younger than his historical counterpart (who was 54 when he met Cleopatra). Egypt is under the joint rule of Cleopatra and her younger brother Ptolemy.

Act I Caesar enters Egypt in pursuit of his rival Pompey, whom he has defeated at Pharsalia. Attended by the tribune Curius, he crosses the Nile and is acclaimed by the Egyptians. Pompey's wife Cornelia (whom Curius once loved) and her son Sextus beg for a reconciliation. Caesar agrees to embrace Pompey, but at that moment the Egyptian general Achillas appears with a message of welcome from Ptolemy; he presents Caesar with a gift of friendship which, to the horror of the Romans, is revealed to be Pompey's severed head. Caesar warns Achillas that he will punish Ptolemy for this act. Cornelia attempts to kill herself, but Curius intervenes. His offer to marry Cornelia is rejected. Sextus vows to avenge his father's murder.

At the Egyptian court, Cleopatra learns from her attendant Nirenus that Pompey has been murdered on Ptolemy's orders. She resolves to seduce Caesar in a bid to be sole ruler of Egypt, while dismissing Ptolemy as fit only for sexual conquests. Achillas tells Ptolemy that the plan to appease Caesar with Pompey's head was counter-productive; he offers to kill Caesar and win Ptolemy sole power over Egypt if he can have Cornelia as his reward.

At his camp, Caesar reflects on human mortality

Design by Jacopo Fabris for the Port of Alexandria in a production of Handel's 'Giulio Cesare in Egitto' at the Theater am Gänsemarkt, Hamburg, in 1725

as he contemplates Pompey's funeral urn. Cleopatra presents herself in disguise: she claims to be Lydia, a noble lady deprived of her fortune by Ptolemy. Caesar and Curius are captivated. Cleopatra and Nirenus observe a further attempt at suicide by Cornelia, this time prevented by Sextus. 'Lydia' tells Cornelia that she serves Cleopatra and engages her help and Sextus's against Ptolemy. Caesar arrives at Ptolemy's palace and warily accepts an offer to be shown the royal apartments. Cornelia and Sextus appear and rail at Ptolemy: Sextus is imprisoned, Cornelia put to tending the seraglio gardens. Achillas makes advances to Cornelia and is rebuffed, leaving mother and son to mourn their fate.

Act 2 Caesar is led by Nirenus into a garden of cedars leading to a view of the Palace of Pleasure on Mount Parnassus. An instrumental symphony is heard and the scene opens to reveal Cleopatra (still disguised as Lydia) on the throne of Virtue with the Muses as her companions. She takes up the melody of the symphony in a ravishing aria, accompanied by instruments on stage. Caesar runs towards her, but the scene closes and Nirenus assures him that 'Lydia' will welcome him later. In the seraglio garden Cornelia is doing menial tasks. She rejects Achillas's advances. Ptolemy tells Achillas to perform what he promised, but reveals in an aside that Achillas will not get his expected reward. Ptolemy himself then accosts Cornelia, but also gets rebuffed. She again contemplates suicide and is again forestalled by Sextus, who has been released by Nirenus. Cornelia

is to appear before Ptolemy, and Nirenus advises Sextus it will be a good opportunity to take his revenge. Cleopatra, in her apartments, feigns sleep as Caesar arrives. Curius arrives with news of a group of conspirators demanding Caesar's death. Cleopatra reveals her true identity and says she will put down the riot, but after assessing the situation advises Caesar to escape. He determines to face the conspirators and leaves the griefstricken Cleopatra. In the seraglio Ptolemy indicates that Cornelia is to share his bed. Sextus attempts to kill him, but is prevented by Achillas. The latter tells Ptolemy that Caesar has fled and has apparently been drowned; meanwhile Cleopatra is raising troops against Ptolemy. Achillas demands the hand of Cornelia for his pains, but Ptolemy refuses, leaving Achillas to hint at a change of allegiance. Sextus, remorseful at his failure, attempts to kill himself, but Cornelia gives him courage for a further assault on Ptolemy.

Act 3 Achillas, at the port of Alexandria, resolves to support Cleopatra. Ptolemy's forces defeat Cleopatra's and Cleopatra is taken prisoner. Caesar emerges from the sea, washed ashore by the waves. He watches as Sextus and Nirenus come upon Achillas, wounded in the battle. Achillas confesses to the murder of Pompey and passes to Sextus a seal which gives command of a troop of warriors. Caesar intervenes, taking the seal and promising to rescue Cornelia and Cleopatra. In the palace Cleopatra is taking leave of her handmaidens, but her sorrow turns to joy as Caesar arrives and drives out

Ptolemy's guards. Elsewhere in the palace Cornelia is defending herself with a dagger against Ptolemy's renewed advances. Sextus appears with drawn sword, challenges Ptolemy and kills him. At the harbour Caesar and Cleopatra appear in triumph, and prepare to reward Nirenus and Curius. Cornelia and Sextus bring the news of Ptolemy's death. Cleopatra offers Caesar Ptolemy's crown and sceptre. Caesar returns them to Cleopatra, and she accepts them as 'a tributary queen to Rome's great emperor'. They declare their love, and all look forward to peace and liberty under Rome's protection.

*

The score of *Giulio Cesare* was by far Handel's most sumptuous to date, not only in its stylistic variety and melodic richness but more specifically in its use of the orchestra, which included two pairs of horns crooked in different keys and a stage band with harp, theorbo and viola da gamba. It is also one of his most dramatically compelling operas, despite the over-frequent suicide attempts and assaults on Cornelia's virtue. The character of Cleopatra in all her 'infinite variety' is painted with special insight and under-standing – a tease in Act 1, turning from seduction to despair in Act 2 and returning to triumph in Act 3. Her two arias of grief, 'Se pietà' and 'Piangerò la sorte mia', are among Handel's finest in that vein, while 'V'adoro, pupille', with its ravishing instrumental sonorities, is surely unsurpassed as an exemplar of seductive song.

Caesar's role includes some fine accompanied recitative (notably the moving 'Alma del gran Pompeo') and the remarkable aria with solo horn, 'Va tacito'. Ptolemy's viperish character is well caught in his three arias. Cornelia and Sextus may seem to have more music than their position in the drama merits – a consequence of the need to reflect the distinction of the original singers – but this will not be seen as a defect if the roles are cast from strength. The use of choral ensembles in the opening scene and off stage for the conspirators in Act 2 is effective and original for its time.   A.H.

Gloriana

Opera in three acts, op.53, by Benjamin Britten to a libretto by William Plomer; London, Covent Garden, 8 June 1953.

The original cast was led by Joan Cross in the title role and Peter Pears as the Earl of Essex, with Monica Sinclair (Frances), Jennifer Vyvyan (Penelope), Geraint Evans (Mountjoy), Frederick Dalberg (Raleigh), Arnold Matters (Cecil), Inia Te Wiata (Ballad-Singer).

Queen Elizabeth I	soprano
Robert Devereux, Earl of Essex	tenor
Frances, Countess of Essex	mezzo-soprano
Charles Blount, Lord Mountjoy	baritone
Penelope, Lady Rich *sister of Essex*	soprano
Sir Robert Cecil *Secretary of the Council*	baritone
Sir Walter Raleigh *Captain of the Guard*	bass
Henry Cuffe *a satellite of Essex*	baritone
A Lady-in-Waiting	soprano
A Blind Ballad-Singer	bass
The Recorder of Norwich	bass
A Housewife	mezzo-soprano
The Spirit of the Masque	tenor
The Master of Ceremonies	tenor
The City Crier	baritone

Citizens, maids of honour, ladies and gentlemen of the household, courtiers, masquers, old men, men and boys of Essex's following, councillors
Dancers: Time, Concord, country girls, rustics, fishermen, morris dancer
Actors: Ballad-singer's runner, Sir John Harington, French ambassador, Archbishop of Canterbury, phantom kings and queens, pages
Setting England in the later years of Elizabeth I's reign

Commissioned by the Royal Opera House, Covent Garden, *Gloriana* is 'dedicated by gracious permission to Her Majesty Queen Elizabeth II in honour of whose coronation it was composed'. It is set in the later years of Elizabeth I's reign, and at the time of the première the opera's emphasis on an aging, ungracious monarch was felt in some quarters to be inappropriate; the work has not been extensively revived, though a successful ENO production (1984; later issued on a video recording) vindicated its quality, as did an Opera North production with Josephine Barstow, later recorded (conducted by Charles Mackerras, 1993). As William Plomer explained, Lytton Strachey's *Elizabeth and Essex* was the opera's starting-point. Moreover, since this was his first attempt at a libretto and time was very short, the work's genesis was a fraught and turbulent one. Work began in earnest only after royal approval for the project was received in May 1952. Britten began the music in August that year, and the full orchestral score was completed in mid-March 1953.

The libretto was deliberately heterogeneous – a mixture of prose and verse, archaic and modern English – and the music (especially Act 2, scenes i and iii) performs a comparably skilful balancing act between Tudor allusions and Britten's own style, as well as between separate numbers and larger-scale continuity. Above all, *Gloriana* establishes strong, effective contrasts between public and private worlds.

*

Act I.i *At a tournament* Robert Devereux, Earl of Essex, is revealed as hot-blooded and jealous of anyone who might win the Queen's favour. He provokes a fight with the tournament victor, Charles Blount, Lord Mountjoy, and is slightly wounded at the moment when the Queen and her entourage arrive. She expresses her annoyance that her bravest champions should fight among themselves and urges them to attend her at court as friends. Essex and Mountjoy are reconciled and Elizabeth is acclaimed in the 'Green leaves' chorus.

I.ii *The Queen's private rooms in Nonesuch Palace* The Queen discusses the rivalry of Mountjoy and Essex with her chief adviser Sir Robert Cecil. She admires Essex's impulsive arrogance, but Cecil warns her of the political dangers of showing affection for him. He also informs her of the reports that a new Armada may be on the way. Essex is announced and, to distract the Queen from cares of state, sings two lute songs: 'Quick music's best' and, in contrast, 'Happy were he', a brilliant fusion of Britten's style and allusions to Elizabethan lute songs. The poem is by the historical Earl of Essex, and Britten uses a motif from John Wilbye's 'Happy, O happy he'. The Queen is moved, but Essex grows impatient. He wants to go to Ireland to suppress the Tyrone rebellion, and accuses Cecil and Sir Walter Raleigh of intriguing against him. The Queen resists and sends him away. The act ends with a restrained soliloquy in which she prays for power 'that I may rule and protect my people in peace'.

Act 2.i *Norwich* In the most overtly ceremonial scene in the opera, the Queen visits Norwich. After a welcome from the Recorder of Norwich and some expressions of impatience from Essex, a masque, in celebration of Time and Concord, and comprising six dances and choral pieces, is performed.

2.ii *The garden of Essex's house* Essex's sister Lady Penelope Rich and Mountjoy meet and sing of their love. Essex and his wife Frances enter, the Earl complaining at the way the Queen thwarts his desire to go to Ireland. The couples meet and, in a quartet, imagine themselves gaining increasing power and influence as the Queen ages: only Lady Essex urges caution.

2.iii *The palace of Whitehall* A ball is in progress, dominated by Lady Essex, who has been instructed by her husband to dress with maximum extravagance, even though she is sure that this will annoy the Queen. After a pavane and galliard the Queen enters. She observes Lady Essex in her finery and orders an energetic lavolta, after which, again at her command, the ladies withdraw to change their linen. During the ensuing morris dance the ladies return one by one. Lady Essex, who reappears in plainer clothes, tells Lady Rich that her dress was stolen while she was changing, and when the Queen returns

it is clear who appropriated it. Elizabeth looks grotesque: Lady Essex's dress is too small for her, and, she says, if it does not become her it certainly cannot become Frances. She soon leaves again, while Essex, Mountjoy and Lady Rich comfort Frances in her humiliation. (This incident has an historical basis.) Essex grows ever more rebellious, but when the Queen, notoriously mercurial, returns, her mood has changed and he is told that he is, after all, to be appointed Lord Deputy in Ireland. He accepts the commission with enthusiasm and leads the Queen in a coranto of celebration.

Act 3.i *Nonesuch Palace* The Queen's maids discuss Essex's failure to put down the Irish rebellion. Essex appears, demanding to see the Queen. When, despite the maids' protests, a curtain is drawn aside, the Queen is seen unadorned, in a dressing gown and without a wig. Though sympathetic to Essex, she cannot overlook his failure in Ireland and his complaints about his enemies at court only make matters worse. After his departure the Queen completes her toilet, and Cecil is admitted, to underline the twin dangers of an Ireland still in revolt and an Essex now making trouble in England. Reluctantly, Elizabeth orders that Essex be kept under guard; he has failed her because she in turn has failed to tame him. As she declares with weary decisiveness, 'it is I who have to rule'.

3.ii *A street in the city of London* A blind balladsinger regales the crowd with the story of Essex's attempt to foment rebellion. Some of Essex's sympathizers try to persuade others to join them, but the City Crier proclaims the Earl a traitor.

3.iii *The palace of Whitehall* Cecil and the councillors try to persuade the Queen to sign the order condemning Essex to death. At first she refuses and, left alone, laments her indecision. Lady Essex, Lady Rich and Mountjoy are admitted and the two women plead in turn for Essex's life. To the humble Lady Essex the Queen responds kindly, but when Lady Rich insolently attempts to argue that the Earl warrants the Queen's pardon because the Queen needs him, Elizabeth calls for the warrant and signs it. Then the Queen is alone in a timeless void. In a sequence of speeches she recalls her relationship with Essex (the music of the second lute song is heard) and reconciles herself to death. The opera ends with the fading strains of the celebratory 'Green leaves' chorus.

*

Britten's imaginative use of allusions to Elizabethan dances and lute songs to create not only local colour but also a sense of ironic distance from the 20th century is one of *Gloriana*'s great strengths. The treatment of the Elizabeth and Essex relationship veers towards the melodramatic, yet there is still a strong sense of two wayward, incompatible temperaments, and the music during the opera's final stages does not shy away from the grandiose, the more firmly to underline the gradual, touching dissolution. Through Plomer's portrayal of the Queen as an 'outsider', Britten was able to transcend irony and create a conclusion of true pathos, worlds away from a conventional operatic death scene and providing a striking counterweight to the opera's earlier emphasis on public ceremonial.

The difficulties Britten experienced with *Gloriana*, and its early reception, may help to explain why Britten failed to compose the much-mooted *King Lear* and tended to avoid 'grand opera'. His great achievements in this more intimate medium cannot wholly dispel a sense of regret for what might have been.   A.W.

Golden Cockerel, The
[*Zolotoy petushok (Le coq d'or)*]

Dramatized fable (*nebïlitsa v litsakh*) in a prologue, three acts and an epilogue by Nikolay Andreyevich Rimsky-Korsakov to a libretto by Vladimir Nikolayevich Bel'sky after the eponymous imitation folk tale in verse by Alexander Sergeyevich Pushkin, based in turn on 'The House of the Weathercock' and 'Legend of the Arabian Astrologer' from *The Alhambra* by Washington Irving; Moscow, Solodovnikov Theatre (Sergey Ivanovich Zimin's private opera company), 24 September/7 October 1909.

Emil Cooper conducted the first stage performance; the production was designed by Ivan Bilibin, and Nikolay Speransky sang King Dodon with Aureliya Dobrovol'skaya as the Queen of Shemakha.

King Dodon	bass
Prince Guidon	tenor
Prince Afron	baritone
Commander Polkan	bass
Amelfa *royal housekeeper*	contralto
Astrologer	tenore altino
The Queen of Shemakha	soprano
The Golden Cockerel	soprano

Boyars, guards, footsoldiers, canoneers, servants,
    the Queen of Shemakha's slave girls and
    entourage, crowd

Setting The imaginary realm of King Dodon

Rimsky-Korsakov's last opera, incorporating (in Act 2) music originally sketched for abandoned projects on *The Barber of Baghdad* (1895) and *Sten'ka Razin* (1905), was very quickly composed between October 1906 and September 1907. Then began a protracted battle with the censor, which prevented the work from reaching the stage until after the composer's

death in 1908. The portrayal of a slothful autocrat engaged in idiotic warfare struck too close to home in the wake of the humiliating Russo-Japanese War (1904–5). The composer, who had suffered indignities during the political disturbances of 1905, did in fact harbour a grudge against the Autocracy, and the censor's sensors were not aroused altogether in vain. Indeed, the autograph full score bore an epigraph, later prudently crossed out, from the role of the Distiller in Rimsky's own *May Night*: 'A fine song, friend! A pity, though, that the head man gets mentioned in it in less than decent words'. The composer refused to alter the libretto, with its reference near the end to 'a new dawn . . . without the Tsar'. (The censor's demands were in any case obtuse, requiring the elimination of lines from the original, long since published Pushkin text.) The only parts of the opera that were performed during Rimsky's lifetime were the Introduction and Wedding Procession, played at a 'Russian Symphony Concert' (alongside Stravinsky's early vocal suite *The Faun and the Shepherdess*) under the auspices of the Belyayev publishing house in February 1908, and the Queen of Shemakha's Hymn to the Sun, sung in concert the next month by the soprano Nadezhda Zabela.

Though the cartoonish mockery of authority is clear enough in a blanket sort of way, the libretto's symbolism – assuming it exists – has resisted coherent explanation. The *envoi*, 'The fable's false, but contains a hint, a lesson for good young lads!', addressed to the reader by Pushkin and to Rimsky's audience by the Astrologer, remains as teasing in the opera as it had been in the tale.

*

Prologue The Astrologer, the opera's framing character and its implied narrator, appears before the curtain to warn the audience that he is about to conjure up a cautionary tale.

Act I *King Dodon's throne room* The king complains that he is tired of warfare but that his neighbours keep on invading. He asks his assembled councillors, including his two sons, how he can avoid engagements in the future. Prince Guidon answers that he should withdraw the army to the capital, because life is more pleasant there than at the frontier. With no army at the border no one will invade. All think this is a marvellous idea until Commander Polkan points out that defending the capital is riskier than defending the frontier. Prince Afron suggests they disband the army and only mobilize it a month before each attack. This idea too is acclaimed until Polkan, whom everyone resents as a killjoy, points out that the enemy is not likely to give a month's notice. Everyone, now baffled, longs for the days when the future could be foretold in beans or in wine-dregs (and all begin to argue as to which is the better method). At this point, accompanied by the same music as in the Prologue, the Astrologer appears with a magic Golden Cockerel who, placed on a high perch, can warn of any border disturbance, and can also tell the king when it is safe to 'reign, lying on your side'. Overjoyed, the king promises any reward the Astrologer can name. The latter says he will claim his reward later, but would like the promise in writing, to make it 'lawful'. The king indignantly refuses ('Lawful? What's that? I never heard of such a thing. My whims and orders – that's the law around here'). Amelfa now brings in the big royal bed, some treats to eat and the king's pet parrot, who, interpreted by Amelfa, sings his praises. The Cockerel gives reassurance and everyone falls asleep. To judge by his music, the king sees a vision resembling the Queen of Shemakha in his dreams. All at once the Cockerel sounds the alarm. Polkan awakens the king, who mobilizes two armies, placing one of his sons at the head of each. Again the Cockerel sounds the alarm. Now the king must go into battle himself. Grumbling, he dons his rusty armour (which he has grotesquely outgrown) and goes off to battle, his people seeing him off with huzzahs.

Act 2 *A mountain gorge* Looking in vain for the battle, the king stumbles upon the bodies of his two sons, whose armies have apparently fought each other to total destruction. He spies a tent which, he reasons, must contain the enemy. Before he can attack it out comes the gorgeous Queen of Shemakha, who sings her famous Hymn to the Sun, 'Otvet' mne, zorkoye svetilo' ('Answer me, bright orb'); she then brazenly announces that she has come to subdue King Dodon, not by force of arms but by her voluptuous charms. At her command, Dodon sends Polkan away, removing his only protection from the evil queen's wiles. The rest of the act is given over to the conquest, which begins with the queen's description of her unclothed body, and ends with a wild dance that exhausts the king and makes him her slave. (In his stern performance note, Rimsky-Korsakov directs that the dance should only look strenuous; 'it must not interfere with the singers' breathing'.) Having exacted Dodon's promise to banish Polkan (he goes even further and orders his loyal commander beheaded), the queen 'agrees' to come back with him and become his consort.

Act 3 *The capital* The crowd is wondering when the army will return. The royal wedding procession approaches; all hail the king and the new queen. Suddenly the Astrologer's music is heard; he materializes and claims his reward – the queen! The king naturally reneges on his promise and has the Astrologer forcibly removed. The Astrologer resists. Dodon strikes him on the head and kills him; at this

the sky darkens. The queen laughs it all off, but when the king tries to embrace her she repulses him with taunts. They dismount and begin to ascend the steps to the palace, but the Cockerel swoops down from its perch and pecks the king on the head, killing him. When light returns, both the Cockerel and the Queen of Shemakha have vanished. The terrified crowd laments.

Epilogue The Astrologer reappears before the curtain, reminding the audience that what they have seen is only a fairy tale and that the bloody denouement should therefore not upset them. He leaves with the cryptic assurance that only he and the Queen of Shemakha were real people – 'all the rest were dream, delusion, pale shade, empty air . . .'.

*

The Golden Cockerel is the only one of Rimsky-Korsakov's 15 operas to have achieved repertory status beyond Russia. This was Dyagilev's doing. At the prompting of the artist Alexandre Benois, the great impresario staged the opera in Paris and London in 1914 (under the title *Le coq d'or*, which has stuck to it in the West), with the singers seated in rows at the sides of the stage, accompanying the movements of dancers and mimes, who enacted the plot according to the conventions of *ballet d'action* (choreography by Fokin). With colourful sets and costumes by Natal'ya Goncharova in the style of primitive Russian broadside prints (*lubki*), this production delightfully enhanced the cartoonish aspect of the opera (although the composer's enraged widow successfully sought a restraining order through the French courts) and vouchsafed it continuing popularity. (A similar production was mounted at the New York Metropolitan Opera in 1918 with choreography by Adolph Bolm and Pierre Monteux conducting.) It also set an important precedent for Stravinsky, whose opera *The Nightingale*, not to mention such later stage works as *Renard*, *The Wedding* and *Pulcinella*, to a greater or lesser extent embodies the same split between singing and movement. It was an important stage in the modernist dismantling of the *Gesamtkunstwerk*, the Wagnerian 'total art work'.

The opera opens with a brash trumpet phrase (later to be identified as the Golden Cockerel's cry) which must remind anyone who knows it of the tag which begins all the scenes of Rimsky's *The Tale of Tsar Saltan*. The trumpet is now muted, yet played *fortissimo* and doubled, which turns the timbre into a musical cartoon, reminiscent of the garish colours and crude draughtsmanship of *lubki*. That vein of parody is characteristic of the opera throughout. It is a study in calculated tawdriness and triviality – again anticipating Stravinsky, this time the composer of *Petrushka*. The orchestra is full of gaudy sonorities, some of them, like the Astrologer's glockenspiel, functioning as 'leit-timbres' (specific sounds, as opposed to themes, to denote characters).

Two of the three traditional melodies quoted in the score are of the paltriest sort imaginable. When the Queen of Shemakha forces King Dodon to sing her a love song in Act 2, he does so to the tune of 'Chizhik, chizhik, gde tï bïl?' ('Birdie, birdie, where've you been?'), the Russian equivalent of 'Pat-a-cake' or 'Ring a ring of roses'. The triumphant Wedding Procession in Act 3 reaches its climax with a snatch of 'Svetit mesyats' ('The moon shines brightly'), a veritable roadhouse number. (The remaining folk tune, the aptly named 'Uzh tï, sizen'kiy petun' ('Oh you little grey-blue cock'), is associated with Amelfa in Act 1.) The chorus that greets the bridal couple is harmonized in a wicked burlesque of the 'folk harmonizations' that ethnomusicologists like Yevgeniya Linyova, armed with phonographs, had been touting as the 'authentic' Russian idiom of the future. (The chorus proves that Rimsky had seen her work, and that he disapproved of it.) The casting of the eunuch Astrologer as a weird *tenore altino* (for which, according to the composer's performance note, a high tenor with a strong falsetto register may substitute) is the ultimate *lubok* coloration. When he claims the Queen of Shemakha, improbably, for a bride, his voice shoots up to an *e''*.

The Queen of Shemakha's Lakmé-ish coloratura music is a *reductio ad absurdum* of the stereotyped 'oriental' idiom associated with many works by the Five (Rimsky and his group) and also of the chromaticism long associated with fantastic characters in Rimsky-Korsakov's earlier operas. Even in the act of parody, Rimsky advanced in spots to virtual atonality, making *The Golden Cockerel* a classic example of early modernism (its most direct issue again being early Stravinsky: compare the title characters' music in *The Firebird* or *The Nightingale*). But, as King Dodon says in Act 3, 'to everything there is a limit'. There was a line, firmly drawn in Professor Rimsky-Korsakov's imagination, that he would not and could not cross. 'There you are, decadents, have a feast', he remarked with nervous testiness in a letter to a friend, 'but still and all, pornographic clowns, to decadence I have not descended!' What kept him 'above' it was precisely the reliance on mechanistic sequences that many analysts and critics now deplore.

Where the fantastic mode had been rigorously segregated in earlier Rimsky-Korsakov from the folkish or diatonic, in *The Golden Cockerel* the two are interwoven to an unprecedented degree, realizing the notion of *nebïlitsa* as embodied in the opera's subtitle – a story in which everything is unreal. The actual cry of the cock, given a 'fantastic' harmonization when it appears as such, also furnishes the

background figuration for the saccharine lullaby music in Act 1, and immediately thereafter, for a folkish chorus.   R.T.

Götterdämmerung ('Twilight of the Gods')

Third day of *Der Ring des Nibelungen* in a prologue and three acts by Richard Wagner to his own libretto; Bayreuth, Festspielhaus, 17 August 1876.

For the original cast *see* Ring des Nibelungen, Der.

Siegfried	tenor
Gunther	bass-baritone
Alberich	bass-baritone
Hagen	bass
Brünnhilde	soprano
Gutrune	soprano
Waltraute	mezzo-soprano
First Norn	contralto
Second Norn	mezzo-soprano
Third Norn	soprano
Woglinde ⎫	soprano
Wellgunde ⎬ *Rhinemaidens*	soprano
Flosshilde ⎭	mezzo-soprano
Vassals, women	

The first draft of *Siegfrieds Tod* (originally spelt *Siegfried's Tod* and later renamed *Götterdämmerung*) is dated (at the end) 20 October 1848. This draft begins in the hall of the Gibichungs, but having been persuaded that too much background knowledge to the story was presupposed, Wagner added a prologue some time before 12 November. He undertook the versification of *Siegfrieds Tod* between 12 and 28 November, but then put it aside, perhaps unsure how to reconcile the diverging strands of the drama: divine myth and heroic tragedy. In the summer of 1850 he made some preliminary musical sketches for the prologue and began a composition draft, which was discontinued after the opening of the leave-taking scene for Siegfried and Brünnhilde. Having then added a preliminary drama, *Der junge Siegfried* (1851), and *Die Walküre* and *Das Rheingold* (1851–2), Wagner found it necessary to subject *Siegfrieds Tod* to revision: Siegfried had already been replaced as the central figure of the cycle by Wotan; the ending was altered; the Norns' scene was completely rewritten; a confrontation between Brünnhilde and the rest of the Valkyries was compressed into the dialogue for Brünnhilde and Waltraute (Act 1 scene iii); and several passages of narrative now rendered superfluous by *Die Walküre* and *Das Rheingold* were removed. The first complete draft of *Götterdämmerung* was begun on 2 October 1869 and finished on 10 April 1872. The second complete draft (short score) was made, as with *Siegfried*, in parallel, between 11 January 1870 and 22 July 1872. The full score was finished in Wahnfried, Wagner's house in Bayreuth, on 21 November 1874.

*

Prologue *The Valkyrie rock (as at the end of 'Siegfried')* The prologue opens with the two chords heard at the awakening of Brünnhilde (*Siegfried*, Act 3), but now in the darker, mellower tonality of Eb minor. The Three Norns, daughters of Erda, are weaving the rope of destiny. The First Norn tells how, long ago, Wotan came to drink at the Well of Wisdom, sacrificing an eye as forfeit. He had cut a spear from the trunk of the World Ash Tree, which had later withered and died. The Second Norn tells how a brave hero broke Wotan's spear; the god then sent heroes from Valhalla to chop down the tree. The Third Norn describes how the chopped logs of the World Ash Tree have been piled round Valhalla; one day they will be ignited and the entire hall will be engulfed in flames. Gods and heroes are awaiting that day. As each Norn in turn passes on both rope and narration, the wind and brass intone the theme of the Annunciation of Death (*Walküre*, Act 2 scene iv). The First Norn sees fire burning round the Valkyrie rock and is told that it is Loge fulfilling Wotan's command. A vision of Alberich and the stolen Rhinegold causes the Norns anxiety. To a baleful statement of the Curse motif on the bass trumpet, followed by that of the Twilight of the Gods, the rope breaks.

In terror and confusion the Norns descend into the earth and an orchestral interlude evokes sunrise.

Ex.1

Ex.2

A pair of themes, exx. 1 (a sturdier form of Siegfried's horn call) and 2 (a new theme associated with Brünnhilde), are worked into a climax as the lovers come out of the cave to which they retired at the end of *Siegfried*. Brünnhilde sends Siegfried off on deeds of glory ('Zu neuen Thaten'), urging him to remember their love. A rapturous duet follows, constructed from exx. 1 and 2 and other themes associated with the pair and their love and heroism. The vocal lines continue the new style evolved in Act 3 of *Siegfried*, richly ornamented with figurations and melismas. Siegfried gives Brünnhilde the ring as a token of his faithfulness; in exchange, she offers him her horse, Grane.

Another orchestral interlude (colourfully scored, with the glockenspiel and triangle adding to the gaiety) depicts Siegfried's Rhine Journey. It begins with a variant of ex. 1, and the hero's progress is suggested by the appearance of the Fire motif and those of the Rhine and Rhinemaidens. In its latter stages, the dark-hued diminished triad of the Ring motif initiates a change of mood (and tonality).

Act I.i–ii *The hall of the Gibichungs* The action proper begins as Gunther, the chief of the Gibichungs, asks his half-brother Hagen whether his reputation is high: 'Nun hör', Hagen' (Hagen is the son of Alberich from a loveless encounter with Queen Grimhilde). The accompanying motif, that of Hagen (ex.3), is a stunted form of the heroic octave leap of Siegfried's Forging Song (*Siegfried*, Act 1). Hagen replies that it would be higher if Gunther were to find a wife and Gutrune, his sister, a husband. The galloping Valkyrie motif and that of the fire god Loge are heard as Hagen tells them about Brünnhilde lying on a rock encircled by fire. He suggests that Siegfried would win the bride for Gunther if Gutrune had won Siegfried's love first. Hagen reminds them of a potion they have that would make Siegfried forget any other woman.

Ex.3

Ex.4

Siegfried's horn is now heard and Hagen calls down to him (scene ii): his 'Heil! Siegfried', with ominous irony, picks out the notes of the Curse motif, sounded simultaneously on a trio of trombones. Such references have become increasingly oblique in the latter part of the *Ring*: a few bars later, the Curse motif sounds again as Siegfried asks whether Hagen knows him – a reminder of what it is that linked their ancestors. Hagen has to tell Siegfried the purpose of the Tarnhelm he is carrying. Gutrune appears, to a tender new motif (ex.4). She offers Siegfried the drugged potion and he, in a gesture pregnant with irony, drinks to the memory of Brünnhilde and their love. An extended trill symbolically shifts the tonality from the Ab of Siegfried's memory to the G of Gutrune's presence. Siegfried is immediately drawn to Gutrune and loses no time in offering himself as her husband. He then offers to win Gunther a wife, and as he is told about Brünnhilde high on a rock surrounded by fire, it is clear that he has only the faintest recollection of her. (Trills and tremolando strings evoke both the fire and the haziness of his memory.)

Siegfried proposes to use the Tarnhelm to disguise himself as Gunther in order to bring back Brünnhilde. The idea of swearing blood brotherhood brings forth the motifs of the Curse, the Sword (in a fast, energetic variant) and, less expectedly, that of Wotan's Spear: the symbol of the original contracts that have brought such trouble and strife. Siegfried and Gunther swear their oath: 'Blühenden Lebens labendes Blut', with its duetting in 3rds and 6ths, the first of several reactionary structures in the work. Motivic reference slows down here but does not disappear: the menacing presence of Hagen in the background accounts for both the Ring and Curse motifs and for the effective juxtaposition of falling perfect and diminished 5ths (the former associated with heroism, the latter with evil) at 'blüh' im Trank unser Blut!' Siegfried sets off up the river again, followed by Gunther. The dour Hagen remains guarding the palace, contemplating the satisfactory progress of his scheme to win power: 'Hier sitz' ich zur Wacht'. The falling diminished 5th is now irrevocably associated with him, and the falling semitone, which can be traced back ultimately to Alberich's cries of woe in *Das Rheingold*, here attains its most anguished harmonization.

An orchestral interlude meditating on salient themes effects a transition from Hagen sitting malevolently on watch outside the palace to Brünnhilde sitting in innocent contemplation of Siegfried's ring outside the cave. The introduction of Brünnhilde's ex.2, with lighter scoring, dispels some of the oppressive atmosphere, but there remain enough pungent harmonies to suggest that trouble lies ahead.

I.iii The Valkyrie rock There is thunder and lightning and Brünnhilde sees her sister Waltraute approach on a winged horse (much use of the galloping Valkyrie motif). In her delight, Brünnhilde fails to notice Waltraute's agitation: has Wotan perhaps forgiven her? Waltraute explains that she has broken Wotan's command in coming, but sadly he is no longer to be feared. She then narrates ('Seit er von dir geschieden'), to a wealth of motivic reference, how Wotan, as the Wanderer, returned to Valhalla with his spear shattered, how he ordered the heroes to pile up logs from the World Ash Tree, how the gods sit there in fear and dread, and how Wotan longs for the ring to be given back to the Rhinemaidens; it is to persuade Brünnhilde to do this that Waltraute has come. Although stunned by this narration (ex.5 with its anguished leaps is eloquent), Brünnhilde refuses to throw away Siegfried's pledge. The final brief exchange between Brünnhilde and Waltraute is enacted to one of the numerous little groups of allusive motifs which distinguish the score

of *Götterdämmerung* (in the earlier parts of the *Ring*, motivic references are generally more sparing and explicit).

Ex.5

Waltraute departs in a thundercloud which passes to reveal a calm evening sky. But the peace is illusory. The flames leap up again round the rock and Brünnhilde hears Siegfried's horn. She rushes excitedly to the edge of the cliff and is horrified to find a stranger: Siegfried disguised by the Tarnhelm as Gunther. Her rapturous welcome is abruptly terminated with a discord, remembered from Hagen's Watch in scene ii, but also identifiable as the '*Tristan* chord' at correct pitch. The significance of the interpolation of that pivotal chord from Wagner's intervening opera (*see* **Tristan und Isolde**) at Brünnhilde's cry 'Verrath!' ('Betrayed!') – the point at which the hero's love (under the influence of a magic potion, be it noted) is perceived to be false – need hardly be laboured. No less notable is the fact that the '*Tristan* chord' turns out to be the G♯ minor of the Tarnhelm motif (*see* **Rheingold, Das**) with the addition of an intensifying diminished 7th (the F). But most extraordinary of all is the fact that the '*Tristan* chord' and Tarnhelm motif – both at their original pitch – effect a return to B minor, the key in which the act will end, as it began: a remarkable example of the interaction of local tonal reference with large-scale structural planning. The disguised Siegfried claims Brünnhilde as wife, violently snatches the ring from her finger and forces her into the cave for the night. He places his sword symbolically between them.

Act 2 On the shore in front of the Gibichung hall Hagen, sitting outside the palace in a half-sleep, is visited by his father, Alberich: 'Schläfst du, Hagen, mein Sohn?' The syncopations of Hagen's Watch reappear here, but in B♭, the key of the Nibelungs. Hagen is urged to acquire the ring, and intends to do so, but will swear faithfulness only to himself. Dawn breaks in a loosely canonic passage scored for eight horns (scene ii) and Siegfried returns, now in his own form once more. Gunther is following with Brünnhilde, he says, and he tells Hagen and Gutrune how he braved the fire and overpowered Brünnhilde. He secretly changed places with Gunther and, using the Tarnhelm's magic, returned in an instant.

Hagen summons his vassals (scene iii) with blasts on his horn; his cries of 'Hoiho!' make frequent use of the ubiquitous falling semitone. The vassals rush in from all directions and are intemperately amused when they find out that Hagen has summoned them not for battle but for celebration. Their chorus in C major, with augmented-triad colouring influenced by Hagen – 'Gross Glück und Heil' – is another example of stylistic regression in *Götterdämmerung*, exciting as it can be in the theatre.

Clashing their weapons together, the vassals hail Gunther and his bride (scene iv), 'Heil dir, Gunther!', the switch to B♭ possibly in recollection of a more celebrated Bridal March (*Lohengrin*) in the same key. To a melancholy reminiscence of the galloping Valkyrie motif, Brünnhilde is led forward, her eyes cast down. Gutrune's motif (ex.4) is prominent as she comes out of the hall with Siegfried. The sound of Siegfried's name provokes a violent reaction from Brünnhilde, her mute amazement forcefully depicted in the sustained diminished 7th chord that stops the music in its tracks. It starts up again with the anguished contortions of ex.4 and, less predictably, the Destiny motif from the Annunciation of Death in *Die Walküre*. Has Siegfried forgotten his bride, Brünnhilde asks? She sees the ring on his finger and asks how he got it, as it was seized from her by Gunther. Siegfried states simply that he won it by slaying a dragon. Raging against the gods for allowing Siegfried to betray her, Brünnhilde borrows a broad phrase from the Valhalla motif, in the original key of D♭. Siegfried tells how he won Brünnhilde for Gunther and claims that his sword lay between them during the night. Brünnhilde asserts that Nothung hung on the wall as its master wooed her. (Both, of course, are right.) Siegfried, pressed by Gunther and the onlookers to declare his innocence, swears on the point of Hagen's spear that he has kept faith with his 'blood-brother': 'Helle Wehr, heilige Waffe!' His innocently ringing perfect 5ths (both rising and falling) are tellingly offset by Hagen's diminished 5th sounded in the bass. The enraged Brünnhilde swears on the same spear-point that Siegfried has perjured himself. Siegfried calls everyone to the wedding-feast and leads Gutrune into the palace.

Brünnhilde, left alone with Gunther and Hagen, laments Siegfried's treachery (scene v). At first she scorns Hagen's offer to avenge her; the hero would soon make him quake, she says. But then she confides that Siegfried's back would be vulnerable; she gave him no protection there as he would never turn it on an enemy. Gunther bemoans his own disgrace, but initially reacts with horror to Hagen's proposal to strike Siegfried dead (the minatory falling semitones on trombones are combined with the tortured ex.5 on bassoons and double basses). He is persuaded by the promise of obtaining the ring and it is decided to tell Gutrune that Siegfried was killed by a boar while out hunting. The trio of the conspirators, a passage of great power, is a stylistic regression that runs contrary to Wagner's stated principles (the libretto for *Götterdämmerung* in fact preceded the theoretical essays), though there is some attempt to integrate the

passage by means of motivic reminiscence: the new oath of vengeance principally recalls the oaths sworn on Hagen's spear earlier in the act. Siegfried and Gutrune reappear from the palace and a wedding procession forms. The celebratory C major is chillingly darkened in the final bars by the intervention of the falling semitone on trombones in combination with ex.5 a tritone away from the main key.

Act 3.i–ii *Wild woodland and rocky valley by the bank of the Rhine* Siegfried's horn call is heard first in the orchestra and then in the distance, supposedly sounded by Siegfried out hunting. It is answered by the horn call of the Gibichungs (an inverted form). The ominous falling semitone and tritone from the end of the previous act are heard, but then the lyrical music of the Rhinemaidens supervenes. They are playing in the river, singing of the lost gold. Siegfried, having lost his way, stumbles on them and they playfully ask him for the ring on his finger; he refuses. Then he relents, but when they tell him of the dangers the curse-laden ring brings he says he will not succumb to threats. The Rhinemaidens abandon the 'fool', leaving Siegfried to meditate on the oddity of women's behaviour.

Hagen's voice and falling semitone are heard, and Siegfried calls the hunting party over (scene ii). He tells them that the only game he has seen was three wild water-birds, who told him he would be murdered that day. Siegfried drinks jovially from a horn, but Gunther can see only Siegfried's blood in his. Siegfried is asked to tell the story of his life, and he begins with his upbringing by the ill-tempered Mime (to the ostinato of the Nibelungs' motif): 'Mime hiess ein mürrischer Zwerg'. The dwarf taught him smithing, but it was his own skills that enabled him to forge Nothung, with which he killed the dragon Fafner (the Sword and Dragon motifs are heard). As yet Siegfried has no trouble in recalling the past. Swirling augmented harmonies conjure the enchantment of the world he is describing. He tells how the taste of the dragon's blood enabled him to understand the song of the Woodbird, and the Forest Murmurs are recalled. The bird had warned him of Mime's treachery and he had despatched the scheming dwarf.

Hagen hands him a drugged drink which he says will help him to remember what happened next. The music, recalling the trills of the potion he was given in Act 1, tells us that memories have indeed been stimulated: where the trills previously led to the theme of Gutrune, now they soar into a theme remembered from the prologue duet, closely followed by the Brünnhilde motif, ex.2. To the appropriate motifs, and in an increasingly ecstatic state as he relives the traumatic but forgotten experience, Siegfried relates how he was led to a high rock surrounded by fire; there he found the

'Götterdämmerung' (Wagner), Act 3: Josef Hoffmann's design for the final scene in the original production at Bayreuth,
17 August 1876

sleeping Brünnhilde, whom he awoke with a kiss. The expected C major resolution is thwarted by Gunther's tritonal expression of dismay. Two ravens fly overhead and, as Siegfried looks up, Hagen plunges his spear into his back. Brass instruments thunder out the Curse motif and Hagen's falling semitone; one of Siegfried's heroic motifs is hurled out by the entire orchestra, but it reaches its climax on a discord and finally collapses on to the repeated-note, tattoo figure that is to become the basis of the Funeral March. The themes and radiant C major tonality of Brünnhilde's awakening (*Siegfried*, Act 3) are recalled, and Siegfried dies with Brünnhilde's name on his lips.

Siegfried's Funeral March represents a motivic pageant of his life and ancestry, as his body is carried off by vassals in a solemn procession. Themes associated with the Volsungs and their love are followed by a grand statement of the Sword motif in its original C major (on a trumpet), and by the motifs of Siegfried and his heroism, ending with a triumphant transformation, in E♭, of ex. 1.

3.iii *The hall of the Gibichungs* Gutrune comes out of her room into the hall. She thinks she hears Siegfried's horn, but he has not returned. She has seen Brünnhilde walking towards the Rhine, and is

anxious. Hagen is heard approaching ('Hoiho!', on falling semitones over ex.5) and Siegfried's corpse is brought in. She accuses Gunther of murdering him, but he blames Hagen, who claims – to the music of the oath-swearing – to have killed him for committing perjury; Hagen steps forward to seize the ring and, when Gunther stands in his way, Hagen murders him. Hagen tries again to take the ring, but as he approaches Siegfried, the dead man's hand rises into the air, to the horror of all. The Sword motif, in its other primary key of D major, makes a quietly noble intervention, but gives way to the motif of the Twilight of the Gods.

Brünnhilde enters with calm dignity and tells how Siegfried swore her an eternal oath. Gutrune, realizing that the drink had obliterated Siegfried's memory of his wife, curses Hagen and prostrates herself over Gunther's body, where she remains, motionless, until the end. Brünnhilde orders logs to be gathered to make a funeral pyre worthy of the hero ('Starke Scheite'). Loge's motif blazes in eager anticipation. She sings of her betrayal by this noblest, most faithful of men. Addressing Wotan in Valhalla, she says that Siegfried's death has atoned for his guilt and has brought her enlightenment through sorrow. This quietly reflective passage is rounded off by a statement, no longer threatening, of the Curse motif and a sublime resolution in D♭, the ultimate goal of the cycle ('Ruhe, ruhe, du Gott!'). She takes Siegfried's ring, promising that it will be returned to the Rhinemaidens, whose carefree music is now heard. She hurls a blazing torch on to the pile of logs, which immediately ignites. Greeting her horse Grane (to recollections of the galloping Valkyrie motif), she mounts it and rides into the flames. The exultant theme sung by Sieglinde in *Die Walküre* on hearing of her future son's destiny ('O hehrstes Wunder') returns now to crown the peroration: Wagner referred to this motif as 'the glorification of Brünnhilde' (ex.6).

Ex.6

The whole building seems to catch fire and the men and women press to the front of the stage in terror. Suddenly the fire dies down and the Rhine bursts its banks, flooding the entire space. On the appearance of the Rhinemaidens, Hagen leaps into the water in pursuit of the ring. To the sound of the Curse motif, they drag him down into the depths and hold up the ring in triumph. The water-level falls again and from the ruins of the palace, which has collapsed, the men and women watch a burst of firelight as it rises into the sky. Eventually it illuminates the hall of Valhalla, where gods and heroes are seen assembled. The Valhalla motif is naturally prominent here, and those of the Rhinemaidens and the Glorification of Brünnhilde are symbolically intertwined. To the sound of the motifs of the Twilight of the Gods and, finally, the Glorification of Brünnhilde in a radiant D♭ major, Valhalla is engulfed in flames: the long-awaited end of the gods has come to pass.

*

The final opera of the *Ring*, a long evening's performance in its own right, provides an appropriately weighty conclusion to the epic cycle. 26 years elapsed from the time Wagner made his first prose draft for the work to the completion of the full score, with inevitable consequences in terms of stylistic unity. Retrogressive elements of grand opera exist side by side with motivic integration representative of Wagner's most mature style. And yet, the stylistic integrity of *Götterdämmerung* is scarcely compromised, so skilfully are the disparate elements welded together and so intense is the dramaturgical conviction. The resources and stamina demanded by

the work (from both singers and orchestra), combined with its sheer length and theatrical potency, make it one of the most daunting yet rewarding undertakings in the operatic repertory.   B.M.

Grand Macabre, Le ('The Grand Macabre')

Opera in two acts by György Ligeti to a libretto by the composer and Michael Meschke after Michel de Ghelderode's play *La balade du Grand Macabre*; Stockholm, Royal Opera, 12 April 1978.

The cast at the première included Sven-Erik Vikström (Piet the Pot), Kerstin Meyer (Amando, then called 'Spermando'), Elisabeth Söderström (Amanda, then called 'Clitoria'), Erik Saedén (Nekrotzar), Arne Tyrén (Astradamors), Barbro Ericson (Mescalina), Monika Lavén (Venus), Gunilla Slättegård (Prince Go-Go) and Britt-Marie Aruhn (Gepopo, then called 'Säpopo').

Piet the Pot	high tenor
Amando	mezzo-soprano
Amanda	soprano
Nekrotzar	baritone
Astradamors	bass
Mescalina	mezzo-soprano
Venus	high soprano
Prince Go-Go	treble/soprano/ high countertenor
Ruffiak	baritone
Schabiack	baritone
Schabernack	baritone
White Minister	spoken
Black Minister	spoken
Gepopo *Chief of the Secret Police*	soprano
People of Breughelland, spirits, echo of Venus;	
offstage boys' chorus	
Silent: detectives and executioners of the Secret	
Police, pages and servants of Prince Go-Go's	
court, Nekrotzar's entourage	
Setting Breughelland, an imaginary country	

The Hungarian Ligeti's relationship with Sweden, where several of his works had their premières and where he taught from 1961, was confirmed by the director Göran Gentele's commission for the Royal Opera. At first an *Oedipus* was planned, with Gentele as librettist; then, after his unexpected death, Ghelderode's *La balade du Grand Macabre* was suggested by Aliute Meczies, eventually the designer of the first production. Michael Meschke, director of the Stockholm puppet theatre, was given the task of condensing the play. But Ligeti changed the text again during composition, which began in December 1974 and lasted until 1977. The libretto was originally

'Le Grand Macabre' (Ligeti), Prince Go-Go (Gunilla Slättegård) with the Black and White Ministers in the original production at the Stockholm Royal Opera, 12 April 1978

written in German as *Der grosse Makaber*, but translated into Swedish by Meschke for its première, under the present title.

*

The plot is simple but all-encompassing, ranging from sex to politics, inebriation and death, and enabling Ligeti to display all he had achieved during the past quarter century. The scene is set in the kingdom of Breughelland, the kingdom of peasants, monsters and apocalypses glimpsed in that master's paintings. An overture in the form of a short palindrome for 12 motor horns introduces the action, and sets a tone of run-down misuse (there are similar preludes to the second and third scenes). Piet the Pot enters singing the *Dies irae*: he is the opera's common man, drunk throughout the action. Soon he is joined by a pair of young lovers, 'very beautiful in a Botticellian way', Amando and Amanda (originally called Spermando and Clitoria). They are vocally as well as physically entwined in each other, singing in gasps of Monteverdian embellishment that suggest their excited state. (Ligeti himself has mentioned *Poppea*, *Falstaff* and *Il Barbiere di Siviglia* as works that lie behind his own, of which he offers distorted snapshots.) But their duet is interrupted by another voice, coming from a tomb. One calling himself Nekrotzar emerges, and declares he has come to

announce the end of the world: he is the 'Grand Macabre' of the title. He sends Piet off to the tomb to fetch his props (coat, hat, scythe and trumpet) then rides off, with Piet as his mount, to bring his message of death and destruction. Amando and Amanda meanwhile have taken themselves off to the tomb to complete their lovemaking.

The second scene is concerned largely with a couple whose sexual needs require more encouragement: Astradamors, the astrologer, and Mescalina – he wearing women's underwear over his trousers, she clad entirely in leather and brandishing a whip. Once their activities have culminated in a 'bum kiss', she dispatches her husband to his telescope. He observes, and utters mumbo jumbo, while she falls into a drunken sleep in which she implores Venus to give her a lover more potent than her husband. Nekrotzar then enters on Piet's back and congratulates Astradamors for having prophesied his coming. Mescalina, coming out of her dream, demands a man who is well hung: Nekrotzar offers himself, and in a violent embrace kills her. The act then climaxes in a demonically exultant trio for the three men before they go off to the palace.

The third scene, beginning Act 2, takes place there. The ruler of Breughelland is the boy prince Go-Go, who is beset by warring politicians, the White Minister and the Black Minister. Gepopo, the Chief of the Secret Police, suddenly arrives with his agents to deliver a warning in nonsense code made the more undecipherable by musical acrobatics. But then the threat is revealed: it is Nekrotzar. He enters during a big orchestral set piece, headed 'Collage', where the ground bass is a disjointed version of that from the finale of the 'Eroica' Symphony (the rhythm is kept as a skeleton, with different pitches). Above this is a gathering mad overlay of cheap dance music and banal fanfares, these eventually taking over and remaining to punctuate Nekrotzar's fuller announcement of the coming doomsday. While there is still some time left, Astradamors and Piet are all for spending it drinking the wine laid out on the palatial table, and Nekrotzar joins them in an alcoholic trio, seemingly believing himself to be drinking human blood already. He then goes off into a distracted reverie, accompanied by music of a fantastic rococo sort, and remembers his satanic destructions of the past. He is, however, recalled to his task by the approach of midnight, and calls down nothingness while the orchestra slowly marches through a sequence of chords, wide-spread, beautiful and ominous. Then, as a canon in the orchestra slowly slips downward, he himself collapses: the end of the world has come, and the only one to die is Death. The curtain descends as another, dense, still, orchestral texture gradually turns into a confused gallop in the brass.

The fourth scene, or Epilogue, has no separate overture but develops straight out of its predecessor, while returning to the setting of the first scene. Astradamors and Piet hover above the ground, believing themselves to be dead; they then float off. Before long all the rest have turned up: Go-Go, Nekrotzar, Mescalina, the Ministers, and finally, emerging from the tomb where they have been settled for two scenes, Amando and Amanda. Have they all really died and been resurrected to find themselves in much the same situation? Or was Nekrotzar merely a powerless charlatan? In the play he is shown up as a fake, but Ligeti leaves the question open, and has his principals sing the amoral moral: 'Fear not to die, good people all! No one knows when his hour will fall. And when it comes, then let it be ... Farewell, till then, live merrily!'

P.G.

Guillaume Tell [*Guglielmo Tell* ('William Tell')]

Opéra in four acts by Gioachino Rossini to a libretto by Etienne de Jouy and Hippolyte-Louis-Florent Bis, assisted by Armand Marrast and Adolphe Crémieux, based on Friedrich von Schiller's play *Wilhelm Tell;* Paris, Opéra, 3 August 1829.

The première was conducted by François-Antoine Habeneck with Henri-Bernard Dabadie in the title role, Adolphe Nourrit as Arnold, Laure Cinti-Damoreau as Mathilde, Alex Prévost as Gesler and Nicolas Levasseur as Walter Furst.

Arnold Melcthal		tenor
Guillaume Tell [William Tell]	*Swiss conspirators*	baritone
Walter Furst		bass
Mathilde *Princess of the House of Habsburg*		soprano
Melcthal *Arnold's father*		bass
Gesler *Governor of the cantons of Schwyz and Uri*		bass
Rodolphe *commander of Gesler's archers*		tenor
Leuthold *a herdsman*		baritone
Ruodi *a fisherman*		tenor
Hedwige *Tell's wife*		mezzo-soprano
Jemmy *Tell's son*		soprano
A Huntsman		baritone

Chorus of peasants of the cantons of Uri, Schwyz and Unterwalden; knights, pages, and ladies of the train of Mathilde; hunters, soldiers, and guards of Gesler; three brides and their bridegrooms

Setting Switzerland in the 13th century, near Altdorf in the canton of Uri

Guillaume Tell, Rossini's last opera, is the new *grand opéra* he had been contracted to write under the terms of the agreement with the French government drawn up in 1824 at the time of his arrival as a resident in Paris. A number of texts were considered for the project, including two by Eugène Scribe, one of which later became Auber's *Gustave III* and Verdi's *Un ballo in maschera*, the other Halévy's *La Juive*. The choice of Schiller's *Wilhelm Tell* (1804) was both adventurous and shrewd. Whether or not Rossini intended this to be his last opera, it brings together elements of his art that he had successfully developed over the previous 17 years. Schiller's original play engages themes in which the mature Rossini showed a special interest: among them, the political ideals of a conservative people who seek independence with peace, and the psychology of paternal relations. It also enabled Rossini to exploit further an underlying interest in the related genres of folk music, pastoral and the picturesque. The libretto, drafted by Etienne de Jouy, was revised by H.-L.-F. Bis, Armand Marrast, Adolphe Crémieux (who helped shape the Act 2 finale) and, most importantly, by Rossini himself.

The publication rights to the opera were acquired, well in advance of the première, by Eugène Troupenas. As a result, a generally accurate contemporary edition of the opera was quickly available.

Henri-Bernard Dabadie in the title role of Rossini's
'Guillaume Tell', which he created at the Paris Opéra,
3 August 1829: portrait (1836) by François-Gabriel Lépaulle

This edition is not, however, entirely reliable since the promptness of publication involved starting the process of engraving while the opera was still in rehearsal. Significant changes to both music and text were made by Rossini and his collaborators during rehearsals and immediately following the first performances. Few of these changes were incorporated into the Troupenas edition; some, absent from the autograph manuscript, appear only in the theatre's own parts. Apart from altering the scale and proportions of the opera, the modifications affect our perception of the character of Arnold and the role of the men of Schwyz. Any theatre production needs to take into account the full range of available options. (These have been clearly set out in M. Elizabeth C. Bartlet's critical edition of *Guillaume Tell*.)

Rossini left Paris within a fortnight of the opening but on his return to the city he prepared an abridged edition of the opera, first seen in 1831. This reduces the work to three acts, with a new finale based partly on the concluding section of the famous overture. During the 1830s it was not uncommon for the Paris Opéra to stage Act 2 by itself, but the most significant French revival of the period came on 17 April 1837 when a revised version of the three-act abridgement was staged with Gilbert Duprez as Arnold. Though Rossini personally disliked the sound of the new

tenore di forza, the emergence of Duprez was a phenomenon that did much to ensure the work's continuation in the repertory. In 1856 the four-act version was restored to the Paris stage. In February 1868, in Rossini's presence, the Opéra celebrated the work's 500th performance, and it remained an integral part of the Parisian stage repertory until 1932. (During some of the centenary performances in Paris in 1929, the role of Arnold was sung by James Joyce's protégé John O'Sullivan.)

Foreign-language versions of the opera, often adaptations or much truncated, appeared in Europe and the USA in the early 1830s. The first New York performance took place, in English, in 1831. London did not see the original French *Guillaume Tell* until it was staged at Covent Garden in 1845. Previous English productions included *Hofer, the Tell of the Tyrol*, adapted by J. R. Planché and arranged by Henry Bishop, at the Drury Lane Theatre in 1830 and the Italian *Guglielmo Tell* at Her Majesty's Theatre in 1839. Though Rossini supervised an adaptation of the opera, *Rodolfo di Sterlinga*, created in Bologna in 1840 partly as a vehicle for the tenor Nichola Ivanoff, he appears to have had no hand in the various Italian versions of the score. The first Italian staging, to a translation-cum-adaptation by Luigi Balocchi, was in Lucca on 17 September 1831 with Duprez as Arnold. Subsequent Italian revivals used Calisto Bassi's fuller and more reliable version, or a conflation of Bassi and Balocchi. It is a sad fact, however, that what major revivals there have been outside France over the years have tended to be of the italianized *Guglielmo Tell*.

La Scala, which had staged a carnival season adaptation in 1837, first staged *Guglielmo Tell* in 1845. Toscanini conducted performances there in 1899, and in the early years of this century Francesco Tamagno was heard as Arnold. His immediate successor in the role was Giacomo Lauri-Volpi who sang it frequently in Italy and the USA. In 1972 at the Florence Maggio Musicale, Riccardo Muti conducted an uncut version of *Guglielmo Tell* with Norman Mittelmann as Tell, Nicolai Gedda as Arnold and Eva Marton as Mathilde; he later led a further uncut revival, using a revised Italian translation by Paolo Cattelan, at La Scala in 1988 with Giorgio Zancanaro as Tell, Chris Merritt as Arnold and Cheryl Studer as Mathilde. In 1990, in their first staging of the opera since 1889, Covent Garden mounted a beautifully considered and eminently naturalistic French-language production by John Cox, with Gregory Yurisich as Tell, Chris Merritt as Arnold and Lella Cuberli as Mathilde. The opera has been recorded, complete and in French, only once: a distinguished set conducted by Lamberto Gardelli with Gabriel Bacquier as Tell, Nicolai Gedda as Arnold and Montserrat Caballé as Mathilde. Of the various Italian language recordings, the finest is Riccardo Chailly's version with Sherrill Milnes as Tell, Luciano Pavarotti as Arnold (a role he declined to sing on stage) and Mirella Freni as Mathilde.

*

The opera is prefaced by a four-movement overture, programmatic in intention and formally different from anything Rossini had previously devised. The opening colloquy for five solo cellos is a rare inspiration, evoking, Berlioz suggests, 'the calm of profound solitude, the solemn silence of nature when the elements and human passions are at rest'. The pastoral scene that follows the storm is also memorable. The use of a traditional Swiss herdsman's melody, a *ranz des vaches*, gives Rossini material for one of the finest of his many english horn solos; it is a melody that undergoes a number of transformations during the course of the opera, giving it something of the character of a leitmotif.

Act I *On the shores of Lake Lucerne* As the curtain rises a triple wedding celebration is to hand while Ruodi the fisherman sings a love song. To William Tell the prospect of festivities is marred by fear of the Austrian regime which, since the loss of influence of the Holy Roman Empire in the region, has become increasingly repressive. Local Swiss customs have been a particular Austrian target; but in the three forest cantons of Uri, Schwyz and Unterwalden resistance to the Austrians is growing, something typified by the decision of a revered elder, Melcthal, to officiate personally at the wedding ceremony. Unfortunately his son Arnold, who has served with an Austrian regiment, has fallen in love with the Austrian princess, Mathilde. When Tell puts to Arnold the urgency and justice of the Swiss cause (duet, 'Où vas-tu ... Ah! Mathilde, idole de mon âme!'), Arnold's private dilemma is eloquently addressed as orchestrally accompanied dialogue gives way to the lyrical 'Ah! Mathilde', the pitch wrenched up from G♭ to A♭ as Arnold's anguish becomes increasingly palpable. After Melcthal has blessed the couples, festivities resume with dancing and an archery competition won by Tell's young son Jemmy. But the idyll is not to last. A local herdsman, Leuthold, has killed an Austrian soldier who was attempting to rape his daughter. With the Austrians in pursuit, he asks to be rowed to safety; but with dangerous waters and a storm brewing the response is muted until Tell volunteers as ferryman. Thwarted by Leuthold's escape and by the people's loyalty to Tell, the Austrians prepare to sack the village while the Austrian Governor's henchman Rodolphe takes old Melcthal hostage. It makes a gripping end to an opening act in which Rossini is far more expansive than Schiller. In particular, Rossini seems concerned to establish the harmonious communal life of the Swiss people as a key factor in the evolving drama.

Central to this strategy is the inclusion in Acts 1 and 3 of a considerable amount of colourful and expertly written choral and dance music. It is often cut in performance; but, far from being extraneous to the drama, it is crucial to it.

Act 2 *The Rütli Heights overlooking Lake Lucerne and the nearby cantons* A hunting chorus is answered by an evening song of Swiss folk working in the hills and fields. Mathilde has glimpsed Arnold and sings of her love for him in 'Sombre forêt', an exquisite strophic aria in the French style, finely orchestrated (the quiet drum roll prefacing each stanza is one of the opera's most affecting instrumental gestures). Their reunion persuades Arnold that he must win military glory with the Austrian army so as to become worthy of Mathilde in the eyes of the world (duet, 'Oui, vous l'arrachez à mon âme'). Tell and Walter have seen the lovers together but their mission is to persuade Arnold to join the anti-Austrian confederates. In the trio 'Quand l'Helvétie est un champ de supplices', the appeal to Arnold is reinforced by the revelation that the Austrians have murdered his elderly father, Melcthal. This is one of Rossini's finest creations, a superbly structured ensemble rich in telling musical and psychological detail; it also marks a significant departure from Schiller's play where old Melcthal is blinded, not murdered, and where Tell, the simple man of action, declines to be involved in the various meetings on Rütli Heights. The men of Unterwalden, Uri and Schwyz now begin to appear, crossing woods, mountains and water to gather for the swearing of an oath of allegiance. Rossini characterizes each group separately, with the good faith of these so-called rebels reflected in the idyllic music he writes for the men of Schwyz. As forces – military and musical – grandly mass, the confederates ask Tell for guidance. At the great oath-swearing ('Jurons, jurons par nos dangers') the trumpets sound; but there is no melodramatic denouement. Day breaks over the mountains, the drum again quietly rolls, and the cry 'Aux armes!' is repeated three times before the orchestra adds a torrential 16-bar coda. ('Ah, it is sublime', remarks Berlioz in his essay on the opera, 'let us take breath'.)

Act 3.i *A secluded chapel in the gardens of the Altdorf palace* In this scene, subjected to various revisions and emendations by Rossini, Mathilde comes face to face with Arnold, her now bereaved lover. He has no option but to renounce her, and in 'Sur la rive étrangère' she bids him farewell.

3.ii *The square at Altdorf* Gesler has ordered enforced festivities to mark one hundred years of Austrian rule. Sensing public hostility, he demands that the people be humiliated by paying homage to his hat. The dances that follow are vividly characterized by Rossini; in particular we sense the festering resentment of the local women who are forced to cavort with the salacious Austrians in the 'Soldiers' Dance'. Tell refuses to pay homage to Gesler; but he is recognized as the man who saved Leuthold and is promptly arrested. He tells his son, Jemmy, to carry the signal for the start of the Swiss revolt, but the boy is also arrested. With both Tell and Jemmy in his grasp, Gesler dreams up his sadistic ploy to test Tell's nerve and marksmanship by ordering that, if he wants to save both his own and his son's life, Tell must shoot an arrow through an apple placed on Jemmy's head. Tell is defiant and appalled – 'Ah! tu n'as pas d'enfant' – and in the great aria 'Sois immobile' he addresses Jemmy before finally drawing his bow. The aria stands at the heart of the opera and is one of the most personal of all Rossini's musical utterances. A solo cello is used at the outset, as it might be in a Bach Passion, but the major–minor oscillations and the lie of the line itself are fashioned in Rossini's own way. Verdi was to follow some of Rossini's cues when he came to portray another grieving father, Rigoletto. Tell hits the apple, but he is rearrested when he confesses that a second bolt, inadvertently revealed, was intended for Gesler if Jemmy had been harmed. Mathilde now intervenes. She demands that Gesler release Jemmy into her care; she also vows to effect Tell's release. But Gesler has other ideas and, amid growing civil unrest, Tell is despatched to the dangerously infested dungeons of the fortress at Küssnacht across the lake.

Act 4.i *Melcthal's house* Returning to the family home, Arnold plans revenge for his father's murder. He also recognizes that, with Tell's capture, he is now the man who must lead the uprising. Berlioz thought Arnold's aria here, 'Asil héréditaire', the finest thing in the score, a filial lament of great finish and beauty. It is also very powerful. As Arnold is joined by men from the cantons, he reveals Tell's and old Melcthal's cache of arms in a violent cabaletta that looks ahead to the more declamatory writing for the tenor voice that Donizetti and Verdi would shortly develop.

4.ii *A rocky shore by Lake Lucerne* Mathilde and Jemmy join Hedwige, Tell's wife, who is desperate for news of her husband. Mathilde is prepared to offer herself to the rebels as hostage for Tell's safe return. Jemmy lights the beacon to signal the uprising. Tell, whose hands were released during the crossing to Küssnacht (he was the only man on board strong enough to steer safely), has managed to seize the Austrian boat and braves the storm to return. On landing he wastes no time in hunting down and shooting Gesler. Meanwhile, Altdorf has been freed. The confederates gather, the skies clear and the mountain landscape is seen again in all its majesty. Moved by the scene before him, Arnold addresses his dead father in lines that are not in Schiller: 'Ah, father, why are you not here in this moment of joy for all Helvetia?' The tribute over, Rossini's hymn to nature and liberty steals forth, the *ranz des vaches* entering softly on the horns with a numinous beauty that Wagner would later match but not surpass.

*

Schiller's *Wilhelm Tell* is neither revolutionary nor tragic. It has been described by Susanne Langer as 'a species of serious heroic comedy'. As such, *Guillaume Tell* is heir to a tradition which Rossini closely embraced in his *opere serie* of the years 1813–23. Langer writes of Schiller's Tell, the character of whom Rossini took into his opera virtually unchanged:

Tell appears as an exemplary personage in the beginning of the play, as citizen, husband, father, friend and patriot; when an extreme political and social crisis develops, he rises to the occasion, overcomes the enemy, frees his country, and returns to the peace, dignity and harmonious joy of his home. The balance of life is restored. As a personage he is impressive; as a personality he is very simple . . . Such are the serious products of comic art; they are also its rarer examples. The natural vein of comedy is humorous – so much so that 'comic' has become synonymous with 'funny'.

By 1829, Rossini had become a master of the comic style in both its aspects: comedy as humour and comedy as a vehicle for expressing vitality, continuity and harmony in human affairs, however strong the potential for disorder in those affairs may be. *Guillaume Tell* is very much the great summarizing work of his career, an astonishing drawing together of the finest elements on offer in both Italian and French music theatre of the time. Here at last was a subject – human and political – grand enough to require the huge formal advances he had made in his final years in Naples, above all his use of the chorus as a multi-faceted protagonist. The opera formed both a consummation and a natural resting-point. Partly because of difficulties over his annuity from the Opéra, possibly also because of illness, Rossini, who lived until 1868, did not attempt to write another opera.   R.O.

H

Halka

Opera in four (originally two) acts by Stanisław Moniuszko to a libretto by Włodzimierz Wolski after a story from Kazimierz Wójcicki's *Stary gawędy i obrazy* ('Legends and Pictures'); concert performance, Vilnius, 1 January 1848 (staged Vilnius, 18 February 1854); standard, revised version, Warsaw, Wielki Theatre, 1 January 1858.

The cast at the première of the standard version included Wilhelm Troszel as Stolnik, Jan Stysiński as Dziemba, Aloizy Żółkowski as Janusz, Cornelia Quattrini as Zofia, Paulina Rivoli as Halka and Julian Dobrski as Jontek.

Stolnik *a nobleman*	bass
Dziemba *Stolnik's steward*	bass
Janusz *a young nobleman*	baritone
Zofia *Stolnik's daughter*	soprano
Halka *a peasant girl*	soprano
Jontek *a mountaineer*	tenor
Piper	baritone
Villager	tenor
Stolnik's guests, villagers	
Setting Southern Poland in the late 18th century	

Moniuszko met the poet Włodzimierz Wolski during a visit to Warsaw in September 1846. He read Wolski's poem *Halska*, based on a story by Kazimierz Wójcicki, and asked the poet to prepare a libretto on the theme of the poem. The original two-act version of the opera was completed in Vilnius in May 1847 but was rejected by the Wielki Theatre in Warsaw, probably because its theme of class conflict was considered politically inflammatory. The first, concert, performance was organized by the composer and given with amateur singers and players.

In 1856 Moniuszko made several changes and additions to the opera, making Jontek a tenor rather than a baritone role and adding the duet for Jontek and Janusz (Act 2 of the standard version) and the Highlander Dances (Act 3 of the standard version). When the Wielki Theatre finally agreed in July 1857 to stage *Halka*, the composer expanded the work to its present four-act version, subdividing each of the original acts into two. The further additions were as follows: Act 1, Stolnik's polonaise aria and a concluding orchestral mazurka; Act 2, an orchestral prelude and Halka's opening aria; Act 3, an orchestral prelude; Act 4, an orchestral prelude and Jontek's opening aria. Wolski again provided the text for the new material. The première of this, the standard version of *Halka*, took place at the Wielki Theatre to immediate acclaim. The director was Leopold Matuszyński and the conductor Jan Quattrini. Its success made Moniuszko a national celebrity and belatedly launched his career. The popularity of *Halka* was such that it was given 36 times in its first year and 500 times by 1900. Productions have been staged in at least eight Polish theatres outside Warsaw. It was given in Prague (conducted by Smetana) in 1868, and has been performed in Moscow, Chicago and Jerusalem among other cities.

*

Act I *The drawing-room of Stolnik's manor house, near Kraków* The overture introduces several of the themes used in the opera. The introductory Andante presents the theme associated with Halka's sorrow and culminates in a *largo* passage which returns in the final act just before her suicide. The main body of the movement (*agitato*) has a two-part structure with concluding Presto, akin to many Rossini overtures. Of the three themes in the exposition, the second appears in the noblemen's drinking chorus in Act 1 and the third accompanies Halka's pleas to Jontek in Act 2. The bridge between exposition and recapitulation introduces a theme from Jontek's G minor aria in Act 2 and the theme associated with Janusz's guilt.

The curtain rises on a betrothal party in Stolnik's manor house. Stolnik's daughter Zofia has become engaged to a young nobleman, Janusz, and the guests wish the couple happiness and long life in a colourful choral polonaise. As the guests move to another room, Janusz and Zofia are left with Stolnik. In a terzetto they ask his blessing on their engagement but are interrupted by a distant voice, which Janusz recognizes as that of Halka, a village girl whom he has seduced and abandoned; she sings a simple Krakovian folksong. Although an ensemble, the terzetto has musical affinities with the typical cavatina-cabaletta designs of early 19th-century Italian opera. Janusz is left alone to give vent to his

Characters from an early production of Moniuszko's 'Halka'

conflicting emotions, fear of the consequences of Halka's arrival and guilt over his treatment of her. This short strophic romance is his only solo item in the opera. Halka enters singing her folksong, as yet unaware of Janusz's betrayal. She questions him about his intentions, but he answers evasively and arranges a further meeting, fearing that they will be discovered. The folksong leads into a multi-sectional duet of considerable formal complexity and dramatic power. The opening Allegro depicts Halka's rapturous greeting and Janusz's evasive response in an extended ternary movement. This leads to an arioso section in which Janusz expresses his remorse through one of the opera's several recurring themes. A *largo* section in a chromatic C major is an expression of tenderness which culminates in affirmations of mutual love in the final cabaletta. The layout of the entire sequence and its skilful dramatic pacing are reminiscent of an extended scena in Rossini or Donizetti. In the last scene, we return to the festivities of the betrothal party, as Stolnik and the guests drink the health of the young couple. The noblemen's drinking chorus, possibly inspired by some of the choruses in *Der Freischütz*, was the final number of the original Act 1. Stolnik's rather conventional polonaise aria and the lively concluding mazurka were added in the 1857 revision.

Act 2 *The garden of Stolnik's manor house* The prelude prefigures much of the early part of the act, referring to Halka's 'sorrow' theme, to the main theme of her opening aria, to the festivities continuing inside the manor house and to Jontek's aria. Throughout the act the music is continuous. Halka has returned to the garden of the manor house, haunted by a sense of Janusz's presence within. Her G minor aria was described by Hans von Bülow as 'a little masterpiece, full of warmth and tenderness'. It is really a double aria, with the opening cavatina enclosing a nostalgic middle section in the major and the cabaletta leading directly into the next number. Jontek, a mountaineer from Halka's village – himself in love with her – appears and warns her of Janusz's deceit, begging her to return to the village. His G minor aria following Halka's recitative is of a folk-bravura character, with *krakowiak* rhythms which are especially strong in the second section.

One of the main dramatic scenes of the opera, the finale begins with a brief impassioned orchestral prelude, followed by three extended ensemble numbers. The first is a duet between Halka and Jontek (repeated with chorus), in which the third overture theme is heard: Halka, in distress, knocks at the door of the manor house. Janusz appears and reprimands Jontek for disturbing the celebrations. As Halka faints, Jontek turns on Janusz and in a powerful multi-sectional duet accuses him of deserting her. (This number was added for the Warsaw première.) Halka recovers and names Janusz as the father of her child. In the final sextet with chorus a crowd gathers, but Janusz persuades them that she is mad. His steward Dziemba is ordered to drive the intruders away.

Act 3 *Halka's village in the Tatra mountains* The first part of the prelude was added for the Warsaw première and consists mainly of elaborations of Halka's folksong. The original prelude follows, a brief movement in which we hear the bells ringing for Vespers. The entire act is really an extended scenic tableau in the manner of French grand opera; there is no significant dramatic action. In the opening chorus the villagers come out from Vespers and discuss the forthcoming wedding of Janusz. The music alternates a solemn style appropriate to the occasion with lively dance-based sections anticipating the festivities. Next follow the Highlander Dances; this ballet, added for the revised version of 1856, is the centrepiece of the act. The dances are based on the distinctive folk music of the Tatra highlands of southern Poland. In a duet with chorus, Jontek and Halka arrive and relate the events at the manor house to a sympathetic crowd. An alternation of solos rather than a true duet, this movement contains some of the most four-square and conventional material in the opera, and is curiously at odds with the vitality of the preceding dances. In the finale, a villager spots a black crow, regarded as a bad omen. To Halka's distress, a wedding procession is heard in the distance. A semi-fugal chorus, with interjections from Jontek, Halka and the Villager, brings the act to a close.

Act 4 *The square in front of the village church* A piper is playing a cheerful melody in the village square. Jontek asks for a *dumka* (lament), and sings of his grief over Halka. The slow mazurka (*kujawiak*) rhythms of this lament are the foundation for some of the most expressive and beautiful solo vocal writing in the opera. The wedding procession arrives; as it passes Zofia sees Halka's distress and innocently questions her. Halka tries to explain her predicament, but the wedding procession then enters the church. The chorus is based on a Polish folksong, and it gives way to a Rossinian quintet accompanied by chorus and a trio for Stolnik, Janusz and Zofia, before resuming as the procession enters the church. There is a short duettino in which Jontek once more tries to convince Halka of Janusz's deceit, while she still proclaims her love for him. As the choir sings Halka resolves to set fire to the church, but relents as she hears the music. She laments her child, who died of starvation, but still declares her love for Janusz. This is an effective scena, powerfully alternating the choral hymn with Halka's increasingly demented dramatic recitatives and her poignant prayer, an italianate cavatina notable for its solo cello accompaniment. Halka now resolves in a cantilena to kill herself and commends her soul to God. She rushes to the edge of a precipice and hurls herself over before Jontek can stop her. As the wedding procession emerges from the church Jontek confronts Janusz with the news of her death. In some ways the opera ends ambivalently. Despite

the tragedy, the final section is an affirmative D major chorus, as the villagers are forced by Dziemba to sing in praise of the Lord and Lady. It is difficult to be sure if this is an ironic play on different levels of meaning or simply a response to the censor.

*

In Moniuszko's mature works the practice of using Polish dances as a basis for arias and ensembles, common in the 19th century, carried a new ideological burden as the chief means of establishing a national operatic idiom. *Halka* is as popular today in Poland as it was over a hundred years ago. It is regularly performed at the Wielki Theatre, Warsaw, and can also be heard periodically at opera houses in the provinces. Clearly this reception transcends issues of musical quality. The work has become for many a powerful national symbol, and its lively dance movements and tuneful arias – choral polonaises and polonaise arias depicting the nobility while mazurka and *krakowiak* arias represent the lower orders – have acquired something of the popularity and even the status of a folk art. Historically it may be regarded as the first Polish 'grand opera', comparable in a way to Glinka's *A Life for the Tsar* and Smetana's *Dalibor*. Yet, unlike those works, *Halka* has remained a product for home consumption only. Its characteristic blend of conservative italianate melodic idioms and Polish national dance rhythms at times results in music of lively charm, but also courts mediocrity, allowing the well-tried formula to act as a substitute for genuine creative vitality.   J.Sn.

Hänsel und Gretel ('Hänsel and Gretel')

Märchenspiel in three acts ('Bilder') by Engelbert Humperdinck to a libretto by Adelheid Wette after a fairy-tale by the Brothers Grimm, Jacob Ludwig and Wilhelm Carl; Weimar, Hoftheater, 23 December 1893.

The original cast included Marie Kayser (Gretel), Ida Schubert (Hänsel), Ferdinand Wiedey (Peter), Luise Tibelti (Gertrud) and Hermine Finck (the Witch).

Gretel	soprano
Hänsel *her brother*	mezzo-soprano
Gertrud *their mother*	mezzo-soprano
Peter *a broom-maker, their father*	baritone
Sandman	soprano
Dew Fairy	soprano
Witch	mezzo-soprano
14 angels, children	
Setting The woods of the Ilsenstein	

*'Hänsel und Gretel' (Humperdinck), scene from the
production at the Vienna Hofoper (18 December 1894) with
Paula Mark (Gretel), Marie Renard (Hänsel), and Marie
Lehmann (Witch)*

In April 1890 Humperdinck was asked by his sister,
Adelheid Wette, to set to music four folksongs from
the Grimm fairy-tale *Hänsel und Gretel* for performance by her children. The work might have rested
there; but at the time Humperdinck was seeking the
text for a comic opera, and his family persuaded him
that the songs might be extended into a small
Singspiel. The piece was performed privately in this
version in the Wettes' house; the delighted response
encouraged Humperdinck to turn the material into a
fully-fledged opera, even though he had doubts
about the fairy-tale being suited to such treatment.

On receiving the completed score in October
1893, Richard Strauss, who was then assistant
conductor at the Weimar theatre, declared the opera
a masterpiece. The première was due to be conducted
by Hermann Levi in Munich, on 14 December 1893;
but the illness of Hanna Borchers (who was to sing
Gretel) caused a postponement and the honour of
conducting the first performance fell to Strauss in
Weimar. Strauss's future wife Pauline de Ahna was
to have sung Hänsel, but she too was ill and Schubert
sang Hänsel in her place, while Schubert's part of
Gretel was taken over at short notice by Kayser. The
overture could not be performed as the parts had
not arrived. Any shortcomings in the première, however, were compensated for by the speed and success

with which the opera was taken up by other
theatres, aided by the *Hänsel und Gretel* touring
company founded by Georg Richard Kruse in
1894. The emperor (Wilhelm II) praised the work
at its Berlin première, conducted by Felix Weingartner on 13 October 1894. Two outstanding
individual performances were given within the
first year, by Hedwig Schako as Gretel in the
Frankfurt première and by Ernestine Schumann-
Heink as the Witch in Hamburg, with Mahler conducting.

The progress of *Hänsel und Gretel* abroad was
equally impressive. The London première took place
as early as 1894: Luigi Arditi conducted the opera in
English at Daly's Theatre, with Marie Elba as Hänsel
and Jeanne Douste as Gretel. The American première, at the Metropolitan in 1905, was conducted by
Alfred Hertz. *Hänsel und Gretel* was the first opera to
be broadcast complete from Covent Garden, in
January 1923. In 1954 the first recording of the opera
was made, Herbert von Karajan conducting, with
Elisabeth Grümmer as Hänsel and Elisabeth
Schwarzkopf as Gretel. In Germany, performances of
Hänsel und Gretel have remained popularly associated with Christmas.

*

Humperdinck referred to the overture as 'Children's
Life'; it sums up much of the poetic and musical
content of the work. Exuberant dances are balanced
by the hymnlike sounds of the 'Evening Prayer'; its
phrases, which spread in extending arches, suggest
the divine providence that will protect the children in
their adventures. As this theme combines polyphoni-
cally with the folklike dances, the music becomes
more rumbustious – but, as Humperdinck said, such
is the way with children and their games.

Act I In the broom-maker's house The curtain rises
to show the children at more serious business, Hänsel
making brooms and Gretel knitting stockings. Gretel
sings a folksong, 'Suse, liebe Suse', to accompany her
work; Hänsel takes over, though a slight interruption
of the gentle flow suggests that their minds are not
wholly on their business. Hänsel then breaks the
thread more decisively by throwing down his work
and complaining of hunger. Even Gretel's reference
to providence, to a phrase of the Evening Prayer,
cannot silence his cries. A dance provides the
diversion needed; Gretel makes a game of sweeping
all Hänsel's grumbling out of the house ('Griesgram
hinaus'). The reappearance of the gentle accompaniment of 'Suse, liebe Suse' at the close of the song
confirms that peace has returned. Gretel is even able
to show Hänsel some milk that a neighbour has given
them for the family's supper. The children's delighted expectation is reflected in the new variations
woven from the 'Suse' folksong; but one fragment
from the original persists, reminding Gretel of the

work they should be doing. It seems the reminder may prove effective until Hänsel mentions the word 'dancing', when thoughts of work vanish and the 'Suse' motif is swept into the dance-song 'Brüderchen komm tanz mit mir'. Unlike 'Suse, liebe Suse' (or the later 'Ein Männlein steht im Walde'), this is not a quoted folksong though it is equally successful in evoking a children's world. The variations stray more and more from the opening as the children are led further and further into their game. The momentum of the dance is halted only by the dramatic entry of Gertrud. As the children attempt to explain why they have done so little work, the forgotten 'Suse' fragment slips back, punctuated by ominous signs of the mother's anger. Gertrud accidentally knocks over the precious milk and in despair chases the children out to pick strawberries. Her solitary lament, 'Da liegt nun der gute Topf', is accompanied by last sorrowful echoes of the 'Suse' motif.

The distant sounds of the broom-maker's song, 'Ral-la-la-la, ral-la-la-la', begin in the minor key as a slightly humorous lament for the poor man in his hunger, but a lilting major version soon follows. At first Gertrud puts such energy down to drinking, but as Peter produces food from his basket the mood of lamentation is forgotten. Even Gertrud's account of the spilt milk fails to damp their spirits and dance fragments continue to punctuate their dialogue. At the height of their jubilation Peter pauses to inquire about the children. When Gertrud reveals that they have been sent into the forest, the rhythms change in character, and Peter warns of the Witch's Ride. At first the music remains spirited, but as Peter settles into his Witch's Ballad it grows in intensity. Finally convinced of the children's real danger in the forest, Gertrud hurries out of the house with Peter to seek them.

Act 2 *In the wood* As the prelude develops the music of the Witch's Ride from folksong to orchestral tone-painting, it seems that Peter has hardly exaggerated the terrors of the gingerbread Witch. With a gradual calming of the Bacchanalian dance figures, the curtain rises on the more peaceful forest scene of Gretel making a garland of rosehips and Hänsel picking strawberries. They sing a cheerful folksong, 'Ein Männlein steht im Walde', to a spare orchestral accompaniment. After the heavy rhythms of the Witch's Ride the children's innocent pleasures are suggested by the weaving of delicate melodic fragments. When a cuckoo picks up their falling interval of a 3rd, they echo its call and absorb it further into their melodies. They also make a game of mimicking his stealing habits with their strawberries, only to find to their horror that they have eaten every one.

From this point the melodic lines and orchestral

texture take on a more opaque quality, as if the wood were darkening around them. From the sudden silence as Hänsel admits he has lost their way, a more mysterious and sustained melodic line emerges, one first heard as a background to the Witch's Ride. It is repeated in shorter note values and chromatically distorted versions as the children's fear of the forest grows. Mists rise, and their imaginations succeed in turning the cuckoo's call into a portent of doom and even in invoking the rhythms of the Witch's Ride. When the mists clear, all that is revealed is the Sandman, a small grey figure with a sack on his back. The heavier sonorities vanish, leaving harmonics from harp and strings to accompany his simple song, 'Der kleine Sandmann bin ich'. As though to indicate that the peaceful sleep the Sandman brings, as he sprinkles his sand on to the children's eyes, is real, his song is carried over into an expansive chorale-like melody. The children respond by singing their Evening Prayer, its reassuring triadic shapes purging their minds of all horrors. The earlier mysterious shape is incorporated into the polyphonic sequences that grow from the Prayer, which is now connected with heavenly mysteries, as in a 'Dream Pantomime' a ladder reaches down from heaven and 14 angels are seen to surround the sleeping children. The symphonic proportions of this ballet-pantomime more than balance the excesses of the Witch's Ride and leave one in no doubt that good will triumph in the coming battle between evil and innocence.

Act 3 *The gingerbread house* The spiky motif for the gingerbread house which begins the third act promises a rude awakening for the children. Its staccato rhythms foreshadow the character of the Witch herself, but the prelude soon weaves them into a smoother texture, as though seeking to prolong the mood of the ballet-pantomime. When the Dew Fairy enters to awaken the children, he sings his own version of the Sandman's song, 'Der kleine Taumann heiss' ich', followed by a melody from the overture closely associated with the Evening Prayer. The suspended melodic lines of Gretel's first words show her still hovering on the borders of sleep; then she wakes Hänsel and a more everyday world returns, as the two children mimic birdsong. Hänsel, however, soon refers back to the music of the Prayer, and Gretel joins him in relating their dream of the 14 angels.

The polyphonic lines of the ballet-pantomime prove so pervasive that they seem to overflow into the moment when the morning mists clear to reveal the gingerbread house, making it seem part of the same dream-imagery, except that barcarolle rhythms now convey a more sensual character. As the children express their delight in the sweets making up the house, a new staccato figure is heard, offering a more obvious contrast to the Prayer. The combination of these two figures creates an irresistible momentum. The children ignore the warnings of the gingerbread house's spiky motif in the orchestra and they remain unaware of the Witch creeping up on them and throwing a noose round Hänsel's neck until the staccato rhythms of her laughter break out from the whole orchestra.

From this point the barcarolle rhythms seem like an ensnaring web, with the Witch singing many new variations to prolong the flow. Although she entices the children with words of endearment, their responses show that they recognize her true nature. Indeed, when Hänsel slips his halter and tries to escape with Gretel, the melodic façade drops and she fixes them with a spell. She shuts Hänsel in a cage, intending to fatten him up, and sends Gretel indoors to set the table: Gretel is already plump enough for cooking. The Witch's power might seem frightening, except that the constant return to the barcarolle rhythms makes her culinary preparations seem like a reckless game. At one point her excitement grows so great that it spills over into a return of the Witch's Ride, 'Hurr hopp hopp'. The children await their moment. As the oven burns hotter and the Witch's excitement continues to rise, Gretel breaks her spell and frees her brother; when the Witch tells her to look into the oven she feigns stupidity and asks the Witch to demonstrate, and the two of them bundle her into the oven. They express their feelings in the Gingerbread Waltz, 'Nun ist die Hexe tot', their own version of the barcarolle figures. The explosion of the Witch's oven heralds a further transformation: the gingerbread figures surrounding the house are revealed as dead children, waiting for the touch of Hänsel and Gretel to bring them back to life. As their subdued song 'O rühre mich an' changes into a dance (the sign of returning life), more of the opera's themes become woven into the fabric, as in the overture. 'Ral-la-la-la' heralds the arrival of Peter and Gertrud, closely followed by the dance-song from the first act. The reappearance of the Evening Prayer confirms its place in the children's triumph.

*

Critics have often debated as to whether the richness of the musical material of *Hänsel und Gretel* and the elaboration of its development are not too much for a simple, traditional fairy story. Yet despite the Wagnerian range of colours and textures that Humperdinck drew from the orchestra, he succeeded in keeping the melodic and rhythmic foundations of his music simple. By indulging in seemingly endless polyphonic variations on his folk melodies, Humperdinck actually remained close in spirit to the carefree sensuousness of children. It was this uninhibited exploitation of Wagnerian musical techniques, without the complexities or philosophical undertones of music drama, that so attracted audi-

ences at the time. The fairy-tale content offered a contrast to the craze for Italian *verismo*, and the opera was compared to Weber's *Der Freischutz* as another German monument in the battle against the influx of Italian opera. Yet perhaps the work's most enduring quality is its melodic appeal, which ties the music directly to folksong and gives reality to Humperdinck's claim of having recreated *Märchenoper* (fairy-tale opera).   **A.G.**

Hans Heiling

Grosse romantische Oper in a prologue and three acts by Heinrich August Marschner to a libretto by Eduard Devrient after legends about the Hans Heiling Cliffs in Bohemia; Berlin, Hofoper, 24 May 1833.

The cast at the première included Eduard Devrient (Heiling), Therese Grünbaum (Anna), Maria Theresia Lehmann-[Löw] (the Queen), Karl Adam Bader (Conrad) and Louis Schneider (Stephen).

The Queen of the Gnomes	soprano
Hans Heiling *her son*	baritone
Anna *his bride*	soprano
Gertrude *her mother*	contralto
Conrad *a baronial hunter*	tenor
Niklas *another hunter*	speaking role
Stephan *the village blacksmith*	bass

Gnomes, peasants, wedding guests, musicians and hunters
Setting The cavernous underground realm of the gnomes; later the village and surrounding woodlands above it

According to various legends, the outcroppings of rock on the cliffs cut by the River Eger (now Ohře) near Karlsbad (now Karlový Varý) in western Bohemia were once members of a wedding procession that was turned to stone by Hans Heiling, king of the gnomes or earth spirits. Although Devrient does not say specifically in his memoirs which legends he studied for the *Hans Heiling* libretto, one likely source was the first published work on the subject, C. H. Spiess's *Hans Heiling, vierter und letzter Regent der Erd-, Luft-, und Wassergeister, ein Volksmärchen des 10. Jahrhunderts* (Leipzig, 1798), which included in a prologue several legends Spiess had collected. Since Spiess's time, many other writers have created works on the same theme. These stories fall into three groups.

In the first group Heiling is a spooky prince of the dwarfs (sometimes a dwarf himself), a troll, or a sovereign of the gnomes. The best known of these is *Die Heilingszwerge*, by the Grimm brothers, in which

Hans Heiling, here an old troll, lives in an ancient house that appears once a century at the foot of the cliffs that bear his name. Tired from picking berries, a woman appears at the house and asks for hospitality. Heiling grants it then disappears to hunt for his dwarfs. The house vanishes and the woman is unable to go back to her village for a hundred years.

In the second group Heiling is a youth who looks into the Eger to be greeted by a beautiful water nymph who promises to teach him many things if only he will remain unmarried. But when the unfortunate Hans falls in love with a girl and prepares to marry her, he is met at the altar by the nymph, who wreaks revenge by turning the whole wedding party into stone.

In the third group Heiling is a man of ill repute who tries to win the heart of a girl betrothed to a virtuous young journeyman carpenter. While the youth is gone, Heiling presses the father for his daughter's hand and is eventually successful; but when the youth returns wealthy the father relents and allows the lovers to reunite. Enraged, Heiling calls on the devil to turn the wedding party into stone in exchange for his soul.

Like Heinrich Heine in *Die verzauberte Zwergenhochzeit* (1834), Devrient combined elements from all three groups with some new material of his own. His Heiling is ruler over the gnomes but not actually one of them; his dominion is limited to the Lower World. Nor is anyone turned to stone here, although this appears to be an important feature of the legends. What sets Devrient's libretto apart from other treatments of the subject, however, is his character development, particularly that of Heiling. Though a supernatural monarch, benevolent and respected, he succumbs to the temptations of men and falls in love with Anna, a mortal girl who appears to return his love. But when she jilts Heiling in favour of an ordinary man, he promises vengeance, and it is only the intercession of his mother that prevents him from unleashing the fury of the subterranean hordes on the wedding party. Thus Heiling displays a dual nature: he is at once tyrannical yet magnanimous, mortally weak yet supernaturally strong – in short, both villain and hero.

Devrient first offered his work to Mendelssohn, who however could not warm to the character of Heiling and regarded such 'supernatural' subjects as out of fashion. Marschner, however, saw in the libretto great possibilities for developing his concept of German opera, and he began work on the music in 1831. The thunderous applause that greeted the Berlin première was soon repeated throughout Europe, and the work, which represents the zenith of Marschner's creative powers, has remained in the repertory of German and Czech houses ever since. Important revivals took place in Prague in 1889 and

1938, in Dresden in 1923 and in Berlin in 1929. For the landmark Dresden performances Pfitzner invented a way of creating Heiling's magic book, with pages that turn progressively faster (plans for its manufacture were published in 1930). Among several modern British productions, two have attempted to modernize the story by transplanting the action to a Swiss bank (1972, Oxford) and a psychiatric ward (1983, Wexford). C. F. Peters published the full score in 1892.

*

Prologue *A cavern under the earth* Accompanied by a relentless, almost Baroque walking-bass pattern set in a chromatically rich harmonic context that by this time had become one of Marschner's trademarks, a chorus of gnomes are mining gold and diamonds. Hans Heiling, their king, declares that he has fallen in love with Anna and will forsake his subterranean kingdom for life on earth with her. A poor country girl, Anna has been cajoled by her mother into consenting to an engagement with this rich stranger whom she respects but does not love. Because Heiling must give up his reign if he decides to live above ground, his mother and the other gnomes entreat him not to go, but in vain. Mother and son part; to accommodate a complex scene change, the overture, its recapitulation modified to serve as an entr'acte, is played next.

Act I.i *A room in a building above the underground realm* Heiling arises from beneath the earth, closing forever the entrance to the gnomes' realm. Met by Anna and Gertrude, he gives Anna a golden chain; adorning herself, she imagines how she will be the envy of her friends. She asks Heiling to accompany her to a festival but he, naturally serious and even bad-tempered, refuses. Anna gets over her disappointment, however, when she sees the pages in his magic book turning automatically. But the commotion begins to terrify her, and Heiling, angered that she has meddled with his belongings, pushes her away. She entreats him to destroy the frightening book, and finally he casts this last vestige of his power into the fireplace. Thunder is heard. Anna thanks him for destroying the fearful book but begins to grow distrustful of him. After what seems to have been a whirlwind courtship, Heiling and Anna are already beginning to react to traits in each other that they find distasteful. Only Heiling's grand tripartite aria 'An jenem Tag' (with an italianate middle section resembling a siciliana) interrupts the ensemble texture to allow him to express his undying love for Anna – a point to emphasize, since the balance of the opera is devoted to the destruction of their love.

I.ii *The village fairgrounds* Peasants celebrate the Feast of St Florian with a rousing march and chorus. Heiling has agreed to accompany Anna to the festival after all, provided she does not dance; but the young men of the village badger her until she consents, thereby breaking her word to Heiling. The youths are jealous of the taciturn older man who has won the hand of the fairest maid in the village. Conrad, who has loved Anna since childhood, chides Heiling mercilessly in his allegorical strophic song with laughing choral refrain, 'Ein sprödes, allerliebstes Kind'. Heiling leaves in despair. For this scene, designed to provide comic relief and develop intrigue, Marschner abandoned much of the extended ensemble writing of the earlier scenes in favour of a simpler style reminiscent of folk music. The opening march and chorus are essentially free of the chromatic harmony and rapid modulation of the earlier sections. The same may be said of Conrad's song, although here the device also serves a psychological purpose, because Conrad uses it to arouse Heiling's jealousy much as Caspar does to Max (*Der Freischütz*) and Iago to Otello. The development of intrigue, which requires a rapid, impassioned interchange of ideas, is carried out in spoken dialogue unencumbered by music.

Act 2.i *A forest* Anna has lost all affection for Heiling, whom she now fears; she loves only Conrad. In the aria 'Sonnst du verfallen', upon whose melody Wagner based his 'Todesverkündigung' ('Annunciation of death') leitmotif (*Die Walküre*), the Queen, who suddenly appears with her gnomes, reveals to Anna the origin of her betrothed and urges her to give him back to his heartbroken mother and her realm. When the gnomes have gone, Anna asks Conrad to help her against the possible revenge of the gnome king. He consents and takes her home.

2.ii *A hut in the forest* The sound effects of a storm outside are multiplied by means of the spoken voice over the orchestra in an ominous melodrama and song ('Ein geiziger, hartherziger Mann') in which Gertrude expresses fear that her daughter is lost; but Conrad brings her inside to safety. Heiling enters with jewels to adorn the bride, but Anna falls back from him in fear. As he leaves he lunges at his rival with a dagger, wounding him.

Act 3.i *A ravine in the mountains* Heiling realizes that he has sacrificed his supernatural powers for life on earth but has gained nothing. He decides to return to the land of the gnomes.

3.ii *A churchyard* To contrast with the heavy drama that has just transpired, Marschner returns to his diatonic folk style to provide a satisfactory conclusion. Having recovered from his wound, Conrad prepares to marry Anna, but Heiling reappears to take revenge on him. Conrad draws his sword, but it mysteriously shatters. Meanwhile, the Queen materializes, begs her son to forgive and forget, and leads him into the kingdom beneath the earth. The peasants breathe a sigh of relief, while Anna and Conrad sing of their love.

*

While his earlier *Der Vampyr* could be described as partly modelled on Weber's *Der Freischütz*, in the first scene here (Act 1.i) Marschner begins to pull away from that mould into one that is musico-dramatically more integrated – one that presages Wagner's *Der fliegende Holländer* – by casting practically everything in ensemble. The four individually numbered sections (an inheritance from Singspiel) have so many subsections whose music is only distantly related that they might best be termed 'ensemble complexes'. This kind of construction grew naturally out of the need imposed on Marschner by the librettist to reinforce the personality transformations he had given the characters of Anna and Heiling.

A.D.P.

Hérodiade ('Herodias')

Opéra in four acts by Jules Massenet to a libretto by Paul Milliet and Henri Grémont [Georges Hartmann] based on the story by Gustave Flaubert (1877); Brussels, Théâtre de la Monnaie, 19 December 1881 (revised version, Paris, Théâtre Italien, 1 February 1884).

The original production featured Blanche Deschamps-Jehin in the title role, with Edmond Vergnet as John the Baptist, Léon Gresse as Phanuel and Mlle Duvivier as Salome.

Salomé [Salome]	soprano
Hérodiade [Herodias]	mezzo-soprano
Jean [John the Baptist]	tenor
Hérode [Herod]	baritone
Phanuel *Chaldean astrologer*	bass
Vitellius *Roman Proconsul*	baritone
High Priest	baritone
Merchants, Romans, Priests, Levites, Pharisees,	
Sadducees, Galileans, Samaritans, Ethiopians,	
Nubians and others	
Setting Jerusalem, in the reign of Herod	
Antipas	

Following the success in France and Italy of *Le roi de Lahore*, Massenet's publisher Georges Hartmann suggested Flaubert's *conte* as the source of his next opera, and he was one of the writers credited with the libretto (Angelo Zanardini was responsible only for the Italian translation, the original plan being for simultaneous premières at the Paris Opéra and La Scala). The score was finished in the summer of 1881 but the new director at the Opéra, Auguste Vaucorbeil, found the plot incoherent and rejected it. The opera was not performed at the Palais Garnier until 1921. In his unreliable memoirs Massenet describes a chance meeting in the street with the director of the Théâtre de la Monnaie, Brussels, who begged for the privilege of presenting the première; more prosaic negotiations were doubtless put in hand by Hartmann. The Monnaie gave the piece a lavish staging, which earned the composer the Ordre de Léopold, and the work ran for 55 performances. The Italian première followed two months later at La Scala on 23 February 1882.

The most significant revival was that at the Théâtre Italien in Paris on 1 February 1884, which marked the start of Massenet's first period of success in Paris. The cast included Victor Maurel (who also directed) as Herod, Jean de Reszke as the Baptist and Edouard de Reszke as Phanuel, and Massenet took the opportunity to change the original three-act, five-scene format of the Brussels première into the four acts detailed below, to expand the role of Phanuel for the bass de Reszke brother (the first scene of Act 3 was added for him), and slightly to rearrange the running order of the remaining scenes. The dramaturgy is marginally tauter, but even the most fervent admirer of Massenet has to admit that Vaucorbeil had a point: dramatic coherence is not *Hérodiade*'s strongest suit. Nevertheless, it was staged frequently on both sides of the Atlantic up to the turn of the century (reaching London in 1904 under the title of *Salomé*) and has never quite lapsed from the repertory. One reason for this is that its five leading roles are rewarding to star singers (Emma Calvé sang both Salome and Herodias), and most recently it has been a vehicle for Montserrat Caballé and José Carreras.

*

Act I *A courtyard in Herod's palace* A caravan of merchants and their slaves greet Jerusalem and the end of their journey. The astrologer Phanuel quells a dispute between Judeans and Samaritans and up-braids the people for failing to make common cause against a greater enemy, the Romans. He prophesies imminent revolt ('Le monde est inquiet'). Salome enters – in this version of the story she is not part of the royal household. Phanuel knows her to be the daughter of Herodias, but she does not, and while searching for the mother who abandoned her as a child she has fallen under the spell of John the Baptist and his preaching ('Il est doux, il est bon'). They leave. Herod enters in search of Salome, for whom he has an illicit passion; he is swiftly followed by Herodias, who tells her husband of the Baptist's insults and insists that he avenge her honour by having him executed ('Ne me refuse pas'), reminding him that she abandoned her family and her child for him. He demurs for political reasons. The Baptist enters with cries of 'Jézabel', and they flee before his wrath. Salome returns and in a three-part duet with the Baptist expresses chaste love for him ('Ce que je veux') but is politely but firmly rejected. The Baptist,

mindful of his mission, encourages her to concentrate instead on the new dawn about to break ('Aime-moi donc alors, mais comme on aime en songe').

Act 2 *Herod's apartments* Herod sings of his obsession for Salome ('Vision fugitive'). Phanuel accuses him of neglecting political considerations in favour of private passion, but Herod remains confident of using the Baptist's popularity to help drive out the Romans and then in turn dealing with such religious agitators. The scene changes to a square in Jerusalem. Herod incites his subjects to revolutionary frenzy, but Roman cohorts are already at the gates of the city. Vitellius enters and quells the people with an angry glance. In Tiberius's name he grants the crowd's demands for religious freedom. A group of Canaanites led by Salome and the Baptist enters, proclaiming the superiority of spiritual power over temporal.

Act 3 *Phanuel's house* The Chaldean tries to fathom the significance of the Baptist – is he human or divine ('Dors, ô cité perverse ... Astres étincelants')? Herodias asks him the identity of the girl who has stolen her husband's love, and he prompts her to recall her abandoned daughter ('Si Dieu l'avait voulu') before telling her that rival and child are one. She refuses to believe him and storms out. The scene changes to the temple, in whose vaults the Baptist is now imprisoned. Salome recalls happier days ('Charmes des jours passés'). Herod enters stealthily, planning to release the Baptist as an act of defiance against Vitellius, but soon forgets the plan when he discovers Salome. His ardent advances are haughtily rejected, and Herod threatens to have them both put to death. The High Priest summons the people to prayer. The priests demand that Vitellius pronounce sentence of death on John, who has been hailed as the new Messiah, and after a brief trial death by crucifixion is confirmed (but in the event not carried out). When Salome offers to share the Baptist's fate, Herod's fury is redoubled.

Act 4 *An underground vault* John prepares for death ('Adieu donc, vains objets'). When Salome appears, he admits his love ('Que je puis respirer') but forbids her to join him in death. The scene changes to a room in the palace. Roman soldiers celebrate the subjugation of Judaea. Vitellius, Herod and Herodias enter, and after a suite of dances Salome begs for mercy for the Baptist. Herodias feels faint stirrings of maternal emotion when Salome sings of the mother who abandoned her. The executioner enters, his sword dripping with the Baptist's blood. Salome draws a dagger and hurls herself at Herodias but, when the latter exclaims 'Grâce, je suis ta mère', turns the blade upon herself.

*

Hérodiade is the best of Massenet's three attempts at traditional *grand opéra*: there is an energy, a masculine thrust that those who know only the later works might find surprising. The musical motifs attached to the various characters are fresh and apposite, and used for much more than purposes of reminiscence: they develop, and there are subtle interconnections between them – the Salome theme, for instance, and one of Herod's or, more properly, Salome-as-desired-by-Herod.

Hérodiade is also the first of his operas in which Massenet's word-setting reaches maturity. Regular phrases are broken up with purposeful mis-stresses and *enjambements* that add their own rhythmic counterpoint (see especially Salome's 'Il est doux' and Herod's 'Vision fugitive'). The instrumentation is heavily perfumed, with pseudo-orientalisms delicately sketched in; Tchaikovsky must have had the second-act ballet at the back of his mind when he wrote the 'Danse arabe' in *The Nutcracker*. (There is also a curious anticipation of Sardou and Puccini's *Tosca* when Phanuel comes across Herod lying in a drugged stupor and remarks 'Voilà l'homme qui fait trembler tout un empire'.)

Despite the well-oiled skill of the public scenes, the strength of the work lies in more familiar Massenet territory: erotic obsession. The musical portrait of Herod, his lustful slaverings vividly suggested by copious use of saxophone, is a powerful one, and that of the hag-ridden Herodias, gradually coming to accept that her husband's affections have been stolen by her daughter, is scarcely less compelling (a modern-dress staging of *Hérodiade* could be quite disturbing). Both are worthy of Flaubert, to whose fine story the depth of Oscar Wilde's debt (*see* Salome) can scarcely be overstressed. If the Baptist and Salome are more conventionally drawn, their duets are beautifully crafted and exude the 'discreet, semi-religious eroticism' for which the composer is famous.

One reason for the opera's dramaturgical incoherence – and an example of the eroticism verging on the indiscreet – is the 'heavy-breathing' identification of the Baptist with Christ. The Priests demand his death because he has proclaimed himself the Messiah; crucifixion is the first sentence passed on him; in his prison aria he addresses a *père* who is plainly Jehovah, not Zachariah. This lends the Baptist-Salome relationship a heady sex-and-religion charge that, even so heavily veiled, must have seemed shocking in 1881.   R.M.

Heure espagnole, L' ('The Spanish Hour')

Comédie musicale in one act by Maurice Ravel after the play by Franc-Nohain; Paris, Opéra-Comique (Salle Favart), 19 May 1911.

The cast at the première included Geneviève Vix as Concepcion, Jean Périer as Ramiro, Hector Dufranne as Don Inigo and Fernand Francell as Gonzalve.

Torquemada *a clockmaker*		tenor ('Trial'†)
Concepcion *Torquemada's wife*		soprano
Gonzalve *a bachelor*		tenor
Ramiro *a muleteer*		baritone ('Martin'‡)
Don Inigo Gomez *a banker*		bass
Setting The interior of Torquemada's shop in Toledo in the 18th century		

† A thin nasal tone like that of Antoine Trial (1737–95)
‡ Named after Jean-Blaise Martin (1768–1837), whose voice encompassed tenor and baritone ranges

Franc-Nohain's comedy *L'heure espagnole* had been a great success at the Odéon in Paris in 1904, and Ravel made only some small cuts and revisions in refashioning it as a libretto for the earlier of his two completed operas. The director of the Opéra-Comique, Albert Carré, had doubts as to whether his clientèle would accept the risqué story-line and on these grounds delayed acceptance for some time after Ravel finished the vocal score in October 1907. He agreed only at the insistence of Mme Jean Cruppi, the wife of a cabinet minister, and Ravel dedicated the work to her. Two days before the première he wrote: 'What I've tried to do is fairly ambitious: to breathe new life into the Italian *opera buffa*: following only the principle . . . the French language, like any other, has its own accents and inflections of pitch.' At the same time he referred to Musorgsky's *Zhenit'ba* ('The Marriage') as the work's only real ancestor.

The casting – Vix was a well-known Carmen, and Périer had been the original Pelléas nine years earlier – emphasized the parodic element in Ravel's score, as did the pairing in a double bill with Massenet's *Thérèse*. Press reaction was mixed. Pierre Lalo found that Ravel's air of detached superiority spoilt his enjoyment, while Reynaldo Hahn, referring to Ravel's technique as 'a sort of transcendent jujitsu', preferred those diatonic moments in the score which the composer had failed to hide beneath the Hispanic chromaticism. The opera reached Covent Garden in 1919, Chicago and New York in 1920, the Paris Opéra in 1921 (with Fanny Heldy) and La Scala in 1929 (with Conchita Supervia). Heldy's recording of 'Oh! la pitoyable aventure!' stands as an unrivalled example of clear diction and sexual verve.

*

During an orchestral introduction clock noises (taken, it appears, from Ravel's projected opera *Olympia*, where they accompany the entry of Coppelius) prepare the audience for the sight of Torquemada at his work-bench, his back to them. The simultaneous ticking of three clocks at different speeds, but coinciding every 15 seconds, acts as a symbol of the struggle between order and chaos which informs the opera at many levels.

Ramiro enters with a watch to be mended which once belonged to his uncle the toreador and saved him from the bull's horns. The explosion of Spanish colour as Ramiro tells his tale not only serves an obvious referential purpose but marks him out as a man of action. Concepcion enters and reminds Torquemada that it is Thursday, the day when he has to spend an hour ('l'heure espagnole', indeed) going round winding up the municipal clocks. He leaves, asking Ramiro to await his return and declaiming importantly 'l'heure officielle n'attend pas' ('official time does not wait') – a phrase which has gestural and psychological similarities with Golaud's 'Je suis le prince Golaud, le petit-fils d'Arkel le vieux roi d'Allemonde' in the first scene of *Pelléas et Mélisande*. Ramiro's continuing presence suits neither Concepcion, who likes to have this hour each week free in order to keep her male friendships in good repair, nor Ramiro, who knows he ought to indulge in light conversation but can't think of anything to say. However, Concepcion takes advantage of having a strong man around the place and asks him to carry a grandfather clock up to her bedroom. As he ascends the staircase with his load, the voice of the poet Gonzalve is heard off stage singing a roulade.

Gonzalve enters, and the roulade turns into a song of no literary merit whatever ('Enfin revient le jour si doux'), to which Ravel responds with equally tired Spanish clichés. This emphasizes the high level of Ravel's hispanicisms so far and, more importantly, informs the audience that Gonzalve is a dolt; though it goes against the composer's wishes to play the part for laughs. Concepcion urges Gonzalve to take advantage of the few moments the muleteer's absence allows them, but Gonzalve is intoxicated with his own poetic images, and before she can bring him down to earth Ramiro returns, his mission accomplished. Astonished by his despatch, Concepcion decides that, after all, she has asked him to move the wrong clock. Would he be kind enough to fetch it down again and take up another one instead? Ramiro is perfectly obliging. As he departs, Gonzalve 'with a disdainful look' says 'les muletiers n'ont pas de conversation' ('muleteers have no conversation'), unwittingly copying the admission Ramiro has already made to Concepcion. Ravel sets Gonzalve's version to almost the same music, not surprisingly, but the effect is very different since Gonzalve's part must be sung (Ravel says in a preface to the score) 'lyrically, with affectation', whereas Ramiro's, like the rest, must be sung in the manner of recitative in Italian *opera buffa*. Gonzalve's bitchy comment comes over as dry and inexpressive within the context of his overall vocal style, Ramiro's admission as lyrical

within the context of his. This is but one example out of many of Ravel's almost abstract game-playing in the opera.

Concepcion persuades Gonzalve to insert himself in the clock that Ramiro will shortly be carrying up to her bedroom. Gonzalve expatiates on the 'sensations neuves' the experience is likely to afford. Don Inigo enters, to a dotted rhythm similar to that of the pompous peacock in Ravel's song cycle *Histoires naturelles*. His oratory is well into its stride when Ramiro returns. Concepcion explains him away to Don Inigo as a removal man. Ramiro lifts the clock containing Gonzalve on to his shoulders and Concepcion goes up the stairs after him, ostensibly to see to its correct placing. Don Inigo decides that his only chance of being alone with Concepcion is to hide, in a clock; he squeezes himself in with difficulty, while the orchestra underlines the ridiculous nature of the exercise with a surrealistically non-chalant waltz (all the more effective because the bar lengths have been constantly changing until this point).

Ramiro descends alone and muses on the complex mechanisms of clocks and women. Concepcion rejoins him, distraught because, she says, the clock now in her room is not functioning properly. Ramiro goes to bring it down again. Don Inigo's cuckoo imitations do not amuse Concepcion, and she pleads with him to come out of his clock; but this is easier said than done. Ramiro returns, bearing both clock and Gonzalve, and soon it is Don Inigo who is on his way upstairs. Gonzalve has still not recovered from his attack of poetry and refuses to leave his clock. Concepcion walks off in a huff. Alone, Gonzalve sings of the delights of imprisonment.

Ramiro returns and sings of Concepcion's charms; if he were not a muleteer he would be a watchmaker. Concepcion enters, and she has only to say 'Monsieur!' for Ramiro to divine her command. With Gonzalve silently immured, Concepcion delivers a tirade against her two established lovers ('Oh! la pitoyable aventure!') as the awful prospect of fidelity for another week stretches before her. Ramiro descends with Don Inigo's clock and offers still further service as a clock remover, but this time Concepcion asks for his services 'sans horloge' and follows him up the stairs.

Don Inigo and Gonzalve are left on stage, each in his clock. Don Inigo is unable to extricate himself and retires inside. Gonzalve emerges easily enough and sings a lyrical farewell to his prison, but he too retires inside on seeing Torquemada returning. Torquemada capitalizes on Don Inigo's close interest in his clock by selling it to him and assures Gonzalve that he has just the clock for him too. Torquemada and Gonzalve try unsuccessfully to set Don Inigo free.

Ramiro and Concepcion descend from her room. After one further attempt, with Concepcion's assistance, Ramiro finally pulls Don Inigo free without apparent effort. Finally, the five characters step forward in a ceremonial gesture to address the audience. The moral is taken from Boccaccio: 'in the pursuit of love there comes a moment when the muleteer has his turn'.

*

The opera forms part of a larger group of Spanish works that spanned Ravel's whole career, and the necessary Spanish colouring provided him with a reason for a virtuoso use of the modern orchestra, which he felt was 'perfectly designed for underlining and exaggerating comic effects'. Brilliant though his orchestration is, there is some truth in the oft-repeated comment that the clocks are more human than the humans. In the theatre, it is often hard to disguise a calculating coldness at the heart of the opera or to resist the charge, so unjustly levelled at many of his other works, that here Ravel was indeed just a little too clever for his own good.   R.N.

Hippolyte et Aricie ('Hippolytus and Aricia')

Tragédie en musique in a prologue and five acts by Jean-Philippe Rameau to a libretto by Simon-Joseph Pellegrin after Jean Racine's *Phèdre*, Euripides' *Hippolytos* and Seneca's *Phaedra*; Paris, Opéra, 1 October 1733.

The cast included Marie-Anne de Cupis de Chassé de Chinais (Theseus) and Claude Antier (Phaedra), with Marie Dupré and Louis Camargo among the dancers.

Aricie [Aricia]	soprano
Hippolyte [Hippolytus] *Theseus's son by a previous marriage*	haute-contre
Phèdre [Phaedra] *Theseus's wife, Hippolytus's stepmother*	soprano
Thésée [Theseus] *King of Athens*	bass
Oenone *Phaedra's confidante*	soprano
Arcas *Theseus's confidant*	haute-contre
Diane [Diana]	soprano
L'Amour [Cupid]	soprano
Jupiter	baritone
Tisiphone *a Fury*	haute-contre
Pluton [Pluto] *King of the Underworld*	bass
Mercure [Mercury]	tenor
Neptune	bass
The High Priestess of Diana	soprano
Three Fates	haute-contre, tenor, bass
A Follower of Cupid	haute-contre
A Priestess	soprano
A Sailor Girl	soprano
A Huntress	soprano
A Shepherdess	soprano
Diana's nymphs, forest dwellers, Diana's priestesses, underworld gods, Troezenians, sailors, hunters and huntresses, shepherds and shepherdesses	

Setting The Spartan city of Troezen; Hades; the Forest of Aricia

Rameau's controversial first opera, which appeared when he was 50, had a troublesome early history. Some of the performers were unable or unwilling to master the work's difficulties. This, along with criticism of the dramatic structure, led to a series of cuts, which severely blunted the work's dramatic impact. The opera sparked off a dispute between Rameau's supporters and Lully's, and aroused professional jealousy from other composers and librettists. Though successfully revived in 1742 and 1757 and again posthumously, it never enjoyed the reputation of Rameau's other *tragédies*. Nowadays, though, it is rightly regarded as one of the peaks of his output.

The first modern staging of *Hippolyte* took place at Geneva on 28 March 1903. The previous year Charles Bordes had organized a concert performance at the Schola Cantorum, Paris, and was eventually to mount the first revival at the Paris Opéra (13 May 1908). Among later productions, that at Birmingham University in 1965 led to the earliest near-complete recording of the work (L'Oiseau-Lyre), a powerful and committed performance conducted by Sir Anthony Lewis with John Shirley-Quirk (Theseus) and Janet Baker (Phaedra) in the cast.

*

Prologue *The forest of Erymanthus* Jupiter persuades Diana to let her chaste forest dwellers serve Cupid on one day each year. Diana pledges to protect Hippolytus and Aricia.

Act I *The temple of Diana* Theseus has secured the Athenian throne, compelling the princess Aricia, the last of his enemy Pallas's line, to take vows of chastity. Aricia expresses her anguish in the monologue 'Temple sacré'. Before the ceremony begins, she and Hippolytus discover their mutual love. As the priestesses perform airs and dances in Diana's honour, Phaedra, who is secretly in love with Hippolytus, arrives to enforce Theseus's order. Outraged at Aricia's defiance and suspecting that Hippolytus loves the princess, Phaedra orders her guards to sack the temple. As the priestesses appeal to the gods thunder is heard, graphically represented by Vivaldian tremolandos and sharp dynamic contrasts. Diana descends; to Phaedra's chagrin, she reaffirms her protection of the lovers. Phaedra learns that Theseus has descended to Hades. Oenone suggests that, now that she is effectively a widow, Phaedra may declare her love to Hippolytus.

Act 2.i *The entrance to Hades* Theseus's comrade Peirithous has tried to abduct Pluto's wife, but has been caught. As Theseus attempts to rescue him, Tisiphone bars his way, his spiteful threats contrasting with Theseus's eloquent pleas. Their altercation includes a terse duet, 'Contente-toi d'une victime'.

2.ii *Pluto's court* Pluto declares that, as Peirithous's accomplice, Theseus must share his suffering. He commands a trial, whereupon he and his court call on the rivers of hell to avenge the outrage ('Que l'Averne, que le Ténare, le Cocyte, le Phlégéton'), their imprecations barked out over a turbulently undulating accompaniment. As the Furies dance, the underworld gods prepare vengeance. When Theseus pleads to be reunited with Peirithous, the Fates reveal that he must await his hour. Their stark, homophonic trio (the first Trio des Parques), 'Du Destin le vouloir suprême', is modelled on the Furies' Trio in Lully's *Isis*. Theseus, his mission clearly hopeless, appeals to Neptune: his prayer 'Puisque Pluton est inflexible', an arioso of Bach-like intensity with a figured accompaniment of rising arpeggios, reveals that Neptune had sworn to assist his son three times. Mercury descends and persuades Pluto that Neptune's oath must be upheld. Before Theseus leaves, however, the Fates warn that he will find hell in his own home. Their second trio, with its sweeping upward scales, aggressive dotted rhythms and sudden silences, is justly renowned for its bizarre enharmonic progressions, introduced by Rameau 'to inspire dread and horror'.

Act 3 *Theseus's palace near the sea* As she prepares to reveal her guilty love to her stepson, Phaedra prays to Venus that Hippolytus might yield to her passion ('Cruelle mère des amours', a monologue in which her conflicting emotions are conveyed by subtle changes of pace and harmonic intensity). When Hippolytus arrives, Phaedra pretends that her former anger was feigned. Taking his expressions of relief and his support for her son's claim to the throne as a sign of tenderness, Phaedra offers him 'throne, son and mother'. Unaware of what she is really offering, Hippolytus rejects the throne: he longs only for Aricia. In her fury, the queen tactlessly describes Aricia as her rival. Appalled, Hippolytus calls down divine retribution, at which point Phaedra realizes her love is hopeless and commands him to pierce her heart. When he refuses, she seizes his sword; he seizes it back. At that moment Theseus enters. Finding his son apparently threatening his wife's honour, the king recalls the Fates' prediction. He is made none the wiser by what follows: Hippolytus is too honourable to accuse his stepmother, Phaedra appears defiant, while Oenone insinuates that Hippolytus had indeed threatened the queen. Theseus is prevented from further questioning by the arrival of his subjects to thank

Neptune for his safe return. During their celebration – a colossal chorus ('Que ce rivage retentisse'), several dances and an air – the king must conceal his anguish. Eventually dismissing his subjects, he prays again to Neptune: for his outrage Hippolytus must die ('Puissant maître des flots', a tortured monologue as powerful as his earlier prayer). The sea boils: Neptune has heard Theseus's prayer.

Act 4 *Diana's grove by the sea* Bewailing his fate ('Ah! faut-il, en un jour'), Hippolytus realizes he cannot reveal the truth to his father. He asks Aricia to share his exile. Hunters and huntresses arrive to give thanks to Diana. Their celebration, characterized by hunting horns, is interrupted by a sea monster which carries off Hippolytus. Aricia, fainting, is led away. As the onlookers react to his apparent death ('O disgrace cruelle'), Phaedra reveals her guilt. Her confession, in which the claps of thunder and the quaking earth that reflect her feelings are vividly painted by the orchestra, leads up to a powerful invocation underpinned by sustained double-stopped strings.

Act 5.i *Diana's grove by the sea* Theseus has learnt the truth from Phaedra, who has committed suicide. He is about to throw himself into the sea when Neptune reveals that, through Diana's intervention, Hippolytus is alive. For too readily accepting his son's guilt, Theseus is condemned never to see him again. Grief-stricken, the king nevertheless accepts his punishment ('Je ne te verrai plus! O juste châtiment!', another Bach-like arioso, with drooping flute arpeggios and poignant suspensions).

5.ii *The forest of Aricia* Awakening to harmonious sounds, Aricia is nevertheless inconsolable. Shepherds and shepherdesses assemble as Diana descends; she announces the arrival of a king who will be Aricia's husband. Initially refusing to look at him, Aricia turns – to discover Hippolytus. The forest dwellers celebrate their reunion, while a shepherdess sings the coloratura *air du rossignol*.

*

In reworking the story of Phaedra's incestuous love, Pellegrin borrowed elements (including several lines) from both Racine's *Phèdre* and his classical models. His setting, however, alters the balance between the characters: it is not the eponymous lovers who dominate the drama but the tragic figures of Theseus and Phaedra. That of Theseus is the more powerful, gaining immensely from the decision to devote Act 2 to his selfless mission and subsequent trial. In Act 3 Pellegrin deliberately places the welcoming *divertissement* to prevent Theseus from learning the truth about what he has witnessed; the fact that the king must therefore suppress his anguish gives greater impact to his eventual outburst, the tragic consequences of which are felt in Act 4. (During the first run the *divertissement* was moved, against Rameau's wishes, to the more conventional but dramatically weaker position at the end of the act.) Theseus's attempted suicide and dignified acceptance of Neptune's punishment provide a fitting end to one of the most monumental characterizations in Baroque opera. The smaller role of Phaedra suffers from comparison with Racine's more subtle study in the psychology of jealousy. Nevertheless, the queen's revelation of her love is certainly worthy of Racine, while her expression of remorse at Hippolytus's apparent death is among the outstanding passages in 18th-century opera.   G.Sa.

Huguenots, Les ('The Huguenots')

Grand opera in five acts by Giacomo Meyerbeer to a libretto by Eugène Scribe and Emile Deschamps; Paris, Opéra, 29 February 1836.

The first Valentine was Cornélie Falcon; Adolphe Nourrit (Raoul), Nicolas Levasseur (Marcel), Julie Dorus-Gras (Marguerite), Jean-Etienne-Auguste Massol (Nevers) and the father and son Ferdinand and Alexis Prévost, both basses, also sang at the première.

Raoul de Nangis *a Huguenot gentleman*		tenor
Marcel *his servant*		bass
Marguerite de Valois *betrothed of*		
Henry of Navarre		soprano
Urbain *her page*		soprano
Valentine *daughter of the Count of*		
Saint-Bris		soprano
Count of Saint-Bris ⎱ *Catholic*		bass
Count of Nevers ⎰ *noblemen*		baritone
De Retz ⎫		bass
Cossé ⎪		tenor
Méru ⎬ *Catholic gentlemen*		bass
Thoré ⎪		bass
Tavannes ⎭		tenor
Bois-Rosé *a Huguenot soldier*		tenor
Protestant and Catholic soldiers, courtiers, and		
burghers		
Setting Touraine, then Paris, August 1572		

Meyerbeer's first French opera project, *Robert le diable* (1831), had scored a great success. On hearing Falcon sing the part of Alice in it during summer 1832, Meyerbeer resolved that she would take a leading role in his next opera. The groundwork for *Léonore, ou La Saint Barthélemy*, as *Les Huguenots* was initially called, was laid in discussions with Scribe and the Opéra director Louis Véron in September 1832. The subject matter was very much in fashion: the period of confrontation between Huguenots (French Protestants) and Catholics in the late 16th century had been

the setting for several plays in the late 1820s, as well as Prosper Mérimée's novel, *Chronique du règne de Charles IX* (1829). Contrary to what has been sometimes suggested, there is little evidence that Scribe modelled *Les Huguenots* upon Mérimée's book. Both novel and libretto do, however, feature prominently a real historical event, the St Bartholomew massacre of over 3000 French Protestants in Paris on the night of 23 August 1572.

Meyerbeer signed a contract, which had a penalty clause for late delivery, with Véron on 23 October 1832 and began composing immediately. For family reasons, including the death of his brother and the illness of his wife, he failed to meet the deadline, and a dispute broke out between him and Véron. Meyerbeer had, however, drafted much of the work before he decided upon major revisions during a trip to Italy in summer 1834: an expansion of the role of the servant Marcel (which he came to consider his most successful characterization up to that time) and the creation of more numbers with female voices. To address the latter problem – and possibly influenced by the leading role of the soprano in the 'Guerra! guerra!' chorus of Bellini's *Norma* – Meyerbeer added the figure of Queen Catherine de Medicis to the Act 4 'Bénédiction des poignards'. He called upon Gaetano Rossi, a previous collaborator, to provide Italian verse so that he could begin at once to compose new music. Because Scribe had little time in autumn 1834 and was reluctant to act as a mere adapter of another's work, Meyerbeer turned to the poet Emile Deschamps, who made substantial contributions to the libretto.

The quarrel with Véron was patched up, and rehearsals at the Opéra began in June 1835. Among the most noteworthy alterations made at this point was a recasting of the slow section of the duet between Valentine and Raoul in Act 4 at the insistence of Nourrit, who was offended by the directness of the language between the adulterous couple. Also significant was an order from the government censor forbidding the appearance of Catherine de Medicis, doubtless to avoid any association of royal authority with intolerance in an era when a middle-of-the-road monarchy was consciously trying to project the opposite image; her music was taken by Saint-Bris. *Les Huguenots* proved an even greater triumph than *Robert le diable* and was the first work to be performed more than a thousand times at the Opéra. The unflattering portrait of Catholic fanaticism caused the libretto to be rewritten in certain towns during its rapid conquest of Germany: in Munich it was first performed as *Anglikaner und Puritaner* and in Kassel as *Die Ghibellinen vor Pisa*.

*

Act I *A hall in the chateau of the Count of Nevers* After a brief overture, based on the chorale 'Ein feste Burg',

Nevers launches a buoyant mood-setting chorus about the pleasures of youth and tells his Catholic comrades that, in the spirit of a recent peace treaty between the Protestant faction and the royal house, he has invited a Huguenot nobleman, Raoul de Nangis, to join their revelry. Raoul's entry is highlighted by a change of musical character and tonality in an extended solo that lies high in the tenor voice, a heartfelt expression of gratitude in a predominantly comic context. The multi-sectional introduction is brought to a close by a drinking chorus ('Bonheur de la table') with a frenzied coda containing a twofold increase in tempo and rapid patter singing. When prodded to reveal past amorous exploits, Raoul responds that he has fallen in love with an unknown woman whom he recently rescued; he describes her beauty in a strophic *romance*, 'Plus blanche que la blanche hermine', the intimacy of which is underlined by a solo viola accompaniment in the changing part of each strophe.

The Catholic gentlemen make light of Raoul's love and of Marcel, his serious and abstemious manservant, who appears soon after to a strain in the bassoons and double basses. Marcel, horrified to see Raoul with Catholics, appeals to his conscience with the chorale 'Ein' feste Burg'. At the request of the bemused company, Marcel sings an old Huguenot song, 'Piff, paff', with a grotesque accompaniment that highlights piccolo, bassoon, cymbal and drums. His macabre account of Catholic misfortune during the battle of La Rochelle evokes nothing more than laughter. A valet enters with news that a beautiful woman has arrived to speak with Nevers. The men fall over themselves with offers to go in his place and then peer through a window to watch the *tête-à-tête* ('L'aventure est singulière'). The comic atmosphere is momentarily dissipated by an orchestral explosion and sudden tonal shift when Raoul himself follows suit: he identifies the woman as the one he rescued but, now convinced that she is one of Nevers' conquests, declares he is no longer enamoured of her. In a monologue Nevers, unheard by Raoul, reveals that the mysterious woman is his betrothed, a lady-in-waiting to the Catholic Queen Marguerite de Valois. She has come to inform him that, by order of the queen, their marriage cannot take place. The queen's page, Urbain, enters with a note requesting Raoul's presence at a secret rendezvous. Nevers and his companions identify the seal as Queen Marguerite's and, in a comical canon, affectedly congratulate him. (A certain poetic licence here allows Marguerite as the queen; she was in fact

'Les Huguenots' (Meyerbeer), Act 2 (the gardens of the chateau of Chenonceaux): design by Edouard Despléchin for the original production at the Paris Opéra, 29 February 1836; lithograph by C. Deshayes

Charles IX's sister and became queen only on her marriage to Henry of Navarre. She is known to history as La Reine Margot.) In a concluding chorus Raoul expresses his bewilderment with a halting melodic line, Marcel delivers a prayer in long notes and the Catholic gentlemen remark upon Raoul's good fortune.

Act 2 *The gardens of the chateau of Chenonceaux* Queen Marguerite sings a multi-sectional entrance aria about her desire to see the heart take precedence over political disputes ('O beau pays de la Touraine'). She then informs Valentine, her lady-in-waiting, that she has asked her to break off her engagement with Nevers in order to marry Raoul and thereby cement the still fragile truce between the factions. Before he arrives the ladies of the court take a swim in the river, while the page Urbain secretly looks on with delight. The *choeur dansé*, 'Jeunes beautés sous ce feuillage', has obvious erotic appeal and, together with the women's chorus sung as the blindfolded Raoul is led into the garden, serves as a counterweight to the male choruses in the first act. When the blindfold is lifted Raoul expresses wonder at his surroundings and the beauty of the queen in the duet 'Beauté divine, enchanteresse'. The stiffness of their encounter, suggested by two parallel strophes sung in succession, gives way to a scherzo-like section where the two voices combine; this is followed by a *cabalette* in which Raoul delivers an impassioned strain, and Marguerite laughingly warns him not to fall in love with her.

In a recitative, she informs him that his hand will be given in marriage to the daughter of the Catholic Count of Saint-Bris as a gesture of reconciliation between the religious groups. Catholic and Protestant notables have been invited to witness the ceremony and both groups appear in her gardens. They swear eternal peace to a dramatic alternation of *a cappella* singing and full orchestral accompaniment, the slow section of a multi-sectional finale. But when Valentine appears with her father, Raoul recognizes her as the woman who visited Nevers and refuses to conclude the pact. The *strette* of the *final* begins quietly in unison, as the entire assembly gives voice to its astonishment, and concludes with boisterous expressions of renewed hatred between the two religious factions.

Act 3 *The Pré-aux-clercs on the bank of the Seine* After an introductory chorus of Parisian pleasure-seekers, the Huguenot soldier Bois-Rosé leads his comrades in a *rataplan*. The wedding procession of Valentine and Nevers, accompanied by a choral litany, is seen making its way to the chapel. *Rataplan* and litany are combined and superimposed upon a chorus of the Catholic populace who demand that the Huguenots show respect for their ritual. Huguenots and Catholics adopt a menacing posture

towards each other, but tension is unexpectedly relieved by the appearance of a colourful band of singing and dancing gypsies.

Marcel intercepts Saint-Bris as he leaves the chapel and presents him with a challenge for a duel from Raoul. The signal for the nightly curfew is given, a passage coloured evocatively by chimes, horn octaves and woodwind chords. As night descends, Valentine and Marcel appear, unaware of each other's presence at first (duet, 'Dans la nuit où seul je veille'). The situation is treated comically at the outset, with popping octave leaps in bassoons and horns and Marcel's exaggerated (and therefore suspect) claim that he does not fear women. Valentine reveals to him the Catholics' plan to ambush Raoul before the duel; during the slow section of the duet she sings of her will to save Raoul's life and Marcel gives voice to his agitation with rapid declamation beneath her lyrical line. In the *cabalette* she expresses her distress at having betrayed her father and, with a shift to the major mode, Marcel attempts to comfort her.

Raoul and Saint-Bris appear with their witnesses and prepare for the duel during a septet propelled by a motor rhythm in dotted figures suggestive of the determination of each party ('En mon bon droit j'ai confiance'). Raoul's life is saved because, just as Saint-Bris's henchmen arrive, a band of Huguenot soldiers is unexpectedly heard in the distance singing the *rataplan*; knowing that an ambush is imminent, Marcel calls out to them. Bloodshed between the two groups is prevented by the equally unexpected arrival of Queen Marguerite. From her Raoul discovers the real purpose of Valentine's earlier visit to Nevers. As a nuptial march sounds in the distance, Saint-Bris tells Raoul with great satisfaction that a wedding between Nevers and his daughter has already taken place. Nevers arrives in a sumptuously decorated and illuminated boat to escort Valentine; Catholic students and Protestant soldiers exchange insults.

Act 4 *Outside Valentine's bedroom in Nevers' residence* Valentine sings a *romance*, 'Parmi les pleurs', about her continuing love for Raoul. Suddenly he appears, prepared to give up his life by trespassing in a rival Catholic household. When others are heard approaching she begs him to hide.

Saint-Bris, Nevers and a group of Catholic gentlemen enter and discuss plans to massacre the Protestant population of Paris. This scene of the Consecration of the Swords is in two large sections. The first, in E major, ends when Nevers, after refusing to participate in the massacre, is led off. At its core lie two renditions of the ensemble 'Pour cette cause sainte', separated by Nevers' symbolic act of breaking his sword. The principal dramatic action of the second section, centred on G♯ minor/A♭ major, is the appearance of three monks bearing white scarves as identification tags for Catholics, and the oath-taking itself, led by Saint-Bris and the monks. This last action stands out through repeated alternation of chords. The end of the second section, in the fastest tempo of the number, comes as the entire assembly advances to the front of the stage brandishing swords ('Dieu le veut, Dieu l'ordonne'). This ensemble opens into a reprise – in unison and even more fully scored than before – of 'Pour cette cause sainte', a spectacular conclusion to the number.

When the conspirators depart, Raoul emerges and runs to warn the Protestants. But Valentine stops him in his tracks and in the duet 'O ciel! où courez-vous?' she begs him not to leave; for the first time she declares her love directly to him. This gives rise to the slow section of the duet, Raoul's impassioned *cavatine*, 'Tu l'as dit'. He is awakened from his amorous reverie by the sound of bells, the signal for the start of the massacre, and, mirroring the plunge to reality, the music abruptly turns from G♭ to C major. In the *cabalette* he declares his intention to join his co-religionists, and though he vacillates once again following that section, he finally dashes off.

Act 5.i *A ballroom in the Hotel de Nesle* Protestants have gathered to celebrate the marriage of Marguerite to Henry of Navarre. Raoul bursts in bearing news of the massacre and urges the Protestants to take up arms in defence of their brethren.

5.ii *A Protestant cemetery, with a church in the background* The wounded are taken into the church. Raoul meets Marcel and both are soon joined by Valentine, who tells them that Nevers is dead. She urges Raoul to save himself by donning a white scarf. When he refuses she declares, in a passage of true heroic stature ('Ainsi je te verrai périr?'), that she will adopt his faith – an example of the dramatic cogency Meyerbeer was capable of at his best moments: recitative merges seamlessly into declamatory measured writing as the melodic line rises gradually to a♭'', is transformed, *pianissimo*, and in a final burst of energy rises to c''' and descends two octaves within the space of a single bar. Marcel performs an impromptu marriage ceremony to the sparing and mournful accompaniment of a single bass clarinet.

As Catholic murderers enter the church, Marcel is seized with a vision of heaven; Valentine and Raoul are themselves transported by Marcel's ecstatic music and the passage culminates in a unison rendition by all three of 'Ein feste Burg'.

5.iii *A street* Valentine and Marcel support Raoul, who is mortally wounded. Saint-Bris appears and orders his soldiers to execute the three immediately. Only after the shots have been fired does he realize that he has ordered the execution of his own daughter. Finally, Queen Marguerite arrives to put a stop to the massacre.

*

In *Les Huguenots* Meyerbeer successfully grafted the formula of a highly variegated succession of scenes connected by a well-integrated plot on to a historical setting that prominently features public turmoil. In the first three acts some of the most effective scenes blend comedy into the mix, for example the Valentine–Marcel duet in Act 3: first the two grope in the dark and then Marcel very quickly moves from comic gynophobia to staunch loyalty and paternal solicitude. Neither Valentine nor Raoul is as richly drawn in the music. As often with Meyerbeer, the most remarkable sequence in the opera, the fourth-act Consecration of the Swords and the ensuing duet for the lovers, does not depend on effective characterization: in a bold stroke he reversed the usual progression towards the massed finale by placing the large choral set piece at the middle of the act. This produces a tinder-box setting for the duet, in which the love music is projected as an escapist reverie in a distant key; and Raoul's subsequent hesitations, though they have never earned him many admirers, create the sparks that kept generations of opera-goers enthralled. Even Meyerbeer's detractors (such as Wagner, later in his career) grudgingly admired this act. In its juxtaposition of reverential Protestant victims and fanatical Catholics – both invoking the name of the Lord – the fifth act is a classic example of the vivid ironical contrasts characteristic of Meyerbeerian grand opera.

S.Hr.

I

Idomeneo, re di Creta
('Idomeneus, King of Crete')

Dramma per musica in three acts, κ366, by Wolfgang Amadeus Mozart to a libretto by Giovanni Battista Varesco after Antoine Danchet's *Idoménée*; Munich, Residenztheater, 29 January 1781.

The original cast included Anton Raaff (Idomeneus), Dorothea Wendling (Ilia), Elisabeth Wendling (Electra), Vincenzo dal Prato (Idamantes) and Domenico de Panzacchi (Arbaces).

Idomeneo [Idomeneus] *King of Crete*	tenor
Idamante [Idamantes] *his son*	soprano castrato
Ilia *Trojan princess, daughter of Priam*	soprano
Elettra [Electra] *princess, daughter of*	
Agamemnon	soprano
Arbace [Arbaces] *confidant of the king*	tenor
High Priest of Neptune	tenor
Oracle	bass
Trojan prisoners; sailors; people of Crete	
Setting Mycenaean Crete: the Royal palace at Kydonia (Sidon), by the sea, and the temple of Neptune	

Mozart received the commission from the Munich Intendant, Count Seeau, during the summer of 1780. Danchet's five-act libretto of 1712 was adapted by the Salzburg cleric Varesco in three acts, on the pattern of the 'reformed' operas of Jommelli and Gluck, balancing the introduction of Italian arias by retaining a strong choral element, ballet, a high proportion of orchestrated recitative, scenic effects, and some ensemble writing. The influence of Gluck's *Alceste* is felt in hieratic scenes, particularly the speech for the High Priest and the utterance of the oracle, but also in the prevailing seriousness. Mozart had witnessed the synthesis of French forms and Italian music in Piccinni's *Roland*, the effect of which, and perhaps of Jommelli, was to encourage what Gluck tended to repress: highly developed aria forms with the bloom of italianate lyricism.

Raaff may have been instrumental in obtaining the commission for Mozart, and other singers, as well as the orchestra, were known to Mozart from Mannheim. He was therefore able to start work before leaving Salzburg on 5 November. His completion of the work in Munich is documented in letters home; his father, besides supplying trumpet mutes, had to act as intermediary between composer and librettist. Mozart is constantly concerned with theatrical effect and timing. The libretto required severe pruning: the oracle must have fewer words; the recitatives were too long; there were too many arias (at the last minute, two were dropped from the third act).

Mozart also reported the singers' reactions, and the elector's approval of the music in rehearsal. The first performance, attended by Leopold Mozart, was well received. The designs were by Lorenzo Quaglio and the ballet-master was Le Grand, who in the absence of the librettist may have acted as director. Raaff, by then 66, was tactfully nursed by the composer; Idomeneus's music contrives to be brilliant and expressive without placing exceptional demands on breath-control. The Wendling sisters-in-law were capable and experienced; Elisabeth, the younger, must have been a formidable singer to have inspired Electra's music. Unfortunately the Idamantes was relatively inexperienced – Mozart had to teach him his part 'as if he were a child'; and the Arbaces insisted on the unnecessary development (with two arias) of his role.

There were three performances in 1781. In September of that year Mozart wrote to his father from Vienna that he would like to revise *Idomeneo* 'more in the French style', but with a German text (by J. B. von Alxinger, who had translated Gluck's *Iphigénie en Tauride*). Idomeneus must be a bass (Ludwig Fischer). Various numbers were included in concerts in his first year in Vienna, as if sowing seeds for a new production; but the only other performance in Mozart's lifetime, at Prince Auersperg's palace in Vienna, was given by amateurs. The chief alteration actually made was to recast Idamantes as a tenor. Mozart added two new numbers, rewrote the ensembles involving Idamantes, produced a simplified version of Idomeneus's showpiece ('Fuor del mar'), and made further cuts including Arbaces' arias and a good deal of recitative: so much, indeed, that at times intelligibility was endangered.

Idomeneo was not performed again until the 19th century, when various translations appeared in the repertory of German companies. The first of these was in Kassel (1802), followed by Vienna and Berlin (1806). The music was occasionally employed in 19th-century *pasticcios*, but there were few recognizable performances outside Austria and Germany until the 20th century, the first in Paris (in concert form) being in 1902, in Britain (Glasgow) 1934, in Italy and the USA 1947. The 150th anniversary (1931) was mostly recognized by productions in German, still more or less 'arranged', notably Richard Strauss's version for Vienna (published in vocal score). In the last 30 years most major companies have produced *Idomeneo*, but as an opera in need of perpetual revival rather than a repertory item.

*

The Trojan war is over; the legendary misfortunes of the returning Greek chieftain Idomeneus closely parallel the biblical story of Jephtha. Ilia and other Trojan captives have been sent to Crete ahead of him. Electra is there, following the murder of Agamemnon by her mother. Both have fallen in love with Idamantes.

The overture, in D major, is a boldly truncated sonata movement expressing majesty and suffering. It ends with a diminuendo making repeated use of a significant motif first heard in the ninth bar, which occurs throughout the opera and has been identified as a 'Sacrifice' or 'Idamantes' motif. The cadence prefigures the tonality of the first aria and allows Ilia to sing without further introduction.

Act I *Ilia's apartment in the palace* Ilia bewails her fate: orphaned, a prisoner, in love with her captor's son and certain that he must prefer his compatriot Electra to a foreign slave. She explores her dilemma in a subdued lament in G minor, its moderate tempo as characteristic of her as an Allegro is of Electra (recitative and aria, 'Padre, germani, addio!'). When Ilia considers her own disloyalty to her father, Priam, in loving a Greek, Mozart introduces the 'Idamantes motif' in the cellos.

Idamantes enters with words of comfort and even affection, but she proudly rejects him. In a short, majestic Adagio Idamantes protests that he has committed no fault, and in a driving Allegro he blames the gods for his suffering ('Non ho colpa'). As evidence of his kindly intentions, he frees the Trojan prisoners (chorus, 'Godiam la pace'). Electra protests at this action and is suspicious of his motives. Arbaces brings news of Idomeneus's shipwreck and Idamantes rushes off. In obbligato recitative, Electra gives vent to her jealousy: with Idomeneus dead, who will prevent his son marrying Ilia? Her D minor aria ('Tutte nel cor vi sento') writhes between fury and self-pity. The daring reprise in C minor not only symbolizes her mental disturbance but anticipates the storm of the next scene: although decorum is restored in that the aria ends in D, the music continues without interruption or change of speed.

The sea-shore, strewn with wreckage A distant chorus of sailors echoes the chorus on shore ('Pietà! Numi, pietà'). In pantomime Neptune is seen calming the waters; the king lands and dismisses his followers. He can think only of the impending sacrifice, for the price of his survival is that Neptune must be offered the first person he meets; he imagines himself haunted by the innocent victim ('Vedrommi intorno'). The 'Idamantes motif' reappears in the Andantino, as do images of the storm in the Allegro. The victim appears: it is Idamantes searching for his father. At the latter's ecstatic recognition simple recitative explodes into orchestral figures. But Idomeneus breaks away in horror as realization dawns, leaving Idamantes a prey to fear and longing; the atmosphere of the storm again affects Idamantes' aria ('Il padre adorato'). The Cretan soldiers land and the populace comes to greet them (ballet sequence with choral chaconne, 'Nettuno s'onori').

Act 2 *A royal apartment* [1786 only: orchestrated dialogue and aria. Ilia yields Idamantes to Electra but asks to be remembered: he sings 'Ch'io mi scordi di te?', and rondò, 'Non temer, amato bene', with obbligato violin.]

Idomeneus tells Arbaces everything; he resolves that Idamantes must escape sacrifice by taking Electra back to Argos. Arbaces responds sententiously, in an energetic Allegro ('Se il tuo duol', omitted in 1786). Ilia approaches the king. In Mozart's most tenderly poised melodic vein, she accepts Idomeneus as a second father ('Se il padre perdei'). He now sees that the sacrifice will ruin two lives beyond that of the victim; his recitative underlines his concern by its orchestral use of motifs from her aria. His own aria ('Fuor del mar'), majestic in D major (the opera's home key), exists in a simplified (1786) version as well as the more flamboyant original destined for Raaff. Freed from the sea, he finds a worse storm in his own heart. In the middle section he asks why a heart so near to shipwreck cannot find it; Mozart risked a heart-stopping enharmonic modulation before the full reprise. Electra is transformed by the thought of Idamantes escorting her home; her aria is a serene invocation of love ('Idol mio, se ritroso'), accompanied by strings only, and utterly unlike the remainder of her role. A distant march, beginning with muted brass, grows to *fortissimo* to mark the change of scene.

The port of Kydonia Electra and the chorus welcome the propitious calm ('Placido è il mar, andiamo'). Idomeneus bids farewell to his sorely perplexed son (trio, 'Pria di partir, o Dio!'). As they are about to embark, a tempest breaks out (represented in music of barely repressed violence) and a terrible sea-monster appears (storm, with chorus,

'Qual nuovo terrore'): the people demand who has brought this upon them by angering the gods. Without naming Idamantes, Idomeneus publicly confesses (obbligato recitative) that he is the sinner; he has the temerity to accuse the gods of injustice. Terrified at the revelation, the crowd flees in confusion ('Corriamo, fuggiamo').

Act 3 The palace garden In a tender E major aria, Ilia bids the winds bear her message of love to Idamantes ('Zeffiretti lusinghieri'). When he appears she is unable to suppress her feelings, and they declare themselves (duet, 'S'io non moro' – probably omitted at the première; replaced in 1786 by a shorter duet with some of the same material, 'Spiegarti non poss'io'). Idomeneus and Electra find the lovers. The varied emotions of all four are embodied in the harrowingly beautiful harmonic and contrapuntal web of one of Mozart's supreme achievements, the quartet ('Andrò, ramingo e solo'). Ilia's heart is still divided; Electra is full of suppressed jealousy; Idamantes, again banished without learning the reason, is deeply saddened, and Idomeneus wishes the gods would kill him instead. Each has reached the limit of suffering; their voices unite at 'soffrir più non si può'. Idamantes repeats his opening phrase, an emblem of loneliness and misery, and leaves the stage. Arbaces begs the king to help his suffering people and laments the condition of his country in a magnificent obbligato recitative ('Sventurata Sidon!'), usually retained when the role is reduced. His aria ('Se colà ne' fati è scritto', omitted in 1786) is more conventional, a broadly conceived piece accompanied by strings.

A large public place before the palace The high priest confronts the king (recitative, 'Volgi intorno la sguardo, o Sire'): the monster has devoured thousands and laid the country to waste. Only Idomeneus can save them by naming the sacrificial victim. To the longest development of the 'Idamantes motif' he confesses the truth; the Cretans are awed and deeply moved ('O voto tremendo'). The collision of triplet violin quavers with the duple rhythms of the voices, the ominous fanfares of muted brass, and a melancholy chromatic fragment, form a picture of desolation without equal in 18th-century music.

The temple of Neptune, both exterior and interior being visible The king and priests process to the temple (march) and prepare the sacrifice (chorus of priests with Idomeneus, 'Accogli, o re del mar'). A jubilant cry is heard (fanfare); Idamantes has slain the monster. Idomeneus fears worse will befall them, but Idamantes enters robed for sacrifice. Interrupted only by the first of the arias Mozart planned to omit before the 1781 performances, but may ultimately have included (Idamantes's 'Nò, la morte io non pavento': he has no fear of death but dies willingly), these scenes unfold in orchestrated recitative of

unprecedented length and expressiveness. At the moment of sacrifice Ilia enters and offers herself instead; the confusion is ended only when the oracle commands the abdication of Idomeneus in favour of his son, who is to marry Ilia. Electra invokes the Furies (her stupendous rage aria, 'D'Oreste, d'Ajace', was replaced in 1781 by a recitative powerful even by the standards of *Idomeneo*). Idomeneus welcomes his retirement (recitative, 'Popoli! a voi l'ultima legge'). His exquisitely beautiful aria ('Torna la pace al core') was also cut in 1781, but its serene glow perfectly concludes the action. The brisk final chorus ('Scenda Amor, scenda Imeneo') is followed by an extended ballet.

*

Idomeneo is divided from its French model by the spread of Enlightenment. Danchet's libretto includes another love tangle (Idomeneus loves Ilia), and involves Electra closely in the plot (jealous of Ilia, she reveals to the priests Idomeneus's scheme to save Idamantes). It also ends tragically, with Idamantes dead and Idomeneus driven mad by Nemesis. Varesco, undoubtedly influenced by Metastasio, made myth into *opera seria*, an allegory of enlightened monarchy; flawed by his vow, rather than his failure to fulfil it, Idomeneus is unfitted to reign, but the god permits the organic transfer of power to the new generation and the reconciliation of former enmities by dynastic marriage. This restoration of harmony is movingly captured in Idomeneus's final aria, so that Mozart's omission of 'Torna la pace' is particularly regrettable. This theme also reflects the father-son relationship which is considered to have been the source of much creative tension in Mozart.

The letters to his father, and the cuts on which he insisted, demonstrate Mozart's growing theatrical judgment as well as the powers of persuasion he exercised upon the singers. Most remarkable is his willingness at the last moment, following the dress rehearsal, to sacrifice superlative music for a theatrical end. In view of his intended and actual reworkings, it seems safe to say that *Idomeneo* never reached a form with which he would have been completely satisfied. Unfortunately some performances with tenor Idamantes ignore not only the 1786 aria and duet in Act 2 but also Mozart's careful revision of the great Act 3 quartet, whose texture is ruined if the original line is simply placed an octave too low.

Even within the repertory of 'reform' opera (Italian, French and German), *Idomeneo* is remarkable for its orchestration. Mozart used clarinets here for the first time in an opera, and four horns, but the music for flutes, oboes, bassoons and trumpets is equally striking, as are the brass mutes in the Act 2 march and the scene where the Cretans learn that the sacrificial victim must be Idamantes. The varied but almost continual use of all the wind instruments creates an unprecedentedly rich palette, although trombones are confined to the oracle's speech (and may have been omitted: Mozart made four different settings of it). Most remarkable is the deployment of wind instruments during critical passages of recitative, notably those preceding the two final arias. The strings are treated with equal resourcefulness; for instance the tremolando in the High Priest's recitative, the hammering in 'O voto tremendo', responding to the muted trumpet calls, and the harplike pizzicato in the invocation of Neptune at the beginning of the last scene.

Instrumental inventiveness is matched by harmonic daring; even the simple recitatives make expressive use of enharmonic progressions and remote tonalities. *Idomeneo* is also notable for its continuity, again beyond what was normal in 'reform' operas. Several numbers have no final cadence but move into the next recitative as if to avoid leaving time for applause; Mozart added such an ending to the simpler version of 'Fuor del mar'.

Idomeneo is also the first Mozart opera in which the arrangement of tonalities seems deliberately calculated. Recognition of certain recurring keys is not only assisted by instrumentation but by the use of distinct motifs; the use of these is more highly developed than in any previous opera. Although it is unlikely that every instance was intentional, Mozart cannot have overlooked the 'Idamantes motif': from the overture to the sacrifice scene its most clearly identifiable recurrences all relate to the young hero. Nevertheless, most of the opera consists of discrete numbers which reflect Mozart's determination that music should govern the poetry. With this end in view, he did not reject virtuosity, but turned its musical qualities to dramatic ends. Despite detectable influences within it, and from it (for instance in *Don Giovanni* and *La clemenza di Tito*), *Idomeneo* stands on its own, occupying a special place in the affections of its composer who went on to other achievements as vital and significant, but never returned to its dignified, heroic, yet thoroughly human world.   J.Ru.

Incoronazione di Poppea, L' [*Coronatione di Poppea, La*] ('The Coronation of Poppaea')

Dramma musicale in a prologue and three acts by Claudio Monteverdi and others to a libretto by Giovanni Francesco Busenello primarily based on Tacitus's *Annals* (books 13–16) but also Suetonius, *The Twelve Caesars* (book 6); Dio Cassius, *Roman History* (books 61–2); and pseudo-Seneca, *Octavia*; Venice, Teatro SS Giovanni e Paolo, 1643.

Prologue

La Fortuna [Fortune]	soprano
La Virtù [Virtue]	soprano
Amore [Cupid]	soprano

Opera

Ottone [Otho] *most noble lord*	mezzo-soprano
Poppea [Poppaea] *most noble lady, mistress of Nero, raised by him to the seat of empire*	soprano
Nerone [Nero] *Roman emperor*	soprano
Ottavia [Octavia] *reigning empress, repudiated by Nero*	soprano
Drusilla *lady of the court, in love with Otho*	soprano
Seneca *philosopher, preceptor to Nero*	bass
Arnalta *aged nurse and confidante of Poppaea*	alto
Nutrice *nurse of the empress Octavia*	alto
Lucano [Lucan] *poet, intimate of Nero, nephew of Seneca*	tenor
Valletto *page of the empress*	soprano
Damigella *lady-in-waiting to the empress*	soprano
Liberto *Captain of the praetorian guard*	tenor
Two Praetorian Soldiers	tenors
Lictor *officer of imperial justice*	bass
Pallade [Pallas Athene] *goddess of wisdom*	soprano
Mercurio [Mercury] *the gods' messenger*	bass
Venere [Venus]	soprano
Friends of Seneca, consuls, tribunes, Graces, Cupids	

Setting Rome, AD 65

This was Monteverdi's last opera, probably his last work altogether. Although the identity of only one of the original singers, Anna Renzi, in the role of Ottavia, is known for certain, several others can be tentatively identified from the cast of the opera with which *L'incoronazione di Poppea* shared the stage of the Teatro SS Giovanni e Paolo during the 1642–3 season, *La finta savia*, with music by several different composers on a libretto by Giulio Strozzi. These include the soprano Anna di Valerio (possibly as Poppaea), and the castratos Stefano Costa (possibly Nero) and 'Rabocchio' or 'Corbacchio' (possibly the Page). The only documented revival took place in Naples in 1651, for which a libretto was published. Both of the surviving manuscript scores can be associated with that revival. Only one, possibly two, of the remaining sources reflect the original Venetian production: a scenario published in 1643 and a manuscript libretto recently dlscovered at Udine. The other libretto sources include five manuscripts and one print, published in a collection of Busenello's works (*Le hore ociose*, 1656), which was evidently supervised by the librettist and represents his final –

though not necessarily original – version of the text. The differences among the various sources are extensive enough to require historical explanation, and they must be resolved before a definitive performance text can be established. Inconsistencies in the scores, in particular, which clearly post-date Monteverdi's death, have raised questions about the authenticity of the music they contain. It is now generally agreed that some sections were written by other, younger composers such as Francesco Sacrati, Benedetto Ferrari and Francesco Cavalli. The score has been edited numerous times since the beginning of this century, usually in connection with performances, by among others Vincent d'Indy (1908), Gian Francesco Malipiero (1931), Raymond Leppard (1966) and most recently by Alan Curtis (1990), whose edition is the first to attempt a scholarly collation and rationalization of the sources. The opera can be said to have entered the operatic mainstream in the early 1960s with performances at, among other places, Aix-en-Provence (1961), Glyndebourne (1962) and La Scala, Milan (1967).

*

Prologue *In the heavens* Fortune, Virtue and Cupid contest their primacy; in a closing duet, Fortune and Virtue grant the victory to Cupid, who responds that they will have occasion to observe his powers this very day.

Act I.i *Outside Poppaea's palace* At daybreak, Otho, returning from abroad, stands outside his beloved Poppaea's palace and sings of his love, first in a brief aria ('E pur io torno') that in form (*ABA*) and musical material (circling around the tonic) portrays the idea of returning, then in a longer aria ('Apri un balcon') whose third strophe terminates abruptly and pathetically in recitative as he sees Nero's sleeping soldiers and understands that Nero is inside and that Poppaea has betrayed him.

I.ii Overhearing him, the soldiers awaken, curse the love of Poppaea and Nero, and gossip about the court. Monteverdi increases the naturalism of this scene by overlapping its opening with the end of Otho's monologue.

I.iii Poppaea and Nero come out into the early morning light, where they bid passionate farewell to one another. Monteverdi intensifies the sensuality of their relationship by interlacing their texts where the librettist had given them successively. Musical elaboration of particular keywords, languid chromaticism and aria-like lyricism portray the lovers' pleasure in one another. But by judicious repetition of words and interrupted lines, Monteverdi manages to portray the nature of Poppaea's power over Nero.

I.iv Poppaea talks with Arnalta about her ambitions for the crown, boasting that Cupid will assure her success ('Speranza, tu mi vai . . . per me

guerreggia Amor'), but her old nurse warns against trusting great men, Love or Fortune.

I.v *Rome [the imperial apartments]* In one of the musical peaks of the opera, the recitative lament 'Disprezzata regina', Octavia bewails her fate: rejected by Nero, she is furious at the danger she faces of losing both husband and kingdom. She firmly dismisses her nurse's advice that she distract herself by taking a lover, and vows to remain steadfast in her sorrow.

I.vi Seneca attempts to console Octavia, urging her to stand firm. The page, remarking on the impotence of Seneca's advice, ridicules him for his pedantry; Octavia leaves to pray in the temple.

I.vii Seneca muses on the pain caused by the trappings of royalty.

I.viii He is joined by Pallas Athene, who, from the heavens, foretells his impending death, promising to warn him again through Mercury. In an unusually florid passage, Seneca expresses his willingness to embrace death whenever it comes.

I.ix Seneca is then joined by Nero, who insists, against his old tutor's advice, that he will do exactly as he wishes: he will send Octavia into exile and crown Poppaea empress. This is one of the most dramatic moments in the opera as the two men, the one mature, thoughtful and moral, the other immature, headstrong and passionate, pit their wits against each other. Monteverdi escalates the conflict by once again interlacing the characters' lines rather than presenting their speeches successively throughout, and he portrays the intensity of the conflict with his characteristic *stile concitato* (or warlike style), consisting of rapid repeated notes and forceful arpeggios. Nero finally dismisses Seneca, but the philosopher has the last word: the worst is to be expected when power wages war against reason.

I.x In a succession of sensual evocations of their pleasure in one another, Poppaea and Nero, overheard by Otho, discuss their happiness; he promises to make her empress and she, manipulating his weakness, insinuates that he is ruled by Seneca, whereupon Nero orders one of his soldiers to carry a death sentence to the philosopher, closing the scene with an echo of Cupid's message in the prologue: today Poppaea will see what Cupid can do.

I.xi In a strophic aria ('Ad altri tocca in sorte') Otho, overheard by Arnalta, reveals to Poppaea his despair at having been replaced in her affections by Nero, and she answers each of his strophes with one of her own, on the same bass line, justifying her change of heart as the effect of Fortune's favour. A more intense recitative exchange, which Monteverdi heightens through repetition and intercalation of Otho's and Poppaea's final lines, concludes abruptly with Poppaea's curt dismissal: 'No more, no more. I am Nero's.'

I.xii Left alone, Otho vents his despair and rage against Poppaea in recitative bursts. He even contemplates murdering her.

I.xiii He is overheard by Drusilla, who complains that he is still obsessed by Poppaea. He assures her that he will henceforth cast Poppaea from his mind and heart and think only of *her*, but he expresses himself in a lyrical aria style that seems forced and artificial when compared with the recitative of the previous scene. Although Drusilla is suspicious, she is finally reassured and departs. But Otho, knowing he cannot maintain his vow, confesses that his lips may say Drusilla but that Poppaea is in his heart.

Act 2.i *The garden of Seneca's villa outside Rome* Mercury, sent to earth by Pallas Athene, announces to Seneca that the day of his death has arrived. Seneca rejoices in the news, and Mercury departs on the wings of his highly elaborate, melismatic song.

2.ii Liberto haltingly attempts to inform Seneca of Nero's death sentence, but unnecessarily. Seneca assures him that he is ready to die and asks him to inform Nero that he is already dead and buried.

2.iii Seneca gathers the members of his household around him and in a poignant lyrical effusion ('Amici è giunta l'ora') informs them of his decision. They urge him to reconsider in a strikingly expressive madrigal chorus whose first section ('Non morir Seneca') is built on the imitative treatment of an ascending chromatic scale but whose much more cheerful, diatonic second section ('Questa vita è dolce troppo') suggests a certain lack of sympathy with his gesture. He is unaffected by their pleas and orders them to prepare his fatal bath.

[A scene for Seneca and a chorus of Virtues is given here in some of the libretto sources, including Busenello's print of 1656, but it is not set in either of the scores or mentioned in the published scenario of 1643 and thus was probably never set to music.]

2.iv *Rome* Relieving the dramatic intensity generated by Seneca's impending death, and providing the time necessary for the death to take place, the page and lady-in-waiting exchange a series of flirtatious arias. He begins with two strophes in lively duple metre ('Sento un certo non so che'); she responds with a single strophe in compound metre ('Astutello garzoncello'), and they join in a final lascivious duet ('O caro, o cara') featuring short imitative phrases and longer passages in a style similar to that of the closing duet of the opera (see below).

2.v Nero, having heard of Seneca's death, joins with his friend Lucan in an extended, sensuous duet of continuously overlapping lines in praise of Poppaea's beauty. The second section of the duet, 'Bocca, bocca', is built on the same bass line as that of the closing duet of the opera (see below); in both cases it is surely the traditional association with sexual love that is being invoked. This duet is one of the erotic peaks of the opera. Nero ends the scene alone, with an aria ('Son rubin preziosi') that is musically something of a let-down. (The sources disagree on the extent of this aria.)

2.vi Otho berates himself for thinking of harming Poppaea. In a rather subdued three-strophe aria ('Sprezzami quanto sai') he recognizes that his passion for her will remain hopeless.

2.vii He is joined by Octavia, who commands him to kill Poppaea and to disguise himself as a woman so as not to be apprehended. When he initially rejects her command, she threatens him with blackmail. Although they both speak entirely in recitative, Monteverdi distinguishes powerfully between Otho's unfocussed hesitancy and Octavia's forceful determination.

2.viii Reassured by Otho's declaration of love, Drusilla rejoices in an aria-like section enclosed by a refrain ('Felice cor mio'). The page teases Octavia's nurse about her age, taunting her with the vision of Drusilla in love. In a two-strophe aria ('Il giorno feminil') the nurse philosophically agrees that spring is the season for love.

2.ix Otho reveals that Octavia has ordered him to kill Poppaea and asks Drusilla to lend him her clothes so that he can disguise himself. Although disturbed by Otho's willingness to commit so heinous an act, she readily agrees, responding with two reprises of her joyful refrain from the previous scene (a convincing dramatic touch added by Monteverdi that underscores Drusilla's love for Otho).

2.x *Poppaea's garden* Poppaea, rejoicing at the death of Seneca, whom she recognized as the last obstacle to her ambitions, prays that Cupid ensure her marriage to Nero ('Amor, ricorro a te'). She expresses undying affection to her nurse Arnalta, who, characteristically, cautions her mistress against too much ambition. Feeling drowsy, Poppaea repeats her prayer to Cupid and is lulled to sleep by Arnalta's lullaby, whose circular melody and frequent, extended cadences actually produce a soporific effect.

2.xi Cupid, descended from Heaven to prevent Poppaea's death, hides near her. He sings an extended aria ('O sciocchi, o frali'), the four strophes of which elicit three different musical settings. Except for its added string accompaniment, the fourth strophe is the same as the first; it thus creates one of the most extended arias in the opera.

2.xii Disguised as Drusilla, Otho enters the garden and reluctantly attempts to kill the sleeping Poppaea, but Cupid stays his hand. Poppaea awakens in time to identify the fleeing Otho as Drusilla, Arnalta calls the guards to pursue 'her', and Cupid declares that he has saved Poppaea and wishes to make her empress.

Act 3.i *Rome* Drusilla rejoices in the hope that her rival will soon be dead and that Otho will be hers alone. The expansive enthusiasm of her refrain, 'O felice Drusilla', ironically underscores her ignorance of the outcome of the previous scene.

3.ii Arnalta, the lictor and a number of his colleagues come to seize Drusilla, who sadly recognizes that her enthusiasm was mistaken and that she must now pay for lending Otho her clothes.

3.iii Drusilla is brought before Nero and, when questioned about the murder attempt, decides to shield Otho and pleads guilty. Nero furiously sentences her to death.

3.iv Otho, refusing to allow Drusilla to accept the blame for his act, confesses to the crime and blames Octavia for instigating it. This gives Nero the excuse to repudiate Octavia, whom he orders to leave Rome in a ship. He spares Otho's life and commutes Drusilla's sentence, allowing them to go into exile together.

3.v After informing her of Octavia's guilt and exile, Nero joyfully tells Poppaea that they will be married this very day. This highly lyrical scene culminates in an expansive duet in which the two lovers sing together for the first time ('Ne più s'interporà').

3.vi Octavia sadly divests herself of the imperial garments and bids farewell to Rome in a highly expressive recitative monologue, 'Addio Roma'.

3.vii Arnalta exults in Poppaea's success and in her own improved station but remarks that she would have preferred to be born a lady and die a servant so that death would be more welcome.

3.viii *Nero's palace* After a lengthy expressive conversation between Nero and Poppaea filled with lyrical outpourings of love and contentment, Poppaea, hailed by the tribunes and consuls in chorus, is crowned empress. Then Cupid, descending from heaven with Venus, the Graces and the Cupids, crowns her as goddess of beauty on earth. The opera concludes with a duet for the lovers built on a descending tetrachord ostinato, 'Pur ti miro'. With melodic lines that are very close to one another and continually overlap, this duet has been considered the perfect embodiment of the eroticism of the opera. Although it is generally agreed that the text of this duet is not by Busenello and the music not by Monteverdi – the text is certainly by Benedetto Ferrari, and the music may be too – it was probably introduced soon after the première of the opera. To a 17th-century Venetian audience no less than a modern one, it evidently served a crucial dramatic function.

*

The historical context of the opera helps to explain its extraordinary glorification of lust and ambition at the expense of reason and morality. Its libretto was the product of a libertine intellectual movement in Venice that was specifically concerned with the relative value of religion and sensuality. But the intellectual issues in the libretto become charged with feeling in Monteverdi's music. He portrays the characters as human beings with strong emotions, fears and desires, who express themselves in distinctly different ways: Poppaea and Nero are prone to hedonistic lyricism in arioso, aria and duet; Octavia speaks only in strongly etched recitative; Otho's music lacks focus, is hesitant and is limited in range; Seneca's is bold and strongly directional. And their conflicts touch the very depth of their beings. For its broad moral compass and its psychological conviction, *L'incoronazione di Poppea* stands as the first in a long, if broken, tradition of operatic monuments that includes *Don Giovanni* and *Don Carlos*.   E.R.

Indes galantes, Les ('The Amorous Indies')

Opéra-ballet in a prologue and four entrées by Jean-Philippe Rameau to a libretto by Louis Fuzelier; Paris, Académie Royale de Musique (Opéra), 23 August 1735.

The cast at the première included the following singers in the various roles: Pierre de Jélyotte (haute-contre), Mlle Eremans (soprano), Jean Dun (haute-contre), Mlle Petitpas (soprano), Marie Pelissier (soprano), Denis-François Tribou (haute-contre), Claude Chassé de Chinais (bass).

Le turc généreux	
Hébé [Hebe]	soprano
L'Amour [Cupid]	soprano
Emilie	soprano
Osman	bass
Valère	haute-contre
Les Incas du Pérou	
Huascar	bass
Phani	soprano
Don Carlos	haute-contre
Les fleurs	
Tacmas	haute-contre
Ali	bass
Zaïre	soprano
Fatima	soprano
Atalide [revised version only]	soprano
Les sauvages	
Don Alvar	bass
Damon	haute-contre
Zima	soprano
Adario	tenor

Cupids, Turks, Incas, Persians, Indians

The vogue at the Opéra during the 1730s was for *opéras-ballets* on mythological themes. *Les Indes galantes*, Rameau's first work in this genre, reverts to a type involving believable modern characters, a type initiated by Campra's *L'Europe galante* (1697) and fashionable during the first 20 years of the century. At its première it consisted only of a prologue and two entrées, 'Le turc généreux' and 'Les Incas du Pérou', the entrée 'Les fleurs' being added at the third performance. After criticism of what was seen as the absurdity of disguising the hero as a woman, this entrée was replaced with a version in which the plot and all the music except the *divertissement* was new. With the addition of a final entrée 'Les sauvages' (10 March 1736), the work took on something like a definitive form. In the course of many revivals, however, the number and order of entrées was frequently altered. The last complete contemporary performance was in 1761; at subsequent revivals, individual entrées were replaced with those from other works, not all by Rameau. The prologue stayed in the repertory until 1771, 'Les Incas' and 'Les sauvages' respectively until 1772 and 1773. The first complete modern revival of *Les Indes galantes* was at the Paris Opéra on 18 June 1952, and was notable for the lavishness of its staging.

＊

The prologue retains its allegorical character in introducing the work's theme, aspects of love in far-flung lands: the young men (dancers) of four allied European nations forsake the goddess Hebe and, despite the advice of Cupid, are led off to war. The Cupids, realizing that Europe is deserting them, decide to fly to the various 'Indies' (a generic term at that time for any exotic land).

These Indies become the settings for the ensuing entrées. 'Le turc généreux' is set on an island in the Indian Ocean. A French girl, Emilie, has been sold as a slave to the pasha Osman, who has fallen in love with her. When Emilie's beloved Valère is ship-wrecked and captured, Osman recognizes him as the one who freed him from slavery. Though envious of the lovers' happiness, Osman shows his gratitude by releasing them.

'Les Incas du Pérou' takes place during a Sun Festival in the shadow of a Peruvian volcano. Huascar, the Incan master of ceremonies, loves the princess Phani, though she loves the Spaniard Don Carlos. To convince Phani that the Sun god disapproves of her love, Huascar causes the volcano to erupt. When Carlos foils Huascar's attempt to abduct her, the frenzied Incan causes a further eruption and is crushed by molten rocks.

In the original version of 'Les fleurs', the young Persian prince Tacmas and his confidant Ali are each in love with the other's slave – Tacmas with Zaïre, Ali with Fatima. On the day of the flower festival, the four meet in a confusing encounter where Tacmas is disguised as a woman and Fatima as a Polish slave; but when Zaïre and Fatima reveal that each loves the other's master, the men exchange slaves and all take part in the festival. In the revised version, Fatima (here Sultana rather than slave) suspects her husband Tacmas of infidelity with Atalide. Disguised as a slave, she gains Atalide's confidence and discovers that her suspicions are unfounded. The happy couple take part in the festival.

In 'Les sauvages' a tribe of North American Indians prepares to make peace with its European vanquishers. The Spaniard Don Alvar and French-man Damon vie for the hand of the chief's daughter Zima. But she, declaring that the jealous Spaniard loves too much and the fickle Frenchman too little, follows her innocent 'savage' instincts and chooses an honourable Indian brave, Adario. The shamefaced Europeans join the Indians in the Great Peace-Pipe ceremony.

＊

Fuzelier's libretto, though much criticized in Rameau's day, has considerable merits. Each entrée has its distinctive character, while except in the prologue there are no supernatural interventions. Fuzelier generates the necessary visual and dramatic interest by means of his cleverly chosen locations and the indigenous ceremonial they provide. (Certain details of the latter were culled from published reports of recent events or from first-hand experience.) In the process he manages to contrast European and other cultures, not always to the former's advantage, as the episode of the generous Turk and the lighthearted but moving tribute to the 'noble savage' demonstrate.

Rameau's magnificent response to this material raised the traditionally lightweight genre of *opéra-ballet* to a new level. To 'Les Incas' he brings an intensity no less than that of the *tragédies*: from the start of the eruption to the end of the entrée is an almost unbroken sequence of 350 bars, during which voices and orchestra interact with extraordinary vehemence. The entrée is dominated by Huascar, whose fanatical but wholly credible character Rameau establishes with a sureness not found outside *Hippolyte*. Elsewhere it is the grace and variety of the *airs* and dances that impress most. 'Les sauvages', which proved particularly popular, includes a reworking of Rameau's harpsichord piece *Les sauvages*, inspired by the dancing of two American Indians in Paris in 1725.   G.Sa.

Infedeltà delusa, L' ('Deceit Outwitted')

Burletta per musica in two acts by Joseph Haydn to a libretto by Marco Coltellini, possibly revised by Carl Friberth; Eszterháza, 26 July 1773.

The first cast featured Maddalena Friberth (Vespina), Barbara Dichtler (Sandrina), Carl Friberth (Filippo), Leopold Dichtler (Nencio) and Christian Specht (Nanni).

Vespina *a girl of spirit, sister of Nanni, and in love with Nencio*		soprano
Sandrina *a simple girl, in love with Nanni*		soprano
Filippo *an old peasant, father of Sandrina*		tenor
Nencio *a well-to-do peasant*		tenor
Nanni *a peasant, in love with Sandrina*		bass
Setting A small village in the Tuscan countryside in the 18th century		

For nearly 30 years Haydn was responsible for directing operatic performances for his employer, Prince Nikolaus Esterházy, and composed the work (*Lo speziale*) that opened the new opera house at the Prince's estate in 1768. The first documented performance of *L'infedeltà delusa*, the earliest of Haydn's major stage works, was on the name-day (26 July) of the Dowager Princess Esterházy, as the first edition of the libretto – printed at Ödenburg (Sopron) by Joseph Siess – indicates. The libretto was reprinted with a new title-page, 'nell'occasione del gloriosissimo arrivo quìvi de Sua Maestia L'Imperatrice Maria Theresia ... nel mese di Settembre dell'Anno 1773'. This famous performance ('If I wish to hear a good opera, I go to Eszterháza', as Maria Theresa is supposed to have said) took place on 1 September, and the work was revived once more, on 1 July 1774, during the visit of two distinguished Italians. No other revivals are known during Haydn's lifetime.

L'infedeltà delusa has enjoyed considerable esteem, even popular success, since World War II. Before the war it had been arranged as a Singspiel, *Die Liebe macht erfinderisch*, with a German text by Hermann Goja, and the music edited by Gottfried Kassowitz (Vienna, *c*1930). Performances in its original form began with a broadcast by Hungarian Radio in 1952 and a production at the State Opera, Budapest, in 1959. Since publication of the editions by H. C. Robbins Landon (1960) and by Dénes Bartha and Jenö Vécsey (1964) it has been staged at the Holland Festival, and several times in Germany, Britain, France, Sweden and the USA. It has also been easily the most favoured Haydn opera in both number and quality of recordings: conducted by Antonio de Almeida (1969) – still perhaps the finest of all Haydn operatic recordings – Frigyes Sándor (1976), Antal Dorati (1980) and Sigiswald Kuijken (1989).

*

Act I *Outside Filippo's house* Filippo, Vespina and her brother Nanni, and Nencio are enjoying the beauty of a summer evening, but Vespina senses that Nencio is hatching a plot with Filippo, and Nanni is concerned about Sandrina's absence. Sandrina enters, perturbed by her father's plan to marry her to Nencio. The F major quintet, 'Bella sera ed aure grate', that opens the work is by far the largest number in the opera; it is also the most beautiful of all Haydn's opera ensembles. Structurally, it consists of two sections, a Moderato followed by an Allegro in 3/8 time, the change in tempo and time signature coinciding with Sandrina's entrance and plea to her father. In an imaginative touch Haydn has her solo accompanied solely by strings, her father's otherwise identical music accompanied solely by winds. Brother and sister, then all the characters, take up the same melody. Filippo drags out of Sandrina her reluctant agreement to marry Nencio and rebuff Nanni, to whom, when her father leaves, she admits her predicament in an uncharacteristically vehement *presto* aria in A major ('Che imbroglio è questo!'). Nanni's anger finds expression in a brilliant aria, 'Non v'è rimedio' (Allegro di molto, 3/4 time, F minor), virtually a challenge to the absent Filippo: one or the other of them must die. The number ends with frenetic rising violin figuration and vivid flourishes from oboes and horns.

The kitchen of Nanni's house Vespina, preparing supper, sings of the grief brought on by love. When her brother returns, equally dejected by the loss of Sandrina, they express their desire for vengeance in a dashing D major duet ('Son disperato').

Outside Filippo's house Nencio serenades Sandrina in a very long and slow-moving aria, with pizzicato strings suggesting his guitar; his theme is the flirtatious unsatisfactoriness of town girls compared with those of the countryside; a poignant dissonance at the word 'guai' ('woe'; bar 114) reveals something more than a stock response to a conventional idea. While Vespina and Nanni listen from the shadows, Nencio tries in vain to persuade Sandrina to love him. It is all too much for Vespina, who steps forward and slaps Nencio, thus setting the finale in motion, a busy G major ensemble of perplexity (Allegro di molto, followed by Presto).

Act 2 *Outside Filippo's house, the following morning* Vespina has a plan and, disguised as a frail old woman, begins to put it into action. Her brother slips away as Filippo and Sandrina come out, the former intent on lodging a complaint against Nanni. With feigned reluctance Vespina tells them that Nencio married her daughter and then abandoned her; the long scene of *secco* recitative is exquisitely lightened by five passages of accompanied recitative as the distraught 'old woman' tries to find consolation in resorting to proverbs. Her mock-pathetic Adagio aria, 'Ho un tumore', lists her infirmities. (Haydn deleted 38 bars from it, presumably for the performance the empress attended; the musical loss is more than offset by the dramaturgical gain.) Seeing Nencio approach, father and daughter re-enter their house and lock the door. The bemused Nencio is told to look after his wife and children; Filippo berates him soundly in a *presto* outburst, 'Tu sposarti alla Sandrina?', offset by tender phrases that reveal his love for his daughter. The bewildered Nencio suspects a trick, but before he can knock on the door, a tipsy German manservant (Vespina, in her second disguise) tells him in pidgin Italo-German that 'his' aristocratic master is going to marry Sandrina that day. In a rollicking F major aria in 6/8 time, 'Trinche vaine allegramente', Vespina urges Nencio to enjoy the celebrations. This is the shortest, and also the wittiest, number in the opera. Nencio now thinks he understands Filippo's changed attitude, but he hardly gets his breath back before Vespina enters again, this time as the pretended bridegroom, the Marchese di Ripafratta, who tells Nencio that Sandrina is to be fobbed off with his servant. Nencio, wanting to see Filippo's discomfort, agrees to act as witness at the wedding, and in an aria gleefully anticipates his revenge. Vespina emerges to tell Nanni that Filippo has taken the bait, and in an E major aria, 'Ho tesa la rete' (Allegretto, 2/4), which makes charming use of muted violins, she tells him that if she is careful she will lure more than one bird into the net. (As in the aria earlier in the act, Haydn again cut 38 bars.)

A room in Filippo's house All of Filippo's attempts to convince his daughter of the advantages of her fine match are vain; Sandrina wants only a simple life with Nanni (aria, 'È la pompa un grand'imbroglio'). Nanni enters, announcing himself as the Marquis's servant, accompanied by the notary (Vespina, in her fourth and last disguise) to prepare the contract; the Marquis will join them when he has completed arrangements for his bride's wardrobe and the honeymoon. The finale (C major, Poco adagio, Presto) opens with the notary drawing up the contract, which Nencio and Nanni sign as witnesses. Nanni reveals himself to the 'notary' as proxy for the bridegroom. Vespina, singing snatches from two of her disguised roles, explains her part in the proceedings – she has changed the names on the contract – and there is nothing Filippo, or for that matter Nencio, can do other than accept the double wedding of Sandrina and Nanni, Vespina and Nencio.

*

This work marks an important step forward in Haydn's development as an opera composer. Com-

pared with its predecessor, *Le pescatrici* (1769), *L'infedeltà delusa* reveals a marked degree of concentration: the five characters are all from the peasant class, the chorus is excluded and the work is limited to two acts of equal length. The orchestra is of modest size, including oboes, horns and strings, augmented by bassoons (specified only in the opening quintet). Timpani are used only in the three C major pillars of the structure (where they are combined with horns): the overture, Filippo's aria early in Act 2 and the finale. A gift of 25 ducats from Prince Nikolaus to Haydn at the end of May was probably a thank-offering for the new opera, and it may have received a private performance in the early summer. **P.B.**

Intermezzo

Bürgerliche Komödie mit sinfonischen Zwischenspielen in two acts by Richard Strauss to his own libretto; Dresden, Staatsoper, 4 November 1924.

The first singers in the roles of Christine and Robert were Lotte Lehmann and Joseph Correck. Fritz Busch conducted.

Christine	soprano
Robert Storch *her husband, a conductor*	baritone
Anna *their maid*	soprano
Franzl *their eight-year-old son*	spoken
Baron Lummer	tenor
The Notary	baritone
His Wife	soprano
Stroh *another conductor*	tenor
A Commercial Counsellor	*Robert's Skat partners*	baritone
A Legal Counsellor		baritone
A Singer	bass
Fanny *the Storchs' cook*	spoken
Marie and Therese *maids*	spoken
Resi *a young girl*	soprano

Setting Partly in Grundlsee, partly in Vienna

In the spring of 1916 Strauss was still composing *Die Frau ohne Schatten*, as well as finishing the new prologue for the full-opera version of *Ariadne auf Naxos*, but an idea struck him for a new opera of his own. This was not to be another collaboration with Hofmannsthal, nor a substantial art-work at all: rather, it would be a light domestic comedy, almost operetta, with a story based on a marital *contretemps* of his own (in 1903), and leading roles modelled upon himself and his wife Pauline. For a libretto he approached the critic and playwright Hermann Bahr, who made sketches but found the composer so intent upon strict verisimilitude that he finally

'Intermezzo' (Richard Strauss), design by Adolf Mahnke for Act 1 scene v (based on a room in the Strauss family villa in Garmisch) for the original production at the Dresden Staatsoper, 4 November 1924

suggested that Strauss should be his own librettist – a role he had abandoned after his first opera, *Guntram*. He took it up again with delight, if not much urgency; the whole opera was completed, during a South American tour, only in the summer of 1923.

Intermezzo proved to be something more than a self-regarding jest – though the composer did have Lehmann visit his family to observe Pauline's ways, the Dresden sets copied their Garmisch home, and Correck wore a Strauss-mask. There was of course gossip about 'doubtful taste', especially because the volatile, petulant Pauline was faithfully drawn, and her husband depicted as buoyantly sensible and generous. Yet Strauss could hardly have seen that as a *risqué* new departure: for 30 years he had portrayed himself in his music, along with Pauline in *Ein Heldenleben* and the *Sinfonia domestica*, and in the latter their son Franz as the noisy baby-in-the-bath (he appears in *Intermezzo*, like their maid Anna, under his own name).

The opera has had a fitful career. Its three-hours-plus probably exceed Strauss's original intention. Though his modest strings, double winds and standard percussion are reinforced by harp, piano, harmonium and a third horn, they must work hard and sonorously. The opera demands much from its stage hands too, for part of the theatrical joke is the rapid succession of contrasted settings briefly

glimpsed. Above all, it depends upon an appealing pair of character-comedians who can sing: like Hermann Prey and Hanny Steffek, for many years the ideal Storch couple.

*

Act I.i *The dressing-room at home in Grundlsee* Robert is packing for a two-month engagement in Vienna while Christine fusses, bridles, berates the servants and bemoans her lot. When Robert has gone, the maid Anna tries in vain to placate her; but a telephone invitation to go skating improves her mood. A brisk orchestral interlude develops her voluble tunes and ends with glissando sweeps: toboggans whizzing downhill.

I.ii *The ski slopes* On the slope is young Baron Lummer on skis; Christine on her toboggan runs him over. She blames him vociferously, but then discovers that their parents know each other. The interlude mingles the Baron's slight tune with Robert's and Christine's before settling into a lengthy waltz (tongue-in-cheek plainly visible).

I.iii *The Grundlsee inn* A ball is in progress. The Baron and Christine stop dancing – she is theatrically exhausted; they chat, agree to meet next day, and go back refreshed for the next waltz. The orchestra continues with suave passion in D♭, fades away and drops suddenly into blunt C major . . .

I.iv *A furnished room in the Notary's house* Christine is vetting the room for her new protégé and in minute, peremptory detail she enjoins the Notary's wife to take motherly care of him. Interlude: the Baron's and Christine's tunes, cautiously and decorously romantic.

I.v The Storchs' dining-room Christine is writing a letter to Robert, mentioning her penurious new protégé, the migraines which have delayed his university studies, and her promise to help him. He pays his daily visit, dropping unsubtle hints about how useful a loan (or gift) would be – but Christine's prudent instincts are subliminally aroused, and she confines her response to praising her husband's dependable kindness (brightly in A, then devoutly in B♭). After the Baron departs she falls to mellow musing, and the orchestra warms the idyll into an elaborate rhapsody.

I.vi The Baron's lodgings The Baron, alone, smokes a cigarette and considers whether he should press the Frau Hofkapellmeister harder. Indiscreetly, his girl-friend Resi arrives; he sends her out while he drafts a note to Christine. His tone of bland bluster is continued in the interlude.

I.vii The Storchs' house Christine expostulates about the Baron's stupid letter, with its shameless request for 1000 marks. He enters, and is duly and loftily rebuked. But then the maid Marie brings a note addressed to the Hofkapellmeister Robert Storch. It proves to be a plea from a certain Mitzi Meier for opera tickets, with a promise to meet her 'angel' afterwards in the bar as usual. Christine explodes with anger and the Baron retreats. She dispatches a telegram to her faithless husband announcing that she knows about Mitzi and is leaving forever – and orders poor Anna to pack everything at once. There are orchestral paroxysms (of saintly trust betrayed) in F minor, the basic key for the rest of the act.

I.viii Franzl Storch's bedroom Descending tearfully upon their son, Christine explains that his wicked father has betrayed her; he will never see him again, because they are going away. Little Franzl ('Bubi') obstinately defends Papa. His mother stays to pray for this fatherless child, and herself, until he is asleep again. (Opinions differ about which is the more embarrassing, this scene or the Act 2 finale; here, Strauss supplies a poignant lyrical plaint without any saving hint of irony.)

Act 2.i *The house of the Commercial Counsellor* The Commercial Counsellor is playing Skat (Strauss's beloved betting game with cards, something between bridge and poker: the orchestra represents the shuffling and dealing) with the Legal Counsellor, an opera singer and the conductor Stroh, and they discuss Storch's daunting wife. Robert, arriving late from rehearsal, protests that her abrasive temperament is just what he needs, and sings a little eulogy to her – whereupon her telegram reaches him. Dumb-

founded, without any idea (unlike Stroh) who Mitzi Meier might be, he rushes off; his friends continue serenely with their *Skatpartie*. There is a frantic orchestral interlude.

2.ii The Notary's offices Christine descends upon the Notary to demand a divorce. First he suspects her relationship with his lodger the Baron to be germane; then he doubts her evidence against his friend Robert to be adequate. She flounces out. In the interlude, a violent thunderstorm blows up.

2.iii The Prater Wet and distraught, Robert wanders in the Prater. Stroh rushes up to confess: it is *he* who knows Mitzi Meier – but she was vague about his name, and hit upon the wrong Kapellmeister when she consulted the telephone directory. Robert insists absolutely that Stroh must tell this to Christine in person. Interlude: joyous, hyper-excited relief in honest C major, subsiding into gentle confidence.

2.iv The Storchs' house Amid volatile chromatics, the packing up proceeds in some disarray. Christine has sent the Baron off to Vienna to play detective. As she discusses that with the maids, a telegram comes from Robert: unfortunate confusion, Stroh on his way to explain it all! – and indeed the unlucky Stroh is at the door. She doubts whether she wants to be persuaded, but the last interlude – an exuberant 6/8 affair – recycles the main themes with an air of finality.

2.v The same Robert arrives, expecting complete exoneration; but it is Christine who demands apologies. He goes off in a fury and she declares that she always knew it would end like this.

2.vi The same The Baron reports upon his mission, but his vague findings have been pre-empted. Christine dismisses him brusquely. Though Robert, back again, makes fun of her illusions about him, she accepts the teasing almost meekly: like Barak's Wife in Strauss's previous opera, *Die Frau ohne Schatten*, she has been deeply stirred by the sight of her husband in real anger. They bill and coo at length in A, with a rapturous F♯ coda.

*

If the cheerful triviality of the *Intermezzo* story is in radical contrast to the lofty concerns of *Die Frau ohne Schatten*, so is its musical form, which is much more interesting than the fact that the opera is auto-biographical. Hofmannsthal's dramaturgy for *Die Frau* had dictated long Wagnerian paragraphs and continuous development; in *Intermezzo* Strauss gave himself room to play with the mercurial conversation style he had devised for the *Ariadne* prologue, and to veer away from through-composed music drama towards a new kind of number opera. There are at least as many distinguishable themes in *Intermezzo* as in any other of his operas, and assiduously de-veloped as always – but in a string of bright, separate little inventions, each with a neat theatrical point, and each scene in quick alternation with vivid orchestral interludes. (The score is also spiced with jokey quotations, from his own and other composers' music.) With a feather-light plot, anecdotal detail had to provide the life of the piece. Given the strictly naturalistic text, no vocal 'numbers' were feasible beyond the odd lyrical effusion; otherwise, the distinct set pieces had to be orchestral, and mostly between the scenes. They supply more than just a frame: *Intermezzo* depends upon them for due variety of colour and rhythm (and some of its better jokes), as both its title and its subtitle imply. Often longer than some of the scenes, the orchestral interludes are more lyrically elaborated, and variously ironic, cartoon-pictorial (the toboggan scene) or vehemently impassioned. The latter passages have been thought 'excessive', as if Strauss ought to have trimmed the emotional storms to a bourgeois scale of propriety; but his adored Pauline never did, and he would have scorned the notion that mythical opera-heroes were entitled to stronger feelings than middle-class musicians.

Among the singing roles, the Christine/Pauline character is brilliantly fixed by her music (full of irascible leaps like the part of Barak's Wife, which Pauline had also inspired unawares). Robert/Richard is pleasantly idealized; the Baron is no more than a languid cartoon, and the lesser characters fare worse. For the next two decades Strauss would attempt nothing remotely like this piece – until his last opera, *Capriccio*, which capitalized upon lessons learnt from the *Intermezzo* experiment.   **D.M.**

Iolanta ('Iolanthe')

Lyric opera in one act by Pyotr Il'yich Tchaikovsky to a libretto by Modest Il'yich Tchaikovsky after Henrik Hertz's play *Kong Renés Datter* ('King René's Daughter'), translated from the Danish by Fyodor Miller, adapted for the Malïy Theatre (Moscow) by Vladimir Rafailovich Zotov; St Petersburg, Mariinsky Theatre, 6/18 December 1892.

The first performance was conducted by Eduard Nápravník, with Nikolay Figner as Vaudémont and Medea Mei-Figner in the title role.

Iolanta *blind daughter of King René*		soprano
René *King of Provence*		bass
Vaudémont *Count, Burgundian knight*		tenor
Ibn-Hakia *Moorish physician*		baritone
Robert *Duke of Burgundy*		baritone
Alméric *armour-bearer to King René*		tenor
Bertrand *doorkeeper to the castle*		bass
Martha *Bertrand's wife, Iolanta's nursemaid*		contralto
Brigitta } *Iolanta's friends*		soprano
Laura		mezzo-soprano

Iolanta's servant-girls and girl friends, the king's retinue, the duke's regiment, men-at-arms
Setting The mountains of southern France, 15th century

Tchaikovsky began work on *Iolanta* on 28 June/10 July 1891 with the decisive confrontation between Iolanta and Vaudémont, culminating in their big duet in praise of light. Although he complained to his librettist brother of a loss of facility after the huge access of inspiration that carried him through *The Queen of Spades*, the opera was finished in short score by 25 August/5 September and the orchestration was completed on 8/20 November. The composer was not entirely happy with the result. He accused himself of self-repetition (notably of *The Enchantress*), and a passage in a letter he wrote to a would-be librettist in February 1892 ('medieval dukes and knights and ladies capture my imagination but not my heart') is often taken as evidence of his attitude to his last opera. Rimsky-Korsakov, who attended the dress rehearsals, recalled it scathingly in his memoirs. Yet at the première, so the composer reported, *Iolanta* fared much better with the audience than the ballet *The Nutcracker* (as a companion-piece to which it had been commissioned by the Imperial Theatres).

*

A lush garden with hedge roses and fruit trees, its gate at the rear overgrown with green The introduction, scored for woodwind and horns, is intensely chromatic, evocative of Iolanta's world of darkness. The opening of the scene, like that of *Yevgeny Onegin*, pits vocal *parlante* against background music, in this case a solo string quartet (muted) and harp, which serenade the blind princess and her companions as they pick fruit in the garden. Iolanta confides in Martha that she senses she is lacking something, but does not know what (her father has forbidden any revelation that she is handicapped). The musicians are silenced and she expresses her doubts more fully in an arioso ('Otchego eto prezhde ne znala': 'Why did I not know this before'). Her girl friends and ladies-in-waiting try to comfort Iolanta with flowers. Finally Brigitta, Laura and Martha, followed by the chorus, sing Iolanta to sleep. All exit except Iolanta who sleeps at the rear of the stage, behind the overgrowth, through the next pair of scenes.

Alméric enters, having presented credentials to Bertrand. He announces the impending arrival of King René, accompanied by the Moorish physician Ibn-Hakia, who will see whether Iolanta's blindness may be cured. They enter, and after Ibn-Hakia has been led off to examine the sleeping Iolanta, the king prays for his daughter's recovery ('Gospod' moy, yesli greshen ya': 'O Lord, if I have sinned'). Ibn-Hakia returns and informs the king that it may be possible to restore Iolanta's sight, but only if she is made aware of her misfortune and desires a cure. The king is unwilling to risk his daughter's unhappiness. To 'modal' oriental strains (compare the 'Arabian Dance' in *The Nutcracker*), the physician gives the king some ancient metaphysical advice: he is unwise to consider the world of the flesh apart from the world of the spirit; Iolanta can only be made whole if her spirit grasps the idea of light and prepares her eyes to receive it. They make for the castle.

Robert and Vaudémont wander into the garden, lost. They have no idea that they are in the grounds of King René or that Iolanta sleeps nearby. In fact Robert is preparing to ask to be released from his childhood betrothal to Iolanta because he has fallen in love with Countess Mathilde of Lorraine, to whom he sings an impassioned encomium ('Kto mozhet sravnit'sya s Matil'doy moyey': 'Who may compare with my Mathilde'). Vaudémont declares that he is uninterested in physical charms but rather looks for a woman of perfect purity; this romance, composed during rehearsals at Nikolay Figner's request, is optional.

The two intruders begin looking around and Vaudémont stumbles on the nook where Iolanta is sleeping. He is immediately thunderstruck, recognizing the answer to his just-uttered prayer. Robert takes fright at what he perceives to be an enchantment. He insists that they leave. The ensuing quarrel awakens Iolanta. She comes out, meets the two knights, and rushes off to fetch some wine to entertain them. While she is off stage Robert leaves, so that when she returns Vaudémont is alone. He sings to her of his infatuation and asks for a rose the colour of her cheeks. She picks him a white one. He points out her error and asks specifically for a red one; she does not know what that means. He asks her how many roses he is holding; when she answers that she cannot tell without touching them, he knows that she is blind. He extends sympathy; she is uncomprehending. He describes to her what she is missing; she understands at last but insists that she does not need light in order to praise the Creator (duet, 'Chudnïy pervenets tvoren'ya': 'Wondrous firstling of creation').

The stage fills with the remaining characters, except Robert. When King René finds out that Iolanta has learnt of her blindness in the course of finding love he is at first in despair, but Ibn-Hakia points out that his condition has now been met, and nothing stands in the way of a cure. The assembled characters join voices in a brief octet expressing hope, at the end of which the king, believing in the cure at last, threatens Vaudémont with execution if the operation is unsuccessful. Ibn-Hakia understands that the king is providing Iolanta with the incentive she needs to gain her sight. She leaves to undergo the cure.

Vaudémont asks for Iolanta's hand in marriage, but King René informs him that she is pledged to another. Robert, returning with his retinue (who at last provide a male chorus), requests release from his promise of marriage in favour of Vaudémont, a request the king is now only too happy to grant. Iolanta returns, cured. All raise their voices in praise of light and its creator, partly to a reprise of the main tune whose resemblance to Anton Rubinstein's song *Zhelaniye* ('Longing'), after Lermontov, so annoyed Rimsky-Korsakov. The resemblance was probably a deliberate double homage: the first line of Lermontov's poem – 'Open up my gaol cell, let me see the light of day!' – is singularly apt to the dramatic situation.

*

The dramatic confrontations and arias in *Iolanta*, despite the fact that several of the latter (Iolanta's opening arioso, King René's prayer, Robert's aria) achieved an independent recital-stage popularity, are fairly routine and in at least one case, the king's, downright trite. Ibn-Hakia's monologue-aria, too, is pretty much thrown-off; the mysterious East did not beckon Tchaikovsky as it did his teacher Rubinstein or his contemporaries of the Five, nor did the composer respond in any special way to the libretto's metaphysical trappings. The magic in this opera is to be found in its decorative colours.   R.T.

Iphigénie en Aulide ('Iphigenia in Aulis')

Tragédie in three acts by Christoph Willibald Gluck to a libretto by Marie François Louis Gand Leblanc Roullet after Jean Racine's *Iphigénie en Aulide*, itself after Euripides; Paris, Académie Royale de Musique (Opéra), 19 April 1774.

The original principals were Henri Larrivée (Agamemnon), Mlle du Plant (Clytemnestra), Sophie Arnould (Iphigenia), Joseph Legros (Achilles), Durand (Patroclus), Nicolas Gélin (Calchas) and Beauvalet (Arcas).

Agamemnon *King of Mycenae and*	
Argos	baritone
Clitemnestre [Clytemnestra] *his wife*	soprano
Iphigénie [Iphigenia] *their daughter*	soprano
Achille [Achilles] *a Greek hero in love with*	
Iphigenia	tenor
Patrocle [Patroclus] *a Greek chieftain and*	
friend of Achilles	bass
Calchas *High Priest*	bass
Arcas *Captain of Agamemnon's guards*	bass

Three Greek women	sopranos
Slave from Lesbos	soprano

Greek officers, warriors and people, guards,
Thessalian warriors, women from Argos and
Aulis, slaves from Lesbos and priestesses of
Diana

Setting Aulis, a town on the island of Euboea
off the coast of Greece at the time of the
Trojan War

Iphigénie en Aulide was the first of the seven operas
that Gluck composed for Paris, although it was not
actually commissioned by the Académie Royale de
Musique. After *Paride ed Elena* failed to meet with
success in Vienna in 1770, Gluck's thoughts turned
elsewhere. He had already written and adapted
several French *opéras comiques* for Vienna and he had
admired and studied the *tragédies lyriques* of Lully
and Rameau; their influence can certainly be seen in
Gluck's three Viennese 'reform' operas, *Orfeo ed
Euridice*, *Alceste* and *Paride ed Elena*. It was inevitable
that, having incorporated many features of French
opera into his latest works, Gluck should be drawn to
the French stage itself.

So, in the early 1770s, with no certainty of a
production, Gluck set the libretto of *Iphigénie en
Aulide* written by Roullet, an attaché to the French
Embassy in Vienna. The two men then began to plan
their conquest of Paris, a matter involving artistic
politics and diplomatic letters to the Académie
Royale and the French press. The directors of the
Académie Royale, fearing that *Iphigénie en Aulide*
would drive existing French operas off the stage,
were reluctant to accept the work unless Gluck
agreed to write five more operas for them. However,
with the support of the Dauphine, Gluck's former
singing pupil Marie Antoinette, the composer
arrived in Paris in 1773 and, after six months of
strenuous rehearsals, during which Gluck's
demands on his performers were exigent, sometimes
abrasive, occasionally furious, *Iphigénie en Aulide*
finally reached the stage.

Gluck revised the opera after the first run of
performances, introducing the goddess Diana
(soprano) at the end of the opera as a *dea ex machina*,
and altering and expanding the *divertissements* for a
1775 revival. So, broadly speaking, there are two
versions of the opera; but the differences are by no
means so great or important as those between *Orfeo
ed Euridice* and *Orphée et Eurydice* or between the
Italian and the French *Alceste*. The Gluck collected
edition (1987) opts for the later version, with the
omitted 1774 music printed in the second volume.
The differences are indicated in the synopsis below.

Iphigénie en Aulide was much performed in France
in the 18th century and in the first part of the 19th,
since when it has not been revived as regularly as, for

example, *Orphée et Eurydice* or *Iphigénie en Tauride*.
Wagner realized the importance of the work and
made his own version in German for performances in
Dresden in 1847, with Wilhelmine Schröder-Devrient
in the title role. He rescored the opera, made
numerous cuts and added recitatives and other
music of his own – he also changed Act 3 and gave it a
new ending, with Diana (called Artemis, her Greek
name, by Wagner) ordering Iphigenia to go to Tauris
as her High Priestess there, thus effecting a link
between *Iphigénie en Aulide* and *Iphigénie en Tauride*
which was certainly not Gluck's intention. This
version of the opera was often performed in
Germany; Mahler conducted a famous revival of it in
Vienna in 1907, the year Lucienne Bréval scored great
success in the title role in Paris. *Iphigénie en Aulide*
was not performed in England until 1933, in Oxford.
In a revival at the Maggio Musicale Fiorentino in
1950 Boris Christoff sang Agamemnon, repeating
his performance in 1959 at La Scala with Giulietta
Simionato as Iphigenia. Christa Ludwig sang the title
role at the Salzburg Festival in 1962; Elisabeth
Söderström sang it at Drottningholm in 1965. It was
conducted by Sir Charles Mackerras at the Vienna
Staatsoper in 1987. A performance at the Spitalfields
Festival, conducted by Richard Hickox, took place in
London in 1987 with Isabelle Poulenard as Iphigenia
and John Aler as Achilles, a role he recorded that year
with Lynne Dawson (Iphigenia), Anne Sofie von
Otter (Clytemnestra) and José van Dam (Agamemnon); conducted by John Eliot Gardiner, this is the
first recording of the 1775 version of the opera. There
has also been a recording of Wagner's version
conducted by Kurt Eichhorn with Anna Moffo and
Dietrich Fischer-Dieskau, but to date there has been
no recording of the original 1774 version. A series of
performances of this version by Opera North is
scheduled for 1996.

*

Act I *The Greek camp on one side in the background,
a wood on the other* The Greek fleet, led by Agamemnon, is becalmed on its way to Troy. The High
Priest Calchas has consulted the oracle and says that
to obtain favourable winds Agamemnon must
sacrifice his daughter Iphigenia to appease the
goddess Diana, whose favourite stag he killed.
Agamemnon has sent to Greece for Iphigenia on the
pretext of marrying her to Achilles but, after a change
of heart, he has also sent Arcas to turn her back on the
pretext that Achilles has been unfaithful to her.

The overture suggests the violently contrasting
emotions to be encountered in the opera itself, and at
the point where its opening bars return Agamemnon
sings – a surprising, highly dramatic gesture which
hastens on the action and anticipates the very fluid
style of the opera, which moves from air to recitative
to dance or chorus with few breaks in the action or

44. 'The Golden Cockerel' (Rimsky-Korsakov), set design by Ivan Bilibin for Act 2 (the tent of the Queen of Shemakha) for the original production at the Solodovnikov Theatre, Moscow, in 1909

45. 'Götterdämmerung' (Wagner, 1876), Brünnhilde (Deborah Polaski) is brought to Gunther (Alan Held) in Act 2 of the production by Richard Jones (designed by Nigel Lowery) at the Royal Opera House, Covent Garden, in 1995

Aperçu du Décor du 3ᵉ acte.

Guillaume Tell

Paysans

N.º 9.

Chœurs

Bands

Above: 46. *'Guillaume Tell'*
(Rossini, 1829), Act 3 scene ii
(the square at Altdorf); water-
colour, probably by Franz Peirot,
from a manuscript mise-en-scène
(c1840) designed to convey
details of the original Paris
production to provincial (and
foreign) theatres intending to
stage the opera

Left: 47. *'Guillaume Tell'*
(Rossini), one of the costume
designs by Hippolyte Lecomte
(for a peasant) for the original
production at the Paris
Opéra in 1829

Right: *48. 'L'incoronazione di Poppea' (Monteverdi, 1643), Janet Baker as Poppaea and Robert Ferguson as Nero in the 1971 production at Sadler's Wells, London*

Below: *49. 'Idomeneo' (Mozart, 1781), quartet from Act 3 in the production by Michael Hampe (designed by Martin Rupprecht) at Drottningholm, with Stuart Kale (Idomeneo), David Kuebler (Idamante), Ann-Christin Biel (Ilia) and Anita Soldh (Electra)*

Above: 50. 'Les Indes galantes' (Rameau, 1735), La Fête du Soleil, from the co-production between the Paris Opéra, Teatro Comunale, Florence, and Montpellier Opéra (directed by Jean-Marie Villégier, with sets by Carlo Tommasi and costumes by Patrice Cauchetier), performed by Les Arts Florissants at the Teatro Metastasio-Prato, Florence, in 1986

Left: 51. 'L'italiana in Algeri' (Rossini, 1813), design for a costume for Isabella in a production at La Scala, Milan, in 1823

52. 'Jenůfa' (Janáček, 1904), scene from Act 3 in the production by Nikolaus Lehnhoff (designed by Tobias Hoheisel) at Glyndebourne Festival Opera in 1989, with Anja Silja (the Kostelnička), Roberta Alexander (Jenůfa) and Philip Langridge (Laca)

53. 'Kát'a Kabanová' (Janáček, 1921), Act 1 scene ii of the production by Nikolaus Lehnhoff (designed by Tobias Hoheisel) at Glyndebourne Festival Opera in 1988, with Nancy Gustafson (Kát'a) and Felicity Palmer (Kabanicha)

54. 'King Priam' (Tippett, 1962), scene from a revival (1985) of the original production by Sam Wanamaker (designed by Sean Kenny) at the Royal Opera House, Covent Garden, with Kim Begley (Achilles) and Robert Dean (Patroclus)

55. 'Lady Macbeth of the Mtsensk District' (Shostakovich, 1934), scene from the 1994 revival of the 1992 production by André Engel (sets Nicky Rieti, costumes Nicky Rieti and Nicole Galerne) at the Paris Opéra (Bastille), with Anatolij Kotscherga (Boris) and Paolo Barbacini (Zinovy)

56. 'Legend of the Invisible City of Kitezh' (Rimsky-Korsakov, 1907), scene from the Kirov Opera production at the Edinburgh Festival, 1995

57. 'Lohengrin' (Wagner, 1850), scene from Act 1 of the Werner Herzog production (designed by Henning von Gierke) at Bayreuth, 1980, with Paul Frey (Lohengrin), Nadine Secunde (Elsa), Manfred Schenk (King Henry), Ekkehard Wlaschika (Telramund) and Gabriele Schnaut (Ortrud)

58. 'The Love for Three Oranges' (Prokofiev, 1921), scene from the production by Frank Corsaro (designed by Maurice Sendak) at Glyndebourne Festival Opera in 1982, with Ryland Davies as the Prince

Sophie Arnould as Iphigenia in Gluck's 'Iphigénie en Aulide': bust by Jean-Antoine Houdon (1741–1828)

the music. In this opening arioso Agamemnon calls defiantly to Diana that he will not sacrifice his daughter: it leads into his air 'Brillant auteur de la lumière'. The music remains fluid, with tempo changes and passages of recitative within the air. Agamemnon has done all he can, and admits that if Iphigenia comes to Aulis nothing can save her.

The Greeks ask Calchas how the gods may be placated. Calchas and Agamemnon sing of the severity of the necessary sacrifice; a prayer to Diana ensues. The Greeks demand to know the victim; without disclosing Iphigenia's name, Calchas promises that the sacrifice will be made that very day.

Alone with Calchas, Agamemnon asks if the gods can really command a father to kill his daughter (air, 'Peuvent-ils ordonner qu'un père'). Calchas's reference in the ensuing recitative to Iphigenia's already being on her way is immediately answered by a brief chorus of Greeks announcing the arrival of Clytemnestra and Iphigenia. In a march-like air, 'Au faîte des grandeurs', Calchas reflects on the feebleness of mortals, even at the height of splendour; and in a minuet-like chorus the Greeks welcome Iphigenia and her mother ('Que d'attraits, que de majesté'). An expression of grief is heard from Agamemnon under the beginning of the chorus: Arcas has failed to prevent Iphigenia from coming. Agamemnon leaves just before Clytemnestra and Iphigenia enter. After Clytemnestra's short air of gratitude ('Que j'aime à voir ces hommages

flatteurs'), there is a *divertissement*, a series of dances and choruses (shorter and more succinct in the 1775 version than in the original), during which Iphigenia herself has a short air, 'Les voeux dont ce peuple m'honore'.

Clytemnestra interrupts: she has been told by Agamemnon, in a last desperate measure to save his daughter, that Achilles has been unfaithful to Iphigenia, and Clytemnestra, in a fierily indignant da capo aria, 'Armez-vous d'un noble courage', urges her to prepare to leave. Left alone, Iphigenia is at first incredulous, then laments that she ever loved Achilles (air, 'Hélas! mon coeur sensible et tendre'). Achilles now enters, amazed to see Iphigenia in Aulis, and even more so to hear of his supposed infidelity. He refutes her accusations and assures her of his love in a dialogue in recitative and arioso, incorporating an air for each of them before a final duet in which they call on the god of marriage to unite them that very day ('Ne doutez jamais de ma flamme') .

Act 2 (as Act 1) Iphigenia's attendants reassure her that Achilles will marry her, although he has been told that Agamemnon suspected he had scorned her love (chorus, 'Rassurez-vous, belle Princesse'; in the 1774 version a short simile air follows for one of the Greek women, 'L'indomptable lion ardent', and the chorus is repeated). Iphigenia responds reflectively but becomes more animated when she sings of her changing emotions, Agamemnon's pride and Achilles' anger ('Par la crainte et par l'espérance').

Clytemnestra tells Iphigenia that preparations are being made for her marriage, to which Agamemnon has now consented. Achilles enters with his friend Patroclus and after a march for the Thessalians Achilles presents Patroclus to Iphigenia and leads the Thessalians in a rousing military chorus in her praise: 'Chantez, célébrez votre reine!' A *divertissement* follows (much longer in the 1775 revision, where the dances and choruses are a celebration of Achilles' valour, during which Iphigenia frees the slaves whom he has brought from Lesbos). After a ceremonial quartet and chorus to Diana ('Jamais à tes autels'), Arcas enters and, unable to control himself any longer, tells them that Agamemnon is waiting at the altar not to marry Iphigenia to Achilles but to sacrifice her. Arcas's words at the crucial disclosure (unaccompanied, so that they are clearly heard) are greeted with outbursts of horror from the other principals and the chorus. Clytemnestra poignantly begs Achilles to save Iphigenia (air, 'Par un père cruel à la mort condamnée'), then Iphigenia herself leads a trio in which she expresses her love for her father while Clytemnestra and Achilles rant against him, the three of them finally uniting in an appeal to the heavens ('C'est mon père, Seigneur').

Clytemnestra and Iphigenia leave, and in a short air which veers between anger and tenderness (Allegro and Lento) Achilles sends Patroclus to tell Iphigenia that he will contain his fury and respect her father ('Cours, et dis-lui'). But in the next scene Achilles' confrontation with Agamemnon becomes more and more heated until it erupts into a fiery duet ('De votre audace téméraire'). Achilles tells Agamemnon that he will have first to kill him before he sacrifices his daughter.

Alone, Agamemnon wavers between his duty to Greece and his love for his daughter. He sends Arcas to take Iphigenia and Clytemnestra to Mycenae; then follows an arioso with abrupt changes of mood and tempo, leading to an air whose sighing phrases and desolate minor key express Agamemnon's love for his daughter ('O toi, l'objet le plus aimable'); this extended scene ends with Agamemnon resolute and defiant as he tells the goddess to take his life rather than Iphigenia's.

Act 3.i (as Act 1) The assembled Greeks brutally demand the sacrifice in a diatonic, homophonic chorus which returns several times in this act. Iphigenia has refused to leave with Arcas and tells him to take care of Clytemnestra during the sacrifice. Achilles hurries in and calls on Iphigenia to leave with him. She replies that she must submit to her destiny ('Il faut de mon destin') and, after further pleas from Achilles, she declares her love for him and bids him farewell ('Adieu, conservez dans votre âme'). But Achilles is still determined to save her, as he makes clear in a heroic bravura air, with prominent horns and trumpets: 'Calchas, d'un trait mortel percé'.

Alone, Iphigenia reflects, but is interrupted first by the impatient Greeks and then by Clytemnestra, who also expresses her willingness to die for her daughter. Iphigenia's farewell to her mother ('Adieu, vivez pour Oreste') is also twice interrupted, by Clytemnestra herself and by the Greeks. She goes, and Clytemnestra gives vent to her rage in a recitative; an extraordinary arioso follows in which she has a vision of the sacrifice. She begins hesitantly, 'Ma fille! Je la vois', becoming more impassioned, her voice rising with the oboe phrases, until she sees Agamemnon about to kill Iphigenia; then she bursts into a passionate plea to Jupiter, her father, to send his thunderbolts into the Greek camp ('Jupiter, lance la foudre!'). When she has finished, she hears off stage the Greeks singing a processional hymn on their way to the sacrifice; her anguished comments are heard over the chorus, much as Agamemnon's were in Act 1.

3.ii *A seashore with an altar* Iphigenia is kneeling on the altar steps; behind her is the High Priest holding the sacred knife, his hands stretched out towards the heavens. The Greeks' hymn is broken off at the arrival of Achilles and his Thessalians, determined to save Iphigenia, who nevertheless begs the gods to take their victim ('Grands Dieux! Prenez votre victime!'). Most of the music of this scene is based on the Greeks' chorus heard earlier. Calchas interrupts the skirmish between Greeks and Thessalians: he tells them that Diana has changed her mind and a sacrifice is no longer required. (Gluck replaced this denouement in the 1775 revision by having the goddess herself appear, thus removing the ambiguity of Calchas' change of heart in the face of a challenge to his divine powers by Achilles; the only gain in the 1775 version is that Diana gives her blessing both to the wedding of Achilles and Iphigenia and to the Greeks' voyage to Troy.) There is a quartet of rejoicing for Iphigenia, Clytemnestra, Achilles and Agamemnon ('Mon coeur ne saurait contenir'), which leads to a chorus ('Jusques aux voûtes étherées').

The original version ended with a lengthy *divertissement* including an air for a Greek woman ('Heureux guerriers') and a chaconne, interrupted just before the end by Calchas, exhorting the Greeks to great conquests. The opera ended with a sinister war chorus, 'Partons, volons à la victoire', with stark, bare octaves and crude thumps on the bass drum, perhaps with a hint of irony; this was omitted from the 1775 version, which had an expanded final *divertissement* including the magnificent passacaglia from the Act 1 *divertissement* of 1774.

*

While *Iphigénie en Aulide* may lack the unity of conception, construction and style of *Iphigénie en Tauride*, in its original version it is one of Gluck's most powerful dramas; to an extent the revision, with its alterations to suit French taste, can be regarded as something of a compromise. The continuity of the opera's action is ensured by the long stretches of continuous music as Gluck elides in a masterly fashion the free forms of recitative and arioso with arias and ensembles. The three extended *divertissements* are not integrated into the drama as thoroughly as in some of Gluck's other Paris operas, but the dramatic irony of that in Act 1 is highly effective.

Of the opera's characters, Agamemnon and Clytemnestra are no less important than Iphigenia, and all of them are among Gluck's most memorable creations: Agamemnon with his two great monologues in the first two acts which are without precedent in the history of opera, Clytemnestra with her passionate arias and her visionary scene in Act 3, and Iphigenia herself, whose growth from the young lover of Act 1 to her heroic exaltation at the thought of dying for her father and her country in the third is so effectively conveyed in her music. The music broke new ground too with its combination of Italian lyricism and melody and French declamation, a formula Gluck was to use in various ways in all his Paris operas and of which he was justifiably proud. 'I have found a musical language fit for all nations', he wrote to the *Mercure de France* in February 1773, 'and hope to abolish the ridiculous distinctions between national styles of music'.   J.H.

Iphigénie en Tauride ('Iphigenia in Tauris')

Tragédie in four acts by Christoph Willibald Gluck to a libretto by Nicolas-François Guillard after Guymond de la Touche's *Iphigénie en Tauride*, itself based on Euripides; Paris, Académie Royale de Musique (Opéra), 18 May 1779.

The principals in the first performance were Rosalie Levasseur (Iphigenia), Henri Larrivée (Orestes), Joseph Legros (Pylades) and Moreau (Thoas).

Iphigénie [Iphigenia] *High Priestess of Diana*	soprano
Oreste [Orestes] *King of Argos and Mycenae, Iphigenia's brother*	baritone
Pylade [Pylades] *King of Phocis, Orestes' friend*	tenor
Thoas *King of Tauris*	bass
Diane [Diana] *goddess of hunting*	soprano
First Priestess	soprano
Second Priestess	soprano
A Scythian	bass
A Minister	bass
A Greek woman	soprano

Priestesses, Scythians, Eumenides (Furies), guards and Greeks
Setting Tauris (modern Crimea), after the Trojan War

Iphigénie en Tauride was the sixth of Gluck's seven operas for Paris. While it is a 'sequel' to *Iphigénie en Aulide* in that it deals with events following Iphigenia's supposed sacrifice, at the end of the earlier opera there is little indication of the coming violence – the Trojan War, the homecoming of Agamemnon and later of Orestes – which is over by the time the present one begins. Iphigenia has been transported to Tauris by Diana and has become a priestess; Orestes has avenged the death of his father by killing his mother and her lover. The subject, a popular one, had already been used for several French and Italian operas including a 'reform opera' by Tommaso Traetta which Gluck had conducted in Vienna in 1763. By a strange coincidence Goethe's play *Iphigenie auf Tauride* was first performed in Weimar the year Gluck's opera had its première in Paris. The first known reference to Gluck's setting is

in a note he drafted before signing his contract with the Académie Royale de Musique in 1775; two of his letters from that year make it clear that Marie François Louis Gand Leblanc Roullet, his collaborator for *Iphigénie en Aulide* and the French *Alceste*, was at work on the libretto. It is not clear why or at what stage Roullet passed it on to the young Parisian poet Guillard. The evidence suggests that it was in 1776, but it is impossible to be certain, partly because Gluck's behaviour concerning the libretto and the music appears to have been secretive to the point of deviousness. This was probably to keep secret the subject of his next opera from Niccolò Piccinni, who had been brought to Paris by the directors of the Académie Royale de Musique as a rival to Gluck. In the event the Académie gave Piccinni a different libretto on the Iphigenia in Tauris story, by A. de Congé Dubreuil, but this opera was a comparative failure when it was first performed in 1781 while Gluck's had been an unqualified success two years before.

Gluck made a German version of the opera for performance in Vienna on 23 October 1781. The translation was made by the young Viennese writer Johann Baptist Edler von Alxinger; Gluck altered the music to fit the new German libretto and amended the orchestration where the text required it. The major revisions were the transposition of the part of Orestes from baritone to tenor and the replacement of Iphigenia's last recitative and the chorus of priestesses at the end of Act 2 by an instrumental sinfonia.

Iphigénie en Tauride has always been one of Gluck's most frequently performed operas. It was first seen in London in 1796 in Lorenzo da Ponte's Italian translation. One of the most important interpreters of the title role in the 19th century was Wilhelmine Schröder-Devrient. Richard Strauss made his own version for the Weimar Hoftheater in 1889, rewriting many of the recitatives, altering certain of the numbers in Act 1, joining the third and fourth acts together and revising the end of the opera; he linked many of his elaborate revisions by a new musical motif of his own. Like Wagner's revision of *Iphigénie en Aulide*, Strauss's of *Iphigénie en Tauride* is of interest as one great composer's view of another, but although it was quite often performed at the beginning of the century (it was the version used for the work's première at the Metropolitan Opera in 1916), it is now rarely heard. It was recorded in 1961 with Montserrat Caballé in the title role.

Revivals of *Iphigénie en Tauride* in the 20th century have included performances conducted by Carlo Maria Giulini in Aix-en-Provence in 1952 with Patricia Neway as Iphigenia and Léopold Simoneau as Pylades, later recorded. Another famous production which also found its way on to record, albeit 'privately', was that directed by Luchino

'Iphigénie en Tauride' (Gluck): drawing by Gabriel de Saint-Aubin showing the appearance of the goddess Diana at the denouement of Act 4 in the original production at the Paris Opéra (Académie Royale de Musique, Palais-Royal), 18 May 1779

Visconti at La Scala in 1957 with Maria Callas (sung in Italian). In 1961 Rita Gorr sang Iphigenia at Covent Garden with Sir Georg Solti conducting; that year she recorded excerpts from it conducted by Georges Prêtre. Régine Crespin sang it at the Paris Opéra in 1965; a new production there in 1984 featured Shirley Verrett as Iphigenia and Thomas Allen as Orestes. Productions in Britain have been conducted by Roger Norrington at the Edinburgh Festival (1979) and John Eliot Gardiner at Covent Garden (1973, with Sena Jurinac); Gardiner also conducted it in Lyons in 1983 with Diana Montague and this production was subsequently recorded. Diana Montague also sang the title role in Welsh National Opera's 1992 production.

*

Act 1 *The sacred wood of Diana with the entrance to her temple in the background* The opera begins with a gentle minuet (called 'Le calme'), suddenly interrupted by a tempestuous Allegro which depicts the approaching storm. The orchestral tumult is crowned by the entry of the piccolo, and then – when the storm is at its height – by the voice of Iphigenia, soon joined by her priestesses, begging the gods to help them. This is one of the most remarkable openings in the

history of opera. In the preface to *Alceste*, Gluck and Ranieri de' Calzabigi had said that the overture should forewarn the audience of the nature of the drama to follow; although he had done this in *Alceste* and *Iphigénie en Aulide*, Gluck went much further in *Iphigénie en Tauride* by introducing the voice in the middle of what seems to be an instrumental overture with a slow introduction. The orchestral tempest symbolizes Iphigenia's inner torment, as she explains in the recitative that follows when the storm has died away. She describes her dream the previous night in which she saw first her father, Agamemnon, fleeing from his murderer, her mother Clytemnestra; then she saw her brother Orestes, but a fatal power forced her to kill him. So, in a succinct recitative, Gluck explains the events so far, as well as preparing for what is to follow. After a short lament for the priestesses, Iphigenia bewails the hopelessness of her situation, and then in an intense, almost serenely despairing air, begs the goddess Diana to take her life so that she can be with Orestes once again ('O toi qui prolongeas mes jours').

After another sorrowful chorus for the priestesses, Thoas rushes in. He too has been frightened by the storm and, having consulted the oracles, demands that Iphigenia does her duty and sacrifices a stranger to appease the gods. Thoas's air 'De noirs pressentiments', with its restless dotted rhythms and almost incessant semiquavers in the bass, depicts his obsession. The Scythians crowd in and press their king's demands for a sacrifice. One of them reveals that two Greeks have been cast up on to their shore during the storm, and despite Iphigenia's protests Thoas sends her to prepare for their sacrifice. The Scythians' choruses and the short dances that follow are in the exotic, so-called Turkish style so popular in the 18th century, with piccolos, tambourine, triangle and cymbals to the fore.

Orestes and Pylades are brought in. Thoas tells them of their fate; as they are led away, Orestes, in an expressively harmonized phrase, blames himself for bringing Pylades to his death.

Act 2 *A chamber in the temple set aside for victims; on one side is an altar* Orestes and Pylades are in chains. Orestes is prey to guilt and remorse: the music of his exclamation, 'Dieux! à quelles horreurs m'aviez-vous réservé', echoes Iphigenia's entry in the first act. Orestes' recitative culminates in an agitated air, 'Dieux qui me poursuivez', with horns, trumpets, timpani and tremolando strings, in which he begs the gods to cast him into hell for his crime. Pylades responds with a serene, lyrical air in which he assures Orestes of his undying friendship ('Unis dès la plus tendre enfance').

A minister of the sanctuary enters and takes Pylades away. Believing that Pylades has gone to his death, Orestes calls furiously on the gods to strike him down; his anguished recitative is restless in rhythm and unstable in harmony. This yields to more tranquil music before his arioso 'Le calme rentre dans mon coeur!'; that the calm is illusory is made clear by the violas' uneasy ostinato rhythm, on the same note for 28 bars.

Orestes sinks into sleep, only to dream that he is possessed by the Eumenides, come to torment him for killing his mother (Gluck specifies that the Furies should be seen on the stage; they appear to the same music as began Orestes' previous recitative, but enriched by the addition of three trombones, and sing a chorus which seems like a parody of Baroque polyphony: 'Vengeons et la nature'). Orestes begs them to have pity; then, at the climax of the scene, he awakens thinking that he sees his mother. But it is actually Iphigenia (a dramatic masterstroke, Gluck's idea rather than Guillard's). So many years have passed that neither recognizes the other. Iphigenia asks Orestes for news of Mycenae: he tells her of the murder of Agamemnon by Clytemnestra and how Orestes in turn killed his mother – adding that at last Orestes had found the death he had looked for. Iphigenia, overcome, tells him to leave her; after a short chorus for the priestesses she sings a grief-laden air, 'O malheureuse Iphigénie'. Like several other laments by Gluck (including that from *Orfeo*, 'Che farò senza Euridice'), it is in a major key. Again there are persistent accompaniment figures in the orchestra, and the syncopated first violins are as obsessive here as the violas were, in a different context, earlier in the act. Iphigenia and her priestesses now perform funeral rites for Orestes in a ceremonial chorus.

Act 3 *Iphigenia's apartment* Iphigenia tells her priestesses that she will yield to their wishes and send one of the captives to Greece to tell her sister Electra of their sufferings in Tauris. She is struck by the resemblance of one of the prisoners to her brother Orestes, and laments that she will be reunited with her brother only when she dies (air, 'D'une image, hélas!'). Orestes and Pylades are brought in; Iphigenia is moved by their mutual devotion. In the trio 'Je pourrais du tyran', the three characters express different emotions: Iphigenia her indecision, and the two friends their eagerness to die for each other. Finally Iphigenia announces that Orestes will take the message to Greece, and leaves the men arguing for the right to die ('Et tu prends encore').

The music of the Furies returns as Orestes begs Pylades to let him be the one to die, so that he can escape the Furies. In a more lyrical air ('Ah, mon ami'), Pylades begs Orestes to abide by Iphigenia's decree, but when she returns Orestes threatens to kill himself unless she changes her mind and sends Pylades instead of him. She has to agree; as Orestes is led away, Iphigenia gives Pylades the letter for

Electra. He ends the act with a rather conventional, heroic, bravura air ('Divinité des grandes âmes').

Act 4 *The interior of the temple of Diana; the statue of the goddess is mounted on a dais, and to one side is the sacrificial altar* Iphigenia, in anguish, prays to Diana to give her strength to perform the sacrifice ('Je t'implore et je tremble': a virtuoso, italianate aria based on the Gigue from J. S. Bach's Partita no.1 in B♭). The priestesses, singing to Diana, lead Orestes in. The proximity of the relief of death has given him a new serenity which finds expression in a short, very French air ('Que ces regrets touchants'). The priestesses sing a processional hymn to Diana ('Chaste fille de Latone') as they prepare him for the sacrifice.

Orestes is led to the altar. Iphigenia once more calls on the gods to give her strength, and takes the sacrificial knife. 'Iphigénie, aimable soeur! C'est ainsi qu'autrefois tu péris en Aulide' ('My beloved sister Iphigenia, thus did you too perish in Aulis'), mutters Orestes as she is about to strike the fatal blow. 'Mon frère' ('My brother'), she replies, followed by an outburst of astonished joy from the priestesses. This recognition takes merely a few bars of recitative, lightly accompanied; and Iphigenia's air of jubilation is then cut short when a Greek woman comes to warn them of the approach of Thoas who has heard that one of the captives has left Tauris.

In the confusion that follows, Thoas determines to sacrifice Orestes himself, even when he knows his true identity; but then Pylades returns with an army of Greeks and kills Thoas. To the music of the tempest from Act 1, there is a brief skirmish between the Greeks and Thoas's army of Scythians; then Diana herself appears, halts the fighting, and tells the Scythians to return her statues to the Greeks. She tells Orestes that his remorse has effaced his guilt, and sends him to rule as King of Mycenae, taking Iphigenia to Greece with him. Orestes offers his thanks in a brief, minor-key arioso 'Dans cet objet charmant'. The opera ends with a chorus of departure and a return (or allusion) to the calm sea of the opening, 'Les Dieux, longtemps en courroux'. Gluck wrote no music for the customary concluding ballet, which was supplied by François-Joseph Gossec.

*

Iphigénie en Tauride was the crowning achievement of Gluck's career, a result of the combination of his lifelong experience as an opera composer and a libretto which is arguably the best he ever set. The opera is one of Gluck's most tightly constructed, and although the action moves quickly and the tension is seldom relaxed for long, he still left room for dramatic and lyrical expansion. Each of Gluck's late operas is unique; even in his 60s he was a tireless experimenter. *Iphigénie en Tauride* has an unusual number of ensembles, and although there are more arias than, for example, in *Armide*, he strikes a balance between these more italianate set pieces and the French declamation and short airs, leading to a comparable fluidity of musical structure which always serves the development of the drama. Of all Gluck's operas, *Iphigénie en Tauride* is the one in which he was most successful in bringing his theories of operatic reform to life in a memorable combination of music and drama in which every detail is subordinate to the whole.   J.H.

Iris

Melodramma in three acts by Pietro Mascagni to a libretto by Luigi Illica; Rome, Teatro Costanzi, 22 November 1898.

Hariclea Darclée was Iris and Fernando De Lucia sang Osaka at the first performance.

Iris	soprano
Her Father	bass
Osaka	tenor
Kyoto	baritone
Citizens, geishas, samurai	
Setting Japan in the 19th century	

In 1896 Mascagni met Luigi Illica, from whom he had commissioned a new libretto and who suggested a tragedy set in Japan, a country which until then had inspired only Gilbert and Sullivan's operetta *The Mikado* in spite of the current vogue for exotic subjects. Mascagni asked him for a tragedy that could be treated realistically but in which the setting could colour the music. The libretto was ready as requested in the following April; fired by the subject, Mascagni completed the opera a year later. It was then performed, with minor revisions, at La Scala with considerable success, inaugurating the vogue for *fin-de-siècle* exotic opera.

Act 1 begins with the Hymn to the Sun as the citizens welcome the dawn. Iris, a young, poor and innocent girl, looks after and is the only support of her aged, blind Father. She appears from their simple house and relates a dream she has had. She has been noticed by Osaka, a rich young man who enlists the help of the brothel-keeper Kyoto to enable him to satisfy his passion. Under cover of a travelling theatre show which Osaka and Kyoto set up outside her house Iris is carried off; a payment is left in lieu for her Father, so legalizing the 'transaction' according to custom. The old man is given to understand that she has gone of her own free will, and rages at his absent daughter. In Act 2 she is confined to the brothel quarter, where Osaka tries vainly to arouse a passionate response from her: she

is frightened to take pleasure. Osaka leaves, bored, but Kyoto tries to lure him back by exposing Iris in public. Osaka's passion is again aroused, but the girl's Father arrives and she calls to him in relief. The old man, still unaware that she was forced to go, curses her as he flings ordure at her. She leaps from the window into an open sewer below. In Act 3 the sewer is being picked over by scavengers, who find Iris close to death. They steal her finery and run off as the sun rises. She dies in the warmth of the sunlight, as the Hymn to the Sun is heard once more.

*

Mascagni said that he did not want the music of *Iris* to be only 'arid comment' on the drama but that it should 'develop it with its own inexorable force'. This ingenuous declaration fails to conceal the true problem with the subject, the thinness of the action. In the third act, a protracted depiction of Iris's anguish in its symbolic relationship with the egoism of the three male characters, there is virtually none. The almost inevitable consequence is the introduction of an excessive number of character-pieces, among which is the grandiloquent Hymn to the Sun, a sort of orchestral-choral prologue with dances, arias and serenades. The static nature of the plot in relation to the exoticism of the setting was to pose a number of problems for Puccini in *Madama Butterfly* (1904), and it is obvious that some solutions common to both were first found by Mascagni. In the search for realistic orchestral sounds he made use of the shamisen, a long-necked Japanese lute with a piercing tone, and enriched the percussion with several Japanese instruments (bells, tam-tam, gong). All of these are used in the travelling-theatre scene in the first act. This, together with the beginning of Act 2, is the most colourful part of the whole score, when a Japanese play is performed on the stage, a theatrical device often used after *Pagliacci*. It is neatly interwoven with the abduction of Iris, using the dancers as an allegory of what is happening and at the same time serving as cover for the deed. The dominant features of the writing are the dynamic nuances, lyrical vocal texture and harmonic blends of unusual delicacy and originality, although Mascagni could not match what Puccini's greater skill and shrewdness were later to accomplish. His unremitting search for inspired melodies does not, however, fall into empty mannerism but serves the subject, on the lines of *Cavalleria rusticana*, and contributes to the success of the work as a whole.   M.G.

Italiana in Algeri, L' ('The Italian Girl in Algiers')

Dramma giocoso in two acts by Gioachino Rossini to a libretto substantially derived from Angelo Anelli's libretto for Luigi Mosca's *L'italiana in Algeri* (1808, Milan); Venice, Teatro S Benedetto, 22 May 1813.

The singers at the first performance were Marietta Marcolini (Isabella), Filippo Galli (Mustafà), Luttgard Annibaldi (Elvira), Annunziata Berni Chelli (Zulma), Giuseppe Spirito (Haly), Serafino Gentili (Lindoro) and Paolo Rosich (Taddeo).

Mustafà *Bey of Algiers*	bass
Elvira *wife of Mustafà*	soprano
Zulma *slave, confidante of Elvira*	mezzo-soprano
Haly *Captain of the Algerian Corsairs*	bass
Lindoro *young Italian, favourite slave of*	
Mustafà	tenor
Isabella *Italian lady*	contralto
Taddeo *companion of Isabella*	bass
Eunuchs of the harem, Algerian corsairs, Italian	
slaves, pappataci; women of the harem,	
European slaves, sailors (supernumeraries)	
Setting Algiers, about 1805	

The opera is Rossini's first *buffo* masterpiece in the fully fledged two-act form. It quickly won widespread popular acclaim in Italy and it was the first Rossini opera to be produced in Germany (1816, Munich) and France (1817, Paris). Paradoxically, it was the failure with Venetian audiences of Rossini's own *La pietra del paragone* (which had scored such a hit in Milan and elsewhere) that prompted a crisis in the schedule of the Teatro S Benedetto in late April 1813, a crisis exacerbated by the non-appearance of a promised opera by Carlo Coccia. To fill the gap, Rossini was commissioned to rework Anelli's libretto for *L'italiana in Algeri*, first set to music by Luigi Mosca for La Scala, Milan, in August 1808. Rossini completed the work in 27 days, in time for the première on 22 May 1813. Predictably, there were those in the audience during the opera's initial run ready to proclaim that the opera was a rehash of Mosca and secondhand Rossini. In fact, nothing could be further from the truth, as informed Venetian critical opinion rapidly acknowledged. This is not only one of Rossini's most brilliant scores but also one of his most original, with most of the music, including the famous overture, freshly written by him. The only parts of the score farmed out to his anonymous collaborator are the secco recitatives, Haly's Act 2 aria 'Le femmine d'Italia' and, possibly, the original Act 2 cavatina for Lindoro, 'Oh come il cor di giubilo'. It is not known for certain who helped Rossini adapt Anelli's libretto. What is clear is that the changes reflect Rossini's desire to strengthen and modify the character of the heroine Isabella and to bring to the big ensembles – the Act 1 finale, the stretta to the Act 2 quintet – the kind of manic verbal onomatopoeia that he delighted in setting to music.

Marcolini and Galli were leading artists for whom Rossini had already written important roles. The strength of the cast was said to have been an important factor in the opera's initial success; indeed, it was Marcolini's decision on 19 June to use the occasion of a charity night gala to sing Mosca's setting of 'Pensa alla patria' as well as Rossini's that finally scotched all talk of plagiarism by Rossini. When the production transferred to Vicenza in the summer of 1813, Marcolini commissioned from Rossini a new Act 1 cavatina, 'Cimentando i venti e l'onde', more closely aligned to the demands of her voice and technique than 'Cruda sorte!'; it has not, however, supplanted the original cavatina. For the Milanese première in 1814 Rossini made changes to the orchestration of 'Cruda sorte!' and substituted an obbligato flute for an obbligato cello in Isabella's Act 2 cavatina 'Per lui che adoro'. The Act 2 cavatina for Lindoro, 'Concedi, amor pietoso', partly based on music from *Tancredi* and also new to the score, is a more substantial piece than 'Oh come il cor di giubilo' and is more certainly a genuine Rossini composition than its predecessor. Rossini's final modification to the score came in Naples in 1815 when the politically inflammatory Rondo for Isabella in Act 2, 'Pensa alla patria' ('Think of your country'), was replaced by 'Sullo stil de' viaggiatori'; this, incorporating the overture's second theme, is certainly by Rossini himself – though nowadays there is little likelihood of 'Pensa alla patria' being banned by the censor. All Rossini's variants can be found in the appendices to Azio Corghi's definitive critical edition published in 1981 by the Fondazione Rossini, Pesaro.

The opera was frequently performed in Europe, and in the USA, in the period up to 1830 and rarely left the repertory even in the later years of the 19th century when Rossini's reputation was in widespread decline. Its revival in modern times dates from 1925 and a Turin production, conducted by Vittorio Gui, with Conchita Supervia as Isabella. Richard Strauss was among those reported to have been 'mad with enthusiasm' about the opera and Supervia's performance of the title role, something she repeated with equal success during famous revivals in Paris in 1929 and at the Royal Opera House, Covent Garden, in 1935. She recorded Isabella's three arias and part of the Act 1 finale ('O che muso') in 1927. Gui was also the conductor when the opera was produced at Glyndebourne in 1957 with Oralia Dominguez in the title role. Distinguished Isabellas of more recent times have included Teresa Berganza, Marilyn Horne, Lucia Valentini-Terrani and Agnes Baltsa. During the 1970s and 80s the opera was directed a number of times by Jean-Pierre Ponnelle, whose ability to reproduce on stage the patterns and rhythms of Rossini's score was as gratifying as it was amusing.

*

Title-page of the first edition of the vocal score of Rossini's 'L'italiana in Algeri', with a scene from the opera engraved by Cöntgen (Mainz: Schott, c1819; this copy bears the stamp of the selling agent Ricordi)

Act I.i *Mustafà's palace – a small hall in the Bey's apartments* Elvira laments the decision of her husband, the Bey Mustafà, to reject her. Zulma and the court eunuchs try to comfort her but the arrival of Mustafà confirms their worst fears. His Andantino 'Delle donne l'arroganza', full of grotesque intervals and elaborate coloratura, shows him to be arrogant and domineering. Mustafà orders Haly to arrange for Elvira to be married to Lindoro, his Italian slave; he also orders Haly, on threat of instant impalement, to find him an Italian girl to replace Elvira. Lindoro, meanwhile, laments his separation from the beautiful Isabella (cavatina, 'Languir per una bella'). In their duet 'Se inclinassi a prender moglie', Mustafà and Lindoro swap opinions on the desirability of the proposed match.

I.ii *The seashore* Haly and his men have sunk a ship and captured the survivors, among them an Italian girl, Isabella. In her cavatina 'Cruda sorte!' she grandly mourns her ill-fortune. But at Rossini's insistence a further element is added to the text of the cavatina; in the fleeting 'Già so per pratica' we encounter the wily, feline side of Isabella's nature. Isabella is determined to find her beloved Lindoro

and is irked by the constant amorous attentions of her travelling companion Taddeo. In the duet 'Ai capricci della sorte' they begin by wrangling but come to the reluctant conclusion that their present parlous state is not best served by arguing, and they should adopt the roles of uncle and niece. The duet is a perfect early example of Rossini's genius for using musical forms and conventions as the springboard of his comedy; the contrast between this and the almost unrelieved patter of the earlier Mosca setting is especially instructive.

I.iii *A small hall in Mustafà's palace* Haly reports the capture of a beautiful Italian girl and Lindoro is told he can return to Italy provided he takes Elvira with him. Mustafà's aria 'Già d'insolito ardore' reveals him aroused to fever-pitch as he contemplates the arrival of the Italian girl.

I.iv *A magnificent hall in Mustafà's palace* The philandering Mustafà is brought face to face with Isabella. As Isabella enters the hall the music makes a furtive step-by-step ascent from C to E♭, as if following Isabella's gaze as it travels upwards to Mustafà's face. A slow round begins with the words 'O che muso' ('My god, what a mug!'), a line that

Conchita Supervia made as memorable as Edith Evans's exclamation about the handbag in Wilde's *The Importance of Being Earnest*. In the music that follows, wonder, solemnity and barely suppressed laughter wittily coexist. Taddeo, intervening, narrowly escapes death by impalement. When Lindoro, Elvira and Zulma come to make their farewells, Isabella and Lindoro sing a minuet-like Andantino in G major, leading to a transition of Mozartian poignancy as the lovers, astonished, recognize each other. It is a transition that stands at the very heart of the opera, the lovers' suppressed ardour touchingly juxtaposed with Mustafà's bumbling expression of earthbound bemusement. Isabella guilefully announces that she could never love a man who treated his wife as Mustafà is treating Elvira. She also insists that Lindoro, being Italian, should be detailed to remain with her. The announcement sends the entire company into a state of delirium, their heads full of the sounds of bells ('din din', the women), a hammer ('tac tac', Lindoro), crowing ('cra cra', Taddeo) and a cannon ('bum bum', Mustafà).

Act 2.i *A small hall* (as Act 1.i) Everyone is amused at the antics of Mustafà, who has become a besotted lover. But Zulma is confident that things could work to Elvira's advantage, and it is Elvira who informs her apparent rival that Mustafà has invited Isabella to take coffee with him. Having convinced Isabella of his absolute fidelity to her, Lindoro is overjoyed when she agrees to attempt to escape (the alternative versions of his cavatina are discussed above). Further to ingratiate himself with Isabella, Mustafà proposes to appoint Taddeo to the position of Kaimakan, protector of the Muslims. Taddeo finds both the idea and the lavish costume quite unbearable ('Ho un gran peso sulla testa') but prudence in the face of Mustafà's anger persuades him to accept the position.

2.ii *A magnificent ground-floor apartment; behind it a loggia opens to the sea* Isabella tells Elvira to follow her advice. While she dresses in anticipation of her reunion with Lindoro she is secretly watched by Mustafà, Taddeo and Lindoro; but in fact she is aware of their presence, and her aria 'Per lui che adoro' is both a love song to Lindoro and a deception at Mustafà's expense. In the quintet 'Ti presento di mia man' Mustafà vainly tries to be alone with Isabella, but Lindoro and Taddeo refuse to leave. When Isabella invites Elvira to coffee in an attempt to

reconcile her with her husband, Mustafà is beside himself with anger and frustration. In an interlude, Haly sings of the wiles of Italian women. Isabella now plays her master card. As a token of her love, she offers to bestow upon Mustafà the Order of Pappataci, an order whose members lead a life exclusively given over to eating, drinking and sleeping. They also take a vow to keep silent, whatever dramas are playing around them. The 'Pappataci' trio for Mustafà, Taddeo and Lindoro is a splendid piece of foolery and one of the score's most diverting episodes. Isabella now rallies Mustafà's Italian servants, appealing to their sense of patriotism so that they become accomplices in her escape. Her rallying call, the recitative and rondo 'Pensa alla patria', has great power and a glorious, long-breathed solemnity of utterance, though she is also able to cope on the side with the cackling Taddeo. The asides to Taddeo apart, this is the kind of highly effective *opera seria* piece that no Italian composer before Rossini would have had the wit to include in a *buffo* entertainment. Lindoro announces that the Pappataci ceremony is about to begin. Mustafà's capacity for silence is tested as Isabella openly flirts with Taddeo; he fails and is quickly reprimanded. The scene is now set for Isabella and Lindoro to make their escape. A ship is to hand and under cover of the Pappataci ceremony Mustafà and Taddeo are easily duped as the lovers board it. Realizing too late what is happening, Taddeo tries to alert Mustafà, who recognizes that Italian girls are too clever for him. He begs forgiveness of his wife, gives the lovers his blessing and leads the company in wishing them a safe journey home as the boat is waved off.

*

L'italiana in Algeri is a work of great richness and sophistication. Formally it is an innovative piece, drawing Rossini's experience from his early single-act *farse* into a larger context. It is also, despite being written at speed, notably free from any kind of self-borrowing. The numbers that were farmed out to another composer, gracious and decorous in an 18th-century style, are by contrast a reminder of how fiercely the flame of Rossini's own comic invention burns in this remarkable opera, which transcends Mosca's earlier effort as surely as Rossini's *Il barbiere di Siviglia* was shortly to transcend Paisiello's.

R.O.

J

Jenůfa [*Její pastorkyňa* ('Her Stepdaughter')]

Opera in three acts by Leoš Janáček to his own libretto after Gabriela Preissová's play *Její pastorkyňa*; Brno, National Theatre, 21 January 1904. (*Pastorkyně* – in dialect, *pastorkyňa* – means simply 'not own daughter'; in the play and the opera, Jenůfa is both stepdaughter and foster-daughter to the Kostelnička. Janáček, when approving the German translation, was anxious to promote *Stieftochter*, 'stepdaughter', rather than *Ziehtochter* or *Pflegetochter*, 'foster-daughter'. 'Stepdaughter' and 'stepmother' have consequently been used in this article.)

At the first performance Jenůfa was sung by Marie Kábeláčová, the Kostelnička by Leopolda Svobodová, Laca by Alois Staněk-Doubravský and Števa by Bogdan Procházka (Theodor Schütz).

Grandmother Buryjovka *retired mill owner and now housekeeper at the mill*	contralto
Kostelnička Buryjovka *a widow, her daughter-in-law*	soprano
Jenůfa *stepdaughter of the Kostelnička*	soprano
Laca Klemeň *half-brother to Števa*	tenor
Števa Buryja *grandson of Grandmother Buryjovka*	tenor
Foreman *(at the mill)*	baritone
Jano *a herdboy*	soprano
Barena *servant girl at the mill*	soprano
Herdswoman	mezzo-soprano
Mayor	bass
Mayor's Wife	mezzo-soprano
Karolka *their daughter*	mezzo-soprano

Recruits, musicians, people from the mill, mill workers, country-folk, children

Setting A remote village in Slovácko (Moravian Slovakia), with a stream and a mill; some time between 1868 and 1890

As an opera composer Janáček was a late developer. *Jenůfa*, his first distinctive opera, was given only in his 50th year, and his greatest operas were written after the age of 65. His reputation was equally slow in coming, but he is now accepted as one of the 20th century's most substantial, original and immediately appealing opera composers.

Gabriela Preissová's play *Her Stepdaughter* was first given in Prague in 1890. The next year, Janáček set a libretto made from one of her short stories as his second opera, *The Beginning of a Romance*, and by 1893 seems to have been considering *Her Stepdaughter* as a possible libretto. He began preliminary work on 18 March 1894; by the end of the year he had written the overture 'Žárlivost' ('Jealousy'), originally conceived to open the opera though never used that way during Janáček's lifetime. Act 1 was probably written in full score between 1895 and 1897 but Janáček then dropped the opera for several years. When he took up the work late in 1901 it went faster; he completed Act 2 by summer 1902 and the whole opera by March 1903. He was able to play it to his daughter Olga on her deathbed; it is dedicated to her memory.

Janáček first offered it to the Prague National Theatre in March 1903. It was immediately rejected, possibly because of an antagonism towards him by the head of opera, Karel Kovařovic. The opera, however, was performed in Brno early the next year, conducted by Janáček's pupil Cyril Metoděj Hrazdira. Despite a tiny orchestra of 34, it achieved some popular success, and continued to be played in Brno and on provincial tours up to 1913. Prague, however, refused to take it up until 1915, when under great pressure from several friends of Janáček, Kovařovic's resistance weakened, and he consented to stage the work subject to his revisions (chiefly cuts and some reorchestration). Janáček agreed (he was 61, and had waited long enough), and the work was given a fine performance under Kovařovic on 26 May 1916. Soon afterwards, *Jenůfa* was translated into German by Max Brod (who thereafter translated most of Janáček's operas) and was given in Vienna in 1918. It was, however, the Berlin Staatsoper production of 1924 under Erich Kleiber which really established the work's reputation in Germany and which led to over 50 more performances before Janáček's death in 1928.

The vocal score (1908) incorporated revisions made by Janáček in 1906–7 (including several cuts suggested by Hrazdira). After the Prague production, the Czech publishing firm Hudební Matice issued a vocal score (May 1917) based on the original plates but also indicating Kovařovic's cuts. The German score issued by Universal Edition (December 1917) reproduced only the Kovařovic version.

It is in this form that the opera was known until Charles Mackerras's reconstruction of the Brno score, which was recorded by Decca in 1982. Universal Edition published a new edition of the score (1969) which restored an aria omitted by Janáček in 1904 and kept Kovařovic's revisions. In 1996 Universal Edition finally published the 'Brno (1908)' version, edited by Charles Mackerras and John Tyrrell, which opened the many cuts made by Kovařovic and returned to Janáček's original orchestration.

*

Act I *The Buryjovka mill, towards evening* The turning of the mill-wheel is represented at the beginning of the short prelude by a repeated xylophone note, a sound Janáček returned to several times during the act. The mill and what it represents is an important element in the motivation of the characters. After the death of his parents, the mill now belongs to Števa, while his elder half-brother Laca, having only a small inheritance, is forced to work there as a common labourer. Both are in love with their cousin Jenůfa, an orphan brought up by her stepmother. Jenůfa loves Števa, by whom she is pregnant, and as the curtain goes up she is seen waiting anxiously for his return from the annual conscription ceremony, 'Už se večer chýlí' ('Night is already falling'). If Števa is drafted into the army Jenůfa will not be able to marry him and her pregnancy will be revealed. Laca watches her suspiciously and in a bitter aria, 'Vy stařenko' ('You, Grandmother'), expresses his frustration and jealousy at the better lot, in love and in fortune, of his half-brother.

This opening scene also introduces three minor figures connected with the mill. There is Grandmother Buryjovka, its former owner, now living at the mill as a pensioner. She is harsh towards Laca but indulgent towards her two actual grandchildren, Števa and Jenůfa, and is easily pacified by Jenůfa when the latter apologizes for being unable to concentrate on her work, 'Stařenko, nehněvejte se!' ('Don't be cross, Grandmother!'). Next the herdboy Jano, whom Jenůfa has taught to read, runs on to announce this achievement. Finally there is the mill Foreman, a sympathetic older man, who gives Laca the opportunity to talk about Jenůfa (Laca denies, naturally, that he likes her at all). The Foreman also sharpens Laca's blunt knife for him, an incident whose significance is made clear only at the end of the act. At the end of this dialogue the Foreman announces the dramatic news that Števa has not, after all, been conscripted.

This produces a hubbub of reaction: Jenůfa is overjoyed, Laca furious. And soon the recruits can be heard approaching, singing a familiar anti-conscription song, 'Všeci sa ženija' ('All are getting married'), to a stage-band accompaniment, Janáček's skilful

and authentic evocation of Moravian folk instrumental ensembles.

At the climax of this ensemble, Števa enters. However glad she is to see him back, and not recruited, Jenůfa cannot help reproaching him for being drunk. This makes him show off, boasting of his conquests, and throwing money around for more music. He demands to hear Jenůfa's favourite song, 'Daleko široko' ('Far and wide'), here set as three stanzas sung by the chorus with instrumental music for dancing in between. The pace quickens and turns into a wild dance. At the climax a stern figure comes forward and with a single gesture silences the musicians. This is Jenůfa's stepmother, known as the Kostelnička. This word describes her honorary office at the local chapel, where she serves as sacristan. She is a woman of little means, but immense moral authority. She orders Jenůfa to wait a year before marrying Števa, during which time he must not get drunk. In an aria 'Aji on byl žlutohřívý' ('He too was golden-haired') that Janáček cut before it could be published in 1908 but was printed in the Universal score of 1969 and reinstated in several productions since, the Kostelnička explains her reasons. She had married Jenůfa's widowed father, the ne'er-do-well but attractive brother of the miller. Her husband soon squandered their wealth and died, leaving her to bring up his young daughter. The Kostelnička saw parallels between Jenůfa and herself and was anxious to spare her stepdaughter this fate. She leaves as abruptly as she entered. Grandmother Buryjovka sends away the musicians, tells Števa to get some sleep, and attempts to comfort Jenůfa with the thought that every young couple has to endure hard times. This gives rise to one of the more old-fashioned elements of the score, a full-scale slow concertato ensemble for four soloists and chorus composed on the Grandmother's words 'Každý párek si musí svoje trápení přestát' ('Every couple must get over its problems'). At its end the sound of the xylophone is heard once again, now rather more urgently and ominously.

The rest of the act is a series of confrontations between Jenůfa and her two admirers. The first is with the drunken Števa, who, scarcely penitent or aware of the full implications of the Kostelnička's ban, reacts angrily to Jenůfa's reproaches, even when they settle into a pleading Andante, 'Beztoho bude od mamičky těch výčitek dost, dost' ('Even so, there will be many, many reproaches from my mother'). His anger, however, soon dissolves into praise of Jenůfa's rosy cheeks ('Už pro tvoje jablúčkovy líce'), a lyrical moment in which Grandmother Buryjovka's voice joins those of Števa and Jenůfa for a brief trio before she hauls her grandson off to bed.

All this has been observed by Laca who, after another xylophone intervention, spitefully reminds

Jenůfa of how Števa boasted of his conquests. She refuses to be upset and Laca, goaded to distraction, takes out the knife the Foreman had been sharpening earlier. If all Števa cared for was Jenůfa's rosy cheeks how might he react if her beauty were disfigured? In a flash his knife does its work and her cheek is slashed. Laca is immediately horrified by his action, and in a brief ensemble his slow lyrical pain is poured out above the faster reactions of Barena the servant girl, and the Grandmother. The final voice is that of the mill Foreman, who declares that Laca did this on purpose.

Act 2 *A room in the Kostelnička's cottage, half a year later* The gloomy prelude (two meandering bassoons provide its chief melodic content) is punctuated by sharp chords and leads to a *fortissimo* outbreak before sinking back again – an evocation of despair and fear in the depths of winter. The Kostelnička has hidden Jenůfa away at her cottage where, eight days previously, she has given birth to a son. She is still weak and, after a short appearance notable for its tender 'baby music' (as Jenůfa contemplates her child) and a rare moment of duetting between the two women, Jenůfa is sent to bed with a sleeping draught. Alone, the Kostelnička sets to work. Her first plan is to beg Števa to marry Jenůfa. He reluctantly appears at her command and is subjected to urgent and even tender pleading, 'Pojď se, Števo, přece naň podívat' ('Come, Števa, do look at him'). She even kneels to him. But Laca's knife has done its work too well: Števa no longer thinks Jenůfa beautiful. He is going to marry the Mayor's daughter instead. He offers money, but not marriage, and hurries out.

The next visitor is Laca. He has come to see the Kostelnička frequently during the past months, to inquire about Jenůfa, whom he believes, like the rest of the village, to be in Vienna. Only now does he learn that Jenůfa has been at home all this while and has given birth to a child – Števa's child. Laca still wants to marry Jenůfa, but is so dismayed to hear about the child that the Kostelnička, in a fateful moment of decision, tells him that it died. She then sends him away on an errand. She must now prove her lie correct. After a highly dramatic monologue, one of the key moments of the opera in which she wrestles with her conscience and screws up her courage, 'Co chvíla' ('In a moment'), she runs from the cottage, carrying the child with her. Almost immediately Jenůfa wakes up from her drugged sleep and notes the absence of both her stepmother and the baby. She concludes that the Kostelnička must have taken him to show to the people at the mill. Calm at last, she offers up a prayer to the Virgin, a touching setting of the *Salve regina* in Czech ('Zdrávas královno').

The Kostelnička returns alone from her expedition to the icy millstream. She tells Jenůfa that the girl has been delirious for two days, during which the child died, a fact that Jenůfa accepts with tender resignation, 'Tož umřel' ('So he died'). And when Laca arrives soon after, she similarly accepts unresistingly his earnest proposal of marriage, urged on by the Kostelnička. As she blesses the union and then curses Števa, the window is forced open by the wind and, filled with foreboding, she cries out in terror. The five-note rhythm of her final word 'načuhovalo' ('[as if death] were peering in') forms the basis for an ominous postlude to the act.

Act 3 *A room in the Kostelnička's cottage, two months later* It is early spring and the cottage is filled with preparations for Jenůfa's wedding to Laca. Jenůfa has recovered her strength, whereas the Kostelnička is only a shadow of her former self and is helped out by a Herdswoman. The Mayor and his wife arrive and while the Kostelnička shows them the trousseau, Laca and Jenůfa are left alone: a deep relationship is beginning to form between the two. Števa arrives with his betrothed – the Mayor's daughter Karolka – and Jenůfa adroitly manages a reconciliation between the half-brothers. Finally a group of girls from the village bring flowers and sing a wedding song 'Ej, mamko, mamko' ('Hey mother') for Jenůfa. Grandmother Buryjovka gives her blessing to the pair and as the Kostelnička is about to add hers, a tumult is heard outside. Jano runs in with the news that workmen from the brewery sent to cut ice from the stream have discovered the frozen corpse of a little child. Jenůfa thinks it is her child, and the gathering crowd suspect her of murder. Laca holds off the mob but it is the Kostelnička who silences the people with her own confession of guilt, 'To můj skutek' ('It's my deed'). At first appalled, Jenůfa begins to understand the motives behind the Kostelnička's terrible action. In one of the great moments of opera she forgives her stepmother, who is then led off to stand trial (and under Austrian law of the time, to her death). The crowd follows, leaving Laca and Jenůfa alone on the stage. Jenůfa thinks that Laca can no longer want her in these circumstances, but she is wrong, and as he pleads with her, the stubborn dissonant note that has clouded the tonality throughout this scene suddenly disappears – a token of Jenůfa's hard-won acceptance of his love.

*

This final scene is known in two forms, the canonic apotheosis that Kovařovic elaborated from it, and Janáček's more sober orchestration, much more in keeping with the spiritual growth that is depicted in the opera. It is wrong to emphasize the violent actions of the opera – Laca's slashing of Jenůfa's cheek, the Kostelnička's murder of Jenůfa's baby – in an attempt to link the opera to the wave of *verismo* works written at the same time by Czech composers. Nor should too much be made of the folkish scenes in the outer acts; Janáček was keen to stress that though the words were authentic, the music was in fact his own. This is not a folklore opera, as was its predecessor, *The Beginning of a Romance*, and modern productions have sometimes dispensed with the traditional Moravian folk costumes to underline this. The opera instead belongs to a line in which the spiritual development of the characters is paramount, a line that can be seen running through Smetana's late operas and before that in Mozart's *Die Zauberflöte*. Laca and Jenůfa have quite visibly grown through the opera from obsessed and self-centred individuals in the first act to generous and understanding human beings in the last. The shocking course of events is not there for gratuitous violence, but as a depiction of the hard lessons they have had to learn. The Kostelnička has the hardest lessons of all and it is fitting that Janáček's title for the work should reflect that she is the main character.

J.T.

Jolie fille de Perth, La ('The Fair Maid of Perth')

Opéra in four acts by Georges Bizet to a libretto by Jules-Henri Vernoy de Saint-Georges and Jules Adenis after Walter Scott's novel *The Fair Maid of Perth*; Paris, Théâtre Lyrique, 26 December 1867.

The role of Catharine was composed for the coloratura of Christine Nilsson, although in the event it was Jeanne Devriès who sang it. Auguste-Armand Barré sang the Dove, Alice Ducasse was Mab and Henry was sung by Massy.

Catherine [Catharine] Glover	soprano
Henri [Henry] Smith	tenor
Simon Glover *Catharine's father*	bass
Mab *Queen of the gypsies*	soprano
Ralph *an admirer of Catharine*	bass or baritone
Duc de Rothsay [Duke of Rothesay]	baritone
A noble in Rothesay's service	tenor
Major-domo	bass
Citizens, gypsies	
Setting Perth, Scotland	

La jolie fille de Perth was commissioned by Carvalho, director of the Théâtre Lyrique, in July 1866, the choice of libretto being fixed by the terms of the contract. The commission confirmed Carvalho's faith in Bizet following *Les pêcheurs de perles* in 1863 and the unfinished *Ivan IV* in the intervening years. The librettists were experienced men of the theatre, especially Saint-Georges, yet the libretto is notoriously free in its treatment of Scott's novel and loose in its dramatic structure. Bizet was well aware of its faults and was unenthusiastic about the verse, yet he set to

work with great energy and completed the score before the end of 1866. The opera reached a public dress rehearsal on 10 September 1867, but for a variety of reasons the performances were postponed until December. Although it was well received, it did not draw good audiences and had only 18 performances, the same number as *Les pêcheurs de perles* had received in the same theatre four years before. A persistent criticism, with which Bizet privately agreed, was that the music had been 'sacrificed to the false gods of the quadrille, the *roucoulade*' and the 'concessions' of coloratura. The opera was played in Brussels in April 1868 but not revived until 1883, when it was subjected, like Bizet's other operas, to substantial posthumous disfigurement.

*

Act 1 takes place in the forge of Henry Smith. He is in love with Catharine, daughter of Simon Glover, whose name also indicates his profession. But Catharine is coquettish and likes to tease her admirers. Mab, the gypsy queen, suddenly rushes in. She sings some *couplets* ('Catherine est coquette'). Smith shelters her from her pursuers and hides her when Catharine, her father, and another admirer, Ralph, all enter. Smith and Catharine are alone together when the Duke of Rothesay arrives to have his dagger-blade repaired. Catharine, to make Smith jealous, pretends to flirt with the Duke. Smith is about to strike him when Mab emerges from hiding and thus arouses Catharine's jealousy.

At the start of Act 2 Glover and his friends are on patrol in Perth's city square. The Duke and some revellers are celebrating the carnival. There is a gypsy dance. The Duke enlists Mab's aid in getting Catharine to come masked to the ball that night. Mab, who was once the Duke's lover, sings more *couplets* ('Les seigneurs de la cour') and swears to be avenged on him. Smith does not share everyone's joy, but sings a doleful Serenade ('A la voix d'un amant fidèle'). He is drawn into a tavern as midnight strikes. Ralph, also drinking, falls asleep in the street but wakes to see a woman, actually Mab dressed as Catharine, being led to the Duke's palace. He finds Smith and tells him what he has seen, causing Smith to run off in pursuit. Ralph then hears Catharine singing Smith's Serenade from her house and realizes his mistake.

In Act 3 the Duke entertains his guests with a cavatina ('Elle sortait de sa demeure'). When Mab is brought in she refuses to unmask until the lights are out. Smith arrives, convinced of Catharine's faithlessness even when she appears with her father and denies it furiously. When he sees the Duke wearing a silver rose which he, Smith, had given her (it had passed through Mab's hands) his convictions are redoubled.

In the first tableau of Act 4 Ralph and Smith

dispute Catharine's honour and agree to fight. In the second tableau, Mab reports that the Duke stopped the fight. But Catharine has gone mad, singing a ballad ('Echo, viens sur l'air embaumé'). She thinks Smith is dead, but is brought to her senses when he sings his Serenade. Mab appears at the window in Catharine's clothes, and the whole imposture is revealed. Catharine thinks it was all a dream.

*

This libretto must be severely criticized not only for its remoteness from Scott and its garbling of his original characters but also for its dependence on such worn-out devices as mistaken identity, coincidence and wholly irrational events. It is hard to read the changing motivations and actions of Mab and Ralph, for example, although Smith, Glover and the Duke are all more consistent in character. Making Catharine coquettish justified her treatment as a coloratura, which in turn required a mad scene in the last act. It is hardly surprising that Bizet's dramatic gifts are given little scope, although he applies some deft motivic treatment at salient points. Nor did he attempt any Scottish colour at all, offering Bohemian and polonaise idioms instead. The strength of the opera lies in the vitality of its set pieces and individual numbers. Scenes of drinking and festivity, ensembles of bewilderment or challenge, duets and solos of different types: all this draws out the best from Bizet's muse, full of wonderful melodic, harmonic and instrumental invention. It is hard to accept that such a fresh score belongs to an unstageable opera, but its fate is always more likely to be in the form of extracts than as a dramatic continuum. Smith's Serenade, the best-known piece from the opera and well worthy of its celebrity, was borrowed from *Don Procopio*.   H.M.

Jonny spielt auf ('Jonny Strikes Up')

Oper in two parts by Ernst Krenek to his own libretto; Leipzig, Neues Theater, 10 February 1927.

The original cast, conducted by Gustav Brecher, included Paul Beinert as Max, Fanny Eleve as Anita, Max Spilcker as Jonny, Theodor Horand as Daniello and Clare Schulthess as Yvonne.

Max *a composer*	tenor
Anita *an opera singer*	soprano
Jonny *a negro jazz-band fiddler*	baritone
Daniello *a virtuoso violinist*	baritone
Yvonne *a hotel chambermaid*	soprano
Artists' Manager	tenor
Hotel Director	tenor
Railway Employee	tenor
Policeman 1	tenor
Policeman 2	baritone
Policeman 3	bass

Hotel guests, travellers and audience, glacier (chorus)

Setting A central European city, Paris and the Alps during the mid-1920s

In its first season *Jonny* was produced at 42 opera houses, including the Metropolitan, and performed 421 times in Germany alone, a record unmatched in a single season. By 1929 the libretto had been translated into 14 languages. Productions were lavish, with many special effects such as real cars and trains and film projection. The opera was eventually revived in Florence in 1963, and eight other productions have followed, notably the first British one, an English version by Opera North in 1984.

*

Part I.i *On top of a glacier in the Alps* Max, a melancholic intellectual composer (either a self-portrait of Krenek when young or a caricature of Webern), meets Anita, a glamorous singer who has performed a leading role in one of his operas. Max's hymn to the glacier is full of bland Romantic clichés. Anita finds the atmosphere of these rarefied heights sterile and morbid and Max is obliged to rescue her, significantly neglecting to press on to the summit.

I.ii *Anita's house in the city* Anita has melted the heart of her 'Glacier man' and they have been having an affair. He presents her with the manuscript of his latest opera, which she is about to sing in Paris. They rehearse a sentimental aria 'Ich suchte mein Heim in der Träume Land' ('I sought my home in dreamland'). A car arrives and she almost forgets her banjo, a vital prop for the opera.

I.iii *A hotel corridor in Paris* Yvonne is tidying Daniello's room, to a shimmy in a quick 'gramophone tempo', when Jonny, the symbolic manifestation of the new man free from sexual and musical inhibitions, and with whom she is in love, arrives with his golden saxophone; he, however, seems more interested in Daniello's Amati violin. Daniello, a virtuoso womanizer, returns in a throng of admirers and Yvonne joins them. Daniello persuades Anita to invite him to her room. Meanwhile Jonny steals the precious violin and hides it in Anita's banjo case.

I.iv *The following morning* Anita prepares to depart for home, leaving Daniello her ring as a keepsake, but taking Yvonne, dismissed after the theft of the violin, as her maid. Daniello, his ego bruised by Anita's confession that she is already attached to Max, persuades Yvonne to deliver the ring to Max, ostensibly as payment following a bet. Jonny resigns from his employment in Paris to pursue the banjo case. The Artists' Manager arrives and offers Anita a contract to tour America.

'Jonny spielt auf' (Krenek), Part 1, scene iii (a hotel corridor in Paris): scene from the original production at the Neues Theater, Leipzig, 10 February 1927

Part 2.i *Anita's house that evening* Max has received a telegram from Anita and longs for her return. Her failure to arrive as promised prompts a tortured psychological monologue, which parodies the expressionism of Schoenberg's monodrama *Erwartung.*

2.ii *The next morning* Anita finally arrives, altered by the Parisian experience, and greets Max nervously. The 'gift' of Anita's ring from Daniello confirming that she has been unfaithful badly upsets Max, who rushes off. Jonny reclaims the violin with Yvonne's help and celebrates triumphantly with a cross between a negro spiritual and a Lutheran chorale.

2.iii *The glacier* The mysterious solace of the mountains induces in Max thoughts of suicide as he realizes that nature can no longer provide him with sufficient inspiration. Spurred on by the singing glacier, which reiterates its message, he realizes he must respond to life itself if his music is to be vital. Just then a broadcast of Anita singing the aria from his opera is relayed by loudspeaker from the hotel terrace below. Admitting the extent of his need for Anita's life-force, Max resolves to seek his salvation in her. Significantly, the next item, to the great relief of the audience, is Jonny's jazz band, starring the stolen violin, which Daniello, by now a guest at the hotel, recognizes. The contrast of styles represents the past and future of music, in which the new appropriates the best of the European tradition in the form of Daniello's violin.

2.iv *A city street* Jonny is on the run with the violin, heading for America; in his haste he drops his train ticket.

2.v *The railway station* The discovery of Jonny's lost ticket leads the police to the station, where Max and Anita are also about to leave for America. Jonny places the violin among Max's luggage and Max is arrested instead. Assuming Anita and Yvonne to be accessories to the crime, Daniello tries to prevent them from leaving but falls on to the track and is crushed by the oncoming train.

2.vi *Outside the police station* With Jonny's help Max escapes by car.

2.vii *At the railway station* Max and Anita are reunited and with Yvonne and the Manager they board the train, singing optimistically in a simple tonal and homophonic idiom, punctuated by the strains of the violin from Jonny, who is straddling the revolving globe on the station clock. In striking up the new note it is he who leads the people in the dance towards a new life, where nothing is to be taken too seriously.

*

Jonny is one of the most characteristic products of the Weimar Republic, embodying the mythology and fashions of its time and reflecting a growing conviction that music should be entertaining and relevant. Its overwhelming popular success established it as a model for a spate of 'Zeitopern' (operas of their time), although it is fantastic and escapist compared with the more realistically ordinary settings of Hindemith. The plot, involving an opera, is laden with symbolism; it presents contradictions in psychology, lifestyle and temperament between the old world (East) and the new (West). Although the opera is largely set in Paris (the work is Krenek's response to his experiences there in the early 1920s), it is the image of America that focusses the European longing for a new land of freedom and promise. *Jonny* appeared to indicate a change of direction for Krenek, but in fact its kaleidoscopic nature draws on earlier compositions such as the jazz elements of *Der Sprung über den Schatten* (1923) and the world-weariness of his 1925 Rilke settings. Krenek, however, objected to the label 'jazz opera' for *Jonny* as the jazz in it was idiomatically superimposed rather than absorbed in any integral way. His usage is closer to that of Milhaud and Stravinsky than to Weill's. Krenek's eclecticism, particularly the return to tonality and Puccinian lyricism, reveals his sceptical attitude towards the role of contemporary music as assigned by the Second Viennese School.

The tremendous success of *Jonny* put Krenek firmly at the forefront of European culture between the wars. This was not least because as sheer entertainment it created an unprecedented impact on the contemporary operatic scene, but also because it exposed key issues about musical modernism and brought them to public attention. It raises questions about the relative validity of different sorts of music; whether these will remain as pertinent to future audiences as they did to Krenek himself at the time will affect the extent to which the work may transcend its original historical context and continue to succeed in revival. There is, however, little doubt that the expertly crafted eclecticism and period flavour of the opera will continue to attract admirers.

C.Pu.

Juive, La ('The Jewess')

Opéra in five acts by Fromental Halévy to a libretto by Eugène Scribe; Paris, Opéra, 23 February 1835.

The cast at the première included Cornélie Falcon as Rachel, Julie Dorus-Gras as Princess Eudoxie, Adolphe Nourrit as Eléazar and Nicolas Levasseur as Brogni.

Eléazar *a Jewish goldsmith*	tenor
Rachel *his daughter*	soprano
Cardinal Brogni *president of the Council*	bass
Léopold *prince of the Empire*	tenor
Princess Eudoxie *the Emperor's niece*	soprano
Ruggiero *the city provost*	baritone
Albert *sergeant in the Emperor's army*	baritone
Courtiers, clergymen, officers, soldiers, guards,	
heralds, town crier, hangman and citizens	
Setting Konstanz, Switzerland, in 1414	

The first production of *La Juive*, in 1835, was one of the most spectacular ever seen at the Opéra. The Act

1 procession and the Act 3 festival became famous for their splendour. One newspaper thought the procession, with all the leading figures on horseback, was the eighth wonder of the world.

Nothing is missing in this prodigious resurrection of a distant century. The costumes of the warriors, civilians and ecclesiastics are not imitated but reproduced in the smallest detail. The armour is not paste-board, it is real metal. One sees men of iron, men of silver, men of gold! The Emperor is a glittering ingot from head to foot! The Opéra may become a power capable of throwing its armies into the balance of power in Europe.

The role of Eléazar was written in response to Nourrit's request for a tenor role that was for once not a faultless hero. It has been a vehicle for many famous tenors and was a favourite part of Caruso's. The work – Halévy's first serious grand opera – won admiration from both Berlioz and Wagner; one of its greatest admirers was Mahler, who declared: 'I am absolutely overwhelmed by this wonderful, majestic work. I regard it as one of the greatest operas ever created'.

*

Act 1   A Te Deum is heard from the church at one side of the city square while the jeweller Eléazar and his workmen are hammering in their workshop at the other. The citizens object to Jews working on a Christian festival. Rachel, Eléazar's daughter, is in love with a man she knows as Samuel, who is in fact Prince Léopold pretending to be a Jew (he has fallen in love with her and so has found employment with her father). She is puzzled by his evident authority over the Emperor's soldiers in protecting the Jews from molestation by Ruggiero, the city provost, and by angry citizens.

Act 2   Léopold has joined Eléazar and Rachel in celebrating the Passover, although Rachel becomes anxious when he discards the unleavened bread. Princess Eudoxie comes to buy a gold chain as a gift for her husband (Léopold) to mark his victory over the Hussites. Léopold, who escapes notice by his wife, confesses to Rachel that he is in fact a Christian. She decides to give up everything for him even so, and Eléazar, though horrified at first, agrees to give him his blessing. To Rachel's distress, Leopold hints at other difficulties.

Act 3   At a fête in the Emperor's palace Léopold is honoured for his victory. Eléazar comes with Rachel to deliver the gold chain for Eudoxie to present. Rachel realizes that 'Samuel' is none other than Prince Léopold and publicly denounces him. For loving a Jewess he may be sentenced to death, and she would die too. Cardinal Brogni goes further by including Eléazar in his anathema for questioning the justice of this law, and has all three led away for trial.

'La Juive' (Halévy), Act 1 (procession through the city of Konstanz): design by Charles Séchan, Léon Feuchère, Jules Dieterle and Edouard Despléchin for the original production at the Paris Opéra (Salle Le Peletier), 23 February 1835; lithograph

Act 4 Eudoxie pleads with Rachel to save Léopold by retracting her charge; Brogni pleads with her to save them both by renouncing her faith; but she refuses. Eléazar, tormented by the thought that Rachel will die, but steadfast in his beliefs, also refuses. Brogni's daughter, he explains darkly, was saved many years before by some Jews; though he knows where she is, his revenge on Brogni will be to go to his death without revealing the information.

Act 5 Eléazar and Rachel are led to the scaffold. She has saved Léopold after all by swearing his innocence, to Eléazar's horror. Despite her father's pleas Rachel refuses to renounce her Jewish faith. Brogni begs Eléazar to reveal where his (Brogni's) daughter is. As Rachel is hurled into the boiling cauldron, he cries 'La voilà' ('There she is') and goes himself to his death. Rachel was thus not a Jewess at all.

*

The sensational dramaturgy of the libretto perfectly exemplifies Scribe's theatrical style. The plot is spring-loaded with inherently improbable facts (Rachel being in fact not Eléazar's daughter but Brogni's; her lover being in fact not a Jewish artisan but a Christian prince), the revelation of each of which creates a general *frisson* expressed normally by a large static ensemble. The background conflict between Christians and Jews provides a sense of menace sharpened by the emphasis on ceremony and spectacle; and, in Brogni and Eléazar, Scribe created two fanatics whose wills are doomed to end in collision. The success of *La Juive* must be attributed to these uninhibitedly stagy elements as well as to Halévy's music. He treated the Jewish scenes as local colour, not in any way identifying with them as a Jew himself. His orchestration is bold throughout, calling for left-hand pizzicatos in the violins and chromatic brass. The new valve trumpet has some prominent solos, including the melody in Rachel's 'O mon Dieu, que j'implore' in the finale of Act 1. Brogni's anathema in Act 3 is pronounced with valve trumpets and valve horns outlining his sombre descending scales. Anvils are heard from Eléazar's workshop. Halévy was to some extent hampered by Scribe's metric regularities and facile rhymes, but his melodic invention is strong and he proved himself well able to conjure up an atmosphere of desperate agitation (as in Eléazar's scene with Brogni in Act 4) or genial romantic passion (as in Léopold's Serenade in Act 1). Eléazar's great air, 'Rachel, quand du Seigneur' at the close of Act 4, is one of the opera's unforgettable scenes, a fine portrayal of Eléazar's tormented, fanatical soul.   H.M.

K

Kaiser von Atlantis, Der [Der Kaiser von Atlantis, oder Der Tod dankt ab ('The Emperor of Atlantis, or Death Abdicates')]

'Legend' in four scenes by Viktor Ullmann to a libretto by Petr Kien; Amsterdam, Bellevue Theatre, 16 December 1975.

The cast for the intended performance in 1944 included Marion Podolier, Hilde Aronson-Lindt, David Grünfeld (Pierrot and Soldier), Walter Windholz (Emperor Überall) and Karel Berman (Death). At the 1975 première the singers were Roberta Alexander (Girl), Inge Frölich, Adriaan van Limpt (Pierrot), Rudolf Ruivenkamp (Soldier), Meinard Kraak, Tom Haenen.

Emperor Überall	baritone
Death	bass-baritone
Pierrot	tenor
Loudspeaker	bass-baritone
Drummer	mezzo-soprano
Girl	soprano
Two female dancers	

The work was composed in 1943 in the Nazi concentration camp Theresienstadt (Terezín). Two versions of the libretto, one handwritten, the other typed, were made on the reverse side of prisoner information forms. The work is scored for seven singers and a medium-sized ensemble of available instruments.

In the Prologue (melodrama) the Loudspeaker, after introducing the characters, describes the situation in which the living no longer laugh, the dying no longer die, and life and death have lost their customary meanings. Death finds this repulsive and goes on strike: henceforth no one is allowed to die. Death regrets the passing of the old ways of dying and the coming of the new, mechanized methods of death; the Drummer announces, in the Emperor's name, that total war shall prevail. Scene ii (following an intermezzo, 'Dance of Death') is set in the Emperor's office, where he tries to discover if anyone has died, only to receive the same answer each time: no one can. In scene iii a Girl and Soldier from opposing camps fall in love, as the Drummer tries to uphold the Emperor's authority. Scene iv follows the second intermezzo ('The Living Death'). The

Emperor is again in his office, enraged at his impotence, although Pierrot and the Drummer try to soothe him. He finds Death standing behind a mirror and begs him to restore the status quo. Death agrees on condition that the Emperor is the first to die. He is at first unwilling, but finally consents and is led through the mirror by Death as the others sing a chorale.

The opera comprises recitatives, arias and ensembles (duets and trios), and the prelude and two intermezzos are danced. Ullmann's music and Kien's text inevitably mirror much of the tension and anxiety which the Terezín inhabitants felt in the face of an unknown but threatening fate. As with Ullmann's music generally, the style of the work is eclectic, ranging from that of Weill to the Second Viennese School. With its rich harmonic and contrapuntal textures, and its varied instrumentation and idiomatic vocal writing, a convincing sense of theatre emerges. The quotation of music known to the Terezín audience would no doubt have had a powerful impact had the work been presented there. Ullmann quotes the 'Angel of Death' motif from Josef Suk's *Asräel* symphony and uses a distortion of *Deutschland über Alles*. The final chorale, sung to the melody of *Ein' feste Burg ist unser Gott*, urges that life's end should be through the dignity of natural death and not through meaningless killing. Although rehearsals began in Terezín in September 1944, both censorship of the clear allusion to Hitler (the Emperor) and the increasing transports to Auschwitz prevented a production. (Ullmann himself was sent to Auschwitz the following month, where he died immediately. The same fate was suffered by Kien.) Since the opera's 1975 première, however, performances have been given in Europe, Israel and North and South America. **D.B.**

Kát'a Kabanová

Opera in three acts by Leoš Janáček to his own libretto after Alexander Nikolayevich Ostrovsky's play *Groza* ('The Storm') in the Czech translation by Vincenc Červinka; Brno, National Theatre, 23 November 1921.

The first Kát'a was Marie Veselá; Karel Zavřel (Boris), Jarmila Pustinská (Varvara), Marie Hladíková (Kabanová), Valentin Šindler (Kudrjáš) and Pavel Jeral (Tichon) also sang at the première, which was conducted by František Neumann.

Marfa Ignatěvna Kabanová (Kabanicha)
   a rich merchant's widow   contralto
Tichon Ivanyč Kabanov *her son*   tenor
Katěrina (Kát'a) *Tichon's wife*   soprano
Varvara *a foster-child in the*
   Kabanov household   mezzo-soprano
Savël Prokofjevič Dikoj *a merchant*   bass
Boris Grigorjevič *Dikoj's nephew*   tenor
Váňa Kudrjáš *teacher, chemist and engineer*
   employed by Dikoj   tenor
Glaša *a servant in the Kabanov*
   household   mezzo-soprano
Fekluša *a servant*   mezzo-soprano
Kuligin *friend of Kudrjáš*   baritone
Woman from the Crowd   contralto
Passer-by   tenor
Late-night Passer-by   silent
Townspeople, offstage chorus
Setting The town of Kalinovo on the bank of
   the Volga in the 1860s

Vincenc Červinka's translation from Russian of Ostrovsky's play appeared in the spring of 1918; it may have been this, or the production of the play in Brno in March 1919, that drew Janáček's attention to it as a possible opera, but it was not until the autumn of 1919 that he began to inquire about permission to set it. He acquired the rights from Červinka early in January 1920 and began composition on 9 January. Janáček's autograph score was complete by 17 April 1921, though he continued to make small revisions up to the Brno première, on 23 November 1921. The work was subsequently dedicated to the woman who inspired it, his beloved Kamila Stösslová, 38 years his junior and a married woman.

The vocal score (made by Janáček's pupil Břetislav Bakala) was published in February 1922 and incorporated a few minor changes suggested by Max Brod, who provided the German translation. More substantial additions derived from Janáček's insistence on seamless joins between the two scenes in Act 1 and Act 2, and the briefness of the music he originally provided for the scene changes. In November 1927 Janáček solved the problem by extending the interludes in these acts. For Act 1 he extended existing material, but for Act 2 he wrote fresh music. The new interludes were first heard on 21 January 1928 at the Prague German Opera under William Steinberg, who also played the first two acts through without a break (a procedure enthusiastically endorsed by Janáček). Janáček did not attend the

German première of the opera (under Otto Klemperer in Cologne) in 1922 but was present at the much more successful Berlin première in 1926 under Fritz Zweig. *Kát'a Kabanová* was Janáček's first opera to be performed in Britain (under a very young Charles Mackerras) in 1951 and in 1976 it initiated Mackerras's cycle of recordings for Decca, with Elisabeth Söderström in the title role.

*

The overture has one of the most evocative openings in opera. A long-held chord on the lower strings swells into a short melodic phrase and comes to rest on an eight-note timpani motif (ex.1). In the follow-

Ex.1 Moderato
trbn (with mute)

ing Allegro ex. 1 is speeded up and given to the oboe against the jingle of sleigh-bells and a whirling flute figure. This music will be associated with Tichon's departure: Kát'a's fate is sealed during his absence. The contrasting *espressivo* theme has associations with Kát'a. Each time it is heard it is quelled by the timpani theme – the course of the opera in miniature.

***Act I.i** A park on the bank of the Volga in front of the Kabanovs' house: afternoon* Kudrjáš invites Glaša to admire the view of the afternoon sunlight on the Volga. They are soon distracted by the approach of Dikoj, rebuking his nephew Boris for his apparent idleness. Dikoj is looking for Kabanicha (the widowed matriarch of the Kabanov household) and, told that she is in the park, goes off to find her.

Left alone with Boris, Kudrjáš asks him why he is so submissive to Dikoj. Boris explains that following the death of his parents, his grandmother's will has provided for him and his sister on condition that he lives with his uncle Dikoj and shows him respect. Boris accepts these humiliating conditions for his sister's sake. After a brief interruption as Fekluša praises Kabanicha's charity to Glaša, Boris reveals to Kudrjáš that he has fallen in love with a married woman. During an orchestral interlude they briefly observe from a distance the object of his passion, Kát'a Kabanová, as she returns from church with her husband Tichon, her mother-in-law Kabanicha and the Kabanovs' foster-daughter Varvara.

This short interlude (Janáček's response to Puccini's entrance music for Butterfly) is the first lyrical moment in what has been an expository and rather wordy introduction; it suggests Kát'a's gentle nature. The mood abruptly changes. Kabanicha orders Tichon to make the traditional trip to the market at Kazan', complaining that Tichon now neglects her for his wife. Tichon denies this, as does Kát'a, whose first words (in regular, warmly-harmonized phrases) contrast strongly with Kabanicha's (in jagged recitative-like passages, accompanied by whole-tone chords). Kát'a goes indoors leaving Kabanicha to complain further. When Kabanicha herself leaves, Varvara defends Kát'a to a petulant Tichon and expresses sympathy for her. A brief interlude leads into scene ii.

I.ii In the Kabanovs' house Janáček moved this scene indoors to provide a more intimate setting for Kát'a's confession, in which she tells Varvara of her happier, carefree life before she married; she now longs to be free again, like a bird in the air. She remembers her daily routine, and especially her visionary trances in church. At this moment a regular lyrical melody forms, but the pace quickens and the pitch rises as Kát'a's reminiscences become feverish and she describes how she feels herself to be on the brink of some disaster. Varvara wonders if Kát'a is ill. Kát'a replies that she would be less troubled if she were only ill, as the pace now relaxes. A more ominous depiction of her conflict begins: a sinuous theme initially on the english horn punctuated by *sforzando* stabs as Kát'a describes how the Devil seems to be whispering to her. When Varvara asks about her dreams Kát'a, in one of the great lyrical phrases of the opera, declares she cannot sleep ('Varjo! Nemohu spát'). She imagines that someone keeps on whispering in her ear, as if he were embracing her, and that she goes off with him. Varvara urges her to tell her more, but Kát'a is ashamed.

With a repeat of the sleigh-bell music from the overture Tichon comes in, preparing to leave. Kát'a flings herself into his arms and begs him either not to go or to take her with him. He refuses, unable to understand her distress. At this point ex.1 is heard continually in the orchestra, soon to be joined by another, even more ominous theme ending in a semitone clash. After another lyrical appeal Kát'a, believing some misfortune will happen (the semitone ostinato), begs Tichon to make her swear an oath never to speak to, look at, or think of any stranger while he is gone. Low trombone chords heighten the sense of catastrophe.

As Tichon remonstrates, Kabanicha comes in announcing that everything is ready for his departure (the sleigh-bell music again). Through the mildly protesting Tichon Kabanicha dictates humiliating instructions as to how his wife should behave while he is away: she must be polite, obey Kabanicha, find work to do, and not look at other men. As in Act 1 scene i, the two women are sharply contrasted; Kabanicha gives her instructions against a whole-tone motif, Kát'a receives them from Tichon against a

lyrical theme (on the viola d'amore), which at the end expands into a brief but radiant interlude. Left alone by Kabanicha, husband and wife have nothing to say. The ostinato begins again, and a complex of the sleigh-bell theme, semitone clash and ex. 1 make up the increasingly tense orchestral background as Kabanicha returns. She forces Tichon to his knees to say goodbye to her and rebukes Kát'a for publicly embracing her husband. With a final word to Varvara, Tichon leaves against a triple *forte* version of ex.1.

Act 2.i A room in the Kabanovs' house, late afternoon As they sit together, embroidering, Kabanicha reproaches Kát'a for not observing the tradition of displaying her sorrow publicly while her husband is away. The older woman retires, leaving orders not to be disturbed. The mood changes with the first significant appearance of a theme associated with Varvara (on the viola, against sensuous flute and celesta off-beat chords). Before Varvara goes for a walk she gives Kát'a the garden gate key (which she has stolen from Kabanicha's hiding place). If she sees 'him', she tells Kát'a, she will ask him to come to the gate.

Kát'a's crisis of conscience is powerfully depicted in an alternation of moods. It is interrupted by a conversation off stage between Kabanicha and Dikoj, who has just arrived. Kát'a unthinkingly hides the key. When she is sure that she is alone again she realizes that fate has made up her mind for her. She goes out, longing for nightfall.

Kabanicha enters with Dikoj, who is slightly drunk. While he proclaims his own soft-heartedness, telling of a worker whom he insulted and then begged for forgiveness, Dikoj suggestively sidles up to Kabanicha but is repulsed by her. The vigorous and cheerful interlude which Janáček added here in 1927 throws a comic slant on this encounter. It leads into scene ii.

2.ii Outside the Kabanovs' garden gate, a summer night A short prelude consists of the alternation of a hesitant theme and a lyrical one. Kudrjáš arrives with a guitar and as he waits for his sweetheart Varvara he sings a two-stanza song, 'Po zahrádce děvucha' ('Early one morning a girl went walking in the garden'), against a light, guitar-like accompaniment. The words (about a young woman courted by a handsome suitor but who has eyes for another) were a late substitution for Ostrovsky's original lyric, a grisly song about a Cossack who is contemplating killing his wife. Boris arrives and tells Kudrjáš that he met a girl who asked him to come to this spot: he has come in the hope of meeting Kát'a. Kudrjáš warns him of the risks for a married woman. Varvara comes out of the gate singing the words 'Za vodou, za vodičkou' ('Over the river my Váňa is standing') to the viola theme heard in the previous scene. Kudrjáš responds with a second verse and the two go off to the river.

Left alone, Boris compares himself to the departing lovers, uncertain of his own situation. Soon Kát'a appears – to the hesitant first theme from the prelude – and guiltily repulses Boris's attempt to take her hand. But Boris declares his love for Kát'a; as the lyrical theme from the prelude is heard, Kát'a relents. To a soaring orchestral theme (and a vocal top C) Boris declares his passion. She is deeply troubled by her sense of sin but guardedly admits her love for him. Kudrjáš and Varvara return and discuss their hoodwinking of Kabanicha while in the distance Boris and Kát'a, who have gone for a walk, are heard declaring their love for one another. It is late and Kudrjáš soon calls the others back. He and Varvara then sing alternate verses of another song, 'Chod' si dívka, do času' ('So go here soon, my girl'). Boris and Kát'a return. To a *fortissimo* version of the soaring theme Kát'a goes in through the garden gate leaving Boris behind. On a radiant chord – E major gently alternating with E minor – the curtain comes down.

Act 3.i *Two days later, a ruined building overlooking the Volga; towards evening* An ostinato background with pattering chords suggests the beginnings of a storm. Kuligin and Kudrjáš shelter from the rain and are soon joined by others. Kuligin notices that the walls of the ruin are covered with barely discernible paintings depicting the punishment of the damned in Hell. Dikoj also takes shelter and is accosted by Kudrjáš. The two men clash about the nature of storms; Kudrjáš considers them 'electricity' (he has just urged the need for lightning conductors) while for Dikoj they are punishments sent from God. The rain stops and Dikoj walks out into the open air.

Varvara appears, and when Boris arrives she urgently attracts his attention. She tells him that Tichon has returned and that Kát'a has gone to pieces and is threatening to confess everything to her husband. When Kát'a enters, Boris and Kudrjáš hide from her while Varvara attempts to calm her. Her behaviour attracts the attention of passers-by (the only onstage chorus in the piece) and as Dikoj, Kabanicha and Tichon arrive the storm builds up (ex.1 is heard prominently). Kát'a falls on her knees and confesses her infidelity publicly. Kabanicha forces Kát'a to name her lover and finally she does so against a *fortissimo* version of ex.1. Kát'a collapses into Tichon's arms but immediately tears herself away and rushes out into the breaking storm. The storm music leads straight into scene ii.

3.ii *A bank of the Volga, dusk turning to night* Tichon and Glaša hurry in, searching for Kát'a, who is missing. No sooner have they left than Kudrjáš and Varvara arrive. She complains of being locked in her room by Kabanicha. Kudrjáš advises her to run away with him to Moscow. They leave together.

In the distance Tichon and Glaša can be heard calling for Kát'a. She enters alone. Against a lyrical theme on the oboe and viola d'amore Kát'a regrets her confession, seeing it as futile as well as humiliating for Boris. She dreads the emptiness of nights alone and longs for death (she interprets the brief wordless offstage chorus as a funeral lament) but her life continues, bereft of meaning except for her longing to see Boris. Suddenly he enters and embraces her silently against a gentle orchestral interlude. He is being sent to a trading post in Siberia; Kát'a, on the other hand, remains at the mercy of her vindictive mother-in-law and drunken husband. She has a special message for Boris: he must give alms to the beggars he meets on his journey. The wordless chorus returns, sounding here, in Janáček's instructions, like 'the sigh of the Volga' (its music was in fact heard during Kát'a's public confession). This theme and a recurring, searing *fortissimo* trill dominate the farewell as Boris's voice trails off in the distance. Then against a repeated timpani beat and a chirruping motif, Kát'a imagines her grave visited by birds and covered with flowers. She crosses her arms and throws herself into the river. Hearing the noise, a search party enters, followed by Kabanicha. Dikoj retrieves Kát'a's corpse against an excited orchestral background deriving from the sleigh-bell theme. Tichon blames his mother for Kát'a's death and flings himself on to her lifeless body. Kabanicha impassively thanks those assembled for their efforts. The wordless chorus is heard once more, *fortissimo* combined with ex.1.

*

Kát'a Kabanová initiated the great final period of Janáček's career. With the confidence gained by the success of *Jenůfa* in Prague in 1916, he first dealt with unfinished business: the completion of his previous opera, *The Excursions of Mr Brouček*, and the radical revision of his first opera *Šárka*. He then proceeded, at the age of 65, to crown his career with the composition of four final operas, on which his reputation now rests. Of these the first, *Kát'a Kabanová*, is the most conventional as far as its libretto is concerned, but it is also his most tender, as he was to tell its dedicatee, Kamila Stösslová, a few months before he died. Janáček's passion for her inspired the central portrait of Kát'a and is evident throughout the opera, welling up almost from nothing at the beginning of the overture and quelled only in the final notes of the opera by the brutal timpani theme and its connotations of fate and authoritarian repression.   J.T.

Khovanshchina ('The Khovansky Affair')

'National music drama' (*narodnaya muzïkal'naya drama*) in six scenes, traditionally given in five acts, by Modest Petrovich Musorgsky to his own libretto, compiled with Vladimir Vasil'yevich Stasov from historical sources; St Petersburg, Amateur Musical-Dramatic Club in Kononov Auditorium, 9/21 February 1886, in Rimsky-Korsakov's version (given by Imperial Theatres, St Petersburg, Mariinsky Theatre, 7/20 November 1911; Ravel-Stravinsky version, Paris, Théâtre Champs-Elysées, 5 June 1913 [with Stravinsky's final chorus, 16 June 1913]; Shostakovich version, Leningrad, Kirov Theatre, 25 November 1960).

Albert Coates conducted the 'official' première in 1911, with Fyodor Shalyapin as Dosifey, Ivan Yershov as Golitsïn and Yevgeniya Zbruyeva as Marfa.

Prince Ivan Khovansky *head of the Strel'tsï*	
(*musketeers*)	bass
Prince Andrey Khovansky *his son*	tenor
Prince Vasily Golitsïn	tenor
The Boyar Shaklovity	baritone
Dosifey *leader of the schismatics ('Old*	
Believers')	bass
Marfa *a schismatic, a young*	
widow	mezzo-soprano
Susanna *an old schismatic*	soprano
A Scrivener	tenor
Emma *a girl from the German quarter*	soprano
Pastor	bass
Varsonof'yev *Golitsïn's attendant*	bass
Kuz'ka *a musketeer*	baritone
Streshnev *a young boyar*	tenor
Three *Strel'tsï*	basses
Golitsïn's Minion	tenor

Refugees, musketeers, their wives, Old Believers, immured maidens and Persian slave girls of Ivan Khovansky, Tsar Peter's guard, crowd

Setting Various locations in and near Moscow at a time roughly corresponding to that of the second 'revolt of the *Strel'tsï*' (1689)

Musorgsky conceived the work in 1872 and began its composition the next year; it was left unfinished, and (except for two fragments) unorchestrated at his death in 1881. A vocal score transmitting Musorgsky's manuscripts as he left them was published in 1931, edited by Pavel Lamm. The first performing edition was made by Rimsky-Korsakov (published 1883) and this was the version given at the 1886 première, under Eduard Goldshteyn, and at the Mariinsky Theatre in 1911. A variant of this version by Ravel and Stravinsky was used for the Paris performance in 1913, directed by Dyagilev, under

Emil Cooper, with Shalyapin and with Yelizaveta Petrenko as Marfa. In 1952 Shostakovich orchestrated the scenes omitted by Rimsky for the Kirov Theatre, and in 1958 he re-orchestrated the rest of the opera for a film version (1959, with Mark Reyzen as Dosifey and Yevgeny Kibkalo as Shaklovity, conducted by Yevgeny Svetlanov). Shostakovich's score was published in 1963; at the stage première Boris Khaikin conducted, with Boris Shtokolov as Dosifey.

It is significant that Musorgsky's second historical opera was conceived in Tsar Peter I's bicentenary year, for it reflects the moral controversy that has always swirled around 'Peter the Great', the first Russian Emperor, through whose reforms the modern Russian state was created after Western European bureaucratic models; who built his capital, in which Musorgsky lived, on marshes at the cost of untold thousands of indentured lives; and who has been regarded by a divided posterity as either the best thing that ever happened to Russia or the worst. The letter to Vladimir Stasov in which Musorgsky first mentioned being 'pregnant' with the new opera (16–22 June/28 June–4 July 1872) also contains enigmatic musings about 'the power of the black earth' and its resistance to ploughing 'with tools wrought of alien materials'. These dark ruminations are virtually all we have to go on if we want to understand, as a work of history, the sprawling, unprecedented opera-chronicle that gestated over the nine years that remained to the composer, since his early death from alcoholism left crucial holes in the scenario. There is reason to believe that the faint note of hope subsequently built into the opera by its revisers was not the one intended by its creator.

It was inevitable that Musorgsky, in writing an opera that would contain a judgment of Peter, should have concentrated on the period of the so-called 'Strel'tsï Revolts', the convulsions out of which the modern Russian state emerged. It was impossible to base a libretto on the life and actions of the tsar himself; the Russian censorship prohibited the representation of any member of the Romanov dynasty on the dramatic stage. His opponents (with one royal exception) could be shown in action, however, and it was on them that Musorgsky fastened.

In order to assert full power, Peter had to overcome opposition from three quarters. First there were the *strel'tsï* (musketeers), the crack Moscow militia, represented in the opera by their leader Ivan Khovansky and his son Andrey. A crisis of succession was created in 1682 by the death of Tsar Fyodor Alexeyevich (Romanov) at the age of 20, leaving a sickly and half-witted 16-year-old brother Ivan, and also his half-brother Peter, then not quite ten. The families of the two royal mothers competed viciously for the throne. The *strel'tsï* backed Ivan's

'Khovanshchina' (Musorgsky): design by Apolinary Vasnetsov for scene vi (secluded hermitage in a pine forest; the Old Believers' immolation) in the first Moscow production by Mamontov's Private Opera Company at the Solodovnikov Theatre, 12/24 November 1897

family and secured the installation of the two young heirs as joint sovereigns, with Ivan's sister Sophia as regent. Khovansky now tried to use his troops to force the new régime to abrogate the recent church reforms; some thought he coveted the throne either for himself or for Andrey. This threatened revolt was the 'Khovansky affair' (Khovanshchina). Sophia, formerly the strel'tsï's protégée, now turned around and had both Khovansky and his son beheaded. Her agent in this perfidy was a boyar, Fyodor Shaklovity, whom Sophia installed as Khovansky's successor at the head of the strel'tsï. (In the opera, as in history, Shaklovity eliminates Khovansky, but seemingly as Peter's agent rather than Sophia's.)

Peter's second opponent, Sophia herself, is represented in the opera by Prince Vasily Golitsïn, Sophia's chief minister (and former lover), himself an eager reformer who envisaged the abolition of serfdom and the institution of mass education. These plans were doomed when a second strel'tsï revolt, organized by Shaklovity at Sophia's behest to murder Peter and his family and install the regent as actual hereditary ruler, failed. As a result of this offensive against the 17-year-old tsar, Sophia was sent off to a convent, Shaklovity was executed and Golitsïn was exiled. By 1696 Peter's mother and half-brother had died and the 24-year-old tsar assumed his full responsibilities as head of the Russian church and state.

The last of Peter's opponents were the so-called Old Believers, religious recusants who had been persecuted from the time of Peter's father Alexey. Their representative in the opera, Dosifey, had to be invented, for they had no organized clergy. The libretto identifies Dosifey with Prince Mïshetsky, an Old Believer of noble birth whose narrative Glib' ('The Depths') explicitly identified Peter as Antichrist. The Old Believers, never a serious threat to the royal power, responded to the events herein recounted with an epidemic of mass suicides, chiefly by burning.

One major character remains to be accounted for. In order to make their assemblage of historical portraits jell into some semblance of a plot, Musorgsky (and Stasov, his collaborator) resorted to the most conventional, and in this case blatantly anachronistic, sort of operatic glue: romantic love. Andrey Khovansky's love interest (though he is chiefly seen betraying her) is his fiancée Marfa, a figment of the libretto but its most important prop. She is an Old Believer, a specially favoured member of Dosifey's spiritual community; she is linked by amorous bonds to the strel'tsï; and she is a soothsayer with a fatal influence on Prince Golitsïn, to whom she foretells Sophia's downfall and his own. She alone, in other words, inhabits all the worlds of the opera and links them. Her constant tone of keening lamentation symbolizes the doom that overhangs everything and everyone, the doom that is the core and essential message of this most pessimistic of historical operas.

Khovanshchina accumulated gradually in vocal score scene by scene, but not in order. Until 1879, when Musorgsky finally wrote out a fair copy of the existing texts (it is called the 'blue notebook') and linked them as a guide to completing the opera (and, possibly, for submission to the censor), there was no libretto, properly speaking. Only two tiny excerpts from the third scene were ever orchestrated by the composer. When the manuscripts were finally put in blue-notebook order after the composer's death, it was found that two scenes remained unfinished: Act 2 lacked a conclusion and Act 5 was little more than a sheaf of sketches. No wonder the action has seemed to exude an air of pointless confusion and ambiguity, and has been so susceptible to contradictory readings – though one interpretation, arguably at variance with the composer's, has been gradually built into the opera by its revisers. A brief account of this process must be included here, since unlike *Boris Godunov* (which has two), *Khovanshchina* has no complete 'original' version to which one can revert.

The standard interpretation of the Petrine reforms is one that casts all of the variously contending political and social factions portrayed in the opera – Sophia's regency, the *strel'tsï*, the Old Believers – into the dustbin of history. All of them, but particularly the Old Believers, were viewed as the symbol of everything that was outmoded and antiquated, 'petty, wretched, dull-brained, envious, evil and malicious' (as Stasov put it of the character Susanna in a letter to Musorgsky). This view was fixed once and for all by Rimsky-Korsakov, who had to fill the gaps in *Khovanshchina* as well as orchestrate (and cut and 'correct') it. His method was that of symbolic reprise. At the end of Act 2, he followed the break-up of the colloquy at Golitsïn's, involving representatives of all three anti-Peter factions, with an impressively developed reprise of the melody of the opera's prelude ('Dawn over the Moskva River'). At a stroke all ambiguities were resolved: Peter is 'day', the Muscovite opposition, in all its manifestations, is 'night', a view driven home again at the very end of the opera, where Rimsky trumped his own final chorus (composed on an Old Believers' melody Musorgsky had transcribed and designated for the opera's conclusion) with a brassy reprise of the March that had represented the unseen Peter in the Act 4 finale. Shostakovich, when it came his turn to revise *Khovanshchina*, ratified Rimsky's view and even managed to strengthen it. Retaining Rimsky's final chorus, he replaced Rimsky's ending for Act 2 with a foreshadowing of the Act 4 march, and transferred Rimsky's reprise of the 'Dawn' theme to the very end of the opera, where it casts an even more conclusively optimistic judgment on the whole of the opera's action.

Without all these reprises, first of Peter's march and then of the 'Dawn', the Old Believers would have the fifth act of *Khovanshchina* all to themselves, and, as they trudge off to their mass suicide, accompanied by the sober strains of their psalm, the opera would end on a note of quiet pessimism, a sense of loss. Act 5, as Musorgsky evidently intended it (and as realized uniquely in the version of the opera Sergey Dyagilev presented to Paris in 1913 with the help of Ravel and Stravinsky), acts as a gloss on the rest of the drama – a conservative and nationalistic judgment that calls the necessity of the political events portrayed in the other four acts severely into question, implying that what for some may have been a dawn was for others the veritable end of the world.

The cluttered action of *Khovanshchina* can best be grasped by conceptualizing the six scenes in the blue notebook in two groups. (Musorgsky himself never specified a grouping; the conventional five-act format was Rimsky-Korsakov's idea.) The first three scenes are chiefly centred on each of Peter's opponents in turn: *strel'tsï* (Khovansky), Golitsïn (representing the unseen Sophia) and Old Believers. The last three then show them eliminated in the same order. Soviet researchers have proposed regrouping the scenes to make this scheme clearer: Scene i = Act 1; Scenes ii and iii = Act 2; Scenes iv–vi = Act 3. The division is attractive for the further reason that both intervals, as well as the final curtain, follow choruses. In the synoptic table that follows, the constituent units are the individual manuscripts. Their dates are given ('Old Style') so that the opera's creative history may be reconstructed.

*

Prelude *'Dawn over the Moskva River'*
Scene i *Red Square, Moscow*

a   *Strel'tsï* keep watch; after singing an old marching tune the sentry Kuz'ka dozes off, is awakened and reprimanded.

b   A scrivener arrives and sets up shop; Shaklovity dictates denunciation of the Khovanskys (its text is from an actual historical document).

c   Settlers violently compel the scrivener to read them a posted notice detailing penalties imposed by the *strel'tsï* on perfidious nobles; they lament that punishing the rich does not help the poor (the offstage opening chorus is based on a folksong from the Villebois collection, 1860).

d   Ivan Khovansky enters to thunderous acclaim and vows to crush Sophia's enemies and punish treason.

e   Emma, a young Lutheran from the German quarter, rushes in pursued by Andrey Khovansky; Marfa intercedes and is threatened with a dagger.

f   Ivan Khovansky returns and demands Emma; Dosifey enters, puts an end to the quarrel and entrusts Emma to Marfa for protection.

g   Dosifey prays, with chorus, for preservation of the faith.

Scene ii *Golitsïn's study*

a Golitsïn reads Sophia's love letter (its text is derived from a historical document) and wonders if he can still trust her.

b He reads a letter from his mother.

c A Lutheran pastor arrives and pleads for Emma and a Lutheran church.

d Marfa enters and reads Golitsïn's fortune in a bowl of water, predicting imminent disgrace and exile (Divination, 'Silï potaïnïye': 'O mysterious forces') .

e Golitsïn dismisses Marfa, whispering instructions to his attendant Varsonof'yev that she be drowned. Ivan Khovansky arrives and they quarrel over the boyars' hereditary rights.

f Dosifey enters; he reveals his past identity as Prince Mïshetsky (offstage, the Old Believers sing a folksong, from the 1866 Balakirev collection). He exhorts Golitsïn and Khovansky to join forces with him to restore old ways.

g Marfa returns, in fright, telling of the attempts on her life and its thwarting by passing bodyguards of Peter.

h Shaklovity enters and announces that a denunciation (his own) has been received and acted upon by Peter, who has vowed to clean up the 'Khovansky mess' (*Khovanshchina*).

Scene iii *Strel'tsï quarter, across the Moskva River*

a The Old Believers sing (the Balakirev-derived melody cited above).

b Marfa laments her lost love ('Iskhodila mladyoshen'ka vse luga i bolota': 'A girl went out walking in the fields and marshes' – based on a folksong in the Villebois collection).

c Susanna reproaches Marfa for her unclean passion.

d Dosifey intervenes, sending Susanna away; Marfa confesses her love for Andrey and her wish to immolate herself with him; Dosifey counsels patience.

e Shaklovity, alone, muses on Russia's troubled history (aria, 'Spit streletskoye gnezdo': 'The nest of strel'tsï sleeps').

f The *strel'tsï* awaken, with hangovers, and immediately start thinking about wine.

g Their wives nag them about their drinking.

h Kuz'ka sings to his balalaika, with chorus (the Rumour Song).

i The scrivener rushes in with news of mercenary attacks on the *strel'tsï*.

j The *strel'tsï* appeal to Khovansky, who declines to fight Peter, and they pray for deliverance.

Scene iv *Refectory on Ivan Khovansky's estate*

a Khovansky is at home, awaiting news; his servant girls entertain him (the choruses of immured maidens are based on folksongs from the Melgunov collection, 1879). A warning arrives from Golitsïn; Khovansky ignores it, calling for more entertainment.

b Khovansky's Persian slave girls dance for him.

c Shaklovity arrives with a summons to a meeting with Sophia; as Khovansky dons his robes the girls sing a chorus in praise of their master (based on a chorus Musorgsky learnt from Shishko, lighting director of the Mariinsky Theatre, included in Rimsky's

1876 collection). At the doorway, Shaklovity stabs Khovansky, then gloats over the corpse by continuing the interrupted song.

Scene v *Red Square, before St Basil's shrine*

a Golitsïn's exile is mourned by Moscow settlers.

b Dosifey laments (in an aria) the fate of Khovansky and Golitsïn; he and Marfa decide the time has come for immolation.

c Andrey confronts Marfa over Emma; she tells him the girl has been sent beyond the frontier. Andrey calls for the *strel'tsï*.

d The *strel'tsï* enter with axes and blocks, ready for execution; Marfa offers Andrey asylum and they depart.

e In a double chorus, the *strel'tsï* pray for divine mercy and their wives plead against their husbands' pardon.

f Peter's guard enters, to a march with onstage band; his pardon of the *strel'tsï* is announced.

Scene vi *Secluded hermitage in a pine forest; moonlight*

a Dosifey mourns the outcome of his struggle with Peter and appeals to his followers to prepare for death.

b Andrey enters, disconsolate; Marfa lovingly leads him to the pyre ('Lyubovnoye otpevaniye': 'Love Requiem').

c Dosifey leads the faithful into the hermitage.

A final chorus, unwritten, was to have been based on an Old Believer melody Musorgsky had taken down from the singing of his friend Lyubov' Karmalina.

*

Khovanshchina is an aristocratic tragedy, and this is reflected in its musical style. But for the scenes involving the low-born scrivener, it is full of 'noble' melody in place of the radically realistic speech-song one finds in Musorgsky's songs or in the earlier version of *Boris*. In part this is a continuation of a tendency, already noticeable in the revised *Boris*, towards a more heroic scale and a more authentically tragic tone – in short, towards a more traditionally operatic style. But Musorgsky refused to call it a retrenchment; on the contrary, in one of his late letters to Stasov he pointed with pride to his *advancement* towards what he called 'thought-through and justified melody', meaning a kind of melody that would embody all the expressive potential of speech. Yet these sinuous melodies, unlike the idiosyncratic recitatives of his earlier manner, are curiously impersonal. The characters who sing them (Marfa throughout, Shaklovity in Scene iii, Dosifey in Scenes iii and vi) do not speak, it seems; rather, something akin to a Tolstoyan notion of impassive historical forces (what Musorgsky, in his sphinx-like way, had called 'the power of the black earth') speaks through them. And this is perhaps the central message of an opera in which personal volition is everywhere set at nought; in which everyone plots and strives and everyone loses; in which the final stage picture shows the last survivors of the old order, the opera's only morally undefiled characters, resolutely stepping out of history and into eternity, where Peter cannot touch them.   R.T.

King Priam

Opera in three acts by Michael Tippett to his own libretto after Homer's *Iliad*; Coventry, Belgrade Theatre (Royal Opera, Covent Garden), 29 May 1962.

The cast at the première included Forbes Robinson (Priam), Marie Collier (Hecuba), John Dobson (Paris), Margreta Elkins (Helen) and Richard Lewis (Achilles).

Priam *King of Troy*	bass-baritone
Hecuba *his wife*	dramatic soprano
Hector *their eldest son*	baritone
Andromache *Hector's wife*	lyric dramatic soprano
Paris *Priam's second son*	boy soprano/tenor
Helen *wife to Menelaus of Sparta, then wife in adultery to Paris*	mezzo-soprano
Achilles *a Greek hero*	heroic tenor
Patroclus *his friend*	light baritone
Nurse	mezzo-soprano
Old Man	bass
Young Guard	lyric tenor
Hermes *messenger of the gods*	high light tenor

Hunters, wedding guests, serving women

Setting The royal palace, walls, environs and plain of Troy, and the royal palace at Sparta

King Priam (1958–61), Tippett's second opera, was in many respects a carefully considered reaction to *The Midsummer Marriage*, which had been composed, without any real prospect of production, between 1946 and 1952. The experience of a prolonged gestation and period of composition, and an unfavourable response when it was eventually produced at Covent Garden in 1955, did not deter Tippett. His mind had already turned to considering Greek theatre in some radio talks in 1953 about the effect of music in the theatre. Three years later he read a book by Lucien Goldmann, *Le dieu caché*, which, he wrote, 'determined the tragic nature of my new opera *King Priam*' through its analysis of tragedy in the dramas of Jean Racine. He was also influenced by Bertolt Brecht's concept of epic theatre, the visit to London in 1956 of the Berliner Ensemble and the Barrault production of Paul Claudel's *Christophe Colomb*.

In 1957 a commission from the Koussevitzky Foundation in America for a large-scale choral and orchestral work brought from Tippett an initial idea of a work in 'eight, somewhat unrelated scenes'

concerned with man's progress from birth to death. He was persuaded that this was in reality an operatic scenario and advised to discuss the project with the director Peter Brook. In the aftermath of *The Midsummer Marriage*, in which Tippett had created his own heavily symbolic scenario, it was suggested that he should now take a familiar story and present it simply. He found his ideal material in Homer's *Iliad*, though it is characteristic that, given his instinctive pull towards the Greek world, he should view the scenario from the Trojan perspective. His declared aim was to focus on the 'mysterious nature of human choice'. He was able to change the scope of the commission to one for an opera, and it was later agreed that it would be produced by the Royal Opera, Covent Garden; the company gave the première at the Coventry Festival of 1962 which marked the consecration of the new cathedral. *King Priam*, one of the most war-torn of all operas, was thus heard for the first time a day before the première of Britten's *War Requiem*.

*

Prelude As in *The Midsummer Marriage*, *King Priam* opens with a vivid musical 'frame' for the orchestra and chorus. In this instance the piercing trumpets of war speak for themselves, as do the fusillades of timpani-fire. According to authoritative commentators, the offstage cries of the chorus represent the anguished sounds of labour, taken over by the lower brass as a jolting pattern of contractions.

Act I.i *The royal palace at Troy* A final heave and a gentle oboe introduces a baby in his cot – we have been present at the birth pangs of Paris. The musical drama is stark and uncompromising and, though harsh, has a sense of visceral excitement. Tippett's command of grand dramatic gesture is here at its most impressive, and just as brilliantly calculated is the intimacy of the darkened nursery and the gentle sounds of a nurse calming the crying baby.

It is in this domestic context that Tippett introduces King Priam and his Queen, Hecuba. She is troubled by a dream and cannot attend to the child. Her musical line is jerky and haughty, in distinct contrast to the soothing tone of the nurse and the regal entry of Priam. This initial scene comes to a point of focus when the King summons an Old Man to interpret the dream. He reads it as a premonition that the child Paris will in time cause his father's death. Hecuba's reaction, violent and hysterical, is to call for the child to be killed immediately. Her frenzied singing is accompanied by a wild, insistent ostinato from the violins, which is to be her characterizing musical gesture. When Priam is asked to react he sings against a warm and deeply moving chordal pattern from the lower strings, and his attitude is initially one of torn humanity – 'a father and a King'. It is clear from the music that his conscience tells him one thing, but that his duty as a king compels him to follow a ruthless course, and the child's death is ordered. In his response Priam touches on what is for Tippett the central theme of the opera – the conflict between human choice and the actions of Fate: 'O child who cannot choose to live or die, I choose for you'. The origin of this topic has been pointed out in a passage from *The Midsummer Marriage*: 'Fate and freedom propound a paradox/ Choose your fate but still the god/Speaks through whatever acts ensue'.

Interlude 1 begins as the King and Queen leave to the sound of a royal fanfare. Tippett now introduces one of the most significant dramatic devices of the opera. The Nurse, Old Man and Young Guard (who goes briefly off stage with the child as if to dispose of him, though in fact he ensures his survival) come to the front of the stage and address the audience directly. They comment on the action in the manner of a Greek chorus but also adopt a Brechtian trait in examining the moral and philosophical (but in no direct sense political) issues raised so far. By implication, we are invited to ponder these issues ourselves, at a subtle remove from the enmeshed world of the opera's protagonists. This is Tippett's adaptation of the technique of alienation, and the interjection also serves to move the action forward.

I.ii The countryside outside Troy The pastoral timbre of woodwind punctuated by bucolic horn calls conjures up a world of 'hunting and the arts of peace'. Priam and his eldest son, Hector, are seen at their recreation. Attention focusses on an alluring young boy discovered by Hector, who performs dazzling feats. His ambition is to leave his shepherd father and graduate to Troy as a 'young hero' like Hector. Priam accepts him and on asking his name is answered 'Paris'. As at the foretelling of the Old Man in scene i, time momentarily stands still, for which Tippett finds a clipped, dislocated sound from woodwind and gentle chiming percussion. This momentous discovery enables Priam to release the feelings he had clearly felt when making his initial choice: 'So I'd hoped it might be; that accident or god reversed the choice'. Priam now has an extended monologue of reflection and consideration of his position. Haunted by echoes of his earlier contemplation, he decisively accepts Paris as his son, whatever the consequences.

Interlude 2 (like the first interlude) serves a dual purpose. As Chorus, the characters reflect on life as 'a bitter charade', and their tone, as was true of Priam's monologue, is here intensified. They then go on to fill in a stretch of the story with the help of a chorus of wedding guests who report on Hector's wedding to Andromache. Paris's growth from boy, to youth, to beautiful young man is sketched, and we learn of his rift with his father and brother and that he has

sailed to Greece, 'where Menelaus keeps open house in Sparta with his wife, Daughter of Zeus, Queen Helen'.

I.iii Menelaus's palace at Sparta In one of Tippett's most vivid dramatic coups the onward flow of this narrative is cut short by the unmistakable sounds of ecstatic love-making. The male voice has a line derived from the birth pangs of the opening, and the same frisson of physical excitement is uncannily created. This adulterous passion of Paris and Helen is soon put in context by her invocation of her husband Menelaus. Paris is outraged that she could possibly return to him and so asks her to choose between them. She indicates that she chooses Paris, if he so wishes. His reflection is suffused with the acceptance that if he sails with her back to Troy there will be a grim avenging war. As he prays to Zeus for guidance, the god Hermes suddenly appears in his role as a messenger of the gods. Another striking theatrical moment is now prepared – the Judgment of Paris – in which he is asked to choose between three goddesses, Athene, Hera and Aphrodite. He relates the first two to Hecuba and Andromache (though she has not yet appeared to us in the opera) and Aphrodite, as if by reflex action, to Helen. He chooses her, is cursed by the others and takes her away to Troy. This decisive end to Act 1 is dramatically very effective: a crucial personal choice has been made which will trigger an irrevocable war and a further chain of seemingly inevitable events.

Act 2.i Troy We are plunged directly into this climate of conflict and violence. Act 2 has been described as a 'war' act, scored only for men's voices and an ensemble of wind, brass and percussion, with a prominent role for the piano. This is a theatrically telling deployment of resources, and it creates a fine dramatic balance. Tension mounts as Hector and Paris quarrel. Hector is the embodiment of the Trojan 'young hero' annoyed by 'Prince handsome Paris', whose adulterous affair is the cause of the war. Troy's very masculinity and sovereignty are at stake, and the accompanying music has a hectoring muscular quality – its memorability enhanced by extensive quotation in the Second Piano Sonata (1962) and the Concerto for Orchestra (1962–3). Priam emerges to command the situation, and his sons run off to fight.

2.ii Achilles' tent The first interlude of this act sees Hermes taking the Old Man from the walls of Troy through to the Greek battle lines. The clear threat to Troy is the Greek war-hero Achilles, who however has retreated to his tent because of a trivial snub administered by Agamemnon. He is now seen ensconced with his friend Patroclus, and it is implied that their emotional relationship is of the closest, Patroclus being the key to Achilles' heart. In musical terms Tippett manages the most effective contrast.

As if intensified by the surrounding barrage of warlike noises, the episode in the tent has a moving intimacy – Achilles sings to the accompaniment of his guitar, and Patroclus is moved to tears by his song. They decide to dress Patroclus in Achilles' celebrated armour and to send him to battle in order to confound the Trojans, who imagine Achilles, for a time, to be passive.

2.iii *Troy* A second 'war' interlude reversing the journey of the first leads to a final scene of reportage. Paris tells Priam of Hector's fight with a figure in Achilles' armour; Patroclus is killed, and Priam, Paris and Hector enact a gruesome ceremony of blood-lust over the dead body, only to be overshadowed by the far more blood-curdling sound of Achilles' war-cry of revenge, which closes this central act.

The shaping of this act as an independent entity was an addition and revision to the original two-act scenario, as is revealed by Eric Walter White, who corresponded with the composer at the time of composition. Others prefer the two-act structure and see the final result as afflicted by 'structural imbalance' and 'faults in construction'. The composer's judgment however seems theatrically and dramatically acute. Act 3 may be lengthy, but its purpose is not so much one of action, of which there has been plenty, as of restitution and contemplation.

Act 3.i *The royal palace at Troy* In a suitable counterbalance to the counterpointing of women and goddesses at the end of Act 1, the final act opens with a tableau for the women – as wives and mistress. Andromache is visited by a premonition of Hector's death at the hand of Achilles, and with her mother-in-law Hecuba she berates the adulterous Helen, who is indirectly the instrument of his death. In an imposing aria, 'Let her rave', Helen asserts her authority and near-divinity, and the three women join in a trio addressed to their associated goddesses.

3.ii *The royal palace at Troy* After Interlude 1, in which a chorus of serving women briefly confirm the death of Hector, scene ii is a graphic and revealing treatment of King Priam's reaction to this blow. Paris breaks the news and is severely rebuked for his trouble – he goes to kill Achilles in further revenge. An extended monologue allows Priam to reflect on the tricks of Fate.

3.iii *Achilles' tent* The profound and purely instrumental Interlude 2 which precedes this scene shifts the action back to Achilles' tent. Achilles is disturbed by Priam, who brings the body of Achilles' beloved Patroclus to trade for that of his own beloved son Hector. This is the overwhelming moment of human emotion in the opera: the two enemies, united in grief, find a bond of common humanity. The almost schematic pattern of deaths is outlined as if in premonition: Paris will kill Achilles, Agamemnon will kill Paris, and Neoptolomus (Achilles' son) will

kill Priam. In making these seem like gratuitous events, Tippett concentrates the final stages of his opera on two extended moments. In Interlude 3 Hermes, as Messenger of Death, sings a lyrical hymn to the divine power of music as an instrument of healing and love. It has been objected that this holds up the action, but the objection misses the point that the 'action' is now secondary.

3.iv *Troy* The final scene focusses on the withdrawal of Priam into a private world of grief and preparation for death. He refuses to speak to the avenging Paris, his wife Hecuba and daughter-in-law Andromache. Only Helen melts his heart, as if in acknowledgment of her mysterious near-divinity. He is killed as if inevitably, but in acknowledgment of his humanity the opera's last gesture reflects our tears of compassion for the nobility of his suffering. The musical and dramatic gesture, as throughout this opera, is uncannily meshed.

*

King Priam is in some respects an exception among Tippett's five operas in that it is set in the past and based on a familiar story. But it is entirely characteristic in the way in which he presents his carefully honed scenario as a paradigm of chequered humanity. The eternal conflict of love in the shadow of death and violence is present in one form or another in every Tippett opera, and the probing of the individual psyche and of human interaction in *King Priam* is as profoundly explored as in any of the others. With this opera it seemed that Tippett had almost entirely changed his musical personality. The instrumental expression is spare and angular, counterpoint has gone, the tonal foundation is fragmented, and the lyricism is now highly rhetorical and sharply differentiated from the lyrical luxuriance of *The Midsummer Marriage*. This sea-change in Tippett's style mirrors profoundly the tragic nature of the work. The opera's musical language, directly related to the heroic subject it serves, has a compelling unity of purpose which Tippett was later to eschew. *King Priam* is one of the most powerful operatic experiences of the modern theatre and a landmark in the history of British opera. **G.Le.**

King Roger [*Król Roger; Pasterz* ('The Shepherd')]

Opera in three acts by Karol Szymanowski to a libretto by Jarosław Iwaszkiewicz and the composer very loosely based on Euripides' *Bacchae*; Warsaw, Wielki Theatre, 19 June 1926.

The composer's sister, Stanisława Szymanowska, sang Roxana at the première. King Roger was sung by Eugeniusz Mossakowski and the Shepherd by Adam Dobosz.

Król Roger II [King Roger] *King of Sicily* — baritone
Shepherd — tenor
Roxana *Queen of Sicily* — soprano
Edrisi *Arabian sage* — tenor
Archbishop — bass
Deaconess — contralto
Priests, monks, nuns, acolytes, courtiers, guards, eunuchs, Shepherd's disciples
Setting Sicily in the 12th century

The earliest discussions about *King Roger* took place in the summer of 1918 when the poet Jarosław Iwaszkiewicz visited Szymanowski at Yelisavetgrad (now Kirovograd). The first version of the libretto was completed by Iwaszkiewicz (partly following sketches prepared by Szymanowski) in June 1920, but in the course of composition Szymanowski made substantial alterations to the libretto, in particular rewriting the whole of the last act. He had originally intended to call the opera *Pasterz* ('The Shepherd'), and the changes he made reflected the shift of focus from the Shepherd to the King. Work on the music began in 1920, but the opera was completed only in August 1924. The first performance was conducted by Emil Młynarski, produced by Adolf Popławski and designed by Wincenty Drabik. Several productions have been given, including one in London in 1975. A vocal score was published in 1926, with a German libretto appearing two years later, and the full score was published in 1973. The opera has been recorded under Mieczysław Mierzejewski.

*

The work ostensibly concerns the conflict between the Christian church and a pagan creed of beauty and pleasure proclaimed by a young Shepherd. Queen Roxana is seduced by the allurements of the Shepherd and his faith; King Roger at first follows him as a pilgrim, but in the end stands alone. This provides a framework for a Nietzschean reworking of Euripides' *Bacchae*, which Szymanowski knew in translation.

Act 1 *The interior of a church* In some ways *King Roger* is as close to oratorio as to opera and the first act has the character of a static tableau stylizing the Byzantine religious and cultural world. The music is continuous, but the act falls into three distinct formal units, somewhat in the nature of very extended set numbers. The atmosphere is tellingly conveyed by Szymanowski's notes on the stage setting: 'Golden mosaics, shadows. Marble . . . an early Roman ceiling – as in the Palatina . . . choirs – the clergy in gilded robes, stiffly hieratic – incensories. A severe, formal splendour with oriental overtones'. A solemn mass is taking place as the curtain rises, and against the background of choral incantations (the importance of the chorus strengthens the work's oratorio connec-

tions) the Archbishop and Deaconess describe how the people are being led away from the church towards a new faith. The Arabian sage Edrisi describes to King Roger the Shepherd who advocates this new faith. As the Archbishop demands retribution the voice of Roxana the Queen is heard interceding on the Shepherd's behalf and suggesting that he be summoned to the church to explain himself.

The arrival of the Shepherd immediately transforms the scene and the music, and the choral archaisms are replaced with a song of serene and limpid beauty in which he proclaims his creed of love and beauty. This represents the second of the three major formal units of the act, and its opening phrase becomes one of the Shepherd's two leitmotifs. The motivic links between this phrase and the earlier Byzantine themes help to clarify the symbolic meaning of the opera and of its characters. It is apparent already that the conflict between the Church and the Shepherd – between medieval scholastic conventions and the Dionysian cult of self-abandoning joy – is really an externalization of opposing forces within Roger himself. Much of the opera works on this symbolic level. Edrisi, for instance, might be viewed as a symbol of wisdom or rationality and Roxana as an embodiment of the allurements of love.

As Roxana is increasingly captivated by the Shepherd's song the third and final formal unit in the act begins. The voices of Roxana and the Shepherd soar above the choral music in a mounting ecstasy of expression which is dramatically interrupted by Roger's call for silence. For the first time the King is characterized musically by an independent theme, later to be associated with him, and the contrast between the restless urgency of this theme and the suavity and sensuous appeal of the Shepherd's music epitomizes the dramatic and symbolic conflict at the heart of the work. The act ends as Roger asks the Shepherd to return that night to stand trial.

Act 2 *The inner courtyard of the palace* The second act is an oriental (Arab-Indian) tableau centred on two extended set numbers: Roxana's aria, in which she pleads for clemency for the Shepherd, and the ritual dance of the Shepherd's followers. In general the richly dissonant harmonic language, the oriental stylizations and the sumptuous orchestral impressionism (recalling the Ravel of *Daphnis et Chloé*) give to this act a quality of sustained ecstasy which is in sharp contrast to the Byzantine archaisms of Act 1. Szymanowski's tone painting in the opening section is masterly, conveying the heavy heat of the Sicilian night by dense, slowly moving harmonies supporting melodic strands of faintly oriental hue. The curtain rises on Roger and Edrisi, with Roger's music already betraying the unsettling influence of the Shepherd. The latter's imminent arrival, heralded

'King Roger' (Szymanowski), Act 1 (the interior of a church) of the original production at the Wielki Theatre, Warsaw, 19 June 1926, with sets designed by Wincenty Drabik

by the distant sound of tambourine and zither, immediately evokes a response from Roxana, whose hauntingly beautiful aria, strophic in design, has become the best-known music from the opera (familiar above all in the violin transcription by Pawel Kochański).

The appearance of the Shepherd is a moment of considerable dramatic intensity, as the orchestra works the Shepherd's two leitmotifs into an impassioned climax. As he describes his faith and origins his themes mingle with Roxana's in yet another ecstatic climax, culminating in his call for music and dancing. The dance of the Shepherd's followers is the clearest example of oriental stylization in the opera, its wordless chorus, percussion ostinatos and metrical irregularities directly reminiscent of the central sections of Szymanowski's Third Symphony (1916). As the dance becomes ever more abandoned, the voices of Roxana and the Shepherd rise above the chorus and orchestra, their ecstasy once more interrupted by Roger. An attempt to seize the Shepherd and chain his hands proves unsuccessful, and he leaves, followed by Roxana and eventually by Roger himself.

Act 3 *In the ruins of an ancient theatre* All three acts of the opera are built around a confrontation between Roger and the Shepherd. In Act 3 this takes place in the ruins of a Greek amphitheatre: 'Rows of semicircular benches towering above each other ... then the sky with brilliant stars ... in the centre the altar of Dionysus'. Here the symbolism of the opera is

made even more explicit as the Shepherd appears to Roger as Dionysus and the King makes a sacrifice to him, no longer suppressing the Dionysian within himself. In the passage that follows the voices of Roxana and the Shepherd once more soar above the chorus in the most powerful and sustained climax of the opera, before they depart and leave the King alone.

For the most part the third act is centred on Roger's character, and it is significant that his is the only part in the opera which truly grows musically, in contrast to the archetypes of Roxana and the Shepherd. He emerges only inconclusively in the first act, then travels through his 'dark night of the soul' in the second to his final hymn to the sun at the end of Act 3, when the 'dream is over ... the beautiful illusion passed'. In the final pages, as Roger salutes the rising sun, his vocal line achieves a dignity and strength that had formerly eluded it. In a departure from Euripides' play obviously influenced by Nietzsche, he emerges 'strong enough for freedom', enriched and transformed by the truths of Dionysus but no slave to them. At the end he stands alone as a powerful symbol of modern Nietzschean man.

*

The ending, in which Roger alone resists the Shepherd's influence, marked a crucial modification by Szymanowski himself of the original version of the libretto (where Roger follows the Shepherd as a disciple), and the change was symptomatic of a change in the composer's attitude to the hedonistic private world of his own earlier music. In *King Roger* that private world is symbolized above all by the 'Bacchic singing and dancing' of the second act. Yet the seductions of this act are given distance and perspective by means of a gentle stylized counterpoint, arising naturally out of specific stylizations of Byzantine, Arabic and Hellenic elements in the opera. It is indeed possible to view the three acts as three vast scenic tableaux, Byzantine, oriental and Hellenic respectively. The archaisms of the first and third acts contrast with the revelries of the second act, where the attractions of Dionysus are presented without dilution in a musical language which recalls the most opulent of Szymanowski's middle-period works.   J.Sn.

König Hirsch ('The Stag King')

Opera in three acts by Hans Werner Henze to a libretto by Heinz von Cramer after the fable by Carlo Gozzi; Berlin, Städtische Oper, 23 September 1956 (severely cut); revised as *Il re cervo, oder Die Irrfahrten der Wahrheit*, Kassel, Staatstheater, 10 March 1963; first performance of complete score, Stuttgart, Staatsoper, 5 May 1985.

The cast at the Berlin première included Sándor Kónya as the king, Helga Pilarczyk as Costanza, Tomislav Neralic as Tartaglia and Nora Jungwirth as Scolatella I. For the Kassel revision the first cast included Claude Heater (Leandro), Felicia Weathers (Costanza), Hans Günter Nöcker (Tartaglia) and Ingeborg Hallstein (Scolatella I). The Stuttgart staging was conducted by Dennis Russell Davies and produced by Hans Hollmann with a cast led by Toni Krämer, Julia Conwell, John Bröcheler and Karin Ott.

(Characters named as in *Il re cervo*; see below)

Leandro *the king*	tenor
Costanza *his lover*	soprano
Tartaglia *the chancellor*	bass-baritone
Scolatella I	coloratura soprano
Scolatella II	soubrette
Scolatella III	mezzo-soprano
Scolatella IV	contralto
Checco *a melancholy musician*	tenor buffo
Coltellino *an unsuccessful murderer*	tenor buffo
Six Alchemists	silent
Two Statues	contraltos
Cigolotti *a magician*	spoken
The Stag	spoken

Voices of the wood, voices of the people, voices of the wind, courtiers, pages, wild animals, people from the city, soldiers, huntsmen

Setting Near Venice, between sea and forest, in antiquity

Henze began discussions on a successor to his first stage opera, *Boulevard Solitude*, in 1952; Cramer's libretto was prepared by the following year and the composition of *König Hirsch* occupied Henze between 1953 and 1955. It was the first of his works to be composed during his self-imposed exile in Ischia, and its teeming, many-hued textures reflect the optimism of this period in his life. The original score contained more than five hours of music, and its arias in particular were severely cut by the conductor Hermann Scherchen for the Berlin première in 1956, which was directed by Leonard Steckel. The same version was also presented at Darmstadt in 1959 (conducted by Hans Zanotelli and directed by Harro Dicks) and at Bielefeld the following year. In 1962 Henze prepared a revised version, reducing the score to approximately half the original length and restoring the italianate names of Gozzi's fable. The revision involved substantial recomposition: new blocks of material replaced larger structures (the original finale of Act 2 became Henze's Fourth Symphony) and Cramer and the composer created a speaking role, the magician Cigolotti, to 'ensure that the plot remains comprehensible even though it is compressed'. In general it was the supernatural, 'magical' aspects of the score that were excised. The Kassel première of *Il re cervo* was conducted by Henze himself and the same production by Hans Hartleb was also seen in Munich two years later, conducted by Christoph von Dohnányi. In 1985 the uncut, original version of *König Hirsch* was at last performed, in Stuttgart. The following synopsis is of the version published in 1963 as *Il re cervo*.

*

Act I: 'The Castle'

I.i Everything is being prepared for the coronation of the new king, Leandro, who has been raised in the forest among the animals. As a storm rages (depicted in the orchestral introduction), Scolatella complains that the weather has ruined her clothes; she nurtures ambitions to become queen. Though the thunder terrifies her, she does not lose her self-confidence or her ambition, and from the looking-glass she summons her double, Scolatella II, who emerges equally full of complaints and closely followed by Scolatella III and Scolatella IV; all are intent on winning the hand of the new king.

I.ii ('The Coronation Procession') Scolatella I dispatches her doubles and hides herself as the sounds of a carillon and a chorus of celebration herald the beginning of the ceremony. Tartaglia appears, also looking for a hiding place, from where he delivers a long sardonic commentary on the absurd sycophancy of the ceremony ('a lamb led to the slaughter') and rails against his own unjust treatment. From his imperious manner Scolatella assumes Tartaglia to be the king.

'König Hirsch' (Henze), Act 2 (the wood): scene from the original production at the Städtische Oper, Berlin, 23 September 1956, with Checco and the alchemists disguised as animals

I.iii Scolatella takes the opportunity to introduce herself just before Costanza is brought in by guards. Tartaglia offers her freedom, but she refuses to leave; she is keen to discover what the new king is like, but assumes that he has had her arrested and therefore must be far less compassionate than Tartaglia. The chancellor eagerly agrees with this assessment; he gives her a dagger and tells her to kill Leandro with it. When Costanza hesitates, he forces her to hide the weapon and orders her to remain outside.

I.iv As the sound of the bells that dominated the previous scene dies away, the animals of the forest gather around Leandro to say goodbye; he delivers his farewell in a slow-moving, expressive aria. When he is left alone, two statues, singing in rhythmic unison and accompanied by harp and celesta, warn him of the dangers of the human world he is joining; they promise to warn him (by laughing) whenever anyone lies to him.

I.v ('Finale') Fanfares announce Tartaglia's entrance; he tells the new king that he must choose a bride. He is followed by a vivid carnival procession that also includes the four Scolatellas, each of whom is already confident she will be crowned queen. Leandro questions them, assisted by the statues; none of them meets his exacting standards.

I.vi Tartaglia introduces Costanza, and Leandro is immediately intrigued; the silence of the statues convinces him that she is suitable, and the couple begin a long, slow love duet. As it ends, Leandro breaks the statues so they cannot reveal his lover's

untruths, but Tartaglia 'discovers' Costanza's hidden dagger, and insists that she must be executed. Leandro decides he must abdicate, and is led back to the forest by Cigolotti, disguised as a parrot.

I.vii Tartaglia's plan has succeeded: he is triumphant. The spirits of the wind whirl around the stage, and Tartaglia orders Coltellino to follow Leandro and kill him; he will not accept the excuse that the spirits have blown away the assassin's dagger and pistol, and provides him with replacements. The act ends with the sounds of a percussion band and the entry of six alchemists, who have arrived, belatedly, to welcome the new king.

Act 2: 'The wood'

2.i An orchestral prelude of 'magical' textures – woodwind, horns, celesta – evokes the living, breathing sounds of the forest, and the voices of the woods warn of the presence of a stranger among them; suddenly the forest is full of men. Leandro is dogged by Scolatella, who clings to the idea that she is queen, though he tries to shake her off. Everyone – human, animal and the alchemists disguised as animals – appears to be both predator and prey; in the general confusion that culminates in a violent stretta, Tartaglia attempts to stab Leandro, but fails.

2.ii Cigolotti wishes to give Checco the secret of magical transformation; he can then pass it on to the king and save his life. As the sounds of the voices of the wood die away, Checco begins a beautifully expressive aria accompanied by solo guitar.

2.iii Tartaglia wounds a stag, but the animal

escapes, and the chancellor demands that Checco tell him where Leandro is hiding.

2.iv They have a magical vision of the stag's death, but Tartaglia also learns of the transformational spell, which he uses to change into the king's shape while Leandro himself is turned into the stag. Checco and Cigolotti are horrified by the events they have inadvertently set in train.

2.v Tartaglia now assumes the powers of the king; in a fierce declamation he imposes his dictatorial rule on the country, and organizes a stag hunt that will finally destroy Leandro, as a storm breaks over the forest.

Act 3: 'The City'

3.i Under Tartaglia's despotic rule the city has become a ghost town. While an offstage chorus cries for deliverance, Leandro, still transformed as the Stag King, wanders the streets. He receives no response to his calls, which are set against Coltellino's lament for his failure as an assassin.

3.ii Percussion again heralds the alchemists, who find themselves as hounded as the rest of the population.

3.iii Costanza enters the city searching for Leandro and, in an aria of high-lying legato lines over the sounds of the chorus, recalls her short-lived love for him.

3.iv Costanza finds the Stag King, and they manage to sing a second love duet, before the stag flees as Tartaglia arrives.

3.v Tartaglia pretends to be Leandro, but Costanza is not deceived and rejects his advances; the false king, now thoroughly paranoid, summons his soldiers to repel the enemies he sees on every side.

3.vi The people have become aware of the presence of the stag; an ancient legend holds that the arrival of a stag will restore peace to the city. Tartaglia still demands the animal be shot on sight, but just as he is about to do the deed himself he is shot by Coltellino, who mistakes him for the king. Leandro is transformed back to his real self, and the work ends with a general choral celebration, framing a short duet in which Leandro and Costanza are finally united.

*

In both its versions, but especially the original, *König Hirsch* is the most luxuriant of all Henze's operatic scores. Henze has acknowledged the italianate flavour of much of his writing, citing Bellini's example for some of the scoring. At the beginning of the opera, he wrote: 'rudiments of serial technique can still be found. They seem to mobilize the harmony, and rhythm, in order to release the material with greater freedom'. The opera is made up of self-contained numbers, highly varied – arias and cabalettas, duets and ensembles, music for the hunts and for the mimes – but it is connected by vivid bridge passages into a continuous whole, so that each act gives the impression of being through-composed.

A.C.

L

Lady Macbeth of the Mtsensk District
[*Ledi Makbet Mtsenskogo uyezda*]

Opera in four acts, op.29, by Dmitry Shostakovich to a libretto by the composer and Alexander Preys, after the short story by Nikolay Leskov; Leningrad (now St Petersburg), Malïy Opernïy Teatr, 22 January 1934 (revised as *Katerina Izmaylova*; Moscow, Stanislavsky–Nemirovich-Danchenko Music Theatre, 8 January 1963).

At the première the cast included A.I. Sokolova (Katerina), Georgy Nikiforovich Orlor (Boris), Stepan Vasil'evich Balashov (Zinovy) and Pyotr Ivanovich Zasetsky (Sergey).

Katerina L'vovna Izmaylova *wife of*	
Zinovy Borisovich	soprano
Boris Timofeyevich Izmaylov	
a merchant	high bass
Zinovy Borisovich Izmaylov *his son,*	
a merchant	tenor
Millhand	baritone
Sergey *the Izmaylovs' worker*	tenor
Coachman	tenor
Aksin'ya *the Izmaylovs' worker*	soprano
Shabby Peasant	tenor
Steward	bass
Porter	bass
Three Workers	tenors
Priest	bass
Apparition of Boris Timofeyevich	bass
Chief of Police	baritone
Policeman	bass
Teacher	tenor
Drunken Guest	tenor
Old Convict	bass
Sentry	bass
Sonetka *a convict*	contralto
Woman Convict	soprano
Officer	bass
Workers, policemen, guests, convicts	

Setting The Russian provinces in the mid-19th century

Shostakovich began the composition of his second opera in autumn 1930, as his first opera, *The Nose*, was completing its short run at the Malïy Theatre, Leningrad. Turning once again to 19th-century Russian literature for a subject, he chose Leskov's tale of the passion, greed and brutality of a provincial merchant's wife. The composer and his co-librettist Alexander Preys made small but significant alterations to Leskov's story, all designed to humanize the central character of Katerina, to find justification for her crimes and make her a positive, sympathetic figure. Shostakovich referred to his opera as a 'tragedy-satire'; his chief technique in winning the spectator's sympathy for his heroine was to caricature those around her with excessively grotesque and parodistic music. With the conspicuous exception of the convicts in the final act, Katerina is the only character in the opera treated to music of genuine lyrical feeling.

Shostakovich completed *Lady Macbeth* in December 1932, dedicating it to his new bride Nina Varzar. The work was projected as the first of a trilogy or tetralogy of operas, a cycle dealing with the fates of women from different periods of Russian history. Interest in staging *Lady Macbeth* came from both the Malïy Theatre in Leningrad and from the Nemirovich-Danchenko Music Theatre in Moscow. In the event, the Leningrad production, staged by Nikolay Smolich, designed by Vladimir Dmitriyev and conducted by Samuil Samosud – the same team responsible for producing *The Nose* – beat its Moscow rival to the première by two days: Vladimir Nemirovich-Danchenko's production, which took a less satirical reading of Shostakovich's work and made some cuts and alterations, opened under the title *Katerina Izmaylova* on 24 January 1934.

The opera, in both its productions, was an immediate critical and, especially, popular success; its earthy approach to sex, its graphic language and extreme violence gave it the powerful appeal of realism. The composer's confident mastery of the musical and dramatic idiom was indisputable. Despite minor criticisms, *Lady Macbeth* was widely hailed as the first major opera of the Soviet period. Over the next two years it received nearly 200 performances in Moscow and Leningrad. During the same period, it was exported and performed, either in concert or staged versions, in many cities including Buenos Aires, Cleveland, London, New York, Philadelphia, Stockholm and Zürich. In December

1935, a new production, similar to that of Leningrad's Malïy Theatre, was staged in the Bol'shoy Theatre's offshoot in Moscow. For a brief period in early January 1936, when the Malïy theatre company was on tour in Moscow, the city played host to three different productions simultaneously.

On 26 January 1936, Stalin, accompanied by a delegation of high-ranking government officials, attended a performance of the Bol'shoy production. The dignitaries did not stay for the fourth act. Two days later, an unsigned editorial, 'Sumbur vmesto muzïki' ('Muddle instead of Music'), an uncompromising attack on Shostakovich's opera, appeared unexpectedly in the government newspaper *Pravda*: 'From the very first moment, listeners are stunned by the deliberately dissonant and confused stream of sounds . . . singing is replaced by screaming . . . the music quacks, hoots, pants and gasps in order to express the love scenes as naturally as possible . . .'. The editorial censured the opera's pretensions as social satire, its rejection of the principles of classical opera and of 'a simple, accessible musical language'. It equated the opera's flaws with petty-bourgeois, leftist distortions in the other arts, contrasting this with the realistic, wholesome character of the 'true' art demanded by the people.

The timing and context of the editorial – its proximity, for instance, to Stalin's highly publicized approbation of Dzerzhinsky's opera *Quiet Flows the Don* earlier in the month – left no doubt in the artistic community that this was a strategically planned official assault whose sights extended well beyond this particular opera, or indeed the field of music. It was the opening salvo in a campaign that resulted in the explicit subjugation of the individual creative freedom of Soviet artists to the repressive control of the Communist Party and State, through their obligatory adherence to the aesthetic doctrine of Socialist Realism.

Shostakovich's opera quickly disappeared from the repertory, not to return for nearly 30 years and then only in a significantly revised version. In the mid-1950s, after Stalin's death, Shostakovich made revisions to his opera but it was not approved for production until 1963, when it was rehabilitated, as *Katerina Izmaylova* op.114, at the Stanislavsky–Nemirovich-Danchenko Music Theatre in Moscow on 8 January 1963. Ironically, perhaps, some of the most controversial aspects of the first version – the crude, naturalistic language and musical effects, especially the musically explicit seduction scene (1.iii) – had already been sanitized in the vocal score published in 1935, before the opera was repressed. In the revised version Shostakovich took the sanitizing process still further, modifying the extremes of tessitura and replacing two of the orchestral entr'actes.

In the late 1970s, the original 1932 version of *Lady Macbeth* was reinstated; it was staged, published and recorded in the West to great acclaim. Since then, the original version has replaced the revised *Katerina Izmaylova* in the repertory of Western opera houses. In the Soviet Union, however, where the composer's substitution of the revised version was accepted at face value, the revised version was recognized as definitive.

The following synopsis corresponds to the original 1932 version of the opera.

*

Act I.i *Katerina's bedroom* Katerina, the young wife of the provincial merchant Zinovy Izmaylov, tries to fall asleep, but gives up. She reflects instead on the source of her perpetual boredom and depression. In a brief arioso, she reveals her feeling of uselessness. The arrival of her father-in-law, Boris Timofeyevich, is announced by a steady, ominous pulse that punctuates an awkward bassoon melody. He asks if they will have his favourite dish of mushrooms for supper and Katerina nods curtly. Bridling at Katerina's apathy, Boris berates her for laziness and for failing to produce a child after nearly five years of marriage. Katerina defensively blames her husband but Boris accuses her of frigidity and (somewhat illogically) warns her not to try to cuckold his son. As he departs, he tells her to prepare some rat poison. To his back, she retorts that he is the rat.

Informed that the dam at the mill has broken, a reluctant Zinovy decides he must oversee repairs himself. Boris scolds the tittering workers and bullies them into a choral apotheosis of their master, 'Zachem, zhe, tï uyezzhayesh', khozyain?' ('Why are you leaving us, master?'), its patent hypocrisy underscored by coarse waltz rhythms. As Zinovy prepares, at a gallop, for his departure, he points out to his father the new worker Sergey. Boris cruelly officiates the otherwise tender farewell between husband and wife, convincing the guileless Zinovy that Katerina must swear her fidelity in public. Her humiliation reaches its pinnacle as Boris forces her to her knees. The brief, somewhat ominous, entr'acte between scenes grovels in the low range of cellos and basses.

I.ii *In the Izmaylovs' yard* The scene begins abruptly with the high-pitched screams of Aksin'ya as a group of male workers roughly manhandle and molest her. In the seething turmoil, Sergey takes command of the assault and is cheered on by his companions. The arrival of their mistress, Katerina, puts an immediate end to the abuse; she delivers a proud defence of women's value in her arioso 'Mnogo vï, muzhiki' ('You men are all so conceited'), and threatens to beat them. Sergey persuades her instead to wrestle. Almost overwhelmed by desire, he pins Katerina down; Boris Timofeyevich arrives,

'Lady Macbeth of the Mtsensk District' (Shostakovich, 1934), scene from the film of the revised version, 'Katerina Izmaylova',
directed by Mikhail Shapiro (1966), with Alexander Sokolov as Boris Timofeyevich and Galina Vishnevskaya in the title role

discovers them in this compromising position and demands an explanation. Katerina invents a story to protect Sergey and Boris barks at everyone to get back to work. In stark contrast to the tone of the music that immediately precedes and follows it, the entr'acte is a rollicking, circus-like romp.

I.iii Katerina's bedroom Katerina prepares for bed, lonely and bored. Making his rounds, Boris keeps tabs on her. In her aria, 'Zherebyonok k kobïlke toropitsya' ('The foal runs after the filly'), a lyrical and emotional effusion central to the perception of the heroine as a sympathetic figure, Katerina gives vent to the full measure of her frustrated passion and despair. Over an ominous drum roll, Sergey knocks at the door, throwing Katerina into fear and confusion. He persuades her to admit him and asks to borrow a book. He searches awkwardly for topics to prolong the conversation, admitting to his own boredom and sympathy for her position. Sergey's refusal to depart marks the beginning of a gradual, but inexorable, build-up of dramatic tension. He suggests that they wrestle again and, disregarding her protestations, embraces the struggling Katerina. She eventually succumbs to his seduction, and the union is consummated boisterously in a brassy instrumental interlude. The graphic musical representation of the sexual act in this lengthy passage, in particular the explicit trombone slides, proved the opera's most notorious feature in its first productions. In the languorous aftermath of lovemaking,

Katerina half-heartedly tells Sergey to leave, but she acknowledges him now as her only husband. The curtain falls with a brief reprise of the rollicking music of the previous entr'acte.

Act 2.iv A courtyard in the Izmaylovs' house The sleepless Boris patrols for burglars, and reminisces about his youth. As the music breaks into a brisk galop, he remembers fondly his prowess at the seduction of married women. When Boris notices a light on in Katerina's bedroom, the music shifts to a crude parody of a Viennese waltz; Boris persuades himself that, with Zinovy absent, he himself should go to her. At that moment he overhears Sergey and Katerina as they exchange tender farewells. Furious at the betrayal, Boris seizes Sergey as he departs and raises a rumpus. The workmen gather and Boris sends for a whip, calling Katerina to observe the relentless, rhythmic thrashing. Locked in her room, Katerina is unable to defend her lover. Finally she climbs down the drainpipe to intercede, but it is only his exhaustion which causes Boris to stop. He has Sergey locked in the storeroom and orders Katerina to bring him some of the leftover mushrooms, meanwhile sending someone to fetch Zinovy. Against a romantic obbligato for solo violin, Boris greedily consumes the mushrooms, unaware that Katerina has laced them with rat poison. Soon his stomach begins to burn but Katerina defiantly rejects his order to bring water. As Boris writhes on the ground and calls for a priest, Katerina removes his keys and runs to free Sergey. A chorus of passing labourers sing as they go to the fields, 'Vidno, skoro uzh zarya' ('See, the dawn is almost breaking'), and Boris sends one of them to fetch the Priest. In his confession, Boris tells the Priest about the rat poison and points to Katerina as he dies, but all think he is merely raving. The hypocrisy of Katerina's grief shows through her grotesque parody of the supplication music from the prologue to Musorgsky's *Boris Godunov*. As the Priest tries to comprehend the cause of death, he launches into jaunty, and utterly inapt, dance music. By contrast, the massive chordal tutti which opens the entr'acte, and the extended passacaglia which gradually builds and peaks in intensity, are more tragic in tone.

2.v *Katerina's bedroom* Katerina wakes Sergey and begs him to kiss her passionately. Sergey warns her that soon her husband will return; he whines that he is not content to be her secret lover, that he wants her as his wife; then he drifts back to sleep. She vows to make him both a merchant and her husband. Her resolve and new sense of courage, underscored by a resolute pulse, evaporate when she spies the threatening ghost of Boris Timofeyevich in the corner. He curses her. Katerina wakes Sergey in fear, but he cannot see the ghost and calms her. They sleep until, sensing the approach of her husband, Katerina wakes Sergey and whispers to him to hide. Trumpets herald Zinovy as he knocks insistently at the door and demands entry. Katerina delays him as long as she can. When she finally admits him, she responds to his suspicious questions with sarcasm in a heated, fast-paced exchange. When Zinovy begins to beat her, Katerina calls upon Sergey to protect her. Zinovy tries to escape, but Katerina strangles him while Sergey holds him down. Zinovy dies after Sergey strikes him over the head with a candlestick. To a vamp-like accompaniment, Sergey carries the body to the cellar as Katerina lights the way. She then embraces Sergey as her husband.

Act 3.vi *The Izmaylovs' house* On their wedding day, while standing outside the cellar, Katerina confesses to Sergey that she is afraid. He tells her not to fear the dead, only the living. Looking to the future, they depart for the church. The shabby Peasant enters and, in a grotesquely comic song punctuated with drunken hiccups, 'U menya bïla kuma' ('Once I had a ladyfriend'), he expounds in characteristically Russian fashion the joys of drinking. His desire for a drink prompts him to break the lock on the cellar; the stink at first repels him, but then, to the bouncy, dance-like accompaniment of trumpets and drums, he discovers the corpse of Zinovy and runs off to the police. The entr'acte extends the sprightly, colourful atmosphere.

3.vii *At the police station* In a song in conspicuous strophic form, 'Sozdan politseyskiy bïl vo vremya ono' ('The police were created in the days of old'), the Chief of Police impresses on his men the significance of their profession. In the lilting waltz refrain, the chorus of policemen lament the low pay and the scarcity of bribes. The Chief is annoyed that Katerina has not invited him to her wedding and promises to get even. Saying he has caught a socialist, a policeman drags in a Teacher who has been experimenting to see if frogs have souls. He is thrown in jail. The bored Chief resumes his song. The shabby Peasant arrives and informs them that there is a corpse in the Izmaylovs' cellar, news which is greeted with enthusiasm. The policemen make haste to depart. The entr'acte alternates the police's bustling music with unrelated dance-like episodes.

3.viii *In the Izmaylovs' garden* In fugal entries, the wedding guests wish the married couple long life, health and happiness. According to Russian custom, the Priest periodically calls for the couple to kiss. In a rather tipsy manner, he extols Katerina's beauty. Gradually the drunken guests fall asleep. Suddenly Katerina notices that the lock on the cellar has been broken. Terrified, she tells the reluctant Sergey that they have not a minute to waste. Sergey fetches some money, but their escape is cut off by the march of the approaching police. Impatient with the Chief's self-important dawdling, Katerina begs Sergey's forgiveness and extends her hands for the handcuffs. Sergey, however, tries to escape and is beaten. Both are led away.

Act 4.ix *On the banks of a river* A column of convicts settles down for the night, separated into the sexes and guarded by sentries. In an affecting, folk-inspired lament in Musorgskian vein, 'Verstï odna za drugoy' ('Verst by verst, one after another'), an Old Convict reflects philosophically on the endless road; his resignation to a cheerless fate is reinforced by the chorus of convicts. Slipping the sentry a bribe, Katerina makes her way to Sergey and snuggles up to him tenderly. Initially ignoring her, Sergey snaps at her for ruining his life. Tormented by his rejection, Katerina begs his forgiveness and returns to her place. In counterpoint with solo english horn, she intones a plaintive lament 'Nelegko posle pochyota da poklonov' ('It's hard after being honoured and respected'). Sergey steals up to the pretty young convict, Sonetka, and flirts with her. They make fun of Katerina. If he wants to win her favour, Sonetka demands that Sergey get her a new pair of stockings. Sergey fawns on Katerina, pretending that without the stockings he will not be able to travel further. Selflessly, she takes off and gives him her own pair, which he promptly delivers to Sonetka. Katerina watches helplessly as Sergey carries Sonetka off in triumph; she is forced to endure the shrill mockery of the other women. Over an ominous, low sustained tremolo, the heroine, numb with grief, examines her black conscience in the arioso 'V lesu, v samoy chashche yest' ozero' ('In the forest, right in a thicket, there is a lake'). Sergey and Sonetka return from their tryst and jauntily tease Katerina. A steady drumbeat is heard and the sentries muster the column of convicts for departure. Slowly, Katerina approaches Sonetka on the bridge and pushes her, screaming, into the river, throwing herself in after. Both women are swept away by the strong current. The convicts are quickly formed back into ranks and are marched away, to a reprise of the Old Convict's lament.

*

Musically and dramatically, *Lady Macbeth* is more immediately accessible than *The Nose*. It shares with the earlier opera a dynamic, fast-paced momentum – unified by instrumental interludes that connect the scenes within each act – as well as frequent, often comic, allusions to the aesthetic of music hall, theatre and circus. Here, however, Shostakovich places these features within a realistic plot and grounds them in a more conventional tonal idiom. He makes it difficult not to empathize with the suffering and downfall of Katerina, a misguided but, in the context of her social milieu, singularly strong and noble spirit.

Although *Lady Macbeth* has finally and firmly established itself among the few operatic master-pieces of the 20th century, its fate as tragic victim of Soviet political repression also caused an irreparable loss for the history of opera. Still under the age of 30 and one of the most naturally gifted theatrical composers of his generation, after the work's con-demnation Shostakovich abandoned his ambition to create a tetralogy of operas about women. Despite a lifelong attraction to the genre and frequent fitful starts, he never completed another opera.

L.E.F.

Legend of the Invisible City of Kitezh and the Maiden Fevroniya, The [*Skazaniye o nevidimom grade Kitezhe i deve Fevronii*]

Opera in four acts by Nikolay Andreyevich Rimsky-Korsakov to a libretto by Vladimir Nikolayevich Bel'sky conflated from the so-called Kitezh Chronicle of I. S. Meledin, the novel *V lesakh* ('In the Woods') by Pavel Ivanovich Mel'nikov (Pechersky), songs and epics collected by Kirsha Danilov and several traditional tales, including *The Life of Peter, Prince of Murom, and his Wife Fevroniya* (as set down in 1547, the year of their canonization); St Petersburg, Mariinsky Theatre, 7/20 February 1907.

The première was conducted by Felix Blumenfeld; the sets and costumes were by Apollinary Vasnetsov and Konstantin Korovin, and the cast included Andrey Labinsky as Vsevolod,

Mariya Kuznetsova as Fevroniya, Ivan Yershov as Grishka Kuter'ma, Vladimir Kastorsky as the Bard, Nadezhda Zabela as Sirin and Yevgeniya Zbruyeva as Alkonost.

Prince Yury Vsevolodovich *ruler of Kitezh*		bass
Princeling Vsevolod Yur'yevich *his son*		tenor
Fevroniya		soprano
Grishka Kuter'ma		tenor
Fyodor Poyarok		baritone
A Boy *Prince Yury's page*		mezzo-soprano
Two Upper-Crusters		tenor, bass
Bard *(psaltery player)*		bass
Bear Trainer		tenor
Singing Beggar		baritone
Bedyay	*Mongol warriors*	bass
Burunday		bass
Sirin	*vatic birds*	soprano
Alkonost		contralto

The Prince's musketeers, wedding party, domra players, upper-crusters, mendicant brothers, miscellaneous crowd, Tatars

Setting The Volga woods near Lesser Kitezh, in Lesser and Greater Kitezh, on Lake Svetlïy Yar, in the woods of Kerzhenets and in the Invisible City, in the year 6751 from the creation of the world

The 16th-century *zhitiye* (hagiography) of St Fevroniya of Murom has always been a prime document of Russian religious syncretism, in which Christian elements coexist with remnants of pre-Christian Slavonic mythology. The libretto of Rimsky-Korsakov's penultimate opera (composed in 1903–4), combining history (the Mongol invasion of 1223), pantheistic folklore and Christian mystery, is another such document. In setting it, Rimsky drew on a lifetime of experience in imitating a wide variety of traditional musical genres, now including church chant. Bel'sky, the librettist, had originally planned a dramatization of the *zhitiye* itself, but this Rimsky-Korsakov disallowed. His own reverent sentiments, already memorably embodied in *The Snow Maiden*, were pantheistic (and not so much metaphysical as aesthetic). These, bolstered with a strong dose of patriotism, dominated the opera to the extent that it held the stage in Soviet times with only minimal alterations to its text.

*

Act I *A forest* After a prelude entitled 'In Praise of the Wilderness', the curtain rises on a dense forest, where Fevroniya lives with her brother, a woods-man. She sings of its mysteries and communes with the birds and beasts, her song culminating in a jubilus: 'A-oo!', the traditional folk-poetic ejaculation of wordless nature ecstasy. Suddenly she spies a stranger who has lost his way on a hunt. They immediately fall in love, he with her spiritual wisdom and beauty, she with his heroic mien. He claims her for his bride but, hearing hunting horns approach, leaves her to join his party, promising to send matchmakers to her brother. His men enter in pursuit of him, and Fevroniya learns from the huntsman Fyodor Poyarok that she has become betrothed to his master, Vsevolod, son of Prince Yury of Kitezh.

Act 2 *The town of Lesser Kitezh* A holiday crowd turns out to greet Princess Fevroniya as her wedding procession passes through Lesser Kitezh on the way to Greater Kitezh. A trained bear entertains them. An old bard sings a prophetic song to his psaltery, foretelling woe. A group of rich citizens express their discontent with Vsevolod's choice of a low-born bride and persuade the drunken Grishka Kuter'ma to mock her on her arrival. A group of mendicant brothers sing a song of praise to the rich citizens, a song of mockery at Grishka. The bridal party enters, announced by Poyarok; the ritual of the 'bride's ransom' is performed, followed by a song of praise to the bride. Suddenly the Tatars attack. They take two prisoners: Fevroniya, as a prize, and Grishka, who in fear for his life agrees to guide them to Greater Kitezh. The populace disperses in horror. Fevroniya prays for a miracle: that Greater Kitezh be made invisible to the enemy.

Act 3.i *The Cathedral Square of Greater Kitezh* The people are assembled at dead of night. Poyarok, whom the Tatars have blinded, comes with news of their pillage. Prince Yury leads his people in prayer. A page is sent up to a tower to watch for the advancing host; when he spies them Prince Yury appoints a militia, headed by his son, to defend the city. As the soldiers march off, singing, a golden mist descends on Kitezh, accompanied by the ringing of the church bells.

The bloody battle of Kerzhenets is depicted in the entr'acte, which pits the soldiers' song against the Tatars' leitmotifs, all accompanied by a musical motif suggesting wild hoofbeats.

3.ii *Lake Svetliy Yar* Grishka leads the Tatars, with Fevroniya, to the banks, where Greater Kitezh should be visible on the opposite shore. Since there is nothing to be seen but golden haze, the Tatars accuse him of deception, tie him up, and threaten death by torture the next day. They muse on the day's events, regretting that the noble Vsevolod, though he sustained 40 wounds, would not allow himself to be taken as an honoured prisoner but preferred to perish on the battlefield. They make fires and fall to dividing their booty. In a dispute over Fevroniya the Tatar warrior Burunday slays his companion Bedyay. The group finish their division of spoils while singing a gruesome song about the ravens flocking over the field of carnage. The Tatars fall

asleep. Grishka, raving with guilt and remorse, implores Fevroniya to untie him. Although he has not only betrayed Kitezh but has blamed her for his own misdeed, Fevroniya shows him kindness. Grishka's head is ringing with the Kitezh church bells. To put an end to their ear-splitting sound he runs to the lake to drown himself but stops short as the first rays of dawn come up and show the reflection of the invisible city in its waters; he runs off in terror, taking Fevroniya with him. The Tatars, awakened by his cries, see the reflected city and disperse in fright.

Act 4.i *A forest; the next night* Fevroniya and Grishka are struggling through the wilderness (the opening forest music returns, dissonantly harmonized). Grishka is still raving; Fevroniya tries to comfort him with scriptural verses, but he finally goes mad, does a violent dance and runs off howling. Fevroniya, left alone, falls asleep, and as she does so the forest is transformed into a magical place: lighted candles appear in the trees and illuminate the night; fantastic flowers blossom forth and unearthly birds begin to sing, among them Alkonost, who tells Fevroniya that she is to die. The ghost of Vsevolod appears to lead her to the Invisible City. The prophet-bird Sirin foretells her eternal life.

The transfiguration of Fevroniya's soul on the way to the Invisible City is portrayed in the entr'acte, a magnificent orchestral carillon.

4.ii *The Invisible City* Fevroniya is greeted by Prince Yury and her wedding party, who resume the ceremony broken off in Act 2. Vsevolod leads her to the altar. She remembers Grishka, asks that he too be saved, but is told that he is not ready. She sends a message of consolation to him to inspire him to achieve eternal life with her in the Invisible City.

*

Although the miracle by which the city of Kitezh was saved from the 'Tatars' is clearly wrought by the Christian God (and is announced by the spontaneous ringing of church bells), the only supernatural agencies to appear in the opera are Sirin and Alkonost, the traditional prophet-birds of Slavonic mythology. Fevroniya herself is turned into an apostle of pantheism: when asked in Act 1 whether she attends church she answers, 'Is not God everywhere? You may think [my forest] is an empty place, but no – it is a great church, where day and night we celebrate the Eucharist'. And the music to which she sings these lines comes back in Act 4 to accompany her transfigured soul – after an apotheosis that harks deliberately back to the Snow Maiden's nature ecstasies – into the Invisible City. There, the mystical rites are inextricably bound up with a folk wedding ceremony – the very one that had been interrupted by the Tatars in Act 2, of which the melody is recapitulated. Thus Christian religion

'Legend of the Invisible City of Kitezh and the Maiden Fevroniya' (Rimsky-Korsakov), final scene (the invisible city, with the prophet-birds Sirin and Alkonost, centre right): design by Apolinary Vasnetsov for the original production at the Mariinsky Theatre, St Petersburg, 7/20 February 1907

is treated in *Kitezh* as an aspect of folklore, which is probably how Rimsky-Korsakov, an enthusiastic positivist, viewed it.

Kitezh is often called the 'Russian Parsifal', and this is justified insofar as Wagner's last opera was clearly among its models. The miracle music in Acts 3 and 4 resonates with the basso ostinato from the Good Friday Spell, and there is even a sort of Dresden Amen in the last scene, which takes place in the transfigured realm, having been foreshadowed when Fevroniya had spoken to Grishka of God's mysterious greatness, and again when she partakes of the Eucharistic bread offered her by the ghost of Vsevolod and is spiritually transformed. The opera's opening scene, of which the music is often reheard later, is rightly compared with the Forest Murmurs in *Siegfried* (although it is organized around a Balakirevesque key scheme, B minor alternating with D♭ major, and although it contains the same typically Russian cadences that inform much of the vocal writing); the appearance of Alkonost and Sirin to Fevroniya as disembodied voices in Act 4 was probably inspired by the Forest Bird episode in the same scene from Wagner's opera. Another ostensible echo from the *Ring* is the episode where the oafish Burunday kills Bedyay, as Fafner kills Fasolt, in a dispute over spoils.

Of course, there are also many resonances in *Kitezh* from earlier Russian opera, of which there was

by the early 20th century a distinguished body of 'classics'. Chief among them was Glinka's *A Life for the Tsar*; the collision of national forces in Rimsky's opera was modelled on Act 3 of Glinka's, in which the Poles break in on a betrothal ceremony just as the Tatars do in *Kitezh*, their approach being telegraphed to the audience by a preliminary snatch of their leitmotif between the strains of a wedding song. The other important Russian model was Musorgsky, from whom Rimsky derived, or attempted to derive, the declamatory style in which he cast the role of Grishka Kuter'ma, whose music is full of resonances from the role of the Pretender (another Grishka!) in the Cell and Inn Scenes from *Boris Godunov*. Since Rimsky's musical imagination was heavily dependent on parallel rhythmic periods and melodic sequences, the imitation is flawed, and Grishka's music came out sounding (surely inadvertently) as if modelled on that of Pyotr Il'ich, the tormented anti-hero of Serov's *The Power of the Fiend*, an opera Rimsky did not hold in very high esteem. A third musical precedent from earlier Russian opera is that of the Republican Council scene in Rimsky-Korsakov's first opera, *The Maid of Pskov*, on which the final chorus in Act 2 is modelled, showing the inhabitants of Lesser Kitezh in a state of panic. Here Rimsky's choral writing is of a 'realistic' declamatory complexity he had not attempted since his early days as a member of the Kuchka, the Five. While the opera is conceived from first to last as a stylization of folk art, both as to sound and as to structure, of actual quoted folksongs there are only two: the song of the mendicant brothers in Act 2 and the famous historical song 'Pro tatarskiy polon' ('On the Mongol Captivity', published by Balakirev and also used by Tchaikovsky and Taneyev), which, suitably dressed up with augmented 2nds, provided one of the leitmotifs of the invaders, the other being a descending tone-semitone (octatonic) scale, long associated in Rimsky's work with exotic, usually supernatural, evil.

The music of the opera is wholly continuous. While it is essentially composed in lyric set pieces, they are never allowed to come to full closes and are never extracted (hence they are not listed individually in the synopsis above). Even the pairs of scenes that make up the third and fourth acts are connected by the entr'actes in such a way that there is no musical close before the end of the act – and not even then in the case of Act 2, which fades out on an unresolved tritone.   R.T.

Life for the Tsar, A [Zhizn' za tsarya; Ivan Susanin]

'Patriotic heroic-tragic opera' in five acts (or four acts with epilogue) by Mikhail Ivanovich Glinka to a libretto by Baron Yegor Fyodorovich Rozen, Vladimir Sollogub, Nestor Vasil'yevich Kukol'nik and Vasiliy Andreyevich Zhukovsky; St Petersburg, Bol'shoy Theatre, 27 November/9 December 1836 (as Ivan Susanin, with a new libretto by Sergey Gorodetsky, Moscow, Bol'shoy Theatre, 21 February 1939).

The original Ivan was Osip Petrov; Sobinin was the debutant Lev Ivanovich Leonov, natural son of John Field; Mariya Stepanova sang Antonida; Anna Vorob'yova sang Vanya; and Catterino Cavos conducted the première.

Ivan Susanin *a peasant from the village of*	
Domnino	bass
Antonida *his daughter*	soprano
Bogdan Sobinin *her fiancé*	tenor
Vanya *an orphan, Susanin's ward*	contralto
Head of a Polish Detachment	baritone
Head of a Russian Detachment	bass
Polish Messenger	tenor
Russian and Polish choruses; soldiers, gentry,	
peasants, crowd	
Setting Russia and Poland, 1613	

A Life for the Tsar was hatched in the aristocratic literary salon of the poet Vasiliy Andreyevich Zhukovsky, to which Glinka became attached imme-

diately on his return to St Petersburg from Italy in 1834. 'When I declared my ambition to undertake an opera in Russian', Glinka recalled in his memoirs, 'Zhukovsky sincerely approved of my intention and suggested the subject of Ivan Susanin'. It was a predictable choice at a time in Russian cultural history when 'national' in the context of high art inevitably connoted 'patriotic', and 'folk' inevitably connoted 'peasant'. Ivan Susanin was the quasi-legendary hero of popular resistance to Polish infiltration in the wake of the False Dmitry's triumph over Boris Godunov in the early 17th century. A volunteer militia, financed by Kuz'ma Minin, a merchant from Nizhnïy-Novgorod, and commanded by Prince Dmitry Pozharsky, was challenging the Polish forces abroad in the land in the name of Mikhail Romanov, the 16-year-old scion of an old boyar family, who had been elected tsar by a popular assembly in February 1613 and who immediately went into hiding in a monastery near his family estate in Kostroma. Susanin, a local peasant, concealed from a Polish search party the whereabouts of the young tsar, the founder of the last Russian dynasty, under torture and at the eventual cost of his life. The event was first recorded in a crown charter granted to the martyr's son-in-law Sobinin in 1619, and renewed in the name of Susanin's heirs by every Romanov ruler down to Nikolay I. The name entered historical literature in 1792 and was immortalized by Sergey Glinka (the composer's cousin) in his *Russian History for Purposes of Upbringing* (1817), since which time it went into all children's textbooks and became part of every Russian's patriotic consciousness.

Parallels with Susanin's deed were suggested by the activities of peasant partisans in the Patriotic War of 1812 against Napoleon; in the aftermath of that war 'Ivan Susanin' became a fixture of Russian Romantic literature (e.g. the eponymous ballad, or 'duma', by Kondraty Rïleyev) and the Russian stage, including the musical stage (e.g. Catterino Cavos's eponymous Singspiel, to a libretto by Alexander Shakhovskoy; Glinka's opera, too, was originally to have been called *Ivan Susanin*: its eventual title was conferred upon it by Tsar Nikolay I in return for the dedication). Before suggesting the subject to Glinka, Zhukovsky had tried to interest the historical novelist Mikhail Zagoskin in it. By the time of Glinka's association with Zhukovsky, moreover, ideas of national and patriotic art had been given a new context as part of the doctrine of Official Nationality associated with the reign of Nikolay I. Zhukovsky, not only a great poet but also an official of Nikolay's court and tutor to the tsarevich (the future Alexander II), was one of its most enthusiastic proponents, and the self-sacrifice of the peasant Susanin in the cause of establishing the Romanov dynasty epitomized the official doctrine's ideals.

Except for the epilogue, which he wrote himself (it remains a prime historical document of Nikolayan state ideology), Zhukovsky farmed out the actual task of composing the text to his court colleague Baron Rozen, the German-born secretary to the tsarevich, who, after augmenting the title character's household so far as necessary to obtain a standard operatic quartet, seems for the most part to have followed Rïleyev's treatment of the Susanin legend with its dramatic scene in the woods. Before Rozen's involvement in the project Vladimir Sollogub wrote the texts for the opening choruses and for Antonida's cavatina and rondo in Act 1. Nestor Kukol'nik, one of Glinka's closest friends, contributed the text for Vanya's scene at the monastery gates, which was composed at Peterhof in August 1837 (that is, ten months after the première) as a vehicle for Vorob'yova, who had had a sensational success in the part; it was first performed on 18 October, and since then has usually replaced the heroic aria for Sobinin that originally opened Act 4. A detailed scenario, modelled largely on the formal conventions of the contemporary Italian opera, was drawn up late in 1834 and guided the composer and librettist(s) as they worked independently, the music frequently outrunning the text. Glinka relied as well on an unusually complete and well thought-out musical plan that reflected not only his acquaintance with French rescue operas and an aspiration to achieve 'a single shapely whole', but also his enthusiastic commitment to the state ideology and his determination to embody it in symbolic sounds.

The music was in Soviet times divorced from its original context and made the bearer of a new libretto by Gorodetsky that replaced the notion of nationhood to which the composer subscribed with one that separates the idea of nation from the idea of a divinely sanctioned monarchy. The implicit claim was that music, being transcendent, is ideologically adaptable. But the claim was contradicted by the opera's critical reception, as witness the difficulties both Soviet and Western scholars had in identifying and justifying the opera's national character.

Although the Gorodetsky libretto is the one to which the opera has been most frequently performed and recorded since 1939 (Mark Reyzen sang Ivan under Samuil Samosud at the première), the original libretto was revived – in the spirit, one gathers, of *glasnost'* – at the Bol'shoy in 1989. Performance materials are no doubt forthcoming, and one may assume that the days of the ersatz libretto are numbered. The following synopsis is based on the original.

*

Act I *The village of Domnino on the river Shacha* Groups of male and female peasants enter from opposite sides, the men singing of their devotion to tsar and country, the women of the coming of spring. Antonida enters and sings of her longing for Sobinin, then of her approaching wedding day ('V pole chistoye glyazhu': 'I gaze over the broad field'). Susanin enters and quashes his daughter's happy daydreams: there can be no talk of weddings while the country's fate remains uncertain. Boatmen are heard on the river; their boat appears bringing Sobinin. He brings news of Pozharsky's resistance and (supported by the chorus) asks for permission to wed Antonida forthwith; Susanin says only when there is a lawful tsar on the throne will he permit it; Sobinin says it will not be long, for the assembly has already elected Mikhail Romanov; all rejoice at this.

Act 2 *A ball given by the Head of the Polish detachment; guests of both sexes* Couples are dancing a polonaise. They express confidence in their victory over the Russians in a chorus. The dancing continues with a krakowiak and a Pas de quatre (waltz). A messenger rushes in with news of the election of Mikhail, who would displace the Polish prince Wladyslaw as chief claimant to the throne. A group of soldiers immediately sets out towards Kostroma, where Mikhail is known to be hiding, so as to kidnap the tsar-elect and prevent his installation (mazurka and finale).

Act 3 *Susanin's hut* After an entr'acte, the curtain goes up on Vanya, who is singing of his happy life in the bosom of Susanin's family. Susanin enters and tells Vanya the news of Mikhail's election. Vanya expresses his fear that the Poles might come after Mikhail; Susanin reassures him that they would never succeed in finding him, for no one would betray the tsar. Peasants stop by on their way to work to offer congratulations on Antonida's wedding. Sobinin enters, then Antonida; all four members of the family express their joyous anticipations in a quartet. Sobinin goes out to attend to final arrangements. Susanin gives thanks that he has lived to see his daughter married; he and Antonida reassure Vanya that one day he will have the same good fortune as his sister. Their musing is interrupted by the sound of approaching horses. The Poles burst in. They pose as a 'deputation' and ask to be led to the tsar. At first Susanin refuses indignantly, but after threats (and after reflecting that if he refuses another might not) he feigns agreement. He tells Vanya that he will attempt to lead the Poles astray and that Vanya must hasten to the monastery and warn the tsar's people of the imminent danger. Antonida realizes the Poles will kill her father; she begs him not to go. The Poles pull them apart and leave with Susanin. Antonida falls on a bench weeping. At this point Antonida's friends arrive for the bridal party, singing a ritual song of comfort; they break off singing when they see that Antonida is genuinely weeping. She tells them what has happened ('Ne o

'A Life for the Tsar' (Glinka): watercolour by Grigory Gagarin showing a scene from Act 3 (in Susanin's hut) of the original production at the Bol'shoy Theatre, St Petersburg, 27 November/9 December 1836

tom skorblyu, podruzhen'ki': 'Not for that do I grieve, dear friends'). Sobinin comes back with peasants, having heard that the Poles have been in the village; the peasants swear vengeance.

Act 4.i *A forest glade; night* After an entr'acte, Sobinin enters with the peasants, armed. They have lost their way in the dark. Sobinin encourages them (aria, 'Brattsï, v metel'': 'Brothers, into the storm!').

4.ii *The monastery gates* Vanya arrives on foot, exhausted; he beats on the door for a long time before anyone stirs. He identifies himself, explains the situation, and bids everyone leave with him (aria, 'Bednïy kon' v pole pal': 'My poor horse has fallen in the field').

4.iii *A dark, snow-bound forest* The Poles curse Susanin for not finding the high road to the monastery; they decide to light a fire and rest. They fall asleep, and Susanin reflects on his fate: the Poles have begun to sense the truth; will he be able to hold them off till dawn (aria, 'Tï priydyosh', moya zarya': 'You will come, my dawn')? Susanin reminisces about his family and bids them a vicarious farewell. A storm blows up. The Poles stir. They question Susanin, who finally reveals his ruse with a taunt. The Poles fall upon Susanin and kill him, but not

before he has seen the first rays of sun and knows that he has succeeded. Immediately, Sobinin and his peasants enter and fall upon the Poles.

Act 5 (Epilogue) *Red Square, Moscow* After an entr'acte, a vast crowd is seen rejoicing at Mikhail's coronation, among them Antonida, Sobinin and Vanya. Susanin's heirs lament him passionately; soldiers tell them the tsar will not forget their father's sacrifice. Bells ring out as the tsar approaches. All are caught up in the hymn (finale, 'Slav'sya, slav'sya, nash russkiy Tsar'': 'Glory to thee our Russian Caesar').

*

The earliest Russian opera to achieve permanent repertory status (hence the cornerstone of the Russian national repertory) and the first to be performed abroad (in Prague under Balakirev, 1866), *A Life for the Tsar* was, quite simply, the first Russian opera that was truly an opera (not a Singspiel), competitive with yet stylistically distinct from its most advanced Western European counterparts. For these reasons its historical significance is impossible to overrate: in Yury Keldïsh's memorable phrase, the opera 'marked the boundary between the past and the future of Russian music', and it was immediately so perceived (especially, at first, by literary men such as Pushkin and Gogol).

The composer's root conception of the drama underlying his first completed opera lay in the opposition of Russian music *v* Polish, a structural antithesis that has many surface manifestations. The Poles (the 'other') are at all times and places represented by stereotyped dance genres in triple metre (polonaise, mazurka) or highly syncopated duple (krakowiak); they express themselves only collectively, in impersonal choral declamation. The Russian music is at all times highly lyrical. Its chief identifying traits are predominance of duple (or compound-duple) time, though duple bars are often grouped very irregularly, as in Vanya's song with its seven-bar phrases; cadential terminations by (sometimes heavily embellished) falling 4ths or 5ths (what Glinka called the 'soul of Russian music'); and a very free, seemingly unstable interplay of relative major and minor keys (reflecting what ethnomusicologists call the 'mutable mode' of Russian melismatic songs). The prime examples of Russian style are from Act 1: Antonida's cavatina and the first part of the concluding trio. The second act is entirely given over to Polish dances. Thereafter the rhythm of the musical contrast becomes more rapid: the Poles' approach in Act 3 is signalled by a few strategic allusions to the Act 2 polonaise; their colloquies with Susanin both in that act and in Act 4 are always couched (on both sides) in stereotyped generic terms. At the tensest moment in Act 3, where the Poles forcibly seize Susanin and he cries out 'God, save the Tsar!', Polish (triple) and Russian (duple) rhythms are briefly superimposed. The symbolic battle of styles is also played out in the overture, which (contrary to usual practice) was the first number from the opera to be composed.

Derivations from actual folklore in *A Life for the Tsar* are few. Susanin's first replique in Act 1 is based on a coachman's song Glinka had taken down from life, while a very famous song, *Vniz po matushke po Volge* ('Downstream on the Mother Volga'), reduced to a characteristic motif, accompanies the denouement in Act 4 as an ostinato. The bridesmaids' chorus in Act 3 (a brilliant adaptation of an old Russian decorative stage convention to a novel dramatic purpose), while set to an original melody, is composed in the authentic pentasyllabic hemistichs of Russian wedding songs, which Glinka was the first artist-composer to set in an actual quintuple metre instead of adapting it to a more conventional one. (The result is another form of 'Russian' compound duple, precisely as in the famous Allegro con grazia from Tchaikovsky's Sixth Symphony.) Wholly, if very skilfully, feigned are the choruses in Act 1, including the one for boatmen in which an elaborate pizzicato accompaniment in imitation of balalaika strumming cunningly pits the theme of the earlier women's chorus in counterpoint against the boatmen's tune.

Far more important than the sheer amount of folk or folk-like material in the score is the use to which that material is put. This was Glinka's great breakthrough: he was able to prove that Russian melody could be elevated to the level of tragedy. In other words, he had without loss of scale integrated the national material into the stuff of his 'heroic' drama instead of relegating it, as was customary, to incidental decorative numbers. Of the dramatic crux, including Susanin's Act 4 scena in which the national style is particularly marked, one commentator wrote: 'One must hear it to be convinced of the feasibility of such a union, which until now has been considered an unrealizable dream'. One reason why it had been so considered, of course, was that before Glinka Russian composers had never aspired to the tragic style at all. What made it feasible was that the main characters in Glinka's opera were all peasants, hence eligible, within the conventions of the day, to employ a folkish idiom.

But that hardly made the opera 'democratic'. The most advanced of all Glinka's musico-dramatic techniques was one that enabled him to harp from beginning to end on the opera's overriding theme of zealous submission to divinely ordained dynastic authority. The epilogue, which portrays Mikhail Romanov's triumphant entrance into Moscow, is built around a choral anthem (Glinka called it a 'hymn-march') proclaimed by massed forces, including two wind bands on stage, to the following quatrain by Zhukovsky:

> Slav'sya, slav'sya nash russkiy Tsar',
> Gospodom dannïy nam Tsar'-gosudar'!
> Da budet bessmerten tvoy tsarskiy rod!
> Da im blagodenstvuyet russkiy narod!
>
> (Glory, glory to thee our Russian Caesar,
> Our sovereign given us by God!
> May thy royal line be immortal!
> May the Russian people prosper through it!)

(In the 1939 Gorodetsky text, this reads: 'Slav'sya, slav'sya tï, Rus' moya! Slav'sya tï, russkaya nasha zemlya! Da budet vo veki vekov sil'na Lyubimaya nasha, rodnaya strana!': 'Glory, glory to thee, my Russia! Glory to thee, our Russian land! May our beloved, our native land be strong throughout all ages!')

Glinka's setting is in a recognizable 'period' style – that of the 17th- and 18th-century *kantï*, three- or four-part polyphonic songs that were the oldest of all 'Westernized' Russian repertories (ironically, and perhaps unknown to Glinka, their ancestry was part Polish), and which in Peter the Great's time were often used for civic panegyrics (in which form they were known as 'Vivats'). The *Slav'sya* theme is related to that of the opening chorus in Act 1, and through that relationship to the opening phrase of the overture. But that only begins to describe its unifying role. The *Slav'sya* theme (which in Nikolayan and Alexandrine Russia became virtually a second national anthem) is foreshadowed throughout the opera wherever the topic of dynastic legitimacy is broached. Thus A *Life for the Tsar* is thematically unified in both verbal and musical dimensions by the tenets of Official Nationality – a congruence that is sundered if the libretto is replaced. The irony, of course, is that Glinka adapted the techniques by which he achieved this broadly developed musico-dramatic plan from the rescue operas of the revolutionary period and applied them to an opera where rescue is thwarted (though in Cavos's version it had been provided), and in which the political sentiment was literally counter-revolutionary.   R.T.

Lohengrin

Romantische Oper in three acts by Richard Wagner to his own libretto; Weimar, Grossherzogliches Hoftheater, 28 August 1850.

The première, under Liszt's direction, included Carl Beck (Lohengrin), Rosa Agthe (Elsa), Hans Feodor von Milde (Telramund), Josephine Fastlinger (Ortrud), and Höfer (King Henry).

Heinrich der Vogler [King Henry the Fowler]	bass
Lohengrin	tenor
Elsa of Brabant	soprano
Duke Gottfried *her brother*	silent
Friedrich von Telramund *a count of Brabant*	baritone
Ortrud *his wife*	mezzo-soprano
The King's Herald	bass
Four Noblemen of Brabant	tenors, basses
Four Pages	sopranos, altos

Saxon and Thuringian counts and nobles, Brabantine counts and nobles, noblewomen, pages, vassals, ladies, serfs

Setting Antwerp; first half of the 10th century

Wagner's acquaintance with the Lohengrin legend dates back to the winter of 1841–2, when he encountered it in the form of a synopsis and commentary in the annual proceedings of the Königsberg Germanic Society. In the summer of 1845 he became engrossed in the legend of the Holy Grail, reading Wolfram von Eschenbach's poems *Parzivâl* and *Titurel* in editions by Simrock and San-Marte, and the anonymous epic *Lohengrin* in an edition by J. Görres.

By 3 August of that year a prose scenario had been outlined and by 27 November the versification

completed. Wagner then made his first complete draft, on two staves (completed 30 July 1846), followed by the second draft with elaboration of instrumental and choral parts. Various changes were made to the poem during composition, especially in Act 3. Probably for this reason the second complete draft for Act 3 was made before those for Acts 1 and 2, but there is no evidence to suggest that the acts were originally composed in anything other than the usual order. The full score was written out between 1 January and 28 April 1848.

Wagner, by 1850 in exile in Switzerland, was unable to be present at the first performance. The work was well received in Germany, but he was unable to hear it until 1861, when it was given in Vienna. The first performance in Bayreuth did not take place until 1894, when Mottl conducted a cast including Ernest van Dyck and Lillian Nordica. The performances at Bologna in 1871 were the first of any Wagner opera to be given in Italy. The work was first performed in Great Britain in 1875 in Italian, in 1880 in English and in 1882 in German; before World War I *Lohengrin* was by far the most popular of Wagner's operas in Britain. Notable exponents of the title role have included Albert Niemann, Jean de Reszke, Leo Slezak, Lauritz Melchior, Set Svanholm, Jess Thomas, Peter Hofmann, Placido Domingo, Siegfried Jerusalem and Ben Heppner. Elsa has been sung by Emma Eames, Nellie Melba, Johanna Gadski, Emmy Destinn, Maria Jeritza, Elisabeth Rethberg, Lotte Lehmann, Kirsten Flagstad, Astrid Varnay, Elisabeth Grümmer, Anna Tomowa-Sintow, Jessye Norman and Cheryl Studer.

Unlike *Holländer* and *Tannhäuser*, *Lohengrin* was not subjected to revision by Wagner, except for the excision of the second part of Lohengrin's Narration (Act 3), a cut carried out at his request at the first performance and ever since (a recording under Leinsdorf reinstating the passage bears out Wagner's conviction that it would have an anti-climactic effect). The double male-voice chorus 'In Früh'n versammelt uns der Ruf' in Act 2 is often cut in performance, despite its imaginative antiphony. A cut traditionally made after Lohengrin's Narration (from Elsa's swoon to 'Der Schwan!') is particularly regrettable in that it gives Elsa no chance to express remorse.

*

The prelude opens with the sounds of a body of divided strings high up in their compass, alternating with four solo violins and a chorus of flutes and oboes: a striking aural image for the shimmering of the Holy Grail. In contrast to all Wagner's earlier overtures, it is conceived like a single breath, as a unified movement, rather than in the traditional sections, yet with references to forthcoming thematic ideas. According to Wagner, the prelude represented

'Lohengrin' (Wagner), Act 1 scene ii (the arrival of Lohengrin) in the original production at the Grossherzogliches Hoftheater, Weimar, 28 August 1850: engraving from the 'Illustrirte Zeitung' (Leipzig, 12 April 1851)

the descent from heaven of a host of angels bearing the Grail, and their return to heaven.

Act I *A meadow on the banks of the Scheldt near Antwerp* King Henry (the historical Henry the Fowler) has come to Antwerp to exhort the Brabantines to join him in defending Germany against the imminent invasion by the Hungarians in the east. The curtain rises on two groups of people: the king, under the Oak of Justice, surrounded by Saxon counts and nobles, and opposite them the Brabantine counts and nobles headed by Friedrich von Telramund, by whose side stands his wife Ortrud. The Herald summons the Brabantines to arms and they respond with fervour. But there is dissension in the air. Telramund, charged to give account, accuses Elsa, in a quasi-recitative, of murdering her brother Gottfried, the heir to the dukedom of Brabant, and claims the succession for himself.

The king summons Elsa and she comes forward timidly (scene ii). The subdued wind chorus, contrasting with the clashing brass of the previous scene, suggests her vulnerability. At first she is silent, but then she tells how she had prayed to God in her distress, 'Einsam in trüben Tagen', falling into a sweet sleep. The king urges her to defend herself, but her trance-like state gives way only to an exultant account of a vision of a knightly champion. The latter is prefaced by the Grail music on high strings and

accompanied with extreme delicacy on wind and strings, with harp arpeggios and a magical touch on a solo trumpet. The king and bystanders are much moved, but Telramund is unimpressed. He demands judgment through combat; Elsa invokes her visionary champion.

Herald and trumpeters twice sound the call. There is no response, but when Elsa sinks to her knees in prayer, a modulation from A♭ (the tonality associated with her) to A major (that associated with Lohengrin), combined with an increase in tempo and agitated tremolando strings, signifies the distant approach of the knight, in a boat drawn by a swan. The arrival is greeted by excited choral ejaculations, which at the beginning of scene iii coalesce into a hymn of welcome. Lohengrin bids farewell to the swan and, after making his obeisance to the king, offers himself as Elsa's champion. Shifting into her tonality of A♭, he makes her promise that she will never ask his name or origin, sounding a phrase (ex.1) that will act as a motif of reminiscence. They pledge themselves to each other and Telramund, ignoring entreaties to desist, braces himself for battle.

Ex.1

Nie   sollst du mich   be - fra - gen

['Never may you question me']

The ground is measured out and the Herald announces the rules of combat. In a passage in triple time – the only such example in the entire work – the king invokes the blessing of heaven, 'Mein Herr und Gott'. His prayer is taken up by the chorus and built to a climax. Onstage trumpeters sound the call to battle and, after the king has struck three times with his sword on his shield, the two men fight. Lohengrin defeats Telramund but spares his life. Elsa is overcome with joy, while the crowd acclaim Lohengrin victor in a triumphant finale. Ortrud wonders who the stranger is that renders her magical powers useless. Telramund, crushed and humiliated, falls at her feet.

Act 2 *The fortress at Antwerp* The curtain rises to reveal the palace at the back and the kemenate at the front (the dwellings of respectively the knights and the womenfolk). The minster stands to the right and on its steps are seated Telramund and Ortrud. It is night. A sustained, muted drum roll and a baleful theme given out on the cello evoke the presence of dark, malignant forces. In the 12th bar an ominous-sounding theme based on the traditionally 'supernatural' chord of the diminished 7th, and associated specifically with Ortrud (ex.2), is announced by cellos and two bassoons. The motif of the 'forbidden question' (ex.1) is also heard on the english horn and bass clarinet. Telramund rouses himself, launching into a bitter tirade punctuated by an aggressively dotted string figure and a rushing, rising semiquaver scale in the bass, blaming Ortrud for his disgrace, 'Durch dich musst' ich verlieren'. The underlying eight-bar structure of this 'aria' is only slightly varied. But after a recitative exchange, in which Ortrud promises a way to undermine Lohengrin's heavenly protection, a more freely structured section begins, 'Du wilde Seherin', in which Ortrud tells Telramund that Lohengrin's power would be nullified if Elsa were to ask him about his name and origins. It is this passage in particular that has caused the scene as a whole to be regarded, with justification, as the most stylistically advanced by Wagner to date. A descending chromatic phrase (a pre-echo of the 'magic sleep' harmonies in the *Ring*) sounded at 'Du wilde Seherin' is the first of a nexus of themes (associated with Ortrud, her sorcery and the 'forbidden question') which have more than an ornamental function: they form the substance of the musical argument. Quasi-recitative and arioso here alternate and merge imperceptibly. The scene ends with a dramatically effective if stylistically regressive revenge duet for the two voices in unison over tremolando strings.

An ethereal wind chorus opens the second scene, heralding the appearance of Elsa, dressed in white, on the balcony of the kemenate. Ortrud, dismissing Telramund, calls up to Elsa (oboes and stopped horns

producing a sinister sound next to Elsa's flute) and hypocritically appeals to her generous nature. As Elsa disappears to descend to ground level, Ortrud invokes the pagan gods in a powerful outburst. Affectedly prostrating herself before Elsa, Ortrud listens while the bride-to-be sings of her naive matrimonial bliss in a succession of untroubled diatonic harmonies. Gradually Ortrud instils the poison. First her diminished 7th theme (ex.2) sounds

Ex.2

on the bassoons; then, to the accompaniment of the 'forbidden question' motif, she comments darkly on Lohengrin's mysterious origins and appearance. Elsa shudders with dread (tremolando diminished 7th chords), but recovers her composure. In a brief duet, both express their feelings, though Ortrud's vengeance is subjugated musically to the ecstasy of Elsa's line, which is also reinforced by mellifluous strings. As day breaks, Elsa and Ortrud go inside; Telramund reappears briefly, gloating over his expected triumph.

Scene iii opens with an antiphonal exchange between two trumpets blowing the reveille from the tower answered by two in the distance. As the rest of the orchestra joins in, the palace gates open and four royal trumpeters cause a brief, dramatic plunge into C major (from and back into D major) with their onstage fanfares. The filling of the stage is matched by gathering momentum in the orchestra, leading to the double chorus for male voices 'In Früh'n versammelt uns der Ruf'. Though belonging to the grand operatic tradition soon to be abjured by Wagner, this and subsequent choruses show skill in their part-writing and can be exhilarating in performance. The Herald announces that Telramund is banished; anyone who consorts with him suffers the same fate. The stranger sent by God, he continues, wishes to take as his title not Duke, but Protector of Brabant; today he celebrates his wedding, tomorrow he will lead them into battle. These announcements are punctuated by choral acclamations, following which four disgruntled nobles, formerly liegemen of Telramund, detach themselves from the crowd and are recruited by Telramund, who has been skulking in the shadows.

The fourth scene initiates the wedding procession to the minster, but as Elsa reaches its steps, Ortrud interposes herself (on a dramatically interrupted cadence, leading to diminished 7th agitation) to claim precedence. In a regularly phrased 'aria' she goes on to taunt Elsa for her ignorance of her champion's origins, 'Wenn falsch Gericht'. Elsa's reply is forthright and confident, supported by a full wind chorus in exultant sextuplets. Ortrud's next onslaught is interrupted by the arrival of the king, Lohengrin and the Saxon nobles from the palace (scene v). Lohengrin consoles Elsa and begins to lead her to the minster once more. This time the procession is interrupted by Telramund, who vehemently accuses Lohengrin of sorcery. His demand that the knight reveal his name is brushed aside by Lohengrin. No king or prince can command him, he replies, only Elsa. But as he turns to his bride, he sees with dismay that she is agitated: the motifs of Ortrud and the 'forbidden question' tell us why. The following ensemble ironically juxtaposes Elsa's doubt, expressed to herself, with the unquestioning trust of the onlookers.

The king expresses his satisfaction and, as the nobles crowd round Lohengrin to pledge their allegiance, Telramund prevails on Elsa to allow him to expose the sorcerer by spilling just a drop of his blood. Lohengrin repulses Telramund and Ortrud, and the procession sets off once again. A climax built by sequential means brings the act to a rousing conclusion. But there is a final *coup de théâtre*. As Elsa and Lohengrin reach the top step of the minster, she looks down to see Ortrud raising her arm in a gesture of triumph. The motif of the 'forbidden question' rings out on trumpets and trombones, its F minor colouring casting a menacing shadow over the radiance of the predominating C major.

Act 3.i–ii *The bridal chamber* The celebrated orchestral introduction to Act 3, which has become a concert piece in its own right, is notable for its metric displacements – in contradistinction to the regular common-time periods elsewhere, dictated by the conventional poetic metres adopted. The curtain rises on the bridal chamber. To the strains of the even more celebrated bridal march, 'Treulich geführt', two processions enter from behind: Elsa escorted by the ladies, and Lohengrin by the king and nobles. The couple embrace and are blessed by the king. The attendants retire, to a repetition of the march.

With an enharmonic modulation from B♭ to E major an atmosphere of tender devotion is immediately established for scene ii, 'Das süsse Lied verhallt'. Muted strings provide the background for a profusion of melodic ideas, launched by first a solo clarinet, then a solo oboe. Except for a few brief bars, the voices are heard in succession rather than combination. Elsa's first suggestion that Lohengrin share with her the secret of his name is deflected, but she becomes more and more insistent, despite his alternate warnings and protestations of love.

Attempting to reassure her, he says that he renounced glorious and blissful delights to woo her. But Elsa is far from reassured: he may tire of her and return to the joys he left behind. The tempo quickens. Ortrud's theme (ex.2) is ubiquitous: at one point Elsa's line becomes a diatonic version of it, in E minor. Finally, as the motif of the 'forbidden question' rings out, Elsa asks outright who he is. Telramund and his henchmen break into the chamber. With Elsa's assistance, Lohengrin fells Telramund at a stroke; the henchmen kneel before Lohengrin. He orders Telramund's body to be taken to the king's judgment seat; there he will answer Elsa's question.

3.iii *The banks of the Scheldt; daybreak* Brabantines appear from all sides, stirringly heralded by trumpets. Telramund's covered body is brought in. Then Elsa enters, followed by Lohengrin, who tells the king that he can no longer lead his troops into battle. He explains how he killed Telramund in self-defence and goes on to denounce Elsa for breaking her vow. Now he is forced to reveal his origins. The shimmering Grail music of the work's opening introduces Lohengrin's Narration, 'In fernem Land'. He tells how he came as a servant of the Grail; such knights are granted invincible power on condition of anonymity. Now that his secret is revealed, he must return to Monsalvat. His father is Parzival and his name is Lohengrin. The Narration begins with conventionally balanced phrases but develops into a freer structure more appropriate to narrative as the unfolding of the tale seizes the imagination of teller and listener. Elsa momentarily swoons; then, to Lohengrin's remonstrations, she begs forgiveness. The king and chorus add their pleas, Elsa's voice soaring above them all. But the laws of the Grail are immutable. The swan appears, drawing an empty boat. After addressing the swan, Lohengrin turns to Elsa and tells her that had they lived together for just a year, her brother Gottfried would have been restored to her. He entrusts her with his sword, horn and ring, to be given to Gottfried should he return one day. Ortrud comes forward declaring that she recognizes the swan, by the chain round its neck, as Gottfried, whom she bewitched; now he is lost to Elsa for ever. To the radiant music of the Grail, Lohengrin kneels silently in prayer. A white dove descends and hovers over the boat. Seeing it, Lohengrin loosens the chain round the swan, which sinks. In its place appears a boy in shining silver: Gottfried. Lohengrin lifts him to the bank, proclaiming him Duke of Brabant. Ortrud collapses, while Gottfried advances first to the king and then to Elsa. Her joy turns to sorrow as she watches Lohengrin depart. As the Grail knight vanishes from sight, Elsa falls lifeless to the ground.

*

Lohengrin is the last of Wagner's works that can fairly be described as an opera rather than a music drama. It contains, however, the seeds of future developments and is a powerfully conceived, imaginatively scored work in its own right.   **B.M.**

Lombardi alla prima crociata, I
('The Lombards on the First Crusade')

Dramma lirico in four acts by Giuseppe Verdi to a libretto by Temistocle Solera after Tommaso Grossi's poem *I Lombardi alla prima crociata*; Milan, Teatro alla Scala, 11 February 1843. Revised in French as *Jérusalem* to a libretto by Alphonse Royer and Gustave Vaëz; Paris, Opéra, 26 November 1847.

The original cast included Giovanni Severi (Arvino), Prosper Dérivis (Pagano), Carlo Guasco (Oronte) and Erminia Frezzolini (Giselda). The first cast of the revised version, *Jérusalem*, included Gilbert Duprez (Gaston), Charles Portheaut (the Count), Adolphe-Joseph-Louis Alizard (Roger) and Esther Julian-Van-Gelder (Hélène).

Arvino	} *sons of Folco, Lord of Rò*	tenor
Pagano		bass
Viclinda *Arvino's wife*		soprano
Giselda *her daughter*		soprano
Pirro *Arvino's squire*		bass
Prior of the City of Milan		tenor
Acciano *tyrant of Antioch*		bass
Oronte *his son*		tenor
Sofia *Acciano's wife, a secret Christian convert*		soprano

Nuns, priors, populace, hired ruffians, armigers in Folco's palace, ambassadors from Persia, Media, Damascus and Chaldea, harem women, knights and crusading soldiers, pilgrims, celestial virgins, Lombard women
Setting Milan, in and around Antioch, and near Jerusalem in 1097

In the 11 years from March 1842 (the première of *Nabucco*) to March 1853 (the première of *La traviata*), Verdi wrote 16 operas, an average of one every nine months. As with *Nabucco*, there seems to be hardly any surviving information about the genesis of his next one, *I Lombardi*. No records exist of negotiations with La Scala, although popular rumour has it that, after the huge success of *Nabucco*, Bartolomeo Merelli (the impresario there) left to the composer's discretion the fee for the new opera, and that Verdi took advice on a proper sum from his future wife, Giuseppina Strepponi. Nor is there any surviving correspondence between Verdi and Solera. They were both in Milan during the period of composition

(presumably the second half of 1842) and, if we are to trust Verdi's later recollections, he altered very little of Solera's initial draft. The opera was apparently frowned upon by the religious censors in Milan but eventually escaped with only a few unimportant changes. The first night was a wild public success. For a revival in Senigallia in July 1843, Verdi composed a new cabaletta in Act 2 for Antonio Poggi (as Oronte).

*

The prelude (the first Verdi wrote) is very short and follows the conventional strategy of attempting a kind of radical synopsis of the ensuing action.

Act I: 'The Vendetta'

***I.i** The piazza of S Ambrogio, Milan* To a stage-band accompaniment, the opening chorus celebrates new friendship between the brothers Arvino and Pagano ('Oh nobile esempio!'); the two have been enemies ever since Pagano jealously attacked Arvino during the latter's wedding to Viclinda 18 years ago. Pagano and Arvino appear with their family and supporters to announce publicly their reconciliation. This leads to a large-scale concertato movement, 'T'assale un tremito! ... padre che fia?', which is led off by Arvino's daughter Giselda, who anxiously asks why her father seems so ill at ease; as the ensemble develops, all the principals are musically differentiated. A Prior of the city announces that Arvino will lead a group to the Crusades. All join in a bellicose chorus, 'All'empio che infrange', and process off to a robust march. An offstage chorus of nuns introduces Pagano, who, in the Andante movement of a double aria, 'Sciagurata! hai tu creduto', informs us that he can never forget Viclinda. A group of supporters enters, swearing to help him against Arvino, and he finishes the scene with a fierce cabaletta of revenge, 'O speranza di vendetta'.

***I.ii** A gallery in the Folco palace* Viclinda and Giselda are still uneasy. Arvino enters to inform Viclinda that his elderly father, Folco, is in the adjoining room. Giselda offers a prayer for divine assistance, the subtly scored and harmonically bold preghiera 'Salve Maria!' As the women go off, Pagano and his henchman Pirro appear. Pagano enters Arvino's room, to emerge a little later, bloody dagger in hand, dragging Viclinda after him. But, as flames are seen through the windows, Arvino and his followers intercept the villain. The discovery that Pagano has killed his own father in mistake for his brother precipitates the central Andante mosso, 'Mostro d'averno orribile'. Arvino demands his brother's death while Giselda counsels mercy; Pagano tries unsuccessfully to kill himself, and all join in pronouncing his banishment in a final stretta, 'Va! sul capo ti grava'.

Act 2: 'The Man of the Cave'

***2.i** A room in Acciano's palace in Antioch* Months

have passed; Viclinda has died and the Crusaders are at the gates of Antioch. Acciano and his supporters remain defiant in the chorus 'È dunque vero?' The stage empties to leave Acciano's wife Sofia (who has converted to Christianity) and their son Oronte. Oronte has fallen in love with Giselda, who has been taken prisoner, and recalls her in an Andante ('La mia letizia infondere') remarkable for its motivic economy. With his mother's prompting, Oronte agrees to convert, celebrating his decision in the gentle cabaletta, 'Come poteva un angelo'.

2.ii *The mouth of a cave at a mountain peak* A suitably sombre orchestral prelude introduces Pagano (now called 'The Hermit'), who emphasizes his new-found faith in the minor–major *romanza* 'Ma quando un suon terribile'. Pirro enters and, failing to recognize his old accomplice, confesses his sins and seeks to atone by revealing to the Crusaders Antioch's defences. A distant stage-band march heralds the Crusaders, who appear with Arvino at their head. Arvino tells 'The Hermit' that Giselda has been captured, and Pagano swears to aid them in battle. The scene closes with a brash, warlike chorus, 'Stolto Allhà!'

2.iii *Inside the harem at Antioch* A female chorus, complete with rather bland musical gestures towards 'eastern' local colour, introduces Giselda, who closes the act with a full-scale double aria billed as a 'Rondò-Finale'. In the first movement, 'Se vano è il pregare', she prays to her dead mother. The *tempo di mezzo* (middle section) sees the stage suddenly filled with fleeing women and pursuing Crusaders: Sofia tells Giselda that Arvino has killed her husband and son, and in the closing cabaletta, 'No! . . . giusta causa non è d'Iddio', Giselda turns on her father for his ungodly violence.

Act 3: 'The Conversion'

3.i *The valley of Jehoshaphat* A group of Crusaders and their followers cross the stage, singing the noble chorus, 'Gerusalem!', one of the simplest but most effective pieces in the opera. Giselda appears and is soon joined by Oronte, whom she had believed dead. The lovers' decision to escape danger by running off together is played out in a traditional four-movement duet, notable for its second movement, 'Oh belle, a questa misera', in which the couple bid farewell to their homelands; and for an unusually curtailed cabaletta, 'Ah, vieni, sol morte', punctuated by offstage warlike cries from the Lombard soldiers.

3.ii *Arvino's tent* Arvino has discovered the disappearance of his daughter and calls down a curse on her. A group of Crusaders report that Pagano has been seen nearby and in a driving aria with chorus, 'Sì! del ciel che non punisce', Arvino vows to search Pagano out and kill him.

3.iii *Inside a cave* An elaborate orchestral prelude with solo violin, divided into three contrasting

sections, begins the scene. Giselda helps on Oronte, severely wounded by the Crusaders. Railing against God, she launches the first movement of an ensemble, 'Tu la madre mi togliesti'; but she is interrupted by Pagano (still 'The Hermit'), who brings holy water with which to bless the dying Oronte. The solo violin is still much in evidence (a sure sign that Oronte is destined for heaven) in the second, lyrical movement, the richly melodic Andantino 'Qual voluttà trascorrere'.

Act 4: 'The Holy Sepulchre'

4.i *A cave near Jerusalem* A brief dialogue in the original printed libretto, not set to music, explains that Giselda has been brought back to her father by 'The Hermit', and that Arvino has forgiven his daughter. The scene then opens with Giselda, overtaken in sleep by a chorus of celestial spirits. A vision of Oronte appears to sing the Andante 'In cielo benedetto', in which he tells his beloved that the Crusaders will find much-needed water at Siloim. When the vision vanishes, Giselda breaks into a brilliant cabaletta of joy, 'Non fu sogno!' – apparently one of the most popular numbers in the opera with contemporary audiences.

4.ii *The Lombard camp near Rachel's tomb* The Lombards, dying of thirst, conjure up visions of their distant homeland in the famous chorus 'O Signore, dal tetto natio', a number whose hymn-like slowness and predominantly unison texture suggest it was modelled on 'Va pensiero' from *Nabucco*. Giselda announces that the Lombards can find water at Siloim, and they prepare for battle with the warlike chorus 'Guerra! guerra!', first heard in Act 2 as 'Stolto Allhà!'

4.iii *Arvino's tents* 'The Hermit', gravely wounded, enters supported by Giselda and Arvino. Pagano reveals his true identity and, on the point of death, leads off the final ensemble, 'Un breve istante'. The tent is thrown open to reveal Jerusalem, now in the hands of the Crusaders, and the opera ends with a grand choral hymn, 'Te lodiamo, gran Dio di vittoria'.

*

I Lombardi has often been compared to *Nabucco*, the immensely successful opera that preceded it in the Verdi canon. It is easy to see how such comparisons usually find the later opera less satisfactory. *I Lombardi* has a wider-ranging action than *Nabucco*, but Verdi, at this stage of his career, was less able or willing to depict various sharply contrasting locales, and many of the opera's choral sections (which traditionally carried the weight of such depictions) are pallid and routine. The great exception is the chorus 'O Signore, dal tetto natio', which rightly stands beside 'Va pensiero' as representative of Verdi's new voice in Italian opera. The opera's musical characterization is strangely uneven: the presence of two leading tenors seems to divide attention where it might usefully have been focussed; but the leading soprano, Giselda, stamps her personality on the drama at a very early stage and succeeds in emerging with impressive effect.

The Paris Opéra had been making overtures to Verdi for some two years when, in the summer of 1847, he signed a contract to supply the theatre with a 'new' work. As had Rossini and Donizetti, Verdi offered for his début at the Opéra a revision of one of his earlier Italian operas: *I Lombardi*, not previously seen in Paris. The librettists retained little of the original plot apart from its basis in a crusade: in vocal terms, the lovers Giselda and Oronte become Hélène and Gaston, the warring brothers Arvino and Pagano become the Count of Toulouse – now a baritone rather than tenor – and Roger. As well as adding the obligatory ballet, Verdi decided on some wide-ranging structural changes, adding much new music, cutting what he considered weak or inappropriate and leaving only a few of the original numbers in their former positions. *Jérusalem* was well received in Paris, but in spite of being in many ways superior to *I Lombardi*, the opera failed to establish itself in either the French or the Italian repertory (although it was published in Italy as *Gerusalemme*) and is today only occasionally revived. This is in some ways regrettable, as the opera simplifies somewhat the complex action of the original, adds convincing new music (in particular the fine crowd scene of Act 3 scene ii), cuts some of the weaker portions and, by converting Arvino from a tenor to a baritone, solves one of the original problems of vocal distribution. *Jérusalem* serves as a fascinating first document in charting Verdi's relationship with the French stage, to become increasingly important during the next decade.

R.P.

Louise

Roman musical in four acts by Gustave Charpentier to a libretto by the composer or by Saint-Pol-Roux; Paris, Opéra-Comique (Salle Favart), 2 February 1900.

Marthe Rioton was the first Louise, Adolphe Maréchal the first Julien; the Mother was sung by Blanche Deschamps-Jéhin, the Father by Lucien Fugère. Albert Carré directed, André Messager conducted, and the sets were by Lucien Jusseaume: the team who two years later were to inaugurate Debussy's *Pelléas*.

Julien *a young artist*	tenor
Louise	soprano
Her Mother	contralto
Her Father	bass
A Young Rag Picker	mezzo-soprano
A Coal Gatherer	mezzo-soprano
A Noctambulist *later dressed as the king of the Fools*	tenor
A Newspaper Girl	soprano
A Rag Picker	bass
A Milkwoman	soprano
Two Policemen	baritones
An Arab Street Vendor	soprano
A Street Sweeper	mezzo-soprano
A Painter	bass
A Songwriter	baritone
A Student	tenor
A Young Poet	baritone
Two Philosophers	tenor and bass
A Sculptor	baritone
An Apprentice	baritone
Blanche	soprano
Marguerite	soprano
Suzanne	contralto
Gertrude	contralto
Irma	soprano
Camille	soprano
An Errand Girl	soprano
Madeleine	contralto
An Old-clothes-man	tenor
A Dancer	silent
An Old Bohemian	baritone
A Forewoman	mezzo-soprano
Elise	soprano

Street vendors, vegetable sellers, beggars, Bohemians, working girls, women etc.

Setting The Montmartre district of Paris

Charpentier began *Louise* in Rome while, as winner of the Prix de Rome, he was at the Villa Medici, having reluctantly departed from his beloved Montmartre in 1887. Originally, it was planned that Hartmann, the music publishers, would obtain a libretto on which he could write an opera, but, tired of waiting, Charpentier began writing a text himself. Although he vehemently denied suggestions that others had collaborated, there is now strong evidence to suggest that the poet Saint-Pol-Roux, godfather to his eldest son, was paid outright by the composer to supply the complete text. Whatever the case, Charpentier was advised to incorporate more lyrical elements beside the extended realistic scenes. It is this Zolaesque naturalism, transferred into operatic terms, that most strongly characterizes the work: Charpentier himself explained that he wished to capture the thought of his generation. He finally completed the work in 1896, and though timid in promoting it, he made several attempts to interest opera houses in it.

Léon Carvalho, director of the Opéra-Comique,

'Louise' (Gustave Charpentier), Act 2 scene i of the original production at the Opéra-Comique (Salle Favart), 2 February 1900, with sets designed by Lucien Jusseaume: from 'Le théâtre' (April 1900)

disliked the sordid realism of the Montmartre setting, suggesting a substitution of the epoch of Louis XV and the incorporation of a happy ending, where Julien would suddenly appear through a window to embrace Louise, to the accompaniment of a benediction by her father. Charpentier, however, would accept no such compromises. In 1898 Carvalho's successor Albert Carré accepted the work unaltered, scheduling it as the first production of the new century. Marthe Rioton was succeeded in the title role by Mary Garden, who made it one of her greatest successes. The work itself was a success, performed a hundred times during the first season and a thousand times by 1935.

*

Act I *A room in the mansard of a working man's tenement*
Through the window is the balcony of a neighbouring house where a young poet, Julien, sings lyrically of spring in Paris and of his love for Louise. Louise soon enters and sees him, and he explains that he has written to her parents asking for her hand. If they refuse again, he says, she must elope with him. But Louise is torn: 'I love you so much', she tells Julien, 'but I love them too'. Julien accuses her of timidity, and encourages her to be brave and free. As

each tells how they fell in love with the other, the music becomes more lyrical. 'There's no madonna of Vinci who has a smile like you', says Julien. As they sing together in octaves, her mother enters, shuts Louise in the kitchen, and goes to the window to scold Julien.

In scene iii Louise's mother mocks the loving words of Julien and scolds Louise, calling Julien a good-for-nothing, a drunkard and a debaucher. Louise's remark that he might go to the bar less often if he had a woman provokes bitter laughter from her mother. Taunting her mother, Louise prides herself on having won Julien's heart and inflames her still further in an exchange highlighted by Charpentier with unconventional chromatic harmony.

In scene iv Louise's father returns from work with words which characterize him as the archetype of the French working-class husband: 'La soupe est prête?' ('Is the soup ready?'). He has a letter which he lays on the table. Louise's mother brings up the subject of idlers, rich enough to fall in love and spend all their lives on holiday. 'L'égalité, les grands mots' ('Equality? Just big words'), says her father, in the first of many such statements with political overtones: 'when you don't have an income, you have to be content to earn one for someone else'. But underneath he seems happy, affectionately calling his wife an old goose, dancing with her and kissing Louise. Louise finds the letter, which she knows to be from Julien, and confronts her father with it. A row ensues, in which Charpentier gradually increases the musical tension, as the father admires the eloquence of the letter while Louise's mother pours scorn on Julien. Louise collapses in tears: the pretext for a tender scene between father and daughter. 'How does one choose a good husband?', asks Louise. 'Experience', replies her father, adding the remark, shocking for its time, that 'second marriages are generally happier'.

Act 2 *An open thoroughfare at the foot of Montmartre* The prelude to the act is entitled 'Paris awakes' and is bound together by a simple motif heard at the outset. The various street vendors and waste gatherers form the basis of the scene. The Noctambulist dwells on the readiness of the poor working girls for better things, love included. More political questions are put into the mouths of the various vendors: 'shouldn't soft beds and fine clothes, like the sun, belong to everyone?' The Milkwoman has never had time for love. Others talk of paradise. 'Give me the address', asks the Arab. 'Why', comes the reply, 'it's Paris'.

In the next two scenes Julien and his Bohemian friends look for the place where Louise works. Julien plans to catch her when her mother isn't looking, while the others have the idea of making her their muse. A discussion on class ensues. 'The one hope in life', explains a philosopher, 'is to become middle-class'. The street vendors reappear, and Julien is once again drunk with the beauty of Paris. Coming out of work, the girls chatter about their fancies and conquests. Eventually Louise arrives with her mother, who is suspicious, but Julien manages to pull Louise aside. With the street vendors' cries as a background they once again argue, Louise still attached to her parents, Julien encouraging her to break free.

After an interlude, the scene changes to a seamstress's workroom, where the girls are busy at work, singing to the sound of the sewing-machine. Louise looks sick with love. The girls provocatively remark that she is too much under her mother's thumb and that when she is slapped she should slap her in return. One of the errand girls, in Paris slang, explains how, when her father spanks her, she tells him to try her mother, who has a larger behind. They extol the virtues of love and the delirium of kissing. Julien appears in the courtyard and sings a serenade, accompanied by a guitar. The girls and Louise are delighted, but after a little flirting they all get bored with the ardour of his song. Louise, overcome, decides to leave work. The act ends with the

stupefaction of the girls and forewoman at this gesture of defiance.

Act 3 *A little garden on the side of Montmartre* The act begins with a prelude, 'Towards the distant city', followed by Louise's romance, 'Depuis le jour'. Louise sings to Julien of her love for him: she seems to have broken free and she recalls the constraints of her home. 'Each soul has a right to be free', says Julien, with conviction and dignity, again extolling the wonders of the city of Paris as they contemplate its lights from the hill: 'city of joy, city of Love'. An extended love scene ensues, followed by the entry of children, Bohemians and the people of the *quartier* following a carnival procession. The noctambulist is dressed as the King of the Fools.

In scene iii Louise is crowned muse of Montmartre. After a while, her mother appears, looking unhappy and falling into Julien's arms. She explains that she has not come to quarrel but to announce that Louise's father is ill and needs to see his daughter before he can be cured. Louise explains to Julien that when she returns she will have her freedom. Reluctantly she leaves, handing back the shawl with which she has been crowned.

Act 4 *As Act I* Louise's father, who has been idle for 20 days, has become bitter, 'crushed beneath a yoke imposed by fate'. Louise looks out of the window to a tenderly orchestrated reminiscence of 'Depuis le jour'. Her father continues by recounting the pain a family feel when their daughter, whom they have cared for, runs off with a stranger, taking away their one joy in life and changing her too into a stranger. Her mother, calling her into the kitchen, tells her that, despite her promise, she cannot go back to Julien. 'Free love', mocks her mother, 'just an excuse to get out of marriage'. Her father pretends she is a little girl again. 'Baby would be quiet', sings Louise, 'if her father had not caused so much sorrow'. She talks of his 'misguided affection'. Voices are heard; 'Paris is calling', says Louise, preparing to leave. Her father, angry, tries to bar the way, but eventually she breaks out, and her father, now distraught, curses Paris, shaking his fist.

*

Even before the première, the work had become something of a *cause célèbre*: rumours circulated about the immorality of the subject matter as well as about the revolutionary nature of the score. In fact it is far from unconventional, owing much to Gounod and Massenet; and Massenet admired it. There are, however, moments of originality, such as the highly effective end to the first tableau of Act 2, where the voice of the Street Vendor, plying his fresh green artichokes, perfectly captures the continuity of Montmartre street life. The work's allegiance to the realist cause, its rich orchestral palette – which includes instruments as different as the viola d'amore (perhaps used by a sentimental Montmartre busker) and the sewing-machine (foreshadowing the use of everyday 'instruments' such as the typewriter in Satie's *Parade*) – and the memorability of the set-piece 'Depuis le jour' have assured it a unique place in the repertory.

Charpentier planned several sequels to this work but completed only *Julien*, which deals with the artistic aspirations of Louise's suitor and, like its predecessor, is loosely autobiographical; it did not achieve success. Another discarded idea was *Marie* (about Louise's daughter). In 1936 the composer was involved in a film version of *Louise*.   R.L.S.

Love for Three Oranges, The
[Lyubov' k tryom apel'sinam; L'amour des trois oranges]

Opera in a prologue and four acts, op.33, by Sergey Prokofiev to his own libretto after Carlo Gozzi's *fiaba L'amore delle tre melarance* (1761), adapted (1913) by Vsevolod Meyerhold, Vladimir Solov'yov and Konstantin Vogak; Chicago, Auditorium, 30 December 1921 (as *L'amour des trois oranges*, French translation by the composer and Vera Janacopoulos).

The first cast included Jose Mojica (the Prince), Octave Dua (Truffaldino), Nina Koshetz (Fata Morgana), Hector Dufranne (Celio), Irene Pavlovska (Clarice) and Jeanne Dusseau (Ninetta), conducted by the composer.

The King of Clubs *king of an imaginary kingdom where everyone dresses as a playing-card*	bass
The Prince *his son*	tenor
Princess Clarice *the king's niece*	contralto
Leander *prime minister, costumed as the King of Spades*	baritone
Truffaldino *jester*	tenor
Pantalone *courtier, the king's confidant*	baritone
Celio *sorcerer, the king's protector*	bass
Fata Morgana *witch, Leander's protector*	soprano
Linetta } *princesses in*	contralto
Nicoletta } *the oranges*	mezzo-soprano
Ninetta }	soprano
Cook	hoarse bass
Farfarello *a devil*	bass
Smeraldina *a black slave girl*	mezzo-soprano
Master of Ceremonies	tenor
Herald	bass
Trumpeteer	bass trombone

Ten Cranks (five tenors, five basses), Tragedians (basses), Comedians (tenors), Lyricists (sopranos, tenors), Empty Heads (altos, basses), imps (basses), doctors (tenors, baritones), courtiers (full chorus)

Silent roles: monsters, drunks, gluttons, watchmen, servants, four soldiers

Setting The world of make-believe, once upon a time

Prokofiev's second completed opera (juvenilia apart) and the first to achieve performance was written in New York, where the composer had settled after emigrating from Russia in the wake of the revolution. Immediately before his departure, in spring 1918, Vsevolod Meyerhold, the great director, made Prokofiev a gift of the first issue of his journal *The Love for Three Oranges*, containing a Russian adaptation (by Meyerhold with two collaborators) of the eponymous theatrical tale by the Venetian nobleman and satirist Carlo Gozzi (1720–1806). Gozzi had cast the work in the form of a *commedia dell'arte* scenario, seeing in the slapstick comedy of masks an antidote to the heavy melodrama and the petty naturalism that were (he thought) degrading the contemporary theatre. A century and a half later Meyerhold felt the same way. He expressed the hope that Prokofiev would derive a prose libretto from the scenario and set it in the fleet, flexible and resolutely 'anti-operatic' manner of his earlier opera, *The Gambler*, which Meyerhold had hoped to produce in the last pre-revolutionary Petrograd season. By the time Prokofiev docked in San Francisco he had a draft libretto in hand.

Gozzi had derived his *fiaba*, a ludicrous parody of the standard quest motif, by conflating two stories in Giambattista Basile's *Pentamerone*, subtitled *Lo cunto de li cunti* ('The Tale of Tales'), the earliest (1634) printed collection of European folk and fairy-tales. Having launched a pamphlet war on both the reigning dramatists of the mid-18th-century Venetian stage – Carlo Goldoni, the paragon of bourgeois realism, and Pietro Chiari, a specialist in highflown melodrama – Gozzi was challenged by Goldoni to do better. He boasted that he could ruin his antagonists by dramatizing the most ridiculous story in the world in the very manner Goldoni and Chiari most despised. As enacted by the celebrated troupe of Antonio Sacchi during the Venetian carnival of 1761, *L'amore delle tre melarance* redeemed its author's boast: Goldoni beat a retreat the next year to Paris.

Owing to the conventions of the *commedia dell'arte*, Gozzi made room in his adaptation for a large number of traditional masks: Tartaglia (the Prince), Pantalone, Smeraldina, Brighella (a character dropped by Prokofiev) and above all Truffaldino, a species of Arlecchino, the mask worn by Sacchi himself. Erudite burlesque reached its height in a little set piece in Act 2, entitled the 'quarrel trio' (*contrasto in terzo*), in which three characters fall into a dispute about dramatic values. Clarice declares her preference for 'tragic performances, in which you find characters hurling themselves from windows or turrets'; Leandro plumps for comedies of manners; Brighella pleads for 'the improvised comedy of masks, an innocent popular diversion'.

This little quarrel trio grew in Meyerhold's adaptation to become, both temporally and spatially, the frame of the entire play. The spatial frame was to consist of twin turrets on opposite sides of the stage, housing a collection of clowns representing aesthetes of various antagonistic persuasions. The action was to begin with a parade, in which the actors portraying the aesthetes, divided into 'Realistic Comedians' and 'High Tragedians', would enter duelling with quills; the fight was to be broken up by a trio of Cranks. Thus joined, the battle would continue in an undertone, with frequent eruptions, throughout the play; the aesthetes' constant comment on the action, and their strenuous exhortations to the actors, would furnish the temporal frame. This was one of the very earliest applications of illusion-destroying 'art as art' gimmickry, soon to become such a modernist cliché. What makes it historically significant is the clarity of its descent from an 18th-century aristocratic model. Even if Prokofiev had never set it, Meyerhold's *Love for Three Oranges* would have been a prime document of the emergent modernist sensibility and of its sources.

Thanks to Prokofiev, it is more than a document. Having secured a commission from Cleofonte Campanini, the director of the Chicago Grand Opera,

Title-page from the first issue of Vsevolod Meyerhold's journal, 'The Love for Three Oranges' (the theatrical tale which gave the journal its name inspired Prokofiev's opera)

who had wanted to produce *The Gambler* but was unable to obtain the materials from revolutionary Petrograd, the composer went to work on the music early in 1919 and delivered the completed score on 1 October. But it took more than two years before the opera achieved production, first because of Campanini's sudden death but second because of Prokofiev's impossible demands (he insisted on compensation for the delay in implementing the contract). Mary Garden, who took over the directorship of the Chicago company, finally agreed to his terms, and it was given in a French translation. The linguistic handicap notwithstanding, the opera could make its way because of its profusion of visual gags, and its high proportion of illustrative orchestral music; it is the single Prokofiev opera that could be called a success in his lifetime. Its enormously successful Soviet premières took place in 1926 (Leningrad, Academic Theatre, formerly and now the Mariinsky, with Ivan Yershov as Truffaldino) and 1927 (Moscow, Bol'shoy Theatre under Golovanov, with Nadezhda Obukhova as Clarice and Antonina Nezhdanova as Ninetta). These triumphs played a significant role in persuading Prokofiev to return to his homeland in the 1930s.

*

Prologue *A grand proscenium with towers on either side, each with little balconies and balustrades* The opening skirmish between the Cranks on the one hand and the Tragedians, the Comedians, the Lyricists and the Empty Heads on the other. As the Cranks announce the beginning of the play, the Trumpeteer gives the signal (bass trombone in the orchestra) for the curtain to go up. (This scene provides the material for the first movement, 'Cranks', in the concert suite from *The Love for Three Oranges, 1919.*)

Act I.i *The royal palace* The King consults with his physicians over the Prince's hypochondria. Only laughter, he is advised, will cure his son. He decides, with Pantalone and Leander (the latter secretly plotting with Clarice against the Prince), to arrange entertainments and charges Truffaldino to oversee them.

I.ii *Before a cabbalistic drop curtain* Celio and Fata Morgana, protectors respectively of the King of Clubs and his arch-enemy the King of Spades (Leander), play three rounds of cards while their attendant imps frolic about. Celio loses all three hands, to the Cranks' dismay. (This scene provides the material for the second movement, 'Infernal Scene', of the suite.)

I.iii *The royal palace* Leander and Clarice plot to worsen the Prince's hypochondria, thus paving Clarice's way to the throne. She advises 'opium or a bullet'; Leander retorts that booming 'Martellian verses' (the one surviving – and possibly unwitting – reference in Prokofiev's libretto to the old Venetian disputes) will do.

Act 2.i *The bedroom of the hypochondriac Prince* Truffaldino tries in vain to get the Prince to laugh by dancing, then forcibly rouses him for the entertainments (heralded offstage by the first of several versions of the March; the fully elaborated March that forms the third movement in the suite is a conflation of all the versions heard in the opera, but is based chiefly on the reprise that forms the entr'acte between this scene and the next).

2.ii *The great courtyard of the royal palace* The Prince is singularly unamused by Truffaldino's entertainments (a mock battle of monsters with enormous heads, and a pair of fountains pouring forth oil and wine – the latter a survival from Gozzi's scenario, where the oil and wine, both rancid, had stood for Goldoni and Chiari. Fata Morgana enters to make sure the Prince does not laugh. Truffaldino collides with her, causing her to fall back and expose her knobbly knees and withered behind. At this the Prince goes into gales of laughter represented in the music by a little set piece over an ostinato (and with the Prince's 'Ha-ha-ha-ha' inevitably parodying the opening unison in Beethoven's Fifth). Enraged, Fata Morgana curses the Prince with a fatal passion for three oranges, which he must seek to the ends of the earth. He rushes off with Truffaldino to find them, the devil Farfarello propelling them with his magic bellows.

Act 3.i *A desert* Celio intervenes on the Prince's behalf. He conjures up Farfarello, who blows the Prince and Truffaldino on stage. Celio informs them that the oranges they seek are in the kitchen of the palace of the witch Creonta, guarded by a cook with a lethal ladle. He gives Truffaldino a ribbon to distract the cook, and warns that when the oranges have been secured they must be opened only in the presence of water. Farfarello blows up a storm, which carries the pair off towards Creonta's palace. (The orchestral scherzo symbolizing their flight serves as an entr'acte in the opera and as the fourth movement of the suite.)

3.ii *The courtyard of Creonta's palace* Having distracted the cook with Celio's ribbon, the Prince and Truffaldino sneak into the kitchen (offstage) and make off with the oranges. They are transported back to the desert (so the next entr'acte tells us) by a reprise of the scherzo.

3.iii *The desert* The oranges have grown to enormous size. Weary of lugging them, the Prince and Truffaldino lie down to sleep. Truffaldino is too thirsty to sleep. He cuts one of the oranges to get some juice. Instead a fairy princess emerges, calling for water. Truffaldino opens a second orange to get juice for the two of them. A second princess emerges, also calling for water. The two princesses die of thirst; the horrified Truffaldino rushes offstage in a panic. The Prince awakens and finds the bodies. He nonchalantly orders four passing soldiers to bury

them. Then he cuts into the third orange. Princess Ninetta emerges and is about to share the fate of her predecessors, but the Cranks lower a pail of water from their turret and save her life. A great love duet seems imminent, only to be spoilt by the Lyricists, who break into a paean in praise of love duets. (The thirst music, the recognition music and the aborted love music furnish the materials for the fifth movement, 'The Prince and the Princess', of the suite.) Ninetta refuses to go with the Prince without suitable clothes. He goes off to fetch them for her. Fata Morgana now enters with Smeraldina in tow. By means of a magic pin they turn Ninetta into a rat and Smeraldina takes her place. The King and his retinue accompany the Prince back to the desert to the strains of the familiar March. They are dismayed to discover Smeraldina, but the King commands his son to proceed with the wedding.

Act 4.i *The drop curtain (as I.ii)* Celio and Fata Morgana have it out: the latter gets the upper hand, but the Cranks come once again to the rescue, abduct her to their tower and bid Celio turn the rat back into Ninetta.

4.ii *The throne room of the royal palace* The King and his retinue enter to one last reprise of the March. When the curtains around the Princess's throne are drawn back the rat is discovered. Pandemonium ensues, during which Celio manages to turn the rat back into Ninetta. Truffaldino arrives out of nowhere to expose Smeraldina; she is sentenced to hang, along with Clarice and Leander. As the rope is prepared, they all make a run for it. (The music accompanying their breakout forms the basis of the final suite movement, entitled 'Flight'.) Fata Morgana appears and opens a trap door for them into which they (and she) disappear. The remaining *dramatis personae* hail the Prince and the Princess.

*

Like *The Gambler*, *The Love for Three Oranges* is basically in what Prokofiev called a 'declamatory' style; but ('taking American tastes into account', as he put it in his autobiography) the composer provided a few more obviously lyrical moments cast in fugitive rounded forms, and there are a couple of diverting instrumental showpieces (the March in Act 2, the Scherzo in Act 3). The musical style as such derives from Rimsky-Korsakov's *Golden Cockerel* by way of Stravinsky's *Petrushka*.

Compared with Meyerhold's scenario, Prokofiev's opera shows the usual streamlining and minor alterations. The most noteworthy difference is the hugely expanded role Prokofiev accorded the 'Greek chorus' of onstage spectators – the very thing Meyerhold and his colleagues had already so significantly expanded from Gozzi's little 'quarrel trio'. To Meyerhold's Comedians, Tragedians and Cranks (the latter numbering three in the scenario, ten in the opera), Prokofiev added groups of 'Lyricists', forever demanding 'romantic love, moons, tender kisses', and 'Empty Heads', bent on 'entertaining nonsense, witty double-entendres, fine costumes'. In this way he thought to cover every sort of standard operatic situation and cliché (what in Russian is still called *vampuka* after a famous grand-opera lampoon first produced at a St Petersburg cabaret in 1909). The Comedians, Tragedians, Lyricists and Empty Heads are continually breaking in on the action of Prokofiev's opera as it approaches one or another of their pet stereotypes to egg it on. His Cranks, eager to foil all factions (but particularly the Tragedians), do more than that: they actually intervene in the plot, Pirandello-fashion (but before Pirandello!), change its course and utterly destroy all stage illusion. The play, literally, is their plaything. (And art, the composer implies, is ours.) When Prokofiev's forgotten opera was given its earliest post-war revivals (especially the Ljubljana revival of 1956 that travelled to the Holland Festival and was recorded there), critics were struck by the affinity between the ironically detached, constantly interrupted antics on stage and the discontinuous structure of the music. That remains the most authentic of the opera's virtues.   R.T.

Lucia di Lammermoor ('Lucy of Lammermoor')

Dramma tragico in three acts by Gaetano Donizetti to a libretto by Salvadore Cammarano after Walter Scott's novel *The Bride of Lammermoor*; Naples, Teatro S Carlo, 26 September 1835.

The première was given by a remarkable cast, including Fanny Tacchinardi-Persiani (Lucia), Gilbert Duprez (Edgardo), Domenico Cosselli (Enrico) and Carlo Porto (Raimondo).

Lucia	soprano
Enrico Ashton *Laird of Lammermoor,*	
Lucia's brother	baritone
Edgardo *Laird of Ravenswood*	tenor
Lord Arturo Bucklaw *Lucia's bridegroom*	tenor
Raimondo Bidebent *a Calvinist chaplain*	bass
Alisa *Lucia's companion*	mezzo-soprano
Normanno *huntsman, a retainer of Enrico*	tenor
Retainers and servants, wedding guests	

Setting The grounds and hall of Lammermoor and of Ravenswood, and the graveyard of the Ravenswoods; Scotland, during the reign of William and Mary (late 17th century)

Before Cammarano adapted Scott's novel, it had been the basis of three earlier Italian librettos – by Giuseppe Balocchi for Michele Carafa's *Le nozze di*

Lammermoor (1829, Paris), Calisto Bassi for Luigi Rieschi's *La fidanzata di Lammermoor* (1831, Trieste) and Pietro Beltrame for Alberto Mazzucato's *La fidanzata di Lammermoor* (1834, Padua). Like nearly all the Scott operas, Donizetti's *Lucia* departs from its model in several ways. Cammarano made the original characters Frank Hayston, Laird of Bucklaw, Ailsie Gourlay and the Reverend Peter Bide-the-Bent into, respectively, Lord Arturo Bucklaw, Alisa and Raimondo Bidebent, conflating Lucy's father Sir William Ashton and her elder brother Colonel Sholto Ashton into Enrico Ashton. (Some English adaptations use the names Sir Arthur Bucklaw, Alice, Raymond Bide-the-Bent and Sir Henry Ashton.) Although Scott's most memorable villainess, Lucy's mother, is left out altogether, much of the powerful plot survives.

Donizetti produced *Lucia* on his return to Naples from Paris. Arguably his finest score, it is deeply in tune with the romantic sensibility of the age – indeed, it is generally considered the archetype of Italian Romantic opera. Following the successful première in Naples, Adelaide Kemble and Napoleone Moriani sang in the first performance at La Scala, on 1 April 1839; at the French première (Paris, Théâtre Italien, 12 December 1837) Tacchinardi-Persiani and Antonio Rubini sang, as they did at the English première (London, Her Majesty's, 5 April 1838). The French version by Donizetti himself (to a translation by Alphonse Royer and Gustave Vaëz, with the music adjusted and altered at many points) was first given at the Théâtre de la Renaissance, Paris, on 6 August 1839, with Sophie Anne Thillon and Achille Ricciardi. This version entered the Opéra repertory in 1846, with Maria Nau and Duprez, and became a staple of the repertory of French provincial theatres; and it was in this version that the opera was introduced to the USA, at New Orleans, with Julia Calvé and Auguste Nourrit, on 28 December 1841. The Italian original's first hearing in the USA was also at New Orleans, given by a touring company from Havana, on 1 March 1842. Since these beginnings the role of Lucia has been central in the repertory of every soprano with a gift for *fioritura*; among the most famous are Adelina Patti, Etelka Gerster, Ilma Di Murska, Emma Albani, Marcella Sembrich, Nellie Melba, Luisa Tetrazzini, Amelita Galli-Curci, Toti dal Monte, Lily Pons, Maria Callas, Joan Sutherland, Beverly Sills and Edita Gruberová.

*

Act I.i *The grounds of Ravenswood Castle* After a short B♭ minor prelude, punctuated by ominous drum-rolls, mournful horn phrases and a dirge-like march, the curtain rises on Normanno and the other huntsmen, who are about to explore the nearby ruins of the castle belonging to Enrico's hated enemy Edgardo (chorus, 'Per correte le spiagge vicine'). The

Luisa Tetrazzini in the title role of Donizetti's 'Lucia di Lammermoor'

huntsmen leave, and Normanno, seeing that Enrico is troubled, learns from him that the Lammermoor fortunes are in jeopardy; only Lucia can save them, by means of an expedient marriage. The chaplain reminds Enrico that she is still grieving for her mother, who has recently died, and that the girl is not ready to love. At that, Normanno declares that she has been on fire with love for Edgardo, meeting him every morning ever since he rescued her from a rampaging bull. Enrico is enraged (Larghetto, 'Cruda, funesta smania'). The huntsmen return to report that Edgardo is nearby; Enrico swears to destroy his enemy (cabaletta, 'La pietade in suo favore'). The chorus and the double aria for the baritone form the impetuous climax to this scene.

I.ii *The park at Lammermoor Castle, with a fountain* The scene begins with an elaborate harp solo (which at least one Lucia, Ernesta Grisi, was enterprising enough to perform herself). Impatiently, Lucia awaits a tryst with Edgardo. She looks at the fountain, where an ancestor of the Ravenswoods jettisoned the corpse of a Lammermoor lass he had slain in a jealous rage; she is frightened because she has recently seen the girl's ghost. She describes the episode vividly to Alisa (Larghetto, 'Regnava nel silenzio'), mentioning that the water had turned blood-red. This aria is a fine example of Donizetti's gift of using vocal ornament to dramatic ends: the

embellishments he wrote out vividly convey the heroine's unstable mental state. Alisa declares that Lucia's love for Edgardo is beset with difficulties and urges her to renounce him. Lucia, however, believes in his constancy (cabaletta, 'Quando rapito in estasi'; Tacchinardi-Persiani was not fond of Lucia's entrance arias and substituted ones from the role of Rosmonda from Donizetti's *Rosmonda d'Inghilterra*, 1834, which had been written for her – that Donizetti approved of the substitution is evident from his incorporation of the *Rosmonda* scena into the French *Lucie de Lammermoor*).

Edgardo arrives and Alisa goes to watch for intruders. He tells Lucia that he has been called to the Stuart cause in France and must leave next morning. Before he goes he wants to extend the hand of friendship to Enrico, despite the long-standing feud between their families. Lucia, frightened of her brother's furious temper, begs Edgardo to keep their love secret. He reminds her that he swore, by his father's grave, that he would be avenged, and although their love has quenched his anger his oath remains unfulfilled. Lucia calms him, and he places a ring on her finger, claiming that henceforth they are as married; Lucia accepts this, giving him a ring in return. She begs him to write to her, telling him that he will hear the echo of her sighs, even in France, and he reassures her before he departs (duet, 'Verranno a te sull'aure', a melody that will be of strategic importance in her later mad scene as she imagines her formal marriage).

Act 2.i *Enrico's apartments in Lammermoor Castle* Enrico discusses with Normanno the marriage he has hastily arranged between Lucia and Arturo Bucklaw, and is worried that she may oppose it. Normanno has been intercepting Edgardo's letters and, with Enrico's connivance, has forged one to say that Edgardo loves another woman – leaving her no reason to hold back from the proposed marriage. Taking the forged letter, Enrico sends Normanno to welcome Arturo. Lucia enters, listless; Enrico comments on her pallor, to which she responds that he knows why she grieves (duet, 'Il pallor funesto'). She protests at his inhuman severity, but he claims that his strong fraternal feelings prompt his wish to see her appropriately married. When she says that she already considers herself Edgardo's wife, Enrico hands her the forged letter; the shock of reading it causes her to stagger as though she had received a blow. Enrico reproaches her with folly, but Lucia is numbed at the thought of Edgardo's infidelity. Sounds are heard of the welcome for Arturo. Lucia wants only to die, not to marry; but Enrico stresses the perils of his political situation, from which only an alliance with the Bucklaws can save him. He ruthlessly tells her that without her cooperation he will surely be executed, and she will be responsible.

This powerful duet scene with its three contrasting sections represents a touchstone of Donizetti's skill as a musical dramatist, in his characterization of the successive stages of the estrangement between brother and sister.

Enrico hurries out to greet Arturo. Lucia turns to Raimondo, who tells her that, although he knows her letters to Edgardo were intercepted, he managed to have one of them securely delivered. Believing Edgardo has never replied, the chaplain is convinced of his infidelity and tells Lucia that the exchange of rings has no validity in God's eyes. Despite his persuasiveness, Lucia confesses she loves Edgardo still. He urges the impressionable girl to remember a sister's duty and her obligation to her dead mother (aria, 'Ah! cedi, cedi'), and goes on to assure her that her reward will be in heaven. (This episode was traditionally omitted, but its importance in charting Lucia's crumbling resistance is now generally recognized.)

2.ii *The Great Hall of Lammermoor Castle* Wedding guests are assembled to greet Arturo ('Per te d'immenso giubilo': a rousing unison chorus with a solo interlude); Arturo smugly claims that the fortunes of the house will now undoubtedly improve. Enrico tells him not to be surprised at Lucia's sad demeanour as she is still grieving for her mother. Arturo questions Enrico about the rumours of Edgardo, but Lucia's entrance saves him from answering. The marriage contract awaits the requisite signatures: half-fainting, Lucia signs her name, but to her the document is like her own death warrant. Suddenly there is uproar as Edgardo unexpectedly appears: he wonders what power restrains him as he confronts his enemy, and Enrico fears that he has betrayed his sister. The famous sextet in D♭, 'Chi mi frena in tal momento', expands the shock of Edgardo's arrival, developing a groundswell of conflicting emotions, twice rising to climaxes. Its structure is simple (*A–A'–B–B'*), but no small measure of its effectiveness comes from the skilful *crescendo* of forces: first tenor-baritone, then soprano-bass with tenor and baritone in the background, and only in the B sections engaging all six soloists and chorus. Lucia is bereft; Raimondo is touched by her pitiable state. Their swords drawn, Arturo and Enrico order Edgardo away, but he defies them, insisting on his right to be present: Lucia, he claims, is his bride. Raimondo now shows him the contract; Edgardo asks if Lucia herself has signed it and when she confesses he tears off her ring and tramples on it, cursing the moment he fell in love with her and vowing eternal hatred. Enrico, Arturo and the guests demand his instant departure. Lucia sinks to her knees, praying for deliverance; but Edgardo throws down his sword, bares his breast and declares he has no more desire to live. The

transitional passage of this concerted finale brings back, in Rossinian fashion, the accompanying tune that had underlain the earlier conversation between Arturo and Enrico in its opening section. This uneasy attempt at civilized discourse breaks down when Raimondo produces the marriage contract, an episode accompanied by misremembered echoes of Lucia's entrance music earlier in this scene, providing thereby a clue to her mental agitation. Edgardo's curse (a moment made famous by Duprez) precipitates the D major stretta, which develops in the usual fashion: a thrusting unison for the furious Enrico and his followers, succeeded by a shift in texture dominated by the soprano and tenor, leading through an interlude of harmonic restlessness to a reinforced statement of the earlier material, capped by an emphatic coda.

Act 3.i *The dilapidated hall of the Ravenswoods* A fierce storm rages; Edgardo, alone, expresses the wish that the storm foretell the end of the world. Unexpectedly, Enrico enters; he gloats that, even as he speaks, Lucia is entering her bridal chamber with Arturo (duet, 'Qui del padre ancor respira') and declares that he has come to challenge Edgardo to a duel the following dawn in the Ravenswoods' graveyard. (In the mid-19th century this Tower Scene was regarded as one of the great dramatic moments of the opera; and there was once a near-riot at the Théâtre Italien when it was omitted because of a singer's indisposition. The scene was later often omitted as the opera came to be regarded primarily as a prima donna's vehicle and the rest of the cast was second string; but with singers who understand the art of dramatic declamation in bel canto opera, the Tower Scene can still produce a strong impression.)

3.ii *The Great Hall at Lammermoor* The wedding guests dance to celebrate Lucia's wedding (chorus, 'D'immenso giubilo'). Suddenly Raimondo, badly shaken, appears, ordering them to stop their merriment. In a grisly narrative (Larghetto, 'Dalle stanze ove Lucia', over a restlessly modulating accompaniment), he tells that he heard a cry from the bridal chamber; hastening there, he was aghast to see Arturo dead on the floor, with Lucia, holding a bloodstained dagger, smiling at him, enquiring where her bridegroom was. The guests are stunned (chorus, 'Oh! qual funesto avvenimento!').

At Lucia's entrance her mental disorder is suggested by the flute (Donizetti had originally planned to use a glass harmonica here) playing a distorted variant of 'Regnava nel silenzio'. She is wearing a white gown now spattered with blood, and believes she is ready for her wedding to Edgardo. Trembling, she urges him to let her rest by the fountain in the park (the melody of 'Verranno a te' makes it clear that in her confusion she thinks their exchange of rings was a true plighting); then she remembers the ghost that arose from the fountain. Next, imagining they are before an altar, she believes she hears their wedding hymn, and sees the ceremony taking place ('Ardon gl'incensi'). This is the Larghetto of the Mad Scene; her hallucination is appropriately cast as a theme and variations, and it is capped today by an extensive cadenza with flute obbligato. That this now traditional effect does not appear in the score (it is a disfiguring addition by or for Teresa Brambilla) indicates that Donizetti evidently trusted Tacchinardi-Persiani, whose powers of improvisation were legendary, to insert her own cadenza at this point.

Enrico, returning from his encounter with Edgardo, is at first furious at her apparent vindictiveness, but Raimondo points out that her mind has failed. Her declaration that she is the victim of her brother's cruelty fills Enrico with contrition; foreseeing her death, Lucia assures the imagined Edgardo that heaven will be beautiful for her only when he joins her there (cabaletta, 'Spargi d'amaro pianto'). Enrico bids Alisa lead his stricken sister away and urges Raimondo to attend her. Raimondo sternly rebukes Normanno for the bloodshed he has caused.

3.iii The graveyard of the Ravenswoods Edgardo appears, early for his appointment to duel with Enrico. The thought of dying on Enrico's sword is not unwelcome to him, as the whole universe seems a desert. He thinks of Lucia as a joyous bride as he confronts the prospect of his death. He bids farewell to the earth, thinking of his own neglected, unmourned grave (Larghetto, 'Fra poco a me ricovero') and wishing Lucia would at least pay heed to the tomb of one who died for love of her.

The Lammermoor retainers approach, remarking how a day that dawned in gladness has ended in grief. Edgardo demands their meaning: they tell him that Lucia lies near death and is calling for him. A funeral knell tolls. Edgardo is determined to try to see her once more but Raimondo restrains him, assuring him that Lucia is indeed already dead. Edgardo thinks of her in heaven; although they were separated on earth, they shall be united before God (cabaletta, 'Tu che a Dio spiegasti l'ali'). He is resolved to die. Raimondo and the others try to restrain him, but he draws his dagger and stabs himself. His dying thoughts are of Lucia.

*

In the days of exigent prima donnas, the famous Mad Scene was regarded as the sole raison d'être for *Lucia*'s survival, but today, thanks to the example of Callas as much as anyone, its eerie persuasiveness, heightened by melodic and harmonic allusions to earlier parts of the score, as well as its musico-dramatic distinction, have gained for it recognition as a good deal more than a soprano's warhorse. Besides

allowing a soprano to demonstrate her technical prowess, the Mad Scene is extraordinarily forward-looking and filled with adroit psychological touches. It gives the effect of being through-composed, although in fact it consists of two major episodes: the choruses before and after Raimondo's narrative, and the extended recitative and double aria for the soprano. But so cannily are the sections joined and overlapped (for instance, Lucia continues the recitative while the orchestra introduces the melody of her Larghetto) that the segments of the traditional sequence succeed each other without any sense of disruption. Most surprising of all, perhaps, is the mirroring of Lucia's disorientation in the distorted versions of melodies heard earlier in the opera. Significantly, the one melody she manages to keep straight in her muddled head is 'Verranno a te'.

The Tomb Scene is in effect a second aria-finale, but it conveys a true Romantic frisson with its setting, its atmosphere of foreboding succinctly created in a brief prelude with prominent horn parts. Both of Edgardo's solos, in D major, and the B major chorus that separates them evoke a sense of tragic loss that seems inconsistent with the major mode. One fine touch (which Duprez claimed he suggested to Donizetti) was to have the initial phrases of the repetition of the *moderato* cabaletta, following Edgardo's stabbing himself, divided between the cello and the voice. For many the Tomb Scene is the high point of the whole score.

Both historically and artistically, *Lucia* deserves its reputation. When it was new it was regarded as the apogee of high Romantic sensibility. The clear plot, which trims away much of Scott's accessory detail, possesses the stark tautness of a tale by Poe. It is no coincidence that Flaubert employed it as an important point of reference in the downward course of Emma Bovary, that quintessential victim of Romantic illusions.

Although all the principal roles are vocally challenging, their music is uniformly grateful. The score contains scant sign of the unevenness that afflicts a number of Donizetti's works. Cammarano's libretto moved him deeply and, inspired by his recent first exposure to Paris, Donizetti produced what is certainly his masterpiece. That *Lucia* used to be regarded as an unlikely survivor of an outmoded style derives from the fact that it was usually performed with many damaging cuts (sometimes even the Tomb Scene would be omitted). Today the value of the work is more easily grasped as it has fortunately become customary to perform it complete, and the many revivals of other bel canto operas in recent years have helped in the appreciation of its true stature.   **W.A.**

Lucio Silla ('Lucius Sulla')

Dramma per musica in three acts, K135, by Wolfgang Amadeus Mozart to a libretto by Giovanni De Gamerra; Milan, Regio Ducal Teatro, 26 December 1772.

The original cast was: Bassano Morgnoni (Sulla), Venanzio Rauzzini (Cecilius), Anna de Amicis-Buonsolazzi (Junia), Felicità Suardi (Cinna), Daniella Mienci (Celia) and Giuseppe Onofrio (Aufidius).

Lucius Sulla *dictator of Rome*	tenor
Giunia [Junia] *daughter of Caius Marius,*	
betrothed to Cecilius	soprano
Cecilio [Cecilius] *exiled Roman*	
senator	soprano castrato
Lucio [Lucius] Cinna *his friend,*	
a conspirator	soprano
Celia *sister of Sulla*	soprano
Aufidio [Aufidius] *tribune, friend of Sulla*	tenor
Guards, nobles, senators, people of Rome	
Setting Rome, 79 BC	

The contract for *Lucio Silla*, dated 4 March 1771, required Mozart to deliver the recitatives in October 1772 and to be in Milan by November to compose the arias and rehearse 'with the usual reservations in case of theatrical misfortunes and Princely interventions (which God forbid)'.

The primo uomo (Cecilius) arrived only on 21 November, the prima donna (Junia) still later. Morgnoni was a last-minute replacement (so his role is relatively simple). Mozart had to make alterations in the light of Metastasio's comments on the libretto. Archduke Ferdinand's letter-writing delayed the première two hours; it was immensely long (there were three ballets), but nevertheless was followed by 25 more performances, a major triumph. The libretto was set by other composers including J. C. Bach (1775, Mannheim), but Mozart's opera was not revived until 1929 (Prague, in German).

*

The successful general Lucius Sulla seized total power in Rome but unexpectedly laid it down the year before his death. Some of the characters are historical, but the plot is fiction.

Act I *A neglected grove* The banished Cecilius reappears secretly in Rome and learns from Cinna that Sulla, declaring him dead, proposes to marry Junia. Cecilius may see her when she goes to mourn her father; love promises a better future ('Vieni ov'amor t'invita'). Cecilius is prey to fear and joyful anticipation (the first of many fine obbligato recitatives) as well as feelings of tenderness ('Il tenero momento').

In Sulla's palace Celia agrees to persuade Junia to accept Sulla (in minuet style, 'Se lusinghiera speme'); no girl will resist for the sake of the dead. Junia rejects the tyrant who has deposed her father and banished her lover. Sulla, at first not unkind, says the price of obstinacy may be death. Junia responds ('Dalla sponda tenebrosa'): in an *adagio* section she invokes her father and lover, then (*allegro*) pours scorn on his love. Sulla decides he must overcome the weakness of affection and, like a true tyrant, condemn her (obbligato recitative and aria, 'Il desio di vendetta').

The mausoleum The rest of Act 1 uses no simple recitative. After the fiery D major of Sulla's aria, Mozart sets the new scene by sombre music which modulates obliquely to C minor. Cecilius's mixed feelings bring varied figurations and rapid tempo changes. Junia enters with mourners; within their funeral chorus she sings a G minor lament ('O del padre ombra diletta'). Cecilius is at first taken for a ghost. Their duet ('D'Eliso in sen m'attendi'), a moving Andante and brilliant Allegro, ends the act on a note of hope.

Act 2 *A military arch* Aufidius tells Sulla that, as Junia has many supporters in Rome, he should publicly declare her his wife ('Guerrier, che d'un acciaro'). Sulla permits Celia's betrothal to Cinna. Cecilius pursues Sulla with a sword but Cinna restrains him; rashness will gain nothing. Cecilius mingles hope and despair in snatches of obbligato recitative, but his aria ('Quest'improviso tremito'), a concise Allegro in D, shows his fierce desire for revenge. Celia tries to declare her love for Cinna but is tongue-tied (an appealing Grazioso, 'Se il labbro timido'). Cinna is more concerned with plotting; but Junia refuses to marry Sulla and murder him in bed. He must care for Cecilius (obbligato recitative), whose danger freezes her heart. Her aria ('Ah se il crudel periglio') is a grandiose Allegro of stunning virtuosity. Cinna decides that he must undertake communal vengeance himself (obbligato recitative and a vigorous aria, 'Nel fortunato istante').

Hanging gardens Struggling with contradictory feelings, Sulla again assures Junia that refusal means death. His aria ('D'ogni pietà mi spoglio') explodes: drained of pity, he will assuage his hurt by killing. In a short middle section he is overcome by tenderness towards her, quickly suppressed. Cecilius tells Junia that he must kill the tyrant; if he dies his shade will watch over her ('Ah, se a morir mi chiama'). Exceptionally, the main section is Adagio, nobly arching in wide leaps, and the middle section a tender Andante. Celia urges Junia to marry Sulla ('Quando sugl'arsi campi'). Her cheerful A major is followed by the tragic D minor of Junia's soliloquy on the conflict of duty and love. She will kill herself rather than submit, and gasps out her despair in an agitated aria ('Parto, m'affretto') with a daring harmonic shift at the reprise.

'Lucio Silla' (Mozart), first scene of Act 1 (a neglected grove): design by Fabrizzio Galliari for the original production at the Regio Ducal Teatro, Milan, 26 December 1772

The Capitol The chorus hopes that Sulla's glory will be crowned by love ('Se gloria il crin ti cinse'). Sulla publicly claims Junia as the token of civil peace; she is prevented from killing herself when Cecilius vainly attacks Sulla. In a trio ('Quell'orgoglioso sdegno') Sulla declares that he will humble his enemies, Cecilius is defiant, and Junia, joined by Cecilius, anticipates the consolation of death.

Act 3 *Before the prison* Cinna excuses his failure to support a futile assassination attempt. He agrees to marry Celia if she can persuade her brother to have mercy; she promises to achieve this whatever storms arise ('Strider sento la procella'). Cinna expresses optimism (Cecilius has supporters) in a heroic aria in D ('De' più superbi il core'). Junia appears for a last farewell; she will not save Cecilius by yielding to Sulla. Aufidius comes to take Cecilius to public judgment; in a melting, rondo-like aria ('Pupille amate') in minuet tempo he says her tears will make him die too soon; his soul will return, dissolved in a sigh. Junia is left to her premonitions, her obbligato recitative richly scored and anticipating the motif of the aria ('Frà i pensier più funesti'), in which she imagines Cecilius dead, lamenting over a throbbing muted accompaniment; then with a determined Allegro she runs after her lover.

A hall in the palace The denouement takes place in simple recitative. Even as Sulla condemns Cecilius, Junia publicly proclaims her betrothal. Baffled, even

moved, the tyrant decides to forgive her and permit the two couples to marry. He retires from public life (finale); the chorus praises his devotion to Rome, and the soloists sing of love and freedom.

*

Mozart constructed the first two acts cleverly, gradually abandoning the conventionally formed and very long arias preferred in Milan for more flexible designs perhaps suggested by Gluck's *Alceste*. Despite the magnificent mausoleum scene, *Lucio Silla* remains an unreformed type of *opera seria*. Several D major arias with trumpets and drums are contrasted with remarkable richness of expression in the splendid roles of Cecilius and Junia, while Celia's lightly scored music provides relief. Although its plot is turgid and its denouement unconvincing, *Lucio Silla* is musically the finest work Mozart wrote in Italy, and ranks with examples of *opera seria* by the greatest masters of the time.   J.Ru.

Lucrezia Borgia

Melodramma in a prologue and two acts by Gaetano Donizetti to a libretto by Felice Romani after Victor Hugo's play *Lucrèce Borgia*; Milan, Teatro alla Scala, 26 December 1833.

The cast at the première included Henriette

Méric-Lalande as Lucrezia, Marietta Brambilla as Orsini, Francesco Pedrazzi as Gennaro and Luciano Mariani as Alfonso.

Lucrezia Borgia	soprano
Gennaro	tenor
Maffio Orsini	mezzo-soprano
Duke Alfonso	bass-baritone
Liverotto	tenor
Vitellozzo	bass
Nobles, guests, guards	
Setting Venice; Ferrara	

One of the major successes of Donizetti's career, *Lucrezia Borgia* reflects his interest in powerful melodramatic tragedy. He was attracted to the subject by the scene in Hugo's play in which the six coffins of Lucrezia's victims were suddenly revealed. The Milanese censors refused to allow the inclusion of this episode in the opera; indeed, the subject was at first regarded as so suspect that three years elapsed between the successful opening run at La Scala and the next production. For a time the work was given under a number of aliases; in one version the action was transferred to a non-Christian country.

For its second production at La Scala, in January 1840, Donizetti revised the final scene, adding an arioso for the dying Gennaro and eliminating Lucrezia's final cabaletta, as he thought it dramatically incongruous for a mother to sing a brilliant aria over a son whose death she has, albeit unwittingly, caused. From 1840 on, *Lucrezia Borgia* became one of the central works of the repertory, its vogue lasting until the end of the century. Famous Lucrezias have included Karoline Unger, Giulia Grisi, Therese Tietjens and, more recently, Montserrat Caballé. A number of complete recordings have reawakened interest in this powerful, if dated, work.

*

In the prologue Gennaro has come to Venice with his friends, among them Maffio Orsini, Liverotto and Vitellozzo, to celebrate Carnival. His companions leave Gennaro behind; he lies down on a bench to rest. A masked woman enters and admires the sleeper affectionately (aria, 'Com'è bello!'), revealing that he is her son, although he is unaware of their relationship. When he awakens she questions him about his past; but when Gennaro's friends return he is horrified to learn from them that this beautiful creature is the infamous Lucrezia Borgia.

In Ferrara (Act 1), Duke Alfonso, Lucrezia's fourth husband, hopes to avenge his honour, having learnt from a spy that Gennaro is suspected of being Lucrezia's lover. Gennaro and his friends have come to Ferrara for adventure, but when he sees Lucrezia's crest on the façade of her palace he lops off the 'B', causing the emblem to read *orgia*. Indoors Lucrezia,

furious at this insult but unaware of who has perpetrated it, bids Alfonso avenge her. When Gennaro is brought in, Lucrezia fears for his safety, but she pretends to go along with her husband's plan of poisoning Gennaro, knowing that she has an antidote. When Alfonso leaves, Lucrezia gives her son the antidote and orders him to leave Ferrara at once. Before he can go, Maffio Orsini insists (Act 2) that he attend a ball at the Princess Negroni's. There Orsini's carefree drinking song (brindisi, 'Il segreto per esser felice') is interrupted by sinister voices singing of death. Gennaro and his companions rush to the doors to escape but discover they are locked in. Clad in black, Lucrezia suddenly appears, declaring she has poisoned their wine to avenge the insult to her family crest. Believing that he had left Ferrara, she is horrified to see Gennaro among her victims. The others are led off, leaving Lucrezia with her son. She swears she never meant to harm him and pleads with him to drink an antidote (aria, 'M'odi, ah, m'odi'); Gennaro refuses, even when she reveals their relationship to him. He dies, and she swoons by his corpse.

*

In a number of significant ways *Lucrezia Borgia* anticipates Verdi. A dialogue duet over a sombre melody anticipates the scene between Rigoletto and Sparafucile. The interplay of the voices in the trio for Lucrezia, Gennaro and Alfonso looks forward to a number of Verdian terzettos, and the arioso for the dying Gennaro, 'Madre, se ognor lontano', prefigures the phrases of the dying Ernani.

W.A.

Luisa Miller

Melodramma tragico in three acts by Giuseppe Verdi to a libretto by Salvadore Cammarano after Friedrich von Schiller's play *Kabale und Liebe*; Naples, Teatro S Carlo, 8 December 1849.

The first cast included Marietta Gazzaniga (Luisa), Achille De Bassini (Miller), Antonio Selva (Walter) and Settimio Malvezzi (Rodolfo).

Count Walter	bass
Rodolfo *his son*	tenor
Federica *Duchess of Ostheim,*	
Walter's niece	contralto
Wurm *Walter's steward*	bass
Miller *a retired old soldier*	baritone
Luisa *his daughter*	soprano
Laura *a peasant girl*	mezzo-soprano
A Peasant	tenor
Federica's ladies-in-waiting, pages, retainers,	
archers, villagers	

Title-page of the first edition of the vocal score of Verdi's 'Luisa Miller', showing the end of Act 3 (Milan: Ricordi, 1850)

Setting The Tyrol, in the first half of the 17th century

Verdi's relationship with Naples, never entirely happy, continued inauspiciously during the late 1840s: in 1848, despite his efforts to withdraw, the Neapolitan authorities held him to a longstanding contract for a new opera at the S Carlo. The librettist was to be Salvadore Cammarano, resident poet at the theatre and a man of vast experience in both the practical and the artistic side of operatic production. Verdi's first idea was for a setting of Francesco Guerrazzi's recent historical novel, *L'assedio di Firenze*, a large-scale subject designed to suit the dimensions of the S Carlo and, one imagines, intended to follow the line of Verdi's current preoccupation, *La battaglia di Legnano* (première January 1849). However, by April 1849 this idea – hardly surprisingly given the counter-revolutionary political climate engendered by the previous 'year of revolutions' – had been rejected by the Neapolitan censors. Cammarano then suggested using Schiller's *Kabale und Liebe*, a play Verdi himself had earlier considered. The composer accepted, although not without asking for a considerable number of structural alterations to the synopsis Cammarano sent

him (not all of which the poet, who was no Piave in matters of acquiescence, agreed to).

Negotiations had thus far been undertaken with Verdi in Paris, where he had set up house with Giuseppina Strepponi while supervising the première of *Jérusalem*. In the late summer of 1849 he returned to Italy to work on *Luisa Miller* (as Schiller's play had been retitled); he arrived in Naples in late October to supervise the staging of the opera, first performed some five weeks later. The première was probably a success (press reports are lacking), but even though the opera received a respectable number of revivals it never attained the popularity of *Nabucco* or *Ernani* and faded from the repertory later in the century. *Luisa* was 'rediscovered' in the 1920s as part of the Verdi 'renaissance' in Germany and has subsequently become – with *Nabucco*, *Ernani* and *Macbeth* – one of the few Verdi scores written before 1850 to enjoy a firm place in the international repertory.

*

The overture, in C minor, is unlike any other Verdi wrote in that it is monothematic rather than a succession of contrasting melodies; the composer's clear intention was to emulate a Germanic, 'symphonic' movement rather than the usual, Italian potpourri type. The modulations and other symphonic devices show that Verdi was perfectly able to understand and reproduce this style when the mood took him.

Act I: 'Love'

I.i A pleasant village A pastoral atmosphere is immediately created by the orchestra's 6/8 movement and prominent wind writing, and is confirmed by the chorus's simple, rocking melody 'Ti desta, Luisa', which bids Luisa awake on a beautiful April dawn. Miller and Luisa enter, Miller casting doubts on his daughter's relationship with 'Carlo', an unknown young man who has arrived with the new Count. Luisa expresses her naive love in the cavatina 'Lo vidi, e 'l primo palpito', which is simple and cabaletta-like, continuing elaborate woodwind effects in the accompaniment. Villagers present Luisa with flowers and 'Carlo' (Rodolfo in disguise) emerges from the crowd. The lovers join Miller in a closing terzetto, 'T'amo d'amor ch'esprimere', Miller avoiding the main melody to mutter his suspicions and discontent in a staccato counter-theme.

As the stage clears, Miller is detained by the Count's steward Wurm, who angrily demands Luisa's hand in marriage. In the spacious, conventionally organized Andante, 'Sacra la scelta è d'un consorte', Miller insists that his daughter will make her own choice of husband. But Wurm reveals the true identity of 'Carlo' and Miller bursts into a cabaletta of rage and grief, 'Ah! fu giusto il mio sospetto! '

I.ii A room in Walter's castle Walter and Wurm are in mid-conversation, Wurm having told the Count of Rodolfo's involvement with Luisa. When Wurm leaves, Walter releases his confused paternal feelings in the minor–major *romanza* 'Il mio sangue, la vita darei', another expanded form in which the major section takes an unexpected plunge back into minor reflections. Rodolfo appears and his father orders him to marry the recently widowed Duchess Federica. Before Rodolfo can explain his predicament Federica appears, heralded by a delicate chorus, 'Quale un sorriso d'amica sorte'. Federica and Rodolfo are left alone, and the Duchess admits her love in the first movement of a two-movement duet ('Dall'aule raggianti'), which begins lyrically but diverts into fragmentary dialogue as Rodolfo admits he loves another. The ensuing cabaletta, 'Deh! la parola amara', confirms their divided position.

I.iii A room in Miller's house An offstage chorus tells of a hunt in progress. Luisa is anxiously awaiting 'Carlo' but is instead confronted by her father, who reveals her lover's true identity and his forthcoming marriage. Rodolfo intervenes to swear his continuing love, telling Miller he knows a terrible secret that will protect them from the Count's wrath. Walter himself arrives to precipitate the first movement of the concertato finale, an Allegro dominated by a driving violin melody reminiscent of the overture theme. Walter summons soldiers and orders the arrest of Miller and his daughter, ignoring both the protests of Miller and Rodolfo and the entreaties of Luisa. The ensuing Andantino, the central lyrical movement 'Fra' mortali ancora oppressa', allows the principals to present their differing reactions with unusual definition. The act then quickly comes to a close: in an arioso of gathering intensity Rodolfo pleads with his father and, at the climax, threatens to reveal the dreadful secret. Walter immediately frees Luisa, the chorus thanks heaven, and the curtain falls with no concluding stretta.

Act 2: 'The Intrigue'

2.i A room in Miller's house (as I.iii) Villagers rush on and in a formal narrative tell Luisa that her father has been taken to prison. As they disperse Wurm enters and tells Luisa that, to save her father, she must write a letter that he, Wurm, will dictate, saying that she never loved Rodolfo and now wishes to elope with Wurm. Before signing the letter, Luisa offers a prayer, the famous 'Tu puniscimi, o Signore', remarkable for its lack of formal repetition. Wurm continues his demands: that she will swear the letter is her own and that she loves him. She closes the scene with a cabaletta, 'A brani, a brani, o perfido', that swings from minor to major as she moves from anticipation of death to the thought that her father will be at hand to minister to her final moments.

2.ii Walter's room in the castle Walter, brooding, is joined by Wurm, who tells him of the progress of their plot against Luisa. They join in a narrative duet, 'L'alto retaggio non ho bramato', recalling their murder of the old Count and Rodolfo's discovery of the secret. The duet begins with an objectivity typical of operatic narrative, but becomes increasingly fragmented as the description of events unfolds, culminating in the cabaletta-like 'O meco incolume' in which Walter vows to protect Wurm or accompany him to the gallows.

Federica appears and Wurm is dismissed. Walter tells her that Rodolfo is now ready to marry, and produces Luisa who, in a dialogue movement controlled by orchestral melody, denies Rodolfo and declares her love for Wurm. This last statement precipitates the lyrical Andante 'Come celar le smanie', unusual in its complete lack of orchestral accompaniment.

2.iii The castle gardens Rodolfo now has Luisa's infamous letter, and sorrowfully reminisces in the famous Andante 'Quando le sere al placido', an early example of Verdi's use of the French *couplet* form. Wurm appears and Rodolfo challenges him to an immediate duel, which Wurm evades by firing his pistol into the air and rushing off. Walter appears with some followers and, after Rodolfo has told him of Luisa's 'betrayal', persuades his son to marry Federica as revenge. Rodolfo, in a confusion of distress, closes the act with the cabaletta 'L'ara, o l'avello apprestami'.

Act 3: 'The Poison'

A room in Miller's house (as I.iii) An orchestral reminiscence of past themes introduces 'Come in un giorno solo', in which the villagers lament Luisa's sorrowful countenance. Luisa, who exchanges words with the chorus while writing a letter, is joined by Miller, who has learnt from Wurm the true nature of her sacrifice. Their ensuing duet is in the usual four movements, during the first of which Miller discovers that Luisa's letter proposes a suicide pact with Rodolfo. In the second movement, 'La tomba è un letto', Luisa returns to her naive, first-act musical style as she looks forward to an innocent grave while Miller counters with an impassioned plea in the parallel minor. The movement ends with Luisa tearing up the letter; there is a heartfelt reconciliation, and father and daughter join in a cabaletta, 'Andrem, raminghi e poveri', in which they look forward to leaving the village to live a simple, wandering existence.

As Miller departs, Luisa hears an organ from a nearby church; she kneels in prayer. Rodolfo enters and in a long, passionate recitative full of violent orchestral interjections forces her to admit to writing the letter; then he shares with her a drink which he has surreptitiously poisoned. The duet moves into regular musical periods at the Andante, 'Piangi, piangi, il tuo dolore', whose lyricism seems all the more intense for having so long been denied in the duet. Rodolfo admits that he has poisoned them both; knowing this, Luisa at last feels free to confess her deception, and they join in the stretta, 'Maledetto il dì ch'io nacqui', Rodolfo cursing the day he was born, Luisa trying to comfort him. The arrival of Miller, who quickly discovers all, leads to a terzetto finale, 'Padre, ricevi l'estremo addio', at the close of which Rodolfo, seeing Luisa fall dead, kills Wurm before himself collapsing by the side of his beloved.

*

For that perceptive early critic of Verdi, Abramo Basevi, *Luisa Miller* marks the beginning of Verdi's 'second manner', one in which he drew more on Donizetti's example and less on Rossini's, and in which his musical dramaturgy took on a more subtle and varied form. Modern commentators have sometimes endorsed this judgment, signalling the opera as an important step towards *Rigoletto*. However, while the rustic ambience of the opera undoubtedly called forth from Verdi a new and compelling attention to local colour, it is difficult to see in the formal aspect of *Luisa* an essential stylistic turning-point, particularly when compared with *Macbeth*, which had appeared two years earlier. Nevertheless, few would argue

about the opera's important position among pre-*Rigoletto* operas: not so much for its formal experiments as for its control of conventional musical forms, especially the grand duet. And in this respect, the middle-period work *Luisa* most resembles is not *Rigoletto* but *Il trovatore*, whose driving energy within conventional contexts is apparent through much of the earlier opera, in particular in its final act.

R.P.

Lulu

Opera in a prologue and three acts by Alban Berg to his own libretto after Frank Wedekind's plays *Erdgeist* and *Die Büchse der Pandora*; Zürich, Stadttheater, 2 June 1937 (Acts 1 and 2); Paris, Opéra, 24 February 1979 (three-act version, completed by Friedrich Cerha).

At the first performance, conducted by Robert Denzler, Nuri Hadzic sang the title role, Maria Bernhard was Geschwitz, Asger Stig, Dr Schön and Peter Baxevanos, Alwa.

Lulu	high soprano
Countess Geschwitz	dramatic mezzo-soprano
A Theatrical Dresser/A High-School Boy/	
A Groom	contralto
The Professor of Medicine (spoken)/The	
Banker/The Professor (silent)	high bass
The Painter/A Negro	lyric tenor
Dr Schön *editor-in-chief*/	
Jack the Ripper	heroic baritone
Alwa *Dr Schön's son,*	
a composer	young heroic tenor
Schigolch *an old man*	high character bass
An Animal Tamer/	
An Athlete	heroic buffo bass
The Prince/The Manservant/	
The Marquis	buffo tenor
The Theatre Manager	low buffo bass
A Clown	silent
A Stagehand	silent
The Police Commissioner	spoken
A Fifteen-year-old Girl	opera soubrette
Her Mother	contralto
A Woman Artist	mezzo-soprano
A Journalist	high baritone
A Manservant	lower baritone
Setting A German city, Paris and London, in the late 19th century	

Berg began to prepare an operatic treatment of Wedekind's two Lulu plays in 1928, when his negotiations to secure the rights to Gerhart Hauptmann's *Und Pippa tanzt* came to nothing. His affair with Hanna Fuchs-Robettin appears to have directed his search for the literary source for a second opera (*Wozzeck* being the first) towards a subject through which he could explore both the life-enhancing and the destructive properties of erotic love. He had known the text of *Erdgeist* at least since the early 1900s, and in 1905 had attended a private production by Karl Kraus in Vienna of *Die Büchse der Pandora*. Although Berg did not finalize his agreement with Wedekind's widow until the following year, the libretto of *Lulu* was completed by the end of 1928 together with musical drafts of early scenes, which carried over some of his sketches for *Und Pippa tanzt*. Work on the opera occupied him more or less continuously until his death in 1935.

By 1934 the short score of *Lulu* was virtually complete, but under the Nazi regime the possibility of a German or Austrian opera house's daring to mount the première became increasingly remote. To encourage a production further afield Berg prepared a five-movement concert suite from the opera, the *Symphonische Stücke aus der Oper 'Lulu'*, consisting of the rondo, Film Music and Lied der Lulu from Act 2, together with the interlude between Act 3 scenes i and ii, and the final Adagio; these became the first portions of the score to be orchestrated, and the suite received its first performance, conducted by Erich Kleiber, in Berlin on 30 November 1934. Berg then began to orchestrate *Lulu* from the beginning, incorporating those sections already scored for the suite. By the time of his death Acts 1 and 2 were complete, as well as the first 360 bars of Act 3, together with its interlude and the final Grave taken over from the Adagio of the suite. Of the remaining short score four brief passages (87 bars out of a total of 1326 in Act 3) remained to be fully notated, with accompanimental or subsidiary vocal lines still to be added.

After Berg's death his widow, Helene, was at first keen to see the opera completed; it was generally agreed that such a completion would be possible without the need for any new music to be composed. Schoenberg and Webern were asked to carry out the task but both declined, and after the première of the first two acts in Zürich Helene Berg became increasingly unwilling to allow the score to be finished by another hand; in 1937 political pressure halted the engraving of the vocal score of Act 3.

After World War II concert performances in Vienna in February and April 1949 were followed in September by a staging at La Fenice, Venice. Productions at Essen in 1953 and at Hamburg in 1957 renewed the debate over the completion of the score, and during the next decade strong arguments were raised in favour of such a treatment. But by 1960 Helene Berg's prohibition had become complete: no one was to be allowed access to the Act 3 material, a decision repeated in her will made in 1969 and

published after her death in 1976. In 1962, however, shortly after the Viennese stage première on 9 June (conducted by Karl Böhm with Evelyn Lear as Lulu, Gisela Litz as Geschwitz, Rudolf Schock as Alwa and Paul Schöffler as Schön), Universal Edition had allowed Friedrich Cerha to begin a study of the sketches and short score with a view to completing the work. After Helene Berg's death the Alban Berg Foundation took legal action to prevent the performance of Cerha's version, but the première of the three-act *Lulu* eventually took place in Paris in February 1979, conducted by Pierre Boulez and staged by Patrice Chéreau. Teresa Stratas sang Lulu, Yvonne Minton Geschwitz; Kenneth Riegel was Alwa and Franz Mazura Schön. The same forces subsequently made a commercial recording. There followed a rapid sequence of new productions of the three-act version. The American première took place at Santa Fe in July 1979 in English translation (by Arthur Jacobs) and conducted by Michael Tilson Thomas, with Nancy Shade in the title role. Covent Garden staged the British première on 16 February 1981, conducted by Colin Davis and directed by Götz Friedrich; Karan Armstrong was Lulu.

*

Prologue To a flourish in the orchestra the Animal Tamer welcomes the audience and invites them to inspect his menagerie. As each animal is introduced the orchestra identifies it thematically with a character in the opera. The snake appears last; assistants carry Lulu on, and the orchestra introduces the music that will accompany each of her entrances in the opera.

Act I.i *A spacious but shabby painter's studio* Dressed as a pierrot and watched by Dr Schön, Lulu is having her portrait painted. Alwa arrives to take his father to the dress rehearsal of his new ballet, asking after Lulu's husband, the Professor of Medicine (Recitative). The Painter seduces Lulu; he calls her 'Nelly' and later 'Eva' (Introduction–Canon–Coda). The Professor is heard knocking at the door; he enters and collapses with a heart attack (Melodrama). While the Painter goes to fetch help, Lulu tries unsuccessfully to urge her husband back to life, accompanied by a saxophone (Canzonetta). On his return, the Painter questions Lulu's motives (Recitative–Duet): does she love anything or anyone? Lulu's response is always the same: she does not know. She goes off to change her clothes, and the Painter worries about what a future with her might hold (Arioso). An orchestral interlude then develops the music first heard in the Canzonetta and Canon.

I.ii *An elegant salon in the Painter's house* Lulu and the Painter have married. They discuss the morning's mail; Lulu is astonished by the announcement of Dr Schön's engagement. The Painter celebrates Lulu's beauty and his good fortune in marrying her

(Duettino); the sound of the doorbell (a vibraphone tremolando) interrupts them. The visitor is a beggar, and the Painter leaves Lulu to deal with him. It is Schigolch, an old friend of Lulu's – perhaps her father, perhaps a former lover (Chamber Music I, for wind nonet). He calls her Lulu; she says, 'I have not been called Lulu in the memory of man'. The doorbell sounds again, and Schigolch leaves as Dr Schön enters.

The remainder of the act is dominated by a large-scale sonata-form movement (first subject, exposition, second subject, coda, development, recapitulation), the elements of which symbolize Lulu's relationship with Schön. Its first theme is introduced with Schön's opening words as he shows his distaste for Schigolch. He is surprised by the Painter's blindness to Lulu's behaviour, but the purpose of his visit, expressed in the second subject, a gavotte and musette, is to insist that Lulu stop seeing him. Lulu's love for Schön is crystallized in a Mahlerian slow theme that forms the coda of the exposition, all the elements of which are repeated as their argument goes back over the same ground. The Painter returns and Lulu leaves. The reprise of the coda is interrupted by a passage dominated by an obsessive, steadily accelerating rhythmic figure (Monoritmica), the main rhythmic feature of the opera, which signifies death and destruction; it had previously appeared at the death of the Professor of Medicine. Schön tells the Painter of Lulu's past; appalled, the latter rushes off and cuts his throat. Lulu reappears and Schön realizes what has happened; Alwa arrives and together they discover the body. The music now begins to decelerate as Schön telephones the police to report the suicide. The doorbell announces their arrival, and Lulu tells Schön that she will still marry him. The orchestral interlude picks up the sonata coda at the point at which it was broken off; it gives way to the sound of a jazz band to introduce the following scene.

I.iii A theatre dressing room Lulu is changing for her performance as a cabaret dancer. She asks Alwa whether Dr Schön will be in the audience and tells him of her latest admirer, a prince, who wants to take her to Africa as his wife. When she goes on stage Alwa wonders whether he could write an opera about her, but decides it would be too incredible. The Prince's conversation with Alwa (Chorale Variations) is interrupted by an alarm, and Lulu storms in (Ragtime): she has seen Schön in the audience with his fiancée. Schön soon follows and tries to make her return to the stage (Sextet); the Theatre Manager gives Lulu five minutes to compose herself, and everyone leaves except Schön.

The sonata movement resumes with a development section as Schön pleads with Lulu not to stop his forthcoming marriage. But when she tells him of

her plan to marry the Prince, he realizes that he is incapable of severing his links with her. As the sonata finally reaches its recapitulation Schön breaks down, and Lulu, triumphant, dictates a letter for him to send, breaking off his engagement.

Act 2.i A large living-room in Schön's house Lulu has married Schön but continues to attract admirers. She welcomes one of them, the lesbian Countess Geschwitz, who invites her to a ball for women artists (Recitative). As she leaves, Schön regrets that such people are now part of his 'family circle' (Ballade). Against Lulu's wishes he goes off to the Stock Exchange (Cavatina); Geschwitz returns, followed by the Athlete, Schoolboy and Schigolch (Ensemble). As they settle down for the day, Lulu greets them. All three declare their love for Lulu and their wish to marry her (Canon); they panic when 'Herr Doktor Schön' is announced (Recitative) and rush to hide, but it is Alwa who enters, not his father.

Alwa's declaration of love for Lulu begins the rondo that will dominate this act (just as the sonata form dominated the first one), representing his own obsessive dependence on her. The main theme, highly lyrical, is heard first as Alwa enters. Its course is constantly interrupted, first by two Chorales as the Manservant brings hors d'oeuvres and returns to clear the plates. Schön's return goes unnoticed, until the Athlete sees him brandishing a gun (Tumultuoso); Alwa is taken off by his father, and the Athlete takes the opportunity to hide again. In a five-strophe aria Schön then rounds on Lulu, accusing her of disgracing him and offering her the revolver to kill herself and save his face. He searches the room, discovering Geschwitz's hiding-place. Before his final strophe Lulu offers her first apologia: in her Lied, whose high tessitura and elaborate figuration encapsulate her vocal character in the opera, she disclaims responsibility for the men who have died for love of her. Schön knew her character when he married her, and she has never pretended to be other than she is; he may have sacrificed his position for her, but she has offered her youth to him. Resuming his aria, Schön threatens Lulu with the gun, but a noise from the Schoolboy distracts him, and Lulu fires five shots into her husband. As he dies he catches sight of Geschwitz – 'the devil!' Lulu begs Alwa to save her from arrest (Arietta); the scene ends as the police knock on the door.

The palindromic orchestral interlude is the turning-point in the opera, the division in Wedekind's drama between Erdgeist and Die Büchse der Pandora; Lulu's remorseless climb to success and social status in the first half will be mirrored by her fall in the second. The music accompanies a silent film that portrays her arrest, trial for Schön's murder and imprisonment, and then the plans for her escape (to be effected by catching cholera from Geschwitz and changing places with her in an isolation hospital).

2.ii *The same living-room, a year later* Alwa, Geschwitz and the Athlete await Schigolch (Recitative). He brings plans for Lulu's rescue and leaves with the Countess, who is to take Lulu's place in the hospital (Largo). The Schoolboy arrives, having escaped from a correction centre. He has his own plan to rescue Lulu but the Athlete convinces him that she has died in prison and throws him out. Lulu appears with Schigolch and slowly descends the stairs; the Athlete is appalled by her wasted appearance and leaves, threatening to betray her to the police. When Lulu is finally left alone with Alwa, she regains her former vitality and celebrates her freedom (Melodrama). The music of the rondo surfaces again as Alwa declares his love, praising her beauty in minute detail and musical metaphors (Hymn). As the couple fall on to the sofa, Lulu observes that it might be the very spot where his father bled to death.

Act 3.i *Paris, a spacious salon* The Athlete proposes a toast to the assembled company in honour of Lulu's birthday in the first of three large-scale ensembles that dominate the scene (each with material based on the circus music of the Prologue, which returns on each occasion with increasing frenzy). The Banker is questioned about the prospects for the Jungfrau Railway shares that everyone has bought, and the crowd drifts off to the gambling tables. Lulu is threatened by the Marquis: he is blackmailing her, but instead of demanding money intends to install her in a Cairo brothel (Concertante Chorale Variations I and II). In his Procurer's Song (Intermezzo I) a solo violin quotes for the first time a Wedekind cabaret song (the *Lautenlied*), which will form the basis of the subsequent orchestral variations and articulate the final scene. Lulu refuses (Intermezzo II) in an aria that recapitulates her Lied from Act 2 scene i, and the Marquis threatens to reveal her to the police as the murderer of Dr Schön (Variations III–XII).

The crowd returns, on its way to supper; the Jungfrau shares are booming (Ensemble II). The Athlete also tries to blackmail Lulu, and as the Banker is told of the collapse of the Jungfrau shares, Schigolch too asks Lulu for money; together they make plans to dispose of the Athlete (Pantomime). In a spoken dialogue over a cadenza for solo violin and piano the Marquis warns off the Athlete, and in a dialogue that mixes speech, Sprechgesang and lyrical arioso Lulu first convinces the Athlete that Geschwitz is in love with him, then persuades Geschwitz (who is horrified by the prospect) to spend a night with him. The Athlete and Geschwitz leave for Schigolch's lodgings, while Lulu arranges to exchange clothes with the Groom. There is uproar

as the news spreads of the Jungfrau collapse: everyone is ruined (Ensemble III). In the chaos Lulu manages to escape just before the Marquis brings the police to arrest her.

The orchestral interlude is a set of four variations on Wedekind's *Lautenlied*, first heard during the Marquis's Procurer's Song in the preceding scene. At the end of the interlude the tune is crudely harmonized and played on seven woodwind to simulate the sound of a barrel organ. The tune will reappear three times in the course of the next scene.

3.ii *London, a windowless garret in the East End* Alwa and Schigolch await Lulu's return on her first night as a prostitute. They hide as she enters with her first client, the Professor; the music associated with her first husband, the Professor of Medicine – the Melodrama and Canzonetta of Act 1 scene i – returns. As Lulu and her silent client go into an adjoining room Alwa and Schigolch rifle his pockets, finding nothing but a devotional book. They hide again as he leaves, but the next visitor proves to be Geschwitz, carrying Lulu's pierrot portrait which has dogged her throughout the opera. When it is nailed to the wall, Lulu and her three admirers contemplate its beauty and how their fate has been bound up with it (Quartet). Lulu is unable to bear the memory of her past and leaves again for the street, followed by Geschwitz, as the fourth variation from the interlude is recalled in the orchestra.

A reprise of the second variation accompanies the conversation of Schigolch and Alwa, who hide again as Lulu returns with her second client, a Negro. As they argue about money, the music associated with the Painter in Act 1 (the Monoritmica and Duettino) is evoked; Alwa intervenes and the Negro clubs him to death. Lulu leaves again; Schigolch drags off Alwa's body as the third variation is heard. Geschwitz considers suicide, but Lulu appears with another client: Jack the Ripper. Music associated with Dr Schön from the Act 1 sonata and Act 2 Cavatina is recalled as Lulu begs Jack to stay the night and then argues about money. As the couple go off into the next room there is a final quotation of the music that has accompanied Lulu's entrances throughout the opera. Geschwitz contemplates Lulu's portrait and a return to Germany (Nocturno). There is a scream off stage, and a death cry (to a 12-note chord) as Jack kills Lulu. He then stabs the Countess as she goes to help her. Jack washes his hands and leaves the dying Countess to her *Liebestod*, and to a final cadence based upon chords associated with Alwa, Schön and herself.

*

The large-scale structure of *Lulu* is completely reliant on closed forms in a way that invokes the 19th-century 'number opera', even though those formal divisions do not always coincide with the dramatic divisions into acts and scenes. Each scene is built up from more or less self-contained units, carefully defined in the score; Berg's terminology is not wholly consistent, and the unfinished Act 3 left some of the forms untitled. The first two acts are dominated by the sonata and rondo structures respectively, the third by the theme and variations that first appear in its orchestral interlude; the entire structure is unified further by the increasing tendency of the music to recapitulate earlier material until the final scene contains little that has not been heard earlier in widely differing dramatic contexts.

Berg's use of 12-note technique in *Lulu* is very much tailored to his own dramatic ends. Although all its note rows are ultimately derived by permutation from the single basic set that represents Lulu's innate sexuality, in practice the score is based on a collection of interrelated rows whose distinct melodic shapes function as character motifs throughout the opera: they portray Lulu's protean nature (indicating how each of her admirers has a different concept of her), Schön's conformist inflexibility, Alwa's lyrical idealism, Geschwitz's selfless love and so on.   A.C.

Lustigen Weiber von Windsor, Die
('The Merry Wives of Windsor')

Komische-fantastische Oper in three acts by Otto Nicolai to a libretto by Salomon Hermann Mosenthal after William Shakespeare; Berlin, Königliches Opernhaus, 9 March 1849.

The cast at the first performance included August Zschiesche (Falstaff), Leopoldine Tuczek (Mrs Ford), Pauline Marx (Mrs Page), Louise Köster (Anne Page), Julius Krause (Ford), Julius Pfister (Fenton) and Eduard Mantius (Slender).

Frau Fluth [Mrs Ford]	soprano
Frau Reich [Mrs Page]	mezzo-soprano
Herr Fluth [Ford]	baritone
Herr Reich [Page]	bass
Jungfer Anna Reich [Anne Page]	soprano
Junker Spärlich [Slender]	tenor
Dr Caius	bass
Fenton	tenor
Sir John Falstaff	bass
First Citizen	tenor
Innkeeper, Waiter, Second, Third and Fourth Citizens	spoken
Citizens, women and children	

Setting Windsor in the early 17th century

In 1841, after a period of several years in Italy during which he wrote four Italian operas with mixed success, Nicolai took up the post of Kapellmeister at the Vienna Hofoper, where he was expected to

compose German opera. He seems to have searched continuously for a suitable libretto for a German opera, but was unable to find a subject that satisfied him. In the meantime he revised two of his Italian operas, *Il proscritto* (as *Die Heimkehr des Verbannten*, 1844) and *Il templario* (as *Der Tempelritter*, 1845). In about 1845 he finally decided on *The Merry Wives of Windsor*, though not without misgivings about his ability to do justice to it. When he offered *Die lustigen Weiber von Windsor* for production at the Hofoper it was turned down and he resigned his post. In 1847 he went to Berlin as Kapellmeister at the cathedral and at the Hofoper; there he conducted the highly successful première of *Die lustigen Weiber von Windsor* two years later. Nicolai did not live long to enjoy his triumph, dying of a stroke just two months after the première, at the age of 38; however, the opera has never lost its place on the German stage, and the charming overture is still popular in the concert hall. The work was first heard in the USA at Philadelphia in 1863, and in London the following year.

*

Act I.i *Between the houses of Ford and Page* Mrs Ford is reading a love letter from Falstaff; Mrs Page joins her and they realize that he has sent them identical letters. The repeated quaver patterns in their duet 'Nein das ist wirklich doch zu keck!' neatly characterize their reaction to the effrontery of the fat old knight, and delightedly they plan to take revenge on him. In the following dialogue Page tells Ford, Slender and Dr Caius that he hopes to wed his daughter, Anne, to Slender, though Dr Caius and Fenton both want to marry her. In the recitative and duet 'So geht indes hinein', young Fenton, whose feelings Anne reciprocates, urges his suit in vain; his ardent melodic line is effectively contrasted with Page's busy semiquaver patterns as he gloats over Slender's wealth.

I.ii *Inside Ford's house* Mrs Ford considers what she will say to Falstaff when he visits her; the fine recitative and aria 'Nichts sei zu arg' skilfully develops her character as a quick-witted, resourceful and charming woman. Mrs Page enters and in dialogue they discuss their plan to make Falstaff hide in a washing basket and then have him thrown into the river. Mrs Page conceals herself and as the finale begins Falstaff arrives. His portliness contrasts amusingly with the tripping figures that Nicolai gives him to sing as he begins his courting of Mrs Ford. Mrs Page bursts in as planned with the news that Ford is coming, and the two women get Falstaff into the basket. Ford, accompanied by his neighbours, enters in a fury and searches the house (he has been informed, anonymously, by his own wife of Falstaff's assignation with her). Meanwhile, the washing basket is removed by two servants, Falstaff receives a ducking, and Mrs Ford and Mrs

Page laugh together, in a delightful duet, at the lessons they are teaching the men. When Ford returns from the search, his wife roundly scolds him for his unworthy suspicions; as the curtain falls, she simulates a fainting spell.

Act 2.i *The Garter Inn* In a dialogue scene Falstaff, now recovered from his involuntary swim, is gossiping with his cronies; he has been invited to a further meeting with Mrs Ford, ostensibly to take up where they left off. He and his friends sing a tuneful drinking song, 'Als Büblein klein'. In another short section of dialogue the Waiter tells Falstaff that a certain Sir Brook (or 'Bach' in the German), actually Ford in disguise, is waiting to speak to him. The following recitative and comic duet 'O! Ihr beschämt mich', in which Ford tries to discover the truth about Falstaff's relationship with Mrs Ford, amusingly depicts the increasingly furious Ford's struggles to maintain the character of Sir Brook while Falstaff boasts of his success with Mrs Ford.

2.ii *Page's garden* It is evening and Anne's three suitors have the idea of serenading her. Nicolai blends this succession of scenes into a musically continuous number. Slender enters with comic fearfulness ('Dies ist die Stunde') but hides on the arrival of Dr Caius, whose comical mixture of French and mispronounced German adds to the humour of the situation. Hearing Fenton approaching, he too hides. Fenton, thinking he has the garden to himself, sings the Romanze 'Horch, die Lerche singt im Hain!', which is full of charming melodic invention with a smooth, expressive string accompaniment and bird-like trills on piccolo and flute. When Anne appears, they sing the duettino 'Kannst du zweifeln'; an elaborate violin solo enriches the orchestral colour and the section closes with an ingenious cadenza for the two voices and solo violin. In the concluding quartettino, the lovers pledge themselves to each other while Slender and Dr Caius comment in suppressed fury from their hiding places.

2.iii *Inside Ford's house* In a dialogue scene Falstaff is again courting Mrs Ford. As before, Mrs Page interrupts them with the news that Ford is coming. This time they disguise Falstaff as an old woman. Ford and his wife confront each other in the duet 'So jetzt hätt' ich ihn gefangen' and she mocks his jealous fury. The finale follows without a break as Slender, Dr Caius and Page arrive; Falstaff is smuggled out under their very noses and they again search the house fruitlessly.

Act 3.i *Page's house* The scene begins in dialogue. Mrs Ford and Mrs Page have explained the situation to their husbands; Ford is penitent. They plan to teach Falstaff a lesson he will not forget, and Mrs Page sings the ballad of Herne the Hunter, 'Vom Jäger Herne'. Mrs Page privately tells Anne (in dialogue) that she has arranged for her to marry Dr

Caius that night: then Page tells Anne that he has arranged for her to marry Slender. Anne, alone, vows to confound both of them and marry Fenton, affirming her determination to outwit them in the aria 'Wohl denn! Gefasst ist der Entschluss'.

3.ii *Windsor Park* The moon rises during the orchestral introduction and Ford, Page and their neighbours sing the chorus 'O süsser Mond' as they prepare for Falstaff's arrival. Falstaff enters dressed as Herne the Hunter and in the terzettino 'Die Glocke schlug schon Mitternacht' Mrs Ford and Mrs Page flirt teasingly with him. Then follows a ballet and chorus of the neighbours dressed as elves ('Ihr Elfen weiss und rot und grau'), and a harp solo announces the arrival of Anne dressed as Titania and Fenton as Oberon. Page appears dressed as Herne, and in the *Mückentanz* (Midges' Dance) 'Mücken, Wespen, Fliegenchor' the terrified Falstaff is further tormented. In the meantime, Slender and Dr Caius go off with each other, disguised as elves, both thinking that they are with Anne, and Anne and Fenton hurry away to get married; there is then a general dance and chorus, 'Er gesteht noch immer nicht'. In a final dialogue, Anne reconciles her parents to her marriage with Fenton, and the opera concludes with a charming terzettino for the 'merry wives', Mrs Ford and Mrs Page, with Anne.

*

The criticisms of Italian influence in Nicolai's work, which had been levelled at his earlier operas by German writers, continued to be directed against *Die lustigen Weiber von Windsor*, though less aggressively. A reviewer of the overture, writing in the *Neue Zeitschrift für Musik* in 1850, appreciated its 'obvious avoidance of trivialities', but also noted that 'Italian reminiscences, even if only distant and somewhat ennobled, are clearly recognizable'. However, it is arguable that such criticism was motivated by narrow nationalistic feeling, and that in this opera Nicolai had found a highly effective balance between the German and Italian elements in his musical makeup; it was a balance which the young Wagner, almost 20 years earlier, seems to have envisaged in his first published article, 'Die deutsche Oper' (1834), and which he tried unsuccessfully to achieve in *Das Liebesverbot* (1836). In *Die lustigen Weiber von Windsor*, Nicolai's German background is apparent in the importance given to the orchestra, in his concern to match form and structure to the dramatic situation, and in the range of the harmonic language. The Italian element shows in his liking for vocal decoration and in the nature of much of the melodic material; his Italian experience enabled him to treat the comic elements in the opera with a lightness and charm which few German composers of his generation were able to rival.   **C.B.**

M

Macbeth

Opera in four acts by Giuseppe Verdi to a libretto by
Francesco Maria Piave (with additional material by
Andrea Maffei) after William Shakespeare's play;
Florence, Teatro della Pergola, 14 March 1847
(revised version, with libretto translated by Charles-
Louis-Etienne Nuitter and Alexandre Beaumont,
Paris, Théâtre Lyrique, 21 April 1865).

The first Macbeth was Felice Varesi; the first Lady
Macbeth, Marianna Barbieri-Nini.

Duncano [Duncan] *King of Scotland*		silent
Macbeth ⎫ *Generals in*		baritone
Banco [Banquo] ⎬ *Duncan's army*		bass
Lady Macbeth *Macbeth's wife*		soprano
Lady-in-waiting to Lady Macbeth		mezzo-soprano
Macduff *a Scottish nobleman, Lord of Fife*		tenor
Malcolm *Duncan's son*		tenor
Fleanzio [Fleance] *Banquo's son*		silent
A Servant of Macbeth		bass
A Doctor		bass
A Murderer		bass
The Ghost of Banco [Banquo]		silent
A Herald		bass
Hecate		mime

Witches, messengers of the King, Scottish nobles
and exiles, murderers, English soldiers, bards,
aerial spirits, apparitions

Setting Scotland and the Anglo-Scottish border

Verdi's contract of 1846 with the impresario
Alessandro Lanari and the Teatro della Pergola of
Florence stipulated no particular opera, and in the
summer various possibilities, including *I masnadieri*
and *Macbeth*, were under consideration. The final
decision, Verdi made clear, would depend on the
singers available. *Macbeth* would have no tenor lead
but needed a first-class baritone and soprano; *I
masnadieri*, on the other hand, was dependent on a
fine tenor. By late September the cast had been
secured, notably with the engagement of Varesi, one
of the finest actor-singer baritones of the day;
accordingly, the choice fell on *Macbeth*. By this time,
Verdi had already drafted the broad dramatic lines of
the opera and had written encouraging letters to his
librettist, Piave, emphasizing that this, his first
Shakespearean subject, was to be a special case: 'This
tragedy is one of the greatest creations of man! If we
can't do something great with it, let us at least try to
do something out of the ordinary . . . I know the
general character and the *tinte* as if the libretto were
already finished'.

As the première drew near, Verdi again and
again demonstrated his particular interest in the
opera: by bullying Piave into producing exactly the
text he required; by engaging his friend Andrea
Maffei to retouch certain passages; by taking unusual
time and care in making sure the production was
well rehearsed and true to his intentions; and by
endlessly coaching the leading singers – in particular
Varesi and Barbieri-Nini – to ensure that their every
nuance was as he wished. The première was a great
success and the opera soon began to be performed
around Italy; Verdi often advised those responsible
for revivals of the special attention that the opera
needed.

In 1864 the French publisher and impresario Léon
Escudier asked Verdi to add ballet music for a revival
of the opera at the Théâtre Lyrique, Paris. The composer agreed but also stated that he wanted to make
substantial changes to some numbers that were 'either
weak or lacking in character'. As well as the additional
ballet and major or minor retouchings to various
numbers, this revision eventually included: a new aria
for Lady Macbeth in Act 2 ('La luce langue'); substantial alterations to Act 3, including a new duet for
Macbeth and Lady Macbeth ('Ora di morte'); a new
chorus at the beginning of Act 4 ('Patria oppressa');
and the replacement of Macbeth's death scene with a
final 'Inno di vittoria'. The Paris première, which included Jean-Vital Ismael Jammes (Macbeth) and
Amélie Rey-Balla (Lady Macbeth), was largely unsuccessful. The reception puzzled Verdi and, although
the original version of the opera continued to be performed for some time in Italy, it is clear that he wished
the 'Paris' version to supersede it. In spite of a recent
revival of interest in the 1847 version, and in spite of
the fact that it is clearly more unified stylistically, the
later version is the one generally heard today. In the
discussion below, the most substantial revisions will
be considered as they appear.

*

The prelude is made up of themes from the opera. First comes a unison woodwind theme from the witches' scene at the start of Act 3, then a passage from the apparition music in the same act. The second half is taken almost entirely from Lady Macbeth's Act 4 'sleepwalking' scene.

Act I.i *A wood* The witches' chorus that opens the act divides into two parts, the first ('Che faceste?') in the minor, the second ('Le sorelle vagabonde') in the parallel major. Both partake of the musical 'colour' associated throughout with the witches, among which are prominent woodwind sonorities (both dark and shrill), mercurial string figures and a tendency for rhythmic displacement. Macbeth and Banquo enter and are hailed by the witches with their threefold prophecy (Macbeth shall be thane of Cawdor; he shall be king; Banquo's descendants shall be kings), darkly scored and with prominent tritones in the harmonic progression. A brisk military march then introduces messengers, who inform Macbeth of Cawdor's death and hence the fulfilment of part of the prophecy. As Verdi admitted to his principal baritone, Varesi, this sequence would traditionally have called for a double aria for Macbeth, but instead the composer supplied a one-movement duettino for Macbeth and Banquo, 'Due vaticini', full of broken lines and suppressed exclamations as the two men examine their consciences. The witches' closing stretta, 'S'allontanarono', is far more conventional, though it does find room for yet more 'characteristic' colour.

I.ii *A room in Macbeth's castle* Lady Macbeth's cavatina generates great dramatic power from a conventional outward form. After a stormy orchestral introduction, she enters to read a letter from her husband describing the events we have just witnessed. The first part of her double aria, 'Vieni! t'affretta!', bids Macbeth hurry home so that she can instil in him her bloody thoughts; it is remarkable for its avoidance of formal repetition and for its tightly controlled but distant harmonic excursions. A messenger announces that Macbeth and Duncan are expected that night, and Lady Macbeth exults in the cabaletta 'Or tutti sorgete', whose moments of agility are tightly woven into the restricted formal structure. The cabaletta over, Macbeth appears and in a brief recitative Lady Macbeth unfolds her murderous plans for Duncan. The couple are interrupted by the arrival of the King himself, whose parade around the stage is accompanied by a 'rustic' march from the stage-band.

The 'Gran Scena e Duetto' that follows begins with Macbeth's extended arioso 'Mi si affaccia un pugnal?!', during which he sees a vision of a dagger and steels himself to murder Duncan. The passage is extremely rich in musical invention, as sliding chromatic figures jostle with distorted 'religious'

harmonies and fugitive reminiscences of the witches' music; it will set the tone for the great free recitatives of Verdi's later career. Macbeth enters the King's room, and Lady Macbeth appears, soon to be rejoined by her husband. Macbeth's motif at 'Tutto è finito!' ('All is finished!') furnishes the accompaniment material for the first movement of the four-movement duet, the Allegro 'Fatal mia donna! un murmure'. This first movement involves a rapid exchange between the characters, with musical continuity mostly supplied by the orchestra. As Macbeth describes the inner voice that has forever denied him sleep, the second, more lyrical movement, 'Allor questa voce', begins: the singers again have dissimilar musical material, although they eventually come together for an extended passage. A short transitional movement, 'Il pugnal là riportate', sees Lady Macbeth return the dagger to the King's room and emerge with blood on her hands which she has smeared on his sleeping servants. The duet closes with a short cabaletta, 'Vieni altrove! ogni sospetto', which in the 1847 version quickly turns to the major mode but which in 1865 Verdi revised to keep subdued and in the minor throughout.

The first-act finale begins with the arrival of Macduff and Banquo, the latter singing a solemn apostrophe to the night. Macduff calls everyone together and announces the murder of Duncan. The news launches the Adagio concertato, 'Schiudi, inferno': a tutti outburst of group anguish, a quiet unaccompanied passage in which all pray for God's guidance, and a final soaring melody in which divine vengeance is called down upon the guilty one. Following the pattern of the preceding duet, the final stretta is extremely short, functioning more as a coda than as a movement in its own right.

Act 2.i *A room in the castle* An orchestral reprise of part of the Act 1 grand duet leads to a recitative between Macbeth and his wife. Malcolm has fled and is suspected of Duncan's murder, but Macbeth, obsessed by the witches' prophecy that Banquo's sons will be kings, decides that more blood must flow. In the 1847 version, Lady Macbeth closes the scene with the cabaletta 'Trionfai! securi alfine', a conventional two-verse aria in the manner of Elvira's music in *Ernani*. In 1865 Verdi replaced this with 'La luce langue' ('The light is fading'), a multi-sectional aria whose advanced chromaticism is consistently that of his later style.

2.ii *A park* The quiet, staccato chorus of murderers, 'Sparve il sol', in Verdi's traditional manner of depicting sinister groups, leads to a *romanza* for Banquo, in the coda of which the assassins strike him down but cannot prevent his son Fleance from escaping.

2.iii *A magnificent hall* Lively festive music underpins the assembling of noble guests, after which Macbeth summons his wife to sing a brindisi (drinking song). She obliges with 'Si colmi il calice', and (as will happen in Act 1 of *La traviata*) is answered by the unison chorus. The closing strains of the song still echo in the orchestra as Macbeth learns from an assassin of Banquo's death and Fleance's escape. The festive music resumes, but Macbeth has a horrible vision of Banquo at the banquet table (this and the second hallucination were revised and chromatically intensified in the 1865 version). Lady Macbeth calms him and repeats her brindisi, but the vision returns. The king's terror precipitates the concertato finale, 'Sangue a me', which is led off and dominated by Macbeth, though with frequent interjections from his wife, who tries to quieten him. There is no formal stretta, the act ending with the general sense of stunned surprise still intact.

Act 3 *A dark cavern* After a stormy orchestral introduction, the witches' chorus, 'Tre volte miagola', brings back the opening idea of the prelude as the first of a series of increasingly lively, rhythmically bumpy 6/8 melodies, ones clearly intended to depict the 'bizarre' element of the supernatural. The ballet that follows, written for the 1865 Paris version, is broadly in three movements. In the first, various supernatural beings dance around the cauldron to an Allegro vivacissimo. Hecate is called forth and, in an Andante second movement full of the rich chromaticism of Verdi's later style, mimes that Macbeth will come to ask of his destiny and should be answered (Verdi insisted that this section be mimed rather than danced). The final movement is a sinister waltz, the spirits dancing even more wildly around the cauldron.

The Apparition Scene, substantially revised in the 1865 version to intensify its harmonic and orchestral effect, has little sustained melodic writing and consists of brief but telling musical episodes. The first introduces the three apparitions, who make their predictions of Macbeth's fate: the armed head is that of Macbeth himself, the bloody child represents Macduff 'from his mother's womb untimely ripp'd', the crowned child holding a bough is Malcolm with the trees of Birnam Wood, with which his soldiers will advance on Macbeth's stronghold. Then, to Macbeth's arioso 'Fuggi, regal fantasima', come the eight kings, the last of whom is in the form of Banquo and precipitates Macbeth's 'Oh! mio terror! dell'ultimo', at the end of which he faints. A gentle chorus and dance of the aerial spirits, 'Ondine e silfidi', precedes the finale, which was completely rewritten for 1865. In the 1847 version the act finished with a fast cabaletta for Macbeth, 'Vada in fiamme', very much in the early Verdi mould though with an unusual minor–major key scheme. In 1865 the composer replaced this with a duettino for Macbeth and Lady Macbeth, 'Ora di morte e di vendetta', in which, however, the added subtlety of articulation results in a loss in sheer rhythmic power.

Act 4.i *A deserted place on the borders of England and Scotland* The original 1847 version of the opening chorus, 'Patria oppressa', not least in its lamenting of the 'lost' homeland, is somewhat reminiscent of the 'patriotic' choruses that became so famous in Verdi's early operas, although the minor mode gives it a different colour. The 1865 replacement is one of the composer's greatest choral movements, with subtle details of harmony and rhythm in almost every bar. Macduff's 'Ah, la paterna mano', which follows, is a conventional minor–major *romanza*, and the scene is rounded off by a cabaletta-like chorus, 'La patria tradita', as Malcolm's troops prepare to descend on Macbeth.

4.ii *A room in Macbeth's castle (as I.ii)* Lady Macbeth enters, sleepwalking. Her famous aria, 'Una macchia' ('Out, damned spot'), is justly regarded as one of the young Verdi's greatest solo creations. Preceded by an atmospheric instrumental depiction of Lady Macbeth's guilty wandering, the aria itself is distinguished by its expanded formal and harmonic structure and – most important – by a marvellously inventive orchestral contribution.

4.iii *Another room in the castle* A noisy orchestral introduction leads to Macbeth's confessional 'Pietà, rispetto, amore', an effective slow aria with some surprising internal modulations. The aria concluded, soldiers rush on to announce the seeming approach of Birnam Wood; a pseudo-fugal orchestral battle ensues during which Malcolm overcomes Macbeth in single combat. In 1847 the opera ended with a short, melodramatic scene for Macbeth, 'Mal per me', full of declamatory gestures that recall motivic threads from earlier in the drama. For 1865 Verdi replaced this with a choral Victory Hymn, 'Macbeth, Macbeth ov'è?', a number in his most modern style with more than a hint of Offenbach in its dotted rhythms, and perhaps even a hint of the *Marseillaise* in its final bars.

*

There is no doubt that Verdi's frequently voiced perception of the 1847 *Macbeth* as an especially important work, ennobled by its Shakespearean theme, was one that he successfully converted into dramatic substance. Much of the opera shows an attention to detail and sureness of effect unprecedented in earlier works. This holds true as much for the 'conventional' numbers, such as Lady Macbeth's opening aria or the subsequent duet with Macbeth, as for formal experiments like the Macbeth-Banquo duettino in Act 1. What is more, the new standard set by *Macbeth* was one that Verdi rarely retreated from in subsequent works.

The 1865 revisions undoubtedly enrich the score, supplying several of its most effective pieces, notably

'La luce langue' and the opening chorus of Act 4. Clearly the sense of stylistic disparity the revisions create did not concern Verdi; indeed, for the most part he made little attempt to match the replacement numbers with the main body of the score, instead producing pieces that are among the most harmonically advanced of his later career. Nor should such disparity unduly concern us: we may well overestimate the importance of stylistic consistency in opera, and the 1865 revision will surely continue to be the most commonly performed version of this magnificent work.   R.P.

Madama Butterfly ('Madam Butterfly')

Tragedia giapponese in two acts by Giacomo Puccini to a libretto by Giuseppe Giacosa and Luigi Illica after David Belasco's play *Madame Butterfly*, itself based on John Luther Long's short story, which in turn was based partly on Pierre Loti's tale *Madame Chrysanthème*; Milan, Teatro alla Scala, 17 February 1904 (revised Brescia, Teatro Grande, 28 May 1904; definitive version, though in French, Paris, Opéra Comique, 28 December 1906).

The cast at the première included Rosina Storchio (Butterfly), Giovanni Zenatello (Pinkerton) and Giuseppe de Luca (Sharpless). The conductor was Cleofonte Campanini.

Cio-Cio-San [Madam Butterfly]		soprano
Suzuki *her maid*		mezzo-soprano
F. B. Pinkerton *Lieutenant in the United*		
States Navy		tenor
Sharpless *United States consul at*		
Nagasaki		baritone
Goro *a marriage broker*		tenor
Prince Yamadori		tenor
The Bonze	*Cio-Cio-San's uncles*	bass
Yakuside		bass
The Imperial Commissioner		bass
The Official Registrar		bass
Cio-Cio-San's mother		mezzo-soprano
The Aunt		soprano
The Cousin		soprano
Kate Pinkerton		mezzo-soprano
Dolore ('Trouble') *Cio-Cio-San's child*		silent

Cio-Cio-San's relations and friends and servants
Setting Nagasaki at the beginning of the 20th
century

Puccini was seized with the subject after seeing Belasco's play performed in London in June 1900, and he immediately applied to Belasco for the rights. These, however, were not officially granted until September of the following year. In the meantime Puccini had sent a copy of Long's story to Illica, who drew up a scheme in two parts. The first, originally intended as a prologue, derived from Long (with comic embellishments in the spirit of Loti) and showed the wedding of Pinkerton and Cio-Cio-San (called Butterfly by her friends); the second covered the action of Belasco's play and was divided into three scenes, the first and last being set in Butterfly's house and the second in the American consulate. As Giacosa proceeded with the versification the prologue expanded into Act 1 and the first scene of the second part into Act 2, while Illica's intention of retaining Long's ending (with Butterfly's suicide interrupted by the arrival of her child and the maid Suzuki who bandaged her wounds) was overruled in favour of Belasco's final catastrophe. Not until November 1902 was the libretto complete, whereupon Puccini decided in spite of strenuous opposition from Giacosa to abolish the scene in the American consulate, and with it the contrast between a Japanese and a Western ambience desired by Illica. Instead the two remaining scenes of the second part were to be fused into a single act lasting an hour and a half.

The composition was interrupted in February 1903 by a motor accident from which Puccini made a long and painful convalescence. The score was completed by December and the première fixed for February the following year, with an outstanding cast. Although the singers and orchestra showed much enthusiasm, the first night was a disaster; the opera was subjected to what Puccini described as 'a veritable lynching'. That the audience's hostility was deliberately engineered has never been doubted; all the evidence points to Ricordi's chief rival, Sonzogno, as the prime mover. Puccini was also accused of plagiarism of himself and other composers. He at once withdrew the opera, and although convinced of its merits he made alterations to the score before allowing it to be performed elsewhere. He discarded several details involving Butterfly's relations in Act 1, divided the long second act into two parts separated by an interval and added the arietta 'Addio, fiorito asil' for Pinkerton. The second performance took place on 28 May that same year at the Teatro Grande, Brescia, Salomea Krusceniski replacing Rosina Storchio among the original cast. This time the opera enjoyed a triumph.

Further modifications were to follow, however, mainly affecting Act 1. These ended with the Paris première, which was given by the Opéra-Comique on 28 December 1906, and formed the basis of the definitive printed edition. At the suggestion of Albert Carré, the theatre director and husband of the prima donna Marguerite, Puccini further softened Pinkerton's character, eliminating his more xeno-

*Rosina Storchio as Cio-Cio-San and Giovanni Zenatello as
Pinkerton in the original production of Puccini's 'Madama
Butterfly' at La Scala, Milan, 17 February 1904*

phobic utterances, and avoided the confrontation
between Butterfly and Kate, who thus emerges as
a more sympathetic character. Earlier that year,
however, Ricordi had already brought out a vocal
score in which many of the original passages can be
found. Three of them, all from Act 1, were reinstated
with Puccini's sanction for a revival at the Teatro
Carcano, Milan, shortly after World War I (they were
not, however, reprinted). Joachim Herz's production
of *Madama Butterfly* in 1978 restored some of the
original music from the autograph, and the earliest
version was given complete at La Fenice in 1982 and
at Leeds in 1991. Outstanding exponents of the title
role have included Geraldine Farrar, Toti dal Monte
(Toscanini's favourite interpreter), Victoria de los
Angeles, and later Renata Scotto and Mirella Freni, as
well as several Japanese singers.

*

Act I *A hill near Nagasaki; in the foreground a Japanese
house with terrace and garden* An orchestral passage
sets a scene of bustling activity as Goro leads
Lieutenant Pinkerton out of the house, demonstrating its various appurtenances, in particular the
sliding panels – so ridiculously fragile, the lieutenant
thinks. The domestic staff are presented to him: a
cook, a servant and his future wife's maid, Suzuki,
who at once begins to bore Pinkerton with her
chatter. While Goro is reeling off the list of

wedding guests, Sharpless enters out of breath,
having climbed the hill from Nagasaki. A characteristic motif establishes his benign, good-humoured
presence. At Goro's bidding servants bring drinks
and wicker chairs for Sharpless and his host.
Pinkerton explains that he has bought the house on a
999-year lease which may be terminated at a month's
notice. In his solo 'Dovunque al mondo', framed by
the opening strain of *The Star-Spangled Banner* (later
used as a recurrent motif), Pinkerton outlines his
philosophy – that of the roving 'Yankee' who takes
his pleasure where he finds it ('an easy-going gospel',
observes Sharpless). After sending Goro to fetch the
bride, Pinkerton dilates on her charms and his own
infatuation. Sharpless recollects having heard her
voice when she paid a visit to the consulate. Its ring of
simple sincerity touched him deeply and he hopes
that Pinkerton will never hurt her. Pinkerton scoffs at
his scruples, so typical of unadventurous middle age.
Both drink a toast to America (*The Star-Spangled
Banner* again) and, in Pinkerton's case, to the day
when he will take home an American wife.

Goro announces the arrival of Butterfly and her
friends, heralded by the distant sound of humming
female voices. As the procession draws nearer the
orchestra unfolds a radiant theme that begins with a
series of rising sequences, each phrase ending on a
whole-tone chord, then evolves into an extended
periodic melody to which an essentially pentatonic
motif of Japanese origin (ex.1) forms a hushed coda.

Ex.1

Butterfly, whose voice has been heard soaring above
those of the female throng, has by now appeared. She
bows to the two men. Sharpless questions her about
her family and background. He learns that her
people were once wealthy but have since fallen on
hard times, so that she has been forced to earn her
living as a geisha. She is 15 years old. Sharpless
repeats his warning to Pinkerton. More guests arrive,
including Butterfly's mother, a Cousin, an Aunt and
Uncle Yakuside, who immediately asks for wine.
Meanwhile the women exchange impressions of the
bridegroom (not all of them favourable) until at a

sign from Butterfly they all kowtow to Pinkerton and disperse. Butterfly shows Pinkerton her treasures and mementos, which she keeps concealed in her voluminous sleeves – a clasp, a clay pipe, a girdle, a pot of rouge (which she throws away in response to Pinkerton's mocking glance) and a narrow sheath which she hurriedly carries into the house. Goro explains that it holds the dagger with which Butterfly's father killed himself by the emperor's command. Re-emerging, she produces puppets that represent the spirits of her forebears. But she adds that she has recently visited the American mission to renounce her ancestral religion and embrace that of her husband (ex.1 returns). Goro calls for silence; the Imperial Commissioner proclaims the wedding and all join in a toast to the couple's happiness, 'O Kami! O Kami!' (At this point in the original version there was a drunken arietta for Yakuside, who broke off to chastise a badly behaved child.) The festivities are interrupted by the Bonze, who bursts in denouncing Butterfly for having forsworn her faith. As her relations scatter in horror the orchestra embodies their curse in a whole-tone motif. Alone with his bride Pinkerton comforts her, while Suzuki can be heard muttering her evening prayers to the gods of Japan. There follows an extended duet for the lovers ('Viene la sera') woven from several melodic threads, now rapturous, now tender and delicate. Twice the 'curse' motif intrudes, first as Butterfly recalls how her family has cast her off, then when she remembers how the most beautiful butterflies are often impaled with a pin. The duet concludes with a grandiose reprise of the music which accompanied her first appearance.

Act 2 Part i *Inside Butterfly's house* Three years have gone by. Butterfly is alone with Suzuki, who is praying to the Japanese gods that her mistress's sufferings may soon end. Butterfly retorts that such gods are lazy; Pinkerton's God would soon come to her aid if only he knew where to find her. Their funds are nearly exhausted and Suzuki doubts whether Pinkerton will ever return. Furious, Butterfly reminds her how he had arranged for the consul to pay the rent, how he had put locks on the doors, and how he had promised to return 'when the robins build their nests'. In a celebrated aria ('Un bel dì vedremo') she pictures the scene of Pinkerton's return and her own joy. Goro arrives with Sharpless, who brings a letter from the lieutenant. Butterfly gives him a cordial welcome, and asks him how often the robins build their nests in America. Sharpless is evasive.

Prince Yamadori enters and makes Butterfly an offer of marriage, which she mockingly rejects: she is a married woman according to the laws of America, where divorce, she says, is a punishable offence. Yamadori leaves and Sharpless begins to read the letter, breaking the news that Pinkerton intends to go out of Butterfly's life for ever, but she misunderstands the letter's drift and he abandons the task. He asks what she would do if Pinkerton were never to return, and she replies that she could resume her profession as a geisha, but that she would rather die by her own hand. Sharpless angers her by advising her to accept Yamadori's offer, but then she hurries to fetch her son by Pinkerton; astonished and moved, Sharpless promises to inform the father and leaves. Suzuki drags in Goro, whom she has caught spreading slanderous rumours about the child's parentage. Butterfly threatens to kill him, then dismisses him with contempt. The harbour cannon signals the arrival of a ship. To an orchestral reprise of 'Un bel dì' Butterfly seizes a telescope and makes out the name *Abraham Lincoln* – Pinkerton's man-of-war. She and Suzuki proceed to deck the house with blossom in a duet ('Scuoti quella fronda di ciliegio'). After adorning herself 'as on our wedding day' she, Suzuki and the child settle to a night of waiting, while an unseen chorus of wordless voices, recalling the theme to which Sharpless attempted to read Pinkerton's letter, evokes the slowly fading light.

Act 2 Part ii An interlude, originally joined to the previous humming chorus, depicts Butterfly's restless thoughts; then, to the distant cries of the sailors, the sun rises to disclose Butterfly, Suzuki and the child seated as before. Butterfly sings a lullaby and takes the boy to another room, where she quickly falls asleep. Pinkerton appears with Sharpless. Suzuki catches sight of a woman in the garden and Sharpless tells her that it is Pinkerton's wife, Kate. Their concern, he tells her, is to ensure the child a good American upbringing. He reproaches the lieutenant for his heartlessness. Pinkerton pours out his grief and remorse in the *romanza* that Puccini added for Brescia ('Addio, fiorito asil') and leaves, unable to face the bride he has betrayed. Butterfly enters, to confront Sharpless, Suzuki and Kate. When the situation is explained to her she reacts with great dignity; she bids them retire and return in half an hour. She takes a last farewell of her child and stabs herself behind a screen with her father's dagger. Pinkerton is heard desperately calling her name.

*

No Puccini opera testifies more strongly than *Madama Butterfly* to his ability to discern the possibilities for music drama in a trivial play performed in a language of which he hardly understood a word. Here he and his librettists (working as always under his own direction) fleshed out Belasco's pathetic but ridiculous puppet into a genuine figure of tragedy who proceeds during the action from child-like innocence to an adult understanding and a calm acceptance of the destiny which her code of honour enjoins upon her. Butterfly is the apotheosis of the frail suffering heroine so often encountered in

Puccini's gallery; and he would return to her only once more in the slave-girl Liù in *Turandot*.

By making use of at least seven Japanese folk melodies the composer both evoked the Far Eastern ambience and enlarged his musical vocabulary, since every one of them is assimilated into his own personal and by now highly sophisticated style. The scale of musical thought is likewise grander than ever before, the love duet in Act 1 being the longest and most elaborate that Puccini ever wrote. Though the organization remains for the most part motivic the motifs are no longer always systematically referential in the Wagnerian manner. The whole-tone curse motif is not always associated with the Bonze, while ex.1 receives its fullest treatment where Butterfly tells Pinkerton about her visit to the American mission in order to embrace her husband's religion ('Io seguo il mio destino') – an event that has no bearing on the theme's first appearance. In his later operas Puccini tended more and more to use motifs without hard and fast associations.   J.B.

Maid of Orléans, The [*Orleanskaya deva*]

Opera in four acts by Pyotr Il'yich Tchaikovsky to his own libretto after Friedrich von Schiller's tragedy translated by Vasily Andreyevich Zhukovsky, Jules Barbier's *Jeanne d'Arc* and Auguste Mermet's libretto for his own opera, after Barbier (1876), with various details adapted from Henri Wallon's biography of Joan of Arc; St Petersburg, Mariinsky Theatre, 13/25 February 1881.

The first performance was conducted by Eduard Nápravník, to whom the opera was dedicated; Mariya Kamenskaya sang Joan, Fyodor Stravinsky, Dunois, Ippolit Pryanishnikov, Lionel and Wilhelmina Raab, Agnès.

Joan of Arc	soprano/mezzo-soprano
King Charles VII	tenor
Agnès Sorel	soprano
Dunois *French knight*	baritone
Lionel *Burgundian knight*	baritone
Archbishop [Cardinal in first production]	bass
Raymond *Joan's betrothed*	tenor
Thibaut d'Arc *Joan's father*	bass
Bertrand *a peasant*	bass
Lauret	bass
A Soldier	bass
Voice from the Angelic Choir	soprano

Courtiers and ladies, French and English soldiers, knights, monks, gypsies, pages, buffoons, dwarfs, minstrels, jesters, clowns, crowd

Setting France, 1431

Tchaikovsky's most ambitious opera was written in just nine months beginning in late November 1878. Actual composition took place entirely in western Europe (Florence, Paris, Vaudois Switzerland) and was finished 'down to the smallest detail' by the end of February 1879. Orchestration, which took longer, was carried out during the spring and summer months on various southern Russian and Ukrainian country estates belonging to the composer's friends and relations, and finished in late August. From the beginning Tchaikovsky envisaged the work as 'the one that will make my name popular', and that it did. For the first time he experienced an unqualified success with a first-night audience; not only that, *The Maid of Orléans* was the first Tchaikovsky opera to be performed abroad (1882, Prague). Thereafter the opera's fate was not happy. It fell victim to the curtailment of the theatrical season following the assassination of Tsar Alexander II, only two weeks after the première, and in the ensuing austerity it was not revived. It did not see the stage again until the 20th century, by which time it was something of a historical curio.

The role of Joan exists in two versions (both included in the composer's complete works): as originally written, for dramatic soprano, and as revised for Kamenskaya, a mezzo. Ever since the first production the role has been regarded primarily as a vehicle for star mezzos, notably Irina Arkhipova, for whose sake the opera was given a revival at the Bol'shoy in the 1970s, and recorded.

*

The overture, a portrait of Joan as pure and virginal being epitomized by a flute cadenza, culminates in a preview of the angelic music from the Act 1 finale.

Act 1 *A forest near Domrémy* Maidens are celebrating a village festival. Thibaut enters with Raymond and upbraids them for making merry at a time of war; he urges Joan to marry Raymond for protection (*scena* and trio). Joan refuses, claiming to be following heaven's wish; Thibaut accuses her of alliance with the devil. Fire is seen; the tocsin rings; Bertrand enters with fleeing peasants and warns the villagers that an English attack is imminent. Joan reassures the crowd with a prophecy, asserting that the English commander, Salisbury ('Salis-býu-ri'), has been slain. A French soldier rushes in and confirms this news and Joan is acclaimed a seer. All join her in a hymn of thanksgiving. Obedient to her calling, the Maid of Orléans sings farewell to her native region (aria, 'Prostite vÿ, kholmÿ, polya rodnïye': 'Farewell, O native hills and fields'– best known in French translation, 'Adieu, forêts'). Attended by a heavenly choir, she sets out to save France.

Act 2 *The Castle of Chinon* After an entr'acte, based chiefly on the main theme of the hymn, minstrels entertain the anxious Charles VII (the chorus is Tchaikovsky's interpolation, based on the melody of *Mes belles amourettes*, included as 'Mélodie antique française' in his *Children's Album* for piano, op.39). Unconsoled, the king calls for his gypsies, dwarfs and clowns; each group does a dance. When Charles orders the entertainers be given rich rewards, his vassal Dunois reminds him that the treasury is empty; his mistress Agnès promises assistance and goes off to collect her jewels. Dunois exhorts the voluptuary monarch to renounce Agnès and lead an attack and briefly succeeds in rousing him. The dying Lauret rushes in with news of another French defeat, then expires; Charles, terrified, decides to retreat beyond the Loire, and Dunois, disgusted, forswears his allegiance and departs (compare their duet with that in Act 2 scene i of *Don Carlos*). Agnès returns and consoles the king (arioso and duettino; compare the latter with 'Tu m'aimes' in Act 4 of *Les Huguenots*). A chorus is heard off stage in praise of 'the maiden saviour' and Dunois comes rushing back with the news that the English have been miraculously defeated. The Archbishop enters and tells how a young girl took command of the battle and routed the enemy; the king changes places with Dunois to test her. Joan enters at the head of a throng; she picks out the king and to prove her divinatory powers repeats to him his secret prayers; at the Archbishop's request she tells her story (Joan's narrative, 'Svyatoy otets, menya zovut Ioanna': 'Holy Father, they call me Joan' – compare Pimen's narrative in *Boris Godunov*, Act 4). Charles, believing in her, puts her at the head of the army amid general thanksgiving.

Act 3.i   A battlefield near Reims   After a short introduction representing a battle with the English, Lionel rushes on stage pursued by Joan; they fight, and he yields, but, on the point of slaying him, she sees his face and is overcome with love. After at first taunting her weakness Lionel also falls in love. Dunois enters, Lionel surrenders to him and changes his allegiance to the French while Joan sinks back as if wounded.

3.ii   The cathedral square at Reims   Charles and his retinue enter the cathedral for his coronation. He reappears crowned, with Joan at his side. Thibaut, still persuaded that his daughter is in league with the devil, announces to Raymond his determination to expose her. King and crowd hail Joan as saviour; Thibaut accuses her of sorcery. She is silent; thunder is heard; the Archbishop demands that she affirm her holy mission and her purity. She remains silent, there is a louder thunderclap, and all express horror. During the ensuing ensemble with chorus Joan's voice is heard – to the audience alone – admitting guilt and requesting punishment. Lionel urges Joan to flee; she does so, but not before turning on him and calling him her enemy and destroyer.

Act 4.i   A thick forest   Joan, distraught, admits her love for Lionel ('Kak! Mne lyuboviyu pïlat'?': 'What! me, inflamed with love?'). Lionel enters and after a short resistance she yields to his embrace; heavenly voices, heard by her alone, reproach Joan for failing and foretell pain and martyrdom, but eventual redemption. English troops enter, slay Lionel and take Joan prisoner.

4.ii   A square in Rouen   Joan is led to the stake to the strains of a lugubrious march. Onlookers at first mock the witch, but are then overcome with pity at her pale, luminous expression – English soldiers ward them off. Joan asks for a cross and a soldier breaks a stick in two, binds the pieces, and gives them to a priest for her (this episode was prohibited by the censor at the first production). The fire is lit and grows; the angels invite the transfigured Joan to her heavenly abode.

*

Compared to its chief literary source, *The Maid of Orléans* shows an enormous effort to popularize and simplify. Schiller's scenes of dissension and intrigue – and valour – among the English are eliminated; the English do not in fact exist in the opera except as an onrushing crowd in Act 4. On the other hand, the fleeting episode with Lionel is grossly magnified to provide the pretext for a love duet; indeed, Joan's infatuation with him becomes the central intrigue, fatally compromising her and disqualifying her from her mission in the eyes of heaven. The beginning of the opera, a decorative genre scene, is borrowed from Mermet; the conclusion (Joan's martyrdom at the stake rather than on the battlefield as per Schiller) comes from Barbier. Along the way the composer made various alterations and interpolations on his own initiative: Lauret in Act 2, the final encounter with Lionel in Act 4 and virtually all the choral repliques.   R.T.

Makropulos Affair, The
[*The Makropulos Case*; *Věc Makropulos*]

Opera in three acts by Leoš Janáček to his own libretto after Karel Čapek's comedy *Věc Makropulos*; Brno, National Theatre, 18 December 1926.

The first cast included Alexandra Čvanová (Marty), Zdeněk Otava (Baron Prus and Emil Olšovský (Gregor); the conductor was František Neumann.

Emilia Marty *a famous opera singer*	soprano
Dr Kolenatý *a lawyer*	bass-baritone
Albert Gregor *Dr Kolenatý's client*	tenor
Vítek *Dr Kolenatý's clerk*	tenor
Kristina *Vítek's daughter, a young opera*	
singer	soprano

Baron Jaroslav Prus *a lawyer and*	
Gregor's legal adversary	baritone
Janek *Prus's son*	tenor
Cleaning Woman	contralto
Stage Technician	bass
Hauk-Šendorf *an old, half-witted*	
ex-diplomat	tenor
Chambermaid	contralto
Doctor	silent role
Offstage male chorus	

Setting Prague in 1922: Kolenatý's chambers, the empty stage in a theatre, a hotel room

Janáček saw Karel Čapek's play on 10 December 1922 in Prague a few weeks after its première and was immediately struck by it. His approaches to Čapek in February 1923 were discouraged because of possible copyright problems, but nevertheless he took a copy of the play with him on his holiday in Slovakia in July that year. By the time he returned to Brno he had decided firmly on *Makropulos* for his next opera. Further negotiations with Čapek in August and September found a way round the problems and on 11 November 1923 Janáček began work on his eighth opera.

Janáček adapted the text himself, adhering to Čapek's three-act plan, but avoiding the scene change in Act 3. He completed the opera on 12 November 1925. His pupil Ludvík Kundera made the vocal score, which was sent to Universal Edition on 19 June 1926 and published a few days before the Brno première on 18 December; the Prague première under Otakar Ostrčil took place on 1 March 1928. Despite the great demands of the piece, both productions were successful and Janáček was delighted with the warm reception of what was to be his last new opera given during his lifetime. However, he took exception to the freedom with which Max Brod translated the text into German and insisted on many changes before the final text was approved. The German première took place at Frankfurt under Joseph Krips on 14 February 1929, six months after Janáček's death.

*

Čapek's play is essentially a thriller: the gradual uncovering of the mystery surrounding the opera singer Emilia Marty, who is in possession of detailed information about events long past, and who exerts a strange fascination on all who meet her. Her arrival in Prague coincides with the final stages of the protracted lawsuit between Albert Gregor and Jaroslav Prus. The overture is one of Janáček's most formal.

Act I *A room in Dr Kolenatý's chambers* Vítek's ruminations on the Gregor–Prus case are interrupted by the plaintiff, Albert Gregor, asking for news of it. Gregor is optimistic about the outcome; the clerk, who has seen Gregor's father shoot himself, less so. The arrival of Vítek's daughter Kristina breaks into their arguments. A quiet, richly harmonized chordal motif evokes her bemused state: she is infatuated with the beauty and the artistry of the singer Emilia Marty, whom she has just heard rehearsing at the theatre. Suddenly (and simultaneously with Dr Kolenatý) Emilia appears in the chambers (a stage direction specifies a 'strange light'). Kristina and her father withdraw. Emilia wishes to hear details of the case, and at a rattling speed (sometimes no more than a single-note parlando) Kolenatý proceeds to expound it. The case concerns the attempt of the Gregor family to prove their claims to the profitable Loukov estate, which they believe Ferdinand Karel Gregor should have inherited from Baron Josef Ferdinand Prus, who died intestate and without issue in 1827. Prus had indicated his intention to leave his estate to Gregor; Prus's relatives contested this on the grounds that no written will was found and that on his deathbed Baron Prus had proclaimed he was leaving his estate to a certain 'Mach Gregor'. Emilia startles Kolenatý by asserting that 'Mach Gregor' was in fact Ferdinand Gregor, the son of the Scottish singer Elian MacGregor, and that a will does exist – she describes its whereabouts in the present Baron Prus's house. The reluctant and disbelieving Kolenatý is sent off there.

Emilia and Albert Gregor are left alone together. The substantial scene between them, one of the many virtuoso dialogues of the opera, shows Gregor bewitched by her and tantalized by her revelations. His passion is depicted in a new surging motif in the orchestra and by his high-lying tenor part. Emilia Marty is immune to his ardour, treating him like a child, though she softens a little when asked about Elian MacGregor. She becomes strangely perturbed, however, when he knows nothing about a 'Greek document' that she believes he has inherited.

Kolenatý returns with Prus. They have found the will, though Prus dampens excitement by insisting that more evidence is needed to prove that Josef's 'son Ferdinand' is in fact Ferdinand Gregor. Emilia offers to provide it, to the further bemusement of Kolenatý. An orchestral postlude – one of Janáček's longest – concludes the act.

Act 2 *The empty stage of a theatre after a performance* A Stage Technician and a Cleaning Woman discuss Emilia Marty's triumph and the effect the singer has had on them. Prus comes on, looking for her. Hearing that she will soon return, he stands on one side. The Technician and the Cleaning Woman leave, and Kristina and Prus's son Janek steal on to the stage, Kristina alternately teasing and encouraging her tongue-tied admirer. When he attempts to kiss her, his father comes forward. Emilia enters; her questions to Janek make him even more silent and embarrassed. Gregor appears, followed by Vítek, and gives Emilia a bouquet containing a present. She discards both and insults him further by giving him money. When Vítek offers his congratulations by comparing her to 'Strada', Emilia delivers her contemptuous opinion of Strada and other long-dead singers. She then turns her attention to Janek and Kristina, cuddling in the corner, and asks if they have been 'in paradise' yet. Emilia declares that it is not really worth it, to a striking passage (ex.1) based on a four-note motif (taken from the postlude to Act 1) against a side-drum roll. When asked what is

Ex.1   Meno mosso

worth it, she replies, chillingly: 'Nic! zhola nic!' ('Nothing, absolutely nothing!').

The group is joined by Hauk-Šendorf, to a fidgety little flourish in the orchestra. He has come to see the woman who has reminded him of his lover of 50 years earlier. Against a dance motif with castanet rhythms, he describes the Spanish gypsy Eugenia Montez: since losing her he has also lost his reason. Emilia Marty, who has comprehensively insulted everyone else, is strangely kind-hearted towards the madman, kisses him and addresses him in Spanish to a fast, grotesquely scored version of the dance tune. Suddenly the flourish returns and Hauk withdraws. Emilia asks all to leave her except Prus, suggesting to the eager Gregor that he return later.

In her crucial encounter with Prus, Emilia learns two things: that in addition to the will he has found a sealed envelope; and that in the parish register 'Ferdinand' is referred to not as 'Ferdinand Gregor', but as 'Ferdinand Makropulos', his mother given as 'Elina Makropulos'. The mention of this name sets off a version of ex.1 in the orchestra, and Emilia's angry surprise cuts into the courteous pace of the interview. Unless a 'Mr Makropulos' comes forward, the sealed document will remain with Prus. When she suggests he might sell it to her, he turns away.

Prus is followed by Gregor. He must go, she says, to Kolenatý to get back the document she gave him, to be replaced with another in the name of Makropulos. She is totally indifferent to his passionate declarations; in fact she falls asleep. Gregor's frustration is only averted by the entrance of the Cleaning Woman. When Emilia wakes up it is Janek who stands before her. Like the others, he is bewitched by her. She persuades him to do a 'heroic deed': to steal the envelope for her. But the scene has again been witnessed by his father, who imperiously

dismisses him. Janek retires, crestfallen. Emilia steps up close to Prus and again asks for the envelope in return for her sexual favours. To a brief but powerful climax – a dotted rhythm ending in a cymbal roll – Prus agrees to hand it over that evening.

Act 3 *A hotel room* A lively prelude accompanies 'motions of dressing', shadows thrown on the transparent curtain of the bedroom. Emilia Marty emerges in a peignoir, Prus in evening dress, but without a collar. He silently hands over an envelope, which Emilia reads and declares genuine. But Prus feels he has been defrauded: she was like a corpse. They are interrupted by a Chambermaid with the message that Prus's servant urgently needs to speak to him. When Prus returns, he makes Emilia send the girl away: his son has killed himself. The singer is unmoved. As Prus goes off, Hauk comes in. He has stolen his wife's jewels and proposes fleeing to Spain with Emilia. Surprisingly, she consents, but the Chambermaid returns to announce company: Gregor, Kolenatý, Vítek, Kristina, Prus and a doctor, who removes Hauk. The document dated 1836 which Emilia sent Kolenatý turned out to be written with modern ink and is thus a forgery. They have come to interrogate her.

She goes to change, while in a short interlude the others go through her trunk in which they find a variety of documents and names, but all with the initials 'E.M.'. When Emilia Marty returns, elaborately dressed and slightly drunk, she answers their questions by insisting that her name is Elina Makropulos, born in Crete in 1585, and that her father was Hieronymus Makropulos, physician to the Rudolf II, the last Habsburg emperor to keep his court in Prague. She also admits to the alias of Elian MacGregor, the mistress of Josef Prus and the mother of Ferdinand Gregor. She had lent Josef Prus the Makropulos document (now in the sealed envelope) – a formula devised by her father for Rudolf to give him 300 years of life. Rudolf had insisted that Makropulos first try it out on his daughter. Elina fell sick; her father was imprisoned as a charlatan, but Elina recovered and escaped with the formula. Kolenatý continues to insist that she is lying, but Emilia is fast becoming beyond the reach of words and begins to recite the opening of the Lord's Prayer in Greek, her mother tongue. When Kolenatý again demands to know her real name she collapses with the words 'Elina Makropulos' as ex.1 returns. At last Kolenatý believes she is telling the truth. Emilia is carried to the bedroom, and a doctor summoned.

An interlude follows, at first fast and shrill with piccolos and percussion, then slow with high violins as a new lyrical tune emerges. When Emilia appears again, it is 'as a shadow' supported by a doctor. She has felt the hand of death upon her, and 'a green light fills the stage and the theatre'. In chorus the men ask her forgiveness. By now, however, for her they are only 'things and shadows'; living and dying are all the same to her. The other-worldly atmosphere is heightened by an offstage male chorus which repeats Emilia's words. One mustn't live so long, she declares; only for those with a normal span can life have meaning. Then to a final version of ex.1 (now in harmonics) Emilia reaches the climax of her *scena*, sung against a gentle rocking motif in the orchestra, a slow waltz which modulates through several keys against high sustained chords. Asked why she came, she replies that it was for the document, and the pace increases as she reads its opening words. She no longer wants it, and gives it to Kristina – she can live 300 years, she can be famous, she can sing like Emilia Marty. Kristina, however, takes the document and holds it above a flame until it burns. A red light fills the stage. With the words 'Pater hemon' Emilia Marty collapses and dies. The orchestra concludes with a grandiose version of the rocking theme.

*

The Makropulos Affair was his last operatic première that Janáček lived to see; despite the complexities of the score (which caused considerable worries during rehearsals) both the Brno and Prague productions were triumphs. It has only recently come to enjoy the same admiration as his other late operas, although it is his most perfectly constructed. No one doubts the power of the wonderful finale with some of Janáček's grandest music or the virtuosity of the characterization, from its stunning central portrait down to the smallest subsidiary characters, all memorably alive. But the elaborate lawsuit, explained in the first act at some length, the great demands of the orchestral parts and the need for outstanding singing actors have all inhibited performances. When given with total conviction by an outstanding cast, such as the durable Sadler's Wells production with which Charles Mackerras introduced the piece to British audiences (1965), the work with its strange amalgam of passion, mystery and eccentricity comes across as one of the most powerful operas of the 20th century.   J.T.

Manon

Opéra comique in five acts by Jules Massenet to a libretto by Henri Meilhac and Philippe Gille after Antoine-François Prévost's novel *L'histoire du chevalier des Grieux et de Manon Lescaut* (1731); Paris, Opéra-Comique (Salle Favart), 19 January 1884.
   The chief singers at the première were the Flemish soprano Marie Heilbronn (Manon) and Jean-Alexandre Talazac (Des Grieux), with Alexandre Taskin as Lescaut.

Manon Lescaut	soprano
Poussette	mezzo-soprano
Javotte *actresses*	mezzo-soprano
Rosette	mezzo-soprano
Chevalier des Grieux [Des Grieux]	tenor
Count des Grieux *his father*	bass
Lescaut *Manon's cousin*	baritone
Guillot de Morfontaine *a nobleman*	tenor
Brétigny *a tax farmer*	baritone
Innkeeper	baritone
Two Guardsmen	tenor, baritone
A Maid	mezzo-soprano

Citizens of Amiens, travellers, gamblers, the Parisian beau monde, worshippers, soldiers
Setting Amiens, Paris and the road to Le Havre, early 18th century

Massenet suggested setting Abbe Prévost's novel to Meilhac, with whom he had collaborated on the one-act trifle *Bérangère et Anatole* in 1876 (destroyed by the composer); Meilhac was separated from his usual partner Ludovic Halévy, and working at this time with Philippe Gille.
   Prévost (1697–1763) was briefly a member of a strict Benedictine order, and having left it spent the rest of his life in exile. The novel known nowadays simply as *Manon Lescaut* is the seventh and last part of a sequence entitled *Mémoires et aventures d'un homme de qualité*; it was written in London and published in Amsterdam. A narration within a narration – the storyteller meets Des Grieux, who recounts the story of Manon – it is similar in structure to Mérimée's *Carmen*. The action is set during the regency of Philippe d'Orléans, which followed the death of Louis XIV in 1715, a period of notorious corruption in public life; a possible parallel with the Second Empire may have appealed to Massenet and his librettists. Inevitably the plot is simplified (Manon leaves Des Grieux three times in the novel, but only once in the opera) and any element of social criticism is avoided in the interests of providing a conventional, highly competent and lightly licentious libretto acceptable to Opéra-Comique audiences. The main changes are turning Lescaut into Manon's cousin rather than her brother, and transferring the scene of her death from the swamps of Louisiana to the road to Le Havre.
   Massenet worked closely with his librettists in spring 1882, completed the piano score later that year, and finished the orchestration in summer 1883. He had the score printed before rehearsals started at the Opéra-Comique, as was his practice in order to minimize opportunities for interference from Léon Carvalho. The première was a success with the public and most of the press, and *Manon* remained in the Opéra-Comique repertory until 1959, achieving over 2000 performances.

Heilbronn was not the first choice for Manon: Massenet wanted (and rehearsed with) a soprano under contract to another theatre whose manager would not release her, while Talazac pressed the claims of one of his protégées. Heilbronn had sung in Massenet's first piece for the Opéra-Comique, *La grand'tante* (1867), and temporarily retired from the stage following her marriage into the aristocracy. She died aged 35, only two years after the première. Almost exactly a year later (17 January 1885) the Carl Rosa Opera Company gave the British première, in Liverpool, and the work was soon being played throughout Europe and the Americas (December 1885, New York, with Minnie Hauk). In 1887 Massenet met the Californian soprano Sibyl Sanderson, with whom he had the first of his two grand affairs; he coached her for her début in the title role (2 February 1888, The Hague, under the pseudonym of 'Ada Palmer' as a publicity gimmick) and for her he made alterations subsequently incorporated in the 'definitive' score published in 1895. Further post-première additions include the third-act entr'acte, Manon's Gavotte (added in 1884 for Marie Roze, who created the title role in London, and adapted from the song 'Sérénade de Molière' dating from 1880), the reprise of 'N'est-ce plus ma main' in the finale, and in 1894 an alternative to the Gavotte, the 'Fabliau', in all probability composed for Georgette Bréjean-Silver, who sang the role in a major revival at the Opéra-Comique (Carvalho had temporarily dropped *Manon* from the repertory following Sanderson's defection to the Opéra). Since then the leading roles have been sung by all leading singers: Nellie Melba, Mary Garden, Louise Edvina, Maggie Teyte, Fanny Heldy, Ninon Vallin, Victoria de Los Angeles, Sena Jurinac, Fernand Ansseau, Enrico Caruso, Fernando de Lucia, Tito Schipa, John McCormack, Beniamino Gigli, Alfred Piccaver, Nicolai Gedda, Alfredo Kraus and Alain Vanzo are represented in an exhaustive discography.

*

Act I *The courtyard of an inn in Amiens* Guillot, Brétigny and the three 'actresses' impatiently await their dinner. The coach from Arras arrives, and curious townspeople are joined by Lescaut, who is meeting his 15-year-old cousin Manon on her way to a convent on the orders of her parents. She arrives, breathless with wonder at her first journey away from home ('Je suis encore tout étourdie'). While Lescaut leaves to search for her luggage, Guillot sees her and offers her money 'for a word of love', is rebuffed, and mocked by his companions. He nevertheless tells Manon that his coach is at her disposal. Lescaut witnesses the end of the conversation and reproaches Manon for her lack of discretion, which threatens the family honour ('Ne bronchez pas'), before retiring to gamble with his cronies. Left

alone once more, Manon casts envious glances at the actresses and their fine clothes, but realizes sadly that prospects of a life of luxury will be shut off by the convent door ('Voyons, Manon, plus de chimères'). Des Grieux enters to await the coach that will take him to his father ('J'ai marqué l'heure du départ'). He sees Manon and falls in love with her at first sight. She receives his compliments gracefully, and admits that it is her taste for pleasure that has led to her family sending her to the convent. Des Grieux will have none of this, and Manon sees her chance: Guillot's postilion is standing by his coach. The lovers flee joyfully ('Nous vivrons à Paris'). Lescaut and Guillot return to find the bird has flown. Guillot, publicly humiliated, swears revenge.

Act 2 *The apartment of Manon and Des Grieux in the rue Vivienne, Paris* Des Grieux writes a letter to his father asking permission to marry Manon, who reads it back to him ('On l'appelle Manon'). She inquires thoughtfully whether it is not enough for them just to be lovers. Des Grieux asks about a bunch of flowers; Manon answers that it was thrown anonymously through the window from down in the street. The maid announces two soldiers: one is Lescaut and the other, she whispers to Manon, is the wealthy Brétigny in disguise. Brétigny pretends to restrain Lescaut from avenging insults to the family honour – the latter is deflated when Des Grieux shows him the letter – and tells Manon aside that Des Grieux's father is having him abducted that same evening. He also propositions her; she sees her chance of escape to a better life. The intruders leave, and Des Grieux goes to post the letter. Manon tells herself that though she loves Des Grieux, she is not worthy of him, and she knows she is unable to resist Brétigny's offer. She bids sentimental farewell to the domestic scene ('Adieu, notre petite table'). Des Grieux returns and tells her of his dream of the rustic retreat they will share in wedded bliss ('En fermant les yeux'). Noise is heard at the door. Manon begs her lover not to go to it, in vain. He is abducted.

Act 3.i *The Cours-la-Reine* Lescaut and the three actresses are among the tradesmen and pleasure-seekers (Lescaut: 'A quoi bon l'économie ... O Rosalinde'). The actresses pointedly snub Guillot, who in turn provokes the possessive and jealous Brétigny; he has heard that Manon asked her protector to invite the company from the Opéra to perform at her home, and he refused. Guillot makes plans. Manon enters on Brétigny's arm, at the summit of her fame ('Je marche sur tous les chemins'; Gavotte: 'Obéissons quand leur voix appelle'). Manon then overhears a conversation between Brétigny and the Count des Grieux, the Chevalier's father, who reveals that his son is taking holy orders and is to preach his first sermon at St Sulpice later in the day. Manon, unaware that the Count knows who she is, asks him if his son has forgotten the cause of his misery, and he answers in the affirmative. Guillot returns in triumph with the ballet troupe from the Opéra. After the fourth entrée, Manon abruptly orders her coach to take her to St Sulpice. Guillot is publicly humiliated once more.

3.ii *The parlour of the seminary at St Sulpice* Pious female worshippers comment admiringly on the qualities of the new abbé. The Count des Grieux tries to dissuade his son from taking the final step ('Epouse quelque brave fille') and, seeing that he is adamant, promises to make over part of his inheritance. Alone, Des Grieux prays for peace of mind ('Ah! fuyez, douce image'). He leaves for the holy Office. Manon enters and asks the porter if she may see Des Grieux, and while waiting prudently prays God for forgiveness in advance. Des Grieux angrily dismisses her. She admits her guilt, begs for forgiveness, and asks him only to remember their past love ('N'est-ce plus ma main'). Her physical touch overcomes Des Grieux's scruples: the lovers are reunited.

Act 4 *The Hôtel de Transylvanie* Lescaut and the actresses join gamblers and professional card-sharpers. Guillot entertains them with a suggestive ditty about the regent. Manon enters with Des Grieux, a

'Manon' (Massenet), Act 4 (the Hôtel de Transylvanie),
the entry of Manon (Marie Heilbronn) and Des Grieux
(Jean-Alexandre Talazac) in the original production at the
Opéra-Comique, Paris, 19 January 1884; engraving from
'Le théâtre illustré'

fish out of water yet still under her spell ('Manon, sphinx étonnant'). She reminds him that his inheritance has nearly run out: he must gamble for more money. Unwillingly he accepts a challenge from Guillot, while Manon and the actresses sing rapturously of what money will bring them ('Ce bruit de l'or'). Guillot loses repeatedly and suddenly breaks off the game, hinting that Des Grieux has cheated – a charge hotly denied. As Guillot leaves, Manon urges Des Grieux to follow suit, but he feels that if he does, the charge will be believed. Guillot returns with the police and orders the arrest of Des Grieux and his accomplice. The Count des Grieux also enters to lead the final ensemble and support the order for his son's arrest. Manon collapses as she is led away.

Act 5 *On the road to Le Havre* For her loose morals Manon has been sentenced to deportation to the colonies, and Lescaut's and Des Grieux's plot to rescue her has foundered on the desertion of their accomplices. But Lescaut bribes the sergeant of the escort to let him speak to his cousin. He leaves the lovers alone. Manon, broken in body and spirit, begs Des Grieux's forgiveness for the shame she has brought him (duet: 'Tu pleures?' 'Oui, de honte sur moi') before expiring amid a flurry of reminiscences from the earlier acts.

*

Manon may be Massenet's best-known and most popular opera but, an early work, it is by no means unflawed. The Meilhac-Gille libretto is prolix and over-reliant on narrative values; the result is nearly three hours of music – longer than *Carmen* – and the score is seldom performed uncut in the theatre. The first act, especially, takes a long time to get going, a crucial fault. In the interests of producing a conventional libretto tailor-made for Opéra-Comique audiences – opportunities for a church scene, two street scenes and a gambling scene, all stock material at the Favart, must have attracted Massenet to the novel – the authors softened the material significantly. Lescaut, in the novel Manon's brother and pimp, becomes her cousin and is turned into a standard *opéra comique* swashbuckler, blandly characterized by the music. There is some confusion about why he talks so proudly of the Lescaut family honour in the first two acts; in the original version of the novel the Lescauts were of some substance, but in Prévost's revision of 1753 they were taken down a social peg. Massenet and his librettists presumably preferred the original, but the degree of irony intended is not made clear. Des Grieux is similarly watered down. In the novel he does indeed cheat at cards, and is taught how to by Lescaut, who with some awkwardness in the opera has to combine military bluffness with some of the functions of Des Grieux's faithful friend in the novel, Tiberge. In both instances the aura of moral corruption in Prévost's story is compromised, just as no one would know from the opera alone that Brétigny is a rich tax farmer. In post-1871 Paris any hint of social criticism was unwelcome.

The designation 'opéra comique' is misleading: there are only a few lines of spoken dialogue. But in their place there is much *mélodrame*, faultlessly handled at a technical level. The first meeting of Manon and Des Grieux is presented this way under a 9/8 phrase on solo violin later to become the lovers' main motif, and the scene for the Count and his son at St Sulpice, which moves from dialogue to *mélodrame* to arioso and back again, is another perfectly crafted passage. (Massenet left among his papers a score in which both dialogue and *mélodrame* were set vocally without any changes to the accompaniment; this revision was first given at the Metropolitan Opera in New York in 1988.)

Less satisfying are the moments when convention takes over. The sinister atmosphere of the gambling den, laced with the hysterical hedonism of 'Ce bruit de l'or', gives way to the stock concerted finale, complete with the Count des Grieux, who has no business to be there save to underline a calculated echo of *La traviata*; similarly, the desolation of the last act with its perky song for the military escort and swooning 9/8 Andante espressivo for the lovers dissolves into a cynically laid-out series of reprises. Massenet's post-première insertion of the reminiscence of 'N'est-ce plus ma main' effectively sinks the ship, and is one of the rare examples of his second thoughts definitely not being for the better.

Yet in general it is hard not to admire the charm of the 18th-century pastiche, the suavely composed bustle of the crowd scenes, the genuine dramatic power of the St Sulpice confrontation with its potent mixture of sex and religion, or the deft delineation of the principal characters. Des Grieux may remain the undeveloping mooncalf lover – a fault of the adaptation – yet three solos of the varied quality of the second-act Dream, 'Ah! fuyez' and 'Manon, sphinx étonnant' are reward enough for both singer and audience.

But in Manon herself Massenet created a portrait of the eternal feminine to rank with Mélisande and Lulu, and it is on this that the opera's appeal rests. Maupassant wrote of Prévost's heroine's 'instinctive perfidy', describing her as 'sincere in her deception and frank in her infamy', and Massenet caught the contradictions perfectly. This is, to be sure, a male view of seductive womankind: the generous, ambitious, pleasure-loving good-time girl who delivers the goods and expires of nothing so much as sheer exhaustion, but not before having repented of the sins required of her and sworn eternal constancy to her faithful lover. Yet this somewhat one-sided view has not prevented all lyric sopranos of note queuing up to sing the role, encompassing as it does a string of

well-contrasted showpieces, from the shy, hesitant 'Je suis encore tout étourdie' (an example of supremely perceptive musical characterization), through the regretful 'Voyons, Manon', the skittish charm of the Letter Scene, the pure sentiment of the farewell to the *petite table*, the glittering confidence of the Gavotte, the irresistible 'N'est-ce plus ma main' (the shimmering violins at the moment of physical contact is one of operatic literature's great X-rated effects) to the mournful repentance of the finale. They add up to a formidable and teasingly enigmatic whole, and a rewarding challenge to singing-actresses. In the final analysis *Manon* is by way of being a 'highlights' opera, lacking the cohesion and economy of more mature Massenet works, but those highlights were seldom surpassed in the composer's oeuvre.   R.M.

Manon Lescaut

Dramma lirico in four acts by Giacomo Puccini to a libretto by Domenico Oliva and Luigi Illica after Antoine-François Prévost's novel *L'histoire du chevalier des Grieux et de Manon Lescaut*; Turin, Teatro Regio, 1 February 1893 (revised version, Milan, Teatro alla Scala, 7 February 1894).

The first performance was conducted by Alessandro Pomè with Cesira Ferrani (Manon), Achille Moro (Lescaut), Giuseppe Cremonini (Des Grieux) and Alessandro Polonini (Geronte).

Manon Lescaut	soprano
Lescaut *her brother, Sergeant of the Royal* *Guards*	baritone
The Chevalier des Grieux	tenor
Geronte de Revoir *Treasurer General*	bass
Edmondo *a student*	tenor
The Innkeeper	bass
A Singer	mezzo-soprano
The Dancing Master	tenor
A Lamplighter	tenor
Sergeant of the Royal Archers	bass
A Naval Captain	bass

Singers, old beaux and abbés, girls, townsfolk,
   students, courtesans, archers and sailors

Setting France and America during the second
   half of the 18th century

Puccini's first two operas, *Le villi* (1884) and *Edgar* (1889) had little impact on the general public although they did not escape the notice of critics. His third, *Manon Lescaut*, however, triumphantly vindicated his publisher Giulio Ricordi's faith in him. Of all Puccini's operas it had the most tormented genesis. Ricordi, his 'guide, philosopher and friend' until his death in 1912, tried to dissuade him from a subject which had already achieved great popularity in Massenet's setting of 1884, as yet unperformed in Italy (see *Manon*). Puccini remained firm in his decision to undertake it, declaring that 'Manon is a heroine I believe in and therefore she cannot fail to win the hearts of the public. Why shouldn't there be two operas about her? A woman like Manon can have more than one lover.' Dissatisfied with the bizarre pseudo-philosophical pretensions of Ferdinando Fontana, who had written the librettos for his previous operas, Puccini first turned to the playwright Marco Praga as a possible librettist. But Praga had never attempted an opera libretto before and insisted on bringing in the young poet Domenico Oliva, with whom he had already collaborated on a literary and artistic journal, to do the versification. Both authors were contracted by Ricordi during the summer of 1889. By the beginning of the next year they had produced a libretto in four acts set respectively in Amiens, in the lovers' humble apartment in Paris, in Geronte's town house and in the Louisiana desert where Manon dies. Puccini professed himself satisfied and managed to complete the first act by March 1890. But by June he was complaining that the libretto was driving him to despair and that it would have to be redone. He particularly wanted an entire scene at the end of Act 3 showing the embarkation at Le Havre. Rather than alter his original scheme Praga preferred to bow out. Ricordi then turned to Ruggero Leoncavallo, who drafted out a new scheme for Act 2, leaving Oliva to fill out the lines; then he too retired from the project, owing to pressure of other work. Finally, in autumn 1891 Luigi Illica was called in to overhaul the entire text in accordance with Puccini's requirements. He reworked the scene at Le Havre into its present form, adding the song of the Lamplighter, while Ricordi contributed the quatrain in which the ship's captain agrees to take Des Grieux aboard. Puccini himself supplied 11 unmetrical lines for the duet between Lescaut and Manon in Geronte's town house; a further two were provided by Leoncavallo for the conclusion of Des Grieux' solo in the same scene. Some time during the summer of 1892 the original Act 2 was dropped altogether and replaced by what had until then been Act 3 part 1, now suitably expanded. Thus the embarkation scene became a separate act, prefaced by an intermezzo. By this time Oliva no longer wanted to be associated with the opera; but as much of his work exists in the finished product, Illica tactfully withheld his own name from the title-page, so that the published libretto remains to this day without an attribution. Later Oliva maintained that the fourth act was exactly as he had originally written it. The score was finished in October 1892, Act 3 being completed last. Puccini, as

he often did, drew on previous material: the Agnus Dei from his student piece, the so-called *Messa di gloria* (1880) for the 'madrigal' of Act 2; another student exercise, *Mentìa l'avviso* (1883), for the melody of Des Grieux' aria 'Donna non vidi mai'; a minuet for string quartet (1884) speeded up for the opera's opening; and the elegy *Crisantemi* (1890), also for quartet, for certain moments in Act 3 and Act 4.

As La Scala was occupied at the time with rehearsals for Verdi's *Falstaff*, Ricordi chose the Teatro Regio, Turin, for the première. *Manon Lescaut* was Puccini's first and only uncontested triumph, acclaimed by critics and public alike; its success meant that his financial problems were permanently solved. Ricordi took advantage of the favourable reception to link its hire with that of *Falstaff*, so that neither opera could be given without the other. Before the published vocal score appeared Puccini made, at Illica's suggestion, a radical change to the finale of Act 1, replacing a conventional *pezzo concertato*, based on the melody of 'Donna non vidi mai', by an exchange between Lescaut and Geronte and a reprise of the melody of Des Grieux' 'Tra voi belle' entrusted to Edmondo and the students. The new finale was first performed on 7 February 1894 at La Scala, where the cast included Olga Olghini (Manon), Tieste Wilmant (Lescaut), Vittorio Arimondi (Geronte) and the original Des Grieux, Cremonini. The London première (Covent Garden, 14 May 1894), with Olghini (Manon), Antonio Pini-Corsi (Lescaut) and Umberto Beduschi (Des Grieux), prompted Bernard Shaw to hail Puccini as Verdi's most probable heir among Italian composers, noting that 'the domain of Italian opera is enlarged by an annexation of German territory'. The opera established itself at the Metropolitan, New York (18 January 1907), with Lina Cavalieri (Manon), Antonio Scotti (Lescaut) and Enrico Caruso (Des Grieux). Outstanding exponents of the title role have included Lucrezia Bori, who introduced the opera to Paris in 1910, and Lotte Lehmann, who sang it in Vienna in 1923 with Alfred Piccaver as Des Grieux.

Puccini continued to modify *Manon Lescaut*, in particular omitting for many years the heroine's aria in Act 4, 'Sola, perduta, abbandonata'. He finally reinstated it with a slightly altered ending for the 30th-anniversary performance, given at La Scala (1 February 1923) under Arturo Toscanini with Juanita Caracciolo in the title role. Toscanini himself suggested certain alterations to the scoring, all of which have since been incorporated in the current version of the opera.

*

Act I *A public square in Amiens* Outside an inn soldiers, students and townsfolk are enjoying the fine summer evening. Edmondo leads the company in a 'madrigal' ('Ave sera gentil'). The students welcome

'Manon Lescaut' (Puccini), Act 3 (Le Havre, a square near the harbour); a page from the disposizione scenica (production book) for the original production at the Teatro Regio, Turin, 1 February 1893

Des Grieux, who addresses a group of girls with ironical gallantry ('Tra voi belle, brune o bionde'). The young Manon arrives on the stage coach from Arras accompanied by her brother Lescaut and Geronte, who orders lodgings for the night. The cynical Lescaut, aware of the older man's interest in his sister, is happy to collude in his plans for her; the two men go into the inn. The crowd disperse leaving Manon alone with Des Grieux. She tells him that she is bound for a convent, but agrees to meet him later. When she has gone in, Des Grieux pours out his feelings in the soliloquy 'Donna non vidi mai'. Edmondo overhears Geronte summoning a carriage to leave for Paris within the hour – to abduct Manon – and warns Des Grieux. He and Manon sing a love-duet ('Vedete? io son fedele') before making their escape in the carriage. Lescaut assures the mortified Geronte that his sister, who has expensive tastes, will soon need a rich protector as Des Grieux has no money.

Act 2 *An elegant salon in Geronte's house* Manon, installed as Geronte's mistress, is in the hands of her hairdresser when Lescaut enters. She asks for news of Des Grieux, recalling nostalgically the humble apartment in which they were happy together and contrasting it with her present luxurious surroundings ('In quelle trine morbide'). Lescaut tells her that he has turned the young man into a gambler, so that he may win enough money to provide her with the

luxury she cannot do without. A group of singers perform a madrigal in her honour ('Sulla vetta tu del monte'), after which Lescaut goes to fetch Des Grieux. Geronte arrives with friends who offer bouquets and trinkets. A dancing master teaches her the minuet. Manon takes leave of the company with a brief 'pastoral' ('L'ora, o Tirsi, è vaga e bella'), promising to join them later on the boulevards. When she is alone Des Grieux appears at the door. In their duet ('Tu, tu, amore') he begins by reproaching her, but she soon overcomes his resistance and Geronte returns to find them in each other's arms. Manon parries his ironic thrusts by holding a mirror to his face. He retires, threatening that they will meet again. The lovers prepare to flee; but Manon is sad at having to relinquish so much wealth, as Des Grieux observes with dismay ('Ah, Manon, mi tradisce il tuo folle pensier'). To a brisk orchestral fugato Lescaut bursts in to tell them that Geronte is on his way back with the city guards. Manon's insistence on gathering up the jewels causes a fatal delay. As Geronte and the guards enter the jewels spill out of her cloak, and she is arrested for theft.

Act 3 *Le Havre, a square near the harbour* An intermezzo based on previously heard themes covers the time of Manon's imprisonment and the journey to the French port. As a woman of loose character she is housed in a barracks with prostitutes awaiting deportation to America. Lescaut plans to procure her escape by bribing a guard. As Manon appears at a grille, she and Des Grieux exchange words of love and hope while a Lamplighter passes by on his rounds. A shot is heard, indicating that Lescaut's plan has miscarried. One by one the prostitutes and Manon are taken to the ship, while a sergeant-at-arms calls their names and the crowd comment on the appearance of each. Des Grieux prevails upon the ship's captain to take him aboard in a solo, 'Guardate, pazzo son, guardate', and with a reminiscence of the Act 2 duet, he falls into Manon's arms.

Act 4 *A vast desert near the outskirts of New Orleans* Manon, in flight with Des Grieux from the son of the French governor, is at the end of her strength. She sends Des Grieux to look for shelter for the night, then breaks out in an agonized lament, 'Sola, perduta, abbandonata'. Des Grieux returns to find her dying.

*

Manon Lescaut placed Puccini firmly in the front rank of contemporary composers. Bernard Shaw correctly drew attention to the symphonic element in Act 1, while the *grand tableau* of the prostitutes' roll-call in the third act represents something new in Italian musical dramaturgy – a *pezzo concertato* in which time is never frozen. No less remarkable is Puccini's skill in depicting the dawning of young love, first with an orchestral anticipation of Des Grieux' aria 'Donna non vidi mai', then in the course of the duet 'Vedete? io son fedele', in which shy conversational exchanges gradually flower into an ecstatic lyricism. Thematic recurrence is used with a new flexibility, exemplified by the various transformations undergone by the motif associated with the heroine. At moments of high emotion *Manon Lescaut* comes nearer the Wagner of *Tristan* than do any of Puccini's other operas.

On the debit side, the elimination of the lovers' Parisian idyll not only leaves an awkward gap in the action but also precludes a consistent portrayal of Manon's character. Indeed, a letter to Illica, undated but obviously written several years later, shows Puccini toying with the notion of an additional act showing the lovers living happily together in Paris. The chief difficulty lay in finding a sufficiently original ending. Also unsatisfactory is the concentration of all the gaiety into Acts 1 and 2 and all the gloom into Acts 3 and 4. But any such weaknesses are amply made good by the abundance of youthful vitality, which has enabled Puccini's opera to hold its own against Massenet's technically more adroit setting of the same subject.   J.B.

Maria Stuarda ('Mary Stuart')

Tragedia lirica in two or three acts by Gaetano Donizetti to a libretto by Giuseppe Bardari after Andrea Maffei's translation (1830) of Friedrich von Schiller's *Maria Stuart*; Milan, Teatro alla Scala, 30 December 1835.

At the première Maria Malibran sang the role of Mary; others in the cast included Giacinta Pazzi Tosi (Elizabeth), Domenico Reina (Leicester), Ignazio Marini (Talbot) and Pietro Novelli (Cecil).

Elisabetta [Queen Elizabeth I]	soprano
Maria Stuarda [Mary Stuart]	
Queen of Scots	soprano
Earl of Leicester	tenor
Talbot	bass
Lord Cecil	bass
Anna	mezzo-soprano
Courtiers, soldiers, servants	
Setting Westminster and Fotheringhay Castle	

This work was originally intended by Donizetti as a vehicle for his favourite prima donna, Giuseppina Ronzi de Begnis, but when it was in rehearsal at the S Carlo, Naples, the king personally forbade its performance (the depiction of royalty on the stage was always a sensitive subject). Donizetti cobbled much of the score into a work with a different plot, *Buondelmonte*, with new recitatives and other changes, given at Naples on 18 October 1834. But Malibran became enthused with the subject of Mary Stuart and insisted on appearing in the opera at La Scala, where she ignored the censor's changes and caused the opera to be banned by the local authorities. In sanitized form, the work was given occasionally in Italy in the ensuing years. Its first 20th-century revival was at Bergamo in 1958 and it speedily re-entered the repertory. The discovery of the missing autograph in Sweden made possible the preparation of a more authentic edition, in two acts, which was revived at Bergamo in 1989.

The critical edition based on the recovered autograph reveals an interesting example of Donizetti's practice of self-borrowing. Two numbers from *Maria Stuarda*, which Donizetti seems to have given up as a lost cause some time after its suppression in Milan, were later reused in *La favorite*: the opening chorus at Westminster and the stretta to the first finale. After *Stuarda*, this ensemble at one time formed part of an apparently never-completed project, *Adelaide*, and from there it went into *L'ange de Nisida* before coming to rest at the end of Act 3 of *La favorite*. For the reworked version of *Maria Stuarda* at S Carlo in 1865 these numbers were replaced, as they were now familiar from their context in *La favorite*. It is in this inaccurate version that the opera has become widely known in the 20th century.

*

Act 1 opens with Queen Elizabeth mulling over the possibility of marriage to the Dauphin of France, but she cannot forget her love for the Earl of Leicester. When he arrives at court, Leicester is taken aside by Talbot, who gives him a portrait and a letter from Mary Stuart in which she requests an interview with the English queen. Leicester's love and sympathy for the imprisoned Mary are rekindled. Later, Elizabeth confronts Leicester, who hands her the letter, thereby arousing her jealousy; but he persuades her to agree to meet Mary.

Act 1 scene ii (in most 20th-century performances entitled Act 2) is set in the castle at Fotheringhay, where Mary thinks nostalgically of freedom, envying the clouds that can skim towards France (cavatina, 'O nube che lieve'). Leicester arrives to prepare her for Elizabeth's coming but Mary is both resentful and afraid. (Their love duet, added via *Buondelmonte* for the 1835 Milan performance, was later judged 'intrusive' by Donizetti.) Elizabeth, infuriated at the sight of the proud, beautiful Mary, treats her with contempt and disdain; stung, Mary calls Elizabeth a 'vil bastarda' and a stain on the honour of England. Elizabeth summons the guards and swears to be avenged.

In Act 2 (or 3), back at Westminster, Cecil tries to persuade Elizabeth to sign Mary's death warrant while Leicester pleads that she be spared. Offended by Leicester's obvious preference for the Scottish queen, Elizabeth tells him that she has already signed the document and orders him to witness the execution. At Fotheringhay, Mary receives her sentence from Cecil without flinching. Revealing a cassock beneath his cloak, Talbot hears her confession and absolves her. Mary asks her faithful friends to join her in praying for forgiveness for all who have wronged her, and Leicester can only stand helplessly by as Mary is led towards the executioner.

*

There are a number of interesting features in this score. The extended Act 1 finale (the scene of the confrontation – historically untrue, of course – between the two queens) is unusual in that the middle section is longer than the Larghetto and the stretta combined; it shows more clearly perhaps than anywhere else in Donizetti's output his intense interest in dramatic immediacy and potency. The Larghetto of this finale, a canonic sextet, is the source of a remarkably similar passage in Verdi's *Nabucco*. One of the most impressive numbers in *Maria Stuarda* is the eloquent prayer in the final scene; extensively revised, this melody was to form the basis for the ensemble at the end of Act 1 of *Linda di Chamounix*. Mary's confession duet with Talbot and her aria-

finale are among the most affecting moments in the opera – indeed, in Donizetti's entire output.

W.A.

Martha [*Martha, oder Der Markt zu Richmond* ('Martha, or The Market at Richmond')]

Romantic comic opera in four acts by Friedrich Flotow to a libretto by W. Friedrich (Friedrich Wilhelm Riese) after an idea by Jules-Henri Vernoy de Saint-Georges; Vienna, Kärntnertortheater, 25 November 1847.

The cast at the première included Anna Zerr (Lady Harriet), Josef Erl (Lyonel), Carl Just (Lord Tristan), Therese Schwarz (Nancy) and Karl Johann Formes (Plumkett).

Lady Harriet Durham *maid of honour to* Queen Anne	soprano
Lord Tristan Mickleford *her cousin*	bass
Plumkett *a young farmer*	bass
Lyonel *his foster brother*	tenor
Nancy *waiting-maid to Lady Harriet*	mezzo-soprano
Sheriff	bass
Three Manservants	tenor, basses
Three Maidservants	soprano, mezzo-sopranos
Courtiers, pages, ladies, hunters and huntresses, farmers	

Setting In and near Richmond, near London, c1710

It was after the success of *Alessandro Stradella* in Vienna in 1845 that Flotow, who had been resident in Paris since 1831, received a commission from the Vienna Hofoper to write a new opera. He decided to extend his music from the ballet *Lady Harriette, ou La servante de Greenwich* of 1844 into a full-length opera. For the libretto he again approached Friedrich, who had written the text of *Alessandro Stradella*. Friedrich was well versed in the new plot, having already written a libretto on the subject for Eduard Stiegmann's opera *Lady Harriet*, performed in Hamburg in 1846. Working in close collaboration, Flotow and Friedrich created their most successful opera, *Martha*, which has held its place in the repertory until the present day. (The same plot was also set to music that year by the Irish composer Michael Balfe as *The Maid of Honour*, performed in London a month later than *Martha* with no success.) The celebrated aria 'Letzte Rose' is the Irish folksong, 'The last rose of summer', as it appeared in Thomas Moore's *Irish Melodies* in 1813, although the tune was adapted by Moore from earlier sources.

*

'Martha' (Flotow), Act 2 (the spinning scene) with the principals of the original production at the Kärntnertortheater, Vienna, 25 November 1847: engraving by A. Geiger after Cajetan

Act I.i *Lady Harriet Durham's boudoir* Lady Harriet is tired of life at court and longs for true love. Her maid, Nancy, tries in vain to raise her spirits; to make things worse Lady Harriet has to ward off the amorous approaches of her foppish cousin, Lord Tristan. On hearing the local peasant girls singing on their way to the annual Richmond Fair, she decides all three should dress up as peasants and mingle with the common folk to watch the merriment, for it is at this fair that the maids commit themselves for one year to the service of the bidding farmers. To ensure anonymity, Lady Harriet will call herself 'Martha', Nancy will be known as 'Julia' and Lord Tristan must answer to the name of 'Bob'.

I.ii *The market square of Richmond* Plumkett and Lyonel arrive in the hope of finding two servant-girls. They reminisce on how Lyonel's fugitive father had brought him as a child to Plumkett's parents, where they found refuge, until the father died, without ever revealing his name or standing. He did, however, leave Lyonel his ring, saying that if he were ever in danger he should show it to the queen. The Sheriff formally opens the fair and proclaims the royal decree that any maid who takes on service has to remain with her new master for one year. The farmers have no difficulty in finding willing maids, while Plumkett and Lyonel remain undecided. Lady Harriet and Nancy arrive, dragging 'Bob' behind them. He insists they go home immediately, and as

their discord starts to attract attention, Lady Harriet pretends that 'Bob' is trying to force her into service on his farm. The indignant commoners point out that there are enough willing maids to serve him, and a group of girls who have not yet found employment descend on him. Left alone with Plumkett and Lyonel the ladies, highly diverted, hire themselves off as servants for the pittance now paid in advance. The joke over, they try to get Lord Tristan to take them home, but the Sheriff confirms that they have entered into a one-year agreement of service, and their new masters drag them off to their cart while Tristan is held back by the angry farmers.

Act 2 *Plumkett's farmhouse* The farmers try putting the girls to work, but they protest that they are unversed in household chores. While the two exasperated men show them how to spin flax, Nancy flees the room and Plumkett runs after her, leaving Lyonel and 'Martha' alone. Lyonel confesses his tender feelings, offering to overlook her assumed low standing and to marry her. Amused, Lady Harriet declines, but accedes to his request to sing a simple folksong ('Letzte Rose'), in which she hints at her loneliness. It is now midnight. The girls are locked into their room, and the men retire. When all are sleeping a knock is heard on the girls' window. It is Lord Tristan. Overjoyed, Harriet and Nancy escape through the window before their new masters, woken by the noise, can stop them.

Act 3 *A forest near Richmond* Queen Anne is hunting, watched by Plumkett and a group of peasants. Nancy arrives fully accoutred for the royal hunt and accompanied by her huntresses. She and Plumkett recognize each other, and he attempts to take her back to the farm by force. Nancy denies ever having known him and has him chased away by her formidable companions. Lyonel appears, lamenting the loss of Lady Harriet, whom he loves in the guise of his absconded maid Martha, and sings the aria 'Ach, so fromm'. Deep in thought, he fails to notice Lady Harriet enter with Lord Tristan. The latter is still trying to win her heart, but she sends him away, admitting to herself that she is actually pining for Lyonel. On hearing her voice, Lyonel falls to her feet, professing his love, but she disavows him, for fear of the scandal any knowledge of her adventure would cause at court. Lyonel becomes angry and Lady Harriet, alarmed, calls Lord Tristan and the hunting party. Lyonel is not believed when he relates how Lady Harriet had tricked her way into his house by posing as a servant. She declares that he has lost his mind, and he is arrested. The act ends with the quintet with chorus 'Mag der Himmel euch vergeben'. As Lyonel is led away, he gives Plumkett the ring he had received from his father with the request that it reach the queen.

Act 4.i *Plumkett's farmhouse* The ring has now been identified by the queen as that of the unjustly banished Earl of Derby. Lady Harriet comes to reveal to Lyonel who he really is, but also to ask his forgiveness and to offer him her hand in marriage. Lyonel angrily rejects her. Plumkett has already forgiven Nancy, and Harriet now enlists the loving couple's assistance in her plan to win Lyonel back.

4.ii *In front of Plumkett's farmhouse* Peasants and servants set up a replica of the Richmond Fair, with one of the farmers dressed as the Sheriff. Lady Harriet and Nancy appear as 'Martha' and 'Julia' in peasant costume to meet Plumkett as he leads the heartbroken Lyonel to the mock fair. The two girls, re-enacting the events of the real fair in Act 1, offer themselves once again to Plumkett and Lyonel, who can no longer resist their offer of love and dedication. The two couples embrace to the jubilation of the crowd.

*

From the point of view of the intrinsic merit of the work, the success of *Martha* was surely inevitable. The libretto, couched in succinct and witty couplets, tells a tale that is well constructed, exciting, amusing and sentimental. The bustling folk scenes, the rough-and-ready situation at the farm, the magnificence of the royal hunt and the sophistication of court life and, in particular, the depth of emotion of the principal characters, find fitting expression in Flotow's music, in which the Singspiel style is reserved for his

buffoonish and peasant characters (Nancy, Plumkett and the maids of Richmond), with the sustained, bel canto French Romanticism of *opéra comique* for the lovers Martha and Lyonel. Although all this implies a certain degree of eclecticism (which was indeed common in France at the time), the stylistic unity of the work is manifest. For example, the motifs of the theme of the highly operatic and heroic 'Mag der Himmel euch vergeben' are derived from those in the simple folksong 'Letzte Rose'. Flotow also included numerous well-placed repetitions of the reminiscence themes ('Letzte Rose' is repeated five times).

P.C.

Mask of Orpheus, The

Lyric tragedy in three acts by Harrison Birtwistle to a libretto by Peter Zinovieff; London, Coliseum, 21 May 1986.

At the first performance Philip Langridge sang the role of Orpheus Man, Jean Rigby Eurydice Woman, Tom McDonnell Aristaeus Man; Marie Angel was the Oracle of the Dead, and the conductor was Elgar Howarth.

Orpheus:	
The Man	high baritone
The Hero	mime
The Myth/Hades	high baritone
Eurydice:	
The Woman	lyric mezzo-soprano
The Heroine	mime
The Myth	lyric mezzo-soprano
Aristaeus:	
The Man	tenor
The Hero	mime
The Myth	tenor
The Oracle of the Dead/Hecate	high soprano
The Troupe of Ceremony/Judges of the Dead:	
The Caller	bass-baritone
First Priest	bright tenor
Second Priest	baritone
Third Priest	basso profondo
The Three Women/Furies	soprano, mezzo-soprano, contralto
The Troupe of Passing Clouds	mimes
The Voice of Apollo	pre-recorded tape
Setting Mythic Greece	

Birtwistle was first commissioned by the Royal Opera House, Covent Garden, to write an opera on the Orpheus myth after the success of the première of *Punch and Judy* in 1968. He began work on the score in 1973 but the initial project foundered, and the commission passed first to London Weekend Television and then to Glyndebourne before lapsing altogether in 1976, at which point Act 1 and much of Act 2 had been completed. In 1981 the ENO revived the commission, and between 1982 and 1984 Birtwistle, not without a struggle, completed the second act and the whole of the third, as well as compiling the electronic tapes at IRCAM in Paris with the help of Barry Anderson. The staging at the ENO was directed by David Freeman with designs by Jocelyn Herbert. Despite its critical success the work has not been revived since 1986 because of the formidable production costs; a concert performance of Act 2 was given by the BBC Symphony Orchestra at the Barbican, London, in January 1988.

The essence of the dramatic organization of *The Mask of Orpheus* is its rejection of linear narrative: events unfold cyclically rather than with a conventional goal in time. Somewhat in the manner of a medieval altarpiece, Birtwistle's presentation of the bundle of myths surrounding the central story of Orpheus and Eurydice involves the parallel presentation of different, often contradictory, versions of the events; episodes are overlaid and repeated from different perspectives, and the threefold representation of each of the main characters by singer, mime and puppet (whose words are delivered by an offstage singer), allows simultaneous presentation of such perspectives. What is already a highly complex formal structure is interrupted on six occasions by electronic interludes in which a mime troupe enacts myths associated with (but not related directly to) the Orpheus story; these violent 'Passing Clouds of Abandon' and lyrical 'Allegorical Flowers of Reason' are inserted at points of maximum calm or crisis in the main action and while they are being portrayed all other action is frozen.

*

Parados Speaking in his own invented language, Apollo oversees the birth of Orpheus, giving him the gifts of speech, poetry and music. Orpheus's first memory is of voyaging with Jason and the Argonauts.

*

Act I.i Orpheus falls in love with Eurydice; she agrees to their marriage.

(Passing Cloud: Dionysus)

In the wedding ceremony, Hymen is invoked and the Troupe of Ceremony ritually questions the lovers; the omens are bad as Eurydice stumbles over her answers. Orpheus's love song fails to lift the gloom.

I.ii Two versions of Eurydice's death are presented simultaneously.

(Passing Cloud: Lycurgus)

Aristaeus as Man and Hero makes love to Eurydice Woman and Heroine as she walks by the river; in one version she resists, in the other she does not; in both she dies from the bite of a water snake.

(Allegorical Flower: Anemone)

Aristaeus tells Orpheus of his wife's death.

I.iii First time-distortion: Orpheus imagines he, and not Aristaeus, watched Eurydice's death. During the funeral ceremony the Troupe of Ceremony asks Hermes to guide Eurydice to the Underworld, while elements of the earlier love duet are recalled. Orpheus cannot accept that he was powerless to save his wife and consults the Oracle of the Dead. The Oracle offers him three clues to the Underworld in exchange for his gift of music, but when she attempts to imitate his song she produces only screams and shrieks. Orpheus imagines he can find his way to the Underworld. He describes the 17 arches of the aqueduct that connects the mountain of the living to that of the dead; Eurydice is transformed into myth.

Act 2 The structure of Act 2 follows the progress of Orpheus Myth across the 17 arches of the aqueduct, while Orpheus Man watches as in a dream and sings, off stage, a 17-verse Song of Magic. Each arch represents a different attribute of the world of the living which Orpheus is leaving behind, and all the characters he encounters are distorted versions of those he met in Act 1. This act begins, though, with the second time-distortion: Eurydice's death is presented again; she is killed by two giant snakes.

Arch I Countryside Orpheus sings to Charon as he crosses the River Styx.

Arch 2 Crowds Orpheus's music moves the Furies.

Arch 3 Evening Orpheus's death is foretold; he sees a vision of Eurydice.

Arch 4 Contrasts He drinks from the pool of memory but refuses the pool of forgetfulness; he has a second vision.

Arch 5 Dying He sees those tormented in the Underworld.

Arch 6 Wings His magic overcomes all dangers.

Arch 7 Colour Orpheus reaches the centre of the Underworld and confronts its rulers, Hades, Persephone and Hecate. He does not notice that they mirror himself, Eurydice and the Oracle.

Arch 8 Secrecy Orpheus continues his singing.

Arch 9 Glass He makes his escape.

Arch 10 Buildings He is surrounded by shadows of Eurydice.

Arch 11 Weather The shadows dance before him but he does not select one.

Arch 12 Eyes Orpheus begins his return, thinking Eurydice is following him, but it is Persephone.

Arch 13 Knives Persephone stumbles and another Eurydice replaces her. As Orpheus overcomes all the dangers she tries to leave the Underworld, but cannot; Apollo urges Orpheus to sing.

Arch 14 Animals Orpheus crosses the Styx. Charon refuses to carry Eurydice and she falls away.

As Orpheus meets the sunlight the memory of Eurydice fades.

Arch 15 Ropes Orpheus has lost Eurydice for ever.

Arch 16 Order Orpheus realizes his journey was a dream, and re-enacts it as Orpheus Hero.

Arch 17 Fear Orpheus mourns Eurydice, rejecting three offers of marriage.

(Allegorical Flower: Hyacinth)

Orpheus hangs himself.

Act 3 The dramatic structure of the act is based upon the movements of the tides, as it explores Orpheus's reputation, the beginnings of Orphism and his destruction by Apollo. Nine episodes of the myth are presented in a time-sequence that begins by moving backwards, then moves into the future and finally returns to the past. Between the episodes, Orpheus sings the verses of his Song of Magic, eventually challenging Apollo. The act begins with the third time-distortion: Orpheus Hero is rejected by the Underworld and re-created as a myth.

Episode 1 Orpheus Hero re-enacts his return from the Underworld and his suicide.

Episode 2 Orpheus Man sings of his descent to the Underworld.

Episode 3 Eurydice's death is viewed by Orpheus Man and Hero.

(Allegorical Flower: Lotus)

Episode 4 Orpheus Hero re-enacts his journey from the Underworld, with the same result.

Episode 5 Aristaeus is punished by his bees and is consoled by Orpheus; Zeus kills Orpheus with a thunderbolt for daring to reveal divine mysteries through his art.

Episode 6 Orpheus Myth is dismembered by the Dionysiac women.

Episode 7 His head floats down the river Hebrus.

Episode 8 Orpheus Myth has become an oracle, consulted by Aristaeus. Apollo eventually silences him for challenging his own Delphic oracle.

(Passing Cloud: Pentheus)

Episode 9 The sacrifice of Orpheus Myth is resumed from Episode 6, as the women eat his flesh.

Exodus The myth of Orpheus decays.

*

Complicated as the dramatic structure of *The Mask of Orpheus* is, its musical structure is substantially more intricate. Like Birtwistle's *Punch and Judy* it is designed as a 'number opera' but one in which the closed forms are interlocked and superimposed; its components owe very little to traditional notions of operatic structure. In the second act, for example, each verse of Orpheus's Song of Magic is itself broken down into four sections: a dream (aria), fantasy (recitative), nightmare (speech) and finally silence. As the journey progresses, however, the verses contract and their proportions alter, until at the 15th Arch the nightmare element takes over completely. Such careful plotting is built into each section of the opera, and it is underpinned by an independent orchestral structure that is, as Birtwistle describes it, 'through-composed'; 'the orchestra, even though it responds to the events on stage, has a life of its own'. The structures of the stage music and the orchestral music coincide only once, at the climax of the work in the third act, when the principal characters are represented only by puppets. The electronic elements, for the voice of Apollo and the interludes of the mime troupe, add yet another independent layer.   A.C.

Masnadieri, I ('The Bandits')

Melodramma in four acts by Giuseppe Verdi to a libretto by Andrea Maffei after Friedrich von Schiller's play *Die Räuber*; London, Her Majesty's Theatre, 22 July 1847.

At the première Jenny Lind sang Amalia, Italo Gardoni was Carlo, Filippo Coletti was Francesco, and Luigi Lablache sang Massimiliano.

Massimiliano, Count Moor	bass
Carlo *his son*	tenor
Francesco *brother to Carlo*	baritone
Amalia *orphan, the Count's niece*	soprano
Arminio *the Count's treasurer*	tenor
Moser *a pastor*	bass
Rolla *a companion of Carlo Moor*	tenor
Wayward youths (later bandits), women, children, servants	
Setting Germany, at the beginning of the 18th century	

The lucrative contract to compose an opera for Her Majesty's Theatre in London was an important sign of Verdi's burgeoning international reputation, and the occasion allowed him to write for some of the most famous singers of the age. More than that, the librettist was his friend Andrea Maffei, a distinguished man of letters with a reputation far above that of Piave or Solera, who had supplied most of Verdi's earlier librettos. However, all this notwithstanding, *I masnadieri* had a troublesome birth: Maffei's lack of experience in theatrical matters was a considerable trial; Verdi quarrelled with the publisher of the opera, Francesco Lucca (with whom he never had the generally cordial relations he enjoyed with the rival firm, Ricordi); and when he arrived in London to supervise the production, he seems to have been oppressed beyond all reason by the detested English weather. The première was a magnificent gala occasion – Queen Victoria headed the guests of honour – and a triumphant success, aided by the fame of the singers, especially Lind and Lablache, one of the great names of the previous generation of Italian singers. But the enthusiastic reception was short-lived, and the opera fared rather badly in Italy. Modern revivals are not uncommon, but they remain special occasions: it seems unlikely that the work will find a permanent place in the international repertory.

*

A lachrymose cello solo, written expressly for Alfredo Piatti, principal cellist at Her Majesty's Theatre, forms a brief but effective prelude.

Act I.i *A tavern on the frontier of Saxony* In a formally conventional, carefully crafted double aria with chorus, Carlo muses on his distant homeland and his beloved Amalia (the Andante 'O mio castel paterno') before receiving a letter from his brother, who tells him that he is forbidden to return home. He and his friends decide to become bandits and swear an oath of blood brotherhood (the cabaletta 'Nell'argilla maledetta').

I.ii *Franconia: a room in Massimiliano's castle* A rapid change of locale is effected for a second double aria, this time for Carlo's wicked brother, Francesco. In the angular 'La sua lampada vitale' Francesco threatens to hasten the end of his father's life. He then orders that Massimiliano be told of Carlo's death in battle, hoping that shock and grief will finish the old man off. In a forceful cabaletta, 'Tremate, o miseri!', he eagerly looks forward to assuming power.

I.iii *A bedroom in the castle* After a prelude in which solo woodwind are prominent, Amalia looks at the sleeping Massimiliano and thinks back over past joys in 'Lo sguardo avea degli angeli'. The aria was clearly written with Jenny Lind in mind: it is far more highly ornamented than the usual Verdian model and, to accommodate the free flow of decoration, formally far more discursive. Massimiliano awakes and, in a short duet movement with Amalia, 'Carlo! io muoio', laments that he will die without seeing his favourite son. Arminio and Francesco enter to deliver the false news of Carlo's death, saying that Carlo's dying words accused his father and instructed Amalia to marry Francesco. This revelation precipitates the quartet 'Sul capo mio colpevole': Massimiliano is both repentant and furious with Francesco; Amalia (joined by a reformed Arminio) offers religious consolation; Francesco eagerly looks forward to his triumph. It is a powerfully effective clash of emotions, and ends as Massimiliano, seemingly lifeless, falls to the ground.

Act 2.i *An enclosure adjoining the castle chapel* Time has passed, and Francesco is lord of the castle. Amalia visits Massimiliano's grave and in a simple Adagio, 'Tu del mio Carlo al seno', imagines him and Carlo together in heaven. Arminio rushes in to reveal

that Carlo and Massimiliano are both alive. Amalia rejoices in a jubilant and distinctly old-fashioned cabaletta, 'Carlo vive?', which again gave ample opportunity for Jenny Lind to demonstrate her famed agility. Francesco enters to declare his love for Amalia and they launch into a four-movement soprano–baritone confrontation duet, a type of dramatic situation at which Verdi almost always succeeded magnificently. But for once the format proves disappointing: the Andantino 'Io t'amo, Amalia' dissolves too quickly into routine rhythmic unison at the 3rd or 6th, and the cabaletta 'Ti scosta, o malnato', in which Amalia defies Francesco's attempts to take her by force, deals unimaginatively with the clash of tessituras that many of Verdi's best examples exploit so powerfully.

2.ii *The Bohemian forest near Prague* The 'Scena e Coro' offers a typical slice of bandit life, though the choral writing is more complex than Verdi usually ventured. Rolla, condemned to be hanged, is rescued by Carlo and his followers, who rejoice in their carefree life. They leave Carlo alone to lament his outcast state in a fine minor–major *romanza*, 'Di ladroni attorniato'. His companions return to report that they are under attack and all join in a warlike chorus.

Act 3.i *A deserted place adjacent to the forest near Massimiliano's castle* Amalia has escaped from Francesco but is now alone and terrified to hear the sound of bandits nearby. She begs for mercy from the first man she sees: miraculously, he turns out to be Carlo, and the lovers are blissfully united in a duet. The first lyrical movement, 'Qual mare, qual terra', is perhaps a trifle dull, although colouristic vocal effects in part make up for a lack of the usual confrontational tension. Amalia tells Carlo of his father's death, and of Francesco's attempts on her virtue. They join in a closing cabaletta, 'Lassù risplendere', in which Amalia has yet more opportunity to display her trills and agility.

3.ii *Inside the forest* A further, rather jaunty bandits' chorus introduces the 'Finale Terzo'. Carlo wrestles with his Byronic soul and even contemplates suicide, but is interrupted by Arminio, whom he sees delivering food to someone imprisoned in a deserted tower. Carlo intervenes, bringing forth from the tower an emaciated old man who reveals himself as Massimiliano. In an impressive minor–major narrative, 'Un ignoto, tre lune or saranno', Massimiliano (who has not recognized his son) tells how Francesco had him confined there after he recovered from his collapse. Carlo is outraged, and calls on his fellow bandits to join him in swearing a solemn oath of vengeance against Francesco.

Act 4.i *A suite of rooms in Massimiliano's castle* Francesco's 'Pareami che sorto da lauto convito' describes a frightening vision of divine retribution in a movement that prefigures the great soliloquies of Verdi's middle-period operas. He summons Moser and asks forgiveness for his sins: only God can grant forgiveness, the pastor answers. Prompted by signs that the castle is under attack, Francesco rushes off to meet his fate.

4.ii *The forest (as 3.ii)* Carlo will not reveal his identity to Massimiliano but nevertheless asks for 'a father's blessing'. In a gentle duet, 'Come il bacio d'un padre amoroso', father and son are vocally united. The robbers appear, having captured Amalia, and very soon Carlo's identity is revealed. In a final trio 'Caduto è il reprobo!', reminiscent of the parallel number in Act 4 of *Ernani*, Carlo rails against his commitment to the life of crime while Amalia offers to stay with him no matter what may befall. But Carlo's robber companions are near at hand, impossible to ignore: in a final declamatory passage, he stabs Amalia and rushes off to the gallows that await him.

*

I masnadieri is one of the most intriguing of Verdi's early works. It should have been a great success: a foreign commission of great prestige, a high Romantic basis in Schiller (one of the composer's favourite sources), a distinguished man of letters as the librettist, a cast of international standing. What is more, Verdi and his librettist consciously tried to break with certain longstanding traditions in order to make their creation more romantically intense: no other early opera dispenses with an opening chorus, for example, or with a concertato finale. But all these ingredients proved problematic. Verdi felt out of touch and out of sympathy with the English environment and may have been unsure of the audience's taste and requirements; the drama proved somewhat unwieldy, particularly in its lack of opportunities for character confrontation; Maffei, in spite of his poetic skills and willingness to experiment, was unsure of himself in dramatic pacing; and the cast, Jenny Lind in particular, inspired music which, though distinguished enough on its own, proved difficult to subsume under an overall dramatic colour, the achievement of which was so crucial to Verdian success.   R.P.

Mathis der Maler ('Mathis the Painter')

Opera in seven scenes by Paul Hindemith to his own libretto; Zürich, Stadttheater, 28 May 1938.

The cast at the first performance included Asger Stig (Mathis), Peter Baxevanos (Cardinal Albrecht), Judith Hellwig (Ursula), Leni Funk (Regina), Fritz Honisch (Pommersfelden) and Marko Rothmüller (Truchsess von Waldburg).

Mathis *a painter*	baritone
Cardinal Albrecht	tenor
Hans Schwalb *peasant leader*	tenor
Regina *his daughter*	soprano
Sylvester *an army officer*	tenor
Riedinger	bass
Ursula *his daughter*	soprano
Pommersfelden *dean of Mainz Cathedral*	bass
Capito *the Cardinal's counsellor*	tenor
Count Helfenstein	silent
Countess Helfenstein	contralto
Truchsess von Waldburg *army leader*	bass

Setting Mainz in *c*1525, during the Peasants' War

The action takes place at the time of the Peasants' War, an event that followed the Reformation. Mathis is based on the painter Matthias Grünewald, whose major work, the Isenheim altarpiece, is the inspiration for some scenes in the opera. In Scene 1, Mathis is working on a fresco in a monastery when the peasants' leader, Schwalb, who is wounded, bursts in with his young daughter Regina. Schwalb reproaches Mathis for spending his time painting while his fellow beings are fighting for their lives. A cavalry group led by Sylvester comes in search of Schwalb, and Mathis helps him and Regina escape. In Scene 2, the citizens of Mainz, Catholics and Protestants, are quarrelling as they wait in the palace of Martinsburg for the cardinal archbishop's return. Cardinal Albrecht, after acknowledging their greetings, dismisses them, retaining only Riedinger, a rich Protestant citizen, and Ursula, his daughter. Mathis joins them and, while the cardinal is engaged with Riedinger, he and Ursula reveal their love. Riedinger complains to the cardinal of a Catholic order to burn Lutheran books, and Albrecht, who is dependent on Riedinger for money, countermands the order. After Riedinger's departure, however, he is persuaded by the dean of Mainz Cathedral, Pommersfelden, to allow the burning. Sylvester enters and, recognizing Mathis, denounces him for letting the peasant leader escape. When Mathis pleads for the peasants, Albrecht tells him not to meddle in political matters. Mathis, asserting that he cannot paint while his fellow men go in fear, demands his release from Albrecht's service. Pommersfelden orders Mathis's arrest, but Albrecht decides he should be allowed to go in peace.

Scene 3 opens in Riedinger's house where Lutherans are hiding books; a fire can be seen burning outside in the market-place. Their attempts are foiled by Albrecht's counsellor Capito, and soldiers carry off the books. Capito overcomes the Lutherans' anger by producing a letter from Luther to the cardinal, urging him to marry a Protestant, thus bringing reconciliation to his people. Ursula, entering, is asked whether she would be prepared to serve the cause by marrying a man chosen for her. Left alone, Ursula is full of foreboding and, when Mathis enters, she begs him to take her away with him. Despite his love, Mathis declines, since he is going to join the rebel peasants. As they sing their farewells, Lutherans and Catholics in the market-place exchange insults; the books burn.

In Scene 4, set in a ruined village, peasants have captured Count and Countess Helfenstein. As the Count is led off to execution, they threaten the Countess with rape. They scorn Mathis's efforts to restrain them and finally strike him down. Schwalb, entering with Regina, puts an end to the quarrel by warning them of approaching troops. In the ensuing battle Schwalb is killed. The army leader, Truchsess von Waldburg, wants to arrest Mathis, but the Countess pleads for him. Mathis is left alone with Regina, weeping over her father's body. In Scene 5, in the cardinal's office, Capito attempts to persuade Albrecht to marry a rich heiress: the alternative is bankruptcy. Albrecht, discovering that his intended bride is Ursula, reproaches her for taking part in an 'ignoble bargain'. She replies that she consented to the marriage because she saw in him an enlightened prince who alone had the power to reconcile the warring people, and she begs him to devote himself to this cause. Albrecht, his conscience roused, vows to do so, but within his church, eschewing both riches and marriage. Ursula makes a similar renunciation.

In Scene 6 Mathis and Regina, fleeing from the fighting, have taken refuge in a forest. After singing the child to sleep, Mathis muses bitterly on his abject state: he has signally failed to help his fellow men. He experiences a series of visions, in which he, as St Anthony, is confronted with figures from his past: the Countess (representing luxury); Ursula (succes-sively as beggar, prostitute and martyr); Schwalb (warlord); Capito (man of learning); and Pommers-felden (merchant). A chorus of demons, as depicted in the Isenheim altarpiece, torments him, to be succeeded by another scene from the polyptych: the meeting of St Paul and St Anthony. St Paul (Albrecht) encourages Mathis to return to his painting and use the gift God gave him for the betterment of mankind.

In Scene 7 Mathis sits in his studio in Mainz surrounded by his pictures and drawings, while Ursula watches over Regina, who is dying. Her death is followed by an orchestral interlude. When the lights come up, Mathis is alone in his studio, now bare except for a table containing his last few possessions and an empty chest. Albrecht comes to visit him. Mathis tells him that his work is done, and all that now remains for him is 'like a beast in the forest to seek a place to die'. After Albrecht has gone, Mathis begins quietly to pack the chest.

*

Hindemith spent two years (July 1933 to July 1935) composing the words and music of the opera, and its related symphony. It was the result of his desire, already heralded by his *Gebrauchsmusik* period, to write in a more popular way. Consequently *Mathis*, though composed in numbers, is contrapuntally less rigid than *Cardillac*, and the music is based to a large extent on folksong and church choral music, though only occasionally are these quoted directly. Another unifying factor lies in the tonal relationships, based on ideas which Hindemith developed while teaching in Berlin and subsequently expounded in his book *Unterweisung im Tonsatz*. However, there is nothing academic about the opera, which is a powerful expression, clearly autobiographical, of the dilemma of an artist in times of political strife. Both words and music are skilfully used to present the main characters (Mathis, Albrecht, Ursula, Regina) as living human beings, and the lyrical scenes are as touching as the more spectacular ones (the book-burning, the temptation of St Anthony) are dramati-cally exciting. *Mathis der Maler* is without doubt Hindemith's operatic masterpiece. Difficulties with the Nazis prevented its production in Germany until 1946, since when it has become well established in the repertory.   G.Sk.

Matrimonio segreto, Il ('The Secret Marriage')

Melodramma giocoso in two acts by Domenico Cimarosa to a libretto by Giovanni Bertati, after George Colman the elder and David Garrick's play *The Clandestine Marriage*; Vienna, Burgtheater, 7 February 1792.

The original cast included Dorothea Bussani (Fidalma), Irene Tomeoni (Carolina), Giambattista Serafino Blasi (Geronimo), Francesco Benucci (Count Robinson), Giuseppina Nettelet (Elisetta) and Santi Nencini (Paolino), who went to Vienna in 1790 from Eszterháza, where he had performed in several of Cimarosa's operas.

Carolina ⎱	*Geronimo's*	soprano
Elisetta ⎰	*daughters*	mezzo-soprano
Paolino *young clerk to Geronimo*		tenor
Geronimo *a rich merchant*		bass
Fidalma *his sister*		contralto
Count Robinson		bass
Setting Geronimo's house in 18th-century Bologna		

The opera's initial success was partly due to the cast, and the particularly happy combination of Blasi and Benucci in their Act 2 duet 'Se fiato in corpo avete' brought the house down at the première.

The Emperor Leopold II, who attended, was so impressed that, after offering dinner to all the performers, he had them repeat the opera in a private performance on the same day. This was quite a feat considering that, according to contemporary reports, the première lasted close to three hours because of public acclamation and the repetition of arias and ensembles.

Bertati's text found a perfect match in Cimarosa's music. The unfavourable comments of Bertati's fellow poets are clearly biased. A letter from the librettist Giambattista Casti to Lorenzo da Ponte exemplifies the intrigues and back-stabbings prevalent in operatic circles at the Viennese court: 'Last evening came the première of *Il matrimonio segreto*. The music is marvellously beautiful, but the words fell very far below expectations, and everyone is dissatisfied, particularly the singers'. Da Ponte, to whom Casti had also sent a copy of the libretto, replied: 'Bertati's verses are what they might have been expected to be. Let Vienna swallow them' (this from a man who fashioned his own *Don Giovanni* for Mozart after Bertati's text, which was set to music by Giuseppe Gazzaniga).

The plot of *Il matrimonio segreto* derives in part from the elder Colman and Garrick's *The Clandestine Marriage* (1766, London), which in turn was inspired by William Hogarth's series of etchings *Marriage à la mode*. Two earlier operas on the same topic might have influenced Bertati: the French comedy with music *Sophie, ou Le mariage caché* (1768, Paris), with text by Mme Riccoboni and music by Josef Kohaut; and the one-act comic opera *Le mariage clandestin* (1790, Paris), with text by Joseph Alexandre Pierre de Ségur and music by François Devienne.

Cimarosa's opera, given in Vienna exactly two months after Mozart's death, enjoyed a greater success than any of Mozart's operas, with the possible exception of *Così fan tutte*. Up to the end of the century it had over 70 performances in Vienna alone and was still being given there in 1884, with revisions by J. N. Fuchs. Eduard Hanslick wrote that the opera was 'full of sunshine . . . it had that genuine light golden colour, which is the only fitting one for a musical comedy'. By the time he composed it Cimarosa's orchestration had acquired a fuller and richer sonority than in his early works; independent motivic and rhythmic material serves as commentary on the action.

The opera attained instant international fame, and in the first two years after its première was presented in Leipzig, Dresden, Berlin, Paris, Milan, Florence, Naples, Turin, Madrid and Lisbon, among other cities. In the first half of the 19th century it was performed in ten translations, often reworked with titles such as *Die heimliche Ehe*, *Le mariage secret*, *Der adelsüchtige Bürger*, *Il segreto e l'intrigo della lettera*, *Lo sposalizio segreto* and *Il matrimonio notturno*. It was even performed in Calcutta (1870). It was given on 23 April 1933 at the Library of Congress, Washington, DC, and is one of the few late 18th-century *opere buffe* to receive occasional revivals.

Some celebrated singers also furthered its fame throughout the 19th century. The bass Luigi Lablache sang the role of Geronimo at the King's Theatre, London, and the Théâtre Italien, Paris, in 1830. Maria Malibran's Carolina, Antonio Tamburini's Count and Giovanni Battista Rubini's Paolino were also noteworthy. While the opera conquered Paris audiences throughout the 1830s and 40s, Berlioz found it tiring. Schumann considered it masterly in its writing and instrumentation but musically uninspiring.

*

Act I The musical world of Mozart has already been re-created in the Largo of the overture with three initial D major chords. The brilliant orchestration of flutes, oboes, clarinets, horns, trumpets, timpani and strings not only provides a festive atmosphere but shows a melodic effusiveness and inventiveness full of verve, vitality and exuberance. The light, whirling string figures that open the Allegro moderato sections recall the beginning of the overture to *Le nozze di Figaro*.

As the curtain rises Paolino and Carolina, who have been secretly married for several months, are discussing how they will break their news to her father without antagonizing him too much. They hope that Geronimo, who aspires to join the ranks of the nobility, will be appeased through the wedding of his elder daughter, Elisetta, to Count Robinson. Paolino has arranged this match in the hope of pleasing Geronimo so much that, when he learns of the secret wedding of Paolino and Carolina, he will forgive them. The duet 'Cara non dubitar', the following recitative and the duet 'Io ti lascio', present a continuous opening scene, unified by the recurrence of the initial string figures of the overture which are combined with witty interjections for solo oboe. It is a remarkably tender and touching love duet.

Paolino delivers a letter from the Count to Geronimo, whose deafness is a source of humour. Once he realizes that the Count is asking for Elisetta's hand, Geronimo rejoices at the prospect of his daughter becoming a countess in the aria 'Udite tutti, udite'; it begins Andante maestoso, but changes to an Allegro of unbridled enthusiasm, with dotted rhythms and leaps in the orchestral parts depicting Geronimo's joy at the words 'Che saltino i dinari'. The aria is a wonderful portrayal of the varying moods of the dramatic situation, ranging from sections in rapid parlando to a slower pacing at Geronimo's realization that Elisetta does not share his joy, and a sudden recovery of the original joyful mood (with a shift in tonality from A major to ♭ major), with a faster ending at 'La festa si prepara'. This was one of the most popular numbers at the opera's première.

Elisetta, quickly assuming the airs of a countess, accuses her younger sister of treating her with disrespect. The ensuing agitated trio for Carolina, Elisetta and Fidalma, 'Le faccio un inchino', another highlight of the opera, is an excellent characterization of the verbal aggression between the sisters: Carolina ridicules Elisetta in a parlando line, and Fidalma attempts to act as peacemaker. Despite Fidalma's good life with her brother, her state of widowhood does not please her; she too has nuptial intentions, and the object of her affections is Paolino.

The plot is complicated by the Count's pompous entrance and his attempt to identify his bride. He approaches Carolina, then Fidalma and, when he finds out that the least attractive, Elisetta, is to be his spouse, he is shocked and disappointed. The ensuing quartet, 'Sento in petto un freddo gelo', for Carolina, Fidalma, Elisetta and the Count, is an excellent depiction of four disparate sets of thoughts and sentiments. The situation is now quite out of hand for Carolina and Paolino; not only will the Count have nothing to do with Elisetta but he wants to marry Carolina instead. Pandemonium breaks out in the Act 1 finale as Elisetta accuses her younger sister of seducing the Count, while Geronimo's deafness prevents him from hearing or understanding the commotion.

Act 2 A duet for Geronimo and the Count, 'Se fiato in corpo avete', cleverly depicts their differences, as the Count tells Geronimo that he will not marry Elisetta, while Geronimo insists that he will. There is a complete change in the character of the music when the Count's proposal to marry Carolina for only half the original dowry is met with enthusiasm. The young lovers' misfortune worsens with Fidalma's declaration of love for Paolino. In a beautiful bel canto aria with clarinet solo ('Pria che spunti in ciel aurora') Paolino decides that he and Carolina must run away. The finale is a nocturnal scene, in which each character emerges from his or her bedroom and catches the lovers in the act of escaping. Paolino and Carolina admit that they are married; the Count, in a quick about-face, decides to marry Elisetta; and Geronimo accepts and forgives.

*

The directness, exuberance, spontaneity, gracefulness and musical sincerity of this opera gave it an international appeal. With a libretto that presents the action in clear strokes, uncomplicated by disguises and mistaken identities, it successfully depicts the misfortunes of a young couple who dare to contradict the established social codes. A sentimental comedy along the lines of Samuel Richardson's *Pamela*

(1740), it celebrates the naturalness popularized by Rousseau. Though not a satire, it is an expression of contemporary values and social mores. The aristocrat, Count Robinson, is a laughable, comic figure, as is Geronimo, whose aristocratic aspirations override paternal concern for his younger daughter's feelings. The music is at times almost Romantic in expression, especially in Paolino's 'Pria che spunti in ciel aurora'. In its clever use of parlando as a comic device it bridges the gap between the 18th-century *intermezzo comico per musica* and the operas of Rossini and Donizetti.   G.La.

May Night [*Mayskaya noch'*]

Opera in three acts by Nikolay Andreyevich Rimsky-Korsakov to his own libretto after Nikolay Vasil'yevich Gogol's story 'Mayskaya noch', ili Utoplennitsa' ('May Night, or The Drowned Maiden') from his collection *Evenings on a Farm near Dikanka* (i, 1831); St Petersburg, Mariinsky Theatre, 9/21 January 1880.

The first performance was conducted by Eduard Nápravník, with Fyodor Stravinsky as the Village Head and Ivan Mel'nikov as the Charcoal Burner.

Village Head	bass
Levko *his son*	tenor
Hanna	mezzo-soprano
Charcoal Burner	baritone or high bass
Village Clerk	bass
Distiller	tenor
Sister-in-law *of the Village Head*	contralto
Pannochka-Rusalka ('Little Lady Water Nymph')	soprano
Brood-hen ⎫ *water nymphs*	
Raven ⎬ *(coryphées)*	mezzo-sopranos
Stepmother ⎭	

Lads, girls, bailiff's men, water nymphs (spirits of drowned maidens)

Setting A Ukrainian village; the time is unspecified

Gogol's early Ukrainian tales, full of evocative song and dance, and peopled with characters borrowed from the folk puppet theatre and the vaudeville stage, are little operas in search of a composer. *May Night*, in particular, the subject of planned or finished operas by Alexander Nikolayevich Serov and Mykola Vitaliyovych Lysenko in addition to Rimsky-Korsakov, embodies a theme originating in German folklore but well known to urban Russians in the early 19th century in the form of a celebrated Singspiel, Kauer's *Das Donauweibchen*. As Russified – or rather, 'Little-Russianized' – by Stepan Davïdov under the title *Lesta, ili Dnevprovskaya rusalka* ('Lesta, or The Dnepr Water Nymph'), it played the Russian stage in various versions between 1803 and 1854 and was at its height of popularity in the early 1830s when Gogol wrote his tale. The way *May Night* begins already shows how reminiscences of operas and Singspiels were guiding the author's pen:

A ringing song flowed like a river down the streets of the village. It was the hour when, weary from the cares and labours of the day, the lads and girls gather together in the glow of the clear evening to pour out their gaiety in strains never far removed from melancholy. The brooding evening dreamily embraced the dark blue sky, transforming everything into vagueness and distance. It was already dusk, but the singing did not cease. Levko, a young Cossack, son of the Village Head, slipped away from the singers with a bandura in his hands. He was wearing an astrakhan cap. He walked down the street thrumming on the strings and dancing to it. At last he stopped quietly before the door of a cottage surrounded with low-growing cherry trees. Whose cottage was it? Whose door was it? After a few moments of silence, he began playing and singing:

Solntse nizen'ko	The sun is low,
vechir blizen'ko,	the evening's nigh,
Viidi do mene,	Come out to me,
moyo serden'ko!	my little heart!

In the space of a paragraph we have a chorus, a dance to the bandura and a solo song. No wonder, as Rimsky-Korsakov tells us in his memoirs, his wife kept insisting that he compose an opera on this subject, until in 1877 he gave in. Rimsky allowed Gogol for the most part to dictate the succession of musical numbers, and wherever possible he drew on authentic folk materials, particularly the collection of Ukrainian folksongs published in 1872 by his St Petersburg Conservatory colleague Alexander Rubets, from which he chose eight songs. With its feast of folksong, *May Night* was not only a faithful counterpart to its literary prototype. It was also a fulfilment of Gogol's own prophecy – made in 1836, the year of *A Life for the Tsar* – that Glinka's example would lead to opera made out of 'our national life'.

*

Act I *A village street* The curtain rises on a group of lads and lasses enacting a ritual game song about planting ('A mï proso seyali': 'Ah, the millet did we sow', incorporating tunes from three collections, those of Rubets, Balakirev and Rimsky himself). Levko enters, singing to his bandura the song quoted above (set to a Rubets tune). Hanna comes to the door; they banter, Levko announcing his determination to marry her over his father's objections; they confess their love. At Hanna's request, Levko tells the tale of the old Squire's House (narrative, 'Davno eto bïlo': 'It happened long ago'): a widowed lieutenant

had lived there with a beautiful daughter; he took a wife who was a witch; turned out by her stepmother, the little lady had hurled herself into the lake and become a water nymph; with her companions, she dragged the evil stepmother into the lake and drowned her, but the stepmother also became a water nymph, and no one knows which. Levko and Hanna part as the girls' voices are heard off stage singing a Whitsun song (recitative and Trinity song, based on a Rubets tune). The Charcoal Burner staggers out, dead drunk, trying to dance the hopak and find his way home; the girls send him to the Village Head's house instead (hopak, 'Hop! Hop! Hop! Tra-la!'). The Village Head, Levko's father, approaches Hanna's house and tries to woo her; he is rebuffed, but Levko is infuriated and resolves to make a fool of his old dad (trio and chorus). He gathers some lads together and teaches them a scurrilous song about the Head.

Act 2.i *The interior of the Village Head's cottage* The Head, his Sister-in-law and a Distiller, who is to set up shop in the old Squire's House, discuss their affairs (in a trio, based on two Rubets tunes). The Charcoal Burner enters, thinking he is home; he curses the Village Head to himself; the Head is about to throw him out when a stone comes through the window; the Head curses the thrower, but is stopped by the Distiller, who tells a story of a curse that backfired on his mother-in-law. Levko and his friends strike up their 'song about the Head' from the street. The Head rushes out and comes back with Levko, disguised as a devil, with sooted face and sheepskin coat turned inside out, showing the black hide. The light suddenly goes out. Levko's friends rescue him and substitute the Sister-in-law, whom the Head locks up in a store-room. When the Clerk enters (to the strains of a Rubets tune) and informs him that they have captured the black-faced devil, the Head looks inside the store-room and discovers his indignant Sister-in-law, who departs muttering a stream of imprecations. Head, Clerk and Distiller rush out, vowing to settle with the boys.

2.ii *The street, before the village lock-up* After deliberating, the Head, the Clerk and the Distiller decide to burn the lock-up and the devil within. The Clerk decides that if whatever is within agrees to make the sign of the cross then it is not the devil. They open the door and out comes the Sister-in-law again, more furious than ever: she had been seized by the boys and again substituted for Levko. The village bailiffs rush in with the culprit – only it turns out to be the tipsy Charcoal Burner. Beside himself, the Head sends everyone out again in pursuit (finale).

Act 3 *The banks of the lake, before the old Squire's house* After an orchestral prelude evoking night in the Ukraine, Levko enters, pensive, and sings of Hanna ('spi, moya krasavitsa, sladko spi': 'sleep, my

'May Night' (Rimsky-Korsakov): scene from Act 3 of the 1894 production at the Mikhaylovsky Theatre, St Petersburg, with (left to right) M. M. Churprïnnikov (Levko), F. I. Stravinsky (Village Head), N. S. Klimov (Village Clerk), G. P. Ugrinovich (Distiller) and I. K. Goncharov (Charcoal Burner)

beauty, sleep sweetly'). To keep awake he strikes up another song, but is interrupted by Pannochka-Rusalka, soon joined by her water nymph companions, who sing and dance a *khorovod*. She asks Levko's help in discovering her stepmother, which he succeeds in doing by watching them play the game 'Who shall be Raven?' The nymphs turn on the culprit and drag her down. In gratitude, Pannochka-Rusalka hands Levko a letter to the Head. Levko, who cannot read it, wonders what it contains. At sunrise the Head, Clerk, Distiller and bailiffs enter in pursuit and are about to lock Levko up when the Clerk reads the letter, which is in the handwriting of the local commissar and which orders the Head to marry his son to Hanna at once (choral Whitsun songs, *Rusal'nïye*, based on Rubets tunes). Hanna enters in rapture, and the lads and lasses sing the praises of the bridal pair.

*

In its general approach to orchestration – that open-textured, primary-hued idiom that one instantly recognizes as Rimskian (abounding in 'leitmotivic' timbres such as the solo violin for Hanna, the ingénue) – as well as in countless effective details (the combination of piano and harp to represent the hero Levko's bandura, the *buffo* idiom of the Village Head, the sentimental romance style of the love duet, the polonaise rhythms in the Act 2 trio, the whole-tone

harmonies at moments of supernatural horror), the score is a homage to Glinka, particularly direct in the somewhat archaic but telling use of natural brass. While it was through imitating Glinka that Rimsky truly found himself, he added something all his own: a deliberate cultivation of the ritual aspects of folklore as a manifestation of the immemorial Slavonic agrarian religion.   R.T.

Mazepa ('Mazeppa')

Opera in three acts by Pyotr Il'yich Tchaikovsky to a libretto by Victor Burenin, revised by the composer and with an Act 2 insert aria for the title character to words by Vasily Kandaurov, after Alexander Sergeyevich Pushkin's poem *Poltava*; Moscow, Bol'shoy Theatre, 3/15 February 1884.

A simultaneous production by the Mariinsky Theatre had its first performance three days after the première. The Bol'shoy performance was conducted by Ippolit Al'tani, with Bogomir Korsov in the title role and Emiliya Pavlovskaya as Mariya; Eduard Nápravník conducted at St Petersburg, with Ippolit Pryanishnikov in the title role, Ivan Mel'nikov as Kochubey, Fyodor Stravinsky as Orlik and Mariya Kamenskaya as Lyubov'.

Mazeppa *Cossack captain*	baritone
Kochubey	baritone
Mariya *Kochubey's daughter*	soprano
Lyubov' *his wife*	mezzo-soprano
Andrey	tenor
Orlik	bass
Iskra	tenor
A drunken Cossack	tenor

Cossacks, women, servants, monks

Setting Russia at the end of the 17th century

Tchaikovsky's was the second opera to be based on Pushkin's poem about the notorious 17th-century Ukrainian Cossack leader. (The first, by a noble dilettante named Boris Viettinghoff-Schell, had been composed in 1858 and was performed the next year at the St Petersburg Bol'shoy Theatre.) Ivan Mazeppa sought independence from Russia through an alliance with Sweden, but was defeated at the Battle of Poltava. As the champion of a subject people he became a Romantic legend, hero or villain depending on attitudes to the Russian Empire. The libretto, meant originally for the cellist-composer Karl Davïdov, largely ignores the historical and military circumstances. The operatic Mazeppa does his dirt on a personal rather than political plane. He surprises his friend Vasily Kochubey, a Cossack judge, by demanding the hand of the latter's daughter Mariya, with whom he has reached an understanding despite the vast difference in their ages. Andrey tells Mariya he loves her, but realizes that she does not reciprocate his feelings (Act 1 scene i). To avenge what he sees as a dishonouring theft, Kochubey, through the agency of Andrey, denounces Mazeppa's separatist scheme to the tsar (1.ii). Disbelieved, he is remanded by Peter to Mazeppa, who has him tortured and condemned.

Act 2 scene i consists of an extended prison monologue followed by an interrogation by Mazeppa's henchman Orlik, all based in large part on Pushkin's original verses. Act 2 scene ii is also based closely on the poem; after the interpolated Kandaurov aria, it consists of a scene in which Mazeppa hints to Mariya of his ambition and exacts from her a pledge of devotion, followed by one in which Kochubey's wife Lyubov' warns her daughter of the impending execution. In Act 2 scene iii, Kochubey and his friend Iskra are beheaded before a crowd, Mariya and Lyubov' arriving a heartbreaking instant too late to prevent the act.

In Act 3 Andrey makes an attempt on Mazeppa and is mortally wounded. Mazeppa, now in flight from the tsar, finds Mariya deranged and abandons her. Andrey dies in the arms of the crazed girl, who mistakes him for an infant and sings him a lullaby that brings the opera to a striking *pianissimo* conclusion.

While this plot has all the makings of a pompous historical spectacle along the lines of *The Maid of Orléans*, the composer chose to make *Mazepa* a more inward lyric drama. Only the execution scene is handled in the grand manner, replete with military music. Elsewhere, heavy emphasis is placed on an unhappy romantic intrigue that was in part fabricated ad hoc: Andrey, the young Cossack lad in love with Mariya, has no counterpart in Pushkin. The quiet ending was in fact a brilliant second thought, replacing a more conventional finale published in the original vocal score in which Mariya met an Ophelia-like end accompanied by a chorus of horrified onlookers. Another such second thought was Mazeppa's Act 2 aria, in which he leaves no doubt that for all his amorality his love for Mariya is sincere.   R.T.

Médée (i) ('Medea')

Tragédie mise en musique in a prologue and five acts by Marc-Antoine Charpentier to a libretto by Thomas Corneille; Paris, Académie Royale de Musique (Opéra), 4 December 1693.

The title role was sung by Marthe Le Rochois; Creusa was sung by Mlle Moreau, Creon by Dun and Jason by Du Mesny, and Jean Bérain designed the scenery and costumes.

Médée [Medea] *princess of Colchis*	soprano
Nérine [Neris] *her confidante*	soprano
Jason *prince of Thessaly*	haute-contre
Arcas *confidant to Jason*	tenor
Créon [Creon] *King of Corinth*	bass
Oronte *prince of Argos*	baritone
Créuse [Creusa] *daughter of Creon*	soprano
Cléone *confidante to Creusa*	soprano
La Victoire [Victory]	soprano
Bellone *goddess of war*	soprano
La Gloire [Glory]	soprano

Corinthians, Argians, Love's captives, demons, phantoms

Setting Corinth in antiquity

Médée, Charpentier's only work for the Académie Royale de Musique, was perhaps the most important opera produced there in the decade after the death of Lully. The theorist and lexicographer Sébastien de Brossard considered it 'the one opera without exception in which one can learn the things most essential to good composition'. André Campra later included portions of the music in his pastiche opera *Télémaque*. Louis XIV personally complimented Charpentier on the work, and the king's brother and his eldest son attended several performances. The *Mercure galant* favourably mentioned the Italian

songs (2.vii) and praised in particular the performance of Le Rochois:

The passions are so vivid, particularly in Medea, that
when this role was but declaimed it did not fail to make a
great impression on the listeners. Judge for yourself if,
having given rise to beautiful music, Mlle Rochois, one of
the best singers in the world and who performs with
warmth, finesse and intelligence, shone in this role and
made the most of its beauties. All of Paris is enchanted
with the way that this excellent singer performs Medea,
and one cannot fail to admire her.

While Titon du Tillet and others proclaimed *Médée* a
critical success, Brossard pointed out that it was not
successful with the public. The *Journal de l'Opéra* lists
no performances after 15 March 1694, but it was
revived at Lille on 17 November 1700.

*

In the prologue rustics and shepherds praise Louis
XIV. They summon to earth Victory, Bellone,
goddess of war, and Glory. Victory, who has long
lived in France, will not favour those who envy
Louis' fame: they seek to prolong war, while Louis
wishes to bring peace to his kingdom.

Act I *A public place* The sorceress Medea has
gained Jason's love (and has borne him two children)
in return for help in obtaining the golden fleece; they
scheme to have King Pelias of Thessaly murdered,
but are discovered and flee to Corinth. When the act
begins Medea complains that Jason now loves the
princess Creusa who is betrothed to Oronte, prince of
Argos. Medea needs the protection of Oronte and
King Creon of Corinth to fend off the impending
attack by Thessaly. She reveals her plan for a
dreadful revenge should Creusa steal Jason's heart.
Jason tells Medea that their children are safe in the
care of Creusa. In return, Medea agrees to give her
superb robe to the princess. Jason, alone with Arcas,
weighs his debt to Medea against his love for Creusa.
A fanfare heralds Oronte's arrival. The Corinthian
and Argian soldiers enact in song and dance their
battle with the Thessalians.

Act 2 *A vestibule* Creon tells Medea he will fight
her enemies, but she must be banished as her
presence in his city is unsettling. Medea sadly
relinquishes her children into Creusa's care. Once she
is gone, Creon plans to keep both Jason and Oronte
in his service by means of their love for Creusa, to
defend his kingdom. Jason and Creusa sing a love

'Médée' (M.-A. Charpentier), Act 3 scene v: design by Jean Berain for the original production at the Paris Opéra (Académie
Royale de Musique), 4 December 1693

duet; they are joined by Oronte, and a chorus of Love's captives sings of the pains and pleasures of love.

Act 3 *A place set aside for Medea's evocations* Oronte offers asylum in Argos to Medea and Jason, but Medea tells him of Jason's love for Creusa. Medea and Oronte together vow revenge; Jason reassures Medea that he will join her after the battle. In a grand monologue Medea laments her unjust fate. When Creon decrees the marriage of Creusa and Jason, Medea prepares a poison with which to saturate the robe she has given to Creusa.

Act 4 *A palace with a magnificent garden* Medea and Oronte plot their revenge. Creon arrives to confront Medea, who uses her sorcery to summon madness. Left alone, Creon is overwhelmed by delusions.

Act 5 *Medea's palace* Creusa begs Medea to return Creon's reason, but a chorus of Corinthians announces that Creon has murdered Oronte and then turned his sword upon himself. Creusa vows revenge on Medea, but Medea activates the poison contained within her robe and she dies in Jason's arms. Medea then reveals to Jason the full extent of her vengeance: she has murdered their children.

*

Corneille's libretto presents a complicated love quadrangle between Medea, Jason, Creusa and Oronte which, together with a struggle between Corinth and Thessaly, slows the opera's pace for the first three acts. But when Medea begins her holocaust of revenge the dramatic tension intensifies. Especially striking is Charpentier's depth of musical characterization in the monologues of Medea, which run the gamut of passions from seething rage (1.i) to motherly love (2.ii), lamentation (3.iii), vengeance (3.iv and 4.v) and horror at her own actions (5.i). Corneille's libretto includes stock situations common to both French and Italian opera of the time, such as Creon's mad scene (4.ix) and Medea's incantation scene (3.v), alongside elements of the ballet de cour: the divertissement of Love's captives (2.vii) and the choruses and dances of the demons and furies (3.v–vii). Charpentier's music is a virtual compendium of instrumental and vocal forms (overture, *passacaille*, chaconne, recitative, arioso, *air*, lament, ensemble and chorus), and the attention he devotes to details of instrumentation, tempo and dynamics could serve as a guide to 17th-century orchestration.   J.S.P.

Médée (ii) ('Medea')

Opéra comique in three acts by Luigi Cherubini to a libretto by François-Benoît Hoffman; Paris, Théâtre Feydeau, 13 March 1797.

At the première the title role was sung by Julie-Angélique Scio, who was acclaimed for her interpretations of difficult declamatory parts and whose early death from tuberculosis was attributed to excessive vocal gymnastics in roles such as Medea. The first Jason was Pierre Gaveaux, also a renowned composer of *opéras comiques*.

Jason *leader of the Argonauts*		tenor
Médée [Medea] *his wife*		soprano
Néris [Neris] *her confidante*		mezzo-soprano
Créon [Creon] *King of Corinth*		bass
Dircé [Dirce] *his daughter*		soprano
First attendant		soprano
Second attendant		mezzo-soprano
Dirce's attendants, Argonauts, Corinthian citizens		
Setting Creon's palace and its surroundings in Corinth, in mythological ancient Greece		

With his move to France in 1785, the logical continuation of Cherubini's development would be in the direction of *tragédie lyrique*. To his chagrin, however, he was unable to break into the clique which ruled the taste of the Académie Royale [Impériale] de Musique, and consequently his most important contributions to 19th-century opera were made within the framework of *opéra comique*. The two most successful examples were *Médée* and *Les deux journées*. Although it received critical approval, *Médée* enjoyed only a *succès d'estime*, disappearing after 20 performances. Paris did not see another production until the mid-20th century. However, the Germans were taken with the work, performing it on numerous occasions throughout the 19th century. Margarete Schick was Medea in the first Berlin production (17 April 1800), for which the *Allgemeine musikalische Zeitung* published an extensive analysis; it was still being performed there in 1880. Franz Paul Lachner set the spoken dialogue to Wagnerian-style recitative in 1854 for a production in Frankfurt in 1855. This became the opera's standard form until the 1980s. *Médée* was introduced to Vienna in 1803, and it would appear that performances there in 1809 were the occasion for Cherubini to make extensive cuts of about 500 bars which were incorporated into a published edition of the period. It was revived again in 1812 for Anna Milder-Hauptmann and was still in repertory in 1871.

The opera's destiny in England and Italy was less fortunate. It was presented in London at Her Majesty's Theatre, Haymarket, on 6 June 1865 with Thérèse Tietjens in the title role and recitatives by Luigi Arditi. It was repeated on 30 December 1870 at Covent Garden. In Italy, it was not staged until 30 December 1909 at La Scala, in a translation by Carlo Zangarini; the edited score remained the standard Italian version until the 1980s. The reception was lukewarm, and there were no further performances until the 16th Maggio Musicale Fiorentino in 1952, when Maria Callas sang the title role and ensured the opera's renewed success in the 20th century. The original French version, with reduced spoken dialogue, was given at the Buxton Festival on 28 July 1984 and at Covent Garden on 6 November 1989.

*

Act 1 *A gallery in Creon's palace* Dirce's attendants are trying to assure her that she is right to marry Jason. Finally convinced, Dirce calls on Hymen to bless the forthcoming union ('Hymen, viens dissiper une vaine frayeur'). Creon promises Jason protection for his sons and Jason begs Dirce to accept the Argonauts' gifts. The March of the Argonauts follows, but the sight of the Golden Fleece brings back Dirce's earlier forebodings. Rather than stop the music at the end of the march Cherubini maintains the scene's momentum by having Dirce and Jason sing their first words concerning the fleece to musical accompaniment. Jason tries to calm Dirce by stating that Medea is probably dead. Creon incites her to have faith in the gods' generosity, and everyone invokes Hymen to bless the marriage in a hymnlike chorus. A stranger is announced and, entering, reveals herself to be Medea. She claims Jason but incurs the wrath of Creon, who orders her to depart. The act ends with a prolonged duet between Jason and Medea in which Medea alternately cajoles and threatens in an effort to persuade Jason to return to her ('Vous voyez de vos fils la mère infortunée').

Title-page of the full score of Cherubini's 'Médée' (Paris: Imbault, 1797), showing a scene from Act 3

Jason refuses, and both deplore the influence of the Golden Fleece on their lives ('O fatale Toison'). This scene is set almost entirely to music which closely follows the emotions of the participants, contributing to a profound understanding of their characters and motivation.

Act 2 *A wing of Creon's palace* After a short orchestral introduction the enraged Medea enters cursing Jason for preventing her from seeing her children. She summons the deities of Hades to help her wreak vengeance as Neris runs in, imploring her to hide from Creon's wrath. Medea, however, confronts him, pleading with him, in the first vocal music of the act, to allow her one day's respite to take leave of her children ('Ah! du moins accordez un azile'). In an extended ensemble in which the music faithfully mirrors everyone's passions, Creon, after much hesitation, grants Medea's wish. With Medea lost in contemplation, Neris laments the fate of her mistress ('Ah! nos peines seront communes'). Medea revives to plot her revenge. Jason reveals his affection for their sons. She begs to see them one last time ('Chers enfants'), to which Jason agrees as he leaves for pre-marriage ceremonies in the temple. Medea instructs Neris to have her children give a poisoned robe, crown and jewels as presents to Dirce. The curtain descends as the prayerful strains of the offstage ceremony to Hymen ('Fils de Bacchus descend des cieux') are punctuated by the onstage mutterings of Medea's vengeance.

Act 3 *A meadow in front of the temple* The final act is preceded by an orchestral interlude depicting the storm raging both in nature and in Medea's heart. She invokes the help of the gods as Neris enters with the children. Except for the dialogue concerning Dirce's acceptance of the gifts, the rest of the action is set to music of a forcefulness unheard of at this period. After Neris leaves, Medea curses her maternal weakness ('Eh quoi, je suis Médée') and, under cover of cries from the palace, where Dirce is consumed by the flames of the presents, drags the children into the temple to murder them. Jason rushes in with the people of Corinth but too late. Medea, wielding her knife and surrounded by the three Eumenides, appears in the temple doorway. She prophesies that Jason will wander homeless for the rest of his life and will meet her in Hades. As she rises into the air, the temple bursts into flames and the people, terror-stricken, flee as the curtain falls.

*

In its unmitigated horror, this opera has few equals. Its savage fury ties it closely to its Greek ancestry. Hoffman took one sentiment, revenge, and one action, murder, and expanded them into three hours of unrestrained emotion such as the French lyric stage had never seen. He provided excellent characterizations with which Cherubini could work, portraying the two principal characters in depth. Because of the spoken dialogue, *Médée* is classed as an *opéra comique*, although the first edition labels it simply *opéra*. There are no comic interludes, and most of the musical numbers are ensembles (nine, to three arias). In fact, the music of *Médée* gave way to mid-19th-century French and German grand opera, and not until Bizet's *Carmen* did it find a successor in style and form. As Brahms said: 'This *Médée* is the work we musicians recognize among ourselves as the highest peak of dramatic music.'   S.C.W.

Mefistofele ('Mephistopheles')

Opera in a prologue, five acts and an epilogue by Arrigo Boito to his own libretto after Johann Wolfgang von Goethe's play *Faust*; Milan, Teatro alla Scala, 5 March 1868 (revised version in four acts, Bologna, Teatro Comunale, 4 October 1875; second revised version, Venice, Teatro Rossini,13 May 1876).

The cast of the revised version (Bologna) included Erminia Borghi-Mamo (Margherita), Italo Campanini (Faust) and Romano Nannetti.

Mefistofele [Mephistopheles]	bass
Faust *a scholar*	tenor
Wagner *Faust's pupil*	tenor
Margherita *a simple girl*	soprano
Marta *Margherita's neighbour*	mezzo-soprano
Elena [Helen of Troy]	soprano
Pantalis *Helen's companion*	mezzo-soprano
Nereo *a Greek elder*	tenor
Heavenly host, cherubim, penitents, hunters,	
villagers, students, witches, warlocks, coryphaei	
and warriors	

Setting The empyrean, Frankfurt in the 16th century, and the banks of the Peneios

Mefistofele was the first opera at La Scala for which a composer was his own librettist. The first performance was a fiasco for several reasons, among them Boito's inexperience, the unworkable length of his 'reform' libretto and a largely inadequate cast. In addition, the advance promotion of the work by Boito's partisans and a few influential critics hoping for changes in conventional Italian opera antagonized a large sector of the conservative Milanese public and musical press. Only the Prologue in heaven was well received, but that came early in a stormy evening that lasted until well after midnight. Boito, his self-confidence deeply shaken, thoroughly revised and shortened the work. He eliminated two episodes that aroused particular opposition at the première: the scene at the emperor's court and an orchestral Battle Symphony. He recast the women's

chorus, 'La luna immobile', as a duet for soprano and contralto, and shortened the dialogue between Faust and Wagner in Act 1.i; he inserted the duet 'Lontano, lontano' in the Prison Scene, taking it from his discarded score of *Ero e Leandro*; he revised the arias for Faust and Margherita; and with the assistance of Cesare Dominiceti he modified the orchestration. Later he expanded the choral fugue at the end of the Brocken Scene. Indeed, there are few pages of the autograph, a veritable palimpsest, that do not show modifications introduced over the space of a decade or more.

The revised version of 1875, performed at Bologna and sung by a notable cast, aroused enthusiasm. For the next production of the work, at the Teatro Rossini, Venice, in 1876, Boito added, for Borghi-Mamo, Margherita's 'Spunta l'aurora pallida'. It is this definitive four-act version that is described below. The opera was first given in London at Her Majesty's Theatre on 6 July 1880, with Christine Nilsson, Campanini and Nannetti. Its first performance (in English) in the USA was at Boston on 16 November 1880. The work returned to La Scala on 25 May 1881, this time to great approval, sung by Maddalena Mariana-Masi, Marconi and Nannetti and conducted by Faccio. In all these productions the roles of Margherita and Helen of Troy were performed by the same singer, as Boito sought thereby to stress the concept of 'die ewige Weibliche' (the eternal feminine).

Revivals of *Mefistofele* in the 20th century have usually been associated with famous bass singers. The first was at La Scala on 16 March 1901, with Fyodor Shalyapin making his first appearance outside Russia, and with Caruso as Faust. The same role served for Shalyapin's North American début at the Metropolitan on 20 November 1907, with Farrar as Margherita. In the 1920s Nazzareno De Angelis was an impressive Mephistopheles, and he recorded the role. Since 1969 the work has been staged with some regularity at the New York City Opera, where the title role has been associated principally with Norman Treigle and Samuel Ramey.

*

Prologue *The empyrean* After echoing trumpet-calls the phalanxes of heaven praise the Lord. Mephistopheles offers to wager that he can gain the soul of Faust (aria, 'Ave, Signor'). A Chorus Mysticus gives the Lord's assent. Mephistopheles vanishes, whereupon cherubim, penitents and finally the whole heavenly host resume their canticle of praise.

Act 1.i *The square at Frankfurt* As merry-makers celebrate Easter Sunday, the elector and his retinue pass. Contemplating the arrival of spring, Faust is joined by his stuffy student, Wagner, who finds the crowds boring. They watch the dancing of a vigorous *obertas* (a Polish folk-dance). As evening descends,

Fyodor Shalyapin in the title role of Boito's 'Mefistofele'

Wagner superstitiously thinks of evil spirits, but Faust's attention is soon caught by a grey friar (rather than Goethe's poodle), who moves in mysterious circles. Wagner claims it to be a figment of Faust's imagination, but Faust closely observes the friar, who is apparently murmuring prayers, telling his rosary.

1.ii Faust's study, later that evening Faust enters, followed by the friar, who hides. The peaceful evening turns Faust's thoughts to God (aria, 'Dai campi, dai prati'). When he opens the Gospels a cry reveals the presence of Mephistopheles. Faust demands to know who his visitor is, and is informed that this is the Spirit of Denial (aria, 'Son lo spirito che nega sempre'). Mephistopheles offers to serve Faust in exchange for his soul. Faust agrees because if he can once think 'Stop, fleeting moment, you are beautiful' he will die without thought of the hereafter. The pact is quickly signed, the Devil spreads his cloak and off they fly.

Act 2.i Marta's garden Faust courts the shy Margherita while Mephistopheles teases her neighbour, Marta. Margherita asks Faust if he believes in God; he replies that he seeks a deeper truth, an ecstasy that he defines as 'Nature, Love, Mystery'. When he declares his love she replies that she sleeps with her mother, who slumbers lightly, whereupon Faust provides her with a narcotic, assuring her that no harm will ensue. In a breathless, syncopated

quartet the two couples proclaim their contrasting approaches to love.

2.ii A rugged mountain-top in the Harz A blood-red moon illuminates the scene as Faust and Mephistopheles climb up, accompanied by will-o'-the-wisps. Witches and warlocks arrive to celebrate the Witches' Sabbath. Mephistopheles seats himself on a rocky throne, seizes a globe of glass and in his aria, 'Ecco il mondo', tells Faust of the Earth's vileness. Laughing, he shatters the globe. The witches begin a wild dance. Faust sees a vision of Margherita, a blood-red necklace about her throat. The dance in celebration of the Witches' Sabbath grows more frenzied.

Act 3 A prison cell Margherita, her mind wandering, lies in chains. She thinks of the baby she has borne to Faust, which she is accused of drowning, and of her mother, with whose death by poisoning she is charged. Mephistopheles has led Faust to her cell and withdraws as Faust pleads with her to flee. Upset by Faust's impatience, she wonders why he does not kiss her. She confesses her crimes, telling him how she wants the graves of her victims arranged. Again he urges her to escape, and they imagine fleeing to an enchanted isle in the duet 'Lontano, lontano'. When Mephistopheles announces the dawn, Margherita confuses him with the headsman come to lead her to her death; then she recognizes him as the Devil himself. Praying for forgiveness, she rejects Faust as she dies. Heavenly voices proclaim her salvation as Mephistopheles drags Faust away.

Act 4 A flowery mead by the banks of the Peneios Helen of Troy and Pantalis greet the full moon, summoning sylphs and nereids. They withdraw as Faust and Mephistopheles appear, the former enchanted with his surroundings, the latter uneasy and unmoved by the dancing. Helen returns, obsessed by the burning of Troy. Faust addresses her in idealized terms, neatly rhymed, beguiling her with the way he fits sound to sound. They sing of their rapture in the duet 'Amore, misterio celeste' and retire to the grotto.

Epilogue Faust's study The aged Faust thinks of the emptiness of his experience. Now death is nigh he has a final dream: to rule over a prosperous populace in peace (aria, 'Giunto sul passo estremo'). Mephistopheles fears that Faust may yet elude him. While Faust clasps the Gospels, praying for salvation, Mephistopheles spreads his cloak, urging Faust to seek new adventures. As Faust dies, celestial voices welcome his soul to Heaven.

*

Boito's music is curiously uneven, often revealing his difficulty in developing ideas. It attains its greatest momentum in the Prison Scene (Act 3), in its revised form. The chorus of the heavenly phalanxes, 'Ave, Signor', from the Prologue returns at the end of the

Prison Scene and again at the conclusion of the opera, thereby endowing the work with an underlying coherence that it would not otherwise possess. Bernard Shaw summed up his reaction to *Mefistofele* in these terms: 'The whole work is a curious example of what can be done in opera by an accomplished literary man without original musical gifts, but with ten times the taste and culture of a musician of only ordinary extraordinariness.' **W.A.**

Meistersinger von Nürnberg, Die
('The Mastersingers of Nuremberg')

Music drama in three acts by Richard Wagner to his own libretto; Munich, Königliches Hof- und Nationaltheater, 21 June 1868.

At the première Franz Betz sang Sachs, Mathilde Mallinger, Eva; Pogner was sung by Kaspar Bausewein, Beckmesser by Gustav Hölzel, Walther by Franz Nachbaur.

Hans Sachs *cobbler*		bass-baritone
Veit Pogner *goldsmith*		bass
Kunz Vogelgesang *furrier*		tenor
Konrad Nachtigal *tinsmith*		bass
Sixtus Beckmesser *town clerk*		bass
Fritz Kothner *baker*	Mastersingers	bass
Balthasar Zorn *pewterer*		tenor
Ulrich Eisslinger *grocer*		tenor
Augustin Moser *tailor*		tenor
Hermann Ortel *soapmaker*		bass
Hans Schwarz *stocking weaver*		bass
Hans Foltz *coppersmith*		bass
Walther von Stolzing *a young knight from Franconia*		tenor
David *Sachs's apprentice*		tenor
Eva *Pogner's daughter*		soprano
Magdalene *Eva's nurse*		soprano
A Nightwatchman		bass

Citizens of all guilds and their wives, journeymen, apprentices, young women, people

Setting Nuremberg, about the middle of the 16th century

Wagner conceived *Die Meistersinger* in 1845 as a comic appendage to *Tannhäuser*, in the same way that a satyr play followed a Greek tragedy. His first prose draft for the work was written in Marienbad (Mariánské Lázně) in July that year, using Georg Gottfried Gervinus's *Geschichte der poetischen*

National-Literatur der Deutschen of 1835–42 for historical background. Other relevant volumes in Wagner's Dresden library include Jacob Grimm's *Über den altdeutschen Meistergesang* (1811), J. G. Büsching's edition of Hans Sachs's plays (1816–19) and Friedrich Furchau's life of Sachs (1820). The second and third prose drafts date from November 1861 (the former probably 14–16 November, the latter, containing minor revisions, prepared on 18 November for Schott). At this point, Wagner found J. C. Wagenseil's Nuremberg Chronicle of 1697 a particularly rich source of information on the ancient crafts and guilds and on other aspects of Nuremberg. Also evident are motifs from such contemporary stories as E. T. A. Hoffmann's *Meister Martin der Küfner und seine Gesellen*, which is set in 16th-century Nuremberg. Wagner completed the poem of *Die Meistersinger* on 25 January 1862 and began the composition in March or April. The full score was not completed until October 1867.

Even after the immensely successful première under Hans von Bülow in Munich, *Die Meistersinger* was taken up first by theatres of medium size, such as Dessau, Karlsruhe, Dresden, Mannheim and Weimar (all in 1869). The court operas of Vienna and Berlin followed in 1870. The work was first given at Bayreuth in 1888 under Hans Richter. The first performance in England was also under Richter, at the Theatre Royal, Drury Lane, in 1882, and in the USA under Anton Seidl, at the Metropolitan in 1886. Notable exponents of the role of Hans Sachs have included Edouard de Reszke, Anton van Rooy, Friedrich Schorr, Hans Hotter, Theo Adam, Dietrich Fischer-Dieskau, Karl Ridderbusch, Hans Sotin and Bernd Weikl. Walther has been sung by Jean de Reszke, Max Lorenz, Set Svanholm, Jess Thomas, René Kollo, Jean Cox, Placido Domingo, Siegfried Jerusalem and Ben Heppner. Eva has been sung by Emma Eames, Emmy Destinn, Elisabeth Rethberg, Lotte Lehmann, Elisabeth Schumann, Helen Donath, Hannelore Bode and Eva Marton. Notable conductors, besides Richter and Seidl, have included Carl Muck, Felix Mottl, Erich Leinsdorf, Bruno Walter, Reginald Goodall, Thomas Beecham, Rudolf Kempe, Georg Solti, Herbert von Karajan, Eugen Jochum, Silvio Varviso, and Wolfgang Sawallisch.

*

The prelude opens the work in an emphatic, magisterial C major, with a theme that celebrates the dignity of the Masters, at the same time possibly hinting at their air of self-importance (ex.l). A more pensive idea (ex.2) gives way to a pair of themes (exx.3 and 4), the first, of a fanfare-like nature, standing for the Masters and their guild. An elaborate modulation to E major introduces Walther and the theme of his passion (ex.5), later to form a part of his Prize Song. After an episode in E♭ (based on ex.1) depicting the chattering, bustling apprentices, three of these themes (exx.1, 3 and 5) are expansively combined before a grandiloquent coda.

Ex.1

Ex.2

Ex.3

Ex.4

Ex.5

Act I *Inside St Katharine's Church* The act opens with the congregation singing a sturdy C major chorale (of Wagner's invention), the phrases of which are interrupted by ex.2: Walther is urgently trying to communicate with Eva. At the end of the service, the church empties and Walther addresses Eva. He wishes to know whether she is betrothed, and though Eva sends away Magdalene to find first her handkerchief, then the clasp, and then her prayer-book, she never quite manages to stem Walther's impassioned flow with an answer. Magdalene finally tells him that Eva will marry the mastersinger who wins the song contest to be held the next day. Walther is left to be instructed in the rules of the mastersingers by David, Sachs's apprentice, with whom Magdalene is in love. In scene ii David, after some ribbing from his fellow apprentices, proceeds to initiate Walther into the secrets of his own master's art: a properly fashioned song is, after all, he says, like a well-made pair of shoes. His catalogue of the tones that have to be learnt ('Mein Herr!'), along with the appropriate rules (mostly taken by Wagner from Wagenseil) overwhelms Walther, but he sees that his only hope of winning Eva is by composing a mastersong in the approved manner. The apprentices, who have erected the wrong stage, put up the right one under David's supervision, to the accompaniment of their bustling semiquavers.

Eva's father, Pogner, now enters with the town clerk, Beckmesser (scene iii). Two tiny motifs are heard here, later much repeated both together and individually (ex.6). Pogner assures Beckmesser of his goodwill and welcomes Walther to the guild,

Ex.6

surprised as he is that Walther wishes to seek entry. Kothner calls the roll, to a contrapuntal working-out of ex.6. Pogner then announces the prize he intends to award to the winner of the song contest the next day ('Nun hört, und versteht mich recht!'). The first part of his address is based entirely on a new motif, ex.7. Then he changes to the style of an old-fashioned

Ex.7

recitative, accompanied by sustained chords, to tell how burghers such as they are regarded in other German lands as miserly. Returning to ex.7 and to an important idea derived from fig.x of ex.1, he proposes to counter this slander by offering all his goods, as well as his only daughter, Eva, to the winner of the song contest. His proviso that she must approve the man is not welcomed by all the Masters. Sachs's proposal, however, that the winner be chosen by the populace, as a means of renewing the traditional rules with the good sense and natural instincts of the common people, is laughed out of court.

Walther is introduced by Pogner and asked about his teacher. His reply ('Am stillen Herd') is that he learnt his art from the poetry of Walther von der Vogelweide and from nature itself. In formal terms, the song is a piece of gentle mockery, on the composer's part, of the medieval *Bar*-form so prized by the Masters. Of the three stanzas, A-A-B, the last (*Abgesang*) is intended to be a variation of the others (*Stollen*), but in 'Am stillen Herd' the variation is so florid that no one is able to contradict Beckmesser's opinion that it is but a 'deluge of words'.

Beckmesser withdraws into his Marker's box, ready to pass judgment on the young knight's formal attempt to enter the guild. The syncopated motif accompanying him both here and elsewhere is a churlish version of the dotted motif that first introduced Walther, as befits Beckmesser's cantankerous character. The rules of the *Tabulatur* are read out by Kothner in a style that parodies that of Handelian opera, complete with coloratura (given, unusually, to a bass, for comic effect).

For his Trial Song, Walther takes up the command of the Marker: 'Fanget an! So rief der Lenz in den Wald'. A passionate celebration of the joys of spring and youthful love, it again fails to find favour with the Masters. It is, in fact, a complex *Bar*-form in which each *Stollen* is in two parts – *A-B-A'-B'-C* – though Beckmesser interrupts after *A'*, assuming that the form is ternary (*A-B-A*). Beckmesser's critical scratching of chalk on slate provokes Walther's angry outburst about envious Winter lying in wait in the thorn-bush.

Beckmesser leads the chorus of opposition to Walther; only Sachs admires his originality. Walther mounts the singer's chair (a gross breach of etiquette) to complete his song. The hubbub increases as he does so: the Masters, by an overwhelming majority, reject his application to the guild, while the apprentices revel in the commotion. With a gesture of pride and contempt, Walther strides from the stage, leaving Sachs to gaze thoughtfully at the empty singer's chair.

Act 2 *In the street in front of the homes of Pogner and Sachs* The orchestral prelude takes up the main theme of Pogner's Address (ex.7) in a joyous celebration of midsummer's eve: trills and glissandos abound. The curtain rises to reveal a street and a narrower adjoining alley in Nuremberg. Of the two corner houses presented, Pogner's grand one on the right is overhung by a lime tree and Sachs's simpler one on the left by an elder. The apprentices are tormenting David once again.

Magdalene asks him how Eva's paramour fared at the Song School and is vicariously disconsolate at the bad news. Sachs arrives and instructs David to set out his work for him by the window. Pogner and Eva return from an evening stroll and sit on a bench under the lime tree. The new motif (ex.8) to which he expresses his satisfaction with Nuremberg and its customs is reminiscent rhythmically of ex.7. Pogner belatedly realizes that Eva's questions about the knight are no idle curiosity.

Ex.8

As Eva follows her father inside, Sachs has his work bench set up outside his workshop. The tender reminiscences of a phrase from Walther's Trial Song (ex.9) suggest that the knight's celebration of spring

Ex.9

and his embodiment of vital youthful passion have made a great impression on him. Sachs's relishing of the scent of the elder in this solo, 'Was duftet doch

der Flieder', has given it the name of the 'Flieder Monologue': it develops into an exquisite evocation of the joys of spring.

Eva approaches Sachs's workshop (scene iv) and, in a long, delicately woven exchange, tries to elicit from him the likely winner of the next day's contest. Sachs, not unaware of her attractiveness, playfully parries her questions until Magdalene enters to tell her that her father is calling, and that Beckmesser intends to serenade her.

Walther now turns the corner (scene v) and an impassioned duet ensues, based largely on a demonstrative variant of one of the themes from the previous scene. They are at a loss as to how to get round her father's conditions for obtaining her hand. Walther suggests eloping, but he gets carried away by his loathing of the Masters' pedantry until he is interrupted by the sound of the Nightwatchman's horn: a single blast on an F♯ that launches an exquisite transition to the B major of the Midsummer Magic music. Eva has meanwhile followed Magdalene into the house and now re-emerges, having changed clothes with her.

Eva and Walther are about to make their escape when Sachs, who has realized what is afoot, allows his lamp to illuminate the alley they are in. They hesitate and are then pulled up short by the sound of Beckmesser tuning his lute. Walther is for settling his score with the Marker and has to be restrained by Eva: 'What trouble I have with men!', she sighs. She persuades him to sit quietly under the lime tree until Beckmesser has finished his song. But Sachs has other ideas, launching into a noisy, vigorous song of his own ('Jerum! Jerum!'). A simple, ballad-like structure with augmented harmonies spicing the basic B♭ major, Sachs's song is permeated with references to the biblical Eve and to shoemaking that are not entirely lost on the listeners. Beckmesser has less time for the poetic subtleties; seeing what he believes to be the object of his wooing come to the window (in fact Magdalene in Eva's clothes), he begs Sachs to stop his clattering. Reminding him that he had been critical of his workmanship earlier in the day, Sachs suggests that both would make progress if Beckmesser were to serenade while he, Sachs, marked any faults with his cobbler's hammer. (The coloratura of Beckmesser's Serenade 'Den Tag seh' ich erscheinen' is a parody of an old-fashioned bel canto aria. It is also notable for its obvious and stilted rhymes and its grotesque violations of metre and misplaced accents. Clearly Beckmesser provided a target for Wagner's ill-will towards what he perceived as hostile, insensitive critics – not least Eduard Hanslick, whose name was commandeered for the Marker in the 1861 prose drafts – and other reactionary practitioners. But Beckmesser's artistic failings are also precisely those ascribed to the Jews in *Das*

Judenthum in der Musik, and it may be argued that the serenade is also a parody of the Jewish cantorial style.)

The commotion caused by Sachs's hammering and Beckmesser's attempts to make himself heard above it brings the populace out on to the streets. A riot ensues (scene vii), during which David, under the impression that Beckmesser is courting Magdalene, cudgels him. The music of the Riot Scene, which takes up the theme of Beckmesser's Serenade, and which contains more than a dozen polyphonic lines, is notoriously difficult to perform; a simplified version, initiated by Toscanini, is used in many houses. At the height of the pandemonium, the Nightwatchman's horn is heard again. Everybody disperses, and by the time he arrives on the scene the streets are empty; he rubs his eyes in disbelief.

Act 3.i–iv *Sachs's workshop* The prelude to the third act, familiar as a concert item, opens with a broadly phrased theme on the cellos, taken up contrapuntally by the violas and, in turn, second and first violins; the theme (ex.10) has earlier been heard as a counter-melody to Sachs's 'Jerum! Jerum!' in Act 2. The horns and bassoons then intone the solemn chorale that is to become the ode of homage to Sachs sung by the assembled townsfolk at the end of the opera. Announced by the characteristic semiquavers of the apprentices, David enters the workshop. Sachs, deep in thought, at first ignores him but then asks him to sing the verses he has learnt for the festival of St John, celebrated on midsummer's day. His mind still on the events of the previous evening, David begins his ditty to the tune of Beckmesser's Serenade and has to start again: 'Am Jordan Sankt Johannes stand'. David belatedly realizes that it is also his master's name-day (Hans = Johannes). When the apprentice has left, Sachs resumes his philosophical meditation on the follies of humanity: 'Wahn! Wahn! Überall Wahn!' (The concept of *Wahn*, which includes the notions of illusion, folly and madness, lies at the heart of *Die Meistersinger*: by the 1860s, Wagner had come to believe that all human endeavour was underpinned by illusion and futility, though art, he considered, was a 'noble illusion'.) The 'Wahn Monologue', as it is often known, begins with ex.10;

Ex.10

ex.8 is heard as Sachs's thoughts turn to Nuremberg and its normally peaceful customs. The memory of the riot returns, but the agitated quavers are banished by the serene music of the Midsummer Magic. The last part of the Monologue, the dawning of midsummer's day, brings back ex.7.

The end of Sachs's reverie, and the beginning of

scene ii, is signified by a modulation with harp arpeggios, rather in the manner of a cinematic 'dissolve'; similar gestures occur later too in connection with dreams and reveries. Walther appears and tells Sachs of a wonderful dream. Sachs urges him to recount it as it may enable him to win the Master's prize. (Wagner had readily become a convert to the Schopenhauerian view that creativity originates in the dream-world.) Walther's resistance to the demands of the Masters is overcome in the name of love, and he embarks on his Morning Dream Song – what is to become the Prize Song: 'Morgenlich leuchtend in rosigem Schein'. He produces one *Stollen* and then, at Sachs's bidding, another similar, followed by an *Abgesang* (ex.5). Under Sachs's instruction, Walther goes on to produce another three stanzas. The last part of the overall structure (A-A-A), each section of which is in *Bar*-form (A-A-B), is not supplied until scene iv.

In the third scene, Beckmesser appears alone in the workshop. After his beating the night before, he is limping and stumbling, and prey to nightmarish memories and imaginings. All this is depicted in a 'pantomime' notable for its anarchically progressive musical style. Picking up Walther's freshly penned song, he pockets it on Sachs's re-entry. He adduces it as proof that Sachs means to enter the song contest, but Sachs denies such a plan and offers him the song. Beckmesser's suspicions are eventually allayed, and he delightedly retires in order to memorize the song.

Eva enters (scene iv) and under the cover of a complaint about the shoes Sachs has made for her, she expresses her anxieties about Walther and the coming contest. Sachs affects not to understand, and pretends not to notice Walther's arrival, in spite of Eva's passionate cry and a thrilling tonal shift in the orchestra. Walther delivers the final section of his song and Eva, moved to tears, sobs on the shoulder of Sachs, until the latter drags himself away, complaining about the lot of the cobbler. Eva, emotionally torn between the avuncular shoemaker and her younger lover, draws Sachs to her again. Sachs reminds her of the story of Tristan and Isolde and says he has no wish to play the role of King Mark; the themes of the opening of Wagner's *Tristan* and of King Mark are recalled here.

Magdalene and David arrive, and Sachs, with a cuff on his ear, announces David's promotion to journeyman, in time to witness the baptism of 'a child' (the themes of the Masters and of the opening chorale are heard at this point). The progeny turns out to be Walther's new song. The music moves to a plateau of G♭ major, a tritone from the C major of the surrounding scenes, for Eva's introduction to the celebrated quintet, 'Selig, wie die Sonne'.

3.v *An open meadow on the Pegnitz* The themes associated with Nuremberg (ex.8) and midsummer's

'Die Meistersinger von Nürnberg' (Wagner): model of Heinrich Döll's set for Act 3 scene v (an open meadow on the Pegnitz) for the original production at the Königliches Hof- und Nationaltheater, Munich, 21 June 1868

day (ex.7), along with fig.x of ex.l, effect a transition to the fifth scene. The townsfolk are all gathered and, to the accompaniment of fanfares on stage, greet the processions of the guilds: first the shoemakers, then the tailors and bakers. A boat brings 'maidens from Fürth' and the apprentices begin dancing with them; David, at first reluctant, is drawn in.

At last the Masters arrive, to the music of the first-act prelude. Sachs is hailed by the populace with the chorale from the third-act prelude to the words with which the historical Sachs greeted Luther and the Reformation: 'Wach auf, es nahet gen den Tag'. Sachs modestly acknowledges the homage and exhorts people and Masters to accord the coming contest and prize their due worth. Beckmesser, who has frantically been trying to memorize Walther's song, is led first to the platform. His rendering of the song, to the tune of his own Serenade, is marked by grotesque misaccentuations and violations of metre, but it is his garbling of the words, producing an absurd, tasteless parody of the original, that provokes a crescendo of hilarity in the audience. He presses on in confusion, but only makes a greater fool of himself. Finally he rushes from the platform, denouncing Sachs as the author.

Sachs refutes that honour and introduces the man who will make sense of it for them. Walther's Prize Song, 'Morgenlich leuchtend in rosigem Schein', compresses his earlier dry run into a single *Bar*-form of three stanzas (*A-A-B*) but with each stanza expanded. In several details, including the heart-warming plunge into B major (from a tonic of C) in the second stanza, Walther's prize-winning entry is a greater infraction of the rules than ever. But the Masters are evidently swept away by Walther's artistic integrity and impassioned delivery, for he is awarded the prize by general consent.

When Pogner proffers the Master's chain to Walther he impetuously refuses, and Sachs delivers a homily (to exx.l and 3, together with the Prize Song) about the art that the Masters have cultivated and preserved throughout Germany's troubled history: 'Verachtet mir die Meister nicht'. Sachs's address concludes with a celebration of the sovereignty of the German spirit – a theme dear to Wagner's heart in the 1860s; that spirit, it is proposed, can never be exterminated so long as the great German art that sustains it is respected. The salient themes of the opera's prelude, notably ex.4, are recalled for the final choral apostrophe to Sachs and 'holy German art'.

*

On one level, *Die Meistersinger* is a glorious affirmation of humanity and the value of art, as well as a parable about the necessity of tempering the inspiration of genius with the rules of form. The work may also be regarded, however, as the artistic component in Wagner's ideological crusade of the 1860s: a crusade to revive the 'German spirit' and purge it of alien elements, chief among which were the Jews. It can further be argued that anti-Semitism is woven into the ideological fabric of the work and that the representation of Beckmesser carries, at the very least, overtones of anti-Semitic sentiment. That Walther's outburst against Beckmesser in Act 1 scene ii, for instance, is intended as a reference to the Grimm brothers' anti-Semitic folktale *Der Jude im Dorn* is clear from the parallel situation: in the Grimm tale a bird flies into the thorn-bush, in Walther's song it flies out again in an image of liberation. The matter is put beyond doubt by Wagner's pun 'Grimm-bewährt', which suggests both 'guarded with anger' and 'authenticated by Grimm'. The identification here of Beckmesser with the stereotypical Jew of folklore has profound implications for the interpretation of the character and of the work as a whole.

The only comedy among Wagner's mature works, *Die Meistersinger* is a rich, perceptive music drama widely admired for its warm humanity but regarded with suspicion by some for its dark underside. Its genial aspect is immensely enhanced by the technical mastery displayed by Wagner at the height of his powers.   **B.M.**

Midsummer Marriage, The

Opera in three acts by Michael Tippett to his own libretto; London, Covent Garden, 27 January 1955.

The cast at the première included Richard Lewis (Mark), Joan Sutherland (Jenifer), Otakar Kraus (King Fisher), Adele Leigh (Bella), Oralia Dominguez (Sosostris), and Michael Langdon and Edith Coates as the Ancients. Strephon was danced by Pirmin Trecu.

Mark *a young man of unknown parentage*		tenor
Jenifer *his betrothed, a young girl*		soprano
King Fisher *Jenifer's father, a*		
businessman		baritone
Bella *King Fisher's secretary*		soprano
Jack *Bella's boyfriend, a mechanic*		tenor
Sosostris *a clairvoyant*		alto
He-Ancient *Priest of the Temple*		bass
She-Ancient *Priestess of the*		
Temple		mezzo-soprano
Strephon		dancer
Chorus of Mark's and Jenifer's friends		
Dancers attendant on the Ancients		
Setting A clearing in a wood with a ruined		

temple and steps leading away on either side; the present time

Tippett had written a folksong opera in 1934 and two children's operas in 1938–9; a first full-scale opera was to be the goal of his first decade of mature composition and the completion of a long-term strategy. He considered a range of ideas, and others developed during this period but were discarded. A crucial stage in the journey towards his operatic vision was his war-time oratorio *A Child of our Time* (1939–41), for which, acting on the advice of T. S. Eliot, he wrote his own text. With this achievement as a foundation he embarked on the creation of an operatic scenario, again taking inspiration from Eliot (among many other sources). This began as a vision in his mind's eye:

I *saw* a stage picture . . . of a wooded hilltop with a temple, where a warm and soft young man was being rebuffed by a cold and hard young woman . . . to such a degree that the collective, magical archetypes take charge – Jung's *anima* and *animus* – the girl, inflated by the latter, rises through the stage flies to heaven, and the man, overwhelmed by the former, descends through the stage floor to hell. But it was clear they would soon return.

In acknowledging the strong Jungian resonance of his starting-point – he had undergone Jungian analysis in 1938–9 – Tippett points to the crux of the opera: the search for wholeness. In A *Child of our Time* the scapegoat figure sings 'I would know my shadow and my light, so shall I at last be whole', and Tippett later described the sentence as 'the only truth I will ever utter'. *The Midsummer Marriage* (1946–52) is the dramatic realization of this dream achieved by means of a modern comedy with a mythic backdrop.

The opera's initial reception was very mixed, even hostile. The dramatic confusion of the production and the common perception of Tippett's libretto as a clumsy hotchpotch obscured the reaction to the music. Its self-sufficient strength was revealed in a crucial studio broadcast in 1963, which led to a superior production at Covent Garden in 1968; but even this did not entirely rehabilitate the work as a dramatic entity. The production by Welsh National Opera in 1976 finally revealed the score to be a universal masterpiece, and it has since been produced all over the world to general recognition as a source of musical and theatrical enrichment.

*

Act I: 'Morning'

The young man and woman of the initial stage-picture are Mark and Jenifer. He is an orphan, of mysterious birth, a child of nature in touch with the elements and possessed of a warm generous nature. Jenifer is the cold, idealistic daughter of a modern tycoon, King Fisher. The strong Celtic, and specifically Cornish, connotations of these names (Jenifer is a form of 'Guinevere') already touch upon a deeper dimension, which is immediately present in visual terms as the curtain opens on mist; as it clears in the rising sun a ruined temple is revealed. The trigger for the action is the runaway marriage eagerly anticipated by Mark in the opening scene and furiously opposed by King Fisher. This conflict in itself might have delivered only comedy. The key to the opera's sequence of events is Jenifer's arrival and surprising announcement that she wants to postpone the wedding – the rebuff of Tippett's first vision.

The music of these first scenes has a symphonic breadth, and even before Jenifer's dramatic entry the opera's supernatural substructure has emerged. It is immediately apparent that Tippett is in full command of the musico-dramatic stage. The buoyant exhilaration of the orchestral prelude gently recedes and in so doing creates a sense of space and distance to which the offstage voices of the chorus calling to each other lend enchantment.

These are Mark's and Jenifer's friends, who are gathering to celebrate the marriage. When they emerge in full view they sing a radiant hymn to the sun, but as the music fades, mysterious sounds invade the air and the ruined temple becomes the focus of attention. From its portals, to the accompaniment of a charming little march, a procession of dancers emerges. As an audience we seem to be observing, through the eyes of the silent chorus, the actions of another world. This ritual is interrupted by Mark's unexpected arrival. He remonstrates with the guardians of the temple, the He- and She-Ancients, whom he clearly knows of old, and asks for a 'new dance'. They do not oblige him and quickly disappear to the same little march which heralded their mysterious arrival.

Mark now greets his friends and sings a passionate love-reverie ('And like the lark I sing for joy because I love'). At the height of his rapture he sees Jenifer arrive, but his joy fades when he observes that her dress is not that of a bride. Her rejection of Mark is couched in lofty, spiritual terms ('It isn't love I want, but truth . . . For me the light! For you the shadow'). She climbs up some stone steps as if to heaven and disappears. The chorus cannot cheer up the crestfallen Mark, who responds to her challenge by descending through a set of gates, as if to hell. By this climactic gesture the plighted pair begin their journey of spiritual discovery.

Coming in hot pursuit of his daughter the bluff, brazen King Fisher arrives on stage. Having seen Mark run away, he assumes that Jenifer has gone with him. After the accumulation of tension at the end of the previous scene, Tippett now introduces a welcome touch of comedy. King Fisher is accompanied by his charmingly dutiful secretary, Bella. Thwarted by the closure of the gates, King

Fisher demands to have them opened, and so encounters the Ancients, who treat him with aloof contempt. Tippett's delineation of musical characterization is beautifully handled here. Bella eventually suggests that she should get her boyfriend, the mechanic Jack, to open the gates and King Fisher agrees. In the meantime he exhorts the male and female chorus in turn to help him search for Mark and Jenifer. He resorts to offering money, which the men cheerfully accept but the women angrily reject as a bribe. This encounter is cast as a sturdy strophic set-piece which allows for the rejection to emerge very effectively as the upsetting of a musical scheme.

The atmosphere again lightens with the arrival of Jack. He and Bella emerge immediately as the down-to-earth counterbalance to Mark and Jenifer. In some of Tippett's most delightfully loose-limbed writing they sing easily of their comfortable love for each other. But when an attempt is made to break open the gates a powerful unseen voice warns King Fisher not to tamper. His arrogance forces another confrontation which is again thwarted by the voice. An urgent ensemble of confusion ensues in which King Fisher urges Jack to try again, while Bella, frightened by the voice, tries to draw her boyfriend back. As this conflict grows to heights of musical passion, the issue at stake is swept aside by the sudden re-emergence of a transfigured Jenifer at the top of the steps. Time seems to stand still: having now mastered the ebb and flow of his dramatic presentation so far with such skill, it is as if Tippett can summon up from the depths of the psyche whatever music is required.

Jenifer's dazed utterance on 'returning to the world' provokes a confrontation with her father, and this acts as a cue for Mark's return. At length the two relate their separate experiences. Jenifer's aria is an exalted visionary expression of spiritual radiance; Mark sings of earthy passion – it is a conflict of spirit and senses. Ecstatic with spiritual purity, Jenifer asserts her superiority, only to be broken by Mark's revelation. This action provokes a reversal of their earlier journeys, and as they run off in opposite directions to continue their spiritual exploration the threads of the act are stirringly pulled together in a chorus recalling the symphonic opening in key (B♭) and gesture; this comments on the ordeal of individuation to be endured by Mark and Jenifer.

Act 2: 'Afternoon'

Mark and Jenifer are absent throughout this act, yet its crux is an enactment of their trials. Tippett frames the act with a glowing evocation of a balmy summer's afternoon in which the glistening, shimmering heat is virtually palpable. The whole is constructed symmetrically but with an unerring dramatic curve. The chorus inhabit the landscape with madrigal-like bursts of song and wander off

'The Midsummer Marriage' (Tippett), Act 3: final scene from the original production at Covent Garden, London, 27 January 1955, with Joan Sutherland and Richard Lewis as Jenifer and Mark (centre) flanked by Edith Coates and Michael Langdon (standing, left and right) as the Ancients and with the dancer Pirmin Trecu as Strephon kneeling before them (set by Barbara Hepworth)

into the woods, leaving Jack and Bella to sing a love duet in which they map out the course of their married life with touching intimacy and predictability. They also disappear into the woods, and the stage is suddenly alive with unseen presences.

What follows, at the very heart of the opera, is the celebrated sequence of Ritual Dances. Three are enacted here: 'The Earth in Autumn' (in which the hound hunts the hare), 'The Waters in Winter' (where the otter chases the fish) and 'The Air in Spring' (the hawk shadows the bird). This ballet is a predatory struggle between the female and the male. The vulnerable male is represented throughout the animal transformations by Strephon, the leading dancer from the temple, who acts as Mark's 'shadow'. In the third dance the violence of the chase (every move in the music is graphically portrayed) threatens to overwhelm the stage, and the bird is nearly killed. Bella, who is watching, screams, and we are back in the everyday world of the opera. She is comforted by Jack, the chorus pass by merrily, and the act ends as it started, but scarred by the undercurrent of menace.

Act 3: 'Evening and Night'
The act opens at sunset with a choral tableau of rejoicing and festivity. King Fisher arrives to announce that he is bringing a private clairvoyant, Madame Sosostris, to unravel the mystery. Sending the chorus off to greet her, he tangles again with the Ancients, whom he challenges to a contest. He is warned by them again ('You meddle with powers

you cannot gauge, courting a risk you do not understand. Should you persist, there's mortal danger to your person'). But King Fisher is now beyond such sober instruction. The entry of Madame Sosostris seems a bit of a romp, and she turns out at first to be Jack in disguise, a trick which only serves to deepen the apprehension of awe as the presence of Sosostris herself becomes apparent.

She emerges as a 'huge contraption of black veils of roughly human shape, though much more than life-size' – her face is never seen. A crystal bowl is placed before her and there follows a magnificent extended aria which forms the still centrepiece of the final act. Sosostris is not however a mere modern clairvoyant, for Tippett invests her with divine insight – oracular power achieved at the expense of her womanhood. Her aria is a profound exposition of the seer's self-sacrifice; it outlines the ordeal of the oracle in hearing divine inspiration. She is therefore a metaphor for the very source of creativity: 'I am what has been, is and shall be. No mortal ever lifted my garment'. This great apostrophe is the transcendent lodestar of the opera, quoting from an essay by Schiller which Beethoven kept framed over his desk. The aria draws from Tippett his most overwhelmingly moving and visionary music – a supreme moment in the whole literature of opera.

After the aria King Fisher rejects Sosostris's lyrical vision of Jenifer about to unite with Mark, and he is moved to tear the veils which surround her, only to reveal the lotus flower in which Mark and

Jenifer are seen in 'radiant transfiguration, in reds and gold, posed in mutual contemplation. Sosostris has vanished'. Her vision vindicated, King Fisher is blinded by it. When he tries to shoot Mark, he dies himself, as predicted, and we realize that the earlier warning voice had been Sosostris's. The requiem which follows releases the energy of rebirth for the fourth and final ritual dance, 'Fire in Summer' (the voluntary human sacrifice).

Strephon and a fellow dancer prepare for the rite of the summer solstice with ritual fire, and as he holds the 'freely burning stick above his head' we see Mark and Jenifer assume a pose of 'vigour and ecstasy' in symbolic union within the lotus petals. They sing an ecstatic duet as Strephon collapses at their feet in a final gesture of sacrifice, to be wholly consumed as the incandescent spiritual fire transfigures the stage. As the chorus join the celebration of divine and physical love the lotus leaves rise to cover the three figures and the bud finally bursts into flame. Although Strephon is dead, Mark and Jenifer are reborn to their life of fulfilment and psychic equilibrium, and as the fire dies away and the magical 'second dawn' breaks they return to the everyday world to marry at last.

*

The Midsummer Marriage represents the musical and philosophical culmination of Tippett's extended first period of composition. The music's richly coloured harmonic language and its unequivocal tonal foundation embody precisely the opera's visionary goal of spiritual and psychic unity and balance. From the glowing harmonic fabric springs a profusion of lyrical expression unparalleled in Tippett's output. The writing for chorus and orchestra is warmly homogeneous but accommodates an effortless range of Tippett's rhythmic and contrapuntal devices. The distinctive musical world of the opera was to linger briefly in three major works: the Corelli Fantasia (1953), the Piano Concerto (1953–5) and the Second Symphony (1956–7). For many it represents the quintessential Tippett. In spite of the general incomprehension with which the work was initially received, the magnificence of Tippett's conception in every respect has assured it a unique position in 20th-century opera.   G.Le.

Midsummer Night's Dream, A

Opera in three acts, op.64, by Benjamin Britten to a libretto by him and Peter Pears, after William Shakespeare's play; Aldeburgh, Jubilee Hall, 11 June 1960.

The cast for the première included Alfred Deller as Oberon, Jennifer Vyvyan as Titania, Owen

Brannigan as Bottom, April Cantelo as Helena, Marjorie Thomas as Hermia, Thomas Hemsley as Demetrius, George Moran as Lysander and Peter Pears as Flute.

Oberon *King of the Fairies*	countertenor (or contralto)
Tytania [Titania] *Queen of the Fairies*	coloratura soprano
Puck	acrobat, speaking role
Theseus *Duke of Athens*	bass
Hippolyta *betrothed to Theseus*	contralto
Lysander ⎫ *in love with Hermia*	tenor
Demetrius ⎭	baritone
Hermia *in love with Lysander*	mezzo-soprano
Helena *in love with Demetrius*	soprano
Bottom *a weaver*	bass-baritone
Quince *a carpenter*	bass
Flute *a bellows-mender*	tenor
Snug *a joiner*	bass
Snout *a tinker*	tenor
Starveling *a tailor*	baritone
Cobweb ⎫	treble
Peaseblossom ⎪ *fairies*	treble
Mustardseed ⎪	treble
Moth ⎭	treble
Chorus of fairies	

Setting A wood near Athens, then Theseus's palace

A Midsummer Night's Dream was something of a rush job, conceived and created between August 1959 and April 1960 for performance at the 1960 Aldeburgh Festival, in celebration of rebuilding work at the Jubilee Hall, the festival's only theatre until the opening of the Maltings at Snape in 1967. Britten's reputation stood high at that time and the new opera was soon taken up elsewhere. In 1961 alone it was seen at Covent Garden (in the Aldeburgh production) and in Hamburg, Berlin, Milan, San Francisco, Zürich and Tokyo. It was the first Britten opera to be staged at Snape (1967) and among many successful subsequent productions the English Music Theatre Company's 1980 staging, also first seen at Snape, transferred to Covent Garden in 1986. A fine production at Glyndebourne by Peter Hall (1981) was televised; a recording conducted by Britten and with many of the original cast was released in 1967. There is also a recording conducted by Richard Hickox (1990).

*

Act I *The wood, deepening twilight* At the start the orchestra evokes the mystery and magic of the wood by moving through a succession of all 12 major triads, the string glissandos suggesting the breathing of a dreamer in a deep sleep. The fairies appear and their first song, 'Over hill, over dale', has the direct, fresh melodic use of scale patterns that is a familiar yet never hackneyed Britten fingerprint. Puck enters to what will prove his characteristic accompaniment of trumpet and drum, speaking rather than singing, and preparing for the entrance of Oberon and Titania. The King and Queen of the Fairies are angry with each other, their music ('Ill met by moonlight') almost extravagantly intense as they quarrel over possession of the 'lovely boy stol'n from an Indian king'. After Titania's departure, Oberon summons Puck and orders him to fetch a magic herb that will enable him to have his own way. Now the quartet of Athenian lovers approach: first Hermia and Lysander, who swear undying love; then Helena and Demetrius in a very different state, she making frank advances, he spurning them. As the lovers move away, Oberon returns. Puck brings him the flower and Oberon charges him to use it to 'cure' Demetrius of his dislike of Helena. Britten sets Oberon's lines 'I know a bank' to a sinuous melody in a suitably exotic orchestral garb, with celesta prominent. Here the justification for what might have seemed a risk – the choice of the countertenor voice for Oberon – is clear and complete: there is an air of Baroque fantasy in the music, which nevertheless remains entirely Britten's.

Next the Rustics (as Britten designates the Athenian craftsmen) appear, to decide on the cast for the play they are offering for the Duke's wedding celebrations. For the broad comedy of this scene Britten adopts an appropriately jaunty style, with a gawky solo trombone, making sure that the words have every chance of being heard, and that Bottom achieves the necessary prominence, with his desire to 'play the lion'. As the Rustics depart, Lysander and Hermia return, still in love but weary. They fall asleep and Puck, in error, squeezes the herb's juice into Lysander's eyes. Then Helena and Demetrius arrive, still fighting. Left alone, Helena wakes Lysander, whose instant declaration of love she interprets as mockery. They run off, and Hermia awakes alone, bewildered and afraid. The act ends with the events which, in Shakespeare, happen earlier. To a repeat of the initial forest music, Titania asks her attendants to sing her to sleep. After the lullaby ('Ye spotted snakes') has done its work, Oberon enters and squeezes the juice into her eyes, with the final admonition 'Wake when some vile thing is near'.

Act 2 *The wood, dark night* The act begins with four quiet orchestral chords (using all 12 notes) like a chromatic version of the harmonies that begin Mendelssohn's famous overture. Titania is asleep, and does not wake as the Rustics rehearse their play. Puck observes them, resolving to make mischief – so, when Bottom returns after an exit, he wears an ass's head and his colleagues flee in terror. Bottom sings a loud, coarse song ('The woosel-cock, so black of

hue'), waking Titania and inspiring her instant devotion. She summons her fairies with a gentle, florid waltz ('Be kind and courteous') and the fairies, complete with an onstage band of sopranino recorders, small cymbals and woodblocks, entertain the couple until they both fall asleep. Oberon is at first well satisfied with Puck's doings, but when Demetrius and Hermia appear Puck's mistake is all too clear. After Demetrius has fallen asleep Oberon uses the magic herb on him, singing 'Flower of this purple dye' to a reminiscence of 'I know a bank'. But the lovers' main scene of conflict is yet to come. When Lysander and Helena enter, Demetrius awakes and immediately declares his passion for Helena. Hermia returns and there is an extended quartet of argument and recrimination during which the girls insult each other; it reaches a climax when Lysander and Demetrius leave to fight. Oberon is in a rage with Puck, but the trouble-maker makes amends, manoeuvring the lovers about the forest until they collapse exhausted. The fairies sing a touching lullaby to the four 'magic' chords ('On the ground sleep sound') and Puck squeezes an antidote into Lysander's eyes.

Act 3 *The wood, early next morning* Oberon explains to Puck that he now has the Indian boy who was the cause of his dispute with Titania. He releases Titania from the spell, and causes Bottom's ass's head to disappear. To a solemn dance ('quasi Sarabano') the King and Queen of the Fairies anticipate their midnight visit to Theseus's palace. As offstage horns take over from the 'morning lark', the lovers wake and are at last fully reconciled, Helena with Demetrius, Hermia with Lysander. Still in a daze they set off for Athens. Bottom only wakes when the other Rustics come in search of him with the exciting news that 'our play is preferred'. After a lively ensemble they hurry away to make their own preparations. During an orchestral interlude based on increasingly urgent statements of the horn-call music, the scene changes to the ducal palace. Theseus sings the praises of his bride Hippolyta, and after hearing the two pairs of lovers tell of their reconciliation he announces that they shall be married alongside his own wedding. The play is called for, and 'The most Lamentable Comedy and most Cruel Death of Pyramus and Thisby' is presented. Britten's music adds splendid point to this notably unpatronizing farce of confusion and incompetence; even his parody of a Donizetti mad scene with obbligato flute for Thisby makes its point without over-emphasis. The performance ends with a robust Bergomask dance. Then midnight strikes and a more solemn mood supervenes. At Theseus's bidding – 'Lovers, to bed' – the stage empties. Then the fairies appear, with Puck, Titania and Oberon. 'Now, until the break of day' is a haunting song of blessing, as serenely poised as anything in Britten. But, as in Shakespeare, the last words go to Puck, the last sounds to the brisk divisions of his trumpet and drum.

*

The nocturnal theme of Shakespeare's play was an obvious attraction to Britten: only the year before he had concluded his *Nocturne* with a setting of a Shakespeare sonnet. Moreover the play had been a favourite at least since he had played the viola in Mendelssohn's incidental music as a 15-year-old. It was a particular challenge to start with a text other than a custom-made libretto, and Shakespeare's play had to be cut by half. The shift of emphasis is clear in that, while the play begins at Theseus's court, Britten begins in the wood, with the play's Act 2 scene i. Nevertheless, only one line is added to Shakespeare: in Act 1 of the opera Lysander explains Hermia's plight in the face of the ruling, 'compelling thee to marry with Demetrius'. In all three acts the music is continuous and there are no scene-divisions marked in the score, although Act 3 has an extended interlude to facilitate the change of scene.   A.W.

Mireille

Opéra in five acts by Charles-François Gounod to a libretto by Michel Carré after Frédéric Mistral's epic poem *Mirèio*; Paris, Théâtre Lyrique, 19 March 1864.

The first Mireille was Marie Caroline Carvalho, wife of the theatre's director; the first Vincent was François Morini.

Mireille *daughter of Maître Ramon*	soprano
Vincent *son of Maître Ambroise*	tenor
Ourrias *a bull-tamer*	baritone
Maître Ramon *a wealthy farmer*	bass
Maître Ambroise *a peasant*	bass
Vincenette *Vincent's sister*	soprano
Taven *a sorceress*	contralto
Clémence *a friend of Mireille*	soprano
A Ferryman	bass
Andreloux *a shepherd*	contralto
Mulberry gatherers, townspeople, spirits of the Rhône, farmhands, pilgrims to the chapel of the Saintes-Maries	
Setting Provence, 19th century	

The appearance of *Mirèio* in 1859 (in a bilingual edition, with the Provençal text matched by a French prose translation on facing pages) brought the Provençal poet Frédéric Mistral to the attention of the Parisian literary establishment for the first time. Gounod probably knew the epic by the end of 1861 and, after receiving permission from Mistral for an operatic adaptation, began to work seriously on the project at the beginning of 1863, composing most of it on location. Gounod gave the poet regular progress reports, admitting early on that the dramatic requirements of the stage had forced the elimination of much local detail. Shorn of its forays into such things as the intricacies of olive cultivation and silk weaving, the essentials of Mistral's plot are reproduced faithfully by Carré, with some re-ordering of events: Mistral places the great scene in which Mireille confronts her father with her love for Vincent after Vincent is wounded by Ourrias; in the opera that scene occurs before the duel, to create a situation where Vincent's wound provides dramatic justification for Mireille to undertake the dangerous journey to the Saintes-Maries.

Preparations for the first production by the Théâtre Lyrique began in October 1863. A particularly turbulent rehearsal period followed – at one point communication between Gounod and the Carvalhos was effected through an exchange of notarized letters – and the work was radically modified before the première. Changes included the elimination of a duet for Mireille and Ourrias in Act 2, an abbreviation of Mireille's Act 4 'Air de la Crau' and resultant composition of her Act 2 *air* (not, as is frequently said, the Act 4 *ariette* 'Heureux petit berger', which had been planned from the start), and the composition of Andreloux's *chanson* in Act 5. *Mireille* was poorly received at its première, with Carvalho unsuccessful in certain passages and Morini ineffective as Vincent. In an attempt to improve its fortunes, major changes in the order of events in Acts 3 and 4 were hastily improvised after the second performance, but these do not seem to have prolonged the run appreciably. Neither was *Mireille* a success at Covent Garden in July 1864, for which Gounod supplied recitatives in place of the original spoken dialogue and created a happy ending. Further changes were made for a new production at the Théâtre Lyrique in December 1864: the work was regrouped into three acts (with elimination of much material in the original Acts 3, 4, and 5), a new duet for Mireille and Vincent was added to bring down the final curtain, and a *valse-ariette* was written for Carvalho. *Mireille* still did not take hold. An additional unsuccessful attempt to make the work profitable – with numerous new changes not sanctioned by the composer – was made in 1874 at the Opéra-Comique. Finally in 1889 the work was well received in a new production at the Opéra-Comique that used a version very similar to the three-act one of December 1864.

Mireille became a staple of the Opéra-Comique repertory for the next 75 years and the aim of new productions subsequent to that of 1889 became to restore the score as it was first performed in March 1864. This was only partly achieved in 1901 and 1939.

'Mireille' (Gounod): final scene in Act 2 (at the entry to the arena at Arles) of the original production at the Théâtre Lyrique, Paris, 19 March 1864; lithograph by Caillot after Auguste Lamy

The composer-conductor Henri Busser produced an edition of *Mireille* based upon the latter production that purported to be as close to the version of the première as documentation would allow; all complete recordings of the work have used this text. Unfortunately his score is founded on misreadings of the early editions and newly uncovered manuscript source material permits a more accurate reconstruction.

*

Act I *A mulberry orchard* While a group of girls gathers mulberry leaves, the good sorceress Taven sadly notes that some of them will experience sorrow in love. Clémence (originally listed, like the role of Vincenette, as a 'dugazon' voice – a light, expressive soubrette) retorts that this will not happen to her because she will be taken from Provence by a handsome prince to live in a splendid castle. Mireille modestly confesses that she would be satisfied simply if a lad declared love to her in complete sincerity ('Et moi, si par hasard'); her melodic line, in contrast to Clémence's exuberant music, is dominated by conjunct motion and flows naturalistically. Mireille's friends playfully mock her, and after they leave she tells Taven that the rumour of her love for Vincent, a boy below her station, is true. Taven warns her that wealth and poverty are ill-matched. Vincent

himself passes by and Mireille engages him in conversation. He tells her that she is even more attractive than his sister ('Vincenette a votre âge'); this duet starts casually in B♭, but later grows in lyrical intensity with a section in D♭, while an instrumental refrain containing syncopated rhythms in 6/8 supplies Mediterranean colour. Before parting they agree that if misfortune should befall either of them, the other will make a pilgrimage to the shrine of the Saintes-Maries to pray for assistance.

Act 2 *At the entry to the arena at Arles* After a Provençal *farandole*, Mireille appears with her friends, followed shortly by Vincent. When bystanders suggest a love song, Mireille and Vincent oblige with the Chanson de Magali ('La brise est douce et parfumée'), featuring elegant alternation between 6/8 and 9/8 and many musical details that effectively evoke the poem's nature-based metaphors for love. The revellers take up the *farandole* again and enter the arena. Mireille stays behind and is gently warned by Taven that at this time of year she will be approached by suitors (*chanson*, 'Voici la saison mignonne'). In response, Mireille sings of her love for Vincent in a large *air* ('Trahir Vincent') with a heartfelt slow section followed by a mechanistic *cabalette*. Much as Taven predicted, the bull-tamer Ourrias declares his love for Mireille in *couplets* pervaded by dotted rhythms that communicate his resolve. Mireille leaves hastily. When her father, Maître Ramon, steps out of the arena Ourrias complains that Mireille has not been receptive to his suit. At that moment, Vincent and his father, Maître Ambroise, also appear. To a declaimed melodic line, Ramon asserts that fathers must wield an iron fist over their families and that no one in his household would dare defy him (finale, 'Un père parle en père').

Mireille reappears and reveals that she is in love with Vincent. Ramon orders her to forswear her attachment to him. He is about to strike Mireille when, in the ternary slow section of the finale, she falls on her knees to beg for understanding ('A vos pieds hélas me voilà'); she evokes the memory of her mother with a shift from minor to major coloured by an expressive clarinet counterpoint to the vocal line. But her plea falls on deaf ears: Ramon angrily curses Vincent and his father and in the *strette* ('Oui que l'enfer de vous s'empare') vows that he will not let Mireille see the lad again. Mireille and Vincent sing in unison that the attempt to separate them is vain; Ambroise replies to Ramon's verbal abuse in similar terms; the assembled crowd deplores Ramon's insensitivity.

Act 3.i The Val d'enfer, near Taven's cave After an elfin orchestral entr'acte redolent of Mendelssohn, Ourrias tells his friends to return home without him; he is still distressed by Mireille's rejection and intends to take revenge upon Vincent (duet, 'Ils s'éloignent'). Vincent appears and is surprised by Ourrias, who accuses him of having used sorcery to obtain Mireille's affection. Ourrias ignominiously strikes the unarmed lad with his trident. Hearing the moans of the wounded Vincent, Taven rushes out from her cave and curses Ourrias.

3.ii The banks of the Rhône The waters are lit by a full moon. Ourrias, plagued by remorse and fear ('Ah! que j'ai fait!'), calls on the ferryman to transport him to the opposite bank. Suddenly, as the orchestra gives forth eerie chromatic progressions, white phantoms emerge from the depths of the river. A distant bell sounds midnight. String arpeggios evoke the effect of ghosts floating on water. Terrified, Ourrias renews his call to the ferryman. He jumps on to the boat, but as it sets off the waters become agitated. The ferryman reminds Ourrias of Vincent. The boat sinks; Ourrias drowns.

Act 4.i The interior courtyard of Ramon's farm on St John's Eve; bonfires light the scene Ramon and his farm hands celebrate the harvest, but Mireille is despondent and leaves. Her father bemoans the fact that the laws of nature have made his daughter so unhappy. Mireille opens her window and dreamily remembers the Chanson de Magali. As day begins to break, the shepherd boy Andreloux appears playing his pipes (*chanson*, 'Le jour se lève'). Mireille envies

him for his blissful existence (*ariette*, 'Heureux petit berger'). Vincenette rushes on to tell Mireille what has happened to Vincent (duet, 'Ah! parle encore'). To a grand chordal accompaniment in triplets, Mireille resolves to undertake the perilous pilgrimage across the Crau desert to the Saintes-Maries. The music assumes a much more intimate character as she gathers her jewels as a humble offering and the two girls pray for Vincent's recovery.

4.ii The Crau desert – a vast rocky and arid plain; midday Mireille is exhausted and disorientated (*air*, 'En marche'). She sees a mirage of a splendid city on the edge of a lake as the orchestra sounds an augmented version of the 'Sainte ivresse' music (to be heard at the end of the opera). Mireille collapses in despair when it disappears. The shepherd's pipes in the distance revive her and she pushes on to her destination.

Act 5 Outside the chapel of the Saintes-Maries The faithful cross the stage and enter the chapel, calling for divine protection. Vincent appears and looks for Mireille; he prays for her safety (*cavatine*, 'Anges du paradis'). Mireille stumbles in, delirious and on the brink of death. She is ecstatic at being reunited with Vincent and has a vision of the sky opening to receive her ('Sainte ivresse! divine extase'). Ramon and others rush on. Mireille dies of sunstroke, but her soul is beckoned to eternal bliss in heaven by a celestial voice.

*

The role of Mireille stands far above the others in its musical characterization. This is partly because the other characters, with the exception of Vincent, are not developed through sustained presence: Vincenette, Taven, Ourrias, and even Ramon, serve almost as episodic figures in the unfolding story. Vincent sings fine music in the Act 1 duet and the Chanson de Magali (the best-known number from the opera) but a pale *cavatine* in the last act. *Mireille* was noteworthy in its day for presenting class differences entirely within the context of agrarian, rural society and some early reviewers had difficulty accepting that a 'mere' country girl could sing an aria with heroic cut such as 'En marche'.   S.Hr.

Mitridate, re di Ponto
('Mithridates, King of Pontus')

Dramma per musica in three acts, K87/74a, by Wolfgang Amadeus Mozart to a libretto by Vittorio Amadeo Cigna-Santi after Giuseppe Parini's translation of Jean Racine's *Mithridate*; Milan, Regio Ducal Teatro, 26 December 1770.

At the première Mithridates was sung by

Guglielmo d'Ettore; Aspasia by Antonia Bernasconi; Xiphares by Pietro Benedetti; Pharnaces by Giuseppe Cicognani; Marcius by Gaspare Bassano; Ismene by Anna Francesca Varese; Arbates by Pietro Muschietti.

Mitridate [Mithridates] *King of Pontus*   tenor
Aspasia *his betrothed*   soprano
Sifare [Xiphares] *his younger*
    son   soprano castrato
Farnace [Pharnaces] *his elder son*   alto castrato
Marzio [Marcius] *a Roman*   tenor
Ismene *a Parthian princess betrothed*
    to Pharnaces   soprano
Arbate [Arbates] *Governor of*
    Nymphaeum   soprano castrato
Setting Nymphaeum, 63 BC: the palace, a
    temple, the port, hanging gardens and a
    military encampment

Mitridate was commissioned for Carnival 1771; Mozart wrote the recitatives and overture while touring Italy in 1770. Reaching Milan on 18 October, he was forced to write and rewrite the arias quickly; Benedetti caused anxiety by his late arrival (1 December) and someone tried to persuade the prima donna to introduce arias from Gasparini's *Mitridate* (1767, Turin: with the same libretto). As in Vienna in 1768 there were those who condemned the work in advance because of Mozart's extreme youth. They were silenced by the first performance. Despite its length – six hours, with the ballet – *Mitridate* was repeated 21 times. Some music not by Mozart may have been included in the performances, and some lines of recitative are missing in every source. The designs for the scenery by the brothers Galliani were applauded. No further performances are known until the present century.

*

Mithridates, who long defended his empire against the Romans, and his son Pharnaces (who in Racine's play remains treacherous to the end) are historical personages; but the plot is fiction.

Act I Mithridates, twice married and with two sons, is betrothed to Aspasia (Racine's Monime). He is reported dead resisting the Romans. Both his sons, Xiphares and the elder, Pharnaces, are in love with Aspasia; she reciprocates only the love of Xiphares. Thwarted ambition leads Pharnaces to conspire against his father with the Roman Marcius. Defeated by Pompey, Mithridates unexpectedly returns, bringing Ismene, a Parthian princess betrothed to Pharnaces (she does not appear in Racine). Mithridates fears he has returned to two ungrateful sons, but is reassured by Arbates, Governor of Nymphaeum, concerning Xiphares. Mithridates' second aria, in a regal D major, ends the first act.

Act 2 Pharnaces spurns Ismene; she complains to the King who says Pharnaces is worthy to die. Mithridates doubts Aspasia's fidelity; he has to leave to do battle with Pompey, but proposes to marry her first. His aria alternately thanks loyal Xiphares (*andante*) and hurls accusations at Aspasia (*allegro*). Xiphares decides he must leave Pontus and bids Aspasia a moving farewell ('Lungi da te, mio bene': one of the three extant versions has an obbligato horn part). Aspasia laments her fate in a soliloquy (aria in two tempos, 'Nel grave tormento'). When Mithridates accuses Pharnaces of treachery he admits his guilt ('Son reo: l'error confesso'), but betrays Xiphares' love for Aspasia. Mithridates imprisons both his sons; the lovers bid a supposed last farewell (the only duet).

Act 3 Mithridates prepares for his final battle ('Vado incontro al fato'; Gasparini's setting is the one in the standard Mozart scores). Spurned by Aspasia, he sends her poison, which she accepts (monologue: recitative framing a cavatina); but Xiphares prevents her from drinking it. He prepares for worthy death in battle ('Se il rigor d'ingrata sorte', a noble *Sturm und Drang* aria in C minor). As the Romans attack, Marcius frees Pharnaces; in a magnificent scena (aria, 'Già dagli occhi') he resolves to support his father and goes to burn the Roman fleet. Mithridates is victorious but mortally wounds himself; he unites Xiphares with Aspasia, and forgives Pharnaces, who marries Ismene.

*

Fitting the arias for demanding singers did not prevent Mozart introducing ample variety of expression. Aspasia's second aria is a powerful lament in G minor; Xiphares' second combines short *andante* sections with vehement *allegro* passages. All his, Aspasia's and Ismene's music is characterized by extreme virtuosity. Mozart skilfully abbreviated the required ternary forms and used a large number of arias in which contrasting affections are expressed by alternating tempos. The overture is a three-movement sinfonia in D major and the finale a very short 'coro' of soloists. *Mitridate* is an astonishing achievement for a boy of 14; it makes the best use of conventional forms of expression and presents a drama which, if artificial, contains scenes of real intensity.   J.Ru.

Mondo della luna, Il ('The World on the Moon')

Dramma giocoso in three acts by Joseph Haydn to a libretto by Carlo Goldoni; Eszterháza, first known performance, 3 August 1777, but possibly July 1777.

The first cast consisted of Pietro Gherardi (Ernesto), Benedetto Bianchi (Buonafede), Catharina

Poschwa or Poschva (Clarice), Maria Anna Puttler (Flaminia), Leopold Dichtler (Cecco), and possibly Guglielmo and Maria Jermoli (Ecclitico and Lisetta).

Ecclitico *a false astrologer*		tenor
Ernesto *a cavalier*		alto castrato
Buonafede *a protective father*		baritone
Clarice	} *Buonafede's daughters*	soprano
Flaminia		soprano
Lisetta *Buonafede's maidservant*		contralto
Cecco *Ernesto's servant*		tenor

Pupils of Ecclitico, gentlemen, dancers, pages, servants and soldiers

Setting Italy in the 18th century

Il mondo della luna, the first opera of Haydn's to be staged following the institution of a regular opera season at Eszterháza in 1776, was the last of the three Goldoni librettos that he set. The other two were *Lo speziale* (1768) and *Le pescatrici* (1770). The text of Haydn's opera corresponds to Goldoni's libretto up to the first two lines of Act 2 scene xiv, but beginning with the Act 2 finale it follows that of Gennaro Astarita's setting (1775, Venice) with the exception of the closing chorus, whose origin is unknown.

Haydn's opera has a complicated genesis; the autograph materials survive in three partial versions. Early fragments show the parts of Ecclitico, Ernesto and Lisetta notated in alto, tenor and soprano clefs, respectively; but Ecclitico's and Ernesto's vocal ranges were later switched, and Lisetta's part was lowered. Ernesto is the last castrato role Haydn wrote before his ill-fated *L'anima del filosofo* (1791). Buonafede's role lies in a high baritone range, having been tailored to the voice of Bianchi. Poschwa and Puttler, like Bianchi, had been newly engaged in 1776. Dichtler sang in some 60 operas at Eszterháza between 1766 and 1788, and occasionally augmented his meagre salary by copying music. The exact date of the first performance is unknown: receipts from the printer of the libretto are dated 28 June 1777; the work was given in honour of the marriage on 3 August 1777 of Prince Nikolaus Esterházy's second son, Count Nikolaus, and Countess Maria Anna Weissenwolf. According to the libretto, Ecclitico was sung by Guglielmo Jermoli (who also took the role in Astarita's version) and Lisetta by his wife, Maria, but the couple apparently left the prince's service at the end of July. Whether they participated in the wedding performance is unclear. Little is known of other stagings in the 18th century. In the 20th century *Il mondo della luna* has been revived at Schwerin (1932), at the Holland Festival (1959, conducted by Giulini), in London at the Camden Festival (1960) and at Schleswig (1984).

*

Act I.i *A terrace on top of Ecclitico's house* Ecclitico devises a plan to trick Buonafede into allowing Flaminia, Clarice and Lisetta to marry the lovers of their choice: Ernesto, Ecclitico and Cecco, respectively. In a lengthy tripartite intermezzo-recitative-aria sequence, Ecclitico presents three pantomimes representative of life on the moon, which the gullible Buonafede observes through the false astrologer's telescope. Buonafede's longing for the moon is articulated in the tonal ascent from D major to E♭ major, the tonal centre of Ecclitico's aria, 'Un poco di denaro', in which he solicits the help of Ernesto and Cecco in carrying out his scheme.

I.ii *A room in Buonafede's house* Clarice and Flaminia express their desire to marry. Flaminia's coloratura aria in the heroic key of C major, 'Ragion nell'alma siede', quickly establishes her as Ernesto's counterpart. The wilful and less obedient daughter, Clarice, openly confronts authority in her first aria sung to Buonafede ('Son fanciulla da marito'). Ecclitico persuades Buonafede to swallow 'an elixir', actually a sleeping potion, which will transport him to the 'world of the moon'. Imaginative accompanied recitative underscores this event. Since Goldoni excluded *seria* characters from the predominantly comic domain of finales, only Clarice and Lisetta witness Buonafede's supposed ascent to the moon, which they interpret as the old man's demise. His hallucinatory journey, depicted in the assonance and alliteration of Goldoni's text ('Vado, vado, volo, volo'), is reflected in Haydn's evocative 'flight' music.

Act 2 *A delightful garden decorated to look like the world of the moon* On awaking in Ecclitico's garden, Buonafede beholds the moon's many beauties; Haydn depicts its exotic character in several pastoral ballet numbers. Such extended use of instrumental music is found in no other Italian opera by Haydn. Social positions are now reversed: Cecco, disguised as the emperor of the moon, joins Ernesto in teasing Buonafede. Ernesto, pretending to be Hesperus, the evening star, incites Buonafede's curiosity. (In this scene the original Ernesto wore the remodelled costume of Orpheus from the production of Gluck's opera at Eszterháza the previous year.) But the old man remains blissful at being on the moon, as is evident in 'Che mondo amabile', in which he dances and imitates birdcalls.

Lisetta is then brought to the lunar world, followed by Clarice and Flaminia. Now that everyone is assembled, Ecclitico proceeds with his plan. In the finale ('Al comando tuo lunatico') Cecco crowns Lisetta empress. This mock coronation was the only event of Goldoni's Act 2 finale, but the unknown author of Astarita's revisions lengthened the action. The revised text contains frequent comic interjections of nonsense language and several events from Goldoni's Act 3, including the betrothal of

Buonafede's daughters and the old man's discovery of the hoax. With this additional action, the second-act finale is able to accommodate extended musical development. The serious characters, Flaminia and Ernesto, also participate in the comic action, an advance in finale construction since the mid-century.

Act 3 *A room in Ecclitico's house* Goldoni's third act is much eviscerated by the additions made to the second-act finale. In the end, Buonafede consents to the marriages. Clarice and Ecclitico sing of their love in a beautiful two-tempo duet, 'Un certo ruscelletto', and the opera concludes with a chorus of reconciliation ('Dal mondo della luna').

*

Il mondo della luna was pillaged for several self-borrowings. The overture circulated widely in an altered version as the first movement of Haydn's Symphony no.63 (*La Roxelane*); the short intermezzo at the beginning of Act 2 scene xi was rearranged as the Andante of *La vera costanza* published by Artaria in a set of six overtures (Vienna, 1782–3); the same intermezzo appeared, along with several other selections from Act 2, in five trios of 1784; and Ernesto's aria, 'Qualche volta non fa male', with alternating major-minor passages, was adapted as the Benedictus of the 'Mariazell Mass' (1782).

The topsy-turvy world of the moon presented in this Goldonian farce incorporates many absurd situations, exotic locations and opportunities for travesty, all of which appealed to Haydn's creative genius. In his imaginative use of woodwind instruments, balletic interludes and accompanied recitatives, Haydn shows a new mastery, and the finales show a new awareness of large-scale structures.　　　　　　　　　　　　C.C., P.B.

Mosè in Egitto ('Moses in Egypt')

Azione tragico-sacra in three acts by Gioachino Rossini to a libretto by Andrea Leone Tottola after the Old Testament and Francesco Ringhieri's *L'Osiride*; Naples, Teatro S Carlo, 5 March 1818 (revised Act 3, March 1819). Revised version in four acts as *Moïse et Pharaon*, with a new libretto by Luigi Balocchi and Etienne de Jouy; Opéra, Paris, 26 March 1827.

Michele Benedetti first sang the title role, with Isabella Colbran and Andrea Nozzari as the young lovers. At the première of the Paris version the roles were sung by Nicolas Levasseur, Laure Cinti-Damoreau and Adolphe Nourrit respectively.

Faraone [Pharaoh]	bass
Mosè [Moses]	bass
Aronne [sometimes Elisero; Aaron] *his brother*	tenor
Elcia [Anaïs] *a young Jewish girl*	soprano
Osiride [Amenophis] *Pharaoh's son*	tenor
Amaltea [Sinaïs] *Pharaoh's wife*	soprano
Mambre [Auphis] *priest*	tenor
Setting Egypt in Biblical times	

Mosè in Egitto was one of the fruits of Rossini's extraordinarily productive sojourn in Naples as musical director of the S Carlo (18 operas in seven years, nine of them for that theatre). Conceived as a biblical drama suitable for staging during Lent, the work nonetheless grafts on to the Old Testament narrative a love story taken from Ringhieri's drama of 1760. Like Aida and Radames in Verdi's opera, Rossini's heroine, the young Jewish girl Elcia, and the Pharaoh's son Amenophis fall in love despite the conflict between their two peoples. In its original form, the Neapolitan version of 1818–19, *Mosè in Egitto* is one of the freshest and dramatically most effective of Rossini's *opere serie*, and there is a strong case for preferring this version to the somewhat bloated and more arbitrarily structured revision which he prepared for Paris in 1827 under the title *Moïse et Pharaon*. (For its first London performances (1822–3) the opera was given under the title *Pietro l'eremita*.)

By deliberate design, *Mosè in Egitto* has no overture, yet the opening is as effective as any created by Rossini. A plague of darkness covers the land of Egypt. After three summoning chords, a semiquaver figure in C minor ushers in the chorus of distraught and bewildered Egyptians. Despairing for his country's plight, Pharaoh sends for Moses in an attempt to negotiate the freedom of the Israelites. Moses's brother Aaron shrewdly advises caution, recalling earlier acts of deception by Pharaoh, but Moses accepts Pharaoh's word. Moses's magnificent address to the Almighty 'Eterno! immenso! incomprensibil Dio!', accompanied by trumpets, horns and woodwind, recalls the 'Tuba mirum' from Mozart's *Requiem*, just as the brilliant C major transformation which follows – Moses restoring light to Egypt – suggests a debt to one of Rossini's favourite works, Haydn's *The Creation*. News that the Israelites are about to leave Egypt upsets Osiride. More guileful than the gentle, radiant Elcia whom he loves, Osiride plots with the disaffected priest Mambre to sow doubts among the Egyptian people, who stand to lose much by the Israelites' departure. The first act ends with Pharaoh attempting to go back on his word, whereupon Moses invokes a plague of hail and fire on the land.

In Act 2 Pharaoh once again offers the Israelites their freedom. He also proposes an arranged marriage between his son and an Armenian princess. Osiride now determines to abduct Elcia but he is seen by Aaron. Informed of the lovers' intended flight,

Moses enlists the help of Ameltea, wife of Pharaoh but sympathetic to the Jewish cause. In the duet 'Ah! Se puoi così lasciarmi', Osiride proposes to Elcia that they abandon the court and live together in the woods but they are discovered by Amaltea and Aaron, a confrontation that generates the quartet 'Mi manca la voce'. Pharaoh again attempts to go back on his word but this time Moses threatens that the royal prince and all the first-born of the land will be felled by lightning. Pharaoh pronounces Osiride co-ruler and demands that he pass sentence of death on the captive Moses. Elcia reveals her relationship with Osiride; her 'Porgi la destra amata' is a tender, expiatory aria. But Osiride, less wise politically than his vacillating father, insolently condemns Moses who strikes him dead with a lightning shaft. It is a brilliant *coup de théâtre* and its aftermath, Pharaoh's lament for his dead son, draws from the orchestra an eerie *pizzicato strappato*, an effect worthy of Berlioz. Elcia now becomes febrile, a nascent Lucia di Lammermoor. The breaking up of this superb scene is one of the major aberrations of the 1827 Paris revision.

Act 3 provides a coda to these traumatic events. Having travelled to the edge of the Red Sea, the Israelites can go no further. It is at this point that Moses leads them in the famous prayer, written by Rossini for the 1819 Naples revival of the opera, 'Dal tuo stellato soglio'. The prayer is answered; the waters divide at the touch of Moses's rod, and the pursuing Egyptians, led by Pharaoh and Mambre, are drowned as the waters close about them in the wake of the fleeing Israelites.

For the Paris version of his Moses opera, Rossini elaborated and reordered the musical and dramatic structures. In conformity with French taste of the time and the added resources of the Paris Opéra, the work is both grander and more spectacular than the original, at some cost to its essential freshness and cogency. Only three numbers are entirely new: the *scène et quatuor* 'Dieu de la paix' in Act 1, Anaïs's *scène et air* 'Quelle horrible destinée' in Act 4 and the concluding and rarely performed *cantique* 'Chantons, bénissons le Seigneur'. The overture, introduction and Act 3 ballet all draw on material from Rossini's *Armida* (1817), though the ballet is substantially new. Reorderings include the transference of the famous 'Scene of the Shadows' from the start of the work to the opening of Act 2 and the dismembering of the original's important Act 2 finale. The death of Pharaoh's son is postponed and Elcia's 'Porgi la destra amata' is turned into an appeal by Pharaoh's wife to their lovelorn son. The Paris libretto also renames several leading characters: Pharaoh's son, Osiride, becomes Aménophis, Pharaoh's wife, Amaltea, becomes Sinaïde and the young Hebrew

girl Elcia becomes Anaï, daughter of Marie [Miriam] (mezzo-soprano), Moses's sister. Osiride (bass) is the Egyptian High Priest, originally the tenor role of Mambre (not to be confused with Prince Osiride in *Mosè in Egitto*).

Like *Le siège de Corinthe* (1826), *Moïse et Pharaon* can be seen as an experiment in handling the resources of grand opera and, as such, an important stepping-stone towards the creation of Rossini's one wholly original work for the French stage, *Guillaume Tell* (1829). Houses with large choral resources and a ballet will continue to prefer it but the Neapolitan original has been too little noted by smaller houses and companies, to which it is admirably suited. R.O.

Moses und Aron ('Moses and Aaron')

Opera in three acts by Arnold Schoenberg, to his own libretto (Act 3 not composed); *Der Tanz um das goldene Kalb* performed in concert, Darmstadt, 2 July 1951; Acts 1 and 2 performed in concert, Hamburg, Nordwestdeutscher Rundfunk, 12 March 1954; Acts 1 and 2 staged, Zürich, Stadttheater, 6 June 1957.

At the first (concert) performance Hans Herbert Fiedler played Moses and Helmut Krebs sang Aaron. Fiedler again played Moses at the first staged performance, with Helmut Melchert as Aaron.

Moses	speaker (deep voice)
Aron [Aaron] *his brother*	tenor
A Young Girl	soprano
A Young Man	tenor
Another Man	baritone
A Priest	contralto
A Sick Woman	contralto
An Ephraimite	baritone
A Naked Youth	tenor
Another Man	speaker
Four Naked Virgins	sopranos, contraltos
Naked Men	tenors, basses
The Voice from the Burning Bush	semichorus
Twelve Tribal Chieftains	tenors, basses
Beggars	altos, basses
Old Men	tenors
Seventy Elders	basses and silent roles
Six Solo Voices	soprano,
(in the orchestra)	mezzo-soprano, contralto, tenor, baritone, bass

Israelites, dancers, extras of all kinds

The Young Girl is also one of the four Naked Virgins; the Voice from the Burning Bush comprises three to six each of sopranos, trebles, contraltos, tenors, baritones and basses; about a third of the Seventy Elders are sung roles, the rest silent

Setting Egypt, at the time of the Israelites'
bondage

From every point of view, whether musical, religious
or philosophical, the opera is Schoenberg's most
comprehensive religious masterpiece. The ideas that
gave rise to it occupied him for many years before its
composition, and their dramatic expression called
forth music of immense power and diversity. It is in
some respects a sequel to the unfinished oratorio
Die Jakobsleiter (1917), for Moses is required to fulfil
the prophetic mission laid upon the chosen one
in the earlier work; but it is also the product of
Schoenberg's deep concern with questions of Jewish
politics and religion. About 1922–3 he began planning two works in which conflicting aspects of
spiritual revelation were to be symbolized by Moses
and Aaron. In the first, the prose drama *Der biblische
Weg* ('The Biblical Way', 1926–7), which deals with
political aspirations in a modern setting, the downfall
of the chief protagonist comes about through his
attempt to combine the principles of both Moses and
Aaron. The second, a cantata to be called *Moses am
brennenden Dornbusch* ('Moses at the burning
Thornbush'), was expanded to a full-scale oratorio
text entitled *Moses und Aron* (1927–8), and transformed into an opera libretto in 1930. The first two
acts were composed between 1930 and 1932, but the
third hung fire, and although to the end of his life
Schoenberg frequently spoke of setting it, he never
did so.

In consequence the question of performance did
not arise till very late, when he finally accepted that
he would probably not be able to complete the work.
On 2 July 1951, only 11 days before Schoenberg's
death, Hermann Scherchen conducted *Der Tanz um
das goldene Kalb* ('The dance round the golden calf') at
the Darmstadt summer school for new music. It had
to be repeated immediately at the same concert, and
Schoenberg was told by telegram of its great success.
It was another three years before the radio station
Nordwestdeutscher Rundfunk mounted the first
complete performance of the opera, with Hans
Rosbaud conducting at short notice in place of Hans
Schmidt-Isserstedt. A recording was made and later
issued commercially. In 1957 the opera was staged for
the first time in Zürich, without the third act, with the
same Moses and conductor. A 1959 production under
Scherchen in Berlin, which was seen later in various
continental cities, tried the predictably unsuccessful
experiment of speaking the third act against a
recording of the music of Act 1 scene i. Since then it
has become standard practice to omit Act 3 entirely.

*

Act I.i *The calling of Moses* For a brief but
unforgettable moment before the curtain rises,
pianissimo chords sung by Six Solo Voices in the
orchestra suggest a spirituality beyond human
involvement. Moses is then discovered addressing
God in prayer: 'only, eternal, omnipresent, invisible
and unimaginable God' (not 'inconceivable' – a
common mistranslation). The Voice from the
Burning Bush charges him with the task of prophet. It
is represented by a six-part speaking chorus which
cuts across and intermittently obscures the soloists in
the orchestra, so that something of the spiritual
quality of the opening music is already lost as God's
commands are framed in words. Moses foresees the
difficulty of proclaiming the nature of God to his
chosen people, and pleads that he lacks eloquence.
He is told that Aaron will be his mouthpiece, a
dispensation that Schoenberg symbolizes by making
Moses a speaking role and Aaron a tenor. At the end
of the scene the Six Solo Voices, still dominated by
the speaking chorus, sing of God's promise to his
chosen people of a spiritual future.

I.ii *Moses meets Aaron in the wilderness* An agile,
restless prelude introduces Aaron. Moses does not
need to tell him what God demands of them: he
already knows, and expresses his understanding of
God's purpose in the soaring melodic lines that
characterize his music and set the tone of the scene.
Moses gives his own, more austere interpretations
simultaneously. Although they occasionally seem to
unite when echoes from the first scene are heard,
Moses knows, for instance, that God cannot be
swayed by human actions, whereas Aaron sees him
as an arbiter who is susceptible to sacrifices. God is
thereby diminished. As Schoenberg said in the words
to his chorus op.27 no.2: 'You shall make no image.
For an image confines, limits, grasps what should
remain limitless and unimaginable. You must believe
in the spirit directly, without emotion, selflessly.'
Aaron is already setting up images.

I.iii and I.iv *Moses and Aaron bring God's message to
the people* A young girl and two men in a state of
religious exaltation have seen Aaron on his way to
meet Moses. They believe the new god may help in
the freeing of the Israelites from captivity. Their
volatile music infects without convincing the
sceptical people. A Priest, the spokesman for law and
order, resists it in the stiff accents that mark all his
utterances. The people polarize into two groups and
end by shouting at each other before preparing to
resign themselves again to their servitude. Suddenly
Moses and Aaron are seen approaching as though
borne along by an unseen power. The people reunite
in mounting excitement. Apart from the two brothers, who are God's emissaries, they are the only force
in the drama, and a highly inconstant and unpredictable one. Minor characters emerge from among them
from time to time to voice varying emotions or
opinions, but they do not themselves influence the
course of events.

Moses and Aaron arrive. The people promise the new god liberal sacrifices if he can offer them hope. When they are told to fall down and worship an all-powerful but invisible presence they pass from incomprehension to savage derision, each chorus displaying an extraordinarily versatile use of imitation and canon to intensify declamatory power. Moses accepts defeat and blames Aaron, who angrily snatches his staff and turns it into a serpent. This is the first of three miracles by means of which he convinces the people of God's power and their own weakness in allowing themselves to become demoralized in captivity. After each they celebrate their returning courage and new-found belief with a march-like chorus. Moses takes hardly any part in the proceedings, but if Aaron's success is based on images it is not entirely without divine sanction: the voices in the orchestra, silent since the first scene, give his actions some support, and their hymn announcing God's promise is taken up by Aaron and the people (to slightly less exalted words) before the final march.

Interlude The Israelites are encamped in the wilderness. Moses has been absent on the mountain for 40 days receiving God's law. A small chorus, in darkness in front of the curtain, partially whispers its fear that he will not return.

Act 2.i and ii *Aaron and the Seventy Elders before the mountain of revelation* The Priest and the Elders warn Aaron that without laws or intelligible gods the people are growing mutinous. Suddenly there is a sound of tumult and they pour on to the stage threatening to kill their leaders if they do not give them back their old gods. Aaron tells them to bring gold; he will give them the kind of god they long for. Their frustration turns at once to rejoicing.

2.iii and iv *The golden calf and the altar* As the people part to reveal the calf the mountain of revelation becomes visible in the distance. If the cult of the false god leads to an orgy that cannot be presented according to the letter of the stage directions, the music rises to every demand. Offerings of all kinds are brought, including beasts that are slaughtered by butchers who perform a wild dance and throw raw meat to the people. A Sick Woman is cured by touching the calf, and some Old Men kill themselves as a sacrifice. An Ephraimite and Twelve Tribal Chieftains gallop up to pay homage to the calf; they kill a Young Man who denounces their idolatry. A lull ensues during which people exchange gifts till drunken brawling takes over. Four Naked Virgins are sacrificed. Wholesale destruction and suicide break out. Naked Men strip women and carry them off. Gradually the turmoil subsides. Some sleep, others drift away; finally all is still. A voice cries out that Moses is coming down from the mountain. He returns carrying the tables of the law. The golden calf vanishes at his command.

2.v *Moses and Aaron* To music filled with fleeting reminiscences of the first two scenes of the opera Aaron defends himself vigorously against his brother's anger and intransigence. His actions have been prompted, as ever, by Moses's unspoken thoughts. The people respond to the truth when it is presented to them in a comprehensible form; compromise can save them from loss of hope. Even the tables of the law can present only a part of the truth, and hence an image. At this Moses smashes the tables and prays to be relieved of his office. To the hymn of the chosen people, in which Aaron joins, and their march, the Israelites cross the back of the stage following a pillar of fire. Moses is left alone, despairing at their reconversion by yet another image. His idealism too has been no more than an image, for his thoughts cannot and may not be expressed: 'O word, word that I lack'.

*

The version of the third-act libretto that Schoenberg seems in general to have favoured consists of a single brief scene. Aaron has been arrested. Although circumstances have not otherwise changed, Moses is allowed the victory in their debate. Aaron is freed, but falls dead. Moses proclaims a future in which the people will be at one with God. There is also an earlier, slightly longer, version which Schoenberg seems to have remembered as late as 1950, and a later one (1935) ending with an extraordinary vision of the diaspora. He insisted that the opera was in no way concerned with the artist's role, but he certainly saw that role as prophetic. He once wrote that Beethoven, Bruckner and Mahler had not been permitted to write tenth symphonies because they would have revealed more of the ultimate truth than it was given to man to know. To express in music the unity with God achieved in Act 3 would have been to compose a tenth symphony. Yet it was Schoenberg's prophetic duty never to admit to the impossibility of doing so, or to cease to strive towards its attainment. The first two acts, however, provide a parable of his view of man's religious predicament which is both musically and dramatically complete. At some level he must have been aware of that, and indeed have planned it.

O.W.N.

Muette de Portici, La ('The Mute Girl of Portici')

Grand opéra in five acts by Daniel-François-Esprit Auber to a libretto by Eugène Scribe and Germain Delavigne; Paris, Opéra, 29 February 1828.

The cast of the first production included Laure Cinti-Damoreau (Elvire), Adolphe Nourrit

(Masaniello), Henri-Bernard Dabadie (Pietro); with Lise Noblet as Fenella.

Alphonse *son of the Spanish Viceroy*
   of Naples   tenor
Elvire *his fiancée*   soprano
Masaniello *a Neapolitan fisherman*   tenor
Fenella *his sister, a mute*   dancer
Pietro   bass
Borella } *Masaniello's companions*   bass
Moreno   bass
Lorenzo *confidant of Alphonse*   tenor
Selva *officer of the Viceroy*   bass
A Lady-in-waiting to Elvire   soprano
Soldiers, fishermen, conspirators, nobles, Spanish
   women, Neapolitan women, villagers
Setting Naples and Portici in 1647, during the
   rebellion against the Spanish Viceroy

The first version of the libretto, in three acts, was written by Delavigne in 1825, on a subject of great interest at the time. Entitled *Masaniello, ou la Muette de Portici*, it was submitted to the censors, who demanded changes. The second version was reworked by Scribe, but was not completed. In this version Scribe not only changed the conception to meet the demands of the censors, suppressing explicitly revolutionary material, but also created a new type of libretto, for a *grand opéra* in five acts. He added a first act introducing the traditional pair of lovers, which inevitably affected the following acts, but this version differed considerably from his final one. The original revolutionary content, and the attempt to provide logical motivation for the actions of the main characters and chorus, gave rise to inconsistencies which could not be corrected in the final five-act version. The mute girl Fenella's participation only in pantomime – an idea indebted to Walter Scott's *Peveril of the Peak* (1822) as well as the *mélodrame* of the boulevard theatres – was part of the original conception; none of the earlier composers who had treated this story (Keiser, Bishop and Carafa) had employed this device. Auber reportedly set the libretto in the space of three months.

*

The masterly overture, with its concise themes, is associated in spirit with the world of Fenella and the common people. The mood of unrest in its opening bars recurs a number of times, the tension often enhanced by delayed resolutions.

Act I *Naples, the gardens of the palace of the Spanish Viceroy* As the chorus rejoices at the forthcoming marriage of Alphonse to the Spanish princess Elvire, the bridegroom reveals that he is plagued by a guilty conscience for seducing and abandoning the mute fishermaid Fenella. Elvire approaches with a festive procession; her companions perform two Spanish

'La muette de Portici' (Auber), Giovanni Mario as Masaniello and Pauline Leroux as Fenella in the 1862 Covent Garden production: lithograph from a contemporary sheet music cover

dances. The tyrannical Viceroy has had Fenella imprisoned, but she escapes and begs Elvire to protect her from her persecutors. Elvire and her companions enter the church for the wedding ceremony. When it is over, Fenella recognizes Alphonse as her seducer and accuses him in front of Elvire. As the soldiers try to seize Fenella, she manages to escape with the aid of the people.

Act 2 *The beach at Portici* Masaniello, leader of the revolutionary movement, sings a barcarolle ('Amis la matinée est belle') expressing opposition to the Viceroy. Pietro returns from Naples, having failed to find Fenella. The two friends sing a duet, swearing vengeance on their Spanish oppressors. Fenella rushes in and tells them what has happened to her. The indignant Masaniello swears to be revenged, and urges the fishermen to rebel. They all swear loyalty to him.

Act 3.i *A room in the palace* Elvire at first rejects Alphonse, but eventually yields to his pleading and they sing of their mutual happiness.

3.ii *The market-place of Naples* The market is busy; the people dance a tarantella. Selva recognizes Fenella, and his soldiers try to capture her. This is the signal for the rebellion to begin. A soldier who attempts to disarm Masaniello is killed. When the rest of the soldiers have been overpowered the rebels, after praying for divine help, go off to set the palace on fire.

Act 4 *Masaniello's hut in Portici* Masaniello is horrified by the bloodshed and destruction of the revolution, over which he has lost control. He views hospitality as a sacred duty, and when Alphonse and Elvire seek shelter from the mob he takes them in, unaware of their identity. Even after learning that Alphonse is both Fenella's seducer and the Viceroy's son, he defends him against his former friends, who demand his execution. Masaniello finally allows the pair to escape. The representatives of the people solemnly ask him to take the keys of the city of Naples. While the people hail him as victor, his former companions threaten to murder him.

Act 5 *The entrance of the Viceroy's palace; Vesuvius in the background* Pietro reveals that he has poisoned Masaniello. Borella brings the news that Alphonse is approaching the city with a battalion of soldiers. Although Masaniello has gone mad, he is persuaded by Fenella to lead the rebels into battle to prevent the crushing of the revolution. Fenella prays for him. Elvire enters and tells how Masaniello saved her life; because of this he has been murdered by his own men. The people hail Alphonse as the victor. Vesuvius erupts, and Fenella, overcome with grief, flings herself into the lava.

*

The history of *grand opéra* begins with *La muette de Portici*. The characteristics of the genre include a new degree of magnificence in the sets and sensationally dramatic technical stage effects, the culmination of each act in a large tableau and ingeniously staged crowd scenes. The opera provided new opportunities for the director, librettist, set designer and costume designer to work together, and they made a careful study of the historical background of the Neapolitan revolt. The climax of the final scene with the eruption of Vesuvius was a sensation, and its influence was felt in *grand opéra* from Meyerbeer and his contemporaries to Wagner's *Götterdämmerung*. The work's connection with the Belgian revolution of 22 August 1830 made it a general symbol of revolutionary ideas.

On one level, Auber's music is influenced by the *opéra comique* and the popular political song of the time; on another, by the more formal type of operatic aria, ensemble, dance and finale; and on a third (in the pantomime scenes) by the *mélodrame*. The overture's first, turbulent theme returns again at the beginning of Act 4, at the point when Fenella mimes the devastation brought about by the revolution. A further theme from the overture, one unusually chromatic for Auber, and first appearing before the triumphal march, recurs at the end of the opera at Fenella's suicide. Recent commentary on the opera has drawn attention to the apparent conflict between the character of this march, which not only brings the overture to a stirring end but is also heard again at the end of the fourth act, seeming to imply that the revolution is victorious, and the actual outcome of the opera.

Auber's music is conventional where he is composing for conventional love scenes (which only appear in the five-act version): Elvire's 'Plaisirs du rang suprême' and the duet, 'N'espérez pas me fuir', which follow the cantabile–cabaletta pattern. Masaniello's barcarolle in Act 2, with its concealed challenge to tyrants, became popular throughout Europe. The chorus 'Courons à la vengeance' and the duet for tenor and bass, 'Mieux vaut mourir' by Masaniello and Pietro, dominated by the refrain 'Amour sacré de la patrie', were highly congenial to the revolutionary movements of the 19th century. The suggestive power of the music for Fenella's pantomimes and the dances influenced many other works; for instance, the Allegro vivace in the first part of no.4 is echoed in one of Verdi's rising themes, employed in his overture to *Oberto*.

In Masaniello's mad scene Auber employs the commonly encountered device of musical quotation, with the hero repeating themes from the chorus 'Courons à la vengeance' and his barcarolle. Throughout the opera he uses reminiscences to create a network of musico-dramatic relationships supported by deliberate tonal planning. In Act 5, the growing intensity of the finale, where the D minor harmony clearly suggests the Act 2 finale of *Don Giovanni*, is dramatically compelling.

In the vocal score published in England, the Andante of the overture was replaced by the first barcarolle, and the market chorus was inserted after the quotation from the march. In England and the USA, the aria known as 'My Sister Dear', taken from *Le concert à la cour* ('Pourquoi pleurer') to be used as an interlude, was particularly well known and frequently published.   **H.S.**

N

Nabucco [*Nabucodonosor* ('Nebuchadnezzar')]

Dramma lirico in four parts by Giuseppe Verdi to a libretto by Temistocle Solera after Antonio Cortesi's ballet *Nabuccodonosor* and Auguste Anicet-Bourgeois' and Francis Cornu's play *Nabuchodonosor*; Milan, Teatro alla Scala, 9 March 1842.

At the première the cast included Prosper Dérivis (Zaccaria), Giuseppina Strepponi (Abigaille), Giorgio Ronconi (Nabucco), Corrado Miraglia (Ismaele) and Giovannina Bellinzaghi (Fenena).

Nabucco [Nabucodonosor] *King of Babylon*	baritone
Ismaele *nephew of Sedecia, King of Jerusalem*	tenor
Zaccaria *High Priest of the Hebrews*	bass
Abigaille *slave, presumed to be the first daughter of Nabucodonosor*	soprano
Fenena *daughter of Nabucodonosor*	soprano
The High Priest of Baal	bass
Abdallo *elderly officer of the King of Babylon*	tenor
Anna *Zaccaria's sister*	soprano
Babylonian and Hebrew soldiers, Levites, Hebrew virgins, Babylonian women, magi, Lords of the Kingdom of Babylon, populace	
Setting Jerusalem and Babylon, 587 BC	

The story of *Nabucco* began some 18 months before its first performance, soon after the successful première of Verdi's first opera, *Oberto, conte di San Bonifacio* (1839). A contract was drawn up between Verdi and Bartolomeo Merelli, impresario at La Scala, according to which Verdi would write three further operas. The first of these, the comic work *Un giorno di regno* (1840), was a disastrous failure and (at least according to Verdi's own later memories) the humiliation of public rejection caused the composer to give up his professional calling. The tragic loss of his young family must also have affected him deeply (his two children and then his wife Margherita Barezzi died in three successive years, 1838–40). However, in the winter of 1840–41, Merelli persuaded Verdi to take on Temistocle Solera's libretto of *Nabucco*, which had been turned down by the young Prussian composer Otto Nicolai.

The background of *Nabucco* (or *Nabucodonosor* as it was originally called) derives from biblical sources, most extensively from *Jeremiah*; and although Nabucco (Nebuchadnezzar) is the only biblical character to appear, the part of the prophet Zaccaria has strong overtones of Jeremiah. Solera's main source was a French play, first performed in 1836, although some of his alterations can be traced to the scenario of a ballet also derived from the play, given at La Scala in 1838. The lack of documentation concerning the genesis of the opera can be put down to a number of factors: Verdi was relatively unknown at the time, and few of his letters were preserved; he and Solera were together in Milan, and had little need of correspondence; and Solera – unlike some of Verdi's future librettists – was an experienced man of the theatre who apparently needed little help in constructing a dramatically convincing text.

After a number of delays, *Nabucco* was first performed at La Scala in March 1842. Strepponi, with whom Verdi formed a permanent attachment probably beginning around this time, was in poor voice (and her final scene was cut after two performances), but the opera was nevertheless a great success. It was revived at La Scala for the autumn season of 1842 and ran for a record 57 performances. For this revival Verdi made a number of small changes to suit the new Abigaille, Teresa De Giuli Borsi, and added some adjustments to the vocal line of Fenena's preghiera in Part 4. For a Venice revival in the Carnival season 1842–3, he replaced this preghiera with a *romanza* for Fenena. It seems that Verdi wrote ballet music for a revival of *Nabucco* in Brussels in 1848, although no trace of it has survived.

*

The overture, except for the chorale-like opening, is made up of themes from the opera: the main, recurring idea is from the 'Maledetto' chorus in Part 2; there is also a compound-time, pastoral version of 'Va pensiero' and several more martial inspirations.

Part I: 'Jerusalem'

Inside the temple of Solomon The Babylonian army has reached Jerusalem and is at the gates of the temple. The Israelites lament their fate, but the prophet Zaccaria rallies them: he has as a hostage Fenena, daughter of Nabucco, the Babylonian king, and God will assist them. The people follow Zaccaria

Right: 59. 'Lucia di Lammermoor'
(Donizetti, 1835), Lucia and Edgardo in
an early Italian production

Main picture: 60. 'Lucia di Lammermoor'
(Donizetti, 1835), scene from the
production by Graham Vick (sets and
costumes by Paul Brown) for the Maggio
Musicale Fiorentino (shared with the Grand
Théâtre, Geneva), Teatro Comunale,
Florence, in 1996, with Elizabeth Futral
(Lucia) and José Bros (Edgardo)

Above: 61. 'Lulu' (Berg, 1937),
scene from the production by Götz
Friedrich (designed by Timothy
O'Brien) at the Royal Opera
House, Covent Garden, in 1981,
with Karan Armstrong as Lulu

Left: 62. 'Lucrezia Borgia'
(Donizetti, 1833), Joan Sutherland
(Lucrezia) and Stafford Dean
(Alfonso d'Este) in the production
by John Copley (sets John Pascoe,
costumes Michael Stennett) at the
Royal Opera House, Covent
Garden, in 1980

63. 'Macbeth' (Verdi, 1847), scene from the 1987 revival of the 1984 production by Antoine Vitez (designed by Yannis Kokkos) at the Paris Opéra, with Simon Estes (Macbeth) and Elizabeth Connell (Lady Macbeth)

64. 'Madama Butterfly' (Puccini, 1904), scene from the 1974 Sadler's Wells Opera production by Colin Graham (designer John Fraser) at the London Coliseum

65. 'The Makropulos Affair' (Janáček, 1926), set design by Josef Čapek for Act 2 (backstage at the theatre after the performance by the singer Emilia Marty) in the Prague première (1928)

66. 'The Mask of Orpheus' (Birtwistle, 1986), scene from the original production by David Freeman (designed by Jocelyn Herbert) at the English National Opera, London Coliseum, with Philip Langridge as Orpheus, lying slain

67. 'A Midsummer Night's Dream' (Britten, 1960), scene from the 1984 revival of Peter Hall's 1981 production (designed by John Bury) for Glyndebourne Festival Opera, with Elizabeth Gale (Tytania) and James Bowman (Oberon)

68. 'Die Meistersinger von Nürnberg' (Wagner, 1868), painting by Michael Echter showing a scene from Act 1, based on the sets for the original production at the Königliches Hof - und Nationaltheater, Munich

Above: 69. 'Moses und Aron' (Schoenberg, staged 1957), scene from the production by Peter Hall (designed by John Bury) at the Royal Opera House, Covent Garden, in 1965, with Forbes Robinson as Moses and Richard Lewis as Aaron

Left: 70. 'Moses und Aron' (Schoenberg, staged 1957), scene from the production by Herbert Wernicke at the Théâtre du Châtelet, Paris, in 1995, with Philip Langridge (Aaron) and Aage Haugland (Moses)

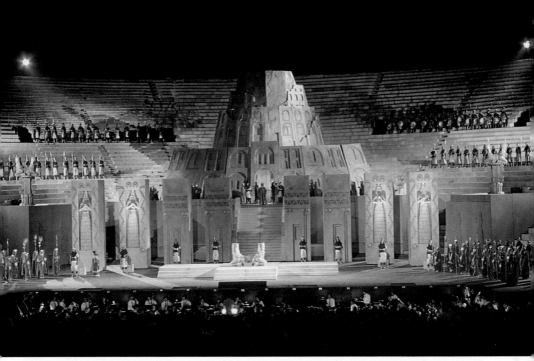

71. 'Nabucco' (Verdi, 1842), the production by Gianfranco de Bosio at the Arena di Verona in 1991

72. 'Norma' (Bellini, 1831), Alessandro Sanquirico's design for the finale of the original production at La Scala, Milan

73. 'Le nozze di Figaro' (Mozart, 1786), scene from Act 1 of the John Copley production (designed by Stefanos Lazaridis and Michael Stennett) at the Royal Opera House, Covent Garden, 1982, with Marie McLaughlin (Susanna), Diana Montague (Cherubino) and Richard Stilwell (Count Almaviva)

74. 'Nerone' (Boito, 1924), set design by Lodovico Pogliaghi for the original production at La Scala, Milan

into battle. The two numbers that encompass this action are linked and in many ways comprise a single unit. The opening chorus, 'Gli arredi festivi', is fashioned on a large scale and draws its effect from the juxtaposition of contrasting blocks: a terrified populace, a group of praying Levites, another of supplicant virgins. Zaccaria responds with a double aria: the Andante, 'D'Egitto là sui lidi', has an unusual two-stanza structure in which the opening of the second stanza is sustained by unison chorus; the cabaletta, 'Come notte al sol fulgente', also features a unison choral interruption.

The stage clears, leaving Fenena and Ismaele alone. We learn in recitative that Ismaele and Fenena fell in love while Ismaele was imprisoned in Babylon, and that Fenena has helped him escape to Israel. They are interrupted by Abigaille, who has stolen into the temple at the head of a band of disguised Assyrian warriors. She had also fallen in love with Ismaele during his captivity and now taunts him with her victory. The accompanied recitative that introduces Abigaille immediately fixes her unusual vocal character, which requires power in the lower register, agility above the staff and a forceful dramatic presence throughout. The ensuing terzetto, 'Io t'amava', is a moment of lyrical relaxation graced with much vocal ornamentation, somewhat out of character with the rest of the score.

The finale of Part 1 begins with a pseudo-fugal chorus, 'Lo vedeste?', as the Israelites panic in defeat. Nabucco arrives on horseback to the triumphant strains of a stage-band march, but Zaccaria threatens to kill Fenena if Nabucco profanes the temple. This tableau precipitates the central, static moment of the finale, 'Tremin gl'insani', which is led off by Nabucco and which characterizes by turn the conflicting attitudes of the principals. When the stage action resumes Ismaele, fearful for Fenena, disarms Zaccaria. Nabucco is now free to act and, in a furious stretta, orders the destruction of the temple.

Part 2: 'The Impious One'

2.i *The royal apartments in Babylon* While Nabucco is away Fenena has been appointed regent. The act opens with a full-scale double aria for Abigaille, who, it turns out, is the daughter of a slave, not the king. After an intense recitative her thoughts turn to Ismaele in the Andante 'Anch'io dischiuso un giorno'. The aria is highly ornamental, with each two-bar phrase rounded by a vocal flourish; but the ornaments, typically for Verdi, are strictly contained, giving their proliferation at the climax a compelling energy. The High Priest of Baal arrives with news that Fenena has freed the Israelites, and reports that the king has been killed in battle; urged on by a warlike chorus, Abigaille decides to assume power herself. Her cabaletta, 'Salgo già del trono aurato', returns to the forceful tone of the recitative and,

although in a far more dynamic context, again succeeds in wedding ornamental gestures to a rigorously controlled structure.

2.ii *A room in the palace, giving on to other rooms* Zaccaria's recitativo and preghiera, 'Vieni o Levita', is an oasis of calm in this generally hectic opera, its accompaniment of six solo cellos deployed with great variety of texture. As Zaccaria leaves by one door, Ismaele arrives by another, only to be shunned by the Levites in the chorus 'Il maledetto': they hold him responsible for their captive state. Then follows another grand finale, similar in its opening sections to that of the first part. Abigaille is declared queen and is about to crown herself when Nabucco, whose death had been falsely reported, reappears to snatch the crown for himself. This precipitates the centrepiece of the finale, 'S'appressan gl'istanti', a quasi-canonic movement that gains its effect not from individual characterization (each of the principals sings the same melody) but from an inexorable increase in textural complexity and sonic power. Nabucco then faces the crowd and declares himself not only their king but their God. A thunderbolt strikes him down for this blasphemy and the crowd murmurs in shocked response. Italian operatic convention would now suggest a fast concluding movement, but instead Solera and Verdi decided on a mad scene for Nabucco during which his discourse distractedly moves between fast and slow tempos before he faints. A triumphant cry from Abigaille brings down the curtain.

Part 3: 'The Prophecy'

3.i *The hanging gardens of Babylon* The routinely cheerful opening chorus, complete with stage-band interpolations borrowed from Part 1 ('E l'Assiria una regina'), is in its orchestration perhaps an early Verdian effort at depicting local colour. It leads to one of the opera's best numbers: the Abigaille-Nabucco duet, in which Abigaille, who has now succeeded in seizing power, dupes the king into signing Fenena's death sentence. After an opening recitative, the duet unfolds in the traditional four-movement pattern. A fast-paced dialogue movement ('Donna, chi sei?'), in which repeated orchestral motifs supply the continuity, leads to a movement of lyrical repose in which the characters develop their opposing attitudes in greater detail ('Oh di qual'onta aggravasi'). The third movement reimposes the outside world, as offstage trumpets announce the death sentence; and then in the final cabaletta ('Deh perdona') Nabucco and Abigaille restate their fixed positions: he begging her to show mercy, she inflexibly maintaining her dominance.

3.ii *The banks of the Euphrates* The closing scene of Part 3 is entitled 'Coro e Profezia' ('Chorus and Prophecy'). The Hebrews' sighs for their lost home-land are violently countered by Zaccaria, who presents a vision of the future in which Babylon will be reduced to ruins. The Hebrews' choral lament ('Va pensiero') is the most famous piece in *Nabucco*, perhaps in all Verdi. It is deliberately simple, almost incantatory in its rhythmic tread, unvaried phrase pattern and primarily unison texture; and by these means it creates that powerful sense of nostalgia which, later in the century, gave the chorus its status as a symbol of Italian national aspirations. In the context of the drama, however, the chorus's attitude is cast aside by Zaccaria, whose two-part minor–major prophecy ('Del futuro nel buio') takes up rhythmic and melodic strands from 'Va pensiero' and places them in a fresh dynamic context.

Part 4: 'The Broken Idol'

4.i *The royal apartments (as 2.i)* The scene opens with Nabucco alone on stage, an orchestral prelude representing the king's distraction through scattered recollections of past themes. He hears a funeral march, sees Fenena on her way to execution, but is powerless to help her. As a last resort, he offers a prayer to the God of Israel; sanity returns and he marshals a band of followers to save his daughter. The scene is structured as a double aria for Nabucco, with his prayer ('Dio di Giuda') as the first part. The ensuing cabaletta ('Cadran, cadranno i perfidi') is highly unusual in beginning with a choral statement of a subsidiary theme.

4.ii *The hanging gardens* To an extended version of the funeral march heard fleetingly in the previous number, Fenena and the Israelites are led towards their deaths. Fenena offers a brief but touching prayer ('Oh dischiuso è il firmamento'), and then, just in time, Nabucco rushes on to save her. He announces his conversion and is restored as king; Abigaille (we learn) has taken poison. All now join in a triumphant hymn to their new God ('Immenso Jeovha'), a grandiose unaccompanied chorus with which, in most 19th-century performances, the opera came to a close. In the score, however, there is a far more restrained ending: the dying Abigaille enters to ask forgiveness, singing a fragmented melody ('Su me . . . morente') to the accompaniment of solo cello and english horn.

*

There are many ways in which *Nabucco*, as the composer himself said, is the true beginning of Verdi's artistic career, the true emergence of his distinctive voice. It is admittedly an uneven score, with occasional lapses into banality and some unsteady formal experiments that we shall rarely see in future works. But the essential ingredients of Verdi's early style are in place: a new and dynamic use of the chorus, an extraordinary rhythmic vitality and, above all, an acute sense of dramatic pacing. Although, unusually for Verdi, *Nabucco* has no important tenor role, Nabucco and Zaccaria present

magnificent opportunities for the baritone and bass, and Abigaille, though always problematic to cast, can prove highly effective for a forceful yet agile soprano. However, as has often been pointed out, the true protagonist of the opera is undoubtedly the chorus, which dominates several of the strongest scenes, and which enters with such stirring effect at climactic points in so many of the solo numbers.   R.P.

Nerone ('Nero')

Tragedia in four acts by Arrigo Boito to his own libretto; Milan, Teatro alla Scala, 1 May 1924.

Aureliano Pertile sang the title role at the première; Marcel Journet was Simon; Rosa Raisa sang Asteria.

Nero *Roman emperor*	tenor
Simon Mago [Simon Magus]	
a magician	baritone
Asteria	soprano
Rubria *a Vestal virgin*	mezzo-soprano
Fanuèl *a Christian apostle*	baritone
Tigellino [Tigellinus] *Nero's henchman*	bass
Gobrias *a follower of Simon*	tenor
Dositèo *a Roman*	baritone
Pèrside *a Christian*	soprano
Cerinto	contralto
Setting Ancient Rome	

Nerone occupied Boito for some 60 years and was originally conceived in five acts, ending with Nero playing the role of Orestes on stage as Rome burns around him. It was shortened at Giulio Ricordi's suggestion. The music is rich but episodic, contrasting the diatonicism of the Christian episodes with the strange harmonies and orchestral colour associated with both Nero and Simon the Paraclete. Boito makes considerable use of recurring themes. The score was worked into performing shape after Boito's death by Vincenzo Tommasini and Antonio Smareglia, working under Toscanini's direction.

*

Act I *The Via Appia, Rome, near the catacombs, by moonlight* Nero appears, haunted by mysterious voices accusing him, justifiably, of matricide. With him is Simon Magus, a priest of a mysterious cult, who promises to rid Nero of his obsession that he is pursued by the Erinyes (Furies). Bearing an urn containing his mother's ashes, Nero hopes to placate her spirit by burying them, and thinks of himself as a new Orestes (aria, 'Queste ad un lido fatal'). Asteria, in the form of an Erinys, seeks to pursue Nero, not from vengeance but for love. Simon detains her. To the Christian tombs comes Rubria, who kneels and says the Lord's Prayer. Asteria is strangely moved by this, but suddenly she dashes off in pursuit of another god. Fanuèl, a Christian apostle, enters; Rubria wishes to confess a sin to him but she is interrupted by Simon and leaves. Simon tells Fanuèl of his vision of the Christians triumphing over decadent imperial Rome, and then offers to buy some of this power. Fanuèl curses Simon, and the two declare their enmity. Nero returns with Tigellinus, who seeks to calm Nero's fears and tells him that he will enter Rome in triumph. The populace hail him as an Apollo.

Act 2 *Simon's subterranean temple* A crowd of devotees has gathered when a curtain parts to reveal Simon in the sanctuary, surrounded by initiates. He holds a flaming beaker from which issue first blood and then a cloud of steam that obscures him from view. The curtains are drawn and the worshippers express their conviction that Simon has ascended into the sky. When the crowd disperses Simon sets Asteria upon the altar in preparation for Nero's arrival. Nero enters and, believing Asteria to be a goddess, worships her. He begs forgiveness, confessing his sins, among them the rape of a Vestal virgin. Emboldened, he kisses Asteria and discovers she is no goddess, but a mortal woman. Enraged by this, he starts to smash the deceptive mechanisms of Simon's bogus temple, summons guards to seize Simon and Asteria and declares himself the new divinity of the temple.

Act 3 *An orchard* Fanuèl recites the Beatitudes to a group of Christians while Rubria and some women weave garlands. Asteria enters, wounded, having escaped from the snake-pit into which Nero had ordered her to be cast. She urges the Christians to escape because Simon, desperate to save his life, has revealed their presence to Nero and his guards. Rubria begs Fanuèl to flee, but he wants to hear her interrupted confession. Disguised as a blind beggar, Simon comes to ask Fanuèl to use his power to assist him; he has been ordered by Nero to give proof of his boast that he could fly. When Fanuèl refuses Simon signals concealed soldiers to arrest him, and Fanuèl bids his followers a moving farewell in the aria 'Vivete in pace'. They accompany their leader to prison leaving Rubria in torment, alone.

Act 4.i *The Oppidium* In this antechamber of the Circus Maximus, between the cells and the arena, Gobrias, Simon's assistant, warns his master that he has arranged a fire in the city to spare Simon from making his 'flight'. Asteria has thought of this way of saving the Christians in the resultant confusion. Nero and Tigellinus have also heard of the intention to raise a fire; the emperor welcomes it as an opportunity to redesign the city. The Christians are forced into the arena, there to enact a sanguinary Greek myth. A veiled Vestal virgin pleads for the Christians, who

are singing a Credo. Nero commands the veil be stripped from the virgin, revealing her to be Rubria; recognizing the girl he had violated, he orders her to be cast into the arena with her fellow Christians. Simon is hurled from the roof and, failing to fly, crashes to his death. The smoke of the fire envelops the Circus, causing panic.

4.ii *The Spoliarium* To this mortuary beneath the Circus come Fanuèl and Asteria, seeking Rubria's body. Fatally wounded but still alive, she confesses her sin at last: how she had served Vesta, been raped by Nero and become a Christian; but she fears she has not truly served her new faith. Fanuèl pardons her and calls her his betrothed as she dies. He and Asteria flee the burning Circus, but Asteria soon returns, jealous that Rubria had been possessed by Nero. Realizing that Rubria is dead, Asteria drops on her corpse a flower which the girl had given her.

One of the most successful passages in the opera is the passacaglia at the beginning of Act 2, with its repeated bass and variations interspersed with brief interludes. Another is Fanuèl's recital of the Beatitudes near the beginning of Act 3. There are, however, a number of passages of empty rhetoric, and others that are merely busy. But in spite of its unevenness, *Nerone* everywhere testifies to Boito's serious, erudite purpose.   W.A.

Nightingale, The [*Solovey (Le Rossignol)*]

Lyric tale in three acts (scenes) by Igor Stravinsky to a libretto by Stepan Mitusov after the tale by Hans Christian Andersen; Paris, Opéra, 26 May 1914.

At the première the Nightingale was sung by Aurelia Dobrovol'skaya; others in the cast included Pavel Andreyev, Yelzaveta Petrenko, Varfolomeyev and Gulayev.

The Nightingale	soprano
The Cook	soprano
The Fisherman	tenor
The Emperor of China	baritone
The Chamberlain	bass
The Bonze	bass
Death	mezzo-soprano
Three Japanese Envoys	two tenors, bass
Courtiers, Emperor's entourage, spectres (offstage	
* chorus of altos), pages, ladies-in-waiting*	
Setting China	

The first act of this touching little Orphic allegory was begun shortly before the death of Stravinsky's teacher Rimsky-Korsakov in 1908 (Acts 2 and 3 were composed in 1913–14). The scenario was worked out in March 1908 (old style) at the apartment of Vladimir Bel'sky, Rimsky's librettist, whose influence may be detected in the use of Andersen's Fisherman as a framing character, appearing at the ends of each scene (like the Astrologer in *The Golden Cockerel*). Stravinsky dedicated the work to its librettist, Mitusov.

When in 1909 Stravinsky began receiving ballet commissions from Sergey Dyagilev, he found himself sidetracked from his operatic project, and eventually turned cold not only to it but (under the influence of Dyagilev and Alexandre Benois) to opera generally. He entitled the first act of *The Nightingale* 'A scene from Andersen's Tale of the Nightingale' and designated it for concert performance. It would have been published as a self-contained tone poem with voices had Stravinsky not been offered an enticing contract by Alexander Sanin (*né* Schoenberg, 1869-1956), a leading Russian operatic stage director. As one of the founders of the Moscow Free Theatre, Sanin proposed to Stravinsky that he write a full-length opera for the theatre's first season. 'My greatest dream', he wrote, 'is to show you off to Moscow, to St Petersburg, indeed to all of Russia.' That was also a dream of Stravinsky's, whose three early ballets had made him famous in Western Europe but had not been seen in his homeland. After some hesitation, he decided to complete *The Nightingale* in return for a very high fee, and on the condition that a 45-minute work in three tiny 'acts' could be substituted for the whole evening's entertainment originally requested.

The Moscow Free Theatre folded before *The Nightingale* could be staged, and the première went to Dyagilev after all, in a marvellously colourful production designed by Benois and conducted by Pierre Monteux, with the voices of the Nightingale (sung by Aurelia Dobrovol'skaya) and the Fisherman emanating from the pit, turning the opera into a virtual pantomime. At Dyagilev's instigation, Stravinsky extracted a ballet score, *Chant du rossignol*, from the music of the second and third acts. Since its 1919 première under Ansermet it has been so much more successful in the concert hall than in the theatre that in his autobiography the composer falsely claimed to have conceived it as a symphonic poem from the start. The original opera did achieve a Russian production shortly after the revolution (Mariinsky Theatre, May 1918, directed by Vsevolod Meyerhold and conducted by Albert Coates); since then, however, its slender stage career has been mostly a Western one, usually in double or triple bills with ballets.

*

Act I *The edge of a wood by the seashore* A Fisherman, mending his net, sings of his nightly pleasure in the Nightingale's song. The bird sings its greeting, but is interrupted by the Chamberlain, the Bonze, the Cook and a retinue of courtiers. After first mistaking the Nightingale for a cow and a chorus of frogs, they invite it to sing before the Emperor. The Nightingale willingly accepts, though it prefers to sing in the forest, and declines all compensation, saying its only reward consists of its listeners' tears. As the courtiers leave with the bird, the Fisherman reflects disconsolately on its departure.

Act 2 *The throne room in the Emperor's porcelain palace* The act opens with a great scurry and bustle (played in silhouette) as the palace is made ready for the Emperor's appearance at a fête. The scrim is lifted on the interior of the porcelain palace, illuminated by countless lanterns and torches. The Emperor is carried in to the strains of the Chinese March. The Nightingale performs its coloratura song, and receives its reward of tears. Three Japanese Envoys present the Emperor with a mechanical nightingale, which is wound up and entrances the court with its whirring air (a travesty of the 'Forest Murmurs' from Wagner's *Siegfried*). The real Nightingale slips away unnoticed. When the Emperor realizes the bird is gone, he banishes it in a fit of pique. The offstage voice of the Fisherman announces the approach of Death.

Act 3 *A hall in the palace containing the Emperor's bedchamber* The Emperor is ill. Death, wearing the imperial crown and holding the imperial sword and banner, sits at his bedside, while a chorus of spectres sings of the Emperor's misdeeds as he writhes in agony. The Nightingale comes to the rescue: by beguiling Death with a three-stanza song, it redeems the banner, sword and crown one by one. Again it refuses all reward save tears, and flies away. A 'solemn procession' accompanies the slow entrance of the Emperor's retinue as they trudge onstage expecting to collect his corpse. Instead he bids them a hearty good morning. The offstage voice of the Fisherman rounds off the opera with a reprise of the opening invocation to the Nightingale's sunrise song.

*

The musical idiom of the first act adheres closely to what Asaf'yev called the 'modest, rationalized impressionism' of the early 20th-century St Petersburg school. Although the orchestral introduction bears the indubitable imprint of Debussy's *Nuages*, there is little in the exuberantly decorative score that cannot be associated with the idiom of such older Rimsky-Korsakov pupils as Anatoly Lyadov and especially Nikolay Tcherepnin. Both musically and dramaturgically, the first act continues the line established by Rimsky's late series of fantasy operas culminating in *The Golden Cockerel*, also about a magical bird, with which *The Nightingale* shared a double bill in its first production. Except for the title character's songs (one in each act) that were, in the

'Nixon in China' (Adams): opening scene from the original production by Peter Sellars at Houston Grand Opera, 22 October 1987, with Carolann Page as Pat Nixon and James Maddalena as Richard Nixon (set by Adrianne Lobel)

event, sung from the pit, the second and third acts, written at a time when Stravinsky was hostile to opera as a genre, are virtual ballets (or better, pageants) in which the action consists largely of stage processions, and the dominant impression comes from the highly coloured décor (matched by Stravinsky's brilliant orchestration).The composer's hesitation over completing the work in response to Sanin's offer had to do not only with his aesthetic estrangement from opera, but with the fact that he had crossed a stylistic Rubicon with *Petrushka* and *The Rite of Spring*, and felt he could no longer return to the gentler impressionistic idiom of the one completed act. He managed to rationalize the resulting stylistic incongruity on the basis of the setting of the second and third acts: the 'artificial' ambience of the Chinese court as opposed to the natural beauty of the opening scene. The music he composed for Sanin ingeniously exploited interactions between the pentatonic 'Chinese' scale and the fully octatonic idiom of *The Rite of Spring*. The orchestration of the new scenes matched the brash harmonic idiom, exploiting striking colour contrasts in place of the rich and subtly blended sonorities of the first act.

Later Stravinsky came to more amicable terms with opera and regarded *The Nightingale* as a curiosity. Approached without preconception, it is an entertaining spectacle, if not a very dramatic one.

R.T.

Nixon in China

Opera in two acts by John Adams to a libretto by Alice Goodman; Houston, Grand Opera, 22 October 1987.

The first cast included James Maddalena (Nixon), Carolann Page (Pat Nixon), John Duykess (Mao Tse-tung), Trudy Ellen Cranley (Chiang Ch'ing), Sanford Sylvan (Chou En-lai) and Thomas Hammons (Henry Kissinger).

Richard Nixon	baritone
Pat Nixon	soprano
Chou En-lai	baritone
Mao Tse-tung	tenor
Henry Kissinger	bass
Chiang Ch'ing	soprano
Nancy T'sang *first secretary*	
to Mao	mezzo-soprano
Second secretary to Mao	mezzo-soprano
Third secretary to Mao	mezzo-soprano
Dancers, militia, citizens of Beijing	
Setting Beijing	

Conceived in 1982 by Peter Sellars and completed in 1987, *Nixon in China* has as its subject the American President Richard Nixon's visit to China from 21 to 27 February 1972, with the differences between Eastern and Western views of the world as a subtext. The work contains little action; rather, it is divided into six tableaux, within which the characters convey their world views – and sometimes find themselves speaking at cross-purposes – in a series of connected conversations and soliloquies.

The opera begins with the arrival of the presidential aircraft at an airport outside Beijing and includes the expected ceremonial welcome from Chou En-lai. Nixon describes the flight, diplomatically, as smooth, while the music conveys the truth: it was bumpy. Nixon, in his 'News' aria, immediately establishes that the priorities of the journey are symbolic; indeed, he likens his landing in Beijing to that of the Apollo astronauts who landed on the moon, and notes that, because it is prime television viewing time in the USA, his arrival will be witnessed by the maximum possible audience. This focus on the superficialities of conveying a public image proves to be Nixon's weakness here. In the second scene, which takes place in Mao Tse-tung's study, Nixon, Mao, Chou and an oafish caricature of Kissinger air various views of history and of the contemporary world, and it becomes clear that the Chinese are operating on a deeper, more philosophical level than the Americans. The first act ends with a banquet scene.

At the start of Act 2, Pat Nixon is taken on a tour of a commune and to the Summer Palace, where she sings her central aria, a touching humanitarian vision, 'This is prophetic!' The next scene brings Nixon, Mao, Chou, Pat and Mao's wife Chiang Ch'ing together to watch a contemporary political Chinese ballet, 'The Red Detachment of Women', in which the villainous landlord, Lao Szu, played by Kissinger, is thwarted by the courageous women soldiers of the State. The scene ends with a monologue in which Chiang Ch'ing, the only Chinese character presented unsympathetically, offers her view of the Cultural Revolution and her place in history.

The final scene takes place on the Nixons' last night in Beijing. The Nixons, Mao and Chiang Ch'ing and Chou En-lai occupy individual beds. The two couples reminisce about the beginnings of their personal mythologies in the 1940s: Mao recalls the struggles of the Revolution, while Nixon's war memories revolve around having his own hamburger stand. Chou, in comparatively few words, offers a more sweeping overview of the era, and ties it to the present: 'How much of what we did was good? Everything seems to move beyond our remedy . . . Outside this room the chill of grace lies heavy on the morning grass'.

Adams's music is minimalist and eclectic, like many of his chamber and orchestral works of the 1970s and 80s. In the orchestral interludes one hears references, both passing and lingering, to everything from Wagner to Gershwin and Philip Glass. The musical characterizations, however, are often quite striking, and Adams's text settings for Richard Nixon in particular reflect the president's speech patterns recognizably.   A.K.

Norma

Tragedia lirica in two acts by Vincenzo Bellini to a libretto by Felice Romani after Alexandre Soumet's verse tragedy *Norma*; Milan, Teatro alla Scala, 26 December 1831.

The demanding role of Norma was written for Giuditta Pasta. Lacking his favourite tenor, Rubini, Bellini had the services of the forceful veteran Domenico Donzelli, whose voice he once described as dark and low; his part rarely rises above g'. Adalgisa, now usually given to a mezzo-soprano, was written for the high soprano Giulia Grisi; she later became a famous Norma herself, and also created Elvira in *I puritani*. Oroveso's role was limited by the insufficiencies of Vincenzo Negrini.

Oroveso *head of the druids*	bass
Pollione *Roman proconsul in Gaul*	tenor
Flavio *friend to Pollione*	tenor
Norma *druidess, daughter of Oroveso*	soprano
Adalgisa *young priestess at the temple of Irminsul*	soprano
Clotilde *Norma's confidante*	mezzo-soprano
Two Children of Norma and Pollione	mime
Druids, bards, priestesses and Gallic soldiers	
Setting The sacred forest and temple of Irminsul, Gaul, during the Roman occupation	

Norma was written as the second of two operas planned in summer 1830 for Milan, for which Bellini was paid an unprecedented 12,000 lire. Romani's libretto uses themes from several earlier works: Jouy's libretto *La vestale* (1807, Paris) for Spontini, Chateaubriand's novel *Les martyrs* (Paris, 1808) and Romani's own earlier librettos, *Medea in Corinto* for Mayr (1813, Naples), also treating infanticide, and *La sacerdotessa d'Irminsul* for Pacini (1820, Trieste). Bellini intervened continuously, revising and trimming the libretto. They did not use Soumet's fifth act, a mad scene where Norma leaps into an abyss, but devised the celebrated final ensemble. The subject was chosen by 23 July 1831 and Romani gave Bellini the text for the *introduzione* on 31 August; the opera went into rehearsal about 5 December. The manuscript evidence affords ample testimony to Bellini's continual revisions. He is reputed to have made eight versions of 'Casta diva', and may have discarded an entire sinfonia before composing the present one. There are many sketches of the Act 1 duet between Adalgisa and Pollione (producing melodies developed in 'Mira, o Norma' and 'Già mi pasco' in Act 2). Bellini made changes to the trio at the end of Act 1, possibly for the performances he directed at Bergamo in 1832. Current scores present many problems, and the Boosey vocal score (London, 1848) offers alternative readings to Ricordi's.

The première was unsuccessful, partly because the first act ends unconventionally with a trio instead of with a more complex ensemble. However, *Norma* quickly became popular; it was staged at Naples, Bergamo and Venice during 1832 and at Rome in 1834 when, because 'norma' was also a liturgical term, performances were given as *La foresta d'Irminsul* with the principals changed to Delia and Galieno. Outside Italy, *Norma* was staged in Vienna (in German) during May 1833, and at the King's Theatre, London, during June of that year, when the cast included Pasta and Donzelli. *Norma* reached New York (in English) in 1841; it was the inaugural opera at the Academy of Music in 1854, with Grisi and Giovanni Mario. The first performance at the Metropolitan was in 1890 (in German) with Lilli Lehmann in the title role; Rosa Ponselle sang her first Norma at the Metropolitan in 1927, while Maria Callas, having made her London début as Norma at Covent Garden in 1952, made her American début at Chicago in 1954 and her first appearance at the Metropolitan, in 1956, in the same role. The exciting partnership of Joan Sutherland (Norma) and Marilyn Horne (Adalgisa) began in 1967 at Covent Garden.

*

Act I.i *The sacred forest of the Druids* The sinfonia uses themes from Norma's duet with Pollione in Act 2 and a section of the chorus 'Guerra, guerra'. Oroveso, in 'Ite sul colle, o Druidi', instructs the Druids to watch for the first sight of the new moon and then to signal, with three strokes on the bronze shield of Irminsul, the start of the sacred rite over which Norma will preside. The Druids call on Irminsul to inspire Norma with hatred against the Romans in the chorus 'Dell'aura tua profetica'. As they leave, Pollione and Flavio enter the grove. Although Pollione once loved Norma (who has borne him two children), his passion for her has cooled and he now loves Adalgisa, who returns his love. Flavio asks if he does not fear Norma's anger – Pollione trembles at the thought and relates his dream of approaching the altar of Venus in Rome with Adalgisa, only to be confronted with a dreadful phantom while the voice of a demon proclaims Norma's revenge. His cavatina 'Meco all'altar di Venere', more robust than those written for Rubini, is interrupted by the sound of the gong and the voices of the Druids, accompanied by a march, announcing that the moon has risen and commanding that all profaners of the sacred grove be gone. After Pollione's cabaletta on a theme inspired by the march, he and Flavio hurry away.

The Druids file into the grove; in the chorus 'Norma viene: le cinge la chioma' they evoke her appearance, with her hair wreathed in mistletoe and a golden sickle in her hand. Norma arrives surrounded by the priestesses. In her recitative, 'Sediziose voci', she criticizes the Druids' warlike

chants; the time is not yet ripe to rise against the Romans, who will be defeated at the appointed hour. Norma cuts a branch of mistletoe from the oak-tree in the centre of the grove; then, raising her arms, she prays to the chaste goddess of the moon in 'Casta diva' (in the autograph MS this cavatina is pitched one tone higher than in Ricordi's printed scores). She asks that there be peace for the present; when the moment arrives to shed the Romans' blood she, Norma, will lead the revolt. The Druids demand that the first victim should be Pollione; Norma realizes that she could not kill him herself, and in the cabaletta, 'Ah! bello, a me ritorna', admits that if he were to return to her, she would defend his life. The melody of this cabaletta is adapted from one used in *Bianca e Fernando* (1828) and the unsuccessful *Zaira* (1829) with a new coda added. When the Druids have left the grove, Adalgisa laments her weakness in succumbing to Pollione, then in 'Deh! proteggimi, o dio', prays for strength to resist him. Pollione returns to find her in tears. At first she professes to have overcome her love for him, but in a duet, 'Va, crudele, al dio spietato', he urges her to fly with him to Rome and finally she agrees to renounce her vows.

I.ii *Norma's dwelling* Norma is troubled because Pollione has been recalled to Rome. She asks Clotilde to hide her children as someone is heard outside. It is Adalgisa, who comes to ask Norma for help and counsel. She confesses that while praying in the sacred grove, she saw a man who seemed to be a

Giuditta Pasta in the title role of Bellini's 'Norma' which she created at La Scala, Milan, in 1831: portrait (painted between 1831 and 1835) by François Gérard

heavenly vision. In 'Sola, furtiva, al tempio', Adalgisa tells Norma how she continued to see the man in secret and at each meeting fell more deeply in love with him. Her confession is overlaid with Norma's nostalgic recollections of her own love affair. Sympathetically Norma agrees to free Adalgisa from her vows (which are not yet final), so that she can depart with her lover. The two voices unite in 'Ah! sì, fa core e abbracciami', whose cadenza in thirds characterizes their warm friendship throughout the opera. Norma asks who Adalgisa's lover might be; the girl indicates Pollione, who enters at that moment. With 'Oh! di qual sei tu vittima' (adapted from the *Ernani* sketches of 1830), Norma launches into the trio that replaces the usual finale ensemble. She enlightens Adalgisa on her own betrayal by Pollione and vehemently denounces him; he admits his love for Adalgisa and begs her to come away with him, but she refuses, while Norma bursts out with even greater fury in 'Vanne, sì: mi lascia, indegno', dismissing him from her sight.

Act 2.i *Inside Norma's dwelling* Norma, clutching her dagger, stands regarding her sleeping children and ponders their fate, in one of Bellini's best-known recitatives, 'Dormono entrambi . . . non vedran la mano', introduced by a cello melody. Deciding that death while they slept would be preferable to the shame that they would endure alive, she considers their innocence in her arioso, 'Teneri, teneri figli', which re-uses the cello melody. She moves to kill them, but cannot bring herself to do so; she embraces them and calls for Clotilde to summon Adalgisa. Norma proposes to the younger priestess that she marry Pollione and accompany him to Rome, on the condition that she take the children with her and care for them after Norma's death. Adalgisa refuses, insisting that she will go to Pollione, but only to persuade him to return to Norma. The expressive duet, 'Mira, o Norma', contains extensive coloratura for both singers and is followed by the brilliant 'Sì, fino all'ore estreme', in which they again sing in thirds as they proclaim their friendship.

2.ii *A lonely place near the Druids' wood* The Gallic warriors discuss Pollione's imminent departure for Rome in 'Non partì? Finora è al campo' (from *Bianca e Fernando* and *Zaira*). Oroveso warns them that freedom is still far away; a more tyrannically oppressive proconsul will certainly replace Pollione, and Norma has given them no guidance. In his aria with chorus, 'Ah! del Tebro al giogo indegno', Oroveso rails against the infamy of the Roman yoke, but bids the Gauls have patience: their chance for revenge will come.

2.iii *The temple of Irminsul* Norma hopes to hear of Pollione's repentance, but Clotilde tells her that he intends to abduct Adalgisa from the temple. Rushing to the altar, Norma strikes the shield of Irminsul

three times, the signal for war; the Gauls respond with the ferocious war hymn 'Guerra, guerra! Le galliche selve'. When Oroveso demands to know why Norma does not complete the sacrificial rite, she replies obscurely that the victim is ready. Clotilde brings news that a Roman has been caught in the cloister of the virgin priestesses. It is Pollione, who is brought in under guard. He refuses to answer Oroveso's questions and Norma raises the sacred dagger, but is unable to kill him. She decides to interrogate him alone and the others withdraw. In their duet, 'In mia man alfin tu sei', Norma offers Pollione his life if he will swear to abandon all thoughts of Adalgisa. When he refuses, she threatens to kill not only Pollione but their children as well, and to punish Adalgisa by fire for breaking her vows.

Norma summons back the Gauls and announces that a guilty priestess must die on the sacrificial pyre. When Oroveso and the Druids demand to know the culprit's name, Norma replies 'Son io' –'It is I'. A huge ensemble builds up, beginning with 'Qual cor tradisti' in which Norma claims that Pollione has not escaped her, for they will die together in the flames; Pollione's love for Norma is reborn in the face of her sublime courage; Oroveso and the Druids, reluctant to believe Norma's confession, gradually accept its truth. In 'Deh! non volerli vittime', Norma beseeches her father to spare her children and to look after them when she is dead. Oroveso at first refuses, then relents, promising to honour Norma's last request. Norma and Pollione are led to the pyre.

*

Norma has always been revered above other Italian operas of the period. Reviews compared it to Spontini's *La vestale*, whose heroine, Julia, is subjected to similarly overwhelming dramatic pressures; but Donizetti's *Anna Bolena* (1830, Milan) perhaps provides a more immediate musical influence. The title role is one of the most taxing and wide-ranging parts in the entire repertory: a noble character whose tragedy lies in her fatal love for an enemy of her people. The many different aspects of Norma's temperament are marvellously drawn by Bellini, not only in the aria 'Casta diva', but also in the superb duets with Adalgisa and Pollione, and in the ensemble in the finale of Act 2, where Bellini reaches his peak as a musical dramatist.   **S.M., E.F.**

Nozze di Figaro, Le ('The Marriage of Figaro')

Opera buffa in four acts, K492, by Wolfgang Amadeus Mozart to a libretto by Lorenzo da Ponte after Pierre-Augustin Beaumarchais' play *La folle journée, ou Le mariage de Figaro* (1784, Paris); Vienna, Burgtheater, 1 May 1786.

The original cast was: Francesco Benucci (Figaro), Nancy Storace (Susanna), Luisa Laschi (Countess), Stefano Mandini (Count), Dorotea Bussani (Cherubino), Maria Mandini (Marcellina), Francesco Bussani (Bartolo and Antonio), Michael Kelly (Basilio and Curzio), and Anna Gottlieb (Barbarina).

Count Almaviva	baritone
Countess Almaviva	soprano
Susanna *her maid, betrothed to Figaro*	soprano
Figaro *valet to Count Almaviva*	bass
Cherubino *the Count's page*	mezzo-soprano
Marcellina *housekeeper to Bartolo*	soprano
Bartolo *a doctor from Seville*	bass
Don Basilio *music master*	tenor
Don Curzio *magistrate*	tenor
Barbarina *daughter of Antonio*	soprano
Antonio *gardener, Susanna's uncle*	bass
Villagers, peasants, servants	

Setting Aguasfrescas near Seville, the Almavivas' country house; the action is contemporary with the play and opera

The operatic version of Beaumarchais' *Le mariage de Figaro* may have been a timely notion of Mozart's own. Although the play was banned from the Viennese stage, it was available in print and Paisiello's opera on the earlier play, *Le barbier de Séville*, had triumphed in Vienna in 1783 (and all over Europe). Mozart evidently studied Paisiello's handling of the same personalities and included deliberate references to it (*see* **Barbiere di Siviglia, Il**). Composition began late in 1785 and the opera may have been drafted in only six weeks; it seems that much of it was composed before Mozart had obtained permission to stage it. After some opposition attributed to the Italian composers resident in Vienna, and (if Da Ponte is to be believed) after the librettist had overcome the emperor's objections, it was produced in May with an outstanding cast whose character and skills, as well as their performance in Paisiello's *Barbiere*, contributed to its conception. Michael Kelly discussed the event in his reminiscences. Mozart may have expected Storace to sing the Countess; he rearranged the Act 2 trio and other passages so that Susanna took the upper line.

Contrary to what is often stated, *Figaro* was generally liked, as is indicated by the emperor's ban on excessive encores (only arias were to be repeated). The opera marks the last watershed of Mozart's career; from now on he was a recognized opera composer. There were, however, only nine performances in 1786; the Viennese preferred other works, such as Martín y Soler's *Una cosa rara*. *Figaro* was next given in Prague, where according to Mozart's report (letter of 15 January 1787) it created a furore and led to the commission for *Don Giovanni*. The successful

Vienna revival (26 performances in 1789) preceded the commission for *Così fan tutte*: Susanna was confirmed as the prima donna's role when Mozart wrote two new arias for Adriana Ferrarese del Bene, Da Ponte's mistress and the first Fiordiligi.

By this time *Figaro* had received isolated performances in Italy (Acts 1 and 2, the rest composed by Angelo Tarchi; 1787, 1788), and had been translated into German for performances in Prague (June 1787), Donaueschingen (1787) and other German centres over the next few years. These performances used spoken dialogue, as did the first performance in France (Paris Opéra, 1793, using Beaumarchais). The London première took place in 1812, in Italian, following interpolations of numbers into other operas by Storace and Benucci; in 1819 it was given in English, reduced to three acts and arranged by Bishop. In New York the first performances were in 1824, in English, and 1858, in Italian. *Figaro* is now Mozart's most popular opera, displacing *Don Giovanni*. No major company allows it to fall out of the repertory for long; Glyndebourne opened with it in 1934.

In production, the vein of rococo nostalgia which was to inspire *Der Rosenkavalier* was displaced by the greater realism of Visconti (1963, Rome) and Hall (1973, Glyndebourne); it is now customary to emphasize the socio-political tensions of the original play which Da Ponte had been obliged to suppress.

*

In the first part of the Beaumarchais trilogy, *Il barbiere*, Almaviva wooed Bartolo's ward Rosina with the aid of Figaro, now his valet. He has also, despite his Don Juanesque tendencies, abolished the *droit de Seigneur* whereby he had the right to deflower every bride among his feudal dependants.

For the overture Mozart abandoned a planned middle section, leaving an electrifying sonata without development which perfectly sets the scene for the 'Crazy Day'.

Act I *An antechamber* The pacing motif and lyrical response in the opening duet ('Cinque, dieci') belong respectively to Figaro, who is measuring the room, and Susanna, who is trying on a new hat for their forthcoming wedding. She finally entices him from his work to admire her, and to sing her motif, suggesting that she may prove to be the stronger personality. When Figaro tells her the Count has offered them this room, conveniently situated between those of the Count and Countess, she reacts with alarm. In the ensuing duet ('Se a caso madama') she mocks Figaro's imitation of the high and low bells of their employers: the room's convenience will also make it easy for the Count, who has designs on her, to visit Susanna when she is alone. Figaro's confidence is shaken, but if the Count wants to dance, it is he, Figaro, who will call the tune; in his cavatina,

'Se vuol ballare', his mind's eye makes the Count dance first a minuet, then a Presto contredanse.

Figaro has obtained a loan from Marcellina, and, never imagining he will have to keep to the bargain, has agreed to marry her if he defaults. Bartolo offers her his help: in this way he will both avenge himself on Figaro (who thwarted his plans to marry Rosina in *Il barbiere*) and rid himself of an embarrassment (Marcellina). His exit aria, 'La vendetta', has a full orchestra with trumpets, in the opera's principal key, D major. His vaunted legal knowledge is expressed with formal counterpoint, but his fury also vents itself in comically undignified patter. Susanna, aware of Marcellina's interest in Figaro, hustles her out, the music poised, the exchange of compliments venomous in their duettino, 'Via resti servito'. Cherubino, who is in trouble with the Count, confides in Susanna. In a lyrical arch of melody over a sensuously muted accompaniment, he impulsively babbles of his love for all women ('Non so più'), an enchanting musical image of confused adolescence. The Count is heard; Susanna hides Cherubino behind a chair. Basilio's voice interrupts the Count who, believing himself alone with Susanna, is making amorous proposals; while he too hides behind the chair, Cherubino nips on to it and Susanna covers him with a dress. Basilio's malicious (but accurate) observation that Cherubino adores the Countess rouses the Count from concealment. Gruffly, in an ascending line, he demands an explanation (trio, 'Cosa sento!'); Basilio, his motif unctuously descending, disclaims knowledge; Susanna threatens to faint, and the men officiously come to her aid. The Count describes his discovery of Cherubino in Barbarina's room, hidden under a cloth . . . at which he is again revealed, to the Count's self-righteous indignation, Basilio's delight and Susanna's horror. Sonata form perfectly matches the action, the recapitulation fraught with irony (or, from Basilio, sarcasm). Figaro ushers in a rustic chorus praising the Count's magnanimity in renouncing his extramarital right, but the Count refuses to be trapped into marrying the couple then and there, and banishes Cherubino with an officer's commission. While apparently sending him on his way, to the bold march rhythm of 'Non più andrai' (no more frolicking and flirting; he is off to death or glory), Figaro detains the page for purposes of his own.

Act 2 *The Countess's chamber* In an achingly tender Larghetto, the neglected Countess prays to the god of love to restore her husband's affections (cavatina, 'Porgi, Amor'). But she listens eagerly to Susanna and Figaro's plotting (Figaro leaves to a snatch of 'Se vuol ballare'). Cherubino is to be dressed as a girl, take Susanna's place, and compromise the Count. Cherubino's ardour is formalized, in a song of his own composition, 'Voi che sapete', sung to Susanna's 'guitar' accompaniment; in this canzona Mozart miraculously suggests, but evades, the clumsiness of youth. Susanna tries to dress him but he keeps turning his gaze towards the Countess ('Venite, inginocchiatevi': an action aria replaced in 1789 by the strophic 'Un moto di gioia'). Alone with the Countess, Cherubino is close to winning her heart when the Count demands admittance: he has returned precipitately from the hunt because of an anonymous letter (part of Figaro's ill-laid plot). In confusion the Countess thrusts Cherubino into her closet; the Count asks questions; Susanna enters unseen. The Countess says Susanna is in the closet. The Count's jealous fury, his wife's terror and Susanna's anxious assessment of the situation again outline a sonata form, although the action does not advance (trio, 'Susanna, or via sortite'). When the Count leaves to fetch tools to break down the door, forcing the Countess to go with him and locking the bedroom door behind them, Susanna thrusts Cherubino through the window (duettino, 'Aprite, presto aprite') and enters the closet.

When they return, the Countess confesses that Cherubino is in the closet, half-dressed, but protests her innocence; the Count is ready to kill. Mozart's most consummate comic finale begins by resuming the fury and anxiety of the trio (E♭, 'Esci omai, garzon malnato'). But it is Susanna who emerges, to a simple minuet which mocks the nobles' consternation. Explanations and further confusion occupy an extended Allegro which deploys its thematic wealth with marvellous inventiveness. Although puzzled, the Count has to ask forgiveness. At the single abrupt key-change of the finale (B♭ to G) Figaro enters, again asking for an immediate wedding. Recovering his sang-froid (C major, gavotte tempo), the Count poses questions about the anonymous letter; Figaro prevaricates. Antonio charges in to complain of damage to his garden caused by the page's precipitate exit (Allegro molto, F major). The Count senses more chicanery; Figaro claims it was he who jumped. The tempo slows to Andante (in B♭) and with measured calm the Count questions Figaro about a paper the page has dropped: the music emerges from an harmonic cloud to a shining recapitulation as Figaro (prompted by the women) identifies it as the page's commission, left with him (he claims) to be sealed. The Count is baffled, but revives when Marcellina, Basilio and Bartolo rush in demanding justice (the home key, E♭).

Act 3 *A large room decorated for the marriage-feast* The Countess urges Susanna to make an assignation with the Count; they will exchange cloaks and compromise him with his own wife. Susanna approaches him, explains her previous reticence as delicacy, and offers to meet him that evening. In a rare outburst in the minor (duet, 'Crudel! perchè finora') the Count reproaches her; changing to major, he sings of his coming happiness with exuberant syncopation. She tries to join in but trips over the right replies ('Yes' for 'No', etc.), correcting herself at a melodic high point. Leaving, she encounters Figaro and carelessly shows her satisfaction: 'without a lawyer we've won the case'. The Count, overhearing, is again suspicious and angry (obbligato recitative and aria, 'Vedrò, mentre io sospiro'). Must he sigh in vain while a mere servant wins the prize? The martial orchestration and key, even the contrapuntal language, recall Bartolo's aria, but the music snarls with aristocratic jealousy, not pompous self-importance: within the social structure of this opera it is a truly menacing utterance.

At the trial of Marcellina's case Curzio is finding for the plaintiff. Figaro protests that he cannot marry Marcellina without his parents' consent. On the discovery of a birthmark on his arm, it emerges that he is the lost son of Marcellina, and Bartolo reluctantly admits paternity. Marcellina embraces Figaro and the three express delight while the Count and Curzio mutter their annoyance in a sextet, 'Riconosci in questo amplesso'. Susanna misinterprets the embrace and boxes Figaro's ears. The comical explanation leads to a quartet of satisfaction against which Curzio and the Count fling out a defiant phrase of anger.

The Countess, waiting for Susanna, muses on the past and wonders if there is hope for her marriage.

'Le mariage de Figaro': engraving by J.-P.-J. de Saint-Quentin showing the final denouement, from the first authentic edition of Beaumarchais' 'La folle journée, ou Le mariage de Figaro' (1785)

This set-piece, an obbligato recitative and rondò, 'Dove sono i bei momenti', which, it has been argued, may originally have been intended to precede the previous scene, shows her as profoundly tender yet impulsive; it reaches a glowing a'' at the climax. Antonio tells the Count that Cherubino is still in the castle. The Countess dictates to Susanna a letter to the Count confirming their rendezvous; in their duettino, 'Che soave zeffiretto', their voices mingle in an expression of the love they feel, each for her own, while the honeyed music shows none of the deviousness of their intentions.

During a choral presentation to the Countess, Cherubino, still in girl's clothing, is unmasked, but allowed to stay for the wedding as he (and Barbarina) show a tendency to make revelations embarrassing to the Count. Throughout the finale, the necessary action is cunningly woven into the sequence of dances. During the march the two couples (Marcellina and Bartolo have decided to regularize their union) are presented to the Count and Countess. The bridesmaids' duet and chorus (contredanse) precede the alluring fandango, during which Susanna slips the letter to the Count, sealed with a pin (to be returned as a sign of agreement); Figaro, who has not been let in on the plot, notices with amusement that the Count has pricked himself.

Act 4 *The garden, at night; pavilions on either side* Barbarina, the go-between, has lost the pin (a mock-tragic cavatina, 'L'ho perduta'). Figaro, hearing her tale, concludes that Susanna is unfaithful; an abyss seems to open beneath him. Marcellina is inclined to warn Susanna; she must have a good reason for meeting the Count, and women should stick together ('Il capro e la capretta'). Barbarina is preparing to meet Cherubino in a pavilion. Figaro summons Basilio and Bartolo to witness the betrayal. Basilio moralizes about the wisdom of not resisting one's superiors, adding a tale of his own hot youth ('In quegl'anni'). Figaro's monologue (obbligato recitative and aria, 'Aprite un po' quegl'occhi') uses raw musical gestures to convey the terrors, for a clever but emotionally simple man, of sexual betrayal. Disconnected phrases reveal his anxiety, and horn fanfares mock him without mercy. He overhears but cannot see Susanna, who is disguised as the Countess and who is aware of his presence (obbligato recitative and aria, 'Deh vieni, non tardar'). The floating line and titillating woodwind cadences with which Susanna confides her amorous longing to the night perfectly capture the blended love and mischief with which she deliberately rouses Figaro's jealous passion (in 1789 Mozart replaced the aria with the elaborate rondò, 'Al desio').

From now on all is confusion; the characters mistake identities and blunder into each other in the dark, receiving kisses and blows intended for others, before nearly all of them end up in the pavilions (finale). Cherubino begs 'Susanna' (actually the disguised Countess) for a kiss; Susanna watches anxiously as the Count and Figaro drive the pest away. The Count begins to woo 'Susanna', who responds shyly; Figaro's impotent rage is highlighted in the bass. He contrives a temporary interruption. As the key changes from G to E♭, a serenade-like melody ironically evokes the peace of the night. Seeing 'the Countess' (actually Susanna), Figaro tells her what is going on; then, recognizing her by her voice, he pays 'the Countess' passionate court. Enraged, Susanna boxes his ears again, blows which he greets with rapture. This scene unfolds to a frantic Allegro, replaced at the reconciliation by pastoral 6/8. Now the two of them enact Figaro pleading passionate love to 'the Countess'; on cue, with a second abrupt key-change (B♭ to G), the Count bursts in on them, calling witnesses, dragging everyone including the false Countess from the pavilion, shouting accusations. As he denounces her and refuses forgiveness, the entry of the real Countess (in Susanna's clothes) leaves the company breathless. The humbled Count's prayer for forgiveness, and her loving response, build into a radiant hymn before the brilliant conclusion brings down the curtain on the crazy day.

*

Figaro is generally agreed to be the most perfect and least problematic of Mozart's great operas. The libretto, despite its complication (to which any synopsis does scant justice), is founded on a carefully constructed intrigue and Mozart draws musical dividends even from a hat, an anonymous letter and a pin. The advance on the sketched *opere buffe* of the immediately preceding years is astonishing, and must be attributed mainly to the effect on his imagination of the play, ably seconded by Da Ponte's adaptation.

The originality of the ensembles has often and rightly been commented upon. Many of them carry the action forward, not at the 'natural' tempo of recitative but under musical control; this makes such moments as the revelation of Figaro's parents to Susanna (the Act 3 sextet) both touching and funny, and creates palpable tension when the Count comes near to murdering his wife's 'lover' in Act 2, although

we know the unseen Susanna will enable the page to escape. The arias are no less original for their brevity and directness. They convey, economically and unforgettably, the essential characterization of Bartolo, Cherubino ('Non so più'), the Countess and the Count. Figaro and Susanna are presented in ensembles and action arias (his Act 1 cavatina, although it is a kind of soliloquy, and 'Non più andrai'; her 'Venite, inginocchiatevi'). Their central place in the intrigue is confirmed when each has an obbligato recitative (normally a sign of high rank) in the last act; these precede the last arias, soliloquies which deepen Figaro's character (although his cynical denunciation of women is not endearing) and reveal the subtlety and tenderness of Susanna. Mozart's replacement of 'Deh vieni' in 1789 by 'Al desio' is a rare case of his damaging his own work by pandering to a singer.

Modern performances often omit Marcellina's Act 4 aria, a stately minuet and melodious Allegro of deliberately old-fashioned cut (with coloratura and strings-only orchestration), and Basilio's, an elaborate and inventively composed narration in three sections (andante, minuet, allegro). Despite their virtues these pieces of moralizing by minor characters create a sequence of four arias inappropriate so near the denouement, and an excess of minuet tempo.

The only other critical reservation about *Le nozze di Figaro* concerns the episodic structure of the third act. It comes precisely where Da Ponte had to depart decisively from Beaumarchais (omitting the extended trial scene). The reordering of scenes has been shown not to represent Mozart's original intention, but the revised sequence avoids two immediately successive entries for the Countess and works well in the theatre. Any non-sequiturs in Act 3, however, count for little in performance and throw into greater relief the ingenious management of its finale. In the great finales of Acts 2 and 4, Mozart reached a level which he could never surpass; indeed, he was hardly to equal the B♭ Allegro of the second act finale for its mercurial play of motifs and the subsequent Andante for the synchronization of dramatic revelation with the demands of musical form.   J.Ru.

O

Oberon [*Oberon, or The Elf King's Oath*]

Romantische Oper in three acts, J306, by Carl Maria von Weber to a libretto by James Robinson Planché after Christoph Martin Wieland's poem *Oberon*; London, Covent Garden, 12 April 1826.

The original Reiza and Huon were Mary Ann Paton and John Braham; Charles Bland sang the title role (without success) and Fatima was sung by Lucia Elizabeth Vestris.

Oberon *King of the Elves*		tenor
Puck		mezzo-soprano
Reiza *daughter of Haroun al Rachid*		soprano
Sir Huon of Bordeaux *Duke of Guienne*		tenor
Sherasmin *Huon's squire*		baritone
Namouna *Fatima's grandmother*		spoken
Fatima *Reiza's attendant*		mezzo-soprano
Haroun al Rachid *Caliph of Baghdad*		spoken
Babekan *a Saracen prince*		spoken
Abdullah *a corsair*		spoken
Two Mermaids		mezzo-sopranos
Roshana *wife of Almanzor*		spoken
Almanzor *Emir of Tunis*		spoken
Fairies, ladies, knights, slaves, mermaids		
Setting Fairyland, the banks of the Tigris,		
Africa and France in medieval times		

On 18 August 1824 Weber received a letter from Charles Kemble in London, inviting him to compose a new opera and to come to Covent Garden to direct it during the following season, along with performances of *Der Freischütz* and P. A. Wolff's *Preciosa* (for which Weber had written incidental music). He was in an advanced stage of consumption and his doctor warned him that if he went to London he could expect only a few more months, or perhaps weeks, of life. But concern for his family's financial future overrode concern for his own health – he was aware that at best he had only a few years longer – and three days later he accepted the commission. Kemble offered him the subjects Faust or Oberon and, having chosen the latter, Weber asked for the libretto to be sent to him as soon as possible. By the beginning of December Planché's libretto had not arrived, and it became clear that the opera would have to be postponed until the 1826 season. Finally,

on 30 December, the first act arrived, to be followed by the second on 18 January 1825 and the third on 1 February. In order to set the text satisfactorily Weber had already begun an intensive course in English in October 1824 (he took 153 lessons in all), and was thus able to correspond with Planché in English. His letters show his concern over the nature of the libretto, so different from those he was used to; on 19 February he wrote to Planché:

The intermixing of so many principal actors who do not sing, the omission of the music in the most important moments – all these things deprive our *Oberon* the title of an opera, and will make him unfit for all other Theatres in Europe; which is a very bad thing for me, but – *passons la dessus.*

He accepted that, given English taste, there was no alternative; but had he lived he would certainly have revised *Oberon*, adding recitatives, to suit the German stage, although he would have needed to do much more than this to make it stageworthy.

By the time Weber left for England in mid-February 1826 he had completed the bulk of the opera. Travelling via Paris, he reached England on 4 March. Rehearsals began on 9 March, but several of the solo numbers were still lacking. He finished the remaining portions amid an exhausting round of rehearsals, concerts and social engagements. On 23 March he wrote the rondo 'I revel in hope and joy' for Braham, an immensely popular tenor; three days later he completed the cavatina 'Mourn thou, poor heart' for Paton and, in another three days, 'O Araby' for Vestris. Having rearranged the chorus 'For thee hath beauty' for female voices, Weber imagined that the opera, apart from the overture, was complete; but Braham requested a substitute for 'From boyhood trained', which he found too high in tessitura, and Weber grudgingly composed 'Ah! 'tis a glorious sight to see' on 6 April. He finished the splendid overture three days before the première. At the last minute, however, he was obliged to write 'Ruler of this awful hour' for Braham, who wanted another piece to show off a different quality in his voice.

The première on 12 April was a triumph, the overture and all the individual numbers were encored and Weber was loudly called for at the conclusion. By this stage, though, his health was

Lucia Elizabeth Vestris as Fatima in Weber's 'Oberon', a role she created at Covent Garden, London (12 April 1826): hand-coloured lithograph

completely shattered, and less than two months later he died, on the night before his planned return to Germany.

Despite the circumstances of its composition, *Oberon* contains some of Weber's most delightful music, which has assured the work a permanent, if peripheral, place in the repertory, even though its overall structure is far from satisfactory. In 1860 Planché produced a revised version in Italian which had recitatives by Weber's pupil Julius Benedict and incorporated some music from *Euryanthe*. There have been many other arrangements, including one with recitative by Franz Wüllner and one by Gustav Brecher with sections of instrumental music by Mahler (based on material from the opera) to accompany the dialogue.

*

The brilliant overture opens atmospherically with Oberon's horn-call, which acts as a motif throughout the work.

Act I *Oberon's bower* A chorus of fairies keeps guard over the sleeping Oberon ('Light as fairy foot can fall'). The number begins with an inversion of the horn-call; syncopation in the voice parts and delicate staccato interjections from wind and strings characterize the chorus. Puck dismisses the fairies and explains that Oberon and Titania have quarrelled over whether man or woman is the more inconstant in love; they have vowed not to be reunited until they find a couple who are constant through adversity. In an impassioned C minor aria, 'Fatal vow', in which the horn-call again underlies the melodic invention, Oberon deplores the situation. Puck informs him that Charlemagne has condemned the knight Huon to go to Baghdad, where he must kill the man on the caliph's right hand, then kiss the caliph's daughter and marry her. Puck discloses the sleeping Huon with his squire, Sherasmin. Oberon shows Huon, in a dream, a vision of the caliph's daughter, Reiza, imploring Huon to come to her. Her short guitar song, 'Oh why art thou sleeping', also begins with the horn-call. The vision fades, and Oberon wakes them. He pledges his help and gives Huon a fairy horn to call him to his aid. He also gives him a magic goblet which will spontaneously fill with wine but will burn the lips of the impure. (The goblet was excised from Planché's 1860 revision of the text.) Fairies are summoned and in the ensuing ensemble, 'Honour and joy', they transport Huon and Sherasmin to Baghdad.

The banks of the Tigris Huon saves Prince Babekan from a lion, but when Babekan drinks from the goblet it burns his lips; he attacks his rescuers but is driven off. Namouna tells them of Reiza's impending marriage to Babekan and of her vision of a knight who is to rescue her from it. (Planché removed the incidents involving Babekan and Namouna in 1860.) Huon reflects that his commitment to knightly honour has now been joined by the emotion of love. He was originally intended to sing 'From boyhood trained' at this point, but in the première this was replaced by the rather bombastic D major aria, 'Ah! 'tis a glorious sight to see'.

The palace of Haroun al Rachid In the harem Reiza tells Fatima she would rather die than marry Babekan, and anxiously waits for the rescuer she has seen in a vision. In the finale, 'Haste gallant knight', she urges speed on her deliverer, her opening phrase once more recalling the horn motif. Fatima returns with news of Huon's arrival, and then the harem guard is heard approaching, chanting to the accompaniment of an Arabian melody which Weber took from Carsten Niebuhr's *Reisebeschreibung nach Arabien* ('Description of a Journey to Araby', 1774). The number ends with Reiza anxiously awaiting rescue.

Act 2 *A magnificent salon in the palace of Haroun al Rachid* The act opens with a chorus of praise, 'Glory to the caliph', to which Weber, using bold orchestral unisons, gives an exotic flavour. After Reiza is brought in for her marriage to Babekan, to the accompaniment of woodwind, triangle and tambourine, Huon and Sherasmin rush in. Babekan confronts Huon, but is killed. Before the slaves can attack, Huon sounds his horn and they are paralysed, allowing Huon and Sherasmin to escape with Reiza and Fatima. When Huon has routed the guards in the palace garden, Oberon appears and conjures up the port of Ascalon and a ship to take them to Greece (in 1860 Planché shortened and rearranged much of the foregoing). Huon and Reiza depart, while Sherasmin woos Fatima; she sings the aria 'A lonely Arab maid'. Huon returns, urging haste, and they sing of their buoyant hopes in the quartet 'Over the dark blue waters', which includes the main *allegro* theme of the overture. In the solo and chorus 'Spirits of air and earth and sea' Puck mischievously summons the spirits of the four elements to wreck Huon's ship; an extensive orchestral postlude illustrates the storm. After the shipwreck Huon prays for Reiza's recovery ('Ruler of this awful hour'). When she revives, Huon goes in search of help. Reiza, awed by the sea, sings the demanding recitative and aria 'Ocean! thou mighty monster', in which orchestral figurations from the storm recur. During the aria a ship comes into sight and she attracts the attention of its crew. However, it is filled with pirates, led by Abdullah, who abduct her, leaving Huon unconscious and bound. Oberon appears, to the sound of the magic horn; he summons Puck and instructs him to take Huon to the house of the gardener Ibrahim in Tunis in seven days' time. (In Planché's 1860 version Oberon sings 'From boyhood trained' over the unconscious Huon at this point, with the text changed from the first to the third person.) In the finale, 'Oh! 'tis pleasant to float on the sea', mermaids and fairies appear and sing irrelevantly, but beautifully, of their joy.

Act 3 *Outside Ibrahim's house in Tunis* The enslaved Fatima bewails her fate, singing nostalgically 'O Araby!' Sherasmin, now married to her, enters and together they sing of their childhood ('On the banks of the sweet Garonne'). Puck causes Huon's appearance. Fatima tells him that Reiza has just been brought to Tunis and Sherasmin urges him to disguise himself; they join in the trio 'And must I then dissemble?'

Almanzor's palace in Tunis Inside the harem Almanzor welcomes Reiza, but she expresses her sadness in the F minor cavatina 'Mourn thou, poor heart'. Reiza communicates with Huon by means of a bouquet of flowers, and Huon gives utterance to his feelings in the rondo 'I revel in hope and joy'. Roshana, who is jealous because of her husband Almanzor's passion for Reiza, tries to induce Huon to kill him and marry her; she summons her slaves to help persuade him in the chorus and ballet 'For thee hath beauty'. He still refuses, and when Almanzor arrives Huon is seized and led away. Meanwhile Sherasmin has found the horn. Just as Huon is about to be burnt at the stake, the horn sounds and the finale 'Hark! what notes are swelling', begins. Weber based the opening section of this number on a *danse turque* from La Borde's *Essai sur la musique*. At first all

the slaves begin to dance and then, at a louder blast on the horn, Oberon and Titania appear and the Tunisians flee. Oberon tells the lovers that their trials are at an end, and they are transported to Charlemagne's palace. An extended instrumental march accompanies a procession of king and courtiers. Huon kneels before Charlemagne and explains that he has accomplished his mission. The opera ends with a chorus of praise for Huon and Reiza.

*

It is a remarkable testimony to Weber's operatic genius that, notwithstanding the unmitigated awfulness of its libretto, *Oberon* has maintained a toe-hold in the repertory. To a very considerable extent he was able to compensate for triviality and inconsequence in the libretto by skilful musical treatment. The imaginative and expressive quality of his writing for the principals invests them with a depth of characterization far beyond the implications of the text, while his sensitivity to colour and atmosphere in the orchestral and concerted numbers lifts the work above the level of shallow pantomime suggested by its libretto. Above all, however, Weber was able to lend an illusion of coherence to the picaresque farrago of nonsense with which Planché had presented him, by his subtle use of the horn-call as a recurrent musical motif; this technique, which he had already applied in *Der Freschütz* and *Euryanthe*, plays an important part in rescuing *Oberon* from the oblivion to which its libretto so nearly consigned it.

Weber died at a critical point in the development of Romantic opera. The rosy future for German opera that seemed to have dawned during the early 1820s with his and Spohr's successes proved illusory; their increasingly ambitious aesthetic aims had begun to drive an ever-widening gulf between them and the taste and capacity of a large proportion of their audience. Had Weber lived the picture might have been different, though even he might have been unequal to the task of combining the high musical ideals of a 'German Artist' with the popular appeal necessary to fill a theatre in the complacent Biedermeier society of the post-revolutionary 1830s.

C.B.

Oedipus rex

Opera-oratorio in two acts by Igor Stravinsky to a libretto by Jean Cocteau after Sophocles; Vienna, Staatsoper, 23 February 1928 (previously performed as an oratorio, Paris, Théâtre Sarah Bernhardt, 30 May 1927).

Oedipe [Oedipus]	tenor
Jocaste [Jocasta]	mezzo-soprano

Dessin de Théodore Strawinsky.

'Oedipus rex' (Stravinsky): Théodore Stravinsky's design for the set which appears in the published score, where it is described by the composer as presenting 'the advantage of having no depth. It avoids the voices becoming lost. Everything takes place on the same level.'

Créon [Creon]	bass-baritone
Tirésias [Tiresias]	bass
A Shepherd	tenor
A Messenger	bass-baritone
'Le Speaker' (narrator)	spoken

Chorus of tenors and basses
Setting Thebes, mythological time

Stravinsky claimed to have been inspired with the idea of composing a hieratic drama in an archaic sacred language ('not dead but turned to stone') by reading a biography of St Francis of Assisi. Having decided on Sophocles' Oedipus play, he turned to Cocteau, who had been trying to secure his collaboration since 1914, and whose highly compressed *Antigone* he had admired. The music was composed in 1926–7; Jean Daniélou translated the sung portions into Latin. The composer insisted on a conventional numbers format, 'opera' and the music-maiming 'music drama' having become antithetical categories in his mind. It was Cocteau's idea to introduce the opera's six episodes with didactic spoken summaries in the vernacular, though in the event their effect was the opposite of illuminating: they added yet another layer of stiff distancing from the action, which had already been paralysed by Stravinsky's insistence that the main characters behave like statues. (A frieze-like set, drawn by the composer's artist son Théodore, is prescribed in the published score.) While the effect of this procedure has been compared to that of Brecht's 'epic theatre', it seems more likely beholden to older Russian-symbolist notions of art as harbinger of a new mythological age and conveyor of spiritual community. These ideas, it seems hardly necessary to add, were lost on the Ballets Russes audience (and even on Dyagilev, to whom it was presented in token of his 20th anniversary as impresario). Following the première, conducted by Lothar Wallerstein, the opera made its way first in Germany, possibly abetted by the Brechtian resonance. Its successful production at the Kroll Opera, Berlin (1928, Klemperer conducting), was immortalized by the uncomprehending Schoenberg in a notorious squib.

*

The prophecy that their son will kill his father and marry his mother has led Laius and Jocasta to expose the newborn child Oedipus on Mount Cithaeron. Rescued and adopted, he has grown to manhood and, through the machinations of the gods, unwittingly fulfilled the prophecy.

Act I The Speaker announces that a trap has been laid for Oedipus and that the ensuing drama will display its closing.

Episode i As the action commences the inhabitants of Thebes call upon their king to save them from pestilence; their first invocation of his name is immediately transformed into a famous three-note ostinato that oscillates a baleful minor 3rd on its repetitions (chorus, 'Kaedit nos pestis'). Accompanied by regal dotted rhythms and giving his words proud melismatic emphasis, Oedipus the king promises to save the city from the plague as he had once saved it from the Sphinx (aria, 'Liberi, vos liberabo').

Episode ii Creon, the king's brother-in-law, sent to Delphi to consult the oracle, now returns with the gods' answer, delivered through a peremptory C major arpeggio (aria, 'Respondit deus'): it is revealed that the murderer of the former king Laius is at large in Thebes and must be driven out. Egged on by the crowd, Oedipus vows that he will solve the crime (aria with chorus, 'Non reperias vetus skelus').

Episode iii He calls upon Tiresias the seer, who, knowing that Oedipus is doomed, holds his tongue (aria, 'Dikere non possum'). When Oedipus, enraged, accuses Tiresias of being the murderer himself, the seer intones a clue over a D major cadence that will return when Oedipus finally sees the light: 'the murderer of the king is a king'. For now, however, Oedipus remains unaware, (self-)deceptively resolving the harsh truth-cadence to his own dulcet E♭ tonality, in which he floridly accuses Tiresias and Creon of a jealous plot against him (aria, 'Invidia fortunam odit'). The loud argument, which culminates in actual shouting, brings Queen Jocasta to the scene; she is hailed by the populace (chorus, 'Gloria, gloria, gloria!').

Act 2 Episode iv Jocasta upbraids the men for quarrelling at a time of plague (aria, 'Nonne erubeskite, reges, clamare'). Accompanied by an orchestral evocation of aulos and kithara (flute and harp), and insinuating her words seductively in a stereotyped 'oriental' vein, she belittles the oracle. Do they not lie? Had it not been foretold that Laius would be killed by a son of hers, while in fact he had been killed by thieves at a crossroads? At the mention of the word 'crossroads' (*trivium*), reiterated mysteriously by the crowd, now figuratively as well as literally a 'Greek chorus', Oedipus is seized with fear: accompanied by an ominous timpani tattoo, he recalls that he did once kill an old man at a crossroads (aria with chorus, 'Pavesco subito, Jocasta'). But he remains undeterred in his prideful quest and resolves to send for an old shepherd, the last remaining witness to the crime.

Episode v Now a Messenger (a role often doubled by the singer playing Creon) appears with news of the death of Polybus, King of Corinth, who had raised Oedipus as his son, but who on his deathbed had admitted that Oedipus had been adopted (aria with chorus, 'Mortuus est Polybus'). The Shepherd now gives reluctant testimony: he

had witnessed the finding of the baby Oedipus, abandoned on a mountainside (aria, 'Oportebat takere'). Jocasta senses what is coming and flees, but the crowd jumps excitedly to the conclusion that their king was of divine birth, and Oedipus, swayed willingly to their opinion, exults in a final melismatic cascade (aria with chorus, 'Nonne monstrum rescituri'). But the Messenger and the Shepherd reveal the awful truth before departing: Oedipus was the son of Laius and Jocasta who abandoned him; he was the slayer of Laius who begot him; and now he is the consort of Jocasta who bore him. Oedipus, suddenly shorn of all musical ornateness, sees the light plain, at last confirming the D major cadence he had diverted before (aria, 'Natus sum quo nefastum est . . . Lux facta est!'). He vanishes.

Episode vi Heralded by pompous fanfares, the Messenger now returns and, with the chorus's help, enunciates what the Speaker calls 'the famous monologue, "Dead is the sacred head of Jocasta"' (aria with chorus, 'Divum Jocastae caput mortuum!'). Three times he pronounces the terrible words, the chorus filling in the details: Jocasta has hanged herself for shame, and Oedipus has put out his eyes with her golden brooch. Oedipus, now literally blinded, reappears, and his former subjects lovingly drive him from Thebes to a reprise of the opening chorus ('Ekke regem Oedipoda . . . Vale miser Oedipus noster, te amabam').

*

The music is the product of Stravinsky's early neoclassic manner at its most extreme: musical materials thought outdated for a century or more – themes formed from arpeggiated triads, diminished 7th chords, formal recitatives – are ostentatiously displayed, and a deliberately offputting *hauteur* is affected. Yet lurking behind the frigid exterior is a very humane conception of the tragedy, centred (the composer's explicit denial notwithstanding) on the person of Oedipus. Thanks to a vivid use of tonality-symbolism, a powerful thematic recapitulation at the climax, and a masterly transmutation of Oedipus's musical idiom, which undergoes a wrenching transformation as he is brought low, the immobilized opera manages against all ostensible odds to achieve stunning catharsis.   R.T.

Orfeo [*L'Orfeo*] ('Orpheus')

Favola in musica in a prologue and five acts by Claudio Monteverdi to a libretto by Alessandro Striggio based mainly on the Orpheus myth as told in Ovid's *Metamorphoses*, though drawing also on the account in Virgil's *Georgics*; Mantua, ducal palace, 24 February 1607.

La Musica [Music] *the prologue*	soprano
Orfeo [Orpheus]	tenor
Euridice [Eurydice]	soprano
Silvia [Sylvia] *the messenger*	soprano
Speranza [Hope]	soprano
Caronte [Charon]	bass
Proserpina	soprano
Plutone [Pluto]	bass
Apollo†	tenor

Nymphs and shepherds, infernal spirits and
  Bacchantes‡
Setting The fields of Thrace (Prologue, Acts 1,
  2, 5); the underworld (Acts 3, 4)

† The role of Apollo occurs in the published score but not
in the librettos for the 1607 Mantua performances
‡ This last chorus occurs in the librettos for the 1607
Mantua performances but not in the published score

Unlike its model, Jacopo Peri's *Euridice* (1600 – the
earliest opera for which the music survives),
Monteverdi's *Orfeo* was not written for dynastic
celebrations, but simply as an entertainment for the
1607 carnival season at the Mantuan court. It was
prepared under the auspices of Francesco Gonzaga,
elder son of the Duke of Mantua, for performance
before the Accademia degli Invaghiti. It is possible
that *Orfeo* owes its existence to nothing more than
sibling rivalry between Francesco Gonzaga and his
brother Ferdinando, who from 1605 had studied at
the university of Pisa and had become closely
involved in musical and theatrical activity at Pisa and
Florence. On 5 January 1607 Francesco wrote to
Ferdinando mentioning the new opera and asking
him to request the loan of a castrato in the service of
the Grand Duke of Tuscany. The singer whom
Ferdinando selected, the young castrato Giovanni
Gualberto Magli, who did not arrive at Mantua until
15 February, was at first expected to sing the
prologue and one other unspecified role (possibly
that of Hope); later, he was also allotted the role of
Proserpina. The other members of the cast, insofar as
they can be identified, were the singer-composer
Francesco Rasi (presumably in the title role) and 'a
little priest' (possibly Girolamo Bacchini) who sang
Eurydice. It seems likely, then, that most, if not all,
the principal female roles of the opera were sung by
castratos. The instrumentalists and chorus were
probably drawn from the court musical establishment. The apparently large and diverse instrumental
ensemble required (related to the rich ensembles of
intermedi, court entertainments of the period) can in
fact be managed by a small group of players.

  Orfeo was first performed in the ducal palace at
Mantua in a room (not apparently a spacious one) in
the apartments occupied by the duke's sister Margherita Gonzaga d'Este. Tradition has it that this
was the Rivers Room, but the location is, in fact,

uncertain. The duke ordered a second performance
on 1 March. Two printings of the libretto survive
from 1607 and presumably correspond to these two
performances. A third performance was projected for
the proposed visit to Mantua in 1607 of the Duke of
Savoy, but the visit was cancelled, and the performance seems not to have taken place. The score of the
opera was published at Venice in 1609, and a second
edition appeared in 1615.

  It has been suggested that *Orfeo* was presented at
various Italian venues outside Mantua soon after its
first performance, but none of these suggestions is
based on sound evidence. A *dramma pastorale* with
the title *Orfeo* was given at Salzburg in 1614, and
another *Orfeo* was given there in 1619; these may
have been performances of Monteverdi's work. A
revival at Genoa before 1646 appears more securely
documented. Thereafter, *Orfeo* seems to have remained unperformed until the early years of this
century. The score was examined and discussed by
the two 18th-century music historians Charles Burney and Sir John Hawkins, and an abridged modern
edition was published in 1881 by Robert Eitner. The
first edition to have been given in a modern
performance, however, was that published by
Vincent d'Indy in 1905. D'Indy had directed concert
performances of this edition, which omits Acts 1 and
5, at the Schola Cantorum, Paris, on 25 February and
2 March 1904, and it was later used for the first
modern stage performance, a charity matinée given
under Marcel Labey at the Théâtre Réjane, Paris, on 2
May 1911, with Robert Le Lubez as Orpheus, and
Claire Croiza in the role of the messenger.

  Modern editions of *Orfeo* (and their associated
performances) have been, broadly speaking, of two
kinds. The first is the free adaptation or modern
arrangement of the original. In this area, composers
have been particularly active. Besides d'Indy, Carl
Orff (1925), Ottorino Respighi (1935), Bruno Maderna
(1967) and Luciano Berio (1984) among others
responded to the opera by making arrangements of
their own; and various editors also prepared versions
in which the original musical text was much adapted.
The second kind of edition and performance is the
one informed by research into the performance
conventions of Monteverdi's own time. Two composers – Gian Francesco Malipiero and Paul Hindemith – are represented here; and Malipiero's edition
of 1930, a faithful transcription of the 1609 edition,
remains valuable today. For the most part, though,
this area has been the province of the scholar and
scholar-performer, from Jack Westrup, whose Oxford University Opera Club performance of 1925 was
revived at the Scala Theatre, London, in 1929, to
August Wenzinger (Hitzacker, Saxony, 1955; recording issued the same year), Raymond Leppard
(London, 1965), Denis Stevens (edition published

1967), Nikolaus Harnoncourt (recording issued 1969), Roger Norrington (Kent Opera, 1976, and Florence, 1984) and John Eliot Gardiner (London, 1981).

Although *Orfeo* is divided into a prologue and five acts, a division which relates it to classical tragedy, it was almost certainly played without breaks between the acts, the scene changes between Acts 2 and 3, and Acts 4 and 5 taking place in front of the audience.

*

Toccata The opera is preceded by a toccata 'to be played three times ... before the raising of the curtain'.

Prologue *The fields of Thrace* The curtain rises to reveal a wood by the banks of a stream before which the personification of Music sings five stanzas – 'Dal mio permesso amato' – set as variations over a repeated bass (strophic variations). She pays compliments to the audience, the Gonzaga family in particular, and introduces herself as the power which can soothe troubled hearts or arouse the coolest minds to love or anger, a reference to the affective power of music mentioned by Greek philosophers and a concept very much in the minds of the creators of early opera. In stanza 4 she introduces the protagonist of the opera, Orpheus, and refers to the mythical power of his singing, which 'drew the wild beasts and made a servant of the Inferno'. Finally, she bids silence for the action which is to follow. The stanzas of the prologue are introduced and punctuated by a five-part ritornello for strings which will be heard again at the end of Act 2 and at the beginning of Act 5, where it can be seen as an emblem of music's power.

Act I *The fields of Thrace* Orpheus and Eurydice enter in the company of a chorus of nymphs and shepherds, who, as in classical drama, introduce and comment on the action, both as individuals and as a group. One of the shepherds reveals that this is the wedding day of Orpheus and Eurydice and urges his companions to celebrate it in song. They do so first in a solemn invocation to Hymen, god of marriage, and then, after a brief introduction by one of the nymphs, with a lively choral and instrumental dance. A shepherd invites Orpheus to sing of his love; he responds with a passionate arioso, 'Rosa del ciel', in which he addresses first the sun (Apollo, his father) and then Eurydice, expressing his happiness that she has at last accepted him. She responds, pledging her heart to him, and the chorus round off this first action symmetrically with a shortened repeat of their dance and invocation. A shepherd reminds the company that they should go to give thanks at the temple, and Orpheus, Eurydice and most of their companions exit to the sound of a processional ritornello for strings.

A small ensemble is left on stage to sing a chorus in which they reflect that no one should abandon himself to despair since after darkness 'the sun displays its bright rays all the more clearly'. The chorus serves to suggest the passage of time while the nuptials of Orpheus and Eurydice are celebrated at the temple. A sinfonia follows, introducing the arioso sung by Orpheus at the beginning of Act 2. The implication is that there should be no break between the acts.

Act 2 *The fields of Thrace* Orpheus responds to the chorus with the words 'Ecco pur ch'a voi ritorno, care selve e piaggie amate' ('Behold, I return to you, beloved woods and river-banks') and initiates a sequence of music in which he and his companions celebrate the pleasures of the day. They do this in a series of strophic arias: first, three arias are sung by the nymphs and shepherds, introduced and separated by ritornellos for which Monteverdi gives precise instrumentation; then Orpheus himself sings an aria of four stanzas, 'Vi ricorda, o boschi ombrosi', telling of the sorrow that he suffered before Eurydice accepted him. This sequence of music conveys a sense of unaffected joy before the sudden reversal of Orpheus's fortune. Following Orpheus's aria, one of the shepherds urges him to continue in the same vein, but before he can do so, a chromatic change in the bass line marks the entrance of the messenger, Sylvia, and words which are to become a refrain during the remainder of the act: 'Ahi caso acerbo, ahi fato empio e crudele!' ('O bitter plight, o wicked and cruel fate!')

In the exchanges which follow, the import of these words is not immediately understood by the chorus, and Monteverdi suggests the two levels of awareness by using different cadence centres for the messenger and the chorus. Only as Orpheus becomes disturbed by the messenger's distress does he sing a line, 'D'onde vieni? Ove vai? Ninfa che porti?', in which he moves to her cadence centre of E. She attempts to give her news, but at the mention of Eurydice's name, Orpheus interrupts in anguish with a line which completely disrupts the prevailing tonality. The messenger, now resolute, forces the tonality back to the prevailing level and announces Eurydice's death. Orpheus utters only the word 'Alas' before falling silent 'like a mute stone, so grieved that he cannot express his grief'. The messenger paints a vivid picture of Eurydice's death. She describes the way in which Eurydice, gathering flowers to make a garland for her hair, was bitten by a snake; she tells how she and her companions made vain efforts to revive her; and, as her narration rises to a climax, she repeats Eurydice's dying invocation of Orpheus's name. As she finishes, a shepherd takes up the cry 'Ahi, caso acerbo', initiating a sequence of reactions to the news. Orpheus rouses himself, and in a brief but poignant lament mourns Eurydice's death and resolves to bring her back from the underworld.

He exits, and the chorus is left to mourn, singing first 'Ahi, caso acerbo' and then turning to reflect upon the transience of human happiness. Sylvia, having acted as messenger, and consumed by self-loathing, banishes herself from human company, and the chorus conclude the act with duet laments punctuated by the refrain 'Ahi, caso acerbo'. As they leave, Music's ritornello is heard once more, as if to bring comfort and hope, and the scene changes as the first of the underworld sinfonias is heard. In contrast to the instrumental music for the upper world, which has been scored mainly for strings, with occasional use of recorders, this sinfonia is scored for cornetts and trombones with continuo played on a regal (reed organ).

Act 3 *The underworld* Orpheus enters, accompanied by Hope, who has guided him to the underworld and now describes the scene in images drawn from Virgil's *Aeneid* and Dante's *Inferno*. She can accompany him no further, for inscribed on a rock at the entrance to Pluto's kingdom are the words (from Dante) 'Abandon all hope, you who enter'. She leaves, and Orpheus is confronted by the awesome figure of Charon, ferryman of the River Styx. He, remembering 'ancient outrages' (the attempted abduction of Proserpina by Theseus and Pirithous, and the theft of Cerberus by Hercules), forbids Orpheus entry to Pluto's domains.

Orpheus responds with an aria, 'Possente spirto', cast in the form of strophic variations, in which he employs all his arts as a singer to persuade Charon to ferry him across the Styx. The importance of this aria is reinforced by its placing almost exactly at the centre of the five-act structure. The aria is preceded by a sinfonia which represents Orpheus playing his lyre and should be scored for strings and organ with wood pipes as Monteverdi indicates when it is repeated later in the act. In the first four stanzas of his aria, Orpheus attempts to impress Pluto by displaying his ability as a virtuoso singer. For these stanzas Monteverdi provided two versions of the vocal line, one which the performer could ornament himself and one which provides a model of the complex ornamentation that he had in mind for a demonstration of Orpheus's power. The stanzas are punctuated by phrases for the three main classes of late Renaissance instruments: bowed strings, wind, and plucked string instruments. In the fifth stanza, as Orpheus's thoughts turn to Eurydice, Monteverdi abandons variations in favour of a simpler, more passionate style of declamation. The variation bass returns, however, for the final stanza, and here Monteverdi surrounds the voice with a halo of strings.

Charon, singing substantially the same music as before, declares himself flattered, but unmoved, and his obduracy provokes a final passionate outburst from Orpheus, culminating in the words 'Rendetemi il mio ben, Tartarei numi'. He plays his lyre, and though his singing has failed, his playing succeeds in lulling Charon to sleep. Seizing his opportunity, Orpheus steals Charon's boat, and as he crosses the Styx he sings again 'Rendetemi il mio ben, Tartarei numi'. He enters Pluto's kingdom. The sinfonia heard at the beginning of the act is repeated twice, and between the playings a chorus of infernal spirits reflect that no enterprise undertaken by man is undertaken in vain.

Act 4 *The underworld* Pluto and Proserpina enter. Although Orpheus's singing failed to move Charon, it has profoundly affected Proserpina, and she pleads with her consort for Eurydice's release. He is moved by her entreaties and sends one of the spirits to announce that he will allow Orpheus to lead Eurydice back to the upper world provided that he does not turn to look upon her until they have left the abyss. The spirit departs, and another reflects that Orpheus will only lead his bride to freedom if he is able to let reason rule his youthful passion. While Orpheus and Eurydice are being informed of Pluto's decision, Proserpina and Pluto play out a short love scene in which Proserpina blesses the day that she was herself stolen away from the earth by Pluto and brought to the underworld. Orpheus enters, leading Eurydice. As they begin their progress from the underworld he sings a lively aria, 'Qual honor di te fia degno', another set of strophic variations, though this time over a 'walking bass' in crotchets, in which he praises the power of his lyre in subjugating the will of Tartarus. After three stanzas, however, doubts assail him. How can he be sure that Eurydice is following him? Is it simply envy that makes Pluto forbid him to look at her? Why should he hesitate to turn? – for what Pluto forbids Cupid demands.

After each of these questions he pauses to listen, and on the last occasion there is a great noise off stage. Imagining that the Furies are carrying off Eurydice, Orpheus turns, and for a few moments looks upon her before the vision is abruptly cut off and a spirit tells him that he has broken the law and is unworthy of grace. Eurydice is heard lamenting his losing her 'for too much love' before she is ordered back to the realms of the dead, nevermore to see the stars (an echo of Dante). Orpheus tries to follow her but is drawn back to the upper world by a force invisible to him. The chorus of spirits sing that only he who can conquer his passions is worthy of eternal glory. A final 'underworld' sinfonia is heard. The scene changes back to the fields of Thrace, and Music's ritornello is heard again as the last act begins.

Act 5 *The fields of Thrace* Orpheus is alone, lamenting the loss of Eurydice. He looks at the familiar scenes which comforted his suffering before Eurydice accepted him. Now, however, there is no hope of regaining her, and he will join the hills and rocks in their grief. As he laments, an echo gives back the final syllables of each phrase, subtly changing their meaning so that it supplies words of sympathy. Lamentation gives way to praise of Eurydice's beauty, and in the final paragraph of his soliloquy Orpheus resolves to reject all other women. At this point the ending of the opera found in the 1607 librettos diverges from that of the 1609 score. In the librettos, which we must assume represent the original ending, Orpheus sees the Bacchantes approaching and withdraws as they erupt on to the stage. They threaten to take revenge on Orpheus for rejecting them and perform an extended finale, with solos and choral refrain, in praise of Bacchus. This finale is close in spirit to the ending of the Orpheus story given by Ovid and Virgil and would certainly have been practicable in the constricted space in which we suppose that *Orfeo* was first performed. The 1609 score substitutes a more spectacular ending, based on Hyginus's *Astronomia*, which allowed for the use of a cloud machine. In this, Apollo descends to Orpheus and chides him for being a slave to his emotions. He invites Orpheus to join him in the heavens, from where he can look upon Eurydice's semblance in the stars. The two ascend to the heavens singing a virtuoso duet, and nymphs and shepherds sing a very brief chorus concluding with a moral drawn from Psalm 126 (Vulgate 125): 'he who sows in tears shall reap the fruit of grace'. The opera closes with a *moresca* (a 'Moorish' dance) performed by shepherds.

*

Various theories have been advanced to explain the changed ending. It has been suggested that the ending found in the score was the original version, altered when it was found that the opera was to be played in a room too small to accommodate a cloud machine. On the whole, though, it seems more likely that the Bacchanalian finale was the original version. This being the case, opinions differ as to whether the more spectacular, but more perfunctory, ending was written in anticipation of the projected performance at Mantua for the Duke of Savoy, or whether the original version was thought by Monteverdi and/or others to be too nearly tragic to provide a suitable ending for an opera. In either case the authorship of the literary text for the 1609 ending is uncertain.

Monteverdi's *Orfeo* is generally regarded as the first work of genius in the history of opera. It presents a rich blend of Greek myth with 16th-century dramatic conventions, and of the varied instrumental and vocal groupings of the *intermedio* and madrigal traditions with the newer expressive medium of Florentine operatic recitative pioneered by Peri. The

flexibility and expressive power of the new style are fully unleashed only in the second act, in which Sylvia relates the death of Eurydice; Orpheus's reaction progresses convincingly from a stunned realization of the finality of death to his angry refusal to accept it. Though it stands somewhat apart from the mainstream by virtue of its being a court opera, *Orfeo* is not simply a courtly entertainment but a work which addresses with economy and passion the most profoundly felt of human emotions.   J.W.

Orfeo ed Euridice
[*Orphée et Eurydice* ('Orpheus and Eurydice')]

Italian version: *Azione teatrale* in three acts by Christoph Willibald Gluck to a libretto by Ranieri de' Calzabigi; Vienna, Burgtheater, 5 October 1762.

French version: *Tragédie opéra* in three acts by Gluck to a libretto by Pierre Louis Moline after Calzabigi; Paris, Académie Royale de Musique (Opéra), 2 August 1774.

The principals in the first performance of the Italian version were Gaetano Guadagni (Orpheus), Marianna Bianchi (Eurydice) and Lucia Clavarau (Cupid). For the première of the French version the singers were Joseph Legros (Orpheus), Sophie Arnould (Eurydice) and Rosalie Levasseur (Cupid).

Italian Version

Orfeo [Orpheus]	alto castrato
Euridice [Eurydice] *his wife*	soprano
Amore [Cupid]	soprano

Shepherds, nymphs, Furies and spectres from
    Hades, heroes and heroines in Elysium,
    followers of Orpheus
Setting Classical Thrace

French Version

Orphée [Orpheus]	tenor
Eurydice *his wife*	soprano
Amour [Cupid]	soprano

Shepherds, shepherdesses, nymphs, demons, Furies,
    happy spirits, heroes and heroines
Setting Classical Thrace

Orfeo ed Euridice was the first of Gluck's three so-called reform operas written with Ranieri de' Calzabigi (the other two were *Alceste* and *Paride ed Elena*) in which a 'noble simplicity' in the action and the music was intended to replace the complicated plots and florid musical style of *opera seria*. Calzabigi had gone in 1761 to Vienna where he was encouraged to collaborate with Gluck by Count Durazzo, the Intendant of Viennese theatres; a further important collaborator was the influential choreographer

Gasparo Angiolini. *Orfeo ed Euridice* was first per-formed on the name-day of Emperor Francis I, when it was a great success; it went on to become the most popular of Gluck's works, as it has remained.

The 1762 production was revived in Vienna the following year, but the work was not then performed until 1769, when Gluck himself conducted it in Parma as the third part of a triple bill, *Le feste d'Apollo*. For this, *Orfeo ed Euridice* was given without an interval and with the alto castrato part originally written for Guadagni transposed up for the soprano castrato Giuseppe Millico. Then, in 1774, Gluck revised the opera for performances at the Académie Royale de Musique (the Opéra), transposing and adapting the role of Orpheus for an *haute-contre*, the type of voice usually used for heroic or amatory roles in French opera rather than the castrato, which had virtually no place in French music and was some-thing of an object of ridicule. Gluck also altered the orchestration of the opera to suit the different forces of the Opéra, and added vocal and instrumental pieces to make the opera much larger, longer and grander. This work, *Orphée et Eurydice*, had a new French text by the young French poet Moline based on Calzabigi's libretto but with additions. The work's success surpassed even that of Gluck's first Paris opera, *Iphigénie en Aulide*, earlier in 1774, and it continued to feature prominently in the repertory of the Opéra.

Performances abroad began with the production of the Italian version at the King's Theatre in London in 1770, but although Guadagni again sang the title role only seven numbers of Gluck's original re-mained and the opera was lengthened with words by Giovanni Bottarelli and music by J. C. Bach. Pro-ductions were soon given at many opera houses throughout Europe, usually of the Italian version, including one conducted by Haydn at Eszterháza in 1776. In the first part of the 19th century the tenor Adolphe Nourrit was celebrated for his portrayals of Orpheus at the Paris Opéra; and in 1854 Liszt conducted the opera at Weimar, writing his sym-phonic poem *Orpheus* to replace the overture and adding some closing music on the same themes.

The first appearance of a female singer in the role of Orpheus was one Demoiselle Fabre in Milan in 1813, but the most famous female interpreter of the role in the 19th century was the contralto Pauline Viardot, for whom Berlioz made his edition of the opera in 1859. For this, Berlioz re-adopted the original vocal register of the Italian Orpheus and combined what he considered to be the best of Gluck's Italian and French versions. Basically, he followed the 1774 French score, rearranging it in four acts, and reverting to the Italian original only where he thought it musically or dramatically superior. In the process he cut several numbers from the French score, including the third verse of Orpheus's first-act lament 'Objet de mon amour', the Act 3 trio and the whole of the final *divertissement*, and replaced the final chorus with that of *Echo et Narcisse*, 'Le Dieu de Paphos et de Gnide'. He also made adjustments to Moline's French text and restored much of the key scheme and some of the original, more subtle orchestration of the Italian version.

During the 19th century the part of Orpheus was sung nearly as often by a tenor as by a contralto; Berlioz's edition is just one of many composite versions of the opera, albeit the most famous and most distinguished. However, the versions of the opera most frequently given since the 1870s are adaptations of Berlioz's version back into Italian, in three acts, still with a contralto as Orpheus, and incorporating music that Berlioz omitted from Gluck's 1774 French score. The most popular of these hybrid Italian versions was published by Ricordi in 1889. Gluck's opera has even been transposed down for a baritone; Dietrich Fischer-Dieskau and Hermann Prey have both sung the role in Germany.

Toscanini was a great champion of *Orfeo ed Euridice*, and conducted it regularly during his seasons at La Scala, Milan. There is a recording of him conducting Act 2 in a concert performance with Nan Merriman and Barbara Gibson and the NBC Sym-phony Orchestra. Clara Butt sang Orpheus in 1920 at Covent Garden, with Sir Thomas Beecham conducting; Kathleen Ferrier took the role at Glyndebourne in 1947 and Covent Garden in 1953. Other notable postwar female interpreters of Orpheus have included Rita Gorr at the Opéra-Comique in Paris in 1959 and Marilyn Horne at the Metropolitan in 1972; she also made a distinguished recording of the opera with Sir Georg Solti conducting. Another, conducted by Renato Fasano, was made in 1965 by Shirley Verrett, who sang the role at Covent Garden in 1972. Janet Baker was also an admired Orpheus, and chose the opera for her Glyndebourne farewell in 1982 conducted by Raymond Leppard; this version too was recorded.

The recordings and most of the performances mentioned above are of a composite version in Italian. Despite its fame, even the Berlioz edition has been little performed this century, an omission which has been rectified by Anne-Sofie von Otter, who recorded a modification of it (changing it back into three acts and restoring the third-act trio) conducted by John Eliot Gardiner in 1989. Recently several countertenors have sung the original Italian version with great success, among them John Angelo Messana, René Jacobs and Derek Lee Ragin; Jacobs made a fine recording of the 1762 version with La Petite Bande conducted by Sigiswald Kuijken in 1982; Ragin recorded the opera with John Eliot Gardiner and the English Baroque Soloists in 1991.

Kathleen Ferrier as Orpheus in Gluck's 'Orfeo ed Euridice'

The 1774 French version has made lamentably few appearances this century either on the stage or in the record catalogues, partly because of the difficulty of finding adequate high tenors. Two of its most distinguished interpreters, however, made recordings: Nicolai Gedda, who sang the role at the Paris Opéra as late as 1973, recorded it in his prime in 1955 conducted by Louis de Froment; and, finest of all, Léopold Simoneau recorded it in 1956 with Hans Rosbaud conducting.

In the synopsis that follows, 'I' stands for the Italian version, 'F' for the French version; see pages 463–4 for a comparison of the two versions.

*

Act I.i *(I), i–ii (F) A pleasant but solitary grove with the tomb of Eurydice in the middle of an avenue of laurel and cypress trees* After a lively overture, nymphs and shepherds enter to a sombre orchestral introduction with garlands of myrtle and antique vases as part of the funeral rites for Eurydice, some burning incense and scattering flowers. The chorus sings a mourning hymn, whose solemnity is intensified by the low pitch of the soprano line and the use of three cornetts (in *Orfeo*; three trombones in *Orphée*). Orpheus, who lies prostrate on a rock, interrupts them three times with an anguished cry of Eurydice's name. He tells them to perform the last rites and strew her grave with flowers; this they do to a dance, full of chromatic inflections, after which the chorus is repeated, the

orchestral introduction now serving as postlude. (The French version has a brief recitative for Orpheus before this postlude, or 'ritournelle', breaking the palindromic symmetry of the original.)

Left alone, Orpheus calls to Eurydice in the aria 'Chiamo il mio ben così'/'Objet de mon amour': this lament is in three verses, separated by two increasingly impassioned recitatives, each beginning with Orpheus's cries of 'Euridice!', akin to those heard during the opening chorus. The echo effects of the opening chorus are also extended here with a second, offstage orchestra of chalumeaux and strings (the *chalumeau* – a clarinet-like instrument – was not to be had in Paris; Gluck replaced it with an oboe). Each verse has different solo instruments: respectively flute, horns and english horns in *Orfeo*, and two flutes, one horn and two clarinets in *Orphée* (again Gluck had to replace an unusual and distinctive timbre with a more ordinary one). After the third strophe Orpheus rages against the cruelty of the gods and determines to wrest Eurydice from them and bring her back to the land of the living.

I.ii *(I), iii–iv (F)* Cupid appears and tells Orpheus that Jove has taken pity and will allow him to descend into Hades; if he can appease the Furies with his singing he can bring Eurydice back. This is all told in recitative in *Orfeo*; for *Orphée*, Gluck shortened it, adding an *air* ('Si les doux accords de ta lyre') for Cupid that covers similar ground to the second part of the original recitative. Orpheus is delighted, but Cupid warns him that if he looks at Eurydice before he has brought her back to earth he will lose her for ever; neither is he allowed to explain this curious behaviour to his wife. Cupid leaves him, singing a little aria in which he warns Orpheus to be silent and control his desire ('Gli sguardi trattieni'/'Soumis au silence'; the livelier sections increase the agony and the irony, with their simple 3/8 rhythm, rather like a serenade).

Orpheus imagines Eurydice's anxiety and distress at his behaviour at their reunion; but he must bow to the will of the gods. Thunder and lightning are heard as he leaves for Hades. In *Orfeo* this is set as recitative, with a brief orchestral coda; for *Orphée* Gluck cut the recitative substantially, removing the simulated encounter between Orpheus and Eurydice, and gave Orpheus a long, heroic bravura aria, a display piece for Legros ('L'espoir renaît dans mon âme'). This virtuoso italianate aria, complete with provision for a cadenza, has provoked much criticism partly because it is inconsistent with Gluck's declared reform principles (although it was very popular in the 18th century). It has not been established for certain whether the music of this aria is in fact by Gluck or by Ferdinando Bertoni, who claimed to have composed it, although Gluck had used it twice before, in his opera *Il Parnasso confuso*

(1765) and in the *Atto d'Aristeo*, one of the companion operas to the 1769 Parma production of *Orfeo ed Euridice*. Lasting over five minutes, the aria is by far the longest piece in Act 1 of *Orphée*; although its length and its style may seem at odds with the music of the rest of the opera, there is no denying that it brings the act to a spectacular conclusion.

Act 2.i *A terrifying grotto beyond the river Cocytus, hidden in the distance by thick smoke billowing out of the grotto* An 'orribile sinfonia' (Calzabigi's description) is heard, a short, terrifying dance with jerky rhythms, chromatic harmony and open-ended phrases (Gluck replaced the two horns of *Orfeo* with a solo trumpet in *Orphée*). Gluck again uses a double orchestra: harp and pizzicato strings accompany Orpheus and represent his lyre, with the rest of the orchestra for the Furies. A brief prelude for the harp indicates that Orpheus is on his way, and immediately the Furies and demons of the underworld threaten him in a chorus whose relentless repeated rhythms, homophonic writing and stark octave lines heighten the tension. The music hurries on into another short dance for the Furies full of rushing scales, which leads to a repeat of the opening chorus, extended now to portray the barking of the multi-headed guard dog Cerberus with quick string glissandos. In *Orfeo* there is a repeat of the opening sinfonia; in *Orphée*, Orpheus actually interrupts the chorus of Furies here with his first attempt to placate them.

'Be moved by my tears', he pleads, to be answered by the Furies' angry cries of 'No!'/'Non!' (Orpheus's wide-ranging line is more ornate in the French revision). The Furies ask Orpheus why he is there: 'Misero giovane, che vuoi, che mediti?'/'Qui t'amène en ces lieux?' (The Furies sing quietly at first, but the obsessive rhythms of the first chorus continue.) Orpheus interrupts, and his brief arias are followed by continuations of the chorus, which however gradually become less fierce until the Furies, finally moved by Orpheus's singing, make way for him to move on into Elysium. The Furies' music dies away and comes to rest (on their first perfect cadence in the act, the surprise of which is increased and strengthened by the major-key ending).

In *Orfeo*, at this point the second scene begins; but when he revised the opera Gluck added an 'Air de Furies', a substantial dance of terror drawn from his ballet *Don Juan* (1761), which also seems to have been the melodic and harmonic inspiration for the five choruses of Furies in the first scene of *Orfeo* the following year. The inclusion of this dance in *Orphée* gives an extra purpose and dimension to the preceding choruses.

2.ii *(I), ii–iii (F) The Elysian Fields; flowery arbours, groves and fountains and grassy areas on which groups of Blessed Spirits are resting* As the scene changes from Hades to the Elysian Fields, so the music, which has been predominantly in the minor mode, turns to the radiance of F major, the traditional pastoral key, for the opening Dance of the Blessed Spirits. In *Orphée*, Gluck expanded this celebrated piece for two flutes and strings, surely the most other-worldly minuet ever written, and indeed made it nearly three times its original length by adding a central section with a solo flute (the D minor piece generally known simply as 'Dance of the Blessed Spirits'), followed by a reprise of the opening; a further extra dance follows, and an *air* for Eurydice and the chorus ('Cet asile aimable et tranquille'), another pastoral piece, in F major and a flowing 6/8 metre, repeated in instrumental form as a dance for the heroes and heroines.

Then follows one of Gluck's most original arias as Orpheus marvels at the beauty of the scene in which he finds himself ('Che puro ciel'/'Quel nouveau ciel'). Its orchestration in *Orfeo* is the most complex that Gluck ever wrote: an oboe melody, with a softly rippling triplet accompaniment from the strings, solo cello and solo flute, with supporting parts provided by solo bassoon horn and continuo. Gluck simplified the solo flute and cello parts when he revised *Orfeo* for Parma in 1769 and retained this less demanding version in Paris in 1774: a great loss, as is Orpheus's brief dialogue with the Blessed Spirits at the end of the aria when they tell him that Eurydice is coming. 'Quel nouveau ciel' has no chorus and ends with Orpheus's words to Eurydice: 'Your attractive glances and gentle smile are the only blessings that I want'. The Blessed Spirits continue with a chorus, 'Vieni a' regni del riposo'/'Viens dans ce séjour paisible', after which there is a slow dance for flutes and strings.

Orpheus, mildly impatient, begs the Spirits to restore Eurydice to him as soon as possible, which they do during a reprise of the previous chorus with different words; the act ends as Orpheus leads Eurydice away, without looking at her.

Act 3.i *A dark labyrinthine grotto surrounded by rocks, thickets and wild plants* The scenes built around choruses, solo voices and dances of the two previous acts are replaced in this act by the encounter between Orpheus and Eurydice alone. And unlike the other two acts this one begins, after a few bars of agitated strings, with recitative, as Orpheus urges Eurydice to hurry up and follow him. She is naturally suspicious of his strange and impatient behaviour which, no matter how much she questions him, he cannot explain. Their exchanges culminate in a duet ('Vieni, appaga il tuo consorte'/'Viens, suis un époux'): here is no sweet, submissive Eurydice but a passionate and jealous wife, as she shows in her following aria, 'Che fiero momento'/'Fortune ennemie'. When Gluck revised this number for *Orphée* he recast its central slower section as a dramatic duet to press the

ITALIAN AND FRENCH VERSIONS OF *ORFEO ED EURIDICE*

N – new to 1774 version; R – revision of number in 1762 version; items in 1774 version neither N nor R are in effect direct transcriptions; italic numerals represent 1774 version

Orfeo ed Euridice, 1762	*Orphée et Eurydice*, 1774
Act I	**Act I**
1 Sinfonia, C	*1* Ouverture, C
Scene i	*Scene i*
2 Coro: Ah, se intorno, c	*2* Choeur: Ah! dans ce bois, c
3 Recit. (Orfeo): Basta, basta	*3* Récit (Orphée): Vos plaintes (R3)
4 Ballo, E♭	*4* Pantomime, E♭
5 *a*) Coro: Ah, se intorno, c	*5* Choeur: Ah! dans ce bois, c (R5a)
b) Ballo (ritornello), c	
	6 Récit (Orphée): Eloignez-vous! (N)
	7 Ritournelle, c (=5b)
	Scene ii
6 *a*) Aria (Orfeo): Chiamo il mio ben così, F	*8* *a*) Air (Orphée): Objet de mon amour, C
b) Recit. (Orfeo): Euridice, Euridice!, f	*b*) Recit (Orphée): Eurydice! Eurydice!, c
c) Aria (Orfeo): Cerco il mio ben, F	*c*) Air (Orphée): Accablé de regrets, C
d) Recit. (Orfeo): Euridice, Euridice!, F	*d*) Récit (Orphée): Eurydice! Eurydice!, C
e) Aria (Orfeo): Piango il mio ben, F	*e*) Air (Orphée): Plein de troubles, C
7 Recit. (Orfeo): Numi! barbari Numi	*9* Récit (Orphée): Divinités de l'Achéron (R7)
Scene ii	*Scene iii*
8 Recit. (Amore, Orfeo): T'assiste Amore	*10* Récit (Amour): L'Amour vient au secours
	11 Air (Amour): Si les doux accords, F (N)
	12 Récit (Orphée, Amour): Dieux! Je la reverrais! (R8)
9 Aria (Amore): Gli sguardi trattieni, G	*13* Air (Amour): Soumis au silence, G
	Scene iv
10 Recit. (Orfeo): Che disse?	*14* Recit (Orphée): Impitoyables Dieux! (R10)
	15 Ariette (Orphée): L'espoir renaît, B♭ (N)
11 Orchestral coda, D	
Act 2	**Act 2**
Scene i	*Scene i*
12 Ballo, E♭	*16* Maestoso, E♭
13 Introduction, c	*17* Prélude, d
14 Coro: Chi mai dell'Erebo, c	*18* Choeur: Quel est l'audacieux, d
15 Ballo, c	*19* Air de Furie, d
16 Coro: Chi mai dell'Erebo, c	*20* Choeur: Quel est l'audacieux, d
17 Ballo (=12), E♭	
18 Orfeo, Coro: Deh placatevi, E♭	*21* Orphée, Choeur: Laissez-vous toucher, B♭ (R18)
19 Coro: Misero giovane, E♭	*22* Choeur: Qui t'amène, B♭
20 Aria (Orfeo): Mille pene, c	*23* Air (Orphée): Ah! La flamme, c
21 Coro: Ah, quale incognito affetto, c	*24* Choeur: Par quels puissants remords, g
22 Aria (Orfeo): Men tiranno, c	*25* Air (Orphée): La tendresse, g
23 Coro: Ah, quale incognito affetto, f	*26* Choeur: Quels chants doux, f
	27 Air de Furies, d (N)

Scene ii
24 Ballo, F

Scene ii
28 Ballet des Ombres heureuses
    a) Lent tres doux, F
    b) Même mouvement, d (*N*)
    c) 28a, F (*N*)
    d) Air, C (*N*)
29 Air (Eurydice, Choeur): Cet asile, F (*N*)
30 Ritournelle, F (*N*)

Scene iii
31 Air (Orphée): Quel nouveau ciel, C (*R*25)

25 Aria (Orfeo, Coro): Che puro ciel, C
26 Coro: Vieni a' regni, F
27 Ballo, B♭
28 Recit. (Orfeo): Anime avventurose
29 Coro: Torna, o bella, F

32 Choeur: Viens dans ce séjour, F
33 Lent, B♭
34 Récit (Orphée): O vous, ombres
35 Choeur: Près du tendre objet, F

Act 3
Scene i
30 Recit. (Orfeo, Euridice): Vieni, segui i miei passi

31 Duetto (Orfeo, Euridice): Vieni, appaga il tuo consorte, G
32 Recit. (Euridice): Qual vita
33 Aria (Euridice): Che fiero momento, c

Act 3
Scene i
36 Récit (Orphée, Eurydice): Viens, viens, Eurydice (*R*30)
37 Duo (Orphée, Eurydice): Viens, suis un époux, F (*R*31)
38 Récit (Eurydice): Mais d'où vient (*R*32)
39 *a)* Air (Eurydice): Fortune ennemie, c
    b) Duo (Eurydice, Orphée): Je goûtais les charmes, E♭ (*R*33, part)
    c) Air (Eurydice): Fortune ennemie, c

34 Recit. (Orfeo, Euridice): Ecco un nuovo tormento

35 Aria (Orfeo): Che farò senza Euridice, C
36 Recit. (Orfeo): Ah finisca e per sempre

40 Récit (Orphée, Eurydice): Quelle épreuve cruelle (*R*34)
41 Air (Orphée): J'ai perdu mon Eurydice, F (*R*35)
42 Récit (Orphée): Ah! puisse ma douleur (*R*36)

Scene ii
37 Recit. (Amore, Orfeo, Euridice): Orfeo, che fai?

Scene ii
43 Récit (Amour, Orphée, Eurydice): Arrête, Orphée! (*R*37)
44 Trio (Eurydice, Orphée, Amour): Tendre Amour, e (*N*)

Scene iii
38 Maestoso, D

*Scene iii**
45 Orphée, Amour, Eurydice, Choeur: L'Amour triomphe, A–D (*R*43)

Ballo
39 Grazioso, A
40 Allegro, a

Ballet
46 Gracieux, A (=39)
47 Gavotte, a (*R*40)
48 Air vif, C (*N*)
49 Menuet, C (*N*)
50 Maestoso, A (*R*38)

41 Andante, D

42 Allegro, D
43 Orfeo, Amore, Euridice, Coro: Trionfi Amore, D

51 Très lentement, D (*R*41)
52 Chaconne, D (*N*)

* In original conducting score, items appear in the order: *50, 46, 47, 48, 49, 45, 51, 52*; between *48* and *49* is a Lent et gracieux, G (Collected Edition, appx, pp.324–5), and *49* is followed by 2 bars of modulation (Collected Edition, appx, p.310)

action forward. In the next recitative, inevitably, Eurydice faints, and as Orpheus turns to look at her she dies (the Paris version is particularly moving here as the two voices unite for one last note). Orpheus gives vent to his desperation first in impassioned recitative, and then in an apparently controlled aria, a lament in the major key ('Che farò senza Euridice?'/'J'ai perdu mon Eurydice'). Gluck added an orchestral postlude to this famous aria when he revised it, greatly intensifying its noble tragedy. Its three verses balance 'Chiamo il mio ben così'/'Objet de mon amour' in Act 1; the two subsidiary sections begin with Orpheus's cries, 'Euridice!', as do the two recitatives that separate the strophes of the first-act aria.

3.ii Orpheus is about to kill himself when Cupid reappears, says that Orpheus has given proof enough of his fidelity and restores Eurydice to life, telling them to enjoy the pleasures of love. Gluck added a trio when he revised the opera, initially a rather sombre piece with its minor key, repeated syncopated rhythms and dark orchestration (low strings with bassoons), but brightening to a faster, major-key ending as the three principals celebrate the power of love.

3.iii *The magnificent temple of Cupid* Orpheus, Eurydice, Cupid and shepherds and shepherdesses celebrate. The symmetry characteristic of the opera is maintained even in the concluding ballet of *Orfeo*, which begins with an instrumental version of the final chorus and, after four dances, ends with a reprise of the chorus. *Orphée*, on the other hand, has a lengthy final *divertissement* which is apt to seem rather over-extended (and is often cut altogether) when it is performed, as in the collected edition, after the final chorus.

The engraved score of *Orphée* published in 1774 after the first performances places the Act 3 trio in the middle of the final *divertissement*, between the Menuet and the Maestoso; but in the Gluck collected edition (1967) it is restored to its original position before the final chorus, as in the 1774 libretto. Recent research on the conducting scores used for the first Paris performances shows that the original order of the Act 3 *divertissement* was different from that in the printed score (see footnote to Table 1).

*

Orfeo ed Euridice is a milestone both in Gluck's work and in the history of opera. It is in effect the first of Gluck's 'reform' operas, although it was not until the publication of the Italian *Alceste* of 1767 that his and Calzabigi's reformist principles and aims were presented in the preface as a manifesto (*see Alceste*). These two, with Angiolini and Durazzo,were united in their desire to revivify the musico-dramatic arts, to free them from the convention-bound complacency by which they were constrained. *Orfeo*, although an

azione teatrale with roots in the dramatic pastoral tradition, embodies all Gluck's reforms except for that of the overture, which instead of apprising the audience of the nature of the opera is a jolly, high-spirited sinfonia in one movement which could well have served as curtain-raiser to a comic opera. But gone are the coloratura and the da capo arias of Italian *opera seria*, together with the regular and restrictive alternation of recitative and aria and the *recitativo secco* accompanied only by the continuo. Instead, in *Orfeo* the chorus assumes a role of much greater importance than was usual in Italian opera, sometimes rivalling that of the protagonist, as at the beginnings of the first two acts. The recitative is very varied and fluid, and often impassioned and colourful, partly because it is orchestrated throughout and partly because it is so attentive to the words and their sense; and the arias themselves are placed at telling dramatic points – each is vital to the drama, the structure and the characterization.

Orfeo owes much to French opera and drama in spite of the fact that it is in Italian. Calzabigi had spent much time in Paris; his experience of French theatre and opera is evident throughout the libretto. Gluck generously declared that he was indebted to Calzabigi for the invention of the new form of Italian opera, but he himself was certainly familiar with both *tragédie lyrique* and *opéra comique*, and the influences of both are manifest in *Orfeo*. The opening scene at the tomb is reminiscent of Act 1 of Rameau's *Castor et Pollux*, and even a lament as profound as Orpheus's 'Chiamo il mio ben così' is related to the three-verse French *romance* of the kind found in *opéras comiques*. Gluck's revision for the Paris performances of 1774 brought the work even closer to the French tradition. However, the transposition and adaptation of the role of Orpheus from alto castrato to *haute-contre* resulted not only in the loss of much of the formal balance and the satisfying tonal sequence (compare in Table 1 the key relationships of the two versions in Act 1 and especially Act 2) but also the change of emphasis in the role of Orpheus from the elegiac, disembodied beauty of the castrato to the much more heroic high tenor.

But there were undoubtedly gains as well as losses in the transformation and expansion of the short, intimate court chamber opera into a full-scale work for a large public opera house. When Gluck made the French revision, some 12 years after the Italian original, he was a much more experienced composer and man of the theatre, and the revision has an added sweep and grandeur; the addition of Eurydice's aria and the ballets in the second act and the trio in the third are undoubted gains. It is ironic that the versions of the opera best known and most widely performed today are based on Berlioz's hybrid edition and in consequence, since the 19th century, Orpheus has nearly always been sung by women 'en travesti'. Nowadays, however, the original Italian role can be sung by a countertenor, and although there are few high tenors who can negotiate the consistently dizzy heights of the French version, the score could be transposed down a tone to correspond with what we believe 18th-century French pitch to have been. Such means would bring us as close as possible to Gluck's originals.

J.H.

Orlando

Opera in three acts by George Frideric Handel to an anonymous libretto adapted from Carlo Sigismondo Capece's *L'Orlando* (1711, Rome), after Ludovico Ariosto's *Orlando furioso*; London, King's Theatre, 27 January 1733.

The roles were originally taken by Antonio Montagnana (Zoroastro), Senesino (Orlando), Anna Maria Strada del Pò (Angelica), Francesca Bertolli (Medoro) and Celeste Gismondi (Dorinda) – the last probably identical with the Neapolitan *buffa* soprano Celeste Resse.

Orlando *a knight*	alto castrato
Angelica *Queen of Cathay, in love with*	
Medoro	soprano
Medoro *an African prince, in love with*	
Angelica	alto
Dorinda *a shepherdess*	soprano
Zoroastro *a magician*	bass
Isabella *a princess*	silent

Orlando was the only new opera of Handel's season of 1732–3. He wrote it during the first weeks of the season (which opened on 4 November with an adaptation of Leo's *Catone in Utica*) and completed the score on 20 November. The libretto is considerably changed from Capece's original, most notably in the introduction of the character of the magician Zoroastro, who becomes the presiding genius of the opera; the role was created for the distinguished bass Montagnana. The princess Isabella, important in Capece's libretto, appears briefly in Act 1 of the opera as a silent role. *Orlando* is the first of the three Handel operas with a text deriving from Ariosto's epic poem (the others being *Ariodante* and *Alcina*) and, despite the extensive variations, remains closest to the spirit of the original.

The opera achieved ten performances, six before a Lenten run of oratorios and four afterwards. Further performances were reported to have been deferred because of the indisposition of a singer. It seems likely that this was a hint of Handel's breach with Senesino (who may have been unhappy with the unusually difficult and irregular role of Orlando), which came to a head in June 1733 with the defection of that singer and most of Handel's company to the newly formed 'Opera of the Nobility'. Sir John Clerk of Penicuik (a wealthy Scottish landowner who was also a skilled amateur musician) saw the last performance of *Orlando* on 5 May and recorded the contrast between the excellence of the opera and the poor attendance, the latter no doubt depleted by hostile machinations against Handel:

I never in all my life heard a better piece of musick nor better perform'd – the famous Castrato, Senesino made the principal Actor the rest were all Italians who sung with very good grace and action, however, the Audience was very thin so that I believe they get not enough to pay the Instruments of the Orchestra ... One Signior Montagnania sung the bass with a noise like a Canon ...

Handel never revived the opera and it remained unheard until the production at Halle on 28 May 1922, in an arrangement by H. J. Moser. The first British revival was at the Unicorn Theatre, Abingdon, on 6 May 1959, in which year it was also given in Florence; it has had numerous revivals since, particularly in the 1980s, when it was heard in Britain, Germany and the Low Countries and in Venice, Paris, Chicago and San Francisco.

*

Act I The time and place of the action are undefined, the scenes ranging from conventional pastoral landscapes to symbolic tableaux created by Zoroastro's magic. (In Ariosto Orlando is attached to the court of Charlemagne, implying a period around AD 800.) The opening scene is the countryside at night, with a view of a mountain on which Atlas is seen supporting the heavens. Zoroastro contemplates the constellations, obscure in meaning to ordinary mortals, but which tell him that Orlando will one day return to noble deeds. Orlando himself appears, torn between conflicting desires for love and glory. Zoroastro rebukes him for his devotion to love, and illustrates the dangers of that emotion by causing the distant mountain to change to the Palace of Love, where heroes of antiquity appear asleep at Cupid's feet. He urges Orlando to follow Mars, the god of war. Orlando, at first shamed by the vision, decides that glory can be obtained in pursuit of love.

The scene changes to a wood with shepherds' huts, Dorinda's domain. Her thoughts, troubled by love, are interrupted as Orlando rushes past with a princess (later identified as Isabella), whom he has rescued. Angelica appears: despite Orlando's attentions to her she has fallen for Medoro, whose wounds she healed while he was being looked after by Dorinda. Medoro overhears and enters with a declaration of his love for Angelica. Dorinda returns;

it is clear that she loves Medoro. To avoid hurting her he pretends that Angelica is a relation of his; Dorinda knows he is lying but his words still enchant her. Zoroastro tells Angelica he knows of her love for Medoro, and warns her of Orlando's likely revenge. When Orlando appears, Angelica cannot tell him what has happened but pretends to be jealous and taunts him about the princess he has rescued. Zoroastro prevents Medoro's untimely approach by causing him to be concealed by a fountain as the scene is transformed into a garden. Angelica tells Orlando he must prove his faith by never seeing the princess again. Orlando agrees; he will fight the most terrible monsters to show his love. Medoro asks Angelica whom she has been talking to; she tells him and persuades him not to fight such a rival. Their embrace is seen by Dorinda, who forces Angelica to explain that Medoro is her betrothed. Angelica thanks Dorinda for her kindness and gives her a piece of jewellery, but Dorinda would sooner have had a gift from Medoro. He begs her to forgive him, but she says she has been hurt and remains inconsolable.

Act 2 In a wood, Dorinda's melancholy reflections on the song of the nightingale are interrupted by Orlando, who learns of Angelica's love for Medoro. Dorinda shows him the jewel, saying it came from Medoro. Orlando recognizes it as a bracelet he once gave to Angelica. Believing himself betrayed, he threatens to kill himself and pursue Angelica into hell.

In a grove of laurels, near a grotto, Zoroastro rebukes Angelica and Medoro for arousing Orlando's anger; mortal minds wander in darkness when led by the blind god of love. Medoro carves his name and Angelica's on the laurel trees to declare their love, and Angelica resolves to return with him to Cathay. Orlando, entering, is enraged at the sight of the names on the trees and rushes into the grotto in pursuit of Angelica. She, however, appears from the opposite side and bids a sad farewell to the trees and the streams. Orlando emerges and pursues her, Medoro following. Zoroastro's magic now intervenes: Angelica is engulfed by a large cloud which bears her away in the company of four genii. Orlando loses his reason. He believes that shades from the underworld have taken Angelica from him; he will follow them, becoming a shade himself, and imagines himself crossing the Styx in Charon's boat and entering Pluto's kingdom. There in his madness he sees a Fury in the form of Medoro, who runs into the arms of Proserpina; her weeping at first rouses his pity. As he runs back into the grotto it bursts open to reveal Zoroastro on his chariot. The magician gathers Orlando up in his arms and flies off with him.

Act 3 Medoro explains to Dorinda that Angelica has sent him to her for refuge; she is glad he is no longer deceiving her. Orlando appears and declares his love for Dorinda. She is at first flattered, but as Orlando becomes more ardent and addresses her as Venus it becomes obvious he is still raving; in a fit of delusion he squares up for unarmed combat with an imagined enemy and leaves. Dorinda, telling Angelica of Orlando's madness, delivers her thoughts on love as a wind that sets the brain spinning, bringing as much pain as joy. Zoroastro appears and orders his genii to change the scene to a dark cavern; he promises to restore Orlando's former glory. Dorinda tells Angelica that Orlando has destroyed her house and buried Medoro in the ruins. Orlando appears, addresses Angelica as the sorceress Falerina and threatens to kill her; grief-stricken at the news of Medoro's death, she defies him. As Orlando throws her into the cavern, it changes into a beautiful temple of Mars. Orlando claims he has rid the world of its monsters; sleep overcomes him. Zoroastro declares that the time has come to restore the madman; he pours liquid over the face of Orlando, who awakens, his senses returned. Dorinda tells him he has murdered Medoro in his frenzy. Full of remorse, he decides to kill himself, but Angelica begs him to live on. Medoro was saved by Zoroastro, who now implores Orlando to accept the lovers' betrothal. A statue of Mars, with fire burning on an altar, rises as Orlando proclaims victory over himself. He wishes joy to Angelica and Medoro, who promise to be true to each other. Dorinda, inviting them to her cottage, says she will forget her sorrows. All join in praise of love and glory.

*

Though *Orlando* shares characteristics with both earlier and later Handel operas involving supernatural effects, it is unique in its mix of characters and in its flouting of Baroque operatic conventions to depict the deranged state of the hero's mind. Angelica and Medoro are on the whole conventional lovers, their best music being in their slower numbers (notably Medoro's exquisite 'Verdi allori') and in the moving trio at the close of Act 1 when they vainly try to console the distraught Dorinda. The lovelorn shepherdess herself never becomes a comic role, despite the quirky rhythms of her arias. The gentle pathos of her unrequited love is always present, and there is a slightly manic ring to her solo in the final ensemble as she invites the company to the home she previously declared to be destroyed. Zoroastro, a striking figure, has three magnificent arias, of which the last ('Sorge infausta una procella') is well known (and long held a place in 19th-century versions of the oratorio *Israel in Egypt* as 'Wave on wave congeal'd with wonder'). Orlando is a highly original creation, and a role which makes few concessions to the expectations of an operatic primo uomo. There are only three regular da capo arias, two in Act 1 and the impassioned 'Cielo! se tu il consenti' in Act 2.

Irregular forms then predominate, including the astonishing Mad Scene ('Ah! stigie larve') at the close of Act 2, in which a mixture of accompanied recitative and measured passages in various tempos depicts Orlando's imaginary journey to the underworld, taking in a lament over a chromatic ground bass and ending with a haunting rondo in gavotte rhythm. In this scene occur the notorious bars of 5/8 time, but they appear only briefly between sections of unmeasured recitative and their impact on the ear is slight. Orlando's final aria of slumber ('Già l'ebro mio ciglio'), through-composed and accompanied by the veiled tones of two solo *violette marine* (violas with resonating strings) over a pizzicato bass, is both moving and mysterious.

Orlando makes a special appeal to modern sensibility with its concentration on the psychological states of characters in a fantasy world lending itself to reinterpretation; it is also a splendid exemplar of what the Baroque theatre could achieve in allying stagecraft to drama expressed through music.   A.H.

Orphée aux enfers ('Orpheus in the Underworld')

Opéra bouffon in two acts by Jacques Offenbach to a libretto by Hector-Jonathan Crémieux and Ludovic Halévy after classical mythology; Paris, Théâtre des Bouffes-Parisiens (Salle Choiseul), 21 October 1858 (revised version, as an *opéra-féerie* in four acts, Paris, Théâtre de la Gaîté, 7 February 1874).

The original 1858 production featured Lise Tautin as Eurydice, and Tayau as an Orpheus who genuinely played the violin; Désiré (Amable-Désiré Courtecuisse) sang Jupiter, with Léonce (Edouard-Théodore Nicole) as Pluto.

Pluton [Pluto] *god of the underworld, disguised*		
as Aristée [Aristaeus], a farmer		tenor
Jupiter *father of the gods*		baritone
John Styx *servant of Pluto, formerly King of*		
Bœotia		tenor
Mercure [Mercury] *Jupiter's messenger*		tenor
Orphée [Orpheus] *a musician*		tenor
Bacchus *god of wine*		spoken
Mars *god of war*		baritone
Cerbère [Cerberus] *three-headed watchdog*		
of the underworld		barked
Morphée [Morpheus] *god of sleep*		tenor
Eurydice *wife of Orpheus*		soprano
Cupidon [Cupid] *god of love,*		
son of Venus		mezzo-soprano
Diane [Diana] *goddess of chastity*		soprano
L'Opinion Publique [Public		
Opinion]		mezzo-soprano
Junon [Juno] *wife of Jupiter*		soprano
Vénus [Venus] *goddess of beauty*		soprano
Minerve [Minerva] *goddess of wisdom*		soprano
Gods, goddesses, shepherds, shepherdesses, lictors,		
infernal spirits		

Setting The countryside near Thebes; Mount Olympus; the underworld

Orphée aux enfers marked a significant advance for Offenbach in 1858. He had founded the Bouffes Parisiens three years earlier, when he was restricted by the terms of his licence to producing short works for just a few performers; he was now permitted to use larger casts and chorus and to offer his audiences a full-length work for the first time. Though the idea of parodying Greek mythology was not new, the vehemence with which Offenbach did so, not least by turning a stately minuet into a cancan, caused a good deal of critical comment. However, this merely served to increase interest in the work and ensure its overwhelming success in Paris. In turn this led to international celebrity on an enlarged scale and substantially accelerated the pace of acceptance of his works abroad. *Orphée* was produced in Breslau and Prague in 1859 and, in a new German version by Johann Nestroy, at the Carltheater, Vienna, on 17 March 1860. It was for this version that Carl Binder (1816–60) arranged the familiar overture, which has helped to maintain the work's place as the most widely known of all Offenbach's *opéras bouffes*.

During the 1860s it continued to attract worldwide productions, and in 1874 Offenbach expanded the four scenes into four separate acts for a spectacular production at the Théâtre de la Gaîté. This opened with a new overture ('Promenade autour d'Orphée') and introduced new characters, two ballets and several new vocal numbers, among them (in Act 3) Mercury's saltarello 'Eh hop! eh hop! place à Mercure' and a Policemen's chorus 'Nez au vent, œil au guet'. Subsequent productions have generally made selective pickings from the 1874 additions. A revival of the Théâtre de la Gaîté production in 1878 featured Offenbach's compositional rival Hervé in the role of Jupiter.

*

Act I *The countryside near Thebes, with the house of Orpheus* Public Opinion righteously parades herself as guardian of public virtue ('Qui suis-je? Du Théâtre Antique'), after which Eurydice arrives, singing of her lover, the farmer Aristaeus ('La femme dont le cœur rêve'). Her husband, Orpheus, then enters. Alas, the two can't stand each other, and above all Eurydice can't abide Orpheus's violin playing. Orpheus therefore deliberately taunts her by playing part of his latest violin concerto ('Ah! c'est ainsi'). He goes on to inform her that he has laid a trap for her lover Aristaeus by filling the cornfields with snakes.

The Bacchanal from Act 4 of Offenbach's 'Orphée aux enfers': drawing by Gustave Doré, who designed some of the costumes for the original production at the Théâtre des Bouffes-Parisiens, Paris, in 1858

Aristaeus appears ('Moi, je suis Aristée'), and Eurydice tries to warn him, but he simply encourages her to walk through the field. Of course she is bitten, whereupon Aristaeus reveals himself as Pluto, god of the underworld, which for Eurydice makes the prospect of death much brighter ('La mort m'apparaît souriante'). He duly sets off with Eurydice to his realm, leaving Orpheus to contemplate joyful freedom. However, Orpheus's joy is cut short by Public Opinion, who insists that, for the sake of public decency, he must go to the underworld and bring back his wife.

***Act 2** Mount Olympus in the clouds at dawn* The gods are still sound asleep ('Dormons, dormons que notre somme') when Venus, Cupid and Mars return from their amorous nocturnal pursuits ('Je suis Vénus!'). No sooner have they settled down than a blast on Diana's hunting horn tells them it is time to get up ('Quand Diane descend dans la plaine'). To their chagrin, Jupiter reprimands them for ungodly behaviour. As they disperse to their duties, Mercury enters, having been sent by Jupiter to summon Pluto to appear before the father of the gods; when Pluto then arrives, Jupiter berates him for having kidnapped a mortal woman. They are interrupted by a revolt of the gods, who have finally had enough of Jupiter's hypocrisy and parade his own amorous adventures ('Aux armes, dieux et demi-dieux!'). Just then Public Opinion arrives with Orpheus, reluctant-

ly reclaiming his wife. Jupiter tells Pluto to return Eurydice, and all the gods decide to go with him to the underworld to ensure that the order is carried out.

***Act 3** Pluto's boudoir, in Hades* Eurydice is bored. Her only company is Pluto's servant John Styx, who tells of his sad life since he was King of the Bœotians ('Quand j'étais roi de Béotie'). He has been charged with keeping Eurydice under lock and key, and he hastily returns her to her room at the sound of Pluto coming back with Jupiter. Cupid tells them that Eurydice is a prisoner in the next room. Jupiter is understandably anxious to verify this, which he can finally do when Cupid enables him to get through the keyhole by transforming him into a fly. Eurydice is sufficiently bored to welcome even a fly, which she playfully chases ('Bel insecte à l'aile dorée'). Finally allowing himself to be caught, Jupiter identifies himself and suggests that, in the confusion created by Pluto's forthcoming party, Eurydice should flee with him to Olympus.

***Act 4** Hades and the River Styx* An extravagant party is in full swing, and the gods sing the praises of wine ('Vive le vin! vive Pluton!'). Eurydice is there, disguised as a Bacchante ('J'ai vu le Dieu Bacchus'), and everyone thoroughly enjoys a dance that turns from a stately minuet into an infernal galop or cancan ('Ce bal est original'). Jupiter tries to sneak off with her, but Pluto bars the way and points out that

Orpheus is on his way with Public Opinion. Jupiter is momentarily put out until Cupid thinks of a plan. When Orpheus arrives and demands the return of his wife, Jupiter agrees on condition that, on his exit from Hades, Orpheus leads the way and does not look round. The procession duly starts but, by hurling a thunderbolt just behind Orpheus, Jupiter shocks him into turning round. To the delight of everyone except Public Opinion, he thus forfeits his right to Eurydice, and Jupiter transforms her into a priestess of Bacchus.

*

As with all stage works of the genre, the success of Offenbach's operettas depended a good deal on the librettists and performers. In this respect he was both well served and skilful at discovering talent. His sound theatrical judgment extended to his part in selecting and shaping the subjects he used. Many of these were satirical treatments of familiar stories. The satire of this piece consists largely of portraying the revered figures of antiquity in farcical and incongruous situations (such as the cancan for the gods), the only direct musical satire being a quotation of Gluck's 'J'ai perdu mon Eurydice'. Berlioz's version of Gluck's opera appeared the year after *Orphée aux enfers*.   **A.L.**

Otello ('Othello')

Dramma lirico in four acts by Giuseppe Verdi to a libretto by Arrigo Boito after William Shakespeare's play *Othello, or The Moor of Venice*; Milan, Teatro alla Scala, 5 February 1887.

The première, conducted by Franco Faccio, featured Francesco Tamagno (Otello), Victor Maurel (Iago) and Romilda Pantaleoni (Desdemona).

Otello *a Moor, general of the Venetian army*	tenor
Iago *an ensign*	baritone
Cassio *a platoon leader*	tenor
Roderigo *a Venetian gentleman*	tenor
Lodovico *an ambassador of the Venetian Republic*	bass
Montano *Otello's predecessor as Governor of Cyprus*	bass
A Herald	bass
Desdemona *Otello's wife*	soprano
Emilia *Iago's wife*	mezzo-soprano

Soldiers and sailors of the Venetian Republic, Venetian ladies and gentlemen, Cypriot populace of both sexes, Greek, Dalmatian and Albanian men-at-arms, island children, an innkeeper, four servants at the inn, common sailors

Setting A maritime city on the island of Cyprus, at the end of the 15th century

After *Aida* in 1871, there was to be no Verdi operatic première for 16 years. As the 1870s progressed, Verdi seemed increasingly isolated from current trends in Italian music, in particular by the tendency of both public and composers to look outside Italy (to France and, later, even more to Germany) for new ideas and aesthetic attitudes. It is against this background that we should examine his reluctance to write new works after the Requiem of 1874: Verdi was a composer who, after being at the forefront of Italian musical taste for two decades, suddenly found himself accused of being distinctly old-fashioned, out of touch with the times; and indeed he probably felt so too. Those who sought to lure him out of self-imposed retirement, among whom the prime mover was the young director of the Ricordi publishing house, Giulio Ricordi, had to tread carefully. Ricordi eventually teamed up with Arrigo Boito, the librettist and composer, who in the 1860s had been one of the most visible members of the Italian avant garde, but whose respect for the old maestro was growing with the years. In June 1879 Ricordi and Boito mentioned to Verdi the possibility of his composing a version of Shakespeare's *Othello*, surely a canny choice given Verdi's lifelong veneration for the English playwright and his attempts after *Macbeth* to tackle further Shakespearean topics (notably *King Lear*). Verdi showed cautious enthusiasm for the new project, and by the end of the year Boito had produced a draft libretto, one full of ingenious new rhythmic devices but with an extremely firm dramatic thread.

Although Verdi eventually agreed – with a characteristic show of reluctance – to collaborate with Boito on *Otello*, the project was long in the making. First came two other tasks, the revisions to *Simon Boccanegra* (1881, effected with Boito's help) and to *Don Carlos* (1884), both of which can be seen in retrospect as trial runs for the new type of opera Verdi felt he must create in the changed Italian artistic climate. Verdi also bombarded Boito with alterations to the libretto draft of *Otello*, especially to the Act 3 finale, which he felt must furnish occasion for a grand concertato finale in the traditional manner. The opera was then composed in a series of intensive bursts, the comparative speed suggesting that Verdi had previously sketched the music rather thoroughly. The cast was carefully selected and intensively coached by Verdi himself, and the première was a predictable, indeed a well-nigh inevitable success, although some critics of course lamented the sophistication and lack of immediacy they found in Verdi's new manner. The opera was soon given in the major European capitals and became an important element of the operatic reper-tory. Though it has never reached the level of popularity of the middle-period masterpieces – something hardly surprising considering the severe vocal and orchestral demands made by the score – *Otello* remains one of the most universally respected of Verdi's operas, often admired even by those who find almost all his earlier works unappealing.

For the Paris première at the Théâtre de l'Opéra in 1894 Verdi added a ballet score to the third act and also made some significant revisions to the same act's concertato finale, reducing the musical detail in an effort to bring out the embedded conversations. These revisions were not incorporated into the Italian version and are rarely heard today.

*

Act 1 *Outside the castle* A sudden burst of orchestral dissonance begins the opera with an immediacy Verdi had never before attempted: a clear sign that this work will engage a more realistic notion of musical drama. A violent storm is raging, and the onlookers from the shore, among them Iago, Cassio and Montano, comment on the fortunes of their leader Otello's ship. The crowd's reaction momen-tarily coalesces into 'Dio, fulgor della bufera', a desperate prayer to save the ship, but then all is again confusion until, to cries of 'È salvo!', Otello safely arrives. He greets his followers with a ringing salute, 'Esultate!', proudly announcing that the Turks have been beaten. The chorus then closes this opening 'storm' scene with a triumphant victory chorus, 'Vittoria! Sterminio!'

As the crowd goes about its work, Iago and Roderigo, in the inn, come to the fore. In a texture alternating simple recitative with arioso, the venom-ous Iago assures his friend that Desdemona will soon tire of her new husband, Otello, and thus become available to the besotted Roderigo. Iago then reveals his hatred for Cassio, who he thinks has unjustly overtaken him in rank. Their conversation is fol-lowed by the fireside chorus 'Fuoco di gioia!', a series of contrasting sections tied together by brilliant orchestral effects imitating the crackling flames. As the fire dies down, Iago encourages Cassio to drink, eventually breaking into the brindisi 'Inaffia l'ugola', a three-stanza song with choral refrain, by the end of which Cassio is much the worse for wine. Roderigo provokes him to a fight; this is interrupted by Montano, who himself becomes embroiled with Cassio. Iago skilfully stage-manages the confusion by ordering Roderigo to call the alarm; soon there is general panic. At the height of the disturbance, Otello enters, sword in hand, and with an imperious gesture, 'Abbasso le spade!' ('Lower your swords!'), restores calm. His inquiry finds Cassio guilty and he dismisses him from service (to a stifled cry of triumph from Iago). Desdemona has by now

appeared, and Otello dismisses the crowd, to be left alone with his new bride.

The ensuing love duet, although it bears a certain distant relationship to earlier 19th-century practices, is really *sui generis*, its tendency towards a series of short, contrasting sections all but obliterating vestiges of any larger, multi-movement structure. After a brief orchestral transition as the stage clears, a choir of solo cellos heralds the opening exchange, 'Già nella notte densa'; Otello evokes the nocturnal ambience before Desdemona turns to the past, and in the largest lyrical section, 'Quando narravi l'esule tua vita', recalls with Otello the manner in which his narrations of past exploits first won her over. At the close of this episode the lovers sing a patterned alternation, 'E tu m'amavi per le mie sventure', a paraphrase of Shakespeare's 'She lov'd me for the dangers I had passed, And I lov'd her that she did pity them'. Otello wishes for death at this moment of ecstasy, but soon their mutual feelings spread forth into a final gesture of intimacy: a thrice-repeated kiss ('Un bacio . . . ancora un bacio') whose intensity is reflected in the highly decorated violin melody that underpins the stage action. With a final gesture towards the night, 'Vien . . . Venere splende', Otello leads Desdemona back into the castle. The solo cellos return to effect a tender close.

Act 2 *A room on the ground floor of the castle* After an orchestral introduction suggesting Iago's busy energy, the villain is revealed, assuring Cassio that with help from Desdemona he will regain his place in Otello's estimation. Iago sends Cassio off to attend her and comes forward to deliver his famous soliloquy, 'Credo in un Dio crudel', a kind of evil Credo in which he plays to the hilt his demonic character. As befits Iago's slippery energy, this dynamic Credo hovers between arioso and aria, its devious harmonic and formal twists continuing to the last. Iago now notices Desdemona and Emilia in the garden and offers a *sotto voce* commentary as Cassio approaches them with his suit. Then, seeing Otello approach, he positions himself for the crucial confrontation in which he sets out to arouse Otello's jealousy.

The Otello-Iago duet continues to the end of the act, although interrupted by a series of set-pieces and dialogues that become increasingly caught up in the central action. The first phase of the duet, and its most fragmentary, involves the initial testing of Otello: Iago's teasing questions and repetitions, Otello's angry confusion, and then Iago's first mention of 'jealousy', to a sliding chromatic figure of great harmonic audacity. And the first set-piece interruption is a jarring one: Desdemona is seen again in the garden, and distant voices serenade her in a simple chorus, 'Dove guardi splendono raggi', a piece whose musical atmosphere recalls the choral

'Otello' (Verdi), scene from Act 3 of the original production at La Scala, Milan, 5 February 1887: engraving from the special commemorative edition of 'L'illustrazione italiana'

evocations of Act 1 in both style and tonality. As the chorus ends, Desdemona approaches Otello to intercede on Cassio's behalf. But Otello's response is disturbed: so much so that Desdemona gently asks for pardon in a second set-piece, the quartet 'Dammi la dolce e lieta parola', in which Otello bemoans the loss of his peace of mind while Iago extracts from Emilia a handkerchief of Desdemona's that has been cast aside in the preceding dialogue. As the quartet comes to a close, Otello dismisses Desdemona and Emilia, and is again left alone with Iago. This time the emotional temperature is near boiling point, and a few comments from Iago are enough to precipitate the aria 'Ora e per sempre addio', in which Otello bids farewell to his past life in a closed form that, appropriately given the dramatic situation, has strong hints of the younger Verdi's lyrical style. The aria disintegrates into furious orchestral figures as Otello demands proof of his wife's infidelity, eventually grabbing Iago by the throat and hurling him to the ground. Iago now takes over and gradually leads the atmosphere into those calmer waters where he can begin his story, 'Era la notte', in which – to a musical structure as complex and surprising as Otello's was simple and direct – he offers as 'proof' words he has overheard Cassio mumble in his sleep. From there to the end of the act, all is gathering dramatic energy. Iago cites Desdemona's handkerchief – which he claims to have

seen in Cassio's hands – as a final, visible proof, and Otello unleashes the cabaletta, 'Sì, pel ciel', in which he and then Iago swear to exact a terrible vengeance.

Act 3 *The great hall of the castle* An orchestral introduction derived from Iago's Act 2 description of jealousy shows that his machinations are still working. A herald announces the imminent arrival of Venetian ambassadors and Iago directs Otello to conceal himself and await the arrival of Cassio and further 'proof'. As Iago retires, Desdemona appears for the second of her extended duets with Otello; like the first, it is loosely structured around contrasting sections, with a prominent thematic reminiscence to aid the sense of closure. First comes 'Dio ti giocondi, o sposo', in which the semblance of lyrical normality (a patterned alternation of the voices, and periodic phrasing) soon gives way to agitated, fragmentary music as Desdemona mentions the plight of Cassio. Otello describes with repressed intensity the magical nature of the handkerchief Desdemona has mislaid, his anger rising further as she again attempts to deflect him into talk of Cassio. Finally he hurls out a brutal accusation of infidelity. Desdemona is crushed and at first can only murmur confusedly; but then, with 'io prego il cielo per te', her melody flows into the lyrical centre of the duet as she prays for Otello and bids him look at the first tears she has shed through grief. Otello at first seems calmed by this outburst, but soon his accusations return with added fury. As a cruel parting gesture, he recalls the calmer opening music of the duet, only to break it off with a gross insult and push Desdemona from the room.

Otello returns to centre stage for his most extended solo of the opera, the self-pitying soliloquy 'Dio! mi potevi scagliar', which begins in barely coherent fragments, rises gradually to a controlled lyricism, and again collapses, this time into furious invective. Iago appears and quickly takes charge, leading Otello aside where he can observe and listen to Cassio, and then involving Cassio in discussion of his dalliance with the courtesan Bianca in such a way that Otello thinks the reference is to his wife. The terzetto 'Essa t'avvince coi vaghi rai', set in the form of a scherzo and trio, skilfully counterposes Iago's and Cassio's comic exchange with Otello's anguished commentary. Cassio even produces Desdemona's handkerchief (hidden in his lodgings by Iago), and Iago's elaborate description of this item forms a hectic stretta to the terzetto.

Offstage trumpets announce the arrival of the Venetian ambassadors. As the ceremonial sounds approach, Otello hurriedly discusses with Iago the method of Desdemona's death, which they agree should be strangulation in her bed. As Iago slips off to fetch Desdemona the dignitaries appear, welcomed by a choral salute. Lodovico gives Otello a letter from the Doge, but is disturbed by Otello's violent interruptions to his ensuing conversation with Desdemona, especially to her wish that Cassio be reinstated. Otello reports that the letter calls him back to Venice, with Cassio left in his place. During this speech, Otello directs a series of angry asides to Desdemona and at its close seizes his wife with such violence that she falls to the ground. The general amazement precipitates the Largo concertato, 'A terra! ... sì ... nel livido fango', led off by an unusually long and thematically developed solo from Desdemona, much of it later repeated by the ensemble. As the Largo unfolds, Iago works furiously in the musical background, assuring Otello that he will deal with Cassio and delegating Roderigo for the task. As the movement comes to a close, Otello wildly dismisses everyone, unleashing on Desdemona a final, terrible curse. Left alone with Iago, he can only mutter incoherently before fainting. Iago gestures triumphantly at the body and, with offstage voices still hailing Otello as the 'Lion of Venice', brings down the curtain with a derisive shout of 'Ecco il Leone!' ('Here is the Lion!')

Act 4 *Desdemona's bedroom* A mournful english horn solo with fragmentary phrases sets the tone of this final act. Desdemona discusses with Emilia the present state of her husband's mind and then, with presentiments of death upon her, sings the famous Willow Song, 'Piangea cantando', whose three stanzas with refrain poignantly tell of a young girl abandoned by her lover. After a final, heartfelt farewell to Emilia, Desdemona kneels to offer an 'Ave Maria', softly intoned over a gentle string accompaniment before flowering into 'Prega per chi adorando', her personal entreaty for divine assistance. Accompanied by high strings of the utmost delicacy, Desdemona settles in her bed.

A mysterious, double bass solo introduces Otello to the bedchamber. Miming to an instrumental recitative punctuated by motivic fragments, he lays down his sword, puts out the torch that illuminates the room, approaches the bed and, to a repetition of the 'bacio' music from the end of Act 1, kisses the sleeping Desdemona. On the third kiss she awakens, so beginning the final and in many ways the freest of the Otello-Desdemona duets, a confrontation that reflects through the proliferation and intensification of motivic repetitions an inexorable progress towards Desdemona's death. At the brutal climax of the scene, deaf to Desdemona's protestations of innocence and to her final pleas, Otello suffocates his wife with a terrible cry of 'È tardi!' ('It is too late!').

Romilda Pantaleoni as Desdemona, the role she created in the original production of Verdi's 'Otello' at La Scala, Milan, in 1887

Only then does the orchestral surge finally flow back and attain some stasis. To a succession of weighty chords, Otello admits Emilia, who tells him that Cassio has killed Roderigo and has himself survived. She discovers the dying Desdemona, who with her final gasps desperately attempts to protect Otello. But Emilia guesses the truth and raises the alarm. Soon the room is filled with Lodovico, Cassio, Iago and armed men. Again the free, arioso musical texture takes over as Iago's plot is unravelled, first by Emilia's admission that Iago must have obtained the handkerchief from her, then by the appearance of Lodovico, who reports that the dying Roderigo revealed his part in the conspiracy. Otello, finally understanding his tragic error, grabs his sword and, to slow, solemn chords, begins his final oration, 'Niun mi tema'. He reflects on his past glory, apostrophizes Desdemona in an unaccompanied passage that briefly flowers into lyricism and then, to general horror, stabs himself. His dying words as he drags himself towards Desdemona's body call forth yet another repetition of the 'bacio' music from Act 1.

*

The chronological position of *Otello* in Verdi's long list of tragic operas – the last work, separated from all the others by a considerable time gap – has inevitably made it seem a special case; indeed, for many earlier in the century, perhaps even for some today, it is his only serious opera to merit sustained critical attention. Recent critics have sometimes reacted against this by stressing the many traditional aspects of the score: its reliance, especially in Act 1, on 'characteristic' numbers such as the storm scene, victory chorus and brindisi; the clear remnants of traditional forms in the 'cabaletta substitutes' such as 'Sì, pel ciel'; and of course its most unequivocal gesture to traditional form, the great concertato finale that closes Act 3. Some have gone even further, and suggested for example that passages such as the Act 1 love duet should be regarded as further manipulations of the standard four-movement duet, and that there is in effect an unbroken tradition with Verdi's earlier works.

This last position may swing too far towards the claims of tradition. It is more profitable to regard *Otello* as an opera that attempts a break with the past in an effort to produce a new, more modern conception of musical drama. At some time between *Aida* and *Otello* we might hazard that Verdi passed an intangible divide, and now saw the basis of his musical drama residing in continuous 'action' rather than in a patterned juxtaposition of 'action' and 'reflection'. There may well be gestures towards the traditional, normative structures of earlier in the century – it would be difficult to imagine how any opera could completely avoid them. But for the most part the opera strives for a different, more fluid type of musical drama: one that is closer to prose drama in its willingness to admit a swift succession of emotional attitudes during a series of dramatic confrontations. Of course, no value judgments should be attached to this greater fluidity: musical drama is endlessly protean in the manner and the forms in which it may be expressed, and there is nothing intrinsically superior in a type of opera that approaches the rhythms of the spoken theatre. We should, however, preserve a sense of distance between *Otello* and Verdi's earlier operas, a fact that renders even more remarkable Verdi's creative energy and capacity for self-renewal during the last years of his life. R.P.

Owen Wingrave

Opera in two acts, op.85, by Benjamin Britten to a libretto by Myfanwy Piper after Henry James's short story; BBC television, 16 May 1971 (London, Covent Garden, 10 May 1973).

For the BBC broadcast Benjamin Luxon sang the title role. John Shirley-Quirk was Coyle, with Janet Baker as Kate, Jennifer Vyvyan as Mrs Julian; Peter Pears was Sir Philip, Nigel Douglas sang Lechmere, Sylvia Fisher was Miss Wingrave, Heather Harper was Mrs Coyle.

Owen Wingrave *the last of the Wingraves*	baritone
Spencer Coyle *who runs a military cramming establishment*	bass-baritone
Lechmere *a young student with Owen at Coyle's establishment*	tenor
Miss Wingrave *Owen's aunt*	dramatic soprano
Mrs Coyle	soprano
Mrs Julian *a widow and dependant at Paramore*	soprano
Kate *her daughter*	mezzo-soprano
General Sir Philip Wingrave *Owen's grandfather*	tenor
Narrator *a ballad singer*	tenor
Distant chorus of treble voices	
Setting London and at Paramore, the Wingrave family seat, in the late 19th century	

BBC television commissioned an opera from Britten in 1966, and in 1968 he and Myfanwy Piper began to sketch the scenario of *Owen Wingrave*, a story Britten had known since at least the time of his earlier Henry James opera, *The Turn of the Screw*. The composition, whose style reflects Britten's later interest in aspects of 12-note technique, was sketched between the summer of 1969 and February 1970; the full score was completed by August. The television recording was made at Snape Maltings in November 1970, and a month later a recording was made with the original cast. Britten thought of the work as a chamber opera, although it requires an orchestra of 46. He intended it for the stage as well as television, and although it has been seen relatively infrequently in either medium, it was effectively staged by Glyndebourne Touring Opera in 1995.

*

During the Prelude, a succession of portraits of military ancestors is seen at Paramore. At the end Owen himself is seen, bearing a marked resemblance to the last portrait, that of his late father.

Act I.i *The study of Spencer Coyle's military crammer* Coyle is completing a lesson on tactics for his students Lechmere and Owen Wingrave. Wingrave's distaste for violence is already evident in his response to Lechmere's naive enthusiasm for warfare, and he explains to Coyle that he feels unable to pursue the family tradition. After Owen has left, Coyle expresses his perplexity at Owen's decision.

I.ii *Hyde Park* Owen reflects on the horrors of war, relieved that he has told Coyle of his feelings. This *scena* is intercut with the dialogue between Coyle and Owen's aunt at her residence. Miss Wingrave is enraged at her nephew's refusal to do his family duty.

I.iii *At the Coyles'* Mrs Coyle joins her husband and Lechmere in a last attempt to persuade Owen to change his mind, but without success. As they drink to Owen's future, Coyle gives him his aunt's instructions to go home to the country at once.

I.iv–vii *Paramore* Scene iv introduces Kate Julian and her widowed mother, family friends. Both are worried by the news of Owen's disgrace and when Owen arrives he is dismayed at their evident

hostility. His aunt and his grandfather, General Sir Philip Wingrave, are no more welcoming. Scene v comprises an extended ensemble: 'a week passes during which Owen is under constant attack'. In scene vi the Coyles and Lechmere arrive, all three sympathetic to Owen but still unable to understand his rejection of all they stand for. The family has ordered Coyle 'to make one last appeal', and he and Owen recognize that the qualities of a fighter underlie Owen's refusal to conform. In scene vii, family and guests assemble for dinner. The atmosphere is tense, and when Coyle encourages him to recall his military past Sir Philip launches a new attack on Owen, in which the Julians and Miss Wingrave join. Owen is driven to assert that he would make declaring and waging war a criminal offence, and his grandfather walks out. The others follow, leaving Owen alone.

Act 2 In the Prologue a narrator sings a ballad relating how once a young Wingrave who shamed the family through cowardice was taken to his room and accidentally killed by a blow from his father. Later the father was found dead in the same room 'without a wound', and thereafter the ghosts of father and son have haunted Paramore.

2.i *Paramore* Owen explains to Coyle how real this story remains to him, while Mrs Coyle attempts unsuccessfully to persuade Kate that she is being too harsh with Owen. Sir Philip appears, and summons Owen to his room. The others remain in the hall and comment variously as Sir Philip is heard telling his grandson that he 'must obey'. Owen's replies cannot be heard, but in the end the General exclaims that he must 'never return'. As Owen explains when he emerges, 'I'm disinherited'. Mrs Julian's reaction, to Kate's intense embarrassment, is to bewail the loss of

'Owen Wingrave' (Britten): filming the original BBC television production, directed by Brian Large and Colin Graham, in 1971, with Jennifer Vyvyan (Mrs Julian) and Benjamin Luxon (Owen Wingrave)

her daughter's prospects as Owen's possible bride. Lechmere and the Coyles are more sympathetic, though Lechmere takes his chance to flirt with Kate, and she encourages him. After Miss Wingrave announces that Sir Philip is too upset to reappear that night, the guests disperse, leaving Owen alone. To music recalling the well-nigh atonal material of the Act 1 Prelude, he addresses the family portraits; then, in the opera's most sustained lyrical and diatonic music, affirms that 'in peace I have found my image, I have found myself'. The Wingrave ghosts appear, and when Owen tells them that he is no longer afraid they disappear into the locked room. Kate returns, expressing her sorrow at Owen's resistance to family traditions. He joins her in voicing regret for what they will lose. However, any prospect of reconciliation is dashed when she taunts him with Lechmere's declaration that he would be willing to sleep in the haunted room for her. Furious at the accusation of cowardice, Owen decides to take up the challenge.

2.ii The Coyles discuss their unease, and Lechmere, having overheard the outcome of Owen's scene with Kate, tells Coyle of his worries. As they go to see what has happened, they hear Kate cry out.

She has entered the haunted room and found Owen dead. As everyone freezes in horror the first stanza of the ballad is heard again, its repeated refrain, 'Paramore shall welcome woe!', fading away to end the opera.

*

Owen Wingrave is a less compelling dramatic expression of Britten's pacifist convictions than *Billy Budd*: the story itself has fewer subtleties, and the need to aim for televisual effectiveness may have encouraged the abandonment of that gradual establishment of character in all its aspects on which his best operas depend. As proved by the church operas which precede it and *Death in Venice* which follows it, Britten's work in the last 15 years of his life was at its best when the strongest constraints were imposed on it. *Owen Wingrave* is not as sheerly concentrated as the church operas, yet its forms are often severely foreshortened. Even so, it has considerable musical strengths: the sinisterly simple ballad, Owen's unaffected moment of vision and, overall, the pervasive shadow of threatening martial music.   A.W.

P

Pagliacci ('Players')

Dramma in a prologue and two acts by Ruggero Leoncavallo to his own libretto, based on a newspaper crime report; Milan, Teatro Dal Verme, 21 May 1892.

The original cast included Fiorello Giraud (Canio), Victor Maurel (Tonio) and Adelina Stehle (Nedda); the conductor was the young Arturo Toscanini.

Canio (in the play, Pagliaccio) *leader of the*	
players	tenor
Nedda (in the play, Colombina	
[Columbine]) *Canio's wife*	soprano
Tonio (in the play, Taddeo) *a clown*	baritone
Beppe (in the play, Arlecchino	
[Harlequin])	tenor
Silvio *a villager*	baritone
Two Villagers	tenor, baritone
Villagers, peasants	

Setting Near Montalto, in Calabria, between 1865 and 1870 on the Feast of the Assumption (15 August)

The success of Pietro Mascagni's *Cavalleria rusticana* in 1890 encouraged the music publisher Edoardo Sonzogno to look for other subjects with strong emotional appeal. When Leoncavallo, an acute analyst of market requirements who recognized the potential of realism as the quickest way to win popularity, offered him the libretto of a story of love and jealousy in a company of wandering players, Sonzogno was convinced it would be successful. Leoncavallo tried first to follow Mascagni's example faithfully by making it a one-act opera, but apart from the larger dimensions of the work he found it dramatically necessary to use the curtain to make clear the distinction between the 'real life' first part of the opera, and the second part in which the play is performed. The triumph of *Pagliacci* was helped by the excellent cast: the composer added the Prologue to the original plan specially for Maurel (Verdi's Iago and future Falstaff). The opera was soon widely performed, and in the first two years alone it was translated into all the European languages, including Swedish and Serbo-Croat (also into Hebrew for the

Tel-Aviv production in 1924); the role of Canio has been the prerogative of the great tenors from Enrico Caruso and Fernando De Lucia to the present day.

Leoncavallo, threatened with a lawsuit for plagiarizing the plot, explained in *Le Figaro* of 9 June 1899 that his point of departure had been an incident in Montalto, a village in Calabria, and that it had been his father Vincenzo, then a magistrate at Cosenza, who had delivered judgment. In fact, though Leoncavallo was aware of the drama which was the subject of the proposed action, as well as others on similar themes, and could certainly have had them in mind, it is more relevant that plots based on jealousy with violent results were fashionable in both plays and operas at the time, from *Carmen* to *Otello* and *Cavalleria*. The other notable feature of the opera, the play-within-a-play, also had plenty of precedents and parallels, constituting almost a genre in themselves. But Leoncavallo's undeniable originality lies in the way he was able to combine news item and play in a tragedy of unusually disturbing violence by making 'stage' and 'life' identical. This successful combination of *dramma buffo* and 'reality' was the model for other experiments, from Strauss's elegant *Ariadne auf Naxos* to Mascagni's disastrous *Le maschere*.

*

Prologue Before the curtain rises, the hunchback actor Tonio announces to the audience that the story is about real people. The melody of Canio's famous aria, 'Ridi pagliaccio', is heard here and returns (in the low strings) soon after, transformed into an outline of intervals and rhythm, when the crowd sees the players' company approaching and comments on the sad life of the actors for whom life is performance. But in general the weaving of themes is aimed at preparing the audience to react emotionally to the drama through the words of the singer. Apart from Canio's melody, at the centre of the brief instrumental introduction between the exposition and reprise of a gay and lively theme, a poetic melody is associated with the furtive love of Nedda and Silvio, while Tonio's aria 'Un nido di memorie', a shrewd reference to a world of popular images, is evoked by a melancholy melody.

Act I *The village square* Preparations are afoot for a performance by the troupe of travelling players who have just arrived. Expectation is keen as the four players are enthusiastically greeted. Canio, their leader, invites the villagers to attend the play that evening. If the initial appearance of the chorus (introduced by a discordant fanfare of trumpets, spoilt by too many progressions) is conventional, the character of Canio's arioso announcing 'un gran spettacolo a ventitrè ore' (scene i), is striking, particularly in the mocking trills and the textual alliteration. Someone suggests jokingly that Tonio is attracted to Canio's wife, Nedda; Canio replies grimly that he would not hesitate to knife Tonio if that were true. His cantabile is introduced by a sparkling theme in the violins, and the sudden change to gravity in his words ('Un tal gioco'), at first restrained and ironic and then in the central section an almost sarcastic melody – which reappears later, in the play – is followed by a short chromatic passage in which there is no longer any pretence ('Ma se Nedda sul serio sorprendessi') and which anticipates what happens soon afterwards. The return of the cantabile followed by the *scherzoso* theme concludes a more or less arc-shaped form which serves the development of the drama, with the violent expression of the leading character's jealousy at the centre of its structure. Leoncavallo thus cleverly succeeds in confirming the action through the music, although it is followed as everyone leaves by the banal Bell Chorus 'Din, don, dan' which is unwittingly reminiscent of Verdi's 'Rataplan' chorus (*Forza del Destino*) and Chabrier's orchestral work *España*.

Nedda remains alone (scene ii). Worried by her husband's jealousy, she reflects on the freedom of the birds which she envies. Leoncavallo displays his talent for imitative orchestration in this character passage inspired by birdsong. Tonio enters; he is in love with her, and tries in vain to kiss her, but she drives him away scornfully, slashing at him with a whip. Here too there is the mingling of stage and life, with Nedda referring to the script of the play that they are to perform in the evening. Angrily Tonio goes off, filled with a desire for revenge, as Nedda's actual lover, Silvio, emerges.

In a love duet (scene iii) Silvio urges Nedda to elope with him after the performance that night. This long episode, necessary for the development of the action, temporarily absorbs the tensions that have preceded it; it provides the only really lyrical interlude in the opera. Divided into three parts, all in slow tempos (*Andante amoroso, Andante appassionato* and *Largo assai*), and dominated by long cantabile phrases, it ends with a romantic recapitulation of the love theme on the cello accompanying the lovers' kiss.

As they are taking leave of each other Tonio comes in and overhears their plan; he rushes to fetch Canio (scene iv). The jealous husband returns (to music recalling Verdi's *Otello*) accompanied by Tonio, whose words are underlined by muted brass. Canio is not quite quick enough to catch Silvio; he insists that Nedda tell him her lover's name, but she will not. Tonio assures him that the unknown man is bound to give himself away at the play later. Prevented by Beppe from stabbing Nedda, Canio dresses in his clown's outfit as, grief-stricken, he sings the celebrated arioso 'Vesti la giubba'. The intermezzo which follows contains the most significant references of the opera. The sad melody of the preceding arioso returns in altered form, and the chromatic progressions lead to the melody of the prologue 'Un nido di memorie', another reminiscence implying the unity of life and art, as is the reworking of Canio's first cantabile 'Un tal gioco' which follows.

Act 2 *As Act I* The curtain goes up almost exactly as it does for the first act, with the same festive music suggestive of a wind band attracting the chattering crowd to the entertainment (scene i). This time Leoncavallo uses Verdi's device of gaiety to emphasize tragedy, although this is hardly necessary as the action on the stage repeats what has just been happening among the actors. The play (scene ii) begins with Columbine/Nedda awaiting her lover Harlequin/Beppe while her husband Pagliaccio/Canio is away. The opening *minuet* and its reprise frame Harlequin's famous serenade accompanied by solo flute and oboe. Then comes the comic *scena* in which Taddeo/Tonio tries to force his attentions on Columbine. Harlequin sees him off and is making love to her (duet *a tempo di gavotta*) when Pagliaccio returns unexpectedly. Canio comes on stage to hear the same words and the same music which his wife had used to her lover in the previous act. His repeated fierce demands to know the name of his rival are also accompanied by musical reminiscence. By now Canio is no longer Pagliaccio and is indifferent to the laughter of the crowd, who grow uncomfortable as they gradually realize that he is not acting. Nedda tries in vain to continue the performance, but when Canio seizes a knife she dashes among the audience – to no avail as he chases and kills her. Silvio runs to help her and he too is killed. Canio's terse comment 'La commedia è finita' ('the comedy is ended') completes the combination of reality and pretence.

*

The actor who appears in front of the curtain to announce the author's intentions anticipates the subsequent break in the theatrical illusion; when Tonio (as the Prologue) gives the order for the show to begin the audience knows that a drama is already being enacted. The 'reality' poetically established by this beginning is one layer of verisimilitude; the action of the opera is another, to which the play gives yet a third dimension, and the double murder takes us back to the second. Canio's 'La commedia è finita' closes the circle opened by Tonio's 'Incominciate' (Canio's phrase had originally been assigned to Tonio, but was appropriated by Caruso when singing Canio and has since remained in the role); and the acknowledged fiction announced in the words of the prologue only points up the *verismo* of *Pagliacci*, established by the actors' claim to be real human beings with ordinary feelings. The pairing of *Pagliacci* and *Cavalleria* on the stage, in spite of the individuality of each, is clear evidence of the common purpose of the two composers, and rescues from neglect the only masterpieces produced in the circle of the Giovane Scuola ('young school').

Pagliacci was intentionally directed at the same audience as *Cavalleria*, and the similarity between them is evident not only in the basis of the story (the jealousy and the setting in the south of Italy), but also in the structure of the work. First, there is the division into two parts separated by an intermezzo, with similar proportions between them (the first being longer and setting the scene for the drama). Then there is the initial gesture of breaking the theatrical illusion, with a Sicilian dialect being used by Mascagni (in conformity with 19th-century tradition), while a still greater separation is achieved by Leoncavallo's Prologue, in spite of its clear reference to the *commedia dell'arte*. The two works are further apart in the details of structure, however: Mascagni used traditional 'number opera' technique (although his treatment is original), while Leoncavallo treated each scene as a unity in which the numbers are cleverly used, sometimes as traditional structures (especially in character-pieces such as the Bell Chorus and Nedda's ballade in Act 1 scene ii), sometimes incorporating melodic references and leitmotifs, and sometimes combining both possibilities.

Pagliacci takes the technique of *verismo* to its limits. Leoncavallo's patient reconstruction of his subject is necessarily less immediate than Mascagni's, but he gained from his study of precedents a refinement of detail, a more significant and shrewd use of orchestration, and a more original and expressive harmony. The critic Eduard Hanslick rightly defined Leoncavallo as a less original but better musician than Mascagni. A continuity with the late works of Verdi can be found in the transformation of a peaceful strolling player into a truculent and violent man. The difference lies in the moral perspective: Otello degrades himself by murder, but Canio recovers his dignity. Leoncavallo understood the connection between social values and the market for entertainment. While its effect is perhaps obvious and at times over-emphatic, it is a necessary and

original feature of the opera, whose vitality is still applauded by audiences all over the world.

M.G.

Palestrina

Musikalische Legende in three acts by Hans Pfitzner to his own libretto; Munich, Prinzregententheater, 12 June 1917.

At the première the title role was sung by Karl Erb; others in the cast included Fritz Feinhals (Borromeo), Paul Bender (Pope Pius IV), Gustav Schützendorf (Luna), Maria Ivogün (Ighino), Emmy Krüger (Silla), Paul Kuhn (Bishop of Budoja) and Friedrich Bodersen (Morone).

Pope Pius IV		bass
Giovanni Morone	*cardinal legates*	baritone
Bernardo Novagerio	*of the Pope*	tenor
Cardinal Christoph Madruscht [Madruzzo]		
Prince Bishop of Trent		bass
Carlo Borromeo *a Roman cardinal*		baritone
The Cardinal of Lorraine		bass
Abdisu, Patriarch of Assyria		tenor
Anton Brus of Müglitz *Archbishop of*		
Prague		bass
Count Luna *ambassador of the King of*		
Spain		baritone
Bishop of Budoja [Budua]	*Italian*	tenor
Theophilus, Bishop of Imola	*bishops*	tenor
Avosmediano, Bishop of Cadiz		
Spanish bishop		bass-baritone
Giovanni Pierluigi da Palestrina *maestro di*		
cappella at S Maria Maggiore, Rome		tenor
Ighino *his son, aged 15*		soprano
Silla *his pupil, aged 17*		mezzo-soprano
Bishop Ercole Severolus, *Master of Ceremonies*		
to the Council of Trent		bass-baritone
Five Choristers of S Maria		
Maggiore		2 tenors, 3 basses
Apparitions:		
Lucrezia *Palestrina's deceased wife*		alto
Nine Dead Masters of the Art of Music		
		3 tenors, 3 baritones, 3 basses
Voices of Three Angels		high sopranos
Two Papal Nuncios		silent
Lainez	*Jesuit generals*	silent
Salmeron		silent
Massarelli, Bishop of Telese *secretary to*		
the Council		silent
Giuseppe *Palestrina's old servant*		silent

Choristers from the papal chapel; archbishops, bishops, abbots, heads of orders, ambassadors, procurators for princes spiritual and temporal, theologians, doctors of all Christian nations;

servants; soldiers of the city guard; street-folk;
angels (apparitions)

Setting Rome (Acts 1 and 3) and Trent (Act 2)
in November and December 1563, the year
in which the Council of Trent concluded;
between Acts 1 and 2 about eight days
elapse, between Acts 2 and 3 approximately
two weeks

Pfitzner completed the libretto of *Palestrina* in 1911.
First performed in Munich, while World War I was in
progress, the work established itself as Pfitzner's
masterpiece, not least for its high moral and
philosophical seriousness; it was the most moving
and coherent of all his expressions of idealistic,
'inspiration'-orientated musical conservatism. Its
first conductor, Bruno Walter, regarded the première
as one of the major events of his life. In November
1917 he took the Munich production on what he was
to describe as a 'propaganda tour' of neutral
Switzerland (Basle, Berne and Zurich), to demonstrate the continuing quality of wartime German
musical culture. Vienna and Berlin productions
followed in 1919, and the work continued to be
performed regularly in Germany until World War II.
A fine recording under Rafael Kubelík was made in
1973, with Nicolai Gedda (Palestrina) and Dietrich
Fischer-Dieskau (Borromeo).

                              *

Act I *A room in Palestrina's house* Pfitzner's musico-
dramatic technique in *Palestrina* is such as to allow no
extractable episodes beyond the preludes to each of
the three acts, sometimes performed as an orchestral
suite. The D minor Prelude to Act 1 begins with
music associated with the central character's
introspective nostalgia for a time in which personal
happiness was linked with creative fluency in the
widely cherished manner of 16th-century sacred
polyphony. Although the opera requires a large
orchestra, the opening of the prelude, scored for four
flutes and four solo violins, is characteristic of the
work as a whole, in its chamber-textured evocation
of 16th-century style (although Pfitzner adopted a
pragmatic disregard for strict stylistic mimicry). The
manner is predominantly restrained and halting.

The curtain rises on a gloomy and frugal chamber
containing Palestrina's work-table, portative organ
and a hanging portrait of his deceased wife, Lucrezia.
A single large window affords a distant view of
Rome; it is late afternoon (night falls during the
course of the act). Beside the window sits Palestrina's
pupil Silla, musing on his planned departure for
Florence as he accompanies himself on a viol in a love
song of his own composition. The song is in the
manner of the Florentine innovators with whom Silla
wishes to study. Rome, whose leitmotif includes a
phrase that will be repeatedly associated with the

rhythm of Palestrina's name, Pierluigi, now seems to
him the venerable guardian of restrictive tradition
from which he longs to escape in search of the
'wonderful current of freedom which flows through
our time'. Silla represents Pfitzner's most sympathetic portrayal of a musical 'modernist' (his main
motif is boyishly Straussian), whose nevertheless
respectful affection for his master manifests itself in
the tactful restraint he shows to his friend, the
composer's son Ighino (the other travesty role), who
soon enters, troubled by his father's current mood of
sad resignation.

Palestrina himself arrives with his friend Cardinal Borromeo, who is critical of the 'cacophonous'
song which Silla had begun to perform for Ighino.
Palestrina excuses his pupil's modernist inclinations
after he has sent the boys off to bed. Borromeo
recommends a firm hand, but Palestrina suggests
that what seems right to their generation might, after
all, give way to 'new sounds'. This humility provides
Borromeo with a suitable pretext for explaining the
threat to polyphonic music posed by the Council of
Trent's deliberations, which the Pope requires to be
concluded after 18 years of debate. The final session
will deal with ritual and the Mass itself, which the
purists want sung in future to plainsong. All
polyphonic compositions would be destroyed. The
Emperor Ferdinand, however, has declared his
opposition to the purists; this has enabled Borromeo
to persuade the Pope to permit the question to be
decided by an exemplary demonstration mass,
reconciling conflict in the 'miraculous play of
interweaving sounds'. Palestrina, he ceremoniously
announces, should accept the task of composing this
mass.

Pleading age and declining power, Palestrina
incites Borromeo to accuse him of blasphemy before
the latter storms out. Palestrina is left alone to ponder
his sense of loss and meaninglessness and to recall
the inspiring presence of his wife. Mysterious
apparitions of former masters now gather around
him (they include Josquin and Enrico Tedesco and
are dressed in a variety of historical and national
costumes). In stylized and statuesque music they
counter Palestrina's nihilistic despair with the assurance that he is required to add the final gem or 'last
stone' to the jewelled necklace of the ages. They
disappear, leaving Palestrina in total darkness.
Fearfully, he calls out in prayer.

Unnoticed by him, a shining angel has appeared,
who sings the initial motif of the Kyrie of the
historical Palestrina's *Missa Papae Marcelli*, regarded
in legend as the work which decided the Council in
favour of polyphony. Mechanically, Palestrina begins to write. Other fragments of the mass are sung
by a gathering throng of angels, although their music
develops into an original polyphonic texture featur-

ing only the opening 'Kyrie' motif of the historical original. Palestrina fills page after page as he senses a mysterious new power within him. The apparition of his wife joins the angels, who fill the entire stage as the back wall and ceiling disappear to reveal 'a full glory of angels and heaven'. The chorus concludes in a triumphant C major that is enriched by deep offstage bells, reinforced by two large tam-tams. Representing the dawn bells of Rome, they ring out in a processional crescendo towards a climactic, full orchestral statement of the 'Pierluigi' figure. In a brief epilogue to the act, Silla and Ighino enter the room, now filled with morning sunlight, to find Palestrina sleeping soundly at his desk. They pick up the strewn sheets. Ighino is filled with joy at what he sees. Eight bars of the renewed dawn processional conclude the hour-and-a-half-long act in a mighty crescendo of tolling bells.

Act 2 *The great hall of Cardinal Madruscht's palace in Trent* After a prelude of driving energy and ceremonial brilliance (the Straussian orchestra includes six horns, four trumpets and four trombones), the Master of Ceremonies to the Council of Trent is found preparing for the session, keeping a diplomatic eye on the seating of national groups. The gradually assembling participants include Borromeo, who is anxious for news of the visit to the Emperor Ferdinand by Cardinal Morone (historical 'saviour of the Council'). He is also embarrassed that Palestrina had refused to compose the demonstra-

tion mass, for which disloyalty he has had him imprisoned. Amid growing tension between the Spaniards and the Italians, the splendidly attired Council goes into session. Morone delivers his message from the emperor, who is anxious for unity among Catholic nations. The ensuing discussion about music and the Mass nevertheless degenerates into risibly chaotic factionalism, and the session is adjourned. The members withdraw, leaving their servants to turn their masters' verbal antagonism into physical threats. A crowd of street-folk pour into the hall and join in a violent brawl, which is only brought to an end by the entrance of Cardinal Madruscht, 'German' host to the Council, with soldiers whom he orders to shoot into the mob. He threatens torture as people fall in the gunfire.

Act 3 *The room in Palestrina's house* A meditative prelude introduces the shortest of the three acts, in which artistic inwardness once again prevails over the turmoil of public affairs. It is evening, and Palestrina sits with Ighino and members of his choir. During his imprisonment his mass had been forcibly removed from the house. It is now being performed before the Pope, although Palestrina seems dazed by his suffering. Cries of 'Evviva Palestrina!' shortly herald the arrival of papal singers to congratulate the 'saviour of music'; his mass has so impressed the Pope that he briefly appears to compliment the composer in person and invite him into his service in the Sistine Chapel. Ighino rejoices, and Borromeo,

'Palestrina' (Pfitzner): the angels' scene from Act 1 of the original production at the Prinzregententheater, Munich, 12 June 1917, with Karl Erb as Palestrina; set by Adolf Linnebach

contrite, makes his peace with his friend. Palestrina, left alone as night falls, goes to his portative organ and prays 'Now forge *me*, the last stone on one of your thousand rings, oh Lord, and I will be of good heart and at peace'. Outside, the cries die away, and the opera concludes with the 'last stone' motif. From the final D minor chord, a single soft D from Palestrina's organ improvisation is held as the curtain falls.

*

Among the work's many admirers, mention must be made of the Munich-based novelist Thomas Mann, whose enthusiasm led to his involvement in 1918, with Walter and others, in founding a Hans Pfitzner-Verein für Deutsche Tonkunst. Mann also included a long and searching discussion of *Palestrina* in his *Betrachtungen eines Unpolitischen* ('Reflections of a Non-Political Man') of 1918. This book, completed during the war, was an extended and complex apologia for Germany and German culture and its anti-democratic, idealistic nature. It became a significant focus of postwar debate, not least in the light of Mann's subsequent shift towards democratic republicanism. Pfitzner, by contrast, remained steadfast in the nationalistic, idealistic conservatism of the *Palestrina* period and to the epigraph from Schopenhauer's *Die Welt als Wille und Vorstellung* which prefaces the score and libretto. In it, Schopenhauer set the intellectual life of the individual against the corporate life of mankind and concluded: 'alongside world history there goes, guiltless and unstained by blood, the history of philosophy, science and the arts'. For all its impressive and carefully researched historical atmosphere, Pfitzner thus significantly located *Palestrina*'s debate about modernism and conservatism in musical style within the timely, if troubled, intellectual and political context which gave birth to Mann's novel *Der Zauberberg* ('The Magic Mountain'), published in 1924 but begun in 1914.

Pfitzner played a prominent part in this factional controversy, which split the increasingly politicized musical culture of Germany between the wars. His essays occasioned heated debate and were to be quoted approvingly in publications of the Nazi years. *Palestrina* represents an important, if often ponderously discursive, late application of the techniques of Wagnerian music-drama. Pfitzner himself interestingly regarded it as an autumnal and even valedictory reflection upon *Die Meistersinger*. Some of its musical innovations, particularly the bony linearity of its contrapuntal and harmonic texture and an expanded range of orchestral coloration, depart from Wagner in nature and intention, however, and demonstrate Pfitzner's love for earlier musical styles. The reversion to historical drama is matched by an idiosyncratic manner of affecting

16th-century mannerisms (the anachronistic treatment of quotations from the *Missa Papae Marcelli* is striking). Pfitzner's purpose could be construed as a deliberately 'Germanizing' one: musically reconstructing Palestrina as a north European master. The opera certainly seems to present Cardinal Madruscht as a specifically German *alter ego* of the conservative composer in Act 2. Nevertheless the character of Palestrina himself, particularly in his solo scenes in Acts 1 and 3, draws from Pfitzner his finest music, which achieves passages of elevated and moving pathos.   P.F.

Parsifal

Bühnenweihfestspiel in three acts by Richard Wagner to his own libretto; Bayreuth, Festspielhaus, 26 July 1882.

At the first performances, Parsifal was sung by Hermann Winkelmann, Heinrich Gudehus and Ferdinand Jäger; Gurnemanz by Emil Scaria and Gustav Siehr; Kundry by Amalie Materna, Marianne Brandt and Therese Malten; and Amfortas by Theodor Reichmann. The conductors were Hermann Levi and Franz Fischer.

Amfortas *ruler of the Kingdom of the Grail*	baritone
Titurel *his father*	bass
Gurnemanz *a veteran Knight of the Grail*	bass
Parsifal	tenor
Klingsor *a magician*	bass
Kundry	mezzo-soprano
First and Second Knights of the Grail	tenor, bass
Four Esquires	sopranos, tenors
Voice from Above	contralto
Klingsor's Flower-maidens	6 sopranos
Knights of the Grail, youths and boys, flowermaidens	
Setting The Grail castle 'Monsalvat' and its environs, the northern mountains of Gothic Spain, in mythological times	

Wagner acquainted himself with the relevant source material for his final opera as early as the summer of 1845, when he read Wolfram von Eschenbach's Parzivâl and Titurel poems, in versions by Simrock and San-Marte. The first prose sketch (now lost) was made in 1857 – not, however, on Good Friday, as Wagner poetically recollected in subsequent years. The first prose draft did not follow until 1865, and the second (written mostly in dialogue form) not until 1877. The poem was written between 14 March and 19 April 1877 and the music between August 1877 and April 1879 (Wagner alternating, in his now customary fashion, between two drafts). He orchestrated the prelude (first version, with concert ending) in autumn 1878 and made his full score of the rest between August 1879 and January 1882.

The first performances were given at Bayreuth on 26 and 28 July 1882 for members of the Society of Patrons, followed by 14 further performances in July and August. In an agreement with his patron, King Ludwig II, designed to pay off the deficit incurred by the first Bayreuth festival, Wagner was obliged to employ the Munich Hoftheater personnel to perform the work, which meant that he had to accept the Jewish Hermann Levi to conduct it. Wagner's intention of consecrating the Festspielhaus with *Parsifal* is indicated by the term *Bühnenweihfestspiel*, which may be translated 'festival play for the consecration of a stage'. In spite of the 30-year embargo placed on performances outside Bayreuth, *Parsifal* was occasionally given elsewhere in those years: Ludwig II had it put on privately in Munich in the years after Wagner's death; it was seen by members of the Wagner Society in Amsterdam in 1905, and again in 1906 and 1908; and in the face of bitter hostility from Bayreuth it was mounted by the Metropolitan in 1903 under Alfred Hertz. Various concert performances were given in Europe during the period of the embargo, including two under Joseph Barnby in London in 1884. The first stage performance in Britain was at Covent Garden in 1914, under Artur Bodanzky.

Parsifal has been sung by Lauritz Melchior, Ramón Vinay, Jess Thomas, Jon Vickers, René Kollo, Helge Brilioth, Manfred Jung, Peter Hofmann, Siegfried Jerusalem and Placido Domingo; Gurnemanz by Alexander Kipnis, Ludwig Weber, Hans Hotter, Gottlob Frick, Theo Adam, Martti Talvela, Franz Mazura, Kurt Moll, Hans Sotin and Robert Lloyd; Kundry by Lillian Nordica, Olive Fremstad, Frida Leider, Kirsten Flagstad, Astrid Varnay, Helen Traubel, Martha Mödl, Régine Crespin, Leonie Rysanek, Christa Ludwig, Yvonne Minton and Waltraud Meier and Amfortas by Anton van Rooy, Clarence Whitehill, Herbert Janssen, Friedrich Schorr, Hans Hotter, George London, Dietrich Fischer-Dieskau, Donald McIntyre, Bernd Weikl and Simon Estes. Notable conductors of the work have included Felix Mottl, Anton Seidl, Carl Muck, Felix Weingartner, Hans Knappertsbusch, Wilhelm Furtwängler, Rudolf Kempe, Pierre Boulez, Reginald Goodall, Eugen Jochum, Georg Solti, Herbert von Karajan, James Levine and Daniel Barenboim.

*

The prelude begins with a broadly phrased theme (ex.1), containing three elements of significance, of which (*y*) is generally associated with suffering, and (*z*) with the Spear. A shimmering background

Ex.1

is built up, against which a trumpet (with oboes and violins) reiterates ex.1, establishing the tonality of A♭ major. The whole process is then repeated in C minor, before two new themes, those associated with the Grail (the 'Dresden Amen': ex.2) and with faith (ex.3) are announced. After some chromatic intensification, especially of ex.1, the curtain rises.

Ex.2

Ex.3

Act I.i–ii *A forest glade* Gurnemanz rouses two of the esquires from sleep and together they kneel and pray (ex.3, as extended in the prelude, followed by ex.2). Gurnemanz bids them prepare the bath for Amfortas, approaching on his sickbed (ex.4 makes its first appearance in the bass here). But first the 'wild woman' Kundry rushes in, her arrival signalled by agitation in the orchestra; she is bringing balsam from Arabia for the sick guardian of the Grail.

Ex.4

Amfortas's entrance on his litter is accompanied by ex.4, which eventually introduces a paragraph in which he looks forward to his relief from pain ('Nach wilder Schmerzensnacht'). The sustained dominant pedal suggests a cadence on B♭, but the ultimate resolution is on to an evasive G♭, hinting that the hope of relief is illusory. The esquires make hostile remarks to Kundry, who responds angrily. Amfortas intones the formula of the 'pure fool made wise by suffering' ('durch Mitleid wissend, der reine Thor'), whom he has been promised as a saviour. He is carried away again to the grieving strains of ex.4.

Gurnemanz reprimands the esquires for their harsh words about Kundry; she is perhaps atoning with good deeds for a past sin, he says. Their taunt that she should be sent in quest of the missing Spear draws from Gurnemanz an emotional recollection of how Amfortas was seduced and dealt his terrible wound, losing possession of the sacred Spear to the magician Klingsor ('O, wunden-wundervoller heiliger Speer!': ex.1 *y* and *z*). The esquires ask how Gurnemanz knew Klingsor, and he begins his Narration proper ('Titurel, der fromme Held'). The sacred relics of the Cup used at the Last Supper and the Spear that pierced Christ's side on the Cross had been given into the care of Titurel, then guardian of the Grail. Ex.1 and a new theme, evolved from ex.3, are developed here in a mystical atmosphere conjured partly by the long, flowing phrases and partly by the radiantly translucent scoring. The brotherhood of the Grail, assembled by Titurel to guard the relics, was closed to Klingsor (his motif, ex.5, is now heard) on account of some unnamed sin. Desperate

Ex.5

to quell his raging passions, Klingsor even castrated himself, but was still rebuffed. To avenge himself, he turned to magic and created a garden of delights, where he lies in wait for errant knights, seducing them with 'devilish lovely women' (intimations of the Act 2 flowermaidens' music are heard here). The aging Titurel sent his son Amfortas to defeat Klingsor, with the consequences already described. Gurnemanz ends his narrative with a recollection of the divine prophecy concerning a 'pure fool', echoed homophonically by the esquires.

A flurry of activity is initiated by the opening figure of Parsifal's motif, ex.6. Parsifal has shot down

Ex.6

a swan on the holy ground and is dragged in by the knights. Gurnemanz's rebuke fills him with remorse and he breaks his bow. To Gurnemanz's questions about his name and origins, however, he professes ignorance. The two are left alone with Kundry, and Parsifal tells what he knows about himself: his mother's name was Herzeleide (Heart's Sorrow), he had strayed from home in search of adventure and had made his own arms for protection. When Kundry, who clearly knows more about him than he does himself, announces that his mother is dead, Parsifal attacks her and has to be restrained.

In the distance, the knights and esquires are seen bearing Amfortas back to the Grail castle. As the processional music starts, Gurnemanz offers to lead Parsifal there. The change of scene, from forest to castle, is effected during the Transformation Music,

which builds the dissonances associated with Amfortas's suffering (ex.7) to an immense climax. Bells ring out with the four-note motif of the procession.

Ex.7

I.iii The castle of the guardians of the Grail Gurnemanz and Parsifal enter the Grail hall and the chorus of knights, 'Zum letzen Liebesmahle', firmly establishes C major as the second primary key of the act. A chorus of youths is heard from mid-height and then one of boys' voices from the top of the dome. Amfortas has been borne in, and the Grail, still covered, placed on a marble table.

Amfortas, reluctant to accede to Titurel's request for him to uncover the Grail, breaks into his monologue of torment, 'Wehvolles Erbe'. He seeks atonement for his sin and the motif of his suffering (ex.7) is prominent along with ex.1. His passionate cry for forgiveness ('Erbarmen!') is answered by the chorus repeating the prophecy. At Titurel's insistence, the cover is removed from the golden shrine and the crystal Grail chalice taken from it. Ex.1 returns, as in the prelude, first in A♭ major and then in C minor, as the voices from above repeat Christ's words offering his body and blood: 'Nehmet hin meinen Leib, nehmet hin mein Blut'. Amfortas consecrates the bread and wine and they are distributed to the knights, who take up a sturdy new theme in E♭ started by the boys and youths from above. Exx.2 and 3 are heard and then the processional music and ex.7 as Amfortas is borne out again, his wound gaping anew. Parsifal, who had convulsively clutched his heart at Amfortas's cry of agony, is unable to tell Gurnemanz what he has seen and is roughly shepherded out. A voice from above (contralto solo) repeats the prophecy, answered by ex.2 from other voices in the dome.

Act 2 Klingsor's magic castle, on the southern slopes of the mountains facing Moorish Spain The act opens with a sinister chromatic transmutation of ex.1, introducing a disruptive tritone, followed by Klingsor's theme (ex.5). Klingsor, surrounded by magical and necromantic apparatus, watches over his domains from a tower. Seeing Parsifal approach, he summons Kundry, whose monosyllabic groans are accompanied by unprepared dissonances. Attempting to resist Klingsor's instructions to seduce Parsifal, she taunts her master with his self-enforced chastity. Parsifal's motif (ex.6) announces that he has reached the battlements; Klingsor watches as he fells one guard after another. The tower suddenly sinks and in its place appears a luxuriant magic garden.

Flowermaidens rush in from all sides, their excited questions accompanied by a playful, dotted variant of ex.1 and by a continuous triplet figure in the strings. As Parsifal appears, they squabble over him, but join forces for their alluring, triple-time 'Komm, komm, holder Knabe!' A number of striking parallels between this scene and the Act 3 finale of Meyerbeer's *Robert le diable* suggest that Wagner may have intended to demonstrate here the superiority of the music drama over conventional opera. The flowermaidens caress Parsifal insistently; a series of modulations recalls the love music of *Tristan und Isolde* and the 'Tristan chord' itself is heard. Just as he manages to free himself from their attentions, he is stopped in his tracks by the sound of his long-forgotten name. It is Kundry, now transformed into an enchanting beauty, who calls, her voice emerging seductively out of the orchestral texture. At Kundry's command the flowermaidens reluctantly disperse.

She tells, in a flowing, compound-time narrative, how she saw him as a baby on his mother's breast: 'Ich sah das Kind'. His mother watched over him lovingly, but one day he broke her heart by not returning and she died of grief. Parsifal's distress at the news is reflected in the chromatic intensification both of his line and of the orchestral texture. Kundry consoles him, urging him to show her the love he owed his mother. As she kisses him, the 'Tristan chord' (at pitch, as ever) is outlined by stopped horns and cello. By a clever twist of its tail, the theme associated with sorcery gradually reveals part of the chaste opening theme of the work (ex.8). Parsifal

Ex.8

leaps up, clutching his heart. His cry 'Amfortas! Die Wunde!' indicates his first real identification with Amfortas's suffering, and his first step on the road to self-knowledge. Falling into a trance, he hears Christ the Redeemer himself call on him to save him from 'guilt-tainted hands' and cleanse the polluted sanctuary. The flower-maidens' blandishments are chromatically enhanced as Parsifal realizes that it was caresses such as Kundry is conferring on him now that brought about Amfortas's downfall.

He repels her, but she appeals to him to use his redemptive powers to save her: for her blasphemous mockery of Christ she has wandered the world for centuries. One hour with him would bring her

release, she says. But Parsifal, recognizing that salvation for them both depends on his withstanding her allurements, resists her. She attempts to block his way to Amfortas and calls to Klingsor. The magician appears and hurls his Spear at Parsifal (an upward glissando on a harp). Parsifal seizes the Spear and as he makes the sign of the Cross with it, the castle collapses and the magic garden disappears.

Act 3 The years of anguish and wandering that intervene between the second and third acts are depicted by the heightened chromaticism of the prelude. The curtain rises on an open spring landscape in the domains of the Grail. Gurnemanz, grown very old and dressed as a hermit, emerges from his hut and uncovers Kundry, whose groans, as she lies stiff and apparently lifeless in the undergrowth, he has heard. He revives her, but receives no thanks, just two words: she wants only to serve ('Dienen . . . Dienen!'). A man approaches in a suit of armour and bearing a spear. A sober variant, in the minor, of Parsifal's motif (ex.6) tells us both the stranger's identity and that he is a changed man. Gurnemanz welcomes him but bids him divest himself of his weapons: it is Good Friday and this is holy ground. As Parsifal does so, Gurnemanz recognizes the man whom he once roughly turned away.

He also recognizes the Spear (ex.1 is recalled), but his outburst of joy is undercut by the music associated with Amfortas's suffering (ex.7). Throughout his troubled wandering, Parsifal tells him, he has guarded the Spear safely. Gurnemanz hails its return with an impassioned outburst that again recalls each of the elements of ex.1: 'O Gnade! Höchstes Heil!' The mystical elaboration of ex.3 from Gurnemanz's Act 1 narrative is now recalled. Gurnemanz tells Parsifal that his return with the healing Spear is timely. Amfortas, longing for death, has refused to reveal the Grail, the brotherhood has degenerated and Titurel has died. The elegiac music of the Act 3 prelude, in its original key of B♭ minor, accompanies his words.

Parsifal is almost overcome with remorse. His feet are bathed by Kundry, and Gurnemanz sprinkles water from the spring on his head, asking that he be blessed ('Gesegnet sei'). Kundry then anoints his feet and dries them with her hair. The hesitant reminiscence of the flowermaidens' music suggests that Parsifal may now be aware of Kundry's alter ego. To a grandiose statement of Parsifal's theme, ex.6, in B major, Gurnemanz anoints his head. After an unusually emphatic cadence (twice confirmed) in this key, and before the Good Friday Music begins 27 bars later also in B major, there occurs the incident of Kundry's baptism by Parsifal. The inner significance for Wagner of this act – as an expression of a Schopenhauerian pacification of the will, but also,

The Holy Communion enacted during the Grail scene at the end of Act 3 of Wagner's 'Parsifal': Paul von Joukowsky's design for the original production at the Festspielhaus, Bayreuth, in 1882

probably, as a symbol of the liberation of the world from impure racial elements – is intimated by the divorcing of this passage from the immediate tonal context.

Gazing on the beautiful meadows, Parsifal says that on Good Friday every living thing should only sigh and sorrow. As the Good Friday Music modulates from B to D major (asserting itself, along with D minor, as a primary tonality of the work) Gurnemanz replies that on this day repentant sinners rejoice at the Redeemer's act of self-sacrifice and nature herself is transfigured. In a transformation scene similar to that in the first act (but in the reverse direction), and underpinned by a processional ostinato rhythm, Gurnemanz now leads Parsifal and Kundry to the Grail hall. There one group of knights bears Titurel in his coffin, while a second group carries Amfortas on a litter. When Titurel's coffin is opened, all break into a cry of woe. The cry establishes D minor for Amfortas's final monologue: 'Mein Vater!' He refuses to uncover the Grail, and when the knights become threateningly insistent, he merely invites them to plunge their swords into his heart.

Parsifal has meanwhile appeared unobserved; he holds out his Spear and with its point touches Amfortas's wound: 'Nur eine Waffe taugt'. Amfortas is miraculously healed and his theme (ex.4) gives way to Parsifal's (ex.6), now in a triumphant D major, as he yields his office as lord of the Grail to the new redeemer. D major turns to D minor before a momentous modulation to the final tonality of A♭ major, on the words 'öffnet den Schrein!' ('open the shrine!'). Here the work's central polarity of A♭/D (major and minor) is resolved by an integration of the two, as of two complementary spheres. Parsifal takes the Grail from the shrine and it shines softly, then radiantly as light falls from above. Kundry sinks lifeless to the ground, redeemed at last. As the motifs of faith (ex.3) and the Grail (ex.2) make their final, luminously scored appearance, Parsifal waves the Grail in blessing over the worshipping knights. A white dove descends to hover above his head.

*

In as far as it addressed the 'meaning' of *Parsifal* at all, much of the literature on the opera up to World War II dealt with the question of whether or not it could be regarded as a religious work. An equally strong claim, based on Wagner's acknowledged sympathies, could be made for a Schopenhauerian/Buddhist interpretation, taking the concept of *Mitleid* ('compassion') as the ethical centre of the work. Darker undercurrents of racial supremacism and anti-Semitism have been revealed, but it should be remembered that *Parsifal* was written against an ideological background of anti-Semitism, a new wave of which was sweeping Germany in the 1870s.

The notion that the concepts of racial purity and regeneration formulated by Wagner in his last years were woven into the ideological fabric of *Parsifal* was less readily embraced by directors in the 1980s than the theme of sexuality. Progressive stage interpretations in recent years have attempted to rehabilitate Kundry and womankind generally, allowing them a more prominent role in the final act of redemption.

Parsifal is the most enigmatic and elusive work in the Wagnerian canon. No attempt to elucidate its mysteries can afford to ignore any of its elements, whether its Christian, pagan, Buddhist or Schopenhauerian ideas, or its concepts of racial purity and regeneration. The only one of Wagner's music dramas written with direct experience of the Bayreuth Festspielhaus, the text of *Parsifal* is set to a diaphanous score of unearthly beauty and refinement. The score offers frequent clues to an understanding of the text, but Wagner's characteristically ambivalent treatment of consonance and dissonance, as of pleasure and pain, and his interweaving of diatonicism and chromaticism, resists any oversimplified interpretation. The juxtaposition of sublimity with richly ambivalent symbolism and

The Grail scene in the Wieland Wagner production of 'Parsifal' at Bayreuth, 1954

an underlying ideology disturbing in its implications creates a work of unique expressive power and endless fascination. **B.M.**

Pêcheurs de perles, Les ('The Pearl Fishers')

Opéra in three acts by Georges Bizet to a libretto by Eugène Cormon and Michel Carré; Paris, Théâtre Lyrique, 30 September 1863.

At the première Leïla was sung by Léontine de Maësen, Nadir by François Morini, and Zurga by Jean-Vital Ismaël.

Zurga *head fisherman*	baritone
Nadir *fisherman*	tenor
Leïla *priestess of Brahma*	soprano
Nourabad *high priest of Brahma*	bass
Fishermen, Indians, Brahmins	
Setting Ceylon in ancient times	

Les pêcheurs de perles, which Bizet composed very rapidly in the summer of 1863 when he was 24, was his second opera to be staged but probably the sixth he had composed. It was commissioned by Carvalho for the Théâtre Lyrique, and the contract was signed in early April 1863. The original setting was Mexico, later changed to Ceylon, and the original title was *Leïla*. The central dilemma of Act 2, a priestess torn between love and her sacred vows, was based, as was observed from the beginning, on Spontini's *La vestale*, Bellini's *Norma* and other operas. The problem of how to resolve the drama remained a point of contention right up to the 1863 performances and has continued to cause misunderstanding through the variants found in corrupt posthumous scores.

Bizet wrote the music as an *opéra comique* with spoken dialogues, which were replaced by recitative shortly before the work opened. The original date planned for the opening, 15 September, was postponed for two weeks owing to the soprano's illness. The cast was not a strong one, but the work was enthusiastically received by the audience and played 18 times during the autumn of 1863, thus proving to Bizet that he was capable of writing an opera that combined an exotic background with strong dramatic conflicts, his most enduring talent as a composer. The opera public was for the first time made aware of his lyrical gifts, his harmonic audacity and his acute ear for orchestral sound. The opera was nonetheless poorly treated by the press, who had little ear for Bizet's talent and no patience with his personal appearance for a curtain call. Berlioz, writing his last article for the *Journal des débats*, was almost the only critic to study the work seriously and treat Bizet with respect.

Poster by Prudent Leray for Bizet's 'Les pêcheurs de perles'
printed for Choudens at the time of the original production
at the Théâtre Lyrique, Paris, in 1863

The opera was not played again in Bizet's lifetime. In 1886–9, following the belated success of *Carmen*, it was played in a dozen cities outside France, and there was a performance in Paris in Italian in 1889. This led to its revival by the Opéra-Comique in 1893, with Carvalho again directing, 30 years after the première. Its success has grown steadily to the point where it has become almost a repertory work in the last 30 years, an interest stimulated by the appearance of an authentic vocal score in 1975 to replace the many corrupt editions issued by Choudens since 1886. Since the autograph manuscript has disappeared, some passages of the 1863 version survive in vocal score only.

Interpreters have included Emma Calvé, Luisa Tetrazzini and Christiane Eda-Pierre in the role of Leïla, and Enrico Caruso, Ferruccio Tagliavini, Alfredo Kraus and Nicolai Gedda in the role of Nadir. At Covent Garden in 1887 the baritone role of Zurga was sung by Paul Lhérie, the original Don José in *Carmen*.

*

Act I *A wild seashore on the island of Ceylon* The curtain rises after a short, serene prelude. Some fishermen are working on their nets; others are drinking, dancing or playing Hindu instruments. The ruins of an old Hindu temple are seen. The opening chorus ('Sur la grève en feu'), with its beautiful middle section for men's voices alone, is one of the most striking numbers in the opera, fully characteristic of

Bizet's lyrical style. Zurga reminds the fishermen that they have to choose a leader. Their immediate choice is Zurga himself, whom they beg to become their king. Next arrives Nadir, a young fisherman who has been wandering in the forest. Zurga welcomes his former friend, and a resumption of the dancing closes the scene.

Left alone, Zurga and Nadir recall their days together. 'Have you been faithful to your vow?', Zurga asks. Their duet ('Au fond du temple saint') recalls the beautiful girl they both once set eyes on in Candy; both were simultaneously enslaved by her beauty, and both then swore to renounce her and to remain friends for ever. This duet is the best-known piece in the opera. It is a noble melody scored, on its first appearance, for flute and harp, always a symbol of sanctity in French opera of that time. The correct version of the duet ends with a section in 3/4 ('Amitié sainte'), replaced in all the corrupt versions by a reprise of the main melody for 'Oui, c'est elle, c'est la déesse!'

A boat arrives carrying a veiled woman. She has been chosen to pray for the fishermen on their annual pearl-fishing expedition and to ward off evil spirits. This is Leïla, who is accompanied by Nourabad, the high priest of Brahma. The music which accompanies her entrance has already been heard as the prelude. 'C'est elle!', the chorus murmur, while the orchestra tells us what we have already guessed: 'C'est la déesse'. Neither Nadir nor Zurga is yet aware of this. The chorus offer her flowers ('Sois la bienvenue'), and from Zurga, who does not recognize her, she takes an oath of obedience. Nadir however does recognize her and cries out; she too recognizes Nadir. But in response to Zurga's questioning she reaffirms her vows of chastity, and a solemn hymn to Brahma rings out.

Leïla and Nourabad enter the temple; Zurga and the chorus go off. Nadir, alone, confesses that he has long dreamt of Leïla and has followed her here (*romance*, 'Je crois entendre encore'). He falls asleep. To the distant sound of fishermen's voices Nourabad leads Leïla in. Her incantation to Siva, full of *fioriture*, is interrupted by Nadir's voice. She briefly draws aside her veil and the hymn is transformed into a declaration of love.

Act 2 *The ruins of an Indian temple at night* An offstage chorus, with a piquant accompaniment for two piccolos, greets the dark. Nourabad leaves Leïla to watch out the night. She tells him in a dramatic recitative how she once saved a stranger's life, protecting him from capture. He gave her a necklace and begged her to wear it for ever. Nourabad goes out and the offstage chorus briefly concludes the scene.

Leïla sings a cavatina ('Comme autrefois dans la nuit sombre'), full of joy that her admirer is near. A solo oboe, recalling Nadir's *romance* (a 'guzla'), is heard, and then Nadir's voice approaching. The lovers are reunited in a breathless Allegro leading to a broad duet ('Ton cœur n'a pas compris le mien') in which Bizet's melodic gift is in full flood. In a recitative Nadir promises to return the next night, and slips away. A shot is heard. Nourabad summons the guards and rushes off in pursuit of the intruder. The people, though agitated at this violation of their priestess's sacred vigil, sing a magnificent brief chorus of distress and prayer. Nadir is led in. In a ferocious finale he and Leïla are about to be put to death by the angry crowd when Zurga intervenes. With his new authority as their king he orders their lives to be spared and whispers to them to leave at once. But Nourabad tears aside Leïla's veil, forcing Zurga to recognize her. His mercy now turns to rage, and he condemns them both to death. As they are led away, both captors and captives invoke Brahma's aid.

Act 3.i *Zurga's tent* Zurga, alone, sings tenderly of his agony, having ordered his friend to his death ('O Nadir, tendre ami de mon jeune âge'). Leïla appears, under guard. She has begged to see him. At first they sing together, both deploring their own distress. She then pleads for Nadir's life, saying he is innocent. But when Zurga realizes that she loves Nadir, his jealousy is inflamed against them both. Nourabad and the fishermen come to lead away their victims. Leïla hands her necklace to a young fisherman and asks him to take it to her mother. Zurga snatches the necklace as the curtain falls.

3.ii A pyre has been erected beneath a statue of Brahma. The chorus are singing, dancing and drinking in bloodthirsty anticipation, while Nadir prays that he may save Leïla. She is led in by Nourabad and some fakirs. She and Nadir sing a hymn-like duet in the face of death. As the dawn finally arrives Nourabad and the men raise their daggers and are about to strike when Zurga intervenes and stops them. Flames from their burning camp have deceived them that it was already dawn. All rush off to save the camp while Zurga frees the captives. He tells them that he set the camp on fire and shows Leïla the necklace. They all embrace. Zurga urges them to escape while he watches Nourabad and the Indians fleeing from the flames.

*

Various alternative endings for the opera were current before the original was restored. One version had Zurga dying in a grand conflagration, another had him stabbed in the back by an Indian as he calls 'Je t'aimais' after the departing Leïla; the lovers appear on a distant rock singing the melody of 'Oui, c'est elle, c'est la déesse'. The melody has entered the consciousness of millions, yet it would be unfair to credit the opera's success to that melody alone. It is, in any case, deliberately exotic in its orchestration and harmony. The drama is inevitably weakened by its dependence on two separate vows pledged many years before, and the potential for conflict between jealousy and brotherly feeling is not given full scope, partly because space had to be found for the conventional apparatus of priests, dancing and incantation. The action strains credulity at times. Yet the three principal roles are some of the best in French opera of its time, and the opera's success is now assured.   H.M.

Pelléas et Mélisande ('Pelléas and Mélisande')

Opera in five acts by Claude Debussy after Maurice Maeterlinck's play; Paris, Opéra-Comique (Salle Favart), 30 April 1902.

At the première, Mary Garden sang the role of Mélisande and Jean Périer that of Pelléas (originally a baritone role but later adapted for tenor); Hector Dufranne sang Golaud, Félix Vieuille, Arkel, and Jeanne Gerville-Réache, Geneviève. André Messager conducted and Albert Carré was the producer. The realistic, detailed sets were by Lucien Jusseaume and Eugène Ronsin.

Arkel *King of Allemonde*		bass
Geneviève *mother of Pelléas and*		
Golaud		contralto
Pelléas ⎱ *grandsons of*		baritone ('Martin')
Golaud ⎰ *Arkel*		baritone
Mélisande		soprano
Yniold *Golaud's son from*		
a former liaison		boy treble or soprano
The Doctor		baritone
The Shepherd		baritone
Unseen chorus of sailors (male voices); serving-women, paupers (silent)		
Setting The kingdom of Allemonde and its surroundings; the time unspecified but presumably medieval		

Maeterlinck established his reputation as a leading exponent of symbolist theatre in the early 1890s; his launch on to the Paris literary scene came with his play *La princesse Maleine* (1890). Debussy, who all his life was constantly planning theatrical projects, had considered setting this play, the first in a series of symbolist works set loosely in medieval times and praised by *Le Figaro* as 'superior in beauty to what is most beautiful in Shakespeare'.

Published in May 1892, Maeterlinck's *Pelléas* was first performed at the Théâtre des Bouffes-Parisiens on 17 May 1893. Debussy attended the single matinée

'Pelléas et Mélisande' (Debussy): Act 1 scene i (a forest; design by Lucien Jusseaume) from the original production at the Opéra-Comique (Salle Favart), Paris, 30 April 1902, from 'Le théâtre' (June 1902)

but had already read the work, as he recounted in a short article, 'Pourquoi j'ai écrit Pelléas', in 1902. In this article he also explained his attraction to the play, revealing his confirmed allegiance to the tenets of symbolism:

The drama of Pelléas which, despite its dream-like atmosphere, contains far more humanity than those so-called 'real-life documents', seemed to suit my intentions admirably. In it there is an evocative language whose sensitivity could be extended into music and into the orchestral backcloth ['décor orchestral'].

Debussy had obtained Maeterlinck's permission to use the play in August 1893, and the following month he began work on the opera – the only true example of the genre that he completed; he started, curiously, with the climactic love scene between Pelléas and Mélisande in Act 4 scene iv. The initial process of composition, when he worked mainly on one act at a time, went on for two years.

It was probably relatively early on that Debussy decided to cut four scenes from the play, a procedure endorsed by Maeterlinck. The opening, with its perhaps over-obvious symbolism of the serving-women trying to open the door of the castle and wash an indelible stain from the entrance, is difficult to imagine as the opening of an opera. The other cut scenes cause some detail to be lost but do not affect the essence of the drama. Perhaps the most notable effect of the transition from play to opera is the

reduction of the serving-women to one silent appearance in the last act.

In addition to the excised scenes, Debussy made many cuts in Maeterlinck's text, several times eliminating repeated phrases, and also reducing the descriptive details that Maeterlinck intentionally incorporated into the dialogue rather than into the almost non-existent stage directions; in Act 1 scene ii of the opera, for example, Geneviève's description of Mélisande as 'always dressed like a princess, even though her clothes were torn by brambles' is removed, although it is clearly the sort of detail that stage designers can incorporate into the visual aspect of a production.

Throughout the early period of intense composition Debussy revealed to several correspondents the difficulties he found in portraying the mysterious and elusive nature of Maeterlinck's characters. To Ernest Chausson, he wrote of the difficulty of capturing the 'nothingness' ('de ce "rien"') he found in Mélisande's character, and the 'beyond-the-grave' ('outre-tombe') impression made by Arkël (originally spelt Arkel), as well as his 'gentleness', which is 'of those who are going to die'. Such ideas clearly reveal Debussy's deep response to the text; they also reflect Maeterlinck's ideas as expressed in his essays, which first appeared while Debussy was working on the opera and were later published in the collection Le trésor des humbles. Other letters from the period of composition reflect Debussy's personal identification with the characters. He saved Act 2 until last. Here he found new challenges, more to do with communicating the impending sense of mystery and catastrophe than with characterization. On 17 August 1895 he could claim to have finished the opera.

In accordance with his normal method of working, he had written the initial text in short score with ideas for orchestration indicated, often in coloured inks. It was not until its acceptance at the Opéra-Comique in 1898 that Debussy was spurred on to produce the vocal score necessary for rehearsal purposes and the full score. In these he continued to make revisions, on occasion adding and subtracting the appearances of principal motifs.

More radical revisions became necessary when the work went into rehearsal. It emerged that several of Debussy's original interludes were too short for the stage to be reorganized between scenes. Under pressure, and with some reluctance, Debussy hastily extended several of them. The original interludes are preserved in the first vocal score, in French only, published in 1902, while the full score and the French–English vocal score give the newer, longer interludes. Also from the rehearsal period date several cuts, notably an exchange in Act 3 scene iv where Golaud asks Yniold, who is spying on Pelléas and Mélisande, if the couple are near the bed. Despite the publication in 1905–6 of a full score, Debussy continued to refine the orchestration. Some alterations were incorporated into a second published edition (the study score in 1950 and the full score in 1966), but further alterations are preserved only in Debussy's personal copy.

At the dress rehearsal a brochure satirizing the plot was distributed and this caused much levity during the performance. Mary Garden claimed that Maeterlinck himself, angered by Debussy's refusal to allow his mistress Georgette Leblanc to sing the role of Mélisande, was responsible.

Critical reaction to the première was divided. One critic found the music 'sickly' and 'lifeless'. Others criticized the 'impressionism' of the work. Among the most perceptive reactions were those of Dukas and d'Indy. Dukas found that 'each bar exactly corresponded to the scene it portrayed … and to the feelings it expressed'; while d'Indy elaborated on Debussy's own comments on his work, finding in it 'simply felt and expressed *human* feelings and *human* suffering in *human* terms, despite the outward appearance the characters give of living in a mysterious dream'.

Until 1914, *Pelléas* was revived almost every year at the Opéra-Comique. The casts included, from 1908, Maggie Teyte as Mélisande. Owing to the difficulty of finding a boy treble for Yniold, a precedent was soon established (contrary to Debussy's wishes) of giving the part to a woman. The

first performances outside France took place in Brussels and Frankfurt in 1907. The following year the work was given in New York (with the Paris cast), at La Scala under Toscanini, in Prague, Munich and Berlin, and at Covent Garden. After 1918 the work was many times revived, but it hardly accorded with the anti-symbolist Cocteau-esque aesthetics of the interwar era. In the 1930s Valdo-Barbey produced a new, less realistic set, merely suggesting where Jusseaume had defined. Possibly drawing inspiration from Maeterlinck himself, his decors paved the way for many future productions in laying stress on the symbolic significance of everyday or natural objects: windows, doors and trees.

A significant event in the opera's history was the 1942 performance under Roger Désormière, captured in the classic recording that many consider unsurpassed. Irène Joachim sang the part of Mélisande and Jacques Jansen Pelléas. Postwar productions have often treated Maeterlinck's setting with considerable freedom, transferring the setting to the present day or, as in the 1985 Opéra de Lyon production, to the Edwardian era (with a short-haired Mélisande).

The performances and recording under Pierre Boulez were the first consciously to break with the accepted, somewhat muted approach to the score. Rhythms were tightened up, contrasts enhanced. Since the 1960s, several conductors – for better or worse – have revived the original shorter interludes, among them Mark Elder in two English National Opera productions. In 1985 John Eliot Gardiner incorporated some of the changes in Debussy's manuscript full score into the Opéra de Lyon performances.

*

Act I.i *A forest* The orchestral prelude outlines three principal themes: the first – modal and ecclesiastical with its bare 5ths and plainsong-like outline – is allied not to a character but rather to the sense of timelessness, or perhaps the forest itself. Mainly confined to the first act, it contrasts with the following two, which are clear character motifs pervading the whole opera: that of Golaud, with its distinctive dotted rhythm, and that of Mélisande, a pentatonically curved phrase. Rhythmic and harmonic transformations mirror the actions and symbolic development of the play.

Golaud has been out hunting but has lost his hounds and the boar he was pursuing. He lights upon a maiden weeping by a well. She is nervous and rebuffs Golaud's approaches ('Ne me touchez pas! Ne me touchez pas!'). Debussy captures the scene with the three motifs of the prelude, varying them harmonically and rhythmically to reflect the detailed emotions and symbols of the text. Golaud's energy for hunting is denoted in the dotted rhythm which marks his motif, while the loss of his quarry is reflected in the motif's loss of its dotted-rhythm element. The sadness and fragility of Mélisande are suggested by the harmonizing of her essentially pentatonic motif with half-diminished ('Tristan') chords. The awakening of Golaud's desire is represented by more conventional added-note harmony. It is more through the questions that are posed than by the answers given that Mélisande's character is developed: we learn that someone has done her wrong ('Tous! Tous!') but we never learn who it was, nor from where Mélisande has come ('Je me suis enfuie! enfuie! enfuie!'). Here Debussy's attention to pacing becomes evident. To underline important dialogue, he stretches it out towards arioso, while leaving more mundane remarks to be quickly declaimed. He uses whole-tone chords in predominantly tonal surroundings to convey a sense of being lost or confused.

Maeterlinck stresses the contrast between Mélisande's youth and Golaud's age: Golaud is taken with Mélisande's eyes, which never close, while she is repelled by his grey hair and giant-like quality. Her oblique answers to his questions increase her air of mystery, which is echoed in the orchestra: 'Quel âge avez-vous?' ('How old are you?'), he asks. 'Je commence à avoir froid' ('I'm beginning to feel cold'). Golaud bids Mélisande accompany him; she agrees only reluctantly, after a comment whose significance – like many such remarks about the weather – clearly goes deeper than its literal meaning: 'La nuit sera très noire et très froide' ('The night will be very dark and very cold'). The scene ends with Golaud's admission that he too is lost, and his motif is for the first time imbued with the modality of the opening one: the strongest forces are not those of the characters but in some power above and beyond, contained perhaps within the dark forest itself.

In the first interlude, highlighted on a trumpet, comes a motif hinted at only once before, when Golaud announced that he was Arkel's grandson. Its importance is evident, but it extends beyond the idea of a mere character-motif, demonstrating how Debussy could extend Maeterlinck's theatre of implication rather than direct expression by adding recurrent motifs intentionally unspecific in their frame of reference.

I.ii *A room in the castle* Geneviève reads Arkel a letter from Golaud to Pelléas, telling him that he has married Mélisande. In depicting her character he adds to her mystery: 'some great terror has evidently befallen her', he writes, going on to recount how she will 'suddenly burst into tears like a child'. Debussy sets the scene with utter simplicity, using medieval modes on E. Arkel, the silent sage, listens without interrupting. At the end of the letter, as Mélisande's

motif is heard, Golaud expresses his anxiety about Arkel's acceptance of her. If Arkel accepts, a lamp must be lit.

Emphasizing the character's inner strength, Debussy prepares for Arkel's first statement with the trumpet motif of the interlude, now played in the cellos 'avec une grande expression' and harmonized with a half-diminished chord at once linking Arkel's musical language with Mélisande's. His response to Geneviève's question 'Qu'en dîtes-vous?' ('What do you say about this?') at the end of the letter clearly marks him as a man who is passive when faced with the force of destiny. The E modes have now opened out to a clear E major and Debussy literally underscores the import of Arkel's utterances with held pedal notes: 'Je n'en dis rien' ('I have nothing to say') is his response, and he goes on to point out that human beings can only ever see 'the underside of fate'.

Pelléas enters and Arkel, emphasizing his paradoxical blindness (since metaphorically he sees more than most), asks who has come in. Geneviève explains that it is Pelléas, remarking that 'he too has been in tears', linking him in our minds with Mélisande. Initiating a symbolic framework that will become increasingly important, Arkel asks Pelléas to 'move into the light'. The final phrase of the scene forms a link between the external events of the play and a more symbolic level: 'Aie soin d'allumer la lampe dès ce soir' ('Take care to light the lamp before this evening'), Geneviève reminds Pelléas, alluding to the prearranged signal to indicate Arkel's acceptance of Golaud's new wife. But we surmise from Debussy's setting that the remark has a deeper significance.

I.iii *Outside the castle* Prefaced in the interlude by appearances of Mélisande's motif, a different level of response is required in this scene. Almost nothing happens. Instead there is a dialogue about darkness and light, seeing and half-seeing, with objects appearing as mists clear or disappearing as night falls. The gardens and forests are dark, and are portrayed with the key of C major, while the coast where Geneviève and Mélisande have been seeking more light is portrayed with its diametrical opposite, F♯ major. A ship passes, with a chorus of sailors, but cannot be seen clearly in the mist. Mélisande sees a guiding beacon out to sea. It grows dark, and she fears a shipwreck. Geneviève leaves Pelléas and Mélisande alone for the first time: they see more guiding beacons, but the wind rises and they have to leave. As we learn that they have a steep path to descend, and that Pelléas must support Mélisande by the arm, we may again suspect a symbolic significance. The act cadences, as yet tentatively in F♯ major, as Mélisande perhaps flirtatiously expresses her hopes that Pelléas will not go away. The key is significant. It has formed a link between the 'light' and the growing bond between Pelléas and Mélisande.

Act 2.i *By a well in the park* The well's magic powers are remarked upon by Pelléas: 'it used to cure the blind', he observes, extending the symbolism of 'seeing' initiated in the first act. Mélisande leans over from the cold marble beside the well, and her hair, longer than herself, dangles into the water. Pelléas notices, and it seems to awaken a desire in him to know about Golaud's first meeting with her. Did Golaud try to kiss her, he asks, and did she want him to? She answers with a simple 'Non'. Suddenly distracted, she plays with her wedding ring above the water. As inevitably it falls in, a harp arpeggio is heard, outlining the chord that had introduced the weeping Mélisande in Act 1. By using it here, Debussy subtly indicates that a chapter in her life has been closed. 'The ring is lost', she remarks, 'nought but a circle of water remains'. Pelléas innocently remarks that if it cannot be recovered they can get another one. Mélisande persuades herself that she lost it 'in spite of herself', 'throwing it up too high into the sunlight'. Pelléas remarks that it was striking noon as it fell; to Mélisande's question as to what they should tell Golaud he replies 'the truth'. In an interlude, Golaud's motif interrupts the flowing semiquavers which have permeated the scene.

2.ii *A room in the castle* Golaud is wounded (as the dislocation of his dotted rhythm portrays: as noon struck, his horse inexplicably bolted, ending up on top of him. He felt his 'heart had been torn in two'). Debussy introduces chiming discords perfectly capturing both the bells and Golaud's stifling pain. Mélisande is tender to Golaud, offering him water and a change of pillow. Suddenly, as the music continues with the plaintive oboe phrases and half-diminished harmonies of her first-act weeping, Mélisande dissolves into tears. By no means the cardboard villain, Golaud is sensitive and compassionate, understanding Mélisande's complaint about the darkness and antiquity of the castle. But suddenly the mood is broken as he notices that her ring is missing. He erupts, demanding that she go and find it at once. He adds that she should take someone – Pelléas – with her. She leaves, weeping.

2.iii *Outside a grotto* Pelléas and Mélisande enter the grotto, and the music, in contrast to the scene by the well, moves to the 'dark' areas of C and F with minor-key A♭s. But as the moonlight floods into the cavern, a luxuriously orchestrated burst of the 'light' key of F♯ is heard. Its beauty is, however, short-lived, giving way to stark 5ths reminiscent of *Nuages* from Debussy's *Nocturnes*. Three paupers can be discerned in the moonlight, and this time, as they leave, Mélisande rejects Pelléas's offer of a helping hand.

Act 3.i *One of the towers of the castle* After a

grooming-song reminiscent of a trouvère chanson, Mélisande lets her hair down from the tower. She has opened the window to let in the warm night air. Pelléas has never seen so many stars. Noticing her hair, he tells her that he finds her beautiful, for the first time addressing her with the familiar 'tu'. He wants to kiss her hand, since he has to leave the next day. A fleeting symbol appears, a rose: Mélisande sees it, but Pelléas cannot. As her hair cascades over him, Debussy gives us the nearest we have had to an aria, but the melody is in the orchestra. The vocal lines curve more lyrically than before, more like an expressive *mélodie* than a real aria. At the end of the scene Mélisande notices that her doves have flown away. Pelléas must leave her, she remarks, 'or else they will never come back'. A long pedal note C (the tonic of the 'dark' key) heralds their disturbance by Golaud. It is nearly midnight, he points out, underlining the contrast with their previous midday meeting. Angrily he warns them to stop behaving like children.

3.ii–iii *The castle vaults* The key of C forewarns of the symbolic darkness of the scene (which Debussy considered particularly original). Golaud leads Pelléas down to the stagnant water where he may 'smell the stench of death'. Encapsulating, for the second time, the 'dark–light' contrast in immediate juxtaposition, the interlude directly portrays his escape into the sea air: 'Je respire enfin'. As he remarks that the gardens have been watered, the music moves into F♯ major. But Golaud now warns Pelléas that he suspects there may be something between him and Mélisande and tells him to avoid her.

3.iv *Outside the castle* Yniold is introduced for the first time. Considerable dramatic tension is built up as Golaud gradually increases his physical and emotional pressure on the child to tell him what he knows of Pelléas and Mélisande's activities together. As he becomes increasingly frustrated by Yniold's innocently uninformative answers, the music rises to a feverish pitch, mirroring the dramatic irony of the situation. At its climax, Golaud remarks that 'he is like a blind man searching for treasure on the ocean bed'. He recovers, and begins to interrogate Yniold afresh. He asks him whether he has seen Pelléas and Mélisande kissing. Yniold replies that he has, and shows Golaud how with a peck on the mouth, but recoiling at the prickliness of his beard as Mélisande had done when she first met Golaud. Finally, employing a sinister ruse, 'Veux-tu voir petite mère?', he gets Yniold to spy into the room where Pelléas and Mélisande are gazing silently at the light.

Act 4.i *A room in the castle* To the sound of the semiquavers that had accompanied the 'hair' scene (3.i) but now with more foreboding harmonies, Pelléas and Mélisande make an assignation to meet

'Pelléas et Mélisande' (Debussy), Act 4 scene ii (a room in the castle, designed by M. Ronsin), with Hector Dufranne (Golaud), Mary Garden (Mélisande) and Félix Vieuille (Arkel) in the original production at the Opéra-Comique (Salle Favart), Paris, 30 April 1902: photograph from 'Le théâtre' (June 1902)

again by the well. 'It will be [our] last night', Pelléas remarks ominously.

4.ii *The same* Arkel enters with Mélisande, his music clearly in E major. He foresees the return of joy and light to the kingdom and remarks that Mélisande will be the agency of renewal. However, he has been watching her, and explains that he has pitied her, for she has seemed like 'someone waiting for some dreadful doom in the sunlight of a beautiful garden'. In a scene of great poignancy he explains the need of an old man 'to touch the brow of a maid or the cheeks of a child': 'one has a need for beauty alongside death'. The rich added-note chords, in unusual orchestration, are the closest to conventional cadences of operatic love music thus far in the opera.

Again, Maeterlinck used the poignancy of the scene to contrast with the violence of what happens next. Golaud enters, at once angry with Mélisande, whom he will not have touch him. He takes his sword from the prayer stool, inspecting the blade as the music nervously hints at motifs without any real continuity, jumping from feigned calm to outbursts of violence. He looks into Mélisande's eyes, remarking, with heavy irony, upon their innocence: 'You would think that the angels of heaven were bathing there'. He bursts out that her flesh disgusts him and seizes her by her hair, forcing her to her knees. As he regains his composure, he tells Mélisande that she may do as she pleases: he will not play the spy. Arkel, in a line weightily set by Debussy, remarks 'If I were God, I would have pity on the hearts of men'. His

utterance resonates into an interlude of extended power, full of double-accented passing notes and middle-register brass.

4.iii *By a well in the park* Again in direct contrast, this scene is a symbolic one, with Yniold playing. Debussy responds with a lightly scored, playful, off-beat rhythm to unify it. Two symbols are introduced: first, Yniold's golden ball is trapped and he cannot move it – a hopeless struggle against destiny, perhaps; secondly, a flock of sheep passes. The shepherd remarks that they are not on their way to the stable. 'Where will they sleep for the night?', asks Yniold pathetically.

4.iv *The same* In this, the final love scene, Pelléas, suddenly eloquent in his imagery, realizes 'I have been playing and dreaming with the snares of destiny round about me'. As he remarks that he has not yet really looked at Mélisande, her motif is heard for the first time in this act. If he does not look, it will be like 'fetching water in a muslin bag'. Several times, perfectly capturing the nervous intensity of their tryst, Debussy withdraws the orchestra: they meet, as it were, in total silence. Immediately the dialogue returns to questions of light and dark. The couple hesitate, not knowing whether to seek the light and shun the dark or vice versa. It is Pelléas who first declares his love: a moment where again Debussy refrains from any orchestral accompaniment. 'We have broken the ice with red-hot irons', he exclaims. With a new motif characterized by a quintuplet figure, Debussy again introduces a quasi-aria, clearly in the 'light' key of F♯ major. But ominous shadows threaten, and the sound of the drawbridge closing is heard. Debussy's portrayal of the contrary emotions experienced by the couple is masterly: 'All is lost! All is won!', says Pelléas, 'How beautiful it is here in the darkness'. The two embrace passionately, but then Golaud falls on Pelléas with his sword and kills him.

Act 5 *A bedroom in the castle* The act begins at once with a new sound, with bare harmony. Mélisande is dying and the doctor is in attendance. He raises hopes of her recovery but Arkel knows better, sensing that those in the room are quiet in spite of themselves. Golaud is full of remorse, persuading himself that the love between Pelléas and Mélisande was like that 'of little children'. Mélisande asks for the window to be opened. 'Which window?', asks Arkel. Mélisande replies, significantly, that she means 'la grande fenêtre'. The 'light–dark' imagery is now to be resolved, since the sun she and Pelléas sought is now to set. United with Arkel, 'she knows, but she does not know what she knows'. Golaud is again doubting and, soon after she realizes his presence, his desire to interrogate her again overcomes him and he asks Arkel and the doctor to leave. His first intense question – 'do you pity me as I pity you?' – is again highlighted by silence in the orchestra. He asks whether she loved Pelléas. 'Mais oui', she replies, innocently asking whether Pelléas is there. Golaud has learnt nothing, and Arkel and the doctor return. Mélisande is cold and asks if the winter is coming. She has recently given birth to a little girl and Arkel asks her to hold her daughter. Suddenly the serving-women enter in silence, not answering when Golaud demands to know why they have come. Mélisande speaks no more; her eyes, too, are full of tears. Golaud still wants to speak to her, but Arkel, accompanied by the final appearance of his motif, prevents him, remarking that 'the human soul needs to go away alone'. The serving-women fall to their knees. 'They are right, they know', says the doctor. Golaud sobs, and Arkel remarks that it is now the turn of the little child. Finally, as the curtain falls, the music moves into the key of C♯ major – sharper still than the F♯ major associated with light and love. The slow four-beat rhythm of the opening completes the tragic circle of life, love and destiny as the curtain falls.

*

However it is produced or performed, the external events that form the plot of *Pelléas* are only part of the point of the play. Maeterlinck's symbolism, couched in seemingly insignificant dialogue, demands a response far removed from that required for conventional 19th-century opera. A more central question is the opera's debt to Wagner. Whatever Debussy claimed, there are strongly Wagnerian elements in *Pelléas*, notably in the harmony which reflects *Tristan* and *Parsifal*, and in the system of leitmotifs portraying characters, themes and symbols. In an article in *Le théâtre* in 1902, Debussy himself wrote out motifs, identifying one of them as the 'thème initiale de Mélisande', and in a rare technical comment about his opera, he interestingly referred to his conscious treatment of Mélisande's motif to emphasize the view he held of her character:

Notice that the motif which accompanies Mélisande is never altered. It comes back in the fifth act unchanged in every respect because in fact Mélisande always remains the same and dies without anyone – only old Arkel, perhaps – ever having understood her.

R.L.S.

Pénélope ('Penelope')

Poème lyrique in three acts by Gabriel Fauré to a libretto by René Fauchois; Monte Carlo, Opéra, 4 March 1913.

At the première Penelope was sung by Lucienne Bréval, Ulysses by Charles Rousselière, Eurycleia by Alice Raveau and Eumaeus by Jean Bourbon; the conductor was Léon Jéhin.

Pénélope [Penelope] *Queen of Ithaca*		soprano
Ulysse [Ulysses] *King of Ithaca*		tenor
Euryclée [Eurycleia] *Ulysses' nurse*		mezzo-soprano
Eumée [Eumaeus] *an old shepherd*		baritone
Antinous		tenor
Eurymaque [Eurymachus]	*Penelope's suitors*	baritone
Léodès [Laertes]		tenor
Ctésippe [Ctesippos]		baritone
Pisandre [Peisander]		baritone
A Shepherd		tenor

Attendants, servants, dancers, flautists, shepherds, people of Ithaca

Setting The island of Ithaca after the Trojan war

When Fauré, with some theatrical but no specifically operatic experience, was searching for a libretto, the singer Lucienne Bréval recommended a text by René Fauchois on the subject of Penelope and Ulysses. Fauré started work in 1907. His directorship of the Paris Conservatoire meant that composing was virtually restricted to the summer break: it took him five years to complete the opera. He called on a young musician, Fernand Pécoud, to orchestrate (for final revision by himself) much of the second act and part of the finale. The shaping of the libretto is competent if conventional; the language tends to be stiff. Fauré's progress is fully documented in letters to his wife (see *Lettres intimes*, ed. P. Fauré-Fremiet, Paris, l951).

Although he admired the conductor, Jéhin, Fauré regarded the Monte Carlo première as a try-out for the Paris production two months later (Champs-Elysées), again with Bréval but with Louis Hasselmans conducting; this started well but was overshadowed by a Dyagilev season with the premières of Debussy's *Jeux* and Stravinsky's *The Rite of Spring*. When, in 1919, *Pénélope* reached the Opéra-Comique, it was no longer, by Parisian standards, an interesting novelty.

*

Act I *In the palace* While they spin, Penelope's attendants discuss their mistress's determination to await the long-delayed return of her husband Ulysses from the war. For more than ten years the palace has been infested with suitors clamouring in vain for her hand. Eurymachus, Antinous and the other three suitors burst in to renew the pressure. The old nurse Eurycleia rebukes them. Penelope appears, scorning their pleas, convinced that Ulysses will return. She has undertaken to marry one of the suitors when the shroud she is weaving for Ulysses' father is finished. Wine and dancing-girls are summoned. As Penelope appeals to the absent Ulysses to save her, a voice is heard outside. A vagrant in rags begs for hospitality. To the disgust of the suitors Penelope, moved by sudden compassion, welcomes him. While Eurycleia washes his feet she recognizes a scar; the stranger (Ulysses disguised) pledges her to silence. She leads him out to give him food. Penelope, seated at her loom, unravels the day's work but is observed by the suitors and forced to promise to make her choice next day. The stranger consoles her with the thought of her husband's return. Penelope and Eurycleia prepare for their evening walk to keep watch over the sea. The stranger follows them.

Act 2 *A moonlit night on a hill-top above the sea with a tall column* Penelope recalls how she and Ulysses used to come here after dark to take the air. Now, every evening, knowing that it can be seen from the sea, she garlands the column with roses. The faithful Eumaeus prays that he may be spared to see his master again. Penelope gently questions the stranger, who reveals that Ulysses on his wanderings sought shelter in his home in Crete. As evidence he describes Ulysses' royal cloak and tunic. When Penelope confesses to misgivings about Ulysses' fidelity, the stranger reassures her. He suggests a stratagem – only a suitor who can bend the great bow of Ulysses may win her hand. The women return to the palace. Ulysses reveals his identity to Eumaeus and the shepherds, and calls for their help on the morrow.

Act 3 *The great hall of the palace* Ulysses has spent the night reconnoitring the building. Among his old weapons he has chosen a sword, which he hides under the throne. Eumaeus informs him that the suitors have ordered sheep and cattle to be brought for sacrifice – so the shepherds are armed with knives. The suitors call for preparations to be made for the wedding feast. They summon Penelope, who announces her one condition: only he who can bend the great bow may claim her hand. The suitors are filled with consternation. Three of them try, with humiliating results. The stranger slyly offers to try in his turn. The suitors are scornful, but when he succeeds and shoots an arrow, they are terrified. The second arrow is aimed at Eurymachus. Ulysses declares himself, the suitors are slaughtered and Penelope is finally convinced. The reunited couple sing of their happiness and there is general rejoicing and praise to Zeus, in which the people of Ithaca join.

*

In his carefully constructed score Fauré used leitmotifs of striking quality (those connected with Penelope and Ulysses are fully treated in the fine prelude, sometimes heard as a separate piece), but Wagnerian influence is more evident in pages of quiet intensity than at climaxes, where the lean, cutting texture is quite un-Wagnerian. Although Fauré professed to abhor illustrative music he was remarkably successful in suggesting such incidents as the weaving (and unravelling) of the shroud and

Poster by Georges Rochegrosse for Fauré's 'Pénélope', printed for Maquet at the time of the Paris première (1913), the same year as the Monte Carlo world première

the stranger's description of Ulysses' royal garments. The elliptical style of *Pénélope* is related to the piano music (e.g. the nine Préludes op.103) of the same period. Many solo passages for voice resemble Fauré's later songs rather than recitative and arioso in the French operatic manner, but they are *mélodies* with contours moulded to dramatic ends. It is typical that the heroine's cry in Act 1 'J'ai tant d'amour à lui donner encore . . .' should be marked 'sans ralentir'. In the opera as elsewhere in his music, interpreters should beware of confusing sentiment with sentimentality. The character of Penelope – proud, loyal, passionate, merciless to the suitors, a woman (as her entrances in Acts 1 and 3 show) of formidable presence – is strongly drawn. Ulysses' music, sinewy with a suggestion of ruthlessness, overcomes the inherent improbability of Penelope's having no more than a lurking suspicion of his real identity. The dances in the outer acts, delightful in themselves, are adroitly woven into the fabric. Here as in the general layout one may detect the influence of Saint-Saëns' *Samson et Dalila*. In a letter to his wife (1 October 1909) Fauré complained that the public were moved only by 'the excessive if always justifiable polyphony of Wagner, the *chiaroscuro* of Debussy, or Massenet's contemptibly passionate squirmings', but were indifferent to the 'clear and *straightforward*' music of

Saint-Saëns, a life-long friend, to which he himself felt closest – 'All that gives me shivers down the spine!'

Notable interpreters of the title role have included Germaine Lubin, Claire Croiza, Suzanne Balguerie and Régine Crespin. Like another major opera of the period, Dukas' *Ariane et Barbe-bleue*, *Pénélope* has won high regard among musicians, but has not entered the repertory. Outwardly unsensational and unspectacular, concerned not with doomed love but with a marriage lasting and happy in spite of the strain of external events, composed in a bare, economical, pared-down musical style in which Fauré clothes feelings running at high tension below the surface, *Pénélope* does not try to seduce the wider operatic public. **R.H.C.**

Peter Grimes

Opera in a prologue and three acts, op.33, by Benjamin Britten to a libretto by Montagu Slater after George Crabbe's poem *The Borough*; London, Sadler's Wells, 7 June 1945.

The première was conducted by Reginald Goodall, and the cast was headed by Peter Pears as Grimes and Joan Cross as Ellen Orford, with Edith Coates (Auntie), Owen Brannigan (Swallow), Roderick Jones (Balstrode), Edmund Donlevy (Ned Keene), Morgan Jones (Bob Boles) and Valetta Iacopi (Mrs Sedley).

Peter Grimes *a fisherman*	tenor
Boy (John) *his apprentice*	silent
Ellen Orford *a widow, schoolmistress*	soprano
Captain Balstrode *retired merchant*	
skipper	baritone
Auntie *landlady of 'The Boar'*	contralto
Niece 1 ⎫ *main attractions of*	soprano
Niece 2 ⎭ *'The Boar'*	soprano
Bob Boles *fisherman and Methodist*	tenor
Swallow *a lawyer*	bass
Mrs Sedley *a widow*	mezzo-soprano
Rev. Horace Adams *the rector*	tenor
Ned Keene *apothecary and quack*	baritone
Dr Thorp [Crabbe in some sources]	silent
Hobson *carter*	bass
Townspeople, fisherfolk	
Setting The Borough, a small fishing town on	
the east coast of England, about 1830	

Despite the difficulties attending the composition and production of *Paul Bunyan* (1941), his first fully musical work for the stage, Britten was soon contemplating a more ambitious operatic project. In the summer of 1941, while visiting California with Britten, Peter Pears bought a copy of George Crabbe's *Works*; singer and composer had already read E. M. Forster's article in *The Listener* (29 May 1941), 'George Crabbe: the Poet and the Man', with its evocation of Aldeburgh and the English east coast. Pears and Britten began to sketch out a scenario before they left America in March 1942, and more drafting took place during the voyage itself. As Pears later put it, 'by the time we came back to London, the whole story of *Peter Grimes* as set in the opera was already shaped, and it simply remained to call in a librettist to write the words'. That process of drafting had already transformed Crabbe's essentially evil Grimes into a character who is as much the victim of an uncomprehending society as of his own weaknesses and contradictions. Above all, Britten's Grimes is unstable, swinging unpredictably between the visionary and the violent.

Montagu Slater agreed to provide a libretto, Christopher Isherwood having declined, and a complete draft was ready around the end of 1942. Britten did not begin to compose the music until January 1944, and it was then that various changes to the libretto were initiated. The complete full score, dated 10 February 1945, shows several striking differences from the definitive vocal score published later in 1945, and the full score published in 1963 includes further minor revisions. The 'Four Sea Interludes' were published separately with the descriptive titles 'Dawn', 'Sunday Morning', 'Moonlight' and 'Storm'. At a fairly early stage of the compositional process the Sadler's Wells Opera Company, where Eric Crozier was Stage Director and Pears had been singing various leading roles, decided to re-open their theatre in north London with *Peter Grimes* at the end of the war in Europe.

In terms of productions and performances, *Peter Grimes* is one of the most successful of 20th-century operas after those by Puccini and Richard Strauss. For at least 20 years, performances in English were dominated by the voice and personality of Peter Pears. Pears led the cast in a fine complete recording under Britten's direction (1959); more recent alternatives have been conducted by Colin Davis, with Jon Vickers as Grimes (1978), by Bernard Haitink with Anthony Rolfe Johnson (1993) and by Richard Hickox with Philip Langridge (1996). Langridge's Grimes was also featured in a video recording of the 1994 production at the English National Opera conducted by David Atherton. Within three years of its première the opera had been staged at Covent Garden and in many European and Scandinavian countries. Serge Koussevitzky, who commissioned it, and to whom it is dedicated, relinquished the American première to Leonard Bernstein: this took place at Tanglewood in 1946. After a relatively fallow period in the 1950s the opera gained new popularity, and there were productions in the Soviet Union and South America. It was filmed for BBC television in 1969, with Pears in the title role.

*

Prologue *Interior of the Moot Hall arranged as for a coroner's inquest* This plunges into the action without preliminaries and establishes the essence of the opera's dramatic and musical tension. The main body of the scene is bound together by recurrences and developments of the brusque initial idea representing the Borough's collective impatience with the likes of Grimes, and there is the clearest contrast – rhythmic as well as harmonic – between this material and Grimes's own more lyrical music. The inquest concerns the death at sea of Grimes's boy apprentice. Despite the evident hostility of virtually everyone present to the fisherman, who is obsessed with his work to the point where he is cruelly neglectful, the Coroner Swallow rules that the boy died accidentally, accepting Grimes's explanation that his boat was blown off course as he tried to sail for London, and that the boy died of thirst and exhaustion. Swallow acknowledges that Grimes had earlier saved the boy from drowning, but he tells the fisherman not to hire another young apprentice. Grimes reacts angrily, but only Ellen Orford shows any sympathy, and their brief but highly charged duet first intensifies the Prologue's pervasive dissonances (most basically, the conflicting tonal centres of B♭ and A), then resolves them, though only precariously, since the arching phrase that they sing in octaves is itself too chromatic to express more than a temporary repose. The Prologue is through-composed, with clear evidence of that arioso style that is an important aspect of Britten's operatic

'Peter Grimes' (Britten), scene from the original production at Sadler's Wells, London, in 1945, with Peter Pears in the title role and Joan Cross as Ellen Orford

technique, alongside more formal aria and ensemble, and it demonstrates his instinctive ability to devise pithy, memorable ideas that serve both dramatic and purely musical purposes.

Act I.i *A street by the sea* The Prologue is linked to Act 1 by the first of the orchestral interludes that encapsulate so much of the opera's atmosphere. This 'dawn' music provides the background to a chorus describing and accompanying the early-morning work of the fisherfolk, and within the chorus various characters, many of whom have already been heard briefly in the Prologue, are introduced again: the placid landlady ('Auntie') of 'The Boar' inn, the tippling Methodist local preacher, the Rector, the drably respectable, disapproving widow Mrs Sedley and the retired sea-captain Balstrode.

After this chorus the main part of the scene falls into five distinct but linked sections: first a vigorous ensemble in which, after general reluctance, Balstrode and Keene help Grimes to haul his boat on to land; second, the short gruff song in which Hobson, the carter, refuses to fetch Grimes's new apprentice (an arrangement made by Ned Keene) from the workhouse; third, another short but expansively lyrical aria (interrupting the carter's song) in which Ellen Orford underlines her willingness to help Grimes ('Let her among you without fault cast the first stone'); fourth, a large-scale fugal ensemble and chorus responding to the approaching storm; and fifth, the extended dialogue between Grimes and Balstrode in which the irreconcilable conflicts in Grimes's character between the visionary and the conventional, between his desire to earn a place in society and his absolute determination to behave as he thinks fit, are fully evident for the first time. The process traced in the music of this fifth section, from Peter's anguished narration of the events culminating in the death of the apprentice ('Picture what that day was like') through his agitated explanation of how he intends to win over the Borough ('They listen to money') to the uninhibited eloquence of his final self-analysis ('What harbour shelters peace?') shows Britten's music at its most powerful: instantly expressive and evocative, the depiction of wind and waves never banal, yet bringing genuine depth to the tensions inherent in the opera's central character. The music has a spontaneity and sense of purpose that generously compensate for the drawbacks of what is at many points a rather laborious, selfconsciously poetic libretto. Britten skilfully balances the presence of distinct sections or 'numbers' against pervasive motivic reminiscences and larger-scale tonal recurrences.

I.ii *Interior of 'The Boar' inn* The episodes are linked by the brilliantly resourceful and hectic 'storm' interlude, and the storm continues to rumble in the background, bursting in whenever the door opens throughout the scene, which is built from a mixture of short solos. These are linked by passages of recitative-like dialogue in which the dramatic tension is never allowed to slacken; there is one extended contapuntal ensemble in the later stages. As the regulars brave the storm to assemble in 'The Boar', there are straightforward but splendidly pointed songs for Auntie and Balstrode; the latter, following the drunken Boles's attempt to fondle one of the Nieces, has a refrain ('We live and let live, and look, we keep our hands to ourselves') that is ironic to the extent that the tolerance it apparently peaches (genuine in Balstrode's case) is in truth a mask for indifference and incomprehension of any Grimes-like nonconformity. Mrs Sedley, against her principles, has also come, awaiting a consignment of laudanum from Keene.

As the atmosphere becomes more convivial Grimes bursts in, expecting to collect his new apprentice. In the shocked silence that ensues he sings the aria 'Now the Great Bear and Pleiades' which, although brief, magically conveys the visionary side of his personality. The descending E major scale of his last line ('Who can turn skies back and begin again?') has a directness and poignancy that only the greatest masters of opera can achieve. A substantial ensemble now builds up as the people become increasingly hostile to Grimes. Auntie calls for a song to defuse the tension, and Ned Keene launches the round 'Old Joe has gone fishing', whose seven-beat metre quickly generates a powerful tension of its own. When Grimes tries to join in he breaks the unanimity of the round apart, and at this moment of maximum instability Hobson, Ellen and the new apprentice arrive, drenched by the storm. With no greeting to those who have done him this favour, Grimes hustles the boy away, as the all too transparent irony of Ellen's last line 'Peter will take you home' is derisively taken up by the chorus: 'Home! Do you call that home?' The storm music gives the act its emphatic final cadence.

Act 2.i *A street by the sea; a fine sunny morning, some weeks later* The orchestra evokes a bright Sunday morning, with resonating bells. At first Ellen's mood is tranquil; her song, 'Glitter of waves and glitter of sunlight', echoes the orchestral interlude. She sits with John, the new apprentice, knitting, while the church service proceeds offstage. But her mood soon changes when she notices a tear in the boy's coat, and a bruise on his neck. Her gloom-laden advice to the boy, ending 'After the storm will come a sleep, Like oceans deep', is ironically counterpointed with the worshippers' *Gloria*, and the irony is intensified when Grimes enters and the *Benedicite* interacts with his ruthless determination to exploit the apprentice, because only through hard work will he win the respect of society. As they quarrel Ellen's music

grows more measured and resigned, Peter's more jagged and aggressive; at her 'Peter, we've failed – we've failed!' he lets out a shriek of anger and strikes her, crying in a mocking echo of the church service: 'So be it – and God have mercy upon me!'

As Grimes rushes off with the apprentice, leaving Ellen distraught, the Borough assemble, and an extended chorus and ensemble is built around the sardonic refrain 'Grimes is at his exercise!', set to one of the work's most pervasive motifs, emphasizing a descending octave with prominent central tritone (Bb–E–Bb). Boles turns the crowd's thoughts towards retribution, and a new refrain emerges: 'The Borough keeps its standards up!' Ellen, still eloquent and restrained, attempts to explain Grimes's motives, but no longer to justify them, and the rest mock her words (and her music). Fearing for the apprentice's safety, the men decide to march to Grimes's hut, and they set off to an extravagantly bloodthirsty chant, whose text may seem unconvincing but is set by Britten to music of chilling force. As the procession recedes the four remaining women – Auntie, Ellen and the Nieces – sing a haunting ensemble of tender regret, 'From the gutter', a brief three-part structure with refrain, whose expressive intensity results primarily from the modal ambivalence of its underlying harmony. This promotes a luminous texture in which dissonance seems more significant than the resolving consonance. In this way Britten uses a basic technical feature to link the scene's extreme contrasts: Ellen's eloquence, Grimes's vehemence, the crowd's aggression, the women's reflectiveness.

2.ii *Grimes's hut (an upturned boat on the cliff edge)* The interlude between the scenes of Act 2 is a passacaglia built on the 'Grimes is at his exercise' motif and progressing from the quiet despair of the women's quartet to the unrestrained fury with which Grimes enters in scene ii. The scene is an extended *scena* for Grimes himself, with an epilogue for the town representatives who enter his hut. The *scena* is in three main sections. In the first, whose music in part relates to the 'They listen to money' material in Act 1 scene i, Peter's own confusion, his conflicting impulses of violence and tenderness towards the boy, are vividly displayed. The central section, itself essentially a three-part form, contains Peter's most sustained expression of his vision of happiness with Ellen. But the more he dwells on this the more insistent its impossibility becomes. Peter is haunted, not only by the memory of his dead apprentice, but also by the knowledge that he can never achieve the kind of stability and social acceptability for which he yearns. In a masterly transition the serene dream music curdles and dissolves into the sinister march of the approaching men. In the final part of the *scena* Peter accuses the apprentice of lying to Ellen about him. Despite the move from singing to Sprechgesang, Britten avoids excessive melodrama, and there is genuine horror in the process whereby, in adopting the threatening music of the march himself, the fisherman drives the apprentice to his death. As Grimes, in his haste to avoid the crowd, urges him down to the boat, the boy trips and falls down the cliff. (The stage directions are clear: Grimes does not actually push him.) In the eerie, understated final section of the scene, the Rector and Swallow, finding the hut empty but apparently neat and tidy, decide that all is well. Only Balstrode, looking down the cliff face, knows better, and the act ends with the recall of the viola solo that began the passacaglia.

Act 3.i *A street by the sea; a summer evening a few days later* The orchestral introduction is one of Britten's most subtle nature scenes, a night-piece shot through with luminous shafts of moonlight. Like both scenes of Act 2, this scene counterpoints onstage and offstage events, the various dances heard from the Moot Hall providing an almost surreal background to the sinister events seen enacted. (It is this scene that offers the closest parallel to a scene in Berg's *Wozzeck*, Act 3 scene iii, though there the dance music is played on stage.) The first half of the scene employs subsidiary characters only: Swallow flirting with the Nieces, Mrs Sedley telling Keene of her belief that Grimes has murdered his new apprentice; the creeping chromatics of her 'Murder most foul it is' are a telling blend of grotesque humour and doom-laden menace. A second stanza of the song follows the cheerful exchanges between the Rector and other burgesses, and Mrs Sedley then overhears Ellen and Balstrode in conversation. Grimes's boat has returned, though Peter himself cannot be found. Balstrode has also discovered the boy's jersey at the foot of the cliff, and Ellen, in a short but ornate aria, remembers embroidering the anchor on it. They decide that, although Peter cannot be saved, they can still help him: what this means becomes clear in the next scene.

Meanwhile Mrs Sedley arouses the populace with the news that Peter's boat is back. After a third stanza of her song there is another violent chorus and ensemble, vowing vengeance and reaching a climax as the crowd, bent on a manhunt, shout the name of their prey, 'Peter Grimes!' The music here achieves an uninhibited ferocity rare in Britten's work.

3.ii *The same, some hours later* The final orchestral interlude rapidly establishes a complete change of mood, though the scene itself is unchanged. The only sounds are a distant fog-horn and the distant cries of the chorus. Grimes's final scene is an extended arioso that periodically flowers into more lyrical phrases and reminiscences of earlier moments in the opera. The basic material grows from the two-note fog-horn motif and, in keeping with Grimes's now irrevocably disturbed mentality, there are rapid changes of mood, as when a memory of Ellen (at one stage in the opera's evolution she was heard calling to Peter at this point) turns rapidly to a contemptuous dismissal of both friendship and gossip. At the climax of the scene the choral shouts reach the same octave B♭s used at the end of the previous scene, and Grimes's delirious response, rapid repetitions of his own name, gradually sinks into a hopeless silence. Ellen and Balstrode appear. Ellen seeks to take Peter home, but Balstrode – in speech, not song – tells him in as many words to take his own life. This, after Grimes's movingly restrained recapitulation of 'What harbour shelters peace?', accompanied only by distant choral reiterations of Grimes's name, may seem a harsh effect, and a harsh judgment: but as cold reality, both are appropriate.

The 'dawn' music returns, the orchestra heard for the first time since Act 3 scene i, and there are three further stanzas of the choral song that began Act l; the only remarks of the various subsidiary characters who assemble are that a boat, seen sinking out at sea, is no longer visible. 'One of these rumours', says Auntie. After the final choral stanza the work's purely harmonic resolution is not in doubt, but the texture darkens as if to underline the fact that, despite its apparent ability to carry on as usual, the Borough has experienced a tragedy from which it ought never to recover.

*

For a first opera (as distinct from the operetta *Paul Bunyan*) and despite the occasionally strong associations with other works – notably Gershwin's *Porgy and Bess* – *Peter Grimes* is a remarkably personal and convincing music drama.

The more determinedly commentators seek to emphasize its flaws, particularly in the libretto, the more memorable its musical ideas and the more resilient its formal design appear to be. What tends to distinguish Britten's outsider-protagonists (and their sympathizers) is their greater sensitivity, and it follows that harshness and coarseness, lending themselves to musical realization through parody or even caricature, will be a prime feature of their opponents. The ironically pointed collision between these opposed characteristics is powerfully presented in Act 1 scene ii, where the fisherman's disturbed yet poetic flight of fancy provokes jaunty, aggressive incomprehension in the others. The conflicting states are portrayed with equal musical conviction – Grimes's aria 'Now the Great Bear and Pleiades', the round 'Old Joe has gone fishing' – and the whole opera is ultimately a resourceful, extended working-out of degrees of interaction and confrontation between personal needs and collective convictions.

By comparison with *Kát'a Kabanová*, or *Wozzeck*,

Grimes may seem conventional in structure, conservative in style. Yet the ambivalence of its subject matter – in particular, the way the audience is left to decide whether or not Grimes is to be pitied rather than blamed – and the remarkable vitality of the music, come together to create an experience that rarely fails to grip in the theatre. Britten has always been praised for his ability to set a scene in orchestral preludes and interludes, but his skill at embodying character in an at times florid vocal style is even more memorable, and never more effective than in Grimes. The work can now be seen as expressing Britten's early and abiding doubts about the viability of 'grand opera' as powerfully as it expresses doubts about the motivation and personality of the principal character. It is therefore no cliché to assert that it laid the technical and expressive foundations for Britten's entire operatic career.   **A.W.**

Pirata, II ('The Pirate')

Melodramma in two acts by Vincenzo Bellini to a libretto by Felice Romani after Isidore J. S. Taylor's play *Bertram, ou Le pirate*, a version of Charles Maturin's *Bertram*; Milan, Teatro alla Scala, 27 October 1827.

The first cast included Giovanni Battista Rubini as Gualtiero, Henriette Méric-Lalande as Imogene and Antonio Tamburini as Ernesto.

Ernesto *Duke of Caldora*	bass
Imogene	soprano
Gualtiero *pirate chief*	tenor
Itulbo *Gualtiero's henchman*	tenor
Goffredo *a hermit*	bass
Adele *companion to Imogene*	soprano
Imogene's son	silent
Fishermen, pirates, courtiers	

Setting Sicily, in and around the castle of Caldora, in the 13th century

Bellini had lived in Sicily and Naples until arriving in Milan on 12 April 1827, invited by Barbaia to write for La Scala. *Il pirata* was only his second professional production, and his first collaboration with Romani. Bellini took over six months writing the opera, in order to impress the audience at La Scala. With an excellent cast, the opera was well received and Bellini was hailed as an exciting new voice. When Rubini and his wife, Adelaide Comelli-Rubini, sang in the opera at the S Carlo, Naples, in 1828, the tenor was probably responsible for major adjustments made to the ending.

Il pirata, with its highly Romantic plot, soon won Bellini international success. The opera was staged in Vienna at the Kärntnertortheater (1828) with Rubini and his wife; in London (the first Bellini opera to be heard there) at the King's Theatre (1830) with Domenico Donzelli, Méric-Lalande and Vincenzo-Felice Santini; and in Paris at the Théâtre Italien (1832), with Rubini and Wilhelmine Schröder-Devrient, who interpolated an aria from Pacini's *Amazilia* and insisted on a happy ending. During the 20th century *Il pirata* was revived at Rome in 1935 to mark the centenary of Bellini's death, while a production at Palermo in January 1958 was transferred to La Scala in May, when the cast included Franco Corelli, Maria Callas and Ettore Bastianini. At Florence during the 1967 Maggio Musicale the cast included Flaviano Labò and Montserrat Caballé. *Il pirata* was given at the Wexford Festival in 1972.

Ernesto, Duke of Caldora, a follower of the house of Anjou, has forced Imogene to marry him against her will and despite her love for Gualtiero, formerly Count of Montalto and loyal to the rival house of Manfred. Gualtiero, defeated in battle and proscribed, has become the leader of a band of Aragonese pirates, who have just been conquered by a fleet under the command of the Duke of Caldora.

The overture, adapted from one probably played before the first version of *Adelson e Salvini* (1825) and itself deriving from Bellini's E♭ sinfonia of 1823, follows the Rossinian model, with a crescendo after the second subject. Act 1 begins with a storm that wrecks Gualtiero's ship. He and his crew, washed ashore near the castle of Caldora, are given succour by the fishermen. In Gualtiero's cavatina, 'Nel furor delle tempeste', he describes the vision, constantly in his heart, of Imogene as an angel. Imogene is seen approaching and Gualtiero hides, briefly emerging when she narrates her dream of finding him wounded on the beach, 'Lo sognai ferito, esangue' (shortened by Bellini after the première). Imogene thinks she hears Gualtiero's voice. That night the pirates carouse in an echo chorus. Imogene summons the pirate captain and recognizes Gualtiero. In their duet 'Tu sciagurato! ah! fuggi' she tells him that she was forced to marry Ernesto to save her father's life. The chorus announces the triumphant return of Ernesto, whose declaration of victory over the pirates, 'Sì vincemmo e il pregio io sento', derives from 'Obbliarti, abbandonarti' in *Adelson e Salvini*. Over an accompaniment of increasing agitation, Ernesto tries to discover if Gualtiero is among the surviving pirates. He wishes to imprison them but Imogene begs for their release. The impetuous Gualtiero has to be forcibly restrained from giving himself away and attacking Ernesto. The act closes with music from the main crescendo in the overture, also used to end Act 1 of *Adelson e Salvini*.

Act 2 opens with a chorus of Imogene's ladies, leading to a duet, 'Tu m'apristi in cor ferita', in which

*Giovanni Battista Rubini as Gualtiero (the role he created)
and his wife Adelaide Comelli-Rubini as Imogene in the
1828 Naples production of Bellini's 'Il Pirata'*

Ernesto denounces Imogene as a sinful wife and
mother; she retorts that he knew of her earlier love
for Gualtiero when he forced her to marry him.
Imogene warns Gualtiero that her husband is aware
of his presence in the castle. He pleads with her to
leave with him, but she refuses. Ernesto, at first
unnoticed, turns their duet into a trio. Gualtiero
challenges him to combat and kills him. To the sound
of a Death March, soldiers lament Ernesto's death;
Gualtiero appears to surrender his sword, and in 'Tu
vedrai la sventurata' expresses his hope that Imogene
will forgive him. A cantabile for english horn and
harp introduces the entry of the distracted Imogene
with her son. In 'Col sorriso d'innocenza' she
imagines that the child can win her Ernesto's
forgiveness; on hearing the death sentence
pronounced on Gualtiero, she loses all sense of
reality and sings the dramatic cabaletta 'O sole ti
vela' before being led away. In a final scene, neither
printed in vocal scores nor usually performed,
Gualtiero is surrounded by soldiers, but evades them
by leaping from a bridge to his death.

Il pirata played a significant role in establishing
the style of the Romantic *melodramma* later developed
by Donizetti and Verdi. The tormented, impulsive
hero of Italian Romantic opera is presented for the
first time in Gualtiero's opening cavatina. Bellini
exploited Rubini's talent for flights of passionate
expression, avoiding any break in the melodic line by
decoration until near the end of the long phrases.
However, Bellini maintained the high tessitura of the
Rossinian tenor, ascending to *e''* in the opening
cavatina (for Rubini he wrote much of Gualtiero's
part a tone higher than it appears in printed scores).

Bellini's style was not yet mature and there are
some more conservative sections in the score, such as
the Larghetto of the duet for Imogene and Ernesto in
Act 2, where the voices are in 3rds and dramatically
undifferentiated, and which contains the opera's
clearest survival of Rossinian *canto fiorito*. Certain
features, such as the echo chorus and the complex
vocal counterpoint in the Act 1 finale, were experiments that Bellini did not repeat. More significant for
his development are the ariosos, such as 'Se un
giorno fia che ti tragga' before the duet for Imogene
and Gualtiero in Act 1.   S.M., E.F.

Platée ('Plataea')

Comédie lyrique ('*ballet bouffon*') in a prologue and
three acts by Jean-Philippe Rameau to a libretto by
Adrien-Joseph Le Valois d'Orville after Jacques
Autreau's play *Platée, on Junon jalouse*; Versailles, La
Grande Ecurie, 31 March 1745.

The role of Plataea was created by Pierre de
Jélyotte, with Marie Fel as Folly.

Platée [Plataea] *a marsh-nymph*	haute-contre
Jupiter	bass
Cithéron [Cithaeron]	bass
Mercure [Mercury]	haute-contre
La Folie [Folly]	soprano
Junon [Juno]	soprano
L'Amour [Cupid]	soprano
Clarine	soprano
Momus (Acts 2 and 3)	tenor
Thespis	haute-contre
Thalie [Thalia]	soprano
Momus (prologue)	baritone
A Satyr	baritone
A Naiad	soprano

*Satyrs, Maenads, grape-pickers, frogs, nymphs,
     retinue of Momus and Folly*

Setting A Greek vineyard; a marsh at the foot
     of Mount Cithaeron

Completed for the dauphin's wedding festivities,
Platée was given a single performance at Versailles in
1745. Its theme, derived from the ancient Greek
writer Pausanias, is the mock marriage between
Jupiter and an ugly marsh-nymph. As such, it
appears grotesquely ill-suited to the occasion,
especially as the bride, the Spanish princess Maria
Teresa, was evidently unattractive. This aspect of
the work, however, seems to have provoked little
contemporary comment. Four years later, the opera
was successfully revived at the Paris Opéra, with the
libretto revised by Ballot de Sauvot. A further revival,
in 1754, remained in the Opéra's repertory until 1759.

75. 'Orphée aux enfers' (Offenbach, 1858), poster by Jules Chéret printed at the time of the production of the revised version at the Théâtre de la Gaîté, Paris, in 1874

Main picture: 76. 'Orfeo ed Euridice' (Gluck, 1762), Act 3 scene i, painting by Pehr Hilleström showing a production by the Swedish Royal Opera in 1773

Left: 77. 'Orfeo' (Monteverdi, 1607), a scene from Act 1, with Guy de Mey as Orpheus in the 1986 London revival of the Early Opera Project production (Florence, 1984)

78. 'Otello' (Verdi, 1887),
Placido Domingo (Otello) and
Sergey Leiferkus (Iago) in the
production at the Royal Opera
House, Covent Garden, in 1992

Left: 79. *Cover of the special edition of 'L'illustrazione italiana' issued to commemorate the première of Verdi's 'Otello' at La Scala, Milan, in 1887*

Below: 80. *'Pagliacci' (Leoncavallo, 1892), chromolithograph by Luigi Morgari, 1893*

Above: 81. 'Parsifal' (Wagner, 1882), scene from the production designed and directed by Robert Wilson (costumes by Frida Parmeggiani) at Houston Grand Opera in 1992, with Harry Peeters as Gurnemanz and Monte Pederson as Amfortas

Below: 82. 'Pelléas et Mélisande' (Debussy, 1902), scene from the production by Richard Jones (sets Anthony McDonald, costumes Nicky Gillibrand) for Opera North in 1995, with Joan Rodgers (Mélisande) and William Dazeley (Pelléas)

Above: 83. 'Porgy and Bess' (Gershwin, 1935), the final scene in the production by Trevor Nunn (sets John Gunter, costumes Sue Blane) for Glyndebourne Festival Opera in 1986, with Willard White as Porgy

Below: 84. 'Prince Igor' (Borodin, 1890), scene from the production by Andrei Serban (sets Liviu Ciulei, costumes Deirdre Clancy) at the Royal Opera House, Covent Garden, in 1990, with Sergey Leiferkus (Prince Igor), Anna Tomowa-Sintow (Yaroslavna), Alexei Steblianko, Paata Burchuladze and Elena Zaremba

85. 'Punch and Judy' (Birtwistle, 1968), a scene from the original production by Anthony Besch (designed by Peter Rice) at the Jubilee Hall, Aldeburgh, with John Cameron as Punch and Maureen Morelle as Judy

86. 'The Rake's Progress' (Stravinsky, 1951), Act 3 scene i (the auction) from the revival of the 1975 production by John Cox (designed by David Hockney) at Glyndebourne Festival Opera in 1994, with Robert Tear as the auctioneer

87. 'Das Rheingold' (Wagner, 1869), scene ii (the giants Fasolt and Fafner threaten to abduct Freia) from the production by Alfred Kirchner (designed by Rosalie) at the Bayreuth Festspielhaus in 1994, with Nina Stemme (Freia), René Pape (Fasolt) and Eric Halfvarson (Fafner)

88. 'Rigoletto' (Verdi, 1851), scene from Act 3 of the production by Jonathan Miller (designed by Patrick Robertson and Rosemary Vercoe) revived by the English National Opera at the London Coliseum in 1983, with Arthur Davies as the Duke and Jean Rigby as Maddalena

Although some criticized the 'grossièretés' of the libretto, the work was by now regarded as one of Rameau's finest. Yet only the prologue was subsequently revived: it appeared for the last time in 1773.

The first modern revivals of *Platée* took place at the Kaim-Saal, Munich (26 January 1901, in German) and Monte Carlo (5 April 1917, in French). The earliest recording, made in 1961, is notable for Michel Sénéchal's superb characterization of the title role.

*

Prologue ('La naissance de la comédie') *A Greek vineyard* Thespis, represented as the inventor of comedy, plans with Cupid, Momus (the god of ridicule) and Thalia (the muse of comedy) to give mortals and gods a moral lesson: they decide to re-enact the episode in which Jupiter cures his wife Juno of jealousy. The prologue culminates in an elaborate chorus, with an independent line for Thespis, 'Formons un spectacle nouveau'.

Act I *A marsh at the foot of Mount Cithaeron* After a storm, graphically depicted in the orchestral prelude, Mercury descends. He explains to King Cithaeron that the storm is caused by Jupiter's impatience with Juno's behaviour. The king suggests a ruse to cure her tiresome jealousy: Jupiter is to pretend to court the ugly but inordinately vain marsh-nymph Plataea. Juno will look foolish when she learns that her jealousy is groundless. The conspirators depart as Plataea arrives. She is convinced that Cithaeron's aloofness is a sign of his love. To the offstage sounds of frogs and cuckoos she begins to woo him. Irritated by his renewed coldness, she accuses him of treachery; her indignant 'Dis donc pourquoi!' is taken up by the frogs in an onomatopoeic chorus, 'Quoi? quoi?' Mercury again descends. Bowing many times, he explains that Jupiter is infatuated by Plataea's beauty and wishes to marry her. Sudden lightning presages a storm – a sign, Mercury explains, of Juno's wrath. But Plataea is undaunted; indeed, in a virtuoso aria ('Quittez, nymphes, quittez vos demeures profondes', punctuated with rude syncopations associated with the frogs), she summons her fellow marsh dwellers to enjoy the rain. The ensuing *divertissement* again features frog noises (oboes at the bottom of their range). It is interrupted by another storm symphony, during which Aquilons (North Winds) force the nymphs back into their swamp.

Act 2 *The same* Mercury explains to Cithaeron that he has hoodwinked Juno into going to Athens in the hope of surprising Jupiter and his new love. 'Look, there she goes', he jokes, pointing to a passing cloud. He and the king wait for Jupiter to arrive, and hide as his cloud descends. Plataea cautiously approaches the cloud ('A l'aspect de ce nuage'). She is amazed when the god manifests himself first as a donkey (its braying, which Plataea mistakes for amorous sighs, realistically portrayed by double stoppings), then as an owl. At the sight of the owl, other birds are heard taking panic-stricken flight, a cacophony ingeniously represented by two flageolets and upper strings. Eventually, amid a shower of fire, Jupiter appears in his own form. He declares his love to the frightened nymph and prepares a *divertissement* in her honour. After a laughing chorus, 'Quelle est aima-a-a-able', Folly appears with the 'fous gais' and 'fous tristes', these dressed respectively as babies and Greek philosophers. In a brilliant parody of an italianate coloratura aria, she recounts the story of Apollo and Daphne ('Aux langueurs d'Apollon Daphné se refusa'), accompanying herself on a lyre stolen from Apollo. There follow two dances 'dans le goût de vielle', the hurdy-gurdy represented by sustained double stoppings. Folly then creates 'a masterpiece of harmony', in which the whole assembly calls on Hymen to unite Jupiter and his new Juno. Plataea's excited outburst at being so described, 'Hé, bon, bon, bon!', is taken up in a final round-like ensemble and chorus.

Act 3 *The same* Returning in a fury from her fruitless mission, Juno is persuaded by Mercury to hide and observe the ceremony that is soon to begin. During a lively chorus 'Chantons, célébrons en ce jour' and ensuing march, Plataea appears, heavily veiled, in a frog-drawn chariot flanked by Jupiter and Mercury and preceded by dryads, satyrs and nymphs. Leading her bridegroom by the hand, she observes that Cupid and Hymen are not yet present. (Mercury comments wryly to Jupiter that these two divinities rarely go together.) In the course of a long chaconne, Plataea becomes increasingly impatient. At last Momus appears, dressed to look like Cupid, blindfold and carrying a ludicrously large bow and quiver. Explaining that Cupid himself is otherwise engaged, Momus presents Plataea with the god's wedding gifts: tears, sorrows, cries, languor (string glissandos). Momus is embarrassed by the nymph's rejection of these gifts and is mocked by Folly (in the virtuoso *ariette* 'Amour, lance tes traits, épuise ton carquois'). Three of Momus's retinue, disguised as Graces, dance in comical fashion. Jupiter then takes Plataea's hand and begins the marriage oath. But when Juno fails to appear, he has to repeat 'I swear . . .' several times. At last she strides in, tears off Plataea's veil – and realizes her mistake. The nymph storms out. To the sound of thunder the gods re-ascend, leaving Folly alone. Countryfolk bring Plataea back and begin to mock her ('Chantons Platée, égayons-nous'). The nymph grabs Cithaeron by the throat and threatens revenge. To renewed taunts she runs off to her swamp, while Folly and the assembly celebrate the reconciliation of Juno and Jupiter.

*

In the repertory of the Opéra and of French opera presented at court, comedy had traditionally played little part. Lully, after his first three *tragédies*, had eliminated comic episodes; from then until the appearance of *Platée* only a small number of operas had truly comic themes. The libretto was intended to emulate one of these, the burlesque entrée 'Cariselli' included in André Campra's compilation of *Les fragments de Monsieur de Lully* (1702) and subsequently much revived. The prologue apart, Le Valois d'Orville's revisions leave little of Autreau's work intact and greatly increase the element of comedy.

An outline of the plot gives the impression that the humour of *Platée* is distasteful. Yet the cruelty of laughing at an ugly but vain nymph is kept at a distance, since the part of Plataea is sung by a man. (This was one of the few travesty parts in French opera of the time.) The work's humour comes not just from the extravagant situations and comic stage business (about which the libretto is unusually explicit) but from the numerous parodies of serious opera, its descents and transformations, its musical and poetic language, its structural conventions. For example, the chaconne that precedes Plataea's marriage is comic not just because of its absurd length or because it is danced in 'le genre le plus noble', but because it is misplaced: chaconnes belong at the culmination of the final *divertissement*. Musical parody takes many forms – exaggerated vocalises, misaccentuations, vocal acrobatics; onomatopoeic

Pierre de Jélyotte in the title role of Rameau's 'Platée', the role he created in the original production at La Grande Ecurie, Versailles, 31 March 1745: portrait by Christian-Antoine Coypel

imitations of frogs, cuckoos, frightened birds, Folly's lyre and hurdy-gurdy. The burlesque use of language is seen in Plataea's frequent recourse to a frog-like 'quoi!', her comic alliterations and demotic expressions, including such un-operatic expletives as 'Fi!' and 'Ouffe!'　　　　　　　　　　　　　G.Sa.

Porgy and Bess

Folk opera in three acts by George Gershwin to a libretto by DuBose Heyward after his novel *Porgy* (1925), with lyrics by Heyward and Ira Gershwin; New York, Alvin Theatre, 10 October 1935.

Porgy *a crippled beggar*	bass-baritone
Bess	soprano
Crown *a stevedore, Bess's lover*	baritone
Serena *Robbins's wife*	soprano
Clara *Jake's wife*	soprano
Maria *keeper of the cook-shop*	contralto
Jake *a fisherman*	baritone
Sportin' Life *a dope peddler*	tenor
Mingo	tenor
Robbins	tenor
Peter *the honey man*	tenor
Frazier *a 'lawyer'*	baritone
Annie	mezzo-soprano
Lily *Peter's wife*	mezzo-soprano
Strawberry Woman	mezzo-soprano
Jim *a cotton picker*	baritone
Undertaker	baritone
Nelson	tenor
Crab Man	tenor

Residents of Catfish Row, fishermen, children, stevedores

Setting Catfish Row, a negro neighbourhood in Charleston, South Carolina, in the 1920s

Porgy and Bess was Gershwin's magnum opus, nourished by more than a decade of technical study and a longheld interest in African-American experience. Attracted to ragtime as a teenage pianist, borrowing blues vocabulary for songs as early as 1920 and identified publicly as a 'jazz' composer from the time of the *Rhapsody in Blue* (1924), Gershwin held a substantial stake in black American music long before the day in autumn 1926 when he happened upon Heyward's novel. He responded to his reading of *Porgy* as if to the voice of destiny. Though his earlier experience with through-composed music drama had been limited to *Blue Monday* (1922), a 20-minute opera 'à la Afro-American' written for a Broadway revue, *Porgy* fired him with the vision of a full-length opera, and he wrote to Heyward immediately to propose a collaboration.

Though the project took nine years to complete, Gershwin's intuition was on the mark. (He never did compose *The Dybbuk*, the 'Jewish opera' for which in 1929 he accepted a Metropolitan Opera commission – ample indication that he was much more at home with *Porgy*'s subject.)

Gershwin called *Porgy and Bess* a 'folk opera'. His belief in the need for a label is understandable, for *Porgy and Bess* is a work whose precise nature was questioned from the beginning. Gershwin's own credentials and prior experience caused some contemporaries to doubt that he was technically equipped to write a fully-fledged opera. The show's original venue (it played nightly on Broadway rather than according to an opera house's schedule, though trained opera singers were required) has raised further questions about its operatic pedigree. The massive cuts that took place before the New York première – to shorten playing time, tighten the drama, ease the singers' burden – have fed the belief that the work's essence lies in the appeal of individual numbers rather than the impact of its overall form. The popularity of some numbers as songs outside the show has seemed to confirm this point, although Charles Hamm has argued for the dramatic merits of the original version, revised by Gershwin and Rouben Mamoulian, its first director. Moreover, although the first production was by no means a flop (124 performances), it did fail to return its backers' investment. *Porgy and Bess* stripped of its recitative won its first commercial success when played in 1941 as a drama of separate musical numbers linked with spoken dialogue.

If these matters seemed to undermine the 'opera' part of Gershwin's label, the 'folk' part also proved contentious. Gershwin invoked the word at a time when the concept of 'the folk' as a term denoting respect for 'otherness' was gaining popular acceptance. The US government's public works programmes during the Depression years signalled a growing inclination to preserve, study and value the indigenous practices of different American subcultures, including economically disadvantaged ones. From that perspective, a tale about southern blacks by a white novelist, set to music by a New York-based, Jewish songwriter-lyricist team and played on the Broadway stage, was easy to criticize on grounds of authenticity. In addition, the opera was about African-Americans, whose lives, long after slavery and emancipation, were still affected by racial stereotyping – by being seen as a feckless but violent people, given to singing or brawling their troubles away. A work like *Porgy and Bess*, which confirmed that stereotype, was seen in some quarters as yet another hindrance to the quest of black Americans for social respect.

For these reasons and others, commentators traditionally have viewed *Porgy and Bess* as a flawed effort. Rather than taking the work as Gershwin composed it, seeking clues to the meaning of 'folk opera' in his career and the score itself, critics and historians have been more inclined to put forward their own definitions of 'folk' or 'opera' and then to demonstrate how Gershwin fell short. Not until 1976, when the first production of Gershwin's complete score, given by the Houston Grand Opera, was hailed as an artistic triumph, did the critical tide begin to turn. Now it seems obvious that *Porgy and Bess* deserves consideration as a successful work of art, proved by over half a century of performers' commitment and audience acceptance, and worthy of being studied and appreciated on its own terms. With Gershwin's score as its basis, his 'folk opera' label seems straightforward enough: a staged, fully sung drama, using operatic techniques (recitatives, arias, reminiscence themes, leitmotifs), about an American ethnic community whose music Gershwin felt he understood, though an outsider, and many of whose artistic conventions he had already mastered through long experience as a pianist and composer.

*

Amid the comings and goings of the Catfish Row inhabitants that open Act 1, Clara can be heard singing a lullaby to her baby, 'Summertime'; her husband Jake is engaged in a crap game. The crippled Porgy arrives in his goat cart, followed by the beautiful but dissolute Bess and her lover Crown, who is the worse for drink. Crown joins the game but loses money to Robbins and in a fit of rage kills him; he flees. Porgy takes Bess in and falls in love with her, and she becomes his woman, protected by his care against community opprobrium and the advances of Sportin' Life, the local dope peddler. In scene ii Robbins is mourned by his friends and neighbours, while his wife Serena sings the lament 'My man's gone now'. Act 2 begins as Jake and the fishermen prepare to set out on a fishing expedition, in spite of a storm warning. Porgy's 'I got plenty o' nuttin'' reflects his happier state of mind since he and Bess have been together. Bess is urged by Porgy to join a picnic excursion to Kittiwah Island, in which he cannot participate (scene ii). Bess encounters Crown, who is hiding there, and despite her genuine love for Porgy, Crown overcomes her resistance. After spending the night with him on the island, she returns to Catfish Row in a state of delirium (scene iii). Porgy helps nurse her back to health and, though intuition tells him she has been with Crown, he reaffirms his love for her. A hurricane hits the coast while Jake and the fishermen from Catfish Row are at sea. As the community prays for their safety, Crown reappears, mocks Porgy for being less than a man and then rushes out into the storm in the vain hope of saving the fishermen. Surviving this onslaught of nature (Act 3), he steals back to Catfish Row the next night to reclaim Bess. The waiting Porgy kills him in a brief struggle. When the police find Crown's body, they arrest Porgy as a witness (scene ii). Freed a week later, he reappears triumphantly on Catfish Row (scene iii), only to find that Bess, convinced by Sportin' Life that Porgy is gone for good, has sailed for New York in the dope peddler's company. The opera ends as Porgy leaves by goat cart to search for Bess. ('Which way New York?', he asks. 'It's way up North, past the custom house', his neighbours reply.)

*

Ira Gershwin once described his brother's imagination as 'the reservoir of musical inventiveness, resourcefulness, and craftsmanship George could dip into'. That 'reservoir' – nourished by a prodigious flow of inspiration and years of regular instruction, and disciplined by the habit of trusting a popular audience's judgments – is the source of *Porgy*'s sweep and power. The work is infused at every level with song of remarkable variety. Most obvious are the freestanding songs, whose melodies Wilfrid Mellers has saluted as 'more memorable than those of any twentieth-century opera', including Clara's lullaby ('Summertime', 1.i), Serena's lament ('My man's gone now', 1.ii), Porgy's banjo song ('I got plenty o' nuttin'', 2.i) and the love duet ('Bess, you is my woman', 2.i). In such numbers Gershwin's belief in the emotions of his principal characters leads to the invention of songs that do not need the opera's dramatic setting to make their impact.

But the principals of *Porgy and Bess* are portrayed as members of a larger community whose identity Gershwin creates through communal songs. Virtually omnipresent on stage and given naturally to musical expression, the residents of Catfish Row sing their own richly varied self-portrait. Rather than borrowing 'spirituals', Gershwin composed his own, which range in mood and technique from songful exaltation ('Leavin' for the Promise' Lan'', 1.ii) and consolation ('Clara, Clara', 3.i) to stark desolation ('Gone, gone, gone', 1.ii) and even simultaneously chanted individual prayers ('Oh, doctor Jesus', 2.iv). On the secular side, Catfish Row's uninhibited social mores can be glimpsed in the opening 'Jazzbo Brown' scene, and are more fully revealed in the fisherman Jake's bemused commentary on romance ('A woman is a sometime thing', 1.i) and a barbaric episode, complete with vocables and tom-toms, during the Kittiwah Island picnic ('I ain' got no shame', 2.ii). In that last scene, the amoral Sportin' Life gets the community, softened up by a day of carousing, to join him in a mockery of biblical teaching, sung in call-and-response fashion replete with blue notes ('It ain't necessarily so').

Finally, Gershwin tapped his reservoir of melody

not only in arias and choruses but in recitatives, aptly termed by Lawrence Starr 'potential song' – declamatory passages from which songful moments may be coaxed by understanding performers. Among many such places in the score, Bess's plea that Crown allow her to return from the picnic to Porgy's side is one of the most economically effective. Here, Bess's character stands revealed. Lacking a true moral compass, torn between love for the upright Porgy and lust for the formidable Crown, she moves in just eight bars from reasonable explanation to the edge of despair. Gershwin restricts her to a word-bound vocal line that, as it rises over a static chordal background, calls more and more on the singer's expressive powers. Elsewhere in the work, he sometimes shapes the drama through musical complication, as in Crown and Robbins's battle, fought to a savage, portentous fugue (1.i). Here, he trusts the performer to convey the precise moment in which Bess's good intentions collapse, then supports her confession of defeat with the opera's most tortured song of all ('What you want wid Bess?').   R.Cd.

Prince Igor [*Knyaz' Igor'*]

Opera in a prologue and four acts by Alexander Porfir'yevich Borodin to his own libretto after a scenario by Vladimir Vasil'yevich Stasov largely based on the anonymous (?) 12th-century epic *Slovo o polku Igoreve* ('The Lay of the Host of Igor'); St Petersburg, Mariinsky Theatre, 23 October/4 November 1890.

At the première Ivan Alexandrovich Mel'nikov sang Prince Igor; Mikhail Mikhaylovich Koryakin, Khan Konchak; Mariya Slavina, Konchakovna; Olga Olghina, Yaroslavna.

Igor Svyatoslavich *Prince of Seversk*	baritone
Yaroslavna *his second wife*	soprano
Vladimir Igorevich *his son by his first marriage*	tenor
Vladimir Yaroslavich [Galitsky] *Prince of Galich, brother of Yaroslavna*	high bass
Konchak *Polovtsian khans*	bass
Gzak	silent
Konchakovna *daughter of Khan Konchak*	contralto
Ovlur *a baptized Polovtsian*	tenor
Skula *gudok (rebec) players*	bass
Yeroshka	tenor
Yaroslavna's Nurse	soprano
Polovtsian Maiden	soprano
Russian princes and princesses, boyars and boyarïnyas, elders, Russian warriors, maidens,	

crowd; Polovtsian khans, girlfriends of
Konchakovna, slave girls of Khan Konchak,
Russian prisoners, Polovtsian guards
Setting The city of Putivl' and a Polovtsian
encampment, 1185

Borodin worked on the opera between 1869 and 1887, and left it unfinished. The project had its origin in a scenario prepared by Vladimir Stasov, at Borodin's request but at Stasov's own choice, from Russia's earliest literary classic (supplemented by episodes and descriptions from two Kievan chronicles, the *Ipatiyevskaya* and the *Lavrentiyevskaya*). The possibly spurious 'Lay of the Host of Igor', describing a 12th-century princeling's ill-fated campaign against a nomadic Turkic tribe that was interfering with trade routes to the south, seemed to Stasov to answer to all of Borodin's poetic and musical strengths: 'broad epic themes, national character, the most diversified *dramatis personae*, passion, drama, the Orient in all its varied manifestations'. In short, the opera was to be another *Ruslan and Lyudmila*, the only significant difference being one of tone: earnestly nationalist (as befitted its time and place) rather than innocently 'magical'.

Stasov sketched out the scenario during a soirée at the home of Glinka's sister, Lyudmila Shestakova, on the night of 19–20 April (1–2 May) 1869. Three symmetrically disposed acts were planned. The first act portrays the social disintegration of Igor's domain in his absence. The second treats Igor and his son in captivity, corresponding roughly to the two middle acts of the eventual opera. The third act is again set in Putivl', and there is an epilogue, with no counterpart in the opera, set two years later at the wedding of Vladimir and Konchakovna. This epilogue, a transparent derivation from the *Ruslan* finale without precedent in lay or chronicle beyond the tacked-on final chorus, nonetheless epitomizes the scenario's ideology; for while in captivity Igor would not assent to a marriage that would make his son a Polovtsian, he rejoices at home in the same marriage when it 'annexes' the khan's daughter as a Russian and a Christian. Another manifestation of the same double standard is the egregious Ovlur, wholly Stasov's invention (in the scenario he is Yaroslavna's half-Polovtsian retainer), whose treachery against his father's people is heartily approved along with his appeal to Igor to break the bonds of chivalry for the sake of Russian 'honour'. (In the eventual opera Ovlur's connection with Yaroslavna was severed; he appears only in Acts 2 and 3 as a turncoat-*ex-machina*.) Thus *Prince Igor* made overt the pervasive subtext to 19th-century Russian essays in orientalism: the racially justified endorsement of Russia's militaristic expansion to the east. 'We go with trust in God for our faith, our Russia, our people', the operatic Igor anachronistically proclaims, very much in the spirit of the reigning tsar, Alexander II.

Borodin began composing, in the late summer of 1869, with Stasov's first number 'Yaroslavna's Dream', based in part on sketches for an earlier operatic project on Lev Mey's drama, *Tsarskaya nevesta* ('The Tsar's Bride', later the basis of an opera by Rimsky-Korsakov). According to Stasov, Borodin followed it early in 1870 with its 'oriental' counterpart, Konchakovna's cavatina (it should be noted, however, that the extant autograph material for that number dates from 1874–5), based in principle on Stasov material but not explicitly provided for. Next (again following Stasov rather than the extant manuscripts) came the chorus of khans, probably adapted from an Oprichniks' chorus in *The Tsar's Bride* – a purely decorative number that could fit here or there or anywhere in the middle act. These were early signs that Borodin's musical fantasy (like Glinka's before him) was going to have its head without concern for dramatic consequences. There is irony in this disregard; as early as March 1870, cold feet about the project's dramatic viability coupled with not unreasonable doubts as to his own competence as a librettist (exacerbated by the humiliating failure of Cui's *William Ratcliff*) caused Borodin to suspend work. Some of his musical sketches went into the Second Symphony, begun the next year, and into *Mlada*, the opera-ballet on which four of the Five worked for a while in 1872. It was only after that project aborted without hope of salvage that Borodin returned to *Igor*. The *Mlada* music, parts of the finale excepted, circled back into the work from which it had mainly been drawn.

It is at present fruitless to attempt a detailed chronology of the opera's piecemeal accumulation from this point. This must await further scholarly studies of the MS. The salient points are as follows.

Most of the Polovtsian music (and also Yaroslavna's Lament, which evidently picked up in this way the somewhat oriental flavour that has nonplussed some writers) was written in 1875. Igor's aria, no.13, was originally composed in 1875 as a modest recitative-arioso to an entirely different text; its replacement, based in part on the *Mlada* music, was composed in 1881. In 1878, following another break in his work, Borodin introduced Skula and Yeroshka, the pair of comical rebec players associated with Galitsky. They were obviously modelled on Varlaam and Missaïl, the tenor-bass pair of vagabond monks in *Boris Godunov*. (This correspondence extends to their musical idiom, largely modelled, in the prologue and finale, on the prose recitatives in Musorgsky's Inn Scene.) 1879 saw the composition of the bulk of Act 1; in 1880 Borodin composed a new conclusion for the act (later dropped, either by the composer or by his posthumous collaborators). The prologue, which followed in 1883, was an attempt to fill an obvious lacuna caused in Stasov's scenario by the absence of the title character before Act 2; the narration of the fateful eclipse was now replaced by its direct, if slightly anachronistic, portrayal. The last major decision was taken in 1884, when Borodin detached the escape and made it the basis of a separate act, Act 3, in which some of the overflow Polovtsian music (March, Procession of khans, Konchak's song, etc.) might find a home.

By the time of his sudden death in 1887 Borodin had orchestrated a miscellaneous group of ten numbers from the opera, mostly for concert performances at the Free Music School under Balakirev and Rimsky-Korsakov between 1876 and 1879. Besides the chorus of praise and its reprise in the prologue, the group included nos.2b, 4 and 5 from Act l; 9, 11, 15 and 17 from Act 2; and 25 and 29 from Act 4. Rimsky-Korsakov, who had actually begun a version of the opera in 1885 with the composer's active collaboration (in the process filling some gaps in the prologue), now undertook to complete it. As he had employed his former pupil Lyadov to assist with the orchestration of the Polovtsian dances in 1879, he now enlisted as his assistant the 21-year-old Glazunov – a favourite of Borodin's during the latter's last five years and possessor of a phenomenal musical memory. Rimsky retouched and scored the middle section of the prologue and all the unorchestrated portions of Acts 1, 2 and 4, plus the Polovtsian March in Act 3, adding verbal and musical transitions as needed. Glazunov's role was more creative: he had virtually to compose the bulk of the third act (1252 bars) on the basis of sometimes very fragmentary sketches. The extent of his role in the composition of the overture must remain unsettled, as he evaluated it differently at different times; on the basis of notations on Borodin's manuscripts ('This will do for a first theme', 'Good for a second theme' etc.), it has been asserted that Glazunov composed it outright.

Doubts about the correspondence between the structurally and dramaturgically lopsided performing version thus produced and the composer's final intentions were inevitable. It has been demonstrated that Rimsky and Glazunov had pruned away some 1787 bars of music, amounting to almost one fifth of the total that Borodin had composed. Several alternative performing versions have been put forth, the most substantial being that prepared in the early 1970s by a troika consisting of a young musicologist (Levashov), a veteran composer (Yury Fortunatov) and the chief régisseur of the Moscow Bol'shoy Theatre (Boris Pokrovsky). First produced in Vilnius in 1974, it was given thereafter at the Deutsche Staatsoper in Berlin and published there in 1978. The chief differences pertain to Act 3. In the alternative version a trio of princes, two of them new characters, swear mutual fealty; the familiar trio (no.23) is cut down to a duet (without Igor) to match its counterpart in *Mlada*; the Russian prisoners sing an invocation to the River Don to the music of the *Mlada* finale; most controversially, the 1875 version of Igor's aria is reinstated alongside its 1881 successor, which retains its place in Act 2. In addition, the 1880 ending to Act 1 (Galitsky's rebellion) is restored (culminating in Galitsky's death on the ramparts of Putivl'), and an epilogue corresponding to Stasov's is appended.

*

Prologue *The market place in Putivl'* Igor sets off on his campaign against the Polovtsï despite an ill-presaging eclipse and the entreaties of Yaroslavna, his wife; Skula and Yeroshka desert (no.l).

Act I.i *The court of Prince Vladimir Galitsky* Skula and Yeroshka lead a paean to Igor's profligate brother-in-law and recount how he abducted a maiden for his pleasure (no.2a: chorus, 'Slava, slava Volodimiru': 'All hail, Vladimir'). Galitsky announces his philosophy (no.2b, recitative and song, 'Greshno tait': ya skuki ne lyublyu': "Twere a sin to hide it: I hate a dreary life'). He mocks his sister Yaroslavna's disapproval (no.2c, recitative). A crowd of maidens rushes in to protest at the abduction; Galitsky sends them on their way (no.2d, chorus and *scena*, 'Oy, likhon'ko! Oy, goryushko!': 'Oh, what misfortune, oh, what sorrow'). The men briefly show their fear of Yaroslavna (no.2e) but, turning their attention to wine, resume singing Galitsky's praises: he should be their prince, not Igor (no.2f: Princely Song, 'Chto u knyazya da Volodomira': 'At Prince Vladimir's').

I.ii *Chamber in Yaroslavna's quarters* Yaroslavna, pining for Igor, suffers from evil dreams (no.3, arioso, 'Nemalo vremeni proshlo': 'No little time has passed'). The Nurse announces the arrival of the maidens, who complain of Galitsky's behaviour in a Glinka-esque 5/4 metre (no.4). Galitsky unexpectedly arrives, frightens off the maidens, attempts to laugh off his sister's reproaches, but in the end agrees to release the abducted girl (no.5); he leaves. A party of boyars comes to Yaroslavna with terrible news: Igor and his son Vladimir have been taken prisoner by the Polovtsï. An alarm sounds: a Polovtsian force under Khan Gzak attacks Putivl' (no.6, finale).

Act 2 *The Polovtsian encampment; evening* A chorus of Polovtsian maidens entertain Konchakovna with a hymn to the cool refreshment of evening (no.7, 'Na bezvod'ye, dnyom na solntse vyanet tsvetik': 'In the absence of water the flower withers in the sun by day'), and go into their dance (no.8, 'Dance of the Polovtsian Maidens'). Konchakovna has fallen in love with the son of her father's enemy, Vladimir, and sings of her expected tryst with him (no.9, cavatina, 'Merknet svet dnevnoy': 'The daylight dies'). Russian prisoners march by on their way back from forced labour. Konchakovna bids the maidens refresh them. The Polovtsian patrol, Ovlur among them, make their round. Ovlur furtively remains onstage when they depart (no.l0). Vladimir cautiously makes his way to Konchakovna's tent and sings of their tryst (no.11, recitative and cavatina, 'Gde tï, gde': 'Where art thou, where'). Konchakovna appears, and the lovers sing in ecstasy (no.12, duet, 'Ti li Vladimir moy?': 'Is it you, Vladimir mine?'). They scamper off at the sound of Igor's approach. He sings an elaborate aria in two parts, the first expressing his passionate thirst for freedom, the second his tender thoughts of Yaroslavna (no.13, 'Ni sna, ni otdïkha': 'Nor sleep, nor rest of any kind'). Ovlur seizes the moment: he approaches Igor and proposes a plan of escape. Igor at first refuses to consider such a dishonourable course, but vacillates (no.14); Ovlur disappears. Khan Konchak enters, oozing magnanimity towards his 'honoured guest' (no.l5, aria, 'Zdorov li, Knyaz?': 'How goes it, Prince?'). He offers to grant Igor's freedom in return for a pledge of non-aggression, even suggesting they become allies; to all of this Igor firmly refuses, much to Konchak's admiration (no.16). The khan orders entertainment from his slaves, offering Igor his pick of the maidens (no.17, Polovtsian dance[s] with chorus).

Act 3 *An outpost of the encampment* Khan Gzak returns from Putivl', prisoners in tow, to a tumultuous greeting from Khan Konchak and the Polovtsï, while the Russians look on and seethe (no.18, Polovtsian March). Konchak sings a song of triumph (no.19, 'Nash mech nam dal pobedu': 'Our sword has given us victory'). He orders a feast (no.20a); the khans go off to divide the spoils (no.20b, chorus, 'Idyom za nim sovet derzhat': 'We'll follow him and hold council'); the Russians bewail their defeat and urge Igor to accept Ovlur's offer (no.20c). The Polovtsï drink and dance themselves into a stupor (no.21, chorus and dance, 'Podoben solntsu khan Konchak': 'Khan Konchak is like unto the sun'). Ovlur summons Igor (no.22). Konchakovna, having heard of the plan, runs onstage; she contends with Igor over Vladimir, Igor making his appeal to the tune of his 'freedom' aria. Finally she rouses the camp, and Igor must make off without his son (no.23, trio, 'Ya vsyo, ya vsyo uznala': 'I've found out everything'). The Polovtsï threaten Vladimir, but Konchak, ever magnanimous, spares him and even blesses his union with Konchakovna (no.24, finale).

Act 4 *At the Putivl' town wall* Yaroslavna laments her fate and that of her husband (no.25, Yaroslavna's Lament: 'Akh! plachu ya gor'ko': 'Ah, bitterly I

weep'). Some passers-by sing a lament of their own at the fate of Putivl', a masterly and justly famous stylization of folk heterophonic polyphony (no.26, Chorus of villagers, 'Okh, ne buynïy veter zavïval': 'Oh, it was not a stormy wind that howled'). Yaroslavna's dejected mood is broken by the sound of approaching hoofbeats; she recognizes Igor from afar. When he dismounts she rushes to him and they exchange ecstatic greetings (no.27, recitative and duet, 'On – moy sokol yasnïy!': 'It is he, my bright falcon'). Skula and Yeroshka blunder onstage carousing, recognize Igor with panic from afar, save their skins by ringing the tocsin to announce the prince's return and gratuitously declare their loyalty (no.28, song to the rebec, *scena* and chorus). The opera ends with a joyful chorus of greeting (no.29, 'Znat', gospod' mol'bï uslïshal': 'We know the Lord has heard our prayers').

*

Borodin, a chemist by profession, had very few works performed or published during his lifetime; *Prince Igor* is his magnum opus. The opera's protracted gestation has suggested parallels with *Siegfried* and *Les Troyens*, but the most fitting comparison is with that other great unwieldy Russian torso, Musorgsky's *Khovanshchina*, like *Prince Igor* a historical opera to the composer's own gradually accumulating and ideologically inconstant libretto. Both were left for others to complete; neither can be said to have achieved definitive form within its author's lifetime. Perhaps most importantly, *Khovanshchina* and *Prince Igor* had Vladimir Stasov in common. The great tribune (and christener) of the Mighty Five (Balakirev, Borodin, Cui, Musorgsky and Rimsky-Korsakov), a librarian by profession, Stasov had a hand in the conception of many of the group's most characteristic works, but in none did he play so important a role as in Borodin's opera.

From the perspective of the later 19th century a *Ruslan*-esque opera could not seem anything but anachronistic in concept and design: even Borodin's fellow-member of the Five, César Cui, called it 'an opera in the narrow and, perhaps, outmoded sense'. Its musical beauties have redeemed it, and the 'epic' genre to which it is said to belong has provided a trusty excuse for its glaring structural gaps (the fates of two major characters being unknown at the final curtain) and its superfluities (much of the love and dance music in the middle pair of acts). At the same time, the work's reputation as an 'operatic picture book' has justified the crudest sort of play-doctoring, such as the 'traditional' omission of Act 3.

Like *Ruslan*, Borodin's opera derived its dramatic rhythm from an opposition of national musical idioms: rigorously Russian versus promiscuously 'oriental'. The former, in *Igor*, is based – though perhaps not as strictly as some have maintained – on 'intonations' from epic ballads and on a small repertory of folksongs. The latter ranges in *Igor* from Arabian to Turkic to Finno-Ugric vernaculars.

Act 2, the only one that Borodin may plausibly be said to have completed (though even this was much retouched by Glazunov and Rimsky-Korsakov: the Prisoners' Chorus was reconstructed from memory by the former to a text by the latter), may serve as paradigm of his operatic manner, and also of the way in which a thoroughly static, formal, conventional (and in some ways inept) conception of the genre is enlivened (and, in corresponding ways, redeemed) by music so fresh and alluring as to keep the opera perpetually alive on the fringes of the repertory.

The act is framed by decorative 'oriental' numbers that set the scene and supply the routine choreographic diversion endemic to grand-operatic second acts. The subplot, the romance of Igor's son Vladimir and his captor's daughter Konchakovna, is given a risibly redundant exposition: lengthy da capo cavatinas for each (Konchakovna's, accompanied by the chorus in Rimsky-Korsakov's version, being a virtual replay of the act's decorative opening), separated by a pair of tiny choral numbers which serve to bring Ovlur furtively on stage, and followed by a duet, longer than the two cavatinas combined, that is cast in equally stereotypical format. The lovers having sung, they depart, almost as if in a Baroque opera, to make way for the title character, who enters to sing his aria of remorse and longing, the opera's centrepiece. This, the largest of all the musical structures in *Prince Igor*, is once again in da capo form but with the reprise modified to produce a climax. After a brief *scena*, Igor's aria is followed by another extended aria for another bass soloist, his captor Khan Konchak, who, like Igor, enters for no other purpose than to sing. The only real dramatic confrontation in the act takes place during the little *scena* between the bass arias when Ovlur steps out of the shadows to propose to Igor an escape plan. Otherwise the act is a classic 'concert in costume', one large vocal number following (but hardly motivated by) another.

The second act of *Prince Igor* would no doubt be just as silly as this description has made it seem were it not for the fact that every number in it is a masterpiece. Borodin's exotic idiom, though it followed and enlarged upon the examples of Glinka (the Ratmir scenes in *Ruslan*) and Balakirev (*Islamey*, *Tamara*), and though it to some extent incorporated source tunes culled from books, was an intensely personal yet flexible style, of all Borodinesque idioms the one most instantly identifiable as the composer's, and adaptable to a great range of emotional expression. Borodin's 'orientalism' is the supreme musical expression of *nega*, the lush languor of the orient as viewed through European eyes. More *nega*

is evoked by the tessitura of Konchakovna's contralto, unexpected in an *ingénue* role. When her voice coils around and eventually beneath Vladimir's as the love duet reaches its climax, the effect is startling, redeeming the insipid verbal text. The concluding Polovtsian dances (which, when performed as a suite, begin with the orchestrally inventive maidens' dance, no.8) marked an epoch for French musicians when introduced by Dyagilev in 1909.

The definitive version of Igor's aria was written in 1881, in full accord with the composer's lyric impulse and in manifest emulation of the title character's battlefield soliloquy in *Ruslan*. The stately themes of its vast da capo structure are concerned, respectively, with Igor's freedom to seek personal glory, and with tender thoughts of his waiting wife, Yaroslavna. The composer's belief in 'artistic truth' over the literal variety (what was then known as realism) is affirmed by Yaroslavna's reprise of Igor's love theme – which, so to speak, we have never seen her hear – when she sings of her corresponding longing in Act 4. Withal, Borodin could be an excellent musical dramatist when that, rather than totemic portraiture, was his purpose. The terse final scene with Ovlur between the big bass arias is a masterly study in character and contrast. Ovlur retains an 'oriental' tendency towards insinuating melisma as against Igor's syllabic steadfastness, but the fast tempo and the obsessive ostinato repetitions endow his responses with a suitable dramatic tension, and the tellingly sparse accompaniment in two- or three-part counterpoint manages to retain a whiff of the lush Polovtsian harmonic idiom even as it conveys urgency rather than the usual *nega*.

A few more scenes like that (and there is reason to believe they might have been supplied had the composer lived), and *Prince Igor* would have needed no excuses. As it is, the opera is a magnificent farrago, a smorgåsbord from which all listeners and critics seem to find some morsel to their taste. As Borodin put it in a letter, 'Curiously enough, all the members of our circle seem to come together on my *Igor*: from the ultra-innovatory realist Modest Petrovich [Musorgsky], to the lyric-dramatic innovator César Antonovich [Cui], to the martinet with respect to outward form and musical tradition Nikolay Andreyevich [Rimsky-Korsakov], to the ardent champion of novelty and power in all things, Vladimir Vasil'yevich Stasov. Everyone is satisfied with *Igor*, strongly though they may differ about other things'.   R.T.

Prophète, Le ('The Prophet')

Grand opera in five acts by Giacomo Meyerbeer to a libretto by Eugène Scribe; Paris, Opéra, 16 April 1849.

Pauline Viardot sang Fidès at the premiere; Gustave-Hippolyte Roger (John), Jeanne Castellan (Berthe) and Nicolas Levasseur (Zacharie) were also in the cast.

Jean de Leyde [John of Leyden]		tenor
Fidès *his mother*		mezzo-soprano
Berthe *betrothed to John*		soprano
Jonas		tenor
Mathisen	*Anabaptists*	bass or baritone
Zacharie		bass
Count Oberthal		bass

Peasants, Anabaptists, soldiers, burghers and
   children
Setting The Low Countries and Westphalia,
   1530

Among the opera projects that Meyerbeer contemplated following the première of *Les Huguenots* in 1836 were *L'Africaine* and *Le prophète*, with his seasoned collaborator Eugène Scribe. The first was abandoned after one act had been drafted, when it became clear that the soprano Cornélie Falcon, for whom Meyerbeer had intended the title role, was losing her voice. On 2 August 1838 Meyerbeer and Scribe signed a formal contract for *Le prophète*, by the terms of which the composer agreed to complete the opera within two years.

The first edition of the libretto includes an excerpt from Voltaire's *Essai sur les moeurs* outlining the historical context of the Anabaptist revolt in 16th-century Germany and the role in that uprising of a certain Jean from Leyden. Other possible literary sources for the libretto include a novel, *Die Anabaptisten* (1826), by Franz Carl Van Der Velde and the *Mémoires de Luther*, a collection of letters, anecdotes and articles assembled by the French historian Jules Michelet. In an essay entitled 'Anabaptistes de Münster' Michelet actually refers to Jean as a 'prophète' and suggests that well before the event he had premonitions about being crowned, like the protagonist in Meyerbeer's work. The dramatic highlight of the opera is the encounter between John and his mother during his coronation; the parallel between this episode and the scene in Schiller's *Jungfrau von Orleans* ('The Maid of Orléans') where Joan is confronted by her father was certainly not lost on Meyerbeer, though whether *Jungfrau* actually provided the creative spark for the operatic scene is unclear.

On assuming directorship of the Opéra in 1840, Léon Pillet informed the composer that a production of *Le prophète* was a priority. Meyerbeer, however, harboured doubts about the suitability of the Opéra roster for his new work. At first he thought that Rosine Stoltz, the Opéra's leading contralto and mistress of the director, would not project well the role of Fidès. His increased confidence in her abilities was soon counter-balanced by growing suspicions about Pillet's commitment to his work. In 1843 it became clear that the powers of Gilbert Duprez, the house's leading tenor, were in decline. Subsequently, the selection of a tenor for the title role became the main issue of contention between Meyerbeer and Pillet: Meyerbeer's two preferred candidates, Gaetano Fraschini and Mario de Candia, were never engaged by the Opéra in this period. Meanwhile Meyerbeer had returned to his native Berlin (1842), where he was appointed Generalmusikdirektor and settled down to direct and compose for the court orchestra.

Renewed impetus for a production of *Le prophète* came when Charles Duponchel and Nestor Roqueplan took over as directors of the Opéra in 1847. By that time Rosine Stoltz was no longer a viable Fidès, and Meyerbeer settled upon Viardot, whom he had actually wanted from the start. He agreed to Roger, a veteran singer from the Opéra-Comique, though with some reservations about stamina which were in part borne out, since Meyerbeer found himself having to reduce the role of John for him. Meyerbeer indulged Castellan's request for an entrance aria by supplying the *cavatine* 'Mon coeur s'élance et palpite' in Act 1, which he explicitly excluded from complete vocal scores. *Le prophète* was a great success at its première, due not only to effective musico-dramatic situations but also to the ballet, in which the effect of ice skating was simulated by equipping the dancers with roller-skates, and the sensational effect of the rising sun in Act 3, the first use of electricity on the stage of the Opéra.

*

Act I *Outside Count Oberthal's castle near Dordrecht*
Following a brief instrumental prelude, the scene is set by a pastoral chorus with conventional rustic touches (open 5ths in the low strings and imitation of shepherds' pipes), as well as a more unusual orchestral effect of small sheep bells rendered by triangle, piccolo and pizzicato strings. Berthe meets her prospective mother-in-law, Fidès, and explains that she must obtain authorization from Count Oberthal to marry John. Three Anabaptists enter, intoning Latin words in unison to a dark accompaniment of bassoons and horns. The architecture of the subsequent number mirrors the spread of discontent among the peasants: an exposition of social evils by each of the three Anabaptists is punctuated by statements of 'Ad nos ad salutarem'; individual peasants begin to show interest, the

tempo increases and there is a unison choral rendition of 'Ad nos'; the number closes with an even more rousing march chorus as the peasants arm themselves with pitchforks and axes and assume ranks. This brings the feudal lord Count Oberthal out of his castle. He does not establish a strong musical presence as he dismisses the seditious activities of the Anabaptists in nondescript recitative; from the musical point of view, the stage instructions for peasants to cower before him are scarcely credible. Berthe asks Oberthal for permission to marry John in a strophic *romance*, 'Un jour dans les flots de la Meuse', in which Fidès echoes the end of Berthe's phrases and the two combine in the refrain. Oberthal refuses and orders his soldiers to seize Berthe and Fidès and disperse the peasants; 'Ad nos' is heard in the distance as the two women are led away.

Act 2 *The interior of John's inn at Leyden* A rustic waltz chorus is the musical backdrop for John's expressions of longing for Berthe, and for the discovery by the three Anabaptists that he bears a striking resemblance to an altar painting of King David in Münster. When alone with the Anabaptists, John reveals a recent dream: to music that will be heard in the coronation scene in Act 4 he tells of being heralded as the Messiah and then dragged to hell by Satan. In a strophic pastorale, 'Pour Berthe moi je soupire', he sings of his love for her; between the stanzas the Anabaptists, who see John as politically useful, try to enlist him by suggesting softly with staccato singing that, just as in his dream, he is destined to rule. These words do not strike a responsive chord, but just then Berthe rushes in, begging John to hide her. Oberthal, who wants her for himself, follows and threatens to execute Fidès if Berthe is not given up; disgusted, John throws her into the hands of the soldiers and Fidès is freed. In a tender number with reduced scoring featuring muted cellos, Fidès blesses John. The Anabaptists reappear, and this time John, eager to wreak revenge upon Oberthal, places his faith in them. He is told, however, that in order to assume leadership of their forces he must leave his homeland and his mother for ever. Recalling Fidès's arioso, John balks at first, but cannot resist the call of the Anabaptists after a twofold rendition of a martial ensemble promising the end of feudal tyranny.

Act 3.i *The camp of the Anabaptists in the Westphalian forest* While sounds of battle are heard in the distance and aristocratic prisoners are led in, the Anabaptist forces express their fanaticism with repeated snap rhythms on strong beats and a unison passage in which they voice their hatred. In strophic *couplets* of swaggering bravado Zacharie revels in the apparent might of the Anabaptist forces ('Aussi nombreux que les étoiles'). Men and women bearing

provisions skate towards the camp: a sforzando followed by a rapid diminuendo on a sustained chord in each bar suggests the motion of skating. The soldiers enjoy a moment of repose as they are served food and drink and are entertained with a ballet. (The music for this was to be recycled in 1937 for the Frederick Ashton ballet *Les patineurs*.)

3.ii *Inside Zacharie's tent* Mathisen agrees with Zacharie that Münster must be taken soon and leaves to rouse the soldiers. Oberthal has stumbled into the Anabaptist camp and is brought before Jonas and Zacharie, who do not recognize him in the dark. Seeing a chance to enter Münster, Oberthal declares that he will join the Anabaptist cause. In a trio with ensemble refrains he swears, tongue in cheek, that he would gladly hang assorted aristocrats at the first opportunity; in a lilting 6/8 passage with interspersed 'tra-la-las' Jonas casually tells him that Oberthal *père* has been executed. When Jonas lights a lamp the real identity of the guest is discovered and the final refrain follows, with grim ironic effect: whereas the first two refrains were those of a drinking-song, the third retains the same music but Jonas and Zacharie sing of Oberthal's impending execution and Oberthal expresses unbridled hatred of the Anabaptists. Just as Oberthal is about to be led off, John appears, in deep reflection about the Anabaptists as well as the intertwined fates of the two women in his life: the orchestra sounds the music of his earlier pastorale about Berthe as he actually sings of his mother. Oberthal informs him that Berthe has been seen alive in Münster. John immediately orders that he be spared, and an attack on the city mounted. Mathisen runs in with the news that there is a revolt among Anabaptist soldiers.

3.iii *The Anabaptist camp* A chorus of rebellious soldiers is the first section of a multi-sectional finale; C major veers suddenly to B major to underscore a *fortissimo* 'mort à l'imposteur'. In a remarkable passage of declamation following the chorus, John, now aware of his charismatic power, forces his disenchanted troops to kneel. A prayer led by the prophet forms the slow section of the number. Following a transition in which, to the accompaniment of harps, John tells of a celestial vision, a 'Hymne triomphal' functions as the *strette*. This culminates in a scenic *coup* before the curtain: the sun rising as the troops prepare for battle.

Act 4.i *A public square in Münster* The city has been taken and a chorus of inhabitants alternates *piano* complaints about the oppressive rule of the Anabaptists and the cruelty of their leader with *forte* affirmations of loyalty to the prophet as his patrols pass by. Fidès, unaware of the prophet's identity, comes begging for alms ('Donnez pour une pauvre âme'). The number is strophic, but in the second strophe Meyerbeer brings in the voice part on an E♭, taking the music to G minor after the prevailing E tonic, thereby intensifying Fidès's expression of distress. Berthe appears and recognizes Fidès. In the agitated first section of a duet she tells of her futile search for John and then, to a broadening of the tempo, exudes joy that she is in Fidès's arms. The latter has been tricked by the Anabaptists into believing that John is dead; following a static ensemble in which both commiserate in extensive parallel singing, Fidès attributes his demise to the work of the prophet, who has grown increasingly bloodthirsty. In the *cabalette* of the duet Berthe vows that she will kill this odious tyrant, while Fidès assumes a more passive position in prayer.

4.ii *The cathedral at Münster* A large crowd has gathered to witness the coronation of John the prophet as a new emperor. To a grand processional march, featuring a family of saxhorns and a trumpet melody (foreshadowing that in Act 2 of Verdi's *Aida*), the electors enter with various imperial accoutrements, followed by John himself. The entire populace kneels in prayer. Fidès appears and, in a fine passage marked 'avec exaltation' in which the voice sweeps rapidly between extremes of tessitura, she vows to strike the prophet. A chorus of children hails John as the prophet-king, and with halting *pianissimo* declamation John concludes that he must be the son of God. His personal reverie and the entire public ceremony are abruptly cut off by Fidès's exclamation of 'Mon fils!' in recognition of her own son, the *coup de théâtre* that spawns the slow section of this finale. John, seeing danger, refuses to admit that he knows the woman. In response to a faction that questions his claim of divine origin, John forces Fidès to repudiate her relationship to him: when he offers to give up his life on the spot if her claim can be substantiated, maternal instinct leads Fidès to declare that he is not her son after all.

Act 5.i *A vaulted cellar beneath the Münster palace* In a brief exchange Jonas, Mathisen and Zacharie agree that, to ensure their own safety, they will deliver the prophet to the imperial armies advancing on the city. They depart and Fidès is led in. In the slow section of a *grand air* ('O toi qui m'abandonnes') she pardons her son for his treatment of her; learning that he intends to appear, she expresses hope that he will see reason and relinquish his iron-fisted power, the music of her *cabalette* returning to the heroic sweep of the music marked 'avec exaltation' in the coronation scene. Fidès assumes the dominant position dramatically, as well as in sheer quantity of music, in the subsequent duet. First she unleashes her anger at her son in a driving allegro replete with dotted rhythms. She orders John to give up power and assures him that, if he does this, celestial pardon will be his. John's direct acknowledgement of Fidès as his mother ignites the final *cabalette*. Berthe happens upon the

'Le prophète' (Meyerbeer), Pauline Viardot as Fidès and Giovanni Mario as John of Leyden in the London première (1849) at Covent Garden: lithograph from a contemporary sheet music cover

two and explains that she intends to set fire to the palace in order to destroy the prophet. She is overjoyed to see John alive, not connecting him with the tyrannical ruler; in music that recalls the pastoral vein and tonality of the Act 2 waltz, the three sing of the joy of a humble existence. When an officer enters and addresses John as the prophet, Berthe is horrified; following a *strette* capped by a torrent of coloratura, she stabs herself. John resolves to seek revenge on the three Anabaptists and the advancing forces of order.

5.ii *A large hall in the palace* Those assembled celebrate the glory of the prophet in song and dance. John tells two officers to allow the enemy to enter and warns them that he has ignited the saltpetre in the cellar. Assuming a convivial air, he launches a strophic drinking song; the second strophe is interrupted by the entry of the three Anabaptists, Oberthal and imperial troops. As Fidès joins her son in the final strophe of the song, an explosion is heard, and the walls of the palace collapse.

*

The première of *Le prophète* took place at a time that was particularly propitious for its box office fortunes and offers one example among several of how Meyerbeer's operas benefited from political events. Since the performance occurred less than a year after the popular uprising of June 1848, *Le prophète* could readily be appropriated by authorities as a piece about the dangers of popular sedition ignited by demagoguery. This was possible especially because the evils of aristocratic authority, the ostensible cause of the Anabaptist revolt, receive very little musico-dramatic projection in the work. The sympathies that are engendered lie mainly with Fidès, the most striking character in *Le prophète* and one with little competition from a romantic female lead whose musical personality is sketchy. Fidès can be seen as a forerunner to La Cieca in Ponchielli's *La Gioconda*; she also could not have been far from Verdi's mind as he forged Azucena in *Il trovatore* within three years of Meyerbeer's première (which he witnessed): like *Le prophète*, *Il trovatore* features an intimate scene between mother and son before the final catastrophe is unleashed.   **S.Hr.**

Punch and Judy

'Tragicomedy or comitragedy' in one act by Harrison Birtwistle to a libretto by Stephen Pruslin; Aldeburgh, Jubilee Hall, 8 June 1968.

The original cast included Maureen Morelle, Geoffrey Chara, Jennifer Hill and John Cameron.

Punch	high baritone
Judy/Fortune Teller	mezzo-soprano
Pretty Polly/Witch	high soprano
Choregos/Jack Ketch	baritone
Lawyer	high tenor
Doctor	deep bass

Birtwistle's first opera was commissioned by the English Opera Group for the Aldeburgh Festival; the original production by Anthony Besch, conducted by David Atherton, was subsequently seen in Edinburgh and London. Despite its critical success and an American première in Minneapolis in 1970, the work was not heard again in Britain until 1979, when Atherton conducted a concert performance in London and a subsequent recording. In 1982 David Freeman staged it for Opera Factory London, a version that was widely seen and subsequently televised. In June 1991 the composer directed a new production at the Aldeburgh Festival.

Cast in a prologue, four scenes (each of three sections) and an epilogue, the musical and dramatic structure of *Punch and Judy* contains the stylized violence of the traditional story within a severely formal mosaic of small-scale closed musical forms; it combines the ritualized rigour of classical Greek drama with a continuous structure of self-contained numbers borrowed from Baroque opera and oratorio (Bach's *St Matthew Passion* was a declared model). The character of Polly represents the positive side of Punch's character, the quest for her offsetting his random acts of violence. There are more than 100 separate musical items labelled in the score, grouped in recurring sequences and cycles.

*

Prologue After a parody fanfare the Choregos appears in front of the curtain to welcome the audience. He underlines the work's mixture of comedy and menace: 'Please to enjoy our little play. If we make you laugh then you need not pay.'

Melodrama 1 The curtain rises on Punch, rocking the baby and singing a threatening lullaby, which ends with his war-cry ('Roo-it-too-it-too-it-too-it-too-it!') as he throws the baby on the fire. Judy enters with her own lullaby and discovers her dead baby; after a word game with Punch she is led to the Altar of Murder while the Choregos offers a commentary. The Murder Ensemble is briefly interrupted by the first Passion Aria, sung by the Doctor and Lawyer as chorus, but Punch stabs Judy and the Choregos leads her to the gibbet. Punch sets off on his search for Pretty Polly.

Passion Chorale 1 Framed by short instrumental toccatas, the Choregos with Judy, the Doctor and the Lawyer comment on the crime just committed.

The Quest for Pretty Polly 1 In a sequence of six short numbers (Travel Music, Weather Report, Prayer, Serenade, Pretty Polly's Rhapsody and Moral) that will be repeated three times in the course of the opera, Punch travels on Horsey (a hobby-horse) to seek out Pretty Polly. An astronomical clock shows that Punch is suspended between heaven and earth, under the sign of the Crab on a summer's afternoon; the Weather Report foretells a tempest from the east at three o'clock. Polly is discovered sitting on a pedestal in a green spotlight. Punch serenades Polly but fails to impress her with his offer of a huge sunflower (it is tainted by the fire in which the baby died), and the Choregos is left to offer commiserations: 'Weep, my Punch, Weep out your unfathomable, inexpressible sorrow.'

Melodrama 2 After a short instrumental sinfonia the Doctor and Lawyer confront Punch with his crime: 'The law of the land is the medicine of mankind'. Punch lures them into a game of riddles and eventually leads them both to the Altar; the Choregos announces their deaths, and Punch stabs them both, the Doctor with a giant syringe, the Lawyer with a huge quill pen.

Passion Chorale 2 After they have been taken to the gibbet, Punch resumes his quest for Pretty Polly.

The Quest for Pretty Polly 2 The sequence of events and musical numbers is repeated: Punch is now suspended between heaven and earth under the sign of the Scorpion at twilight in autumn. Pretty Polly is found this time in a red spotlight, and she dismisses Punch's offering of a huge jewel because it is flawed by the suffering of his victims. The Choregos is again ironically sympathetic.

Melodrama 3 After 'A little Canonic Prelude to Disaster', the second half of the work begins with the Choregos entering the action of the opera. He confronts Punch as they celebrate Pretty Polly: 'Let her be praised in singsong and psalm'. But despite Judy's intervention from the Chorus Gibbet in a Recitative and Passion Aria 2, the Doctor and Lawyer proclaim the Choregos's demise and at the height of the jollity Punch saws him to death inside a bass-viol case. But the Choregos's murder has destroyed the ritual symmetries of the action, as the chorus sings his lament.

Nightmare There is no search this time; after a Transition and the third Travel Music and Weather Report, now showing Punch between heaven and hell at midnight, the Choregos and the Chorus describe a nightmare: 'United in fear, man and landscape dissolve into the whiteness of a shriek'. Punch appears at a fortune teller's booth to consult the Tarot cards; after three Tarot games Judy is revealed as the Fortune Teller. There is a Black Wedding: Punch and Judy are led to Pretty Polly's pedestal, now transformed into a wedding altar; Pretty Polly herself is disguised as a witch. Punch is taunted and scourged, and confronted with the details of his crimes in an Adding-song: 'A fractured skull, a bleeding face, a severed limb, an oozing eye, a twisted neck'. At its climax Punch calls out for Horsey and faints.

The Quest for Pretty Polly 3 The quest is shortened to four numbers; Punch is between heaven and earth under the sign of the Goat, at dawn in winter. But Pretty Polly's pedestal is empty under a blue spotlight; again Punch is comforted by the Choregos.

Passion Chorale 3 Framed by toccatas, Punch's four victims envisage the possibility of a redemptive love.

Melodrama 4 Punch is in prison and condemned to death. The Choregos appears disguised as Jack Ketch the hangman, though Punch soon establishes who he really is and persuades him to put his own head in the noose. After a final war cry, he hangs Jack Ketch. This time he has unwittingly done a good deed; Pretty Polly is bathed in brilliant white light.

Punch Triumphans Pretty Polly sings a rhapsody to spring and joins Punch in a love duet. The gallows is transformed into a maypole, as everyone except the Choregos hymns the happy couple.

Epilogue The Choregos brings down the curtain on what he originally announced as a tragedy but has turned out to be a comedy.

*

In the detailed stage directions in the score, as well as in the musical treatment, Birtwistle is at pains to emphasize the ritual aspects of *Punch*: the Choregos is directed to sing from a booth downstage left, Pretty Polly's pedestal is upstage right, and so on. A group of five wind instruments from the 15-piece ensemble is to be seated on stage. Much of the instrumental writing in the score employs extreme tessituras, and

that characteristic gives the opera its distinctive pungency. Yet the vocal writing is widely varied, from rapt ensembles (the Passion Chorales, the Prayers) through fine-spun arias (Punch's Prayer, Judy's Passion Aria 2) to ditties and declamation (Punch's Rules and War Cries); and the music juxtaposes similar contrasts of style. Pruslin's libretto, intricately worked and saturated with alliteration and puns, is extremely effective in conjuring up the stylized world of the opera, in which human weaknesses and emotions are exaggerated to the point of surreal caricature.   A.C.

Puritani, I ('The Puritans')

Melodramma serio in three parts by Vincenzo Bellini to a libretto by Carlo Pepoli after the play by J.-A. F.-P. Ancelot and Xavier (J. X. Boniface *dit* Saintine), *Têtes Rondes et Cavaliers*; Paris, Théâtre Italien, 24 January 1835.

The original cast included Giulia Grisi (Elvira), Giovanni Battista Rubini (Arturo), Antonio Tamburini (Riccardo) and Luigi Lablache (Giorgio), who collectively became known as the *Puritani* quartet.

Lord Gualtiero Walton *Governor General*	
of the fortress	bass
Sir Giorgio *brother of Lord Walton, retired*	
Puritan colonel	bass
Lord Arturo Talbo *Cavalier, Stuart*	
sympathizer	tenor
Sir Riccardo Forth *Puritan colonel*	baritone
Sir Bruno Robertson *Puritan officer*	tenor
Enrichetta di Francia [Queen	
Henrietta Maria] *widow of*	soprano or
Charles I	mezzo-soprano
Elvira *daughter of Lord Walton*	soprano
Puritan soldiers, Arturo's followers, ladies, pages	
and servants	
Setting A fortress near Plymouth (during the	
English Civil War)	

I puritani was Bellini's final opera. He had left Italy for Paris in 1833 and was in negotiations with both the Opéra and the Théâtre Italien during October, signing a contract with the latter by early February 1834. He had broken with his regular librettist, Felice Romani, over *Beatrice di Tenda* the year before; by 11 March Carlo Pepoli was suggesting plots to him. The story and casting were decided by 11 April, and Bellini began composition on about 15 April. The division into three acts was made at the last moment. The title in the Paris libretto is 'I Puritani e i Cavalieri/opera-seria in due Parti', but Bellini referred to it as 'I Puritani' in a letter of 4 September 1834. This form of the title was finally chosen because of the fame of Scott's *Old Mortality* (1816), translated as *Les puritains d'Ecosse* (1817) and *I puritani di Scozia* (1825), with which the opera has otherwise no connection.

On 21 May 1835 the opera was performed in London at the King's Theatre with the original cast. Three days before, the Princess Victoria had heard a preview of the main pieces, sung by the quartet at a private concert at Kensington Palace in celebration of her sixteenth birthday; throughout her life she was to refer to it as 'the dear *Puritani*'. Meanwhile the opera spread rapidly round Europe. It was performed at La Scala in December 1835, possibly in a pirated version. To avoid religious censorship the title was changed to *Elvira e Arturo* (1835, Palermo) and *Elvira Walton* (1836, Rome). At La Fenice in 1836 Elvira was sung by Giuseppina Strepponi, who became a frequent exponent of the role. At the S Carlo, Naples, in 1837 the Elvira was Caterina Barilli-Patti, mother of Adelina Patti, who sang the role at Covent Garden in 1870. *I puritani* was given during 1883, the inaugural season at the Metropolitan, with Marcella Sembrich as Elvira. Maria Callas sang the role for the first time in 1949 at La Fenice; she repeated it at Catania in 1951, the 150th anniversary of Bellini's birth. Joan Sutherland sang Elvira at Glyndebourne in 1960 and at Covent Garden where *I puritani* had not been heard for 77 years, in 1964.

Bellini prepared a separate version for Maria Malibran to sing (as Elvira) at Naples. He had been negotiating to write a new opera for the S Carlo since February 1834, but work on *I puritani* had progressed slowly because of Pepoli's inexperience, and in early October Bellini decided to adapt it for Naples. The 'Malibran' version contains little new music but, because he had to send off the manuscript before the final cuts were made for Paris, it preserves the original division into two parts and contains three sections not in the standard version: a trio in Part 1, a central cantabile to the duet now in Part 3 and a brief concluding cabaletta (reinstated by Sutherland in a 1975 recording). Neapolitan censorship precluded the duet 'Suoni la tromba'. Transpositions made Riccardo a tenor and much of Elvira's music was taken down to the mezzo range, while Elvira, not Arturo, now led the Part 2 finale. The manuscript arrived at Naples too late and the version was not heard until a concert performance at the Barbican Centre, London, on 14 December 1985; it was staged at Bari the following year with Katia Ricciarelli and Chris Merritt.

*

Part 1.i *A large open courtyard in the fortress* There is no overture. The introduction announces several themes used at the end of the opera. Horn-calls sound from the surrounding countryside as the Roundheads hail the dawn and threaten death for the Cavaliers. A bell announces matins, and Bruno leads the soldiers in prayer. The ladies and gentlemen inhabiting the fortress announce the start of the festivities in celebration of Elvira's wedding. Riccardo tells Bruno that he had hoped to marry Elvira himself, though he knows that his love for her is not returned, and that Lord Walton has consented to her wish to marry Arturo instead. His cavatina, 'Ah! per sempre io ti perdei', expresses his grief.

1.ii *Elvira's chambers* Giorgio finds his niece in great distress, afraid that she will have to marry Riccardo. She pours out her feelings in the first part of their duet, 'Sai com'arde in petto mio'. But she now learns from Giorgio that he has persuaded her father to agree to her marriage to Arturo. She does not believe him at first; then horns sound again in the distance, heralding Arturo's arrival. As the soldiers call out his name, Elvira at last gives way to her joy in 'A quel nome'.

1.iii *The Hall of Arms* A chorus welcomes Arturo as Elvira's bridegroom. He makes a grand formal entrance, bearing gifts that include a magnificent white bridal veil. Arturo's cavatina 'A te, o cara, amor talora', becomes a quartet as each of the two verses is taken up by Elvira, Giorgio, Walton and the chorus. Walton gives Arturo a safe conduct for Elvira and himself; he cannot attend his daughter's wedding as he has to escort a female prisoner, believed to be a Royalist spy, to London. The prisoner is brought in and, when left alone with Arturo, she reveals that she is Queen Henrietta Maria, widow of Charles I. Realizing that she will be put to death once she is recognized, Arturo resolves to save her, but is interrupted by the voice of Elvira; she runs in wearing her bridal veil and singing 'Son vergin vezzosa' ('Donzella vezzosa' at Rome), a *polacca* expressing her joyful exuberance. She places the white veil on Henrietta's head to admire it and then runs out again. Arturo decides to use the veil to smuggle Henrietta out of the castle. Riccardo enters, confronts Arturo and challenges him to a duel (the melody is from the 1828 version of *Bianca e Fernando*); this was originally a trio which included a slow central section, preserved in the Naples score. When Riccardo sees that the woman is the Royalist prisoner, he allows them to leave, promising not to give the alarm until they are outside the fortress walls. Elvira comes in, calling for Arturo; there is general consternation when his flight is discovered. Orders are given for the capture of the traitors. Elvira, her reason slipping away, leads the main ensemble with 'Oh vieni al tempio, fedele Arturo', imagining his return to her. Giorgio, Riccardo and the other Puritans express their pity for Elvira and hatred for Arturo.

Part 2 *A hall with side entrances* The ladies and

'I puritani' (Bellini), Part 1 scene iii (the Hall of Arms) designed by Domenico Ferri for the original production at the Théâtre Italien, Paris, 24 January 1835: engraving

gentlemen lament the fate of the distracted Elvira. In 'Cinta di fiori e col bel crin disciolto', Giorgio describes how she wanders about garlanded with flowers, her hair dishevelled. Riccardo enters, declaring that Arturo has been condemned to death and is to be hunted down. Elvira's voice is heard outside and she comes in, her reason obviously gone. In the mad scene, 'Qui la voce sua soave', she imagines Arturo's voice, laments his departure and comforts Giorgio and Riccardo, both of whom weep as they comment on her words; finally she conjures up an ecstatic vision of Arturo. After she has left, Giorgio works on Riccardo's love for Elvira in the duet 'Il rival salvar tu dêi', pointing out that Arturo's death would kill her, in order to persuade Riccardo to help save the cavalier. Riccardo resists at first, but realizes that he could not bear the prospect of her phantom pursuing him. Both agree, however, that Arturo must die if he is with the Cavalier troops when they attack the fortress. A trumpet sounds and in the celebrated 'Suoni la tromba, e intrepido' they proclaim 'libertà' (replaced by 'lealtà' in Milan and 'fedeltà' in Rome).

Part 3 *A loggia in a wooded garden near Elvira's apartments* An orchestral storm rages as Arturo enters, having for the moment eluded his pursuers. He hears a harp, then the voice of the still distracted

Elvira, singing 'A una fonte, afflitto e solo', a song that he once taught her. Her voice fades and he takes up the melody himself. He is interrupted by a posse of Puritan soldiers searching for him and hides until they have gone, then continues with his song. Elvira appears, drawn by the sound of his voice, and, to a reminiscence of Arturo's first cavatina, sadly conjures up happy memories. When she sees and recognizes him the shock momentarily restores her senses. In the duet 'Nel mirarti un solo istante' they sing of their love for each other and of the sorrow brought by three months' separation – more like three centuries, says Elvira. Arturo explains why he left with another woman, a prisoner who would have been executed but for his intervention. The sound of a drum upsets Elvira's fragile sanity and she suffers a relapse. Arturo tries to lead her away, but she will not go and calls for help. Riccardo, Giorgio, the soldiers and inhabitants of the fortress run in and recognize Arturo. Accompanied by a funeral march, Riccardo condemns the traitor. At the pronouncement of the death sentence, Elvira is finally shocked back to sanity. In the ensemble 'Credeasi misera', launched by Arturo, he assures her of his love, while Elvira vows to die with him. The soldiers impatiently call for Arturo's death, and are accused of cruelty by

Riccardo and Giorgio. A hunting horn announces a herald, who brings a message from Cromwell: the Stuarts have been defeated and a general amnesty is declared. All rejoice at Cromwell's victory and wish Elvira and Arturo happiness.

*

Bellini anticipated Verdi in attributing to *I puritani* an individual 'colorito', which he described as 'basically the genre of *La sonnambula* and Paisiello's *Nina* with a touch of military robustness and something of Puritan severity'. In its harmony and scoring *I puritani* is Bellini's most sophisticated opera – a direct consequence, no doubt, of its having been written for a Parisian audience. To the same cause we may ascribe its unusual wealth of thematic recall, which was a regular feature of contemporary French opera. Bellini's concern to establish a spacious time-scale (his chief point of contact with Wagner) is evident in the introduction, with its parade of slow triplets against the beat. The role of Elvira offers a *ne plus ultra* of romantic madness, conceived less as a morbid condition than as the transfiguration – part lyrical, part virtuoso – of fragile womanhood, such as would find an echo in Donizetti's *Lucia di Lammermoor*. Be it noted, too, that in every act Elvira is heard before she is seen, as happens so often in the operas of Puccini. The opera contains two classic instances of Italian romantic lyricism in the quartet 'A te, o cara' and Elvira's cantabile 'Qui la voce sua soave'; on the other hand there is a striking departure from the norm both in Giorgio's 'Cinta di fiori e col bel crin disciolto', a setting of eleven-syllable lines such as were usually reserved for recitative and Venetian serenades, and in the duet-cabaletta 'Vieni fra questa braccia' in which two five-bar phrases are balanced by a concluding period of nine. Each is a tantalizing hint as to how Bellini's melodic style might have developed had he lived longer. The duet 'Suoni la tromba' anticipates the *Risorgimento* spirit of the 1840s, and became the theme on which Liszt and others composed a collective set of piano variations, *Hexaméron*, in 1839.   S.M., E.F., J.B.

Q

Queen of Spades, The
[*Pikovaya dama (Pique Dame)*]

Opera in three acts, op.68, by Pyotr Il'yich Tchaikov-sky to a libretto by Modest Il'yich Tchaikovsky and the composer after Alexander Sergeyevich Pushkin's novella (1833); St Petersburg, Mariinsky Theatre, 7/19 December 1890.

The première was conducted by Eduard Nápravník, with Nikolay Figner as Hermann, Ivan Mel'nikov as Tomsky, Mariya Slavina as the Countess and Medea Mei-Figner as Lisa.

Gherman [Hermann]	tenor
Count Tomsky	baritone
Prince Yeletsky	baritone
Countess * * *	mezzo-soprano
Liza [Lisa] *her granddaughter*	soprano
Pauline *Lisa's confidante*	contralto
Chekalinsky	tenor
Surin	bass
Chaplitsky	tenor
Narumov	bass
Master of Ceremonies	tenor
Catherine the Great	silent
Governess	mezzo-soprano
Masha *Lisa's maid*	soprano
Make-believe Commander	spoken (boy)

In the intermède (Act 2)	
Prilepa/Chloë	soprano
Milovzor/Daphnis (Pauline)	contralto
Zlatogor/Plutus (Tomsky)	baritone

Nursemaids, governesses, wet-nurses, strollers, children, gamblers etc.
Setting St Petersburg at the close of the 18th century

Modest Tchaikovsky's libretto was originally pre-pared for Nikolay Semyonovich Klenovsky (1853–1915), who had received a commission from Ivan Vsevolozhsky, the Intendant of the Bol'shoy Theatre, Moscow. Pyotr Tchaikovsky had expressed an interest in Pushkin's famous story as early as 1885, but once a lesser composer had been offered Modest's libretto by the theatre directorate he had to wait until not only Klenovsky but also Nikolay Solov'yov had exercised their right of refusal before he could tackle it himself.

The entire opera was composed in Florence in 44 days of frenzied inspiration (30 January–14 March 1890), the composer freely supplementing his brother's text at the dictate of his hectic muse. By mid-June the orchestration was complete and the opera had been submitted to the theatre and to Tchaikovsky's publisher Jurgenson. The inordinate speed of composition was matched by an unusually tight construction and a quality of imagination unmatched in its way in the whole of Russian opera. The composer's many letters to his brother abound with expressions of happy amazement at his own powers of disciplined invention: 'Either I am horribly mistaken, Modya, or the opera is a masterpiece' was the final verdict – one which the international operatic audience has ratified. Earlier he had written 'I am so far firmly convinced that *The Queen of Spades* is a good, and mainly, a very original piece, speaking not from the musical point of view but in general'.

Pushkin's novella, at barely 10,000 words a masterpiece of 'cold fury' (Dostoyevsky) and ironic narrative dispatch, might have seemed a natural for brisk one-act treatment, insofar as a study in ugly monomania suggested musical adaptation at all. The libretto Tchaikovsky set, composed on order from the Imperial Theatres and reflecting many of Vsevolozhsky's suggestions and demands, opened up the terse, tense narrative with all kinds of leisurely interpolations that at times appear to dwarf the original plot altogether. It transposed the action into the 19th-century fairyland known as 'the 18th century' so as to provide a pretext for the most sumptuous interpolation of all, the pastoral; it supplemented Pushkin's proto-Poeish 'horror' with an admixture of more typically operatic 'tragedy': instead of the original Hermann's cynical pretence of romantic interest, there is a genuine romantic intrigue between him and Lisa, not as in Pushkin the Countess's impoverished ward but now her granddaughter and his social superior, which ends in their double suicide.

For these deeds the Tchaikovsky brothers have been castigated many times over by guardians of literature, second-guessed by a Soviet produc-tion team under Meyerhold (their attempted 'repushkinization' of the opera was shown at the Leningrad Malïy Theatre in 1935), and rebuked by puritanical but unimaginative critics. What they have been slow to recognize is precisely what the composer meant when he wrote with such uncharacteristic confidence about his originality: Tchaikovsky's penultimate opera is the first and possibly the greatest masterpiece of musical surrealism.

*

Act I.i *Spring: square in the Summer Garden* Nursemaids, governesses and wet-nurses are enjoying the weather along with their charges, who are playing catch, jumping with skipping ropes, playing at soldiers (this last possibly borrowed from *Carmen*, Tchaikovsky's favourite opera) and so on. Two officers, Chekalinsky and Surin, enter discussing the strange behaviour of their friend Hermann, who watches them gamble the whole night through but never plays himself. Hermann enters with Count Tomsky, who asks him why he is so glum. Out of their conversation, prefigured by the solo cello, Hermann's 'arioso' – actually a rather formal aria in two parts – emerges, in which he confesses he has fallen in love with a beauty above his station ('Ya imeni yeyo ne znayu': 'I don't even know her name'). They wander off. The crowd which has been gathering breaks into a paean to the glorious weather. Hermann and Tomsky wander back in time to congratulate the radiant Prince Yeletsky on his engagement, but to himself Hermann broods enviously in a curious little near-canonic duet with his happy friend.

The Countess enters with Lisa; Yeletsky rushes to greet his betrothed and, to his horror, Hermann recognizes her as the object of his hopeless obsession. All the principals now briefly join in individual though simultaneous expressions of dread ('Mne strashno!': 'I'm frightened!'): Lisa and the Countess of Hermann, whose strange behaviour they have noticed; Hermann of the awful old Countess; Tomsky, knowing Hermann, on Lisa's account; Yeletsky on seeing Lisa's unaccountable change of mood. This tiny quintet has aptly been called the opera's dramatic 'knot'. Surin and Chekalinsky ask Tomsky why the old woman, rich as she is, never gambles. Tomsky regales them with the tale, foreshadowed in the orchestral introduction, of 'The Three Cards' – the secret winning combination imparted to the Countess by the Count of Saint-Germain, long ago when she was known to all of Paris as 'la Vénus moscovite', through which she recouped some ruinous losses on condition that she never play again. It is just an old canard (as its setting in three formal strophes with refrain assures us), but Hermann overhears it with great agitation. His friends tease him with the end of the story, a

prophecy that the Countess, who has revealed the secret only to two men in her life, will die at the hands of the third, 'who, full of love's fiery passion, will come to learn the three cards by force'. A thunderstorm breaks out; all run for cover, leaving Hermann alone on stage, oblivious. He vows that he will win Lisa from Prince Yeletsky by means of the cards.

I.ii Lisa's room; a door to the balcony overhanging the garden At the harpsichord (piano in the pit), Lisa accompanies herself and Pauline in a setting of Vasily Zhukovsky's lyric 'Uzh vecher, oblakov pomerknuli kraya' ('Tis evening, the edges of the clouds have darkened', 1806). Lisa asks Pauline to sing a *solo*; she complies, after hesitating, with a gloomy *memento mori* by Konstantin Batyushkov ('Podrugi milïye': 'Dear girls', 1810); bemused at her own choice, Pauline proposes to offset the lowering mood with a merry *russkaya* (to an imitation folk text by the composer) in which all join, clapping and dancing gaily. The noise brings the Governess on stage with a stern reproof from the Countess at the girls' lack of breeding ('Fi, quel genre, mesdames!'). She gives them a little lesson in *noblesse oblige*, then breaks up the party. After the guests leave, Lisa goes out to the balcony and expresses to the night her ambivalent feelings about her bridegroom (arioso: 'Zachem zhe eti slyozï': 'But why these tears'). At its height she is surprised by Hermann, who suddenly appears out of the shadows. A new wave of dramatic tension begins to build. The couple's first exchange is accompanied by music previously heard at the climax of the orchestral introduction, and for that reason obviously the authentic love music of the opera. Still, Hermann must win Lisa over in good conscience; he delivers an arioso on one knee ('Prosti, prelestnoye sozdan'ye': 'Forgive me, adorable creature'). It, too, is broken off at the climax when the Countess knocks on the balcony door from inside the house and orders Lisa to go to bed; at the sound of her voice Hermann thinks obsessively about Tomsky's prophecy regarding the 'third man'. The final portion of the scene, an amplified reprise of the first exchange, ends with Lisa's declaration, 'I am thine!'

Act 2.i *Masquerade ball in a rich house* The scene begins with a chorus, the first of the scene's many 'neo-classical' stylizations. The Master of Ceremonies invites the guests outdoors to see a fireworks display. Left alone, Yeletsky sings to Lisa an aria, to words by the composer ('Ya vas lyublyu bezmerno': 'I love you beyond measure'), interpolated in order to place Yeletsky among the major characters; from the first a popular recital item, it is strongly reminiscent of Prince Gremin's aria in *Yevgeny Onegin*. Hermann wanders on stage, reading a note from Lisa requesting a rendezvous; his agitation is reflected in the syncopations and the

Mariya Slavina as the Countess in the original production of Tchaikovsky's 'The Queen of Spades' at the Mariinsky Theatre, St Petersburg, 7/19 December 1890

sudden halts that characterize the orchestral accompaniment to this scene throughout. Surin and Chekalinsky steal up behind him and tease him with whispers naming him as the 'third' who will wrest the secret of the three cards; Hermann is dumbfounded.

The Master of Ceremonies announces a pastoral play, 'The Faithful Shepherdess', an extended *divertissement* 'à la Mozart' based on the story of Daphnis (Milovzor, sung by Pauline) and Chloë (Prilepa): (*a*) 'Chorus of Shepherds and Shepherdesses', a parody of the peasant chorus from *Don Giovanni*; (*b*) Dance of the Shepherds and Shepherdesses, a 'sarabande' (in 4/4 time!); (*c*) 'Duet of Prilepa and Milovzor', a take-off of 'Plaisir d'amour' (by J.-P.-E. Martini), in which the lovers declare themselves; and (*d*) 'Tempo di minuetto', in which Plutus (Zlatogor, played by Tomsky) arrives, bearing fantastic gifts, in a golden chariot, but cannot entice Chloë from her shepherd love; the intermède concludes with general rejoicing, including reprises of (*c*) and (*a*). There is a brief confrontation between Hermann and his teasing friends, and an encounter with Lisa in which she tells him how to reach the Countess's bedroom on his way to hers, giving him the final proof of his main chance; then the guests burst into frenzied acclamation at the sudden appearance of the tsaritsa herself, Catherine the Great, in their midst.

2.ii *The Countess's bedroom, lit by icon-lamps* Hermann has stolen into the room; his breathless

monologue on the fate that has brought him there is accompanied throughout by a magnificently sustained orchestral ostinato comprising three elements in ever-changing juxtapositions, a strikingly modern concept. Footsteps announce the arrival of the Countess and a bevy of attendants who sing her to her armchair. She waves them off, expressing her irritation at the *mauvais ton* she encountered at the ball, and prepares for bed; Hermann witnesses 'the repulsive mysteries of her toilette' (Pushkin's phrase). Her mind goes back to her youth and she sings herself to sleep to the anachronistic strains of a tune ('Je crains de lui parler la nuit'), which Tchaikovsky copied out of *Richard Coeur-de-lion*, an *opéra comique* by Grétry (1784). For the second time Hermann reveals himself as intruder, this time rousing the Countess, pleading with her, encountering silence, threatening her with his revolver, at last realizing she is dead. Lisa enters, drawn by the noise. Horrified both at the scene she has discovered and at the thought that Hermann was interested in her only as a conduit, she orders him out. Having lost everything, he rushes out in despair, the air heavy with leitmotifs.

Act 3.i *Hermann's barracks room, late at night* After an orchestral fantasy evocative of Hermann's ravings, he is seen tormented by conscience, obsessively recalling the Countess's obsequies and rereading a forgiving letter from Lisa in which she insists on a midnight meeting. He hears footsteps, the audience hears a whole-tone scale, and the Countess's ghost heavily enters the room, telling him she is there against her will, enjoining him to marry Lisa, and finally imparting the secret of the cards: Three, Seven, Ace.

3.ii *An embankment* Lisa is waiting, distraught, fearing Hermann's failure to appear, which will finally establish his depravity and consequently her own; at last, exhausted, she reflects on her lost happiness in a short, perfectly shaped aria that has become a favourite of the Russian recital stage ('Akh, istomilas' ya gorem': 'Ah, I am worn out by grief'). The clock in a nearby fortress tower strikes midnight and Lisa laments the confirmation of her fears in what sounds at first like the cabaletta to the preceding arioso ('Tak eto pravda!': 'So it's true!'). But Hermann arrives and quells her misgivings (she responds to his appearance with a phrase that seems to quote Tatyana's Letter Scene in *Yevgeny Onegin*, when she sings, 'Resolve my doubts'). Their momentary idyll ('O da, minovali stradan'ya': 'Oh yes, the pain is gone', based on a leisurely 9/8 variation of the main love theme) is shattered when Hermann announces he is on his way to the gaming house, having learnt the secret from Lisa's grandmother's ghost. He rushes off and Lisa, knowing him now to be hopelessly insane, jumps from the embankment and drowns herself in the Neva.

3.iii *The gaming house; supper in progress* The assembled players give free rein to their high spirits. They welcome Yeletsky with surprise; he admits he is there to compensate his loss of Lisa. All call for Tomsky to sing; his song 'Yesli b milïye devitsï tak mogli letat' kak ptitsï' ('If pretty girls could fly like birds') is followed by a gamblers' chorus. Hermann arrives, makes straight for the gaming table, to everyone's delighted surprise, and places an unheard-of 40,000-ruble bet. It is reluctantly accepted; his three wins as per the formula. He doubles; his seven wins. Before staking his last card (against Yeletsky, who eagerly volunteers himself as nemesis) Hermann sings a maniacal song whose incipit could serve as the opera's epigraph ('Chto nasha zhizn'? Igra!': 'What is our life? A game!'); finally his 'ace' turns out to be the Queen of Spades, which – he is certain – looks back at him sarcastically with the Countess's face. Mad, he stabs himself; the opera ends with a brief chorus of ritual farewell.

*

The music of *The Queen of Spades* achieves its hallucinatory quality not through harmony but in its orchestration: Tchaikovsky reveals an unparalleled genius for grotesque combinations of instruments which reaches its height in the scene of the Countess's ghostly visitation. His phantasmal romanticism is associated with the incipient symbolist movement through a network of sinister doubles that haunt the opera on every level, and through the

Ex.1

Act 1 scene i, Tomsky's ballad

Od - nazh - dï v Ver - sa - le 'au jeu de la Reine'...
['Once at Versailles 'au jeu de la Reine . . .

[refrain]
...tri kar - - tï, tri kar - tï, tri kar - tï!
. . . three cards, three cards, three cards!']

Introduction
cl, bn

Act 1 scene i, Hermann's arioso
Ya i - me - ni e - yo ne zna - yu
['I do not know her name']

Symphony no. 5, 1st movt
cl, bn

Queen of Spades, Act 1 scene ii, Countess and Lisa, accompaniment

Act 2 scene ii, Hermann steals up to the countess

many subtly drawn correspondences (to use the arch-symbolist poet Baudelaire's word) between the surface action and its occult underpinnings. To analyse Tomsky's ballad from Act 1 scene i as a source of leitmotifs, for example, is to penetrate in unexpectedly ironic fashion from the one level straight to the other. A jovial set piece characterized by an especially 'enlightened' formal symmetry yields up, on the one hand, a phrase ('x') that, tortured and skewed beyond belief (but not beyond recognition), governs all those moments in which Hermann makes contact, through the Countess, with the world beyond (or it, through her, with him), until, in the last scene, it crushes him with the full weight of the orchestra. On the other hand, the ballad's refrain ('y') resonates as a sinister double with Hermann's just-completed cavatina, linking his love for Lisa with the fatal imperative that will doom them both (ex.1).

Another way of invoking malign destiny is by the use of intertextual resonance: for example, the adaptation of Tomsky's ballad to the rhythm of the main theme in the first movement of Tchaikovsky's recently completed Fifth Symphony, whose motto clearly echoes as well through the E minor orchestral music at the beginning and the end of the opera's penultimate scene, which ends in Lisa's suicide. An intertextual linkage within the opera itself comes when Hermann confesses his love for Lisa in Act 1 scene ii to an unwitting echo of Pauline's melancholy romance. All at once the opera's heroine is identified with the dead maiden in the song; fate has left another calling card.   R.T.

R

Radamisto ('Radamistus', 'Rhadamistus')

Opera in three acts by George Frideric Handel to an anonymous libretto adapted from Domenico Lalli's *L'amor tirannico, o Zenobia* (1710, Venice) as revised for Florence (1712); London, King's Theatre, 27 April 1720.

The first cast included Ann Turner Robinson (Polissena), Anastasia Robinson (Zenobia), Margherita Durastanti (Radamisto), Antonio Montagnana (Farasmane), Benedetto Baldassari (Tiridate).

Radamisto *son of Farasmane*		soprano
Zenobia *his wife*		contralto
Farasmane *King of Thrace*		bass
Tiridate *King of Armenia*		tenor
Polissena *his wife, daughter of*		
Farasmane		soprano
Tigrane *Prince of Pontus*		soprano
Fraarte *brother of Tiridate*		soprano
Setting Asia Minor, 1st century AD		

Radamisto was Handel's first opera for the newly formed Royal Academy of Music, the creation of which he was closely concerned with, and the Academy's second production. The wordbook, unusually, bears the composer's own dedication to King George I. Both the King and the Prince of Wales, recently reconciled after an estrangement of nearly three years, attended the first night and the initial run of ten performances was enthusiastically received. A substantially revised version of the opera was produced at the King's Theatre on 28 December 1720 with revisions to suit a much changed cast; though a few recitatives are lost, this version merits a complete score of its own. There were further revivals with revisions the following year and in January 1728. A version of *Radamisto*, under the title *Zenobia*, was produced at Hamburg on 28 November 1722 and was frequently repeated. The first 20th-century revival, in a version by Joseph Wenz, was at Göttingen on 27 June 1927; the first in Britain was by the Handel Opera Society under Charles Farncombe at Sadler's Wells Theatre, London, on 6 July 1960.

Charles Burney's attribution of the libretto to Nicola Haym is plausible but cannot be confirmed. The basis of the story is a passage in Tacitus's *Annals of Imperial Rome* (xii.51), describing an incident in Asia Minor around AD 51. The action takes place in and near an unnamed city on the banks of the river Araxes.

*

Tiridate, King of Armenia, unmoved by the loyalty of his wife Polissena, has become infatuated with Zenobia, the wife of Radamisto. Radamisto is the son of King Farasmane of Thrace and Polissena's brother. In an attempt to capture Zenobia, Tiridate has laid siege to the city, which Radamisto is holding; the king has already taken Farasmane prisoner.

The opera begins with Polissena in despair, praying for divine help. Tiridate's ally Tigrane, Prince of Pontus, who loves her, fails to persuade her to leave her husband. Tiridate orders the destruction of the city, but allows his brother Fraate to take Farasmane to the city walls to speak with Radamisto. When Radamisto appears (scene ii) Fraate tells him that he must yield the city or his father will be executed on the spot. Farasmane urges his son to be defiant, and Fraate gives the signal for his execution; but Tigrane intervenes. Tigrane and Fraate then lead a successful attack on the city. Tiridate, annoyed at the sparing of Farasmane (scene iii), agrees that he may live if Radamisto and Zenobia are brought to him. Fraate remembers his own former love for Zenobia.

Radamisto and Zenobia escape from the city via a subterranean passage (Act 2) and emerge in open country near the Araxes. Soldiers approach, and in despair Zenobia begs her husband to kill her. He makes a reluctant attempt to do so, but merely wounds her. Zenobia tries to fulfil her intentions by throwing herself into the river. The soldiers, under Tigrane's command, capture Radamisto. Fraate saves Zenobia from drowning. Zenobia is brought to Tiridate (scene ii). He learns that he is his brother's rival in love. Zenobia resists the advances of both brothers. Tigrane brings Radamisto, disguised as a soldier, to Polissena. As Tiridate pays court to Zenobia, Tigrane enters with Radamisto's clothes and announces that he is dead; a 'messenger' will report what happened. The messenger, named Ismene, is the disguised Radamisto (scene iii), immediately recognized by Zenobia. Tiridate is annoyed by the messenger's account of Radamisto's supposed dying speech, but feels that Ismene will be useful and asks him for help in gaining Zenobia.

In Act 3 Tigrane and Fraate, wearying of Tiridate's tyranny, plan to make the king see the error of his ways. Tiridate greets Zenobia as Queen of Armenia (scene ii) and offers her a crown and sceptre. She rejects the offer and Tiridate tries to catch hold of her. Radamisto enters, together with Polissena and Farasmane, and threatens Tiridate with his sword, but Polissena intervenes. Farasmane reveals Radamisto's identity. Tiridate orders his execution and refuses to spare him despite Polissena's pleas; she warns him that her sorely tried fidelity may yet change to anger. Tiridate agrees to pardon Radamisto if Zenobia will be his. In the temple (scene iii) Zenobia makes the choice: she rejects Tiridate and will die with her husband. But Polissena announces that Tiridate's army has revolted and, led by Tigrane and Fraate, surrounds the temple. Tiridate is abandoned by his attendants and is held. Tigrane offers the throne of Armenia to Farasmane. Radamisto asks Polissena to pardon the repentant Tiridate and tells them to rule in Armenia as before; his reunion with Zenobia has banished his sorrows.

*

The serious tone and powerfully motivated action of *Radamisto* mark a decisive break from the more carelessly assembled operas that Handel had composed for London in the previous decade. Both the female roles are memorably portrayed in their music, the submissive Polissena showing strength in her unswerving if apparently unmerited love for her tyrannous husband, and Zenobia brave and passionate in her faithfulness to Radamisto. Only in Polissena's 'Sposo ingrato', the lengthy and over-elaborate Act 3 aria in which she turns on Tiridate, does Handel falter; and the fault was to be splendidly corrected in the first revision of the opera. Radamisto's F minor lament 'Ombra cara', sung in Act 2 when he believes Zenobia to be dead, is perhaps the greatest of all the arias, but the standard is consistently high throughout.

For the December 1720 revival, the alto castrato Senesino took over Radamisto, Durastanti transferring to Zenobia and the bass Giuseppe Boschi playing Tiridate; Handel took the opportunity to make several changes for what seem to be purely artistic reasons. Certain features of the earlier score – such as Tiridate's aria with trumpet 'Stragi, morti' – are regrettably lost, but in general the new version improves on the old, especially in Act 3: Polissena turns on Tiridate with the wonderfully dramatic aria 'Barbaro, partirò' (begun without ritornello), and a remarkable quartet marks the climax. Ten arias, a duet and the quartet were newly composed. In 1721 Handel removed the part of Fraate; the revisions for the 1728 revival, to allow the roles of Zenobia and Polissena to be taken over by the rival sopranos Faustina and Cuzzoni, and Tigrane by the alto castrato Baldi, severely weaken the characterization.   A.H.

Rake's Progress, The

Opera in three acts (nine scenes and an epilogue) by Igor Stravinsky to a libretto by W. H. Auden and Chester Kallman after William Hogarth's series of paintings (1732–3); Venice, Teatro La Fenice, 11 September 1951.

At the première Elisabeth Schwarzkopf sang Anne, Robert Rounseville sang Tom, Nick Shadow was sung by Otakar Kraus, and Baba the Turk by Jennie Tourel; the composer conducted.

Tom Rakewell	tenor
Nick Shadow	baritone
Trulove	bass
Anne *Trulove's daughter*	soprano
Mother Goose	mezzo-soprano
Baba the Turk	mezzo-soprano
Sellem *an auctioneer*	tenor
Keeper of the Madhouse	bass
Whores and roaring-boys, servants, citizens, madmen	
Setting 18th-century England	

Stravinsky happened on Hogarth's paintings at the Chicago Art Institute on 2 May 1947; they struck him as a series of scenes from a drama and suggested the subject for the English-language opera he had wanted to write since arriving in the USA eight years before. His California neighbour Aldous Huxley suggested Auden as librettist, and the latter, after working out a draft scenario with the composer in November, called in his friend Kallman as collaborator.

Stravinsky received the text of the first act on 16 January 1948 and went to work in May (the previous December, anxious to get started, he had composed the icy string-quartet introduction to the graveyard scene, 3.ii). The libretto was finished and handed over to the composer in Washington, DC, on 31 March. The place and date are doubly important for the opera, and for Stravinsky's late career generally, because it was also the place and date of his earliest meeting with the conductor Robert Craft, one of whose first duties as musical assistant was to read the text of *The Rake's Progress* aloud so that the composer might learn its proper intonation and accentuation. (True to his established habit, Stravinsky frequently honoured these niceties in the breach; but his music-motivated departures from standard spoken English were informed ones.)

The epilogue was completed on 7 April 1951, but the last music to be composed was the first to be heard: the fanfarish prelude to Act 1. *The Rake* was 'bought' by the managers of the 14th Festival of Contemporary Music at Venice (the 'Biennale'), the composer's old friend Nicolas Nabokov acting as his agent. The orchestra and chorus of La Scala were engaged for the première, as was the conductor Ferdinand Leitner (after Stravinsky's first choice, Igor Markevich, was rejected by the Italians), who conducted all performances but the first. The first commercial recording, under the composer's baton (and with the harpsichord, mainly played by an uncredited Ralph Kirkpatrick, finally in place instead of the piano cautiously employed in earlier performances), followed a production at the Metropolitan (1953), conducted in the house by Fritz Reiner. Among its later productions, that of the Royal Swedish Opera (1961) under Ingmar Bergman's direction deserves mention because of the composer's enthusiastic endorsement, reported by Craft, extending to the director's decision to break for an interval only once, after 2.ii.

*

Act I.i *The garden of Trulove's house in the country on an afternoon in spring* Tom and Anne celebrate the season and their love ('The woods are green'), while Trulove hopes his doubts about Tom will prove unfounded. In a recitative, Trulove dispatches his daughter to the kitchen and proposes that Tom take a position in a friend's counting-house. When Tom refuses, Trulove warns him that he will not allow his daughter to marry a lazy man. Left alone, Tom angrily reflects that he is not made for a life of drudgery but will trust to fortune (recitative and aria, 'Here I stand', 'Since it is not by merit'). He makes the first of the spoken wishes that provide the plot with its mainspring: for money. Nick Shadow materializes instantly, bids him call Anne and Trulove to hear the news, and informs them all that an obscure uncle of Tom's has died and left him a fortune (recitative [so called, evidently, after the draft scenario, despite its well-articulated aria structure], 'Fair lady, gracious gentlemen'). All react gratefully in their various ways, the ensemble taking shape out of an ironic fugato on the words 'Be thanked', set to a dissonant drooping minor 9th; Tom agrees to employ Shadow and at the latter's suggestion decides to establish himself in London before marrying Anne (quartet, 'I wished but once'). Tom and Anne take their tender leave (duettino, 'Farewell for now'). Tom promises Trulove that he will soon send for him and for Anne; he gaily makes off with Nick, having agreed to pay the latter after a year and a day have passed; Anne

suppresses a tear; Trulove expresses misgivings (arioso and terzettino, 'Dear Father Trulove', 'Laughter and light'). Just before the curtain, Nick Shadow turns to the audience – showing that he is not merely Tom's alter ego (shadow) but truly the devil (Nick) – and announces, 'The progress of a rake begins'.

I.ii *Mother Goose's brothel, London* The Roaring-Boys and Whores cavort in the chorus 'With air commanding'. Shadow and Mother Goose catechize Tom in the ways of cynicism, the harpsichord punctuating the lesson with arch cadences. Tom falters meaningly at the mention of love. He makes as if to flee, but is reassured by Nick, who sets the cuckoo clock back an hour to midnight to show that Tom has time on his side ('Fear not. Enjoy. You may repent at leisure'). Tom drinks, the company egging him on (chorus, 'Soon dawn will glitter'). Nick formally presents him and he sings an initiation song (cavatina, 'Love, too frequently betrayed'). Its excessive sincerity discomfits the whores briefly and strangely attracts them ('How sad a song'). But Mother Goose banishes care and claims Tom for herself while the company serenades their withdrawal to a room off stage ('The sun is bright, the grass is green. Lanterloo'). The scene ends in a dreamlike diminuendo, Shadow warning that when his dreams end the Rake will die.

I.iii *Trulove's garden* The scene is given over to a two-part solo *scena* for Anne, in which she refuses to acknowledge Tom's silence as rejection, invoking night and moon as her allies in caring quest of him (aria, 'Quietly, night') and then, reflecting on Tom's greater need, resolves forthwith to leave her father and follow Tom to London (cabaletta, 'I go, I go to him').

Act 2.i *The morning room of Tom's house in a London square* The Rake, disillusioned with his decadent urbanity, longs for the simple country joys he left behind ('Vary the song'). He pronounces the second wish: to be happy. Shadow enters, a broadsheet in hand. It is an advertisement for Baba the Turk, the lady freak on display at the St Giles Fair. Shadow proposes that Tom marry her to assert his freedom from ordinary appetites and constraints and thereby know true happiness (aria, 'In youth the panting slave'). With a loud laugh Tom sees the point and agrees (duet finale, 'My tale shall be told both by young and old').

2.ii *The street in front of Tom's house* Anne is waiting apprehensively for Tom's return (recitative and arioso, 'How strange!', 'O heart be stronger'). She is surprised by a procession of lackeys carrying all sorts of odd packages into the servants' entrance as night falls; last, a sedan chair is carried in and deposited at the main entrance; Tom alights and, all confusion, recognizes Anne; confessing himself unworthy, he bids her go (duet, 'Anne! Here!'). Baba, heavily veiled, pokes her head out from the carriage and expresses her impatience; Tom admits to the astonished Anne that he is married (Anne: 'I see, then, it was I who was unworthy'). They separately reflect on what might have been, while Baba, periodically appearing at the carriage window, waxes ever more indignant at the delay (trio, 'Could it then have been known', 'It is done, it is done', 'Why this delay?'). Anne exits hurriedly; Tom escorts Baba from the sedan chair, identifying Anne to her as 'a milkmaid to whom I was in debt'. A crowd of passers-by recognize Baba and hail her; she turns to receive their plaudits and, 'with the practiced manner of a great artiste', removes her veil, revealing a full and flowing black beard (finale, 'Baba the Turk is here!').

2.iii *The same room as 2.i, except that now it is cluttered up with every conceivable kind of object* Baba is chattering away over breakfast while Tom sulks (aria, 'As I was saying'). Noticing that he is out of sorts she attempts to cajole him (Baba's song, 'Come, sweet, come'), but he shoves her away. Enraged, she strides about breaking anything to hand until Tom covers her head with his wig, which cuts her off mid-roulade (aria, 'Scorned! Abused! Neglected! Baited!'). He falls into an exhausted sleep upon the sofa; Shadow enters, singing to himself and wheeling a 'fantastic baroque machine' with which he seems to turn a shard from one of Baba's broken vases into a loaf of bread; but as he shows the audience, it is just a device with a false bottom (pantomime; the octatonic machine-music recalls that of the mechanical Japanese bird in *The Nightingale*). Tom awakens with his third wish on his lips: that by means of a miraculous machine he has just seen in a dream he might perform a great good deed and (to the melody of the recitative line immediately preceding the cabaletta in 1.iii) 'deserve dear Anne at last' (recitative-arioso-recitative, 'O Nick I've had the strangest dream'); he is elated to find Shadow standing before him with the very machine he had imagined. Tom exults in his impending salvation while Shadow, addressing the audience, mocks his credulity (duet, 'Thanks to this excellent device', 'A word to all my friends'). Shadow reminds Tom that the machine must be mass-produced and marketed, and proposes a stock issue. They go off in pursuit of backers, Tom meanwhile informing Shadow that he has disposed of his wife.

Act 3.i *The same as 2.iii, except that everything is covered with cobwebs and dust* The marketing enterprise having failed and ruined the Rake, his possessions are up for auction. A crowd gathers gossiping for the sale ('Ruin, disaster, shame'). Anne wanders in looking for Tom, but no one can tell her where he is. Sellem, the auctioneer, enters and gets down to business, selling off a stuffed auk, a mounted fish and so on, to the tune of a waltz with an inanely stylized refrain, each sale greeted with idiotic huzzas from the crowd (aria, interrupted by periodic 'bidding scenes', 'Who hears me, knows me . . . La! come bid, Hmm! come buy'). The final object auctioned turns out to be Baba ('An unknown object draws us near'). As soon as the wig is removed from her head she resumes her interrupted roulade from where she left off in 2.iii (aria, with chorus, 'Sold! Annoyed!'). The voices of Tom and Shadow are heard off stage ('Old wives for sale!'), showing them to be at large. Baba advises Anne to pursue Tom, who still loves her (recitative and duet with chorus and Sellem, 'You love him, seek to set him right'). Tom and Shadow are heard again from the street (ballad tune, 'If boys had wings and girls had stings'). Anne rushes off full of hope (stretto-finale, 'I go to him'), while Baba, with Sellem's reluctant assistance, makes a dignified exit ('The next time you see Baba, you shall pay!').

3.ii *A churchyard with tombs on a starless night* It is a year and a day since Tom and Shadow struck their bargain. 'Servant' now reveals his true identity to 'master' and demands the latter's soul in payment. Tom pleads, but his grave is dug, the clock begins to strike midnight, and Shadow offers him no choice but that of his means of suicide (duet, 'How dark and dreadful is this place'). On the ninth stroke, sporting as ever, Shadow relents and proposes a game of cards accompanied by the suddenly (and wildly) soloistic harpsichord: he will cut the deck three times and Tom must guess which card he holds. First, thinking of Anne, Tom correctly guesses the Queen of Hearts; second, startled by a falling gravedigger's spade, he involuntarily shouts 'The deuce!' – again correct. Now Shadow is upset, and cheats: he replaces the Queen of Hearts in the deck and chooses it again; but Tom, hearing Anne's voice singing a reprise of her Act 2 aria, divines the ruse and wins. He wishes a fourth, uncontracted time, for the return of her love. Defeated, Shadow sinks at the twelfth stroke of the clock into the grave meant for Tom ('I burn! I freeze!'), but as he goes he takes away Tom's reason, leaving him to greet the spring dawn believing himself to be Adonis ('With roses crowned I sit on ground'). This dramatic turning-point is underscored by an anthology of thematic reminiscences – Tom's of Anne's cabaletta in 1.iii, Shadow's of his own aria in 2.i, and, finally, the ballad tune in 3.i.

3.iii *Bedlam* Tom/Adonis calls upon the other inmates to celebrate his wedding to Venus (arioso, 'Prepare yourselves, heroic shades'). The others mock him (dialogue with chorus, 'Madmen's words are all untrue'). Anne appears with the Keeper, who points Tom out to her. He takes her for Venus (arioso, 'I have waited for thee so long'). He asks forgiveness (duet, 'In a foolish dream', 'What should I forgive?').

She comforts him and, accompanied by a pair of flutes, lulls him to sleep while the others marvel at her song (lullaby with chorus, 'Gently, little boat', 'O sacred music of the spheres!'). Her father bids her leave with him (duet, 'Every wearied body', 'God is merciful and just'). Tom awakens, looks in vain for Venus, sinks back heartbroken and dies (finale and mourning-chorus, 'Where art thou, Venus?', 'Mourn for Adonis').

Epilogue *Before the curtain, house lights up* Enter Baba, Tom, Nick, Anne, Trulove, the men without wigs, Baba without her beard. They sing a vaudeville culminating in the fable's moral: 'For idle hands/ And hearts and minds/The Devil finds/A work to do'.

*

There is no work by Stravinsky, or by anyone else, that embodies more conspicuously than *The Rake's Progress* the artistic self-consciousness – the consciousness of art in crisis – that is the nub and essence of 'neo-classicism'. On its every level – plot, scenario, text, music – the opera can seem to throw up such a din of unnecessary allusion as to imperil its own dramatic integrity. The plot, ostensibly a device to link Hogarth's painted scenes, makes explicit or implicit reference (and sometimes both at once) to the myths of Venus and Adonis as well as Orpheus (on which Stravinsky had just completed a ballet), to the Faust legend and to the Don Juan tradition, while at the same time embodying the distinctive structure of a fairy-tale, moreover inserting (in place of Hogarth's rich bride and the 'Ugly Duchess' of the draft scenario) a 'homosexual joke' in the person of Baba the Turk that so outraged Stravinsky's lawyer that he counselled the composer to withdraw from the project. Over and above its newsworthy general aspect of revival, resurrecting stilted 18th-century convention right down to harpsichord-accompanied *secco*, the scenario parodies such famous predecessors as *Don Giovanni* (the Epilogue, but also the Graveyard Scene) and even *Carmen* (the Micaëla-like Anne, ever in gentle-hearted pursuit). The libretto language, much criticized for its difficulty of immediate apprehension ('how', wondered Kirkpatrick, 'does one understand across the orchestra pit of an opera house the words, "London, green unnatural mother"?'), was consciously educed from Pope and Congreve.

As for the music, Stravinsky confessed the late Mozart operas to have been his sources not only of inspiration but of style, even specific figurations. Later, more boldly, he was to declare himself 'Mozart's continuer', even though the opera's musical structure is actually far less ambitious than Mozart's, relying to a great extent on the simple verse and refrain of the ballad opera. The list of additional creditors cited by critics would include – at a minimum, and in chronological order – Handel, Gluck, Beethoven, Schubert, Weber, Rossini, Donizetti (*Don Pasquale*) and Verdi. Nor will anyone approaching *The Rake* from a Russian perspective miss the resonances from Tchaikovsky's Pushkin operas (*Yevgeny Onegin* and *The Queen of Spades*) – doubly ironic in that the originals were themselves concerned with period stylization, the latter with its own variety of 18th-century pastiche.

Despite some early disappointment with its retrospective manner (not entirely a philistine reaction, for the composer, embarrassed, quickly sought stylistic renewal in serialism), *The Rake* has staked Stravinsky's unexpected claim to consideration as one of the major opera composers of his time; it has become a stout repertory item, with more productions than any other opera written after the death of Puccini. The crucial factor has surely been its adaptability to the resources of workshop and student theatres. While inevitably jutting out at first, the impression of pastiche has waned as the opera has joined its models in history, has matured in repertory, and as a fluent performing practice for it has evolved. (Now we are more apt to notice affinities with Stravinsky's own earlier output for the stage; compare, for example, the harpsichord flourishes that accompany Shadow's appearances in 1.i and 2.i with the cimbalom arpeggios that herald the title character in *Renard*.)

The best performances of *The Rake* are those that, taking its style(s) for granted, seriously address its moralizing purpose; and that locate the morality not in the epilogue's persiflage but in the traditional if not 'classical' operatic theme of redemption through love. Tom's final madness, though it complicates this interpretation as modernity complicates everything traditional, does not preclude it. The asylum scene, it is worth noting, was the one Hogarthian vestige on which Stravinsky had set his heart from the very beginning, as we learn from his first feeler to Auden; and Auden's answer explains its survival into the finished opera: 'it is the librettist's job to satisfy the composer, not the other way around'.   R.T.

Rape of Lucretia, The

Opera in two acts, op.37, by Benjamin Britten to a libretto by Ronald Duncan after André Obey's play *Le viol de Lucrèce*; Glyndebourne, 12 July 1946.

The cast for the première, conducted by Ernest Ansermet, included Kathleen Ferrier as Lucretia, Joan Cross and Peter Pears as the Chorus, Otakar Kraus as Tarquinius and Owen Brannigan as Collatinus (recordings of excerpts with this cast were issued).

Male Chorus		tenor
Female Chorus		mezzo-soprano
Collatinus		bass
Junius		baritone
Tarquinius		baritone
Lucretia		contralto
Bianca	*her attendants*	mezzo-soprano
Lucia		soprano

Setting Rome in *c*.500 BC

Britten's first chamber opera, for eight solo singers and an instrumental ensemble of 13 players, was written to a Glyndebourne commission soon after *Peter Grimes*, at a time when the composer was particularly conscious of the problems that could arise when working with an established opera company. (The potential and practicality of the chamber medium encouraged Britten to become involved in the foundation of the English Opera Group in 1946.) *The Rape of Lucretia* is rare among Britten's operas in giving the central role to a female singer. Perhaps because of the stylized form and at times rather strained poeticisms of the text, the work has not enjoyed the relatively widespread success and frequent production of most of Britten's operas, but it was successfully revived at Aldeburgh in 1966 with Janet Baker – a recording followed in 1971 – and there was a well-regarded production by the ENO (1983). A recording conducted by Richard Hickox, with Jean Rigby as Lucretia, was issued in 1993.

The opera is in two acts, each divided into two scenes linked by interludes. Act 1 scene i begins with the Male and Female Chorus, who function as narrators and commentators from outside the main action. They describe the unhappy state of Rome under the Etruscan prince Tarquinius, first in brisk recitative (the orchestra includes piano), finally with a strongly-shaped melody that returns twice in Act 2 to words underlining the fact that a pagan tale is being given a Christian perspective. As the action begins Collatinus, Junius and Tarquinius are drinking in their tent at an army camp outside Rome. The night is sultry – magically and economically invoked by flutterings and oscillations in the orchestra – and the men are bemoaning the general unreliability of women. Only Lucretia, the wife of Collatinus, is held to be of unshakable virtue, and Tarquinius is provoked, as he deviously tells Junius, to 'prove Lucretia chaste'. An exciting, uninhibited interlude, narrated by the Male Chorus, depicts Tarquinius's furious ride to Rome, and ends with the reiteration of Lucretia's name to the sinuous chromatic motif consistently associated with it. In scene ii Lucretia is at home with her attendants Bianca and Lucia, spinning. In a haunting, lyrical ensemble they sing of the routine of their lives and in a brief but intense arioso Lucretia declares 'How cruel men are to teach

'The Rape of Lucretia' (Britten), scene from the 1954 revival (Sadler's Wells) of the original Glyndebourne production (1946) with Kathleen Ferrier as Lucretia and Otakar Kraus as Tarquinius

us love!' The Female Chorus recounts how the women prepare for the night; meanwhile, as the Male Chorus's music makes clear, Tarquinius is approaching. When he is admitted to the house and requests a bed for the night, the Choruses describe the atmosphere of strained formality. Only as 'Lucretia leads Prince Tarquinius to his chamber' do the characters in the main action sing again, in a short, ironically decorous ensemble, bidding each other, repeatedly, 'good-night'. The act ends with the orchestra revealing the passionate feelings underlying this deceptive calm.

Act 2 scene i begins with another episode of narration in which the Choruses outline the depredations wrought by the Etruscans in Rome. As in Act 1 scene i this ends with the serene melody pointing the Christian perspective. Then Lucretia is shown asleep, the Male Chorus describing Tarquinius's approach. Tarquinius kisses Lucretia while she is still asleep, and she responds, imagining the presence of her husband. Then she wakes and a terse dialogue begins as she struggles vainly to resist Tarquinius's demands. The text here may be tortuously allusive, but there is genuine anger and passion in the music, leading into an interlude in which the Choruses sing a chorale describing the sorrow of Christ when virtue is 'assailed by sin', and the consolation offered to

Christians by the purity of the Mother of God. During this interlude the music gradually quietens, and Act 2 scene ii begins with Lucia and Bianca ecstatically welcoming the bright sunshine of a summer morning. Their duet illustrates Britten's skill at using a relatively strict compositional technique – close contrapuntal imitation – to create a strongly built yet naturally expressive form. When Lucretia enters the mood changes instantly. Coolly calm, then hysterical, she sends Lucia to summon her husband to witness the full extent of her shame. She then sings a sad, simple aria as she makes a wreath from the flowers the servants had been arranging. Fearing the worst, Bianca seeks to prevent Collatinus's arrival, but it is too late. He enters with Junius and quickly realizes, from what Bianca tells him, what has happened. Lucretia now returns, to processional music of funeral gravity, and despite Collatinus's expression of love, she declares – in an impassioned arioso (a fully-developed aria would be out of proportion here) – that her shame is too great for her to survive. She stabs herself and dies. A final ensemble of mourning, a passacaglia, follows, and gradually intensifies to the point where all six singers cry out the question 'Is this it all?', seeking consolation for the needless death of a pure woman and the unbearable grief of the survivors.

In an epilogue the question is answered by the Choruses with the Christian promises of eternal life and redemption. This ending was not part of Duncan's original scheme. Britten wanted it primarily for musical reasons, since he felt that to end the work with the mourning ensemble, when the whole opera depended on the double perspective of characters in time and narrators outside time, would have been too abrupt. The imagery of the epilogue may seem contrived, but the gradual transformation of the mourning passacaglia into the serene melody to words that refer not directly to Christian values but to 'great love', 'human tragedy' and 'song', proves the rightness of Britten's dramatic instinct. *The Rape of Lucretia* confirms the mastery already displayed in *Peter Grimes*, of the difficult art of giving a personal slant to traditional operatic forms – recitative, arioso, aria, ensemble – and a fresh feeling to the basic linguistic conventions of tonality, without excessive resort to neo-classical features. *Lucretia* may lack the psychological penetration, and the satisfying ambivalence, of Britten's best stage works – the ironies of Act 1 seem awkward alongside the earnestness of Act 2 – but the resourcefulness of its music and the tautness of its structure create a powerful theatrical experience.   A.W.

Rheingold, Das ('The Rhinegold')

Vorabend (preliminary evening) of *Der Ring des Nibelungen*, in four scenes, by Richard Wagner to his own libretto; Munich, Königliches Hof- und Nationaltheater, 22 September 1869 (first performance as part of cycle: Bayreuth, Festspielhaus, 13 August 1876).

The first Wotan was August Kindermann; Fricka was sung by Sophie Stehle. Loge was Heinrich Vogl; Froh, Franz Nachbaur; Mime, Max Schlosser; and Fafner, Kaspar Bausewein. For the 1876 cast, *see Ring des Nibelungen, Der.*

Gods:	
Wotan	bass-baritone
Donner	bass-baritone
Froh	tenor
Loge	tenor
Fricka	mezzo-soprano
Freia	soprano
Erda	contralto
Nibelungs:	
Alberich	bass-baritone
Mime	tenor
Giants:	
Fasolt	bass-baritone
Fafner	bass
Rhinemaidens:	
Woglinde	soprano
Wellgunde	soprano
Flosshilde	mezzo-soprano
Nibelungs	

The first prose sketch for *Das Rheingold*, at that time conceived in three acts, dates from autumn (probably October) 1851. The sketch was then developed into a prose draft (23–31 March 1852) entitled *Der Raub des Rheingoldes/Vorspiel (oder: das Rheingold)?* The verse draft was made between 15 September and 3 November 1852 and the final poem was incorporated into the private printing of the entire *Ring* text in February 1853.

According to Wagner's account in *Mein Leben*, the initial musical inspiration for *Rheingold* – rushing arpeggio figures in E♭ major – came to him as he lay in a trance-like state in an inn at La Spezia. Doubt has been cast on the likelihood of such a 'vision' but it has also been argued that the documentary evidence neither supports nor contradicts Wagner's account. Discounting a handful of musical jottings, the composition of *Rheingold* was begun on 1 November 1853, with the first complete draft, a continuous setting of the poem that occupied him until 14 January 1854. In view of the unprecedented problems of writing for the *Ring*'s expanded forces (including quadruple woodwind), Wagner elaborated the orchestration in a draft of a full score (a procedure he was not to repeat), between 1 February and 28 May 1854. The fair copy of the full score was written out between 15 February and 26 September 1854.

*

Scene i *At the bottom of the Rhine* The simple, protracted E♭ chords that open the tetralogy do more than depict the depths of the Rhine: they also suggest the birth of the world, the act of creation itself. Eight double basses sound a low octave E♭, to which is added the B♭, a 5th higher on bassoons. Eight horns introduce the Nature motif (ex.1), one by one, building up a complex polyphonic texture. The

Ex.1

pp

motion is increased by first flowing quavers and then rushing semiquavers, both rising through the strings from the cellos. The curtain rises towards the end of this orchestral introduction – 136 bars of unadulterated E♭ – to reveal the three Rhinemaidens swimming in the river. Maintaining the E♭ harmony, but now with pentatonic colouring, the sisters enunciate the first lines of text: an alliterating assemblage of primitive-sounding syllables chosen for aural effect rather than linguistic sense: 'Weia! Waga!' The falling-tone motif, heard again a little later in the ensemble cry of the Rhinemaidens (ex.2),

Ex.2

Rhein - gold!

is one of the most frequently recurring motifs, in its many different forms, in the cycle. Flosshilde chides her sisters for failing to watch over the 'sleeping gold'.

From a dark chasm lower down emerges the hunchbacked dwarf Alberich, his crabbed nature and ungainly movements suggested by stabbing semiquavers accented off the beat and by acciaccaturas. The Rhinemaidens decide to reward his lubricious advances by teaching him a lesson. Woglinde leads him on, and his slithering on the rocks and sneezing are graphically portrayed in the music (accented demisemiquaver slides and more acciaccaturas). Both Woglinde and Wellgunde in turn elude him. Flosshilde too seems to offer him love and consolation (against a harmonic background redolent of a traditional love scene), but she also turns out to be mocking him. Alberich's cry of rage and misery (ex.3) turns the Rhinemaidens' motif (ex.2) from major to minor, the form in which

it is to make by far the greater number of appearances.

Ex.3

We - he! ach we - he!
['Woe! oh woe!']

Failing in a last desperate bid to seize hold of the Rhinemaidens, Alberich sees a bright light illuminating the large rock in the centre. Against a background of shimmering strings, the announcement of the Gold motif (perhaps symbolically a brass fanfare) anticipates the Rhinemaidens' joyous hymn to the treasure they guard. To a motif in 3rds tracing the outline of an ellipsis, known as the Ring or World Inheritance motif, Wellgunde tells that a ring conferring limitless power can be fashioned from the Rhinegold. Only he who forswears the power of love can fashion the ring, adds Woglinde, to the solemn Renunciation of Love motif – in which case they have nothing to fear from the lascivious dwarf. But as they watch, Alberich climbs to the top of the central rock, declares his curse on love, and wrests the gold away with terrible force. He scrambles off with it, deaf to the lamenting cries of the Rhinemaidens.

This primeval first scene lies outside the time zone of the main action, just as it lies outside its tonal structure: the chief tonality of *Rheingold* can be seen as D♭ (the beginning of scene ii and end of scene iv, as of the *Ring* as a whole). Thus the formal structure of *Rheingold* (three scenes and a prologue) replicates that of *Götterdämmerung* and of the entire *Ring*.

Scene ii *An open space on a mountain height, near the Rhine* A pair of horns take over the Ring motif, elongating it into something more noble and visionary; this is the transition into the second scene, where Wotan and Fricka are lying asleep on a mountain height. The vision is that of Valhalla, Wotan's newly built fortress, and its grand motif is given out by a chorus of brass instruments, including the Wagner tubas. Fricka, waking first, rouses her husband, who sings a paean to the completed work: 'Vollendet das ewige Werk!' Fricka reminds him that it was her sister, Freia, the goddess of love, who was rashly offered to the giants in payment for the work. Wotan brushes aside her fears. She chides him for trading love and the virtues of woman (echoes of the Renunciation of Love motif) in exchange for power and dominion. Reminding her that he once pledged his remaining eye to court her (a pledge he was not called upon to fulfil), Wotan says that he never intended to give up Freia.

Even as he speaks, Freia enters in terrified haste, followed closely by the giants Fasolt and Fafner. The

'Das Rheingold' (Richard Wagner): (a) Joseph Hoffmann's design for Scene i (at the bottom of the Rhine; the theft of the Rhinegold) in the first Bayreuth production, 1876; (b) stage wagons used in the same production to create the illusion of the Rhinemaidens swimming underwater; note the use of gas lighting in the wings and borders

second part of the accompanying motif (*x* of ex.4), for long mislabelled that of Flight, has been described as Wagner's 'basic love-motive', a theme central not only to the *Ring* but to all his works. When Wotan

Ex.4

refuses to hand over Freia as payment, Fasolt indignantly reminds Wotan that the runes on his spear symbolize his contractual agreements and it is they that legitimize his power. This exchange is punctuated by the measured, stepwise-descending motif (ex.5) that represents Wotan's spear, his

Ex.5

authority and the bargains he has struck. Fasolt's eloquent music alternates between anger at Wotan's dishonourable behaviour and the tenderness he feels towards Freia. Fafner is interested in Freia only as a possible ransom: he knows that without her youth-perpetuating apples the gods will wither and die.

As the giants prepare to take Freia away, her brothers Froh and Donner (the god of thunder) rush in to protect her. Wotan prevents Donner from exercising force and is relieved to see Loge arrive at last. The flickering chromatic semiquavers that accompany him remind us that he is the god of fire; his motif, artfully combining both the falling tone and semitone, hints at his moral ambivalence (ex.6).

Ex.6

Pressed by Wotan, Loge relates how he has circled the world to find out what men hold dearer than the virtues of womankind ('So weit Leben und Weben'). His account begins like a conventional aria in D major, but as he tells of Alberich's capture of the gold, the motifs of the Rhinemaidens and their treasure become coloured by minor tonalities. As Loge repeats the Rhinemaidens' plea for the gold to be returned to the water, the same motifs are heard in their original bright C major.

Loge's explanation of the power of the ring forged from the gold sets everybody thinking. Wotan determines to acquire it and Fafner demands that it then be handed over in payment. The giants trudge away, dragging behind Freia as hostage. A mist

descends on the gods who, denied Freia's golden apples, begin to wilt; a sense of suspended animation is created by muted tremolando strings and a slow tempo. Wotan, accompanied by Loge, descends through a sulphur cleft in pursuit of the gold. A masterly transition passage for orchestra depicts the descent to Nibelheim. Ex.5 alternates with the motif of the Renunciation of Love. As the tempo quickens, the falling semitone (ex.4) suggests the proximity of greed, evil and servitude, while an obsessively repeated perversion of the Love motif (ex.3) warns of the dangerous forces unleashed in Alberich by sexual frustration. B♭ minor gradually emerges through the sulphurous mists as the primary key, which is then reinforced by a symphonic working of the motifs associated with the Nibelungs and servitude. Eighteen anvils behind the scenes thunder out the dotted rhythm of the Nibelungs' motif. The F they sound is not an arbitrary note, but part of a gigantic dominant preparation for the Nibelheim scene.

Scene iii *The subterranean caverns of Nibelheim .* B♭ minor is to dominate this scene, as it does others featuring the Nibelungs later in the *Ring*. In the depths of Nibelheim, Alberich is tormenting his weaker brother Mime, and demands the magic Tarnhelm that he has forced him to make. The Tarnhelm (represented by a mysterious-sounding motif on muted horns) renders its wearer invisible, and Alberich proves its efficacy by disappearing and raining blows on the defenceless Mime. Alberich eventually leaves, and Wotan and Loge arrive. Loge, offering to help Mime, hears from him (against a background of first the Ring motif and then that of the Nibelungs, with the falling semitone now identified with servitude) how the carefree race of Nibelung blacksmiths has been held in thrall by Alberich since he forged a ring from the Rhinegold.

Alberich returns, driving his slaves with whiplashes to pile up the gold. He brandishes the ring, in a climactic eight-bar passage of immensely compressed power, and they scatter in all directions. Alberich now turns his attention to the strangers. Scornfully dismissing Loge's reminders of their earlier friendship, Alberich boasts about his new-found power and threatens one day to vanquish the gods and force his favours on their women. The threat is made in a stark recitative-like passage following a striking appropriation by Alberich of the sumptuous Valhalla music. Loge pretends to flatter him, but asks how, mighty as he is, he would protect himself against a thief in the night. Alberich shows him the Tarnhelm and Loge asks for a demonstration. To a coiling serpentine theme Alberich turns himself into a dragon. Loge feigns terror and goads Alberich into turning himself into something small like a toad. Alberich duly obliges and is trapped by the gods. Each of Alberich's transformations switches the tonality briefly to G♯ minor (the key associated with the Tarnhelm) within a broader context of A major. The latter is the closest the tonally unstable Loge comes to having a key; the chief tonality of the scene remains B♭, that of the Nibelungs. Wotan and Loge tie Alberich and drag him to the surface, to the accompaniment of another transition passage in which many prominent motifs are subjected to symphonic development.

Scene iv *An open space on a mountain height, near the Rhine* Wotan and Loge deride Alberich's pretensions to world domination: if he wants to be free, they tell him, he will have to give up the gold. Intending to keep the ring to generate more gold, Alberich agrees to hand over the treasure. His right hand is untied – a series of demisemiquaver slides illustrate the rope slipping away – and he summons the Nibelungs with the ring. To the obsessive accompaniment of their dotted figure, the Nibelungs drag in the gold; the continually repeated falling semitone alludes both to the servitude of the Nibelungs and to Alberich's fuming disgrace at being seen in captivity by his slaves. Loge adds the Tarnhelm to the pile of gold, and to Alberich's horror, Wotan demands the ring on his finger too. It is eventually wrested from him by force, at which Alberich delivers, against a single, sinister drum roll, his fateful curse, 'Wie durch Fluch er mir geriet': the ring will bring anxiety and death to whoever owns it; those who possess it will be racked with torment, those who do not will be consumed with envy.

Alberich vanishes, the atmosphere clears and, to the sound of divided violins soaring and descending together, it grows lighter. Donner, Froh and Fricka welcome back Wotan and Loge, who show them Freia's ransom: the pile of gold. Freia returns with the giants, but Fasolt, reluctant to relinquish her, insists that the gold be stacked so as to hide her from sight. Loge and Froh pile up the treasure, filling all the gaps. But Fafner can still see Freia's hair: the Tarnhelm has to be thrown on the heap. Fasolt too can see her shining eyes through a chink, and Fafner demands that the ring on Wotan's finger be used to stop the gap. The Rhinemaidens' falling tone (ex.2) is heard as Loge suggests that Wotan will be returning the ring to them. But Wotan refuses to yield the ring, remaining impervious both to the giants, who threaten to take Freia away again, and to the other gods, who beg him to relent. Finally Erda, the earth goddess, appears in a blue light from a rocky cleft. Her motif (ex.7), intoned initially on bassoons and Wagner tubas, is a minor variant of the Nature motif (ex.1). The new tonal area (C♯ minor), slow tempo and sombre colouring of the Erda scene mark it out as one of considerable individuality and importance: 'Weiche, Wotan! weiche!' Erda warns Wotan that

Ex.7

possession of the ring condemns him to irredeemable dark perdition. A dark day is dawning for the gods: he should yield up the ring. The prophecy evokes an inversion of Erda's theme, the descending form being known as the Twilight of the Gods (ex.8).

Ex.8

Erda disappears from sight and Wotan reluctantly decides to heed her advice. He tosses the ring on the pile, but the joyfully expansive phrases greeting Freia's release give way to nagging figures of worry and greed as Fasolt and Fafner bicker over the treasure and Fafner strikes his brother dead. This passage also effects a large-scale modulation to B minor, for the sole purpose of allowing the Curse motif to ring out in its original tonality, on a trio of trombones, at the killing. Thus the tonality of a single motif sometimes determines the key of an entire structural unit. A proliferation of motifs – associated with the curse, the Nibelungs, the ring and Erda – conveys Wotan's agitation.

The gods prepare to enter the fortress. Donner swings his hammer to gather the mists ('Heda! Hedo!'), with brass fanfares over an exhilarating background of swirling string arpeggios. There is thunder and lightning, the clouds lift and a rainbow bridge is visible, stretching across the valley to the fortress. Yet more shimmering effects on strings and winds accompany the theme of the Rainbow Bridge (a radiant transformation of the Nature motif). Wotan greets Valhalla, as a motif later to be associated with the sword rings out on a trumpet. The gods walk in procession to the bridge, though Loge looks on nonchalantly. The wail of the Rhinemaidens, lamenting their lost gold, rises poignantly out of the valley. Wotan, on being told what it is by Loge, dismisses it and as the curtain falls he leads the gods over the bridge to the triumphant strains of the Valhalla motif. The dramatic situation suggests that the triumph will be a hollow one, but there are few intimations of that in the blaze of D♭ major with which the work ends.

*

Das Rheingold, the first dramatic work to be written according to the theoretical principles laid down in Wagner's essay *Oper und Drama* (1850–51), also represents the most rigorous application of those principles – an extreme position which Wagner subsequently modified. If melodic distinction is occasionally sacrificed in the process, there are nevertheless many memorable and accomplished passages in the work, both involving word-setting (Loge's narration in scene ii, for example) and in purely orchestral writing (notably the prelude and the transitions between scenes ii and iii, and iii and iv). Though described as a 'preliminary evening' to the *Ring* tetralogy, *Das Rheingold* is a substantial work in its own right, with characteristics not shared by other works in the cycle.   B.M.

Rienzi, der Letzte der Tribunen
('Rienzi, the Last of the Tribunes')

Grosse tragische Oper in five acts by Richard Wagner to his own libretto after Edward Bulwer-Lytton's novel of the same name; Dresden, Königlich Sächsisches Hoftheater, 20 October 1842.

At the première Rienzi was sung by Joseph Tichatschek and Adriano by Wilhelmine Schröder-Devrient.

Cola Rienzi *papal notary*		tenor
Irene *his sister*		soprano
Steffano Colonna *head of the Colonna family*		bass
Adriano *his son*		mezzo-soprano
Paolo Orsini *head of the Orsini family*		bass
Raimondo *papal legate*		bass
Baroncelli	*Roman citizens*	tenor
Cecco del Vecchio		bass
The Messenger of Peace		soprano

Herald, Ambassadors from Milan, the Lombard
    States, Naples, Bohemia and Bavaria, Roman
    nobles and attendants, followers of Colonna
    and Orsini, priests and monks of all orders,
    senators, Roman citizens (male and female),
    messengers of peace
Setting Rome, about the middle of the 14th
    century

Wagner's reading of Bulwer-Lytton's novel *Rienzi, the Last of the Roman Tribunes* in Blasewitz, near Dresden, in the summer of 1837, shortly before he took up a post as musical director of the theatre in Riga, confirmed his intention of writing an opera on the subject (the idea had apparently been implanted earlier by his friend Apel). He immediately sketched an outline, followed by a prose draft and then, the following summer, a verse draft. A series of fragmentary composition sketches preceded a continuous composition draft, the first two acts of which were completed by 9 April 1839. At this point Wagner and his wife Minna, heavily in debt, left Riga clandestinely for Paris, by way of London, and work on the opera necessarily ceased. Act 3 was begun in February 1840 and the work completed in draft, with

the overture being written last, in October 1840. In the course of Wagner's dismal, penurious sojourn in Paris he was helped by Meyerbeer, who was influential in having *Rienzi* accepted by the Dresden theatre.

The première lasted, according to *Mein Leben*, more than six hours (including intervals), but the work was received with immense enthusiasm, catching as it did the rebellious spirit of the times, and Tichatschek and Schröder-Devrient scored personal successes in their roles. The work was subsequently given both over two evenings and in a truncated version prepared by Wagner himself. The absence of the autograph score (which was in the possession of Hitler) and of any original printed score without cuts has bedevilled the preparation of an authoritative complete edition.

In spite of the practical problems it posed, and somewhat to the composer's embarrassment on account of its stylistic nature, *Rienzi* was one of Wagner's most successful works in the latter years of his life and up to the end of the century. In Dresden alone, 100 performances had been given by 1873 and 200 by 1908. The first production in the USA was at the Academy of Music, New York, in 1878, and in England at Her Majesty's Theatre, London, in 1879.

*

The overture is notable chiefly for the majestically eloquent theme that returns in Act 5 as Rienzi's Prayer and which is succeeded by a vigorous military march.

Act I A street in Rome Rienzi's sister Irene is about to be abducted by Paolo Orsini and his followers when they are confronted by their rivals, the Colonnas. Adriano Colonna, in love with Irene, attempts to protect her in the ensuing brawl. The commanding presence of Rienzi, when he arrives on the scene (with a sudden shift of tonality from D to E♭), quells the fighting; his friends and the crowd all urge him to take power and bring order to the city.

Alone with Irene and Adriano (terzet, 'O Schwester, sprich'), Rienzi tells how he has sworn to avenge his brother, murdered by a Colonna; the motif (sometimes called the Vengeance motif) first heard here is a forerunner of the motif of reminiscence as used in the *Ring*. Adriano atones for his family's guilt by pledging himself to Rienzi; in return, he is entrusted with Irene and they sing of their love in an impassioned duet ('Ja, eine Welt voll Leiden').

A single sustained note is sounded on a trumpet (first heard at the start of the overture, it returns periodically to symbolize Rienzi's revolutionary authority). An excited crowd gathers and acclaims Rienzi as their liberator and saviour from the tyranny of the nobles ('Gegrüsst'). Refusing the title of king, he tells them that the state should be governed by a senate; he himself will be their tribune.

Act 2 *A great hall in the Capitol* An effulgent orchestral introduction heralds the Chorus of the Messengers of Peace: a triumphal song by the patrician youths, clad in white silk, celebrating the success of their peace mission throughout Italy. The Colonnas and Orsini, compelled to obey the law just as the plebeians must, conspire together against Rienzi. Rienzi receives the foreign ambassadors and claims for the Roman people the historic right to elect the German emperor.

A ballet, allegorizing the union of ancient and modern Rome, is performed. Orsini stabs Rienzi with a dagger, but his assassination attempt is thwarted by Rienzi's steel breastplate. Colonna's men have meanwhile attempted to seize the Capitol. Senators and people demand death for the traitors. Adriano and Irene plead for Colonna's life and Rienzi pardons the nobles. In a final ensemble Rienzi's clemency is praised by Adriano and Irene but condemned as weakness by his friends Baroncelli and Cecco; the nobles plot vengeance while the people hail their leader.

Act 3 *The large square in the ancient forum* The nobles are preparing to attack Rienzi, who, with the battle-cry 'Santo Spirito, Cavaliere!', rouses the people to take up arms. Adriano agonizes over his divided loyalty to his father and to the brother of Irene: 'Gerechter Gott!' A grand procession of senators and armed citizens is led by Rienzi, fully armed and on horseback: the battle-cry 'Santo Spirito, Cavaliere!' is re-echoed, and there is some heavily scored military music.

Adriano begs in vain to be sent as an ambassador to his father. He tells Irene that death is calling him, but finally yields to her entreaties to stay and protect her. Irene and the women pray for victory and in due course Rienzi returns in triumph; the bodies of Orsini and Colonna are borne in on litters. Adriano curses Rienzi and vows revenge. Rienzi is borne aloft on a triumphal chariot, crowned with a laurel wreath.

Act 4 *A square in front of the Lateran church* A series of taps on the timpani open the act in an atmosphere of mystery and conspiracy as Baroncelli, Cecco and some citizens discuss the situation. They deplore Rienzi's arrogance in interfering with the election of the German emperor: the Germans have, as a result, withdrawn their ambassador from Rome. The new emperor, moreover, is an ally of the pope, who was Colonna's protector. Cardinal Raimondo has also turned to the pope for protection. Baroncelli alleges that Rienzi sought an alliance with the nobles, offering his sister Irene in return. The crowd demands evidence of this treachery and Adriano, throwing off his disguise, endorses the charge. The conspirators vow to strike at Rienzi during the

'Rienzi' (Wagner): painting by Baron von Leyser showing the finale of Act 2 in an 1843 Dresden production with Henriette Kriete as Adriano and Joseph Tichatschek (who had created the role at the original Dresden production in 1842) as Rienzi

victory celebrations later that day. As they turn to go, they see a procession of priests and monks, led, to their surprise, by Raimondo; they assume they are entering the church in preparation for the celebratory *Te Deum*.

Rienzi enters in festal garb. Adriano baulks at assassinating Rienzi in view of Irene, while the other conspirators are won over by his rhetoric. Suddenly Raimondo appears on the steps of the Lateran to proclaim the excommunication of Rienzi. As his followers desert him, Adriano tries to persuade Irene to abandon him too, but she remains, in her brother's embrace.

Act 5.i–iii *A hall in the Capitol* Rienzi prays to God for strength: 'Allmächt'ger Vater'; the music of his Prayer draws on the dignified, eloquent main theme of the overture. Joined by Irene, he tells her that he has been deserted by everybody; she refuses to leave him for Adriano and they fondly embrace. Rienzi leaves to arm himself and Adriano enters in agitation. As the commotion outside increases, he tries to carry off Irene by force, but she pushes him away and runs out.

5.iv *A square in front of the Capitol* Deaf to Rienzi's pleas, the people, led by Baroncelli and Cecco, try to stone him. They set fire to the Capitol and Rienzi and Irene are seen on the balcony, clasped in each other's arms. Adriano and the nobles attack the people and try to reach Irene. But as he approaches, the building collapses, burying Adriano as well as Rienzi and Irene.

*

Wagner's conception of *Rienzi* was that of a grand opera, one, moreover, that 'should outdo all previous examples with sumptuous extravagance'. Deliberately planned so that it could not be given in a small theatre, *Rienzi* is generously endowed with marches, processions and ballets. The models of Italian and French grand opera are, however, more evident in Acts 1 and 2 than in the remainder of the work, written after a gap during which Wagner had begun to rethink his stylistic principles.   **B.M.**

Rigoletto

Melodramma in three acts by Giuseppe Verdi to a libretto by Francesco Maria Piave after Victor Hugo's play *Le roi s'amuse*; Venice, Teatro La Fenice, 11 March 1851.

The first cast included Raffaele Mirate (Duke), Felice Varesi (Rigoletto) and Teresa Brambilla (Gilda).

The Duke of Mantua	tenor
Rigoletto *his court jester*	baritone
Gilda *Rigoletto's daughter*	soprano
Sparafucile *a hired assassin*	bass
Maddalena *his sister*	contralto
Giovanna *Gilda's duenna*	soprano
Count Monterone	bass
Marullo *a nobleman*	baritone
Borsa *a courtier*	tenor
Count Ceprano	bass
Countess Ceprano	mezzo-soprano
Court Usher	bass
Page	mezzo-soprano
Noblemen	

Walk-on parts: Ladies, pages, halberdiers

Setting In and around Mantua during the 16th century

Verdi first mentioned the idea of setting a version of Victor Hugo's drama as early as September 1849, shortly after he had returned to Italy with Giuseppina Strepponi. He wanted Salvadore Cammarano to be the librettist; but it was a contract with La Fenice, Venice, signed in April 1850, that eventually brought the opera into being. Perhaps encouraged by the presence in Venice of the accomplished baritone Felice Varesi (who had created the title role of *Macbeth* in 1847), Verdi suggested to Piave, by now the resident poet at La Fenice, that they adapt Hugo's *Le roi s'amuse*, 'one of the greatest creations of the modern theatre'. He had fears that there might be problems with the censor, but Piave – after seeking advice in Venice – managed to reassure him and the plan went ahead under the

working title of *La maledizione*. By summer 1850, however, signs from Venice over the suitability of the subject were not encouraging. Verdi insisted on continuing, saying that he had now found the musical colour of the subject and so could not turn back.

By early October 1850 the cast for the première had been fixed and Piave had submitted a draft libretto. Verdi, still involved with *Stiffelio* at Trieste, had little time to begin composition in earnest and probably did not start drafting the score until late November. However, soon after that, the Venetian police censors intervened: calling attention to the 'disgusting immorality and obscene triviality' of the libretto, they imposed an absolute ban on its performance in Venice. Verdi was enraged, blamed Piave and, refusing to consider writing a fresh opera, offered La Fenice *Stiffelio* instead. Piave, whose doglike devotion to the composer never wavered, hastened to make an acceptable adaptation; entitled *Il duca di Vendome*, this accommodated the censor's objections and was officially approved on 9 December. But Verdi remained steadfast. In a long letter of 14 December, he went into great detail about the dramatic essentials of the subject, insisting (among many aspects that *Il duca di Vendome* had obscured or excised) that the principal tenor retain absolute power over his subjects, and that Triboletto (as the protagonist was then called) remain a hunchback. By the end of the month, a compromise had been reached with the authorities at La Fenice – one which in effect allowed Verdi to retain what he considered dramatically essential – and, soon after, the opera acquired a new title, *Rigoletto*.

Verdi spent the first six weeks of 1851 busy with his score, and arrived in Venice in mid-February to begin piano rehearsals with the principals and to complete the orchestration. The première was an enormous success, and the opera, in spite of continuing problems with local censors, almost immediately became part of the basic repertory, being performed more than 250 times in its first ten years. *Rigoletto* has never lost this position and remains one of the most frequently performed operas in the international repertory.

*

The prelude, as was to become common in mature Verdi, is a kind of synopsis of the opera's dramatic essentials. The brass, led by solo trumpet and trombone, intone a restrained motif later to be associated with the curse placed on Rigoletto; this builds in intensity and eventually explodes into a passionate sobbing figure for full orchestra; the figure peters out, the brass motif returns, and simple cadences effect a solemn close.

Act I.i *A magnificent hall in the ducal palace* The opening scene begins with a lengthy sequence of dance tunes played by an offstage band, over which the Duke and his courtiers converse casually. The Duke has seen a mysterious young woman in church and is determined to pursue her. To drive home his libertine character, he sings a lively two-verse ballad in praise of women, 'Questa o quella'. The Duke then turns his attention to Countess Ceprano, courting her to the accompaniment of a graceful minuet, before Rigoletto enters to mock her unfortunate husband. To a reprise of the opening dance sequence, two conversations take place: Marullo tells the other courtiers that Rigoletto has been seen with a mistress; and Rigoletto advises the Duke to banish or even execute Count Ceprano. The ensuing ensemble (Ceprano and others muttering vengeance against Rigoletto, whose mockery they have often endured) is interrupted by Monterone, come to upbraid the Duke for dishonouring his daughter. Rigoletto's sarcastic reply brings down on him Monterone's terrifying anathema; the scene ends in a further ensemble, with Rigoletto visibly shaken by the old man's curse. This opening sequence is clearly based on the traditional *introduzione* format, but with the difference that it boasts an unprecedented level of musical variety: from the brash dances of the stage-band, to the Duke's light, comic-opera ballad, to the elegant minuet, to Rigoletto's grotesque musical parodies, to Monterone's high drama and the stunned reaction it provokes. But there are also connecting devices (for example the descending melodic motif that opens the dance sequence) and a superb sense of dramatic economy; these serve to bind the episode together, making it one of the richest and most complex opening scenes hitherto attempted in 19th-century Italian opera.

I.ii The most deserted corner of a blind alley Rigoletto, returning home, meets the hired assassin Sparafucile, who offers his services. Rigoletto questions him but eventually sends him away. This brief duet, which is preceded by Rigoletto's intoned reminiscence of Monterone's curse, 'Quel vecchio maledivami!', bears no relation to the formal norms of Italian opera. It is in a single movement, and the primary continuity is supplied by an orchestral melody played on solo cello and bass. Over this, the voices converse with the greatest naturalness, indeed with a restraint that belies the violence of the subject matter. The effect is calm, sinister and seductive: a necessary pause after the preceding hectic activity, but one that adds an important new colour to the dramatic ambience.

Rigoletto reaches his house and offers the first of his long, freely structured soliloquies, 'Pari siamo', in which the contrasting aspects of his personality are tellingly explored within the flexibility of recitative but with the potential emotional charge of aria. The ensuing duet with his daughter Gilda returns us to the formal world of early 19th-century opera, with a conventional four-movement sequence. An opening movement dominated by a syncopated violin melody gives way to 'Deh non parlare al misero', in which Rigoletto's increasingly agonized reminiscences of Gilda's mother are answered by his daughter's broken semiquavers and sobbing appoggiatura ornament. The transition section, as will happen increasingly in later Verdi, also develops lyrical ideas, notably 'Culto, famiglia, patria', in which Rigoletto tells Gilda that she is everything to him. But Gilda wishes for freedom to leave the house. Rigoletto, horrified, calls Giovanna and, in the cabaletta 'Ah! veglia, o donna', enjoins her to watch carefully over her charge. This final movement has none of the driving energy of the early Verdian cabaletta, being far more reminiscent of the relaxed, Donizettian type. But there is room for a remarkable intrusion of stage action: having reached the reprise of the main melody, Rigoletto breaks off, hearing a noise outside; as he goes to investigate, the Duke slips in unnoticed. The cabaletta then continues but with a hidden presence that will lead the action forward.

Left alone with Giovanna, Gilda muses on the young man she has seen at church, hoping that he is poor and of common blood. The Duke emerges from his hiding place to announce his feelings and so initiate a further four-movement duet, though one much reduced in scope and duration in comparison with the preceding number. After a hectic dialogue movement in which Gilda begs him to leave, the Duke declares his love in a simple 3/8 Andante, 'È il sol dell'anima', at the end of which he is joined by Gilda in an elaborate double cadenza. In a brief connecting movement he declares himself to be 'Gualtier Maldè', a poor student; Ceprano and Borsa appear in the street outside and Giovanna, who has not taken her employer's injunction very seriously, warns the lovers to part. The cabaletta of farewell, 'Addio . . . speranza ed anima', is extremely condensed, with the principals sharing the exposition of melodic material.

Gilda, again left alone, muses on her lover's name in the famous aria 'Caro nome'. The opening melodic phrases, as befits the character, are of extreme simplicity, but the aria develops in a highly unusual manner, as a contrasting series of strictly controlled ornamental variants, quite unlike the 'open'-structured ornamental arias of the previous generation. The aria is further held together by its delicately distinctive orchestration, in which solo woodwind play an important part. As the opening melody returns in a coda-like ending, Marullo, Ceprano, Borsa and other courtiers again appear outside and can be heard preparing their revenge: Gilda's abduction.

Rigoletto returns to the scene, and briefly recalls

Monterone's curse before Marullo tells him that they are planning to abduct Countess Ceprano, who lives nearby. While fitting Rigoletto with a mask, Marullo succeeds in blindfolding him. The courtiers sing a conspiratorial chorus, 'Zitti, zitti', mostly *pianissimo* but full of explosive accents. Rigoletto holds a ladder as the courtiers emerge with Gilda, her mouth stopped by a handkerchief. He does not hear her cries for help, but soon tires of holding the ladder and takes off the mask to find his house open and Gilda's scarf lying in the street. To an inexorable orchestral crescendo he drags Giovanna from the house but is unable to speak except once more to recall Monterone's curse, 'Ah! ah! ah! . . . la maledizione!'

Act 2 *A hall in the Duke's Palace* First comes a Scena ed Aria for the Duke, in the conventional mode and a necessary close focus on a character who will see no more of the action during Act 2. Having returned to find Gilda, 'Ella mi fu rapita!' ('She was stolen from me!'), he cries, and in a lyrical Adagio pours out his feelings at her presumed loss. 'Parmi veder le lagrime' is formally structured along familiar lines, but is intricately worked, proving not for the first or the last time that formal conventionality in no sense blunted Verdi's musical or dramatic skills. The courtiers enter to announce in a jaunty narrative that they have duped Rigoletto and have his 'mistress' (actually of course Gilda) nearby; this change of perspective immediately allows the Duke, who is aware of her identity, to launch into a cabaletta of joy and expectation, 'Possente amor mi chiama'. This aria's rather backward-looking melodic and orchestral brashness causes it often to be cut in performance, although doing so unbalances both the scene and the characterization of the Duke, who needs the somewhat vulgar catharsis of this moment to be fully convincing in his Act 3 persona.

The Duke leaves to take advantage of Gilda, and Rigoletto enters for a very different kind of Scena ed Aria. Affecting indifference before the courtiers, he mixes a nonchalant, public 'la ra, la ra' – though one in which the 'sobbing' notes are all too apparent – with stifled asides as he searches for his daughter. The innocent questions of a page eventually reveal to him that Gilda is with the Duke, and against the background of a string figure of gathering intensity he reveals that Gilda is his daughter and demands access to her. The courtiers block his way, and in frustration he unleashes a remarkable aria. 'Corti-giani, vil razza dannata', unclassifiable in conventional formal terms, is in three distinct parts, each marking a stage in Rigoletto's psychological progress. First, against an obsessively repeated string figure, he rails against the courtiers with fierce declamatory force. Then comes fragmentation, a breaking of the accompaniment rhythm, and of the voice: a frightening disintegration. And finally, the

'Rigoletto' (Verdi), the opening of Act 3 in the London première at Covent Garden (1853), with Giorgio Ronconi (Rigoletto), Angiolina Bosio (Gilda), Constance Nantier-Didiée (Maddalena) and Giovanni Mario (the Duke): lithograph from a contemporary sheet music cover

third stage, Rigoletto gains a new dignity and continuity: aided by a solo cello and english horn he asks pity for a father's sorrow.

Gilda enters in despair and throws herself into her father's arms, and so begins yet another four-movement duet. Rigoletto solemnly dismisses the courtiers and bids her tell her story. 'Tutte le feste al tempio', unlike the parallel lyrical duet movements of Act 1, is begun by Gilda: it is she who now achieves a new status from the circumstances that have befallen her. And as with Rigoletto's previous monologue, the duet moves through strongly contrasting sections, from her opening narration, a kind of duet with solo oboe, to Rigoletto's obsessively fixed response, and finally to another clarifying third stage, in which Rigoletto bids his daughter weep and in which she joins him with a completely new kind of vocal ornamentation, only superficially resembling that found in Act 1. Monterone passes by on his way to prison, and this time Rigoletto assures him that he will have vengeance. Staring at a portrait of the Duke, the jester joins with his daughter in a cabaletta, 'Sì, vendetta, tremenda vendetta', that brings the act to a close.

Act 3 *A deserted bank of the River Mincio* An orchestral prelude, in Verdi's severe, 'academic' vein, leads to a brief exchange between Rigoletto and Gilda. Time has passed, but Gilda still loves the

Duke. Rigoletto, promising to show her the true man, has her gaze into Sparafucile's inn through a chink in the wall. The Duke appears, asks loudly for wine and the woman of the house (Maddalena), and breaks into a song in praise of women's fickleness. 'La donna è mobile' is certainly the best-known music in the score, perhaps unfortunately, as its brashness and simplicity make their full effect only in the surrounding gloomy context. The Duke's song dies away, to be followed by the famous quartet. Its first half, 'Un dì, se ben rammentomi', is dominated by a violin melody that carries reminiscences of earlier material (in particular Gilda's 'Caro nome'), over which the Duke and Maddalena converse lightheartedly. Then comes the main lyrical section, 'Bella figlia dell'amore', in which Rigoletto and Gilda join them in a static portrayal of contrasting emotional states. The dramatic aptness of this section is made especially powerful by the manner in which the three principals involved all offer a kind of digest of their vocal characters elsewhere in the opera: the Duke (who carries the main melodic thread) ardent and lyrical, Gilda overcome with appoggiatura 'sobbing', Rigoletto declamatory and unmoving.

A storm is gathering as Sparafucile emerges; over fragmentary bursts of orchestral colour he and Rigoletto agree on a price for the murder of the Duke. Rigoletto will return at midnight to throw the body in the river. The hunchback retires and the Duke is conducted to a room, there dreamily recalling 'La donna è mobile' before falling asleep. As the storm gathers force, Maddalena, attracted to the Duke, tries to persuade Sparafucile to spare him. Professional honour forbids that he kill Rigoletto instead, but he agrees that, if another should come along before the time allotted, a substitution can be made. Gilda overhears this and, in a trio characterized by its relentless rhythmic drive ('Se pria ch'abbia il mezzo'), decides to sacrifice herself. She enters the house, and a terrifying orchestral storm depicts the gruesome events that occur within.

The final scene shows great economy of means. The storm recedes as Rigoletto reappears to claim the body, which has been placed in a sack for easy disposal. He is about to dispatch it when he hears the voice of the Duke again singing 'La donna è mobile'. Horrified, he opens the sack to find Gilda, on the point of death. Their final duet, 'V'ho ingannato!', is necessarily brief, leaving time only for Gilda to look towards her arrival in heaven – with the obligatory flute arpeggios – and for Rigoletto to declaim in ever more broken lines. He recalls the curse one last time, and the curtain falls.

*

Rigoletto is almost always placed as the true beginning of Verdi's maturity, the essential dividing line between 'early' works and the succession of reper-

tory pieces that will follow; and this special placing is commonly seen as exemplified in the striking formal freedom of various scenes. But thus to concentrate on such matters risks a certain distortion: most of the opera's formal innovations have been prefigured in earlier works, and many of its most powerful sections exist unambiguously and comfortably within the formal conventions of the time. However, no earlier work is as impeccably paced as *Rigoletto*, nor does any show its overall consistency of style; and perhaps these matters are best seen as linked not so much to formal matters as to a new sense of musical characterization. With Rigoletto and Gilda in particular, Verdi managed to create musical portraits that function for the most part within the formal norms of Italian opera but that nevertheless manage to develop individually as the drama unfolds. This was as much a technical as an emotional advance; it entailed, that is, a kind of mature acceptance of conventional discourse, as well as an acutely developed perspective on precisely when it could be ignored and when exploited. Though this acceptance was to appear in various guises in the works of Verdi's maturity, it was something that rarely left the composer during the remainder of his long career.   R.P.

Rinaldo

Opera in three acts by George Frideric Handel to a libretto by Giacomo Rossi based on an outline by Aaron Hill after Torquato Tasso's *Gerusalemme liberata*; London, Queen's Theatre, 24 February 1711 (revised version, London, King's Theatre, 6 April 1731).

The first cast included the castrato Nicolini (Rinaldo), Isabella Girardeau (Almirena), Elisabetta Pilotti-Schiavonetti (Armida), Valentino Urbani (Eustazio), Francesca Vanini (Goffredo) and her husband Giuseppe Boschi (Argante).

Goffredo *captain of the Christian armies*	contralto
Almirena *his daughter, betrothed to Rinaldo*	soprano
Rinaldo *celebrated Christian hero*	mezzo-soprano
Eustazio *brother of Goffredo*	contralto
Argante *Saracen King of Jerusalem*	bass
Armida *Queen of Damascus, enchantress*	soprano
A Christian Magician	bass
A Herald	tenor
A Siren	soprano
Mermaids, spirits, fairies, officers, guards, attendants	

Setting Near Jerusalem, during the First
Crusade

Rinaldo was not only Handel's first opera for London
but also the first Italian opera specifically composed
for the London stage; previous examples had been
pasticcios or adaptations. The combination of an
elaborate series of scenic effects with a strong cast
and music of great passion and brilliance made it the
sensation of the season, and (despite mocking notices
from Addison and Steele in *The Spectator*) it had 15
performances before the close of the 1710–11 season.
There were four revivals over the next six years, with
many cast changes and consequent revisions. The
changes for the first three revivals are difficult to
establish because of the absence of printed
wordbooks, but the book issued for the 1717 revival
indicates several differences from the 1711 version,
notably to allow the alto castrato Gaetano Berenstadt
to take over the role of Argante; he was given at least
three new arias. There was no further revival in
London until 1731, when Handel made substantial
revisions to the opera, especially in the final act.
These were partly to reduce the extravagant scenic
demands of the original, and partly to accommodate
a much-changed cast, which included the alto
castrato Senesino as Rinaldo, the contraltos Antonia
Merighi and Francesca Bertolli as Armida and
Argante, and the tenor Annibale Pio Fabri as
Goffredo.

Rinaldo was performed in a German translation
by Barthold Feind in Hamburg in 1715, with revivals
in 1723 and 1727. The first performances since the
18th century were given in London in February 1933
by pupils of the Hammersmith Day Continuation
School at the Century Theatre, Archer Street, and the
'Venture' Fellowship Centre, Notting Hill. The opera
was arranged, translated and conducted by Olive
Daunt. The first modern professional performance
was at Halle in June 1954, conducted by Horst-Tanu
Margraf, and the first in Britain was by the Handel
Opera Society at Sadler's Wells Theatre, London, on
17 May 1961, conducted by Charles Farncombe. It
was also the first Handel opera to be seen at the
Metropolitan, in a Canadian production with
Marilyn Horne in 1984.

Tasso's poem is an epic elaboration of the history
of the First Crusade (1096–9) in which Christian
forces led by Godfrey of Bouillon (Goffredo; c1061–
1100) captured Jerusalem from the Saracens. The
operatic version treats the poem's material freely,
with much emphasis on scenic transformations and
other stage effects. The action nominally takes place
outside the walls of Jerusalem while the city is under
siege by the Christian armies, but some scenes have
fantastic settings of no specified location.

*

Act 1 Goffredo is reminded that he has promised the
knight Rinaldo the hand of his daughter Almirena
if the city is captured. A herald announces the
appearance of the Saracen king Argante, who
emerges from the city to demand a three-day truce,
which Goffredo grants. Argante summons the aid of
Armida, Queen of Damascus and a sorceress. She
appears in a chariot drawn by dragons and proposes
to secure victory by seducing Rinaldo away from the
Christian camp. Her first action, however, is to
abduct Almirena from a beautiful grove in which she
and Rinaldo have been exchanging vows of love.
Eustazio, Goffredo's brother, advises Rinaldo to
consult a local hermit, and Rinaldo vows revenge.

Act 2 Rinaldo, Goffredo and Eustazio, in search
of Almirena, arrive at the shore of a sea in which
mermaids are seen playing. A Siren or Spirit tries to
entice Rinaldo into a boat. He is at first held back
by his companions, but breaks free, boards the boat
and sails out of sight. In Armida's enchanted
palace, Almirena receives unwelcome attentions
from Argante. Armida herself rejoices in Rinaldo's
capture. She offers him her love but he scornfully
rejects it; she tries to seduce him by taking the form of
Almirena, but after initial confusion Rinaldo again
avoids her. Argante then resumes his advances to (as
he thinks) Almirena, promising to free her from
Armida's bondage; but it is the disguised Armida he
is addressing. The two part in anger.

Act 3 By his cave, at the foot of the threatening
mountain on which Armida's palace is situated, a
Christian Magician – the hermit mentioned by
Eustazio – tells Goffredo and Eustazio to ascend the
mountain, giving them magic wands to defeat the
monsters that defend it. The brothers reach the top
and strike the castle gate with the wands, at which
the whole mountain vanishes and Goffredo and
Eustazio find themselves amid a turbulent sea on a
rock, which they descend. The scene changes to the
enchanted garden of Armida's palace, where the
sorceress is threatening to kill Almirena, but
Goffredo and Eustazio arrive in time to save her. The
wands cause the garden to disappear and the scene
becomes open country outside the walls of Jerusalem. The Christian heroes are reunited and resolve to
lead the assault on the city. Argante and Armida,
reconciled, review a march of their troops; the
Christian forces also march and the two armies
engage in battle. The Christian assault, led by
Rinaldo, is successful, and Argante and Armida are
captured. Rinaldo and Almirena are joyfully reunited. Armida breaks her enchanted wand and resolves
to turn Christian. She and Argante are released and
they agree to marry.

The changes in the 1731 revivals affect the plot. In
Act 2 Armida does not appear in Almirena's form but
imitates her voice, and her quarrel with Argante is

precipitated by the latter's admiration of Almirena's portrait. Act 3 loses its marches and battle; instead Rinaldo has to contend with the magically generated obstacles of an enchanted grove. Armida and Argante vanish before the final scene on a chariot drawn by dragons, remaining defiantly pagan. The only new music written for this version is the extended accompanied recitative for Rinaldo in which he tackles the magic grove; the other musical changes were created by the incorporation of eight arias from other operas (five from *Lotario*), and by cuts, adaptations or transpositions. In effect the 1731 version is a pasticcio, and, though a tenor Goffredo may be considered an advantage, the characterization is in general enfeebled and much of the brash brilliance of the original is lost.

*

In his preface to the libretto Aaron Hill suggested that the earlier Italian operas heard in London had been 'compos'd for Tastes and Voices, different from those who were to sing and hear them on the *English Stage*', and that they lacked 'the Machines and Decorations which bestow so great a Beauty on their Appearance'. He had therefore 'resolv'd to frame some Dramma, that by different Incidents and Passions, might afford the Musick Scope to vary and display its Excellence, and to fill the Eye with more delightful Prospects, so at once to give Two Senses equal Pleasure'. Handel's music is certainly both varied and excellent, with much resourceful use of woodwind solos and the addition of four trumpets to the score to produce a wide range of instrumental colour; Armida's final aria of Act 2 includes the unusual feature of improvised harpsichord solos. Some of the musical material was taken from works Handel had composed in Italy three or four years earlier, often substantially reworked. Argante's opening aria, 'Sibillar gli angui d'Aletto', taken directly from the part of Polyphemus in the cantata *Aci, Galatea e Polifemo*, is incongruous despite its appropriately bombastic mood, but the other borrowings fit in well. 'Lascia ch'io pianga', Almirena's heartfelt plea for her liberty in Act 2, was originally a seductive song in the allegorical oratorio *Il trionfo del Tempo e del Disinganno*, but the music is far more moving in its new dramatic context.

The dominant character of the opera is Armida, the first of a line of formidable Handelian sorceresses. She gives an immediate impression of fiery passion in her opening cavatina 'Furie terribili'. The mood reappears in the central section of her great lament in Act 2 ('Ah! crudel il pianto mio'), contrasting with the grief-laden Largo of the aria's main section, introduced by plangent solos on oboe and bassoon. Rinaldo makes a lively hero, rescued from conventionality by 'Cara sposa', his own aria of lamentation on the loss of Almirena in Act 1; the

fully worked counterpoint of the string accompaniment, with occasional chromatic touches, gives it a remarkable emotional power. Almirena, despite 'Lascia ch'io pianga', is a slighter figure, but there is great charm in her birdsong aria 'Augelletti', with its solos for sopranino recorder, and in the playful changes of metre in 'Bel piacere' (taken from *Agrippina*). Of the remaining characters only the blustering Argante is specially memorable. The makeweight arias for the ineffective Eustazio are particularly bland, and the character was cut from revivals after 1713.   A.H.

Ring des Nibelungen, Der ('The Nibelung's Ring')

Bühnenfestspiel ('stage festival play') for three days and a preliminary evening by Richard Wagner to his own libretto; Bayreuth, Festspielhaus, first performance as a cycle: *Das Rheingold*, 13 August; *Die Walküre*, 14 August; *Siegfried*, 16 August; *Götterdämmerung*, 17 August 1876.

The principals in the first three cycles included Franz Betz (Wotan/Wanderer), Amalie Materna (Brünnhilde), Georg Unger (Siegfried), Albert Niemann (Siegmund), Josephine Schefsky (Sieglinde), Karl Hill (Alberich), Friederike Sadler-Grün (Fricka) and Luise Jaide (Erda). The conductor was Hans Richter.

Contrary to Wagner's claim that he turned away from historical subjects on discovering the potentialities of myth for his future music dramas, myth and history were interwoven in the *Ring* from the beginning. Not only was he working on his historical drama *Friedrich I*, begun in 1846, as late as 1848–9, but he was also making speculative connections between the stories of the Hohenstaufen emperor and the Nibelung hoard. Those supposed connections were formulated in the essay *Die Wibelungen: Weltgeschichte aus der Sage*. And although it was previously supposed that *Die Wibelungen* preceded the initial prose résumé and libretto for what became the *Ring*, it is now considered more likely that it succeeded them, probably about mid-February 1849.

The chief sources Wagner drew on for the *Ring* are as follows: the Poetic (or Elder) Edda, the *Völsunga Saga* and the Prose Edda by Snorri Sturluson (all three of which were compiled in Iceland, probably in the first half of the 13th century); *Das Nibelungenlied*, an epic poem written in Middle High German *c*1200; and *Thidreks Saga af Bern*, a prose narrative written *c*1260–70 in Old Norse. Wagner also read copiously around the subject and was indebted to the work of such scholars as Karl Lachmann, Franz Joseph Mone, Ludwig Ettmüller and the Grimm brothers.

Greek drama was also a major influence, not least in its use of mythology, its life-affirming idealism and the religious aura surrounding its performance. The *Oresteia* suggested not only the structure of a trilogy (*Das Rheingold* was merely a 'preliminary evening'), but also the confrontations of pairs of characters, the possibility of linking successive episodes with the themes of guilt and a curse, and perhaps even the leitmotif principle (in Aeschylus's use of recurrent imagery). There are also important parallels between the *Ring* and the *Prometheus* trilogy, especially as reconstructed by its German translator, Johann Gustav Droysen.

Wagner outlined a prose résumé for his drama, dated 4 October 1848, which in his collected writings he called *Der Nibelungen-Mythus: als Entwurf zu einem Drama* (the original manuscript is headed *Der Nibelungensage (Mythus)*). In this résumé the drama centres on Siegfried's death, and, at the conclusion, Brünnhilde purges the guilt of the gods by an act of self-immolation, allowing them to reign in glory instead of perishing. The story at this stage largely follows the order familiar from the finished work, but in autumn 1848 Wagner next compiled a libretto for *Siegfrieds Tod*. This created so much back-narration of earlier events, however, that he subsequently, in 1851, wrote *Der junge Siegfried*, and finally *Die Walküre* and *Das Rheingold* (1851–2). Returning to revise *Der junge Siegfried* and *Siegfrieds Tod* in the light of the whole cycle, Wagner replaced Siegfried as the central figure by Wotan, and altered the ending so that the gods and Valhalla are all destroyed by fire. *Der junge Siegfried* and *Siegfrieds Tod* were eventually renamed *Siegfried* and *Götterdämmerung*. Thus the librettos of the constituent parts of the *Ring* cycle were sketched in reverse order, though the original conception was in the 'correct' order, as was the composition of the music.

After its première the tetralogy was not heard again at Bayreuth until 1896, when it was conducted by Richter, Felix Mottl and Siegfried Wagner. Complete cycles were given in Munich in 1878, Vienna in 1879 and Hamburg in 1880. Following the success of his production in Leipzig in 1878, Angelo Neumann took it on a Europe-wide tour with his travelling theatre, beginning in 1882. The first complete cycle in Britain was given at Her Majesty's, London, in 1882, in German, with Anton Seidl conducting, Emil Scaria as Wotan/Wanderer and Albert Niemann as Siegmund. Not until 1908 was it given in London in English, in uncut performances under the baton of Hans Richter. The first complete cycle in the USA was given at the Metropolitan in 1889, with Lilli Lehmann as Brünnhilde; the conductor was Seidl.

Notable Wotan/Wanderers have included Anton van Rooy, Friedrich Schorr, Rudolf Bockelmann, Hans Hotter, Theo Adam, Donald McIntyre, Norman Bailey, James Morris and John Tomlinson. Brünnhilde has been sung by Lilli Lehmann, Lillian Nordica, Eva Turner, Florence Austral, Frida Leider, Germaine Lubin, Kirsten Flagstad, Astrid Varnay, Birgit Nilsson, Rita Hunter, Gwyneth Jones and Hildegard Behrens. Interpreters of Siegfried have included Jean de Reszke, Lauritz Melchior, Max Lorenz, Wolfgang Windgassen, Jess Thomas, Ludwig Suthaus, Alberto Remedios, René Kollo, Manfred Jung and Siegfried Jerusalem. Siegmund has been sung by Niemann, Set Svanholm, Ramón Vinay, James King, Windgassen, Jon Vickers, Remedios, Peter Hofmann and Jerusalem. Sieglinde has been sung by Lilli Lehmann, Nordica, Milka Ternina, Maria Jeritza, Lotte Lehmann, Flagstad, Varnay, Leonie Rysanek, Régine Crespin, Jessye Norman, Cheryl Studer and Nadine Secunde. Notable conductors of the *Ring* have included Richter, Mottl, Seidl, Mahler, Arthur Nikisch, Artur Bodanzky, Albert Coates, Bruno Walter, Thomas Beecham, Wilhelm Furtwängler, Rudolf Kempe, Georg Solti, Herbert von Karajan, Reginald Goodall, Karl Böhm, Pierre Boulez, Colin Davis, Daniel Barenboim, Bernard Haitink and James Levine.

Interpretations of the *Ring*, both literary and dramaturgical, have ranged from those that explore the work's social and political context to those that focus on its imagery and mythological content, denying any political ramifications. Shaw's classic interpretation of the *Ring* (1898) as a socialist allegory has been hugely influential, as has Donington's radically different analysis of the work in terms of Jungian psychology (1963). Taking their cue perhaps from Shaw, a series of radical stagings in the 1970s and 80s attempted to demythologize the work, emphasizing the corruption and debased moral values by which the gods, and in particular Wotan, are tainted. Recent productions have also dwelt on feminist and ecological aspects of the *Ring*.

See also *Götterdämmerung*; *Rheingold, Das*; *Siegfried*; and *Walküre, Die*.   B.M.

Ritorno d'Ulisse in patria, Il
('The Return of Ulysses to his Homeland')

Dramma per musica in a prologue and three acts by Claudio Monteverdi to a libretto by Giacomo Badoaro after Homer's *Odyssey* (books 13–23); Venice, Teatro SS Giovanni e Paolo, 1640.

Four of the singers in the second production at Bologna are known, and they probably also sang in Venice – Giulia Paolelli as Penelope, Maddalena Manelli as Minerva, her husband Francesco, possibly as Ulysses, and son Costantino.

L'Humana Fragilità [Human Frailty]	soprano
Il Tempo [Time]	bass
La Fortuna [Fortune]	soprano
Amore [Cupid]	soprano
Penelope *Ulysses' wife*	soprano
Ericlea [Eurycleia] *Penelope's*	
old nurse	mezzo-soprano
Melanto *Penelope's young maid*	soprano
Eurimaco [Eurymachus] *a courtier,*	
Melanto's lover and conspirator with the	
suitors	tenor
Nettuno [Neptune]	bass
Giove [Jupiter]	tenor
Ulisse [Ulysses]	tenor
Minerva	soprano
Eumete [Eumaeus] *a swineherd, Ulysses'*	
former servant	tenor
Iro [Irus] *a parasite*	tenor
Telemaco [Telemachus] *son of Penelope*	
and Ulysses	tenor
Antinoo [Antinous]	bass
Pisandro [Peisander]	tenor
Anfinomo [Amphinomus]	alto
Giunone [Juno]	soprano

Penelope's suitors } (Antinoo, Pisandro, Anfinomo)

Phaeacians, celestial beings, sea creatures

Setting Ithaca, an island in the Ionian Sea, after
the Trojan War

This was Monteverdi's first opera for Venice,
Badoaro having written the libretto specifically to
tempt him to display his talents on the Venetian
stage. A great success, the opera received ten
performances in Venice and was then taken on the
road to Bologna, where it was performed at the
Teatro Castrovillani, along with another Venetian
import from SS Giovanni e Paolo, *La Delia* by
Francesco Manelli. The work was revived in Venice
the next year (1641), probably at SS Giovanni e
Paolo, although some sources give S Cassiano as the
theatre. The sources include one 17th-century score
and at least nine manuscript librettos, most of them
18th-century copies. The numerous and significant
differences between the librettos and the score,
and the stylistic distinctions between *Ritorno* and
Monteverdi's other late opera, *L'incoronazione di
Poppea*, prompted questions about the authenticity of
the work late in the 19th century, just after the
anonymous score was discovered in Vienna. But
Robert Haas published it as Monteverdi (1922), and
the attribution, though questioned sporadically since
then, still stands.

The differences between librettos and score are
indeed numerous. They include the number of acts
(the score has three, the librettos five), and the text
and characters of the prologue (they are Fate,
Prudence and Fortitude in the librettos). In addition,
several scenes in the librettos do not appear in the
score, and much dialogue is cut and rearranged. But
these differences, rather than casting doubt on
Monteverdi's authorship, tend to support it, since he
was well known for his editorial intervention in the
texts he set. The work has fascinated a number of
composers, several of whom edited – or 'translated' –
the score for performance: Vincent d'Indy (1925,
Paris, probably the first modern revival), Luigi
Dallapiccola (1942, Maggio Musicale, Florence)
and Hans Werner Henze (1985, Salzburg). Gian
Francesco Malipiero's more scholarly edition appeared in 1930. The work can be said to have entered
the operatic mainstream in the early 1970s with
performances in Vienna, in an edition by Nikolaus
Harnoncourt (1971), and Glyndebourne, in a realization by Raymond Leppard (1972), both of which were
recorded.

*

Prologue Human Frailty is taunted by Time,
Fortune and Cupid who claim, in a final trio, to
control man's fate, rendering him weak, poor and
confused.

Act I.i *A room in the palace* Penelope laments
Ulysses' long absence in a passionate monologue, 'Di
misera regina', which is one of the musical peaks of
the opera. Although largely in recitative, it is
structured by two irregularly recurring refrains in
arioso style, both of which emphasize the word
'return', and by Eurycleia's periodic interruptions
as she echoes her mistress's distress. Monteverdi
himself was responsible for creating this piece
through skilful cutting and restructuring of
Badoaro's exceedingly long and shapeless text. The
music consists largely of repeated notes in a low
register and descending motion. In the refrain 'Tu
sol del tuo tornar perdesti il giorno', it rises
chromatically and laboriously to its highest point
over the course of five bars, only to fall back,
exhausted, to the lowest note of the line, an octave
lower, within a single bar. Penelope leaves the stage
even more depressed and without hope than when
she entered.

I.ii Melanto and Eurymachus flirt in canzonetta-
style arias (hers, 'Duri e penosi son gli amorosi',
comprises two strophes with a refrain, which
Monteverdi expands through repetition), and a duet,
'Dolce mia vita sei'; their lascivious concerns and
melodious style provide a vivid and ironic contrast to
Penelope's mournful mood. From this scene we learn
that Eurymachus, allied with the deceitful suitors,
has urged Melanto to persuade Penelope to accept
one of them as her husband.

[**I.iii** Maritime scene with Nereids and Sirens
(missing in the score)]

I.iv *An Ithacan seascape* In pantomime, accompanied by a sinfonia of repeated chords, the
Phaeacians pass in their ship, disembark with the

sleeping Ulysses, and place him close to a naiads' cave with his baggage.

I.v Neptune and Jupiter debate the fate of the Phaeacians, who have disobeyed Neptune's command by returning Ulysses to his homeland. Neptune expresses his anger in martial arpeggios (the *stile concitato* or warlike style) and furious melismatic passages that exploit the extremes of his bass range. Jupiter approves Neptune's punishment of the Phaeacians.

I.vi The Phaeacians, in their ship, arrogantly sing of man's independence of the gods, whereupon Neptune transforms them and their ship into a rock. In intoning the moral of this story, 'Let the Phaeacians learn today that when heaven is against it, the human journey has no return', Neptune emphasizes once more the keyword of the opera, 'ritorno'.

I.vii Ulysses awakens and, in an extended and wide-ranging recitative monologue, expresses his anguish at being abandoned by the Phaeacians in yet another foreign land.

I.viii Minerva appears disguised as a shepherd, singing a cheerful canzonetta, its two strophes separated by Ulysses' hopeful recitative aside expressing his belief that heaven, in the form of this youth, will help him find his way. During the ensuing conversation, Ulysses learns that he is in Ithaca, that she is Minerva and that the suitors have laid siege to his wife and kingdom, but that Penelope has remained faithful. Minerva advises him to insinuate himself into the court, disguised as an old beggar. Ulysses' music becomes increasingly lyrical as he expresses his joy at the good news, with many passages in triple metre. Minerva's music, on the other hand, becomes exceedingly elaborate once she has revealed her true identity. The scene concludes with a dance-like duet, as a group of naiads hide Ulysses' baggage in their cave.

I.ix Minerva sends Ulysses off to find his old servant, the swineherd Eumaeus, while she leaves for Sparta to bring Telemachus home to help his father reclaim his kingdom from the suitors. Ulysses expresses his happiness in an aria built on the refrain 'O fortunate Ulisse', familiar from the previous scene, where he sang it twice in his joyous dialogue with Minerva. More tentative and impulsive there, it is developed here into a considered, full-blown, two-strophe aria with ritornello. Act 1 of the five-act librettos ends here.

I.x *The palace* Melanto, in her typical, seductive, lyrical style, urges Penelope to choose one of the suitors, punctuating her recitative twice with the brief aria 'Ama dunque'. But the queen is adamant in her refusal. And her musical language, stark recitative within a narrow range, likewise remains as austere as ever: she would not risk increasing her suffering by falling in love again.

I.xi *A woody grove* Eumaeus, driven from court by the suitors, delights in his pastoral existence.

I.xii His reveries are interrupted by Irus, the suitors' parasite, who ridicules the pastoral life. His irregular, stuttering music, with its unpredictable repetitions and metric shifts, contrasts markedly with Eumaeus's noble lyricism. Eumaeus chases him away.

I.xiii As Eumaeus wonders aloud about the fate of his master, Ulysses comes on the scene in his beggar's disguise and assures him that his master is alive and will indeed return. Eumaeus, recognizing that beggars are favoured by the gods but not that this one is his master, offers him shelter and, rejoicing in a brief aria in his characteristically simple, pastoral style ('Come lieto t'accoglio'), leads him away.

Act 2.i *In Minerva's chariot* Minerva brings Telemachus back to Ithaca. In a brief aria, 'Lieto cammino', he exults in the knowledge that he will soon see his father. He and Minerva sing a brief duet in praise of the gods' power, 'Gli dei possenti', in which the movement of Minerva's chariot is portrayed by the undulating figure setting the words 'navigan' ('navigate') and 'aure' ('breezes').

2.ii *A woody grove* Eumaeus joyfully welcomes Telemachus in his longest lyrical effusion so far, 'O gran figlio d'Ulisse', concluding with an invitation to rejoice in song. The song that materializes is Eumaeus's lyrical duet with the beggar (Ulysses) on a text full of pastoral imagery ('Verdi spiaggie al lieto giorno'), culminating in yet another emphasis on the keyword, 'ritorno'. After a second duet between Eumaeus and the beggar, Telemachus dispatches Eumaeus to the palace to inform Penelope of his imminent arrival.

2.iii Ulysses sheds his disguise and reveals himself to his son, and they join in a duet of reunion, 'O padre sospirato, o figlio desiato', which gains expressive power through a remarkable freedom of rhythm and melody. It concludes in a forceful, unanimous acknowledgment of the power of the gods: 'Mortals can hope for anything, for when heaven is protector, nature can do nothing, and the impossible often occurs'. Then, in a strikingly linear arioso passage, Ulysses sends his son off to his mother, promising to join him soon, but in disguise. Act 2 of the five-act librettos ends here.

2.iv *The palace* Melanto complains to Eurymachus of Penelope's unwillingness to choose a new husband. They, in contrast, will abandon themselves to love. This scene reinforces the moral polarity between fidelity and hedonism set up in Act 1 scenes i–ii.

2.v As if to confirm Melanto's description of her behaviour, in this impressively symmetrical scene Penelope systematically rejects, one after another, the suits of Antinous, Peisander and Amphinomus. Each suitor argues his case individually in recitative and is joined by the other two in a lyrical refrain: 'Ama, dunque, sì, sì'. Penelope's response, 'Non voglio amar', becomes increasingly emphatic each time it recurs. Her tone is predictably adamant and dour. The suitors decide to try to change her mood with singing and dancing.

[*2.vi* Ballet of Moors (missing in the score)]

2.vii The palace Eumaeus informs Penelope that her son will soon arrive, and perhaps also Ulysses. She responds sceptically that unless her stars have changed their course, such rumours can only increase her grief.

2.viii The suitors overhear Eumaeus's message and conspire to murder Telemachus on his arrival, concluding their deliberations with a trio in the *stile concitato*. But an omen appears in the form of an eagle flying over their heads, which frightens them into renouncing their plan and resolving to try once more to move Penelope, this time with promises of gold. They conclude their scene with another trio, this one in the light style of the *giustiniana*, a popular Venetian dance-song. The use of this patently ironic style in conjunction with the suitors does much to undercut the seriousness of their threat to the kingdom and makes problematic the interpretation of the action that follows.

2.ix A woody grove In her most florid, Olympian recitative style, Minerva assures Ulysses that when he takes his bow in his hand she will enable him to kill the suitors.

2.x Eumaeus reports to Ulysses the suitors' fearful reaction to the news that he might be alive, to which Ulysses, confident in the knowledge that Minerva is with him, responds with a joyful aria ('Godo anch'io'). They set off for the palace in great anticipation. Act 3 of the five-act librettos ends here.

2.xi The palace Telemachus, reunited with his mother, narrates the story of his travels and especially of his encounter with the beautiful Helen, who caused the wars that took his father away to fight. While in Sparta, he reports, a bird flew over his head, which Helen interpreted as an omen that Ulysses would return to slay the suitors and reclaim his kingdom. Telemachus thus reinforces the message Eumaeus delivered and which Penelope rejected four scenes earlier.

2.xii All the characters are present in this beautifully constructed scene, the longest in the opera. It builds gradually and inevitably as the beggar comes closer and closer to the centre of the action. First, along with Eumaeus, he is mocked and vilified by the suitors for his lowly appearance; next, the stuttering, blustering Irus challenges him to a fight and is soundly – and pathetically – defeated, a premonition of the climax of the scene yet to come. Welcomed by Penelope for his bravery, the beggar

then observes each suitor's vain attempt to woo the queen with lavish gifts. Unaware of Minerva's influence, Penelope surprises herself by agreeing to yield to the one who can string Ulysses' mighty bow. The three trials, each more fatuous than the last, end in ignominious failure. Now the beggar, having earned the right by his bravery, humbly asks a turn, assuring the queen that he does not seek the suitor's prize. All are amazed when he succeeds, whereupon, invoking Jupiter and Minerva, he unleashes his pent-up fury and, screaming for their deaths in the *stile concitato* accompanied by strings, he slays the suitors with the bow. Act 4 of the five-act librettos ends here.

Act 3.i In this strange scene, Irus, alone, relives the suitors' defeat in a stark monologue filled with the literal word-imitations of the text for which Monteverdi was so well known. Recognizing that he cannot survive without the suitors, and crazed with fear and hunger, this comic-turned-pathetic character sees death as the only solution, and commits suicide.

3.ii A desert Mercury informs the ghosts of the suitors that they deserved their fate, and they disappear into hell. He then turns to the audience and declares the moral of the tragedy: that death is the end of all things. (Although important for the interpretation of the work, this scene was not set, according to a note in the score, because it was too melancholy.)

3.iii The palace Melanto, whose lover Eurymachus perished with the suitors, urges Penelope to recognize the threat posed by the stranger and to react angrily to the bloody slaughter, but the queen can only continue her lamentation.

3.iv Eumaeus joins them and tells Penelope that the beggar was Ulysses in disguise, but she refuses to believe him.

3.v Telemachus explains that the disguise was provided by Minerva, but Penelope retorts that the gods are merely toying with them and chides Telemachus and Eumaeus for their gullibility.

3.vi The sea Minerva elicits Juno's promise to convince Jupiter that Ulysses should be restored to his rightful place, despite Neptune's objection.

3.vii Juno pleads, Jupiter is convinced, Neptune mollified, and a chorus of heavenly and maritime spirits seals the agreement.

3.viii The palace In a recitative articulated by a lyrical refrain that recurs three times, each time more insistently, Eurycleia considers whether or not to reveal that she has recognized Ulysses in his bath by the scar on his back.

3.ix Penelope continues obstinately to insist to Telemachus and Eumaeus that she cannot accept the beggar as Ulysses, and they continue to argue with her.

3.x Ulysses, in his true form, joins them to plead his case, but she will not listen. Eurycleia now joins their pleas, adding her knowledge of the scar on his back. But Penelope remains adamant. She yields only when Ulysses describes the cover on her bed, which he alone could have known. In yielding, she releases the lyricism that she has kept in check with her emotions throughout the opera, first in an aria ('Illustratevi o cieli') whose extended phrases are echoed by strings, then in a sensuous final duet with Ulysses.

*

The opera builds to its inevitable and expected climax with all the sweep of the Greek epic on which it is based. Its expressive power is intensified by the humanity of its characters, each of them individually drawn by the librettist but even more by the composer. Monteverdi's legendary commitment to moving the affections through the portrayal of real human beings finds its fullest realization here and in his final opera. *Il ritorno d'Ulisse in patria*, however, because of its proximity to its classical source, the realism of its musical language, and its cathartic power, may be the last opera of the period legitimately to offer itself as a re-creation of ancient tragedy. E.R.

Rodelinda [*Rodelinda, regina de' longobardi* ('Rodelinda, Queen of the Lombards')]

Opera in three acts by George Frideric Handel to a libretto by Nicola Francesco Haym adapted from Antonio Salvi's *Rodelinda, regina de' longobardi* (1710, Florence, Pratolino), after Pierre Corneille's play *Pertharite, roi des Lombards* (1651, Paris); London, King's Theatre, 13 February 1725.

The first cast consisted of Francesca Cuzzoni (Rodelinda), the castratos Senesino (Bertarido) and Andrea Pacini (Unulfo), Francesco Borosini (Grimoaldo), Anna Vincenza Dotti (Eduige) and Giuseppe Boschi (Garibaldo).

Rodelinda *Queen of Lombardy,*	
wife of . . .	soprano
Bertarido *usurped by* . . .	alto castrato
Grimoaldo *Duke of Benevento, betrothed*	
to . . .	tenor
Eduige *Bertarido's sister*	soprano
Unulfo *a nobleman, counsellor to*	
Grimoaldo, secretly a friend	
of Bertarido	alto castrato
Garibaldo *Duke of Turin, rebel to Bertarido,*	
friend of Grimoaldo	bass
Flavio *son of Rodelinda and Bertarido*	silent
Setting Milan, in the 7th century	

Rodelinda was Handel's seventh full-length opera for the Royal Academy of Music. It was produced in the same season as *Tamerlano* and with the same singers. The opera was very well received, achieving 14 performances, and was revived with additional arias at the King's Theatre on 18 December 1725 as the second opera of the new season.

Handel gave *Rodelinda* one further revival, on 4 May 1731; cuts and substitutions (the 'new' items all being taken from other operas) make this the weakest of the composer's own versions. A version prepared by Christian Gottlieb Wendt was given in Hamburg on 29 November 1734, with little success, and was repeated in 1735 and 1736. The production at Göttingen on 26 June 1920, in Oskar Hagen's arrangement, was the first revival of a Handel opera in the 20th century (there was a later, more historical revival there in 1953), and was followed by an equally pioneering production in the USA (Smith College, Northampton, MA, 9 May 1931). The first British revival was by the Dartington Hall Opera Group at the Old Vic Theatre on 5 June 1939; it was also given in London by the Handel Opera Society (with Joan Sutherland) on the Handel bicentenary (1959) and by the Welsh National Opera in 1981.

*

The story is based on the account in Paul the Deacon's *Gesta langobardorum* of events in 7th-century Lombardy, and is set in Milan. The Milanese throne, bequeathed to Bertarido by his father, has been usurped by Grimoaldo, Duke of Benevento. In consequence Bertarido was forced to flee to Hungary, leaving behind his wife Rodelinda, his young son Flavio and his sister Eduige, but he has now returned to Milan in disguise, having put out a report of his own death. Grimoaldo, despite being betrothed to Eduige, seeks the love of Rodelinda: marriage to her will confirm his hold on Milan.

Act I The royal palace Rodelinda is mourning the supposed death of Bertarido. Grimoaldo offers himself as a new husband and is decisively rejected. Garibaldo, Duke of Turin and a treacherous ally of Grimoaldo, suggests that matters will be helped if Grimoaldo firmly breaks his promise to Eduige. This he does, and Eduige, encouraged by a declaration of love from Garibaldo, determines to see Grimoaldo brought down. Alone, Garibaldo reveals that he is merely using Eduige as a step to the throne, to which, as Bertarido's sister, she has a claim while Flavio remains a minor.

A cypress grove, with the tombs of the Lombardic kings; among the monuments is one to Bertarido Bertarido, in Hungarian dress, appears, wondering what has happened to Rodelinda. He is joined by Unulfo. The two men hide as Rodelinda brings Flavio to see the new monument to his father. Unulfo keeps Bertarido from revealing himself. Garibaldo appears: he takes

Flavio hostage and threatens the child with death unless Rodelinda consents to marry Grimoaldo. Rodelinda agrees to accept Grimoaldo to save her son, to the distress of the listening Bertarido; but, as she leaves, she warns Garibaldo that she will demand his head as a gift from her new husband. Grimoaldo arrives and assures Garibaldo of his protection. Unulfo and Bertarido emerge from hiding, baffled by the turn of events. Unulfo tries to comfort Bertarido but Bertarido remains angry at his wife's apparent treachery.

Act 2 *A hall in the royal palace* Garibaldo tells Eduige that she has lost Grimoaldo and asks her to marry him instead; her uncertain reply suggests to him that she still loves Grimoaldo. Eduige meets Rodelinda and asks her how she can accept Grimoaldo, now as much a traitor to Eduige as to Bertarido; her former love for him has changed to hate. Grimoaldo greets Rodelinda and asks her to confirm that she will marry him. She demands one favour first – not, as expected, the death of Garibaldo, but the death of her son Flavio, murdered before her eyes by Grimoaldo himself: she cannot be the wife of a usurper while remaining the mother of the rightful king. Grimoaldo recoils from such action. Garibaldo sees this as a sign of weakness, and unguardedly reveals to Unulfo his own ambition for the throne.

The countryside Bertarido is wandering distractedly. His laments are overheard by Eduige, who is amazed to find him alive. She learns with pleasure that his only desire is to rescue his wife and son, not to regain the kingdom (to which she still aspires). Unulfo assures Bertarido that Rodelinda has remained faithful and tells him it is time to reveal himself. Rodelinda, told by Unulfo that Bertarido is alive, longs to see him again; he arrives and embraces her. Grimoaldo appears: is this, he asks, the chaste Rodelinda in the arms of a lover? Bertarido (whom Grimoaldo has never seen) angrily says who he is; but Rodelinda, fearing for his safety, says he is lying to save her honour. Grimoaldo declares that the man will die anyway and leaves the couple to what they believe will be their final parting.

Act 3 *The royal palace* Eduige, concerned to save her brother, gives Unulfo a key to the prison. Garibaldo urges Grimoaldo to kill Bertarido without delay, but Grimoaldo wavers.

A prison cell Bertarido bemoans his fate. His thoughts are interrupted by the sound of a sword dropped into his cell. Hearing someone approaching, he assumes he is about to be executed; he lashes out with the sword and wounds the intruder – but it turns out to be Unulfo, and Bertarido is immediately full of remorse. Unulfo tells Bertarido to take off his cloak (now bloodstained) and gives him a change of clothing; they leave by a secret passage. Eduige, Rodelinda and Flavio arrive to rescue Bertarido: they find the bloodstained cloak and assume that he has been murdered.

The palace garden Bertarido binds up Unulfo's wound and determines to be avenged on Grimoaldo. They hide as Grimoaldo appears, tormented by his crimes; longing for the simpler life of a shepherd, he lies down and sleeps. Garibaldo appears and, taking Grimoaldo's sword from his side, attempts to kill him, but Grimoaldo awakes as Bertarido emerges from hiding; he drives Garibaldo off and kills him. When he returns Rodelinda is amazed to see him alive. Unulfo and Eduige explain that they rescued him. In gratitude Grimoaldo yields the kingdom of Milan to Bertarido and renews his vows to Eduige; she will reign with him in Pavia. All rejoice.

*

Several qualities combine to give *Rodelinda* its deservedly high reputation among Handel's operas: an unusually coherent story, consistent and credible characters, and music of exceptional power invariably apt to the dramatic situation; only Unulfo's arias are of a decorative nature. Rodelinda's rock-like devotion to her husband makes her an especially sympathetic heroine, and the part allows a wide range of emotions: pathos in the mourning arias of Act 1 ('Ho perduto il caro sposo', 'Ombre piante') and in the prison scene of Act 3 ('Se'l mio duol'), defiance ('Morrai, sì', 'Spietati, io vi giurai'), amorous yearning ('Ritorna, oh caro e dolce mio tesoro') and radiant joy ('Mio caro bene'). Bertarido's arias are no less appealing, his first, 'Dove sei?', having rightfully become one of Handel's most famous. The presence of two villainous characters in the cast contributes significantly to the dramatic tension, the more so because the characters themselves are contrasted: Grimoaldo racked by doubts and not wholly without honour, Garibaldo darkly cynical. The confrontation scenes are among the most gripping in all Handel's operas, with the final one of Act 2 perhaps taking the palm: the sense of threat generated by Grimoaldo's explosion of vengeful anger in 'Tuo drudo è mio rivale' gives an almost unbearable poignancy to the grave beauty of the closing duet ('Io t'abbraccio') for Rodelinda and Bertarido.   **A.H.**

Roméo et Juliette ('Romeo and Juliet')

Opéra in five acts by Charles-François Gounod to a libretto by Jules Barbier and Michel Carré after William Shakespeare's play; Paris, Théâtre Lyrique, 27 April 1867.

The cast at the première included Marie Caroline Carvalho, the wife of the theatre's director (Juliet), Pierre Michot (Romeo) and Auguste Barré (Mercutio).

Juliette [Juliet]	soprano
Roméo [Romeo] *son of Montaigu*	
[Montague]	tenor
Frère Laurent [Friar Laurence]	bass
Mercutio *friend to Romeo*	baritone
Stéphano *page to Romeo*	soprano
Capulet	bass
Tybalt *nephew of Lady Capulet*	tenor
Gertrude *nurse to Juliet*	mezzo-soprano
The Duke	bass
Paris *a young count*	baritone
Grégorio [Gregory] *servant to Capulet*	baritone
Benvolio *nephew of Montague*	tenor
Frère Jean [Friar John]	bass

Male and female retainers and kinsfolk of the House of Capulet and the House of Montague, maskers

Setting Renaissance Verona

Gounod first alluded to an operatic *Roméo et Juliette* in correspondence at the end of 1864, and Barbier and Carré produced a libretto in the first three months of the next year; unlike Felice Romani's book for Bellini's *I Capuleti e i Montecchi* (1830), which is only remotely connected with Shakespeare, the libretto for Gounod's opera adheres closely to the great tragedy. As in some of their previous work, Barbier and Carré borrowed directly from their source. Nevertheless, no single French translation of the play out of the many available in the late 1860s may be designated with confidence as the source for the choice of words in the opera.

In April 1865 Gounod began sketching and drafting *Roméo* at Saint-Raphaël in the Midi, a task he finished by July. His progress was impeded by a recurrence of the nervous disorder that plagued him at various times, but over the course of the next year he orchestrated the opera and in September 1866 decided to add a lavish wedding tableau to Act 4. At first he intended the work to be performed with spoken dialogue, but during rehearsals for the first production he filled the interstices between numbers with recitative. The choral prologue, for which Gounod drew on Shakespeare, as did Berlioz in his earlier dramatic symphony *Roméo et Juliette*, was not added until late in the rehearsal period, as was Juliet's *valse-ariette* 'Je veux vivre'. The latter was an obvious concession to Carvalho, who was unable to perform the more dramatic fourth-act *air* 'Amour ranime mon courage' at the first production.

Roméo was Gounod's most spectacular immediate success. Coming as it did during the Exposition Universelle of 1867, when Paris was invaded by visitors from the provinces and abroad, the opera drew full houses for many consecutive nights. It started its rapid conquest of foreign stages at Covent Garden on 11 July 1867 and before the end of the year had been seen at major centres in Germany and

Belgium. After the demise of the Théâtre Lyrique in 1868, *Roméo* found a new Parisian home at the Opéra-Comique (Salle Favart) from 1873 to 1887; variants introduced for this production include an abbreviation of the finale to Act 1, the elimination of the Duke's role in Act 3 and extensive alterations to the finale of that act. The work was finally transferred to the Opéra in 1888, a production for which Gounod penned Romeo's imposing phrase 'Ah! jour de deuil' at the end of Act 3 and a ballet for Act 4. Though not as popular as *Faust*, *Roméo et Juliette* continues to hold the stage internationally.

*

Prologue After a tempestuous orchestral introduction depicting the animosity between the rival Capulet and Montague houses, the curtain opens to a declaimed prologue for the soloists that summarizes the tragedy to follow.

Act 1 *A masked ball at the Capulet residence* The first number is a conventional multi-sectional *introduction* with soloists and framing chorus: in a rousing Second Empire mazurka assembled guests sing of the pleasures that await them; Tybalt assures Paris that he will become enthralled by the beautiful Juliet; Capulet escorts his daughter into the hall and jovially invites his guests to dance in adjacent rooms. When the stage is clear, the masked Romeo and his friends, Mercutio and Benvolio, who in a fit of devilry have penetrated the enemy's house, come out of hiding. Romeo explains that he has recently had a dream that has filled him with foreboding about their adventure. Mercutio dismisses the dream as the work of the fairy Queen Mab, in a three-section piece coloured by delicate violin and flute filigree and many other picturesque orchestral details (ballade, 'Mab, reine des mensonges'). Romeo suddenly catches a glimpse of Juliet and falls in love instantly. He is dragged aside by his friends just as the girl and her nurse Gertrude enter the hall. In response to Gertrude's glowing praise of Paris, Juliet indicates lightheartedly, with appropriate coloratura, that she is not interested in marriage (*valse-ariette*, 'Je veux vivre'). Romeo steps out from a corner and the two realize that their destinies are one in a minuet-like duet, the restrained expression of which mirrors the formality of their first encounter in Shakespeare. Tybalt unexpectedly happens upon them and the two lovers realize their identities. Romeo and his friends beat a hasty retreat but, as the festive music of the opening wells up in orchestra and chorus, Capulet prevents Tybalt from pursuing them.

Act 2 *The Capulet garden by night: to the left, Juliet's balcony* Romeo has stealthily made his way into the Capulet garden. He apostrophizes Juliet as the morning sun in the famous *cavatine*, 'Ah! lève-toi soleil!', where the fading evening star metaphor is developed musically by chromatically descending harmonies against a sustained bass note. Shortly after she appears on the balcony, Romeo reveals his presence to her and declares his love. Their tender words are momentarily interrupted by a comic interlude in which Gregory and other Capulet servants run through the garden in search of a Montague pageboy seen in the grounds. Romeo re-emerges from hiding for a duet ('O nuit divine') in which Juliet confirms that she will marry him at any time and Romeo renews his pledge of affection. When Gertrude interrupts their tête à tête, the two lovers vainly seek to prolong their encounter in an understated *cabalette* ('Ah! ne fuis pas encore!').

Act 3.i The cell of Friar Laurence, daybreak After setting down a basketful of medicinal plants and flowers, Friar Laurence sings of nature's wonders (*cavatine*, 'Berceau de tous les êtres'). Romeo rushes in and reveals his love for Juliet Capulet. She soon follows and the two ask Laurence to marry them. Convinced of the strength of their attachment, he performs the ceremony (trio and quartet, 'Dieu qui fis

'Roméo et Juliette' (Gounod), Act 2 (the Balcony Scene): Adelina Patti as Juliet and Giovanni Mario as Romeo in the first London performance (Covent Garden, 1867)

l'homme à ton image'). The two lovers ritualistically interject a chant-like response between each stanza of his prayer and the three of them are soon joined by Gertrude for a *strette* that extols the bliss of love with an impressive crescendo and melodic sequence.

3.ii A street in front of the Capulet house Romeo's page Stéphano (Balthasar in Shakespeare's play) taunts the Capulets with a song about a turtle-dove held prisoner in a nest of vultures (*chanson*, 'Que fais-tu, blanche tourterelle'), and draws Gregory and other Capulet servants out of the house (finale, 'Ah voici nos gens!'). Stéphano repeats the refrain of his song in their presence and challenges Gregory to a duel. Mercutio and Benvolio come upon them, followed shortly by Tybalt and Paris. Mercutio is indignant over the fact that Gregory is duelling with a child. Tybalt warns Mercutio to mind his words and the two engage in a duel themselves. Romeo appears and asks Tybalt to forget about the hatred between the families. When Mercutio is fatally wounded by Tybalt, Romeo seeks revenge against the latter and in turn mortally injures his rival. A fanfare heralds the arrival of the Duke. The partisans of both houses clamour for justice and, acquainting himself with what has happened, the Duke exiles Romeo from Verona.

Act 4.i Juliet's room; daybreak After an instrumental prelude in which four cellos sensuously translate the essence of the wedding night, Juliet pardons Romeo for having killed one of her relatives (duet, 'Va! je t'ai pardonné'). The two sing of their love in the slow section of the duet ('Nuit d'hyménée!'). Romeo suddenly breaks away from the embrace when he hears the morning lark. Juliet at first refuses to believe him but then comes to grips with reality before a *cabalette* in which they bid each other farewell ('Il faut partir'). Capulet enters after Romeo has left, informing his daughter that she is to marry Paris that very day. Juliet is in despair at this news, and, alone with Friar Laurence, tells him that she would rather die than marry Paris. He suggests a ruse, using a potion by means of which she will appear dead; the Capulets will then transport her body to the family tomb, where Romeo, forewarned, will meet her. Juliet agrees to the plan and summons her courage in an *air* with a heroic melodic cast ('Amour ranime mon courage').

4.ii A magnificent hall in the Capulet palace Juliet is led on with a wedding march. The guests offer their best wishes and present gifts but as Capulet leads her by the arm into the chapel she collapses. Much to the dismay of all, he cries out that she is dead.

Act 5 The underground crypt of the Capulets Juliet lies outstretched on a tomb. Friar Laurence learns from Friar John that Romeo has not received the letter explaining the ruse and instructs him to find another messenger. After a delicate instrumental interlude that evokes Juliet's somnolent state, Romeo appears. Believing Juliet dead, he drinks a vial of poison. At that moment she awakens and the two sing of their love with extensive thematic recollection of past moments in the opera. As he weakens, Juliet uncovers the sword she has hidden in her clothes and, with no musical preparation, abruptly stabs herself. She gives voice to her love once more – in E♭ major, the key of Romeo's initial declaration of love in Act 2 – and with a final monumental effort the lovers ask for divine clemency before they die.

*

Gounod's opera has been the greatest popular success of the many founded upon Shakespeare's play. The four exquisite love duets in the work have drawn particular praise; each has a distinct musico-dramatic ambience and shape. One of the most significant tributes emerged from the pen of Verdi in the *divisi* cello scoring at the beginning of the Act 1 duet in *Otello*, which directly recalls that of the Act 4 duet in *Roméo et Juliette*. In the same duet, the dropping out of the voices during an impassioned orchestral interlude while Romeo and Juliet embrace is particularly effective. The Act 2 duet provides a wonderful instance of the characterization of Juliet, when she gives impassioned utterance to her love but suddenly reverts to soft-spoken delivery with static accompaniment, warning Romeo not to misinterpret her forthrightness as evidence of shallow emotion. Though his famous *cavatine* in that act is in the same mould as Faust's *cavatine* 'Salut! demeure', Romeo is convincing as a romantic lead, especially at such moments as 'Je te l'ai dit, je t'adore' in the duet, where lyricism is enhanced by a change of metre from triple to common time within the prevailing tempo. Act 2 is framed by a similar orchestral passage at beginning and end, in its later version with the voice superimposed in the sort of slow *parlante* over a lyrical strain that Gounod made his own, and of which there are several other examples in the opera. The strengths of *Roméo et Juliette* extend beyond the love music: Mercutio's Queen Mab ballade is highly evocative, and Gounod achieves (what is for him rare) dramatic verve in the great confrontation scene between the families at the end of Act 3. **S.Hr.**

Rondine, La ('The Swallow')

Commedia lirica in three acts by Giacomo Puccini to a text by Giuseppe Adami after a libretto by A. M. Willner and Heinz Reichert; Monte Carlo, Théâtre de l'Opéra, 27 March 1917.

The original cast included Gilda dalla Rizza (Magda), Ina Maria Ferraris (Lisette), Tito Schipa (Ruggero), Francesco Dominici (Prunier) and

Gustave Huberdeau (Rambaldo); the conductor was Gino Marinuzzi.

Magda de Civry	soprano
Lisette *her maid*	soprano
Ruggero Lastouc	tenor
Prunier *a poet*	tenor
Rambaldo Fernandez *Magda's* protector	baritone
Périchaud	baritone/bass
Gobin	tenor
Crébillon	bass/baritone
Rabonnier	baritone
Yvette	soprano
Bianca	soprano
Suzy	mezzo-soprano
A Butler	bass
A Voice	soprano

Members of the bourgeoisie, students, painters, elegantly dressed ladies and gentlemen, grisettes, flower-girls and dancing girls, waiters

Setting Paris and the Riviera during the Second Empire

During a visit to Vienna in October 1913 for a performance of *La fanciulla del West* Puccini was invited by the directors of the Carltheater to compose an operetta. He agreed in principle, later insisting, however, that it take the form of a through-composed comic opera 'like *Rosenkavalier* but more amusing and more organic'. Of two subjects offered successively by Willner and Reichert, Puccini chose the second and entrusted Adami with the task of drawing up the Italian text. Work proceeded slowly over the next two years. In the meantime Italy's entry into World War I necessitated a revision of the contract, whereby the Viennese management resigned their claim to the opera's première while retaining what amounted to half the performing rights. Giulio Ricordi, Puccini's great champion, had died in 1912, and as his son, the younger Tito, showed no interest in the project Puccini contracted with the firm of Lorenzo Sonzogno for the publication. Because of the state of European hostilities it was decided to launch the opera on what was technically neutral territory; hence the choice of Monte Carlo. The first Italian performance took place at Bologna on 5 June the same year.

During 1918–19 Puccini made various modifications to the score, allocating Prunier to a baritone, raising Lisette's role here and there and adding a *romanza* in Act 1 for Ruggero ('Parigi è la città dei desideri'). In Act 2 he reduced the ensemble 'Bevo al tuo fresco sorriso' (based on a lullaby submitted to a periodical in 1912) to a quartet. In Act 3 he eliminated the quarrel between Prunier and Lisette while retaining much of the music, and assigned the final duet to Prunier and Magda. In this form the opera was given in Vienna (9 October 1920) at the Volksoper, where it met with little success. Later, Puccini prepared yet a third version in which the first two acts reverted to their original design, with Prunier once more a tenor. Act 3, however, was altered even more radically than before, introducing a trio of *vendeuses* whose wares Magda cannot afford to buy, restoring the quarrel between Prunier and Lisetta and bringing in Rambaldo, to new music, with a purse of gold for his former mistress. Meanwhile Ruggero, informed of Magda's past by an anonymous letter, drives her away, where previously he had pleaded wth her to stay. Magda would be on stage 'alone and abandoned' as the curtain fell. There is no record of this version's having been performed, nor is there any trace of the material, which was destroyed by bombing in World War II. All subsequent imprints of the score correspond with the original of 1917.

La rondine did not reach the Metropolitan, New York, until four years after the composer's death in 1924. It has never been seen at Covent Garden.

*

Act I   *An elegant salon in Magda's Parisian house*   Prunier is holding forth to his hostess and her guests about the latest fashion for sentimental love. Lisette mocks the idea and is promptly sent about her business. Yet no one except Magda takes the poet very seriously. Prunier illustrates his theory with the story of his latest heroine, Doretta, who spurned a king's ransom for love ('Chi il bel sogno di Doretta potè indovinar'). Taking up a second verse, Magda completes the story, telling how the girl lost her heart to a student; and she repeats the refrain to her own words 'Folle amore!' In every heart, Prunier maintains, there lurks the devil of romantic love. Rambaldo claims that he knows how to exorcise it; and he gives Magda a pearl necklace. She passes it round, to general admiration, but a gentle waltz theme indicates that her thoughts are elsewhere.

Rambaldo retires, having received permission to present to her the son of a childhood acquaintance. Meantime Magda regales her friends with her account of an innocent flirtation with a student at Bullier's Restaurant ('Ore dolci e divine'), to which his words 'Fanciulla, è sbocciato l'amore' form a waltz-like refrain. Rambaldo returns with the visitor, Ruggero Lestouc, as Magda is having her palm read by Prunier, who predicts that, like the swallow of the opera's title, she will fly south to love and happiness. The company are profuse with suggestions as to where Ruggero shall spend his first night out in Paris. The choice falls on Bullier's. As the guests leave Magda decides to remain at home, then thinks better of it and retires to her boudoir to change. Meanwhile Prunier flirts with Lisette to a sly, insinuating orchestral theme. As it is her evening off, they decide to dine out together, Lisette wearing one of her mistress's hats. When they have left Magda emerges dressed as a *grisette*, ready for an adventure at Bullier's, her mind full of Prunier's prophecy and 'Doretta's' secret.

Act 2   *Chez Bullier*   The restaurant is alive with a crowd of students, artists, flower-girls and *grisettes*. Ruggero is alone at a table. Magda appears and to the importunities of the students she replies that she is meeting somebody; whereupon they lead her to Ruggero's table. The young man fails to recognize her, but they converse amicably. Magda teases him about his probable love-affairs; to which he replies that if he should fall in love it would be for ever. He persuades her to join him in a waltz, which grows in grandeur and vivacity, incorporating reminiscences from Act 1. Prunier arrives with Lisette. The dance concluded, Magda and Ruggero return to their table and pledge their newly born love, she giving her name as Paulette. Lisette starts at the sight of her mistress; but Prunier, at a sign from Magda, convinces the girl that it is only a chance resemblance. Both couples begin a slow concertato ('Bevo al tuo fresco sorriso'), which comes to a sudden halt as Rambaldo appears at the head of the stairs. Prunier tells Lisette to keep Ruggero out of sight. Rambaldo asks Magda for an explanation and she replies that she intends to leave him; he bows ironically and retires. Ruggero returns with Magda's shawl, and the two leave to begin a new life together.

Act 3   *The Côte d'Azur*   On the terrace of a pavilion overlooking the Mediterranean Magda and Ruggero are exchanging thoughts about their first meeting and present happiness. But their money is running out. Ruggero is not unduly worried; he says that he has written to his mother for her consent to their marriage and he paints an idyllic picture of his home in the country. Magda is horrified, for Ruggero knows nothing of her past as a *demi-mondaine*. She goes into the pavilion as Prunier and Lisette arrive. The girl is in an uncontrollable state of nerves: Prunier had tried to make her a music-hall singer at Nice, but her début had been disastrous. Magda greets them and gladly agrees to take Lisette once more into service. Prunier subtly delivers a message from Rambaldo: he is ready to welcome her back on any terms. As Lisette goes to resume her duties Prunier leaves, but not before asking to know her evenings off. Magda is joined by Ruggero, joyfully brandishing his mother's reply: she is delighted that her son has found a virtuous bride and looks forward to meeting her. Heartbroken, Magda reveals that she is not a virtuous innocent and declares that she can never be Ruggero's wife. Their last, anguished duet ('Ma come puoi lasciarmi') takes the form of a cabaletta with orchestral peroration over a vocal 'parlante'; Ruggero collapses in tears, while Magda, supported by Lisette, makes her way slowly out of his life.

*

In its musical organization *La rondine* follows a characteristic Puccinian motivic pattern in which there is more room than usual for extended melodies, that are in turn often broken down into recurring motifs. Second Empire Paris is evoked by frequent waltz rhythms of the slower French rather than the Viennese variety; but there are also occasional hints of more modern dances such as the one-step and even (in the lovers' duet in Act 2 'Perche mai cercate') the slow foxtrot. The large orchestral forces are delicately handled, and a number of harmonic audacities worthy of *La fanciulla del West* merely add piquancy to a score of unusual elegance. The main musical weight is thrown into Act 2, where two of the waltz themes are combined vertically, and whose concertato remains the lyrical pinnacle of the opera. In Act 3 the level of invention falls, probably because the theme of renunciation failed to fire Puccini's dramatic instinct. (That the act was written three times to a different plot but (mostly) the same music tells its own story.) Hence, perhaps, the opera's virtual exclusion from the repertory.   J.B.

Rosenkavalier, Der ('The Knight of the Rose')

Komödie für Musik in three acts by Richard Strauss to a libretto by Hugo von Hofmannsthal; Dresden, Königliches Opernhaus, 26 January 1911.

The Marschallin was created by Margarethe Siems, Baron Ochs by Karl Perron, Octavian by Eva von der Osten and Sophie by Minnie Nast; Karl Scheidemantel was Faninal.

The Feldmarschallin [Marschallin], Marie Thérèse, Princess Werdenberg	soprano
Octavian, Count Rofrano ('Quinquin') *her young lover*	soprano/mezzo-soprano
Mohammed *her black page*	silent
Baron Ochs auf Lerchenau *her cousin*	bass
Sophie von Faninal	soprano
Herr von Faninal *Sophie's rich parvenu father*	baritone
Marianne *her duenna*	soprano
Valzacchi *an intriguer*	tenor
Annina *his niece and partner*	contralto
A Notary	bass
An Italian Singer	tenor
A Flautist, a Cook, a Hairdresser and his assistant, a Scholar, an Innkeeper, a Noble Widow	all silent
Three Noble Orphans	soprano, mezzo-soprano, contralto
A Milliner	soprano
A Vendor of Pets	tenor
Faninal's Major-Domo	tenor
A Police Inspector	bass
The Marschallin's Major-Domo	tenor
Four Lackeys	two tenors, two basses
Four Waiters	one tenor, three basses

Servants, hired deceivers, children, constables
Setting Mid-18th-century Vienna, in the reign of the Empress Maria Theresa

This might easily have been Strauss's fourth opera, instead of his fifth: even after securing Hofmannsthal's permission to set his *Elektra* play once *Salome* was composed, he worried whether he ought not to seek instead for a romantic comedy. While the *Elektra* opera took shape, composer and author discussed possible next subjects; Hofmannsthal was anxious to develop a collaboration with Strauss (who fancied a lusty Renaissance scenario). Just weeks after their *Elektra* première in early 1909, the writer announced the idea he had found to fulfil their hopes. It was the romantic-farcical plot that we know, ardent young Octavian outwitting gross, lecherous Baron Ochs for the hand of Sophie – but with the figure of the Feldmarschallin (Field Marshal's Wife), or Marschallin, who would come to tilt the balance of the opera radically, still a mere shadow. (From first to last versions, nubile Sophie was never much more than a desirable pawn.) Much of the action was adapted from the novel *Les amours du chevalier de Faublas* by Louvet de Couvray, a contemporary of Beaumarchais; other ideas were drawn from Molière's comedy *Monsieur de Pourceaugnac*.

Until six months before the première, the title remained the Baron's own mocking one, 'Ochs auf Lerchenau' – literally, 'ox in the lark-meadow'. (His 'auf' is now often changed without licence to a 'von', which would imply a grander status.) From the start, however, Octavian had been conceived as enjoying a liaison with an aristocratic older woman whom he would leave in order to woo Sophie; and as Hofmannsthal came to draw the Marschallin in depth, with Strauss's warm approval, she grew into one of the great soprano roles. Hofmannsthal dignified her further with the Christian names of the historical empress – as if hinting that she really is the empress, tactfully disguised – and a gracious *levée* befitting a Great Lady. The operatic centre of gravity was displaced from the farce to the affairs of the heart. Yet the plot has no further use for her until the denouement, far into Act 3; and before that, as both authors admitted later, the protracted farce palls. To accommodate both strands, the opera planned as a

'Der Rosenkavalier' (Richard Strauss), the arrival of the silver rose in Act 2 of the original Dresden production (1911),
with Minnie Nast as Sophie and Eva von der Osten as Octavian

two-and-a-half-hour light comedy had swollen to three and a quarter hours plus intervals.

The creative collaboration was of the closest – though conducted almost exclusively by correspondence, like every subsequent Strauss-Hofmannsthal project. While the composer insisted upon brisk theatrical effect, the writer stood guard over delicate details of class, propriety and feeling. For this imagined world Hofmannsthal confabulated a marvellous, untranslatable lingo out of Viennese and provincial dialects, frenchified gentility and earthy idioms, antique formal address and pure linguistic fantasy. Strauss not only rose to the prescribed great moments, but invested all the dialogue – sophisticated beyond any purpose-written libretto until then – with subtle lyrical detail. The orchestra for Der Rosenkavalier is nearly as opulent as that for Elektra; a sizable offstage band is specified too, but modern electronics make that thriftier now.

The triumphant Dresden première was conducted by Ernst von Schuch, the first conductor of Strauss's Feuersnot, Salome and Elektra, with Max Reinhardt as producer. The opera travelled quickly (at La Scala Lucrezia Bori sang Octavian, with Tullio Serafin conducting), and soon other singers established stronger titles to the roles: Richard Mayr as a peerless Ochs, Maria Jeritza and Maria Olczewska as Octavian, Elisabeth Rethberg and then – above all – Lotte Lehmann as the Marschallin, followed later by Viorica Ursuleac, Tiana Lemnitz, Elisabeth Schwarzkopf and Régine Crespin. Ludwig Weber and Kurt Böhme were famous Barons. Many a soprano has progressed from Octavian to Sophie (or the other way round) to the Marschallin, notably Lisa

Della Casa. Sena Jurinac made an indelible mark as Octavian. She and Weber sang in Erich Kleiber's faultlessly idiomatic Rosenkavalier on records; Karajan's superbly engineered recording, made together with Paul Czinner's film, boasts Schwarzkopf and (as Octavian) Christa Ludwig.

*

Act I *The Feldmarschallin's bedroom* The orchestral prelude, which notoriously represents a scene of exuberant love-making – complete with climax on whooping horns, and luxurious afterglow – also introduces much of the leading thematic material. (From the outset Octavian's thrusting horn tune suggests the virile swain of the final version, not the light-comedy travesty role that Hofmannsthal first imagined; when the theme crops up later in Octavian's vocal line, it is a rare mezzo who can match the horns in importunate fervour.) Amidst morning birdsong the rising curtain reveals the Marschallin with her 17-year-old 'Quinquin', half in and half out of bed, exchanging satisfied endearments. When little Mohammed arrives (to his own twinkling march) with the breakfast chocolate, Octavian conceals himself so hastily that she has to warn him to hide his sword too. After the page's exit she rebukes him for that ungallant gaffe; they make up over the chocolate, while the music – which has never strayed for long from basic E major – now moves into A for the first waltz of the opera (period-decorous, with a touch of Mozart).

The Marschallin alarms Octavian by recalling an occasion when her military husband came home unexpectedly. (Strauss insisted later that she is no mother-figure – the Lehmann type – but a neglected wife, still young, who has had lovers before and will have others.) They are both alarmed by a commotion and a gruff male voice outside; the youth slips into a screened alcove, while it dawns upon his mistress that the visitor is only her country cousin Ochs. The mischievous 'Quinquin' reappears disguised as a chambermaid, gormless 'Mariandel'. Now the Baron lumbers in, obsequious but self-important, to declare his errand. He needs his fortunes restored, and proposes to marry young Sophie, daughter of the *nouveau riche* Faninal; since his titled status is his trump card, he wants to flash it by having some presentable, well-born emissary deliver his formal proposal with a silver rose. Relaxing in noble company, he regales his hostess with a gross conspectus (often cut, for decency's sake) of his backwoods seduction methods, all the while making crude passes at 'Mariandel'. This panting hunt-monologue becomes a hard, bright trio as his two hearers comment in sarcastic asides. The Marschallin, who has a sense of humour, recommends her kinsman Count Rofrano as envoy, and shows Ochs his portrait in a locket. Spotting a resemblance, Ochs guesses 'Mariandel' to be a half-sister from the wrong side of the blanket (Marie Thérèse does not contradict him), and confides smugly that he keeps his own bastard son, named 'Leopold' after himself, as his body-servant.

He desires also the services of the Marschallin's notary, who arrives – as 'Mariandel' at last escapes – amid the gaggle of household staff and petitioners who gather for the morning *levée*. While Ochs and the asthmatic lawyer confer and the Marschallin's hairdresser gets to work, a trio of genteel orphans solicit alms, an eager pair of social spies (Valzacchi and Annina) find their services brusquely rejected, and an Italian tenor with flute accompaniment hopes to please with 'Di rigori armato' (a slow waltz of a curious cut, vaguely italianate but not remotely Italian). His second verse is cut short by an explosion from Ochs, enraged by the notary's scruples about writing into the marriage contract a hefty 'wedding gift', or Baron-bribe, from Faninal. Gazing sadly into a mirror, Marie Thérèse tells her hairdresser that he has made her look an old woman. The *levée* ends abruptly; but before the Baron goes off he engages the spies to procure 'Mariandel' for him, and his loutish son brings the Marschallin the silver rose.

Alone, she reflects ('Da geht er hin') that she too was married off straight from the convent, like poor Sophie, and that one day soon she will become 'old Princess Resi': a cruel mystery which has to be accepted.

Octavian, returning in his own clothes, is alarmed by her sudden melancholy. She tries to make him understand that time passes inexorably ('Die Zeit, die ist ein sonderbar Ding', with magically delicate instrumentation), though sometimes at night she gets up to stop the clocks; that today or tomorrow ('Heut' oder morgen') he will leave her for a younger woman. (Rocking up and down in wide intervals, the climactic music recalls the 'Recognition' song in *Elektra*, and behind that a confessional passage from Act 2 of *Tristan*.) Octavian protests passionately, feels himself rebuffed, departs chastened and dejected; too late, the Marschallin realizes that she has let him go without a kiss. The lackeys she sends hotfoot after him fail to catch him, as they soon report in a short 'hunting chorus' (which Hofmannsthal detested: it nearly reduces the tender crisis to operetta). She dispatches Mohammed with the silver rose for Octavian, and sinks into a reverie while a high, silvery violin dreams over his virile tune.

Act 2 *The reception hall of Faninal's town house* An excited prelude sets the scene in the household which awaits the rose-bearer – and after him, the noble bridegroom-to-be. Sophie's father and her duenna Marianne are beside themselves with anticipation; she prays to be worthy of the match, reminding herself that her mother's death has left her alone in the world. Amid gleaming pomp Octavian arrives to present the rose, almost stammering over his set speech ('Mir ist die Ehre widerfahren') – from which a rapt duet blossoms: not quite knowing it, he and Sophie succumb to a *coup de foudre*. (With the presentation comes an otherworldly sequence of frosty chords for celesta, harps, flutes and solo violins.) Next on the formal agenda is Informal Chat, in which Sophie's unexpected mettle enchants him still further. The pockmarked Baron makes his entrance with his hayseed entourage, and proceeds to be earthily offensive and patronizing at once. Faninal and Marianne are abjectly grateful while Sophie, to her great distaste, is prodded and pawed like a prize heifer, and Ochs cajoles her with one of his waltzes, 'Mit mir . . .' – 'With me, no night will be too long for you!' (his other one is the rollicking 'Luck of the Lerchenaus').

At last he retires with her father and the notary to settle the contract. The young pair are quickly locked in a tender duologue ('Mit Ihren Augen voll Tränen'), while the Lerchenau louts attempt to press their unwanted attentions upon the Faninal housemaids. As Octavian urges the bride to rebel, the newly hired spies, Valzacchi and Annina, hurry to alert Ochs. General uproar ensues. Octavian announces that Sophie will reject the Baron, who is first amused and then dismayed when a duel is proposed – and bawls wildly when the youth's sword scores a minor flesh wound in his arm. The horrified Faninal requests that Octavian depart forever, and threatens his daughter with relegation to the convent. Eventually calm returns and people disperse, as Ochs is mollified with bandages and wine (and his louts mutter empty threats – in a morose chorus, not at all what Hofmannsthal intended). Annina brings him further cheer: an assignation note from 'Mariandel', which she reads aloud to a waltz version of Octavian's tune (she and Valzacchi are now in the pay of Octavian). Ochs fails to tip her – an egregious error; but the act concludes nonetheless with a swinging, exuberant reprise of 'Mit mir', and a risky low E for the complacent Baron.

Act 3 *A candlelit private room in a cheap hotel, with a curtained alcove containing a bed* The virtuoso orchestral prelude is all hasty, conspiratorial whispers, with much fugato and intermittent punctuation by Octavian's horn motif: a snare is being laid for Ochs. The curtain rises to discover Valzacchi adjusting Annina's false widow's weeds and rehearsing the 'spectres' who are to appear from trapdoors and secret windows. Octavian looks in, wearing his 'Mariandel' dress (but his own riding boots under it), and goes out. Servants make the room ready and light the candles, many of which the Baron extinguishes when he arrives, one arm around 'Mariandel' and the other in a sling, and the unseen hotel band strikes up a new waltz.

Waltz succeeds waltz while supper is served. The solicitous innkeeper and his bustling waiters irritate Ochs, who wants to get on with the seduction. Once he is alone with his prey, it proceeds badly: 'Mariandel' is coyly backward, her face reminds him uncomfortably of the treacherous rose-knight, and at first she declines to drink any wine. (Her refusal is accompanied by an insouciant waltz in C which is later to generate the great soprano trio, much slower. That seems to make no musico-dramatic point, except on the far-fetched guess that both numbers are about 'renunciation'. More probably, Strauss's symphonic instinct demanded that the final crisis-and-resolution be developed from music already heard – not freshly tacked on, as in most Italian operas. Perhaps also he sought to fulfil Hofmannsthal's request, 'Try to think of some old-fashioned Viennese waltz, half sweet, half cheeky, which should pervade the whole Act'.) When she does imbibe, she grows maudlin and vociferous, and to the Baron's further dismay spectral faces loom out of the shadows. Annina bursts in, followed by her 'children', the hotel staff and three policemen, to denounce him as her errant husband. His lofty denial, and his claim to be blamelessly entertaining his fiancée Fräulein Faninal, do not impress the police, for 'Mariandel' loudly bewails her 'shame' – and someone has maliciously summoned Faninal himself, with Sophie in tow. Meanwhile, to high constabulary amusement, 'Mariandel' slips into the bed alcove, changes clothes and re-emerges as Count Rofrano.

Amid the confusion and mutual denunciations, the Marschallin arrives, alerted by one of the alarmed servants. (She seems to bring the real opera back with her, for by now the farce is stretched thin.) Wielding gracious authority, she soothes all the antagonists and puts them firmly in their places; no harm has been done to anyone, Ochs will of course relinquish his claims to Sophie, and the whole affair has been nothing more than a Viennese masquerade (Sophie repeats the phrase ruefully). For the Baron, the penny drops at last – 'Octavian ... Mariandel ... the Marschallin ... Octavian ...!' – but upon a caution from Marie Thérèse he swears silence: it is his moment of real, endearing dignity. Now, however, with most of the crowd rudely thrusting their bills for the soirée at him, he is reduced to ignominious flight with Leopold, while the 'Luck of the Lerchenaus' whirls merrily in the orchestra. (Strauss was determined upon a huge waltz-climax here; unfortunately, the plot-mechanics Hofmannsthal devised are really too frail to support it.)

Faninal staggers off to another room, and only the seriously involved parties remain. The Marschallin interprets Octavian's tongue-tied abashment, and Sophie's baffled distress at believing herself used as part of the 'masquerade'; Marie Thérèse recognizes that now is 'Heut' oder morgen', and comes to terms with that in a poignant, disjuncted trio with the young lovers, who are still on edge and at odds. Discreetly she allows Octavian to understand that the new situation has her blessing, and assures Sophie, after quizzing her like a careful aunt, that her cousin will know the remedy for those pale cheeks. Their great trio begins – in the ultimate Romantic key of D♭, – with her 'Hab' mir's gelobt' ('I vowed to love even his love for another'); Sophie understands that something wonderful has been done for her but prefers not to inquire too far, and the obscure guilt Octavian feels melts away in the glow of new love. By a favourite Strauss sideslip, the music is wrenched into E for a full-voiced, full-hearted climax. 'In Gottes Namen', says the Marschallin, and goes off to coddle Faninal.

Alone at last for the operatic coda, the lovers carol 'Ist ein Traum?' in 3rds and in G major innocence, like babes in the wood. (Strauss hit upon this duet before there were any words ready, and sent his own dummy verses to Hofmannsthal to ensure that the metre was faithfully copied. The inspiration was surely Hänsel and Gretel's 'Fourteen angels' duet, at night in a trackless forest, in Humperdinck's opera; Strauss had conducted its première, and later in the run his future wife sang Hänsel.) The Marschallin and the placated Faninal pass through briefly, on their ways home: he remarks philosophically that young folk just *are* like that, and she replies 'Ja, ja'. Octavian and Sophie embrace again for a reprise of their duet, this time with the end of each line iced by the 'silver rose' chords – chiming intimations of mortality, strangely touching here. After the lovers trip off little Mohammed trips on, in search of the Marschallin's dropped handkerchief, and triumphantly bears it away. Though open questions hang in the air, his modest success ends the story with a wry smile, still in the happy lovers' key of G.

*

The music glories in Hofmannsthal's text, which satisfied Strauss like nothing before. It was cheerful and knowing, fluent and down-to-earth, and yet made room for sumptuous effects and some elevated intensity. His 'symphonic' facility got full scope, but also his modern penchant for inserting chamber-scale music amid his opulent orchestral tapestries. In all previous operas (at least since Monteverdi's time), if there was dialogue with the quick cut-and-thrust of sophisticated conversation it was set as recitative, or else in formal ensembles; but such conversations make the very texture of *Der Rosenkavalier*, and here Strauss outdoes Wagner with dramatic music in which distinctions between recitative, arioso and formal set pieces are continuously blurred. Unaccompanied lines may have as much lyrical force – and even as much weight in the musical argument – as the big tunes, and Strauss tacks mercurially between those modes. Again and again he invests the uttered words with the poignant sense of their unspoken subtext, and in unstinting sympathy with each of Hofmannsthal's characters. With this opera, Opera itself reached a new level of endeavour. Though the score is ripely tonal it has some bold chromatic experiments, too aptly theatrical to attract much notice, but more ingeniously wrought than the bald, sensational ones in *Elektra*.   **D.M.**

Rusalka

Lyric fairy-tale in three acts by Antonín Dvořák to a libretto by Jaroslav Kvapil after Friedrich de la Motte Fouqué's *Undine*; Prague, National Theatre, 31 March 1901.

The first Rusalka was Růžena Maturová; the Prince was sung by Bohumil Pták, Vodník by Václav Kliment, Ježibaba by Růžena Bradáčová and the Foreign Princess by Marie Kubátová.

Rusalka *a water nymph*	soprano
Prince	tenor
Foreign Princess	soprano
Vodník *a water gnome*	bass
Ježibaba *a witch*	mezzo-soprano
Hunter	baritone
Gamekeeper	tenor
Turnspit	soprano
First Wood Nymph	soprano
Second Wood Nymph	soprano
Third Wood Nymph	contralto

Wood nymphs, guests at the castle, the Prince's entourage

Setting A meadow by a lake and the grounds of a castle

Kvapil's libretto for *Rusalka* takes elements from a number of literary sources but derives principally from Fouqué's *Undine* (1811). Hans Andersen's *The Little Mermaid* and the French legend of Melusine were also cited by Kvapil as part of the background to *Rusalka*. In addition, the name if not the nature of Ježibaba is taken from the Czech translation of the play *Die versunkene Glocke* by Gerhard Hauptmann. The debt which Kvapil claimed he owed to K. J. Erben's *Kytice z pověstí* ('A Garland of National Tales') seems to have been more in its generalized national feeling than specific characterization. The libretto is suffused with a fairytale atmosphere which drew from Dvořák (who had used Erben as the basis for four symphonic poems in 1896) music of extraordinary poetry, particularly his evocation of the Bohemian forest. Having written his libretto in the autumn of 1899, Kvapil showed the text to Oskar Nedbal, Josef Foerster, Karel Kovařovic and Josef Suk before Dvořák, who found it entirely congenial. He began work on 21 April 1900 and became absorbed in it, producing one of his most fluent sketches. In the course of composition, he made use of material from his American sketchbooks. By 27 November 1900 the full score was completed. The National Theatre put its finest resources at his disposal, and the work was a resounding success.

Although Mahler (who was conductor of the Vienna Hofoper at that time) took an interest in the work, the first performance in Vienna was given in 1910 by a Czech company. Its German début was on 10 March 1935 in Stuttgart, translated by J. Will. The first professional production in England, at Sadler's Wells on 18 February 1959 (translation by Christopher Hassall), had only a moderate success. A new production by David Pountney in a translation by Rodney Blumer, given by the English National Opera on 16 March 1983, has proved more durable.

*

Act I *A meadow by a lake, surrounded by a forest* In the moonlight three wood nymphs taunt the water gnome (Vodník), who responds good-naturedly. Rusalka calls to him from the willow tree where she is sitting. She asks about the immortality of the human soul and confesses in a brief, exquisite aria, 'Sem často přichází' ('Often he comes here'), that she has fallen in love with a human, the Prince, who swims in the lake. Horrified that she wants to become human, Vodnik sinks into the lake, telling her that she must

Model of the set design by Stefanos Lazaridis for David Pountney's production of Dvořák's 'Rusalka' for the ENO, 1983

ask the help of Ježibaba. Rusalka in 'Měsíčku na nebi hlubokém' ('Song to the Moon') calls on the moon to tell her beloved that she waits for him. She then turns to Ježibaba, who agrees to let her walk on land but warns her that if she does not find love as a human being she will be accursed for ever. Undaunted, Rusalka begs Ježibaba to transform her, and in a humorous conjuration scene ('Čury mury fuk') Ježibaba turns her into a human, except that she cannot speak. As the warnings of Vodník fade with the night, dawn brings the sound of hunting horns. The Prince, feeling strangely drawn to the lake, sends his retinue home. He sees Rusalka; bewitched by her beauty he takes her home to the castle.

The end of this act is one of Dvořák's most effective. He circumvents the difficulty of having no opportunity for a love duet by providing the Prince with lyrical repeated phrases over a magnificently sustained accompaniment.

Act 2 *The grounds of the Prince's castle* The Gamekeeper and the Turnspit, whose music is breathless and has affinities with the idiom of the bagpipe, spin tales of the forest and gossip about the strangeness of the Prince since he met Rusalka in the woods. The Prince is to marry Rusalka, but he is frustrated by her silence and frigidity. During an exchange in which he tells her desperately that he must win her, a visiting Foreign Princess chides the Prince for neglecting his guest. As evening falls other guests arrive for a ballet, dominated by a graceful polonaise. As the merrymaking continues, Vodník appears in the lake, lamenting Rusalka's fate and singing about her future rejection; ironically, this is set against the bridal chorus sung by the guests. Rusalka, who has become gradually more intimidated by her surroundings, rushes into the gardens and, suddenly recovering her voice, begs Vodník to help

her. Her frantic outburst takes the form of an effective though conventional aria, 'Ó, marno to je' ('Oh, useless it is'); rejected by the Prince, she can neither live nor die. The Prince, accompanied by the Foreign Princess, is dissatisfied with Rusalka; he professes his love for the Foreign Princess, whose music has a dotted, perhaps Polish rhythmic quality. Despite the passionate nature of her duet with the Prince, the music remains deliberately cold. At the climax of the duet, Rusalka intervenes and is pushed away by the Prince. Vodník pronounces his vengeance as the Prince appeals to the Foreign Princess for help. In a cruel and cutting couplet, she tells him to follow his love to hell.

Act 3 *The meadow by the lake* Rusalka is mourning her fate. Ježibaba offers her the possibility of returning to her original form if she murders the Prince. In fury and horror Rusalka refuses and sinks sadly into the lake, only to be rejected by her sisters. The Gamekeeper and the Turnspit ask Ježibaba to help the Prince, who has fallen ill since Rusalka left. Enraged by their temerity, Vodník emerges from the lake and chases them away. A *divertissement* follows for the three wood nymphs, who sing of their loveliness and tease Vodník. He responds sadly and in a passage rising to an extraordinary climax tells them of Rusalka's cursed state. The Prince, delirious, comes looking for Rusalka and asks her to return with him. She tells him of her fate resulting from his rejection and that now a kiss from her would kill him. He begs her to kiss him and give him peace. This climactic passage is relatively brief, and although the Prince and Rusalka do not sing simultaneously, the relative simplicity of the music is poignant. Rusalka asks for mercy on his soul and accepting her sad fate disappears into the lake.

*

In many ways, *Rusalka* stood outside the kind of operatic subject favoured by Czech composers in the 1890s and early 1900s, who were more inclined to naturalism. Nevertheless, it soon became Dvořák's most popular opera both in the composer's native land and in other countries. Its success derives from a number of factors. While much of the opera (especially the final act) is static, Dvořák provides music of extraordinarily sensual beauty and genuine depth. The meditative quality of the work offers the perfect vehicle for his blend of the symphonic and the lyric. To a greater extent than in any of his previous operas, the musical texture is through-composed, although there are occasional isolated numbers which may be extracted. Apart from the delicate beauty of such motifs as Rusalka's, which occurs in the prelude and on her first appearance, and is associated with her throughout the opera, the separable numbers provide a focus for exquisite lyricism, notably in the most famous aria in the opera, 'Měsíčku na nebi hlubokém'. Dvořák's word-setting is at its most expressive and most flexible in this work. There was also opportunity for nationally inflected passages in the more vigorous episodes with the wood nymphs at the beginning of Act 1, the first-act aria of Ježibaba, 'Čury mury fuk', and the exchanges between the Gamekeeper and the Turnspit in Acts 2 and 3. Each character has distinctive music reinforced by a consistently used series of motifs. Dvořák's debt to Wagner is apparent not only in the use of personal motifs but occasionally in the harmonic language. *Rusalka* represents Dvořák at the height of his maturity, exercising superb control over musical and dramatic resources. It remains, after *The Bartered Bride*, the most frequently performed Czech opera.   J.Sy.

Ruslan and Lyudmila [*Ruslan i Lyudmila*]

'Magic' opera in five acts by Mikhail Ivanovich Glinka to a libretto by Valerian Fyodorovich Shirkov (with minor contributions by Nikolay Andreyevich Markevich, Nestor Vasil'yevich Kukol'nik, Mikhail Alexandrovich Gedeonov and the composer) after Alexander Sergeyevich Pushkin's narrative poem (1820), incorporating many of the original verses; St Petersburg, Bol'shoy Theatre, 27 November/9 December 1842.

The première was conducted by Karl Albrecht, with Osip Petrov as Ruslan (alternating in subsequent performances with Semyon Gulak-Artemovsky), Mariya Stepanova as Lyudmila, Anfisa Petrova as Ratmir (the role was intended for Anna Vorob'yova, who sang it after the opening night) and Domenico Tosi as Farlaf.

Svetozar *Grand Prince of Kiev*	bass
Lyudmila *Svetozar's daughter*	soprano
Ruslan *a Kievan knight, Lyudmila's*	
betrothed	baritone
Ratmir *a Khazar prince*	contralto
Farlaf *a Varangian prince*	bass
Chernomor *an evil sorcerer, dwarf*	mime role
Gorislava *a maiden in love with Ratmir*	soprano
Finn *a benevolent sorcerer*	tenor
Naina *an evil sorceress*	mezzo-soprano
Bayan *bard*	tenor

Sons of Svetozar, knights, nobles, immured maidens, Giant Head, wet-nurses and nannies, striplings, bodyguards, cupbearers, guests at table, troops, crowd; maidens of the magic castle, blackamoors, dwarfs, slaves of Chernomor, nymphs and watersprites

Setting Kiev and various fantastic locales, legendary times

Glinka conceived the plan for *Ruslan and Lyudmila* in 1836, shortly after the première of his first opera, *A Life for the Tsar*, at the suggestion of Alexander Shakhovskoy, the Intendant of the Imperial Theatres (who had written a dramatic trilogy, *Finn*, based in part on Pushkin's poem). Initially the composer had sought Pushkin's active collaboration. Before they could start work the poet was killed in a duel (29 January/10 February 1837), and Glinka began composing without a libretto. Early in 1838 a writer acquaintance named Nikolay Polevoy, to whom he had played excerpts from the score, wrote (with some exaggeration) that 'the opera is almost finished, but as yet there is no text. A strange way of writing!'

Strange or not, it was Glinka's preferred way, one that had served him well enough in his first opera. The earliest written document of *Ruslan and Lyudmila* to survive is quite in character: a detailed scenario which the composer wrote down in a notebook Kukol'nik had given him for the purpose on 6/18 November 1837. Several numbers are notated in considerable musical detail. A few – both of Lyudmila's arias, the second part of Ruslan's in Act 2, Ratmir's cavatina in Act 3, the trance-induction music in Act 4, the duet in Act 5 – are quite close to their familiar finished form. But in place of text there are only scansion marks to aid the prospective librettist (at this point Kukol'nik), as well as indications of which numbers to base on Pushkin's own words.

Shirkov, a Kharkiv landowner and amateur poet, entered the picture in the spring of 1838, when Glinka requested from him on trial a text for 'Milolika's' (Gorislava's) cavatina in Act 3 and also had him 'underlay words' to the music of Lyudmila's Act 1 cavatina, already sketched in the preliminary plan. Other numbers completed in 1838 were fairly incidental; they included the Persian chorus in Act 3 (to Pushkin's words), Chernomor's March and Finn's ballad (to Pushkin's words, somewhat adapted by Markevich). Then followed 18 months during which domestic trials and the demands of his post as head of the court chapel choir forced neglect of the project. It was upon resumption late in 1840 that Glinka composed the introduction to Act 1 and the finale to Act 5, as well as the long first part of Ruslan's Act 2 aria (the 'apostrophe to the battlefield' on Pushkin's words), and found the uniquely exalted and contemplative 'epic' tone that would eventually characterize the opera. Shirkov having left St Petersburg for his estate in 1841, finishing touches were made with the aid of Gedeonov and Kukol'nik: the former wrote the duet for Ruslan and Finn in Act 2 scene i and also patched the end of the second act; the latter rather messily rewrote the scene for Ratmir and Finn in Act 5 so as to exclude Farlaf's murder of Ruslan, and also supplied the grand finale. The composer himself seems to have been responsible for the text of Act 2 scene ii (Farlaf and Naina). The opera was submitted to the Imperial Theatres in March 1842 and first performed on the sixth anniversary of the première of *A Life for the Tsar*.

Despite the coincidence of dates, the times were not auspicious. The very next year Rubini's Italian opera troupe set itself up in St Petersburg and Russian opera was almost immediately squeezed out of the Russian capital. In its first season *Ruslan and Lyudmila* was played 31 times; in its second, 12; in 1844–5, six; in 1845–6, two; the next season only once. In 1848 the opera was given only in Moscow, and then was dropped until after the composer's death. It has only fitfully held the stage. Denigrated by narrow-minded proponents of opera-as-drama (ever since Alexander Serov, Russia's greatest music critic, called it 'not a drama, not a play, hence *not an opera*, but a randomly assembled gallery of musical scenes'), and cursed with a blessedly complicated score that prevented popular success ('not every operagoer has studied counterpoint', said Count Wielhorski, Glinka's 'friend', who cut the opera to ribbons for the première), Glinka's masterpiece was caught in a crossfire of taste. Performances during the composer's lifetime were never complete (the first such production was given not in Russia but in Prague, under Balakirev, in 1867, and there have been few since; fortunately an uncut recording was made by Bol'shoy forces under Kondrashin in the early 1950s), and as early as 1859 Vladimir Stasov lamented it – in the Lermontovish title to an article written in the aftermath of a fire that destroyed all the scenic and musical materials of the first production, including the autograph full score – as 'A Martyr of Our Time' (more commonly it was referred to as Glinka's *chose manquée*, after an early, influential review by Rafail Zotov). For most, especially in the West, *Ruslan and Lyudmila* has never meant more than a Proms overture (plus, for record collectors, Farlaf's rondo as performed by Shalyapin). But for epicures of the Russian musical stage – and especially for the generations of composers who mined it indefatigably – it has always been (as one of the miners, Tchaikovsky, put it) 'the Tsar of operas'.

It was possibly in response to his swarm of captious critics that Glinka, in his memoirs, had Pushkin vow that he would change a great deal in his youthful poem when it came to transposing it to the musical stage. The aesthetic gulf between the poet's lively, laconic *jeu d'esprit* and Glinka's opulent, slow-moving opera is extreme, going far beyond the oft-reported (and oft-decried) modifications in the plot. (Characters, including another rival suitor, Rogdai, were removed wholesale; Gorislava was added; most of Pushkin's motley anecdotal content, including a vast battle scene, was pruned away; in compensa-

tion, practically the whole *ruses d'amour* intrigue in Act 3 was freshly invented.) Pushkin's racy parody of Ariosto *à la russe* was taken seriously, treated on the one hand universally, as metaphor (the 'Slavonic liturgy of Eros', in Asaf'yev's inspired phrase, symbolizing the life of the heart), on the other 'Ossianically', as national treasure. The result was the quintessential Russian Romantic opera, and the only Romantic opera by a Russian worthy of comparison with the European masterpieces of the genre.

*

Act I *The luxurious assembly hall of the Grand Prince of Kiev: a wedding feast in progress* Svetozar is giving his daughter Lyudmila to the knight Ruslan. Among the guests are Ratmir and Farlaf, Lyudmila's rejected suitors. All listen to Bayan's vatic song, foretelling sore trials followed by renewed happiness won through the strength of love. All sing the praises of the bridal pair and toast Svetozar. Bayan strikes up another song ('Yest' pustïnnïy kray': 'There is a desert land') about a young singer whose lot it is to sing the fame of Ruslan and Lyudmila (Glinka intended this song as a memorial to Pushkin). Lyudmila sings farewell to her father and to her former suitors (cavatina, 'Grustno mne, roditel' dorogoy': 'I am sad, dear father'). Svetozar blesses the nuptial pair, who are then led off to the wedding bed. The chorus sings an epithalamium to Lel', the Slavonic god of love, in the quintuple metre of traditional Russian wedding songs. All at once a thunderclap is heard and the hall is plunged in darkness; with a flash of lightning Chernomor abducts Lyudmila. When the darkness dissipates, all are frozen in a strange thraldom, about which they sing in turn over a pedal. When they come to their senses, all are dismayed at Lyudmila's disappearance. Svetozar promises her hand and half his kingdom to whomever shall rescue her. Ruslan, Ratmir and Farlaf run off in pursuit, egged on by the chorus of guests.

Act 2.i *Finn's mountain cave* Finn greets Ruslan and reveals to him the name of Chernomor, his malefactor. In a lengthy ballad based on a Finnish melody Glinka had recorded *in situ*, Finn recounts the story of his unhappy courtship of Naina, and reveals that she too is wicked. He indicates to Ruslan that good fortune lies to the north.

2.ii *A thicket* Farlaf meets a gnarled old lady and is horrified to learn she is the sorceress Naina. She assures him of her help in defeating Ruslan and sends him home to await her call. Farlaf exults (rondo, 'Blizok uzh chas torzhestva moyego': 'My hour of triumph is near').

2.iii *Foggy night on a deserted battlefield strewn with fragments of weaponry: lances, shields, helmets, swords; also human remains* Ruslan enters, despondent. He has lost his sword and shield in battle; the prospect of the

'Ruslan and Lyudmila' (Glinka), Act 3 (Naina's magic castle): design by Andrey Adamovich Roller for the original production at the Bol'shoy Theatre, St Petersburg, 27 November/9 December 1842

empty field fills him with intimations of failure and mortality, about which he sings the first part of his grandiose aria ('O pole, pole, kto tebya useyal myortvïmi kostyami?': 'O field, who has bestrewn thee with dead bones?'), but gloomy thoughts give way to renewed heroic aspirations as he reaches the faster section ('Day, Perun, bulatnïy mech v ruke': 'Grant me, O Perun, a damask sword to hand'). As the morning fog dissipates, he sees before him the enormous Head of a sleeping giant. The Head (represented by a unison male chorus) awakens and tries to blow Ruslan down. Angered, Ruslan strikes the Head with his lance. The Head, beaten, gives up its sword to Ruslan, thus answering his prayer. 'But who are you, and whose sword is this?' asks Ruslan; whereupon the Head launches into its narrative ('Nas bïlo dvoye, brat moy i ya': 'We were two, my brother and I'), from which Ruslan learns that the Head's brother is none other than Chernomor, that all of Chernomor's strength is in his enormous beard and that the sword he now holds is Chernomor's own, the only weapon that can defeat him.

Act 3 *Naina's magic castle* To distract Ratmir from his quest, Naina sets her magical slave girls singing a Persian song to enchant him ('Lozhitsya v pole mrak nochnoy': 'The dark of night settles over the plain'). Gorislava, abandoned by Ratmir, enters and bewails her fate (cavatina, 'Lyubvi roskoshnaya zvezda': 'O

splendid star of love'). Ratmir enters, exhausted from his long journey (aria with english horn obbligato, 'I zhar, i znoy smenila nochi ten': 'Sultry heat has supplanted shade of night'); the magical maidens awaken memories of his harem (tempo di valse, 'Chudnïy son zhivoy lyubvi': 'Marvellous vision of love astir'). With their dancing the magical maidens plunge Ratmir into a stupor in which he forgets Lyudmila; Gorislava, too, finds him oblivious. Ruslan now wanders in, lured by Naina. Transfixed by Gorislava he too forgets Lyudmila, to Naina's delight. But Finn appears and dispels the charms. The magical maidens disappear, the magic castle turns into a forest, Ruslan is ready to continue his quest, and Ratmir, now that he has found his true love in Gorislava, becomes our hero's ally.

Act 4 *Chernomor's magic gardens, in the distance a river* Lyudmila is tormented by her bondage and by thoughts of Ruslan. She tries to throw herself in the river but the watersprites restrain her. She answers their blandishments with scorn and refuses to submit to Chernomor (aria, 'Vdali ot milogo v nevole': 'Far from my beloved and constrained'). The sorcerer's suite passes by to the strains of a grotesque march, which gives way to a trio of oriental dances – Turkish, Arabian, Caucasian (the 'Lezginka') – with which Chernomor's subjects entertain their master. Military signals announce the arrival of Ruslan. The dwarf puts Lyudmila into a trance and goes off to do battle. The chorus narrates its progress. Ruslan emerges triumphant, accompanied by Ratmir and Gorislava; with the magic sword he has cut off Chernomor's beard. But now he finds to his horror that he cannot awaken Lyudmila. Together with his companions and the whole liberated suite of Chernomor, he speeds homeward.

Act 5.i *Moonlit steppe* Ratmir, standing watch over the caravan by night, sings of his reawakened love for Gorislava (romance, 'Ona mne zhizn', ona mne radost'': 'She is life and joy to me'). The former slaves of Chernomor rush in with terrible news: Lyudmila has been abducted again and Ruslan has gone in pursuit. Finn materializes and explains that Farlaf has stolen her and is bringing her home to claim her from Svetozar. Finn gives Ratmir a magic ring that alone can awaken Lyudmila from her trance. (Ratmir presumably overtakes Ruslan and gives him the ring; this is neither shown nor related.)

5.ii *Svetozar's assembly hall; Lyudmila is stretched out on a bridal bed at rear, surrounded by her father, Farlaf, courtiers, slave girls, nurses and wet-nurses, striplings, bodyguards, troops, crowd* There is a chorus of lamentation: 'Akh ti, svet Lyudmila, probudis', prosnisya!' ('Lovely Lyudmila, come to, awaken!') Farlaf, unable to rouse her despite Naina's help, cowers. From the distance hoof-beats are heard. Ruslan, Ratmir and Gorislava rush in; Farlaf flees. Ruslan awakens Lyudmila with the ring. The hall resounds with rejoicing: the wedding feast is resumed as the walls fall away to reveal a panorama of ancient Kiev and a throng joins in the celebration.

*

The dilatory, seemingly cluttered action, which has occasioned so much critical impatience, is actually a magnificently calculated embodiment of what Mikhail Bakhtin was later to call the epic chronotope: 'closed like a circle, with everything in it totally finished and complete'. On all levels, time is rounded: the outer acts, set in Kiev, frame the magic quest with a single action (a wedding feast interrupted and resumed), in which all the music resonates thematically with Bayan's opening incantation of Pushkin's immortal first couplet: 'Dela davno minuvshikh dney/Predan'ya starinï glubokoy' ('Deeds of long since vanished days/Tales of yore profound'). The overture (written last, during rehearsals) adumbrates the music of the Act 5 finale and provides a musical frame; this cyclic effect is replicated in later acts by the use of entr'actes that quote the respective act finales. The resulting spacious, enclosed, quasi-palindromic structure became a hallmark of Russian opera, applying even to works, like *Boris Godunov*, that on the surface seem far less formal and more conventionally dramatic. 'Epic time' applies on the level of single numbers as

well: Glinka's forms are extremely ample, yet rarely follow sonata or symphonic form (Ruslan's heroic aria being the chief exception). The preferred *modus operandi* is that of 'ostinato variations' ('Glinka variations', as they are called in Russia), in which a melody is repeated with little essential change, while harmony, tonality and tone colour conspire to work a series of 'magic transformations' around it (as in Finn's ballad, the Head's narrative, the Persian chorus, the Act 5 finale). The appropriateness of such a technique to an opera about sorcery is obvious.

Sorcery of a harmonic kind was perhaps the opera's most enduring legacy. Glinka established a convention that lasted at least to the time of *Firebird* and *Petrushka*, whereby human characters are represented by diatonic music and supernatural ones by chromatic. The nature of his chromaticism – involving what are now called interval cycles (circles of major and minor 3rds), scales formed by inserting passing notes into such cycles, and common-tone progressions – remained a potent influence on the Russian harmonic imagination for generations to come (again, up to early Stravinsky). Glinka's open-voiced, primary-hued 'fantastic' orchestration was, through Rimsky-Korsakov, equally influential. Some of his textures and combinations were routinely appropriated by later composers and became generically 'Russian'. (A case in point is the use of piano and harp in tandem to represent Bayan's *gusli* in the introduction, of which the last echo was heard exactly a century later in Stravinsky's Symphony in Three Movements.)

Finally, no inventory of *Ruslan and Lyudmila* as quarry can omit its abundance of vivid national colours, particularly 'oriental' ones that were a veritable craze during the brief Russian Romantic period – a craze that was an immediate consequence of the early 19th-century military expansion into the Caucasus and 'Central Asia'. Glinka's Ratmir is the very embodiment of oriental *nega* (erotic languor – which, once established, could be as aptly expressed in a waltz as in any more authentically Eastern genre), and the archetype for a host of copies culminating in Borodin's Konchakovna (*Prince Igor*) and ending in Rimsky-Korsakov's Queen of Shemakha (*The Golden Cockerel*, 1908). But like harmonic and orchestral colour, national colour in *Ruslan and Lyudmila* is prodigally variegated: besides the colours of the 'Russian orient', the score luxuriates in tunes of Persian, Turkish and Finnish extraction; and there are also powerful residual whiffs of the italianate: *buffo* in the case of Farlaf's rondo, serious in the numbers of the noble characters with their elaborate sequences of tempos – and of course in Lyudmila's coloratura, the summit of virtuosity in the Russian operatic repertory.

R.T.

S

Sadko

Opera-bïlina (operatically treated heroic ballad) in three or five acts (seven scenes, to be grouped 1–2/3–4/5–6–7 or 1/2–3/4/5–6/7) by Nikolay Andreyevich Rimsky-Korsakov to his own libretto, compiled from the *bïlina* 'Sadko, bogatïy gost' ('Sadko, the Rich Trader') and other ancient ballads and tales with the assistance of Vladimir Vasil'yevich Stasov, Vasily Yastrebtsev, Nikolay Shtrup, Nikolay Findeyzen and Vladimir Nikolayevich Bel'sky; Moscow, Solodovnikov Theatre, 26 December 1897/7 January 1898 (Savva Mamontov's Private Russian Opera).

The première was conducted by Eugenio Esposito, with choreography by Loie Fuller; Anton Sekar-Rozhansky sang the title role, with Nadezhda Zabela as Volkhova, the Sea Princess.

Sadko *psaltery player and singer in*		
Novgorod		tenor
Volkhova *beautiful princess, the Sea King's*		
favourite young daughter		soprano
Okean-More *the Sea King*		bass
Lyubava Buslayevna *Sadko's*		
young wife		mezzo-soprano
Nezhata *young psaltery player from*		
Kiev		contralto
Viking	⎫	bass
Hindu	⎬ *foreign traders*	tenor
Venetian	⎭	baritone
Duda	⎫	bass
Sopel'	⎬ *town entertainers*	tenor
First and Second	⎭	mezzo-sopranos
First and Second Wizards		tenors
Apparition *ancient heroic warrior in the*		
guise of a mendicant pilgrim		baritone
Foma Nazar'ich *elder and commander,*		
town father of Novgorod		tenor
Luka Zinov'ich *town father of Novgorod*		bass
Tsaritsa-Vodyanitsa *the Sea King's*		
mermaid wife		ballerina

Men and women of Novgorod from every walk of life, foreign traders from Novgorod and overseas; seamen, Sadko's retinue, minstrel entertainers (merry lads), blind mendicant pilgrims (stern old men); mermaids, beautiful maidens, white swans and wonders of the sea

Corps de ballet: the Sea Queen's 12 older daughters, married to the blue seas; her little grandchildren, the small streams; fish with silver scales and golden feathers and other wonders of the sea

Setting In Novgorod and on the open sea, in half-legendary, half-historical times

Sadko was a historical figure, a wealthy member of a seafaring commercial guild of old republican Novgorod, who in 1167 dedicated a church to St Boris and St Gleb, the first martyrs of the Orthodox Church. He became a legendary figure in the great Novgorod cycle of bardic narratives (*bïlinï*) recovered and recorded by folklorists in the far north of Russia in the 18th and 19th centuries. In most versions, Sadko starts out as a humble *guslyar*, one who entertains the nobility by singing *bïlinï* to the accompaniment of his psaltery. He conceives an ambition to compete with the hereditary merchants of Novgorod, for which he is reviled and exiled. He achieves his ambition by captivating the Sea King with his playing, for which he is rewarded with golden fish, and with the hand of the Sea King's daughter. One way of reading this Slavonic Orpheus tale is as a parable of free enterprise, capitalism *avant le mot*. Such an interpretation resonates wryly with the stage history of Rimsky's opera, his first to be given its première by Savva Mamontov, the Moscow railway tycoon.

The *bïlina* also embodies an interesting metaphor for the collision of Christianity and the older pantheistic pagan religion of the Slavs, when St Nicholas of Mozhaysk (converted into a nameless pilgrim elder in the opera for reasons of censorship) intervenes to end Sadko's sojourn in the Sea Kingdom and sends him back to Novgorod with his bride, who through her metamorphosis miraculously provides the city with an outlet to the sea.

With its musician protagonist and its opposition of 'real' and fantastic worlds, the story was rich material for operatic treatment, a fact recognized by the historian Nikolay Kostomarov as early as 1861. Credit for realizing its potential goes to the musical journalist and historian Nikolay Findeyzen (1868–1928), who prepared the basic scenario in 1894 and sent it to Rimsky-Korsakov, whose tone poem *Sadko* (1867) was by then a concert classic in Russia. (The

Nadezhda Zabela as Volkhova, the Sea Princess, a role she created in the original production of Rimsky-Korsakov's 'Sadko' at the Solodovnikov Theatre, Moscow, 1897/8: portrait by her husband Mikhail Vrubel

tone poem's most characteristic passages all went into the opera, the celebrated opening music with its magnificent evocation of the calmly swelling sea furnishing the introduction, acting as a leitmotif in Scene 5 and crowning the brilliant finale.) Thereupon a great many cooks got to work on the broth (Stasov furnishing the opening feast scene with its depiction of Novgorod society, as well as the tenor-bass pair of entertainers so obviously copied from Skula and Yeroshka in *Prince Igor*; and Bel'sky supplying the poignant figure of Sadko's human wife Lyubava, abandoned and then reclaimed).

*

Scene 1 The merchant brotherhood of Novgorod is feasting. Nezhata, a visiting psaltery player from Kiev, entertains them with a *bïlina* celebrating the exploits of the hero Volkh. This inspires the company to a paroxysm of self-congratulation (chorus, in 11/4 metre). Sadko enters, declines the command to sing, challenges the merchants in a recitative (on an authentic *bïlina* formula) and an aria, 'Kabï bïla u menya zolota kazna' ('If I had a hoard of gold'). His stubborn audacity, when he expresses his belief that if they had access to the sea they could increase their wealth, finally insults the company, who banish him from their midst; after he has gone, the entertainers mock him in a dance-song (based on a prototype in Rimsky-Korsakov's folksong collection).

Scene 2 *The shore of Lake Ilmen* Sadko wanders disconsolately, singing to his psaltery. Suddenly the water stirs, and he beholds a wonder: a flock of white swans swimming on the lake turn into lovely long-necked maidens, daughters of the Sea King, with Volkhova, the beautiful Sea Princess, at their head. Sadko strikes up a joyous *khorovod*, the maidens form circles and disperse into the woods; Princess Volkhova alone remains on the bank. She tells Sadko that her sisters are betrothed to the blue seas, but that she is destined to marry a mortal. Sadko immediately forgets his wife and pledges his love to Volkhova, but as dawn breaks the Sea King rises up from the lake and calls his daughters back. Volkhova gives Sadko the golden fish that make his fortune.

Scene 3 *Sadko's house* Lyubava worries that she has lost Sadko's love. Sadko enters, tells her of his plan to make his fortune on the banks of Lake Ilmen, and leaves her to manage without him.

Scene 4 *The shores of Lake Ilmen* All of Novgorod has assembled (the lines of the blind pilgrims are set to the melody of a spiritual verse imparted to Rimsky-Korsakov by Terty Filippov, Minister of the Imperial Court). The merchants taunt Sadko's latest boast, and wager their fortune against his head that he cannot harvest golden fish from the lake. He casts his net and, with the help of the unseen Volkhova, wins the bet. Now Novgorod's champion, he is celebrated in a narrative tale by the psalterist Nezhata and the entertainer Duda ('Kak na ozere na Ilmene': "Twas on the Ilmen Lake'). Sadko collects a crew and prepares to set sail for distant seas, asking the foreign traders to describe their homelands so that he will know where to go. The Viking trader sings of his country's foggy, gloomy cliffs (Song of the Varangian Trader). The Hindu trader sings of his country's natural wealth (Song of the Indian Trader). Finally the Venetian trader praises his island city's lusty songs (Song of the Venetian Trader). Sadko thanks the singers, takes leave of Lyubava and sets off for parts unknown.

Scene 5 *On Sadko's ship* 12 years later, Sadko and his crew are becalmed. Sadko divines that the Sea King is angry because he has not been paid proper tribute. After casting their cargo overboard to placate the king, to no avail, the crew cast lots to choose a sacrificial victim. Sadko is of course chosen. He takes leave of his crew and is set adrift on a plank, from which he descends with his psaltery to the ocean floor. As he disappears beneath the waves, the wind blows up and the ship sails off.

Scene 6 In the intermezzo between scenes Sadko hears familiar voices (and the audience familiar harmonies). He is greeted by the Sea King with full retinue, angrily. Volkhova intercedes, and persuades her father to ask Sadko to sing. He sings the praises of his host. Delighted, the Sea King grants his daughter's hand in marriage. All the wonders and monsters of the sea assemble for the wedding feast (Procession of the Sea Creatures); they hail the nuptial pair in a Wedding Song. All dance: first, a Dance of the Streams and Rivulets, then a Dance of the Gold and Silver Fish and finally a general dance to Sadko's psaltery. A storm blows up overhead as the result of the dancing. The ghost of an ancient warrior appears in the guise of a pilgrim: he seizes the psaltery from Sadko's hands; the dancing comes to a halt; the ghost commands the Sea King to release his daughter to Sadko and proclaims the end of the reign of nature gods. Sadko and Volkhova seat themselves in a giant sea shell and depart.

Scene 7 *On the green bank of Lake Ilmen* Sadko sleeps. Volkhova sings him a tender lullaby, but when dawn breaks amid the red morning fog Volkhova dissolves and turns into a swiftly running river. Sadko awakes and hears Lyubava's grievous lament; he calls joyfully to her and they are reunited. A fleet of ships now appears on the river Volkhova. All Novgorod gathers and sings the praises of Sadko, the river, the blue sea, the saintly apparition and the Lord (finale, based in part on an authentic *bïlina* tune).

*

This miscellany of highly coloured scenes – a consequence of the way the opera was put together – though open to criticism in terms of dramatic construction, nevertheless conforms to the episodic character of the old epic genre, and Rimsky did all he could to lend his opera an authentic *bïlina* atmosphere. The most imaginative touch was to set Sadko's recitatives to a lection tone reminiscent of the tune to which 'Sadko, the Rich Trader' was actually sung by Leonty Bogdanov, a 70-year-old peasant from the village of Seredka in Karelia, from whom it had been collected by the ethnographer Pavel Nikolayevich Rïbnikov in 1862. Sadko's *gusli* (psaltery), and Nezhata's too, is represented in the opera by the inevitable tandem, inherited from Glinka, of harp and piano.

In terms of Rimsky's stylistic development, *Sadko* brought to its peak the dichotomy established by Glinka in *Ruslan and Lyudmila*, whereby the human world is represented by diatonic and folkloristic music and the fantastic by a highly manipulated chromatic idiom. The second scene, in which Sadko first encounters the Sea King and his daughter, with their scales of alternating tones and semitones, is a classic example of the technique.

The best-known music in *Sadko* is in the fourth scene, when the foreign traders address the Novgorod crowd at the nouveau-riche Sadko's request. The Viking (or Varangian) Trader's song became a recital favourite second to none in the USSR, while the Indian Trader's – known as 'Chanson Indoue' or 'A Song of India' – has long been a staple of 'semi-classical' background music the world over. It is curious that both are paraphrases (knowing paraphrases, one has to think) of popular items from the operas of Alexander Serov (*Rogneda* and *Yudif* respectively). Also Serovian (after the folksong dialogues in *Vrazh'ya sila*) are many of the recitatives. It seems Rimsky-Korsakov was belatedly repaying the long-deceased Serov for his unwontedly warm review of the old Sadko tone poem 30 years before.

R.T.

Salome

Musikdrama in one act by Richard Strauss to Hedwig Lachmann's German translation of Oscar Wilde's play; Dresden, Hofoper, 9 December 1905.

The singers at the première included Marie Wittich (Salome), Karl Perron (Jokanaan), Carl Burrian (Herod) and Irene von Chavanne (Herodias).

Herodes [Herod] *Tetrarch of Judaea*	tenor
Herodias *his wife*	mezzo-soprano
Salome *his step-daughter*	soprano
Jochanaan [Jokanaan] *(the prophet John*	
the Baptist)	baritone
Narraboth *Captain of the Guard*	tenor
The Page of Herodias	alto
Five Jews	four tenors, one bass
Two Nazarenes	bass, tenor
Two Soldiers	basses
A Cappadocian	bass
A Slave	soprano/tenor
Royal guests – Egyptians, Romans – and entourage,	
servants, soldiers (all silent)	
Setting A great terrace in Herod's palace on	
Lake Galilee	

Strauss's first opera, the Wagnerian *Guntram* (1894), was a disastrous failure, and in later years he claimed that this had nearly wrecked his operatic ambitions. However his second opera, *Feuersnot*, with its somewhat earthy subject, was quickly taken up. After its mildly scandalous success, Strauss sought a new subject. Ernst von Wolzogen, his collaborator on *Feuersnot*, worked hopefully at another raffish one-act comedy, drawn this time from Cervantes, but Strauss did nothing with it. Then a young Viennese poet sent him Wilde's *Salomé*, proposing to adapt a libretto from it; the composer was cautiously interested (he imagined it, incredibly, as a possible pendant to *Feuersnot*). Though Wilde's French original had been a failure in Paris, and in England the play was banned by the Lord Chamberlain, a German version had been well received in Breslau in 1901. Using a new translation, Max Reinhardt staged the play in Berlin the following year with spectacular success. Strauss saw it early in 1903 and swiftly decided to set this Lachmann version of the text as it stood, except for judicious trimming (mostly of subordinate clauses, though also of some marginal dialogue and one or two small roles). He began in earnest as he put the last touches to his *Symphonia domestica*, and in little more than a year the entire opera was sketched but for the Dance of the Seven Veils. During the latter months of 1904 he undertook the full score, for a very large orchestra, and completed *Salome* in June 1905.

Though Strauss and the Dresden conductor Ernst von Schuch had to contend with fractious singers, dismayed by the extreme vocal demands (and in the case of the respectable Wittich as Wilde's perverse heroine, by what the producer Willi Wirk expected her to do on stage), the première earned 38 curtain calls. *Salome* was rapidly taken up by opera houses in many countries, despite ecclesiastical disapproval in Vienna which defeated Mahler's hopes of conducting it, and sustained opposition from moralists in England and the USA. Strauss himself conducted the first Austrian and Italian performances, in Graz and Turin, and Toscanini introduced it to La Scala. When at last (1910) the opera was permitted at Covent Garden, it was ornamented by the first soprano with the natural gifts for an all-singing, all-dancing Salome, the Finnish Aïno Ackté. Strauss had imagined 'a 16-year-old princess with the voice of an Isolde', a wildly optimistic formula, and some Salomes have preferred (like Frau Wittich in the première) to let a supple stand-in discard the seven veils.

In fact the multiple facets of the role – always conceived by the composer in terms of vivid dramatic presence, not necessarily choreographic – can be made to gleam by approaches from quite various angles. There have been many famous Salomes, dancing or not, from Emmy Destinn and Mary Garden to Maria Cebotari, Ljuba Welitsch (whose recording of the final monologue set an inspired standard), Birgit Nilsson and Anja Silja. When Strauss decided that the role should be feasible for lighter lyric sopranos, and not only Isoldes, he was hoping that Elisabeth Schumann might undertake it; she never did, but for its Silver Jubilee production in 1930 he effected reductions in the orchestral weight at all the more threatening places. That version is frequently used now. There is also a French-language version – distinct from the 'official' French translation from Lachmann's German – which Strauss himself adapted from Wilde's own idiosyncratic French, with advice from Romain

Rolland; he also made a few striking changes in the vocal lines. It has been reconstructed from its parts and recorded by Kent Nagano with the Lyon Opéra (released 1991).

*

Salome has no prelude; or rather, the whole first scene is the prelude to the action proper, which begins with Salome's entry and ends with her execution. The curtain rises in silence on the terrace of Herod's banqueting-hall – some soldiers at the parapet, a grand staircase at one side, a bronze cistern-lid visible on the other. A clarinet springs up with the first of Salome's motifs, and there is a *pianissimo* thrill of flutes and divided strings (with harps, celesta and harmonium) in C♯. The lovelorn Narraboth sings 'Wie schön ist die Prinzessin Salome heute Nacht!' ('How beautiful the Princess Salome is tonight!'), while the boy Page who worships him has fearful premonitions; a pair of common soldiers discuss the noisy banquet – where Herod's Jewish guests are arguing theology – and their prisoner Jokanaan, whose prophetic voice is heard from the cistern along with three hortatory motifs in the orchestra.

This opera is a continuous 'stage tone-poem', without separate numbers, and Strauss has now presented his symphonic mini-exposition. Most of the main thematic cells have been laid down, if not yet connected up or developed; and a crucial polarity has been fixed between the febrile chromaticism of Salome's world – veering from one sharp key to another momentarily, but magnetized towards a vibrant C♯ tonic – and the prophet's austerely diatonic realm. He began in plain C major, though his music (which will become the vehicle of suprahuman judgment) tends towards the flat-key modulations of Romantic surrender, without the robust tonic-to-dominant thrust of Classical tonality; the opera will end in stern C minor. Now young Salome herself enters petulantly to her own waltz-music, fleeing the feast and Herod's greedy gaze. The invisible prophet's oratory excites her; the soldiers tell her as much as they know about him, but will not let her see him – they have their orders. She turns her wiles upon Captain Narraboth, who to the Page's dismay succumbs and commands that Jokanaan be brought out.

A long, turbulent interlude (all the heavy brass, for the first time, but none of the glittering percussion) tracks Jokanaan's ascent. Emerging, he denounces, with sonorous authority, not only the monstrous sins of Salome's stepfather but those of her mother Herodias – which excites her the more. To his horror she responds by hymning his own attractions, in three rapturous 'verses'. First she praises his ivory body, and he recoils; then she disparages his body but extols his black mane; rebuffed again, she reviles his hair and sings a paean

89. 'Der Rosenkavalier' (Richard Strauss, 1911), a scene from the Visconti production at the Royal Opera House in 1966, with Sena Jurinac as the Marschallin and Michael Langdon as Ochs

Left: 90. 'Salome' (Richard
Strauss, 1905), Catherine
Malfitano as Salome in the
production by Luc Bondy (sets
Erich Wonder, costumes Susanne
Raschig) at the Royal Opera
House, Covent Garden, in 1995

Below: 91. 'Semele' (Handel,
1744), final scene from the John
Copley production (sets Henry
Bardon, costumes David Walker)
at the Royal Opera House,
Covent Garden, in 1982

Above: 92. 'Siegfried' (Wagner, 1876), scene from the Patrice Chéreau production (sets Richard Peduzzi, costumes Jacques Schmidt) at the Festspielhaus, Bayreuth, in 1976, with René Kollo as Siegfried and Heinz Zednik as Mime

Right: 93. 'Siegfried' (Wagner, 1876), scene from the Glen Byam Shaw production by Sadler's Wells Opera (1973) at the London Coliseum, with Derek Hammond-Stroud as Alberich and Gregory Dempsey as Mime

94. 'Simon Boccanegra' (Verdi, 1857), scene from the production designed and directed by Filippo Sanjust at the Royal Opera House, Covent Garden, 1980, with Kiri Te Kanawa (Maria/Amelia) and Sherrill Milnes (Simon Boccanegra)

95. 'La sonnambula' (Bellini, 1831), Act 2 scene ii in an early Italian production; coloured engraving by P. Oggioni

96. 'Stiffelio' (Verdi, 1850), Catherine Malfitano (Lina), Placido Domingo (Stiffelio) and Gwynne Howell (Jorg) in the Elijah Moshinsky production (sets Michael Yeargan, costumes Peter J. Hall) at the Royal Opera House, Covent Garden, in 1995

97. 'Tannhäuser' (Wagner, 1845), model of Heinrich Döll's set for a valley below the Wartburg in the Munich
production of 1867

98. 'Tannhäuser' (Wagner, 1845), Gwyneth Jones (Venus) and Hermin Esser (Tannhäuser) in the production by
Götz Friedrich (designed by Jürgen Rose) at Bayreuth in 1974

99. *Tosca (Puccini, 1900), Maria Callas (Tosca) and Tito Gobbi (Scarpia) in the 1963/4 production by Franco Zeffirelli (sets Renzo Mongiardino, costumes Marcel Escoffier) at the Royal Opera House, Covent Garden*

100. 'La traviata' (Verdi, 1853), Josephine Barstow as Violetta in the 1973 Sadler's Wells Opera production by John Copley (sets and costumes by David Walker) at the London Coliseum

101. 'La traviata' (Verdi, 1853), Angela Gheorghiu as Violetta in the final scene of the production by Richard Eyre (designed by Bob Crowley) at the Royal Opera House, Covent Garden, in 1994

to his red mouth, which she demands to kiss. (Here poor Narraboth stabs himself in fear and despair, virtually unnoticed.) Refusing to look at the princess, the outraged prophet curses her and retreats to his cistern. A still longer and wilder orchestral postlude mingles the prophet's themes and Salome's – notably a flickering triadic figure to which she first sang, prettily, 'Er ist schrecklich' ('He is frightful'), a passionate melody which is to crown her final monologue, and a menacing four-note motif which has carried Jokanaan's final curse and will mark Salome's demands for his head. The music accelerates to a frenzy and then freezes on a C# tremolo, while snapping brass chords and a winding double bassoon follow the prophet down to the depths.

There is a sudden clatter of woodwind (the Tetrarch's disputatious guests resemble the critics in *Ein Heldenleben*) and Herod enters in distracted pursuit of the princess, with his sour consort on his heels. Like Narraboth and Salome earlier, he remarks a special eeriness in the moon tonight; Herodias denies it. He summons torches and wine for his guests, and slips on the blood around Narraboth's corpse: an ominous cold wind springs up and passes away (chromatic swirls over a prophetic motif), like a rustling of great wings, heard only by Herod. He presses wine and fruit upon the princess and implores her to sit by him. To her mother's grim satisfaction, Salome evades his blandishments. From the cistern the prophet's voice is heard again,

prompting a cross theological debate among Herod's Jewish guests, and a pair of Nazarenes report what they know of the Messiah. The voice goes on to prophesy shame and death for 'the daughter of Babylon', to the great annoyance of Herodias, who recognizes that she is his target.

Here a linking portion of Wilde's text was deleted. Abruptly, then, the Tetrarch invites his stepdaughter to dance for him. Her mother disapproves, and Salome flatly declines – until the tantalized, overwrought Herod swears solemnly to give her whatever she chooses. The cold wind rises again, and also for the last time the prophet's warning voice; Salome, her sullenness vanishing, agrees to perform the Dance of the Seven Veils. (Strauss composed it after the rest of the score. Its Hollywood-exotic contours, bedizened with motifs from the opera proper, sometimes tempt directors to make it an elaborate production number, far beyond the rather chaste little scenario that the composer sketched to guide himself.) When the dance is concluded, more or less brazenly according to the whims of director and soprano, Salome demands her prize from the appalled Herod: the head of Jokanaan, on a silver salver. She is implacable, and Herodias fiercely delighted at the prospect of avenging the insults heaped on her. In lyrical desperation the Tetrarch proposes the most extravagant alternatives: fabulous jewels, half his kingdom, even the veil of the temple. The elaborate arioso monologue with luscious

'Salome' (Richard Strauss): scene from the original production at the Dresden Hofoper, 9 December 1905, with Marie Wittich as Salome and Carl Burrian as Herod

orchestral illustration, punctuated by Salome's increasingly vehement refusals, parallels her own amorous assault on the prophet earlier, against his stony rebuffs. At last, defeated and full of forebodings, Herod gives the fatal order.

Herodias snatches the death-ring from his finger, and it is passed to the executioner, who descends into the cistern. Above, Salome listens with anxious impatience. Over long *pianissimo* tremolos and a bass drumroll, a solo double bass emits high, choked whimpers (like a woman's stifled groans, says the score). As she begins to doubt the executioner's resolve and cries for the soldiers to go down too, there is a confused orchestral eruption, and then hammering timpani. Everything stops but the drumroll. From the cistern a gigantic black arm holds up a salver which bears the prophet's head, and the princess seizes it.

The whole orchestra bursts out in a dissonant roar. In fact, the 'recapitulation' has arrived: violins and woodwinds scream the opening motif of the opera, skewed now over a C bass-line. This climactic monologue is itself virtually a self-contained tone-poem-with-voice, planned in long paragraphs and constantly reviewing the motifs of the opera. (Ernest Newman suspected that the finale had been composed first, and the rest of the score generated backwards from it.) 'Ah! du wolltest mich nicht deinen Mund küssen lassen', Salome sings ('You would not let me kiss your mouth, Jokanaan, but now I will') – here is where Strauss originally supposed that nothing less than an Isolde-voice would do – and with her second 'küssen' the music settles uneasily upon a C♯ tonic. After those first exultant cries, she falls to contemplating Jokanaan's dead eyes (he would not see her, and now he cannot) and his now silent tongue, while the tonality shifts restlessly through the sharp keys. His oracular motifs return in C and related flat keys; but when she recalls his beauty it is in tenderest F♯ major, and at last she persuades herself in C♯ that he *would* have loved her, had he looked at her – 'The mystery of love is greater than the mystery of death'. Aghast, Herod calls for the lights to be put out as the princess bends towards the dead lips, a cloud covers the moon and the music is suspended on a long, breathless trill. The flickering figure is reiterated again and again by oboe and piccolo, answered by a low, dark chord (a backstage organ makes it denser) like a prolonged shudder: the effect of utter derangement is palpable. In the obscurity and in atonal chromatics, Salome sings softly that she has kissed Jokanaan's mouth, and that the taste of love is bitter. The moon re-emerges to illuminate her, the music collects itself into a final radiant C♯ and the voice soars in a brief, heroic *Liebestod*. The orchestra echoes her phrase, adding one gross dissonance like an obscene jeer – and then breaks off in frantic alarums as Herod shrieks for his soldiers to kill her. They crush their princess beneath their shields, amid C minor poundings which suggest a brutal, retributive rape.

*

Salome was guaranteed scandalous, culminating as it does in the heroine's love-making to the severed head of John the Baptist – and Strauss's music supplies an erotic charge far beyond the verbal fancies of Wilde's arch, bejewelled text. What makes it work, and not merely titillate, is its superbly achieved musico-dramatic form. *Salome* established Strauss as a major operatic composer. His tone poems had already made him an international reputation, but by now he had exhausted that vein; indeed, though he was to enjoy almost another half-century of creative life he would write nothing more ambitious for orchestra than the Disney-esque *Alpine Symphony*. For large-scale composition he needed the guidance of a text. Neither his own verse-libretto for *Guntram* nor Wolzogen's purpose-built one for *Feuersnot*, however, had offered him more than broad-brush sentiments – enough to hang neo-Wagnerian leitmotifs on, but nothing to prompt the febrile élan of *Don Juan*, still less the mercurial symphonic fluency of *Till Eulenspiegel* or *Ein Heldenleben*.

Wilde's *Salomé* was the happiest possible find. As a pre-existing text it had already proved itself in performance, so there were no dramaturgical problems to solve; furthermore its single act already suggested the shape of a tone poem, and it was in prose – which gave Strauss's symphonic imagination far greater liberty than regular verse – and yet florid enough to invite lyrical setting. It provided a wealth of opportunities for orchestral illustration, as did its pervasively sultry atmosphere. The composer indulged himself in a huge band with quadruple woodwind, including heckelphone, while reducing it frequently to chamber scale. The real drama lay in extreme psychological conflicts, which eminently suited Strauss (he was never comfortable with strenuous stage action, as distinct from set-piece theatrical coups), and it was fraught with the decadence then currently fashionable. It is unlikely that he pondered over the 'morality' of the piece; he simply turned it into an opera, with acute faithfulness and all the professional resource which had been awaiting such an opportunity. Fundamentally tonal, if spiced with bitonal passages, *Salome* does administer some calculated shocks – in the words of Gabriel Fauré, who admired the score as a whole, 'cruel dissonances which defy all explanation'. Strictly musical explanation, that is: their theatrical impact, apt and alarming, embodies the decent reactions of any normal person like the composer himself to these indecent goings-on. Necrophilia is not among the more popular perversions, and Strauss was less concerned to fathom any 'deeper meaning' it might have than to exploit its operatic potential in terms of unbridled invention, lurid but cogent, and also tender – and profoundly effective.   D.M.

Samson et Dalila ('Samson and Delilah')

Opéra in three acts and four tableaux by Camille Saint-Saëns to a libretto by Ferdinand Lemaire; Weimar, Grossherzogliches Theater, 2 December 1877.

At the première Samson was sung by Franz Ferenczy and Delilah by Auguste von Müller; Eduard Lassen conducted.

Samson	tenor
Abimélech [Abimelech] *satrap of Gaza*	bass
The High Priest of Dagon	baritone
First Philistine	tenor
Second Philistine	bass
A Philistine Messenger	tenor
Dalila [Delilah]	mezzo-soprano
An Old Hebrew	bass
Hebrews, Philistines	
Setting Gaza in biblical times	

In 1867, two years after composing his first opera, *Le timbre d'argent*, and with no clear prospect of seeing it staged, Saint-Saëns embarked on an oratorio on the biblical story of Samson and Delilah. The subject was suggested by Voltaire's libretto *Samson* for Rameau. He admired Handel and Mendelssohn and was an enthusiastic supporter of the newly flourishing French choral movement. Saint-Saëns later wrote:

A young relative of mine had married a charming young man who wrote verse on the side. I realized that he was gifted and had in fact a real talent. I asked him to work with me on an oratorio on a biblical subject. 'An oratorio!', he said, 'no, let's make it an opera!', and he began to dig through the Bible while I outlined the plan of the work, even sketching scenes, and leaving him only the versification to do. For some reason I began the music with Act 2, and I played it at home to a select audience who could make nothing of it at all.

Despite many precedents, most people expressed alarm at the idea of a biblical subject on the stage. After one more hearing of Act 2 Saint-Saëns abandoned his opera. Only after the appearance in 1872 of his third opera, *La princesse jaune*, did he feel sufficiently encouraged to resume *Samson et Dalila*. Act 1 was given a concert performance in Paris in 1875, but it aroused little interest and was severely treated by the critics. The score was finished in 1876,

and although no French theatre showed any interest the opera was taken up enthusiastically by Liszt and mounted in Weimar in 1877.

There was still a long gap before the opera was heard in Paris. A second production in German took place in Hamburg in 1882, and it eventually reached France in 1890 when it was given first in Rouen, then in other French centres, finally reaching the stage of the Paris Opéra in 1892. None of Saint-Saëns' later operas suffered the tribulations endured by *Samson et Dalila*, but none ever enjoyed the same enduring success. It has remained in the repertory ever since and has been a vehicle for such singers as Enrico Caruso, Ramón Vinay, Jon Vickers and Guy Chauvet in the role of Samson, and Louise Kirkby Lunn, Julia Claussen, Rita Gorr, Grace Bumbry and Yelena Obraztsova as Delilah.

*

Act I *Gaza city square with the temple of Dagon to the left, at night* While the rest of the Hebrews are bewailing their fate, Samson alone has faith in God's promise of liberty. This first scene gives the clearest signs of the work's origins as an oratorio, with a fine sombre opening for the chorus leading to a fugue on the words 'Nous avons vu nos cités renversées'. Samson steps forward and sings rousingly against a constant choral prayer. The entry of Abimelech, the Philistine satrap, is marked by gross instrumentation (two ophicleides) which Bernard Shaw deplored as too Meyerbeerian, 'with his brusque measures and his grim orchestral clinkings and whistlings'. Abimelech mocks the Hebrews' God, proclaiming the superiority of Dagon, and the Hebrews cower in terror. But Samson's fervour, supported by the sound of the harp, arouses them to defy Abimelech, whereupon the latter attacks Samson with his sword. Samson seizes the sword and strikes him dead. The Hebrews scatter and the High Priest appears, cursing them and their leader. When a messenger reports that the Hebrews are ravaging the harvest, the High Priest utters a curse that hints at his plan to use Delilah to overcome Samson's strength: 'Qu'enfin une compagne infâme trahisse son amour!'

Dawn breaks. The Hebrews return offering a prayer to the Almighty, now in a humble unison, suggesting plainchant. Down the temple steps comes the seductive Philistine beauty Delilah, supported by her women who, in the delicate style of Gounod, sing of the joys of spring. Implying that their former love has revived, she declares that Samson has conquered her heart; she invites him to join her in her retreat in the valley of Sorek. Samson prays for protection from her charms, and an old Hebrew warns him of danger, forming an effective trio. The Philistine priestesses dance a voluptuous dance, with a tambourine to give exotic colour and some dark premonition at the end. Delilah sings her charming song 'Printemps qui commence' and the old Hebrew repeats his warning. Samson wrestles with his desire to meet Delilah's glance, a desire to which she knows he will succumb.

Act 2 The Valley of Sorek The introduction paints a musical picture of the luxuriant foliage that decks Delilah's retreat. She sits on a rock outside the entrance, rejoicing in her erotic power over Samson and certain that he will fall for her malevolent enticement ('Amour! viens aider ma faiblesse!'). Distant lightning is seen. The High Priest arrives, to the accompaniment of his energetic motif in the bass. He reports that Samson and the Hebrews have defeated the Philistines. He offers her gold for Samson's capture, but she refuses it, being inspired purely by hatred because of his earlier abandonment of her, and by loyalty to her gods. They sing an energetic duet of hatred, propelled by a strong symphonic accompaniment, and she promises to unlock the secret of Samson's strength.

Left alone, Delilah wonders if she can succeed, against a highly imaginative orchestral background. Samson soon appears. Distant lightning is still seen. He has come to say his last farewell, knowing that duty calls him to lead the Hebrews to final victory. Inevitably he is drawn by Delilah's protestations of love to acknowledge that he loves her too. His admission 'Je t'aime!' introduces her main aria 'Mon coeur s'ouvre à ta voix', the best-known piece in the opera. At the end of the second verse Samson joins in to make it a duet. There follows a scene of tremendous power in which Delilah pretends to doubt his love and begs him to reveal the secret of his strength, but he refuses. The thunder seems to Samson to be God's wrath. She scorns him and runs into her dwelling. Samson hesitates, but soon follows her. At that moment some Philistine soldiers emerge from hiding. Delilah gives them the signal, and Samson cries out that he has been betrayed.

Act 3.i A prison in Gaza Samson, blinded and bound, his hair shorn, turns a mill-wheel, graphically portrayed by the orchestra. Echoes of the Hebrews' lament from Act 1 are heard. Overcome with remorse, Samson offers his life in sacrifice, while the Hebrews are heard in the distance bewailing his fall.

3.ii Inside the Temple of Dagon Music covers the scene-change to the temple, where the Philistines are preparing a sacrifice to celebrate their triumph. At first they sing in the gentle tones of their song to spring from Act 1, but when the Bacchanale begins a more savage atmosphere develops. This well-known ballet sequence is a fine specimen of the kind of *divertissement* favoured by Meyerbeer and most French opera composers, with prominent augmented 2nds to suggest a Near-Eastern locale and much use of percussion to evoke the barbarism of the Philistines; there is a voluptuous episode also. After the dance Samson is led in, guided by a boy, to be mocked by the High Priest and the crowd, and also, to a trivialized variant of her love song, by Delilah, who reveals that she had sold his secret in advance and had pretended to love him out of hatred and a desire for vengeance. Samson is remorseful. Her betrayal is now plain. The crowd's mockery is enhanced by more and more trivial music, with a tinkling triangle and bells, the Philistines' vacuous frivolity laid bare. Samson prays to recover his strength. The Philistines pour sacrificial libations in honour of Dagon. The High Priest tells the boy to lead Samson to the middle of the temple where all can see him; Samson whispers to the boy to guide him to the two marble pillars that support the building. As the festivities reach their climax Samson calls on God for vengeance, and with a supreme effort 'bows himself with all his might', bringing down the pillars and the whole temple upon the assembled Philistines and upon himself. The score allows little more than five seconds between Samson's mighty exertion and the descent of the curtain.

'Samson et Dalila' (Saint-Saëns), Samson (sung by Jean-Alexandre Talazac) bringing down the Temple of Dagon at the end of Act 3 of the first Paris production at the Eden-Théâtre, 31 October 1890: engraving from 'L'illustration' (8 November 1890)

*

The libretto of *Samson et Dalila*, based on Chapter 16 of the *Book of Judges*, omits Samson's mighty deeds such as the slaughter of a lion and the slaying of one thousand Philistines with the jawbone of an ass which earned his fame and his leadership of the Hebrews. It concentrates instead on the story of Delilah, presenting Samson as an inspiring leader whose heart can be touched by love of a woman and Delilah as a scheming, merciless avenger. The death of Abimelech in Act 1 is an invention. Although the chorus are prominent at the beginning the Hebrews are not seen on stage again, and Saint-Saëns was right not to make an oratorio of this material.

His technique is unmistakably operatic, both in the skilful deployment of a large orchestra and in the application of motifs. At the time of *Samson et Dalila* Saint-Saëns still admired Wagner enormously (although he later came to see him as a malaise to be avoided), and the influence of *Der fliegende Holländer* and *Lohengrin* can be heard in the strong closing scene of Act 2. Echoes of Berlioz's *L'enfance du Christ* and *Les Troyens* are also to be heard, and the work treads paths marked out by Meyerbeer and Gounod too. It owes its success to the exotic colour of the Philistines' music and the fine choral writing; it is certainly Saint-Saëns' most imaginative opera score, and it reveals an instinct for theatrical emotion, particularly in the second act, that any opera composer would be proud of. It allows us to savour some of the brilliance and intellectual vigour that even his enemies admired.   **H.M.**

Satyagraha

Opera in three acts by Philip Glass to a libretto by the composer and Constance DeJong after the *Bhagavad Gita*; Rotterdam, Netherlands Opera, 5 September 1980.

Gandhi	tenor
Miss Schlesen	soprano
Mrs Naidoo	soprano
Kasturbai	mezzo-soprano
Mr Kallenbach	baritone
Parsi Rustomji	bass
Mrs Alexander	alto
Prince Arjuna	baritone
Lord Krishna	bass
Leo Tolstoy	silent
Rabindranath Tagore	silent
Martin Luther King	silent
Armies, crowd, workers, policemen	

Shortly after a 1976 performance of *Einstein on the Beach* in Amsterdam, Glass was asked by Hans de Roo, the director of the Netherlands Opera, to write a 'real' opera, meaning one for orchestra and chorus

with soloists trained and practised in the singing of traditional operas. Glass responded with the two-hour *Satyagraha*, his second opera about an important historical figure. Taking Gandhi as its central character, it concerns the period he spent in South Africa (1893–1914) and his fight to repeal the so-called 'Black Act' – a law that restricted the movement of non-Europeans from place to place and virtually enslaved the substantial Indian community in South Africa. Gandhi developed the concept of *satyagraha* (roughly, 'truth-force') and fought the act with hunger strikes and peaceful demonstrations, eventually achieving a partial triumph, however imperfect, over the hated law. It marked the beginning of Gandhi's political career.

Each act of *Satyagraha* employs a historical figure (silent) as a sort of spiritual guardian, watching the earthly action from above. In Act 1, which has three scenes, the symbol is Leo Tolstoy; the author was one of Gandhi's inspirations throughout his life, and the two men corresponded until the Russian's death in 1910. Glass believes that the same combination of the political and the spiritual is found in the writings of both men. In Act 2, also in three scenes, Rabindranath Tagore, the poet and scholar who was the only living moral authority acknowledged by Gandhi, serves as the guardian. The symbol in the long, continuous third act is Martin Luther King, whom Glass has described as a sort of 'American Gandhi', going on to say that, together, 'Tolstoy, Tagore and King represent the past, present and future of *satyagraha*'.

Although the opera has a clearly defined plot, it is not presented chronologically. After the timeless, purely philosophical opening, in which Gandhi is advised by Prince Arjuna and Lord Krishna from the *Bhagavad Gita*, the scenes are set in 1910, 1906, 1896, 1906, 1908 and 1913 respectively. Every scene is a self-sufficient drama in miniature; connections between each one are established mainly through musical and cumulative means, rather than through a continuity of stage action.

DeJong's selections from the *Bhagavad Gita* are heard in the original Sanskrit, in an attempt to avoid upsetting the rhythm of what is, after all, a sacred text. As Glass has said:

I liked the idea of *further* separating the vocal text from the action. In this way, without an understandable text to contend with, the listener could let the words go altogether. The weight of 'meaning' would then be thrown onto the music, the designs and the stage action. Secondly, since none of the national languages was going to be used, Sanskrit could then serve as a kind of international language for this opera.

Vastly different from traditional music drama, *Satyagraha* is designed on a moral, indeed religious, plane, and as such is closer to ritual than entertainment, to mystery play than standard opera. Few were prepared for its beauty and spiritual propulsion. In scoring it for strings, triple woodwind and organ, Glass used only what he calls 'international' instruments (i.e. those that can be found, in one form or another, in both the West and India). *Satyagraha* nevertheless uses more conventional forces (nine solo voices and a chorus of 40) than the spartan *Einstein*. While *Einstein* challenges ideas about what an opera, even an avant-garde opera, should be, *Satyagraha* fits Glass neatly into the operatic continuum. *Einstein* attempted to break the rules with Modernist zeal; *Satyagraha* adapts the rules to the composer's own aesthetic. It is difficult to find any historical precedent for *Einstein*, but in *Satyagraha* one may find references to many of the composer's forerunners.

For example, in the opening scene, entitled 'The Kuru Field of Justice', an aria becomes a duet, then a trio, set down with a rich, declamatory, near-Verdian directness, over an elaborate chaconne. Other scenes seem to have been written under the spell of Wagner, Berlioz or Glass's beloved Rossini. But at no point does the music descend to parody; the hearer is never in doubt about the identity of the composer. The closing aria is masterly: an unadorned rising scale in Phrygian mode seeming an eloquent melody in itself, repeated as it is some 30 times over shifting musical sands. The rocket-point anxiety of *Einstein* seems far away, with a serene, impelling power in its stead. While the opera was considered a step backwards by some members of the avant garde, which had lionized Glass after *Einstein*, *Satyagraha* won him new listeners, many of whom consider it his most personal and affecting score to date.   T.P.

Sāvitri

Chamber opera in one act by Gustav Holst to his own libretto adapted from an incident in the *Mahābharata*; London (St John's Wood), London School of Opera, 5 December 1916.

The original cast consisted of Mabel Corran, George Pawlo and Harrison Cook as Death.

Death	bass
Sāvitri	soprano
Satyavān	tenor
Chorus of women's voices	
Setting A wood at evening	

Holst became interested in Hindu literature and philosophy in his mid-twenties, towards the end of the 1890s. What appealed to him, according to his daughter and biographer Imogen, was that 'here was

a rational religion'. He was enthralled by the *Rig Veda* and the *Bhagavad Gita* and wanted to set to music some of the hymns in them, but he could not discover an English translation that satisfied him. He determined, therefore, to learn Sanskrit at the School of Oriental Languages. Although he never became fluent – he had to look up every word in the dictionary and compose each sentence with a crib – he nevertheless translated 20 hymns from the *Rig Veda* and the long poem by Kalidasa on which he based his splendid and ambitious choral work *The Cloud Messenger* (1909–10). He also wrote librettos for two operas on Hindu subjects, *Sita* (1900–06) and *Sāvitri* (1908–9).

Holst began to compose *Sāvitri* after returning from a holiday in Algeria. He gave up one of his teaching posts in order to concentrate on it. Much of it was written in a small rented cottage on the Isle of Sheppey where Holst and his wife spent weekends. It is the antithesis of *Sita*, a three-act work composed on a grandiose scale and with little regard for the practicalities of staging, and which Holst later described, with more than a little exaggeration, as 'good old Wagnerian bawling'. *Sāvitri* benefited from the paring of his style during his composition of the *Hymns from the Rig Veda* of 1907–8. Instead of a vast orchestra, only two string quartets, a double bass, two flutes and an english horn are required. The offstage chorus of women's voices sings to the sound of the 'u' in 'sun'. (A mixed chorus was specified in Holst's original score, but when the opera was in rehearsal for its first performance the conductor, Hermann Grunebaum, suggested that women's voices would serve better and Holst rewrote the choral parts almost overnight.) The opera, 30 minutes long, was intended for performance in the open air, 'or else in a small building'.

The opera is set in a wood at evening. The voice of Death is heard calling to Sāvitri: 'I draw nigh to fulfil my work. I come for thy husband'. Sāvitri has been hearing this voice day and night and has come to dread it. Her husband Satyavān, a woodman – in the original story he was a prince – returns from his work singing of his love for Sāvitri ('What wife in all the world is like to Sāvitri?'). He finds her pale and trembling and thinks she is under the sway of Māyā (the illusion of the physical world). But Sāvitri says she has forgotten Māyā; there is someone else.

Satyavān thinks he hears someone lurking in the forest and raises his axe to fell him; but as he does so the axe falls from his grasp and he collapses on the ground. Death has arrived. Sāvitri welcomes him as 'the Just One' and, because she has not shrunk from him, Death grants her a boon, but 'naught for Satyavān; my breath hath chilled his heart'. Sāvitri asks for life in all its fullness. This is granted to her, but she then claims that she cannot have this full life without Satyavān. Death, outwitted, retreats. Satyavān awakes in Sāvitri's arms. She tells him a Holy One has blessed her. Death is heard admitting that he has been conquered by 'one having Life, one free from Māyā . . . for even Death is Māyā'. She is left in quiet ecstasy with Satyavān.

Sāvitri is a remarkable achievement, anticipating many of the stylistic features – particularly polytonality – of Holst's later works. Neither here nor in the *Vedic Hymns* does he attempt to write in a mock-oriental manner, yet there is something of Indian music about it. This can have been achieved only by instinct, for Holst had heard no Indian music at this time. The economy of the scoring does not preclude richness of texture; and although the scale of the piece is at the opposite pole to the contemporary works of Strauss, Mahler and others, there is richness and colour in Sāvitri's aria about Life that anchors the work to its period and still carries distant echoes of Wagner. Satyavān's unaccompanied song as he returns home is imbued with the spirit of English folksong and there are passages at this point in the work where the sound and shape of the music come close to Vaughan Williams's *On Wenlock Edge*, written at the same time.

Much of the vocal writing is in an effortless conversational recitative that follows the rise and fall of natural speech; in this respect *Sāvitri* strikingly anticipates the church parables of Britten of over half a century later, for there, too, the music suggests orientalism while remaining rooted in the English countryside. Perhaps the most dramatic moment in *Sāvitri* is its opening, where Death's voice is heard unaccompanied. Later, the chorus is used with the utmost poetic discretion and certain solo instruments – viola and flute, for example – take on the importance of extra characters.   M.Ky.

Schweigsame Frau, Die ('The Silent Woman')

Komische Oper in three acts by Richard Strauss to a libretto by Stefan Zweig after Ben Jonson's play *Epicoene*; Dresden, Staatsoper, 24 June 1935.

The original cast included Maria Cebotari (Aminta), Friedrich Plaschke (Morosus), Martin Kremer (Henry) and Matthieu Ahlersmeyer (Schneidebart). Karl Böhm conducted.

Sir Morosus *a retired admiral*		bass
Widow Zimmerlein *his housekeeper*		contralto
Schneidebart *a barber*		high baritone
Henry Morosus *the admiral's*		
nephew		high tenor
Aminta *his wife*		coloratura soprano
Isotta ⎫		coloratura soprano
Carlotta ⎪		mezzo-soprano
Morbio ⎬ *members of an*	*operatic troupe*	baritone
Vanuzzi ⎪		deep bass
Farfallo ⎭		deep bass
The Parrot		spoken

Other players, neighbours

Setting The drawing-room of Sir Morosus's house in London, cluttered with mementoes of his naval career; about 1780

With the unexpected death in 1929 of Hofmannsthal, his junior by a decade – midway through their *Arabella* – the 65-year-old Strauss was bereft of the librettist he had counted upon as a lifelong collaborator. Friends proposed new candidates in vain, while he strove to pull the *Arabella* sketches together and then tinkered with their earlier semi-failure *Die ägyptische Helena*. At length he was put in touch with Stefan Zweig, a distinguished younger writer, politicized intellectual and occasional dramatist, who was flattered to the point of obsequiousness. In 1931 Zweig proposed two ideas: a grandiose, humanitarian, multi-media pantomime which Strauss rejected gently but firmly (just as Zweig later declined to write the *Semiramis* libretto Strauss had so long wanted), and a domestic-scale comedy based on Ben Jonson's *Epicoene, or The Silent Woman* (1609). That the composer approved, and when the *Schweigsame Frau* libretto was finished in January 1933 he greeted it as the best comic-opera text since Da Ponte's *Figaro*.

Zweig's attraction to the English playwright had begun several years earlier, when upon reading a summary of Jonson's *Volpone* he wrote forthwith a successful version of his own. For *Die schweigsame Frau* he consulted translations of the *Epicoene* play, which was widely known (at second or third hand it had inspired Donizetti's *Don Pasquale*). Jonson's 'epicene' creature was a mere pageboy, got up as a woman to fool old Morose into a ruinous marriage; Zweig preferred to make him a real woman, as in *Don Pasquale* – indeed the gentle wife of the real schemer, Morosus's nephew. Yet again Strauss promised to write a swift 'operetta'-style piece, and it was agreed that there should be plenty of spoken repartee. In the event most of that went to the conniving barber Schneidebart, an obvious Figaro cousin. By November 1934 the score was complete but for its potpourri overture.

Despite a notable cast the opera had a fraught première. Even in 1935, Strauss had to battle with Nazi officialdom to get his Jewish librettist acknowledged on the Dresden Opera handbills, whereupon Hitler and Goebbels decided not to attend; and the opera was taken off after two or three performances. Its postwar resuscitation has been fitful, long-drawn-out and uncertain. For what amounts merely to 'grand operetta', the demands upon all the principal singers – and long-sitting audiences – are formidable, and the piece cannot work without a Morosus of crustily disarming, larger-than-life personality (Kurt Böhme was one such). Though Strauss composed the role *con amore*, his music remains a little bland without some extra-musical spicing, like the rest of the score.

*

Act 1 There is a prefatory 'potpourri' – little more than four minutes long, but Strauss's first proper overture since his first opera *Guntram*. The label is mock-deprecatory: though based upon tunes from the opera, this bright curtain-raiser is polyphonic and shapely as well as sprightly.

Arriving for his daily appointment with Sir Morosus, the Barber is delayed by the garrulous Housekeeper. She bewails the rich old Admiral's lonely condition, exacerbated by his absolute intolerance of noise, and imagines the comfort a modest, quiet wife would bring him: a mature lady, of course, not a young one. When the Barber becomes impatient, their loud mutual abuse provokes the furious entry of Morosus and the widow's speedy exit. Morosus delivers a long diatribe against rackety modern London – its noisy entertainments (the orchestra cites several guilty operas), even its church bells. Shaving and soothing him, Schneidebart conjures up a vision of a silent, devoted young bride. (In the matching scene of Rossini's *Barbiere* Figaro is already practising a deception upon Don Bartolo, but here a notion for one is just taking form.) Lulled by the barber's innocent *canzone*, Morosus begins to warm to the idea.

A commotion heralds the return of a prodigal, his scapegrace nephew Henry. The old man is touchingly overjoyed; now he has a companionable heir again, and any wife would be redundant. When Henry confesses that he has brought his 'Truppe' with him, the proud uncle expects a squad of soldiers. In fact Henry has become an operatic tenor, and the troupe that enters (to a 'Kleiner humoristischer Marsch') is a gaggle of Italian singers who hope to play the Haymarket; worse still, he has married the leading soprano. Scandalized, Morosus disowns his nephew, orders the barber to find him a silent bride and stamps out, after an ensemble of protests.

With his offended colleagues, Henry is nonplussed: he was hoping for some money. Schneidebart assures him that there is £60,000 or £70,000 in the cellar (a new ensemble, impressed and excited), explains the Admiral's irascibility to the others – a naval explosion disordered his hearing – and urges them not to despair. Henry refuses to give up his beloved Aminta, as she suggests (their duet becomes a septet with chorus); his colleagues Isotta

and Carlotta, in their own ariettas, reject the barber's idea that one of *them* might marry Morosus (Aminta joins them for a ladies' trio). He offers another plan: trick Uncle into a mock wedding with a meek 'bride', who will then prove an ear-splitting termagant; that should make him value the lot of a peaceful gentleman-bachelor with a deserving heir. Though gentle Aminta has a pang of sympathy for the old man, everybody embraces the prospect in a very long, strenuously bright octet-finale, with chorus.

Act 2 After a preludial minuet, the unhappy Housekeeper helps Morosus prepare to interview three prospective fiancées, whom Schneidebart has found and now ushers in with another fluent *canzone*. Signor Vanuzzi's troupe plays the charade to the hilt: Carlotta is a hopelessly thick peasant girl, Isotta flashy and loquacious, Aminta – at considerable length – virginally mild as 'Timidia'. Morosus makes the obvious choice, and Vanuzzi and Morbio, masquerading as priest and notary, set up the 'wedding' (to music Strauss adapted from the Fitzwilliam Virginal Book, by way of period effect). The old man addresses himself to his 'bride' with a simple candour and sweetness that touch her heart. But the charade must go on: once the ceremony is completed (with a heartfelt sextet), and Farfallo – claiming to have served under the Admiral – has crashed in with a large, boisterous 'wedding party' and crashed out again, and after a brief, tender idyll alone with her 'husband', Aminta's cue now is to scream on high C. At the top of her lungs she emits a torrent of outrageous demands and threats, meanwhile assaulting the marine mementoes. Horrified but impotent, Morosus collapses. Henry comes providentially to the rescue; he quells 'Timidia', promises his uncle to arrange an immediate divorce and packs him off to bed, overcome with gratitude and exhaustion. Now Henry and Aminta enjoy their own clandestine idyll, though she has twinges of self-reproach. From his distant bedroom, Morosus calls out his sleepy thanks again.

Act 3 The orchestral introduction starts with a fugato – like the third act of *Der Rosenkavalier*, but here in a brisk, practical C major quite different from those *sotto voce* Mendelssohnian scurryings – and reaches a polythematic climax. The curtain rises upon a domestic upheaval: 'Timidia' has hired workmen to change everything in the house, with maximal hullaballoo. Her raucous Parrot installed and the Housekeeper's faint protests brushed aside, she begins a coloratura lesson with her 'music master' – Henry in disguise of course, as in Rossini's *Barbiere*, with Farfallo at the harpsichord. (For their songs, Strauss raided Monteverdi and Legrenzi.) The Admiral staggers in with his ears stopped, adding his voice to an anxious ensemble with the Housekeeper and the Parrot. Now the barber announces the imminent divorce hearing, and does some preliminary dickering with 'Timidia' and Morosus. While the latter goes off to dress in his official best, Vanuzzi and the company arrive, to more music from the Fitzwilliam Virginal Book (a John Bull 'In Nomine'), as the 'Lord Chief Justice' with cohorts. Finding themselves briefly alone, all the conspirators gloat in a *prestissimo*.

Morosus returns in full fig, and the proceedings begin – duologues, solo outbursts and ensembles. First there are legal questions about whether 'Timidia', who protests her devotion, is the wife he meant to marry. Then Isotta and Carlotta testify that she has 'known' another man. Henry claims to be that man (in a passionate love song and a new disguise), and Aminta swears that she has been strictly faithful to her husband – all of which is indeed true. When the verdict seems to be going in the Admiral's favour, Farfallo reverses it by a fresh quibble: the contract never required 'Timidia' to be *virgo intacta*. Amid a cruel chorus of suggestions that he might still appeal, the old man crumples in despair.

Abruptly, Henry and Aminta expose the whole charade, with heartfelt apologies. The uncle is astounded, then furious, and finally – over a huge orchestral explosion of relief – amused and forgiving. The naughty performers, who will get what they wanted, retire with a paean of praise. 'How beautiful music is', Morosus muses, 'especially when it's over.' With a glass of wine, his pipe, and his dear nephew and wife at hand he drowses off, in simple E♭ and blissful content.

*

There is more 'light music' in *Die schweigsame Frau*, fluent but two-dimensional, than in any other Strauss opera – the comedians' music in *Ariadne* has more sap, and the *Intermezzo* intermezzos more satirical point. The chromatic excursions are second-hand; the house-overturning music instantly recalls the *Rosenkavalier* ructions, and the banter between Morosus and the barber, *Ariadne*. The protracted ensembles invite comparison with Rossini, and lose by it; where Rossini's ensembles dramatize confusion and conflict, too many of the Strauss-Zweig ones are unanimous declarations, operatically redundant. Only a brilliant cast can cover over the dramatic faults: the unprepared change of heart for Morosus at the crux, long character numbers for marginal figures in the drama, a central ruse in which the sympathetic main couple are inexplicably cruel – including a shy, tender heroine who switches to relentless sadism and back again. Yet a vein of kindly, Indian-summer warmth runs through the score, and in a sensitive performance it makes an impression that outlasts the foolery.   **D.M.**

Semele

Opera in three acts by George Frideric Handel to a libretto by William Congreve after Ovid's *Metamorphoses*; London, Covent Garden, 10 February 1744 (concert performance).

The original cast included Elisabeth Duparc ('La Francesina') in the title role, John Beard as Jupiter, Esther Young as Ino and Juno and Henry Reinhold in the bass parts.

Cadmus *King of Thebes*		bass
Semele *his daughter*		soprano
Ino *her sister*		contralto
Athamas *Prince of Boeotia*		countertenor
Jupiter		tenor
Juno		contralto
Iris *Juno's attendant messenger*		soprano
Somnus *god of sleep*		bass
Apollo		tenor

Thebans, priests, augurs, loves, zephyrs, nymphs, swains, attendants

Setting Thebes, in mythological times

In the early 1740s the performance of oratorios at Covent Garden represented Handel's chief concert activity in London, after Italian opera had begun to fall out of favour. His biblical oratorios had some relationship to Greek tragedy and it is perhaps not surprising that he decided to venture into the world of classical drama. It may have been Thomas Arne's recent setting of Congreve's *Judgment of Paris* text that suggested to him *Semele*, of which the original setting by John Eccles had never been performed. He composed the music in June and July 1743. The considerable adjustment that the text required may have been undertaken by Newburgh Hamilton, who had performed a similar service in respect of *Samson*; this involved the provision or adaptation of words for the choruses, new material for the end of Act 2 (where Congreve had prescribed a 'dumb shew' and 'rural sports', presumably a French-style *divertissement*) and changes in the balance and positioning of recitatives and lyrical numbers. The additional words are largely drawn from Congreve's own verse and from Pope's (including the best-known number, 'Where'er you walk'). The work has been interpreted as a parable about social advancement through sexual favours, and specific targets, in Congreve's time and (less plausibly) in Handel's, have been proposed.

Although Congreve, and Eccles, had intended *Semele* to be given on the stage, Handel designed and performed it 'in the Manner of an *Oratorio*': that is, in concert form. It had only modest success; its amorous topic – it is essentially a creation of the late Restoration period – seems not to have pleased those who attended the Lenten seasons for a different kind of uplift, and it irritated the supporters of true (Italian) opera. There were four performances in February, then two more at the King's Theatre in December, with changes and additions, including arias in Italian, and with some of the sexually more explicit lines removed; it had no further revivals in Handel's lifetime and was perhaps unsurely matched to the spirit of the time.

Semele had its first modern stage revival in Cambridge in 1925 and its London stage première in 1954; it had four productions by the Handel Opera Society under Charles Farncombe (1959, 1961, 1964 and 1975) and entered the repertories of the English National Opera (then Sadler's Wells Opera) in 1970 and Covent Garden in 1982, conducted on both occasions by Charles Mackerras. Its stage première in the USA was at Washington, DC, in 1980.

*

Act 1 Cadmus, his family and priests have foregathered in the temple of Juno for the solemnization of the marriage of Semele to Athamas. The omens seem propitious, but Semele invents reasons for delay and, aside, pleads to Jupiter for help. Ino, herself in love with Athamas, is also distressed (quartet, 'Why dost thou thus untimely grieve?'). Thunder is heard, and the flame on Juno's altar grows feeble. All flee save Ino and Athamas; but he takes her affectionate words to him as merely an expression of sympathy. Cadmus returns and tells of the events he has just witnessed: Semele, with 'azure flames' around her head, was snatched heavenward by 'an eagle of mighty size, on purple wings descending', leaving a diffusion of 'celestial odour and ambrosial dew'. The priests and augurs celebrate rather than mourn her translation, and from a distance her voice is heard in a joyous gavotte ('Endless pleasure, endless love, Semele enjoys above'; Congreve had assigned it to a Second Augur), taken up by all present.

Act 2 In a 'pleasant country', Iris tells Juno of the newly erected palace that her errant husband has built for Semele on Mount Cithaeron. The incensed Juno swears vengeance on Semele and her line, and resolves to call on Somnus, god of sleep, to help her gain access to the heavily guarded palace.

Semele, in the palace, attended by Loves and Zephyrs, calls on sleep to return ('O sleep, why dost thou leave me?') and restore her erotic 'visionary joys'. Jupiter enters, in human form, and reassures her; she responds amorously. The chorus sing of the pains and joys of love. But Jupiter, detecting her discontent and her aspirations to immortality ('I must with speed amuse her'), thinks it wise to send for her sister Ino as a companion. Then he turns the scene to Arcadia and celebrates rural delights ('Where'er you walk'). Ino arrives and describes her remarkable journey, conveyed by Zephyrs, and the sweet music she has heard; the sisters and the chorus sing of the joys of music ('Bless the glad earth with heav'nly lays').

Act 3 Juno comes to Somnus's cave to awaken the unwilling god ('Leave me, loathsome light'). When she promises him his favourite nymph, Pasithea, he agrees to do her bidding: he is to put Ino and the palace sentinels to sleep, and to provide Jupiter with an erotic dream that leaves him prey to any demand that Semele might make of him (duet, 'Obey my will').

Semele is alone and discontent ('My racking thoughts') when Juno, disguised as Ino, enters. She has a magic mirror that deceives Semele into thinking herself more beautiful than ever ('Myself I shall adore': the air's reflecting musical figures suggest the mirror). 'Ino' advises her to refuse Jupiter her bed until he promises to grant any wish to her, and then to require that he come not in mortal guise but 'like himself, the Mighty Thunderer', as only then (she says) will Semele become immortal. Semele thanks her; Juno, elated at the prospect of Semele's destruction, retires.

Jupiter enters, inflamed ('Come to my arms'), but Semele keeps him at a distance ('I ever am granting'). He swears an irrevocable oath, calling Olympus itself as witness (distant rumblings are heard), to grant any demand. She asks as Juno bade her: 'Ah, take heed what you press', Jupiter responds, but she stands firm, supposing him unwilling to accord her immortality ('No, no, I'll take no less'). Jupiter bitterly regrets his hasty oath: if he comes to her in his own guise 'she must a victim fall', for all his 'softest lightning' and 'mildest melting bolt'. Juno, observing, gloats over her triumph. Semele sees Jupiter descending, as a fiery cloud, and realizes too late the consequence of her vanity; consumed by his flames, she dies.

Ino, returned to Thebes, joins Cadmus and the priests, who have witnessed the death of Semele as a storm. Ino relates Semele's fate and Jupiter's command that she and Athamas wed. Apollo appears and prophesies that, phoenix-like, Bacchus, god of wine, will rise from Semele's ashes; the chorus celebrates this fortunate outcome ('Happy shall we be').

*

As in Handel's other works written for concert performance, the many and sometimes extended choruses pose serious problems in production; there exists no conventional framework within the aesthetic of Baroque performance for their staging. The tradition to which they belong, in style, form and function, is that of Handel's English oratorios. Yet, as its history in the 20th century demonstrates, Semele invites realization on the stage because of the eminently theatrical quality of much of its music. That Handel thought of it as akin to his Italian operas is attested by the modifications he required in the libretto, and in particular the adjustments that allowed the inclusion of arias in the operatic da capo form (14 of the 25) where none had existed before. But the work also draws on that spirited, wilful vein of melody, distinctively English, familiar from his earlier *Acis and Galatea* and going back at least to Purcell, which so happily catches the vein of humour that pervades the work. Another striking feature of *Semele* is its abundance of accompanied recitatives, which are more numerous than in any other of his extended English works or indeed his Italian operas, and which are also important in intensifying the drama and the characterization.

Of the characters, it is the women who are the more sharply and perceptively drawn; Jupiter himself appears as little more than an eloquent and ardent lover. Juno's cunning and jealousy, and her natural authority, are speedily established from the moment of her peremptory summons to Somnus in an accompanied recitative at the beginning of Act 3, and consistently maintained up to the jubilant da capo aria to which she departs, her quest for vengeance satisfied. But the music for the hedonistic Semele herself, often deeply sensuous, but not without hints of coquetry and vanity when her ambitions are aroused, represents a tour de force of female character drawing; and the principal scene in Act 2, from her 'Sleep Song' to the final celebration of love and music, stands as one of the great musical paeans to the joys of humankind.   **S.S.**

Semiramide ('Semiramis')

Melodramma tragico in two acts by Gioachino Rossini to a libretto by Gaetano Rossi after Voltaire's *Sémiramis*; Venice, Teatro La Fenice, 3 February 1823.

At the first performance Semiramide was sung by Isabella Colbran; the other roles were taken by Rosa Mariani (Arsace), Filippo Galli (Assur), John Sinclair (Idreno), Matilde Spagna (Azema) and Luciano Mariani (Oroe).

Idreno *an Indian king*	tenor
Oroe *high priest of the Magi*	bass
Assur *prince, descended from Baal*	bass
Semiramide *Queen of Babylon, widow of King Nino*	soprano
Arsace *commander of Semiramide's forces*	contralto
Azema *princess, descended from Baal*	soprano
Mitrane *captain of the royal guard*	tenor
Nino's ghost	bass

Satraps, Magi, Babylonians, princesses, cithara players, foreign women, royal guards, temple priests, Indians, Scythians, Egyptians, slaves
Setting Babylon in the 8th century BC

Semiramide was the last opera Rossini wrote in Italy before he moved permanently to Paris. He worked on it at Castenaso, his country house outside Bologna, in the late summer and autumn of 1822 immediately following his spectacularly successful visit to Vienna. In many respects, the opera is an extended, formally stabilized and dramatically more powerful version of the musical and dramatic archetypes first essayed in *Tancredi* (1813), a work similarly based on a drama by Voltaire adapted by the librettist Gaetano Rossi. On this occasion, though, there is evidence of close and thorough collaboration between Rossini and his librettist: Rossi was obliged to live at Castenaso during the principal period of composition. (His comments on this can be found in his correspondence at the time with the young Giacomo Meyerbeer.) The title role was created by Isabella Colbran, the last of many roles written for her by Rossini, whom she had married on 16 March 1822.

The opera quickly reached Milan, Naples and Vienna. Rossini himself supervised the first British performances at the King's Theatre, Haymarket, in the spring of 1824, with Giuditta Pasta in the title role, as well as the Paris première in December 1825 with Joséphine Fodor-Mainville. Maria Malibran made her Paris début in the title role in 1828. In autumn 1829 a production, with which Rossini may have been connected, was mounted in Bologna. The opera was first staged in New York, in abridged form, in 1835 and in full in 1845. In 1847 there was an important revival by the Royal Italian Opera at Covent Garden with Giulia Grisi, Marietta Alboni and Antonio Tamburini, conducted by Rossini's friend and advocate Michael Costa. In 1860 Rossini ceded the French rights to Michele Carafa whose lavish new staging, with additional ballet music, was seen at the Paris Opéra on 9 July. The production starred the sisters Carlotta and Barbara Marchisio as Semiramide and Arsace; Rossini wrote of them at the time 'they are possessors of that song which is sensed in the soul'. In 1894 Melba sang the title role at the Metropolitan Opera. In 1922 Gustav Kobbé announced '*Semiramide* seems to have had its day', but it was spectacularly revived at La Scala, Milan, in 1962 with Joan Sutherland, Giulietta Simionato, Gianni Raimondi and Wladimiro Ganzarolli, conducted by Gabriele Santini. The outstanding Arsace of recent times, however, has been Marilyn Horne. She recorded the role in December 1965 with Sutherland, conducted by Richard Bonynge. One of the classic Rossini recordings, it has remained

'Semiramide' (Rossini), Act 2 scene v (within the monument of King Nino): design by Alessandro Sanquirico for the first Milan production at La Scala, 9 October 1824

unchallenged for over a quarter of a century. Horne also sang in a distinguished revival of the opera at the Metropolitan in December 1990 directed by John Copley and conducted by James Conlon, with Samuel Ramey as Assur and June Anderson and Lella Cuberli alternating in the title role.

The autograph manuscript of the opera, in the archive of the Teatro La Fenice, Venice, is entirely in the composer's hand; changes, mainly cuts, were made by Rossini for the London and Paris performances in 1824–5. For Paris he redrafted the opera's denouement, mitigating the rapidity of Arsace's change from grieving matricide to triumphantly proclaimed king.

*

Act I.i *Within the precincts of the temple of Baal* Semiramide and Prince Assur have murdered her husband, King Nino, and attempted to murder her son. But the boy, now called Arsace, survived, unaware of his true identity. Now, 15 years later and no longer known to his mother or would-be stepfather, he has become a brilliant young commander on one of the kingdom's furthest frontiers.

The opera is prefaced by one of Rossini's finest overtures, a powerfully worked version of the familiar Rossini archetype, containing, unusually for him, thematic material that recurs in the opera. At the

start of the long opening scene sombre orchestral colours determine the mood of gloom and unease as the high priest, Oroe, stands before the altar of Baal. A huge crowd has gathered outside the temple, impatient for the nomination of a male successor to the throne that Semiramide has occupied since the death of Nino. Prince Assur has pretensions to the throne but fears that Oroe has secret information about him. Idreno, an Indian king, appears at the sanctuary to ask the gods' blessing on his love for the princess Azema. But it is Semiramide's arrival that provides the culmination of Rossini's huge 700-bar exposition: as she approaches the altar there is a blinding flash and the sacred flame is extinguished. The people flee but Oroe returns; at the sanctuary he is confronted by Arsace, back in the city by royal summons. He, too, has an interest in the princess Azema, whom he once rescued from bandits; he also carries a casket containing a sword and scrolls, the property of his late father, which Oroe appears to recognize. When Assur meets Arsace, he remonstrates with him for leaving his border post. But it soon becomes clear that Arsace instinctively distrusts Assur; if Assur succeeds in his claim to the throne, Arsace will never accord him recognition as king.

I.ii The Hanging Gardens of Babylon Semiramide is overjoyed that Arsace, the handsome young commander, has returned. Her cavatina 'Bel raggio lusinghier', a famous soprano showpiece, is the score's most dazzling number, a love song that irradiates the queen's entire personality. An ambiguously worded pronouncement arrives from the oracle at Memphis. Believing the gods at last appeased, Semiramide summons Arsace. In a duet of mutual misunderstanding 'Serbami ognor sì fido', she talks of Assur's treachery in the matter of King Nino's death but mistakes Arsace's love for Azema as love for herself; this is one of Rossini's most eloquent duets, an E♭ andantino in 6/8 time. The use of the crescendo subject from the overture as a transition with the cabaletta is less happy, but the coda is gloriously shaped with augmented rhythms in the voice part and seething figurations beneath.

I.iii The throne room of the palace The Act 1 finale is a 900-bar six-movement structure. Semiramide announces that Arsace is to be both king and her consort. Arsace is appalled, Assur furious. Meanwhile, Azema will be given in marriage to Idreno. As the high priest is about to unite them in marriage, the ghost of King Nino rises up. Arsace will be king, he announces, but there are crimes to be expiated and Arsace must descend into the vault and offer up a sacrifice to Nino's ashes. The first episode of the finale, a slow section in E♭, where allegiance is sworn to Semiramide, treats the overture's solemn horn subject in unaccompanied choral form. Later in the finale there are two especially impressive episodes in the minor key. 'Quel mesto gemito', Semiramide's stunned response to the rumblings from Nino's tomb, deploys a sombre ostinato similar to that which Verdi was to use in the 'Miserere' in *Il trovatore*. The later episode in which the ghost of Nino addresses Arsace is equally powerful, in a restless F minor. It has been noted that the terror is created here as much by the rhythm as by the declamation.

Act 2.i *A room in the palace* Semiramide reminds Assur of their past crimes and threatens to expose him. In a magnificent duet of mutual recrimination, 'Quella, ricordati', they quarrel, like the Macbeths, over events that are beginning to overshadow them. In the andantino Assur reminds Semiramide of 'the night of death' in phrases which are both suave and terrifying.

2.ii The palace sanctuary Oroe and the Magi assemble to lead Arsace to Nino's tomb. The priest now reveals to Arsace what he has recognized from the casket and its contents: that the young man is in fact Nino, son of the late king, and that the king was murdered by his mother and Assur. Killing Assur is easily contemplated, but Arsace prays that his father's spirit will show leniency to Semiramide.

2.iii The queen's apartments Arsace reveals to his mother that he knows all. In a scene distantly reminiscent of the closet scene in *Hamlet*, Nino is also

tacitly present; Rossini even accords him a brief theme of his own. The truth revealed, Semiramide offers her life to her son ('Ebben . . . a te, ferisci'), but Arsace's response is generous. However hateful Semiramide is in the sight of the gods, she is his mother. The music is now lyric and serene as she perceives her son's sincerity through his tears.

2.iv The palace, by the tomb of King Nino Assur is determined to kill Arsace but is told that Oroe has revealed his crimes to the people; he is now on the verge of madness. Colours implicit in the opera's first scene are broodingly remixed as Assur becomes subject to terrible visions. The scene, written for the great bass Filippo Galli, is full of fractured declamation and fraught rhythms. Even the transition to the cabaletta brings its rich cargo of effects as Rossini charts Assur's hazy return to consciousness before the stirring *marziale* conveys to us the resolve of the newly restored man. This remarkable scene is a possible inspiration for the great Banquet Scene in Verdi's *Macbeth*.

2.v Within the monument of King Nino Arsace enters the monument as do Assur and Semiramide, who fears for her son's life. Her prayer, 'Al mio pregar t'arrendi', is followed by a trio, the characters circling

Giulia Grisi in the title role of Rossini's 'Semiramide', which she sang at the opening of the Royal Italian Opera, Covent Garden, in 1847: lithograph from a contemporary sheet music cover

one another in the gloom. Arsace, intending to kill Assur, strikes his mother as she interposes herself between them. Her death throes, extended by Rossini in his Paris revision, make Arsace's accession to the throne less abrupt, though no less harrowing, as Assur is led away and the people acclaim their new and rightful king.

*

With *Semiramide*, Rossini brought his Italian career to a spectacular close. After a series of operas in which the primary areas of interest were either vocal or architectural, Rossini once again drew vocal, dramatic, and architectural elements into harmony with one another. The strategic planning is formidable, with an opening movement of over 700 bars and an Act 1 finale of over 900 bars; the work points directly forward to the huge structural spans of *Guillaume Tell* (1829). The *Semiramide* story, popular with composers of the period, is to some extent locked into an 18th-century Metastasian aesthetic, and Rossini has yet to rid himself of the *travesti* contralto hero. But his treatment of key scenes has great musico-dramatic impact, far removed from the kind of musical tinsel served up by Marcos António Portugal in his *La morte di Semiramide* (1801) where vocal display obscures the thrust of those archetypal relationships and situations which Rossini's music powerfully engages.   R.O.

Serse ('Xerxes')

Opera in three acts by George Frideric Handel to an anonymous revision of Silvio Stampiglia's libretto *Il Xerse* (Rome, 1694) based on Nicolo Minato's *Il Xerse* (Venice, 1654); London, King's Theatre, 15 April 1738.

The original cast included the celebrated castrato Gaetano Majorano, known as Caffarelli, in the role of Xerxes, Maria Antonia Marchesini ('La Lucchesina') as Arsamene, Elisabeth du Parc ('La Francesina') as Romilda, Antonia Merighi as Amastre, Margherita Chimenti ('La Droghierina') as Atalanta, and Antonio Montagnana as Ariodate.

Serse [Xerxes] *King of Persia*	mezzo-soprano
Arsamene *his brother, in love*	
with Romilda	mezzo-soprano
Amastre *heiress to the kingdom of Tagor,*	
betrothed to Xerxes	alto
Ariodate *a prince, vassal to Xerxes*	bass
Romilda *his daughter, in love with*	
Arsamene	soprano
Atalanta *her sister, secretly in love with*	
Arsamene	soprano
Elviro *servant of Arsamene*	bass

Setting Abydos, Persia, in ancient times

Handel composed *Serse* between 26 December 1737 and 14 February 1738. It was to be his last opera for the King's Theatre, which he shared with his rival Giovanni Battista Pescetti for the 1737–8 season. He based it not only on the version of the libretto prepared by Stampiglia for Giovanni Bononcini's setting of 1694 but to some extent on Bononcini's score, from which he had been borrowing musical material since 1734. In *Serse* itself he tended to follow Bononcini in matters of tonality and style rather than use direct thematic quotation; indeed, the considerable degree of rewriting in the score attests to a determination to produce a thoroughly original work on Bononcini's model. The libretto is largely fictional, but has a historical background derived from Herodotus's account of the Graeco-Persian wars (*Histories*, vii). The title role represents the Persian king Xerxes I (reigned 485–465 BC), and the action supposedly takes place at the time of his expedition against Greece, about 470 BC. Reference is made to Xerxes' attempt to bridge the Hellespont with boats and (in the famous opening number of the opera) to his reverence for a plane tree. For the most part, however, the action is a court intrigue involving the rivalry between Xerxes and his brother Arsamene for the love of Romilda, and the rivalry of Romilda and her mischievous sister Atalanta for the love of Arsamene. Amastre (a character derived from Xerxes' historical wife), betrothed to Xerxes but abandoned by him, performs a key role in resolving the complications.

Serse was little appreciated by its original audiences and after only five performances was replaced by repeats of the heroic operas given earlier in the season. It was not heard again until the production of Oskar Hagen's arrangement at Göttingen on 5 July 1924, but thereafter soon became one of the most frequently performed of Handel's operas; there were three productions in the USA between 1928 and 1935. The first British revival was at the Pollards Opera Festival, Loughton, Essex, on 15 June 1935. One of the most successful recent productions was that by Nicholas Hytner for the English National Opera, first given at the London Coliseum on the tercentenary of Handel's birth (23 February 1985), which vindicated the use of the uncut score.

The place of the action (unspecified in Handel's libretto) is presumably Abydos.

*

Act I In a garden, with a summer house on one side, Xerxes addresses affectionate praise to the shade of a plane tree ('Ombra mai fù'). Arsamene and his clownish servant Elviro watch as sweet music is heard and Romilda, in the summer house, sings in gentle mockery of Xerxes: he loves a tree, but it responds only with the rustle of its leaves. Arsamene (who, unknown to Xerxes, is Romilda's lover) tells his brother he does not know who the singer is. As Romilda's singing grows livelier Xerxes becomes captivated by her: he loves her, wants her as his wife. He orders the dumbfounded Arsamene to tell Romilda of his wishes, but Arsamene pleads shyness and Xerxes determines to do his own wooing. Arsamene warns Romilda of what is about to happen, so giving hope to Romilda's sister Atalanta that Romilda will yield to Xerxes and leave Arsamene for her. Xerxes bans Arsamene from the court and declares his love to Romilda, but she remains unmoved. Amastre appears, disguised as a man; she is betrothed to Xerxes but, abandoned by him, seeks revenge. Romilda's father Ariodate announces a Persian victory and presents enemy insignia and prisoners to Xerxes; in reward the King promises him a royal husband, 'equal to Xerxes', for Romilda. Arsamene gives Elviro a letter for Romilda, grieving at his separation from her. Atalanta tells Romilda that Arsamene has found a new lover, but Romilda sees through her lie and says her love will remain true.

Act 2 In a public square, Amastre encounters Elviro, who is disguised as a flower seller and speaks in dialect. She questions him and is grief-stricken and angry to learn that Xerxes is to marry Romilda (disapproved of by Elviro as a vassal's daughter). Atalanta appears and Elviro makes himself known to her; she says she will deliver Arsamene's letter, telling Elviro that Romilda has abandoned Arsamene and now loves Xerxes. Elviro curses Romilda and leaves as the King approaches. Xerxes finds Atalanta reading the letter, and asks to see it. It is a declaration of love which Xerxes recognizes to be in Arsamene's hand. Atalanta claims that the letter is hers and it is she whom Arsamene truly loves. Xerxes is delighted, and takes the letter; Atalanta reminds him that Arsamene will deny he loves her. He now confronts Romilda with the letter: she insists she will always love Arsamene. Xerxes is furious but cannot bring himself to reject her. Elviro prevents Amastre from killing herself. He tells Arsamene what Atalanta said about Romilda and Xerxes; Arsamene is heartbroken.

By Xerxes' new bridge joining the shores of the Hellespont, a chorus of mariners congratulates him on the achievement. Xerxes tells Ariodate that he will shortly advance into Europe. He meets the despondent Arsamene and tells him he is no longer angry: he gladly gives Arsamene permission to marry the woman he really loves, Atalanta. Arsamene declares he loves only Romilda and remains determined to win her. Xerxes advises Atalanta to forget Arsamene but she says she cannot. Elviro remarks on the gathering storm, which threatens to wreck the bridge, and seeks solace in drink. Xerxes meets Amastre, still in disguise, who claims to have been wounded while serving him in the wars. Their strained conversation is interrupted by Romilda. The King again asks her to marry him but Amastre intervenes, calls Xerxes a traitor and draws her sword. She is arrested by the royal guards, but released on the orders of Romilda, who delivers a ringing tribute to those faithful in love.

Act 3 Arsamene and Romilda are quarrelling, but are swiftly reconciled when Atalanta admits her deception and resigns herself to finding another lover. Xerxes again presses Romilda to marry him. She tells Xerxes to seek her father's permission; she will obey her father's orders. Reproached by Arsamene, she says it is death, not marriage, that awaits her. Xerxes again asks Ariodate if he is happy for Romilda to marry 'a person equal to us, and of our blood', and Ariodate, assuming that Arsamene is the person in question, gladly agrees. Romilda now resolves to reject Xerxes, telling him that Arsamene is her lover and that they have kissed. Xerxes says this is a ruse to thwart him but orders Arsamene's execution. Amastre offers to help Romilda by giving her a letter to take to Xerxes, and reflects on the grief she has brought on herself by loving one who has betrayed her. Arsamene blames Romilda for his death sentence.

The final scene takes place in the temple of the sun. Romilda and Arsamene enter, still quarrelling, but when Ariodate joins their hands and tells them they are married with Xerxes' consent they are joyfully reconciled. Now Xerxes appears, to marry Romilda, and is furious when Ariodate explains what he has done. His anger is intensified when a page brings a letter from Romilda, upbraiding him for his betrayal in love, and is not assuaged when the letter is revealed to be from Amastre. He draws his sword and orders Arsamene to kill Romilda with it. But Amastre intervenes, asking Xerxes if he truly wishes treachery to be avenged: he agrees, and Amastre, revealing who she is, turns the sword on him. Xerxes begs her pardon, and receives it; his love for her will be renewed. He blesses the marriage of Romilda and Arsamene. All celebrate the union of love and honour.

*

Serse is not Handel's only comic opera, as it has sometimes been described, but it is the finest of his operas with comical or satirical elements and shows the greatest deviation from the standard forms of *opera seria*. Most of the arias are short, and about half are through-composed, without da capo. In many scenes the music is precisely moulded to the action in a manner which seems prophetically modern (notably at the start of Act 1, with its delightful mix of sinfonias, recitative and short arias), though it in fact derives from the early Venetian origins of the libretto. Only Elviro is a wholly comic role: all the other characters exhibit some degree of seriousness and are sharply and sympathetically drawn. Xerxes is a rather absurd figure but never wholly foolish: the threat of his arbitrary power gives an underlying tension to the drama, and his music, with its big set-piece arias, emphasizes his importance. The heart of Act 2 is his exchange with Romilda: in a duet as simple as it is moving he fails to persuade her to relinquish her love for Arsamene, then reacts with the aria 'Se bramate d'amar chi vi sdegna', a stunning outburst of fury and anguish expressed by alternating fast and slow tempos, and harmonic surprise. His amorous address to the plane tree in the opening scene, 'Ombra mai fù', is presumably satirical, but its perfectly shaped melody and grave beauty have made it the most famous of Handel's opera songs (often entitled 'Handel's Largo', though the tempo is actually Larghetto). The deepest emotions are found in the minor-key songs for Romilda, Arsamene and Amastre, and Handel nicely contrasts the music for Atalanta with that for her sister, epitomizing their characters in the closing arias of the first two acts. Atalanta's 'Un cenno leggiadretto', ending Act 1, is charmingly teasing; Romilda's 'Chi cede al furore', at the end of Act 2, has a noble, seamless melodic line aptly expressing her constancy. The occasional choruses, two with solo trumpet and one with a pair of horns, give additional variety to the score. Though other Handel operas may contain greater music, *Serse* is one of the composer's most consistently satisfying scores, moving surefootedly between farce and tragedy and always responding with insight to the emotions of its very human characters.   **A.H.**

Serva padrona, La ('The Maid as Mistress')

Intermezzo in two parts by Giovanni Battista Pergolesi to a libretto by Gennaro Antonio Federico after Jacopo Angello Nelli's play; Naples, Teatro S Bartolomeo, 5 September 1733.

The singers at the first performance were Laura Monti and Gioacchino Corradi.

Uberto *an elderly gentleman*		bass
Serpina *his servant*		soprano
Vespone *another servant*		silent role
Setting A room in Uberto's house		

La serva padrona was first performed between the acts of Pergolesi's *opera seria Il prigioniero superbo*, commissioned for the birthday celebrations of the Empress Elisabeth Christina, consort of Charles VI. It became one of the most popular examples of intermezzo in the 18th century. Federico based his text on a spoken play of the same title written by Nelli (1673–1767), an erudite member of the Accademia dei

Rozzi in Siena. Published in 1731, the play contains the essence of Federico's plot, which uses familiar stock characters of the *commedia dell'arte*.

For two decades after its creation *La serva padrona* survived in the repertory almost intact, with minimal changes; this was most unusual for the genre. During that period it was performed in more than 60 theatres in Italy and throughout Europe, from Malta and Spain in the south to St Petersburg in the north. The only change to the music over those two decades occurred in Act 2, where the original duet, 'Contento tu sarai', was sometimes supplanted by 'Per te ho io nel core' from Pergolesi's comic opera *Flaminio* (1735).

When first performed in Paris on 4 October 1746 the intermezzo passed almost unnoticed. But during its second Paris presentation, in August 1752, when it was coupled with Lully's *Acis et Galatée*, it became the centre of a controversy that was to affect the future development of opera in Paris and the creation of *opéra comique*. *La serva padrona* was one of the 14 Italian works given in Paris between 1752 and 1754 by a group of Italian *buffo* singers led by Eustachio Bambini. The comic Italian style projected in these works was new to the French public, which split into two camps and voiced their opinions in numerous pamphlets and newspaper articles (the Querelle des Bouffons). The Philosophes and Encyclopedists, such as Rousseau, Grimm and Diderot, were supporters of the Italian comic style and were active participants. Pergolesi, called 'divine' by his supporters, was the chief representative of this new musical style, and six of the 14 compositions given by Bambini's company contained his music. They included Gaetano Latilla's *La finta cameriera* (with Pergolesi's duet 'Per te ho io nel core'), Giuseppe Maria Orlandini's *Il giocatore* (with Pergolesi's duet 'Contento tu sarai'), *Il maestro di musica*, which though attributed to Pergolesi was a pasticcio incorporating only some of his music, and *Tracollo, medico ignorante*, a reworking of his intermezzo *Livietta e Tracollo* (1734).

Through Pergolesi's music the French gradually came to terms with the Italian comic idiom, especially after Rousseau used *La serva padrona* as a model for his own French intermezzo, *Le devin du village* (1752). Two years later Pierre Baurans translated and revised Pergolesi's intermezzo as *La servante maîtresse*; new names were given to the characters, new numbers were added and the recitative replaced by spoken French dialogue.

Pergolesi's intermezzo continued to be performed in Paris and London throughout the second half of the 18th century. In London it was translated into English and enjoyed a great success in outdoor performances, especially at Marylebone Gardens in 1759 in a version by Stephen Storace senior (c1725–81) and James Oswald, with an additional act and a

'La serva padrona', scene from part 2 of an early Paris production of Pergolesi's intermezzo: engraving (18th century)

new character. It was also performed at the King's Theatre, Drury Lane, Ranelagh Gardens and Covent Garden, and over the years inspired several English versions, including *The Maid the Mistress* (1770) with a text by Isaac Bickerstaff and entirely new music by Charles Dibdin, which was later revised as *He Wou'd if he Could* (1771). Giovanni Paisiello made a new setting of Federico's libretto in 1781 during his sojourn in Russia.

*

Intermezzo 1 Uberto angrily emerges from his bedroom and launches directly into an aria, 'Aspettare e non venire'. Serpina, who refuses to take orders from him, has been delinquent in bringing him his chocolate; Uberto's dissatisfaction with her is depicted in the opening line, which includes a descending octave jump, and the phrase is repeated three times at successively higher pitches. The ensuing patter is accompanied by repeated figures in the orchestra. Uberto is all the more frustrated with Serpina since, as her guardian, he has cared for her throughout her adolescent years, and now she is behaving in an ungrateful and insolent manner. In his first full-length da capo aria, 'Sempre in contrasti', patter phrases such as 'e qua e la', 'e su e giù' and 'e sì e no' break the continuity of the phrases into short melodic and rhythmic motifs, depicting his relationship with Serpina in a constant battle of words. Uberto decides to improve the domestic atmosphere by marrying; he orders Vespone to go out and find

him a wife. Serpina insists that he marry her instead, and in her aria 'Stizzoso, mio stizzoso' she promises to lock the doors to prevent him from seeking a wife. A duet of conflicting opinions, 'Lo conosco a quegl'occhieti', closes the first part of the intermezzo.

Intermezzo 2 Serpina enlists the aid of Vespone, whom she has frequently mistreated in the past, to help her to marry Uberto. In return she promises him continued employment and a secure future in her household when she becomes its mistress. To arouse Uberto's jealousy she has Vespone disguise himself as a soldier and announces her intention to marry him. In 'A Serpina penserete', a cleverly constructed sentimental aria, Serpina manipulates Uberto's emotions by convincing him that he will miss her when she leaves. The aria is in several sections of contrasting metres and tempos, portraying changes in mood. Throughout the piece Serpina comments in asides on the effect her words are having on Uberto. In his aria 'Son imbrogliato io gia' he begins to weaken as he considers marriage. The final duet of reconciliation, 'Contento tu sarai', was later supplanted by 'Per te ho io nel core'.

*

La serva padrona is a work of true genius. Pergolesi's basic method of portrayal is the *buffo* style, which he developed to an unsurpassed vitality and effectiveness. As the libretto provided him not only with effective *buffo* scenes but also with a plot which develops logically between credibly drawn characters, it was possible both for the characters to express themselves naturally within the idiom of the music and for the music to make clear the characters' motivation. The work calls for a chamber orchestra of strings and continuo. The unison playing of the first and second violins, and the doubling of the bass line by the violas, produces a thin, two-part texture. The work is remarkable for the suppleness of its melodic phrases and for the vivacity of its arias. Syllabic patter songs, octave jumps and frequent repetition of cadential material were not only components of the new comic idiom, developed in the early decades of the century by Pergolesi, Leonardo Leo, Domenico Sarro, Johann Adolf Hasse, Orlandini and others, but also constituted the basis of the pre-classical style.

G.La., H.H.

Siegfried

Second day of *Der Ring des Nibelungen* in three acts by Richard Wagner to his own libretto; Bayreuth, Festspielhaus, 16 August 1876.

For the original cast, *see Ring des Nibelungen, Der*.

Siegfried	tenor
Mime	tenor
The Wanderer	bass-baritone
Alberich	bass-baritone
Fafner	bass
Erda	contralto
Brünnhilde	soprano
Woodbird	soprano†

† Originally 'boy's voice'

The first sketches for *Jung-Siegfried* (the opera's original title, subsequently changed to *Der junge Siegfried*) date probably from 3–24 May 1851. The prose draft followed between 24 May and 1 June, and two days later Wagner began the versification, ending at midday on 24 June. Following the writing of the poems for *Die Walküre* and *Das Rheingold*, Wagner subjected his texts for *Der junge Siegfried* and *Siegfrieds Tod* (later *Götterdämmerung*) to revision (Nov–Dec 1852). The final poem was incorporated into the private printing of the entire *Ring* text in February 1853. *Der junge Siegfried* and *Siegfrieds Tod* were definitively named *Siegfried* and *Götterdämmerung* in 1856.

Some preliminary musical sketches were made for *Der junge Siegfried* in 1851, but the composition proper was begun in 1856 (probably early September) with the first complete draft. To avoid the problems he had experienced with *Die Walküre*, Wagner took each act through from first draft to score before embarking on the next. He also worked

in tandem between the first complete draft (in pencil) and the second (in ink, on at least three staves – two instrumental and one vocal – elaborating details of the orchestral texture). In June 1857 he broke off work on the drafts, with Siegfried resting under the linden tree (Act 2), partly because the *Ring* was becoming a drain on his financial resources, partly because he wished to try out his increasingly chromatic style on the Tristan legend, a subject inspired to some extent by his love for Mathilde Wesendonck. Nevertheless he briefly took up again the composition of Act 2 shortly after, finishing the first complete draft on 30 July 1857 and the second on 9 August. Not until 27 September 1864 was the task of making a fair copy of the score of Act 1 resumed and between 22 December of that year and 2 December 1865 the scoring of Act 2 was undertaken. Work on Act 3 began on 1 March 1869, after the fair copy of the Act 1 and 2 scores had been finished. The scoring of the whole work was completed on 5 February 1871.

*

Act I A cave in the rocks in the forest Opening with a subdued drum roll and a pair of brooding bassoons, the prelude sets the scene in the dark forest, where the dragon Fafner has his lair, at the same time alluding to the crafty scheming of the dwarf Mime. The contrabass tuba joins in with a motif associated (in *Das Rheingold*) with the hoard and then the dotted Nibelungs' motif is introduced as an ostinato accompaniment to it. The tempo becomes more animated and the motifs of the Ring and Sword are heard, the latter on the bass trumpet in its familiar key of C major, though without disturbing the Nibelungs' tonality of B♭ minor in which the prelude as a whole is set. The curtain rises on Mime hammering away at an anvil (to the rhythm of the Nibelungs' motif), cursing his wearisome labour and his hopeless attempts to forge a sword that the boy

'Siegfried' (Wagner): design by Joseph Hoffmann for Act 3 scene ii (Siegfried strikes the Wanderer's spear) for the original production at the Festspielhaus, Bayreuth, 16 August 1876

Siegfried will be unable to break in two. The giant Fafner has transformed himself into a fierce dragon, Mime tells us (a Dragon motif growls low on tubas), the better to guard the Nibelung treasure. If only he, Mime, could forge together the fragments of Nothung, the sword of Siegfried's father, Siegmund, the boy might kill the dragon with it and the ring would come to Mime.

Siegfried enters to the exuberant strains of his motif (ex.1). He is leading in a huge bear and he

Ex.1

laughs all the way to a top C as it chases Mime round the cave. He demands to see Mime's work but on testing it (to the strains of another motif to be associated with his heroism, ex.2), he scornfully

Ex.2

smashes it on the anvil; he berates Mime to yet another motif (ex.3). His annoyance with the prat-

Ex.3

tling dwarf is hardly diminished when Mime tells him (to a modified form of the Nibelungs' motif, ex.4)

Ex.4

that he should show more gratitude to his guardian. He knocks the proffered meat and soup out of Mime's hands, whereupon the latter embarks upon what Siegfried later calls his 'starling song', 'Als zullendes Kind', telling Siegfried how Mime has nurtured him: one of the several self-contained song forms incorporated into the structure of this act. Siegfried's response, a litany of loathing (exx.3 and 4), inspires only a further attempt at ingratiation, the lyrically tender ex.5. If Mime is his father, Siegfried asks, where is his mother? He forcefully extracts the

Ex.5

whole story from Mime, to reminiscences of the themes of the Volsungs and their love. Hearing about the fragments of Nothung, Siegfried excitedly instructs Mime to reforge the sword and rushes off into the forest, leaving Mime sitting dejectedly at the anvil.

The Wanderer (Wotan in disguise) appears and asks for hospitality (scene ii): 'Heil dir, weiser Schmied!' The textural and motivic contrast between his music, with its noble tread, and Mime's forms the Riddle Scene, as it is sometimes called. The Wanderer stakes his head on answering correctly three questions. Mime asks the name of the races that live in the earth, on the face of the earth and in the cloudy heights. The Nibelungs, the giants and the gods ruled by Wotan, come the answers, duly illustrated with the appropriate motifs, often in their original tonality. To Mime's horror, the Wanderer then demands the same in exchange. His first question concerns the tribe treated harshly by Wotan though dearest to him. The Volsungs, replies Mime confidently. As to the name of the sword to be wielded by the hero Siegfried, he correctly replies Nothung. But when asked who will forge the sword, Mime jumps up in alarm: he has no idea. The answer, the Wanderer tells him against the growls of the Dragon motif, is 'one who has never known fear'. He leaves Mime's head forfeit to the fearless one and departs.

The orchestra paints a dazzling picture of flickering lights and roaring flames as the terrified Mime imagines the dragon looming in the forest (scene iii). Siegfried returns and Mime determines to teach him fear (tremolo strings), but Siegfried's curiosity is only whetted. Mime looks on aghast as Siegfried begins to forge the fragments of the sword himself, to the accompaniment of a transformation of ex.1, its vigour enhanced by augmented triad colouring. On being told the name of the sword, Nothung, Siegfried launches his Forging Song with it: 'Nothung! Nothung! Neidliches Schwert!' This song, also coloured by augmented chords, begins as a strophic structure (the second and third stanzas slightly varied), but after interruptions by Mime, the form dissolves under the pressure of the dramatic momentum. Mime plots how he will offer Siegfried a drugged drink after his battle with the dragon, and then kill him with his own sword. At last the forging is done, and Siegfried crashes the sword down on the anvil, splitting it in two.

Act 2 *Deep in the forest* Two motifs are dominant in the prelude to Act 2: the growling of the dragon, outside whose cave the scene is set, and the Curse. Alberich is keeping watch over the cave and is surprised by the appearance of the Wanderer. Bitterly recalling how, as Wotan, he stole the ring from him, Alberich taunts him (to frequent repetitions of the Spear motif) with his ambitions for world

Backstage view of the dragon in Wagner's 'Siegfried' in the first Paris production (Opéra, 1902): from the 'Scientific American' (29 March 1902), supplement 1369

supremacy. Wotan remains quietly philosophical and even warns Alberich of the approach of Siegfried and Mime. He surprises Alberich further by arousing Fafner on his behalf and asking him to yield up the ring.

Mime arrives with Siegfried (scene ii) and describes to him the fearsome dragon; Siegfried is concerned only to know where is the dragon's heart, so that he can plunge in his sword. Mime leaves Siegfried alone and to the mellifluous strains of the Forest Murmurs (shimmering muted strings supporting woodwind solos), the boy expresses his relief that the ugly dwarf is not his father after all. (The rippling movement of the Forest Murmurs is anticipated more than once in the preceding pages of the score, effectively integrating it into the scene as a whole.) He is lonely, though, and would like a friend. Hearing the song of the Woodbird (a character unseen on the stage), Siegfried tries to imitate it with a pipe made from a reed, but after several abortive attempts (comically rendered on the english horn) he gives up. He blows his horn instead (exx.1 and 2) and a somnolent Fafner drags himself out of his cave. After an exchange of banter and a battle depicted by the conflict of their motifs, Siegfried stabs Fafner in the heart with Nothung. Fafner, with his last gasp,

tells Siegfried his history. Putting his burning hand involuntarily to his mouth, Siegfried tastes the dragon's blood. At last he understands the song of the Woodbird: it tells him to take the Ring and Tarnhelm from the cave.

As Siegfried disappears into the cave, Mime and Alberich appear from opposite sides (scene iii). To a shambling, syncopated accompaniment they argue angrily about the rightful ownership of the treasure. Mime offers to relinquish the Ring, provided he be allowed the Tarnhelm. Their argument is halted by the reappearance of Siegfried with both items; a chorus of horns, wafting the Rhinemaidens' motif, reminds us of the origin of the gold. The Woodbird tells Siegfried to beware Mime, who now approaches and hails him unctuously. As Mime cajoles Siegfried and offers him his drugged drink, thinking he is fooling the boy with his flattery, his actual words keep betraying his intention to make an end of him (a comic device which Wagner apparently borrowed from a 19th-century farce on the Faust legend). Finally, Siegfried, in an access of revulsion, kills Mime with a blow of the sword.

He tosses Mime's body into the cave and drags Fafner's over its mouth. Lying down under the linden tree, he listens again to the song of the

Woodbird and asks its advice. The bird tells him of the bride that awaits him on a mountain top surrounded by fire. Siegfried jumps up and follows the bird as it leads the way.

Act 3.i–ii *The foot of a rocky mountain* The prelude is a symphonic development of a number of major motifs, notably the dotted rhythm pervading the prelude, associated with Wotan, the Valkyries and their riding; the Erda motif and its inversion the Twilight of the Gods; the flattened mediant harmonies of the Wanderer; the falling semitone associated in *Rheingold* with Alberich and the baleful power of his ring; and the Magic Sleep. The Wanderer appears and, summoning Erda (the earth goddess) from her slumber, demands to know more of the earth's secrets: 'Wache, Wala!' First she refers him to the Norns as they weave the rope of destiny, and then to the daughter she bore him, Brünnhilde. When he tells her that Brünnhilde is being punished for her disobedience, she expresses surprise that the one who taught defiance is now punishing it. The technical advance represented by this scene, written after the long break during which Wagner composed *Tristan* and *Die Meistersinger*, is immediately evident. Powerfully conceived vocal lines completely abandoning recitative in favour of heightened arioso are supported by an orchestral texture of unprecedented richness and motivic density. The scene takes the form of a dialogue between the Wanderer and Erda, in which the characteristic material of each is subjected to variation. The form threatens to disintegrate as the emotional temperature rises, until a climax is reached with the Wanderer's announcement that he now looks forward to the end of the gods. The gravity of the moment is signalled with a noble new motif (ex.6);

Ex.6

leitmotifs of such expansiveness and autonomy are henceforth to play a major role in the *Ring*. The Wanderer bequeaths his inheritance to the Volsung hero, Siegfried. Erda, deeply troubled that her wisdom is now ineffectual, sinks back into the earth.

As the Wanderer waits by the cave, Siegfried comes into view, led by the Woodbird, which flies off, recognizing the Wanderer as the master of his raven messengers. In answer to the old stranger's questions, Siegfried tells, to the accompaniment of the appropriate motifs, how he killed the dragon, about the deceit of Mime, and how he himself forged the sword. Siegfried, irritated by the stranger, treats him with contempt. In a last attempt to exert his power, the Wanderer is moved to try to block the boy's path, but his spear is shattered by a stroke of

Siegfried's sword; the motif of the Spear, and hence of Wotan's authority, is symbolically fragmented. The Wanderer vanishes and Siegfried plunges into the flames.

3.iii *On the peak of Brünnhilde's rock* During an orchestral interlude constructed from motifs associated with Siegfried and the fire, the scene changes to the rocky summit of the end of *Die Walküre*. The first violins, unaccompanied, scale the heights as Siegfried climbs to the top of the rock. He has never seen a woman, and mistakes the form of the sleeping Brünnhilde for that of a man, even after removing her helmet (his doubts and irresolution prompting a brief return to the quasi-recitative style). His eventual realization, on removing the breastplate, that it is a woman causes a frenzy of fear and excitement (depicted in a series of flourishes characteristic of the post-*Tristan* Wagner). Now for the first time he has been taught fear, yet he longs to waken her. In desperation he kisses her on the lips, at which she opens her eyes and sits up. With a flurry of harps, and in a bright C major, Brünnhilde greets the light: 'Heil dir, Sonne!' She tells him that she has always loved him, even before he was conceived. Siegfried wonders if the woman is in fact his mother, but she tells him how she was confined on the rock for shielding him. This first part of their extended duet introduces a pair of new thematic ideas (exx.7 and 8), which will return to dominate the close of the act.

The confusion engendered by Siegfried's mixed emotions soon gives way to impetuous desire, the excitability of the vocal line being matched by tumescence in the orchestra. These effusions alternate with slower passages of a darker colour as Brünnhilde becomes increasingly conscious of her vulnerability, stripped as she is of her godhead. When Siegfried tries to embrace her, she pushes him away in terror. Now it is she who is prey to conflicting emotions, and motifs associated with Wotan's agony in Act 2 of *Die Walküre* and even the Curse well up from the depths of the orchestra. She begs him not to destroy the purity of their love, embarking on a monologue almost self-contained in its thematic content (the music is familiar from the *Siegfried Idyll*, composed the following year): 'Ewig war ich'. Gradually she is won over by the intensity of Siegfried's passion and is able to accept her new mortal status. To a riotous profusion of themes, including exx.6, 7 and 8, as well as a new one, ex.9, which combines the boyish vigour and falling 4ths of ex.3 with a suggestion of the cycle's principal Love motif (*see Rheingold, Das*, ex.4), they embrace in

Ex.9

ecstasy. Brünnhilde bids farewell to the world of the gods, and, transformed by each other's love, they invoke 'laughing death'.

*

The long span of 15 years over which the composition of *Siegfried* took place accounts for much of the stylistic inconsistency identifiable in the work. Acts 1 and 2 continue the style of *Rheingold* and *Walküre*, but with some interesting experiments in formal structure, while Act 3, written after the composition of *Tristan* and *Die Meistersinger*, demonstrates a new-found flexibility and maturity. The role of Siegfried, in which the singer is required to dominate the stage for the best part of four hours, culminating in a strenuous final scene with the newly awakened Brünnhilde, is one of the most testing in the tenor repertory. B.M.

Simon Boccanegra

Opera in a prologue and three acts by Giuseppe Verdi to a libretto by Francesco Maria Piave (with additions by Giuseppe Montanelli) after Antonio García Gutiérrez's play *Simón Bocanegra*; Venice, Teatro La Fenice, 12 March 1857 (revised version, with additions and alterations by Arrigo Boito, Milan, Teatro alla Scala, 24 March 1881).

The cast at the première included Leone Giraldoni (Boccanegra), Giuseppe Echeverria (Fiesco), Luigia Bendazzi (Amelia) and Carlo Negrini (Gabriele). For the revised version the cast included Victor Maurel (Boccanegra), Edouard de Reszke (Fiesco), Anna D'Angeri (Amelia) and Francesco Tamagno (Gabriele).

Prologue

Simon Boccanegra *a corsair in the service of the Genoese Republic*	baritone
Jacopo Fiesco *a Genoese nobleman*	bass
Paolo Albiani *a Genoese goldsmith*	bass
Pietro *a Genoese popular leader*	baritone
Sailors, populace, Fiesco's servants	

Dramma

Simon Boccanegra *Doge of Genoa*	baritone
Maria Boccanegra *his daughter, under the name Amelia Grimaldi*	soprano
Jacopo Fiesco *under the name Andrea*	bass
Gabriele Adorno *a Genoese gentleman*	tenor
Paolo Albiani *the Doge's favourite courtier*	bass
Pietro *another courtier*	baritone
A Captain of the Crossbowmen	tenor
Amelia's Maidservant	mezzo-soprano
Soldiers, sailors, populace, senators, the Doge's court, African prisoners of both sexes	

Setting In and around Genoa, about the middle of the 14th century; between the Prologue and Act 1, 25 years pass

Verdi was approached to write a new opera for the Teatro La Fenice in Venice (his last première there had been of *La traviata* in 1853) at the instigation of the librettist Francesco Maria Piave in the spring of 1856. By May of that year a contract had been agreed with the theatre, the subject to be Gutiérrez's *Simón Bocanegra*, and Piave set to work according to precise instructions from the composer. In fact, Verdi himself supplied a complete prose sketch of the action, one so detailed that he insisted that his sketch rather than a draft of the libretto be submitted to the censors for approval. From August 1856 Verdi was in Paris, and in part because communication was difficult with the Italian-based Piave, he took on a local collaborator, the exiled revolutionary Giuseppe Montanelli, who drafted several scenes. Verdi began composing in the autumn of 1856 and, as the date of the première approached, showed his usual close concern with the staging and choice of performers. The première was only a moderate success; the libretto in particular received some harsh criticism. Subsequent revivals in the late 1850s were occasionally successful, although the 1859 La Scala première was a complete fiasco.

Doubtless in reaction to this lack of public acclaim, Verdi considered revising the score during the 1860s; but it was not until 1879 that he finally decided to make substantial alterations, in part to test the possibility of working with Arrigo Boito as librettist on the larger project of *Otello*. Looking over the score, Verdi pronounced it 'too sad' and decided that, although the prologue and final two acts could remain more or less unchanged, the first act needed a thorough overhaul, in particular by the injection of contrast and variety. This idea eventually gave rise to the famous Council Chamber scene; but in the end Verdi (somewhat reluctantly) found it necessary to make large adjustments to several other portions of the score (details are given below). The revised version had a resoundingly successful première at La Scala, directed by Franco Faccio.

*

Prologue *A square in Genoa* The 1857 version begins with a prelude in which various themes from the opera are briefly juxtaposed; the opening scene is the barest of declamatory recitatives. In 1881 Verdi underpinned the opening conversation between Paolo and Pietro with an undulating string theme, rich in harmonic inflections and clearly meant to introduce the maritime flavour of the score. The two men discuss who is to be the next Doge, Pietro persuading Paolo to support the corsair Boccanegra. As Pietro departs to rally the plebeian vote, Boccanegra himself appears. He is at first indifferent to assuming high office, but is persuaded to seek it by Paolo's reminder that his position will help win him his beloved Maria – she is imprisoned in her father Fiesco's home as a result of her love affair and Fiesco's strong disapproval of the plebeian Bocca-negra. From here to the end of the prologue the two versions largely correspond, although Verdi made numerous small revisions for 1881. First comes a chorus during which Paolo and Pietro convince the workers that they should vote for Boccanegra. The scene, remarkable for its restraint, centres on 'L'atra magion vedete?', in which Paolo describes the Fieschi's gloomy palace, which holds Maria prisoner.

As the crowd disperses, Fiesco emerges from his home, stricken with grief: his daughter has just died. After a stern recitative he sings the famous 'Il lacerato spirito', a minor–major *romanza* notable for its extreme melodic simplicity but powerful emotional effect. Fiesco is then joined by Boccanegra for the first grand duet of the opera. The first movement shows the usual violent alternation of moods: Fiesco accuses, Boccanegra tries to placate him, the old man agrees to pardon Boccanegra if he will give up the daughter Maria has borne him. But in a second movement, 'Del mar sul lido', again dominated by maritime figures in the orchestra, Boccanegra nar-rates how the little girl has mysteriously disappeared from the remote hiding place where she was lodged during his absence at sea. Fiesco, who contributes little to this movement, turns his back on Boccanegra, pretending to leave, but hides nearby. In a third movement, full of passionately anxious string figures, Boccanegra enters the palace in search of Maria. His cries of anguish at discovering her body are immediately countered by offstage cheers. To a jarring festive theme – a kind of cabaletta substitute – the people enter to hail Boccanegra as their new leader.

Act I.i *The gardens of the Grimaldi palace outside Genoa* 25 years have passed. An evocative orchestral prelude depicting the rising dawn introduces Amelia, whose French-style ternary aria, 'Come in quest'ora bruna', is notable for its delicately varied accompaniment and its injection of narrative mystery in the middle section. Gabriele's offstage voice is now heard in two stanzas of a *Trovatore*-like serenade, 'Cielo di stelle orbato'. In the 1857 version this leads to a cabaletta for Amelia, 'Il palpito deh frena', which

in 1881 was replaced by a few bars of recitative. In the first movement of the lovers' ensuing duet, Gabriele tries to calm Amelia's fears for the future; in the second, the gentle Andantino 'Vieni a mirar la cerula', they pause to admire the sea around Genoa, although thinking too of enemies within the city walls. At the close of the Andantino the pair are joined by Pietro, who asks permission for the Doge to visit later that day. Amelia, sure that he is planning for her to marry Paolo, sends Gabriele away to prepare for their own wedding. In a final cabaletta, 'Sì, sì, dell'ara il giubilo', much reduced in 1881, they swear to defy the whole world.

Amelia hurries into the palace, but Gabriele is detained by Fiesco (who is posing under the name Andrea, and has long been watching over Amelia; he is very fond of her, although unaware of her real identity). Fiesco, informed of Amelia's and Gabriele's marriage plans, warns Gabriele that his intended bride is not of noble birth but an orphan who was adopted in place of the real Amelia Grimaldi, long since dead. In 1857 the episode was rounded off by a duet cursing Boccanegra, thought responsible for the death; in 1881 there is a *religioso* duet in which Fiesco gives a father's blessing to Gabriele.

Offstage trumpets herald Boccanegra. In a brief scene the Doge gives Amelia a paper showing that he has pardoned her presumed brothers (the Grimaldi, who have plotted against him). In the first movement of the ensuing duet, 'Dinne, perchè in quest'eremo', which is underpinned by a sinuous orchestral melody, Amelia admits that she is in love and, feeling gratitude to Boccanegra, decides to tell him of her lowly birth. This she does in a second movement, the narration 'Orfanella il tetto umile', in the last section of which Boccanegra joins her with a gathering sense of her true identity. The third movement, in which Boccanegra confirms that she is his long-lost daugh-ter, quickly gives way to a cabaletta of mutual joy, 'Figlia! a tal nome io palpito', subtly varied in the 1881 version to increase the sense that both individ-uals have distinct musical personalities. Amelia leaves, and Boccanegra roughly tells Paolo to abandon hope of marrying her. When Boccanegra himself departs, Paolo tells Pietro of his plan to abduct Amelia.

I.ii *The Council Chamber of the Doge's Palace* This scene was almost entirely recomposed for the 1881 version. The 1857 finale is set in a large square in Genoa, and is a conventional four-movement con-certato finale, a grand ceremonial scene in which the Doge appears amid festivities and is interrupted by Fiesco and Gabriele who accuse him of abducting Amelia. As the scene reaches its climax Amelia herself appears, protesting the Doge's innocence and thus precipitating the central Andantino. Amelia then narrates her abduction and escape, but she refuses to reveal publicly who was responsible, and all join in a stretta calling for the guilty one to be brought to justice.

In 1881 Verdi altered this traditional plan, vastly expanding the first movement, eliminating the last, and fashioning new music almost throughout. The scene begins with a stormy orchestral introduction, after which the Doge urges the Council to preserve peace between Genoa and Venice. A riot is heard outside as the plebeians demand death for the patricians and the Doge. Boccanegra orders the crowd to be brought in, and they appear with Fiesco and Gabriele as captives, accused of killing Lorenzino, a leader of the plebeians. Gabriele in turn accuses the Doge of having Amelia abducted and is about to stab him when Amelia enters and interposes herself between them. She narrates her abduction and escape in 'Nell'ora soave', but refuses to reveal publicly who was responsible. A new argument develops between the opposing factions, this time forcefully quelled by the Doge, who launches the central Andante mosso, 'Plebe! Patrizi!', a magnificent ensemble movement in which the Doge's and Amelia's pleas for peace calm the crowd. The Andante over, the Doge pronounces a solemn curse on Amelia's abductor, forcing Paolo to repeat the words. As the chorus reiterate the curse, Paolo falls down in horror.

Act 2 *The Doge's room in the Ducal Palace at Genoa* In 1881 Verdi expanded Paolo's brief 1857 scena into a powerful recitative during which he meditates on the curse that has fallen on him and then puts poison in Boccanegra's drink. Fiesco and Gabriele are led in and, in spite of his hatred for Boccanegra, Fiesco refuses to be involved in Paolo's plot against the Doge. Fiesco leaves and Paolo informs Gabriele that the Doge wishes Amelia for himself. Left alone, Gabriele breaks into a fit of jealous anger that culminates in the two-movement aria 'Sento avvampar nell'anima', the first movement driven by a furious orchestral figure, the second a lyrical Largo enhanced by delicate chromatic details in the vocal line.

There follows a highly condensed four-movement duet for Amelia and Gabriele. During the opening movement Gabriele accuses Amelia of betrayal; she denies this but will elaborate no further. In the second-movement Andante, 'Parla, in tuo cor virgineo', Gabriele begs her to explain herself while she continues to protest her innocence. A tiny connecting movement starts as Amelia hears the Doge approaching. Gabriele refuses to leave, but in a short cabaletta she succeeds in making him hide on the balcony. The Doge enters and in a stormy recitative learns that she loves Gabriele, whom he now knows to be conspiring against him. Left alone, he drinks from the poisoned cup and lapses into

sleep. Gabriele reappears and after some deliberation decides to murder the Doge; but he is stopped by the sudden appearance of Amelia. Boccanegra awakes and eventually reveals that Amelia is his daughter, the three principals cementing their newfound connection in the lyrical Andante 'Perdon, perdon, Amelia'. But a warlike chorus is heard in the distance: the people are rebelling against the Doge. Gabriele offers to sue for peace, and vows to fight at Boccanegra's side.

Act 3 *Inside the Doge's Palace* An orchestral introduction and choral cries in praise of the Doge precede the appearance of Fiesco and Paolo. In an impassioned recitative, Paolo reveals that it was he who abducted Amelia and poisoned the Doge. He is led off to execution. A Captain orders that all the lights in the city be extinguished in honour of the dead. The Doge himself appears, a sluggish, chromatic string theme depicting the moving of the poison through his body. In a shimmering arioso, he delights in his beloved Genoese sea, 'Oh refrigerio! . . . la marina brezza!', before being joined by Fiesco. In the first movement of their duet, 'Delle faci festanti al barlume', which contains the usual series of sharply contrasting episodes, Fiesco challenges the Doge and then admits his true identity. As the lights are gradually extinguished, Boccanegra reveals that 'Amelia' is really Fiesco's granddaughter. At this Fiesco breaks into tears, and the lyrical second movement, the Largo 'Piango, perchè mi parla', sees bass and baritone gradually reconciled. But ominous rhythmic figures in the orchestra warn us that Boccanegra is nearing death, and Fiesco tells him he has been poisoned. Amelia and Gabriele appear and Boccanegra blesses them in a final concertato, 'Gran Dio, li benedici'. With his dying breath he nominates Gabriele as his successor.

*

Simon Boccanegra is the mature Verdian opera most thoroughly revised by the composer, and the fact that these revisions were effected more than 20 years after the original version leaves the opera with some startling stylistic disjunctions. The 1857 drama was remarkably forward-looking for its time, particularly from the point of view of conventional operatic characterization: there are no secondary female characters, but a preponderance of low male voices; and though a baritone protagonist was no longer exceptional, Boccanegra has very few opportunities to show vocal brilliance and is assigned no conventional arias. However, this excitingly unusual vocal constellation is connected with, and in part causes, an important problem, one of which Verdi himself was well aware: the opera was, he felt, too consistently dark in colour, too gloomy.

The 1881 revisions do much to improve this aspect of the work. Though the distribution of voices remains the same, in retouching various scenes the mature Verdi invariably added new levels of harmonic and instrumental colour to the opera. And, perhaps most importantly, by adding the new Act 1 finale (the famous Council Chamber scene), he injected into the heart of the work an episode of enormous vividness and power, enriching the character of Boccanegra in such a way that his subsequent death scene gains considerably in impressiveness.

It has been argued, however, that the revisions – especially the addition of the new Act 1 finale – create a further general problem, one of what we might call dramatic balance. The sheer weight of Boccanegra's new presence tends to overpower the other principals, Gabriele in particular, making their concerns seem unimportant or at least underarticulated. But perhaps critics tend to exaggerate the extent to which these essentially 'narrative' matters are crucial to the success of an opera. In recent years, audiences have been in no doubt that *Simon Boccanegra* contains some of the mature Verdi's greatest dramatic music, and there seems little doubt that the opera will retain its new status as one of the composer's most compelling creations.   **R.P.**

Snow Maiden, The [*Snegurochka*]

Springtime tale (*vesennyaya skazka*) in a prologue and four acts by Nikolay Andreyevich Rimsky-Korsakov to his own libretto after the 'springtime fairy-tale' by Alexander Nikolayevich Ostrovsky (1873); St Petersburg, Mariinsky Theatre, 29 January/10 February 1882.

The première was conducted by Eduard Nápravník; Fyodor Stravinsky sang Grandfather Frost and Mariya Kamenskaya The Bonny Spring.

Prologue

Vesna-Krasna [The Bonny Spring]	mezzo-soprano
Ded Moroz [Grandfather Frost]	bass
Devushka-Snegurochka [Snow Maiden] *their daughter*	soprano
Leshiy [Forest Sprite]	tenor
The Shrovetide Straw-Dummy	bass
Bobïl'-Bakula ('Poor Peasant Bakula')	tenor
Bobïlikha *his wife*	mezzo-soprano

Berendeyans of both sexes and all ages; Spring's retinue, birds: cranes, geese, ducks, rooks, magpies, starlings, skylarks etc.

Opera

Snow Maiden	soprano
Lel' *a shepherd*	alto
Kupava *a young maiden, daughter of a wealthy villager*	soprano
Mizgir' *visiting trader from the Berendey settlement*	baritone
Tsar Berendey	tenor
Bobïl'-Bakula	tenor
Bobïlikha	mezzo-soprano
The Bonny Spring	mezzo-soprano
Bermyata *boyar in attendance*	bass
First Crier	tenor
Second Crier	bass
Royal Page	mezzo-soprano
Forest Sprite	tenor

Boyars, their wives, and the tsar's retinue of psalterists, blind bards, minstrels, fiddlers, pipers; shepherds, lads and lasses, Berendeyans, forest sprites, flowers (Spring's retinue)

Setting The land of the Berendeyans in prehistoric times

Although it is seldom remarked, Rimsky-Korsakov's romantic tale of nature made animate may be classified as a 'sung play'. Its libretto is simply the text of its literary source, unaltered but for considerable condensation: whole parts, including the major role of Kupava's father, were dropped from the cast of characters. Perhaps condensation should have gone further: even its greatest admirers – including the composer, who supplanted the original score of 1881 in about 1895 with an abridgment containing recommendations for further cutting – have acknowledged that the opera is overlong.

Yet in every other way Ostrovsky's play was already a virtual libretto. Composed in verse, it contained so many interpolated songs and dances (sometimes to folk texts that had well-known attendant melodies) that performance without music was virtually unthinkable. For the gala first production (at the Maliy Theatre, Moscow, in 1873), an elaborate incidental score had been commissioned from Tchaikovsky (op.12, 19 numbers), which contains many of the same songs and choruses as Rimsky's opera, sometimes set to the same folk melodies, as specified.

*

Prologue *Midnight, the end of winter: a snow-covered landscape at the Red Hill (a river running at its foot and the Berendeyan capital visible on its opposite bank)* The Forest Sprite announces the change of season, the Bonny Spring enters with her entourage of birds. The birds remind her with their shivering that the season is yet chill because the Snow Maiden, the love-child she has borne of Grandfather Frost, has angered the sun god Yarilo. She bids the birds dance to warm themselves (chorus, on two folksongs transcribed by the composer). Frost arrives and sings of his pleasure in spreading cold. Spring asks after the Snow Maiden; Frost calls her out of the forest. The Snow Maiden asks to be allowed to live among humans for the sake of their songs and games; she admits she listens to Lel''s warm songs particularly, which are so beautiful 'you listen and melt'. At 'melt' Frost takes fright and warns the Snow Maiden to avoid Lel', but he grants her request and asks the Forest Sprite to watch over his daughter; Spring promises to help the Snow Maiden if the need arises. Villagers approach with a Shrovetide effigy, who sings of the changing season (the score incorporates three choral songs from Rimsky-Korsakov's own anthology of 1877). Bobïl' and Bobïlikha spy the Snow Maiden, who begs them to adopt her; when they agree, she calls farewell to the forest. The villagers disperse in fright when the forest answers her cry.

Act 1 *Bobïl's hut, evening* The orchestral introduction contains horn calls associated with Lel', based on shepherds' pipe tunes the composer recalled from childhood. Bobïl' welcomes Lel' (his identifying tune is based on a shepherd call given to Rimsky by the composer Anatol Konstantinovich Lyadov) and invites him to sing for the Snow Maiden; unable to understand why he wants something as paltry as a kiss in payment, she offers a flower instead. Lel' sings two songs, the first melancholy, the second merry. Some girls call to Lel'; willingly he runs off to them, tossing the Snow Maiden's flower aside. She is left lamenting the cold heart she has inherited from her father. Kupava enters and comforts the Snow Maiden; she tells of her betrothal to Mizgir'. Mizgir' enters and enacts the wedding ritual of purchasing Kupava from her friends (this scene incorporates three songs from Rimsky-Korsakov's collection). Mizgir' is about to leave with Kupava when he sees the Snow Maiden and falls in love with her (the background chorus is based on a *khorovod* ('The Linden Tree') from Rimsky-Korsakov's anthology); Kupava leaves, distraught. Bobïl' and Bobïlikha tell the Snow Maiden to get rid of Lel' and pursue her rich admirer. The villagers return from the field and question Mizgir' on his fickleness. He insults Kupava and declares his love for the Snow Maiden. Kupava curses Mizgir'. All resolve to take the matter to the tsar.

Act 2 *Tsar Berendey's court* A chorus of blind psalterists sing the tsar's praises. Bermyata complains of the unseasonable cold; the tsar resolves to celebrate a mass wedding ceremony on Yarilo's day (the Kupala) to placate the god. Kupava enters and tells her story to the tsar. The criers call for all to assemble and hear the tsar's decree; the court assembles to an orchestral march. The Berendeyans, led by Kupava and Lel', sing a hymn to their vatic ruler (chorus *a cappella*). Mizgir', confronted with his crime, confesses and is banished. The Snow Maiden arrives; her beauty dazzles the tsar (Berendey's cavatina, 'Polna, polna chudes': 'How full of wonders'). On learning that the Snow Maiden, for all

her beauty, has never loved, he offers a reward to any who may make the Snow Maiden fall in love. Lel' is the favoured candidate, but Mizgir' asks to be released so that he too may try. Berendey, knowing that the Snow Maiden's love will end his kingdom's deep freeze, assents. All sing a hymn to the tsar.

Act 3 *A forest clearing* The villagers sing and dance while their tsar looks on in approval (choral fantasy on 'The Linden Tree', already heard in Act 1). Bobïl' dances in imitation of a beaver (based on a *khorovod* from Rimsky-Korsakov's anthology). The tsar thanks everyone for their contribution, asks his minstrels for a final dance ('Dance of the Skomorokhi', popularly known as the 'Dance of the Buffoons', on a folktune in Stakhovich's collection) and commands Lel' to sing a final song. As reward, Lel' is allowed to claim a kiss from the maiden of his choice; he picks Kupava, to the Snow Maiden's torment. After everyone leaves, Mizgir' returns and protests his love to the Snow Maiden; she flees, assisted by the Forest Sprite, who bars Mizgir''s path with suddenly appearing foliage and misleads him with hallucinations of the Snow Maiden. Lel' and Kupava return and declare their love; the Snow Maiden reappears and reproaches Kupava for stealing Lel', but Lel' rebuffs her, reminding her that her heart is still cold. The Snow Maiden resolves to learn to love.

Act 4 *The sacred valley of the sun, with a lake, surrounded by Yarilo's sacred hill; dawn* The Snow Maiden calls to her mother, who rises from the lake. At her entreaties, Spring grants her the gift of love. Suddenly nature explodes into life; the flowers sing to the Snow Maiden; Spring leaves with her retinue. Mizgir' overtakes the Snow Maiden who, to his amazement, now returns his passion. Remembering her father's warning, she begs Mizgir' to protect her from the sun. The tsar and villagers arrive to celebrate the Kupala and the ordained wedding ceremony (chorus, based on two *khorovod* tunes in Balakirev's collection, also used for the opening chorus in *May Night*). Mizgir' presents the Snow Maiden as his bride. As she confesses her love, the first rays of the sun strike her and she melts away; Mizgir' throws himself in the lake in despair. The tsar interprets these events to his people: they signify their release from the sun's wrath. He orders a hymn in praise of Yarilo (concluding chorus in a famous 11/4 metre).

*

A special glory of *The Snow Maiden* is its orchestra – 'the Glinka orchestra perfected' by the use of chromatic brass. Still following Glinka's preference for bright, transparent hues, with much use of solo instruments to represent characters (e.g. the Snow Maiden's flute and Lel''s clarinet), Rimsky managed to achieve much greater warmth and sonority without ever swamping the voices. Some of the orchestral textures, especially those alive with nature sounds, are so alluringly memorable as to clinch Rimsky's status as the leading orchestral colourist of the 19th century.

The composer, who thought *The Snow Maiden* his finest work, intended to write a book on the opera, analysing it from standpoints both technical and poetic. He only managed, in the summer of 1905, to jot down an outline and a preliminary classification of themes. He divided the characters into four categories: (a) wholly mythological, representative of animated nature (Frost, Spring, Forest Sprite); (b) mixed types ('half-mythological, half-real'), who inhabit the human world as links with the world of nature (the Snow Maiden, Lel', the vatic Tsar Berendey); (c) humans (Kupava, Mizgir'); and (d) the chorus, supplier of the impersonal folk background. Their respective musical idioms differ symbolically. The unalloyed avatars of nature (especially the Forest Sprite) are characterized by tritones and 'artificial' harmonies (chiefly whole-tone), the humans by the conventional idiom of Romantic opera, the chorus by 'modal' folksongs (often in unusual, asymmetrical metres, or simple units grouped into asymmetrical hypermetres). The mixed characters are of course the most varied and unclassifiable, their style responding to the exigencies of the action.

Rimsky classified the musical materials of the opera into three grades, as it were. The first consists of complexes of leitmotifs (Rimsky listed 12) associated with the various characters; unlike Wagnerian leitmotifs, they are not woven into complex symphonic textures to any great extent (although they are very extensively developed and transformed). The second class includes complete and rounded melodies out of which the lyrical and decorative set pieces are constructed. The third comprises themes or motifs that appear transiently, 'serving as temporary characterization of individual moments' rather than as identifying or recalling themes; sometimes they are used as a foundation (in the orchestra) on which a musical structure is erected – thus 'they serve symphonic, not operatic, ends'. (No examples are given, but the sumptuous music accompanying the betrothal kiss in Act 3 must be a prime one.) Rimsky-Korsakov's fragmentary analysis of *The Snow Maiden* is of interest as a rare quasi-theoretical profession of the pragmatic, semi-systematic method of operatic composition for which he has since been revered and reviled in equal measure.   R.T.

Soldaten, Die ('The Soldiers')

Opera in four acts by Bernd Alois Zimmermann, to a libretto by the composer after Jakob Michael's play (1775); Cologne, Opernhaus, 15 February 1965.

The original cast included Edith Gabry as Marie, with Liane Synek, Helga Jenckel, Anton de Ridder, Claudio Nicolai, Zoltán Kelemen and Willi Brokmeier.

Wesener *a fancy-goods merchant in Lille*		bass
Marie	} *his daughters*	dramatic soprano
Charlotte		mezzo-soprano
Wesener's old mother		contralto
Stolzius *a draper in Armentières*		high baritone
Stolzius's mother		contralto
Obrist *Count of Spannheim*		bass
Desportes *a young French nobleman*		very high tenor
A Young Huntsman *in the service of Desportes*		spoken
Pirzel *a captain*		high tenor
Eisenhardt *an army chaplain*		baritone
Major Haudy		baritone
Major Mary		baritone
Three Young Officers		high tenors
Countess de la Roche		mezzo-soprano
The Young Count *her son*		high lyric tenor
An Andalusian Waitress		dancer
Three Cadets		dancers
Mme Roux *hostess of the coffee house*		silent
The Countess's Servant		spoken
The Young Cadet		spoken
A Drunken Officer		spoken

18 officers and cadets, ballet, doubles of the actors and dancers

Setting French-speaking Flanders, yesterday, today and tomorrow

Zimmermann began work on his only opera in 1957; the following year it was formally commissioned by Cologne Opera. The first version was rejected by the opera house as technically impossible, and in 1963–4 Zimmermann prepared a simplified version, scaling down the forces and narrowing the dramatic scope. Although the published score (1966) still prescribes multiple acting levels and three projection screens to preserve the simultaneities of the action, Zimmermann's original concept had involved up to 12 acting areas each with its own instrumental ensemble. The première in Cologne was conducted by Michael Gielen and directed by Hans Neugebauer; the production later formed the basis of a commercial recording. Following the success of the première, when *Die Soldaten* was proclaimed the most significant German opera since Berg's *Lulu*, it received a succession of stagings that varied considerably in

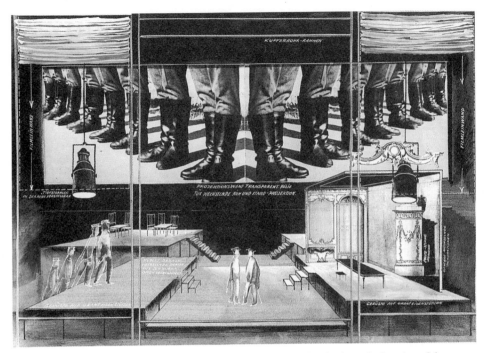

'Die Soldaten' (Zimmermann): set design by Max Bignens for the original production at the Opernhaus, Cologne, 15 February 1965, showing the multiple stages and the three projection screens

their fidelity to Zimmermann's staging instructions: Gerd Albrecht conducted the Kassel production in 1968; Gielen was the conductor for Vaclav Kaclik's staging at Munich in 1969; the 1971 Düsseldorf production, conducted by Günter Wich, was brought to the Edinburgh Festival in 1972. In 1981 at Frankfurt Gielen conducted a production by Alfred Kirchner that stimulated yet more interest in the score; a staging at Stuttgart in 1988, conducted by Bernhard Kontarsky, was the basis of a second commercial recording. The American première in Boston in 1982 was conducted by Sarah Caldwell, and in 1991 the work was staged to much acclaim by the New York City Opera, conducted by Christopher Keene and directed by Rhoda Levine.

*

Act I.i In Lille, Wesener's house After a long, complex and turbulent introduction (Preludio) which unfolds over an insistent rhythmic motif, the first scene shows Marie writing a letter to Madame Stolzius in Armentières. While staying there she has fallen in love with young Stolzius, though she will not reveal her feelings to her sister Charlotte.

I.ii (Ciacona I) In Armentières, Stolzius's house The melancholy Stolzius too has fallen for Marie, and when his mother eventually shows him the letter she has received his mood brightens; Madame Stolzius, however, disapproves of the liaison.

I.iii (Ricercari I) Lille After an interlude of sustained 'colour chords' (Tratto I) Desportes comes to visit Marie; his courtesies are couched in elaborate coloratura, but she rejects his advances, telling him that her father has warned her against men's deceptions. Wesener himself enters, and Desportes uses the opportunity to ask if he can take Marie to the theatre; the father refuses and, when Marie betrays her disappointment, justifies his strictness by pointing out that she is his only delight.

I.iv (Toccata I) Armentières, a public place The army officers – Obrist, Haudy, Mary and Pirzel, with the chaplain Eisenhardt – discuss moral issues with their colleagues. They compare the theatre with the pulpit, and their discussion leads inevitably to the subject of women: does the theatre encourage army officers to seduce respectable girls? Haudy maintains that a whore will always be a whore.

I.v (Nocturne I) Lille, Marie's room To a background of stage percussion Wesener asks Marie whether Desportes can be trusted. She shows her father a love poem the nobleman has sent her, and the prospective match begins to appeal to him. Yet he advises Marie not to sever her connections with Stolzius until Desportes has proposed. Left alone, Marie reveals her continuing love for Stolzius in an increasingly passionate and wide-ranging aria, to which the orchestra provides a violent postlude.

Act 2.i (Toccata II) *Armentières, a café* The officers assemble to drink and play cards; during the scene the score specifies rhythms that they tap out with their cups and spoons. Their banter gives way to a dance full of jazz inflections and led by Madame Roux and her Andalusian waitress. As it subsides Stolzius enters and is immediately teased about Marie; she has been seen around Lille with Desportes. He denies all knowledge of her behaviour or of his rival suitor and leaves.

2.ii (Capriccio, Chorale and Ciacona II) *Lille, Wesener's house* After an interlude (Intermezzo) dominated by organ and onstage percussion, Marie is seen in despair. She has received a reproachful letter from Stolzius, which she shows to Desportes. He pretends anger and dictates Marie's reply, using the opportunity to begin to seduce her. The scene becomes the dramatic and musical pivot of the opera: as the couple's love-making continues the scene simultaneously depicts Stolzius in Armentières, grief-stricken over the letter he has received from Marie and vowing vengeance upon Desportes, and Wesener's mother, watching her granddaughter's downfall and foreshadowing her fate. The grandmother's cynical commentary is set to a folktune, quoted from Lenz, while the orchestra borrows the chorale 'Ich bin's, ich sollte büssen' from Bach's *St Matthew Passion*.

Act 3.i (Rondino) *Armentières* After a short Preludio Eisenhardt and Pirzel are found in the throes of another arcane philosophical debate on the meaning of military life.

3.ii (Rappresentazione) *Lille, Mary's room* Dressed as a soldier, the highly wrought Stolzius successfully applies to be batman to Major Mary.

3.iii (Ricercari II) *Lille, Wesener's house* Charlotte upbraids Marie for transferring her attentions to Mary in Desportes' absence; she refuses to accept her sister's excuses. Mary enters and is greeted with elaborate courtesy by Marie; as the trio prepare to leave, the sisters notice the major's batman and his likeness to Stolzius. The following interlude is an elaborate and extended Romanza which steadily thins down its textures until only a solo guitar remains.

3.iv (Nocturne II) *Lille, the house of the Countess de la Roche* The Countess awaits the return of her son late at night, reflecting in her aria on the pain that sons cause their mothers throughout their lives; her elaborate and wide-ranging set-piece develops into a duet with the arrival of the young Count, her son, as the Countess declares that Marie is an unsuitable partner for him. She herself will oversee the girl's future.

3.v (Tropi) *Lille, Wesener's house* Mary appears to have abandoned Marie, though she disputes this with Charlotte. Their argument is interrupted by the arrival of the Countess, who patronizingly declares herself to be Marie's best ally and advises her to ignore the gossip about the town. She offers Marie a place in her own household, and as the Countess urges her to consider the offer carefully the act ends in an extended trio for the three women, which takes the final scene of *Der Rosenkavalier* as its reference point.

Act 4.i (Toccata III) *Armentières, the café* The final act opens after another orchestral Preludio, with the most ambitious and extensive of Zimmermann's explorations of simultaneity. The scene charts Marie's final downfall and degradation in a nightmarish sequence of tableaux, portrayed on film and by singers, dancers and doubles, in which past, present and future are telescoped. Mary finds Marie at the Countess's house, and after a meeting in a garden is interrupted by the Countess, Marie runs away and cannot be found. Desportes instructs his huntsman to pick up Marie; he does so and rapes her. She becomes a prostitute. Stolzius hears of what has happened, and buys rat poison to exact his revenge. The scene, which begins with a huge, sustained, wordless chord for all the main characters, ends with a densely interwoven chorus on the words 'Must those who suffer injustice tremble, and can only those who do wrong be happy!'

4.ii (Ciacona II) *Armentières, Mary's room* After an interlude (Tratto II) for organ and percussion, Desportes is seen dining with Mary; they are waited on by Stolzius, who overhears their conversation. Desportes is dismissive of Marie's fate: she was only a whore in the first place, and he tells his friend how he had arranged for his huntsman to intercept her before she could find him again. Though Mary protests that he would have married her himself, Desportes is adamant that she got no worse than she deserved. Stolzius poisons Desportes' soup, and as he dies in agony screams Marie's name into his face; Stolzius himself then takes poison.

4.iii (Nocturno III) *A road on the banks of the River Lys* Wesener's final meeting with his daughter is embedded in an aural and visual collage of pre-recorded tape, film footage and musical cross-reference. Offstage voices provide a background of sustained chords and isolated syllables; the officers continue to visit Madame Bischof's café; Eisenhardt is heard proclaiming the Lord's Prayer; the screens show soldiers of many nationalities endlessly marching. A beggar woman accosts Wesener and asks for money; he at first refuses, but then relents, remembering the fate of his own daughter. He has not recognized Marie, who falls to the ground weeping. The sounds of marching become ever louder until everything else is overwhelmed.

*

Though the forces involved in *Die Soldaten* are so

massive – in his score Zimmermann provides the option of siting the percussion in another performing space and conveying its sounds to the stage electronically – they are used with great discrimination and selectivity; chamber sonorities frequently accompany the voices. The vocal lines develop the techniques of Berg's operas – the exceptionally demanding role for Marie, with its high-lying coloratura and expressionist extremes, echoes both her namesake in *Wozzeck* and *Lulu*; elsewhere the parts move freely between speech, parlando, Sprechgesang and unfettered arioso.

As the indications in the summary of the plot suggest, the plan of each scene is based upon a well-defined formal structure, derived again from Berg, within which Zimmermann contains his strictly organized serial material and extensive stylistic borrowings. His use of 'collage' and quotation is more effective dramatically here than in any of his non-operatic works and was arguably the most influential aspect of the opera when it was first performed. A quotation, in his view, was no mere ornament but could symbolize simultaneous musical gestures on different planes. Zimmermann's attempt to convey separate and simultaneous dramatic strands by the use of multiple stages and ensembles appears to have influenced Henze's similar techniques in *We Come to the River* (1976).

A.C.

Sonnambula, La ('The Sleepwalker')

Melodramma in two acts by Vincenzo Bellini to a libretto by Felice Romani after Eugène Scribe and J.P. Aumer's ballet-pantomime *La somnambule, ou L'arrivée d'un nouveau seigneur*; Milan, Teatro Carcano, 6 March 1831.

At the première Amina and Elvino were sung by Giuditta Pasta and Giovanni Battista Rubini; Luciano Mariani sang Count Rodolfo and Lisa was sung by Elisa Taccani.

Lisa *an inn hostess, in love with Elvino*		soprano
Alessio *a villager, in love with Lisa*		bass
Amina *an orphan raised by Teresa,*		
betrothed to Elvino		soprano
Teresa *a mill-owner*		mezzo-soprano
A Notary		tenor
Elvino *a wealthy landowner in the village*		tenor
Count Rodolfo *lord of the village*		bass
Country villagers		
Setting A village in Switzerland in the early		
19th century		

Bellini wrote his sixth professional opera for a remarkable season at the Teatro Carcano which opened with Donizetti's *Anna Bolena*, using the same principals. It was the only occasion on which he was able to write for Pasta and Rubini together. Until a late stage he planned to set *Ernani*, from Hugo's play; he did not start on *La sonnambula* until 2 January, and wrote the second act in two weeks, from about 9 February.

The theme of somnambulism was common; the present libretto has a different plot from those of Foppa's *La sonnambula* (1800) for Paer, Scribe's *La somnambule* (1819) and Romani's *Il sonnambulo* (1824) for Carafa.

Much of the opera is pitched very high. Rubini's part was originally higher than it appears in Ricordi's printed scores (see Boosey's vocal score, 1849), ascending to d'' in the duets and Act 2 aria and rarely falling below a. Bellini may not have intended the original pitches for anyone other than Rubini, who used a mellifluous head voice; transpositions are justifiable, but the current scores produce abrupt key changes. The part of Amina ascends to d''' in the second duet and to $e\flat'''$ (not in the autograph) in the final 'Ah! non giunge uman pensiero'.

The opera was very successful (as Glinka recorded in his *Memoirs*) and was presented with Pasta and Rubini in London (28 July 1831) and Paris (24 October) before being seen again in Italy (1832, Florence). The role of Amina was quickly taken up by Maria Malibran; it was also a favourite role of Giuseppina Strepponi. Famous exponents in England were Jenny Lind (1847) and Adelina Patti, who made her Covent Garden début as Amina (1861). In the 20th century, famous interpreters of Amina included Luisa Tetrazzini, Amelita Galli-Curci and Toti dal Monte, who sang the role at La Scala in 1935, the centenary of Bellini's death. Maria Callas also sang Amina at La Scala and then at the Edinburgh Festival in 1957. On the latter occasion the final performance was sung by Renata Scotto, who was later to make a speciality of the role.

*

Act I.i *The village square with an inn, a mill and hills in the background* There is no overture, but an orchestral introduction supported by offstage band leads to the offstage chorus of villagers, 'Viva Amina'. In a cavatina, 'Tutto è gioia, tutto è festa', Lisa laments that, amid the general rejoicing, she alone is sad, at the prospect of losing Elvino. Alessio rushes in and embraces the unenthusiastic Lisa. As the villagers arrive, he organizes them around Amina's dwelling at the mill and joins in their praises of the girl. Amina comes out of the mill with Teresa and thanks her fellow villagers. She expresses her joy in the cavatina 'Come per me sereno' and the cabaletta 'Sovra il sen la man mi posa', a brilliant show piece of a length unprecedented in Bellini's works; this was his first opportunity to write for Pasta, the great contemporary diva. Amina naively wishes Alessio and Lisa well, and Lisa's sour reaction is noted by Teresa.

A notary enters, announcing the arrival of Elvino, who greets Amina and explains that he has been singing her praises in front of his mother's tomb. Before the notary he pledges her everything he possesses; she replies that she has only her heart to offer him in return. In the duet, 'Prendi, l'anel ti dono', Elvino gives Amina a ring that belonged to his mother and a bunch of wild flowers. The couple are now betrothed and in 'Ah! vorrei trovar parola' Amina wishes she could find words to express her love. The sound of coach wheels is heard, and Count Rodolfo enters; he is on his way to the castle, but accepts Lisa's invitation to stay the night at her inn. Though unrecognized by the villagers, he remembers the mill and the countryside that he left years before, and evokes the memories in a cavatina, 'Vi ravviso, o luoghi ameni'. He is much taken with Amina, whom he compares with a love of his youth (a relic of Romani's complication, specifically rejected by Bellini, whereby Amina is the fruit of an earlier indiscretion).

It is now dusk and Teresa tells everyone to leave promptly, warning Rodolfo of a phantom swathed in white that haunts the area at night. The villagers support Teresa's fears and in the chorus 'A fosco cielo, a notte bruna' describe the ghostly noctambulist to the incredulous Rodolfo. He takes a gallant farewell of Amina, much to Elvino's indignation. Left alone, the lovers quarrel and then make it up again in a duet, 'Son geloso del zeffiro errante', which contains some of Bellini's most delicate exchanges of vocal fioriture.

I.ii A room at Lisa's inn Rodolfo is flirting with Lisa, who informs him that he has been recognized as the new lord of the castle. They are disturbed by a noise and Lisa hurriedly departs, dropping her kerchief. Amina, all in white, comes in by the window; she is walking in her sleep, and Rodolfo realizes that she must be the villagers' 'phantom'. In disjointed phrases Amina speaks of her forthcoming marriage, of Elvino's jealousy and their quarrel. Rodolfo refrains from taking advantage of 'this pure and innocent flower', and goes out by the window, leaving Amina asleep on his sofa. The villagers, arriving to welcome their new lord, are amused to discover a girl in his room; they are about to leave discreetly when Lisa ushers in Elvino and Teresa, triumphantly pointing to the sleeping girl. Everyone exclaims in shocked surprise as they recognize Amina. Woken by the noise, she is confused and completely ignorant of what has happened. She is denounced by all; only Teresa, who picks up Lisa's kerchief (mistaking it for Amina's) and puts it round Amina's neck, believes the girl's protestation of

Giuditta Pasta as Amina and Giovanni Battista Rubini as Elvino in Act 1 scene i of the original production of Bellini's 'La sonnambula' at the Teatro Carcano, Milan, 6 March 1831, with (below) the opening of their duet 'Prendi, l'anel ti dono': lithograph by A. Lanzani

innocence, 'D'un pensiero e d'un accento', with which Amina launches the superb final ensemble. Elvino calls off the wedding and the villagers condemn Amina.

Act 2.i *A shadowy valley between the village and the castle* The villagers rest on their way to the castle to put Amina's case to Count Rodolfo ('Qui la selva è più folta ed ombrosa'). Amina tells Teresa that she is her only support in her grief, and is comforted by her foster-mother. (Bellini cut a long cantilena, mainly for two trumpets, from the orchestral prelude to this scene; it is printed, however, in the Boosey vocal score edited by Pittman and Arthur Sullivan, and is restored on a recording made by Sutherland in 1980.) Elvino soliloquizes on his misery in 'Tutto è sciolto'. Seeing Amina, he reproaches her in 'Pasci il guardo, e appaga l'alma'. When the villagers return, announcing that the Count has exonerated Amina, Elvino furiously snatches his ring from her and in 'Ah! perchè non posso odiarti' regrets that he can neither hate her, nor entirely banish her from his heart.

2.ii *The village square* Brushing off Alessio, Lisa sings of her joy at marrying Elvino ('De' lieti auguri a voi son grata'), who kisses her hand and leads her towards the church. Rodolfo, arriving with the villagers, proclaims Amina's innocence. In the quartet with chorus, 'Signor Conte, agli occhi miei', the Count tries to explain to a disbelieving Elvino that Amina was sleep-walking. Teresa begs the villagers to make less noise as Amina has fallen asleep; she is shocked to see Elvino about to marry Lisa, who points out that she was not found in another man's room. When Teresa produces the kerchief, which she now knows was dropped by Lisa, Elvino realizes that Lisa is a liar.

Amina appears sleep-walking on the eaves of the mill-house roof (it was reputedly Jenny Lind who introduced the bridge across the mill-wheel). The villagers kneel and pray silently for her safety; they sigh with relief in a soothing cadence ('È salva!') as she descends to the ground and, in a typically Romantic 'mad scene' accompanied by reminiscent themes in the orchestra, imagines that she is reunited with Elvino. In the cantabile 'Ah! non credea mirarti' she addresses the flowers, now dead, that he had given her. Elvino awakens her by replacing his ring on her finger. Her happiness restored, Amina gives way to feelings of joy in the brilliant cabaletta 'Ah! non giunge uman pensiero'.

*

Throughout the 19th century *La sonnambula* was regarded in Italy, along with Donizetti's *Linda di Chamounix*, as the epitome of the pastoral genre, which persisted well into the age of Italian grand opera. It was a particular favourite with Victorian audiences. Two of Sullivan's wittiest operatic parodies, the sextet 'A nice dilemma' (*Trial by Jury*, 1875) and 'Carefully on tiptoe stealing' (*H.M.S. Pinafore*, 1878), are modelled on, respectively, the concertato 'D'un pensiero e d'un accento' and the chorus 'Tutto tace: e dorme certo', both from the finale of Act 1. In George Eliot's novel *The Mill on the Floss* Maggie Tulliver's rejected suitor Philip Wakem reproaches her with Elvino's cabaletta 'Ah! perchè non posso odiarti'.

In *La sonnambula* Bellini's mature style appears finally crystallized, a synthesis of heartfelt melody, expressive declamation and coloratura from which all Rossinian hedonism has been banished. The rustic setting together with the subject of an innocent village maiden traduced and finally vindicated would seem to place it in the category of *opera semiseria*, were it not for the absence of the statutory *basso buffo*. The opera is therefore subheaded simply 'melodramma'. The forms are mostly shorter and more flexible than in Bellini's previous works; and there is a plentiful use of orchestral 'parlanti'. The recitatives often take on the quality of arias in low

relief, merging into the formal numbers with the smoothest of transitions. Likewise a considerable dramatic advance is achieved, as in *I Capuleti e i Montecchi* (1830), by the interventions of other singers into solo arias. Among the latter 'Ah! non credea mirarti' stands out as an example of the composer's 'long, long, long melodies' (Verdi's phrase), extending over 36 bars of slow tempo with no element of reprise. At the same time the chorus that opens Act 2, with its strangely Gluckian overtones, bears witness to Bellini's roots in an older, classical tradition.

J.B., E.F., S.M.

Stiffelio

Opera in three acts by Giuseppe Verdi to a libretto by Francesco Maria Piave after Emile Souvestre's and Eugène Bourgeois' play *Le Pasteur, ou L'évangile et le foyer*; Trieste, Teatro Grande, 16 November 1850.

The première cast included Gaetano Fraschini (Stiffelio), Marietta Gazzaniga Malaspina (Lina) and Filippo Colini (Stankar).

Stiffelio *an Ahasuerian preacher*	tenor
Lina *his wife*	soprano
Stankar *an old colonel, count of the Empire and Lina's father*	baritone
Raffaele von Leuthold *a nobleman*	tenor
Jorg *an old preacher*	bass
Federico di Frengel } *Lina's cousins*	tenor
Dorotea	mezzo-soprano

The Count's friends, Stiffelio's disciples, Ahasuerians

Setting Austria, in and around Stankar's castle by the river Salzbach, at the beginning of the 19th century

As was becoming the pattern, Verdi's April 1850 contract for the work that would become *Stiffelio* was signed not with a theatre but with a publisher, in this as in most other cases Ricordi. The librettist was again to be Piave, who himself suggested an adaptation of *Le pasteur*, a French play that had received its première only the previous year but was already available in Italian translation. It was a bold choice, a far cry from the melodramatic plots of Byron (*Il Corsaro*, *I due Foscari*) and Hugo (*Ernani*): modern, 'realistic' subjects were unusual in Italian opera, and the religious subject matter seemed bound to cause problems with the censor.

Giovanni Ricordi decided to have the première staged at Trieste – the theatre that had recently given such a lukewarm reception to *Il corsaro* – and, true to expectation, the local censorship insisted on a number of important changes, in particular muting the action of the final scene so as (in the composer's view) to make it ridiculous. The work's reception was not much better than that accorded *Il corsaro*. *Stiffelio* had occasional revivals in subsequent years, but was continually dogged by censorship difficulties, and in the mid-1850s Verdi decided to 'rescue' his music by revising it to fit a different, less sensitive though similar plot, *Aroldo* (1857), which deals with a 13th-century Saxon knight returned from the Crusades. The original *Stiffelio* disappeared from the repertory and won its first modern revival only in the 1960s. Since then it has received a fair number of performances, including a notable production at Covent Garden in 1993, and is ranked by many as Verdi's most unjustly neglected opera.

*

The overture is of the potpourri type: a sequence of contrasting melodies, some of which return in the subsequent action. Its predominantly martial atmosphere (even the main cantabile melody is scored for solo trumpet) seems, curiously, better suited to *Aroldo* than to the original subject.

Act I.i *A hall on the ground floor of Stankar's castle* The opera immediately pronounces its unusual formal exterior by beginning without the customary introductory chorus. Instead, Jorg offers up an intense chromatic prayer on behalf of Stiffelio, who has just returned from a lengthy mission. Stiffelio appears, surrounded by his family and friends, and in the ensuing narration, 'Di qua varcando sul primo albore', relates that a boatman reported to him how at first light he saw a young man and a woman at an upstairs window of the castle, clearly up to no good, and how the man threw himself from the window into the river, dropping some papers as he did so. Stifled outbursts from Lina and Raffaele suggest their guilty consciences, but Stiffelio puts their fears to rest by magnanimously casting the documents into the fire. All join in a septet, 'Colla cenere disperso', after which Stiffelio's friends sing a welcoming chorus, 'A te Stiffelio un canto', based on a theme heard in the overture.

The crowd disperses, leaving Stiffelio alone with his wife. The first part of his ensuing double aria is a complex, articulated structure, responding as it does to Lina's reactions. First comes 'Vidi dovunque gemere', in which he describes the moral collapse he has seen everywhere on his journey; then he has a reassuring word for his wife in 'Ah no, il perdono è facile'; and finally come the loving words of 'Allor dunque sorridimi' as he takes her hand and asks for a smile such as she gave him on their wedding day. But his melody suddenly breaks off as he sees that her ring is missing. She can give no answer to his inquiries about it and his suspicions burst out in the cabaletta 'Ah! v'appare in fronte scritto'. The final

bars are interrupted by Stankar, who asks Stiffelio to join his friends; with a reminder that he will soon return, the pastor hurries away.

Lina offers a prayer, 'A te ascenda, o Dio clemente', delicately scored and with those elaborate cadential harmonies so characteristic of the later Verdi. She decides to write her husband a letter of confession but is interrupted by Stankar, who reads the first line and is confirmed in his suspicions of her infidelity. Their ensuing duet follows the conventional four-movement pattern. The first movement is dominated by an accusing Stankar, while the second, 'Ed io pure in faccia agl'uomini', is of the 'dissimilar' type, Lina answering his impassioned declamation with obsessively repeated 'sobbing' figures. Stankar, fearful of dishonour for his family, forbids Lina to reveal the truth; she reluctantly agrees and they seal the bargain with the cabaletta 'Or meco venite', sung *sotto voce* almost throughout.

In a brief scena, Raffaele conceals a letter to Lina inside a book, Klopstock's *Messias*. Federico enters to take the book away and is observed by Jorg; he and Raffaele depart.

I.ii *A reception hall in the castle* The jubilant opening chorus, 'Plaudiam! Di Stiffelio s'allegri', fashioned on a waltz-time variant of one of the overture's main themes, is interspersed with fragments of conversation as Jorg tells Stiffelio of the hidden letter and his (mistaken) suspicions about Federico. Stiffelio is called upon to describe his forthcoming sermon, and with bitter declamation says it will concern the evils of betrayal. As if to illustrate his point, he asks Federico for the *Messias*. But the book is locked, and Stiffelio's demand for Lina's key leads to the Adagio of the concertato finale, 'Oh qual m'invade ed agita', a magnificently imposing movement that builds to a climax of rare power. Stiffelio forces the lock; the letter falls out, but Stankar seizes it and, in spite of the preacher's protests, tears it up. Stiffelio's anger bursts on Stankar in the stretta 'Chi ti salva o sciagurato', Lina pleading for her father's protection while Stankar proposes a duel with Raffaele.

Act 2 *An ancient graveyard* The sombre orchestral prelude is one of Verdi's most evocative to date. Lina, drawn by an 'unknown force', comes to find the tomb of her mother and in the Largo 'Ah! dagli scanni eterei' – whose luminous scoring makes a striking contrast to the prelude – begs for divine support. Raffaele appears, refusing to renounce his love for Lina even when she directs at him the imploring cabaletta 'Perder dunque voi volete'. But they are interrupted by Stankar, who provokes Raffaele to the duel he wants by insulting his lineage. They defy each other and begin to clash swords as Stiffelio appears, calling on them to stop in the name of God. The intervention is too much for Stankar, who blurts out that Raffaele is Lina's seducer. This precipitates a magnificent concertato quartet movement, 'Ah no, è impossibile!', one which prefigures the famous quartet in *Rigoletto* in its welding together of strongly contrasting musical material. It is dominated by Stiffelio, who develops an imposing musical presence through his powerful declamatory style. Stiffelio continues to control the next movement, in which he takes upon himself Stankar's challenge to Raffaele. At the height of the action a chorus within the church is heard singing of divine forgiveness. In spite of the others' pleading, Stiffelio cannot renounce his thirst for vengeance, and eventually falls down in a faint at the sight of a nearby cross.

Act 3.i *An antechamber with doors leading to various rooms* First comes a double aria for Stankar in which his sense of dishonour leads him to thoughts of suicide. After an unusually complex recitative, the Andante 'Lina, pensai che un angelo' shows Verdi already along the road to the baritone cantabile movements of his later works, while the cabaletta 'O gioia inesprimibile', performed almost entirely *sotto voce*, approaches the level of suppressed energy so pervasive in *Il trovatore*. As Stankar leaves, Stiffelio appears with Jorg, whom he immediately sends off to warn the congregation of his arrival. He meets Raffaele and, questioning him about Lina's future, leads him to a side room where, Stiffelio says, he will 'hear all'. Lina herself now appears before Stiffelio. This is the key confrontation in the opera: a duet difficult to understand in terms of the standard four-movement pattern, so closely are its various stages fashioned around the rapidly changing reactions of the main characters. First comes Stiffelio's 'Opposto è il calle', in which, to a deceptively simple melody charged with harmonic tension, he demands divorce. Lina's violent response is countered by a yet more restricted phrase from Stiffelio, but then Lina takes over and in 'Non allo sposo' begs him to listen as a priest if not as a husband. Her final plea, 'Egli un patto proponeva', accompanied by solo english horn, is the most touching of all: she declares that her love for Stiffelio has never wavered. Stiffelio, understanding that Raffaele is to blame, goes to the side room to confront him. But Stankar appears, bloody sword in hand, to announce that honour is now satisfied. The closing cabaletta, 'Ah sì, voliamo al tempio', is (as befits the moment) of the 'dissimilar' type, and concludes as Stiffelio is dragged by Jorg towards the church.

3.ii *The interior of a Gothic church* This very brief final scene is remarkable in being based almost entirely on stage effect: there are hardly any sustained melodies, merely declamation and atmospheric choral interpolations. The congregation, Lina included, is at prayer as Stiffelio and Jorg appear. Stiffelio opens the Bible, determined to take inspira-

tion from whatever passage he finds. He reads the episode of the woman taken in adultery and, as he reaches the phrase 'and she rose up, forgiven', the congregation repeats his words in a stirring choral close.

*

Much has been made of *Stiffelio* in recent times, some even claiming that it deserves an equal place beside the operas it immediately precedes, *Rigoletto*, *Il trovatore* and *La traviata*. Its 'modern' plot and subject matter are certainly in tune with contemporary sensibilities, and the tendency of its most powerful moments to avoid or radically manipulate traditional structures has been much praised. There are, though, a few drawbacks, not least the manner in which the progress of the action is occasionally unclear; nor is the reason for Lina's adultery established. And even the 'forward-looking' dramaturgical structures seem at times to lack necessary durational weight, almost as though the composer were working out new formal balances as he progressed. It is, for instance, significant that many of the alterations made for *Aroldo* are not governed by the new plot but are inserted because Verdi felt he could improve the dramatic articulation. However, *Stiffelio* undoubtedly deserves a better fate than its present neglect, and has in its protagonist one of Verdi's finest tenor roles.

R.P.

Stone Guest, The [*Kamenniy gost'*]

Opera in three acts by Alexander Sergeyevich Dargomïzhsky set directly to the verse tragedy of Alexander Sergeyevich Pushkin; St Petersburg, Mariinsky Theatre, 16/28 February 1872 (revised version, Moscow, Bol'shoy Theatre, 19 December 1906/1 January 1907).

The première was conducted by Eduard Nápravník, with Fyodor Komissarzhevsky as Don Juan, Osip Petrov as Leporello, Julia Platonova as Donna Anna and Ivan Mel'nikov as Don Carlos.

Don Juan	tenor
Leporello *his servant*	bass
Donna Anna	soprano
Don Carlos	baritone
Laura	mezzo-soprano
A Monk	bass
First Guest	tenor
Second Guest	bass
Statue of the Commander	bass
Setting Spain; time unspecified	

The opera, unfinished at the time of Dargomïzhsky's death in 1869, was completed by César Cui and orchestrated by Nikolay Rimsky-Korsakov. Rimsky reorchestrated it in 1898–1902, and also retouched the score, in the process rewriting the duel music in Act 2 and Don Juan's arioso 'Kogda b ya bïl bezumets' ('If I were a madman') in Act 3. The prelude, based on a number of themes and leitmotifs from the opera, was added in 1903. This version, now regarded as the standard one, was first conducted by Václav Suk.

Pushkin's 'little tragedy' of 1830 was inspired in part by the first Russian-language production of Mozart's *Don Giovanni*, which had taken place in St Petersburg two years earlier (with the title role transposed for Vasily Samoylov, a popular tenor). Although Pushkin adopted a certain amount from Da Ponte's libretto, including the character Leporello, his treatment of the Don Juan legend differs strikingly from the established tradition of Don Juan plays – a tradition Pushkin must have known, since he revived Tirso de Molina's original subtitle (*El convidado de piedra*; it seems unlikely that the Russian poet would have known the similarly titled operas by Vincenzo Righini or Giuseppe Gazzaniga). Where all previous Don Juan plays had been essentially farcical up to the last scene, Pushkin's is high romantic tragedy, diluted only by the *buffo* role he had taken over from Da Ponte. Everything points inexorably to the horrific expiation. The plot – which is also that of Dargomïzhsky's opera in every detail – is simplicity itself.

*

Act I.i *Before the fence of a monastery, at the gates of Madrid; evening* Don Juan has secretly returned from exile, where he had been sent in punishment for having killed the Commander, Don Alvaro. In the north he had 'all but died of boredom'. With the help of his manservant Leporello he has decided to steal into Madrid, where a rendezvous with the actress Laura awaits him. The familiar sights of the city bring back memories of Inez, an old, dead love. From a chance conversation with a monk, Don Juan learns that Donna Anna, the widow of the slain Commander, comes to the monastery every evening to visit her husband's grave, and that she is beautiful. Don Juan is inflamed with desire to meet her. Catching sight of the woman on her arrival, her face mysteriously hidden behind a black widow's veil, Don Juan is even more strongly drawn to her. Night falls, and while the moon is as yet unrisen Don Juan and Leporello set out under cover of night into the city.

I.ii *Laura's room* Laura is dining, surrounded by her admirers. At their request she sings two songs. One of the guests – the volatile Don Carlos, the Commander's brother – has appealed to her; he reminds Laura of her old love, Don Juan, whom she has not been able to forget. A knock at the door is heard; it is Don Juan. Don Carlos, who has long hated his brother's killer, now challenges him to a duel.

They fight, and Don Carlos is mortally wounded.

Act 2 *In the cemetery, before the Commander's statue* Calling himself 'Don Diego del Calvado', Don Juan, disguised as a monk, has gained entry into the monastery. He meets Donna Anna and with impassioned avowals and artful speeches succeeds in enticing her. She consents to receive him at home the next evening. Drunk with success, Don Juan gives Leporello an impudent order: to invite the Statue of the Commander to stand sentry at Donna Anna's door while he is there. To their horror, Don Juan and Leporello see the Statue nod in assent.

Act 3 *Donna Anna's room* Don Juan reveals his secret to Donna Anna; the widow realizes that before her stands her husband's murderer. And yet she has not the strength to resist him. They agree to meet again the next day and as a sign of forgiveness Donna Anna bestows a kiss upon Don Juan. Suddenly there is a loud knocking at the door; the Statue has come as invited. The stone guest seizes Don Juan's hand and drags him down to hell.

*

The most obvious difference from the familiar libretto – that Donna Anna is the Commander's widow, not his daughter – makes Don Juan's crimes seem that much more odious and the drama's denouement that much more ethically justified. Yet Pushkin's Don Juan, compared with Mozart's, is curiously passive, stalked everywhere by death and attracted to it (he loved Inez for 'her voice so soft and weak, like an invalid's'; he confesses his love to Donna Anna in a cemetery; both his trysts end in death, first Don Carlos's, then his own). His only bold or wilful act is the invitation to the statue, and there, obviously, he does not expect results. Nor does he seek the duel with Don Carlos; when it is over he expresses not triumph but resignation. His meeting with Donna Anna is fortuitous, and he woos her without bravado. Once he sees her he is in the grip of forces beyond his control. One can only explain his revealing his identity to Donna Anna by the fact that (as he says) for the first time Don Juan is truly in love. And no sooner is he touched by true love than he, like all his victims, must perish. He is killed, as it were, by his own sword, wielded by Donna Anna, her husband's inadvertent avenger.

Except for the duel, there is little action in Pushkin's play, and it is generally taken for granted that the poet never meant it for the stage. It is in effect not a tiny play but an extended lyric meditation on love and death. Its merits are precisely those normally shunned by librettists as inimical to music; its beauties are of nuance and detail.

So it was the natural, inevitable choice to serve as basis for the most demonstratively 'reformist' opera ever written. To set a pre-existing play to music as it stands, with no mediating libretto at all, was to reject not only 'numbers' but the whole concept of *dramma per musica*, and to imply that the criteria of opera and those of spoken drama were ideally identical. To ignore the demand that an operatic text make suitable provision for the unfolding of musical structure – whatever the particular structure or the means of its unfolding – was manifestly to devalue musical 'form' and to uphold the idea that (as Nikolay Chernïshevsky put it) 'emotion and form are opposites'. Dargomïzhsky's letters are full of slogans just as categorical ('I want sound directly to express the word; I want truth' – to which Tchaikovsky, in his diary, made rejoinder in kind: 'If there is anything more hateful and *false* than this unsuccessful attempt to introduce *truth* into a branch of art where everything is based on *pseudo* . . . I do not know it').

It is a tricky matter to decide to what extent such a posture was born of commitment to the realist ferment that took hold in Russian art and literature in the 1850s and 60s, and to what extent it was the reaction of an embittered Russian autodidact whose operatic ambitions had been systematically thwarted by the inimical conditions in which he had to work. That the latter fed the former there can be no doubt. But that Dargomïzhsky had professed an early commitment 'to develop the dramatic side of our national character' is no less true, and it is reflected in the remarkable accompanied recitatives that gave his earlier opera *Rusalka* its chief claim to the attentions of the younger generation of Russian composers, whose support comforted, and decisively influenced, Dargomïzhsky in his last decade. In his encyclopedic review of the original production, Alexander Serov singled out for special praise the confrontation of the Miller and the Prince in Act 3 of *Rusalka*, a scene cast entirely in accompanied recitative and set to Pushkin's original verses, or, in other words, composed to the formula that was to characterize the whole of *The Stone Guest*. Dargomïzhsky thanked him by letter for his 'uncommonly deep penetration of my innermost and even unconscious thoughts'. As soon as he had begun 'amusing myself with Pushkin's *Don Juan*', he became a cult object – an honorary member of the Balakirev circle and the focus of a frantic journalistic crusade on the part of Vladimir Stasov and César Cui. Long before the opera was finished it had achieved the quasi-legendary status it has never lost, however infrequent its performances.

It is the infrequency of performances that accounts for the inaccuracy of the legend. For despite its billing, *The Stone Guest* is emphatically not a recitative opera. It is, rather, almost unabatedly lyric in its fundamental impulse – far more so, in fact, than are the recitative scenes in *Rusalka*. The true sources of its style are to be found in the through-composed romances of Dargomïzhsky's late years.

Cui coined the term 'melodic recitative' to describe the romance-like style of Dargomïzhsky's last opera, in which the accompaniments are full of continuous figuration and regular harmonic rhythm, and in which the melodic phrases consist of what Mikhail Druskin termed 'rounded intonational periods', that is, a series of (mostly) quavers surrounded by a pair of crotchets. This is anything but naturalistic reproduction of Russian speech.

A reviewer rightly characterized the idiom of *The Stone Guest* as 'recitative-in-song, much closer to cantilena than to the Italian recitative'. The opera is in effect one gargantuan through-composed romance, the perfect counterpart to Pushkin's text as characterized above. The special 'realist' quality comes from the virtual absence of repetition (hence, absence of 'form'). When the text contains repetitions, the music follows suit, so that minuscule 'arias' do emerge at a couple of points: one for Don Carlos in Act 2; the other, in Act 3, built around a threefold rhetorical repetition by Don Juan: 'Kogda b ya bïl bezumets'. Still, the only detachable numbers in the opera are Laura's two Spanish romances in Act 2, where Pushkin had merely specified 'she sings'. Both were songs already in Dargomïzhsky's portfolio. The first of them, 'Odelas' tumanom Grenada' ('Granada is shrouded in mist'; 1856), has as its ritornello a Spanish tune familiar from Glinka's *Jota Aragonesa*. The second, 'Ya zdes', Inezil'ya' ('Inezilia, I'm here'), is a setting of a Pushkin lyric (after Barry Cornwall). Its ritornello furnished the curtain music for Act 2. (Laroche made the droll prediction that in the new age of realism one of the 'chief tasks [of librettos] will be creating situations and inventing characters to ask one another to sing'.)

Another aspect of Dargomïzhskian realism lay in the studied ugliness of much of the music. Some of this, especially in the gory duel scene, was removed by Rimsky-Korsakov; but the statue music, on which the opera's climax is constructed, consists of novel explorations of whole-tone harmony, striking for the date.   R.T.

Suor Angelica ('Sister Angelica')

Opera in one act by Giacomo Puccini to a libretto by Giovacchino Forzano; New York, Metropolitan Opera, 14 December 1918 (as no.2 of *Il trittico*).

At the première Geraldine Farrar was Sister Angelica, Flora Perini the Princess; the conductor was Roberto Moranzoni.

Sister Angelica	soprano
The Princess *her aunt*	contralto
The Abbess	mezzo-soprano

The Monitress	mezzo-soprano
The Mistress of the novices	mezzo-soprano
Sister Genovieffa	soprano
Sister Osmina	soprano
Sister Dolcina	soprano
The nursing sister	mezzo-soprano
The alms sisters	sopranos
The novices	sopranos
The lay sisters	soprano/mezzo-soprano

Offstage chorus of women, children and men

Setting A convent, towards the end of the 17th century

Forzano's drama about a nun who takes her own life on hearing of the death of her child had originally been planned as a spoken play. In the winter of 1916–17 he offered it to Puccini for his projected 'triptych' (*Il trittico*). The composer accepted without hesitation. Composition proceeded swiftly through the spring and summer of 1917. For local colour Puccini turned to his sister Igenia, Mother Superior at the convent at Vicepelago, and was permitted to visit her establishment and play the score to the assembled nuns, all of whom were moved to tears. Another valuable source of information was Puccini's lifelong friend, the priest Father Pietro Panichelli, who

'Suor Angelica' (Puccini), final scene of the original production (designed by Pietro Stroppa) at the Metropolitan Opera, New York, 14 December 1918, with Geraldine Farrar as Sister Angelica

supplied the text for what the composer flippantly referred to as the 'Marcia reale della Madonna' of the final scene.

The work was completed on 14 September 1917, and was first given along with its two companion-pieces, *Il tabarro* and *Gianni Schicchi*, the following year in America. In the meantime Puccini had extended Angelica's aria, 'Senza mamma, bimbo, tu sei morto' (Without your mother, child, you died') over a reprise of the long orchestra-based melody that heralds the arrival of the Princess's carriage; but this was not heard until the Italian première (11 January 1919), at the Teatro Costanzi, Rome, under Gino Marinuzzi with Gilda dalla Rizza as Angelica and Matilde Blanco Sadun as her antagonist. In subsequent performances Gilda dalla Rizza regularly cut a short aria sung by Angelica as she gathers the flowers from which she distils the poison for her suicide, 'Amici fiori, voi mi compensate' – a remarkably 'modern' piece with polytonal implications. Puccini eventually replaced it with a 16-bar extension of the preceding intermezzo, over which the soprano sings an altered text containing an ironical reference to the 'wasp' episode, oddly indicated in the present score as an optional cut. The aria can still be heard, though dimly, on a recording made by Lotte Lehmann in 1920. The only printed score to carry it is the first edition (1918) of the entire *Trittico*.

*

The garden of the cloister It is a fine spring evening and the air is full of birdsong. From the chapel come the strains of an Ave Maria, in which Angelica's voice can be distinguished. As the nuns emerge into the garden the Monitress assigns condign punishment to two latecomers, to one Sister Lucilla for causing laughter during the service and to Sister Osmina for concealing red roses within her habit. The nuns proceed to disport themselves. Sister Genovieffa notices that the fountain is about to be turned to gold by the rays of the setting sun – a sign of divine grace, says the Monitress, that occurs only on three evenings during May. An air of melancholy descends as they remember the Sister who died a year ago. Surely, Genovieffa exclaims, her spirit would desire a libation from the gilded fountain. In a brief cantabile ('I desideri sono i fiori dei vivi') Angelica declares that desires flower only for the living; those of the dead are fulfilled before they can utter them. The Monitress maintains that to nuns all desires are forbidden; but Sister Genovieffa disagrees. Brought up as a shepherdess, she yearns to fondle a pet lamb ('Soave Signor mio'). Sister Dolcina too has a wish – the sisters reply, laughing, that her wish is for some tasty morsel. And Sister Angelica? She denies wishing for anything. The sisters murmur, shocked, that that is untrue. They know that she is consumed by longing for news of the noble family that has mysteriously forced her to take the veil.

The Nursing Sister hurries in much distressed. One of the sisters has been stung by a wasp and is in agony. Angelica swiftly prepares a floral remedy and the Nursing Sister retires, having praised Angelica's skill. Two Alms Sisters enter with donkey and cart and distribute provisions. The harmonic movement comes to a virtual standstill for 20 bars, until they mention having seen a magnificent coach arrive at the convent; whereupon the orchestra launches the principal melody of the opera, a long, sustained cantilena over which the voices chatter at first casually, then with growing excitement, Angelica showing particular agitation. The nuns go into the cloister as the Abbess comes to summon Angelica to meet an important visitor. The Princess enters, a formidable personage dressed in black and leaning on an ebony stick. Her frigid demeanour is conveyed in the music by a bleak unison figure that winds upward and comes to rest on an unrelated chord. She has come to ask Angelica to sign away her share of her parents' heritage to a younger sister, who is about to be married – to a man who can overlook the dishonour that Angelica has brought upon their family. Angelica protests that her aunt is inexorable. Deeply offended, the Princess tells of frequent visits to her own sister's grave, where their spirits commune ('Nel silenzio di quei raccoglimenti'). But always her thoughts return to her niece's sin and the need for its expiation.

Angelica, duly humble, insists nonetheless that she will never forget her beloved child, only to be brutally told that he has died of a fever. She collapses sobbing, but recovers sufficiently to sign the parchment and when her aunt has left pours out her grief in the aria 'Senza mamma, bimbo, tu sei morto'. Singing of divine grace ('La grazia è discesa dal cielo') the nuns proceed to their cells followed by Angelica, who presently reappears carrying a jar into which she pours a lethal draught distilled from flowers. Bidding the sisters a tender farewell she drinks the poison, and is immediately overcome by guilt at having committed mortal sin. She prays frantically for salvation; the doors of the chapel open revealing a host of angels. In their midst is the Virgin Mary leading Angelica's child by the hand towards the dying mother, as the 'Royal March of the Madonna' swells to a climax.

*

In the dismemberment of the *Trittico* which followed the early performances, *Suor Angelica* was the first to be discarded (much to the annoyance of Puccini, who claimed it as his favourite among the three), although the aria 'Senza mamma' has a plangent beauty which has ensured its continuing popularity. Managements were put off by the problems of an all-female cast. Protestant audiences were alienated by the subject. Even in Italy the prevailing sweetness of the idiom held little appeal for a generation familiar with the explorations of Ildebrando Pizzetti and Malipiero into the austere ecclesiastical traditions of the past. Finally it may be questioned whether Puccini rose adequately to the challenge of the culminating miracle, which ideally calls for the kind of transfiguration that lay outside his range.   J.B.

T

Tabarro, Il ('The Cloak')

Opera in one act by Giacomo Puccini to a libretto by Giuseppe Adami after Didier Gold's play *La houppelande*; New York, Metropolitan Opera, 14 December 1918 (as no.1 of *Il trittico*).

The original cast included Claudia Muzio (Giorgetta), Alice Gentle (La Frugola), Giulio Crimi (Luigi), Luigi Montesanto (Michele), Angelo Bada (Tinca) and Adam Didur (Talpa); the conductor was Roberto Moranzoni.

Michele *a barge-owner (aged 50)*	baritone
Giorgetta *Michele's wife (aged 25)*	soprano
Luigi *a stevedore (aged 20)*	tenor
'Tinca' ('tench') *a stevedore (aged 35)*	tenor
'Talpa' ('mole') *a stevedore (aged 55)*	bass
La Frugola ('the rummager')	
Talpa's wife (aged 50)	mezzo-soprano
Stevedores, a ballad-seller, midinettes, *an organ-grinder and two lovers*	
Setting A bank of the river Seine, Paris, 1910	

Il tabarro is the first item in a triple bill of contrasted one-act operas, a project which Puccini had cherished for many years but from which he had been regularly dissuaded by his publisher Giulio Ricordi as being harmful to the box office. Not until Ricordi's death in 1912 did he feel free to proceed. The first subject was found easily enough: Didier Gold's play *La houppelande*, which Puccini probably saw at the Théâtre Marigny in Paris in autumn that year and which he described to Luigi Illica as 'apache in every sense of the word, and almost, no, more than almost, *Grand Guignol*'. But it was to the young playwright Giovacchino Forzano that Puccini first turned for a suitable text. Forzano, however, was unwilling to adapt someone else's work (in due course he would furnish the other two panels of the 'triptych', *Suor Angelica* and *Gianni Schicchi*, from his own invention) and suggested instead the poet and diplomat Ferdinando Martini. When after a few months he too bowed out, having decided that the profession of librettist was not for him, Puccini approached Giuseppe Adami, who accepted with alacrity his first commission from the composer. Progress was held up for a time by their joint work on *La rondine*, the German text of which Adami was translating and arranging; consequently Puccini did not begin the composition until October 1915.

The opera was completed on 25 November 1916, the subjects of the companion-pieces being still unchosen. However, Puccini was sufficiently pleased with *Il tabarro* to consider giving it the following year in Rome as part of a double bill with *Le villi*; but the absence on military service of Titta Ruffo, his ideal Michele, caused him to abandon the idea. So *Il tabarro* waited to take its place in the *Trittico*, which had its première overseas in the composer's absence a month after the end of World War I. The first Italian production was given at the Teatro Costanzi, Rome, on 11 January 1919, under Puccini's supervision, with Maria Labia as Giorgetta, Matilde Blanco Sadun as La Frugola, Edoardo de Giovanni (Edward Johnson) as Luigi and Carlo Galeffi as Michele; the conductor was Gino Marinuzzi the elder and the director Tito Ricordi (son of Giulio). Late in 1921 Puccini replaced Michele's original apostrophe to the Seine ('Scorri, fiume eterno') with a tauter monologue, strictly geared to the action ('Nulla! Silenzio'), which thereafter became definitive.

*

A quay, with a barge moored alongside Giorgetta is on deck busy with domestic chores, while her husband stands silent, gazing at the sunset. A slow, swirling theme on muted strings, touched here and there with soft woodwind notes, evokes the river Seine (it will recur constantly throughout the opera, so fixing the scene in the listener's consciousness). From time to time a ship's siren sounds. Men pass to and from the hold carrying sacks which they unload on to the quay. Below deck the strains of a shanty can be heard. Giorgetta offers a glass of wine all round; Luigi, Tinca and Talpa gladly accept. Luigi calls to a passing organ-grinder, who obliges by striking up a waltz in discordant 7ths (reminiscent of Stravinsky's *Petrushka*). First Tinca, then Luigi dance with Giorgetta until the reappearance of Michele pulls them up short. He pays off the organ-grinder, who departs. A ballad-seller arrives on the quay and delights the strolling *midinettes* with 'The Story of Mimì' – a sad little ditty which contains a musical reference to *La bohème*. Giorgetta converses awkwardly with Michele, whose reserve she finds

*'Il tabarro' (Puccini), final scene from the original
production at the Metropolitan Opera, New York,
14 December 1918, with Luigi Montesanto as Michele,
Claudia Muzio as Giorgetta and Giulio Crimi as Luigi*

vaguely disquieting. La Frugola arrives in search of her husband, Talpa. She carries a sack full of odds and ends scavenged from the streets, including a titbit for her cat Caporale, the perfect companion of her solitude, and she chatters cheerfully about her activities to a modal melody accompanied by parallel common chords ('Se tu sapessi'). Talpa and the men return, having finished their work. Tinca goes off to a tavern to drown his sorrows, caused by an unfaithful wife. His mocking laughter prompts Luigi to a passionate tirade against the hardships of a stevedore's life ('Hai ben ragione'). La Frugola dreams of a cottage in the country with her husband, basking in the sun with Caporale curled up at her feet ('Ho sognato una casetta'). Giorgetta longs for the happy bustle of the Parisian suburb where she was born. In her lyrical outburst ('È ben altro il mio sogno') she is joined by Luigi, who conjures up similar memories. Talpa and La Frugola retire still absorbed in their pastoral idyll, leaving Luigi and Giorgetta alone together.

At once the atmosphere becomes electric. A tense dialogue proceeds over a tremolando on the violins and a bass ostinato, broken off as Michele appears from the hold, surprised to find Luigi still there. The young man requests to be put off at Rouen, but Michele persuades him to remain aboard. No sooner has her husband gone than Giorgetta asks Luigi why he wanted to leave them. He replies that he cannot bear the thought of sharing her with someone else. They arrange a tryst for that night, the signal for which will be, as usual, a lighted match. The feeling

of unbearable tension is heightened by recurrences of an upward-darting figure first heard on the horn. In a final access of passion Luigi declares that he would sooner stab her to the heart than lose her to another man. When he has gone Giorgetta reflects miserably on the difficulty of finding true happiness. The ostinato figure dissolves into the rocking motion of the Seine theme as Michele returns, and in the course of a long *scène à deux* permeated by a new warmth, melodic and harmonic, he tries to reawaken his wife's affection for him. He recalls the child, now dead, whose cradle they used to tend, and how when the nights were cold he used to enfold them in his cloak (*tabarro*) – and here a faintly sinister motif is heard. He asks Giorgetta why she now seems never to sleep at night and she replies that the air of the cabin suffocates her; she must go on deck to breathe. For the last time Michele begs her to remain with him that night, but she evades his embrace and goes below. Michele utters one word – 'Whore!' A pair of lovers are heard singing in the distance; a bugle call from the barracks sounds the last post; then all is silence. Michele wonders who the adulterer can be. Talpa? Too old. Tinca? Always drunk. Luigi? No, he asked to leave them at Rouen. Still brooding, Michele takes out his pipe and begins to light it. Seeing the flame, which he takes to be the agreed signal, Luigi hastens aboard. To a volley of action music based on the motif first heard when the cloak is mentioned, Michele seizes him by the throat, forces him to admit that he is Giorgetta's lover, then strangles him and wraps the body in his cloak. Giorgetta returns, penitent at having caused her husband pain. She remembers a saying of his: 'Every one of us wears a cloak that hides sometimes a joy, sometimes a sorrow'. 'Sometimes a crime!', Michele cries, opening the garment. Giorgetta screams as Luigi's body rolls at her feet. Michele grasps her by the neck and forces her face against that of the corpse.

*

Of the three works that make up the *Trittico*, *Il tabarro* is the one most frequently performed today. Although it was composed long after the *verismo* movement of the 1890s had run its course, it approaches the canons of literary realism more closely than any of its Italian predecessors, if only by reason of its comparative restraint. The element of Grand Guignol, so blatant in Gold's play, with its double murder, is here softened. *Il tabarro* is arguably the best integrated of Puccini's scores. By far the greater part of it is cast in variants of triple or compound duple rhythm, thereby permitting the Seine theme from the beginning of the work to surface at any point in the action. If the lyrical moments are few, they are the more telling for their rarity.   **J.B.**

Tamerlano ('Tamerlane')

Opera in three acts by George Frideric Handel to a libretto by Nicola Francesco Haym adapted from Agostin Piovene's *Tamerlano* (1711, Venice) and from *Bajazet* (1719, Reggio Emilia), a revised version of the same libretto prepared by Ippolito Zanelli and Francesco Borosini, after Jacques Pradon's play *Tamerlan, ou La mort de Bajazet* (1675, Paris); London, King's Theatre, 31 October 1724.

The first cast consisted of Francesca Cuzzoni (Asteria), Francesco Borosini (Bajazet), Anna Vincenza Dotti (Irene), Giuseppe Boschi (Leo) and the castratos Senesino (Andronicus) and Andrea Pacini (Tamerlane).

Tamerlano [Tamerlane] *emperor of*	
the Tartars	alto castrato
Bajazete [Bajazet] *emperor of the Turks*	tenor
Asteria *his daughter, in love with. . .*	soprano
Andronico [Andronicus]	
Greek prince	alto castrato
Irene *princess of Trebizond, betrothed to*	
Tamerlane	contralto
Leone [Leo] *friend of Tamerlane and*	
Andronicus	bass
Zaida *friend of Asteria*	silent

Setting Prusa [now Bursa], capital of Bithynia, Western Anatolia, 1402

Tamerlano opened the sixth season of the Royal Academy of Music and was Handel's sixth full-length opera for that organization. He drafted the first version of the score, based only on Piovene's 1711 libretto, between 3 and 23 July 1724, but subjected it to extensive revision before the first performance. The revisions, almost certainly prompted by Borosini, make use of the 1719 version of the libretto. There were 12 performances in the first run, suggesting moderate success; Lady Mary Wortley Montagu's offhand verdict ('execrable') was probably untypical. The opera opened shortly before the annual performances of Nicolas Rowe's tragedy *Tamerlane* (1702) at Drury Lane and Lincoln's Inn Fields Theatre on 4 and 5 November, commemorating the birthday of William III and his landing in England. In the play the noble Tamerlane represents William, the ranting Bajazet Louis XIV. It has been suggested that the opera, by presenting Bajazet as the more sympathetic character, carried an alternative (and subversive) political message; but as Borosini's presence in the company fully accounts for the choice of libretto, and as it was normal for the operatic season to open at the end of October, the juxtaposition of opera and play was probably no more than a piquant coincidence.

Handel revived the opera at the King's Theatre on 13 November 1731, again with Senesino, but otherwise with a change of cast; Antonio Montagnana sang Leo. There were four performances. Montagnana received an expansive new aria ('Nel mondo e nell'abisso', adapted from *Riccardo Primo*) but there was no other additional music and several passages (including the Act 2 trio) were cut. An adaptation by Telemann, incorporating ballets in all three acts, was produced in Hamburg on 27 September 1725. The first modern revival, in a version by A. Rudolf and H. Roth, was given at Karlsruhe on 7 September 1924. The first modern British production was at the Barber Institute, Birmingham, on 21 March 1962, conducted by Anthony Lewis. In 1985 Opera North took its production first to Berlin and then, on Handel's 300th birthday, to Halle. The main text of Friedrich Chrysander's Händel-Gesellschaft edition includes all the music of Handel's 1724 performing version, but also incorporates several elements of earlier versions without explanation; his treatment of the final scene is especially misleading (and has unfortunately influenced three recordings of the opera). Though some of the music Handel himself rejected is of high quality, its inclusion in performances of the complete opera has little artistic justification.

*

Act 1 Outside Bajazet's prison house, Andronicus orders the release of Bajazet. On learning that this concession has been granted by Tamerlane, Bajazet determines to kill himself, but he relents when Andronicus suggests that the action will endanger Asteria. Tamerlane puts Andronicus in his debt by offering him the throne of Byzantium, but then reveals he fell in love with Asteria when Andronicus brought her to him to plead for her father's life. He resolves to renounce Irene and give her to Andronicus if the latter will now help him win Asteria. Tamerlane tells Asteria that he wishes to marry her and will spare her father if she consents; he adds that Andronicus is to marry Irene and is attempting to obtain Bajazet's consent to Asteria's marriage. Asteria, appalled at Andronicus's apparent perfidy, recognizes she may have to accept Tamerlane for her father's sake. Bajazet rejects Andronicus's proposal and is told by Asteria that Andronicus has changed his affections, which Andronicus denies. Bajazet tells him to defy Tamerlane and prove his love. Fearing for Bajazet, Andronicus is hesitant, and Asteria remains cold to him. Irene, arriving at Tamerlane's court in company with Andronicus's attendant Leo, finds herself barred from seeing Tamerlane. Andronicus says he will help her gain justice. He advises her to appear as one of her companions bringing a message to Tamerlane; Leo will assist her.

Act 2 Tamerlane informs a startled Andronicus

that Asteria has agreed to marry him (Tamerlane); he will do without Bajazet's consent. Asteria and Andronicus reproach each other. Andronicus vows to object to the marriage and goes to inform Bajazet. Tamerlane, with Asteria at his side, receives the disguised Irene, who upbraids Asteria for taking her place; Tamerlane angrily warns her that he will embrace Irene only if Asteria becomes displeasing to him. After he has left, Asteria mysteriously assures Irene that she does indeed propose to become unpleasing to Tamerlane. Leo promises to support Irene's cause. Andronicus informs Bajazet of Asteria's decision: Bajazet determines to stop her and Andronicus says he will kill himself if Asteria proves unfaithful. In the throne room Tamerlane invites Asteria to sit beside him, but Bajazet intervenes. The guards attempt to force him to bow to Tamerlane, but Bajazet throws himself to the ground and tells Asteria to tread on his neck as she mounts the throne. Tamerlane attempts to drag Asteria to the throne over her prostrate father. She refuses but says she will join Tamerlane if the path to the throne is cleared. The guards pull Bajazet up and, in shame, he disowns his daughter.

Tamerlane offers Andronicus Irene's hand, but Irene herself appears, still disguised, and denounces Tamerlane. Bajazet makes an impassioned plea to his daughter to remember her former vow to be avenged on Tamerlane; he asks her to kill him if she now disowns it. She descends from the throne, and places a dagger before Tamerlane: it was with that weapon, she says, that she intended to murder Tamerlane at their first nuptial embrace. Her defiance enrages Tamerlane, who threatens her and Bajazet with death; but she gains admiring tributes from Bajazet, Andronicus and Irene.

Act 3 Bajazet, imprisoned with Asteria in the seraglio, shares a poison with his daughter: he will use his portion if a rescue attempt he expects does not succeed; she must use hers rather than submit to Tamerlane. Tamerlane tells Andronicus he has relented and orders him to renew his offer to Asteria. Overheard by Asteria, Andronicus is at first reluctant, annoying both Tamerlane and Asteria, but then openly declares he is Tamerlane's rival. Asteria confirms her love for Andronicus and her hatred for Tamerlane. Tamerlane orders the decapitation of Bajazet and says Asteria shall be married to the meanest slave. On her knees Asteria begs mercy for her father, but he enters at that moment and rebukes her for kneeling to the tyrant. Tamerlane orders Bajazet and Asteria to attend him at table and Andronicus to witness their fate. Leo comes to fetch Asteria; she and Andronicus bid each other a tender farewell.

In the imperial hall, Leo urges Irene to seize the throne: Asteria can no longer take her place.

Tamerlane leads in Bajazet, warning of his coming humiliation. Asteria is summoned and ordered by Tamerlane to offer him his cup on bended knees, like a slave. Despite Andronicus's objections she appears to agree, but drops her portion of poison in the cup. This action is seen by Irene, and as Tamerlane exultantly takes the cup she prevents him from drinking. She announces her true identity and Tamerlane is impressed by her concern for him. He orders Asteria to give the cup to either her father or her lover. When she attempts to drink the poison herself, Andronicus dashes the cup from her hand. Tamerlane orders her to be raped by slaves as Bajazet watches. Horrified, Bajazet vows to be free of Tamerlane. Irene and Tamerlane are reconciled. Leo approaches with Asteria, begging a final audience for Bajazet. Calmly Bajazet tells Tamerlane he has taken poison, and will soon be free of his tyranny. Asteria begs Bajazet to kill her with his sword before he dies, but he says he no longer has the power to do so. Bajazet curses Tamerlane, calling on the Furies to rip out his heart and drag him to hell, where Bajazet's ghost will continue to torment him. Asteria and Andronicus escort him out as he is dying, Asteria saying that only her own death remains to complete Tamerlane's triumph. Tamerlane orders the guards to watch her. Andronicus prepares to kill himself, but Tamerlane declares that he is appeased: he will marry Irene, and Andronicus can take the Byzantine throne and marry Asteria. Irene, Tamerlane, Andronicus and Leo look forward to the dawn of a new day after dark night.

                                    *

Tamerlano is among the most consistently serious of all Handel's operas and the only one to end with a real sense of tragedy; the drama generated by the clash of wills between conquering and conquered emperors, compounded by Bajazet's loving concern for his daughter, is sustained throughout with remarkable intensity. Though the primo uomo role is that of Andronicus, the dominant character is, exceptionally, a tenor role, that of Bajazet, a feature to which Borosini clearly made a major contribution (he had sung the role earlier in Francesco Gasparini's 1719 setting of the libretto and prompted many of the revisions to it adopted by Handel). Bajazet's death scene – stunningly realized in a series of accompanied recitatives alternating with arioso passages of varying styles and tempos – forms the climax of the work. In Handel's performing version (reached after much revision of earlier drafts) all that follows is the brief, 22-bar recitative 'Barbaro! or manca solo' and the final *coro*, in which the words anticipating a new dawn are bleakly contradicted by the sombre minor-key tonality. (Asteria is not on stage and her fate is left unclear.) The music nevertheless displays considerable variety within the prevailing mood, there being ample contrast between the calm nobility of Andronicus's most appealing arias ('Benché mi sprezzi' and 'Cerco in vano') and the spiky brilliance of Tamerlane's; Irene's arias, two spirited and one ('Par che mi nasca in seno') touchingly beautiful, similarly offset the pathos of Asteria's music. Ultimately *Tamerlano* is memorable for its great scenes of confrontation rather than for individual arias. One is the death scene; another is the throne-room scene of Act 2, the tension of which is built up and maintained in Handel's longest passage of recitative (plain and accompanied) until it explodes in a fiery trio and unwinds with brief and moving *ariette* for Bajazet, Andronicus and Irene as they acknowledge Asteria's courage. The orchestral scoring is restrained, without brass instruments, though notable for Handel's first use of clarinets (in 'Par che mi nasca in seno'; the indication of 'cornetti' in the autograph is almost certainly an error).

A.H.

Tancredi

Melodramma eroico in two acts by Gioachino Rossini to a libretto by Gaetano Rossi after Voltaire's *Tancrède*; Venice, Teatro La Fenice, 6 February 1813.

Tancredi was first sung by Adelaide Malanotte and Amenaide by Elisabetta Manfredini.

Argirio	tenor
Orbazzano	bass
Amenaide *Argirio's daughter*	soprano
Tancredi *a Sicilian knight*	contralto
Isaura *Amenaide's confidante*	alto
Roggiero *Tancredi's squire*	soprano
Setting The 11th-century city-state of Syracuse	

After the success of *La pietra del paragone* in Milan (1812), Rossini could designate himself a *maestro di cartello*, a composer whose name alone guarantees a public. Tancredi is a further landmark in his career. The work exists in two distinct editions. For the Venice première, Rossini and his librettist engineered a happy ending to the drama; but the following month, for a revival in Ferrara, Rossini worked with the poet and scholar Luigi Lechi to restore the tragic ending of Voltaire's original play.

To understand the far from clear plot-lines of Rossi's text, it is necessary to know something of the drama's pre-history. Like the houses of Montague and Capulet in *Romeo and Juliet*, those of Argirio and Orbazzano are constantly feuding. When the Orbazzani gain the upper hand, Argirio's wife and his daughter Amenaide are exiled to the Byzantine court. There Amenaide is wooed by the powerful Saracen leader Solamir but falls in love with another Sicilian exile, the young knight Tancredi. On her deathbed, Amenaide's mother gives her blessing for a marriage with Tancredi. Meanwhile, the Syracusans, harassed by Solamir and ineptly led by Orbazzano, have put Argirio at the head of their army. As a gesture of reconciliation, he offers to Orbazzano Amenaide's hand in marriage, while agreeing to seize the Tancredi family estates and condemning Tancredi to death in his absence. In the meantime Amenaide, largely ignorant of these events, has sent an anonymous note to Tancredi urging him to return to Syracuse.

*

The opera begins with Argirio and Orbazzano in the process of ratifying their various agreements; but Argirio is astonished and angered when his daughter greets with dismay the idea of marriage with Orbazzano. Tancredi's clandestine arrival is marked by his cavatina 'Tu che accendi questo core', with its buoyant cabaletta 'Di tanti palpiti' (which rapidly became a huge favourite throughout Europe). While Amenaide continues to prevaricate, she is informed by her father of the death sentence that has been passed on Tancredi. When Tancredi appears out of hiding Amenaide (somewhat implausibly) is terror-struck and begs him to go away for ever. In the Ferrara revision, Rossini removes the lovers' Act 1 duet 'L'aura che intorno spira' and brings forward their Act 2 duet 'Lasciami! non t'ascolto'. The intention is economy and added dramatic cogency, but the loss of the original Act 1 duet, spacious and lyrical, is considerable, and the brilliantly confrontational nature of the Act 2 duet makes it inappropriate as a vehicle for the lovers' first reunion. In the long and innovatory Act 1 finale, Amenaide again refuses to marry Orbazzano, but Orbazzano now has in his possession the note Amenaide sent to Tancredi. Convinced by its vague terms and anonymous nature that it is an act of collaboration with the hated Solamir, Orbazzano demands Amenaide's death as a punishment for high treason.

In Act 2 the imprisoned Amenaide is finally condemned to death by her father; but an unknown knight – in reality, Tancredi – comes to champion her cause. Argirio, conscience-stricken over his signing of the death sentence, embraces the champion. In the combat that follows Orbazzano is slain by Tancredi and Amenaide is set free. The leaderless Syracusans now beg Tancredi to help defend them against the Saracens but Tancredi, still convinced of Amenaide's guilt over the anonymous letter and uncertain of the real object of her affections, is not to be persuaded. In the original version, Tancredi reluctantly joins the Syracusan army; the Saracens are defeated, Amenaide's innocence is established, and to repeated cries of 'felicità!' the opera ends with a vaudeville finale. In Voltaire's play, and in the revised Ferrara edition, Tancredi is mortally wounded and dies accepting Amenaide's pleas of innocence and vows of love. The Ferrara revision also brings forward Voltaire's Act 4 scene iv, the lovers' only encounter in the original drama, and shapes it into Tancredi's fine 'Perchè turba la calma', sung to Amenaide before Tancredi's departure to fight the Saracens.

*

Tancredi marks Rossini's coming of age as a composer of *opera seria*. Static forms and limited harmonic horizons are given a new dynamism and reach as Rossini successfully redeploys structural innovations derived from his early one-act operas. It is also one of his most flawlessly lyrical works, a primary example of what Stendhal calls his 'candeur virginale', and reveals his concern for sheer beauty of vocal sound. This preoccupation not only confers on the leading players in his *opere serie* a certain idealized and idealizing quality, but also establishes the aesthetic basis on which the increasingly influential Rossini would judge and advise leading singers over the next 50 years. Although Rossini and his librettist, Rossi, would expand the forms and refine the dramaturgy in *Tancredi*'s sequel *Semiramide* (1823, Venice), the later work cannot lay claim to the mixture of primal innocence and musical sophistication which made *Tancredi* so popular in its day and which it can still reveal when it is staged and sung with a proper degree of refinement and intimacy.   **R.O.**

Tannhäuser [*Tannhäuser und der Sängerkrieg auf Wartburg* ('Tannhäuser and the Singers' Contest on the Wartburg')]

Grosse romantische Oper in three acts by Richard Wagner to his own libretto; Dresden, Hoftheater, 19 October 1845.

The original cast was: Joseph Tichatschek (Tannhäuser), Wilhelmine Schröder-Devrient (Venus), Wagner's niece Johanna Wagner (Elisabeth) and Anton Mitterwurzer (Wolfram).

Herrmann *Landgrave of Thuringia*		bass
Tannhäuser	⎫	tenor
Wolfram von Eschenbach		baritone
Walther von der	*knights*	
Vogelweide	*and*	tenor
Biterolf	*minstrels*	bass
Heinrich der Schreiber		tenor
Reinmar von Zweter	⎭	bass
Elisabeth *the Landgrave's niece*		soprano
Venus		soprano
A Young Shepherd		soprano
Four Noble Pages		soprano, alto

Thuringian knights, counts and nobles, ladies, older and younger pilgrims, sirens, naiads, nymphs, bacchantes. In Paris version, additionally the Three Graces, youths, cupids, satyrs and fauns
Setting Thuringia at the beginning of the 13th century

Wagner's text is a conflation of two separate medieval legends: those concerning Tannhäuser, believed originally to have been a crusading knight from Franconia, and the song contest on the Wartburg – drawing on a number of 19th-century versions, notably those of Ludwig Tieck, E. T. A. Hoffmann, Heinrich Heine, Friedrich de la Motte Fouqué and Joseph Eichendorff.

Wagner worked out a detailed prose draft (28 June–6 July 1842) at Aussig (now Ústí nad Labem) in the Bohemian mountains, and versified it the following spring. After making a number of preliminary sketches for the musical setting, he made his 'fragmentary complete draft' (so called because it survives only in fragmentary form, albeit now largely reconstructed) and a continuous complete draft, the two evolving side by side between the summer or autumn of 1843 and December 1844. The overture was completed on 11 January 1845 and the full score on 13 April. As late as the continuous complete draft, there is evidence of Wagner's conception in terms of traditional numbers, despite his suppression of such designations in the autograph score.

The uncomprehending response of the audience at the first performance on 19 October 1845 was largely due to the inability of Tichatschek, in the leading role, to grasp the principle of *melos* towards which Wagner was progressing. The composer's abnormal vocal demands also took their toll on the other three principal singers. However, by the mid-1850s the work had established itself in the repertory of more than 40 German opera houses. An invitation from Emperor Napoleon III to stage *Tannhäuser* in Paris led to one of the most celebrated débâcles in the annals of operatic history. Revenging themselves on the politically unpopular Princess Pauline Metternich, who had negotiated the invitation, the members of the Jockey Club disrupted three performances at the Opéra in March 1861 with aristocratic baying and dog-whistles before Wagner was allowed to withdraw the production.

Four 'stages' of the work have been identified: (1) the original version as given at the Dresden première in 1845; (2) the edition published by Meser in 1860, incorporating revisions made (notably to the ending of the work) between 1847 and 1852; (3) the version of 1861 (not published), as performed at the Opéra that year; and (4) the version performed under Wagner's supervision in Vienna in 1875, incorporating revisions made subsequent to 1861 (vocal score 1876, full score 1888). There is, however, no reason to abandon the convenient traditional labels of 'Dresden version' (i.e. no.2) and 'Paris version' (no.4), provided it is borne in mind that these terms refer not to what was actually heard in Dresden in 1845 or Paris in 1861 but to revised editions of those performances.

The most noticeable feature of the Paris version (the major differences are described below, and the Paris variants are usefully given in the Dover full score) is the stylistic incongruity arising from the grafting of new sections in Wagner's mature, post-*Tristan* style on to a work of the 1840s. The characterization of Venus was deepened for Paris in a manner prophetic of Kundry in *Parsifal*. Where her somewhat plain declamation was punctuated for Dresden by bare chords, her vocal line for Paris is sensually pliable, with richly scored accompaniments.

The title role in the Opéra performance in 1861 was taken by Albert Niemann, who went on to sing it at the Metropolitan (1886–9). Tannhäuser was the role in which Lauritz Melchior made his Metropolitan début on 17 February 1926; he went on to sing it 51 times in New York, as well as in other major opera houses (144 times in all).

*

Act I.i-ii *Inside the Hörselberg near Eisenach* One of the primary changes for Paris concerned the opening of the opera. The bacchanal in the Venusberg (identified by Wagner and others with the Hörselberg in Thuringia) was extended to provide the ballet demanded by the management and patrons of the Opéra (albeit in the first rather than the traditional second act). In the original version, the stage directions prescribed a rocky grotto with bathing naiads, reclining sirens and dancing nymphs. Venus lay on a couch in a rosy light, with Tannhäuser, half-kneeling, nestling his head in her lap. Urged on by bacchantes, the dancers reached a peak of orgiastic excitement. The Paris version adds the Three Graces and cupids, while satyrs and fauns cause a riotous frenzy by chasing the nymphs. Prompted by the Graces, the cupids quell the riot by raining down love-arrows on all below. The Paris bacchanal is both longer and more frenzied, with the addition of castanets and a third timpani. At the height of the revelry the rising chromatic four-note phrase ubiquitous in *Tristan* is much in evidence. Orchestral textures are richer, more voluptuous, and transitions are negotiated with the assurance of Wagner's mature style.

In scene ii Tannhäuser starts, as though from a dream. He is surfeited with the sensual pleasures of the Venusberg and longs for the simple joys of earthly life. Urged on by the love goddess, he sings his Hymn to Venus, the first stanza in D♭, with harp accompaniment, the second in D with added strings, both ending with a plea to be released. Venus summons a magic grotto and against an accompaniment of ethereal divided strings tempts him to surrender to ecstasy: 'Geliebter, komm!' Tannhäuser seizes his harp again and, to a full orchestral accompaniment, drives his plea to a pitch by singing the third stanza in E♭. Venus angrily releases him ('Zieh hin! Wahnsinniger!': 'Withdraw! Madman!'), prophesying that he will in desperation one day return. When Tannhäuser invokes the Virgin Mary, Venus and her domains instantly disappear. In the Paris version, the voluptuous nature of both vocal line and accompaniment is much enhanced, while two additional passages after Venus's slightly reworded outburst ('Zieh hin! Wahnbetörter!': 'Withdraw! Creature in love with delusion!') reveal new aspects of her character as she gives vent to first angry mockery and then despair.

I.iii-iv *A valley below the Wartburg* Tannhäuser finds himself in a sunlit valley; sheep bells are heard from the heights and a young shepherd is playing his pipe (an irregularly phrased monody started on the clarinet and continued by an english horn on or behind the stage). His simple song, 'Frau Holda kam aus dem Berg hervor', is followed by the chant of the Elder Pilgrims, wafting from the direction of the Wartburg. The second stanza, in which anguished chromaticisms depict the oppression of sin, is a recollection in quadruple time of the corresponding strain of the overture's main theme. As the pilgrims approach, the shepherd greets them and Tannhäuser makes a pious exclamation. The procession passes and Tannhäuser takes up the guilt-oppressed strain of the pilgrims. As the chant dies away, hunting horns are heard, at first in the distance, then closer to.

The Landgrave and minstrels approach (scene iv) and, recognizing Tannhäuser, greet him warmly ('Gegrüsst sei uns'). Tannhäuser's rejection of the past leads to a brief seven-part ensemble, terminated by Wolfram's cry of 'Bleib bei Elisabeth' ('Stay with Elisabeth'), an invocation of talismanic force. Tannhäuser, stopped in his tracks, can only repeat the name. Wolfram goes on to reveal how in their earlier song-contests, Tannhäuser had won the heart of Elisabeth, who had subsequently retired from their company – 'Als du in kühnem Sange uns bestrittest' – followed by the aria proper, 'War's Zauber, war es reine Macht?' The aria, though of conventional cut, has inspired many superlative performances both on stage and on record, often eclipsing those of the singer in the notoriously taxing title role. To Wolfram's pleas for Tannhäuser to stay are added those of the other minstrels in a brief sextet. Tannhäuser yields and embraces his former friends (to an orchestral accompaniment made slightly more exultant in the Paris version). He leads them in a final

The bacchanal in the Venusberg from Act 1 of Wagner's 'Tannhäuser': watercolour by Michael Echter after a performance given at the Munich Hoftheater (using the 1861 Paris version), 1 August 1867

ensemble which brings the act to an end resounding with the blasts of hunting horns.

Act 2 *The Hall of Song in the Wartburg* The act opens with Elisabeth's joyous greeting to the Hall of Song, abandoned by her during Tannhäuser's absence, 'Dich, teure Halle, grüss' ich wieder'. The aria is conventional in phrase structure, but its introduction effectively uses repeated quaver triplets to portray Elisabeth's agitation; an oboe and clarinet also sound the ominous motif first heard when Tannhäuser was dismissed by Venus. Wolfram and Tannhäuser have entered at the back (scene ii); the former remains there discreetly while the latter throws himself at Elisabeth's feet. The chords on pizzicato strings have been said to depict Elisabeth's steps and are followed by a rushing semiquaver figure illustrative of Tannhäuser's gesture.

She begs him to rise and, after regaining her composure, recalls his earlier minstrelsy, 'Der Sänger klugen Weisen', against an accompaniment of sustained, muted strings, with flowing viola and serene wind punctuations. The vocal line becomes disjointed and the accompaniment sparer as she relives the pain of Tannhäuser's departure. Tannhäuser, enraptured, hails the power of love, and the two break into an ecstatic duet in the old-fashioned style, 'Gepriesen sei die Stunde' (often abridged in performance).

Tannhäuser and Wolfram depart, and an abrupt transition introduces scene iii, in which the Landgrave welcomes his niece back to the Hall but finds her unwilling to divulge her thoughts. Trumpets sound from the courtyard, heralding the arrival of the guests (knights, counts, their ladies and retinue) for the song contest (scene iv). March tunes accompany the long procession, eventually with choral parts added, first male, then female, then both together. When everybody has assembled, in a semicircle, the minstrels enter to a more lyrical theme, still in march tempo, but played *sostenuto* on strings alone. In a passage of recitative interspersed with arioso the Landgrave extols the art of song and calls on the minstrels to demonstrate it by singing in praise of love; the worthiest contender will receive his prize from Elisabeth herself. Fanfares and acclamation greet his announcement.

The first contender is Wolfram, who uses the image of a fountain to sing of the purity of love, 'Blick, ich umher'. His simple, unadorned line (which Wagner wanted sung in time, not as free recitative) is accompanied first by harp alone, to which are subsequently added the mellow tones of divided violas and cellos. His song is approved by the assembled company, but not by Tannhäuser, who retorts that the fountain of love fills him only with burning desire. This response was varied in the Paris version, because Wagner also wished to omit the following song for Walther, as the singer assigned the role was inadequate. In the original, Dresden version, Walther picked up the image of the fountain, celebrating it as chastity itself, in an aria similar to Wolfram's in its stiff, formal style and accompaniment, 'Den Bronnen, den uns Wolfram nannte'.

Another minstrel, Biterolf, voices the outraged opinions of the knights and ladies when he challenges Tannhäuser to a combat of more than vocal prowess. He is scorned by Tannhäuser for his inexperience as regards the joys of true love. Wolfram attempts to restore calm with another invocation of pure love, but Tannhäuser responds with what is, in effect, the fourth stanza of his Hymn to Venus from the previous act. The first three stanzas had winched up the tonality successively from D♭ to D to E♭. The E major tonality of the fourth stanza both continues that sequence and contrasts sharply with the E♭ of Wolfram's last utterance.

There is general consternation, and the ladies, with the exception of Elisabeth, leave the hall in shock. The knights round threateningly on Tannhäuser, but Elisabeth steps between them with the cry 'Haltet ein!', a dramatic moment strongly reminiscent of Leonore's 'Töt' erst sein Weib!' in *Fidelio* as she protects her husband from Pizarro's

Albert Niemann in the title role of Wagner's 'Tannhäuser'

knife. The knights are taken aback, but Elisabeth urges clemency, first with some forcefulness, then more touchingly as a woman whose heart has been broken, 'Der Unglücksel'ge'. This section, in B minor and marked *andante*, gives way to an *adagio* prayer in B major whose simple eloquence moves everybody. Tannhäuser himself, overcome with remorse, sinks to the ground with a cry of grief. In a double chorus the minstrels and knights take up the theme of Elisabeth's prayer, hailing this intervention by an 'angel'. Tannhäuser's interjections of 'Erbarm dich mein!' were originally intended to carry over the flood of the entire ensemble; later Wagner allowed the other voices to be omitted if necessary. Finally Elisabeth and the knights take up a melodic idea which is brought to a climax rather in the Italian style; indeed, it has been demonstrated that the whole of scene iv (that is, from the assembly of the guests to the end of the act) follows the typical pattern of a mid-19th-century italianate finale.

The Landgrave steps forward to tell Tannhäuser that his only hope of salvation is to join the band of pilgrims preparing to make their way to Rome. A final chorus, once again in B major, adopts this more optimistic tone and, after the younger pilgrims are heard in the distance, the act ends with Tannhäuser's cry 'Nach Rom!', echoed by Elisabeth, minstrels and nobles.

Act 3 *Valley below the Wartburg* The introduction, depicting Tannhäuser's pilgrimage, is built from themes already associated with the pilgrims and with Elisabeth's plea for Tannhäuser, to which is added a new, chromatically winding idea soon to form the basis of Tannhäuser's Narration. As the curtain rises, Elisabeth is praying in front of a statue of the Virgin. Both she and Wolfram, who loves her silently and has been observing her from a discreet distance, are alerted by the return of the pilgrims from Rome. The pilgrims' chorus moves through a stanza of tortured chromaticism (a vulnerable passage in performance) to an exultant climax, after which it recedes again into the distance.

Elisabeth, seeing that Tannhäuser is not among the pilgrims, falls to her knees and sings her Prayer, 'Allmächt'ge Jungfrau' (in effect another set-piece aria). The use once again of the motif from her Act 2 aria, as she sings of 'foolish longing', invests this phrase with something of the force of a motif of reminiscence. Her prayer ended, Elisabeth notices Wolfram but indicates that he should not speak to her. She leaves; Wolfram remains for scene ii. After an introductory section of arioso, he sings his celebrated Hymn to the Evening Star, 'O du, mein holder Abendstern', a number in the old-fashioned style whose conventionality of phrasing and harmony has done nothing to diminish its evergreen popularity.

The pinched tone of stopped horns and a five-note chromatic phrase in the strings herald the third scene and the reappearance of Tannhäuser; Wolfram initially fails to recognize him. On being told that he has returned from Rome impenitent and unshriven, Wolfram demands to hear the full story. Tannhäuser's Narration, 'Inbrunst im Herzen', is notable on several counts. First, it is the most advanced piece of writing in the opera, in terms of musico-poetic synthesis: that is, the vocal line reflects the natural accentuations of the verse and even changes in character as the narrator's emotional state changes. Second, its formal structure is dictated entirely by the narrative. Third, it is a clear example of the composer's growing recognition of the orchestra's potential for expressive, illustrative purposes. The Narration begins with two stanzas making prominent use of the chromatic winding theme from the act's introduction. A whirr of strings lifts the music into D♭ as Tannhäuser tells how he arrived in Rome, and a celestial wind chorus sounds the 'Dresden Amen'. He describes how he saw the Pope, and the whirring string figure sweeps on into D and E♭ major, the frenzied modulations and formal dissolution aptly reflecting Tannhäuser's state of mind. The climax is reached as he repeats the Pope's words of condemnation: if he has tasted the hellish delights of the Venusberg, he can no more be forgiven than the Pope's staff can sprout green leaves. At these words, the motif heard at Tannhäuser's return sounds once more, the pinched tone of the stopped horns transmuted into the Pope's condemnation.

To Wolfram's horror, Tannhäuser declares his intention of returning to the Venusberg. The orchestral frenzy increases and Venus herself appears in a bright, rosy light, reclining on her couch. (In the original 1845 version Venus did not appear at the end, the Venusberg being suggested by a red glow in the distance; similarly, Elisabeth's death was announced only by bells tolling from the Wartburg. These revisions date from spring 1847.) A struggle ensues for Tannhäuser's soul, resolved by another emphatic enunciation of Elisabeth's name by Wolfram. An offstage chorus announces that Elisabeth has died. But her intercession has redeemed Tannhäuser and Venus disappears, vanquished. Elisabeth's bier is carried on, and Tannhäuser, calling on her saintly soul to intercede for him, falls lifeless to the ground. The final strains of the Pilgrims' Chorus tell of a miracle: the Pope's staff has burst into leaf. Tannhäuser's soul is saved.

*

Tannhäuser, with its frequently abrupt contrasts and rudimentary motivic integration, falls well short of the mature Wagnerian music drama. Yet it marks a considerable advance over *Der fliegende Holländer* in the deployment of the orchestra, continues Wagner's preoccupation with the dramatic conception or 'poetic intent', and shows some awareness of what he later referred to as 'the beautiful, convincing necessity of transition'.   **B.M.**

Thaïs

Comédie lyrique in three acts and seven scenes by Jules Massenet to a libretto by Louis Gallet after the novel of the same title by Anatole France (1890); Paris, Opéra, 16 March 1894.

At the première Thaïs was sung by Sibyl Sanderson, Athanaël by Jean-François Delmas, and Nicias by Albert Alvarez.

Thaïs *actress and courtesan*	soprano
Athanaël *a coenobite monk*	baritone
Nicias *a young sybarite philosopher*	tenor
Palémon *an old coenobite monk*	bass
Crobyle ⎱ *slaves*	soprano
Myrtale ⎰	mezzo-soprano
Albine *abbess*	mezzo-soprano
La Charmeuse *ballet dancer*	soprano
Servant of Nicias	baritone

Actors, philosophers, monks, nuns, citizens of Alexandria

Setting The Thebaid and Alexandria, 4th century AD

The legend of the courtesan-turned-saint Thaïs was written down in the 10th century by the German nun Hrostwitha; a French translation published in the 19th century inspired the Nobel Prizewinner Anatole France (1844–1924) first to a poem (1867) and later to a novel, originally entitled *Paphnuce* after the name of the monk who brings the courtesan back to the bosom of the faith (changed in the opera to Athanaël). The novel was published first as a serial in the *Revue des deux mondes* (1889) and in book form the following year as *Thaïs*. An anti-clerical satire of Voltairean irony, it was savagely attacked by the church. Massenet and Gallet were granted permission to turn it into an opera in 1892. At first France expressed disappointment at the quality and selectiveness of Gallet's libretto (one of the earliest unrhymed examples in France, a 'poème mélique', in the author's words) but after seeing the opera he wrote to Massenet in flattering – and one must assume sincere – terms.

The opera was written for the Californian soprano Sibyl Sanderson, for whom Massenet had a deep *tendresse*. She had sung Manon successfully in France, Belgium and London, and enjoyed a personal success in *Esclarmonde* (1889). *Thaïs* was destined for the Opéra-Comique, but just as Massenet was finishing it, in the spring of 1893, Sanderson signed a contract with the Opéra after a dispute with Léon Carvalho over performance fees, and *Thaïs* was adapted to follow its protagonist to the Palais Garnier; Massenet composed the obligatory ballet during the summer. Despite the controversial nature of the subject matter and the fact that Sanderson 'accidentally' exposed her breasts, the première was not a success, and in effect the work marked the end of her association with the composer; there were only 14 performances of it at the Opéra before Sanderson retired into married life in 1897.

In that year Massenet revised *Thaïs*, adding the scene at the Oasis (Act 3 scene i), suppressing the original ballet and the second-act interlude ('Symphonie des amours d'Aphrodite') and supplying a new ballet for the end of Act 2. It was first given in this form at the Opéra on 13 April 1898, again without conspicuous success. Massenet himself attended the Italian première in Milan with Lina Cavalieri in the title role (1903, Teatro Lirico) – or rather was in earshot, since he seldom actually 'assisted' at his premières – and reported a triumph in a letter to his wife. Cavalieri repeated her success at the 69th performance at the Opéra in 1907, after which the work's popularity was assured: it remained in the repertory of the Palais Garnier until 1956, falling just short of 700 performances. It was popular in the USA in the early part of the century, thanks mainly to Mary Garden and Geraldine Farrar; other famous exponents include Maria Jeritza, Maria Kouznetsov (Kuznetsova), Aïno Ackté, Lilian Berthon, Ninon Vallin, Fanny Heldy and Géori Boué; notable Athanaëls have included its first interpreter, Delmas (also the first French Wotan), Vanni-Marcoux, John Brownlee and Roger Bourdin. There is a substantial discography. *Thaïs* has never entirely lapsed from the repertory but – undeservedly – has never achieved the popularity of *Werther* or *Manon*.

*

Act 1.i *Monks' cells in the Thebaid* Led by Palémon, the monks prepare their evening meal and pray for Athanaël, who has been absent. He enters, scandalized by the life of the courtesan Thaïs in Alexandria, and recalls how as a young man ('Hélas! Enfant encore') he went to her house but was saved by God's intervention on the threshold. He sees her activities as an affront to religion, and despite Palémon's warning ('Ne nous mêlons jamais, mon fils, aux gens du siècle') is determined to win her soul for God. The monks retire to bed. Athanaël is tormented by visions of Thaïs at work, wakes, and in a confident C major outburst sees this as a sign from God to go at once to convert her ('Toi qui mis la pitié dans nos âmes'). Palémon repeats his warning as Athanaël strides off into the desert.

1.ii *The terrace of Nicias's house in Alexandria*

Athanaël greets the city of his birth in a three-part aria ('Voilà donc la terrible cité'), recalling how he has rejected its beauty and its learning, and praying for the protection of angels on his mission. The angels who answer his prayer are Crobyle and Myrtale, who enter with their master Nicias, a friend of Athanaël's youth who greets him affectionately. On learning of his mission, Nicias reveals that he has hired Thaïs's services for a week and that this is his last day: she is even now on her way from the theatre. He advises the monk to change into less forbidding clothes, and in a wittily teasing quartet ('Ne t'offense pas') the slaves fail to remove his habit but at least slip a robe over it and comb and perfume him. Thaïs enters with actors and philosophers. She takes a gentle farewell of Nicias ('C'est Thaïs, l'idole fragile qui vient pour la dernière fois') before inquiring after the stranger with the fierce glances. Nicias warns that he has come to convert her, and she asks Athanaël with lazy mockery why he denies his true nature and the love-light in his eyes ('Qui te fait si sévère'). As she prepares to disrobe, he rushes away, to general amusement, threatening to come to her house. She accepts the challenge.

Act 2.i *Thaïs's house* Suddenly conscious of the emptiness of her life, Thaïs seeks reassurance from her mirror ('Dis-moi que je suis belle et que je serai belle, éternellement') but in growing panic sees signs of approaching old age. She regains her composure as Athanaël enters, and warns him against loving her. He responds with the offer of a type of love unknown to her. She replies that he comes too late: she already knows 'toutes les ivresses'. With growing ardour, he promises that his love will lead to eternal life, which interests her. In preparation, she prays to Aphrodite (and he to God). He suddenly flings aside his robe to reveal his habit, and curses the sins of the flesh. As she cowers, afraid that he may kill her, he repeats his offer of eternal life ('Je l'ai dit: tu vivras') to a rolling, rapturous 9/8 tune. The voice of Nicias off stage reminds her of her past, and as Athanaël promises to wait on her doorstep for her repentance, she collapses in hysteria.

2.ii *Outside Thaïs's house* After the 'Méditation' intermezzo describing her conversion, Thaïs enters humbly, saying that prayer and Athanaël's words have shown her the light. Athanaël promises to take her to Mère Albine's settlement, but orders her first to burn her house and all traces of her past. She pleads, in vain, to keep only an ivory statuette of Eros ('L'amour est une vertu rare') before returning to her house to carry out his orders. Nicias and his companions enter for an elaborate ballet. As it ends, Athanaël announces Thaïs's conversion, and the crowd threaten to stone them both while flames lick at the windows. Nicias saves them by throwing gold to the crowd.

Act 3.i *An oasis, near Mère Albine's settlement* Thaïs, exhausted, begs to be allowed to rest, but Athanaël drives her on, rejoicing in the mortification of her flesh. The sight of blood on her feet eventually moves him to pity, and he goes to fetch water. She praises his kindness ('O messager de Dieu') and blesses him for having brought her to salvation (duet, 'Baigne d'eau mes mains'). Mère Albine and the sisters receive Thaïs, and she bids farewell to Athanaël 'pour toujours'. The significance of the words sinks in, and to the tune of the Méditation Athanaël realizes with horror that he will never see her again.

3.ii *The Thebaid* A storm threatens. In the 20 days since he returned Athanaël has neither eaten nor drunk. He tells Palémon that no amount of self-flagellation brings peace. Palémon merely repeats his warning. Further visions of pre-conversion Thaïs are interrupted by distant voices proclaiming the imminent death of St Thaïs of Alexandria. With the sole thought of seeing and possessing her, Athanaël rushes headlong into the storm.

3.iii *The garden of Mère Albine's settlement* Albine and the sisters pray at Thaïs's deathbed, welcome the distraught Athanaël, and withdraw. The final duet ('Te souvient-il du lumineux voyage') is based on the Méditation and the hymn Athanaël sang as he set out on his journey. She tenderly and gratefully remembers his part in her redemption, sees angels waiting to greet her at the gates of heaven, and at the moment of death is granted a vision of God. Athanaël can only sing of his long-repressed desire for her physical beauty, renounce heaven, and passionately admit his love to her unhearing ears. The curtain falls on his agonized cry of 'Pitié!'

*

Sadly, *Thaïs* has never entirely been taken seriously, since it is one of Massenet's most successful and troubling works. An aura of spurious naughtiness has surrounded it ever since Sanderson's 'accident' at the première, up to Carol Neblett's appearance as the first full-frontally nude opera singer when she sang the title role in New Orleans in 1973. There are countless photographs of Andrée Esposito dressed as if for the Folies Bergère, or of Beverly Sills lounging seductively in an elaborate hammock with mirrors suspended above. Then there is the famous Méditation, submitted over the years to all manner of Palm Court indignities but in fact a marvellous example of self-generating, potentially endless melody and – as no less an authority than Ernest Newman has argued – not inappropriate to the dramatic context. Many, after all, are the *grandes horizontales* – Liane de Pougy, Hortense Schneider – who have found solace in sentimental religiosity after retirement. In the theatre, well played, its effect is extremely powerful even, or perhaps especially, with the optional offstage humming-chorus backing.

Sibyl Sanderson as Thaïs in Massenet's opera, the role she created at the Paris Opéra, 16 March 1894

Gallet's adaptation of Anatole France's anticlerical tirade is skilful. Obviously the discussion of religion at its centre defied operatic setting in 19th-century terms, but otherwise he does justice to the central situation of two characters whose spiritual journeys in opposite directions meet briefly before passing on – the prostitute finding God, the repressed monk being forced to recognize his true nature. The brief meeting of their spirits in the Oasis scene (3.i) is indeed the emotional centre of the work – it is hard to imagine the effect of the piece as a whole before Massenet added it for the 1897 revival. The only important thing missing from the adaptation is the pre-history of the principals. Athanaël's can be surmised on internal evidence: a well-to-do, educated young man who foreswore luxury and education and embraced monasticism. But from the novel we learn of Thaïs's slum childhood, her early Christian baptism, her equally early recourse (Lulu-like) to prostitution and her rise to the top of her profession. Her 'conversion', then, is no such thing; it is rather the classic Roman Catholic 'twitch of the thread', and in the light of that the central duet takes on considerable dramatic truth.

At the end of France's novel, the nuns mistake the deranged monk for a vampire preying on their dead sister and run screaming into the desert; the last words are: 'he had become so repulsive that, passing his hands over his face, he recognized his own repulsiveness'. That is also how Massenet originally ended the opera, but shortly before the première he substituted the simple, abrupt cry of 'Pitié!' That is symptomatic, because what he adds to the novel is compassion for its deluded coenobite, most notably at the moment of realization at the end of the Oasis scene. From the very start, the music reveals the truth behind Athanaël's stern moralistic posturing: as he piously recounts his narrow escape when as an adolescent he went to Thaïs's place of work, the interval of the 7th that tends to denote desire in the language of music is prominent. That conflict between words and notes is maintained throughout the writing for the baritone, especially in the rapture with which he greets Alexandria before remembering himself with a sour little woodwind chord and ritually cursing its luxury, beauty and learning.

The characterization of Thaïs through music suggests a figure far removed from the vamp traditionally represented on stage: there is a cool, calm, teasing confidence to her public persona in the first act; only when she is alone in the second are disillusion and panic at the approach of old age heard, and she is easy prey by the time Athanaël enters. In the third act her childlike simplicity and trust are all the more touching in that the audience has already inferred that the object of her trust is unworthy of it.

Massenet's musical painting reaches full maturity in *Thaïs*, from the open 5ths that portray the vastness of the desert through the coenobite community's chaste diatonic accompaniments and the chromaticism that obviously but effectively suggests the pleasures of the flesh to the carefree hedonistic melodies of Nicias and his companions. The cross-referencing of the thematic material achieves a new subtlety far transcending the bland reminiscences of the earlier works: the Méditation derives both from Athanaël's erotic visions and part of his hymn, which in turn is also derived at one remove from the visions; another vision-fragment is transformed into the lightly sensuous quartet when the slaves tease Athanaël while attempting to undress him, and it turns up in adapted form in Thaïs's Mirror aria. By the time the finale is reached, there is a web of interconnected motifs, chaste and erotic, that starts to match through the music the irony at the heart of France's novel, albeit in gentler, more compassionate form. The human truths contained in *Thaïs* have yet to be revealed either on stage or indeed on record; it is, in many ways, an opera still awaiting its first serious production.

R.M.

Tiefland ('The Lowlands')

Musikdrama in a prologue and two acts by Eugen d'Albert to a libretto by Rudolph Lothar [Rudolph Spitzer] after Angel Guimerá's Catalan drama *Terra baixa*; Prague, Neues Deutsches Theater, 15 November 1903.

Sebastiano *a rich landowner*		baritone
Marta		soprano
Pepa		soprano
Antonia	*in Sebastiano's employment*	soprano
Rosalia		contralto
Pedro *a shepherd*		tenor
Tommaso *the village elder*		bass
Moruccio *a miller*		baritone
Nuri *a little girl*		soprano
Nando *a shepherd*		tenor
Villagers and peasants		

Setting The Pyrenees and the Catalan Lowlands in the early 20th century

Tiefland was d'Albert's seventh opera; after the success of the Prague première, the work was quickly taken up in other major cities in Europe and America, reaching Berlin in 1907, Vienna in 1908 and the Metropolitan, New York, the same year, when the cast included Emmy Destinn as Marta and Erik Schmedes as Pedro. The London première, conducted by Sir Thomas Beecham, was on 5 October 1910, when the girl Nuri was sung by Maggie Teyte, who was making her Covent Garden début. *Tiefland* has remained in the repertory of opera houses in German-speaking countries, but receives only infrequent revivals elsewhere.

*

Prologue *Outside a shepherd's hut, high in the Pyrenees* Pedro greets Nando, another shepherd and the first person he has spoken to for six months. He claims to enjoy his solitary life, though sometimes he prays for a wife. Sebastiano, the local landowner, arrives, accompanied by Tommaso and Marta. He is about to make an advantageous marriage, and intends to give Marta, his mistress, to the unsuspecting Pedro as wife. They can run the mill together. Pedro is overjoyed, though Nando warns him that life in the lowlands is more complicated than the simple existence up in the mountains.

Act I *The main room inside the mill* Pepa, Antonia and Rosalia gossip and question Moruccio about Marta's impending marriage. Marta drives the women out, although she welcomes the child Nuri. Marta, in effect a slave owned by Sebastiano, expresses her misery and shame at being forced to marry a country bumpkin. Moruccio demands to know how Tommaso, the respected village elder, could have got involved in such a wicked arrangement. Cries of 'The bridegroom!' can be heard as Pedro arrives. While Pedro is getting dressed for the wedding, Sebastiano assures Marta that nothing will change between them as a result of her marriage; that evening, if she sees a light in her room, it means that he will be there, waiting for her. Pedro and the villagers come to fetch Marta and they all go off to the church. Tommaso accuses Sebastiano of dishonourable behaviour, but the latter denies it. The wedding procession can be heard returning and Marta and Pedro re-enter. She makes it quite clear to Pedro that he cannot sleep in her room. Upset and bewildered, Pedro offers Marta a wedding present, a silver thaler that he earned, as he explains in 'Wolfserzählung', for killing a wolf that had been preying on the sheep. Although she is touched by his generosity, Marta remains adamant. Suddenly Pedro notices a light in her room; he is about to investigate when it goes out. Marta denies having seen anything, but she agrees to spend the night on a chair in the main room, while Pedro lies down to sleep on the floor.

Act 2 *The same room in the mill, the following morning* Marta is awoken by Nuri's singing and goes to her room. Nuri wakes Pedro, who decides to leave, certain now that there was a man in Marta's room the previous night. When Nuri artlessly says she is sorry that everyone is laughing at him, Pedro at last understands the situation; he knows everything but the name of the man who has dishonoured him. He goes out with Nuri just as Marta, about to follow them, is stopped by Tommaso. Accused by the old man of involving him in the plot to trick Pedro, Marta tells him her story, 'Ich weiss nicht, wer mein Vater war'. She never knew her father; penniless, she and her mother begged for their living. They were joined by a cripple and after the death of her mother she remained with him, earning money by dancing in the street. One day, when she was 14, they came to this valley and she was noticed by Sebastiano. Installing the cripple as miller, he forced Marta to become his mistress. Now she would give anything to be free and worthy of Pedro, whose simplicity has won her heart.

The three women try to question Tommaso as he leaves, but he tells them nothing. When Pedro returns, he demands to know why they are laughing at him, but the women only laugh the more. Pedro, aware that he ought to kill Marta to save his honour but unwilling to hurt the woman he loves, prepares to leave. Marta tells him the wedding guests were laughing at him because they knew she had belonged to another man. Furiously Pedro seizes a knife and stabs her in the arm. Marta, in tears, begs him to kill her. Finally, avowing their mutual love, they plan to go together to the mountains. On Sebastiano's entry, Pedro tells him that he and Marta no longer want the

mill as they are leaving. Sebastiano takes no notice and orders Marta to dance; Pedro orders her to go with him. Realizing that it was Sebastiano in Marta's room the previous night, Pedro attacks the landowner. The villagers drag him away as Marta faints. Tommaso informs Sebastiano that his marriage has been called off; he has told the bride's father about his prospective son-in-law. Sebastiano and Marta quarrel violently and he is about to take her by force when Pedro comes back. There is a fight and Pedro strangles Sebastiano. Calling in the villagers to view the corpse, Pedro tells them that they can laugh now, if they like. Together with Marta he is leaving the hated lowlands to return to his beloved mountains.

*

The violent events of *Tiefland* inspired d'Albert to compose his most effective dramatic work, in which he used an Italian *verismo* idiom to achieve a near-perfect balance between content and style, a balance that he never quite achieved in his other operas. At the same time, the German element of his cultural heritage ensures that the characters and their motivation are drawn with unusual subtlety for a work written in the *verismo* tradition, while the underlying, linked themes of the opera, innocence and guilt (themes again tackled by d'Albert in *Die toten Augen*), are demonstrated to be opposite sides of the same coin.

Marta's complex personality, with the dawning realization that her only chance of happiness lies in the country bumpkin whom she dismissed so derisively at first, is most skilfully mirrored in her music. Though Pedro appears impossibly naive in the earlier scenes, he acquires compassion and understanding as his illusions are shattered one by one. The happy ending, so unlikely at first glance, becomes a genuine possibility as Pedro and Marta discover a new tolerance of each other's weaknesses. The least interesting of the three principals is undoubtedly Sebastiano, a cardboard villain who learns nothing from his experiences, but even he is described in music of an appropriately inflexible strength, while Tommaso, venerable in years but innocent, and the child Nuri, innocent but naturally wise, are sketched with respect and affection by the composer.   E.F.

Tosca

Melodramma in three acts by Giacomo Puccini to a libretto by Giuseppe Giacosa and Luigi Illica after Victorien Sardou's play *La Tosca*; Rome, Teatro Costanzi, 14 January 1900.

The first cast included Hariclea Darclée (Tosca), Emilio De Marchi (Cavaradossi) and Eugenio

'Tosca' (Puccini), scenes from the original production at the Teatro Costanzi, Rome, 14 January 1900, from 'L'illustrazione italiana' (28 January 1900): (top vignette) Act 3, Cavaradossi's execution; (lower left) Act 1, Tosca joins Cavaradossi in the church of S Andrea della Valle; (lower right) Act 2, Cavaradossi is interrogated by Scarpia in the Palazzo Farnese; (below) the final scene in Act 2, Tosca has placed candles beside the body of Scarpia

Giraldoni (Scarpia); the conductor was Leopoldo Mugnone.

Floria Tosca *a celebrated singer*		soprano
Mario Cavaradossi *a painter*		tenor
Baron Scarpia *Chief of Police*		baritone
Cesare Angelotti *former Consul of the*		
Roman republic		bass
A Sacristan		bass
Spoletta *a police agent*		tenor
Sciarrone *a gendarme*		bass
A Gaoler		bass
A Shepherd-boy		alto
Roberti *the executioner*		silent role

Soldiers, police agents, noblemen and women, townsfolk, artisans

Silent: cardinal, judge, scribe, officer, sergeant

Setting Rome, June 1800

Puccini owed his flair for discovering the operatic possibilities of plays to his early familiarity with a wide range of dramatic literature, and to the strong tradition of spoken drama in his birthplace of Lucca. In May 1889, less than a month after the première of *Edgar*, he wrote to the publisher Giulio Ricordi begging him to obtain Sardou's permission to set his play, 'since in this *Tosca* I see the opera that I need: one without excessive proportions or a decorative spectacle; nor is it the kind that calls for a super-abundance of music' – by which he meant that it did not conform to the genre of 'grand opera' which had been in vogue in Italy since the 1870s. For the time being matters went no further and Puccini turned his attention to other subjects. In 1895, however, he saw the play performed in Florence with Sarah Bernhardt (for whom it was written) in the title role. The following year, with *La bohème* behind him, he returned to his idea. Unfortunately Sardou had by now granted the rights to Alberto Franchetti, and Luigi Illica had already written him a libretto, to which Verdi had given his unqualified approval. However, Illica and Ricordi had no difficulty in persuading Franchetti, who was dissatisfied with it, to relinquish it and so leave the field open for their favourite composer. As usual the versification was entrusted to Giuseppe Giacosa, who to begin with was against the project. There was too much plot, he argued, and too little room for lyrical expansion, and, as so often, he continually threatened to withdraw from the partnership. However, by the beginning of 1898 Puccini had the entire libretto in his hands and was able to begin work on the first act. In June of that year he visited Sardou in Paris, who encumbered him with various suggestions ('a fine fellow', Puccini wrote, 'all life and fire and full of historico-topo-panoramic inexactitudes'). Sardou gave his blessing to the libretto, however; and Puccini himself considered it an improvement on the original play.

As always, Puccini was much concerned with authenticity of detail. His friend Father Pietro Panichelli supplied him with information regarding the plainsong melody to which the *Te Deum* was sung in Roman churches, the correct order of the cardinal's procession and the costumes of the Swiss Guard. From Meluzzi, an elderly musician in the employ of the Vatican, he learnt the exact pitch of the great bell of St Peter's; and he made a special journey to Rome to hear for himself the effect of the matins bells from the ramparts of the Castel Sant'Angelo. The Roman poet Luigi Zanazzo provided a suitable text for the song of the Shepherd-boy featured in the prelude to Act 3, the last piece to be composed. By the time the opera was completed in October 1899 two important changes had been made to the libretto. In Act 2 Puccini rejected an aria sung by Cavaradossi under torture which developed into a quartet with Tosca, the Judge and Spoletta, on the grounds that it reverted to the static *pezzo concertato* convention of a bygone age. Likewise he would have none of a 'Farewell to Art and Life' to be sung by the painter as he awaits execution, despite Verdi's avowed admiration for it. Instead he insisted on a lover's anguished lament built around the words 'Muoio disperato'. And, as usual, after much argument with his librettists, he had his way. More disturbing was a letter from Giulio Ricordi complaining of the lack of a transcendental love duet in Act 3 which should form the climax of the drama – doubtless he had in mind the concluding scene of Giordano's highly successful *Andrea Chénier* (1896). Ricordi found the existing dialogue between the lovers intolerably perfunctory, and he regretted the musical quotation from the original version of *Edgar* ('Where indeed is the Puccini of noble, warm and vigorous inspiration?'). The composer stood firm. Tosca, he maintained, would be far too preoccupied with the outcome of events to be able to indulge in a time-wasting effusion. In this, as so often, his theatrical instinct had not betrayed him.

Presumably it was the opera's Roman setting that led Ricordi to arrange the première in the Italian capital. The sets were by Adolfo Hohenstein, chief stage designer of La Scala, and the production was in the hands of Tito Ricordi, Giulio's son. Although the critical reception was mixed – several reviewers took exception to the brutality of the plot – the opera ran for 20 evenings to packed houses. Its success was confirmed two months later in Milan, at La Scala, where it was conducted by Arturo Toscanini with Giuseppe Borgatti as Cavaradossi and the other principals as at Rome. The first foreign performance was given at Buenos Aires in June the same year, followed on 12 July by the London première, at Covent Garden, with Milka Ternina as Tosca ('a true creation' according to Puccini), Fernando De Lucia as Cavaradossi and Antonio Scotti as Scarpia (a role in which he specialized until the end of his career 33 years later). He and Ternina appeared in the New York première (4 February 1901), together with Giuseppe Cremonini (Puccini's first Des Grieux) as Cavaradossi. Since then outstanding Toscas have included Geraldine Farrar, Maria Jeritza (who sang 'Vissi d'arte' lying prone), Maria Caniglia and, later, Maria Callas, whose performances with Tito Gobbi as Scarpia became legendary.

*

Act I *Interior of the church of S Andrea della Valle* The curtain rises to a progression of three chords, the last producing a violent tonal wrench (ex.1, a motif that connotes the villainous police chief Scarpia throughout the opera). The fugitive Angelotti hurries into the church, searches frantically for a key concealed in a shrine of the Madonna and slips into the private chapel of the Attavanti family. The Sacristan enters to a characteristic *buffo* motif. He carries a bundle of

Ex.1

paintbrushes which he proceeds grumblingly to wash. They belong to Cavaradossi, who arrives to put the finishing touches to his portrait of the Magdalen. He contemplates his canvas, in which he has succeeded in blending the dusky, southern charms of his beloved Tosca with the blonde beauty of an unknown woman whom he has often observed at prayer in the church ('Recondita armonia'). The aria is punctuated by asides from the Sacristan. The Sacristan leaves, whereupon Angelotti emerges from hiding; he is recognized by a shocked Cavaradossi, who hastily locks the church door. Angelotti explains that he has just escaped from the Castel Sant'Angelo, where he had been imprisoned by order of Scarpia.

Their conversation is interrupted by the sound of Tosca's voice outside the church. Angelotti again retreats into the chapel, while Cavaradossi admits the singer, who enters in a mood of jealous suspicion – she is sure she heard voices – though her accompanying music conveys a dignified and beautiful presence. Reassured with some difficulty by Cavaradossi, she suggests that they should go to his villa in the country after her evening performance. Cavaradossi, his mind on Angelotti, responds absently. Tosca is further disturbed by the painting, with its resemblance to someone other than herself – the Marchesa Attavanti. For the moment she accepts the painter's explanation and joins him in a tender love duet whose principal theme, occurring at the words 'Mia gelosa', functions as the motif for their mutual passion. Their dialogue is not set as a conventional duet until, at the words 'Qual'occhio al mondo', a typically long-arched Puccini melody leads to a brief unison passage (four bars), but dissolves once more into conversation as Tosca leaves, to a delicate wind and harp accompaniment.

Cavaradossi and Angelotti now plot the latter's escape. After dark he must make for Cavaradossi's villa in female disguise and in the event of danger hide in a well in the garden. A cannon shot from the Castel Sant'Angelo warns that Angelotti's flight has been discovered. At the same time the Sacristan re-enters with the news (false, as it turns out) of Napoleon's defeat at Marengo. The church fills with a joyous throng. At the height of the tumult Scarpia himself appears with Spoletta and other police agents. He rebukes the crowd for desecrating the atmosphere of a church and orders the Sacristan to make ready for a *Te Deum* in honour of the victory. Meanwhile he orders his men to look for clues to Angelotti's presence, which are soon found: a key, a basket empty of provisions which Cavaradossi, the Sacristan tells him, had left untouched; and a fan belonging to the Marchesa Attavanti, Angelotti's sister. When Tosca returns, Scarpia uses the fan to arouse her jealousy, always easily excited. To a recollection of the love-duet she hurries away in tears to the villa to surprise, as she thinks, the guilty pair. Scarpia gives orders for her to be followed, and in a monologue, over a characteristically obsessive pattern of alternating chords, accompanied by bells, organ, drum-beats to simulate cannon-fire and again the growling bassoons, gloats at the prospect of capturing the fugitive and enjoying the prima donna's favours; as the *Te Deum* swells to a climax he exclaims, 'Tosca, you make me forget God!'

Act 2 *Scarpia's apartment in the Palazzo Farnese* Scarpia is dining alone, while below at an entertainment given by Queen Caroline a gavotte is being danced. Spoletta enters to report on his fruitless search of Cavaradossi's villa for traces of Angelotti. Scarpia's fury is mollified when he hears that his men have arrested Cavaradossi himself and brought him to the palace. During the singing of a cantata in the Queen's honour, led by Tosca, Scarpia interrogates the painter in the presence of the executioner, Roberti, and a judge of the criminal court. The choir, with Tosca's voice rising above it, provides an occasionally dissonant, tense background to Scarpia's opening interrogation, accompanied only by low strings and woodwind. As the cantata finishes Scarpia becomes more insistent, then, at Tosca's entrance, sings 'con forza e sostenuto', 'Mario Cavaradossi, the Judge awaits your testimony'. Cavaradossi denies all knowledge of Angelotti, at which Scarpia gives orders for him to be tortured in an adjoining room. Tosca also refuses to reveal Angelotti's whereabouts until, overcome by Cavaradossi's groans, she mentions the well in the garden. Scarpia suspends the torture. Apprised of her betrayal Cavaradossi curses her for her weakness. Sciarrone comes in with the news that the Battle of Marengo had in fact been won by Napoleon.

Cavaradossi breaks out in a paean to liberty, for which Scarpia has him again put under arrest and marched to prison to be shot at dawn. He then promises to have the painter set free on condition that Tosca yield to his embraces. This prompts from Tosca the aria 'Vissi d'arte', into which Puccini weaves the motif that accompanied her first appearance. Spoletta enters and announces that Angelotti has killed himself. Since Tosca has accepted his terms, Scarpia bids Spoletta set up a mock-execution, carefully specifying 'as in the case of Palmieri'. Tosca insists that he write her and Cavaradossi a safe-conduct. While he does so she catches sight of a knife lying to hand. A sinister motif indicates the thought going through her mind. No sooner has Scarpia finished writing than she stabs him and as he expires the 'knife' theme is played on full strings. Before leaving with the safe-conduct she places candles at his head and feet and a crucifix on his breast in conformity with her religious upbringing, and sings on a repeated middle C (although the words are often spoken instead) 'E avanti a lui tremava tutta Roma!' ('And before him all Rome trembled!').

Act 3 *A platform in the Castel Sant'Angelo* A prelude evokes the breaking of dawn. A Shepherd-boy is heard singing as he drives his flock. The sound of sheep-bells gives way to the mingled chimes of matins. Cavaradossi enters accompanied by the melody of the aria he will sing, heard here for the first time, 'con molta anima', on the strings. To a reminiscence of the Act 1 love-duet played on solo cellos Cavaradossi asks for pen and paper with which to write a farewell letter to Tosca. His anguish at leaving her for ever is expressed in the aria 'E lucevan le stelle', a recollection of past bliss before the final darkness, with a mournful clarinet taking the main line before he sings it at the words 'O dolci baci, languide carezze'. Spoletta arrives with Tosca, then retires. Tosca produces the safe-conduct and explains to a suspicious Cavaradossi how she obtained it and how she repaid the giver. Cavaradossi is astonished and delighted. Their tender exchanges are continually overshadowed by Tosca's concern for her lover – will he be able to act his part convincingly during the mock-execution? But when the firing squad arrives he plays his part all too well, for the rifles are loaded, and Tosca finds herself addressing his lifeless body. Meanwhile the news of Scarpia's murder has broken. Spoletta, Sciarrone and the other agents are heard calling for Tosca's blood. She climbs on to the battlements and, crying that she and Scarpia will meet before God, she leaps to her death, to an orchestral peroration of Cavaradossi's 'E lucevan le stelle'.

*

None of Puccini's operas has aroused more hostility than *Tosca*, by reason of its alleged coarseness and brutality (the musicologist Joseph Kerman referred to it, notoriously, as a 'shabby little shocker'); yet its position in the central repertory has remained unchallenged. Not only is it theatrically gripping from start to finish: it presents the composer's most varied and interesting soprano role, hence its perennial appeal for the great operatic actress. In contrast to Sardou's heroine, against whose ignorance and simplicity the playwright can never resist tilting, Puccini's Tosca is a credible woman of the theatre, lacking neither intelligence nor humour, and capable of genuine dignity. Nowhere is she more moving than in Act 3, in which she imagines herself to be in command of the situation and that all she has to do is to teach Cavaradossi how to act. All the more heart-rending is her discovery of the truth.

Tosca is the most Wagnerian of Puccini's scores in its use of motifs, every one of which refers to a single object, person or idea, though none of them is developed or modified. But, like Wagner, he sometimes used them to give us information about a character's unexpressed thoughts. An instance of this occurs in Act 1 where Tosca asks Cavaradossi to meet her that evening. 'This evening?', he queries in alarm, and the orchestra plays a snatch of the motif associated with Angelotti. Likewise Scarpia's interrogation of the painter is punctuated by a motif connoting the well, which Cavaradossi refuses to mention, but of which he is obviously thinking. The only weakness in the drama is Puccini's inept handling of the political element; but issues of this kind held no interest for the composer of *La bohème*, *Tosca* and *Madama Butterfly*.   J.B.

Traviata, La ('The Fallen Woman')

Opera in three acts by Giuseppe Verdi to a libretto by Francesco Maria Piave after Alexandre Dumas *fils'* play *La dame aux camélias*; Venice, Teatro La Fenice, 6 March 1853.

The première cast included Fanny Salvini-Donatelli as Violetta, Ludovico Graziani as Alfredo and Felice Varesi as Giorgio Germont.

Violetta Valéry *a courtesan*	soprano
Flora Bervoix *her friend*	mezzo-soprano
Annina *Violetta's maid*	soprano
Alfredo Germont	tenor
Giorgio Germont *his father*	baritone
Gastone, Vicomte de Letorières *friend of Alfredo*	tenor
Baron Douphol *Violetta's protector*	baritone
Marchese D'Obigny *friend of Flora*	bass
Doctor Grenvil	bass
Giuseppe *Violetta's servant*	tenor
Flora's Servant	bass
Commissioner	bass

Ladies and gentlemen, friends of Violetta and Flora, matadors, picadors, gypsies, servants of Violetta and Flora, masks

Setting In and around Paris, about 1700

By April 1852 Verdi had agreed to write a new opera for the Carnival 1853 season at the Teatro La Fenice in Venice, with Francesco Maria Piave as librettist. But even as late as October no subject had been decided upon: the unusually tight schedule was due in part to Verdi's continuing work on *Il trovatore*, whose première in Rome eventually took place less than two months before that of *La traviata*. By the beginning of November, however, Verdi and Piave had elected to base their opera on Dumas *fils'* play, which had first been performed in Paris earlier that year. The working title of the opera, later changed at the insistence of the Venetian censors, was *Amore e morte* ('Love and Death'). As Verdi wrote to his friend Cesare De Sanctis on 1 January 1853, it was 'a subject of the times. Others would not have done it because of the conventions, the epoch and for a thousand other stupid scruples'. The composer even proposed that, contrary to custom, the opera should be performed in modern costume; but again the Venetian authorities would not agree, and the period was put back to the beginning of the 18th century.

La traviata, it seems, was written in something like record time. Even though the above-quoted letter to De Sanctis dates from just over two months before the première, it is primarily concerned with compositional problems surrounding the still unfinished *Trovatore*; it is clear that *La traviata* was largely unwritten at the time. Its première was the most celebrated fiasco of Verdi's later career, a circumstance probably attributable more to the singers – Salvini-Donatelli was physically unsuited to Violetta and Varesi was too far past his prime to tackle such an exposed role – than to problems the audience may have had with the musical style. Verdi was reluctant to allow further performances until he could find a more suitable cast, but eventually allowed a second staging (on 6 May 1854) at the Teatro S Benedetto, Venice, making various alterations to the score, the most important of which were to the central Act 2 duet between Violetta and Germont. This time success was unequivocal, and the opera soon became one of the composer's most popular works. It has retained this position into modern times, in spite of the fact that the heroine's role is one of the most feared in the soprano repertory.

*

The prelude to *La traviata* is a curious narrative experiment: it paints a three-stage portrait of the heroine, but in reverse chronological order. First comes a musical rendering of her final decline in Act 3, with high, chromatic strings dissolving into 'sobbing' appoggiaturas; then a direct statement of love, the melody that will in Act 2 become 'Amami, Alfredo'; and finally this same melody repeated on the lower strings, surrounded by the delicate ornamentation associated with Violetta in Act 1.

Act I *A salon in Violetta's house* It is August. In a festive atmosphere, the action underpinned by a sequence of lively orchestral dances, Violetta and friends greet their guests, among whom is Alfredo Germont, a young man who has loved Violetta from afar for some time. Eventually all sit down to supper and Violetta calls for a toast. Alfredo takes up the cup to sing the famous brindisi 'Libiamo ne' lieti calici', a simple, bouncing melody repeated by Violetta and finally (with judicious transposition) by the entire chorus. A band in an adjoining room now starts up a succession of waltzes and the guests prepare to dance; but Violetta feels unsteady (the symptoms suggest she is consumptive) and begs the others to go on without her. Alfredo remains behind and, with the dance music still sounding, warns Violetta that her way of life will kill her if she persists. He offers to protect her and admits his love in the first movement of the duet: 'Un dì felice, eterea' begins hesitantly but builds to the passionate outpouring of 'Di quell'amor ch'è palpito', a melody that will reappear later as a kind of emblem of Alfredo's devoted love. Violetta answers with an attempt to defuse the situation, telling him he will soon forget her, and surrounding his passionately insistent melody with showers of vocal ornamentation. The dance music (which unobtrusively disappeared during the duet) now returns as Violetta playfully gives Alfredo a flower, telling him to return when it has faded. To round off the scene the returning guests, seeing dawn approaching, prepare to leave in the concluding stretta, 'Si ridesta in ciel l'aurora'.

Left alone, Violetta closes the act with a formal double aria. She muses fondly of her new conquest in the Andantino 'Ah fors'è lui', which – like Alfredo's declaration – begins hesitantly but then flowers into 'Di quell'amor'. This sequence is then repeated before Violetta violently shrugs off her sentimental thoughts and resolves that a life of pleasure is her only choice. She closes the act with the cabaletta 'Sempre libera degg'io', full of daring, almost desperate coloratura effects. But in the closing stages her melody is mixed with 'Di quell'amor', sung by Alfredo from below the balcony.

Act 2.i *A country house near Paris* It is the following January; three months have passed since Violetta and Alfredo set up house together in the country. Alfredo sings of his youthful ardour in 'Dei miei bollenti spiriti', an unusually condensed Andante with no repetition of the initial melodic phrase. Annina then hurries in to inform Alfredo that Violetta has been selling her belongings to finance their country life together. Alfredo immediately decides to raise money himself and rushes off to Paris after expressing his remorse in the conventionally structured cabaletta 'Oh mio rimorso!' (often cut in modern performances).

Violetta appears and is joined by a visitor who turns out to be Giorgio Germont. Their ensuing grand duet is unusually long; typically for Verdi, the formal expansion is concentrated on the opening section of the conventional four-movement structure. After an initial passage of recitative this first movement involves three main subsections: a kind of lyrical dialogue between the principals. First comes an Allegro moderato ('Pura siccome un angelo') in which Germont describes the plight of his daughter, whose forthcoming marriage is threatened by Alfredo's scandalous relationship with Violetta. After a brief transition Violetta reveals the seriousness of her illness and protests that Alfredo is all she has in the world (the breathless 'Non sapete quale affetto'). But Germont is adamant and in 'Bella voi siete, e giovane' assures Violetta that she will find others to love. Eventually Violetta capitulates: the second movement of the duet, 'Dite alla giovine', begins with her heartbroken agreement to leave Alfredo, and gives ample opportunity for the voices to interweave. The final two movements are relatively brief and conventional: Violetta agrees to break the news to Alfredo in her own way, begging Germont to remain to comfort his son; and then in the cabaletta 'Morrò! la mia memoria' she asks Germont to tell Alfredo the truth after her death.

As Germont retires, Violetta begins to write a letter to Alfredo, but cannot finish before her lover appears. He is disturbed by her agitation, but she answers his questions with a simple, passionate declaration of love, 'Amami, Alfredo' (the melody that served as the basis for the opera's prelude) before rushing out. The remainder of the scene might well, of course, focus on Alfredo, but operatic convention requires a formal double aria for the baritone (who has no other opportunity for an extended solo), so Alfredo's reactions are sandwiched into the transition passages. Soon after Violetta has left, a servant brings Alfredo her letter saying that she must leave him forever, and his anguished reaction is immediately countered by Germont's lyrical Andante, 'Di Provenza il mar, il suol', which conjures up a nostalgic picture of their family home. But Alfredo will not be consoled and at the end of Germont's cabaletta, 'No, non udrai rimproveri', his anger boils over: knowing that she has received an invitation to a party in Paris, he assumes that Violetta has deserted him to return to her old friends.

2.ii *A salon in Flora's town house* A boisterous orchestral opening, over which Flora and her new lover discuss the separation of Violetta and Alfredo, is followed by a two-part *divertissement* as a chorus of gypsies (with more than an echo of the musical world of *Il trovatore*) and then of matadors dance and sing. Alfredo enters and, to an obsessively repeated motif on the lower strings and wind, begins playing recklessly at cards, apparently uncaring when Violetta appears on the arm of Baron Douphol. As

'La traviata' (Verdi): design by Giuseppe and Pietro Bertoja for the second production, at the Teatro S Benedetto, Venice, in 1854

Alfredo and the Baron bet against each other with barely concealed hostility, Violetta repeatedly laments her position in an anguished rising line. Supper is served, and Violetta manages to see Alfredo privately. In answer to his accusations she desperately claims that she now loves the Baron, at which Alfredo calls the guests together and, in a declamatory passage of rising fury, denounces Violetta and throws his winnings in her face as 'payment' for their time together. This precipitates the concertato, which begins with a rapid passage of choral outrage before Germont, who has just arrived, leads off the main Largo. This large-scale movement depicts the contrasting moods of the main characters: Germont reproachful and lyrically contained; Alfredo upset and remorseful with a fragmentary line; and Violetta, privately begging Alfredo to understand her distress with a line which eventually dominates through its simplicity and emotive power. Such is the charge of the movement that the act can end there, without the conventional concluding stretta.

Act 3 *Violetta's bedroom* It is February. The orchestral prelude opens with the idea that began the entire opera, and then develops into an intense solo for the first violins, full of 'sobbing' appoggiaturas. In the spare recitative that follows we learn from a doctor that Violetta is near death. To a restrained orchestral reprise of 'Di quell'amor', Violetta reads a letter from Germont, telling her that Alfredo (who fled abroad after fighting a duel with the Baron) now knows the truth about her sacrifice and is hurrying back to her. But she knows that time is short, and in the aria 'Addio, del passato' bids farewell to the past and to life, the oboe solo adding poignancy to her painfully restricted vocal line. A chorus of revellers

heard outside underlines the gloom of Violetta's isolation, but then, to a sustained orchestral crescendo, Alfredo is announced and arrives to throw himself into Violetta's arms. After the initial greeting Alfredo leads off the Andante movement of the duet, 'Parigi, o cara': a simple waltz-time melody reminiscent of Act 1, in which the lovers look forward to a life together away from Paris. It is significant, though, that Violetta's attempts at Act 1-style ornamentation are now severely restricted in range. Violetta decides that she and Alfredo should go to church to celebrate his return, but the strain even of getting to her feet is too much and she repeatedly falls back. This painful realization of her weakness precipitates the cabaletta 'Gran Dio! morir sì giovane', in which Violetta gives way to a despair that Alfredo can do little to assuage. Germont appears, and a brief but passionate exchange between him and Violetta leads to the final concertato, 'Prendi: quest'è l'immagine', in which Violetta gives Alfredo a locket with her portrait, telling him that, should he marry, he can give it to his bride. The movement begins with an insistent full-orchestra rhythmic figure, similar to that used in the 'Miserere' scene of *Il trovatore* and clearly associated with Violetta's imminent death; later, Violetta develops the simple, intense vocal style that has characterized her in this act. A last orchestral reprise of 'Di quell'amor' sounds as the final blow approaches. Violetta feels a sudden rush of life, sings a final 'Oh gioia!', but then collapses dead on to a sofa.

*

As we have seen, *La traviata* was written in great haste and its genesis was thoroughly entangled with the creation of Verdi's previous opera, *Il trovatore*. Perhaps not surprisingly, there is a series of startling musical resemblances between the two operas. But these similarities are on what one might call the musical surface; in dramatic structure and general atmosphere the two works are remarkably different, in some senses even antithetical. *La traviata* is above all a chamber opera: in spite of the 'public' scenes of the first and second acts, it succeeds best in an intimate setting, where there can be maximum concentration on those key moments in which the heroine's attitude to her surroundings is forced to change. Perhaps for this reason, the cabalettas, those 'public' moments which are so inevitable and essential to the mood of *Il trovatore*, tend to sit uneasily; we remember *La traviata* above all for its moments of lyrical introspection.

It is nevertheless easy to see why *La traviata* is among the best loved of Verdi's operas, perhaps even *the* best loved. In many senses it is the composer's most 'realistic' drama. The cultural ambience of the subject matter and the musical expression are very closely related: no suspension of disbelief is required to feel that the waltz tunes that saturate the score are naturally born out of the Parisian setting. And, perhaps most important, this sense of 'authenticity' extends to the heroine, a character whose psychological progress through the opera is mirrored by her changing vocal character: from the exuberant ornamentation of Act 1, to the passionate declamation of Act 2, to the final, well-nigh ethereal qualities she shows in Act 3. Violetta – Stiffelio, Rigoletto and Gilda notwithstanding – is Verdi's most complete musical personality to date.   R.P.

Tristan und Isolde ('Tristan and Isolde')

Handlung (drama) in three acts by Richard Wagner to his own libretto; Munich, Königliches Hof- und Nationaltheater, 10 June 1865.

The conductor at the première was Hans von Bülow; Isolde was sung by Malvina Schnorr von Carolsfeld, and Tristan by her husband, Ludwig Schnorr von Carolsfeld, who died only three weeks after the final performance. The cast also included Anna Deinet (Brangäne), Ludwig Zottmayr (King Mark) and Anton Mitterwurzer (Kurwenal).

Tristan	tenor
König Marke [King Mark]	bass
Isolde	soprano
Kurwenal *Tristan's servant*	baritone
Melot *a courtier*	tenor
Brangäne *Isolde's maid*	soprano
A Shepherd	tenor
A Steersman	baritone
A Young Sailor	tenor
Sailors, knights and esquires	
Setting At sea, in Cornwall and Brittany during the Middle Ages	

The ancient Tristan legend, probably of Celtic origin, achieved its first literary form in the 12th century. The version used by Wagner as the basis for his drama was that of Gottfried von Strassburg (*fl* 1200–20). Wagner conceived the idea of writing an opera on the Tristan subject in the autumn of 1854, but the earliest dated surviving sketch (an elaboration of two fragments) is from 19 December 1856, at which point he was still engaged on Act 1 of *Siegfried*. The work celebrates and idealizes the love affair – probably never consummated – between Wagner and Mathilde Wesendonck, the wife of his patron.

Wagner began his prose scenario the following summer, on 20 August 1857, and the poem was completed on 18 September. Like *Siegfried* – but unlike all the other music dramas – each act was drafted and elaborated, in sequence, the full score

being reached before the next act was embarked on in sketch. Indeed, because the publishers were eager to have the new work ready for public consumption, the score was actually engraved one act at a time. The fair copy of the full score of Act 1 was completed on 3 April 1858 in Zürich, of Act 2 on 18 March 1859 in Venice, and of Act 3 on 6 August 1859 in Lucerne.

Epoch-making as *Tristan* proved to be, the work had some notable antecedents. There are frequent pre-echoes in the sultry chromaticism of Spohr's *Jessonda*, while the rising chromatic phrase that characterizes the opening of *Tristan* is prominent in Liszt's song *Die Lorelei*. The celebrated 'Tristan chord' (see ex.1) is presaged (though never given in that precise form) in the Liszt song, as well as by earlier composers as various as Mozart, Spohr and Gottschalk. Berlioz's *Roméo et Juliette*, of which Wagner was a staunch admirer, contains a number of melodic inspirations that found their way into *Tristan*, in particular a theme which was developed into that of the so-called Liebestod; the sighing chromatic phrases and general atmosphere of the 'Scène d'amour' from *Roméo et Juliette* foreshadow the love scene in Act 2 of *Tristan*. A further remarkable antecedent of *Tristan* is Hans von Bülow's orchestral fantasy *Nirwana*, the score of which Wagner was studying at precisely the time of his conception of *Tristan* (autumn 1854). When he came to compose the opera three years later, he took over from *Nirwana* (possibly unconsciously) several ideas, both general and specific. *Nirwana* provides not only another, more immediate, source for the rising chromatic phrase that opens *Tristan*, but also a parallel sublimation of it at the close.

The prelude to *Tristan* (with Wagner's own concert ending) was included in a series of three concerts in Paris early in 1860, intended to pave the way for a possible performance of the opera in France by German singers. That scheme came to nothing, as did plans to produce the work in Karlsruhe and Vienna. Providentially, the young King Ludwig II of Bavaria came to Wagner's aid, embracing his work with almost febrile passion, and his support enabled the production to go ahead. The day eventually fixed for performance in Munich, 15 May 1865, was the day chosen by Wagner's creditors to send in the bailiffs; in the afternoon Schnorr lost her voice. The long-delayed première finally took place on 10 June, with three subsequent performances. Uncomprehending hostility in some quarters was matched by unbridled enthusiasm in others; the work was to exert an extraordinary influence over future generations.

Felix Mottl conducted the first performance at Bayreuth in 1886, which was also the year of the first production in the USA (Seidl conducting at the Metropolitan, with Niemann and Lilli Lehmann). The first production in England was at the Theatre

'Tristan und Isolde' (Wagner): model of Angelo Quaglio (ii)'s design for Act 1 (the deck of Tristan's ship) of the original production at the Königliches Hof- und Nationaltheater, Munich, 10 June 1865

Royal, Drury Lane, in 1882. Notable exponents of the role of Tristan have included Jean De Reszke, Lauritz Melchior, Max Lorenz, Set Svanholm, Ludwig Suthaus, Ramón Vinay, Wolfgang Windgassen, Jon Vickers, Peter Hofmann and Siegfried Jerusalem. Isolde has been sung by Lillian Nordica, Olive Fremstad, Eva Turner, Frida Leider, Germaine Lubin, Kirsten Flagstad, Astrid Varnay, Martha Mödl, Birgit Nilsson, Catarina Ligendza, Gwyneth Jones, Hildegard Behrens and Waltraud Meier. Notable conductors of the work, in addition to Mottl and Seidl, have included Mahler, Arthur Nikisch, Bruno Walter, Thomas Beecham, Albert Coates, Erich Kleiber, Wilhelm Furtwängler, Karl Böhm, Rudolf Kempe, Georg Solti, Herbert von Karajan, Reginald Goodall, Carlos Kleiber and Daniel Barenboim.

*

The titles of Prelude and Liebestod for the opening and closing sections of the work are firmly established by tradition, though Wagner referred to them as respectively Liebestod and [Isolde's] Transfiguration. The prelude introduces several of the work's principal motifs. The descending chromatic phrase that begins it (ex.lx) is typical in that, although it has been given such labels as 'Tristan', 'Tristan's suffering', 'grief' and 'the confession', it ultimately defies categorization. Its inversion, the rising four-note phrase with which it is combined (ex.ly), is ubiquitous in *Tristan* and a potent musical image of the work's preoccupation with yearning. The chord occurring at their conjunction in bar 2 is known as the 'Tristan' chord; it returns at various points of significance in the drama.

Ex.1

Act I *At sea, on the deck of Tristan's ship, during the crossing from Ireland to Cornwall* The curtain rises to reveal a construction like a tent on the foredeck of a ship (scene i); Isolde is seen on a couch, her face buried in the cushions. A young sailor sings, 'as if from the masthead', an unaccompanied song about the Irish lover he has left behind in the west ('Westwärts schweift der Blick'). Isolde, who is being brought from Ireland to Cornwall by Tristan to be the bride of his uncle, King Mark, starts up, assuming that the reference to an 'Irish maid' is an insult to her. When her maid and confidante Brangäne tells her that they are soon to land in Cornwall, Isolde launches into a furious outburst against her own 'degenerate race' who have succumbed so easily to the enemy. Brangäne attempts in vain to calm her.

For the second scene the whole length of the ship becomes visible; in the stern stands Tristan, thoughtfully, with folded arms, his faithful retainer Kurwenal reclining at his feet. The young sailor strikes up again, this time accompanied by a tremolando in the bass. Her eyes fixed on Tristan, Isolde sings the enigmatic words 'Mir erkoren, mir verloren' ('Chosen to be mine, lost to me') to motif ex.1*y*, followed by 'Todgeweihtes Haupt! Todgeweihtes Herz!' ('Death-devoted head! Death-devoted heart!') to a chord change from A♭ to A major, the poignant effect of which is enhanced by the switch from woodwind to brass (ex.2), a switch repeated on subsequent occurrences of the motif.

Mark to collect her as bride, and (*x*) undergoes an angry metamorphosis as she curses Tristan.

Brangäne's response makes much use of a tender appoggiatura figure – derived from (*y*); after another gnomic utterance from Isolde, Brangäne switches to triple time in an even more lyrical attempt to console her mistress. The opening bars of the prelude are recalled as Brangäne reminds Isolde of her mother's magic potions. But Isolde has only vengeance in mind (ex.2 intervenes) and she selects the draught of death, at which point the tension suddenly rises as the sailors are heard again, preparing to land.

Kurwenal boisterously calls the ladies to make ready (scene iv), but Isolde insists on speaking to Tristan before they land, in order to 'forgive' him. Her excited farewells to Brangäne, however, and the death-portending motif (ex.3) in the bass (heard previously when she selected the draught) betoken

['Death-devoted head! Death-devoted heart!']

her real intention. Brangäne's pleas are in vain, as is confirmed by the close succession of exx.3 and 2.

Tristan's approach is awaited (scene v) with a striking instrumental passage consisting of a new idea (ex.4) answered by a series of *martellato* chords

Isolde tells Brangäne to instruct Tristan to attend on her. Brangäne's timid request to Tristan is courteously turned aside by him, but when she repeats Isolde's command – to the same imperious chord sequence as her mistress used – Kurwenal makes his own bluntly negative reply, in the firmly diatonic idiom that is to characterize him. He goes on to revel in the slaying by Tristan of Morold, Isolde's betrothed, who came from Ireland to exact tribute from Cornwall. The mockery of Kurwenal's song is reinforced by its self-contained, ballad-like nature; its refrain is picked up by the sailors. Brangäne returns in confusion to Isolde who is barely able to control her anger (scene iii). With both (*x*) and (*y*) of ex.1 repeatedly in attendance, Isolde's Narration tells how the wounded Tristan, disguised as 'Tantris', came to her to be healed and how she recognized him as Morold's killer: 'Wie lachend sie mir Lieder singen'. Isolde's determination to slay Tristan in revenge dissolved as he looked pitifully into her eyes – (*y*) is meltingly transformed here – but now she bitterly regrets that she let the sword drop. With heavy irony she mimics Tristan's 'insulting' offer to

on full strings; this theme has been variously labelled 'Tristan's honour', 'Morold' and 'Isolde's anger' – an indication of the flexibility Wagner allowed himself in the deployment of motifs in *Tristan*. The ominous ex.3 is heard as Tristan approaches. Isolde tells him that she saw through his disguise as 'Tantris' and demands vengeance (exx.2 and 4). Tristan offers her his sword, but Isolde signals to Brangäne for the potion, ex.3 and the offstage sailors' cries again raising the tension. After more ironic mimicry, Isolde hands Tristan the cup (exx.4 and then 2 are prominent). Tristan lifts the cup and drinks. Fearing further betrayal, Isolde wrests it from him and drinks in her turn: Brangäne, in desperation, has substituted the love for the death potion. The climactic chord, played by the full orchestra, is the 'Tristan chord'. (Its association with betrayal, as the obverse of faithful love, resonates beyond *Tristan*, occurring at Brünnhilde's discovery of her betrayal by Siegfried (see **Götterdämmerung**, Act I.iii); in *Parsifal* the ambivalent properties of the chord are exploited by its dual association with temptation and redemption. After they have both drunk, they are seized with a succession of conflicting emotions, all portrayed in the music: rapt wonderment by the prolongation of the 'Tristan chord', agitation by tremolando cellos with muffled drum roll, breathless frenzy by a brief, snatched phrase on unison winds and strings, and finally yearning for each other by the music from the beginning of the prelude. Tristan and Isolde embrace ecstatically, offstage salutations to King Mark again raising the emotional temperature, while Brangäne looks on in horror. The lovers express their passion, first in alternating fragments of phrases, then, in defiance of Wagner's earlier theoretical principles, in conjunction. Only half jolted back to reality by Kurwenal's innocent breeziness and by the jubilant shouts of the onlookers, Tristan and Isolde struggle to comprehend what has happened to them. The act comes to an exhilarating end with the impassioned rising chromatic motif, ex.1y, threading its way through exultant brass fanfares.

Act 2   *In Mark's royal castle in Cornwall*   The orchestral introduction to Act 2 introduces several new principal motifs: exx.5, 6 and 7, each of which

Ex.5

Ex.6

Ex.7

resists definitive categorization, though ex.5 is generally associated in the ensuing act with 'day' (in Schopenhauer's terms the outer material world of phenomena, as opposed to the noumenal sphere of inner consciousness represented by 'night'). Ex.1y also assumes a more urgent form: the lovers' yearning has intensified. The curtain rises to reveal a garden with high trees; Isolde's chamber is to one side and a burning torch stands at the open door. A volley of horn calls gradually receding into the distance signifies the departing hunt of King Mark and his courtiers. The cautious Brangäne warns her mistress that the horns are still audible, but all Isolde can hear are the sounds of the balmy summer night: the horn calls are transmuted into a shimmering orchestral texture by clarinets, second violins and violas, a sweet sound to the lovers ('Nicht Hörnerschall tönt so hold').

Brangäne further warns Isolde that in her impatience to see Tristan she should not be oblivious to the devious Melot, Tristan's supposed friend, who, she alleges, has arranged the nocturnal hunt as a trap. Isolde brushes these fears aside and requests

Brangäne to extinguish the torch: the signal for Tristan to approach. Brangäne demurs, bewailing her fateful switching of the potions. Over glowing orchestral colours, Isolde extols the powers of the love goddess, Frau Minne, which are then celebrated in a new theme (ex.8), the second bar of which includes the shape characteristic of Wagner's main love themes (cf *Walküre, Die*, Act 1). This new theme is

Ex.8

developed sequentially, its ever-intensifying repetitions finally finding release in Isolde's expansive phrase 'dass hell sie dorten leuchte', before her extinguishing of the torch; the climactic power of that phrase is enhanced by the sudden cessation of rhythmic and harmonic motion.

Isolde throws the torch to the ground and, sending Brangäne to keep watch, waits impatiently for Tristan. Her agitated expectation is depicted by ex.6 (with a breathlessly syncopated accompanimental figure); together with another brief figure, that motif is subjected to remorseless sequential repetition, building to a frenzied climax as Tristan finally bursts in (scene ii). They greet each other ecstatically; a breathless exchange follows, in which each brief, snatched phrase (both musical and textual) of Isolde is impetuously appropriated by Tristan: 'Bist du mein?/Hab' ich dich wieder?' After further rapturous effusions, their minds turn to the long-delayed extinction of the torch, a train of thought which soon enters the metaphysical realm of the night–day, noumenon–phenomenon polarity. (An extensive cut (324 bars) is often made at this point, from 'bot ich dem Tage Trutz!' to 'wahr es zu sehen tauge'.) Ex.5, the motif associated with 'day', is prominent here, but most of the others already cited also appear in one form or another.

Tristan draws Isolde to a flowery bank for their central love duet: 'O sink hernieder, Nacht der Liebe', approached by a masterly transition passage that effects a gradual reduction in tension by dynamic, harmonic and rhythmic means. The tonality of A♭ gradually establishes itself out of the tonal flux of the preceding duet, but the transition to some extent disguises the fact that 'O sink hernieder' has aspects of the traditional operatic duet, the singers sharing phrases of music and text.

An interlude is provided by Brangäne's Watchsong from the tower: 'Einsam wachend in der Nacht'. Ravishingly scored, this passage also exemplifies a trait new in *Tristan*: syllables of the text become so distended that the vocal line is treated as an instrument rather than as the carrier of semantic meaning. The exquisitely prolonged cadence of

Brangäne's Watchsong resolves on to ex.9 (an elaboration of an earlier idea) on hushed strings

Ex.9

alone, for Isolde's 'Lausch, Geliebter!' This is much developed, leading to a new melodic idea (ex.l0),

Ex.10

So   stür - ben   wir, um   un   -   ge - trennt

['Then we should die, undivided']

taken up first by Tristan then by Isolde, on the thought of union in death ('So stürben wir, um ungetrennt'); this theme is to provide the main material both for the latter part of this duet and for the Liebestod.

Brangäne's song returns, in curtailed form. Tristan echoes Isolde's earlier words with 'Soll ich lauschen?' From this point the duet gathers momentum. The final stage is launched with 'O ew'ge Nacht', the two singing in harmony of eternal night. The long approach to the final climax is shaped by a series of peaks; sequential repetitions and a sustained dominant pedal raise the tension to an unbearable level, which eventually reaches the point of no return.

The cadence, like the coitus, is *interruptus* (scene iii). A savage discord on the full orchestra (topped by shrieking piccolo) is accompanied by a scream from Brangäne, as King Mark, Melot and the courtiers burst in on the scene. The orchestra graphically depicts the subsiding of the lovers' passions as morning dawns (ex.5). King Mark, much moved, addresses Tristan and, receiving no direct answer, embarks on his long monologue of questioning reproach: would Tristan do this to him ('Mir dies?')? The king's motif, ex.11, announced on his characteristic instrument, the bass clarinet, is an inverted form

Ex.11

of the motif sometimes described as 'Tristan's honour' (ex.4). To King Mark's questions there can be no reply, Tristan responds. His feeling that he no longer belongs to this world is captured in a magical modulation from the music of the opera's opening to ex.9. He invites Isolde to follow him into the realm of night; she assents and he kisses her on the forehead. At this, Melot, whose actions (according to Tristan) have been motivated by his jealous love for Isolde,

draws his sword. Tristan also draws, but allows himself to be wounded. The act ends with King Mark's motif pealing out on brass instruments in D minor.

Act 3 *Tristan's castle in Brittany* The prelude to the final act opens with a doleful, diatonic transformation of ex.1y in a desolate F minor. When the curtain rises, Tristan is seen lying asleep under a lime tree, with Kurwenal bending over him, grief-stricken. A melancholy shepherd's song is heard on the english horn, offstage. The shepherd appears over the castle wall. Kurwenal tells him to play a merry melody if Isolde's ship should come into sight. The sea is empty and desolate ('Öd und leer das Meer!'), responds the shepherd, continuing with his mournful tune. To the joy of Kurwenal, expressed in his characteristically hearty rhythms and melodic lines, Tristan revives and asks where he is. Kurwenal replies that he is in his family castle, Kareol.

Tristan's slow, painful return to consciousness is reflected in his fragmented vocal line. He is dimly aware that he has been brought back from the distant realm of endless night, where he had glimpsed oblivion. Isolde remains in the bright light of day (ex.5) but he looks forward to the final extinction of the torch and their union. This first phase in Tristan's delirium is reflected in the wild lack of control in his music: the complexity of the chromatic harmony, the lurching tempo changes and the undisciplined line.

Kurwenal tells him that he has sent for Isolde, and Tristan, in his fevered imagination, sees the ship approaching; a motif (ex.12) first heard in a sombre

Ex.12

form in the prelude to the third act returns here in obsessive sequential repetition. Tristan's frantic cries to Kurwenal to look for the ship are answered by the english horn playing the mournful shepherd's song. In the next phase of his delirium, Tristan remembers how he heard that song ('Du alte ernste Weise') in his childhood, when his mother and father died. The strains of the song are now woven into a fantasy, to be joined by the falling chromatic phrase heard in Act 1 as Isolde recalled her tending of the sick Tristan. Another frenzied climax follows, in which Tristan curses the love potion, for which he senses he is somehow responsible.

He sinks back in a faint. Kurwenal listens anxiously for signs of life. Tristan revives and the music moves to E major for the final, sublime phase of his delirium, in which he imagines Isolde coming to him across the water: 'Wie sie selig'. Tristan's vocal line, introduced by the mellow ex.9 on horns, is now infinitely, ecstatically protracted – sometimes to ten

'Tristan und Isolde' (Wagner), Act 3 in Wieland Wagner's 1962 production at Bayreuth (1966), with Wolfgang Windgassen as Tristan

slow-moving bars. Gradually the lines begin to fragment as Tristan again imagines he sees the ship approaching. This time a sprightly C major tune on the english horn confirms that it has been sighted. Kurwenal rushes to the watchtower and reports on its progress. He sees Isolde come ashore and goes down to assist (scene ii). Tristan, meanwhile, anticipates her arrival in feverish excitement, tearing the bandages from his wounds.

Isolde enters in haste (ex.7) but Tristan, to a recapitulation of music from the opera's prelude, expires in her arms. Isolde is distraught; her fragmented line includes the opening of ex.10, subsequently to form the basis of the Liebestod.

The music becomes reanimated as the shepherd tells Kurwenal that a second ship is arriving (scene iii); they try to barricade the gate. Brangäne appears, and then Melot, whom Kurwenal strikes dead. King Mark and his followers also appear and, oblivious to the king's pleas, Kurwenal sets upon them, sustaining a fatal wound; he dies at Tristan's feet. King Mark, who had come to yield Isolde to Tristan, laments the scene of death and destruction. The Liebestod, or Isolde's Transfiguration, now begins, with ex.10: 'Mild und leise' ('Gently and softly'). In its latter stages, the conclusion of the Act 2 love duet is also recalled, but passion is now sublimated and the climax of the Liebestod is insistent rather than

frantic. Isolde sinks, as if transfigured, on to Tristan's body, mystically united with him at last. A final statement of ex.1y, achieving its long-awaited resolution on to a chord of B major, brings the opera to a radiant close.

*

Tristan und Isolde is regarded as a milestone in the history of music, largely on account of its pervasive emancipation of the dissonance. The far-reaching influence of the work in technical terms is matched by the overwhelming effect the extremity of its emotional expression has had on generations of artists in all media. On one level, *Tristan* is the ultimate glorification of love: 'a monument to this loveliest of all dreams', as Wagner put it. But on another level, the work goes beyond emotional experience and enters a metaphysical realm. Human existence and the outer material world of phenomena are ultimately transcended and salvation found in the embrace of the noumena, the ultimate reality.

B.M.

Trovatore, Il ('The Troubadour')

Dramma in four parts by Giuseppe Verdi to a libretto by Salvadore Cammarano (with additions by Leone

102/103. 'Tristan und Isolde' (Wagner, 1865), scenes fom Acts 1 and 2 in the production by Jean-Pierre Ponnelle at the Festspielhaus, Bayreuth, in 1981, with René Kollo (Tristan), Johanna Meier (Isolde), Hanna Schwarz (Brangäne) and Hermann Becht (Kurwenal)

Left: 104. 'Il trovatore' (Verdi, 1857), scene from an early Italian production; chromo-lithograph by Luigi Morgari

Below: 105. 'Les Troyens' (Berlioz, 1863), scene from the 1969/70 production by Minos Volonakis (designed by Nicholas Georgiadis) at the Royal Opera House, Covent Garden, with Josephine Veasey as Dido and Jon Vickers as Aeneas

106. 'Turandot' (Puccini, 1926), scene from the
production by Andrei Serban (designed by Sally Jacobs)
at the Royal Opera House, Covent Garden, in 1984,
with Gwyneth Jones in the title role

107. 'Die Walküre' (Wagner, 1870), scene from the production by Patrice Chéreau (sets Richard Peduzzi, costumes Jacques Schmidt) at the Festspielhaus, Bayreuth, in 1976, with Hans Sotin (Wotan) and Roberta Knie (Brünnhilde)

108. 'Die Walküre' (Wagner, 1870), scene from the production by Harry Kupfer (sets Hans Schavernoch, costumes Reinhard Heinrich) at the Staatsoper, Berlin, in 1993, with Deborah Polaski as Brünnhilde

109. 'War and Peace' (Prokofiev), scene from the 1984 revival of the 1972 English National Opera production by Colin Graham (costumes by Margaret Harris) at the London Coliseum

110. 'Wozzeck' (Berg, 1925), scene from the production by David Pountney (designed by Stefanos Lazaridis) at the English National Opera, London Coliseum, 1992, with Donald Maxwell (Wozzeck) and Alan Woodrow (Captain)

111. 'Yevgeny Onegin' (Tchaikovsky, 1879), scene from the Kirov Opera production by Yuri Temirkanov at the Royal Opera House, Covent Garden, with Lyubov Kazarnovskaya as Tatyana and Lyudmila Filatova as Filipyevna the nurse

112. 'Yevgeny Onegin' (Tchaikovsky, 1879), scene from the 1994 production by Graham Vick (designed by Richard Hudson) at the Glyndebourne Festival Opera, with Elena Prokina (Tatyana), Louise Winter (Olga) and John Fryatt (Monsieur Triquet)

113. 'Die Zauberflöte' (Mozart, 1791), backstage preparations for a production at the Weimar Court Theatre (1794): watercolour by Georg Melchior Kraus, director of the scenic workshop at the theatre

114. 'Die Zauberflöte' (Mozart, 1791), designs by Karl Friedrich Schinkel for Act 1 (rocky country, with trees and mountains; in the foreground a temple) for the 1816 production at the Berlin Royal Opera

115. 'Die Zauberflöte' (Mozart, 1791), final scene in the production by John Cox (designed by David Hockney) at the Metropolitan Opera House, New York, 1991, with Kathleen Battle (Pamina), Francisco Araizo (Tamino) and Kurt Moll (Sarastro)

116. 'Die Zauberflöte' (Mozart, 1791), the Jérôme Savary production (designed by Michel Lebois) at the Bregenz Festival, 1985

Emanuele Bardare) after Antonio García Gutiérrez's play *El trovador*; Rome, Teatro Apollo, 19 January 1853 (revised version, *Le trouvère*, Paris, Opéra, 12 January 1857).

The première cast included Giovanni Guicciardi (Luna), Rosina Penco (Leonora), Emilia Goggi (Azucena) and Carlo Baucardé (Manrico).

Count di Luna *a young nobleman of Aragon* baritone
Leonora *a lady-in-waiting to the Princess of Aragon* soprano
Azucena *a gypsy* mezzo-soprano
Manrico *an officer in the army of Prince Urgel, and the supposed son of Azucena* tenor
Ferrando *a captain in the Count's army* bass
Ines *Leonora's confidante* soprano
Ruiz *a soldier in Manrico's service* tenor
An Old Gypsy bass
A Messenger tenor
Leonora's female attendants, nuns, servants and armed retainers of the Count, gypsies, followers of Manrico
Setting Biscay and Aragon, in 1409

Verdi was still in Venice enjoying the success of *Rigoletto* (in March 1851) when he wrote to Cammarano suggesting García Gutiérrez's play (first performed in 1836) as a subject for his next opera. It is clear from his early letters that he saw the drama as a sequel to *Rigoletto*, this time with an unconventional female character, the gypsy Azucena, at the centre of the action. Azucena, like Rigoletto, was to be fired by two opposing passions: maternal love and a desire for vengeance. More than this, it is clear that Verdi wished to develop further the formal freedoms he had experimented with in parts of *Rigoletto*. In an early letter to Cammarano, for example, he urged:

As for the distribution of the pieces, let me tell you that when I'm presented with poetry to be set to music, any form, any distribution is good, and I'm all the happier if they are new and bizarre. If in operas there were no more cavatinas, duets, trios, choruses, finales, etc. etc., and if the entire opera were, let's say, a single piece, I would find it more reasonable and just.

But, as so often with Verdi, his revolutionary statements in his writings were considerably toned down when it came to practical matters. Cammarano's draft libretto turned out to be fashioned along conventional lines, and Verdi made little objection.

In part owing to personal difficulties, work on the new opera moved along rather slowly. Verdi and Strepponi also moved in 1851 to a permanent home at the farm of Sant'Agata near Busseto. Verdi, who had become the most famous and frequently performed Italian composer in Europe, and who could by now

write for more or less whichever theatre he chose in Italy, considered a number of places for the première, being particularly concerned with the availability of a first-rate Azucena. Eventually, in the middle of 1852, the Teatro Apollo in Rome was decided upon. But then, in July 1852, Cammarano died, leaving a draft of *Il trovatore* with many details in need of attention. Bardare was brought in, and was particularly involved in the expansion of Leonora's role, which Verdi had originally wished to minimize but now fashioned as a dramatic equal to Azucena, thus forming a symmetry with the pair of opposed male roles, Manrico and the Count. The opera was a huge success. It very soon became the most popular of Verdi's works, both in Italy and around the world. In the mid-1850s Verdi created a revised version for a performance at the Paris Opéra, in part to ensure his French rights to the score. This revision, in a translation by Emilien Pacini, and entitled *Le trouvère*, included a ballet (placed after the opening chorus of Part 3), omitted Leonora's Part 4 cabaletta, 'Tu vedrai che amore in terra', and involved a substantial rewriting of the end of the opera (during which the 'Miserere' music returns in a lengthy coda).

*

Part I: 'The Duel'

I.i *A hall in the Aliaferia palace* There is no overture or formal prelude, merely a series of martial arpeggios and horn calls to set the scene. Ferrando bids the sentries and servants keep alert: the Count fears that the troubadour who has sometimes been seen in the garden is his rival in love. At the chorus's bidding, Ferrando narrates the story of Garzia, the Count's brother. One day, when still a baby, Garzia was found with an old witch at his cradle. She was driven off, but the boy sickened and was thought to have been given the evil eye. The witch was sought out and burnt at the stake, but her daughter exacted a terrible revenge: on the day of the execution young Garzia disappeared, and the charred remains of a baby were found in the embers of the witch's funeral pyre. All this is told in a two-stanza narrative, each stanza divided into a relatively free introductory passage ('Di due figli'), and then a more formal 'aria' ('Abbietta zingara') in which violins double the voice in octaves (a typical trait of 'gypsy' style). The chorus rounds off each stanza with horrified comments. In freer recitative, run through with a good deal of winding chromaticism, Ferrando continues his narration. The old Count fell into a decline and died; nothing more was heard of the gypsy's daughter, though the old witch herself is said still to roam the skies at night. The chorus joins Ferrando in 'Sull'orlo dei tetti', a rapid stretta that conjures up the ghostly forces around them. At the climax, the chiming of the midnight bell causes universal panic, and all hurriedly disperse.

I.ii The palace gardens Leonora, restlessly wandering, tells her maid Ines how she fell in love with a mysterious knight at a tournament and how he vanished when civil war broke out between the house of Aragon and Prince Urgel of Biscay's supporters. This is for the most part delivered in the spare, functional recitative typical of the opera, a style that makes the moments of arioso all the more effective. Leonora continues her story in the formal mould of a two-stanza Andante, 'Tacea la notte placida', a piece that moves from minor to major, flowering into an angular rising line as she describes how her lover has now returned as a troubadour to serenade her with melancholy songs. Ines suggests that Leonora should forget her lover, but in a highly ornamental cabaletta, 'Di tale amor', Leonora swears that she will die rather than lose him.

The ladies depart and the Count enters to declare his consuming passion for Leonora. He is about to climb up to her apartment when he hears a distant serenade: Manrico's 'Deserto sulla terra', a simple two-stanza canzone. Leonora hurries down to greet the troubadour, in the darkness mistakenly addresses the Count, and is then accused of treachery by Manrico. The three principals finish the act with a two-movement trio, first an Allegro agitato ('Qual voce!') dominated by a breathless, disjointed figure from the violins, and then – ignoring the usual lyrical slow section – straight to a furious stretta ('Di geloso amor sprezzato'). The final curtain sees the Count and Manrico striding off to fight a duel as Leonora falls senseless to the ground.

Part 2: 'The Gypsy'

2.i A ruined hovel on the lower slopes of a mountain in Biscay The tonality, rhythms and melodic gestures of the orchestral introduction bring us back to the musical world of Part 1 scene i as the gypsies celebrate their return to work with the famous 'anvil' chorus, 'Chi del gitano i giorni abbella?' This is immediately juxtaposed with Azucena's canzone, 'Stride la vampa', an invocation of fire and destruction that hovers obsessively around the note *b'*. The gypsies retire (to a muted reprise of their chorus); Azucena tells Manrico of her mother's death at the stake, and of how she planned to take revenge by casting the old Count's son on to the embers of the fire. Her narrative 'Condotta ell'era in ceppi' starts out formally controlled; but as the tale unfolds the music breaks from its tonal and rhythmic confines, coming to an intense declamatory climax as Azucena admits that she mistakenly threw her own baby on to the fire.

Manrico asks whether he is, then, Azucena's son, but the gypsy diverts him with assurances of love and encourages him, in turn, to tell a story. Manrico's 'Mal reggendo' recounts his duel with the Count and how a strange voice commanded him not to deal the fatal blow; but with Azucena's answer it turns into the first lyrical movement of a Verdian 'dissimilar' duet (in which each singer has different musical material). They are interrupted by Ruiz, who bears a letter revealing that Leonora, thinking Manrico dead, is about to enter a convent. Manrico resolves to go to her immediately, and so begins the duet cabaletta, 'Perigliarti ancor languente', in which Azucena begs him in vain not to court danger yet again.

2.ii The cloister of a convent near Castellor The Count is resolved to steal Leonora away from the convent and apostrophizes her in 'Il balen del suo sorriso', an 'aristocratically' graced Largo that exposes the baritone's full expressive range. A bell from the convent urges action, and the Count and his followers disperse to hide, the male chorus's 'Ardir, andiam' serving as a frame for the Count's vigorous cabaletta of expectation, 'Per me ora fatale'. A chorale-like chant from offstage nuns, which mingles with a restrained reprise of the chorus's 'Ardir, andiam', introduces Leonora. Her affecting arioso is cut short by the Count and then, to general amazement, by Manrico, whose sudden appearance precipitates the main lyrical section of the concertato finale, 'E deggio e posso crederlo?' Led off by a breathless Leonora, continued by the patterned opposition of the two male principals, the movement comes to a magnificent climax with Leonora's rising line, 'Sei tu dal ciel disceso, o in ciel son io con te?' Action once more boils up as Manrico's followers surround the Count's men. With a final reprise of 'Sei tu dal ciel' (whose lyrical power functions in place of the usual stretta movement), Leonora rushes off with Manrico.

Part 3: 'The Gypsy's Son'

3.i A military encampment The Count's men are eager to mount an attack on Castellor, where Leonora is safely ensconced, and when Ferrando tells them they will move at dawn the next day they celebrate with the famous chorus 'Squilli, echeggi la tromba guerriera'. The Count is still in agony over his loss of Leonora when Ferrando brings in Azucena, who has been captured nearby. To divert attention under interrogation, Azucena lapses into her 'gypsy' mode, singing 'Giorni poveri vivea', a simple minor-mode song that unexpectedly flowers into the major as she mentions the love she has for her son. But Ferrando has guessed her true identity and in a concluding stretta, 'Deh! rallentate, o barbari', she begs for mercy, the Count exults and Ferrando and the chorus look forward to her death at the stake.

3.ii A room adjoining the chapel at Castellor, with a balcony at the back We move to the rival camp where Leonora and Manrico are about to be married. Manrico calms his bride's fear with the Adagio 'Ah sì, ben mio, coll'essere', in which the tenor approaches most closely the 'aristocratic' musical world of Leonora and the Count. The lovers indulge in a brief duet before Ruiz interrupts to inform Manrico of Azucena's capture. Manrico immediately summons his followers and prepares to mount a rescue operation, pausing only to sing the cabaletta 'Di quella pira'. This movement, which rudely casts Manrico back into the more direct musical world of the gypsies and is probably best known for its (unauthentic) high C's, hides within its blunt exterior a good number of those subtle harmonic and orchestral gestures that Verdi seemed so effortlessly to integrate with his most energetic music.

Part 4: 'The Execution'

4.i *A wing of the Aliaferia palace* It is now too late in the drama for even brief narratives, and we must grasp by deduction that Manrico's attack has failed and that he is now a prisoner of the Count. Leonora arrives to try to save him, and from outside the prison sings of her love in the Adagio 'D'amor sull'ali rosee', which retains her 'aristocratic' ornamental style, but now colours it with dark instrumental sonorities and a predominantly falling line. The ensuing *tempo di mezzo*, perhaps the most famous in Italian opera, magnificently combines three contrasting musical ideas: a solemn 'Miserere' sounding from within; Leonora's fragmented response, underpinned by a quiet yet insistent 'death' rhythm from the full orchestra; and Manrico's farewell to his beloved, 'Ah che la morte ognora', a simple melody that recalls his Act 1 serenade. The number concludes with Leonora's reiteration of her love in the cabaletta 'Tu vedrai che amore in terra' (often omitted in performance for fear of overtaxing the soprano).

The Count appears, determined to execute both Manrico and Azucena. The arrival of Leonora initiates a conventionally structured though powerfully condensed four-movement duet. The first movement involves rapid dialogue over an orchestral melody; then the opponents move to a formally fixed statement of their positions ('Mira di acerbe lagrime'), Leonora begging for the life of Manrico, the Count obstinate in his desire for revenge. But then, in the third movement, Leonora strikes a Tosca-like bargain: herself in exchange for her lover's life. The Count jubilantly agrees, failing to see that Leonora has secretly taken poison. They join in the celebratory cabaletta 'Vivrà! . . . Contende il giubilo'.

4.ii *A grim prison* The closing finale finds Manrico and Azucena languishing in prison. Azucena has a frightening vision of the death that awaits her, the orchestra recalling her 'Stride la vampa' of Part 2. With reassurances from Manrico, sleep gradually overcomes her. They join in the narcotic duet 'Sì, la stanchezza', which begins in the minor but moves to the parallel major for Manrico's 'Riposa, o madre' and Azucena's picture of the simple gypsy life, 'Ai

nostri monti'. Leonora appears, telling Manrico that he is free to go; but he quickly guesses the nature of her bargain with the Count. He accuses her in the concertato 'Parlar non vuoi?', which includes Leonora's frantic attempts to defend herself and, in the later part, Azucena's somnolent reprise of 'Ai nostri monti'. Leonora collapses at Manrico's feet as the ensemble finishes; the poison begins to take effect, and soon the truth is out. In a second formal ensemble, 'Prima che d'altri vivere', Manrico and Leonora bid each other a tender farewell, the Count entering to add his comments in the later stages. As Leonora dies, the Count assumes control: Manrico is led off to the scaffold, and Azucena is forced to watch his execution. As the fatal blow falls, she tells the Count that he has just killed his own brother, and brings down the curtain with a final, exultant cry: her mother has been avenged.

*

Il trovatore, though without doubt one of the two or three most popular Verdi operas, has until recently fared rather badly with critics and commentators, mostly because of its unabashedly formalistic exterior in comparison with the works on either side of it, *Rigoletto* and *La traviata*. This attitude at last shows signs of changing, perhaps as our criteria for judging Verdi's musical dramas alter with time. Indeed, many of the most important stages in the critical rehabilitation of this opera have concentrated attention on just those aspects that were earlier castigated. The libretto, for example, with its immovable character types and 'unrealistic' stage action, has recently been seen as one of the work's great strengths, its economy of dramatic means and immediacy of language forming the perfect basis on which to build Verdian musical drama. Similarly, the extreme formalism of the musical language has been seen as serving to concentrate and define the various stages of the drama, above all channelling them into those key confrontations that mark its inexorable progress.

But if one trait can be singled out that best accounts for the opera's success, it is probably the sheer musical energy apparent in all the numbers. Time and again we find a relentless rhythmic propulsion in the accompaniment, and a tendency for the melodic lines to be forced into a restrictive compass, freeing themselves rarely but with consequent explosive power. This internal energy often runs through entire numbers, making a sense of progress across the various formal stages – from arioso to cantabile to cabaletta – that is just as convincing as the more radical, 'external' experiments with form encountered in the adjoining operas.   **R.P.**

Troyens, Les ('The Trojans')

Opéra in five acts by Hector Berlioz to his own lib-
retto after Virgil's *Aeneid*; Paris, Théâtre Lyrique, 4
November 1863 (Acts 3–5, as *Les Troyens à Carthage*);
Karlsruhe, 6 December 1890 (complete).

At the 1863 première of the second part, Anne
Charton-Demeur sang Dido; Jules-Sebastien
Monjauze sang Aeneas. Luise Reuss-Belce sang
Cassandra at the 1890 complete première, with
Alfred Oberländer as Aeneas.

Enée [Aeneas] *Trojan hero, son of Venus*	
and Anchises	tenor
Chorèbe [Coroebus] *Asian prince,*	
betrothed to Cassandra	baritone
Panthée [Panthous] *Trojan priest, friend of*	
Aeneas	bass
Ascagne [Ascanius] *15-year-old son of*	
Aeneas	soprano
Cassandre [Cassandra] *Trojan prophetess,*	
Priam's daughter	mezzo-soprano
Priam *King of Troy*	bass
A Greek Chieftain	bass
Ghost of Hector *Priam's eldest son*	bass
Helenus *a Trojan priest, Priam's son*	tenor
Two Trojan Soldiers	basses
Mercure [Mercury]	baritone/bass
A Priest of Pluto	bass
Polyxène [Polyxena] *Cassandra's sister*	soprano
Hécube [Hecuba] *Queen of Troy*	soprano
Andromaque [Andromache] *Hector's*	
widow	silent
Astyanax *her 8-year-old son*	silent
Didon [Dido] *Queen of Carthage,*	
widow of Sichée [Sychaeus]	
Prince of Tyre	mezzo-soprano
Anna *Dido's sister*	contralto
Narbal *minister to Dido*	bass
Iopas *Tyrian poet to Dido's court*	tenor
Hylas *a young Phrygian sailor*	tenor/contralto
Trojans, Greeks, Tyrians, Carthaginians, nymphs,	
satyrs, fauns, sylvans, invisible spirits	
Setting Troy (Acts 1 and 2) and Carthage (Acts	
3–5) in classical antiquity	

Berlioz was encouraged to undertake an opera on the
Aeneid by Liszt's mistress, the Princess Carolyne
Sayn-Wittgenstein, during his visits to Weimar in
1855–6; indeed, she told him not to return if he shrank
from the task. His *Mémoires*, compiled for the most
part between 1848 and 1854, trace the lure of Virgil to
the 'budding imagination' of his childhood. The
scene of Dido on her funeral pyre was but the most
vividly remembered of these 'epic passions for which
instinct had prepared me'. In his writings Berlioz
often cites the *Aeneid*, in Latin and from memory (and

often, therefore, with errors). Yet his correspondence
lacks the references to compositional ferment over
Les Troyens that exist for the funeral and Napoleonic
works, the Shakespearian compositions and *Faust*.
The implication is that until then he had considered
Virgil too hallowed for operatic setting, especially in
view of the shoddy treatment an operatic *Aeneid*
might receive in production. In any case it was the
sort of project best reserved for one's seniority. When
in 1856 he began to compose the libretto and some
of the music, Berlioz had just been elected to the
Institute and was enjoying the pinnacle of his success
as a conductor. His domestic situation was stable at
last; in 1854 he had married his mistress of 12 years,
Marie Recio. His health, on the other hand, had
begun its long decline: anything he wrote he might
not live to see performed. Conditions favoured a
valediction. (In fact he lived to 1869.)

Les Troyens was essentially completed by April
1858. Berlioz devoted much of the next half-decade,
unsuccessfully, to securing its production at the
Opéra. But he was unable to attract the patronage
of Napoleon III, who was more interested in
Tannhäuser. Even the three acts staged as *Les Troyens à
Carthage* at the Théâtre Lyrique in 1863 lasted
unadulterated but a single night, following which
number after number was trimmed away, beginning
with the Royal Hunt and Storm. Transmission of the
source materials was compromised accordingly.
Only 15 copies of the complete vocal score were
made – at the composer's expense – before the
mutilations began.

In successive generations *Les Troyens* circulated
in the flawed, misordered and incomplete vocal
scores of *La prise de Troie* and *Les Troyens à Carthage*
published by Choudens in conjunction with the 1863
production. In his will of 29 July 1867 Berlioz
complained bitterly of Choudens' unmet contractual
obligation to engrave the full score (and that of
Benvenuto Cellini), but left to his executors the
responsibility of seeing that it 'be published without
cuts, without modifications, without the least suppression of the text – in sum, exactly as it stands'. The
firm was subsequently enjoined by lawsuit to meet
the provisions of the contract. Full scores of *La prise de
Troie* and *Les Troyens à Carthage*, along with orchestral
parts and an improved vocal score, appeared in the
late 1880s. Of these only the vocal score was offered
for sale, access to the more significant sources being
limited to short-term hire.

Such chaos inevitably meant the slow assimilation of *Les Troyens* into the canon of the century's
great operas. A more or less complete version was
presented in Karlsruhe in December 1890 under Felix
Mottl and elsewhere in Germany in the decade
following; shortened versions began to be presented
in Paris in 1921. Momentum towards a serious

performance tradition for *Les Troyens* was established by the 1957 Covent Garden production under Rafael Kubelík, an event which in many respects fostered the renaissance in Berlioz studies of the 1960s. The Berlioz centennial year, 1969, saw the publication of a definitive score, a new production at Covent Garden and the release of a now famous recording, part of the Colin Davis Berlioz cycle. The 1983 production at the Metropolitan Opera, New York, was televised nationally and issued as a video. In March 1990 a *Les Troyens* billed as 'intégrale', but in fact lacking the ballets, opened the new Opéra Bastille in Paris.

*

Act I *The site of the former Greek encampment on the Trojan plain* The Greeks have lifted their siege of ten years, and the Trojans rejoice near the tomb of the Greek hero Achilles, discovering on the plain the debris of battle and, offstage, the enormous wooden horse that has been left behind. Three shepherds perched on the tomb play their 'antique flutes' (the same as the 'flutes of Dindymus' called for elsewhere in the score), their recurring motif rendered by the orchestral oboes. There has been no overture, and the accompaniment of the first scene is primarily for winds; the full string choir is delayed for Cassandra's entry. Alone, she is agitated by dark premonitions; she has seen the ghost of Hector wandering the ramparts of Troy. Neither King Priam nor the Trojan people, she complains in her aria 'Malheureux roi!', will heed her warnings of the disaster to befall that very night. Even her suitor Coroebus thinks she has lost her reason. His tender *cavatine* implores her to abandon her visions of catastrophe and return to her senses, but to no avail. Nor is she able, in their frantic duet, to convince him that he should flee the city. Instead she gives Coroebus her hand and the chaste kiss of a bride. Death will prepare their nuptial bed.

A march and solemn hymn of thanksgiving for the end of the war signal the processional entry of the Trojan court. The wrestling and games that follow are interrupted by the appearance of Hector's widow, Andromache, and their son, Astyanax, each dressed in the white mourning costume of Trojan tradition. A dolorous clarinet solo accompanies their mute progress downstage. Astyanax, heir to the throne of Troy, lays a basket of flowers at the altar as his mother kneels and prays; she then presents the frightened child to Priam and Hecuba. Andromache, overcome with emotion, lowers her veil to hide her tears. The crowd parts before them and, as they disappear, murmurs a mournful sigh. Descended in spirit from the trombone invocation of the *Symphonie funèbre* and the concluding bars of the *Marche funèbre pour la dernière scene d'Hamlet*, this pantomime is one of Berlioz's most ravishing passages.

Aeneas bursts in with news of Laocoön's death. (This is an error of stagecraft – Aeneas had already entered during the processional march and hymn.) Laocoön, having hurled his javelin into the horse and exhorted the Trojans to set it afire, was set upon and devoured live by two monstrous sea-serpents. The horrified company reacts in a majestic fugal octet and double chorus: such awful chastisement of Laocoön, a priest, is taken to be the vengeance of Pallas, to whom it is now imagined the Greeks must have offered the horse as an act of contrition. Priam and Aeneas, to beg pardon of the goddess for Laocoön's sacrilege, order the huge idol to be brought through the city gates to the Palladium. Cassandra weeps at the thought of her proud nation charging mindlessly towards its destruction. In the distance begins the Trojan march, sacred hymn of Ilium; the *cortège* eventually reaches the stage, but in neither Berlioz's libretto nor the autograph score is there an indication that the horse is seen by the audience. Suddenly there is confusion: the rattle of arms is heard inside the horse. But the people regard this as a good omen, and the helpless Cassandra at length follows the procession into Troy – there, she knows, to die in its ruins.

Act 2.i *A room in the palace of Aeneas* Aeneas has fallen asleep in his armour. Ascanius, terrified by the sounds of battle, hurries towards his father, but when the din subsides he is embarrassed to wake him and runs away. Out of the darkness materializes the bloody and dishevelled ghost of Hector. The collapse of a building rouses Aeneas. In cadaverous recitative Hector announces that the Greeks have taken the walls of Troy and begun to burn the city. To Aeneas are entrusted his nation's children and sacred idols; in Italy, after long wanderings at sea, he will establish a mighty empire and die a hero's death. Panthous brings the idols, and he and Aeneas are soon joined by Ascanius, Coroebus and their warriors. Together they go off to defend the citadel protecting Priam's palace.

2.ii *A gallery in the palace* The sack of Troy is under way. The Trojan women pray before the sacred flame of Vesta-Cybele, their incantations penetrated from time to time by the trumpets of encroaching battle. Aeneas, Cassandra tells them, has liberated those trapped at the citadel and taken Priam's treasure; his force is marching towards Mount Ida, called by destiny to Italy, the new Troy. Coroebus has been killed. When the women cry that nothing can save them from the Grecian rape, Cassandra proffers her dagger and indicates as similar instruments of suicide the silken belts of their garments and a parapet over the square. The women take lyres and begin an ecstatic hymn, 'Complices de sa gloire'; a few cowards are driven away in shame. Cassandra, too, takes a lyre, and it is during this awesome bacchanale that Greek soldiers enter to demand the treasure. Scorning them, Cassandra stabs herself and

Polyxena follows suit. As the Greeks discover that Aeneas and his band have escaped with the treasure, the women turn towards Mount Ida and salute the retreating Trojans with the prophetic 'Italy! Italy!' Some leap from the parapet, others stab themselves or draw the silken belts around their necks. Cassandra, unable to reach the parapet, falls dead on the last cry of 'Italy!'

Act 3 *Dido's throne-room at Carthage* The Carthaginians celebrate the return of good weather and sunshine after a violent tempest. Dido and her retinue arrive during the Carthaginian national anthem, her subjects waving palm fronds and tossing flowers towards their queen. In her recitative and aria we learn that seven years have passed since Dido fled with her people from Tyre and the tyrant who murdered her husband. Now their city flourishes, but they must prepare for war, for the arrogant Numidian Iarbas seeks to impose marriage on her. The multitude, aroused, vow to drive the Numidians back to the desert. Dido, however, has commanded this festival to celebrate the works of peace, and builders, sailors and farmers come forward to receive gifts. Resolved to become military heroes, they leave Dido and Anna to themselves.

In their duet Dido confesses to feelings of uneasiness she cannot understand. Anna, sensing the issue at hand, assures her she will again be loved and suggests that Carthage needs a king. But Dido's marriage vows require her fidelity to the memory of Sychaeus, whose ring remains on her finger. Iopas interrupts them to announce that representatives of an unidentified fleet, driven towards Carthage during the recent storm, seek an audience. Dido bids them welcome. The Trojan March, now in the minor mode, accompanies the entry of Ascanius, Panthous and the Trojan chieftains. Among them is Aeneas, disguised as a sailor. In exchange for shelter Ascanius brings Dido tribute: Iliona's sceptre, Hecuba's crown, Helen's veil – proof that they are Trojans.

Dido instructs the youth to assure Aeneas that his band may take refuge in her city. But the promised repose must wait, for the Numidian invasion has begun. The Carthaginians, though valorous, are short of weapons, and the odds are against them. Aeneas, casting off his cloak, identifies himself and offers his men and arms to Carthage. Dido is smitten at once by this legendary hero, now dazzling in his tunic and breastplate. Pausing to embrace Ascanius and entrust him to Dido's care, Aeneas summons the new allies to battle. The Carthaginians trade their scythes and slings for Trojan armament as the curtain falls.

Act 4.i *A forest near Carthage* In the Royal Hunt and Storm, a ballet-pantomime, water nymphs dart about the pool, and then are frightened by sounds of the hunt. Hunters enter with their dogs, but disperse when a storm gathers; their calls echo through the forest. Dido, dressed as Diana the huntress, and Aeneas enter on foot and take refuge in a cave. In the tumult one can distinguish voices and then cries of 'Italy! Italy!' The stream overflows and waterfalls form, a tree is struck by lightning and catches fire. The storm abates. The clouds disperse.

4.ii *Dido's garden on the shore* Since the defeat of the Numidians, Narbal observes, Dido has neglected the enterprises of her kingdom in favour of hunting and feasting. The Trojans, moreover, stay on. Anna responds that in conflicts between destiny and the heart the greater of the gods is Love. Narbal's fears of impending disaster contrasted with Anna's delight in the state of things come together in a typically Berliozian *réunion des thèmes*. As the orchestral winds play a restrained version of the national anthem over unsettling figuration in the violins, Dido takes her seat for the evening's *divertissement* by Egyptian girls, slaves and Nubian slave women. Unimpressed, she reclines on her couch and directs Iopas to sing a simple song of the fields.

Dido's anxieties are unrelieved, and she turns to Aeneas, asking him to finish his sad tale of the miseries of Troy and to tell her the fate of the beautiful Andromache. Andromache, he begins, was taken in slavery by Pyrrhus, but at length succumbed to her captor and married him. Startled by this precedent of remarriage, Dido senses circumstance conspiring to make her abandon her grief for her late husband. Here begins the great quintet: Ascanius, leaning against his bow like a statue of Cupid, draws the wedding ring from Dido's finger as Anna, Iopas and Narbal look on. Aeneas, rising, turns Dido's attention from melancholy stories to the enchanted Mediterranean night, and in following him she leaves the ring behind on the couch. A shimmering, palpitating magic settles over the scene. During the nocturne for septet and chorus, 'Tout n'est que paix et charme autour de nous', the company slips away. In the celebrated love duet, 'Nuit d'ivresse', Dido and Aeneas compare their love to other epic passions in the same terms as Jessica and Lorenzo in Act 5 of *The Merchant of Venice*. Towards the end they retire, arm in arm, their last refrain heard from the wings. Suddenly Mercury appears in a ray of moonlight, crosses to the column where Aeneas's breastplate hangs, and strikes it with his caduceus. Stretching his arm towards the sea, he intones the now familiar, and suddenly urgent, 'Italy! Italy! Italy!', and vanishes.

Act 5.i *The Trojan camp at the harbour* It is night. While two sentinels patrol the shore, the Phrygian youth Hylas sings wistfully of the homeland to which he will never return. Panthous and the Trojan captains, preparing to leave, note the parallels with that fatal night in Troy: once again the ghost of

'Les Troyens' (Berlioz): design by Philippe Chaperon for the grand floral hall in Dido's palace at Carthage (the throne-room) in the original production of 'Les Troyens à Carthage' ('Les Troyens', Acts 3–5) at the Théâtre Lyrique, 4 November 1863

Hector has been seen, now followed by a retinue of shades. A ghostly chorus of 'Italy! Italy! Italy!' sends them hurrying into their tents. The sentries continue their watch, grumbling to each other at having to leave Carthage for the boredom of the sea. They withdraw before Aeneas, who in his single extended recitative and aria, 'Inutiles regrets', determines to postpone his sacred mission long enough to exchange a last, supreme adieu with his beloved queen. Yet when the ghosts of Priam, Coroebus, Hector and Cassandra command him to delay no longer, he wakes the Trojans and hurries them to their ships to embark before daybreak. He directs a terse but noble farewell towards the palace, then turns to answer his destiny. A thunderstorm rises as the ships begin to move. In the confusion Dido rushes frantically onstage, powerless to arrest this sudden and, to her, inexplicable turn of events. Over strains of the Trojan March she curses Aeneas and the Trojan gods, then flees. From Aeneas and the Trojans comes a last, lusty chorus, 'Italy! Italy! Italy!'

5.ii *A room in Dido's palace at dawn* Some of the vessels have reached the high sea. Dido's first thought is of sending Anna and Narbal to beg Aeneas to grant her a few days more; then, enraged, she gives the futile order to pursue and burn his ships. Finally she dismisses her attendants, telling them to construct a pyre on which the hateful souvenirs of their love might melt in flames. In her monologue, 'Je vais mourir', she resolves to die as well. She bids adieu to her proud city, to Anna, to Africa, the music and text momentarily recalling the love duet.

5.iii *The palace gardens* A pyre has been erected; on its platform are a bust of Aeneas, his toga, helmet and sword, and the bed he had shared with Dido. The priests of Pluto enter with Narbal and Anna, who, in the ritual of sacrifice, loosens Dido's hair and removes her left shoe. Dido climbs to the platform and throws Aeneas's toga and her own veil – symbols of an unhappy love – on to the bundles of wood, but at the sight of Aeneas's armour swoons on the bed. With the prophetic gifts of those about to meet their death, she foresees her memory avenged by the Carthaginian hero Hannibal. Thereupon she draws Aeneas's sword from the scabbard and stabs herself. She rises three times, now seeing all too clearly Carthage vanquished by eternal Rome. At the moment of her death the people curse Aeneas and his race, but the music is that of the Trojan March and in the distance one perceives an apotheosis: at the Roman Capitol victorious legions pass in review before the emperor, his poets and his artists.

*

Berlioz intended from the beginning that *Les Troyens* should be on an epic scale, but he was equally determined to limit its length to four and a half hours. In its duration, therefore, the opera is not especially unusual. The question of length did, however, lead Berlioz to adopt the short and rather abrupt finale that replaces the more ambitious tableau he had originally written.

Les Troyens is technically speaking a number opera, yet within the scenes the advance of the long, intricate story is aggressive and seldom interrupted. Berlioz crafts the seams between the movements with particular finesse, often using shifts of tonality (for instance, the rise from F to G♭ between the septet and love duet) and texture (the sudden *a cappella* fugue for 'Châtiment effroyable') to articulate new turns of dramatic intent. And while *Les Troyens* has strong roots in past operatic practice, Berlioz is less interested in traditional recitative and aria than in freer structures such as monologue, *scène* and pantomime. Dialogue and narrative often seem to be set down over primarily orchestral movements: the sentinels' march in Act 5, for example, and much of the *cérémonie funèbre*, a dirge with mournful winds. The prominent role the orchestra can play in establishing imagery had, of course, been a lesson of the dramatic symphonies; in some respects Berlioz's practice is not so different from Wagner's of the same period.

Orchestral commentary enriches the dramatic impact of *Les Troyens* at every turn. One of its threads is the kind of thematic recall common in Romantic music: the frequent allusion to, and transformation of, the Trojan March, for example, or the surging string figures that convey Cassandra's distress, or the semitone oscillations of the flutes of Dindymus (recalled, from the opening scene, in both the finale of Act 1 and the Royal Hunt and Storm). In the closing bars of Act 3, conversely, Berlioz foreshadows the opening of the Hunt and Storm. Orchestral representations of heartbeats, sighs and other agitations of the spirit are as typical of *Les Troyens* as of the *Fantastique* and *Faust*. Stopped horns and ghostly string harmonics evoke the supernatural world. In the Hunt and Storm virtually every stage action has an orchestral equivalence, and here, too, occurs a mixture of mythical, sexual and atmospheric symbolism that shows Berlioz's Romanticism at its most vivid.

In short, Berlioz's understanding of sonority as a poetic device is profound, beginning with the choice of the mezzo-soprano voice for each of the heroines.

The clarinet solo for the pantomime of Andromache and Astyanax is of wrenching loneliness, as is the two-bar reference to it when, in Act 3, Ascanius begins to weep while bidding his father farewell; of similar impact is the singular appearance of the bass clarinet during the funeral ceremony for Dido. Percussion, oboes and harps approximate what Berlioz understood to be the sounds of classical antiquity. Antiphonal and offstage effects lace the work and lend it its epic size; of these the most substantial is in the finale of Act 1, with its three offstage bands placed to suggest the long, slow approach of the Trojan Horse. The orchestra is typical of the large Berlioz force, with piccolos, english horn, four bassoons, trumpets and piston cornets, a half-dozen or more harps, and another two dozen players off stage – and, of course, the immense chorus. Yet, as in the Requiem, the full complement is summoned only now and again: it is in the division and permutation of his legions that Berlioz most revels.

A central tenet of his artistic creed was that the union of music and poetry held incomparably greater power than either art alone. In writing his own libretto, he gave himself the freedom to perfect both the story and the lyrics as part of the compositional process. (The poetry, though *passé* for the 1860s, is always serviceable and often lovely, and both writing it and setting it certainly stimulated his imagination more than anything a professional librettist had ever provided for him.) By *Les Troyens* he had become a master of design, imagery and multi-dimensional architecture, and what resulted from his particular sense of the composer as hero was a marked solidarity of overall structure. It is not just Aeneas who elides Cassandra's world and Dido's, but the Trojan March, the chorus, the ghosts and the gods -- too much, in short, for *Les Troyens* to survive being divided in two. *Les Troyens à Carthage* was after all a compromise, accepted as a necessity by a composer who imagined his weeks to be numbered; *La prise de Troie* was never more than a title of convenience. To imagine *Les Troyens* as a succession of two self-contained operas is not merely to embrace a historical accident but to miss the opera's point.

D.K.H.

Turandot

Dramma lirico in three acts by Giacomo Puccini to a libretto by Giuseppe Adami and Renato Simoni after Carlo Gozzi's dramatic fairy-tale; Milan, Teatro alla Scala, 25 April 1926.

The outstanding first cast included Miguel Fleta (Calaf), Rosa Raisa (Turandot), Maria Zamboni (Liù), Carlo Walter (Timur) and Giacomo Rimini (Ping).

Princess Turandot	soprano
The Emperor Altoum *her father*	tenor
Timur *the dispossessed King of Tartary*	bass
Calaf *his son*	tenor
Liù *a young slave-girl*	soprano
Ping *Grand Chancellor* ⎤	baritone
Pang *General Purveyor* ⎬ *(Masks)*	tenor
Pong *Chief Cook* ⎦	tenor
A Mandarin	baritone
The Prince of Persia	silent role
The Executioner (Pu-Tin-Pao)	silent role

Imperial guards, the executioner's men, boys,
*   priests, mandarins, dignitaries, eight wise men,*
*   Turandot's handmaids, soldiers, standard-*
*   bearers, musicians, ghosts of suitors and a*
*   crowd*
Setting Peking, in legendary times

The notion of basing an opera on Gozzi's most celebrated *fiaba* (fairy-tale) – one that should 'modernize and bring human warmth to the old cardboard figures' – arose during a meeting in Milan between Puccini, Adami and Simoni in winter 1919–20. Adami supplied the composer with a copy of Schiller's adaptation of the play in the Italian translation of Andrea Maffei. Puccini returned it to him with the instruction to make it the basis of the libretto, adding 'but on it you must rear another figure; I mean – I can't explain!' (clearly he was groping his way towards the conception of the slave-girl Liù). His first instinct was to exclude Gozzi's 'masks' but almost immediately afterwards he wrote: 'It is just possible that by retaining them *with discretion* we should have an Italian element which, in the midst of so much Chinese mannerism . . . would introduce a touch of our life and, above all, of sincerity.' By August 1920 the poets' original scheme had been reworked to Puccini's temporary satisfaction. Of the three acts, the first was to end with Calaf's solving of the riddles and his offer to release Turandot from her obligation provided she could find out who he is. The second would begin with her attempts to do so, including the interrogation and torture of Liù, and end with a long duet, at the climax of which Calaf would reveal his name and thus apparently seal his own fate. Act 3 would open with the preparations for Calaf's execution. At the last moment Turandot would deny all knowledge of his identity and proclaim her love for him. By the beginning of 1921 Puccini had already begun sketching the music with the help of a Chinese musical box belonging to his friend Baron Fassani and some folk music supplied by the firm of Ricordi.

Meanwhile, of the two librettists Adami seems to have assumed the usual role of Luigi Illica, working out the dialogue, and Simoni that of Giuseppe Giacosa, versifying the result. By September Puccini was convinced that the last two acts should be run together, so as to avoid a slackening of interest after the riddle scene. The librettists, however, were against a two-act format; and in December it was decided to bring down the curtain on Act 1 at the point where Calaf, not dissuaded by Timur, Liù and the masks, strikes the gong that announces his challenge. During the early months of 1922 Puccini worked on a new scene for the masks which would open the second act. In October he was engaged with Turandot's aria, 'In questa reggia', which follows. In November, after briefly reverting to the idea of an opera in two acts, Puccini took the unfortunate decision to have Liù die under torture. For the next two years the final duet between Calaf and Turandot proved the great obstacle. None of the versions supplied by Simoni satisfied him. By the time of his death after an operation for throat cancer on 29 November 1924 only a few scarcely legible sketches for it existed. At Toscanini's suggestion these were handed over to Franco Alfano for completion. But at the première 17 months later Toscanini laid down his baton after the death of Liù, the last music composed by Puccini. The score was published with Alfano's ending, shortened in a second edition (the one in regular use). Alfano's conclusion (which has since been given in full in concert performance) fails to redeem the inevitable anticlimax. Clearly the man who can persist in his wooing of a woman of whom he knows nothing, and whom he has every reason to dislike, immediately after a slave-girl has killed herself for his sake, is bound to forfeit our sympathy. Puccini hoped that the librettists would be able to solve the problem for him; but even if they had succeeded it is likely that, as in *Suor Angelica*, he would not have found the appropriate note of transfiguration on which to end.

The title role is one of the supreme challenges for a dramatic soprano. Outstanding exponents have included Claudia Muzio, Lotte Lehmann, Maria Jeritza, Maria Németh, Eva Turner and, later, Maria Callas, Birgit Nilsson and Gwyneth Jones.

*

Act I *A public square in Peking beneath the city ramparts, with the imperial palace to one side* From a bastion a Mandarin proclaims the Emperor's decree: the Princess Turandot shall wed the first suitor of royal lineage who succeeds in solving her three riddles; all who fail will be executed. The Prince of Persia 'whom fortune has not favoured' is due to be beheaded when the moon rises. The crowd surges forward in eager anticipation, only to be brutally repulsed by the imperial guards. As their shouts turn to groans and lamentations, the stark, bitonal flourishes of the orchestra give way to a broad, characteristically Puccinian, drooping melody. In the scrimmage an old blind man is knocked to the ground. The girl

'Turandot' (Puccini), scene from Act 1 (a public square in Peking beneath the city ramparts, with the imperial palace to one side) in the original production at La Scala, Milan, in 1926: from the 'Illustrated London News' (1 May 1926)

accompanying him calls for help. Their rescuer is the disguised Prince Calaf, who recognizes the old man as his father, Timur, exiled King of Tartary. Both are in flight from their country's enemies. Timur's companion is the slave-girl Liù, who decided to share the family's sufferings when Calaf bestowed a smile on her long ago. The hectic motion is resumed as the Executioner's men arrive and begin sharpening the axe. The general blood-lust is conveyed in a fierce ostinato of varied phrase-lengths, yielding to a mood of rapt reverie as all pray for the moon to appear. Slowly the scene fills with a silvery light, reflected in a diaphanous tissue of harmony and scoring. As the culminating cry of 'Pu-Tin-Pao' (the Executioner) subsides, a chorus of boys is heard approaching. Their chant ('Là, sui monti dell'est') is a version of the Chinese folksong 'Moo-Lee-Vha' and will stand for Turandot in her official capacity. Next comes the procession that escorts the Prince of Persia to the scaffold. The young man's looks and dignified bearing move the crowd to pity and they call on the Princess to spare his life, but she confirms his sentence with a silent gesture and the procession moves on.

Timur, Calaf and Liù are left alone in the square. From far off the Prince of Persia invokes the name of Turandot as the axe falls. But Calaf has been so overwhelmed by the Princess's icy beauty that he is determined to try his fortune with her, despite his father's remonstrances. He is about to strike the gong

and issue his challenge when the masks, Ping, Pang and Pong, rush in and restrain him. To fragments of the Chinese national hymn set out in alternations of duple and triple time, they try to deflect Calaf from his purpose. From the balcony the Princess's hand-maidens call for silence – their mistress is sleeping. The masks pay no heed and continue their persuasions. The ghosts of former suitors materialize on the battlements, each bewailing his unrequited love. The masks point to where the Executioner appears bearing the Prince of Persia's severed head. Timur joins his plea to theirs. In her pentatonic arietta ('Signore, ascolta') Liù makes a last appeal, to which Calaf, deeply moved, replies ('Non piangere, Liù'), recommending Timur to her care should he himself fail the test. As he continues to hold out, the music develops into a broadly swaying tug-of-war based on alternating chords and reinforced by the full chorus singing off stage. At the climax Calaf strikes the gong three times. Liù and Timur are in despair.

Act 2.i *A pavilion* Ping, Pang and Pong are preparing for either eventuality – a wedding or a funeral. They reflect on China's misery ever since Turandot came to power. From ministers of state they have become servants of the Executioner. In an andantino of nostalgia ('Ho una casa nell'Honan') each recalls his home in the peace of the countryside. Memories of Turandot's past victims, evoked by an unseen chorus, give way to hopes that the man has been found who can tame her and restore tranquillity to the land. To the sound of trumpets the palace wakes to life, and the music continues without a break into scene ii.

2.ii *The palace courtyard* Gradually a crowd assembles. The various dignitaries take their places, among them the eight wise men, each bearing three scrolls. High up on an ivory throne sits the Emperor Altoum. In an old man's quavering voice he tries in vain to dissuade Calaf from his enterprise. A solemn choral hymn wishes him 10 000 years of life. Once again the Mandarin reads aloud the imperial decree regarding the Princess; and again the boys' chorus is heard, a prelude to the appearance of Turandot herself. Her show-stopping aria 'In questa reggia', with its thrilling exploitation of high notes as the soprano climbs to the top of her register, tells the story of her ancestress Lo-u Ling, who was ravished and murdered by a foreign army, and whose memory she has sworn to avenge on any man foolhardy enough to woo her. A pattern of three chords introduces each of her riddles, to which Calaf gives the correct answers ('Hope', 'Blood' and 'Turandot'). The music of the boys' chorus, entrusted to full chorus and orchestra, now celebrates Calaf's victory. Turandot, in great distress, begs Altoum to release her from her vow, but he refuses. It is Calaf who offers her a way of escape. If by the following dawn she can discover his name, he will consent to be beheaded. Everyone hails Altoum, who hopes to be able to welcome Calaf as his son-in-law.

Act 3.i *The palace gardens, at night* Distant heralds repeat the Princess's command that none shall sleep on pain of death until the Prince's name be revealed. In his celebrated *romanza* 'Nessun dorma', whose principal strain testifies to Puccini's undiminished lyrical gifts, Calaf echoes their words, resolving that his secret shall never be disclosed. The three masks emerge from the shrubbery and offer Calaf various bribes – young half-naked girls, jewels, promises of renown – but he rejects them all. The crowd that has meantime gathered menace him with their daggers, when suddenly the imperial guards appear dragging in Timur and Liù, who were spotted with Calaf. The Princess is summoned. She orders the interrogation of Timur, but it is Liù who steps forward, claiming that she alone knows the Prince's name. Turandot has her bound and Ping tries to make her talk. In words of Puccini's own devising Liù tells the mystified Princess that love has given her the power to resist ('Tu che di gel sei cinta'). Her mournful melody continues throughout the painful scene that follows with an insistence that recalls the roll-call of the prostitutes in *Manon Lescaut*. The Executioner arrives; he and his men torture Liù. At the end of her strength she snatches a dagger from one of the guards and stabs herself. Timur, being blind, has to be told of her death; he joins the lugubrious

procession that bears her body away. At this point Alfano's reconstruction takes over, beginning with a duet ('Principessa di morte') between Calaf and Turandot, in which the Princess, at first haughty and unyielding, succumbs when Calaf embraces her. Humiliated, she begs him to leave, taking his secret with him. But he now feels sufficiently confident to tell her that he is Calaf, son of Timur. At once she recovers her pride, realizing that she still holds his life in her hands. A female chorus punctuated by brass flourishes leads into the final scene.

3.ii *The palace courtyard* Once again the Emperor, his courtiers and the people have assembled. Advancing with Calaf, Turandot declares that at last she knows his name – it is 'Love'. Chorus and orchestra unite in a triumphant reprise of the 'Nessun dorma' motif.

*

Despite its unfinished state *Turandot* is rightly regarded as the summit of Puccini's achievement, bearing witness to a capacity for self-renewal

Rosa Raisa as Turandot, the role she created in the original production at La Scala, Milan, in 1926

unsurpassed by that of still greater composers and demonstrating his unsurpassed mastery of stagecraft. The style remains true to the composer's 19th-century roots, but it is toughened and amplified by the assimilation of uncompromisingly modern elements, including bitonality and an adventurous use of whole-tone, pentatonic and modal harmony. The resulting synthesis commands a new range of expression (the pentatonic scale, no longer a mere orientalism as in *Madama Butterfly*, conveys the full depth of Liù's pathos in 'Signore, ascolta'). The music is organized in massive blocks, each motivically based – a system which shows to particular advantage in Act 1, arguably the most perfectly constructed act in Puccini's output; while the scoring shows a rare imagination in the handling of large forces (the writing for xylophone alone immediately attracts the attention). These attributes, combined with Puccini's unfailing ability to communicate directly with an audience, have established *Turandot* as a classic of 20th-century opera.   J.B.

Turco in Italia, Il ('The Turk in Italy')

Dramma buffo in two acts by Gioachino Rossini to a libretto by Felice Romani after Caterino Mazzolà's *Il turco in Italia*, set by Franz Seydelmann (1788, Dresden); Milan, Teatro alla Scala, 14 August 1814.

The first cast included Francesca Maffei-Festa (Fiorilla), Pietro Vasoli (Prosdocimo), Giovanni David (Narciso), Filippo Galli (Selim), Luigi Pacini (Geronio) and Adelaide Carpano (Zaida).

Prosdocimo *a poet*	bass
Zaida *a slave*	soprano
Prince Selim	bass
Fiorilla	soprano
Don Geronio *her husband*	bass
Don Narciso	tenor
Albazar *Selim's henchman*	tenor
Setting Naples in the 18th century	

The poet Prosdocimo is in search of a subject for a comedy drawn from real life. At a gypsy camp near Naples he encounters Zaida who, as a slave girl in the Erzèrum harem, once loved the prince Selim but was forced to flee after slanders by jealous rivals had led Selim to sentence her to death. The poet tells Zaida that a Turkish prince is expected to visit Italy shortly and that news of her continued fidelity to Selim can then be sent to Turkey. In fact, the prince is Selim himself. To the delight of the poet, whose plot is badly in need of incident and intrigue, the first girl Selim sees and falls for is the overly flirtatious Fiorilla, shrewish wife of the irascible and frustrated

Don Geronio, whose skirmishes with her are abetted by his friend, the lady-killing Don Narciso. During the remainder of the first act the poet takes increasing delight in events: the flirting of Selim and Fiorilla, the anger of Geronio and Narciso (who is himself not unmoved by Fiorilla's charms), the bedlam that ensues when Selim and Zaida finally meet, recognize one another, and are discovered in an affectionate embrace by the remainder of the company.

In Act 2, Selim offers to buy Fiorilla from her husband but Geronio indignantly refuses. Fiorilla and Zaida confront Selim, who manages to insult both ladies by his indecision: he has, in fact, laid plans to abduct Fiorilla at a masked ball, a ploy the all-knowing poet reveals to Zaida, who resolves to go to the ball disguised as Fiorilla. Meanwhile, the poet advises Geronio to masquerade as Selim in order to forestall the abduction. To add to the confusion Narciso, overhearing the plotting, decides to attend in Turkish guise as he too wishes to make off with Fiorilla. There follows confusion on a grand scale; and though Selim and Zaida do eventually find one another and set sail for Turkey, leaving the various Italian parties decently reconciled and Fiorilla's roving eye firmly suppressed, the comedy, particularly at the expense of the hapless Geronio, is often tinged with cruelty. This is particularly the case in the Act 2 quintet, 'Oh, guardate che accidente', with the bemused Geronio involved in a sinister game of ballroom hide-and-seek with two Selims and two Fiorillas.

That quintet is representative of Rossini's preoccupation here with ensembles as opposed to solo numbers. What solo numbers there are occur mainly in Act 2 and are largely 'arias of obligation' written, not always by Rossini, to satisfy the demands of individual singers. (The aria for Selim's henchman Albazar is not by Rossini.) Even Fiorilla, cavilling hussy and sophisticated woman of the world, is characterized more by her role-playing in ensembles than by either of her cavatinas. Significantly, the poet – the detached Rossinian observer – has no aria or duet. He sings only in recitatives, the fine Act 1 trio and in the ensembles within the Act 1 finale where Rossini has cheekily scrawled on the autograph manuscript: 'Well, at least you have a chance to do something here!' This exquisite and witty *dramma buffo*, on a smaller scale than its predecessor *L'italiana in Algeri*, is dominated by ensembles and conversations, etched in with the most delicate strokes, in a style entirely appropriate to the drawing-room chatter of a piece full of 'double meanings, hypocrisy, smothered anger, forced smiles, and asides through clenched teeth'.

                                        R.O.

Turn of the Screw, The

Opera in a prologue and two acts, op.54, by Benjamin Britten to a libretto by Myfanwy Piper after Henry James's tale; Venice, La Fenice, 14 September 1954.

At the première the cast included Peter Pears as Quint, Jennifer Vyvyan as the Governess, Joan Cross as Mrs Grose, Arda Mandikian as Miss Jessel, Olive Dyer as Flora and the young David Hemmings as Miles.

The Prologue	tenor
The Governess	soprano
Miles ⎫ *children in her charge*	treble
Flora ⎭	soprano
Mrs Grose *the housekeeper*	soprano
Miss Jessel *a former governess*	soprano
Peter Quint *a former manservant*	tenor

Setting Bly, a country house, about the middle of the 19th century

This chamber opera – the orchestra comprises 13 players – was the result of a commission for the Venice Biennale of 1954. The subject had been in Britten's mind for some years, after a suggestion by Myfanwy Piper, and her ideas for its operatic treatment encouraged Britten to request a libretto from her rather than from William Plomer, whom he had initially thought of approaching. A complete scenario was arrived at during the summer of 1953 and the libretto began to reach Britten from early in 1954. However, it was the end of March before he was able to begin composing the music, less than six months before the date fixed for the première. The opera was completed in full score by the beginning of August, but various changes were introduced at relatively late stages, notably the addition of the Prologue and of material to the closing scene.

The première had a mixed reception, though the predominant reaction was that the work was one of Britten's finest to date, and remarkably successful in its use of small forces to create memorable dramatic effects. It has received a substantial number of productions worldwide: the first independent production was in Darmstadt in 1958; the American première was in Boston in 1961; the ENO staged a successful new production in 1979. *The Turn of the Screw* was the first of Britten's operas to be recorded complete, relatively soon after the première, under the composer's own direction (1955); a second recording, under Colin Davis (1984), was associated with a television performance, and a third, under Steuart Bedford, was issued in 1994.

*

Prologue Though not part of the original plan, and added for the mundane reason that the opera risked being too short, the Prologue now seems the ideal

way to create an expectant, uneasy atmosphere. On paper it may look like little more than a prosaic, convenient means of filling in the background, telling how the Governess – whose name we never learn – finds out about, and finally decides to accept, the post at Bly, despite the curious circumstance that the uncle of the two children to be in her charge is an absentee guardian and insists that she shall not bother him once she is installed. Britten's musical shaping of the prose text into an arioso (for tenor and piano – the tenor often doubles as Prologue and Quint) balances justified apprehensiveness and unjustified calm to perfection; the vocal line is too shapely and expressive to be termed recitative. Above all, the way in which the orchestra unobtrusively enters at the Governess's moment of decision produces one of those powerful dramatic frissons with minimal means of which Britten is a master.

Act I.i (Theme) *On the journey* Each of the relatively brief, separate scenes is linked to its predecessor by the statement or variation of a 12-note theme, whose intervals rotate in screw-like fashion. This, and the organization of the work's tonal centres around a sequence from A to A♭, for Act 1, which is inverted for Act 2, reaching A at the end by a different route, suggests a high degree of structural control. The work loses nothing of vividness or vitality through this framework, and indeed it has a remarkable variety of form and mood to balance its evident coherence. In Act 1.i the Governess is travelling to Bly, and the music that depicts the rattling motion of her coach also reflects her deep anxiety about the task she has undertaken. The most ornate phrase, a melodic shape that will recur as one of the opera's principal motifs, is set to the words 'O why did I come?'

I.ii (Variation I) *The welcome* As they wait on the porch at Bly, the children chant exuberantly, teasing the Housekeeper. After all three greet the Governess, Britten weaves the four high-register voices into a ravishing ensemble. The Governess is completely at her ease, and declares that 'Bly is now my home'.

I.iii (Variation 2) *The letter* After a fleet-footed variation that continues the lively mood of scene ii, the first signs of trouble appear. The housekeeper gives the Governess a letter stating that Miles has been expelled from school: the 'Why did I come?' theme, with its anxious chromaticism, returns, but the two women cannot accept that Miles is at fault. As the children sing an innocent nursery rhyme, 'Lavender's blue', the women add countermelodies whose poised shape and dissonant harmony encapsulate their hopes and fears.

I.iv (Variation 3) *The tower* All is peaceful and serene on a warm summer evening. The Governess walks in the grounds, expressing her contentment and claiming to have conquered her fears in a miniature da capo aria. Suddenly, on the tower of the house, she sees the shape of a man, and the change of mood is total. She is agitated, afraid, not knowing who he is.

I.v (Variation 4) The window The linking variation leads from the music of the Governess's agitation to the children's most strident and sinister rhyme, 'Tom, Tom, the piper's son'. As they move away the Governess again sees the menacing male figure, and Britten's use of celesta and harp to represent the apparition is chillingly apposite. The Governess describes the man to Mrs Grose and gradually, to music of eerie, implacable power, the housekeeper explains her realization that the man must be Peter Quint, the former valet of the house's absent master, who was sent away for his association with the previous governess, Miss Jessel, and for his evil influence on the children: moreover – as the music settles into numb patterns of horror – both Quint and Miss Jessel are dead. Despite the horror, the Governess rallies, declaring that she must protect the children and, as instructed, not trouble their guardian. Even at this stage it is clear that her precarious sense of confidence is misplaced.

I.vi (Variation 5) Lessons Like scene iv, scene vi embodies a single, extreme change of mood. First Miles and Flora sing a nursery-rhyme-like list of Latin nouns. But when the Governess, after praising Miles, asks him what else he remembers, he sings a very different song, each line giving a new translation of the Latin word 'malo', and expressing his longing for change. The boy's sudden, gloomy remoteness is poignant in its simplicity, though the music, as usually with Britten, balances motivic economy and rhythmic clarity with harmonic ambivalence.

I.vii (Variation 6) The lake Walking with Flora in the grounds, the Governess encourages her to name as many seas as she can (to a variant of the previous scene's Latin list), then to sing a lullaby to her doll. The association between death (the Dead Sea) and sleep is underlined in both the lullaby's text and its uncannily 'limp' music. The Governess does not ask Flora where she learnt such a strange song, but the probable answer arises in the apparition of Miss Jessel, whom the Governess suddenly sees across the lake. In despair she urges Flora to run back to find Miles, and, alone, she pours out her anguished recognition that she can do nothing to save the children. Here the verbal repetitions, packed into a small-scale musical form, show Britten relishing the unavailability of large forces and of an extended time scale to create and sustain a mood.

I.viii (Variation 7) At night In the act's final scene the music is more expansive, though tightly focussed

both in form and texture by the emphasis on relatively high voices – tenor, treble, soprano. Now the ghosts are not only seen but also heard, and the full extent of their malign power over the children is revealed. Quint's highflown poetic imagery is scarcely realistic for a corrupt valet, but it has expressive truth, an other-worldly fantasy suggesting that he is the mouthpiece for deep-seated forces of evil. There is an appropriately ornate quality to the melodic lines of Quint and Miss Jessel, especially in their duet 'On the paths'. Eventually the voices of the ghosts and the children, who have come to their call, coalesce into a haunting ensemble of incantation and response, with the Governess and the housekeeper joining in as they approach. When they enter, the ghosts suddenly disappear, and Miles tells the Governess, using the perfect-4th interval basic to much of the work's material, especially the 'screw' theme and the 'malo' song, that he is, indeed, 'bad'. This disconcerting blend of innocence and knowingness gives a strong ending to the act.

Act 2.i (Variation 8) Colloquy and soliloquy The story is not so neatly symmetrical that it can end with the restoration of the situation with which it began. But the opera underlies the complementary relationship between the acts by beginning Act 2 with the scene most similar to that which ends Act 1.

Quint and Miss Jessel reappear; their purpose now is not to display their control over the children but to explain their own motives, their desire for a power that will compensate for their previous servile status, a power that will reach its culmination when, in Yeats's line used by Myfanwy Piper, 'the ceremony of innocence is drowned', and the children are destroyed. (The setting of the Yeats line to a version of the 'Why did I come?' motif also indicates the Governess's involuntary complicity in the corruption of Miles and Flora.) The scene ends with a short aria for the Governess, 'Lost in my labyrinth', that lends strength to the confidence of the ghosts in its expression of despair and failure; she has no idea how to save the children.

2.ii (Variation 9) The bells This scene does much to explain the Governess's continued, crippling indecision. On the surface the children are 'charming', singing a modified *Benedicite* that never slips into outright mockery. Mrs Grose tells the Governess that if she believes the children are really in danger she should write to their uncle, and although the Governess is at first unwilling, still insisting that the uncle is not to be bothered, her unnerving exchange with Miles as the others leave for church spurs her into action. The bells that dominate the scene now seem more brazen than celebratory, and the Governess's instinct is to flee from Bly.

2.iii (Variation 10) Miss Jessel The Governess

returns to the schoolroom, still intent on escape, but she finds Miss Jessel there, lamenting her own tragedy and threatening revenge. This assertion of possession – over the room, but also over the children – drives the Governess to retaliate, to abandon her selfish plan of flight and take the only step she believes will help the children. She writes to their guardian, accompanied by agitated music that is heard in a calmer version as she reads the letter over. Some commentators have seen this as a declaration of love as much as a plea for help; more obviously, it simply confirms the Governess's crippling ineffectiveness. She is still unable to take the children away. Somehow, as the darker interpretations of the story suggest, there is a part of her that also wills their destruction.

2.iv (Variation 11) *The bedroom* Miles is singing his 'malo' song when the Governess comes in to see if he is ready for bed. She reproaches him for failing to confide in her, and he still refuses to answer her questions about what happened at school, or at Bly before her arrival. Instinctively she knows that a frank confession will free Miles from Quint's power. She tells him that she has written to his guardian, but he hears only the seductive calls of Quint, and refuses to respond to her. The scene is crucial in its psychological insight, and the music, with the nocturnal musing of alto flute and bass clarinet disturbed by occasional flickers and shudders, is highly atmospheric.

2.v (Variation 12) *Quint* To music of febrile intensity and sinister charm, Quint urges Miles to steal the letter from the Governess's desk before it can be posted. After brief resistance, Miles does so.

2.vi (Variation 13) *The piano* Miles is playing the piano, the music a skilful parody of a classical sonata, to the praise of the Governess and Mrs Grose. Flora sings a cat's-cradle rhyme, lulling Mrs Grose to sleep. Flora then slips away, and the Governess quickly wakes the housekeeper, convinced the girl has gone in search of Miss Jessel. As the scene ends, Miles continues to play the piano with increasing flamboyance. The women hurry off to find Flora.

2.vii (Variation 14) *Flora* The Governess and housekeeper find Flora by the lake, and Miss Jessel promptly appears; Mrs Grose does not see her, and seeks to comfort Flora as the girl rails at the Governess in foot-stamping, bad-tempered music. The Governess realizes that it is Miss Jessel who has taught Flora to hate her.

2.viii (Variation 15) *Miles* Mrs Grose approaches the Governess, convinced that Flora is possessed by evil, having heard her pour out 'things I never knew nor hoped to know' in her sleep. The women agree that Mrs Grose should take Flora to her uncle, though the housekeeper says that he will not have had the letter: it was not where the Governess had left it. Now

'The Turn of the Screw' (Britten), scene from the original production at La Fenice, Venice, 14 September 1954, with Peter Pears as Quint and Jennifer Vyvyan as the Governess

the Governess is alone with Miles, and the passacaglia that underpins the rest of the final scene begins. It is a form that ensures a gradual increase of tension and momentum, and the rhythmic profile of the opera's recurring theme expresses the Governess's resolution. The theme also brings with it a degree of harmonic stability, in the 'home' key of A major, which is suddenly and severely disrupted as Quint begins his last attempt to prevent Miles from betraying him by speaking his name. The progress of the confrontation is brilliantly managed by Britten, though this was not achieved without some trial and error, as surviving sketches reveal. The combined lines of Quint and the Governess were not originally included, but they increase the dramatic and musical tension to breaking point. The crux is reached as Miles at last cries out 'Peter Quint, you devil!' Quint is defeated, and his voice dies away on a restatement of his most seductive melisma; but Miles, despite the Governess's immediate, optimistic reaction – 'you are saved, now all will be well' – collapses and dies. As she realizes what has happened, the Governess sings the 'malo' song as a lament. Her final question, 'What have we done between us?', is rhetorical to the extent that the consequences of her actions (and those of the children's guardian) are all too evident – if we assume that with proper care the children need never have been exposed to the corrupting influence of

Quint and Jessel. But there are larger doubts – about whether evil forces, when unleashed, can ever be contained – and the music underlines the doubt to the very end, the vocal line fading on a chromatic dissonance.

*

With its tightly controlled response to James's tale, Britten's opera runs the risk of seeming to shirk depth of expression as decisively as it shuns technical elaboration. Yet there is a spontaneity and naturalness in the musical ideas, and a compact solidity in the form-schemes of each scene, which give the lie to arguments that Britten's response was thin or inhibited. Like its predecessor, *Gloriana*, though for totally different reasons, *The Turn of the Screw* takes risks, not least with the demands it makes on young singers: Miles must be sung by a treble, even if Flora is rarely sung by a young girl. Above all the music reveals its absolute rightness in the way it brings to convincing life the extraordinary Jamesian blend of starchy social conventions and turbulent emotional forces which those conventions promote, while seeking their suppression. Britten gives substance to James's psychological insights without in any way distorting them. *The Turn of the Screw* marked a decisive change in Britten's development. After it, his main concern would be opera which shunned the large-scale effects of *Peter Grimes*, *Billy Budd* or *Gloriana*, and the chromatic intensity obtainable from the acknowledgment of some aspects of 12-note principles a central technique. What did not change, in essence, was the type of subject Britten favoured in his dramatic works.   A.W.

U

Ulisse ('Ulysses')

Opera in a prologue, two acts and an epilogue by Luigi Dallapiccola to his own libretto after Homer's *Odyssey*; Berlin, Deutsche Oper, 29 September 1968.

The original cast included Erik Saedén (Ulysses), Catherine Gayer (Nausicaa), Jean Madeira (Circe), Hildegard Hillebrecht (Anticlea), Loren Driscoll (Eumaeus) and Helmut Melchert (Tiresias/Demodocus); the conductor was Lorin Maazel.

Calypso	‡soprano
Ulisse [Ulysses]	baritone
Princess Nausicaa	high soprano
King Alcinoo [Alcinous]	bass-baritone
Demodoco [Demodocus]	*tenor
Circe *enchantress*	†mezzo-soprano
Tiresia [Tiresias]	*tenor
Anticlea *Ulysses' mother*	soprano
Telemaco [Telemachus] *Ulysses' son*	counter-tenor
Antinoo [Antinous] ⎫ *Penelope's*	baritone
Eurimaco [Eurymachus] ⎬ *suitors*	tenor
Pisandro [Peisander] ⎭	baritone
Melanto	†mezzo-soprano
Eumeo [Eumaeus] *a shepherd*	tenor
Penelope *Ulysses' wife*	‡soprano
Lotus-eaters	boys' voices

*†‡ These roles are doubled

Dallapiccola's last (and only full-length) opera, *Ulisse* was composed over eight years. It is the culmination of a series of works about death and was deliberately conceived as a summation of his oeuvre. The prologue consists of three episodes. In the first, the goddess Calypso gazes out to sea from the island of Ogygia, lamenting that Ulysses has left her, even though she offered to make him immortal. The second episode, depicting Poseidon's angry persecution of Ulysses, is for orchestra alone. As the sound of the stormy sea dies away, the scene changes to a wooded beach on the island of Phaeacia, where a group of young girls are playing as they wait for their washing to dry. Only the Princess Nausicaa sits apart. She is remembering a dream, a vision of a bridegroom who came to her from the sea. The girls resume their game, but break off suddenly when a

man appears from the wood, wearing only a few twigs and leaves. They throw a robe round his shoulders, and Nausicaa, without knowing his identity, welcomes him as the bridegroom of her vision. The stranger is overcome with wonder at Nausicaa's beauty, and kneels at her feet. She tells him to rise and accompany her to the palace of her father, King Alcinous.

Act 1 consists of five scenes: the first and last take place in the King's palace, and they act as a frame for the inner three, in which Ulysses narrates some of his past adventures. Alcinous is holding court in the great hall of his palace when Ulysses enters with Nausicaa. The bard Demodocus sings of what befell the Greek heroes after the fall of Troy and then begins musing on Ulysses' fate. As Demodocus becomes more impassioned, Ulysses can restrain himself no longer and breaks down. The King, noticing his tears, asks his name. Ulysses identifies himself, and agrees to tell them his story. The scene immediately dissolves, revealing (scene ii) Ulysses' ship about to drop anchor off the island of the Lotus-eaters. His crew are near to mutiny, but they agree to beach the ship when they hear the sound of the Lotus-eaters in the distance. The islanders then appear, drugged into euphoric lassitude through eating the blossoms and fruits of the lotus. They offer these to Ulysses' crew, some of whom, despite his exhortations to the contrary, accept. When Ulysses finally re-embarks, only a few of his companions go with him.

After an orchestral interlude, scene iii opens on the island of Aeaea, home of the enchantress Circe. Ulysses has spent more than a year with her, and he is anxious to move on. At first she refuses to let him, and when finally she does give way, she revenges herself by pointing out that all the horrors he encountered on his wanderings were reflections of his own inner nature. He will eventually return to Ithaca, she assures him, but he will find no repose there; his heart – unquiet to the last – will crave the sea again.

Following a brief interlude depicting the sirens' song, scene iv opens on a desolate riverbank in Hades where the souls of the damned wander for eternity in torment. Ulysses has come to Hades to question the ghost of the seer Tiresias about his future destiny. But first, to his horror, the shade of his mother Anticlea appears. She reproaches him for leaving Ithaca: his long absence broke her heart, and her existence in the afterlife is a continual torment. Ulysses tries to embrace her, but she vanishes before he can do so. Tiresias then appears, to tell Ulysses that he will see Ithaca and his wife and son again, but his homecoming will be a bloody one. Tiresias goes on to confirm Circe's prophecy: even after Ulysses has returned to Ithaca, he will set out again on his wanderings. Scene v reverts to Alcinous's palace where Ulysses winds up his narrative, briefly indicating his other adventures. Alcinous promises to help him, and Act 1 ends as Nausicaa bids him farewell, asking him not to forget her.

In the first scene of Act 2 the suitors of Penelope, Ulysses' wife, have set a trap for Telemachus, Ulysses' son, who is returning by sea from Sparta. Antinous, Eurymachus and Peisander, together with their whore, the maidservant Melanto, are waiting on a clifftop on Ithaca, to see whether their plans have succeeded. After a while the suitors depart, and Ulysses arrives, disguised as an old beggar, asking the shepherd Eumaeus for hospitality. His eyes frighten Melanto, and when she sees beacons (announcing Telemachus's safe arrival) flare up on the neighbouring hill, she rushes, terrified, back to the palace. Telemachus then runs in, describing his escape, and he, like everyone else, fails to recognize the disguised Ulysses.

In scene ii Ulysses is standing outside the royal palace listening to Penelope (soprano; often doubling Calypso) singing as she weaves. Inside, the suitors are holding a banquet, but Melanto is worried because she feels that some terrible danger threatens. She leaves the palace, and re-enters only when Antinous assures her that all will be well.

As scene iii opens, the feast is in full progress. The suitors make Melanto dance, giving her the bow of Ulysses as inspiration. Her savage dance is interrupted by the arrival of Telemachus, whom the suitors believed dead. They have not recovered from their surprise when Ulysses enters, and reveals his identity. He orders the guards to hang Melanto, strings the great bow that only he can use and strikes down the suitors one by one. As the crowd disperses Penelope appears.

The epilogue follows after a symphonic intermezzo. Once more at sea and far from Ithaca, Ulysses contemplates the stars, knowing that his knowledge and experience have not brought him repose or wisdom. He prays for some word that will make everything clear. The opera ends as he is vouchsafed a prophetic vision of God. He is alone no more.

*

With this ending Dallapiccola hoped to answer the question posed at the end of his earlier opera *Il prigioniero*. His understanding of the Ulysses myth, while following the outline of Homer's narrative, owes much to subsequent, more philosophical, less dramatic interpretations of the *Odyssey*, e.g. those of Dante, Pascoli, Tennyson and of course Joyce, and makes the Greek hero a searcher after truth. Both musically and philosophically *Ulisse* has much in common with Schoenberg's *Moses und Aron*. The music is in Dallapiccola's late, very refined style and uses 12 closely related 12-note rows that are leitmotifs in themselves and from which a large range of symbols is derived. Dallapiccola's earlier theatre pieces took as their central idea the struggle of man against a force stronger than he, but Ulysses' struggle is above all a struggle against himself, inasmuch as he aspires to penetrate the mystery of the world. The opera is structured as a large, symmetrical arch. In the centre is Ulysses' descent into Hades where, gazing into the abyss, he realizes that he is utterly alone. On either side of this, through his encounters with women and with the Homeric monsters, Ulysses is made to search into himself – an attitude encapsulated in the words 'Guardare, meravigliarsi, e tornar a guardare' ('To search, to wonder, and to search again and again'), with which the opera opens. The vision of God which Ulysses is vouchsafed at the end of the opera enables him to put aside his doubts. It also enabled Dallapiccola to do the same, and to express the certainty in God which had often eluded him throughout his own life. In this respect, Dallapiccola conceived *Ulisse* as the summation of his life's work, and he incorporated into it fragments of many of his earlier scores. **A.Se.**

V

Vampyr, Der ('The Vampire')

Grosse romantische Oper in two acts by Heinrich August Marschner to a libretto by Wilhelm August Wohlbrück after plays based on John W. Polidori's story *The Vampyre*, itself a revision of Lord Byron's *Fragment of a Novel*, sometimes called *Augustus Darvell*; Leipzig, Stadttheater, 29 March 1828.

The cast at the première included Köckert (Davenaut), Wilhelmina Streit (Malwina), Wilhelm Höfler (Aubry), Eduard Genast (Ruthven), Vogt (Dibdin), Dorothea Devrient (Emmy), Wilhelm Fischer (Blunt) and Madame Köckert (Suse).

Lord Ruthven *Earl of Marsden, the vampire*		baritone
Sir John Berkley *Laird of the House of Berkley*		bass
Janthe *his daughter*		soprano
Sir Humphrey Davenaut *Laird of the House of Davenaut*		bass
Malwina *his daughter*		soprano
Edgar Aubry *member and employee of the House of Davenaut*		tenor
The Vampire Master		spoken
John Perth *superintendent on the Marsden estate*		spoken
Emmy *his daughter, George Dibdin's fiancée*		soprano
George Dibdin *a servant of Davenaut*		tenor
Berkley's Manservant		bass
James Gadshill	*peasants on the Davenaut estate*	tenor
Richard Scrop		tenor
Robert Green		bass
Toms Blunt		bass
Suse Blunt *Toms's wife*		mezzo-soprano

Demons, witches, hobgoblins and other creatures from the underworld; hunters and servants of Berkley and Davenaut; peasants from the estates of Davenaut and Marsden; ladies and gentlemen of the nobility

Setting The castle and grounds of Sir Humphrey Davenaut, Scotland, in the 18th century

The original literary source for Marschner's *Vampyr* was the fragment of a novel that Byron's doctor, John W. Polidori, worked up from sketches Byron had abandoned. Attributed to Byron and published in 1819 in the *New Monthly Magazine* under the title *The Vampyre*, the story created a sensation. Plays on the vampire theme became popular in France. The most favoured among them proved to be *Le vampire* (Paris, 13 June 1820) by P. F. A. Carmouche, C. Nodier and A. de Jouffroy, but when J. R. Planché transplanted the action to Scotland, added fresh intrigue, and adapted the work for English audiences as *The Vampire, or The Bride of the Isles* (London, 9 August 1820), he achieved equal success. The same may be said of *Der Vampyr, oder Die Todten-Braut* (Karlsruhe, 1 March 1821), by the elusive H. L. Ritter, who lengthened but simplified the drama and modified the cast. While Ritter's work appears to have been Wohlbrück's immediate model, the latter interpolated additional material, mainly from Ritter's predecessors.

Although the vampire craze spread quickly in the realm of the novel and spoken play, it was slow to creep into opera. Before Wohlbrück's effort, only two one-act works (one produced in Naples, the other in Ghent) enjoyed any popularity. Contemporary with the Marschner-Wohlbrück work was another entitled *Der Vampyr* (Stuttgart, 21 September 1828) with music by Peter Joseph von Lindpaintner and a libretto by C. M. Heigel. Though less tightly constructed dramatically and less convincing psychologically, Lindpaintner's work did have a following and effectively prevented Marschner's from reaching certain stages, notably those in Vienna, until late in the century.

During the century after its première, nonetheless, Marschner's *Vampyr* was given in most major centres in Europe, including Moscow, St Petersburg, Copenhagen, London and Budapest. In a 1924 revision of the score, Pfitzner turned the first half of the first act into a prologue in order to avoid an awkward scene change. This is the version used in performances today, of which there were a number in the 1970s and 80s, primarily in the UK, Germany and the USA.

*

Act I.i *A deserted clearing in the forest on the Berkley estate, with the vampires' cave on the left* Summoned by a chorus of witches and hobgoblins, the Vampire Master appears with Lord Ruthven, a newly created vampire. Ruthven has petitioned for another year on earth before being dragged into hell for eternity. The Vampire Master consents, provided Ruthven can sacrifice three young brides by the following midnight. As Ruthven sings his opening aria, 'Ha! welche Lust!', full of sinister chromatic writing, about the delights of divesting his victims of their blood, the unsuspecting Janthe, his latest conquest, collapses into his arms. Ruthven escorts her into the vampires' cave and sucks her veins dry. Immediately afterwards, Berkley's search party enter the cave to drag out Ruthven, whom Berkley stabs and leaves for dead. On his way back from London, Aubry sees the almost lifeless Ruthven, who asks to be taken to a plateau above the cave to be healed by the rays of the moon. In a melodrama, similar to Weber's Wolf's Glen scene in *Der Freischütz*, Aubry accedes to his wishes. Aubry now realizes that Ruthven must be a vampire, and is aghast; but Ruthven, who once saved Aubry's life, swears him to secrecy. As Ruthven's body slowly revives, Aubry runs off in terror. Sparse at first, the musical fabric becomes more agitated, and more chromatic, as Ruthven recovers.

1.ii A tastefully decorated hall in the castle of Davenaut From an upstairs window, Malwina sees her sweetheart Aubry approaching; she rushes out to

'Der Vampyr' (Marschner), the final scene of Act 2
(Ruthven is dragged down to hell): engraving by
C. A. Schwerdgeburth after H. Ramberg from the
'Orphea-Taschenbuch' (Leipzig, 1831)

meet him. Sir Humphrey, unaware of his daughter's love for Aubry, announces plans for her to marry before midnight the Earl of Marsden, laird of a neighbouring estate. Malwina implores him to reconsider, but Davenaut is adamant. When the Earl of Marsden enters, Aubry pales as he recognizes Ruthven; the vampire quietly reminds him of his oath of silence.

The most significant characteristic of this half of Act 1 is that the music is almost entirely in ensemble. The action is swift, involves close interaction among several characters, and individuals are rarely allowed to impede the dramatic flow with arias that concentrate on a single topic or emotion. Marschner's tendency to integrate the action musically in this way, an important departure from his predecessors' procedures, was to become even more pronounced in *Hans Heiling* (1833).

Act 2.i *A square in front of the castle of Marsden* Guests have arrived for the wedding in the afternoon of the peasants George and Emmy and, as if summoned by Emmy's allegorical *Romanze* about vampires, 'Sieh, Mutter, dort den bleichen Mann', Ruthven appears and begins to woo her. Unable to talk the vampire out of his hideous plans, Aubry resigns himself to hopelessness in the aria 'Wie ein schöner Frühlingsmorgen' (to which Wagner appended a stretta in 1833) and leaves in despair as Ruthven leads Emmy off to claim her as his second victim. The tipsy Scrop, Blunt, Green and Gadshill shuffle in to provide some comic relief with their quartet 'Im Herbst da muss man trinken'. Incensed at their drunken lethargy, Suse jumps on to a table to castigate them, but a shot off stage interrupts her. George runs in to relate that he found Emmy murdered by the vampire, whom he has shot.

Marschner continues here to emulate Weber but provides new effects of his own. The dramatic digression provided by Emmy's *Romanze* matches in general musical style that of Ännchen in *Der Freischütz*, although Marschner does not accompany her with the exotic instrumental countermelody that characterizes the genre in the works of Mozart, Kreutzer and Weber. The spontaneous men's drinking quartet, an operatic innovation of Marschner's (it was encored at all early performances), comes directly from the German *Gesangverein* (choral society) tradition and was calculated to appeal to the popular taste of audiences as well as to provide some relief from the gruesome, emotionally charged narrative.

2.ii *A hall in the castle of Davenaut* It is now evening. Guests assemble for Malwina's wedding. Although despondent, she has resigned herself to marrying Ruthven; but she has no idea that he is a vampire. As midnight nears Davenaut orders the ceremony to begin, but Aubry, prepared to sacrifice himself, divulges Ruthven's secret. Immediately, the vampire is dragged into hell amid the raucous laughter of its unholy denizens. Davenaut gives his consent for his daughter to marry Aubry.

*

Marscher was the most important exponent of German Romantic opera in the generation between Weber and Wagner. His aim in 1828 was to continue the tradition established by Weber in *Der Freischütz*, and he created *Der Vampyr* in its image. The inter-mingling of mortals with supernatural characters from native folklore (rather than Greek mythology), an inheritance from Singspiel, matched Weber's practice as did the general musical construction of the work, and though *Der Freischütz* is more expertly crafted musically and with a tighter dramatic structure than *Der Vampyr*, Marschner advanced structurally, harmonically and dramatically beyond what Weber had achieved. Both works possess a tripartite overture (placed at the end of Act 1 scene i in Pfitzner's revision of *Der Vampyr*) that associates a lyrical second theme with the heroine (Agathe in *Freischütz*, Malwina here). While Weber favoured a predominantly diatonic harmonic idiom closely allied with folksong, Marschner began to introduce chromatic progressions and melodic lines (partly inherited from Spohr) to produce a feeling of foreboding and to increase dramatic tension. The effect of this chromaticism is immediately apparent in such movements as Ruthven's opening aria and in the untitled melodrama that accompanies Aubry's placement of Ruthven's body in the moonlight.

A.D.P.

Vêpres siciliennes, Les
[*I vespri siciliani* ('The Sicilian Vespers')]

Opéra in five acts by Giuseppe Verdi to a libretto by Eugène Scribe and Charles Duveyrier after their libretto *Le duc d'Albe*; Paris, Opéra, 13 June 1855.

The first cast included Marc Bonnehée (Mont-fort), Louis Guéymard (Henri), Louis-Henri Obin (Procida) and Sophie Cruvelli (Hélène).

Guy de Montfort (Montforte) *Governor*		
of Sicily under Charles d'Anjou,		
King of Naples		baritone
Le Sire de Béthune	} *French officers*	bass
Count de Vaudemont		bass
Henri (Arrigo) *a young Sicilian*		tenor
Jean Procida *a Sicilian doctor*		bass
Duchess Hélène (Elena) *sister of Duke*		
Frédéric of Austria		soprano
Ninetta *her maid*		contralto
Daniéli *a Sicilian*		tenor

Thibault (Tebaldo)	} *French soldiers*	tenor
Robert (Roberto)		baritone
Mainfroid (Manfredo) *a Sicilian*		tenor

Sicilian men and women, French soldiers, monks,
　corps de ballet
Setting In and around Palermo, 1282

Following the première of *La traviata* in March 1853, the pace of Verdi's operatic production slowed considerably, from 16 operas in 11 years to six in the next 18 (although these tended to be longer, and much time and creative energy were devoted to revising various works). Verdi now spent an increasing amount of time away from the theatre, and on at least one occasion seems to have decided to stop composing altogether. He had quarrelled with the directors of La Scala, and did not visit Milan for 20 years after a dramatic return in 1848. His attention now turned to Paris. After the performances of *Jérusalem* (the revised version of *I Lombardi*) at the Opéra in 1847 he had intended to produce an entirely new opera for the first theatre of the French capital, but the revolutions of 1848 caused the plan to be shelved. He renewed negotiations with the Opéra, however, in 1852, and a contract was drawn up for a full-scale French grand opera in five acts, with a libretto by Eugène Scribe, the acknowledged poetic master of the genre. After various subjects had been proposed, poet and composer eventually agreed to use a revised version of an existing libretto, *Le duc d'Albe*, written by Scribe and Charles Duveyrier for Halévy (who did not use it) and partly set to music by Donizetti in 1839.

Verdi spent most of 1854 working at the score, making a reluctant Scribe undertake some important revisions and complaining about the sheer length demanded by audiences at the Opéra. The première was well received, even by such severe critics as Berlioz, but the work failed to enter the standard repertory of the Opéra. Its revolutionary subject caused difficulties with the Italian censors and it was first performed in Italian in 1855 at Parma in a bowdlerized version translated by Eugenio Caimi and entitled *Giovanna de Guzman*. Later performances as *I vespri siciliani* retained most aspects of Caimi's translation and it is almost invariably in this Italian version that the opera is encountered today. For a revival at the Opéra in 1863, Verdi replaced 'O jour de peine' in Act 4 with the tenor *romance* 'O toi que j'ai chéri'.

*

The overture, the longest Verdi wrote and still sometimes revived in the concert hall, follows convention in being made up of themes drawn from the opera. It falls into two movements: a Largo, full of rhythmic 'death' figures, even in its more lyrical, major-mode section; and an Allegro agitato, whose main theme is taken from the Henri-Montfort duet in Act 3 and is repeated twice before a noisy Prestissimo brings the piece to a close.

Act I *The main piazza in Palermo* The opening chorus, 'Beau pays de France!' ('Al cielo natio'), musically juxtaposes the victorious French soldiers with the resentful Sicilian people and includes a brief episode in which a drunken soldier, Robert, looks forward to claiming his share of the vanquished Sicilian women.

Hélène enters dressed in mourning; Béthune explains to Vaudemont that she is a hostage of Montfort and has come to pray for her brother Duke Frédéric, executed by Montfort a year ago. Robert staggers up, asking her for a song; she complies with a freely structured aria made up of three brief episodes and a closing cabaletta, 'Courage! ... du courage!' ('Coraggio, su, coraggio'), in which she rallies the Sicilians around her. As the cabaletta draws to a close, the Sicilians advance on the French; but they are interrupted by the appearance of Montfort. He precipitates a largely unaccompanied quartet 'Quelle horreur m'environne!' ('D'ira fremo all'aspetto'), in which Hélène and Montfort explore their conflicting positions. Henri now arrives and, unaware of who Montfort is, explains to Hélène that he has inexplicably been released from prison by the Governor of Sicily but would dearly love to meet the tyrant face to face. At this Montfort reveals his identity and dismisses the women, thus preparing the ground for the closing duet finale. Like Hélène's aria, the duet passes through a number of short contrasting sections (as Montfort learns of Henri's history, offers him a commission in the French army and advises him to avoid Hélène) before closing with a cabaletta, 'Téméraire! téméraire!' ('Temerario! qual ardire!'), in which the characters' mutual defiance is reflected in a clash of strongly contrasting individual themes.

Act 2 *A delightful valley near Palermo* An orchestral introduction suggesting the movement of a boat accompanies the disembarcation of the fanatical patriot Procida. He greets his homeland in a brief recitative before beginning the famous Andante, 'Et toi, Palerme' ('O tu, Palermo'), fashioned in ternary form with a striking level of orchestral detail in the middle section. Procida's followers appear and together they sing the cabaletta 'Dans l'ombre et le silence' ('Nell'ombra e nel silenzio'), in which a stealthy, staccato choral passage precedes the main solo melody. Henri and Hélène arrive and are told by Procida that Spanish forces have agreed to aid the Sicilian cause, but that the Spaniards will not act unless there is a local uprising. Procida departs, to allow Henri and Hélène a two-movement duet. In the Allegro 'Comment, dans ma reconnaissance' ('Quale, o prode'), rapid dialogue precedes Henri's declara-

tion of love; in 'Près du tombeau peut-être' ('Presso alla tomba') the couple sing together (though with highly differentiated lines), Hélène agreeing to accept Henri if he will avenge her brother's death.

Béthune appears, summoning Henri to a ball at Montfort's house that evening; when Henri refuses he is surrounded and dragged away. Hélène explains to Procida what has happened, but he is nevertheless determined to continue his plan of attack. To the strains of a festive tarantella, the stage fills with young Sicilian men and women, among them 12 brides and their prospective husbands. Some French soldiers arrive and Procida, keen to foment trouble, encourages them to take advantage of the local women – to such good effect that at the end of the dance the soldiers abduct the young brides at swordpoint. The chorus of outrage that follows, 'Interdits, accablés' ('Il rossor mi coprì!'), again obsessively repeating rhythmic 'death' figures, is interrupted by offstage voices singing a barcarolle: a boat is seen in the distance carrying French officers and Sicilian women. In a brief interlude, Procida decides that Montfort will be assassinated that very night; and the two very different choruses join in cleverly worked counterpoint to bring the act to a close.

Act 3.i *A study in Montfort's palace* A brief orchestral prelude introduces Montfort, alone and brooding on his past: the woman he abducted many years ago has died, but she brought up their son Henri (who does not know his father's identity) to hate Montfort. The governor summons Henri to his presence before singing the famous 'Au sein de la puissance' ('In braccio alle dovizie'), a freely structured aria full of surprising harmonic excursions, in which he muses on his outward power and inward emptiness. Henri, entering, begins a lengthy duet, 'Quand ma bonté toujours nouvelle' ('Quando al mio sen'), which departs notably from standard Italian formal practice. There is a rapid alternation of tempos and moods in which Montfort presents Henri with proof of their relationship and, to a statement of the main theme of the overture (a melody that also dominates the final section of the duet), rejoices in his revelation. Henri is shocked, fears he must now lose Hélène and, in spite of Montfort's continued pleading, rejects the embrace of his father.

3.ii *A magnificent hall laid out for a grand ball* The long ballet that begins this scene is entitled 'Les quatre saisons' ('Le quattro stagioni') and, at least at the first production, entailed an elaborate mixture of mime and dance, with gods, zephyrs, naiads, fauns and a final dance to Bacchus. Verdi's succession of brief contrasting movements shows the requisite instrumental invention and rhythmic vitality, though it is perhaps too one-dimensional to be of much interest outside its immediate context.

The Act 3 finale is a large choral tableau, typical of French grand opera in its setting of private emotions within a public frame. The festive opening chorus, 'O fête brillante' ('O splendide feste!'), is interrupted by various dance tunes as Procida and Hélène approach Henri to tell him of the plot to murder Montfort. Henri warns Montfort of the danger but still refuses to side with his father. However, when Hélène tries to stab Montfort, Henri defends him and the conspirators are immediately arrested. The ensuing Adagio concertato, 'Coup terrible' ('Colpo orrendo'), which closes the act, is made up of two contrasting musical segments: first, a section of stunned surprise in which a tiny rhythmic motif is isolated and repeated; and then, its antithesis, a long lyrical melody in which all participants join to effect a stirring close.

Act 4 *The courtyard of a fortress* A robust orchestral introduction presents Henri, who shows a pass allowing him to visit the prisoners. He laments his position in 'O jour de peine' ('Giorno di pianto'), a strophic aria whose angular melodic arch and harmonic underpinning are quite unlike the Verdian norm and which ends with a fast coda. Hélène then enters to precipitate the first movement of the grand duet, 'De courroux et d'effroi' ('O sdegni miei'), in which fragmentary responses coalesce into a patterned melody as Henri begs for understanding, the melody momentarily breaking into recitative when Henri admits the identity of his father. The second movement, 'Ami! . . . le coeur d'Hélène' ('Arrigo! ah parli a un core'), is a miniature minor–major *romanza* for Hélène, in which she reconciles herself to Henri, though with no hope of their union; and the duet closes with a curtailed cabaletta, 'Pour moi rayonne' ('È dolce raggio').

Procida enters; he has been informed that Spanish forces are ready to aid the revolutionaries. He is quickly followed by Montfort, who orders the prisoners' immediate execution. Procida then leads off the quartet, 'Adieu, mon pays' ('Addio, mia patria'), in which the principals explore their differing emotions. Montfort offers clemency if only Henri will call him 'father'. A *de profundis* is heard off stage, the place of execution is revealed and eventually, to a slow, high violin melody, Henri submits. The prisoners are released; the marriage of Hélène and Henri is even allowed by Montfort as a symbol of reconciliation, and all join in a final stretta.

Act 5 *Luxurious gardens in Montfort's palace in Palermo* The final act begins with three 'atmospheric' numbers in which the plot is barely advanced but local colour is richly explored. First comes the chorus to honour the wedding pair, 'Célébrons ensemble' ('Si celebri alfine'), quickly followed by Hélène's *sicilienne*, 'Merci, jeunes amies' ('Mercè, dilette amiche'), a *couplet* form entailing considerable

virtuosity. Finally, there is Henri's lightly scored *mélodie* 'La brise souffle au loin' ('La brezza aleggia'), a song in praise of the evening breezes. Procida, his fanatical hatred undimmed, enters to announce the imminent uprising, which will begin at the sound of the wedding bells. He upbraids Hélène when he sees her love for Henri; she is horrified at the coming massacre. Henri leads off the first movement of the terzetto finale, 'Sort fatal!' ('Sorte fatal!'). Hélène tries to stop the progress of events by refusing to go through with the wedding, but in spite of her pleading Henri refuses to leave the scene and in the closing stretta of the trio, 'Trahison! imposture!' ('M'ingannasti, o traditrice'), the principals' conflicting positions are again explored. Montfort enters and signals for the wedding bells to sound. The Sicilians rush in with daggers drawn and fall on Montfort and the French.

            *

Les vêpres siciliennes, in common with almost all French grand operas, has fallen to a great extent from the repertory, its sheer length and the complexity of its vocal and scenic demands placing severe pressure on modern opera-house economics. There may also be purely musical reasons for the opera's comparative neglect: with a very few exceptions, its main lyrical numbers lack the melodic immediacy of the trio of Italian operas (*Rigoletto*, *Il trovatore* and *La traviata*) that immediately preceded it. However, for those wishing to understand Verdi's musical development during the 1850s, *Les vêpres siciliennes* is of enormous importance. In both strictly formal terms and in larger matters of operatic structure, it marks a decisive turn away from the language of the middle-period Italian operas and the emergence of many stylistic features we associate with the later Verdi. There is no subsequent Verdi opera in which the experience of *Les vêpres* will not be recalled and refined.   **R.P.**

Village Romeo and Juliet, A [*Romeo und Julia auf dem Dorfe*]

Lyric drama in six pictures (or scenes) by Frederick Delius to his own libretto after Gottfried Keller's novel; Berlin, Komische Oper, 21 February 1907.

The première was directed by Hans Gregor and conducted by Fritz Cassirer; the main singers were Willi Merkel (Sali), Lola Artôt de Padilla (Vreli) and Desider Zador (Dark Fiddler).

Manz ⎫	*rich farmers*	baritone
Marti ⎭		baritone
Sali *son of Manz as a child*		soprano
Sali *son of Manz as a man*		tenor

Vreli *daughter of Marti*	soprano
The Dark Fiddler *rightful heir to the*	
wood	baritone
Two Peasant Men	baritones
Three Peasant	
Women	soprano, soprano, contralto
Gingerbread Woman	soprano
Wheel of Fortune Woman	soprano
Cheap Jewellery Woman	mezzo-soprano
Showman	tenor
Merry-go-round Man	baritone
The Slim Girl	soprano
The Wild Girl	mezzo-soprano
The Poor Horn-player *vagabonds*	tenor
The Hunchbacked	
Bass-player	bass
Three Bargees	baritone, baritone, tenor

Vagabonds, peasants, bargees

Setting In and around Seldwyla, Switzerland,
in the middle of the 19th century

Work on the libretto for Delius's fourth opera began in 1897, when he first asked Charles Keary to produce an English text. Unhappy with the result, he turned to Karl-August Gerhardi in 1898 for a draft in German. He then resumed negotiations with Keary before deciding to attempt an English libretto himself, which was completed in 1899. The German translation for the first edition of the vocal score (*c*1906), with piano part by Florent Schmitt, was made by Delius's wife Jelka.

Keller based his story on a report in the *Zürcher Freitagszeitung* of 3 September 1847. It told how a young man of 19 and girl of 17 had fallen in love but failed to win their parents' consent because of mutual enmity. The young couple had danced one evening in a local inn; the next day they were found dead in a nearby meadow. Keller elaborated the story, making much of the parents' quarrel over land belonging rightfully to an illegitimate fiddler who could not inherit under Swiss law. Delius used the parental enmity only in so far as it made the marriage of the young couple impossible. The Dark Fiddler was given an altogether more sinister role, as the embodiment of the cruel fate that brings about the suicide of the lovers. At the end Delius has unseen bargemen emphasize the frailty of earthly happiness. Delius did concentrated work on the music during 1900–01, but the orchestral 'Walk to the Paradise Garden', often played separately, was composed in 1906 for the Berlin première.

The first London performance (Covent Garden, 22 February 1910) was conducted by Thomas Beecham, with Walter Hyde, Ruth Vincent and Robert Maitland; the Beecham recording (1948) had René Soames, Lorely Dyer and Gordon Clinton. Performances in Bradford, London and Manchester

to mark the Delius centenary (1962) were conducted by Meredith Davies, with John Wakefield, Elsie Morison and Neil Easton. The Davies recording (1973) featured Robert Tear, Elizabeth Harwood and John Shirley-Quirk. The American première was in Washington, DC, at the John F. Kennedy Center on 26 April 1972, directed by Frank Corsaro and conducted by Paul Callaway, with John Stewart, Patricia Wells and John Reardon. The Swiss première was at the Zürich Opernhaus, 20 December 1980, conducted by Charles Mackerras, with Gösta Winbergh, Ursula Reinhardt-Kiss and Jozsef Dene.

*

Scene 1 *September; a piece of woodland luxuriously overgrown on a hill* Manz and Marti are out ploughing on either side of the disused land. Marti decides to take in an extra furrow from the waste ground, sure that Manz will be doing the same. Sali and Vreli, son and daughter of the farmers, come with lunch and go off to play in the wood while the farmers eat. The children return when they hear a distant voice. It is a lame man with a violin, the Dark Fiddler, rightful owner of the waste ground who cannot inherit because of his doubtful parentage. The children fear him, but he assures them they can play in safety on his land so long as it remains unploughed. If it is ever worked, they must beware. Perhaps time will avenge him, he tells the farmers. The land is to be sold; at once the farmers wrangle about the extra furrows, and with rising tempers drag the children apart and forbid their play.

Scene 2 *Six years later. Outside Marti's house; around it everything has run wild with neglect* The farmers' feud led to a lawsuit which ruined them both. Sali enters, now a young man, drawn irresistibly to see again where Vreli lives. Together they lament the hatred that has wrought such havoc. Sali asks if he may stay awhile, but Vreli fears her father may soon return. They realize their childhood friendship is turning to love and agree to meet that evening on the waste land.

Scene 3 *The wild land overgrown with poppies in bloom, surrounded by cornfields; snow mountains in the distance* Sali lies waiting, and Vreli enters unnoticed. She calls him and hides; he runs eagerly after her. They forget their cares in the delight of being together again. The Dark Fiddler limps down from his ground, reminding them of his former appearance in their lives and the troubles caused by the disputed land. They are all beggars now, and the young people can join his wanderings if they wish. He assures them they will meet again. Sali comforts Vreli in her anxiety and they resume their play. This is interrupted by Vreli's father Marti, who has been spying on her and angrily confronts the young couple. Sali strikes him to the ground, and the scene ends in despair with Vreli imagining her father dead.

Scene 4 *Interior of Marti's house; everything is bare: only a bedstead and a bench are left* Vreli is alone. Marti has lost his reason, and she has taken her father away; the house is to be sold. Sali comes in, having heard the news. The young lovers agree they must never part; they will wander together like larks in springtime. Quietly they settle by the fire and sleep in each other's arms. They dream they are being married in the old church at Seldwyla. As dawn breaks they realize they have shared the same dream. Now they long for a happy day together. Peasants yodel in the distance, and Sali remembers it is the day of the Berghald fair. Vreli must forget her worries and join him in the merrymaking.

Scene 5 *The fair; an inn in front of which booths are erected* The hucksters cry their wares as the town bells peal. A show is about to begin in a tent, and the crowd sings as the circus band strikes up. Sali and Vreli enter, enchanted by all they see. Sali would buy everything for her and bewails his lack of money. As they wander past the inn, a man and woman recognize them as the children of Manz and Marti, now poor and friendless. Sali purchases a cheap ring for Vreli, but more and more they are embarrassed by the insistence of the hucksters. Sali decides this is no place for them and suggests they make for the Paradise Garden, a public park with an inn, where they can be alone and no one will know them. As the crowd emerges from the tent, the young lovers make their escape and begin their walk, hand in hand, towards the garden.

Scene 6 *The Paradise Garden. An old dilapidated house, with snow mountains in the distance, is now used as an inn; a river flows by, with a hay barge moored to the bank* Vagabonds are drinking round a table, and the Dark Fiddler stands gazing at the mountains. He joins his companions and continues the tale of his dispossessed lands: the parents hate, the children love, and no one knows the end. At that moment Sali and Vreli enter. The Dark Fiddler urges them to join his friends,

who extol the vagabond life. The lovers wonder whether happiness might not lie that way. One of the women eyes Sali intently, pointing out that there will be many alternatives when they tire of each other. The Dark Fiddler suggests they think it over, but Sali and Vreli know they will find no contentment there. A bargeman is heard afar on the river, singing of passing strangers drifting by. Sali understands the meaning of the song, and they decide to drift away for ever. They sing their love-death: the hay barge shall be their marriage bed and, as the Dark Fiddler plays a wild accompaniment, Sali casts off, removes the plug from the barge and falls into Vreli's arms. The Fiddler points to the bend in the river as the boat sinks and the young travellers pass out of sight.

*

By the time of *A Village Romeo and Juliet*, Delius was musically fully formed and his idiom had become idiosyncratic and personal; he now had the artistry to invest the young lovers' helplessness with an almost unbearable poignancy. The calm and diatonic opening of the work gradually clouds to the harsh chromatics of the quarrelling farmers. The lovers' duet in Scene 4 is as touching a tribute as any to the influence of Wagner, impossible to conceive without *Parsifal* and 'Ich sah das Kind' (from Act 2); yet the descending semitones of the bass are a Delian hallmark. Delius employs a handful of leitmotifs, using them with masterly flexibility until he gathers the most important of them to form the magical tone poem of 'The Walk to the Paradise Garden'. In his libretto Delius played down the immediacy of the Keller story, so that the young Sali and Vreli are distanced from reality and act out their ill-starred love in trance-like isolation. The Dark Fiddler, too, is an outsider figure such as Delius himself was. The result is an operatic masterpiece with drama and music marvellously integrated, a *Tristan und Isolde* for the young and innocent.   R.A.

Walküre, Die ('The Valkyrie')

First day of *Der Ring des Nibelungen* in three acts by Richard Wagner to his own libretto; Munich, Königliches Hof- und Nationaltheater, 26 June 1870 (first performance as part of cycle: Bayreuth, Festspielhaus, 14 August 1876).

The first Wotan was, as in *Das Rheingold*, August Kindermann; the first Brünnhilde, Sophie Stehle (Fricka in *Rheingold*). Siegmund and Sieglinde were sung by Heinrich and Therese Vogl. For the 1876 cast, *see* Ring des Nibelungen, Der.

Siegmund		tenor
Hunding		bass
Wotan		bass-baritone
Sieglinde		soprano
Brünnhilde		soprano
Fricka		mezzo-soprano
Helmwige		
Gerhilde		
Siegrune		
Grimgerde	*Valkyries*	sopranos and
Ortlinde		contraltos
Waltraute		
Rossweisse		
Schwertleite		

The first prose sketch for *Die Walküre* dates from autumn (probably November) 1851. In a letter to Uhlig of 11 November 1851 Wagner referred to the new work as *Siegmund und Sieglind: der Walküre Bestrafung*, but by 20 November (letter to Liszt) he had renamed it with the familiar title *Die Walküre*. The sketch was developed into a prose draft (17–26 May 1852) and then into a verse draft (1 June–1 July 1852). The final poem was incorporated into the private printing of the entire *Ring* text in February 1853.

The first musical sketches for *Die Walküre* date from the summer of 1852 and include an early version of the Spring Song. The first complete draft was made between 28 June and 27 December 1854. Unlike the comparable draft for *Das Rheingold*, which for the most part consisted of one vocal staff and one instrumental, that for *Walküre* shows some degree of orchestral elaboration, often with one vocal staff and

two instrumental. In spite of the difficulties he experienced – on account of many delays and interruptions – in expanding that first draft into score, Wagner did not find it necessary to make a second draft as for *Rheingold*, since he was now familiar with the expanded orchestral forces. Instead he went straight into a draft of the full score (January 1855–20 March 1856); the fair copy was made in parallel between 14 July 1855 and 23 March 1856.

*

Act I *Inside Hunding's dwelling* The turbulent prelude that opens the work depicts at once a raging storm and the emotional convulsions that are soon to shake the participants in the drama. A tremolo on a single repeated note is maintained by the second violins and violas for 60 bars, while underneath cellos and double basses rampage up and down a series of notes clearly intended to recall the motif of the Spear (*see* **Rheingold, Das**, ex.5): that symbol of Wotan's power and authority is evoked because this entire act is contrived, in a sense, at the instigation of his will. The motif sung by Donner, the god of thunder, at the end of *Rheingold* to the words 'Heda! Hedo!' rings out on the brass, first on the Wagner tubas. Despite the different harmonic context it begins in B♭, exactly as in *Rheingold*; however, it is winched up sequentially through a series of modulations until the tension breaks in a thunderclap, after which the storm begins to subside.

As the curtain rises and Siegmund, collapsing with exhaustion, bursts into the forest dwelling, a cello takes up the Spear motif but turns its end accommodatingly back on itself (ex.1): a hint that an alternative to sheer naked power is being proposed.

Ex.1

Sieglinde enters, and as she bends over Siegmund's sleeping figure that idea is taken up again in conjunction with a phrase expressive of her tenderness (ex.2). The two melodic ideas are worked

Ex.2

to a small climax as Sieglinde fetches him water. Then ex.1 opens out into a fully-fledged Love theme, ex.3 (derived from Freia's theme in *Rheingold*), the music as yet anticipating events on the stage.

Ex.3

Sieglinde now fetches a horn of mead for Siegmund to the accompaniment of an effusively lyrical passage in A major, bassoons, horns and clarinets lending a bloom to the strings. The pair gaze at each other in unspoken affirmation of love, the two halves of the Love motif sounding in reverse order. The minor triad of the motif (ex.4) for the Volsungs (the children of Wälse or Wolfe) evokes the ill luck that dogs Siegmund; the motif is combined with ex.2 as he decides to stay and await his fate.

Ex.4

The arrival of Hunding (scene ii) is heralded by a sharp, abrupt motif on the Wagner tubas. He roughly extends his hospitality and asks where Siegmund has come from and what is his name. Siegmund says he should be called Woeful, describing how one day he returned from hunting with his father, Wolfe, to find their home burnt down, his mother murdered and his twin sister brutally abducted. At Sieglinde's prompting he then narrates how he went to the aid of a young woman forced into a loveless marriage, killing her savage kinsmen in the fight. Hunding now realizes that he is harbouring his kinsmen's foe. The laws of hospitality compel him to give Siegmund shelter for the night, but in the morning he will have to fight for his life.

As she prepares Hunding's night drink, Sieglinde drugs it. Realization of their identity is now dawning on both of them. She leaves the room with a lingering gaze, first at Siegmund and then at a spot in the trunk of the ash tree that stands in the middle of the hut: the Sword motif sounds presciently on the bass trumpet.

In the third scene Siegmund, left alone, meditates on the fever of excitement stirred up by Sieglinde and on his weaponless plight, recalling that his father had promised that there would be a sword for him in his time of need ('Ein Schwert verhiess mir der Vater'). He calls on his father: 'Wälse! Wälse!' (the octave leaps of the Sword motif without the tail-piece are traditionally regarded, by singers and listeners alike, as a test of virility). They launch Siegmund on a

heart-warming soliloquy, richly orchestrated, the rippling harp arpeggios mirroring the gleaming of the sword in the ash tree.

Sieglinde enters. She tells how an old man dressed in grey had thrust the sword into the tree at the wedding ceremony of herself and Hunding. This narration, 'Der Männer Sippe sass hier im Saal', is a choice example of the musico-poetic synthesis – the practical application of Wagner's principles of word-setting – that finds its most consistent expression in *Die Walküre*. Particularly noteworthy are the low-lying vocal line depicting the old man's low-brimmed hat, the shape of the melodic line portraying the flash of his eye and then its 'threatening glance', the falling chromatic intervals for his lingering look of yearning, the expressive appoggiatura on 'Tränen' ('tears') and the final rise to a top G for the physical act of implanting the sword in the tree. The sounding of the Valhalla motif by horns and bassoons, announcing the real identity of the stranger, is one of the classic uses of leitmotif to comment on the action.

With startling suddenness the door of the hut flies open, letting in the spring night (and solving the problem of how the two will escape). Their duet, true to Wagner's theoretical principles, does not allow the couple to sing together. Even Siegmund's Spring Song, 'Winterstürme wichen dem Wonnemond', celebrated as a tenor song extracted from its context, is not as conventional as at first appears. It begins like a ternary aria, but after only nine bars of the middle section the continuation of the Love motif bursts in and disrupts the form. Incomplete and hybrid structures of this kind are typical in Wagner's music dramas. Siegmund speaks of spring and love as brother and sister, to which Sieglinde replies that he is the spring for whom she has so longed. The remainder of the act is an ecstatic declaration of their love, with an unashamed acknowledgment that they are also brother and sister. He admits that Woeful is no longer an appropriate name and Sieglinde renames him Siegmund ('guardian of victory'). To her delight he pulls the sword out of the tree, naming it 'Nothung' ('Needful'). They embrace rapturously and the curtain falls with decorous swiftness.

Act 2 *A wild, rocky, mountain ridge* The music of the prelude anticipates the Ride of the Valkyries in the third act; its vitality is generated by dotted rhythms in 9/8 time, and augmented 5ths heighten the tension. Wotan instructs his favourite daughter, Brünnhilde, the Valkyrie of the title, to ensure that Siegmund wins the ensuing battle with Hunding. She revels in the Valkyrie battle cry, but warns Wotan that he has another battle on hand: his wife Fricka is furiously approaching, in a ram-drawn chariot. Brünnhilde disappears as Fricka, angrily but with dignity, tells how, as guardian of wedlock, she has

'Die Walküre' (Wagner), design by Carl Emil Doepler for a lantern slide for the Ride of the Valkyries in Act 3, in the first complete 'Ring' cycle at Bayreuth, 1876

been invoked by Hunding to punish the adulterous Volsung pair. To her complaint that they have flouted the vows of marriage Wotan replies that he has no respect for vows that compel union without love. Fricka turns her attack to the twins' incest, but Wotan's reply, to the tender accompaniment of the Spring Song and Love themes, indicates that not even this breach of conventional morality shocks him. Fricka continues her indignant protest in an arioso passage in G♯ minor, in which the stock of leitmotifs momentarily gives way to new and distinctive melodic material. At first glance a reversion to an old-style form, 'O, was klag' ich um Ehe und Eid' in fact displays considerable subtlety in its variety of pace and irregular phrase-lengths.

Fricka complains that Wotan has brought disgrace on the gods by fathering these incestuous twins on a mortal woman. He replies that the gods need a

hero free from their protection, who will be able to do the deed they are prevented from doing: restore the ring to its owners and thereby institute a new world order. But Fricka devastatingly exposes the flaw in the guilty god's argument: Siegmund is not able to act as a free hero so long as he is protected by Wotan. As Wotan thrashes about in despair, without a moral leg to stand on, much use is made of a motif (ex.5)

Ex.5

labelled 'Dejection' by Ernest Newman but whose contorted melodic shape and kinship to the Spear motif suggest something more specific: the frustration of Wotan's will. Fricka extracts from him an oath that he will no longer protect his son.

'Die Walküre' (Wagner), back projection, using a lantern slide, for the 'Ride of the Valkyries' in Act 3 of the first Paris production (Opéra, 12 May 1893): from 'L'exposition internationale des arts décoratifs et industriels modernes' (Paris, 1925)

In scene ii Wotan continues to writhe in mental agony (ex.5) and Brünnhilde reappears to receive the full brunt of his outburst of grief and frustration, 'O heilige Schmach'. A powerful climax is generated by the dissonant piling up of motifs, initiated by a new one that is primarily an inversion of ex.5, though also related to that of Wotan's authority (the Spear motif). The notes to which Wotan sings of his endless rage and grief ('Endloser Grimm! Ewiger Gram!') are in fact those of the Love motif (ex.3), a poignant reminder that it is lack of love that is the cause of his troubles.

The ensuing long narration of Wotan, 'Als junger Liebe Lust mir verblich', is a key passage in the work, and one intended not only for the information of Brünnhilde or even of the audience, but as an act of self-revelation, in which we see Wotan in a new light. He begins by confessing how he attempted to fill the vacuum of lovelessness in his life by acquiring power. His hushed reliving of the story is the closest thing in the whole work to pure recitative, but it is by no means oblivious to Wagner's stated principles of wordsetting and in any case it acquires a special aura of suspense from the accompaniment – double basses alone, *pianissimo*. The characteristic motifs appear as Wotan recalls Alberich's forging of the ring, the building of Valhalla and Erda's prophecy; how in the quest for wisdom he sought out Erda again and fathered Brünnhilde on her. The prominence of ex.5 attests to Wotan's sense of frustration, and the motifs of the Curse and the Sword drive the narration to a

tremendous climax: he now longs for only one thing – 'das Ende'. He instructs Brünnhilde to protect not Siegmund in the coming battle but Hunding. Aware that his heart is not in this command, she tries to change his mind, but he is implacable.

The third scene opens with an orchestral interlude making a symphonic development out of agitated repetitions of the Love motif. Siegmund and Sieglinde enter breathlessly. She, tormented by guilt, begs him to abandon her, but he merely vows to avenge the wrong done her by killing Hunding. Horns are heard echoing round the forest, and Sieglinde, feverishly imagining Hunding's dogs tearing at Siegmund's flesh, falls into a faint.

There follows another scene of key significance in the cycle: the Todesverkündigung (Annunciation of Death). Brünnhilde appears, announcing to Siegmund that he must follow her to Valhalla. The Wagner tubas intone a solemn motif whose interrogatory melodic shape and unresolved dominant 7th have generally earned it a label such as 'Destiny' or 'Fate' (ex.6). It is heard throughout the scene, as is a

four-bar theme whose latter half corresponds with it (ex.7). Three distinct brass groupings are used to conjure a mood of quiet, noble heroism: Wagner

Ex.7

tubas, trumpets and trombones, horns with bassoons. When Siegmund hears that he cannot take his sister-bride with him to Valhalla, he declines to go. Brünnhilde tells him that his fate is unalterable but, distressed by his evident devotion to Sieglinde and his threat to kill her rather than be separated, she finally relents and promises to protect him, in defiance of Wotan's command.

Siegmund bends affectionately over the sleeping Sieglinde (scene v). Hunding's horn is heard, and in the ensuing fight Brünnhilde attempts to protect Siegmund with her shield, only for Wotan to appear and shatter Siegmund's sword with his spear. Hunding kills Siegmund, but is himself despatched by Wotan with a contemptuous wave of his hand. Wotan, enraged, then sets off in pursuit of the disobedient Brünnhilde.

Act 3 *On the summit of a rocky mountain* In the Ride of the Valkyries that opens Act 3, the war-maidens gather, collecting heroes for Valhalla. Although hackneyed, the piece has much to recommend it, especially when sung and staged. The scoring illustrates a characteristic device of Wagner's: a brass theme in unison cutting across a dense texture, in this case of trilling, antiphonal woodwind and swirling string arpeggios. The Valkyries notice that Brünnhilde is missing; eventually she is sighted carrying on her saddle not a hero but a woman. They fearfully refuse to protect her from the fury of Wotan. Sieglinde longs to die, but on being told that a Volsung stirs in her womb, she implores Brünnhilde to protect her. She is urged to make her escape to the forest in the east, a place that Wotan avoids, and is given the fragments of Siegmund's sword from which one day his son will forge a new weapon. This announcement is made with an expansive theme (later to be associated with Siegfried's heroism) whose intrepid ring prompts Sieglinde to react with the work's most enraptured melodic inspiration, 'O hehrstes Wunder!' (ex.8). The motif returns at the very end of the cycle, where it is often taken to symbolize the redemption of the world, though Wagner referred to it as 'the glorification of Brünnhilde'.

Ex.8

O hehr - - stes Wun - der!

Herr - - li - che Maid!
['Sublimest of wonders! Glorious woman!']

Wotan storms in (scene ii) and the Valkyries in vain try to shield Brünnhilde. She is told that she can no longer be a Valkyrie, and that she is to be confined in sleep on the mountain-top, a prey to the first man to find her. The Valkyries, horror-struck, protest in eight-part counterpoint, but under threat of the same punishment if they interfere, they separate and scatter.

Left alone with Wotan (scene iii), Brünnhilde begs for mercy ('War es so schmählich'); she asks whether it was so shameful if, though contravening Wotan's orders, she was in fact carrying out his inward wishes. The theme she uses is derived from that of the Spear, the symbol of Wotan's authority, but its severity is turned, by octave displacement, into an eloquent melody (ex.9). She recounts how the

Ex.9

Volsung touched her heart, and a new melody, similarly derived from the Spear motif, blossoms forth in a transported E major: Brünnhilde's compassionate love thus stands opposed to Wotan's tyrannical wielding of power, but also, in motivic terms, grows organically out of it.

Brünnhilde pleads that at least she be spared the disgrace of an ignoble union: let her be surrounded by a circle of fire that will deter all but the bravest of heroes. Deeply moved, Wotan embraces Brünnhilde and, laying her down on a rock, he kisses her shining eyes closed, divesting her of her divinity. Throughout the unfolding of this scene more and more motifs are recalled from the past as emotionally charged memories are brought to the surface. Two new motifs remain to be mentioned: that of the Magic Sleep, evoked by a sinking semitonal melodic line and trance-like mediant progressions, and ex.10, which is

Ex.10

heard in an ominous minor key as Brünnhilde dreads being woken by a coward, but which in its major form acquires a luminous, hypnotic quality in the closing pages of the score.

The last part of this scene is a succession of carefully controlled climaxes, none of which is more affecting than that following Wotan's grief-stricken farewells to Brünnhilde: 'Leb' wohl'. Finally the god summons Loge, who appears not in person but in the music and the flames. The sea of fire that spreads to enclose the whole mountain in flames is depicted by a richly orchestrated texture created from the themes of Loge and others. Wotan sorrowfully departs.

*

Die Walküre is the music drama that most satisfactorily embodies the theoretical principles Wagner set out in his essay *Oper und Drama*. A thoroughgoing synthesis of poetry and music is achieved without any notable sacrifice in musical expression. Indeed, many of the most powerful passages of the work achieve their effect precisely through the organic relationship of music and text. *Die Walküre* is generally regarded as the most approachable of the *Ring* operas, and it has certainly proved the most susceptible to performance in extracts. **B.M.**

Wally, La

Dramma musicale in four acts by Alfredo Catalani to a libretto by Luigi Illica after Wilhelmine von Hillern's story *Die Geyer-Wally*; Milan, Teatro alla Scala, 20 January 1892.

The first cast included Hariclea Darclée (Wally) and Adelina Stehle (Walter), with Ettore Brancaleoni (Stromminger), Manuel Suagnes (Haghenbach), Arturo Pessina (Gellner) and Adriana Guerrini (Afra).

Stromminger *a landowner*	bass
Wally *his daughter*	soprano
Haghenbach	tenor
Gellner	baritone
Walter	light soprano
Afra *a tavern owner*	mezzo-soprano
Messenger	tenor
Setting The Tyrol, about 1800	

In the village of Hochstoff (Act 1) the rich landowner Stromminger taunts Haghenbach, who comes from the rival village of Sölden and is the son of Stromminger's enemy, deriding his success on his return from a hunting expedition. They tussle and Stromminger's daughter Wally tries to make peace between them. She sends away the young huntsman, for whom she shows an obvious partiality; this in turn annoys the factor Gellner, secretly in love with her, who reveals his feelings to the still angry Stromminger. When her father insists that she must marry Gellner, Wally refuses and he banishes her. She goes off into the mountains with her friend Walter.

Act 2 is set in Sölden. A year later Wally has returned to claim the estate she has inherited from her now deceased father. She attends the festival at Sölden and sees Haghenbach, who takes little notice

of her. Gellner is also there, and she tries to get him to leave. In a fit of jealousy she insults Afra, the tavern owner, having been wrongly led to believe by Gellner that Afra is betrothed to the man Wally loves. To avenge the insult, Haghenbach consents to dance with Wally and mocks her passion with a kiss, swearing falsely that he loves her. The bystanders are amused that Haghenbach has humiliated Wally, and through their reaction she is made aware of the truth. She promises to marry Gellner if he will kill Haghenbach.

Act 3 takes place on the same evening. Wally is now beginning to have second thoughts about her pact with Gellner. Haghenbach, who in spite of his mockery realizes that he loves her after all, goes to Hochstoff to see her. Before he can reach her house he is attacked by Gellner, who hurls him into a ravine. Wally, overcome by remorse, rushes to save him. He is found unconscious and she gives him into the care of Afra, to whom she leaves all her wealth.

In Act 4 Wally returns to her refuge in the mountains, contemplating suicide. She is eventually joined by Haghenbach, who tells her of his love; she does not at first believe him, but the couple are finally reconciled. As they seek the path back in the foggy dark the young man is carried away by an avalanche. Calling his name in vain, Wally flings herself into the abyss.

In this work, recognized as his masterpiece, Catalani shows himself halfway between *verismo* opera and Puccini (who was to triumph with *Manon* the following year) and in harmony with Italian decadentism, in particular the poetry of Giovanni Pascoli and Guido Gozzano. If many lyrical passages, vocal and orchestral, anticipate features of *verismo*, and the harmonic organization shows that he had learnt from Wagner, Catalani's real achievement here is the fusion of these heterogeneous factors into a unified and original whole. The opera's merits lie in its fine control of orchestration and expressive melodies, and at some points the musical characterization is very successful. Its weakness is a lack of dramatic interest in the plot, the development of which is too protracted and lacking in intensity. Although it has no great or unforgettable character, dramatic intuition or linguistic craftsmanship such as there is in Puccini, the small world of *La Wally* is real and finely chiselled and this microcosm becomes a creation worthy of a place among the operas that characterize European *fin-de-siècle* music drama. **M.G.**

War and Peace [*Voyna i mir*]

Opera in 13 'lyrico-dramatic scenes' and a choral epigraph by Sergey Prokofiev to a libretto by the composer and Mira Alexandrovna Mendelson (Prokof'yeva) after Lev Nikolayevich Tolstoy's novel (1869); for premières see Table 1.

Numbers refer to the scenes of the final version (see Table 2 and synopsis) in which the character appears

Prince Andrey Bolkonsky (1, 2, 8, 12)	high baritone
Natasha Rostova	lyric-dramatic
(1, 2, 3, 4, 6, 12)	soprano
Sonya (1, 2, 4, 6)	mezzo-soprano
Host of the Ball *an old grandee of Catherine's day* (2)	tenor
Major-Domo at the ball (2)	tenor
Mariya Dmitriyevna	powerful
Akhrosimova (2, 6)	mezzo-soprano
Peronskaya (2)	soprano
Count Il'ya Andreyevich Rostov (2, 3, 4)	bass-baritone, soft quality
Pierre Bezukhov (2, 6, 7, 8, 11, 13)	dramatic tenor
Hélène Bezukhova (2, 4, 7)	contralto
Anatol Kuragin (2, 4, 5, 6, 7)	tenor
Dolokhov (2, 5, 6)	bass
Alexander I (2)	silent
Old Footman to the Bolkonskys (3)	baritone
Housemaid to the Bolkonskys (3)	mezzo-soprano
Valet to the Bolkonskys (3)	bass
Princess Mariya (Bolkonskaya) (3)	mezzo-soprano
Prince Nikolay Andreyevich Bolkonsky (3)	basso profondo, sarcastic quality
Balaga *a coachman* (5)	high, spirited bass
Joseph *a footman* (5)	silent
Matryosha *a gypsy girl* (5)	contralto (not very low)
Dunyasha *young housemaid to the Rostovs* (6, 11, 13)	soprano (not high)
Gavrila *Akhrosimova's footman* (6)	baritone or bass
Metivier *a French doctor* (7)	soft, velvet baritone or bass
A French Abbé (7)	tenor (no high notes)
Denisov (7, 8, 13)	bass-baritone
Tikhon Shcherbatïy (8, 13)	bass (no low notes)
Fyodor (8, 13)	tenor (no high notes)
Vasilisa *a village elder's wife* (8, 13)	mezzo-soprano
Matveyev (8, 11)	baritone
Trishka (8)	contralto (travesti)
Two German Generals (8)	spoken
Orderly to Prince Andrey (8)	low tenor
Field Marshal Mikhail Illarionovich Kutuzov (8, 10, 13)	bass
Adjutant to Kutuzov (8, 13)	tenor (shrill quality)
First Staff Officer (8)	tenor (possibly baritone)
Second Staff Officer (8)	bass or baritone
Napoleon (9, 11)	baritone
Adjutant to General Compans (9)	tenor
Adjutant to Marshal Murat (9)	contralto (travesti)
Marshal Berthier (9)	bass-baritone
Marshal Caulaincourt (9)	silent
General Belliard (9)	crude bass (no low notes)
Adjutant to Prince Eugène (9)	tenor
Offstage Voice (9)	high tenor
Adjutant from Napoleon's Suite (9)	high bass
De Beausset, Minister of the Court (9)	comic tenor
General Bennigsen (10)	bass
General Barclay de Tolly (10)	tenor
General Yermolov (10)	bass
Konovnitsïn (10)	tenor
General Rayevsky (10)	baritone
Song Leader (*zapevala*) (10)	baritone
Malasha *a little girl* (10)	silent
Captain Ramballe (11, 13)	bass
Lieutenant Bonnet (11, 13)	tenor
Jacquot (11)	bass
Gerard (11)	tenor
Young Factory Hand (11)	tenor (possibly baritone)
Shopkeeper (11)	low soprano
Mavra Kuz'minichna *the Rostovs' old housekeeper* (11)	contralto
Ivanov (11)	piercing tenor
Marshal Davout (11)	bass (dark, rich, no low notes)
French Officer (11, 13)	baritone
Platon Karatayev (11, 13)	tenor (soft quality)
Three Lunatics (11)	tenor, high bass, silent
Two French Actresses (11)	soprano, mezzo-soprano
Military Escort (13)	silent

Guests at the ball, Muscovites, peasant militiamen, Russian soldiers, partisans, French soldiers

Setting Russia (Otradnoye, St Petersburg, Moscow, Borodino, Fili nr Smolensk), 1805–12

Prokofiev's operatic masterpiece and one of the tiny handful of post-1945 operas to achieve repertory status, *War and Peace* had an exceptionally complicated creative history that reflected not only the composer's artistic decisions and those of his close advisers, but also the extremely difficult circumstances that attended the opera's gestation.

TABLE 1: PREMIÈRES

version	venue	date	notes
original (11 scenes)	Moscow, Actors' Club	16 Oct 1944	concert perf., 7 scenes with pf
	Moscow, Conservatory	7 June 1945	concert perf., 9 scenes, cond. S. Samosud
	Prague, National Theatre	1948	stage première
expanded (two-evening, 13 scenes)	Leningrad, Malïy Theatre	12 June 1946	Part I (8 scenes), cond. Samosud; Part II, dress rehearsals in July and Dec 1947, cancelled
abbreviated (10 scenes)	Florence, Maggio Musicale	26 May 1953	cond. A. Rodzıński
	NBC TV (New York)	13 Jan 1957	cond. P. H. Adler
final (13 scenes)	Leningrad, Malïy Theatre	1 April 1955	11 scenes, much cut; cond. E. Grikurov
	Moscow, Stanislavsky–Nemirovich-Danchenko Musical Theatre	8 Nov 1957	13 scenes, many cuts; cond. A. Shaverdov
	Moscow, Bol'shoy Theatre	15 Dec 1959	first relatively complete perf., incl. Epigraph; cond. A. Melik-Pashayev

TABLE 2: ORIGINAL LIST OF SCENES

1 [3] The Rostovs and their visit to old Bolkonsky.
2 [4] Natasha meets Anatol at Hélène's (Hélène and Natasha. The Count: 'Let's go, Natasha'. Hélène distracts the Count. Anatol. The kiss. Natasha alone. The old Count.)
3 [5] Anatol and Dolokhov before the elopement.
4 [6] Unsuccessful elopement. Natasha's despair. Pierre.
5 [7] Pierre shakes Anatol.
6   Vilna. Balashov informs Alexander that war has been declared [Tolstoy, III/1/4].
7   Balashov with Napoleon [Tolstoy III/15–7].
8 [8] Before the Battle of Borodino. Kutuzov, Andrey. Pierre, Andrey.
9 [11] Moscow. Execution scene. Pierre a prisoner.
10 [12] Natasha with the wounded Andrey.
11 [13] The French retreat. Pierre freed.

Five separate authorial versions can be distinguished, of which four have been the basis of staged performances and three exist in discrete written form.

First version: According to Prokofiev's widow Lina, as early as 1935 the composer, then living abroad, referred to an opera on Tolstoy's *War and Peace* as a plan of long standing, awaiting only the opportunity for long and concentrated work without interruption. It has been discovered, moreover, that the first theme of the overture (associated in the opera with Kutuzov) was first jotted down in a notebook dating from the early months of 1933. Nevertheless, the earliest concrete evidence of work on the opera dates from April 1941. The composer was living by then with Mira Mendelson, whom he recognized as his second (common-law) wife. She was reading Tolstoy's novel aloud to Prokofiev, according to her memoirs, when he became enthusiastic over the operatic possibilities of the episode in which Natasha Rostova visits the bedside of the delirious Andrey Bolkonsky (Book III, Part 3, chapter 32 [III/3/32]). He drew up an initial list of scenes on 12 April 1941, as in Table 2 (numbers in brackets refer to the scenes of the final version; Scene 5 was an insertion that caused the renumbering of those succeeding).

That the main action of the first part of the opera would centre on the ill-starred elopement of Natasha and Anatol Kuragin was clear from the start. The main action of the second part, as envisaged at this early stage, centred on Pierre Bezukhov and his experiences on the fringes of battle and in the hands of the occupiers.

There is no reason to assume that, having made this plan, Prokofiev would have immediately set to work on the music or even that the opera would have been the next he composed. The year before he had outlined a similar plan for an opera based on Tolstoy's novel *Resurrection*, and had made a far more detailed scenario for an opera on Nikolay Leskov's *The Wastrel*. What decided the matter inevitably in favour of *War and Peace* was of course the German invasion of the Soviet Union a couple of months after Prokofiev had drawn up his outline. Current events were paralleling in unexpected and uncanny fashion 'those pages [of Tolstoy's] recounting the Russian people's struggle against Napoleon's hordes in 1812', the composer wrote. He drew up a new plan. The first five scenes of the original plan became Scenes 2–6, with an ineffably peaceful initial scene based on the chapter in the novel in which Andrey and Natasha are first brought into (unwitting) conjunction (II/3/2; in the scenario it is called 'Night at the Rostov estate, Otradnoye'). The second half of the opera, depicting the French invasion and its resistance, now began more nearly to resemble its ultimate form; a scene 'At Napoleon's Headquarters', corresponding to the eventual ninth scene, took the place of the old Scenes 6 and 7.

The opera was composed very quickly, between 15 August 1941 and 13 April 1942, during Prokofiev's and Mendelson's period of wartime evacuation, first at Nal'chik, near Stavropol' in the Russian Caucasus, then in Tbilisi, the Georgian capital. It consisted of an overture and 11 scenes (corresponding to the final version less the epigraph and Scenes 2 and 10). For the early scenes of aristocratic romance, Prokofiev mined an old abandoned score of incidental music to an aborted 1936 dramatization of Pushkin's *Yevgeny Onegin* for appropriate themes and leitmotifs, and drew as well upon music he was simultaneously composing for a film biography of the poet Lermontov. A copy of the vocal score in Pavel Lamm's hand survives in the Glinka Museum, Moscow. This version of the opera, though complete to the composer's satisfaction, would never be performed.

Second version ('original' in list of premières): Lamm's piano score was dispatched to Moscow for evaluation by the All-Union Committee on Art Affairs whose approval had to precede acceptance by any Soviet theatre. After an audition in May 1942, in which the opera was read through from Lamm's manuscript by the pianists Anatoly Vedernikov and Svyatoslav Richter, Prokofiev received a list of stipulated revisions, which he finished by November. A convenient enumeration of these revisions is found in a letter the composer wrote from his third evacuation domicile (Alma-Ata, in Soviet Central Asia [now Kazakhstan]) to Yevgeny Radin, director of the Kirov Theatre in Leningrad, on 25 March 1943, shortly before completing the opera's orchestration. It is clear from their nature that the committee's chief concern was to underscore the opera's topical relevance, and to ensure that Russia's first 'Great Patriotic War' of 1812 would be memorialized in a fashion consistent with attitudes towards the second, in which the country was then engaged.

Thus, to the 11 scenes of the first version, a choral Epigraph was added, taking off from the famous opening sentence of III/3/2 ('The forces of a dozen European nations burst into Russia'), but continuing in a vein of bombast reminiscent of the jingoistic conclusion of *Alexander Nevsky* (and no wonder: Sergey Eisenstein, the director of *Nevsky*, with whom Prokofiev was then collaborating on *Ivan the Terrible*,

was on hand in Alma-Ata and actively discussing the *War and Peace* revisions with the composer; he was also scheduled to direct the première at the Moscow Bol'shoy Theatre during the 1943–4 season). In his letter to Radin, Prokofiev confesses ambivalence as to whether the Epigraph should serve as prologue to the entire opera or just to the war scenes; this question was never resolved.

Except for two tiny cuts in Scene 4, all the revisions to existing music involved the war scenes. Anecdotal detail was curtailed, characteristic recitative in two instances (one involving Andrey, the other Denisov) was replaced by heroic arioso; the concluding scene reached its culmination in 'a grand choral apotheosis with military orchestra on stage'. The tendency towards impersonal monumentality in the treatment of the war is already noticeable. Most telling were the changes involving the figure of Field Marshal Kutuzov. A lighthearted exchange between the commander and Dolokhov in the scene on the Borodino battlefield was eliminated, and his joking address to the partisans in the last scene was transferred to Denisov. Instead, Kutuzov was given (in preparation for the Moscow concert premiere in 1945) a minuscule da capo aria to sing on the battlefield ('Zheleznaya grud' ne boitsya surovosti pogod': 'The iron breast fears no storm'), the most 'classical' piece of its kind Prokofiev had ever written, and – something absolutely unprecedented in Prokofiev's work to date – based on the melody of a folksong. While the Field Marshal was not yet quite the dominating figure he would become, he was already being divested of ordinary human qualities and transformed into a quasi-deific embodiment of the nation, exactly paralleling the way in which the image of Stalin was being promoted in the prosecution of the actual Patriotic War.

The second version was published in mimeographed vocal score in 1943. A combination of wartime conditions and backstage politics frustrated plans for a Bol'shoy production that year; and although the Metropolitan Opera had expressed interest in producing the work, the Committee on Art Affairs would not countenance a foreign première. Within Russia the second version, though definitive at the time of its completion, would have only concert performances, none complete.

Third version ('expanded' in list of premières): From the time of the original audition before the Committee on Art Affairs, the great champion of Prokofiev's opera had been the conductor Samuil Abramovich Samosud (1884–1964), a powerful figure in Soviet music, who had been chief conductor of the Bol'shoy Theatre since 1936. It was his loss of that position in 1943 that meant the cancellation of *War and Peace*. When he was appointed artistic director of the Malïy Theatre in Leningrad he made the production of Prokofiev's opera a condition. He also insisted on completeness, which created a problem, for the score exceeded the normal length of an operatic evening. Samosud's radical solution was further to expand the opera, which already fell into two relatively discrete and self-contained portions, by adding two more scenes (one to each half), and performing the resulting four-hour-plus spectacle on two evenings.

Samosud not only persuaded Prokofiev to add the scenes; he also chose the scenes to be added. For the first evening he fastened on II/3/14, the chapter in which Natasha and Andrey first 'officially' meet and fall in love. This now became Scene 2 of the opera, 'New Year's Eve Ball, 1810', a brilliant sequence of dances and choral odes against which a great deal of essential plot exposition is ingeniously superimposed. For the second evening, Samosud proposed III/3/4, describing the makeshift war council at Fili, where the decision was taken to abandon Moscow to the enemy. The idea was not only to fill a gap in the plot but to provide a pretext for giving Kutuzov (in Samosud's words) 'an aria such as in [Glinka's] *Susanin* or [Borodin's] *Igor* – central, eloquent, crucial', by means of which Kutuzov and the monumental historical and national forces he embodied, and not Pierre Bezukhov's personal fate, would become the true focus of the evening. After many tries and arguments with the conductor, Prokofiev (who had wanted to limit Kutuzov's big number to a short arioso linked up with the arioso on the battlefield by shared leitmotivic material) finally adapted a folk-epic style melody from his film score for *Ivan the Terrible*. This then provided the great leitmotif of exalted heroism for eventual apotheosis in the concluding chorus of the last scene (now the 13th).

Besides these, Prokofiev made numerous changes great and small on the way to the monumentally expanded version of his opera. One of the most notable, for which Samosud again claimed credit, was the reprise of the Waltz theme from Scene 2 in the opera's penultimate scene, that of Andrey's reunion with Natasha. Most of the others involved a vastly expanded role for the chorus (mostly glorifying the Leader of the People), for which purpose the composer and Mira Mendelson found texts in anthologies at the Tolstoy Museum in Moscow, as well as in Soviet publications. Prokofiev never actually wrote out a definitive score of the expanded version. Its contents must be pieced together from Samosud's detailed memoirs and from the composer's manuscripts, now at the Central State Archives of Literature and Art in Moscow.

Part I of the new *War and Peace* enjoyed a spectacular success, becoming the crown of the Malïy Theatre repertory. It was given a total of 105 times during the 1946 and 1947 seasons. Part II met with disaster. After a fully staged dress rehearsal in July 1947 it was vetoed (in Samosud's grim recollection) by 'certain individuals, to whom it seemed that [its] historical conception was incorrect'. Just what the objections were has never been explicitly revealed, but they were known to have centred on the ninth scene ('Napoleon at the Shevardino Redoubt') and the 11th ('Moscow Aflame'). Perhaps 'fears' is a better word than 'objections'. During 1946, Party decrees, at once Draconian and arbitrary, had been issued on political education, literature and cinema, and many leading artists, including Eisenstein, had been disgraced (music's – and Prokofiev's – turn would come early in 1948). In such an atmosphere, no one dared take responsibility for approving a work dealing with a historical subject that had so many sensitive parallels with the uncertain present.

Fourth version ('abbreviated' in list of premières): By now, as Samosud bleakly recounted, 'Prokofiev's desire to see *War and Peace* was so urgent, so compelling, that he was prepared to go literally to any lengths of editorial changes, abbreviations or cuts if only it would be produced'. Accordingly, in a document dated 5 December 1948 (published for the first time in the 1958 vocal score), Prokofiev proposed a radical condensation of the opera, ostensibly to achieve a 'one-evening' spectacle, in reality to forestall ideological objections, when it was already much too late. The two scenes that had provoked the censors in 1947 were eliminated outright, along with the Epigraph and what was now the seventh scene ('Pierre shakes Anatol'). (The desperate composer also offered producers the option of deleting the overture, the scene at the Bezukhovs' soirée, and even the scene at Fili.) The mutilated ten-scene version thus proposed under duress, for all that it enjoyed a factitious authorization, should not be considered an authentic version, even though it was the form in which the opera first became known in the West (and though it carries the endorsement of some influential Western critics who mistakenly took it to represent, in the words of one, 'Prokofiev's last thoughts').

Fifth version ('final' in list of premières): Prokofiev's actual last thoughts are now represented in the 1958 published score. It is a restored 13-scene spectacle, with additions. Among the items unique to the fifth version are the duet for Natasha and Sonya in the first scene (composed in April 1949), to the continuation of a text by Zhukovsky that Tchaikovsky had set in part as a duet for Lisa and Pauline in *The Queen of Spades*, and a new middle section for Kutuzov's grand aria in the council scene, composed in November 1952, after which Prokofiev did not return to the score. (The widely circulated conceit that this last item was composed two weeks before the composer's death is untrue.)

*

Part I *Epigraph (III/3/2)*

A choral cry of defiance against the foe, adapted from the preface to Tolstoy's account of the Battle of Borodino with all specific references to persons and locales removed so as to make the words fully applicable to World War II.

Scene 1 *(II/3/2) House and garden on the Rostov estate (Otradnoye); May; a moonlit night; Prince Andrey, visiting the Rostovs on business, is reading by the window* Andrey, a widower, muses pessimistically on a gnarled oak he had encountered that day among leafy birches and elms. His thoughts are interrupted by the sound of the young Natasha and her cousin Sonya, rapturously conversing and singing about the beautiful night. Andrey is solaced; he muses on Natasha's attractive qualities.

Scene 2 *(II/3/14–17) A ball at the home of an old grandee of Catherine's time* It is New Year's Eve (1809). A footman announces the arrival of Count Rostov and his daughter Natasha, Andrey Bolkonsky, Pierre and Hélène Bezukhov, Hélène's brother Anatol Kuragin and his friend Lieutenant Dolokhov. Mesdames Akhrosimova and Peronskaya comment acerbically to Natasha about the other guests. Tsar Alexander I deigns to appear and dances a mazurka. A waltz is announced. Pierre Bezukhov, seeing Natasha ignored and disconsolate, asks Prince Andrey to dance with her. They become deeply attracted to one another. Natasha is delighted to hear her father invite Prince Andrey to visit them at home. Andrey, for his part, catches himself dreaming of making Natasha his wife.

Scene 3 *(II/5/7) A small receiving room in the old, gloomy town house of Prince Bolkonsky (the elder) in Vozdvizhenka Street, Moscow; a huge built-in mirror, ancient furniture, footmen in powdered wigs* Count Rostov and Natasha arrive to pay a call following her betrothal to Prince Andrey. The old man will not receive them, sending his daughter Mariya instead. All at once the old prince barges in in nightcap and dressing-gown, offers a sarcastic pseudo-apology for what was actually a deliberate insult, and withdraws with Princess Mariya. Left alone, Natasha muses on her wounded dignity and her abiding love for Andrey.

Scene 4 *(II/5/9–15) A sitting-room in the home of Pierre and Hélène Bezukhov; in the main hall, joined to the sitting-room by an arcade, dancing couples are seen* Hélène offers congratulations to Natasha on her betrothal. She hints, to Natasha's consternation, that her brother Anatol is also in love with Natasha. Count Rostov tries to cut the evening short but Hélène spirits him off. Anatol arrives, confesses his love, boldly kisses Natasha on the lips, and presses a card into her hand, on which he has threatened to die

if he cannot have her. Despite her love for Andrey and Sonya's stern advice, Natasha finds herself fascinated. (Tolstoy had set the early stages of Anatol's seduction at the Opera, prime symbol to him of all that is false.)

Scene 5 *(II/5/16–17) At Dolokhov's: a study hung with Persian rugs, bearskins and arms; Anatol Kuragin in an unbuttoned uniform is lying on a divan, leaning his head on his arm, smiling abstractedly; Dolokhov, in a quilted jacket and boots, is sitting before an open bureau, on which accounts and banknotes can be seen* Anatol tells Dolokhov of his scheme to elope with Natasha, and will not let his friend dissuade him. He exacts an oath of assistance in this exploit from his eager coachman Balaga and, bidding farewell to his gypsy girlfriend Matryosha, sets off into a blizzard.

Scene 6 *(II/5/17–19, 22) A room in Mariya Akhrosimova's town house (where the Rostovs are staying) in Staraya Konyushennaya Street, Moscow; a great glass door leads to a veranda and thence to the garden* Natasha awaits Anatol. When the latter arrives he is intercepted by a servant, Akhrosimova having been forewarned, and flees. Akhrosimova admonishes Natasha for her behaviour and her association with the likes of Hélène and her brother with their 'French' habits and morals. Pierre Bezukhov arrives and, having been told what has happened by Akhrosimova, gives Natasha the terrible news that Kuragin was married all along. Humiliated and disgraced, she knows that she has lost Andrey for ever. Pierre tells her that, were he free, he would gladly marry her himself.

Scene 7 *(II/5/3, 20) Pierre Bezukhov's study; Hélène, Anatol, the Abbé and Dr Metivier* Pierre's furious arrival home interrupts a frivolous conversation with the Frenchmen in which Dr Metivier reveals that the old Prince Bolkonsky had once taken him for a spy. The large but usually mild-mannered Pierre demands Anatol's departure from Moscow and the return of Natasha's letters, threatening violence and actually shaking his brother-in-law by the lapels. After Anatol agrees (though without repenting) and goes off, Pierre's reflections are interrupted by the arrival of Denisov with the news that Napoleon has invaded and 'it looks like war'.

Part II *Epigraph (alternative position).*

Scene 8 *(III/2/15, 20) Before the Battle of Borodino; bulwarks are being prepared* Denisov (Natasha's first fiancé) meets Prince Andrey in the course of military affairs, prompting tender recollections on both sides. Pierre appears, saying he wishes to observe the battle. He and Andrey bid each other a fond farewell. The troops sing a series of choruses in praise of their commander Kutuzov, who upon arrival sings them a pair of tributes in return, 'Bespodobnïy narod' ('O matchless folk') and 'Zheleznaya grud' ne boitsya surovosti pogod' ('The iron breast fears no storm'). He asks Andrey to join his staff, but the latter requests leave to stay with his men. Another military chorus is interrupted by the first shots.

Scene 9 *(III/2/35) Shevardino Redoubt during the Battle of Borodino; Napoleon stands atop a hill looking through his glass; not far from him stand Marshals Berthier and Caulaincourt, M. de Beausset and the emperor's entourage* Napoleon imagines being received in Moscow, but gets bad news about the progress of the battle. He is asked to send reinforcements, which he does with the greatest reluctance. He expresses perplexity at the fortitude of the Russians and his own impotence. From off stage one of the choruses in praise of Kutuzov is heard again.

Scene 10 *(III/3/4) A hut in Fili: the end of the council of war; Kutuzov, Barclay, Bennigsen, Rayevsky, Yermolov, Konovnitsïn and others; the little Malasha, whose head Kutuzov absentmindedly strokes* After each of the generals has expressed an opinion on the question of whether Moscow shall be given up, Kutuzov pronounces his decision that this extraordinary measure is required to save the army and hence the country. He dismisses the others and expresses his feelings about Moscow in a grand aria, 'Velichavaya, v solnechnïkh luchakh, mater' russkikh gorodov' ('Stately, sunlit, mother of Russian cities'). The aria is preceded and followed by another offstage chorus in praise of the commander.

Scene 11 *(III/3/13, 17, 19, 24–5, 33–4; 4/1, 12–13) A street in French-occupied Moscow* This sprawling, episodic scene takes in the most territory from the novel (some of it very freely adapted), proceeding in panoramic, non-narrative fashion. Among the events portrayed are Napoleon's arrival in vain expectation of a receiving delegation, Pierre's encounter with the Rostovs' housekeeper and his arrest under suspicion of arson, the release of the inmates of the lunatic asylum, the flight of the French actors, Pierre's encounter with the peasant soldier Platon Karatayev (the author's proxy in the novel), the outbreak of multiple fires and the inevitable patriotic chorus.

Scene 12 *(III/3/32) A dark hut by night: in the far corner is a bed, on which Prince Andrey is lying; on a stool is a candle, snuffed with a big mushroom* The mortally wounded Andrey, who has unknowingly been lodged with the evacuated Rostovs to await the inevitable, wakes from his delirium (represented by an offstage chorus chanting Tolstoy's 'pi-ti-pi-ti-pi-ti . . .') to behold Natasha. She begs forgiveness; he bears no grudge. They relive happier times, evoked by a multitude of reprises, before he expires.

Scene 13 *(IV/3/12–14, 4/6) The Smolensk road, in a savage blizzard: along the road the French army is retreating; a few soldiers, clothed and shod in whatever came to hand, huddle together for warmth; along the road are cast-off weapons, broken-down carriages* Ramballe and Bonnet,

two French officers, assess the hopelessness of their situation. Together with the retreating convoy march some prisoners, including Pierre and Platon Karatayev. The latter, exhausted, is executed. A partisan detachment under Denisov attacks the convoy and frees the surviving prisoners. Marshal Kutuzov arrives and is greeted by all with a grandiose choral reprise of his Scene 10 aria; it is only one of many reprises that give this scene, like the one preceding it, the character of a summation.

*

Like many works by great but unconventional artists – indeed, like its literary forebear – Prokofiev's *War and Peace* has a perfection of form that is perhaps more readily apprehended by audiences than by critics. Just as Tolstoy's 'baggy monster' of a novel incorporates attributes of other genres (epic, chronicle, sermon, historical tract), Prokofiev's opera, like the operas of Glinka and Borodin, incorporates conspicuous elements of oratorio. Like the most famous operas of Tchaikovsky and Musorgsky, moreover, *War and Peace* is a medley of scenes from a familiar source rather than a trimly plotted drama. These traits, while typical of Slavonic operas (indeed, essential to the definition of the genre), have impeded the opera's progress in the West. Even in Part 1, scenes are rarely dynamic enough to meet conventionally sophisticated notions of dramatic calibre, and this has led to misplaced allegations of naivety on the part of the composer.

The best proof that he knew better than his critics can be found in the very area that has incited the most complaint: that is, the seemingly disjointed selection and sequence of scenes. Prokofiev's decision to focus the early action on the seduction of Natasha Rostova (to the extent that in the early drafts of the libretto every one of the pre-Borodino scenes had derived from Book II Part 5 of the novel) has met with incomprehension and indignation. It has seemed one-sided, both in its representation of the novel's plot (absent, for example, is Natasha's brother Nikolay Rostov, the novel's key character according to many) and in its portrayal of the beloved heroine, who is shown behaving in reprehensibly selfish fashion.

One way of explaining Prokofiev's selection is simply to note that only a complete account of Natasha's seduction and attempted elopement can fully motivate Scene 12, the scene whose operatic potential had instigated the entire project. But that does not suffice. Prokofiev's true accomplishment was to give the two halves of his work, so often regarded as excessively discrete and even antagonistic, a hidden, mutually reinforcing correspondence. (Tolstoy himself hinted at this correspondence when once, rather enigmatically, he referred to the episode of Natasha and Anatol as the 'knot' in which all the themes of his work came together.) They are parallel parables of betrayal compounded: Natasha/Russia, having become infatuated with Anatol/France (note Akhrosimova's strictures in Scene 6) and betrayed her true love Andrey/the people, is in turn betrayed by her seducer. Even Pierre, in the words of one commentator 'a lumbering and implacable force, threatening but not given to unnecessary violence', and who refers to Natasha in Scene 2 as 'my protégée', has a place within this restricted scheme as counterpart to Kutuzov. The double denouement, with the two reprise-laden summation scenes (Natasha's forgiveness, Russia's victory) placed side by side, makes an impact even the opera's most fastidious detractors reluctantly acknowledge.

A full accounting of the opera's stylistic affinities and its musical construction would have to detail both its intricate network of leitmotifs, reminiscences and reprises, and its canny exploitation of contrasting, dramatically pertinent resonances with Russian operatic tradition. Scenes 2 and 4, played against a scintillating backdrop of ballroom music (some of it, like the common-time polonaise in Scene 2, of a calculated unreality) are in as apposite a line of descent from Tchaikovsky's Pushkin operas as are Scenes 8, 11 and 13 in Part II from Musorgsky's historical tableaux. As Prokofiev deliberately underscored the link with *The Queen of Spades* by his choice of text for the Scene 1 duet, so the epic scene of Moscow aflame is veritably a second Kromï Forest (*Boris Godunov*), replete with pointed musical allusions and with a surrogate Holy Fool in Karatayev.

R.T.

Werther

Drame lyrique in four acts by Jules Massenet to a libretto by Edouard Blau, Paul Milliet and Georges Hartmann, based on Johann Wolfgang von Goethe's novel *Die Leiden des jungen Werthers* ('The Sorrows of Young Werther', 1774); Vienna, Hofoper, 16 February 1892.

The first performance was sung in German with a cast led by the Belgian tenor Ernest Van Dyck (a famous Parsifal and Lohengrin) as Werther and Marie Renard, a soprano who had also sung Manon in Vienna, as Charlotte; Sophie was sung by Ellen Brandt-Forster, Albert by Franz Neidl and the Bailli by Carl Mayerhofer. The conductor was Hans Richter.

Werther *aged 23*	tenor
The Bailli *aged 50*	bass or baritone
Charlotte *his eldest daughter,*	
aged 20	mezzo-soprano
Sophie *her sister, aged 15*	soprano
Albert *aged 25*	baritone
Schmidt } *friends of the Bailli*	tenor
Johann	bass or baritone
Brühlmann *a young man*	tenor
Käthchen *a young girl*	soprano
The Bailli's six remaining children	children's voices

Inhabitants of Wetzlar, guests, servants (silent roles)

Setting The outskirts of Frankfurt (Wetzlar, over 50 km distant, is specified); July to December 178 . . .

Goethe's novel, an early and crucial document of the Romantic movement, was both based on fact and, coincidentally, autobiographical. In 1772 the 23-year-old writer fell in love with Charlotte Buff, daughter of the Bailli of Wetzlar, who married instead Johann Christian Kestner; at the same time a mutual friend, Karl Wilhelm Jerusalem, shot himself for love of a married woman with pistols belonging to Kestner (the note he sent asking to borrow them survived and is quoted verbatim in both novel and opera). The publication of *Werther*, with its implicit condonation of suicide, caused a sensation; it is said that an entire Italian edition was suppressed – that is to say, sedulously bought up – by the church authorities. It was soon dramatized, and there was an opera on it as early as 1792.

In his ever-unreliable memoirs, Massenet recalls how his publisher Georges Hartmann accompanied him to Bayreuth for *Parsifal* in 1886 and gave him a copy of Goethe's novel when they stopped at Wetzlar on the return journey. With picturesque circumstantial detail the composer describes starting to read it in a noisy, smoke-filled beer hall and finding especial inspiration in the quotation from Ossian that was to form the emotional climax of the opera. In fact, the idea of a Werther opera is mentioned in a letter as early as 1880, and it was germinating even while Massenet was engaged on *Manon* in 1882. In 1885 he started composition; Hartmann had in all likelihood sketched the scenario but the libretto was by Blau and Milliet, and the inclusion of the publisher's name on the title page had more to do with percentages than authorial responsibility. It is also possible that Hartmann's bankruptcy and the absorption of his business by another firm the year before the première led both to this and to Massenet's generous, if fanciful, account of *Werther*'s genesis.

The score was finished in 1887. Léon Carvalho, director of the Opéra-Comique, turned it down as being too gloomy for his audiences. Shortly afterwards, the theatre burnt down. *Werther* remained in the composer's drawer while he busied himself with *Esclarmonde* and his infatuation with

Sibyl Sanderson. There was a further opportunity for a première in 1889, but this was the year of another international exposition and *Esclarmonde* was thought more suitable. Following the successful Vienna première of *Manon* in 1890, the management there asked for a new Massenet opera and were given *Werther*.

The opera was first given in Paris on 16 January 1893 by the Opéra-Comique in its temporary home at the Théâtre Lyrique, with Guillaume Ibos and Marie Delna. It was not a conspicuous success. In 1894 it was withdrawn from the repertory; the same year saw performances in New York, Chicago, New Orleans and Milan, and throughout the French provinces. There was a single performance at Covent Garden, also in 1894; a dispute between Jean de Reszke and Sir Augustus Harris, as well as lukewarm audience response, prevented further airings. Albert Carré revived the piece at the Opéra-Comique in 1903, and its worldwide popularity dates from then – it has been performed over 1300 times in Paris alone. In recent years it has vied with *Manon* as Massenet's most popular work. In 1902 Massenet himself made a baritone arrangement of the title role for Mattia Battistini, which is still occasionally performed (as at Seattle in 1989, with Dale Duesing).

*

Act 1 *The garden of the Bailli's house, July* The Bailli (roughly Mayor, or Steward) rehearses his unruly younger children in a Christmas carol. Johann and Schmidt call to encourage him to join them at the inn, to discuss the evening's ball, and in particular Charlotte's partner for the occasion, the urbane and melancholy poet Werther, who enjoys the Prince's favour and is destined for a diplomatic post. They also inquire after the return of Charlotte's fiancé, Albert, from a journey, and look forward to celebrating their wedding. When they have left, Werther enters and sings of the beauty of the surroundings ('Invocation': 'O Nature, pleine de grâce, reine du temps et de l'espace'; some commentators have noted the mild blasphemy of these lines, which echo the 'Ave Maria' and express a typical Romantic pantheism). He asks Nature to receive him as a human devotee and the sun to envelop him in its warmth. He then watches as Charlotte, dressed for the ball, gives the children their supper of bread and butter in the house. They are introduced; two others destined for the ball, the starry-eyed Brühlmann and Käthchen, can only utter the word 'Klopstock', the name of the poet, and pass on, to the bemusement of the Bailli. As Charlotte consigns the children to Sophie's care, Werther apostrophizes (aside) this vision of ideal love and innocence. As all leave, the Bailli, encouraged by Sophie, decides to join his friends at the inn.

Albert returns unexpectedly, and asks Sophie if he is still remembered after his six-month absence. She reassures him that all the family's thoughts are of preparation for the marriage, and they go off. Time passes. Charlotte and Werther return from the ball ('Clair de lune'). To a hushed, rocking melody in 12/8 Werther's fatal love is born (not insignificantly the scene's opening words are Charlotte's 'Il faut nous séparer'). She protests that he knows nothing of her, but he cites the children as witnesses to her beauty of spirit. She tells him of the burden of responsibility placed upon her by their mother's early death, and of how they still ask why 'the men in black' took *maman* away, to which Werther can only reply with a passionate declaration of love. As he asks if they may meet again, the Bailli's voice is heard from indoors proclaiming the news of Albert's return. Charlotte tells Werther that this is the man she promised her dying mother she would marry, and admits that for a moment she was in danger of forgetting her oath. Werther enjoins her to keep it, knowing that it will mean his death.

Act 2 *The square in Wetzlar, with the church, the parsonage and the inn, autumn* From the inn, Johann and Schmidt watch townspeople on their way to church to help celebrate the Pastor's golden wedding. Albert asks Charlotte if she has any regrets after three months of marriage. She sweetly reassures him as they enter the church. Werther appears and gives vent to an outburst of jealous fury ('Désolation': 'Un autre est son époux . . . J'aurais sur ma poitrine'). A disconsolate Brühlmann is assured by Johann and Schmidt that Käthchen, his fiancée of seven years, will return to him. Albert comes out of church and in a brief dialogue with Werther, in which there is much between the lines, confesses that his own happiness reminds him of the pain Werther might feel, having met Charlotte when she was still free, and that he understands and sympathizes. Werther replies that if there were any bitterness in his heart, he would leave the town for ever; as it is, he feels only friendship for them both. Sophie enters with a bouquet for the Pastor, reserves Werther for the first minuet at the celebrations, and sings blithely of the happiness that has descended on the town ('Du gai soleil'). Left alone, Werther admits that he was lying to himself: the honourable course would be to leave. Charlotte enters. As Werther nostalgically recalls their first meeting – as does the music – she reminds him of her wifely duty, a duty that would make it prudent for him to depart.

While he should not forget her, she continues, a trial separation would soften his pain; he could return, perhaps, at Christmas. Alone, Werther muses on the notion of suicide, using a variant of the parable of the Prodigal Son ('Lorsque l'enfant'): if a child returned unexpectedly from a journey, would not his father welcome him all the more warmly? He calls

Ernest Van Dyck in the title role of Massenet's 'Werther' which he created at the Vienna Hofoper, 16 February 1892

laden with presents, instinctively senses her sister's distress and tries to cheer her ('Ah! le rire est béni'). When she mentions Werther, whom she plainly loves as well, Charlotte breaks down ('Air des larmes', with saxophone obbligato): tears unshed engulf and destroy the human heart. Sophie tries to persuade her to spend Christmas with their father and the children. Charlotte, alone, prays to God for strength in remembering her duty.

Werther suddenly appears. At first Charlotte and the music attempt to keep the conversation at the level of social pleasantries, about how the children look forward to seeing him, and how nothing has changed in her room, the harpsichord, the books, Albert's pistols, all in the same place. To distract him from the last-named, Charlotte fatally points out the volume of Ossian that Werther once started to translate, and he sings the 'Lied d'Ossian'. 'Pourquoi me reveiller': why answer the call of spring when it only presages the season of storms? The passionate melody forms the basis of the rest of the scene: Charlotte's reserves fail her and they fall briefly into each other's arms. But she recovers herself and leaves the room, saying they will never meet again. Shattered, his mind made up, Werther asks nature to mourn her erring son (to a reminiscence of the first-act 'Invocation') and rushes away. Albert enters, having heard of Werther's return, and grimly starts to interrogate his wife. A servant enters with a message from Werther: he is going on a long journey and asks to borrow Albert's pistols. The husband coldly orders his wife to hand them over. Once alone, she hurries away, praying that she will not be too late. An intermezzo, at once violent and full of foreboding, leads without break into the last act.

Act 4 *Werther's study* Charlotte finds the dying Werther. He prevents her from summoning help, preferring not to be separated from her in this first moment of happiness. To a reminiscence of 'Clair de lune' she admits that she has always loved him and in an embrace they forget momentarily the pain that has intervened. From outside the children's voices are heard singing the first-act carol, and Werther asks to be buried under the lime trees at the far end of the cemetery or, if that is forbidden by the church, then in unhallowed ground, where the priests may pass by but at least one woman will weep at his grave. He dies as children's voices celebrate Christ's birth.

*

on the God he does not recognize to summon him home. Sophie enters; he tells her brusquely that he is leaving for ever and rushes out. The golden wedding procession emerges from the church. Sophie bursts into tears as she gives Charlotte and Albert the news. Both understand the significance of the words 'for ever'.

Act 3 *The drawing-room of Albert's house; Christmas Eve* Charlotte, her heart full of love for Werther, re-reads the letters she should have destroyed ('Air des lettres'), remorseful at having suggested his exile. The third letter warns her that if he does not return at Christmas, she should weep for him. Sophie enters,

Quite why Massenet should have decided to set Goethe's story nearly a century after the sensation of its publication is something of a mystery. If he saw it as a companion piece to *Manon* – both deal with an amorous entanglement in an 18th-century setting – we may be thankful that musically they are sharply dissimilar and, more significantly, that the libretto of *Werther* is an infinitely more skilful adaptation of a novel than that of the earlier work: unnecessary detail is expunged, there is no chorus, and all is concentrated on the central relationship. The novel is cast in the form of letters, with Goethe intervening as 'editor' to describe the protagonist's suicide; for the opera a final duet was needed rather than the lonely death of the original (in which Werther never regains consciousness), and the text makes clever use of elements from the novel. There are other differences: in the novel, as in real life, Charlotte has not promised her dying mother to marry Albert, but does so out of choice, and similarly Albert has no idea why Werther/Jerusalem demands the pistols. The character of Sophie is much expanded in the opera, both as a musical foil and as the unfortunate victim of fallout from the central relationship.

Werther is a fine example of a middle-period opera by a composer who was able to enjoy a full life-span (*La traviata* and *Lohengrin* are useful analogues); there may be rough edges and problems of form, but there is also a nice balance between the vigour and freshness of the inspiration and the growing maturity of technique. In this respect it is interesting that, contrary to Massenet-inspired legend, *Werther* had a seven-year gestation period rather than just one year. The libretto is one of the best Massenet was given. While paying Gallic lip-service to the Romantic hyperbole of Goethe, there is a corresponding spareness of syntax that leaves the music plenty to do other than just illustrate and intensify. There is a lightly sketched-in and satisfying time-structure, from summer to winter, from lightness to dark, from the sun that Werther invokes at his first entry to the moon that sheds light on his first meeting with Charlotte and his death. Pantheism and bourgeois Christian values are interestingly enmeshed.

Werther is still basically a number opera, like *Manon*, as the titles quoted in the synopsis would suggest, but there are very few passages in which voices are heard together, and the numbers themselves are skilfully placed in the seamless flow of what is to all intents and purposes a through-composed conversation piece. There is also a spareness of orchestral texture, an overall darkness of colour in the frequent use of lower brass and woodwind that some have seen, perhaps facilely, as Wagnerian; be that as it may, Massenet never again risked so sombre a pervasive tone, perhaps conscious of *Werther*'s uncertain reception in Paris both before and immediately after the first performance there.

In no other Massenet opera is the melodic inspiration so rich. The 'Invocation' may be inspired by 'Salut, demeure' in Gounod's *Faust*, but it is thoroughly worthy of its model; both the 'Clair de lune', with its shy, filigree instrumentation, and the surging, neo-*verismo* 'Lied d'Ossian' are masterly, and it should be noted that when they are reprised

they are slightly but significantly altered – something that does not happen in *Manon*. The sequence of Charlotte's 'Air des lettres', 'Air des larmes' and 'Prière' adds up to an overwhelmingly grand *scena* for mezzo (it is hard to imagine a soprano, a Manon, coping with it at the Vienna première, since it needs a Berlioz Dido at the very least) on the scale of that for Desdemona in the last act of *Otello*, to which Massenet pays passing homage in Charlotte's sudden cry of farewell to her sister. That this should be followed by the 'Lied' makes the third act one of the most inspired and powerfully sustained in all French opera, let alone in Massenet.

The violent 'Désolation', added after the completion of the score at, it has been suggested, the behest of Van Dyck, may be comparatively obvious, but the uncanonic version of the Prodigal Son later in the act is at once a supremely tactful and deeply felt setting of a potentially mawkish passage, and underlines what has been seen as a manic pattern in the protagonist's music, swinging from extremes of ecstasy to extremes of despair. It could be argued that Sophie's music is too relentlessly cheerful, but she is only 15 and the effect of her undeclared love for Werther as well as the instinctive understanding of a teenager for her elder sister's distress is artfully signalled in the swooning 3/4 tune that underpins the conversation on either side of the 'Air des larmes'.

Indeed, it is the psychological penetration through words and notes that impresses the most. Werther's passion noticeably intensifies once he realizes that his love for Charlotte is doomed (the whole 'Clair de lune' sequence shows extraordinary shrewdness of observation, not least in that neither character actually listens to what the other is saying) and there is something almost sinister in the way that for her own purposes Charlotte declines to release Werther from thraldom; the words 'Pourquoi l'oubli?' when she has already ordered him to leave verge on cruelty, and it is she who suggests Christmas as a possible time for meeting again. Here, one feels, are two people who in the interests of their own personal needs are determined to make each other as miserable as they possibly can, and they certainly succeed.

The significant changes to the original material show how the central misery is liberally spread around. Albert has few notes to sing, but a resourceful baritone can show how the iron enters his soul, how he is changed from a simple, virtuous man confident of his love into a husband who can order his wife to hand over the instruments of her lover's death. Similarly, young Sophie's life is blighted beyond recall by the unbridled and supremely selfish passions of her elders. *Werther* is on the surface a simple, almost commonplace story of love and death, but the composer's insights shed an uncomfortable light on the workings of the human psyche in a fashion that is, quite surprisingly, worthy of Goethe. Massenet may have matured subsequently as a composer, certainly in matters of form and technique, but he wrote nothing greater or more heartfelt than *Werther*.   R.M.

Wozzeck

Opera in three acts by Alban Berg to his own libretto, after Georg Büchner's play *Woyzeck;* Berlin, Staatsoper, 14 December 1925.

Erich Kleiber conducted the première, with Leo Schützendorf in the title role, Sigrid Johanson as Marie and Fritz Soot as the Drum Major in a staging by Franz Ludwig Horth.

Wozzeck	baritone*
Marie *his common-law wife*	soprano
Marie's son	treble
Captain	buffo tenor
Doctor	buffo bass
Drum Major	heroic tenor
Andres *Wozzeck's friend*	lyric tenor*
Margret *Marie's neighbour*	contralto
First Apprentice	deep bass*
Second Apprentice	high baritone
Madman	high tenor

Soldiers, apprentices, women, children

Setting A garrison town and the neighbouring countryside, *c*1830

* Sprechstimme roles

Berg began work on an operatic treatment of Büchner's play in 1914, after he had attended its first Viennese performance at the Residenzebühne on 5 May. It had been given in Landau's revision of K. E. Franzos's 1879 edition of the text and entitled *Wozzeck* because of a misreading of the almost illegible manuscript; Berg prepared his libretto from the Landau edition and hence preserved the misspelling in the opera. By the end of 1914 he had prepared a draft libretto and made some musical sketches, but he then set it aside to finish the Three Orchestral Pieces op.6. Conscription and subsequent service in the Austrian War Ministry prevented his returning to work on *Wozzeck* until 1917, by which time his military experiences had deepened his sense of identification with the central character of the tragedy. He reported progress by autumn the following year, but even after the end of World War I it remained slow. Act 1 was completed by July 1919, Act 2 not until August 1921, and the entire work was finished in short score by October that year. The full score occupied Berg until April 1922; his pupil Fritz

Heinrich Klein prepared the piano reduction. Shortly after his marriage to Helene Nahowski in 1911 Berg had earned his living making vocal scores of Schoenberg's *Gurrelieder* and Schreker's *Der ferne Klang;* the influence of the latter has been detected in the orchestration of *Wozzeck*.

Schoenberg had recommended that Universal Edition take on publication, but Berg initially published the vocal score privately in December 1922; although he signed a contract with Universal the following April no staging was immediately forthcoming. At the suggestion of Hermann Scherchen he prepared for concert performance the *Drei Bruchstücke aus 'Wozzeck'*, consisting of part of Act 1 scene iii, Act 3 scene i and the orchestral interlude between Act 3 scenes iv and v, leading into scene v itself; Scherchen conducted the first performance in Frankfurt in 1924. By then, however, Kleiber had accepted the opera for production at the Berlin Staatsoper, where the first performance aroused much controversy.

Performances in Prague (1926) and Leningrad (1927) followed; the first German production since the première took place at Oldenburg in 1929, conducted by Johannes Schüler, and demonstrated that *Wozzeck* was not beyond the capabilities of provincial houses. Leopold Stokowski conducted the American première in Philadelphia in March 1931. Kleiber's second production, in Berlin in 1932, was the last occasion on which *Wozzeck* was seen in a German house until 1948: Berg was to be officially proscribed by the Nazi regime. The British stage première took place at Covent Garden in January 1952 conducted by Kleiber, with Marko Rothmüller as Wozzeck and Christel Goltz as Marie. Pierre Boulez conducted the French stage première at the Paris Opéra in 1963. The first commercial recording was of a concert performance in Carnegie Hall, New York, in 1951, conducted by Dimitri Mitropoulos with Mack Harrell and Eileen Farrell; the first studio recording was conducted by Karl Böhm in 1965, with Dietrich Fischer-Dieskau and Evelyn Lear.

Berg himself characterized the large-scale dramatic and musical planning of *Wozzeck* as a ternary *ABA* structure in which the highly wrought 'symphonic' central act was flanked by the more loosely constructed outer acts. But the self-contained musical structure of each scene is precisely tied to its dramatic function. Thus the five scenes of Act 1, an exposition that introduces the five main characters in turn and delineates Wozzeck's relationship to them, are designated as a series of five character-pieces; Act 2, the opera's dramatic development, is a symphony in five movements, while the five scenes and final orchestral interlude of Act 3 ('catastrophe and epilogue') are a sequence of six inventions on single musical ideas.

*

Act I.i *(Suite) The Captain's room, early morning* There is
a brief introduction (Prelude: obbligato wind
quintet), three bars in which the english horn
introduces the Captain's theme; Wozzeck is seen
shaving the Captain, who urges Wozzeck to work
more slowly. His words 'Langsam, Wozzeck,
langsam!' define the tritone motif B–F that permeates
the opera. After Wozzeck's numbed response on a
single pitch the Captain continues with his lecture
(Pavane: obbligato timpani and harp), but despite his
enthusiastic contemplation of eternity Wozzeck is
unmoved. 'A good man doesn't rush about', he is
counselled (Cadenza 1: obbligato viola), and his
refusal to react leads the Captain into derision
(Gigue: obbligato flutes and celesta); Wozzeck agrees
with everything he says. The Captain is delighted
with his teasing and continues (Cadenza 2: obbligato
double bass, leading to Gavotte: obbligato brass):
Wozzeck has no moral sense because he has an
illegitimate child (the Captain quotes the regimental
chaplain in a parody falsetto). Wozzeck is finally
provoked into a lyrical response: 'the Lord will think
no less of him because of it' (Double 1: obbligato
horns), and the Captain is confounded (Double 2:
obbligato trombones). Wozzeck then expands on his
theme (Air: obbligato strings), 'Poor folk like us, who
have no money', and his first phrase, 'Wir arme
Leut!', introduces the opera's most significant motif.
The Captain tries to calm him (postlude) and the
remainder of the scene then recapitulates the earlier
conversation and its associated obbligatos. The
following orchestral interlude continues to review
the material of the suite and builds to a *fortissimo*
climax.

I.ii *(Rhapsody) An open field outside the town, late
afternoon* Andres and Wozzeck are cutting sticks,
but Wozzeck is disturbed both by the brooding
atmosphere, represented musically by the sequence
of three chromatic chords on which the scene is
based, and by what he perceives as the threatening
natural world. Andres is untroubled and sings a
folksong, 'Das ist die schöne Jägerei', to counteract
Wozzeck's paranoia, but the scene ends with
Wozzeck hearing noises under the ground and
seeing the sinking sun as engulfing the world in
flames. The orchestral interlude gradually dispels the
atmosphere of menace with the first stirrings of the
military band.

I.iii *(Military March and Lullaby) Marie's house,
evening* Marie, her child in her arms, is watching the
military band march by. The Drum Major acknowledges her, and the march provides the background to
a conversation between Marie and Margret in which
the neighbour remarks on Marie's interest in him.
Marie slams shut her window and the march is
replaced by a lullaby, 'Mädel, was fangst Du jetzt
an?', as Marie sings of her life to her child. Wozzeck

interrupts them. Ignoring the boy, he tries to
articulate the fears he experienced in the fields, as the
music quotes altered motifs from Act 1 scene ii; Marie
is terrified, quoting Wozzeck's own 'Wir arme Leut!'
(but to a different figure), and rushes out. The
interlude portrays her agitation by developing
material from scenes ii and iii into a 12-note figure.

I.iv *(Passacaglia) The Doctor's study, a sunny afternoon*
The 12-note theme of the passacaglia is heard as a
cello recitative. The Doctor, who has secured
Wozzeck's cooperation in his scientific experiments,
accuses him of coughing in the street ('pissing' in
Büchner's original) and goes on to question him
about his diet (variations 1–5). The Doctor feels
betrayed by Wozzeck's lack of commitment but
calms himself, since anger is unscientific. Wozzeck
remembers Marie and recounts his visions in the
fields (variations 6–12) to music derived from scene
ii; the Doctor seizes on an insight into Wozzeck's
mental state (variations 13–21) and pronounces his
diagnosis, 'eine schöne fixe Idee', to a slow waltz
introduced by the first appearance of the Doctor's
motif in the violins. As the tempo quickens he
becomes more and more carried away with his
dreams of scientific immortality. In the subsequent
interlude fragments of the passacaglia are gradually
replaced by music associated with the following
scene.

I.v *(Rondo) The street outside Marie's house, twilight*
Marie continues to admire the Drum Major from her
doorway. The ritornello theme, related to the
opening of the march, represents Marie's desire both
for the soldier and for a new, better life; the Drum
Major's boasting occupies the first episode, his
attempts at seduction the following two sections. The
curtain falls as they rush into the house.

Act 2.i *(Sonata) Marie's room, a sunny morning*
Marie is admiring the earrings the Drum Major has
given her (exposition). When the child stirs Marie
sings him back to sleep with a song about a gypsy
who will take her back to his native land: the two
themes of her guilt (heard in the orchestra) and her
slightly sinister lullaby (derived from Act 1 scene iii)
form the subjects of the sonata movement. Wozzeck
enters, and Marie tries to hide the earrings (development): she says she found them in the street. He is
unconvinced and leaves after briefly contemplating
the child. Marie is overtaken by remorse (recapitulation). The interlude, framed by a pair of harp
glissandos, is a violent development of the themes of
the sonata movement.

2.ii *(Fantasia and Fugue) A street, daytime* The
Captain and the Doctor, Wozzeck's two exploiters,
meet. The Captain now counsels the Doctor not to
rush; the latter (to the same waltz theme as in Act 1
scene iv) diagnoses the Captain's breathing difficulties as symptoms of 'apoplexia cerebria' and gives

him four weeks to live. When Wozzeck appears they turn their attention to him and in a triple fugue – its first subject the Captain's theme, its second the Doctor's, its third (representing Wozzeck) derived from the preceding scene – begin to taunt him about Marie and the Drum Major. Deathly pale, Wozzeck rushes off. An interlude for chamber orchestra introduces the material of the following scene.

2.iii *(Largo) The street outside Marie's house, a gloomy day* To chamber-orchestral accompaniment (precisely the scoring of Schoenberg's First Chamber Symphony) Wozzeck confronts Marie with his suspicions. The music is derived almost entirely from reminiscences of previous scenes, especially Act 1 scenes iii and v. This slow movement at the centre of the opera is in three sections, the first devoted to Wozzeck's accusations, the second (as Wozzeck's jealous rage almost boils over in a knife attack) to Marie's defiance: here the chamber orchestra and the full orchestra are cross-cut, and a descending series of chromatic chords represents the knife. She leaves, and in the last part of the Largo Wozzeck is left to reflect on his existence: 'Der Mensch ist ein Abgrund' ('Man is an abyss'). The music that introduces the scene returns and is gradually transformed into a slow Ländler that forms the main material for the next scene.

2.iv *(Scherzo with two trios) A tavern garden, late evening* Soldiers, apprentices and local girls are dancing to the accompaniment of a stage band. Two apprentices deliver drunken soliloquies (Trio 1), and when the scherzo is resumed (with fleeting references to earlier motifs) the company is joined by Marie and the Drum Major. Wozzeck watches them and is about to launch an attack when the dancing is interrupted by an unaccompanied six-part Hunting Chorus in 7/4 (Trio 2), itself interrupted by another folksong from Andres. When the Scherzo is resumed, a madman observes to Wozzeck: 'Everybody is happy, but it smells of blood!' Wozzeck begins to see the scene swallowed up in blood-red mist. The dance music continues, increasingly grotesque, through the interlude, until it is abruptly cut short.

2.v *(Introduction and Rondo) A guardroom in the barracks, night* To the sounds of snoring soldiers Wozzeck wakes to nightmarish memories of the scene in the tavern. He hears voices, as material from Act 1 scene ii is recalled, and tries to pray. The rondo begins with the arrival of the drunken Drum Major, boasting of his conquest; with each statement of the ritornello he drinks from his bottle. He and Wozzeck fight (to music first heard during Marie's struggles in Act 1 scene v); Wozzeck is knocked down, and when he struggles up he quotes Marie's 'Einer nach dem Andern!' to a whole-tone phrase from Act 2 scene iii. The two alternating chords that closed Act 1 and opened Act 2 fade away to leave an isolated B.

Act 3.i *(Invention on a theme) Marie's room, night, candlelight* Still plagued by guilt, Marie is reading in her Bible the story of the woman taken in adultery. The music unfolds in a series of seven variations on the theme heard in the opening bars as she comforts her child by telling him a fairy story and returns to the Bible to find the passage about Mary Magdalen. Marie's prayer for mercy is accompanied by a three-part fugue, which continues into the interlude, dying away in subdued orchestral colours and arpeggios for harp and celesta.

3.ii *(Invention on a note) A forest path by a pool, dusk* Marie and Wozzeck are walking together. The music of the scene unfolds freely over reiterated B's, sometimes heard as a pedal or in inner parts, sometimes in the high treble. Wozzeck first talks with heavy irony of beauty and fidelity, then tells Marie that he loves her. As the blood-red moon rises, over muted brass Wozzeck draws his knife. To a prolonged crescendo on B he stabs Marie. Images from her life are swiftly recalled in the orchestra – the seduction, lullaby, earrings, march – and as Wozzeck leaves, the opera's fateful tritone is heard. The following interlude builds up to a huge climax on B, cut off by a *fortissimo* chord (which will form the basis of Act 3 scene iv), the opera's *Hauptrhythmus* hammered out by the bass drum.

3.iii *(Invention on a rhythm) A low tavern, dimly lit, night* The rhythm of the polka, heard first on a honky-tonk piano, dominates the scene. Wozzeck is trying to bury his crime in drink. He attempts to silence the pianist by singing a folksong (to a variant of the Act 1 lullaby) but it serves only to remind him of Marie. He persuades Margret to sing, but that also is too painful; Margret notices blood on Wozzeck's hands and goes to tell the other customers. Wozzeck rushes out. The interlude is built from the rhythm of the previous scene.

3.iv *(Invention on a six-note chord) The forest path by the pool, night* Wozzeck has returned to the pool to try to recover his knife. As the orchestral hexachord is put through a spectrum of changes he falls against Marie's corpse, and as the moon rises again, blood-red, he finally loses all reason. Imagining himself covered in Marie's blood he wades ever deeper into the pool to wash himself clean, until he drowns. The Doctor and the Captain pass by hurriedly, scared and not wishing to concern themselves with others' misfortunes, while the scene returns to unearthly calm, with wind instruments simulating the sound of croaking frogs and toads. The final interlude, an invention on a key (D minor), now recapitulates the work's main themes and characters (except Marie); it builds massively on the 'Wir arme Leut!' motif, and its climactic 12-note chord resolves into unambiguous D minor for the Epilogue.

3.v *(Invention on a regular quaver movement) Outside*

Marie's house, bright morning sunshine Over a *perpetuum mobile* symbolizing the continuity of normal life, Marie's child is playing on an imaginary hobby-horse, unaware of what has happened. Another child brings news of the discovery of Marie's body, and after a moment's pause her child follows his friends to see it, as the orchestra recalls fragments of themes associated with her. The opera ends on the pair of alternating chords that closed Acts 1 and 2.

*

Wozzeck is a work of immense structural complexity in which musical devices and dramatic constructs are tightly integrated. Its composition marked the culmi-nation of the first phase of Berg's development; the initial sketches were made while he was completing the Three Orchestral Pieces op.6, and the opera deploys the same language and even some of the same material: elements of the march from op.6 are quoted in Act 1 scene iii. In its use of atonality, whole-tone writing and other devices alongside passages of Mahlerian diatonicism, as well as in the vocal writing (which moves between speech, parlando, Sprech-gesang and arioso), *Wozzeck* represents the most substantial achievement of the Schoenberg school before serialism.   A.C.

Y

Yevgeny Onegin ('Eugene Onegin')

Lyric scenes in three acts by Pyotr Il'yich Tchaikovsky to a libretto by the composer and Konstantin Stepanovich Shilovsky after Alexander Sergeyevich Pushkin's novel in verse (1833); Moscow, Malïy Theatre, 17/29 March 1879 [students of the Moscow Conservatory]; professional première, Moscow, Bol'shoy Theatre, 11/23 January 1881.

The première of the opera was given by students, under Nikolay Rubinstein, with Mariya Klimentova as Tatyana; at the professional première the conductor was Enrico Bevignani and Onegin was sung by Pavel Khokhlov.

Larina *a landowner*		mezzo-soprano
Tat'yana [Tatyana]	*her*	soprano
Ol'ga [Olga]	*daughters*	contralto
Filipp'yevna [Filipyevna] *an old*		
nursemaid		mezzo-soprano
Yevgeny Onegin		baritone
Lensky		tenor
Prince Gremin		bass
A Company Commander		bass
Zaretsky		bass
Triquet *a Frenchman*		tenor
Guillot *valet de chambre*		silent

Peasants, ballroom guests, landowners, officers

Setting A country estate and St Petersburg, 1820s

The idea of transposing the most beloved work of Russian fiction to the musical stage was not Tchaikovsky's to begin with. It was proposed to him, during a social call on 25 May/6 June 1877, by the contralto Yelizaveta Lavrovskaya (1845–1919), and, according to an oft-cited letter to his brother Modest, at first it struck the composer as 'wild'. The drawbacks were obvious: Pushkin's novel was loved for the telling, not the tale. The plot as such was slender and banal, but the book was loved for its divine details: the verbal dazzle, the wry social commentary, the perfectly exact descriptions, the endlessly subtle and nuanced characterizations, the ironized interrelationship of literary and social conventions – all that comes under the heading of narrative quality.

What Tchaikovsky shortly perceived – and what critics (not audiences) have failed to perceive for over a century – was that music of a sort he was uniquely inclined and equipped to write could perform exactly those functions for which Pushkin's narrative voice was prized. The result was a *chef d'oeuvre* of stylized operatic realism: the Russian counterpart to *Traviata* or *Manon*, except that it stands higher in its national tradition than they in theirs, and its realism more fundamentally determined its style.

Tchaikovsky spent a sleepless night after his visit to Lavrovskaya's, at the end of which he had a scenario in hand that differs only slightly from that of the finished opera. On 27 May he sought out his friend Konstantin Shilovsky, who had been pestering him with ideas for biblical and historical grand operas, and persuaded the latter to focus with him on *Onegin*. Together the two of them worked out a text that preserves a maximum of Pushkin's original verses. Shilovsky's major contribution to the libretto consisted of Monsieur Triquet's couplets (both French and ruptured-Russian versions) in Act 2 scene i; the composer was responsible for Lensky's arioso in Act 1.i and that of Prince Gremin in Act 3.i.

He began composing straight away with Tatyana's letter (1.ii), on Pushkin's unaltered text. This self-contained passage, which all educated Russians know by heart, was something Tchaikovsky had planned to set long before conceiving the operatic project. (During this initial period of ardent imaginative work, identifying strongly with Tatyana and full of indignation at the title character, her unworthy love object, the composer unexpectedly found himself the recipient of a similar confessional letter from an unremembered former pupil named Antonina Milyukova; this suggestive coincidence set in motion the chain of events that led to Tchaikovsky's brief, disastrous marriage.) The first four scenes of the opera were written during the month of June (Old Style) on Shilovsky's country estate. Then followed the calamitous events connected with the composer's wedding and its aftermath, when he came to realize that physical contact with a woman repelled him; he returned to *Onegin* during his extended recuperative stay in Western Europe, and only after embarking upon the Fourth Symphony, which would compete for his time for the rest of the year. Act 1 was fully scored by the end of October (in Clarens, Switzerland, where 36 years later Stravinsky composed *The Rite of Spring*). By 13/25 January 1878, all of the opera was complete in score except for the duel scene (2.ii). This, the last vocal music in the opera to be composed, was written in the hills outside San Remo, Italy. The orchestral introduction followed. The whole work was completed in full score on 20 January/1 February. Even with the distractions of personal disaster and major competing projects, it had taken only eight months to write.

Tchaikovsky later revised the third act and this version was first given at the Mariinsky Theatre, St Petersburg, on 19 September/1 October 1885; Eduard Nápravník conducted, with Emiliya Pavlovskaya the sensational Tatyana, Mariya Slavina as Olga, Ippolit Pryanishnikov as Onegin and Mikhail Koryakin as Gremin. The schottisches (écossaises) in Act 3 were added for this production at the request of Ivan Vsevolozhsky, Intendant of the Imperial Theatres.

In the following synopsis, numbers in parentheses refer to Pushkin's novel (chapter and stanza); direct quotations from the novel are from Vladimir Nabokov's translation (1963).

The introduction is based on Tatyana's main leitmotif, establishing her as the opera's central character.

*

Act I.i *The garden of the Larin estate* To the strains of a duet based on Pushkin's early verse *The Poet* ('Slïkhalil' vï ... vdokhnulil' vï': 'Have you not heard ... have you not sighed'), sung by Olga and Tatyana, wafting out from the house like an invocation to the muse, Mme Larina reminisces with Filipyevna about her courtship and marriage, and the relationship of literature to her emotional life, concluding with a maxim paraphrased from Chateaubriand (ii.29–36). The chorus and Dance of the Peasants that follow are a decorative insertion of Tchaikovsky's devising: Mme Larina's serfs return singing from the field bearing the last sheaf, and sing and dance for her to celebrate the harvest. Tchaikovsky did not take these songs from printed anthologies; the second (dance song, 'Uzh kak po mostu-mostochku': 'Across the little bridge') has been identified in oral tradition, but the first (*protyazhnaya*, 'drawn-out song', 'Bolyat moi skorï nozhen'ki so pokhodushki': 'My nimble feet are sore from walking') is evidently original. Attempts have been made to invest the song texts with portent, but unconvincingly. For the *scena* and aria that follow, the librettists extracted a characterization of the two Larin sisters from the verses in which Pushkin contrasted them (ii.23–8) and put it all in Olga's mouth ('Ya ne sposobna k grusti tomnoy': 'I am no good at languid melancholy'). The peasants take their leave. Mme Larina expresses concern at

Tatyana's bookish pensiveness; Filipyevna announces Lensky's approach with a stranger.

Lensky and Onegin are introduced; in the quartet, which Tchaikovsky compared to the quartet in Act 2 of Gounod's *Faust*, the men and the Larin sisters stand in respective pairs and sing a skilful concatenation of phrases from the novel (iii.5–8), the men casually appraising the girls and the entranced Tatyana recognizing in Onegin the 'somebody' for whom her soul had been waiting. Thereupon they form two couples; Onegin and Tatyana stroll off. In an arioso Lensky confesses his feelings for Olga, not for the first time ('Ya lyublyu vas, Ol'ga': 'I love you, Olga'). Onegin and Tatyana, the latter now clearly enamoured, stroll back on stage, the former regaling the company with the famous opening stanza of the novel, in which the young rake cynically recalls the uncle whose timely death had brought him into ownership of the estate bordering on the Larins'.

I.ii *Tatyana's bedroom* The introduction is based on an extended version of Tatyana's leitmotif. Tatyana interrogates the uncomprehending Filipyevna about love and asks her to recount her own courtship and marriage; the nursemaid's story, about ancient and unromantic peasant rituals, strikes no chord within the infatuated girl (iii.17–21). She asks Filipyevna to arrange her writing-desk with pen and paper and sends her away. Tatyana composes her letter to Onegin in a huge (12-minute) aria, the Letter Scene ('Puskay pogibnu ya': 'Even if it means I perish'; its text corresponds to iii.31). Dawn breaks, and a shepherd's pipe is heard (the oboe melody here is in the manner of documented Russian shepherd tunes). Filipyevna comes to wake Tatyana and is surprised to find her up; Tatyana asks her old nanny to send her grandson with the letter to Onegin (iii.32–5).

I.iii *Another part of the Larin estate* Berry-picking peasant girls, singing an imitation folksong drawn from the novel (iii.39) and overheard by Tatyana as she waits for Onegin's response, act in the opera as a frame to the action of this scene, returning at the end. Onegin shows up and reproves Tatyana as gently as he can for her lack of self-control, meanwhile confessing himself incapable of anything more than a brother's love (iv.12–17). Tatyana is stunned into silence.

Act 2.i *A brightly lit room in the Larin house* The entr'acte is based on the central theme of the Letter Scene. To the strains of a waltz, played by a military band courtesy of the Company Commander with whom the ladies flirt, the guests assembled for Tatyana's name-day chatter and gossip (v.25–6, 28). Onegin, bored, flirts and dances with Olga (v.41). Lensky jealously confronts Olga but is rebuffed (v.44–5). Monsieur Triquet, a local Frenchman, sings some name-day doggerel he has composed (v.27, 33).

Mariya Klimentova as Tatyana in the Letter Scene from Act 1
of Tchaikovsky's 'Yevgeny Onegin', the role she created in the
original production by students of the Moscow Conservatory
at the Malïy Theatre, Moscow, 17/29 March 1879

Shilovsky's text begins 'A cette fête conviée', or, in
'Russian', 'Kakoy prekrasnïy etot den' ('What fine
today!'). Olga having promised the cotillon to
Onegin, Lensky confronts his rival, forswears their
friendship and challenges him to a duel; the latter
accepts (v.42; vi.8–12: in the novel, Lensky leaves the
ball at the cotillon and issues his challenge the next
day through Zaretsky, his second). In the largest
ensemble in the opera, the quintet (Tatyana, Olga,
Larina, Lensky, Onegin) with chorus, the assembled
company express their horror at what has happened
(this scene departs the furthest from Pushkin's plot,
since the novel contains no public scandal at the ball;
even so, many of the principals' repliques do roughly
correspond to thoughts and expressions in the novel,
especially vi.1–3).

2.ii *A rustic watermill in the countryside at dawn; winter*
The introduction is based on the first section of
Lensky's aria. Lensky and his second Zaretsky
impatiently await their tardy opponent at the
appointed duelling place. Zaretsky stomps off to
scout for Onegin, while Lensky sings a farewell to
Olga (vi.21-6, a letter-in-verse in the novel, meant as
a parody: 'Kuda, kuda vï udalilis': 'Whither, ah!
whither are ye fled'). Onegin arrives, casually
apologizes for the delay, but insults Zaretsky by
presenting his valet as his second. The paces are
marked off, Onegin fires and, to his horror and
remorse, kills Lensky with the first shot (vi.26–31, 35).

Act 3.i *A side room of a rich noble house in St
Petersburg* A polonaise is in progress. Onegin, having
returned from a long sojourn abroad where he had
tried without success to forget the tragic consequences of his ennui, and bored as ever, encounters
the Princess Gremina, a celebrated beauty, at a fancy-
dress ball and is astounded to recognize Tatyana
(viii.13–20). A schottische is danced. Tatyana's
husband, Prince Gremin, confides to Onegin, an old
acquaintance, what happiness his marriage has
brought him and how gratefully he loves his wife
('Lyubvi vse vozrastï pokornï': 'To love all ages are
obedient', words by Tchaikovsky except for the
incipit, which comes from viii.29). Tatyana pleads
fatigue and leaves with the Prince, and Onegin
realizes that he is now in love with her (viii.21-2, 30).
His aria ('Uvï, somnen'ya net': 'Alas, there is no
doubt') is an ironic recapitulation in music, and
partly in words, of the rapturous opening section
of Tatyana's Letter Scene. A further schottische
is danced. (In place of the foregoing scene Tchaikovsky's original draft scenario had one roughly
based on the concluding section of Pushkin's chapter
vii, in which, shepherded by her mother through
the Moscow 'marriage market', Tatyana meets her
unnamed general and receives his proposal.)

3.ii *A reception room in Prince Gremin's house*
Tatyana has received a confession from Onegin and
does not know how to deal with it. Suddenly Onegin
bursts in and confronts her with his newly kindled
passion. He forces from her the admission that she
loves him still, but cannot shake her resolve to stay
with her husband. She rushes tearfully away, leaving
him behind, shattered (viii.32, including Onegin's
letter to Tatyana, 42–8). (In the original version of this
scene Tatyana's exit was preceded by an embrace on
which Gremin unexpectedly enters; in removing this
melodramatic conclusion, Tchaikovsky made only
textual, not musical, alterations.)

*

Of all the supreme repertory operas, *Yevgeny Onegin*
has surely been treated with the most condescension.
In part this has merely reflected general
condescension towards Tchaikovsky, typically regarded as a wholly naive, spontaneous creator who
could not function vis-à-vis his subjects and tasks
except on the basis of infantile personal identification. True, his endlessly quoted letters to his brother
and his patron contain a mountain of material for
such a reading, and nowhere more so than in those
relating to *Yevgeny Onegin*, full of seemingly ingenuous mooning over Tatyana. To the perceptive
musician, however, the self-concealing sophistication of Tchaikovsky's technique is a miracle every bit
as bracing and shaming as Pushkin's to the literary.

Beyond the general, two special problems have
attended the opera. It has always disconcerted those

for whom the value of Russian music can only inhere in an aura of 'Russianness' and who can discern Russianness only in the presence of folksongs. By that standard Tchaikovsky has been irrelevantly dismissed, and just as irrelevantly vindicated, many times over. In *Yevgeny Onegin*, where the folkish is obviously nothing more than an aspect of decor, 'Russianness' is nevertheless especially crucial, forming the basis of the opera's essential realism and therefore pervasive. But it is Russianness of an urbane sort most Western ears cannot descry as such.

The other problem, perhaps the chief one, involves the opera's relationship to its literary source. The solecism according to which an opera derived from pre-existing literature is judged by a simple yardstick of fidelity – correspondingly exigent as the source is valued – has happily been losing ground; but in the case of *Yevgeny Onegin*, the most revered source of all, it adamantly persists. The opera has been the bane of Pushkin-lovers from the beginning (Turgenev to Tolstoy: 'Undeniably notable music . . . But what a libretto!'). By now, on the authority of the militantly tone-deaf Vladimir Nabokov, denigration of Tchaikovsky's work is literary dogma. The novel's greatness is assumed to lie in its irony, vouchsafed by the intrusive narrative voice – 'a kind of spiritual air conditioner', as it has been – called. Literary critics have not always understood what the music in an opera actually does – particularly in this opera, where the music, quite simply, is the narrator. From the very first notes sung, Olga's and Tatyana's duet to the harp, the music acts as a very busy and detached mediator of situations and feelings. Tchaikovsky 'sings' his opera in an idiom intensely redolent of the domestic, theatrical and ballroom music of its time and place – its, not his – and in so doing he situates it, just as Pushkin situates the literary prototype, in the years 1819–25. And just as Pushkin's characters achieve their 'reality' by virtue of a multitude of precisely manipulated codes, so Tchaikovsky's express themselves through a finely calculated filter of musical genres and conventions.

Moreover, where the novelist must arrange things in a temporal sequence, the musician can simultaneously present and comment without recourse to digression. To pick one example, the comically exaggerated courtly flourishes in the orchestra that accompany Lensky and Onegin on their first appearance instantly sketch their foppish histories, accomplishing much of the work of Pushkin's chapter i, the absence of which is so often and so severely held against the opera's libretto. In their startling anticipation of *Pulcinella*, these '18th-century' curlicues also call attention to Tchaikovsky's under-appreciated mastery of the grotesque.

These points apply not only to the characters' public behaviour and to the obviously 'generic' ballroom scenes, but even, or especially, to their most private and personal utterances. Tatyana's Letter Scene, the most private and personal in the opera, is in effect a string of four romances linked by recitatives. The resonances between the music of this scene and the opening duet-romance are many, conspicuous and calculated: they are the resonances between Tatyana's inner and outer worlds. The most obvious is the fact that both incorporate Tatyana's leitmotif (it is the last line of each strophe in the duet, the middle section of the last romance in the Letter Scene). The leitmotif itself begins on the sixth degree of the minor scale, and initiates a descent to the tonic, thus describing the interval that more than any other defines the idiom of the Russian domestic or household romance of the early 19th century: Russian scholars have gone so far as to coin the term *sekstovïy* ('sixthy') to denote that defining quality. Tatyana's part is, with Lensky's, surely the 'sixthiest' in all of opera.

The melodic-harmonic idiom is only one of many genre resonances that tie Tatyana's Letter Scene to the opening duet and thence to the whole world of the domestic romance. The harp-heavy orchestration of the first two sections is no less potent. But the harp does more than evoke the sounds of domestic music-making. The inspired chords (non-arpeggiato) that punctuate the woodwind phrases in the actual letter-writing music (second of the four romances) take their place within a marvellously detailed sound-portrait of the lovesick girl, in which Tchaikovsky shows himself to be an adept practitioner of Mozart's iconic methods (or 'body portraiture') as outlined in the famous letter to his father about *Die Entführung aus dem Serail*. As in the case of Mozart's Belmonte or Osmin, we can 'see' and 'feel' Tatyana – her movements, her breathing, her heartbeat – in her music. This, too, comes under the heading of narration, and shows off music's advantages: what the novelist must describe, the composer can actually present. As to irony, did Pushkin ever make more trenchant comment than Tchaikovsky, when he mocks Onegin's passionate confession to Tatyana in Act 3 with a fleeting reference to the music by which he had rejected her in Act 1? It is not simply a matter of showing that the boot is on the other foot: that much had already been accomplished by setting Onegin's arioso at the end of Act 3 scene i to the melody of the first romance in the Letter Scene (equally ironic in that Onegin, not having 'heard' that music on its earlier appearance, cannot be 'quoting' it now; the reference is entirely a narrator's aside). The allusion to the rejection music shows him fickle and erratic; it takes the place of the lengthy passage in the novel (vii.19–24) in which Tatyana visits the absent Onegin's library and discovers, by peeking at the annotations in his books, the shallowness of his soul.

The concluding confrontation between Onegin and Tatyana has been described as a duet in the grand style, but even here the method of construction remains that of stringing romances (a technique Tchaikovsky evidently picked up from his teacher Anton Rubinstein: compare the third act of the latter's *Demon*). Tatyana's chief melody apes her husband's aria in the preceding scene, thus telegraphing her answer to Onegin. Only twice, fleetingly, do the two voices mingle. It is hardly a duet at all. Like Tatyana's total silence in response to rejection (1.iii, and except for her participation in ensembles, in 2.i as well) the scene flies in the face of operatic convention, underscoring by omission – another ironic narrator's aside – the futility of the dramatic situation.

The fact that *Yevgeny Onegin* contains no love duets testifies to its singular affinity with Pushkin's novel. This is not to say that there are no divergences between Tchaikovsky's treatment and Pushkin's: in the case of Lensky, in particular, whose Act 2 aria is a very serious moment, the opera does reflect a later, more sentimental age. But even with Lensky, the use of the modest romance form is more than just evocative, it sets distinct limits on his emotional scale. All the characters in the opera remain denizens of a novel (one of the very earliest to be given operatic treatment), not a historical romance or a well-made play.

It is striking to find Tchaikovsky, who professed to despise *The Stone Guest* for its literalistic pretension to 'truth', virtually parroting some of Dargomïzhsky's pronouncements when it came to describing his own equally eccentric work. 'Its content is very unsophisticated', he wrote of his opera to Mme von Meck, 'there are no scenic effects, the music lacks brilliance and rhetorical effectiveness'. That – not, as often supposed, the fact that it consists of extracts from a larger story – is why Tchaikovsky preferred the term 'lyric scenes' to 'opera' in subtitling the score. The most he could hope for, he thought, were 'a few *chosen* listeners', who would discover *Onegin* for themselves at home, and who would create demand for it 'from below'. That certainly happened; within decades of the composer's death his 'lyric scenes' played on all the biggest operatic stages of the world. He even adapted them somewhat to make this possible. But, like *The Stone Guest*, *Yevgeny Onegin* makes its strongest impression in plainer surroundings.

R.T.

Z

Zar und Zimmermann
[*Czaar und Zimmermann, oder Die zwei [beiden] Peter* ('Tsar and Carpenter, or The Two Peters')]

Komische Oper in three acts by Albert Lortzing to his own libretto after Georg Christian Römer's comedy *Der Bürgermeister von Saardam, oder Die zwei Peter*, itself based on Mélesville, E. C. de Boirie and J. T. Merle's *comédie-héroïque Le bourgmestre de Sardam, ou Les deux Pierres*; Leipzig, Stadttheater, 22 December 1837.

At the first performance Lortzing himself sang the role of Peter Ivanov.

Peter the Great *Tsar of Russia*	baritone	
Peter Ivanov *a young Russian carpenter*	tenor	
General Lefort *Russian ambassador*	bass	
Van Bett *burgomaster of Saardam*	bass	
Marie *his niece*	soprano	
Widow Browe *master carpenter*	contralto	
Lord Syndham *English ambassador*	bass	
Marquis de Chateauneuf *French ambassador*	tenor	

Inhabitants of Saardam, Dutch officers, carpenters, town officials, sailors
Setting Saardam in the Netherlands, 1698

In the wake of his first success as a theatrical composer – *Die beiden Schützen*, given in February 1837 – Lortzing worked enthusiastically to complete another comic opera. Before the end of the year he had finished and mounted *Zar und Zimmermann*, in which he himself sang the part of Peter Ivanov, gaining a measure of acclaim and confirming his position as the leading German comic-opera composer. The principal factor in Lortzing's success was his perfect matching of libretto and music; indeed, it was his carefully crafted librettos that were seen by contemporaries as his great strength. As the reviewer for the *Allgemeine musikalische Zeitung* remarked of the première:

At a time when murder, plague, horror and misery of all kinds have to be served up to us from the stage as the piquant fare of opera lovers, often in outrageous dissonances so that we will actually feel something, a comic opera is on the one hand very welcome; on the other, though, it is difficult for it not to disappear without trace. The difficulty lies more in the text than in the music. If there were more well-made comic opera texts there would be more good comic operas.

Zar und Zimmermann was rapidly taken up by other theatres and has retained to the present day a leading place in the German repertory.

*

Act I *A shipyard in Saardam* Tsar Peter the Great is seen disguised as a carpenter under the name Peter Michaelov to learn the art of shipbuilding. Peter Ivanov, a fellow Russian working in the shipyard who has made friends with the Tsar (unaware of his real identity), is in love with the burgomaster's niece, Marie. In the arietta 'Die Eifersucht ist eine Plage' Marie tries to quiet Ivanov's jealousy of other admirers; her charming song is punctuated by short spoken interjections from him. In the following dialogue, the Tsar is informed by General Lefort that there is unrest in Moscow led by his sister. He instructs Lefort to return immediately and gives vent to his anger in the recitative and aria 'Verrathen! von euch Verrathen!', which Lortzing, to underline the Tsar's superior status, treats as an extended number including, unusually, recitative. Van Bett, the burgomaster, arrives and establishes himself as a figure of fun in the aria 'O sancta justitia, ich möchte rasen', which contains prominent solo passages for a bassoon (which has also to supply Van Bett's inaudible bottom F in a cadenza). The burgomaster has received instructions to discover the whereabouts of a foreigner called Peter who is working in the shipyard; he asks to see all Widow Browe's workers, and discovers that though many of them are called Peter, only Michaelov and Ivanov are foreigners; his suspicions settle on Ivanov. When in the following dialogue Lord Syndham, the English ambassador, offers him £2000 to find out what Peter's plans are in respect of England, Van Bett begins to suspect that Peter must be a man of some importance, and when Ivanov reappears the burgomaster begins, to Peter's astonishment, to treat him with exaggerated respect: in the duet 'Darf ich wohl den Worten trauen' Van Bett goes so far as to offer Ivanov his niece's hand in marriage if he will give him information about his plans. The French ambassador, Chateauneuf, arrives on the scene, and in the finale, during preparations for the marriage feast of Widow

Browe's son, he quickly decides that Peter Michaelov is the Tsar and makes contact with him.

Act 2 *An inn* The feast is in full swing. Lefort and Chateauneuf, disguised as sailors, meet with the Tsar to make plans. To distract attention from them Chateauneuf entertains the guests with a song, 'Lebe wohl, mein flandrisch Mädchen'; there is effective participation by Marie and the chorus at the end of each verse. Syndham appears, dressed as a Dutch sailor, and approaches Van Bett to ask whether he has discovered anything. In the following sextet, 'Zum Werk das wir beginnen', Van Bett and Syndham are occupied in making approaches to Ivanov, while at another table Chateauneuf, deep in discussion with the Tsar and Lafort, is on the verge of accomplishing his diplomatic triumph. As in other ensembles Lortzing shows his skill in deriving comic effect from the sharp contrast of characters and situations. The wedding feast proceeds with Marie's bridal song 'Lieblich röthen sich die Wangen', but is suddenly interrupted by the arrival of a Dutch officer and soldiers with orders to inspect the credentials of all foreigners; this leads to the unmasking, in the finale, of the three ambassadors and to Van Bett's further confusion as Syndham and Chateauneuf each identify their own Peter as the Tsar. The act ends in general tumult.

Act 3 *The great hall of the town hall* Van Bett, who still believes Ivanov to be the real Tsar, has assembled a choir to practise a cantata in his honour. In 'Den hohen Herrscher würdig zu empfangen' Lortzing achieves a splendid union between a humorous text and lively music. Marie is unhappy with the idea that Ivanov is the Tsar, since she is convinced that marriage with him will be impossible; the real Tsar promises her that everything will be all right. Left alone, the Tsar reflects on his high position, in the simple and appealing 'Sonst spielt' ich mit Scepter, mit Krone und Stern' (which has now almost gained folksong status in Germany). In the duet 'Darf eine nied're Magd es wagen' Marie begins by treating the bewildered Ivanov as the Tsar, but they end by declaring their love for each other. After she has left the Tsar returns, cursing the fact that the harbour has been blockaded. Ivanov, however, produces a pass given to him by Syndham, which guarantees him safe conduct, and explains that the English ambassador has also furnished him with a yacht, sailors and money. The Tsar takes the pass and gives Ivanov a document, which he makes him promise not to open for an hour. Chateauneuf and Lefort arrive and the finale begins. The Tsar and the two ambassadors hasten to the harbour, leaving the confused Ivanov to receive the advancing deputation of honour led by Van Bett. Still believing that Ivanov is the Tsar, Van Bett again addresses him with comic deference and treats him to an extended clog dance

(for which Lortzing provides a charming waltz). Cannon fire and shouting eventually interrupt the celebration; the main doors of the hall are opened, revealing the Tsar in uniform on a ship leaving harbour. Ivanov opens his document and reads that he has been made Imperial Overseer, with the Tsar's permission to marry Marie. The opera ends with a gracious farewell from the Tsar and a chorus of general rejoicing.

*

Lortzing's comic operas show a vivid personal vein of sentimental humour which, although limited in range, was popular in appeal and made him the most inventive composer of the genre in mid-19th-century Germany. In several respects *Zar und Zimmermann* marks an advance on *Die beiden Schützen*. The earlier opera had to some extent lacked homogeneity; the contrast in style between the song-like numbers and comic ensembles, and the more formal arias and duets derived from German Romantic opera, had been noted by contemporary critics. In *Zar und Zimmermann*, the Tsar's aria is the only one which looks back to the other tradition, but it is justified as a piece of characterization, and in the opera as a whole Lortzing achieved a much more consistent style.

C.B.

Zauberflöte, Die ('The Magic Flute')

Singspiel in two acts, K620, by Wolfgang Amadeus Mozart to a libretto by Emanuel Schikaneder; Vienna, Theater auf der Wieden, 30 September 1791.

Schikaneder himself sang Papageno at the première; Benedikt Schack was Tamino; the Queen was Mozart's sister-in-law Josepha Hofer; Pamina was Anna Gottlieb (the first Barbarina, still only 17); Monostatos was Johann Joseph Nouseul; Sarastro, Franz Gerl.

Sarastro *Priest of the Sun*	bass
Tamino *a Javanese prince*	tenor
An Elderly Priest ['Sprecher'; Orator, Speaker]	bass
Three Priests	bass, tenor, spoken role
The Queen of Night	coloratura soprano
Pamina *her daughter*	soprano
Three Ladies *attendants to the Queen*	2 sopranos, mezzo-soprano
Three Boys	2 sopranos, mezzo-soprano
Papagena	soprano
Papageno *a birdcatcher, employed by the Queen*	baritone
Monostatos *a Moor, overseer at the Temple*	tenor
Two Men in Armour	tenor, bass
Priests, attendants, acolytes, slaves	

Die Zauberflöte is an allegory set in no real locality or historical period. Ancient Egypt is evoked by the mysteries, but early productions also showed Islamic influence on the costumes, with neo-classical architecture appropriate to the Enlightenment. The exotic costumes and setting (and Tamino's nationality) are a mask; Mozart and Schikaneder intended a coded representation of Freemasonry.

Carl Ludwig Gieseke (who originally played the First Slave) said many years later that he had contributed as much as Schikaneder to the libretto, but his claims are now generally discredited. The sources of the libretto are diverse. Christoph Martin Wieland provided the title (*Lulu, oder Die Zauberflöte* from *Dschinnistan*) and the source of Gieseke and Wranitzky's opera *Oberon* (both 1789). Egyptological sources include Gebler's *Thamos, König in Ägypten*, for which Mozart had written incidental music anticipating the style of *Die Zauberflöte*. But in the main the libretto is original and contemporary in its significance.

It has been suggested that the Queen represents Maria Theresa, Sarastro Ignaz von Born (formerly Master of a masonic lodge) and Tamino Joseph II. Fortunately there is no reason why different significations should not coexist. The masonic allegory (evident in the Egyptian/mystic devices which illustrate the printed libretto) is transparent except for the role of Pamina (see below), and in the rapidity of Tamino's rise from initiate to ruler-designate. *Die Zauberflöte* was mostly composed before *La clemenza di Tito* which, however, was performed first. Mozart entered the 'Introduction' [sic] in his catalogue in July, but the March of Priests and Overture are dated 28 September, two days before the première. Schikaneder had successfully presented popular 'machine-comedies' at the out-of-town Theater an der Wieden since 1789. Although it was not a fashionable venue, audiences were substantial and embraced all ranks; Salieri attended a performance and complimented Mozart warmly. Mozart tested Schikaneder's improvisatory powers by fooling with the glockenspiel part in his Act 2 aria. Schack himself played the flute in the finales. Minor parts were taken by members of the theatre company including Schikaneder's brother and the wives of Schack and Gerl.

In Vienna, there were 20 performances in the first month, and publication of extracts began in November; Schikaneder had given over 200 performances by 1800. The first Hoftheater performance was in 1801. Soon after Mozart's death *Die Zauberflöte* was given in Prague and in all other centres of German opera (including Warsaw and St Petersburg) before 1798. Goethe projected a sequel; one by Schikaneder, *Das Labyrinth*, was set by Peter Winter (1798). The first British performances were in Italian (1811), and

it was frequently played as *Il flauto magico*. English versions reached London and New York in 1833. No major operatic centre was without a production in the 19th century and, while understanding of it may alter, the popularity of *Die Zauberflöte* has never waned. Among recent presentations Ingmar Bergman's sensitive film, sung in Swedish, has reached an international audience.

*

Overture: three chords (a masonic number: five if the short upbeats are counted) establish and question the tonic E♭, before a deliberate but mysterious progression to the dominant. The Allegro is monothematic. The B♭ cadence is marked by three times three tutti chords, the 'dreimalige Akkord'. The development is a *tour de force* and the recapitulation miraculously transforms elements by new dynamics and counterpoint.

Act I *Rocky country, with trees and mountains; in the foreground a temple* Tamino is pursued by a monstrous serpent, his terror evoked by *Sturm und Drang* gestures (Introduction, 'Zu hilfe! sonst bin ich verloren'). Three Ladies arrive; they kill the monster and triumph in the first of many delectable multisectioned ensembles. They take stock of the unconscious Prince and quarrel over which of them will guard him while the others tell the Queen. In mutual spite (a skipping 6/8) they all decide to go, and make a lingering farewell.

High-pitched piping announces Papageno, and punctuates his folk-like song ('Der Vogelfänger bin ich ja', in three strophes). In the first extended dialogue Tamino asks who he is. His answer hints at one of the work's themes: 'a man, like you'. He lives by eating and drinking, and by catching birds for the starry Queen. Despite the Ladies' warning, Papageno happily takes the credit for killing the serpent, whereupon the Ladies bring water and a stone instead of wine and bread, and padlock his mouth. They give Tamino a portrait of Pamina, the Queen's daughter. He contemplates its beauty and falls in love; can he be destined for her (aria, 'Dies Bildnis ist bezaubernd schön')? The tender appoggiaturas and pulsations bespeak his wonder and his racing heart. The Ladies tell him that Pamina has been kidnapped by the tyrant Sarastro. To turbulent transformation music the mountains are sundered, revealing a sumptuous chamber; the Queen is discovered on a starry throne (recitative, 'O zitt're nicht, mein lieber Sohn!': 'Do not fear, dear son'). Her aria is a melting G minor Larghetto, the first music in triple time ('Zum Leiden bin ich auserkoren': her daughter's loss torments her), followed by a fiery Allegro ending in giddy coloratura ascending to *f'''* ('Du, du, du wirst sie zu befreien gehen'). It forms Tamino's commission to rescue her daughter; its passion and brilliance leave him no room to suspect ulterior motives. The finale to the first scene is a quintet ('Hm hm hm hm'), another blend of comedy and numinous beauty. Papageno can only grunt until the Ladies unlock his mouth. All sing the moral: if liars were gagged, brotherly love would prevail. Tamino receives a magic flute, which protects him and can change sorrow to joy. Papageno, instructed to accompany Tamino, in whom he has no confidence, is horrified at the thought; Sarastro will surely eat them. He is given a chime of silver bells for his protection. To a final Andante of transcendent simplicity, the Ladies tell them that three wise and lovely boys will guide them.

A fine Egyptian-style chamber in Sarastro's apartment Slaves discuss Pamina's escape from the lust of Monostatos; but he has caught her (trio, 'Du feines Täubchen, nur herein!'). In the brisk *buffo* style which characterizes him throughout, the Moor has the protesting maiden bound. As she faints, Papageno appears; he and Monostatos catch sight of each other and, terrified, each runs away. Papageno recovers (if birds are black, why not a man?), identifies and frees Pamina, and tells her of the Prince who loves her. He, for his part, alas, has no mate. Princess and birdcatcher reflect on the mutual dependence of wife and man: united by love, they approach the divine (duet, 'Bei Männern, welche Liebe'). This duet epitomizes the opera's moral, as well as its musical directness. With the simplest accompaniment, it consists of no more than two almost identical 16-bar strophes (each lightly touching on the dominant) and a coda of the same length. The pastoral 6/8 nevertheless brings E♭, the 'Masonic' tonic, also the key of love (compare Tamino's first aria). Only Pamina's serene ornamentation differentiates the voices: it is a vision of classless, as well as domestic and sexual, harmony.

A grove, with three beautiful temples: at the back, 'Wisdom'; on the right, 'Reason'; on the left, 'Nature' The holiness of the place is evoked by the sturdy rhythms of the trombones, silent since the overture, at the opening of the finale. The Three Boys leave Tamino, urging him to be steadfast, patient and silent – the first clear hint of masonic practice. Tamino, in a recitative, assimilates his surroundings: surely a place of virtue. His purpose is honest; let the tyrant tremble! But his approaches to Reason and Nature (to music reminiscent of the Priest's speech in *Idomeneo*) are rebuffed by unseen voices. The old Priest (Orator, sometimes rendered as 'Speaker') emerges from the temple of Wisdom and in an awe-inspiring dialogue enlightens Tamino as to Sarastro's true and noble nature; he finds Tamino's sentiments worthy but his mind clouded by prejudice; he should not trust a woman's tears. He can say nothing of Pamina 'Sobald dich führt der Freundschaft Hand / Ins Heiligtum zum ew'gen Band' ('Until sacred friendship leads

you by the hand to join the eternal Order'). Tamino asks when light will come to him; the unseen chorus, while the cellos repeat the Orator's arioso cadence, replies: 'Soon, or never'. But Pamina is alive, he hears. In an outburst of gratitude he plays the magic flute: wild animals come to listen, but not Pamina. Then he hears Papageno's pipe, answers it, and runs after the sound. Pamina and Papageno are caught by Monostatos, as he sarcastically completes their cadence. As the slaves bring chains, Papageno is inspired to set them dancing with his bells, and they celebrate freedom with the folk-like 'Könnte jeder brave Mann' (remembered by Schubert in 'Heidenröslein'). Trumpets announce Sarastro, in a chariot drawn by lions; he is acclaimed, in the first substantial chorus. Papageno trembles but Pamina tells the truth: her flight was not from him but from the Moor. Sarastro reassures her, but her mother's pride is beyond forgiveness, and Pamina must stay to learn the ways of virtue from men. Monostatos brings in Tamino; he and Pamina embrace, to the chorus's surprise and Monostatos's fury. Sarastro rewards the Moor with a beating for his attempt on Pamina's virtue (the chorus again sings Sarastro's praise, but sotto voce) and orders the strangers to be veiled and led to the temple for purification. The act ends with a masonic chorus ('Wenn Tugend und Gerechtigkeit') which anticipates the end of *Fidelio*: virtue and justice will make a paradise on earth.

Act 2 *A palm grove, with 18 seats: on each, a pyramid and a horn* The priests enter bearing palm-fronds, to strains of a solemn march, coloured by flutes, basset horns and trombones. Punctuated by the 'dreimalige Akkord', Sarastro tells the Priests that Tamino awaits their consent to undergo the ordeals. Pamina is his destined bride and their union a defence against the malice of Night. The Orator inquires whether Tamino will endure the trial: he is, after all, a prince. More, replies Sarastro: he is a man. The scene closes with a noble invocation by Sarastro of the Egyptian gods ('O Isis und Osiris, schenket der Weisheit Geist').

A small forecourt, in darkness: thunder The Orator tells Tamino he can still withdraw, but he is determined to seek the light. Papageno, terrified of the dark, is told he will find no wife without undergoing the trials ('I'll stay single'). But he agrees to try when he learns that he will have his reward in Papagena, whom he has not yet seen. The piquant contrast of Tamino's quest through obedience to priestly instruction, and the popular-theatre gags of Schikaneder as Papageno, continues throughout the trials. They are warned by the two priests to mistrust women's arts, and meet them with silence ('Bewahret euch vor Weibertücken'). The Three Ladies ask why the companions are in this place of death; they are lost if they disobey the Queen, who is already within

'Die Zauberflöte' (Mozart): scene from Act 2, one of a series of engravings by J. and P. Schaffer from the Brno monthly magazine 'Allgemeines Europäisches Journal' (1795). The designer has closely followed the stage directions: 'the scene changes to two great mountains; in one of them is a waterfall from which the sounds of roaring water can be heard; the other spits out fire; in front of the mountains is a grille through which the fire and water can be seen; where the fire is burning the backcloth must be bright red, and where the water is a black mist lies; the sets are rocks, each closed off by an iron door'.

the sacred precinct (quintet, 'Wie? wie? wie? Ihr an diesem Schreckensort?'). Papageno is ready to believe everything, but Tamino silences him. The Ladies try a softer approach, but admit defeat and vanish (thunder and offstage chorus), leaving Papageno fainting to a minor-mode cadence. After the threefold chords they are led to new trials.

A garden The Moor prepares to rape the sleeping Pamina (aria, 'Alles fühlt der Liebe Freuden'). Mozart asked the orchestra to sound remote; the piccolo and lightning tempo suggest Turkish music. Why cannot a black slave share the delights of love? but the moon can close its eyes. The Queen's arrival sees him off, but now to her daughter she exposes her true motivation. She wants the power conferred by the sevenfold circle of the Sun, which her dying husband confided to the initiates, and she demands that Pamina kill Sarastro with a dagger that she supplies: Tamino and Pamina will both be cursed unless hell's fury is assuaged by his blood (aria, 'Der Hölle Rache'). Surpassing her Act 1 aria in brilliance (though not in difficulty), this Allegro reaches *f'''* four times, and adds a flood of triplet figuration; yet in

addition to agility it demands the passion of a Donna Anna, with similar chromatic harmony in a vengeful D minor. Monostatos has overheard, and offers Pamina death or submission; but Sarastro intervenes. Pamina begs mercy for her mother who, he says, is punished by her own actions. His aria ('In diesen heil'gen Hallen') expresses his humanistic creed; the two verses, in E major, have the purity of folksong, the authority of wisdom. In these sacred halls, they govern not by vengeance but by love, which alone can overcome tyranny.

A large hall The two candidates are left alone, bound to silence. Papageno grumbles; his desire for a drink is answered by a very old lady bringing water. She is 18 (surely she means 80) and her boyfriend is . . . Papageno! A thunderclap covers the sound of her own name as she hurries off. The Three Boys bring real refreshments ('Seid uns zum zweiten Mal willkommen'). Their exquisite E major trio is a warning of imminent crisis. Tamino plays the flute, leaving Papageno to eat. Pamina enters, joyful at finding them; Tamino, mindful of instructions, turns away. Her hurt is palpable in Mozart's most

'Die Zauberflöte' (Mozart): design by Simon Quaglio for Act 1 (the Queen of Night), performed at the Hof- und Nationaltheater, Munich, 1818: pen, ink and watercolour

haunting G minor aria ('Ach, ich fühl's'), its ornate melody arched over the simplest accompaniment so that every note bears its weight of pathos. The threefold chord summons them; Papageno remains behind to continue eating.

The vault of a pyramid. Two priests carry an illuminated pyramid; others hold pyramidal lamps The happy outcome of Tamino's trials is anticipated in a radiant D major chorus ('O Isis und Osiris, welche Wonne!'). Sarastro brings Pamina to him; they must say a last farewell before the greater trials (trio, 'Soll ich dich, Teurer, nicht mehr sehn?'). Sarastro is reassuring; Tamino expresses confidence, but Pamina is full of fears, for him rather than herself. Papageno comes running but the Orator tells him he will never reach enlightenment; he would settle for a drink, and is given wine. Ringing the bells (their part more elaborate with each of the three verses), he sings his second Volkslied: all he wants is a little wife ('Ein Mädchen oder Weibchen').The power of the bells brings her dancing in, still looking 80, but when, somewhat reluctantly, he promises to be true, she is revealed as the lovely Papagena and whisked away.

A small garden The finale is preceded by an introduction for wind band. The Three Boys evoke sunrise, which banishes darkness and death; without change of tempo, the homophonic trio develops into a dramatic quartet. The boys watch the grief-stricken

Pamina greet her mother's dagger as bridegroom. At the last moment they intervene to save her from suicide (Allegro, 3/4), restoring E♭, and with affectionate assurances lead her to Tamino.

Rocky landscape with two mountains, one gushing forth water, the other fire After a solemn introduction two Men in Armour sing a penitential chorale melody ('Ach Gott, vom Himmel sieh' darein') over nervous counterpoint, but the text foretells the triumph of the brave. Tamino, in ritual garb (shoeless), declares himself ready. Pamina calls; they respond with rapture; even death cannot separate them now. The tonality having settled into A♭, F major has the luminosity of a much sharper key, and it brings Pamina ('Tamino mein! o welch' ein Glück') with the rising major 6th which seems especially significant in Mozart (as at the Count's plea for forgiveness in *Figaro*). She takes Tamino's hand: he must play the flute, which her father carved in a magic hour of violent storm, deep in an ancient wood. The disarmingly simple C major of the slow march for flute, brass, and timpani forms a complement to what should be magnificent scenic effects. Tamino plays them through fire and water; the chorus acclaims their triumph.

The small garden Papageno blows his pipe but cannot bring back Papagena. His agitated rondo seizes the attention despite the preceding sublimity.

He is about to hang himself, in true pantomime style enlisting the aid of the audience to delay the event, when the boys remind him of the bells; their magic brings Papagena in feathered youthfulness, and their stammering duet becomes an excited hymn to domesticity and children. Monostatos leads the Queen and Ladies beneath the temple ('Nur stille, stille', a sinister little march). The Queen, bereft of high notes, stoops to offering the defector her daughter. But the sun beams forth, Sarastro appears on high with Tamino and Pamina in priestly robes, and at this transfiguration the demons are exorcised. The Armed Men's introduction recurs, radiant in the E♭ major Andante 'Heil sei euch Geweihten!': 'Hail chosen ones, who have overcome Night . . . [Allegro] Steadfastness conquers and grants the crown to beauty and wisdom'.

*

For the allegory, the end is strikingly unorthodox. Masons left their wives at home, whereas Pamina undergoes tests of constancy (the Queen's temptation; Tamino's rejection) equal to the man's, before joining him in trials by fire and water. Like *Così, Die Zauberflöte* has been accused of hostility to women. This is to confuse the attitudes of characters, including the absurdly misogynist priests in their duet at the beginning of Act 2 (itself a stage in Tamino's trials rather than dogma), with the meaning of the drama. If the Queen is the source of evil, Pamina is the strongest force for good and a necessary complement to Tamino: their union is divinely ordained. However alien to Freemasonry, the implication that women should become initiates is the opera's title to true Enlightenment.

There is no evidence to support the often-reiterated claim that the authors changed the plot, and that the Queen was originally good and Sarastro evil. If even Mozart's music cannot unequivocally distinguish hypocrisy from sincerity it is a condition (not a deficiency) of the art. That the flute and bells come from the Queen is a problem more apparent than real. By tradition such objects are neutral, or can only help the righteous; but the Queen believes in the justice of her cause. She takes a greater risk in offering the guidance of the wise Boys, but it is the Orator who begins the process of enlightenment. Monostatos, the untrustworthy servant, represents ordinary nature going bad; as cowardly as Papageno, the other representative of Everyman, he chooses evil and seeks power (over Pamina, by misused sexuality and by joining the Queen). He is punished, whereas Papageno, falling short of enlightenment, is nevertheless good-hearted and achieves domestic contentment.

Die Zauberflöte possesses attributes of pantomime, but is not ramshackle. It unfolds in many short scenes, a Shakespearian dramaturgy which effectively contrasts the grave with the comical, the austerely hieratic with the earthily improvisational. The only possible weakness is Tamino's second rejection of Pamina. This scene may be an addition to the original plan, and was perhaps misplaced from earlier in Act 2; even disguised as a formal farewell ('Soll ich dich, Teurer') it appears redundant, coming between 'Ach, ich fühl's' and Pamina's attempted suicide.

The full dialogue should be retained; even the slaves' scene adds to our understanding, and the priestly debates are indispensable (Mozart snubbed a booby who seemed to find them funny). The musical numbers function by contrast, employing an unprecedented stylistic range. Yet interconnections exist (such as the echo of the Queen's 'O zitt're nicht' in Tamino's 'O ew'ge Nacht', first finale) as does architecture through distinctive instrumentation (emblematic flute, bells, trombones) and tonality (the E♭/C axis which gives unusual prominence to C minor). Diversity and discontinuity do not deprive the score of the right to be considered as an entity, the masterpiece of Mozart's late style.   J.Ru.

Glossary

Act One of the main divisions of an opera, usually completing a part of the action and often having a climax of its own. The classical five-act division was adopted in early operas and common in serious French opera of the 17th and 18th centuries, but in Italian opera a three-act scheme was soon standard, later modified to two in *opera buffa*. From the late 18th century, operas were written in anything from one act to five, with three the most common; Wagner's ideal music drama was to consist of three acts.

Action musicale (Fr.) A translation of Wagner's 'Handlung für Musik', used by French Wagnerians to suggest something more elevated than a mere opera.

Afterpiece An English opera or pantomime of the 18th or early 19th century, usually about an hour long, designed for performance after a play or other theatrical work.

Air French and English term for 'song' or 'aria'. In French opera of the 17th and 18th centuries it was applied both to unpretentious, brief pieces and to serious, extended monologues, comparable to arias in Italian opera.

Aleatory Term for music in which some element of choice in composition or realization is left to chance or to whim.

Alto *See* Castrato; Contralto; Countertenor; and Haute-contre.

Appoggiatura (It.). A 'leaning note', normally one step above the note it precedes. Appoggiaturas were normally introduced by performers, in recitatives and arias in 18th-century opera, to make the musical line conform to the natural inflection of the words and (in arias) to increase the expressiveness.

Aria (It.) A closed, lyrical piece for solo voice, the standard vehicle for expression on the part of an operatic character. Arias appear in the earliest operas. By the early 18th century they usually followed a da capo pattern (*ABA*); by Mozart's time they took various forms, among them the slow-fast type, sometimes called rondò. This remained popular in Italian opera during most of the 19th century (the 'cantabile-cabaletta' type); even longer forms, sometimes in four sections with interruptions to reflect changes of mood, appear in the operas of Donizetti and Verdi. The aria as a detachable unit became less popular later in the century; Wagner wrote none in his mature operas, nor Verdi in *Otello* or *Falstaff*; in Puccini, too, an aria is usually part of the dramatic texture and cannot readily be extracted. Some 20th-century composers (notably Stravinsky, in the neo-classical *Rake's Progress*) have revived the aria, but generally it has been favoured only where a formal or artificial element has been required.

Arietta (It.), **Ariette** (Fr.) A song, shorter and less elaborate than a fully developed aria or air.

Arioso (It.) 'Like an aria': a singing (as opposed to a declamatory) style of performance; a short passage in a regular tempo in the middle or at the end of a recitative; or a short aria.

Atonal Term for music that is not in a key; it is particularly applied to the Second Viennese School (Schoenberg, Berg and Webern).

Aubade (Fr.) 'Dawn song': term for a song performed in the morning.

Azione teatrale (It.) A serenata-type genre of the late Baroque period, cultivated particularly at the Viennese court. Gluck's *Orfeo ed Euridice* was originally so described.

Ballabile (It.: 'suitable for dancing') A movement intended for dancing; Verdi used the term in Act 3 of *Macbeth* for the song and dance of the witches.

Ballad opera English 18th-century form, consisting of a play, usually comic, in which spoken prose dialogue alternates with songs set to traditional or currently popular melodies. The most famous example is *The Beggar's Opera*.

Ballata (It.) A dance-song; Verdi used the term for 'Questa o quella', in *Rigoletto*.

Ballet-héroïque (Fr.) A genre of the French lyric stage in the first half of the 18th century. It is a type of **Opéra-ballet**, consisting of a prologue and three or four acts or entrées, each with a plot of its own, using heroic or exotic characters. The outstanding example is Rameau's *Les Indes galantes*.

Barcarolle A piece with a lilting rhythm suggesting the songs of Venetian gondoliers; the most famous operatic example is in Act 3 of Offenbach's *Les contes d'Hoffmann*.

Baritone A male voice of moderately low pitch, normally in the range A-f'. The voice became important in opera in the late 18th century, particularly in Mozart's works, although the word 'baritone' was little used at this time ('bass' served for both types of low voice). Verdi used the baritone for a great variety of roles, including secondary heroic ones.

Bass The lowest male voice, normally in the range F-e'. The voice is used in operas of all periods, often for gods, figures of authority (a king, a priest, a father) and for villains and sinister characters. There are several sub-classes of bass: the *basso buffo* (in Italian comic opera), the *basso cantante* or French *basse-chantante* (for a more lyrical role) and the *basso profondo* (a heavy, deep voice).

Bass-baritone A male voice combining the compass and other attributes of the bass and the baritone. It is particularly associated with Wagner, especially the roles of Wotan (the *Ring*) and Sachs (*Die Meistersinger*).

Bel canto (It.) 'Fine singing': a term loosely used to indicate both the elegant Italian vocal style of the 18th and early 19th centuries and the operas (especially those of Bellini) designed to exploit that style.

Bitonality The simultaneous use of two different keys.

Breeches part [trouser role] Term for a man's or boy's character sung by a woman. The central examples are Cherubino in *Le nozze di Figaro* and Oktavian in *Der Rosenkavalier*, but there are many more, among them Verdi's Oscar (Edgar) in *Un ballo in maschera*, Fyodor in *Boris Godunov*, Hänsel, and the Composer in *Ariadne auf Naxos*. In Baroque opera numerous male parts were written for women but, with the issue confused by the castrato singers, casting was less sexually specific.

Brindisi A song inviting a company to raise their glasses and drink. There are examples in Donizetti's *Lucrezia Borgia*, Verdi's *Macbeth*, *La traviata* and *Otello* and Mascagni's *Cavalleria rusticana*.

Burlesque, Burletta A light opera embodying elements of parody. Pergolesi's *La serva padrona* was described as a burletta at its London première.

Cabaletta (It.) Term for the concluding section, generally in a fairly rapid tempo and with mounting excitement, of an extended aria or duet, sometimes dramatically motivated by an interruption after the slower first part (the 'cantabile' or 'cavatina'). The most famous example is Violetta's 'Sempre libera degg'io' (the final section of 'Ah fors'è lui') in Act 1 of Verdi's *La traviata*.

Cadenza A virtuoso passage inserted in an aria, usually near the end, either improvised by the singer or, as in Verdi's later operas, written out by the composer.

Cantabile (It.) 'In a singing style': usually the first, slower part of a two-part aria or duet; it can also indicate an aria in slow or moderate tempo, with a broadly phrased vocal line.

Cantilena Term used for a sustained or lyrical solo vocal line.

Canzone (It.) Term used in opera for items presented as songs, sung outside the dramatic action, for example Cherubino's 'Voi che sapete' in *Le nozze di Figaro* (although Mozart called it simply 'Arietta'). Verdi used it several times, notably for Desdemona's Willow Song in *Otello*.

Canzonetta (It.) A diminutive of Canzone, used in the same sense as that term; an example is Don Giovanni's serenade 'Deh vieni alla finestra'.

Castrato (It.) A male singer, castrated before puberty to preserve the soprano or contralto range of his voice. The castrato figured in the history of opera from its beginnings: Monteverdi's *Orfeo* includes a eunuch in the cast. In the papal states, where women were banned on stage, castratos sang all female roles. They performed the heroic male roles which until the late 18th century were nearly always for high voices: Monteverdi's Nero, Cavalli's Pompey, Handel's Julius Caesar and Gluck's Orpheus were all sopranos or altos.

Castratos dominated the stage during the era of Metastasian *opera seria*. The singers were mostly Italian, but many achieved international reputations in England and the German-speaking lands. They often behaved with the capriciousness of prima donnas. Many, including most of those for whom Handel composed, were of contralto rather than soprano range. Mozart composed Idamantes (*Idomeneo*) and Sextus (*La clemenza di Tito*) for castratos. In the early 19th century castrato roles appeared in a few operas by Rossini and Meyerbeer; thereafter the production of castratos came to be frowned upon. The last known was Alessandro Moreschi (1858–1922) who in 1902–3 made recordings in which the passionate yet curiously disembodied quality of his voice is apparent. The best castratos had high voices of great power, agility and penetration, and intense expressiveness; no one took exception to the use of castratos not only for heroic roles but also amorous ones.

Cavatina (It.) In 18th-century opera a short aria, without da capo, often an entrance aria. Mozart used the term three times in *Le nozze di Figaro*. Later examples are Rosina's 'Una voce poco fà' in Rossini's *Il barbiere di Siviglia* and Lady Macbeth's 'Vieni! t'affretta' in Verdi's *Macbeth*. Cavatinas often concluded with a Cabaletta.

Chaconne (Fr.) A Baroque dance in triple metre and moderate tempo, often involving a ground bass, used in French opera, particularly as the final dance of a group (or of the entire work) in the late 17th century. Later examples appear in Gluck's *Orfeo ed Euridice* and Mozart's *Idomeneo*.

Coloratura Florid figuration or ornamentation. The term is usually applied to high-pitched florid writing, exemplified by such roles as the Queen of Night in Mozart's *Die Zauberflöte*, Violetta in Verdi's *La traviata* or Zerbinetta in Strauss's *Ariadne auf Naxos*, as well as many roles by Rossini and other early 19th-century Italian composers. The term 'coloratura soprano' signifies a singer of high pitch, lightness and agility, appropriate to such roles.

Comic opera A musico-dramatic work of a light or amusing nature. The term may be applied equally to an Italian *opera buffa*, a French *opéra comique*, a German Singspiel, a Spanish zarzuela or an English opera of light character. It is also often applied to operetta or *opéra bouffe* and even musical comedy. Most non-Italian comic operas have spoken dialogue rather than continuous music.

Commedia dell'arte (It.) A comic stage presentation, developed in 16th-century Italy, characterized by the use of masks (or fixed parts), earthy buffoonery and improvisation. Its stock characters (Harlequin, Scaramouche etc), or characters developed from them, have often been introduced into comic operas such as Pergolesi's *La serva padrona*, Mozart's *Le nozze di Figaro*, Busoni's *Arlecchino* and Strauss's *Ariadne auf Naxos*.

Comprimario, comprimaria (It.) 'With the principal': term used for a singer of secondary or minor roles in an opera.

Continuo The continuous bass part used in works of the Baroque period and serving as a basis for the music, supporting the harmony. In opera, a continuo part will normally be played on a sustaining instrument (cello, double bass, viola da gamba, bassoon) and a harmonic instrument (harpsichord, archlute, theorbo, organ). Figures next to the notes indicated to the player what harmonies he should add. The use of continuo persisted in opera up to the end of the 18th century.

Contralto (It.) A voice normally written for in the range *g-e"*. In modern English the term denotes the lowest female voice, but the term could also denote a male Falsetto singer or a Castrato.

In opera, true contralto (as distinct from mezzo-soprano) roles are exceptional. They occurred in the 17th century for old women, almost invariably comic, but in the 18th century composers came to appreciate the deep female voice for dramatic purposes. In Handel's operas several contralto roles stand in dramatic contrast to the prima donna, for example Cornelia in *Giulio Cesare*, a mature woman and a figure of tragic dignity. Rossini's important contralto (or mezzo) roles include Cinderella in *La Cenerentola*, Rosina in *Il barbiere di Siviglia* (original version), and the heroic part of Arsaces in *Semiramide*. In later opera, contraltos were repeatedly cast as a sorceress-like figure (Verdi's Azucena and Arvidson/Ulrica,

Wagner's Ortrud) or an oracle (Wagner's Erda) and sometimes as an old woman.

Countertenor The English term for a male alto singer, often a falsettist. The voice has been rarely used in opera; roles include Oberon in Britten's *A Midsummer Night's Dream* and Glass's *Akhnaten*.

Da capo (It.) An instruction (usually abbreviated D.C.) to return to the head of a piece of music and repeat the first section. The 'da capo aria' was the standard aria form of the late Baroque and early Classical periods, especially in *opera seria*; it was generally understood that the repeated section would be ornamented. It was superseded by the 'dal segno' aria ('from the sign'), in which a sign part-way through the aria indicates the point at which the recapitulation should begin.

Divertissement (Fr.) Term used in early French opera for a section in a group of vocal solos, ensembles and dances usually ancillary to the work's main action, for example in Rameau's *tragédies*. The term is also used for self-contained musical entertainments, usually on a pastoral or allegorical theme, in single or multiple acts.

Drame lyrique (Fr.) 'Lyric drama': the term is used to distinguish a genre of late 19th- and early 20th-century French opera that grew out of the more serious sort of *opéra comique*. Epitomized by many of the operas of Massenet, it encompassed a wide variety of subject matter but used a more intimate dramatic treatment than grand opera, though it was richer in style than the simpler and lighter *opéra comique*.

Dramma giocoso (It.) Term used on Italian librettos in the late 18th century for a comic opera, particularly for the type favoured by Carlo Goldoni and his followers in which character-types from serious opera appeared alongside those traditional to comic opera. The *dramma giocoso* was not regarded as a distinct genre and the title was used interchangeably with others; Mozart's *Don Giovanni*, for example, is described on the libretto as a 'dramma giocoso' and on the score as an 'opera buffa'.

Dramma [drama] **per musica** [dramma musicale] (It.) 'Play for music': a phrase found on the title-page of many Italian librettos, referring to a text expressly written to be set by a composer.

Duet (It.) An ensemble for two singers. It was used in opera almost from the outset, often at the end of an act or when the principal lovers were united (or parted). Later the duet became merged in the general continuity of the music (Verdi, Puccini etc) or dissolved into a musical dialogue in which the voices no longer sang simultaneously (later Wagner, R. Strauss etc). The love duet had become characterized by singing in 3rds or 6ths, acquiring a mellifluous quality of sound appropriate to shared emotion. Often the voices are used singly at first and join together later, symbolizing the development described in the text.

Mozart described 'Via resti servita' in *Le nozze di Figaro* and 'Là ci darem' in *Don Giovanni* with the diminutive *duettino*, though neither is particularly short.

Entr'acte (Fr.) Music written for performance between the acts of a play; in opera the term has been applied to interludes between the acts of the *comédie-ballets* of Lully or the instrumental interludes between those of Bizet's *Carmen* and Debussy's *Pelléas et Mélisande*.

Entrée (Fr.) In 17th-century French ballet, a group of dances unified by subject; later the term was applied to the acts of the *opéra-ballet*. The term was also used for the march-like music heard at the beginning of a *divertissement* of dances and songs.

Falsetto (It.) The treble range produced by most adult male singers through a slightly artificial technique whereby the vocal cords vibrate in a length shorter than usual. It is rarely used in opera. *See* **Countertenor**.

Farsa (It.) A type of opera, generally in one act, popular in Venice in the late 18th and early 19th centuries.

Favola in musica (It.) 'Tale in music': a phrase found on the title-pages of 17th-century scores and librettos.

Festa teatrale (It.) A serenata-type genre of the high Baroque period, cultivated especially in Vienna; typically the subject matter was allegorical and the production part of a celebration of a court event.

Finale (It.) The concluding, continuously composed, section of an act of an opera. The ensemble finale developed, at the beginning of the second half of the 18th century, largely through the changes wrought in comic opera by Carlo Goldoni (1707–93), who in his librettos made act finales longer, bringing in more singers and increasing the density of the plot.

Fioritura [canto fiorito] (It.) 'Flourish': the embellishment of a melodic line, either improvised by a performer or written out by the composer.

French overture A festive musical introduction to an opera, with a slow opening (marked by stately dotted rhythms) and a lively fugal section; one or more dances may follow. It originated with Lully's ballet overtures of the 1650s and quickly became the standard pattern in France; it was copied elsewhere, notably by Handel.

Gesamtkunstwerk (Ger.) 'Total art work': term used by Wagner for his music dramas, in which all the arts (music, poetry, movement, design etc) should combine to the same artistic end. The concept was not original to Wagner, but the term was.

Grand opéra A term used to signify both the Paris Opéra and the operas performed there. Later it tended to be applied more narrowly to the specially monumental works performed at the Opéra during its period of greatest magnificence, including Rossini's *Guillaume Tell*

and several operas composed to librettos of Eugène Scribe by Meyerbeer and others during the 1830s (including *Les Huguenots*). The term also applies to operas by Donizetti, Gounod, Verdi and Massenet.

Ground bass A device used by Purcell, Lully and other composers of the late 17th century in which a piece of music is constructed above a repeating bass part.

Handlung für Musik (Ger.) 'Action in music': term used by Wagner in the libretto for *Lohengrin*.

Haute-contre (Fr.) A high tenor or countertenor voice, cultivated in France until about the end of the 18th century. The *haute-contre* was the voice to which most of the important heroic and amorous male roles in the operas of Lully and Rameau were entrusted.

Heldentenor (Ger.) 'Heroic tenor': a robust tenor voice of clarion timbre and unusual endurance, particularly suited to Wagner's heroic roles (Tannhäuser, Tristan, Siegmund, Siegfried); it was an extreme manifestation of the new dramatic tenor that appeared in the 1830s and 1840s. The term has become standard in the Wagner literature though not used by the composer himself.

Interlude Music played or sung between the main parts of a work.

Intermezzo, intermezzi (It.) Comic interludes sung between the acts or scenes of an *opera seria* in the 18th century.

Italian overture A type of overture favoured in Italian operas from the 1680s and used into the second half of the 18th century. It is in three movements, fast–slow–fast (the last usually in dance rhythm), normally played without a break. It is usually thought to have originated with A. Scarlatti.

Key The quality of a musical passage or composition that causes it to be sensed as gravitating towards a particular note, called the keynote or the tonic.

Lehrstück (Ger.) 'Teaching piece': a term, associated with the work of Bertolt Brecht, for a theatrical genre for amateurs whose function was to teach the participants rather than to engage an audience. Brecht's *Lehrstücke* attempt to teach political attitudes; music plays an important part in those by Weill, Hindemith and Eisler.

Leitmotif (Ger. Leitmotiv) 'Leading motif': a theme, or other musical idea, that represents or symbolizes a person, object, place, idea, state of mind, supernatural force or some other ingredient in a dramatic work. It may recur unaltered, or it may be changed in rhythm, intervallic structure, tempo, harmony, orchestration or accompaniment, to signify dramatic development, and may be combined with other leitmotifs. The concept is particularly associated with Wagner, who used it as a basis for his musical structures, but the idea is older.

Libretto (It.) 'Small book': a printed book containing the words of an opera; by extension, the text itself. In the 17th and 18th centuries, when opera houses were lit, librettos were often read during performances; when an opera was given in a language other than that of the audience, librettos were bilingual, with parallel texts on opposite pages.

Lieto fine (It.) 'Happy ending': term for the normal, almost obligatory happy ending found in virtually all serious operas of the late Baroque and the Classical periods. Often it involved the appearance of a *deus ex machina* (the intervention of a benevolent deity) to resolve a dilemma happily.

Maestro di cappella (It.) 'Chapel master': term used for the head of a musical establishment, secular as well as sacred.

Masque An English genre of the 16th and 17th centuries, based on allegorical or mythological themes and involving poetry, music and elaborate sets. The theatre masque reached its highest development in the dramas and semi-operas of the Restoration (1660–c1700), especially in the works of Dryden and Purcell.

Melisma A passage of florid writing in which several notes are sung to the same syllable.

Melodrama A kind of drama, or a technique used within a drama, in which the action is carried forward by the protagonist speaking in the pauses of, or during, orchestral passages, similar in style to those in operatic accompanied recitative. Its invention is usually dated to J.-J. Rousseau's *Pygmalion* (c1762). Georg Benda was its chief exponent in Germany; Mozart, influenced by him, wrote melodrama sections in his *Zaide*. Beethoven used melodrama in the dungeon scene of *Fidelio*; Weber used it, notably in *Der Freischütz*. Most 19th-century composers of opera have used it as a dramatic device, for example Verdi, for letter scenes in *Macbeth* and *La traviata*, and Smetana in *The Two Widows*. It has been much used by 20th-century composers, among them Puccini, Strauss, Berg, Britten and Henze.

Melodramma (It.) Term for a dramatic text written to be set to music (*see* **Dramma per musica**), or the resultant opera. It does not mean **Melodrama**. Verdi's second opera, *Un giorno di regno*, with a libretto by Felice Romani, was termed a *melodramma giocoso*; the term reappeared on *I masnadieri* and *Macbeth*, as well as *Rigoletto*, *Un ballo in maschera* and the revised *Simon Boccanegra*, but it is hard to attach any special significance to it as terms were used interchangeably.

Mezzo-contralto Term for a particular type of female voice; it was used of Rosine Stoltz (1815–1903), usually categorized as a mezzo-soprano or even soprano, and implied a specially strong lower register.

Mezzo-soprano Term for a voice, usually female, normally written for within the range a-f♯″. The distinction between the florid soprano and the weightier mezzo-soprano became common only towards the mid-18th century. The castrato Senesino, for whom Handel composed, was described as having a 'penetrating, clear, even, and pleasant deep soprano voice (mezzo Soprano)'. The distinction was more keenly sensed in the 19th century, although the mezzo-soprano range was often extended as high as b♭″. Mezzo-sopranos with an extended upper range tackled the lower of two soprano roles in such operas as Bellini's *Norma* (Adalgisa) and Donizetti's *Anna Bolena* (Jane Seymour). Both sopranos and mezzo-sopranos sing many of Wagner's roles.

The mezzo-soprano was often assigned a **Breeches part** in the era immediately after the demise of the **Castrato**, such as Arsace's in *Semiramide*; at all periods they have taken adolescent roles such as Cherubino (*Le nozze di Figaro*) or Oktavian (*Der Rosenkavalier*). The traditional casting however is as nurse or confidante (e.g. Brangäne in *Tristan und Isolde*, Suzuki in *Madama Butterfly*) or as the mature married woman (e.g. Herodias in Strauss's *Salome*). Saint-Saëns's Delilah is an exception to the general rule that the principal female role (particularly the beautiful maiden) is a soprano.

Modulation The movement out of one key into another as a continuous musical process. It is particularly used in opera as a device to suggest a change of mood.

Monodrama A Melodrama for one character. Schoenberg used the term for *Erwartung* (an opera with only one character), although the notated vocal line and continuous score hardly accord with the original juxtaposition of speaking voice and orchestral commentary.

Motif A short musical idea, melodic, rhythmic, or harmonic (or any combination of those); *see* **Leitmotif**.

Musical comedy, Musical Term for the chief form of popular musical theatre in the English-speaking world. It developed from comic opera and burlesque in London in the late 19th century and reached its most durable form in the 1920s and 30s, particularly in the USA.

Music drama, Musical drama The term 'Musical Drama' was used by Handel for *Hercules* (1745), to distinguish it from opera and Sacred Drama. In more recent usage, the meanings attached to 'music drama' derive from the ideas formulated in Wagner's *Oper und Drama*; it is applied to his operas and to others in which the musical, verbal and scenic elements cohere to serve one dramatic end. In 1869, Verdi distinguished between opera of the old sort and the *dramma musicale* that he believed his *La forza del destino* to be. Current theatrical practice tends to qualify this unity by performing music dramas with the original music and words but freshly invented scenic elements.

Musico (It.) 'Musician': term applied in opera, from the 17th century to the early 19th (usually in the form 'primo musico'), to the leading male singer. Normally it signified, like 'primo uomo', the principal castrato; later it could mean the tenor or, in the early 19th century, a female singer in a Breeches part, singing a heroic role at mezzo pitch of the type traditionally assigned to castratos.

Music theatre A catch-phrase, common in the 1960s among composers, producers and critics who had artistic or social objections to traditional grand opera, to designate musical works for small or moderate forces that involve a dramatic element in their presentation. Such works have included small-scale operas, song cycles that are 'staged' and pieces such as Ligeti's *Aventures* and *Nouvelles aventures* that resist precise definition.

Number opera Term for an opera consisting of individual sections or 'numbers' which can be detached from the whole, as distinct from an opera consisting of continuous music. It applies to the various forms of 18th-century opera and to some 19th-century grand operas. Under Wagner's influence the number opera became unfashionable, and neither his operas nor those of late Verdi, Puccini and the *verismo* school can be so called. Some notable 20th-century works can be considered number operas, such as Berg's *Wozzeck* and Stravinsky's deliberately archaic *The Rake's Progress*.

Opéra-ballet (Fr.) A French genre of lyric theatre, cultivated between the death of Lully in 1687 and the mid-18th century. *Opéra-ballets* usually consist of a prologue and three or four acts or *entrées*, each with its own set of characters and independent action but loosely related to a collective idea. Among its exponents are Campra and Rameau, whose *Les Indes galantes* is the outstanding example.

Opéra bouffe (Fr.) A form of satirical operetta derived from the *opéra comique*; the earliest example is Offenbach's *Orphée aux enfers* (1858), written for the Théâtres des Bouffes Parisiens.

Opera buffa (It.) 'Comic opera': a term commonly used to signify Italian comic opera, principally of the 18th century, with recitative rather than spoken dialogue. Though now applied generically, it was one of several such terms used in the 18th century.

Opéra comique (Fr.) Term for French stage works with spoken dialogue interspersed with songs and other musical numbers; it does not necessarily signify a comic opera. The genre was specially associated with the Paris theatre company known as the Opéra-Comique. Some works to which it is now applied were at the time called 'comédie mêlée d'ariettes'. Early masters of the genre include Grétry and Philidor; the supreme *opéra comique* is by general consent Bizet's *Carmen*.

Opera semiseria (It.) 'Half-serious opera': a type of Italian opera falling into neither of the classical genres of tragedy or comedy. Derived from the 18th-century French *comédie larmoyante*, it used serious subject matter, treated with strong melodramatic and sentimental colouring, with subsidiary comic elements, usually in a contemporary middle-class setting. The type began to appear in the 1780s but the designation became widespread only in the second decade of the 19th century; before that, terms such as 'dramma eroicomico', 'dramma tragicomico' and 'dramma di sentimento' were used.

Opera seria (It.) 'Serious opera': term applied to serious Italian operas, on a heroic or tragic subject, of the 18th century and the early 19th ('dramma per musica' is the more usual contemporary description). Defined primarily by music historians out of sympathy with its musical and dramatic principles, 'opera seria' is often used in a derogatory sense. The classical *opera seria* is in three acts, has six or seven characters, consists primarily of arias in Da capo (or shortened da capo) form in which characters express their emotional state, and recitatives, in which the action takes place, with occasional orchestral recitatives at dramatic highpoints and sometimes duets; the topic traditionally involves a moral dilemma, typically a variant of 'love *v*. duty', and is resolved happily, with due reward for rectitude, loyalty, unselfishness etc. The most famous librettist was Pietro Metastasio, whose texts were set many times over.

Operetta (It.) Diminutive of 'opera': a light opera with spoken dialogue, songs and dances. The form flourished during the late 19th century and the early 20th. Earlier it was applied more generally to shorter, less ambitious works. It is still used on the Continent for new works akin to the Musical comedy, into which the operetta evolved in English-speaking countries.

Ostinato (It.) Term used to refer to the repetition of a musical pattern many times over; the Ground bass is a form of *ostinato* used in early opera.

Overture A piece of orchestral music designed to precede a dramatic work (see French overture and Italian overture). By the mid-18th century the Italian type prevailed and the first movement had become longer and more elaborate; there was a tendency to drop the second and third movements. In serious opera there was sometimes an effort to set the mood of the coming drama, as in Gluck's *Alceste* and Mozart's *Idomeneo*; the famous preface to *Alceste* (see p. 18) emphasizes the importance of this. In Mozart's *Don Giovanni, Così fan tutte* and *Die Zauberflöte* the overture quotes musical ideas from the opera. Between 1790 and 1820, there was usually a slow introduction. The notion of tying the overture to the opera in mood and theme was developed in France and also appealed to the German Romantics. Beethoven made powerful use of dramatic motifs in his *Leonore* overtures, while in Weber's *Der Freischütz* and *Euryanthe* overtures almost every theme reappears in the drama. Composers of French grand opera tended to expand the overture. For Bellini, Donizetti and Verdi the short prelude was an alternative, and it became normal in Italian opera after the mid-century. Wagner, in the *Ring*, preferred a 'prelude' fully integrated into the drama, as did Richard Strauss and Puccini, whose prelude to *Tosca* consists simply of three chords (associated with a particular character). In comic operas and operettas the independent overture lasted longer; the structure based on themes from the drama became a medley of tunes. The 'medley' or 'potpourri' overture used by Auber, Gounod, Thomas, Offenbach, Johann Strauss and Sullivan can still be traced in musical-comedy overtures.

Pantomime A dramatic representation in dumb show; the term was also used for a form of mixed-media theatrical entertainment, primarily English, in the 18th century, related to the *commedia dell'arte* and to French ballet traditions. There was also a pantomime tradition in 18th-century Vienna. A French tradition lived on in the famous mute title-role of Auber's *La muette de Portici*; and the ballet sequence in Wagner's *Rienzi* is often referred to as a pantomime because of the relevance of the dancers. The Olympia act of Offenbach's *Les contes d'Hoffmann* also has pantomimic elements. There is a notable pantomimic scene for Beckmesser at the beginning of Act 3 of *Die Meistersinger von Nürnberg*.

Parlando, Parlante (It.) 'Speaking': a direction requiring a singer to use a manner approximating to speech.

Passacaglia Originally, in the 17th century, the term for a song *Ritornello*, and later a dance, with a fixed bass pattern. In opera the term is unusual, but there are notable examples in Act 1 of Berg's *Wozzeck* and Act 2 of Britten's *Peter Grimes*, both on repeated bass figures.

Pasticcio (It.) Term for a work made up, at least in part, from existing works by a variety of composers; the practice, which began in the late 17th century and persisted for most of the 18th, arose from the need for commercial success, which was better assured if singers could be given their tried favourites. A pasticcio was normally put together by a 'house' composer and librettist. Virtually all composers accepted the practice and partook of it, including Handel, Gluck, Haydn and Mozart.

Pastorale A literary, dramatic or musical genre that depicts the characters and scenes of rural life or is expressive of its atmosphere. The pastoral tradition was important in early opera, such as Monteverdi's *Orfeo*, and Handel's *Acis and Galatea*; later it was parodied, as in Offenbach's *Orphée aux enfers* and Sullivan's *Iolanthe* (1882).

Patter song A comic song in which the humour derives from having the greatest number of words uttered in the shortest possible time. The technique came into common use in the late 18th century, when composers introduced the idea into *buffo* solos (e.g. Bartolo's aria 'La vendetta' in Mozart's *Le nozze di Figaro*). There are examples in the works of Haydn, Rossini (notably the 'confusion' ensemble in the Act 1 finale of *Il barbiere di Siviglia*), Donizetti (whose patter duet 'Chieti, chieti' in *Don Pasquale* is a classic example) and Sullivan – whose patter song in *Ruddigore* includes the lines: 'this particularly rapid, unintelligible patter isn't generally heard and if it is it doesn't matter'.

Pertichini (It.) The interventions by other characters during a musical number, who by their actions or the news that they bring affect the progress of the drama and give rise to a musical contrast – for example at the end of the slow section (the cantabile) of a two-part aria, so provoking the fast part (cabaletta).

Pezzo concertato (It.) 'Piece in concerted style': a section within a finale in Italian 19th-century opera in which several characters express divergent emotions simultaneously, as it were a 'multiple soliloquy'. It is usually in slow tempo and is sometimes called 'largo concertato'.

Preghiera (It.: 'prayer') a number common in 19th-century opera in which a character prays for divine assistance in his or her plight. Moses's 'Dal tuo stellato soglio' in Rossini's *Mosè in Egitto* (1818) is perhaps the best-known *preghiera* actually so titled; Desdemona's 'Ave Maria' in Verdi's *Otello* is a late example of the traditional gentle *preghiera*.

Prelude *See* Overture.

Prima donna (It.) 'First lady': the principal female singer in an opera or on the roster of an opera company, almost always a soprano. The expression came into use around the mid-17th century, with the opening of public opera houses in Venice, where the ability of a leading lady to attract audiences became important. Singers who became prima donnas insisted on keeping that title; when conflicts arose, managerial ingenuity devised such expressions as 'altra prima donna', 'prima donna assoluta' and even 'prima donna assoluta e sola'.

Some prima donnas made it a point of status to be difficult. Adelina Patti (1843–1919), at the height of her career, stipulated that her name appear on posters in letters at least one-third larger than those used for other singers' names and that she be excused from rehearsals. The need to meet a prima donna's demands shaped many librettos and scores, particularly because her status was reflected in the number and character of the arias allotted to her.

Primo uomo (It.) 'First man': the principal male singer in an opera or on the roster of an opera company. Just as a leading lady had been given the title 'prima donna', so a famous **Castrato** would claim the title 'primo uomo'. His importance is evident in the roles he sang, which were generally on a par with those for the prima donna. In Handel's *Giulio Cesare* Cleopatra and Julius Caesar each have eight arias. At first 'primo uomo' referred to a castrato, but during the 18th century it came also to be applied to tenors.

Prologue The introductory scene to a dramatic work, in which the author explains, either directly or indirectly, the context and meaning of the work to follow. In early opera, an allegorical prologue may pay homage to the author's patron. Prologues were a usual feature in early Baroque opera; in the late 18th century and the early 19th they were rare. Wagner's *Das Rheingold* may be seen as a prologue to the *Ring* since it presents the background to the plot. There are significant prologues to Gounod's *Roméo et Juliette*, Boito's *Mefistofele* and Leoncavallo's *Pagliacci* (the last modelled on those of ancient drama and with an exposition of the theory of *verismo*). In the 20th century various kinds of literary prologue have preceded operas, as in Stravinsky's *Oedipus rex*, Prokofiev's *Love for Three Oranges* and Berg's *Lulu*.

Quartet An ensemble for four singers. Quartets appear as early as the 17th century; Cavalli's *Calisto* ends with one and A. Scarlatti wrote several. There are quartets in Handel's *Radamisto* and *Partenope*. They appear in many *opéras comiques*. In *opera buffa* of the Classical era, when ensembles are sometimes used to further the dramatic action, quartets sometimes occupy that role: examples are the Act 2 finale of Mozart's *Die Entführung aus dem Serail*, where the sequence of sections shows the consolidation of the relationships between the two pairs of lovers, and in Act 1 of his *Don Giovanni*, where 'Non ti fidar' draws together the dramatic threads. The quartet in the last act of *Idomeneo* is however more a series of statements by the characters of their emotional positions, as is the quartet for the 'wedding' toast in the finale of *Così fan tutte*. Another canonic quartet is 'Mir ist so wunderbar' from Beethoven's *Fidelio*. Verdi wrote a quartet in *Otello*, but his best-known example is the one from *Rigoletto*, an inspired piece of simultaneous portrayal of feeling.

Quintet An ensemble for five singers. Quintets, except within ensemble finales, are rare in the operatic repertory. Notable examples are the two in Mozart's *Così fan tutte*. The only substantial ensemble in the sense of a number where the characters sing simultaneously in Wagner's late operas is the famous quintet in *Die Meistersinger von Nürnberg*, a rare moment in his operas where the dramatic action is suspended and the characters take emotional stock.

Rappresentazione sacra (It.) A religious play with music, in Italian, cultivated chiefly in Florence and often elaborately produced. The *rappresentazione sacra* is a significant forerunner of opera; Emilio de Cavalieri apparently intended his opera *Rappresentatione di Anima,* *et di Corpo* (1600) as a renewal of the genre, by then outmoded.

Rataplan Term used onomatopoeically for a type of chorus based on the martial life, with flourishes of drums, fanfare-like figures, etc.

Recitative A type of vocal writing which follows closely the natural rhythm and accentuation of speech, not necessarily governed by a regular tempo or organized in a specific form. It derived from the development in the late 16th century of a declamatory narrative style with harmonic support, a wide melodic range and emotionally charged treatment of the words. During the 17th century, recitative came to be the vehicle for dialogue, providing a connecting link between arias; the trailing off before the cadence (representing the singers being overcome with emotion), leaving the accompaniment to provide the closure, became a convention, as did the addition of an **Appoggiatura** at any cadence point to follow the natural inflection of Italian words.

By the late 17th century a more rapid, even delivery had developed, a trend carried further in *opera buffa* of the 18th century. Recitative was sung in a free, conversational manner. Plain or simple recitative, accompanied only by **Continuo**, is known as *recitativo semplice* or *recitativo secco* (or simply *secco*), to distinguish it from accompanied or orchestral recitative (*recitativo accompagnato*, *stromentato* or *obbligato*), which in the 18th century grew increasingly important for dramatic junctures. In France, the language demanded a different style, slower-moving, more lyrical and more flexible.

Recitative with keyboard accompaniment fell out of use early in the 19th century. Recitative-like declamation, however, remained an essential means of expression. Even late in the 19th century, when operas written with spoken dialogue were given in large houses where speech was not acceptable (like the Paris Opéra), recitatives were supplied by house composers or hacks (or the composer himself, for example Gounod with *Faust*) to replace the dialogue: the most famous example is Guiraud's long-used set of recitatives for Bizet's *Carmen*. With the more continuous textures favoured in the 20th century, the concept of recitative disappeared (as it did in Wagner's mature works), to be replaced by other kinds of representation of speech. **Sprechgesang** may be seen as an Expressionist equivalent of recitative.

Reform Term applied to Gluck's operas, from *Orfeo ed Euridice* onwards, in which, influenced by the librettist Raniero de Calzabigi, the choreographer Angiolini and French musico-dramatic traditions, he applied new principles to Italian (and later to French) opera, to rid it of what he saw as abuses; these principles are stated in the preface to his *Alceste* (see p. 18). Several other composers had already worked along similar lines.

Rescue opera Term used for a type of opera, popular in France after the 1789 Revolution, in which the hero or heroine is delivered at the last moment either from the cruelty of a tyrant or from some natural catastrophe, not by a *deus ex machina* but by heroic human endeavour. It reflected the secular idealism of the age and often carried a social message. Some rescue operas were based on contemporary real-life incidents, among them Gaveaux's *Léonore, ou l'amour conjugal* (1798) and Cherubini's *Les deux journées* (1800), both to librettos by J. N. Bouilly. The former was the source of Beethoven's *Fidelio*.

Ritornello (It.) A short recurring instrumental passage, particularly the tutti section of a Baroque aria.

Romance Term used in 18th- and 19th-century opera for a ballad-like type of strophic song. It suited the sentimentalism of *opéra comique*, and in Germany was used in the Singspiel, notably by Mozart (Pedrillo's 'Im Mohrenland' in *Die Entführung aus dem Serail*) and later Weber ('Nero, dem Kettenbund' in *Der Freischütz*); Italian examples include several by Verdi, notably Manrico's 'Deserto sulla terra' (*Il trovatore*) and Radamès's 'Celeste Aida' (*Aida*).

Rondò Term for a type of Aria popular in the late 18th century, consisting of two sections, one slow and one fast (sometimes repeated). The form originated in the 1760s; the best-known examples are by Mozart, including 'Non mi dir' (*Don Giovanni*) and 'Per pietà' (*Così fan tutte*). The rondò is a precursor of the cantabile–cabaletta scheme of the early 19th century. (The spelling 'rondò' was common, but 'rondo' and 'rondeau' are also found.)

Sainete (Sp.) A one-act dramatic vignette, comic and popular in character, which from the mid-18th century was often played at the end of Spanish theatrical entertainments. Later it developed into a variety of Zarzuela.

Scena (It.), **Scène** (Fr.) Term used to mean (1) the stage (e.g. 'sulla scena', on the stage; 'derrière la scène', behind the stage), (2) the scene represented on the stage, (3) a division of an act (*see* Scene). In Italian opera it also means an episode with no formal construction but made up of diverse elements. The 'Scena e duetto' is a typical unit in opera of the Rossinian period. A *scena* of a particularly dramatic character, often (though not invariably) for a single character, may be described as a 'gran scena', e.g. 'Gran scena del sonnambulismo' in Verdi's *Macbeth*.

Scene (1) The location of an opera, or an act or part of an act of an opera; by extension, any part of an opera in one location. (2) In earlier usage, a scene was a section of an act culminating in an aria (or occasionally an ensemble); any substantial (in some operas, any at all) change in the characters on the stage was reckoned a change of scene, and the scenes were numbered accordingly.

Schuloper (Ger.) 'School opera': a German opera written in the 20th century for didactic use in schools.

The pedagogic content concentrated on the teaching of music, drama and community spirit. Important examples are Weill's *Der Jasager* (1930) and Hindemith's *Wir bauen eine Stadt* (1930). A distant predecessor is the religious (usually Jesuit) *Schuldrama* ('school drama') practised especially in central Europe in the 16th, 17th and 18th centuries.

Secco (It.) 'Dry': short for *recitativo secco*. A 19th-century term for Recitative with continuo accompaniment.

Seconda donna (It.) 'Second lady': term for the secondary female singer in 18th- and 19th-century opera. The role, usually for soprano or mezzo-soprano, would normally be assigned fewer arias than the prima donna's.

Secondo uomo (It.) 'Second man': term for the secondary male singer in 18th- and 19th-century opera. The role, usually for castrato but sometimes tenor, would normally be assigned fewer arias than the primo uomo's.

Semi-opera A type of English Restoration drama, spectacularly staged and with extensive musical scenes of a masque-like character. The outstanding examples are those by Purcell: *Dioclesian* (1690), *King Arthur* (1691), *The Fairy Queen* (1692) and *The Indian Queen* (1695). There are later examples set mainly by Daniel Purcell and Jeremiah Clarke.

Septet An ensemble for seven singers. Septets are rare in the operatic repertory; a famous example is 'Par une telle nuit', from Berlioz's *Les troyens*, based on a text from Shakespeare's 'On such a night as this' (*The Merchant of Venice*).

Serenata (It.) A dramatic cantata, akin to a short opera, usually on a pastoral, allegorical or mythological topic and given in honour of a person or an occasion. From *sereno* (It.), 'a clear night sky', referring to the usual performance circumstances, the term was used in the 17th and 18th centuries for works performed in courtly or aristocratic surroundings, lavishly set and in a quasi-dramatic manner. The serenata was popular in Venice and Rome, and outside Italy in Vienna.

Set piece An aria or other number clearly demarcated from its context.

Sextet An ensemble for six singers. Sextets are rare in the operatic repertory, except within act finales, but there are two notable Mozart examples: the recognition scene in Act 3 of *Le nozze di Figaro* and the central scene of Act 2 of *Don Giovanni*. The most celebrated operatic sextet is that at the climax of Donizetti's *Lucia di Lammermoor*.

Siciliana (It.) An aria type of the late 17th and early 18th centuries, normally in a slow 12/8 or 6/8 rhythm; it was associated particularly with pastoral scenes and melancholy emotion.

Simile aria A type of aria popular in the 17th and 18th centuries in which the text draws a simile between the singer's situation and some natural phenomenon or activity; such arias offered the composer an opportunity to introduce colourful imagery, for example invoking birds, streams or tempests. Handel, in 'Va tacito e nascosto' (*Giulio Cesare*), introduces hunting music and the sound of the horn, justified by words that parallel Ptolemy's underhand behaviour with the hunter stalking his prey. In *The Beggar's Opera* the Beggar claims to have 'introduc'd the similes that are in all your celebrated *Operas*'; the text includes such parodies as 'I'm like a skiff on the Ocean tost'. The convention continued to be criticized in the 18th century and had nearly died out by the end of it.

Singspiel (Ger.) Literally, a play with songs; the term was used in 18th-century Germany for almost any kind of dramatic entertainment with music. In operatic usage, Singspiel means a German comic opera of the 18th or early 19th centuries, with spoken dialogue. The genre was particularly popular during the late 18th century in Vienna and in Northern Germany (especially Leipzig). In its early days it was influenced by the English Ballad opera. The most significant examples are Mozart's *Die Entführung aus dem Serail* and *Die Zauberflöte*.

Soprano (It.) The highest female voice, normally written for within the range *c'-a"*; the word is also applied to a boy's treble voice and in the 17th and 18th centuries to a Castrato of high range. The soprano voice was used for expressive roles in the earliest operas. During the Baroque period it was found to be suited to brilliant vocal display, and when a singer achieved fame it was usually because of an ability to perform elaborate music with precision as well as beauty. The heroine's role was sung by the most skilful soprano, the Prima donna; to her were assigned the greatest number of arias and the most difficult and expressively wide-ranging music. The highest note usually required was *a* and little merit was placed on the capacity to sing higher.

The development of different categories of the soprano voice belongs to the 19th century, strongly foreshadowed in the variety of roles and styles found in Mozart's operas (although type-casting was not at all rigid: the singer of Susanna in 1789 created Fiordiligi the next year). It was a consequence of the divergence of national operatic traditions and the rise of a consolidated repertory. Italian sopranos of the age of Rossini and Bellini developed a coloratura style and the ability to sustain a long lyrical line (the coloratura soprano and the lyric soprano); later, in Verdi's time, with larger opera houses and orchestras, the more dramatic *spinto* and *lirico spinto* appeared. In Germany the dramatic or heroic soprano was already foreshadowed in Beethoven's Leonore and Weber's Agathe; Wagner's Brünnhilde, demanding great power and brilliance, was the climax of this development. French *grand opéra* developed its own style of lyric-dramatic soprano. The operetta repertory too produced a light, agile voice of its own.

Soubrette (Fr.) 'Servant girl': a stock character of 18th-century French opera and by extension the kind of voice appropriate to a shrewd and spirited young woman. Examples include Serpina in Pergolesi's *La serva padrona*, Susanna in *Le nozze di Figaro*, Despina in *Così fan tutte* and Adele in *Die Fledermaus*. The type of voice called for is light and sharp in focus, with clear diction.

Spieloper (Ger.) A German 19th-century comic opera with spoken dialogue betwen set musical numbers. Examples include Lortzing's *Der Wildschütz* (1824) and *Zar und Zimmermann*, Flotow's *Martha*, Nicolai's *Die lustigen Weiber von Windsor* and Cornelius's *Der Barbier von Baghdad*; similar in type are Berlioz's *Béatrice et Bénédict* and Smetana's *The Bartered Bride*. The term has also been used for an all-sung opera as opposed to one (a *Sprechoper*) with spoken dialogue.

Spinto (It.) 'Pushed': term for a lyric voice, usually soprano or tenor, that is able to sound powerful and incisive at dramatic climaxes. The full expression is 'lirico spinto'. The term is also used to describe roles that require voices of this character, for example Mimì in Puccini's *La bohème* and Alfredo in Verdi's *La traviata*.

Sprechgesang (Ger.) 'Speech-song': a type of vocal enunciation intermediate between speech and song. Notated Sprechgesang was introduced by Humperdinck in *Königskinder* (1897), though he later replaced it by conventional singing. It was exploited by Schoenberg in *Die glückliche Hand* (1910–13) and *Moses und Aron*. Schoenberg wrote that it should 'give [the pitch] exactly, but then immediately leave it in a fall or rise'; Sprechgesang should neither resemble natural speech nor recall true singing. Berg used Sprechgesang in *Wozzeck* and *Lulu*, and introduced a new shade, 'half sung', between Sprechgesang and song.

Stretta, Stretto (It.) Term used to indicate a faster tempo at the climactic concluding section of a piece. It is common in Italian opera: examples include the end of the Act 2 finale of Mozart's *Le nozze di Figaro* and Violetta's aria at the end of Act 1 of Verdi's *La traviata*.

Strophic Term for a song or aria in which all stanzas of the text are set to the same music. The term 'strophic variations' is used of songs where the melody is varied from verse to verse while the bass remains unchanged or virtually so. That form was popular in early 17th-century Italy; 'Possente spirto', sung by Monteverdi's Orpheus, is an example, and Cavalli occasionally used the form.

Tempo d'attacco (It.) Term used in Italian opera of the 19th century for the fast movement of a duet (or an aria) following the recitative.

Tempo di mezzo (It.) 'Middle movement': term used in Italian 19th-century opera for a fast transitional passage separating the two principal sections of an aria (such as the Cantabile and the Cabaletta).

Tenor The highest natural male voice, normally written for within the range *c-a'*. Although the tenor voice was valued in early opera — a tenor, Francesco Rasi (1574–after 1620), sang Monteverdi's Orpheus (1607) — heroic roles in middle and late Baroque opera were assigned to the castrato. Tenors took minor roles, such as the old man (sometimes with comic overtones), the lighthearted confidant, the mischievous schemer or the messenger, or even a travesty role of the old nurse. By the 1720s, important roles were occasionally given to tenors, and by the Classical era the voice was more regularly used in central roles. Such roles as Mozart's Basilio, Ottavio, Ferrando and Titus — comic, docile lover, more virile lover, benevolent monarch — define the scope of the voice at this period.

A creation of the early 19th century was the *tenore di grazia*, a light, high voice moving smoothly into falsetto up to *d''*, called for by many Rossini roles. With the increasing size of opera houses, and the changes in musical style, the *tenore di forza* was called for. The tendency continued as, with Verdi's operas, the *tenore robusto* developed. For the German heroic tenor roles of the 19th century, especially Wagner's, a more weighty and durable type was needed, the **Heldentenor**. The lighter tenor continued to be cultivated for the more lyrical French roles. Many of the great tenors of the 20th century have been Italians, and made their names in Italian music, from Enrico Caruso (1873–1921) to Luciano Pavarotti; to these the Spaniard Plácido Domingo should be added.

Tenor-altino [tenor-contraltino] (It.) A high, light tenor voice, called for by Rimsky-Korsakov for the Astrologer in *The Golden Cockerel*.

Terzet, Trio An ensemble for three singers. Terzets or trios have been used throughout the history of opera. There is an example in Monteverdi's *L'incoronazione di Poppea*; Handel used the form several times, notably in *Tamerlano*, *Orlando* and *Alcina*, and Gluck wrote examples in the closing scenes of his Italian reform operas. Mozart's include three (one in *Don Giovanni*, two in *La clemenza di Tito*) which are akin to arias with comments from two subsidiary characters. There are two in Weber's *Der Freischütz* and several for very high tenors in Rossini's serious operas. The form was much used by the Romantics, among them Verdi, who wrote three examples in *Un ballo in maschera*.

Tessitura (It.) 'Texture': the part of a vocal compass in which a piece of music lies — whether high or low, etc; it is not measured by the extremes of range but by which part of the range is most used.

Théâtres de la Foire (Fr.) 'Fair theatres': term for the theatres at the two Paris fairs, the Foire St Germain and the Foire St Laurent. They represent an important stage in the early history of the **Opéra comique** genre.

Through-composed Term for an aria in which the music for each stanza is different.

Tonadilla (Sp.) In the 18th century, a short stage piece. Usually satirical or political, it was either for a single character or for up to about five. It flourished particularly from about 1770 to 1810. By the middle of the 19th century it had given way to the **Zarzuela**.

Tonal Term used for music in a particular key, or a pitch centre to which the music naturally gravitates. The use of tonalities, or the interplay of keys, can be an important dramatic weapon in the opera composer's armoury.

Tragédie en musique, tragédie lyrique (Fr.) Names for serious, though not necessarily tragic, French opera of the 17th and 18th centuries. The genre was inaugurated by Lully and Quinault (*Cadmus*, 1673); their works, on subjects from mythology or medieval chivalry, each had a prologue and five acts. It was pursued particularly by Rameau (his first was *Hippolyte et Aricie*); its last great exponent was Gluck, whose French reform operas, like his rival Piccinni's, belong in the same tradition.

Travesti (Fr.). *See* **Breeches part** 'Travesty' is sometimes used of a role in which a singer wears the clothes of the opposite sex.

Trio *See* **Terzet**.

Twelve-note The system of musical structure expounded in the 1920s according to which a note-row or series, consisting of the 12 notes of the scale arranged in a fixed order, serves as the basis of all aspects of the composition. Among the operas using this principle are Schoenberg's *Moses und Aron* and Berg's *Lulu*.

Vaudeville (Fr.) A French poem or song of satirical or epigrammatic character common in the 17th and 18th centuries; vaudevilles made up much of the repertory at the annual Paris fairs of St Germain and St Laurent. As the *opéra comique* developed from these ventures, more original music was added. The French *comédie en vaudeville* had an international influence.

Vaudeville final (Fr.) Placed at the end of an act or play, the *vaudeville final* reassembled on stage all the important characters and required each to sing one or more verses of a vaudeville, usually with a choral refrain. This style was common to French opera and *opéra comique*. The influence of the *vaudeville final* may be seen in other genres, and continued into later periods, as in Gluck's *Orfeo*, Mozart's *Die Entführung aus dem Serail*, Rossini's *Il barbiere di Siviglia*, Verdi's *Falstaff*, Ravel's *L'heure espagnole* and Stravinsky's *The Rake's Progress*.

Verismo (It.) 'Realism': name for the Italian version of the late 19th-century movement towards naturalism in European literature, of which Emile Zola in France was the dominant figure. In Italy the novelist Giovanni Verga occupied a similar position; his *Cavalleria rusticana* was the basis for Mascagni's opera (1889), whose tremendous success spawned a series of similar one-act *verismo* operas in Italy and elsewhere of which only Leoncavallo's *Pagliacci* (1891) remains in the repertory. These followed the general naturalistic tendencies towards introducing characters from the lower social strata, strong local colour and situations centring on the violent clash of fierce, even brutal passions, particularly hatred, lust, betrayal and murder. The term is sometimes more broadly used for Italian operas generally of the same period.

Vocalise (Fr.) The type of singing in which several notes are sung to the same vowel; originally designed as a vocal exercise, vocalise has occasionally been used as an expressive device in opera.

Vorspiel (Ger.) 'Prelude': the term appears frequently in German operatic scores from Wagner's *Lohengrin* onwards. *See* **Overture**. The Prologue to Act 1 of *Götterdämmerung*, marked 'Vorspiel', embraces two extended scenes, and may have been influenced by the opening of Marschner's *Hans Heiling*, where a Vorspiel, consisting of choruses flanking a solo for Heiling, precedes the overture.

Zarzuela (Sp.) A Spanish form of light opera, involving the alternation of singing and dancing with spoken dialogue. It reached its peak of popularity in the second half of the 19th century.

Zauberoper (Ger.) 'Magic opera': term for the kind of opera that relies to an unusual extent on stage machinery and spectacular effects; Mozart's *Die Zauberflöte* is the most famous example.

Index of Role Names

This appendix is an index of names of the principal roles in some 264 operas. Shown against each name is the voice type for which the role is written, the title (sometimes short title) of the opera and the name of the composer; where the same role name appears in several operas, the operas are listed successively, in alphabetical sequence of titles (chronological where two or more are identical; where an opera exists in more than one language version, e.g. *La favorite*, only the title of the original is given). Role name forms in general reflect the usage within articles throughout the dictionary.

Two procedures are particular to this appendix. First, names with prefatory titles (King, Princess, Countess, Sir, Lady, Bishop, Don, Rev., Mr, Dr, Madame, Captain etc.) are given inverted, under the name or place rather than the title, thus: 'Ruritania, Queen of', 'Ethelred, King', 'Smith, Sir John', 'Clement VII, Pope'. 'Smith, Sir John' might however appear as 'John Smith, Sir', if in the opera concerned he is normally known by his given name rather than his surname. That principle applies too to untitled persons; 'Mary Brown' will appear in that form, under M, rather than as 'Brown, Mary', under B, if in the opera she is normally spoken of as Mary rather than Miss or Mrs Brown (if she is regularly referred to there as 'Mrs Brown', she will be entered, under B, as 'Brown, Mrs'). Prefatory titles are generally given in English. Where it seems helpful, for example where roles are known equally in one form or another, a cross-reference is supplied (full dual role names are entered in special circumstances, twice over: for example Renato/Anckarstroem). We have endeavoured to enter each name in the form that the user is most likely to seek it first of all, but he or she should be prepared to try an alternative in cases where our selection differs from his or hers. The exigencies of operatic usage demand that no overriding consistency be applied, and will even dictate on occasion the alphabetical splitting of families: husband and wife, such as the Pinkertons (Pinkerton, Lieutenant; Kate Pinkerton), mother and son, as with the Herrings (Herring, Mrs; Albert Herring), father and son, with the Germonts (Germont; Alfredo Germont), father, mother and daughter with the Fords (Ford; Alice Ford; Nannetta) and uncle and nephew with the Morosuses (Morosus, Sir; Henry Morosus) – to cite only a few.

Secondly, with classical and some historical names, an established English form is given as the principal one. Applicable alternative forms are shown, in alphabetical sequence, separated by oblique strokes: Admetus/ Admète/Admeto, Hippolytus/Hippolyte. Where alternative forms do not fall close to the principal one, they are separately entered as cross-references. The form of the name particular to each opera in a sequence is not indicated but should not be difficult to infer (or to ascertain by reference to the entry on the opera concerned). Parentheses are used to indicate the name under which a character is for a time disguised.

This is an index of names, not of people: an entry may be shared by two or more characters bearing the same name, though in the case of bearers of alternative name forms (such as Helen/Elena/Hélène of Troy) a separate entry is given where one (or more) of those names applies to a quite different fictional character. The oblique stroke is occasionally used for characters appearing under two names and for doubled roles; in such cases a cross-reference from the secondary form may be supplied, especially if it would not have been a neighbouring entry.

Abbreviations: **a** – alto; **b** – bass; **bb** – bass-baritone; **bt** – baritone; **ct** – countertenor; **hc** – haute-contre; **ms** – mezzo-soprano; **s** – soprano; **sp** – spoken role; **t** – tenor; **tr** – treble; **x** – silent role

A

Aaron/Aronne/Aron/Eliéser/Elisero **t** *Mosè in Egitto/Moïse et Pharaon* Rossini; **t** *Moses und Aron* Schoenberg

Abbé **t** *Andrea Chénier* Giordano

Abbess **ms** *Suor Angelica* Puccini

Abigail **s** *Lucrezia Borgia* Donizetti

Abigaille **s** *Nabucco* Verdi

Abimelech/Abimélech **b** *Samson et Dalila* Saint-Saëns

Abul Hassan/Barber **b** *Der Barbier von Bagdad* Cornelius

Acciano **b** *I Lombardi* Verdi

Achillas/Achilla **b** *Giulio Cesare in Egitto* Handel

Achilles/Achille **t/bt** *La belle Hélène* Offenbach; **t** *Iphigénie en Aulide* Gluck; **t** *King Priam* Tippett

Acis **t** *Acis and Galatea* Handel

Actor **bt** *Der ferne Klang* Schreker

Adalgisa **s** *Norma* Bellini

Adario **t** *Les Indes galantes* Rameau

Adelaide **ms** *Arabella* Strauss, R.

Adele **s** *Die Fledermaus* Strauss, J.

Adèle, Countess **s** *Le comte Ory* Rossini

Adhemar de Monteil **b** *Jérusalem/I Lombardi* Verdi

Adina **s** *L'elisir d'amore* Donizetti

Admetus/Admète/Admeto **hc** *Alceste* Lully; **t** *Alceste* Gluck

Adolar, Count of **t** *Euryanthe* Weber

Adonis: *see* Captain of the Royal Guard

Adorno, Gabriele: *see* Gabriele Adorno

Adriana Lecouvreur **s** *Adriana Lecouvreur* Cilea

Adriano Colonna **ms** *Rienzi* Wagner

Aegeus/Egée/Egeo **t** *Giasone* Cavalli

Aegisthus/Aegisth **t** *Elektra* Strauss, R.

Aeneas/Enée **bt** *Dido and Aeneas* Purcell; **t** *Les Troyens* Berlioz

Aennchen **ms** *Der Freischütz* Weber

Afanasy Ivanovich **t** *The Fair at Sorochintsï* Musorgsky

Afra **ms** *La Wally* Catalani

Afron, Prince **bt** *The Golden Cockerel* Rimsky-Korsakov

Agamemnon **bt** *La belle Hélène* Offenbach; **bt** *Iphigénie en Aulide* Gluck

Agathe **s** *Der Freischütz* Weber

Agave **ms** *The Bassarids* Henze

Agnès Sorel **s** *The Maid of Orléans* Tchaikovsky

Agnese del Maino **ms** *Beatrice di Tenda* Bellini

Agnese: *see* Alaide

Agrippa, Dr **t** *The Fiery Angel* Prokofiev

Agrippina **s** *Agrippina* Handel

Aida **s** *Aida* Verdi

Ajax I **t/bt** *La belle Hélène* Offenbach

Ajax II **t/bt** *La belle Hélène* Offenbach

Akhnaten **ct** *Akhnaten* Glass

Akhrosimova, Mariya **ms** *War and Peace* Prokofiev

Aksin'ya **s** *Lady Macbeth of the Mtsensk District* Shostakovich

Alaide/Agnese **s** *La straniera* Bellini

Alaskawolfjoe: *see* Joe

Alberich **bb** *Götterdämmerung* Wagner; **bb** *Das Rheingold* Wagner; **bb** *Siegfried* Wagner

Albert **bt** *Werther* Massenet

Albert Herring **t** *Albert Herring* Britten

Albiani, Paolo: *see* Paolo Albiani

Albine **ms** *Thaïs* Massenet

Albrecht, Cardinal **t** *Mathis der Maler* Hindemith

Alcestis/Alceste **s** *Alceste* Lully; **s** *Alceste* Gluck

Alcides/Alcide: *see* Hercules

Alcina **s** *Alcina* Handel

Alcindoro **b** *La bohème* Puccini

Alcinous/Alcinoo, King **bb** *Ulisse* Dallapiccola

Alessio **b** *La sonnambula* Bellini

Alexandr Petrovič Gorjančikov **bt** *From the House of the Dead* Janáček

Alfio **bt** *Cavalleria rusticana* Mascagni

Alfonso, Don **b** *Così fan tutte* Mozart

Alfonso, Duke **bb** *Lucrezia Borgia* Donizetti

Alfonso XI: *see* Alphonse XI

Alfred **t** *Die Fledermaus* Strauss, J.

Alfredo Germont **t** *La traviata* Verdi

Ali **b** *Les Indes galantes* Rameau

Alice **s** *Le comte Ory* Rossini

Alice Ford, Mrs **s** *Falstaff* Verdi

Alidoro **b** *La Cenerentola* Rossini

Alinda **s** *Giasone* Cavalli

Alisa **ms** *Lucia di Lammermoor* Donizetti

Aljeja **ms** *From the House of the Dead* Janáček

Alkonost **a** *Legend of the Invisible City of Kitezh* Rimsky-Korsakov

Alladine **x** *Ariane et Barbe-bleue* Dukas

Almaviva, Count (Lindoro) **t** *Il barbiere di Siviglia* Rossini

Almaviva/Almaviva, Count **bt** *Le nozze di Figaro* Mozart

Almaviva, Countess **s** *Le nozze di Figaro* Mozart

Alméric **t** *Iolanta* Tchaikovsky

Almirena **s** *Rinaldo* Handel

Aloes **ms** *L'étoile* Chabrier

Alphonse **t** *La muette de Portici* Auber

Alphonse XI/Alfonso XI, King **bt** *La favorite* Donizetti

Altoum, Emperor **t** *Turandot* Puccini

Alvar, Don **t** *L'Africaine* Meyerbeer; **b** *Les Indes galantes* Rameau

Alvaro, Don **t** *La forza del destino* Verdi

Alvise Badoero **b** *La Gioconda* Ponchielli

Alwa **t** *Lulu* Berg

Amadis/Amadigi **hc** *Amadis* Lully

Amahl **tr** *Amahl and the Night Visitors* Menotti

Amalia **s** *I masnadieri* Verdi

Amaltea: *see* Sinais

Amanda **s** *Le Grand Macabre* Ligeti

Amando **ms** *Le Grand Macabre* Ligeti

Amantio, Ser **bt** *Gianni Schicchi* Puccini

Amaranta **ms** *La fedeltà premiata* Haydn

Amastre **a** *Serse* Handel; **s** *Xerse* Cavalli

Ambrogio **b** *Il barbiere di Siviglia* Rossini

Ambroise, Maître **b** *Mireille* Gounod

Amelfa **a** *The Golden Cockerel* Rimsky-Korsakov

Amelia **s** *Un ballo in maschera* Verdi; **s** *Simon Boccanegra* Verdi

Amenaide **s** *Tancredi* Rossini

Amenophis/Aménophis **t** *Mosè in Egitto/Moïse et Pharaon* Rossini

Amenophis/Osiride **t** *Mosè in Egitto/Moïse et Pharaon* Rossini

Amfortas **bt** *Parsifal* Wagner

Amina **s** *La sonnambula* Bellini

Aminta **s** *Die schweigsame Frau* Strauss, R.

Amneris **ms** *Aida* Verdi

Amonasro **bt** *Aida* Verdi

Amor, Amore, Amour: *see* Cupid

Amphinomous/Anfinomo **a** *Il ritorno d'Ulisse in patria* Monteverdi

Anaïs/Anaï/Elcia **s** *Mosè in Egitto/Moïse et Pharaon* Rossini

Autonoe **s** *The Bassarids* Henze
Avito **t** *L'amore dei tre re* Montemezzi
Azema **s** *Semiramide* Rossini
Azucena **ms** *Il trovatore* Verdi

B

Baba Mustapha **t** *Der Barbier von Bagdad* Cornelius
Baba the Turk **ms** *The Rake's Progress* Stravinsky
Babekan **sp** *Oberon* Weber
Baby Doe **s** *The Ballad of Baby Doe* Moore
Bacchis **s** *La belle Hélène* Offenbach
Bacchus **sp** *Orphée aux enfers* Offenbach
Bacchus/Tenor **t** *Ariadne auf Naxos* Strauss, R.
Badger **b** *The Cunning Little Vixen* Janáček
Bailli **bb** *Werther* Massenet
Bajazet/Bajazete **t** *Tamerlano* Handel
Balducci **b** *Benvenuto Cellini* Berlioz
Ballad-Singer **b** *Gloriana* Britten
Balstrode, Captain **bt** *Peter Grimes* Britten
Balthazar **b** *Amahl and the Night Visitors* Menotti; **b** *La favorite* Donizetti
Bánk bán **t** *Bánk bán* Erkel
Banker: *see* Professor of Medicine
Banquo/Banco **b** *Macbeth* Verdi
Barak **bb** *Die Frau ohne Schatten* Strauss, R.
Barak's Wife/Dyer's Wife **s** *Die Frau ohne Schatten* Strauss, R.
Barbarina **s** *Le nozze di Figaro* Mozart
Barbe-bleue: *see* Bluebeard
Barber: *see* Abu Hassan, Schneidebart
Bardolph/Bardolfo **t** *Falstaff* Verdi
Barena **s** *Jenůfa* Janáček
Barnaba **bt** *La Gioconda* Ponchielli
Baron **b** *Der ferne Klang* Schreker
Baroncelli **t** *Rienzi* Wagner
Bartolo/Bartolo, Dr **bt** *Il barbiere di Siviglia* Rossini; **b** *Le nozze di Figaro* Mozart
Basilio, Don **b** *Il barbiere di Siviglia* Rossini; **t** *Le nozze di Figaro* Mozart
Bayan **t** *Ruslan and Lyudmila* Glinka
Beatrice/Béatrice **s** *Béatrice et Bénédict* Berlioz
Beatrice di Tenda **s** *Beatrice di Tenda* Bellini
Beckmesser, Sixtus **b** *Die Meistersinger von Nürnberg* Wagner
Begbick, Leokadja: *see* Leokadja Begbick
Beggar **sp** *The Beggar's Opera*
Belcore **bt** *L'elisir d'amore* Donizetti
Belfiore, Count **t** *La finta giardiniera* Mozart
Belinda **s** *Dido and Aeneas* Purcell
Bella **s** *The Midsummer Marriage* Tippett
Bellangère **s** *Ariane et Barbe-bleue* Dukas
Belmonte **t** *Die Entführung aus dem Serail* Mozart
Benedick/Bénédict **t** *Béatrice et Bénédict* Berlioz
Beneš **b** *Dalibor* Smetana
Benoit **b** *La bohème* Puccini
Benvolio **t** *Roméo et Juliette* Gounod

Beppe/Arlecchino **t** *Pagliacci* Leoncavallo
Beppo **t** *Fra Diavolo* Auber
Berendey, Tsar **t** *The Snow Maiden* Rimsky-Korsakov
Bergère: *see* Louis XV Chair
Berkenfeld, Marquise/Marchesa **ms** *La fille du régiment* Donizetti
Berkley, Sir John **b** *Der Vampyr* Marschner
Beroe **ms** *The Bassarids* Henze
Bersi **ms** *Andrea Chénier* Giordano
Berta **ms** *Il barbiere di Siviglia* Rossini
Bertarido **a** *Rodelinda* Handel
Berthe **s** *Le prophète* Meyerbeer
Bertrand **b** *Iolanta* Tchaikovsky
Bess **s** *Porgy and Bess* Gershwin
Besso **b** *Giasone* Cavalli
Béthune, Sire de **b** *Les vêpres siciliennes* Verdi
Betto di Signa **b** *Gianni Schicchi* Puccini
Bianca **ms** *The Rape of Lucretia* Britten
Biancafiore **s** *Francesca da Rimini* Zandonai
Biberach **bt** *Bánk bán* Erkel
Bide-the-Bent: *see* Raimondo Bidebent
Big Prisoner/Nikita **t** *From the House of the Dead* Janáček
Billows, Lady **s** *Albert Herring* Britten
Bill/Sparbüchsenbill **bt** *Aufstieg und Fall der Stadt Mahagonny* Weill
Billy Budd **bt** *Billy Budd* Britten
Billy Jackrabbit **b** *La fanciulla del West* Puccini
Biterolf **b** *Tannhäuser* Wagner
Blanche de la Force **s** *Dialogues des Carmélites* Poulenc
Blind, Dr **t** *Die Fledermaus* Strauss, J.
Blonde **s** *Die Entführung aus dem Serail* Mozart
Bluebeard/Barbe-bleue **b** *Ariane et Barbe-bleue* Dukas; **bt** *Bluebeard's Castle* Bartók
Blunt, Toms **b** *Der Vampyr* Marschner
Bob: *see* Tristan Mickleford, Lord
Bobïl'-Bakula **t** *The Snow Maiden* Rimsky-Korsakov
Bobïlikha **ms** *The Snow Maiden* Rimsky-Korsakov
Boccanegra, Simon **bt** *Simon Boccanegra* Verdi
Bois-Rosé **t** *Les Huguenots* Meyerbeer
Boles, Bob **t** *Peter Grimes* Britten
Bolkonsky: *see* Andrey Bolkonsky
Bolkonsky, Prince Nikolay **b** *War and Peace* Prokofiev
Bonny Spring/Spring Fairy/Vesna-Krasna **ms** *The Snow Maiden* Rimsky-Korsakov
Bonze **b** *Madama Butterfly* Puccini; **b** *The Nightingale* Stravinsky
Borella **b** *La muette de Portici* Auber
Boris Godunov **bt/b** *Boris Godunov* Musorgsky
Boris Grigorjevič **b** *Kát'a Kabanová* Janáček
Boris Izmaylov **b** *Katerina Izmaylova/Lady Macbeth of the Mtsensk District* Shostakovich
Borromeo, Cardinal Carlo **bt** *Palestrina* Pfitzner
Borsa **t** *Rigoletto* Verdi
Bostana **ms** *Der Barbier von Bagdad* Cornelius
Bosun **bt** *Billy Budd* Britten
Bottom **bb** *A Midsummer Night's Dream* Britten

Bouillon, Prince of b *Adriana Lecouvreur* Cilea
Bouillon, Princess of ms *Adriana Lecouvreur* Cilea
Bradamante a *Alcina* Handel
Brangäne s/ms *Tristan und Isolde* Wagner
Brétigny bt *Manon* Massenet
Brighella t *Ariadne auf Naxos* Strauss, R.
Brogni, Cardinal b *La Juive* Halévy
Brouček, Mr t *The Excursions of Mr Brouček* Janáček
Brown bt *Die Dreigroschenoper* Weill
Brünnhilde s *Götterdämmerung* Wagner; s *Siegfried*
     Wagner; s *Die Walküre* Wagner
Bruno Robertson, Sir t *I puritani* Bellini
Budd, Superintendent b *Albert Herring* Britten
Budivoj bt *Dalibor* Smetana
Buonafede bt *Il mondo della luna* Haydn
Butterfly/Cio-Cio-San s *Madama Butterfly* Puccini
Bystrouška/Vixen s *The Cunning Little Vixen* Janáček

C

Cadmus b *The Bassarids* Henze; b *Semele* Handel
Caesar: *see* Julius Caesar
Caius, Dr t *Falstaff* Verdi; b *Die lustigen Weiber von
     Windsor* Nicolai
Calaf t *Turandot* Puccini
Calatrava, Marchese di b *La forza del destino* Verdi
Calchas bt *La belle Hélène* Offenbach; b *Iphigénie en
     Aulide* Gluck
Caliph bt *Der Barbier von Bagdad* Cornelius
Calkas b *Troilus and Cressida* Walton
Callisto/Calisto s *Calisto* Cavalli
Calypso s *Ulisse* Dallapiccola
Canio/Pagliaccio t *Pagliacci* Leoncavallo
Capellio b *I Capuleti e i Montecchi* Bellini
Capito t *Mathis der Maler* Hindemith
Captain t *Wozzeck* Berg
Captain of the Royal Guard/Adonis bt *The Bassarids*
     Henze
Capulet b *Roméo et Juliette* Gounod
Cardillac bt *Cardillac* Hindemith
Carlo t *I masnadieri* Verdi
Carlo, Don bt *Ernani* Verdi
Carlo di Vargas, Don bt *La forza del destino* Verdi
Carlos, Don hc *Les Indes galantes* Rameau; bt *The Stone
     Guest* Dargomïzhsky
Carlos/Carlo, Don t *Don Carlos* Verdi
Carlo VII: *see* Charles
Carlotta ms *Die schweigsame Frau* Strauss, R.
Carmen ms *Carmen* Bizet
Carolina s *Il matrimonio segreto* Cimarosa
Carolina, Countess of Kirchstetten a *Elegy for Young
     Lovers* Henze
Caronte: *see* Charon
Čaroskvoucí: *see* Würfl
Caspar b *Der Freischütz* Weber
Cassandra/Cassandre ms *Les Troyens* Berlioz
Cassio t *Otello* Verdi

Castor hc *Castor et Pollux* Rameau
Catharine/Catherine s *La jolie fille de Perth* Bizet
Catherine the Great x *The Queen of Spades* Tchaikovsky
Cavalier t *Cardillac* Hindemith
Cavaradossi, Mario t *Tosca* Puccini
Cecco t *Il mondo della luna* Haydn
Cecco del Vecchio b *Rienzi* Wagner
Cecil b *Maria Stuarda* Donizetti
Cecil, Sir Robert bt *Gloriana* Britten
Cecilia, St s *Four Saints in Three Acts* Thomson
Cecilius/Cecilio s *Lucio Silla* Mozart
Čekunov b *From the House of the Dead* Janáček
Celaenus/Celenus bt *Atys* Lully
Celia s *Lucio Silla* Mozart; *see also* Fillide
Celio b *The Love for Three Oranges* Prokofiev
Cellini t *Benvenuto Cellini* Berlioz
Cendrillon/Lucette s *Cendrillon* Massenet
Cenerentola/Angelina a *La Cenerentola* Rossini
Céphise s *Alceste* Lully
Ceprano, Count b *Rigoletto* Verdi
Ceprano, Countess ms *Rigoletto* Verdi
Cerberus/Cerbère b *Orphée aux enfers* Offenbach
Čerevin t *From the House of the Dead* Janáček
Chamberlain b *The Nightingale* Stravinsky
Chaplitsky t *The Queen of Spades* Tchaikovsky
Charcoal Burner bt/b *May Night* Rimsky-Korsakov
Charles/Carlo VII t *Giovanna d'Arco* Verdi
Charles VII t *The Maid of Orléans* Tchaikovsky
Charlotte ms *Die Soldaten* Zimmermann; ms *Werther*
     Massenet
Charmeuse, La s *Thaïs* Massenet
Charon/Caronte bt *Alceste* Lully; b *Orfeo* Monteverdi
Chateauneuf, Marquis de t *Zar und Zimmermann*
     Lortzing
Chavez, St t *Four Saints in Three Acts* Thomson
Chazeuil, Abbé of t *Adriana Lecouvreur* Cilea
Checco t *König Hirsch* Henze
Chekalinsky t *The Queen of Spades* Tchaikovsky
Chénier: *see* Andrea Chénier
Cherevik, Solopy b *The Fair at Sorochintsï* Musorgsky
Cherubino ms *Le nozze di Figaro* Mozart
Chevalier t *Der ferne Klang* Schreker
Chiang Ch'ing s *Nixon in China* Adams
Chief of Secret Police: *see* Gepopo
Child ms *L'enfant et les sortilèges* Ravel
Chimene/Chimène s *Le Cid* Massenet
China, Emperor of bt *The Nightingale* Stravinsky
Chocholka s *The Cunning Little Vixen* Janáček
Chorèbe: *see* Coroebus
Choregos bt *Punch and Judy* Birtwistle
Chou En-lai bt *Nixon in China* Adams
Christian/Silvano b *Un ballo in maschera*
     Verdi
Christine: *see* Storch, Christine
Chrysothemis s *Elektra* Strauss, R.
Chub b *Christmas Eve* Rimsky-Korsakov
Cid: *see* Rodrigue

Demetrius **bt** *A Midsummer Night's Dream* Britten
Demo **t** *Giasone* Cavalli
Demodocus/Demodoco **t** *Ulisse* Dallapiccola
Demon (Lucinde) **s** *Armide* Gluck
Demon (Mélisse) **s** *Armide* Gluck
Denisov **bb** *War and Peace* Prokofiev
Des Grieux, Armand: *see* Armand des Grieux
Des Grieux, Chevalier **t** *Manon* Massenet; **t** *Manon Lescaut* Puccini
Des Grieux, Count **b** *Manon* Massenet
Desdemona **s** *Otello* Verdi
Despina **s** *Così fan tutte* Mozart
Desportes **t** *Die Soldaten* Zimmermann
Devil **t** *Christmas Eve* Rimsky-Korsakov
Dew Fairy **s** *Hänsel und Gretel* Humperdinck
Diana/Diane **s** *Calisto* Cavalli; **s** *Hippolyte et Aricie* Rameau; **s** *Orphée aux enfers* Offenbach
Diana Orsini **a** *Bomarzo* Ginastera
Diana Trapes **s** *The Beggar's Opera*
Dibdin, George **t** *Der Vampyr* Marschner
Dido/Didon **s** *Dido and Aeneas* Purcell; **ms** *Les Troyens* Berlioz
Diégo, Don **b** *L'Africaine* Meyerbeer
Diègue, Don **b** *Le Cid* Massenet
Dikoj, Savël Prokofjevič **b** *Kát'a Kabanová* Janáček
Diomedes/Diomede **bt** *Troilus and Cressida* Walton
Dionysus/Voice/Stranger **t** *The Bassarids* Henze
Dirce/Dircé **s** *Médée* Cherubini
Distiller **t** *May Night* Rimsky-Korsakov
Djura **sp** *Arabella* Strauss, R.
Dmitry: *see* Pretender
D'Obigny, Marchese **b** *La traviata* Verdi
Doctor **bt** *Pelléas et Mélisande* Debussy; **b** *Punch and Judy* Birtwistle; **b** *Wozzeck* Berg
Dodon, King **b** *The Golden Cockerel* Rimsky-Korsakov
Doge: *see* Francesco Foscari
Doktor Faust: *see* Faust
Dolcina, Sister **s** *Suor Angelica* Puccini
Dolokhov **b** *War and Peace* Prokofiev
Dolore: *see* Trouble
Dominik, Count **bt** *Arabella* Strauss, R.
Domšík: *see* Sacristan
Donald **bt** *Billy Budd* Britten
Donner **bb** *Das Rheingold* Wagner
Dorabella **s** *Così fan tutte* Mozart
Dorinda **s** *Orlando* Handel
Doris **s** *Atys* Lully
Dorotea **ms** *Stiffelio* Verdi
Dorothée **ms** *Cendrillon* Massenet
Dosifey **b** *Khovanshchina* Musorgsky
Douphol, Baron **bt** *La traviata* Verdi
Doyen de la Faculté **t** *Cendrillon* Massenet
Dreieinigkeitsmoses: *see* Trinity Moses
Drum Major **t** *Wozzeck* Berg
Drummer **ms** *Der Kaiser von Atlantis* Ullmann
Drunk Prisoner **t** *From the House of the Dead* Janáček
Drusilla **s** *L'incoronazione di Poppea* Monteverdi

Duda **b** *Sadko* Rimsky-Korsakov
Duke: *see* Mantua, Duke of
Dulcamara, Dr **b** *L'elisir d'amore* Donizetti
Dulcinée **ms** *Don Quichotte* Massenet
Duncan/Duncano **x** *Macbeth* Verdi
Dunois **bt** *The Maid of Orléans* Tchaikovsky
Dutchman **bb** *Der fliegende Holländer* Wagner
Dyer's Wife: *see* Barak's Wife
Dziemba **b** *Halka* Moniuszko

E

Eboli, Princess **ms** *Don Carlos* Verdi
Ecclitico **t** *Il mondo della luna* Haydn
Edgardo **t** *Lucia di Lammermoor* Donizetti
Edmondo **t** *Manon Lescaut* Puccini
Edrisi **t** *King Roger* Szymanowski
Eduige **s** *Rodelinda* Handel
Egeo: *see* Aegeus
Eglantine **s** *Euryanthe* Weber
Egypt, King of **b** *Aida* Verdi
Eisenhardt **bt** *Die Soldaten* Zimmermann
Eisenstein, Gabriel von **t** *Die Fledermaus* Strauss, J.
Eisslinger, Ulrich **t** *Die Meistersinger von Nürnberg* Wagner
Elcia: *see* Anaïs
Elderly Prisoner **t** *From the House of the Dead* Janáček
Eléazar **t** *La Juive* Halévy
Electra/Elektra/Elettra **s** *Elektra* Strauss; **s** *Idomeneo* Mozart
Elemer, Count **t** *Arabella* Strauss, R.
Elena: *see* Helen of Troy
Eliéser, Elisero: *see* Aaron
Elisabeth **s** *Tannhäuser* Wagner
Elisabeth de/Elisabetta di Valois **s** *Don Carlos* Verdi
Elisabeth Zimmer **s** *Elegy for Young Lovers* Henze
Elisetta **s** *Il matrimonio segreto* Cimarosa
Elizabeth I/Elisabetta, Queen **s** *Gloriana* Britten; **s** *Maria Stuarda* Donizetti
Ellen Orford **s** *Peter Grimes* Britten
Elsa of Brabant **s** *Lohengrin* Wagner
Elvino **t** *Il pirata* Bellini; **t** *La sonnambula* Bellini
Elvira **s** *Ernani* Verdi; **s** *L'italiana in Algeri* Rossini; **s** *I puritani* Bellini
Elvira, Donna **s** *Don Giovanni* Mozart
Elvire **s** *La muette de Portici* Auber
Elviro **b** *Serse* Handel
Emilia **ms** *Otello* Verdi
Emilia Marty **s** *The Makropulos Affair* Janáček
Emilie **s** *Les Indes galantes* Rameau
Emma **s** *Khovanshchina* Musorgsky
Emmie **s** *Albert Herring* Britten
Emmy **s** *Der Vampyr* Marschner
Emperor **t** *Die Frau ohne Schatten* Strauss, R.
Emperor Überall **bt** *Der Kaiser von Atlantis* Ullmann
Empress **s** *Die Frau ohne Schatten* Strauss, R.
Endre II **bt** *Bánk bán* Erkel

Endymion/Endimione a *Calisto* Cavalli

Enée: see Aeneas

Enrichetta di Francia: see Henrietta, Queen

Enrico: see Henry VIII

Enrico Ashton **bt** *Lucia di Lammermoor* Donizetti

Enzo Grimaldi **t** *La Gioconda* Ponchielli

Ephraimite **bt** *Moses und Aron* Schoenberg

Ercole: see Hercules

Erda **a** *Das Rheingold* Wagner; **a** *Siegfried* Wagner

Ericlea: see Eurycleia

Erik **t** *Der fliegende Holländer* Wagner

Ernani **t** *Ernani* Verdi

Ernesto **t** *Don Pasquale* Donizetti; **a** *Il mondo della luna* Haydn

Ernesto, Duke of Caldora **b** *Il pirata* Bellini

Escamillo **bb** *Carmen* Bizet

Esmeralda **s** *The Bartered Bride* Smetana

Essex, Earl of, Robert Devereux **t** *Gloriana* Britten

Essex, Countess of, Frances **ms** *Gloriana* Britten

Etherea: see Málinka

Eudoxie, Princess **s** *La Juive* Halévy

Eugene Onegin: see Yevgeny Onegin

Eumaeus/Eumée/Eumeo/Eumete **bt** *Pénélope* Fauré; **t** *Il ritorno d'Ulisse in patria* Monteverdi; **t** *Ulisse* Dallapiccola

Eumelus/Eumelo **s** *Alceste* Gluck

Euryanthe **s** *Euryanthe* Weber

Eurycleia/Ericlea/Euryclée **ms** *Pénélope* Fauré; **ms** *Il ritorno d'Ulisse in patria* Monteverdi

Eurydice/Euridice **ms** *The Mask of Orpheus* Birtwistle; **s** *Orfeo* Monteverdi; **s** *Orfeo ed Euridice/Orphée et Euridice* Gluck; **s** *Orphée aux enfers* Offenbach

Eurymachus/Eurimaco/Eurymaque **bt** *Pénélope* Fauré; **t** *Il ritorno d'Ulisse in patria* Monteverdi; **t** *Ulisse* Dallapiccola

Eustazio **a** *Rinaldo* Handel

Eva **s** *Die Meistersinger von Nürnberg* Wagner

Evadne/Maid **ms** *Troilus and Cressida* Walton

Evander/Evandre **t** *Alceste* Gluck

Ezio **bt** *Attila* Verdi

F

Fabrizio Vingradito **b** *La gazza ladra* Rossini

Fafner **b** *Das Rheingold* Wagner; **b** *Siegfried* Wagner

Fairy Godmother: see Fée

Falcon **s** *Die Frau ohne Schatten* Strauss, R.

Falke, Dr **bt** *Die Fledermaus* Strauss, J.

Falstaff **bt** *Falstaff* Verdi; **b** *Die lustigen Weiber von Windsor* Nicolai

Faninal **bt** *Der Rosenkavalier* Strauss, R.

Fanuèl **bt** *Nerone* Boito

Faraone: see Pharaoh

Farasmane **b** *Radamisto* Handel

Farfallo **b** *Die schweigsame Frau* Strauss, R.

Farfarello **b** *The Love for Three Oranges* Prokofiev

Farlaf **b** *Ruslan and Lyudmila* Glinka

Farnace: see Pharnaces

Fasolt **bb** *Das Rheingold* Wagner

Fata Morgana **s** *The Love for Three Oranges* Prokofiev

Father **b** *Louise* Charpentier, G.

Father Confessor **bt** *Dialogues des Carmélites* Poulenc

Father/Peter **bt** *Hänsel und Gretel* Humperdinck

Fatima **s** *Les Indes galantes* Rameau; **ms** *Oberon* Weber

Fatty/Willy **t** *Aufstieg und Fall der Stadt Mahagonny* Weill

Faust, Dr **bt** *Doktor Faust* Busoni; **t** *Faust* Gounod; **b** *The Fiery Angel* Prokofiev; **t** *Mefistofele* Boito

Federica, Duchess **a** *Luisa Miller* Verdi

Federico di Frengel **t** *Stiffelio* Verdi

Fée/Fairy Godmother **s** *Cendrillon* Massenet

Feklusa **ms** *Kát'a Kabanová* Janáček

Female Cat **ms** *L'enfant et les sortilèges* Ravel

Female Chorus **ms** *The Rape of Lucretia* Britten

Fenena **s** *Nabucco* Verdi

Fenton **t** *Falstaff* Verdi; **t** *Die lustigen Weiber von Windsor* Nicolai

Fernand/Fernando **t** *La favorite* Donizetti

Fernando, Don **b** *Fidelio* Beethoven

Fernando Villabella **bb** *La gazza ladra* Rossini

Ferrando **t** *Così fan tutte* Mozart; **b** *Il trovatore* Verdi

Fevroniya **s** *Legend of the Invisible City of Kitezh* Rimsky-Korsakov

Fiakermilli **s** *Arabella* Strauss, R.

Fidalma **s** *Il matrimonio segreto* Cimarosa

Fidès **ms** *Le prophète* Meyerbeer

Fieramosca **bt/t** *Benvenuto Cellini* Berlioz

Fiesco, Jacopo (Andrea) **b** *Simon Boccanegra* Verdi

Figaro **bt** *Il barbiere di Siviglia* Rossini; **b** *Le nozze di Figaro* Mozart

Filch **t** *The Beggar's Opera*

Fileno **t** *La fedeltà premiata* Haydn

Filipp'yevna/Filipyevna **ms** *Yevgeny Onegin* Tchaikovsky

Filippo **t** *L'infedeltà delusa* Haydn; see also Philip II

Filippo Maria Visconti, Duke **bt** *Beatrice di Tenda* Bellini

Filka Morozov: see Luka Kuzmič

Fillide/Celia **ms** *La fedeltà premiata* Haydn

Finn **t** *Ruslan and Lyudmila* Glinka

Fiora **s** *L'amore dei tre re* Montemezzi

Fiordiligi **s** *Così fan tutte* Mozart

Fiorello **b** *Il barbiere di Siviglia* Rossini

Fiorilla **s** *Il turco in Italia* Rossini

Fisherman **t** *The Nightingale* Stravinsky

Flamand **t** *Capriccio* Strauss, R.

Flaminia **s** *Il mondo della luna* Haydn

Flavio **t** *Norma* Bellini

Fleance/Fleanzio **x** *Macbeth* Verdi

Fléville: see Pietro Fléville

Flint, Mr **bb** *Billy Budd* Britten

Flora **s** *The Turn of the Screw* Britten

Flora Bervoix **ms** *La traviata* Verdi

Flora/Flore **s** *Atys* Lully

Florence Pike **a** *Albert Herring* Britten

Florestan **t** *Fidelio* Beethoven

Flosshilde **ms** *Götterdämmerung* Wagner; **ms** *Das Rheingold* Wagner

Flute **t** *A Midsummer Night's Dream* Britten

Fluth, Frau: *see* Ford, Mrs

Fluth: *see* Ford

Folly/Folie, La **s** *Platée* Rameau

Foltz, Hans **b** *Die Meistersinger von Nürnberg* Wagner

Ford **bt** *Falstaff* Verdi

Ford/Fluth **bt** *Die lustigen Weiber von Windsor* Nicolai

Ford, Mrs/Fluth, Frau **s** *Die lustigen Weiber von Windsor* Nicolai; *see also* Alice Ford

Foreign Princess **s** *Rusalka* Dvořák

Foreman **bt** *Jenůfa* Janáček

Forest Sprite/Leshiy **t** *The Snow Maiden* Rimsky-Korsakov

Foresto **t** *Attila* Verdi

Fortune-Teller **s** *Arabella* Strauss, R.

Fouquier Tinville **bb** *Andrea Chénier* Giordano

Four Villains: *see* Coppélius, Dapertutto, Lindorf and Miracle

Fox/Golden-mane **s** *The Cunning Little Vixen* Janáček

Fraarte **s** *Radamisto* Handel

Frances: *see* Essex, Countess of

Francesca **s** *Francesca da Rimini* Zandonai

Francesco **bt** *I masnadieri* Verdi

Francesco Foscari/Doge **bt** *I due Foscari* Verdi

Francis **bt** *Boulevard Solitude* Henze

Frank/Warden **bt** *Die Fledermaus* Strauss, J.

Frantík **s** *The Cunning Little Vixen* Janáček

Frantz **t** *Les contes d'Hoffmann* Offenbach

Frasquita **s** *Carmen* Bizet

Freia **s** *Das Rheingold* Wagner

French Abbé **t** *War and Peace* Prokofiev

Fricka **ms** *Das Rheingold* Wagner; **ms** *Die Walküre* Wagner

Fritz **t** *Der ferne Klang* Schreker

Frog **tr** *The Cunning Little Vixen* Janáček; **t** *L'enfant et les sortilèges* Ravel

Froh **t** *Das Rheingold* Wagner

Frosch **sp** *Die Fledermaus* Strauss, J.

Frugola **ms** *Il tabarro* Puccini

Fyodor **ms** *Boris Godunov* Musorgsky

G

Gabriele Adorno **t** *Simon Boccanegra* Verdi

Galatea/Galatée **s** *Acis and Galatea* Handel

Galitsky, Vladimir **b** *Prince Igor* Borodin

Gamekeeper **t** *Rusalka* Dvořák **bt** *The Cunning Little Vixen* Janáček; Wife **a** *The Cunning Little Vixen* Janáček

Gandhi **t** *Satyagraha* Glass

Garcias **s** *Don Quichotte* Massenet

Garibaldo **b** *Rodelinda* Handel

Gaspar, Don **t** *La favorite* Donizetti

Gaston **t** *Jérusalem/I Lombardi* Verdi

Gastone, Vicomte de Letorières **t** *La traviata* Verdi

Gedge, Mr **bt** *Albert Herring* Britten

Gellner **bt** *La Wally* Catalani

Geneviève **a** *Pelléas et Mélisande* Debussy

Gennaro **t** *Lucrezia Borgia* Donizetti

Genovieffa, Sister **s** *Suor Angelica* Puccini

Gepopo, Chief of the Secret Police **s** *Le Grand Macabre* Ligeti

Gérard **bt** *Andrea Chénier* Giordano

Gerhilde **s** *Die Walküre* Wagner

Germont: *see* Alfredo Germont

Germont, Giorgio **bt** *La traviata* Verdi

Geronimo, Don **b** *Il matrimonio segreto* Cimarosa

Geronio, Don **b** *Il turco in Italia* Rossini

Geronte de Revoir **b** *Manon Lescaut* Puccini

Gertrud **a** *Bánk bán* Erkel; *see also* Mother

Gertrude **a** *Hans Heiling* Marschner; **ms** *Roméo et Juliette* Gounod

Geschwitz, Countess **ms** *Lulu* Berg

Gesler **b** *Guillaume Tell* Rossini

Gherardino **a** *Gianni Schicchi* Puccini

Gherardo **t** *Gianni Schicchi* Puccini

Giacomo **bt** *Giovanna d'Arco* Verdi

Gian Conrado Orsini **b** *Bomarzo* Ginastera

Gianciotto: *see* Malatesta, Giovanni

Giannetta **s** *L'elisir d'amore* Donizetti

Giannetto **t** *La gazza ladra* Rossini

Gianni Schicchi **bt** *Gianni Schicchi* Puccini

Giasone: *see* Jason

Gilda **s** *Rigoletto* Verdi

Ginevra **s** *Ariodante* Handel

Gioconda, La **s** *La Gioconda* Ponchielli

Giorgetta **s** *Il tabarro* Puccini

Giorgio **b** *La gazza ladra* Rossini

Giorgio, Sir **b** *I puritani* Bellini

Giovanna **s** *Ernani* Verdi; *see also* Joan of Arc

Giovanna Seymour: see Jane Seymour

Giovanni **b** *Il corsaro* Verdi

Giovanni, Don **bt** *Don Giovanni* Mozart

Giove: *see* Jupiter

Girl **s** *Der Kaiser von Atlantis* Ullmann

Girolamo **bt** *Bomarzo* Ginastera

Giselda **s** *I Lombardi* Verdi

Giulietta **s** *I Capuleti e i Montecchi* Bellini; **s** *Les contes d'Hoffmann* Offenbach; *see also* Juliet

Giulio Cesare: *see* Julius Caesar

Giunone: *see* Juno

Glaša **ms** *Kát'a Kabanová* Janáček

Gloriana: *see* Elizabeth I

Gobrias **t** *Nerone* Boito

Goffredo **a** *Rinaldo* Handel

Go-Go, Prince **tr/s/ct** *Le Grand Macabre* Ligeti

Golaud **bt** *Pelléas et Mélisande* Debussy

Gold Dealer **b** *Cardillac* Hindemith

Golden Cockerel **s** *The Golden Cockerel* Rimsky-Korsakov

Golden-mane: *see* Fox

Golitsïn, Prince Vasily t *Khovanshchina* Musorgsky

Gonzalve t *L'heure espagnole* Ravel

Gorislava s *Ruslan and Lyudmila* Glinka

Gormas, Count of b *Le Cid* Massenet

Goro t *Madama Butterfly* Puccini

Gottardo/Podestà bb *La gazza ladra* Rossini

Governess s *The Turn of the Screw* Britten

Grand Brahmin: *see* High Priest of Brahma

Grand Inquisitor b *Don Carlos* Verdi

Grand Inquisitor of Lisbon b *L'Africaine* Meyerbeer

Grandfather Frost/Ded Moroz b *The Snow Maiden* Rimsky-Korsakov

Grandmother Buryjovka a *Jenůfa* Janáček

Grasshopper tr *The Cunning Little Vixen* Janáček

Graumann b *Der ferne Klang* Schreker

Graumann's Wife ms *Der ferne Klang* Schreker

Gregor, Albert t *The Makropulos Affair* Janáček

Gregory/Grégorio bt *Roméo et Juliette* Gounod

Gremin, Prince b *Yevgeny Onegin* Tchaikovsky

Gretchen bt *Doktor Faust* Busoni

Grete/Greta Graumann s *Der ferne Klang* Schreker

Gretel s *Hänsel und Gretel* Humperdinck

Grigory: *see* Pretender

Grimes, Peter t *Peter Grimes* Britten

Grimgerde a *Die Walküre* Wagner

Grimoaldo t *Rodelinda* Handel

Grishka Kuter'ma t *Legend of the Invisible City of Kitezh* Rimsky-Korsakov

Grits'ko t *The Fair at Sorochintsï* Musorgsky

Grose, Mrs s *The Turn of the Screw* Britten

Günther bb *Götterdämmerung* Wagner

Gualtiero t *Il pirata* Bellini

Guardiano: *see* Padre Guardiano

Guccio b *Gianni Schicchi* Puccini

Guglielmo b *Così fan tutte* Mozart

Guidon, Prince t *The Golden Cockerel* Rimsky-Korsakov

Guillot de Morfontaine t *Manon* Massenet

Gulnara s *Il corsaro* Verdi

Gunther bt *Götterdämmerung* Wagner

Gurnemanz b *Parsifal* Wagner

Gustavus III/Riccardo t *Un ballo in maschera* Verdi

Gutrune s *Götterdämmerung* Wagner

Gypsy b *The Fair at Sorochintsï* Musorgsky

H

Hagen b *Götterdämmerung* Wagner

Haghenbach t *La Wally* Catalani

Halka s *Halka* Moniuszko

Haly b *L'italiana in Algeri* Rossini

Hanna ms *May Night* Rimsky-Korsakov

Hans Heiling bt *Hans Heiling* Marschner

Hans Sachs bb *Die Meistersinger von Nürnberg* Wagner

Hans: *see* Jim Mahoney

Hänsel ms *Hänsel und Gretel* Humperdinck

Harasta/Poacher b *The Cunning Little Vixen* Janáček

Harlequin bt *Ariadne auf Naxos* Strauss, R.

Harriet Durham, Lady (Martha) s *Martha* Flotow

Harry tr *Albert Herring* Britten

Háta ms *The Bartered Bride* Smetana

Haudy, Major bt *Die Soldaten* Zimmermann

Hauk-Šendorf t *The Makropulos Affair* Janáček

He-Ancient b *The Midsummer Marriage* Tippett

Hebe/Hébé s *Les Indes galantes* Rameau

Hecate/Hécate: *see* Oracle of the Dead

Hector bt *King Priam* Tippett

Hector's Ghost b *Les Troyens* Berlioz

Hecuba/Hécube s *King Priam* Tippett; s *Les Troyens* Berlioz

Hedwige ms *Guillaume Tell* Rossini

Heinrich der Schreiber t *Tannhäuser* Wagner

Heinrich der Vogler b *Lohengrin* Wagner

Heinz/Sparbüchsenheinrich bt *Aufstieg und Fall der Stadt Mahagonny* Weill

Helena s *A Midsummer Night's Dream* Britten

Helen/Elena/Hélène of Troy s *La belle Hélène* Offenbach; ms *King Priam* Tippett; s *Mefistofele* Boito

Hélène s *I Lombardi/Jérusalem* Verdi

Hélène Bezukhova a *War and Peace* Prokofiev

Hélène/Helena, Duchess s *Les vêpres siciliennes* Verdi

Helenus t *Les Troyens* Berlioz

Helfenstein, Countess a *Mathis der Maler* Hindemith

Helmwige s *Die Walküre* Wagner

Henry/Arrigo t *Les vêpres siciliennes* Verdi

Henrietta, Queen/Enrichetta di Francia ms *I puritani* Bellini

Henry/Henri Smith t *La jolie fille de Perth* Bizet

Henry Morosus t *Die schweigsame Frau* Strauss, R.

Henry the Fowler, King: *see* Heinrich der Vogler

Henry VIII/Enrico b *Anna Bolena* Donizetti

Herald b *Lohengrin* Wagner

Hercules/Ercole/Hercule/Alcides/Alcide bt *Alceste* Lully; b *Alceste* Gluck; b *Giasone* Cavalli

Herdswoman ms *Jenůfa* Janáček

Hérisson de Porc-Epic bt *L'étoile* Chabrier

Hermann t *The Queen of Spades* Tchaikovsky

Hermes t *King Priam* Tippett

Hermia ms *A Midsummer Night's Dream* Britten

Hermit b *Der Freischütz* Weber

Hero/Héro s *Béatrice et Bénédict* Berlioz

Herod/Hérod/Herodes bt *Hérodiade* Massenet; t *Salome* Strauss, R.

Herodias/Hérodiade ms *Hérodiade* Massenet; ms *Salome* Strauss, R.

Herring, Mrs ms *Albert Herring* Britten

Herrmann, Landgrave b *Tannhäuser* Wagner

Hidraot bt *Armide* Gluck

High Priest bt *Hérodiade* Massenet

High Priest of Baal b *Nabucco* Verdi

High Priest of Brahma/Grand Brahmin bb *L'Africaine* Meyerbeer

High Priest of Dagon bt *Samson et Dalila* Saint-Saëns

John, Friar/Jean, Frère **b** *Roméo et Juliette* Gounod
John of Leyden **t** *Le prophète* Meyerbeer
John Sorel **bt** *The Consul* Menotti
John Styx **t** *Orphée aux enfers* Offenbach
John the Baptist/Jean/Jochanaan/Jokanaan **t** *Hérodiade* Massenet; **bt** *Salome* Strauss, R.
Johnson, Dick/Ramerrez **t** *La fanciulla del West* Puccini
Jokanaan: *see* John the Baptist
Jonas **t** *Le prophète* Meyerbeer
Jonny **bt** *Jonny spielt auf* Krenek
Jontek **t** *Halka* Moniuszko
Jorg **b** *Stiffelio* Verdi
José, Don **t** *Carmen* Bizet
José Castro **b** *La fanciulla del West* Puccini
Josef Lettner: *see* Joe
Josef Mauer **sp** *Elegy for Young Lovers* Henze
Journeyman **t** *Cardillac* Hindemith
Jouvenot, Mlle **s** *Adriana Lecouvreur* Cilea
Juan **t** *Don Quichotte* Massenet
Juan, Don **t** *The Stone Guest* Dargomïzhsky; *see also* Giovanni
Judge/Armfelt **t** *Un ballo in maschera* Verdi
Judith/Judit **ms/s** *Bluebeard's Castle* Bartók
Judy **ms** *Punch and Judy* Birtwistle
Julia: *see* Nancy
Julia Farnese **s** *Bomarzo* Ginastera
Julian, Mrs **s** *Owen Wingrave* Britten
Julien **t** *Louise* Charpentier, G.
Juliet/Juliette **s** *Roméo et Juliette* Gounod
Julius Caesar/Giulio Cesare **a** *Giulio Cesare in Egitto* Handel
Junia/Giunia **s** *Lucio Silla* Mozart
Junius **bt** *The Rape of Lucretia* Britten
Juno/Giunone/Junon **a** *Agrippina* Handel; **s** *Calisto* Cavalli; **s** *Orphée aux enfers* Offenbach; **s** *Platée* Rameau; **a** *Semele* Handel
Jupiter/Giove **b** *Calisto* Cavalli; **b** *Castor et Pollux* Rameau; **bt** *Orphée aux enfers* Offenbach; **b** *Platée* Rameau; **t** *Semele* Handel

K

Kabanicha/Marfa Ignatevna Kabanova **a** *Kát'a Kabanová* Janáček
Karolka **ms** *Jenůfa* Janáček
Kaspar **t** *Amahl and the Night Visitors* Menotti
Kate **ms** *Owen Wingrave* Britten
Kate Pinkerton **ms** *Madama Butterfly* Puccini
Kát'a/Katya/Katěrina **s** *Kát'a Kabanová* Janáček
Katerina Izmaylova **s** *Katerina Izmaylova/Lady Macbeth of the Mtsensk District* Shostakovich
Katya: *see* Kát'a
Kecal **b** *The Bartered Bride* Smetana
Kedruta **a** *The Excursions of Mr Brouček* Janáček
Khan Konchak: *see* Konchak, Khan
Khivrya **ms** *The Fair at Sorochintsï* Musorgsky
Khovansky: *see* Andrey Khovansky, Ivan Khovansky

Khrushchyov **t** *Boris Godunov* Musorgsky
Kilian **bt** *Der Freischütz* Weber
King **bt** *Cendrillon* Massenet
King Fisher **bt** *The Midsummer Marriage* Tippett
Kissinger, Henry **b** *Nixon in China* Adams
Klingsor **b** *Parsifal* Wagner
Klytemnästra: *see* Clytemnestra
Kochubey, Vasily **bt** *Mazepa* Tchaikovsky
Kolenaty, Dr **bb** *The Makropulos Affair* Janáček
Konchak, Khan **x** *Prince Igor* Borodin
Konchakovna **a** *Prince Igor* Borodin
Konstanze **s** *Die Entführung aus dem Serail* Mozart
Kostelnička Buryjovka **s** *Jenůfa* Janáček
Kothner, Fritz **b** *Die Meistersinger von Nürnberg* Wagner
Krishna, Lord **b** *Satyagraha* Glass
Kristina/Krista **s** *The Makropulos Affair* Janáček
Krušina **bt** *The Bartered Bride* Smetana
Kudrjáš, Váňa **t** *Kát'a Kabanová* Janáček
Kuligin **bt** *Kát'a Kabanová* Janáček
Kum **bt** *The Fair at Sorochintsï* Musorgsky
Kundry **ms** *Parsifal* Wagner
Kunka: *see* Málinka
Kupava **s** *The Snow Maiden* Rimsky-Korsakov
Kurwenal **bt** *Tristan und Isolde* Wagner
Kutuzov, Field Marshal **b** *War and Peace* Prokofiev
Kuz'ka **bt** *Khovanshchina* Musorgsky
Kyoto **bt** *Iris* Mascagni

L

Laca Klemen **t** *Jenůfa* Janáček
Lady **s** *Cardillac* Hindemith
Laertes/Léodès **t** *Pénélope* Fauré
La Force, Chevalier de **t** *Dialogues des Carmélites* Poulenc
La Force, Marquis de **bt** *Dialogues des Carmélites* Poulenc
La Haltière, Madame de **ms** *Cendrillon* Massenet
Lamoral, Count **b** *Arabella* Strauss, R.
Landgrave: *see* Herrmann
Laoula, Princess **s** *L'étoile* Chabrier
Lapák **ms** *The Cunning Little Vixen* Janáček
Larina, Madame **ms** *Yevgeny Onegin* Tchaikovsky
Larkens **b** *La fanciulla del West* Puccini
La Roche **b** *Capriccio* Strauss, R.
La Roche, Countess de **ms** *Die Soldaten* Zimmermann
Laura **ms** *Luisa Miller* Verdi; **ms** *The Stone Guest* Dargomïzhsky
Laura Adorno **ms** *La Gioconda* Ponchielli
Laurence, Friar/Laurent, Frère **b** *Roméo et Juliette* Gounod
Lauret **b** *The Maid of Orléans* Tchaikovsky
Lauretta **s** *Gianni Schicchi* Puccini
Lawyer **t** *Punch and Judy* Birtwistle
Lazuli **ms** *L'étoile* Chabrier
Leander **bt** *The Love for Three Oranges* Prokofiev
Leandro, King **t** *König Hirsch* Henze

Major-Domo **b** *Capriccio* Strauss, R.
Malatesta, Dr **bt** *Don Pasquale* Donizetti
Malatesta, Giovanni/Gianciotto **bt** *Francesca da Rimini* Zandonai
Malatestino **t** *Francesca da Rimini* Zandonai
Malcolm **t** *Macbeth* Verdi
Male Chorus **t** *The Rape* of *Lucretia* Britten
Málinka/Etherea/Kunka **s** *The Excursions of Mr Brouček* Janáček
Malwina **s** *Der Vampyr* Marschner
Mama McCourt **a** *The Ballad of Baby Doe* Moore
Mambre: *see* Auphis
Mamma Lucia: *see* Lucia, Mamma
Mandryka **bt** *Arabella* Strauss, R.
Manfredo **bt** *L'amore dei tre re* Montemezzi
Manfredo: *see* Mainfroid
Manon Lescaut **s** *Boulevard Solitude* Henze; **s** *Manon* Massenet; **s** *Manon Lescaut* Puccini
Manrico **t** *Il trovatore* Verdi
Manservant: *see* Prince
Mantua, Duke of **t** *Rigoletto* Verdi
Manz **bt** *A Village Romeo and Juliet* Delius
Mao Tse-tung **t** *Nixon in China* Adams
Marcel **b** *Les Huguenots* Meyerbeer
Marcellina **s** *Le nozze di Figaro* Mozart
Marcello **bt** *La bohème* Puccini
Marcius/Marzio **t** *Mitridate* Mozart
Marco **bt** *Gianni Schicchi* Puccini
Mařenka **s** *The Bartered Bride* Smetana
Marfa **ms** *Khovanshchina* Musorgsky
Marfa Kabanová: *see* Kabanicha
Margherita **s** *Mefistofele* Boito
Margiana **s** *Der Barbier von Bagdad* Cornelius
Margret **a** *Wozzeck* Berg
Marguerite **s** *Faust* Gounod
Marguerite de Valois **s** *Les Huguenots* Meyerbeer
Marianne **s** *Der Rosenkavalier* Strauss, R.
Maria Stuarda: *see* Mary Stuart
Marie **ms** *Mosè in Egitto/Moïse et Pharaon* Rossini; **s** *Die Soldaten* Zimmermann; **s** *Wozzeck* Berg; **s** *Zar und Zimmermann* Lortzing
Marie/Maria **s** *La fille du régiment* Donizetti
Marie of the Incarnation, Mother **ms** *Dialogues des Carmélites* Poulenc
Marie's Son **tr** *Wozzeck* Berg
Marina Mniszek **ms/s** *Boris Godunov* Musorgsky
Mariya **s** *Mazepa* Tchaikovsky
Mariya Bolkonskaya **ms** *War and Peace* Prokofiev
Mark **t** *The Midsummer Marriage* Tippett
Mark, King/König Marke **b** *Tristan und Isolde* Wagner
Marquis **x** *Cardillac* Hindemith; *see also* Prince
Mars **bt** *Orphée aux enfers* Offenbach
Marschallin **s** *Der Rosenkavalier* Strauss, R.
Marschallin's Major-Domo **t** *Der Rosenkavalier* Strauss, R.
Marta **ms** *Mefistofele* Boito
Martha: *see* Harriet Durham, Lady

Marthe **s** *Faust* Gounod
Marti **bt** *A Village Romeo and Juliet* Delius
Marullo **bt** *Rigoletto* Verdi
Mary **a** *Der fliegende Holländer* Wagner
Mary, Major **bt** *Die Soldaten* Zimmermann
Mary Stuart/Maria Stuarda **s** *Maria Stuarda* Donizetti
Marzelline **s** *Fidelio* Beethoven
Masaniello **t** *La muette de Portici* Auber
Masetto **b** *Don Giovanni* Mozart
Massimiliano, Count Moor **b** *I masnadieri* Verdi
Master of Ceremonies **t** *The Love for Three Oranges* Prokofiev
Mathieu **bt** *Andrea Chénier* Giordano
Mathilde **s** *Guillaume Tell* Rossini
Mathilde, Sister **ms** *Dialogues des Carmélites* Poulenc
Mathis **bt** *Mathis der Maler* Hindemith
Mathisen **bb** *Le prophète* Meyerbeer
Matt of the Mint **bb** *The Beggar's Opera*
Matteo **t** *Arabella* Strauss, R.
Maurizio **t** *Adriana Lecouvreur* Cilea
Max **t** *Der Freischütz* Weber; **t** *Jonny spielt auf* Krenek
Mayor: *see* Gottardo
Mazal/Blankytný/Petřík **t** *The Excursions of Mr Brouček* Janáček
Mazeppa/Mazepa **bt** *Mazepa* Tchaikovsky
Medea/Médée **s** *Giasone* Cavalli; **s** *Médée* Charpentier, M.-A.; **s** *Médée* Cherubini
Médor/Medoro **a** *Orlando* Handel
Medora **s** *Il corsaro* Verdi
Mefistofele **b** *Mefistofele* Boito
Meg Page, Mrs **ms** *Falstaff* Verdi
Melanto **s** *Il ritorno d'Ulisse in patria* Monteverdi; **ms** *Ulisse* Dallapiccola
Melchior **bt** *Amahl and the Night Visitors* Menotti
Melcthal **b** *Guillaume Tell* Rossini; *see also* Arnold Melcthal
Melibeo **b** *La fedeltà premiata* Haydn
Mélisande **s** *Ariane et Barbe-bleue* Dukas; **s** *Pelléas et Mélisande* Debussy
Mélisse **s** *Atys* Lully; *see also* Demon (Mélisse)
Melisso **b** *Alcina* Handel
Melitone, Fra **b** *La forza del destino* Verdi
Melot **t** *Tristan und Isolde* Wagner
Melpomene/Melpomène **s** *Atys* Lully
Menelaus/Ménélas **t** *La belle Hélène* Offenbach
Mephistopheles/Méphistophélès **b** *Faust* Gounod; **t** *The Fiery Angel* Prokofiev; *see also* Mefistofele
Mercédès **s** *Carmen* Bizet
Mercury/Mercure/Mercurio **t** *Calisto* Cavalli; **t** *Orphée aux enfers* Offenbach; **hc** *Platée* Rameau; **bb** *Les Troyens* Berlioz
Mercutio **bt** *Roméo et Juliette* Gounod
Mescalina **ms** *Le Grand Macabre* Ligeti
Messenger **bb** *Oedipus rex* Stravinsky
Micaëla **s** *Carmen* Bizet
Mícha **b** *The Bartered Bride* Smetana
Michele **bt** *Il tabarro* Puccini

Norina **s** *Don Pasquale* Donizetti

Norma **s** *Norma* Bellini

Normanno **t** *Lucia di Lammermoor* Donizetti

Norns **a** *Götterdämmerung* Wagner

Norwich, Recorder of **b** *Gloriana* Britten

Notary **b** *Don Pasquale* Donizetti

Nourabad **b** *Les pêcheurs de perles* Bizet

Novice **t** *Billy Budd* Britten

Nureddin **t** *Der Barbier von Bagdad* Cornelius

Nurse/Nutrice **ms** *Boris Godunov* Musorgsky; **ms** *Die Frau ohne Schatten* Strauss, R.; **a** *L'incoronazione di Poppea* Monteverdi

O

Oberon **ct** *A Midsummer Night's Dream* Britten; **t** *Oberon* Weber

Oberthal, Count **b** *Le prophète* Meyerbeer

Oberto **tr** *Alcina* Handel

Obrist **b** *Die Soldaten* Zimmermann

Ochs auf Lerchenau, Baron **b** *Der Rosenkavalier* Strauss, R.

Octavia/Ottavia **s** *L'incoronazione di Poppea* Monteverdi

Octavian, Count Rofrano **s/ms** *Der Rosenkavalier* Strauss, R.

Odabella **s** *Attila* Verdi

Odoardo **t** *Ariodante* Handel

Oedipus **t** *Oedipus rex* Stravinsky

Oenone **s** *Hippolyte et Aricie* Rameau

Officer **t** *Cardillac* Hindemith

Okean-More/Sea King **b** *Sadko* Rimsky-Korsakov

Old Convict **b** *Lady Macbeth of the Mtsensk District* Shostakovich

Old Hebrew **b** *Samson et Dalila* Saint-Saëns

Old Prioress: see Croissy, Madame de

Old Woman **ms/a** *Der ferne Klang* Schreker

Olga **a** *Yevgeny Onegin* Tchaikovsky

Olivier **bt** *Capriccio* Strauss, R.

Olympia **s** *Les contes d'Hoffmann* Offenbach

Opera Singer **s** *Cardillac* Hindemith

Opinion Publique **ms** *Orphée aux enfers* Offenbach

Oracle **b** *Idomeneo* Mozart

Oracle of the Dead/Hecate **s** *The Mask of Orpheus* Birtwistle

Orator: see Speaker

Orbazzano **b** *Tancredi* Rossini

Orestes/Orest/Oreste **ms** *La belle Hélène* Offenbach; **bt** *Elektra* Strauss, R.; **b** *Giasone* Cavalli; **bt** *Iphigénie en Tauride* Gluck

Orestes' Tutor **b** *Elektra* Strauss, R.

Orfeo: see Orpheus

Orlando **a** *Orlando* Handel

Orlik **b** *Mazepa* Tchaikovsky

Orlofsky, Prince **ms** *Die Fledermaus* Strauss, J.

Oroe **b** *Semiramide* Rossini

Orombello **t** *Beatrice di Tenda* Bellini

Oronte **t** *Alcina* Handel; **t** *I Lombardi* Verdi; **bt** *Médée* Charpentier, M.-A.

Oroveso **b** *Norma* Bellini

Orpheus/Orfeo/Orphée **bt** *The Mask of Orpheus* Birtwistle; **t** *Orfeo* Monteverdi; **a** *Orfeo ed Euridice/Orphée et Eurydice* Gluck; **t** *Orphée aux enfers* Offenbach

Orsini, Gian Conrado: see Gian Conrado Orsini

Orsini, Maffio: see Maffio Orsini

Orsini, Paolo **b** *Rienzi* Wagner

Orsini, Pier Francesco: see Pier Francesco Orsini

Ortel, Hermann **b** *Die Meistersinger von Nürnberg* Wagner

Ortensio: see Hortensius

Ortlinde **s** *Die Walküre* Wagner

Ortrud **ms** *Lohengrin* Wagner

Ory, Count **t** *Le comte Ory* Rossini

Osaka **t** *Iris* Mascagni

Oscar **s** *Un ballo in maschera* Verdi

Osiris/Osiride **b** *Mosè in Egitto/Moïse et Pharaon* Rossini

Osman **b** *Les Indes galantes* Rameau

Osmin **b** *Die Entführung aus dem Serail* Mozart

Osmina, Sister **s** *Suor Angelica* Puccini

Ostasio **bt** *Francesca da Rimini* Zandonai

Otello/Othello **t** *Otello* Verdi

Otho/Ottone **a** *Agrippina* Handel; **ms** *L'incoronazione di Poppea* Monteverdi

Ottavia: see Octavia

Ottavio, Don **t** *Don Giovanni* Mozart

Otto **t** *Bánk bán* Erkel

Ottokar **bt** *Der Freischütz* Weber

Ottone: see Otho

Ouf I, King **t** *L'étoile* Chabrier

Ourrias **bt** *Mireille* Gounod

Ovlur **t** *Prince Igor* Borodin

Owen Wingrave: see Wingrave, Owen

Owl **a** *The Cunning Little Vixen* Janáček

Oxana **s** *Christmas Eve* Rimsky-Korsakov

P

Padre Guardiano **b** *La forza del destino* Verdi

Pagano **b** *I Lombardi* Verdi

Page **bt** *Amahl and the Night Visitors* Menotti

Page, Mrs/Reich, Frau **ms** *Die lustigen Weiber von Windsor* Nicolai

Page/Reich **b** *Die lustigen Weiber von Windsor* Nicolai

Pagliaccio: see Canio

Painter/Negro **t** *Lulu* Berg

Palémon **b** *Thaïs* Massenet

Palestrina, Giovanni Pierluigi da **t** *Palestrina* Pfitzner

Pallas/Pallante **b** *Agrippina* Handel

Pamina **s** *Die Zauberflöte* Mozart

Panas **b** *Christmas Eve* Rimsky-Korsakov

Pandarus **t** *Troilus and Cressida* Walton

Pandolfe **b** *Cendrillon* Massenet

Pang **t** *Turandot* Puccini

Pompeo **bt** *Benvenuto Cellini* Berlioz

Pong **t** *Turandot* Puccini

Poppaea/Poppea **s** *Agrippina* Handel; **s** *L'incoronazione di Poppea* Monteverdi

Porgy **bb** *Porgy and Bess* Gershwin

Posa, Marquis of/Rodrigo/Rodrigue **bt** *Don Carlos* Verdi

Poussette **s** *Manon* Massenet

Poyarok, Fyodor **bt** *Legend of the Invisible City of Kitezh* Rimsky-Korsakov

Premier Ministre **b** *Cendrillon* Massenet

Pretender/Grigory/Dmitry **t** *Boris Godunov* Musorgsky

Pretty Polly **s** *Punch and Judy* Birtwistle

Preziosilla **ms** *La forza del destino* Verdi

Priam **bb** *King Priam* Tippett; **b** *Les Troyens* Berlioz

Priest **b** *The Cunning Little Vixen* Janáček; **bt** *From the House of the Dead* Janáček; **b** *Moses und Aron* Schoenberg

Prilepa **s** *The Queen of Spades* Tchaikovsky

Prima Donna/Ariadne **s** *Ariadne auf Naxos* Strauss, R.

Prince **t** *The Love for Three Oranges* Prokofiev; **t** *Rusalka* Dvořák

Prince Charmant/Charming **s** *Cendrillon* Massenet

Prince/Manservant/Marquis **t** *Lulu* Berg

Princess **s** *L'enfant et les sortilèges* Ravel; **a** *Suor Angelica* Puccini

Prison Governor **b** *From the House of the Dead* Janáček

Procida, Jean **b** *Les vêpres siciliennes* Verdi

Professor of Medicine/Banker/Professor **sp/b/x** *Lulu* Berg

Prosdocimo **b** *Il turco in Italia* Rossini

Proserpina, Proserpine: *see* Persephone

Prostitute **ms** *From the House of the Dead* Janáček

Prunier **t** *La Rondine* Puccini

Prus, Baron **bt** *The Makropulos Affair* Janáček

Ptolemy/Tolomeo **a** *Giulio Cesare in Egitto* Handel

Publius/Publio **b** *La clemenza di Tito* Mozart

Puck **x** *A Midsummer Night's Dream* Britten; **ms** *Oberon* Weber

Punch **bt** *Punch and Judy* Birtwistle

Pylades/Pilade **t** *Iphigénie en Tauride* Gluck

Q

Queen of Night **s** *Die Zauberflöte* Mozart

Queen of the Earth Spirits **s** *Hans Heiling* Marschner

Quichotte, Don **b** *Don Quichotte* Massenet

Quickly, Mistress **ms** *Falstaff* Verdi

Quinault **b** *Adriana Lecouvreur* Cilea

Quince **b** *A Midsummer Night's Dream* Britten

Quinquin: *see* Octavian

Quint, Peter **t** *The Turn of the Screw* Britten

R

Rachel **s** *La Juive* Halévy

Radames **t** *Aida* Verdi

Radamisto **s** *Radamisto* Handel

Raffaele von Leuthold **t** *Stiffelio* Verdi

Ragonde **ms** *Le comte Ory* Rossini

Raimbaud **bt** *Le comte Ory* Rossini

Raimondo Bidebent **b** *Lucia di Lammermoor* Donizetti

Raimondo, Cardinal **b** *Rienzi* Wagner

Rakewell, Tom **t** *The Rake's Progress* Stravinsky

Raleigh, Sir Walter **b** *Gloriana* Britten

Ralph **b/bt** *La jolie fille de Perth* Bizet

Rambaldo Fernandez **bt** *La Rondine* Puccini

Ramerrez: *see* Johnson, Dick

Ramfis **b** *Aida* Verdi

Ramiro **t** *La Cenerentola* Rossini; **ms** *La finta giardiniera* Mozart; **bt** *L'heure espagnole* Ravel

Ramia, Emir of **b** *I Lombardi/Jérusalem* Verdi

Ramon, Maître **b** *Mireille* Gounod

Rance, Jack **bt** *La fanciulla del West* Puccini

Rangoni **b** *Boris Godunov* Musorgsky

Raoul de Nangis **t** *Les Huguenots* Meyerbeer

Ratcliffe, Lieutenant **b** *Billy Budd* Britten

Ratmir **a** *Ruslan and Lyudmila* Glinka

Raymond **t** *I Lombardi/Jérusalem* Verdi; **t** *The Maid of Orléans* Tchaikovsky

Rector: *see* Horace Adams, Rev.

Red Whiskers **t** *Billy Budd* Britten

Redburn, Mr **bt** *Billy Budd* Britten

Regina **s** *Mathis der Maler* Hindemith

Reich, Frau: *see* Page, Mrs

Reich: *see* Page

Reinmar von Zweter **b** *Tannhäuser* Wagner

Reiza **s** *Oberon* Weber

Remendado **t** *Carmen* Bizet

Renata **s** *The Fiery Angel* Prokofiev

Renato/Anckarstroem **bt** *Un ballo in maschera* Verdi

Renaud **t** *Armide* Gluck

René, King **b** *Iolanta* Tchaikovsky

Resi **s** *Intermezzo* Strauss, R.

Ribbing/Samuel **b** *Un ballo in maschera* Verdi

Riccardo, Don **t** *Ernani* Verdi

Riccardo Forth, Sir **b** *I puritani* Bellini

Riccardo/Gustavus III **t** *Un ballo in maschera* Verdi

Rich, Lady: *see* Penelope

Riedinger **b** *Mathis der Maler* Hindemith

Rienzi, Cola **t** *Rienzi* Wagner

Rigoletto **bt** *Rigoletto* Verdi

Rinaldo **t** *Armida* Haydn; **ms** *Rinaldo* Handel

Rinuccio **t** *Gianni Schicchi* Puccini

Rizzardo del Maino **t** *Beatrice di Tenda* Bellini

Robert **bt** *Iolanta* Tchaikovsky; *see also* Storch, Robert

Roberto/Nardo **bt** *La finta giardiniera* Mozart

Robert/Roberto **bt** *Les vêpres siciliennes* Verdi

Robert Devereux: *see* Essex, Earl of

Robinson, Count **b** *Il matrimonio segreto* Cimarosa

Rocco **b** *Fidelio* Beethoven

Rochefort **b** *Anna Bolena* Donizetti

Rodelinda **s** *Rodelinda* Handel

Roderigo **t** *Otello* Verdi

Index of Incipits of Arias, Ensembles, etc.

This appendix is an index of first lines of arias, duets and other ensembles and choruses, designed to enable the user to look up the opening words of any item from an opera and find its source. Each entry gives the singer (or singers, for an ensemble), the short title of the opera, the act (if an opera with scene numbers but not acts, the number is in small roman type) and the composer. The arrangement is strictly alphabetical, including the definite or indefinite article and disregarding any punctuation; where two numbers have the same incipit they are alphabetized by the titles of the operas they come from.

This index is inevitably highly selective. The objective here has been to include well-known 'detachable' numbers from the basic repertory operas and a generous selection of the more significant items from fringe-repertory works. For arias (or duets etc.) comprising more than one section, first lines may be given of later sections (such as cabalettas) where these are familiar; so may the first lines of introductory recitatives. Numbers known by titles (Bell Song, Anvil Chorus) are also included, usually as cross-references. Numbers are normally cited in their original language but a few familiar translated first lines are also given.

The list is mostly confined to English, French, German and Italian; no transliterated Russian, nor other Slavonic works, are included, though – bearing in mind that this list is intended primarily for the English-speaking reader – a selection of well-known items from this repertory is included where a familiar English translation exists.

A

Abendlich strahlt der Sonne Auge (Wotan) *Das Rheingold* iv Wagner

Abends will ich schlafen gehn (Gretel, Hänsel) *Hänsel und Gretel* 2 Humperdinck

Aber der Richtige (Arabella, Zdenka) *Arabella* 1 Strauss, R.

Above measure is the pleasure (Juno) *Semele* 3 Handel

A brani, a brani, o perfido (Luisa) *Luisa Miller* 2 Verdi

Abscheulicher! . . . Komm Hoffnung . . . Ich folg' dem innern Triebe (Leonore) *Fidelio* 1 Beethoven

Abuso forse . . . Mira, di acerbe lagrime . . . Vivrà! Contende il giubilo (Leonora, Luna) *Il trovatore* 4 Verdi

Accablé de regrets (Orpheus) *Orphée et Eurydice* 1 Gluck

Accogli, oh re del mar (Idomeneus, chorus) *Idomeneo* 3 Mozart

A celui que jamais (Elvire) *La muette de Portici* 1 Auber

A ce mot seul s'anime (Marguerite de Valois) *Les Huguenots* 2 Meyerbeer

Acerba voluttà, dolce tortura (Princess of Bouillon) *Adriana Lecouvreur* 2 Cilea

A cette fête conviée (Monsieur Triquet) *Yevgeny Onegin* 2 Tchaikovsky

A cette heure suprême (Werther, Charlotte) *Werther* 4 Massenet

Ach Belmonte! ach mein Leben (Konstanze, Belmonte, Blonde, Pedrillo) *Die Entführung aus dem Serail* 2 Mozart

Ach, das Leid hab' ich getragen (Nureddin) *Der Barbier von Bagdad* 1 Cornelius

Ach! du bist wieder da (Marschallin, Octavian) *Der Rosenkavalier* 1 Strauss, R.

Ach Herr, dass ich es offen sag (Aminta) *Die schweigsame Frau* 2 Strauss, R.

Ach, ich fühl's (Pamina) *Die Zauberflöte* 2 Mozart

Ach, ich liebte (Konstanze) *Die Entführung aus dem Serail* 1 Mozart

Ach, so fromm (Lyonel) *Martha* 3 Flotow

Ach wir armen, armen Leute (Peter) *Hänsel und Gretel* 1 Humperdinck

Ach! wo war ich? (Ariadne, Nymphs) *Ariadne auf Naxos* Strauss, R.

Adamastor, roi des vagues profondes (Nélusko) *L'Africaine* 3 Meyerbeer

Addio, del passato (Violetta) *La traviata* 3 Verdi

Addio, dolce svegliare (Mimì, Rodolfo, Marcello, Musetta) *La bohème* 3 Puccini

Addio, fiorito asil (Pinkerton) *Madama Butterfly* 2 Puccini

Addio Firenze, addio, cielo divino (Gianni Schicchi, ensemble) *Gianni Schicchi* Puccini

Addio, mia vita (Italian Singers) *Capriccio* Strauss, R.

Addio, speranza ed anima (Duke, Gilda) *Rigoletto* 1 Verdi

Adieu, conservez dans votre âme (Iphigenia) *Iphigénie en Aulide* 3 Gluck

Adieu, fière cité (Dido) *Les Troyens* 5 Berlioz

Adieu mon beau rivage (Inès) *L'Africaine* 1 Meyerbeer

Adieu, notre petite table (Manon) *Manon* 2 Massenet

Adina, credimi (Nemorino, Adina, Belcore) *L'elisir d'amore* 1 Donizetti

Ah quel respect madame (Ory, Adèle) *Le comte Ory* 2 Rossini

Ah, scostati! . . . Smanie implacabili (Dorabella) *Così fan tutte* 1 Mozart

Ah se a morir mi chiama (Cecilius) *Lucio Silla* 2 Mozart

Ah, se fosse intorno (Titus) *La clemenza di Tito* 1 Mozart

Ah! segnar invano io tento (Argirio) *Tancredi* 2 Rossini

Ah, segnasti la tua sorte (Don Carlo, Don Alvaro) *La forza del destino* 4 Verdi

Ah! segnata è la mia sorte (Anne Boleyn, ensemble) *Anna Bolena* 1 Donizetti

Ah! seguirti fino agl'ultimi confini (Don Alvaro, Leonora) *La forza del destino* 1 Verdi

Ah se il crudel periglio (Junia) *Lucio Silla* 2 Mozart

Ah! se la speme . . . Figlia! a tal nome io palpito (Amelia, Boccanegra) *Simon Boccanegra* 1 Verdi

Ah! se un giorno (Mary, Leicester, ensemble) *Maria Stuarda* 2/3 Donizetti

Ah! se un'urna è a me concessa . . . Ah la morte (Beatrice) *Beatrice di Tenda* 2 Bellini

Ah sì, ben mio, coll'essere . . . Di quella pira (Manrico) *Il trovatore* 3 Verdi

Ah! sì, fa core e abbracciami (Adalgisa, Norma) *Norma* 1 Bellini

Ah! si la liberté me doit être ravie (Armide) *Armide* 3 Gluck

Ah! si maledetto, sospeno fatale (Philip II, Posa, Eboli, Elisabetta di Valois) *Don Carlo* 3/4 Verdi

Ah! speranza dolce ancora (Lucrezia Contarini, Jacopo Foscari) *I due Foscari* 2 Verdi

Ah taci, ingiusto core (Don Giovanni, Leporello, Donna Elvira) *Don Giovanni* 2 Mozart

Ah! the world's not what it was . . . Je crains de lui parler (Countess) *Queen of Spades* 2 Tchaikovsky

Ah! veglia o donna (Rigoletto, Gilda) *Rigoletto* 1 Verdi

Ah! vivre deux (Hoffmann) *Les contes d'Hoffmann* 2 Offenbach

Ai-je dit vrai . . . Ah! qu'il est loin (Werther, Charlotte) *Werther* 2 Massenet

Ai nostri monti (Azucena, Manrico) *Il trovatore* 4 Verdi

Air des larmes: *see* Va! laisse couler mes larmes

Alabama Song: *see* O moon of Alabama

A la faveur de cette nuit (Ory, Adèle, Isolier) *Le comte Ory* 2 Rossini

A l'aspect de ce nuage (Plataea) *Platée* 2 Rameau

A la voix d'un amant fidèle (Henry Smith) *La jolie fille de Perth* 2 Bizet

Albert the Good (ensemble) *Albert Herring* 2 Britten

Alcide est vainqueur du trépas (chorus) *Alceste* 5 Lully

Al dolce guidami castel natio . . . Cielo, a miei lunghi spasimi . . . Coppia iniqua (Anne Boleyn, ensemble) *Anna Bolena* 2 Donizetti

Alfin son tua . . . Spargi d'amaro pianto (Lucia, ensemble) *Lucia di Lammermoor* 3 Donizetti

Al lampo dell'armi (Julius Caesar) *Giulio Cesare* 3 Handel

Alla vita che t'arride (Renato [Captain Anckarstroem]) *Un ballo in maschera* 1 Verdi

Allein! Weh, ganz allein (Electra) *Elektra* Strauss

Alle più calde immagini (Arsace, Semiramide) *Semiramide* 1 Rossini

All'idea di qual metallo (Figaro, Almaviva) *Il barbiere di Siviglia* 1 Rossini

Allmächt'ge Jungfrau (Elisabeth) *Tannhäuser* 3 Wagner

Allmächt'ger Vater (Rienzi) *Rienzi* 5 Wagner

Allons, allons, accourez tous (Attis, chorus) *Atys* 1 Lully

Allor che i forti corrono . . . Da te questo (Odabella) *Attila* prol. Verdi

Al mio piè, perchè . . . Di qual anzor (Don Carlo, Elisabetta di Valois) *Don Carlo* 1 Verdi

Al mio pregar t'arrendi (Semiramide) *Semiramide* 2 Rossini

A lonely Arab maid (Fatima) *Oberon* 2 Weber

Als Büblein klein (Falstaff) *Die lustigen Weiber von Windsor* 2 Nicolai

Als du in kühnem Sange . . . War's Zauber, war es reine Macht (Wolfram) *Tannhäuser* 1 Wagner

Als ein Gott kam Jeder gegangen (Zerbinetta) *Ariadne auf Naxos* Strauss, R.

Als junger Liebe Lust mir verblich (Wotan, Brünnhilde) *Die Walküre* 2 Wagner

Al suon del tamburo (Preziosilla) *La forza del destino* 2 Verdi

Als zullendes Kind (Mime) *Siegfried* 1 Wagner

Alzati . . . Eri tu (Renato [Captain Anckarstroem]) *Un ballo in maschera* 3 Verdi

Amai, ma un solo istante . . . Or del padre benedetta (Joan of Arc, Giacomo) *Giovanna d'Arco* 3 Verdi

Amami, Alfredo (Violetta) *La traviata* 2 Verdi

Ama, sospira, mà non ti offende (Morgana) *Alcina* 2 Handel

Amenaide . . . serbami tua fé (Tancredi) *Tancredi* 2 Rossini

Ami! . . . le coeur d'Hélène (Hélène) *Les vêpres siciliennes* 4 Verdi

Amis, la matinée est belle (Masaniello) *La muette de Portici* 2 Auber

Amis, l'amour tendre et rêveur, erreur! (Hoffmann) *Les contes d'Hoffmann* 3 Offenbach

Am Jordan Sankt Johannes stand (David) *Die Meistersinger* 3 Wagner

A moi les plaisirs (Faust, Méphistophélès) *Faust* 1 Gounod

Amore misterio celeste (Faust, Helen of Troy) *Mefistofele* 4 Boito

Amor è qual vento (Dorinda) *Orlando* 3 Handel

Amore, vieni a me (Glaucus) *Medea* 1 Cherubini

Amour, lance tes traits (Folly) *Platée* 3 Rameau

Amour! viens aider ma faiblesse (Delilah) *Samson et Dalila* 2 Saint-Saëns

Am stillen Herd (Walther, ensemble) *Die Meistersinger* 1 Wagner

Anch'io dischiuso un giorno . . . Salgo già del trono aurato (Abigaille) *Nabucco* 2 Verdi

Ancor non giunse? . . . Regnava nel silenzio . . . Quando rapito in estasi (Lucia) *Lucia di Lammermoor* 1 Donizetti

And do you prefer the storm to Auntie's parlour (Balstrode, Peter Grimes) *Peter Grimes* 1 Britten

And now we summon from this leafy bower (Spirit of the Masque, chorus) *Gloriana* 2 Britten

Andrem, raminghi e poveri (Luisa, Miller) *Luisa Miller* 3 Verdi

Andrò, ramingo e solo (Ilia, Electra, Idamantes, Idomeneus) *Idomeneo* 3 Mozart

Ange adorable (Romeo, Juliet) *Roméo et Juliette* 1 Gounod

Anges du paradis (Vincent) *Mireille* 5 Gounod

Ange si pur (Fernand) *La favorite* 4 Donizetti

Anges purs, anges radieux (Marguerite, Faust, Méphistophélès) *Faust* 5 Gounod

A nous les amours et les roses (Manon) *Manon* 4 Massenet

Answer me, bright orb (Queen of Shemakha) *The Golden Cockerel* 2 Rimsky-Korsakov

Anvil Chorus: *see* Vedi! le fosche notturne

Apparvi alla luce (Maria, Sulpizio) *La figlia del reggimento* 1 Donizetti

Apri la tua finestra! (Osaka) *Iris* 1 Mascagni

Aprite, presto aprite (Susanna, Cherubino) *Le nozze di Figaro* 2 Mozart

Aprite un po' quegl'occhi (Figaro) *Le nozze di Figaro* 4 Mozart

A quanto peni! ma pur fa core (ensemble) *La traviata* 2 Verdi

A quoi bon l'économie . . . O Rosalinde (Lescaut) *Manon* 3 Massenet

Arbitre d'une vie (Elvire) *La muette de Portici* 4 Auber

Arbitre suprême du ciel et de la terre (Moses) *Moïse et Pharaon* 2 Rossini

Ardon gl'incensi . . . splendon le sacre faci . . . Alfin son tua . . . Spargi d'amaro pianto (Lucia, ensemble) *Lucia di Lammermoor* 3 Donizetti

Ardo, sospiro e piango (Diana) *Calisto* 1 Cavalli

Arrêtez, ô mes frères (Samson) *Samson et Dalila* 1 Saint-Saëns

Arrigo! ah parli a un core . . . È dolce raggio (Arrigo, Elena) *I vespri siciliani* 4 Verdi

Art thou troubled: *see* Dove sei, amato bene

Asile héréditaire (Arnold Melcthal) *Guillaume Tell* 4 Rossini

As I said to you [Jak vám pravím pane kmotře] (Kecal, Ludmila, Krušina) *The Bartered Bride* 1 Smetana

Aspetta, aspetta, cara sposina (Malatesta, Don Pasquale) *Don Pasquale* 3 Donizetti

Assassini! (Enzo) *La Gioconda* 1 Ponchielli

Astres étincelants (Phanuel) *Hérodiade* 3 Massenet

A suoi piedi, padre essangue (Bajazet) *Tamerlano* 2 Handel

As when the dove laments her love (Galatea) *Acis and Galatea* 1 Handel

A tanto amor (Alfonso XI) *La favorita* 3 Donizetti

A te Furie, volate a me (Medea) *Medea* 3 Cherubini

A te grave cagion m'adduce . . . Rivedrai le foreste imbalsamate . . . Su dunque! . . . Padre! a costoro (Amonasro, Aida) *Aida* 3 Verdi

A te, o cara (Arturo, Elvira, ensemble) *I puritani* 1 Bellini

A terra . . . sì . . . nel livido fango (Desdemona, ensemble) *Otello* 3 Verdi

Atys est trop heureux! (Sangaride) *Atys* 1 Lully

Au bonheur dont mon âme est pleine . . . Mais celle qui devint ma femme (Albert, Werther) *Werther* 2 Massenet

Au bruit de la guerre (Marie, Sulpice Pingot) *La fille du régiment* 1 Donizetti

Auf, Gesellen, greift zur Axt (Peter the Great) *Zar und Zimmermann* 1 Lortzing

Auf hohem Felsen (Erik) *Der fliegende Holländer* 2 Wagner

Au fond du temple saint (Nadir, Zurga) *Les pêcheurs de perles* 1 Bizet

Augelletti che cantate (Almirena) *Rinaldo* 1 Handel

A un dottor della mia sorte (Bartolo) *Il barbiere di Siviglia* 1 Rossini

Au palais des fées (Eboli) *Don Carlos* 2 Verdi

Aure, deh, per pietà (Julius Caesar) *Giulio Cesare* 3 Handel

Au revoir dans un monde (Elisabeth de Valois, Don Carlos) *Don Carlos* 5 Verdi

Au sein de la puissance (Montfort) *Les vêpres siciliennes* 3 Verdi

Aussi nombreux que les étoiles (Zacharie) *Le prophète* 3 Meyerbeer

Aux langueurs d'Apollon (Folly) *Platée* 2 Rameau

Avant de quitter ces lieux (Valentin) *Faust* 2 Gounod

Ave Maria (Desdemona) *Otello* 4 Verdi

Ave signor (Mefistofele, chorus) *Mefistofele* prol. Boito

Avete torto . . . Firenze è come un albero fiorito (Rinuccio) *Gianni Schicchi* Puccini

A voti così ardente (Maria, Tonio) *La figlia del reggimento* 1 Donizetti

Avvezza al contento (Orpheus, Eurydice) *Orfeo ed Euridice* 3 Gluck

A woman is a sometime thing (Jake) *Porgy and Bess* 1 Gershwin

B

Bagnato dalle lagrime (Gualtiero, Imogene) *Il pirata* 1 Bellini

Bambina, non ti crucciar (Michonnet, Adriana) *Adriana Lecouvreur* 4 Cilea

Bannis la crainte (Admetus) *Alceste* 2 Gluck

Barbara! io ben lo sò (Oberto) *Alcina* 3 Handel

Barbaro! partirò (Polissena) *Radamisto* 3 Handel

Barcarolle: *see* Belle nuit, ô nuit d'amour

Basta che sol tu chieda (Claudius) *Agrippina* 2 Handel

Basta che sol tu chieda (Argante) *Rinaldo* 2 Handel

Batti, batti (Zerlina) *Don Giovanni* 1 Mozart

Beauté divine, enchanteresse (Raoul, Marguerite de Valois) *Les Huguenots* 2 Meyerbeer

Beckmesser's Serenade: *see* Den Tag seh' ich erscheinen

Bei Männern (Pamina, Papageno) *Die Zauberflöte* 1 Mozart

Bella Asteria, il tuo cor (Andronicus) *Tamerlano* 1 Handel

Bella figlia dell'amore (Duke, Gilda, Maddalena, Rigoletto) *Rigoletto* 3 Verdi

Bella Italia (Selim) *Il turco in Italia* 1 Rossini

Bella siccome un angelo (Dr Malatesta) *Don Pasquale* 1 Donizetti

Belle nuit, ô nuit d'amour (Giulietta, Nicklausse) *Les contes d'Hoffmann* 4 Offenbach

Bel piacere e godere (Poppaea) *Agrippina* 3 Handel

Bel piacere e godere (Almirena) *Rinaldo* 3 Handel

Bel raggio lusinghier (Semiramide) *Semiramide* 1 Rossini

Bel sogno beato (Riccardo) *I puritani* 1 Bellini

Benchè mi sprezzi (Andronicus) *Tamerlano* 1 Handel

Ben io t'invenni . . . Anch'io dischiuso un giorno . . . Salgo già del trono aurato (Abigaille) *Nabucco* 2 Verdi

Bess, you is my woman (Porgy, Bess) *Porgy and Bess* 2 Gershwin

Bethörte! (Eglantine) *Euryanthe* 1 Weber

Bimba dagli occhi pieni di malià (Pinkerton, Butterfly) *Madama Butterfly* 1 Puccini

Bin Akademiker (Barber, Nureddin) *Der Barbier von Bagdad* 1 Cornelius

Birdcatcher's Song: *see* Der Vogelfänger bin ich ja

Bleib und wache bis sie dich ruft (Emperor, Nurse) *Die Frau ohne Schatten* 1 Strauss, R.

Blick' ich umher (Wolfram) *Tannhäuser* 2 Wagner

Blickt sein Auge doch so ehrlich (Lady Harriet, Lyonel) *Martha* 2 Flotow

Blühenden Lebens labendes Blut (Siegfried, Gunther) *Götterdämmerung* 1 Wagner

Bolero: *see* Mercè, dilette amiche/Merci, jeunes amies

Bramo di trionfar (Ruggiero) *Alcina* 1 Handel

Brangäne's Watch: *see* Einsam wachend in der Nacht

Bridal March: *see* Treulich geführt

Brillant auteur de la lumière (Agamemnon) *Iphigénie en Aulide* 1 Gluck

Brillant soleil (Huascar) *Les Indes galantes* 2 Rameau

Brillez, astres nouveaux (Planet) *Castor et Pollux* 5 Rameau

Brindisi: *see* Libiamo ne' lieti calici; Viva il vino spumeggiante

Brisons tous nos fers (chorus) *Castor et Pollux* 3 Rameau

Brothers, into the storm (Sobinin) *A Life for the Tsar* 4 Glinka

Brüderchen komm tanz mit mir (Gretel, Hänsel) *Hänsel und Gretel* 1 Humperdinck

Brünnhilde's Immolation: *see* Starke Scheite

Buona sera, mio signore (Rosina, Almaviva, Figaro, Don Basilio, Bartolo) *Il barbiere di Siviglia* 2 Rossini

But hark! the heavenly sphere turns round (Ino) *Semele* 2 Handel

By the walls of Kazan (Varlaam) *Boris Godunov* iv/1 Musorgsky

C

Cade il mondo soggiogato (Claudius) *Agrippina* 2 Handel

Caduto è il reprobo! (Amalia, Carlo, Massimiliano) *I masnadieri* 4 Verdi

Calchas, d'un trait mortel percé (Achilles) *Iphigénie en Aulide* 3 Gluck

Calore! Luce! Amor! (chorus) *Iris* 1 Mascagni

Cara è vero (Rinaldo) *Armida* 2 Haydn

Cara non dubitar . . . Io ti lascio (Carolina, Paolino) *Il matrimonio segreto* 1 Cimarosa

Cara patria, già madre (Foresto) *Attila* prol. Verdi

Cara sposa, amante cara (Rinaldo) *Rinaldo* 1 Handel

Cara sposa, amato bene (Radamisto) *Radamisto* 1 Handel

Carlo! io muoio (Amalia, Massimiliano) *I masnadieri* 1 Verdi

Carlo vive? (Amalia) *I masnadieri* 2 Verdi

Caro! bella! più amabile beltà (Cleopatra, Julius Caesar) *Giulio Cesare* 3 Handel

Caro nome (Gilda) *Rigoletto* 1 Verdi

Cassio's Dream: *see* Era la notte

Casta diva . . . Ah! bello, a me ritorna (Norma) *Norma* 1 Bellini

Catalogue aria: *see* Madamina, il catalogo è questo

Cease to beauty to be suing (Polyphemus) *Acis and Galatea* 2 Handel

Cease your funning (Polly) *Beggar's Opera* 2

C'è a Windsor una dama (Ford, Falstaff) *Falstaff* 2 Verdi

Cedo al destin orribile (Imogene, Gualtiero, Ernesto) *Il pirata* 2 Bellini

Ce fauteuil (King Ouf I) *L'étoile* 1 Chabrier

Celeste Aida (Radames) *Aida* 1 Verdi

Cercherò lontana terra (Ernesto) *Don Pasquale* 2 Donizetti

Cerco il mio ben così (Orpheus) *Orfeo ed Euridice* 1 Gluck

Cerco in vano di placare (Andronicus) *Tamerlano* 2 Handel

Ces lettres! (Charlotte) *Werther* 3 Massenet

Cessa di più resistere . . . Ah il più lieto (Almaviva) *Il barbiere di Siviglia* 2 Rossini

Con rauco mormorio (Bertarido) *Rodelinda* 2 Handel

Consider, fond shepherd (Damon) *Acis and Galatea* 2 Handel

Consolati, o bella (Dorinda, Angelica, Medoro) *Orlando* 1 Handel

Contente-toi d'une victime (Theseus, Tisiphone) *Hippolyte et Aricie* 2 Rameau

Contro un cor (Rosina) *Il barbiere di Siviglia* 2 Rossini

Convien partir (Maria) *La figlia del reggimento* 1 Donizetti

Coperta la frode di lana servile (Polinesso) *Ariodante* 1 Handel

Coppia iniqua (Anne Boleyn, ensemble) *Anna Bolena* 2 Donizetti

Coraggio, su, coraggio (Elena) *I vespri siciliani* 1 Verdi

Cor di padre e cor d'amante (Asteria) *Tamerlano* 3 Handel

Cor ingrato, ti rammembri (Rinaldo) *Rinaldo* 1 Handel

Cortigiani, vil razza dannata (Rigoletto) *Rigoletto* 2 Verdi

Cosa sento (Count Almaviva, Susanna, Don Basilio) *Le nozze di Figaro* 1 Mozart

Could it then have been known (Anne, Tom, Baba) *The Rake's Progress* 2 Stravinsky

Couplets du pal: *see* Ce fauteuil

Courage! . . . du courage (Hélène) *Les vêpres siciliennes* 1 Verdi

Credeasi, misera (Arturo, Elvira, ensemble) *I puritani* 3 Bellini

Credete alle femmine (Fiorilla, Selim) *Il turco in Italia* 2 Rossini

Credete al mio dolore (Morgana) *Alcina* 3 Handel

Credo a una possanza arcana (Andrea Chénier) *Andrea Chénier* 2 Giordano

Credo in un Dio crudel (Iago) *Otello* 2 Verdi

Cruda, funesta smania . . . La pietade in suo favore (Enrico) *Lucia di Lammermoor* 1 Donizetti

Cruda sorte! (Isabella) *L'italiana in Algeri* 1 Rossini

Crude furie degl'orridi abissi (Xerxes) *Serse* 3 Handel

Crudele? . . . Non mi dir (Donna Anna) *Don Giovanni* 2 Mozart

Crudeli, fermate (Sandrina) *La finta giardiniera* 2 Mozart

Crudel! perchè finora (Count Almaviva, Susanna) *Le nozze di Figaro* 3 Mozart

Cruelle mère des amours (Phaedra) *Hippolyte et Aricie* 3 Rameau

Csárdás: *see* Klänge der Heimat

D

Da geht er hin (Marschallin) *Der Rosenkavalier* 1 Strauss, R.

Dagl'immortali vertici . . . È gettata la mia sorte (Ezio) *Attila* 2 Verdi

Dai campi, dai prati (Faust) *Mefistofele* 1 Boito

Dai più remoto esilio . . . Odio solo, ed odio atroce (Jacopo Foscari) *I due Foscari* 1 Verdi

Dal crudel che m'ha tradita (Irene) *Tamerlano* 1 Handel

Dal fulgor di questa spada (Achillas) *Giulio Cesare* 3 Handel

Da lieg' ich! Was einem Kavalier (Ochs, Annina, Servants) *Der Rosenkavalier* 2 Strauss, R.

Dal labbro il canto (Fenton) *Falstaff* 3 Verdi

Dalla sponda tenebrosa (Junia) *Lucio Silla* 1 Mozart

Dalla sua pace (Don Ottavio) *Don Giovanni* 1 Mozart

Dall'aule raggianti . . . Deh! la parola amara (Federica, Rodolfo) *Luisa Miller* 1 Verdi

Dalle basse e dall'alte regioni (Macbeth, Witches) *Macbeth* 3 Verdi

Dalle stanze ove Lucia (Raimondo) *Lucia di Lammermoor* 3 Donizetti

Dall'orror di notte cieca (chorus) *Alcina* 3 Handel

Dal tuo stellato soglio (Moses) *Mosè in Egitto* 3 Rossini

Dammi la dolce e lieta parole (Desdemona, Emilia, Otello, Iago) *Otello* 2 Verdi

D'amor sull'ali rosee (Leonora) *Il trovatore* 4 Verdi

Dans ce beau pays, pur d'hérétique levain (Grand Inquisitor, Philip II) *Don Carlos* 4 Verdi

Dans ce lieu solitaire (Raimbaud, chorus) *Le comte Ory* 2 Rossini

Dans ce séjour (Adèle, Ragonde) *Le comte Ory* 2 Rossini

Dans l'ombre et le silence (Procida) *Les vêpres siciliennes* 2 Verdi

Da quel dì che lei perduta (Percy) *Anna Bolena* 1 Donizetti

Da qual dì che t'ho veduta (Don Carlo, Elvira) *Ernani* 1 Verdi

Da quel dì . . . Vieni fra queste braccia (Arturo, Elvira) *I puritani* 3 Bellini

Das süsse Lied verhallt (Lohengrin, Elsa) *Lohengrin* 3 Wagner

Das war sehr gut, Mandryka (Arabella, Mandryka) *Arabella* 3 Strauss, R.

Date almen per pietà (Medea, Creon) *Medeà* 2 Cherubini

Da tempeste il legno infranto (Cleopatra) *Giulio Cesare* 3 Handel

Da te questo (Odabella) *Attila* prol. Verdi

Da tutti abbandonata (Mary, Leicester) *Maria Stuarda* 1/2 Donizetti

Daylight is fading (Vladimir) *Prince Igor* 2 Borodin

Dear children (Susanin, Antonida, Vanya, Sobinin) *A Life for the Tsar* 3 Glinka

De cet aveu si tendre (Marie, Tonio) *La fille du régiment* 1 Donizetti

Deggio dunque, o Dio, lasciarti (Zenobia) *Radamisto* 3 Handel

D'Egitto là sui lidi . . . Come notte al sol fulgente (Zaccaria) *Nabucco* 1 Verdi

Deh! fuggi un traditore (Tigrane) *Radamisto* 1 Handel

Deh! la parola amara (Federica, Rodolfo) *Luisa Miller* 1 Verdi

Es ist kein Laut zu vernehmen . . . Ah, du wolltest mich nicht (Salome) *Salome* Strauss, R.

È sogno? O realtà? (Ford) *Falstaff* 2 Verdi

Espoir si cher et si doux (Cybele) *Atys* 3 Lully

Est-ce la paix que vous donnez au monde? (Posa, Philip II) *Don Carlos* 2 Verdi

È strano! è strano! . . . Ah fors'è lui . . . Sempre libera degg'io (Violetta) *La traviata* 1 Verdi

Esultate! (Otello) *Otello* 1 Verdi

E Susanna non vien! . . . Dove sono i bei momenti (Countess Almaviva) *Le nozze di Figaro* 3 Mozart

Eterno! immenso! incomprensibil Dio (Moses) *Mosè in Egitto* 1 Rossini

Et je sais votre nom (Des Grieux, Manon) *Manon* 1 Massenet

Et toi, Palerme . . . Dans l'ombre et le silence (Procida) *Les vêpres siciliennes* 2 Verdi

È un folle, è un vile affetto (Oronte) *Alcina* 2 Handel

Evviva la Francia (Maria, ensemble) *La figlia del reggimento* 2 Donizetti

Ewig war ich (Brünnhilde) *Siegfried* 3 Wagner

F

Fabliau: *see* Oui, dans les bois

Faites-lui mes aveux (Siébel) *Faust* 3 Gounod

Falke, Falke, du wiedergefundener (Emperor) *Die Frau ohne Schatten* 2 Strauss, R.

Fama! si: l'avrete (Jane Seymour, Henry VIII) *Anna Bolena* 1 Donizetti

Fammi combattere (Orlando) *Orlando* 1 Handel

Fanget an! So rief der Lenz in den Wald (Walther, ensemble) *Die Meistersinger* 1 Wagner

Farewell my son, I am dying (Boris, Fyodor) *Boris Godunov* vii/4 Musorgsky

Farewell, O forests (Joan of Arc) *The Maid of Orléans* 1 Tchaikovsky

Farewell to Arms: *see* Ora e per sempre addio

Far from my beloved and constrained (Lyudmila) *Ruslan and Lyudmila* 4 Glinka

Fatal mia donna! un murmure (Macbeth, Lady Macbeth) *Macbeth* 1 Verdi

Fatal vow (Oberon) *Oberon* 1 Weber

Fear no danger (Belinda, Second Woman) *Dido and Aeneas* 1 Purcell

Felice cor mio (Drusilla) *L'incoronazione di Poppea* 2 Monteverdi

Ferma, crudel, estinguere (Elvira, Ernani, Silva) *Ernani* 4 Verdi

Fernand, imite la clémence du ciel (Léonor, Fernand) *La favorite* 4 Donizetti

Figlia! a tal nome io palpito (Amelia, Boccanegra) *Simon Boccanegra* 1 Verdi

Figlia che reggi il tremulo piè (La Gioconda, La Cieca, Barnaba) *La Gioconda* 1 Ponchielli

Figlia! . . . Deh non parlare al misero . . . Ah! veglia o donna (Rigoletto, Gilda) *Rigoletto* 1 Verdi

Figlia mia, non pianger, nò (Bajazet) *Tamerlano* 3 Handel

Figli miei, miei tesori (Medea, Jason) *Medea* 2 Cherubini

Fille des rois (Nélusko) *L'Africaine* 2 Meyerbeer

Fin ch'han dal vino (Don Giovanni) *Don Giovanni* 1 Mozart

Fin dall'età più tenera (Anne Boleyn, Percy, Henry VIII) *Anna Bolena* 2 Donizetti

Flieder Monologue: *see* Was duftet doch der Flieder

Flower Duet: *see* Tutti i fior

Flower Song: *see* La fleur que tu m'avais jetée

Fontainebleau! foresta immensa e solitaria . . . Io la vidi (Don Carlo) *Don Carlo* 1 Verdi

Fontainebleau! forêt immense et solitaire . . . Je l'ai vue (Don Carlos) *Don Carlos* 1 Verdi

Forging Song: *see* Nothung! Nothung! Neidliches Schwert

Forgive me, my angel sent from Heaven (Hermann) *Queen of Spades* 2 Tchaikovsky

Forma ideal purissima . . . Amore misterio celeste (Faust, Helen of Troy) *Mefistofele* 4 Boito

Forse la soglia attinse . . . Ma se m'è forza perderti (Riccardo [Gustavus III]) *Un ballo in maschera* 3 Verdi

Forse un dì conoscerete (Ninetta, Giannetto) *La gazza ladra* 2 Rossini

Forte e lieto a morte andrei (Bajazet) *Tamerlano* 1 Handel

Fortune ennemie (Eurydice) *Orphée et Eurydice* 3 Gluck

Fountain Aria: *see* Regnava nel silenzio

Fra gli amplessi (Fiordiligi, Ferrando) *Così fan tutte* 2 Mozart

Fra i pensier (Junia) *Lucio Silla* 3 Mozart

Fra le tue braccia amore (Manon Lescaut, Des Grieux) *Manon Lescaut* 4 Puccini

Franco son io . . . So che per via di trioli (Giacomo) *Giovanna d'Arco* 1 Verdi

Fra poco a me ricovero . . . Tu che a Dio spiegasti l'ali (Edgardo) *Lucia di Lammermoor* 3 Donizetti

Frà tempeste funeste a quest'alma (Grimoaldo) *Rodelinda* 3 Handel

Fratricidii!!! Plebe! Patrizi! (Boccanegra, ensemble) *Simon Boccanegra* 1 Verdi

Fredda ed immobile (Rosina, ensemble) *Il barbiere di Siviglia* 1 Rossini

Frisch zum Kampfe (Pedrillo) *Die Entführung aus dem Serail* 2 Mozart

From boyhood trained (Huon) *Oberon* 1 Weber

From the gutter, why should we trouble (Nieces, Ellen, Auntie) *Peter Grimes* 2 Britten

Fuggiam gli ardori inospiti . . . La tra foreste vergini . . . Sì: fuggiam da queste mura (Aida, Radames) *Aida* 3 Verdi

Fuggi, crudele, fuggi! (Donna Anna, Don Ottavio) *Don Giovanni* 1 Mozart

Fu la sorte dell'armi (Amneris, Aida) *Aida* 2 Verdi

Il mio tesoro (Don Ottavio) *Don Giovanni* 2 Mozart

Il nous frappait dans sa colère (Old Hebrew) *Samson et Dalila* 1 Saint-Saëns

I love you beyond measure (Yeletsky) *Queen of Spades* 2 Tchaikovsky

I love you, I adore you (Lensky) *Yevgeny Onegin* 1 Tchaikovsky

Il padre adorato (Idamantes) *Idomeneo* 1 Mozart

Il pallor funesto ... Soffriva nel pianto languia (Enrico, Lucia) *Lucia di Lammermoor* 2 Donizetti

Il reviendra, j'en suis certaine (Penelope, ensemble) *Pénélope* 1 Fauré

Il rival salvar tu dêi ... Suoni la tromba, e intrepido (Giorgio, Riccardo) *I puritani* 2 Bellini

Il russo Mencikoff (Maurizio) *Adriana Lecouvreur* 3 Cilea

Il santo nome di Dio ... La Vergine degli angeli (Leonora, Padre Guardiano, Franciscan friars) *La forza del destino* 2 Verdi

Il segreto per esser felici (Maffio Orsini) *Lucrezia Borgia* 2 Donizetti

Il Tricerbero umiliato (Rinaldo) *Rinaldo* 2 Handel

Il va venir! et d'effroi je me sens frémir (Rachel) *La Juive* 2 Halévy

Il vecchiotto cerca moglie (Berta) *Il barbiere di Siviglia* 2 Rossini

Il vostro maggio (Siren) *Rinaldo* 2 Handel

I'm like a skiff on the ocean tost (Lucy) *Beggar's Opera* 3

Immolation: *see* Starke Scheite

I'm not disposed to meditation (Olga) *Yevgeny Onegin* 1 Tchaikovsky

Improvviso: *see* Un dì, all'azzurro spazio

Im Walde entschlief ich (Grete) *Der ferne Klang* 2 Schreker

Inaffia l'ugola (Iago) *Otello* 1 Verdi

In braccio alle dovizie (Montforte) *I vespri siciliani* 3 Verdi

Inbrunst im Herzen (Tannhäuser) *Tannhäuser* 3 Wagner

In cielo benedetto (Oronte) *I Lombardi* 4 Verdi

In diesen heil'gen Hallen (Sarastro) *Die Zauberflöte* 2 Mozart

Infelice, che ascolto (Hypsipyle) *Giasone* 3 Cavalli

Infelice, delusa, rejetta ... Venite fidente alla croce (Leonora, Padre Guardiano) *La forza del destino* 2 Verdi

Infelice! e tu credevi (Silva) *Ernani* 1 Verdi

In fernem Land (Lohengrin) *Lohengrin* 3 Wagner

In Früh'n versammelt uns der Ruf (chorus) *Lohengrin* 2 Wagner

In mia man alfin tu sei (Norma, Pollione) *Norma* 2 Bellini

In Mohrenland gefangen war (Pedrillo) *Die Entführung aus dem Serail* 3 Mozart

Inneggiamo, il Signor non è morto (Santuzza, chorus) *Cavalleria rusticana* Mascagni

In pure stille (Iris) *Iris* 1 Mascagni

In qual fiero contrasto ... Tradito, schernito (Ferrando) *Così fan tutte* 2 Mozart

In quali eccessi ... Mi tradì (Donna Elvira) *Don Giovanni* 2 Mozart

In quelle trine morbide (Manon Lescaut) *Manon Lescaut* 2 Puccini

In questa reggia (Turandot) *Turandot* 2 Puccini

In si barbara sciagura ... Ah! ella è mia madre (Arsaces) *Semiramide* 2 Rossini

In uomini (Despina) *Così fan tutte* 1 Mozart

Inutiles regrets! ... Ah! quand viendra l'instant (Aeneas) *Les Troyens* 5 Berlioz

Invano Alvaro! ti celasti al mondo ... Col sangue sol cancellasi ... Le minaccie, i fieri accenti ... Ah, segnasti la tua sorte (Don Carlo, Don Alvaro) *La forza del destino* 4 Verdi

Io di Roma il Giove sono (Claudius) *Agrippina* 3 Handel

Io già t'amai, ritrosa (Grimoaldo) *Rodelinda* 1 Handel

Io la vidi (Don Carlo) *Don Carlo* 1 Verdi

Io l'ho perduta (Don Carlo) *Don Carlo* 1 Verdi

Io non chiedo (Alcestis, Eumelus, Aspasia) *Alceste* 1 Gluck

Io no son che una povera fanciulla (Minnie, Dick Johnson) *La fanciulla del West* 1 Puccini

Io so che alle sue pene (Sharpless, Suzuki, Pinkerton) *Madama Butterfly* 2 Puccini

Io son l'umile ancella (Adriana) *Adriana Lecouvreur* 1 Cilea

Io son ricco e tu sei bella (Dulcamara, Adina) *L'elisir d'amore* 2 Donizetti

Io son sua per l'amor (Adriana, Princess of Bouillon) *Adriana Lecouvreur* 2 Cilea

Io t'abbraccio; è più che morte (Rodelinda, Bertarido) *Rodelinda* 2 Handel

Io t'amo Amalia ... Ti scosta, o malnato (Francesco, Amalia) *I masnadieri* 2 Verdi

Io ti rivedo ... Ah! se un giorno (Mary, Leicester, ensemble) *Maria Stuarda* 2/3 Donizetti

Io vengo a domandar ... Perduto ben ... Qual voce a me dal ciel ... Sotto al mio piè (Don Carlo, Elisabetta di Valois) *Don Carlo* 1/2 Verdi

I revel in hope and joy (Huon) *Oberon* 3 Weber

I sacri nomi ... Numi, pietà (Aida) *Aida* 1 Verdi

Is Cressida a slave? (Troilus) *Troilus and Cressida* 1 Walton

Is it so strange if I resent (Jenifer) *The Midsummer Marriage* 1 Tippett

Is it you, Vladimir mine (Konchakovna, Vladimir) *Prince Igor* 2 Borodin

Is this the very same Tatyana (Yevgeny Onegin) *Yevgeny Onegin* 3 Tchaikovsky

Ist mein Liebster dahin (Empress, Falcon) *Die Frau ohne Schatten* 1 Strauss, R.

It ain't necessarily so (Sportin' Life, chorus) *Porgy and Bess* 2 Gershwin

Ite sul colle, o Druidi! (Oroveso) *Norma* 1 Bellini

It happened long ago (Levko) *May Night* 1 Rimsky-Korsakov

It is he, my bright falcon (Yaroslavna, Igor) *Prince Igor* 4 Borodin

I've found out everything (Igor, Konchakovna, Vladimir) *Prince Igor* 3 Borodin

J

Jägerin, schlau im Sinn (Nancy) *Martha* 3 Flotow

J'ai des yeux (Coppélius) *Les contes d'Hoffmann* 2 Offenbach

J'ai gravi la montagne . . . La victoire facile (High Priest, Delilah) *Samson et Dalila* 2 Saint-Saëns

J'ai perdu mon Eurydice (Orpheus) *Orphée et Eurydice* 3 Gluck

Jak možná věřit: *see* How can he believe

Jako matka: *see* Like a mother

Jak vám pravím pane kmotre: *see* As I said to you

Ja, seit früher Kindheit Tagen (Lyonel, Plumkett) *Martha* 1 Flotow

J'avais fait un beau rêve . . . Oui, voilà l'héroisme . . . Au revoir dans un monde (Elisabeth de Valois, Don Carlos) *Don Carlos* 5 Verdi

Je crains de lui parler (Countess) *Queen of Spades* 2 Tchaikovsky

Je crois entendre encore (Nadir) *Les pêcheurs de perles* 1 Bizet

Je dis que rien ne m'épouvante (Micaëla) *Carmen* 3 Bizet

Je goûtais les charmes (Orpheus, Eurydice) *Orphée et Eurydice* 3 Gluck

Je l'aime donc (Beatrice) *Béatrice et Bénédict* 2 Berlioz

Je l'ai vue (Don Carlos) *Don Carlos* 1 Verdi

Je marche sur tous les chemins (Manon) *Manon* 3 Massenet

Je me sens, hélas, toute chose (King Ouf I, Siroco) *L'étoile* 3 Chabrier

Je ne pourrai plus sortir (Golaud, Mélisande) *Pelléas et Mélisande* 1 Debussy

Je ne te verrai plus (Theseus) *Hippolyte et Aricie* 5 Rameau

Jenifer, Jenifer, my darling (Mark, Jenifer) *The Midsummer Marriage* 1 Tippett

Jerum! Jerum! (Hans Sachs, Beckmesser) *Die Meistersinger* 2 Wagner

Je suis encore toute étourdie (Manon) *Manon* 1 Massenet

Je suis Lazuli! (Lazuli) *L'étoile* 1 Chabrier

Je t'implore et je tremble (Iphigenia) *Iphigénie en Tauride* 4 Gluck

Jetzt, Schätzchen (Jaquino, Marzelline) *Fidelio* 1 Beethoven

Je vais le voir! . . . Il me revient fidèle (Hero) *Béatrice et Bénédict* 1 Berlioz

Je vais mourir . . . Adieu, fière cité (Dido) *Les Troyens* 5 Berlioz

Je vais revoir (Isolier, Ory) *Le comte Ory* 1 Rossini

Je veux vivre dans ce rêve (Juliet) *Roméo et Juliette* 1 Gounod

Je viens célébrer la victoire (Delilah, Samson, Old Hebrew) *Samson et Dalila* 1 Saint-Saëns

Je viens solliciter . . . O bien perdu . . . Par quelle douce voix . . . Que sous mes pieds (Don Carlos, Elisabeth de Valois) *Don Carlos* 2 Verdi

Jewel Song: *see* Ah! je ris de me voir

Jochanaan, ich bin verliebt (Salome, Jochanaan) *Salome* Strauss, R.

Johohoe! (Senta) *Der fliegende Holländer* 2 Wagner

Jour et nuit je me mets en quatre (Frantz) *Les contes d'Hoffmann* 3 Offenbach

Juliet's Waltz Song: *see* Je veux vivre dans ce rêve

Jupiter, lance la foudre (Clytemnestra) *Iphigénie en Aulide* 3 Gluck

Jurons, jurons par nos dangers (William Tell, ensemble) *Guillaume Tell* 2 Rossini

Just think, my son, about the tsars (Pimen, Grigory) *Boris Godunov* 1 Musorgsky

K

Kein Andres, das mir so im Herzen loht (Count, Clairon) *Capriccio* Strauss, R.

Klänge der Heimat (Rosalinde) *Die Fledermaus* 2 Strauss, J.

Komm denn (Eglantine, Lysiart) *Euryanthe* 2 Weber

Komm, mein Bub . . . Eia popeia (Marie) *Wozzeck* 1 Berg

Kommt ein schlanker Bursch' gegangen (Aennchen) *Der Freischütz* 2 Weber

Konstanze, dich wiederzusehen . . . O wie ängstlich (Belmonte) *Die Entführung aus dem Serail* 1 Mozart

L

Là-bas, là-bas dans la montagne (Carmen, Don José) *Carmen* 2 Bizet

Labbro di foco! (Nannetta, Fenton) *Falstaff* 1 Verdi

La bocca vaga: quell'occhio nero (Ruggiero) *Alcina* 1 Handel

La brise et douce et parfumée (Mireille, Vincent) *Mireille* 2 Gounod

La calunnia è un venticello (Don Basilio) *Il barbiere di Siviglia* 1 Rossini

Lachst du mich aus? (Marschallin, Octavian) *Der Rosenkavalier* 1 Strauss, R.

Là ci darem la mano (Don Giovanni, Zerlina) *Don Giovanni* 1 Mozart

Là dal Gange, a te primiero (Idreno) *Semiramide* 1 Rossini

La dolcissima effigie sorridente (Maurizio) *Adriana Lecouvreur* 1 Cilea

Oh! quante volte, oh! quante (Giulietta) *I Capuleti e I Montecchi* 1 Bellini

Oh, se sapeste (Minnie) *La fanciulla del West* 2 Puccini

Oh sole ti vela (Imogene) *Il pirata* 2 Bellini

Oh sommo Carlo (Don Carlo, ensemble) *Ernani* 3 Verdi

Oh the pleasure of the plains (chorus) *Acis and Galatea* 1 Handel

Oh, tu che in seno agli angeli (Don Alvaro) *La forza del destino* 3 Verdi

Oh what pain it is to part (Polly) *Beggar's Opera* 1

Oh what pain . . . That dream of love [Och, jaký žal . . . Ten lásky sen] (Mařenka) *The Bartered Bride* 3 Smetana

Oh, you dark forest (Sadko) *Sadko* 2 Rimsky-Korsakov

O inferno! . . . Sento avvampar nell'anima (Gabriele) *Simon Boccanegra* 2 Verdi

O Isis und Osiris, schenket der Weisheit Geist (Sarastro) *Die Zauberflöte* 2 Mozart

O jour de peine (Henri) *Les vêpres siciliennes* 4 Verdi

O légère hirondelle (Mireille) *Mireille* 1 Gounod

O Lola, ch'ai di latti (Turiddu) *Cavalleria rusticana* Mascagni

O Lord, if I have sinned (René) *Iolanta* Tchaikovsky

Oltre quel limite (Attila) *Attila* 1 Verdi

O lumière sainte (Leïla, Nadir) *Les pêcheurs de perles* 3 Bizet

O ma chère compagne (Elisabeth de Valois) *Don Carlos* 2 Verdi

O ma femme! ô ma bien aimée (Romeo) *Roméo et Juliette* 5 Gounod

O malheureuse Iphigénie (Iphigenia) *Iphigénie en Tauride* 2 Gluck

Ombra cara di mia sposa (Radamisto) *Radamisto* 2 Handel

Ombra mai fù (Xerxes) *Serse* 1 Handel

Ombre, larve (Alcestis) *Alceste* 1 Gluck

Ombre pallide, lo so, mi udite (Alcina) *Alcina* 2 Handel

Ombre, piante, urne funeste (Rodelinda) *Rodelinda* 1 Handel

O meco incolume (Wurm, Count Walter) *Luisa Miller* 2 Verdi

O mein Leid (Eglantine) *Euryanthe* 1 Weber

O messager de Dieu . . . Baigne d'eau mes mains (Thaïs, Athanaël) *Thaïs* 3 Massenet

O mio babbino caro (Lauretta) *Gianni Schicchi* Puccini

O mio castel paterno . . . Nell'argilla maledetta (Carlo) *I masnadieri* 1 Verdi

O mio Fernando (Leonora) *La favorita* 3 Donizetti

O mon Fernand (Léonor) *La favorite* 3 Donizetti

O monumento (Barnaba) *La Gioconda* 1 Ponchielli

O moon of Alabama (Jenny, Girls) *Aufstieg und Fall der Stadt Mahagonny* 1 Weill

O muto asil: *see* Asile héréditaire

O My Beloved Father: *see* O mio babbino caro

O Nadir, tendre ami de mon jeune âge (Zurga) *Les pêcheurs de perles* 3 Bizet

O namenlose Freude (Leonore, Florestan) *Fidelio* 2 Beethoven

O Nature, pleine de grâce (Werther) *Werther* 1 Massenet

Once a gnat was cutting wood (Nurse) *Boris Godunov* 2 Musorgsky

One fine day: *see* Un bel dì

Onegin, I was then far younger (Tatyana, Yevgeny Onegin) *Yevgeny Onegin* 3 Tchaikovsky

On l'appelle Manon (Des Grieux, Manon) *Manon* 2 Massenet

O noble lame étincelante (Rodrigue) *Le Cid* 1 Massenet

On rivalries 'tis safe for kings (Elizabeth I) *Gloriana* 1 Britten

On the banks of the sweet Garonne (Sherasmin, Fatima) *Oberon* 3 Weber

O nube! che lieve per l'aria . . . Nella pace nel mesto riposo (Mary) *Maria Stuarda* 1/2 Donizetti

O nuit d'amour (Faust, Marguerite) *Faust* 3 Gounod

O nume benfico (Ninetta, Fernando Villabella, Gottardo) *La gazza ladra* 1 Rossini

On with the motley: *see* Vesti la giubba

O paradis sorti de l'onde (Vasco da Gama) *L'Africaine* 4 Meyerbeer

O patria mia (Aida) *Aida* 3 Verdi

O patrizi, tremate L'Eterno (Lucrezia Contarini) *I due Foscari* 1 Verdi

O prêtres de Baal (Fidès) *Le prophète* 5 Meyerbeer

Ora a noi (Sharpless, Butterfly) *Madama Butterfly* 2 Puccini

Ora di morte e di vendetta (Macbeth, Lady Macbeth) *Macbeth* 3 Verdi

Ora e per sempre addio (Otello) *Otello* 2 Verdi

Ora soave (Maddalena de Coigny, Andrea Chénier) *Andrea Chénier* 2 Giordano

Or che più non vedrò (Jason) *Medea* 1 Cherubini

Or che siete speranze tradite (Amastre) *Serse* 2 Handel

Or dammi il braccio tuo (Osaka, Iris) *Iris* 2 Mascagni

Or del padre benedetta (Joan of Arc, Giacomo) *Giovanna d'Arco* 3 Verdi

Ore dolci e divine (Magda de Civry) *La rondine* 1 Puccini

O rendetemi la speme . . . Qui la voce sua soave . . . Vien, diletto (Elvira) *I puritani* 3 Bellini

Orest! Orest! Orest! (Electra, Orestes) *Elektra* Strauss

Orfanella il tetto umile . . . Ah! se la speme . . . Figlia! a tal nome io palpito (Amelia, Boccanegra) *Simon Boccanegra* 1 Verdi

O rich-soiled land, O land of Phthia (Achilles) *King Priam* 2 Tippett

Or la tromba in suon festante (Rinaldo) *Rinaldo* 3 Handel

O Roi! j'arrive de Flandre . . . Est-ce la paix que vous donnez au monde? (Posa, Philip II) *Don Carlos* 2 Verdi

O Rosalinde (Lescaut) *Manon* 3 Massenet

Orrida a gl'occhi miei (Ginevra) *Ariodante* 1 Handel

Quel torrente che cada dal monte (Julius Caesar) *Giulio Cesare* 3 Handel

Quel vecchio maledivami! (Rigoletto, Sparafucile) *Rigoletto* 1 Verdi

Que sous mes pieds (Don Carlos, Elisabeth de Valois) *Don Carlos* 2 Verdi

Questa o quella (Duke of Mantua) *Rigoletto* 1 Verdi

Queste innocenti lagrime (Jacopo Foscari, ensemble) *I due Foscari* 2 Verdi

Questo è il cielo di contenti (chorus) *Alcina* 1 Handel

Que tout gémisse (chorus) *Castor et Pollux* 1 Rameau

Qui chiamata m'avete? (Laura, Alvise Badoero) *La Gioconda* 3 Ponchielli

Quick music is best (Essex) *Gloriana* 1 Britten

Quietly, night . . . I go to him (Anne Trulove) *The Rake's Progress* 1 Stravinsky

Qui la voce sua soave . . . Vien, diletto (Elvira) *I puritani* 2 Bellini

Qui m'accolse opresso, errante (Filippo) *Beatrice di Tenda* 2 Bellini

Qui Radames verrà . . . O patria mia (Aida) *Aida* 3 Verdi

Qui te fait si sévère (Thaïs) *Thaïs* 1 Massenet

Quittez, nymphes (Plataea) *Platée* 1 Rameau

Quoi? quoi? (chorus) *Platée* 1 Rameau

Qu'une première amour est belle (Sangaride, Doris, Idas) *Atys* 4 Lully

R

Rachel, quand du Seigneur (Eléazar) *La Juive* 4 Halévy

Rataplan (Preziosilla, chorus) *La forza del destino* 3 Verdi

Recondita armonia (Cavaradossi, Sacristan) *Tosca* 1 Puccini

Re dell'abisso . . . È lui, è lui ne palpiti (Ulrica [Mam'zelle Arvidson]) *Un ballo in maschera* 1 Verdi

Redoutez la fureur d'un Dieu (Balthazar) *La favorite* 2 Donizetti

Regardez-moi bien dans les yeux (Lescaut) *Manon* 1 Massenet

Regnava nel silenzio . . . Quando rapito in estasi (Lucia) *Lucia di Lammermoor* 1 Donizetti

Régnez, Amours (Emilie) *Les Indes galantes* 1 Rameau

Reine, je suis Enée (Aeneas, ensemble) *Les Troyens* 3 Berlioz

Resta immobile: *see* Sois immobile

Resta vicino a me (Michele, Giorgetta) *Il tabarro* Puccini

Reste au foyer, petit grillon (Cendrillon) *Cendrillon* 1 Massenet

Reverenza! . . . Buon giorno buona donna (Mistress Quickly, Falstaff) *Falstaff* 2 Verdi

Reviens à toi, vierge adorée (Coroebus, Cassandra) *Les Troyens* 1 Berlioz

Riconosci in questo amplesso (Susanna, Marcellina, Don Curzio, Count Almaviva, Figaro, Bartolo) *Le nozze di Figaro* 3 Mozart

Riddle scene: *see* Heil dir, weiser Schmied!

Rien! en vain j'interroge (Faust) *Faust* 1 Gounod

Rienzi's Prayer: *see* Allmächt'ger Vater

Riot Scene: *see* Zum Teufel mit dir

Ritorna, oh caro e dolce mio tesoro (Rodelinda) *Rodelinda* 2 Handel

Ritorna vincitor! . . . L'insana parola . . . I sacri nomi . . . Numi, pietà (Aida) *Aida* 1 Verdi

Rivedrai le foreste imbalsamate . . . Su dunque! . . . Padre! a costoro (Amonasro, Aida) *Aida* 3 Verdi

Roi du Ciel et des anges (John of Leyden) *Le prophète* 3 Meyerbeer

Rome Narration: *see* Inbrunst im Herzen

Rosa del ciel (Orpheus) *Orfeo* 1 Monteverdi

Rossignols amoureux (Shepherdess) *Hippolyte et Aricie* 5 Rameau

Rozmysli si, Mařenko!: *see* Think it over, Mařenka

Ruler of this awful hour (Huon) *Oberon* 2 Weber

S

Sacra la scelta è d'un consorte . . . Ah! fu giusto il mio sospetto (Miller) *Luisa Miller* 1 Verdi

Sai com'arde in petto mio . . . Piangi o figlia (Giorgio, Elvira) *I puritani* 1 Bellini

Salgo già del trono aurato (Abigaille) *Nabucco* 2 Verdi

S'altro che lacrime (Servilia) *La clemenza di Tito* 2 Mozart

Salut à la France (Marie, ensemble) *La fille du régiment* 2 Donizetti

Salut! demeure chaste et pure (Faust) *Faust* 3 Gounod

Salve Maria! (Giselda) *I Lombardi* 1 Verdi

Salvezza a la Francia (Maria, ensemble) *La figlia del reggimento* 2 Donizetti

Samson, ô toi mon bien-aimé (Samson, Delilah) *Samson et Dalila* 2 Saint-Saëns

Sangue a me (Macbeth, ensemble) *Macbeth* 2 Verdi

Saper vorreste (Oscar) *Un ballo in maschera* 3 Verdi

Saria possibile (chorus) *L'elisir d'amore* 2 Donizetti

Sa voix fait naître dans mon sein (Dido, Anna) *Les Troyens* 3 Berlioz

Scacciata dal suo nido (Bertarido) *Rodelinda* 2 Handel

Schelm, halt fest (Aennchen, Agathe) *Der Freischütz* 2 Weber

Scherza infida, in grembo al drudo (Ariodante) *Ariodante* 2 Handel

Schiudi, inferno (ensemble) *Macbeth* 1 Verdi

Schläfst du, Hagen, mein Sohn? (Alberich, Hagen) *Götterdämmerung* 2 Wagner

Schweig, schweig (Caspar) *Der Freischütz* 1 Weber

Schweigt doch, ihr Stimmen (Barak's Wife) *Die Frau ohne Schatten* 3 Strauss, R.

Schwüles Gedünst (Donner) *Das Rheingold* iv Wagner

Scintille, diamant (Dapertutto) *Les contes d'Hoffmann* 4 Offenbach

Scuoti quella fronda di ciliegio . . . Tutti i fior (Butterfly, Suzuki) *Madama Butterfly* 2 Puccini

Si la rigueur ou la vengeance (Brogni) *La Juive* 1 Halévy

Si, la stanchezza m'opprime . . . Ai nostri monti (Azucena, Manrico) *Il trovatore* 4 Verdi

Si le bonheur à sourire t'invite (Siébel) *Faust* 4 Gounod

Sì l'eroismo è questo . . . Ma lassù ci vedremo (Elisabetta di Valois, Don Carlo) *Don Carlo* 4/5 Verdi

Si les doux accords (Cupid) *Orphée et Eurydice* 1 Gluck

Si les filles d'Arles (Ourrias) *Mireille* 2 Gounod

Sì, mi chiamano Mimì (Mimì) *La bohème* 1 Puccini

Sì, morir ella de'! (Alvise Badoero) *La Gioconda* 3 Ponchielli

Since it is not by merit (Tom Rakewell) *The Rake's Progress* 1 Stravinsky

S'io non moro (Ilia, Idamantes) *Idomeneo* 3 Mozart

Sì, pel ciel (Otello, Iago) *Otello* 2 Verdi

Si può? Si può? (Tonio) *Pagliacci* prol. Leoncavallo

Sì, quello io son, ravvisami (Odabella, Foresto) *Attila* 1 Verdi

Si ridesti il Leon di Castiglia (chorus) *Ernani* 3 Verdi

Sirius rising as the sun's wheel (Mark, Jenifer) *The Midsummer Marriage* 3 Tippett

Sì: son quella (Alcina) *Alcina* 1 Handel

Si, sperate (Assur) *Semiramide* 1 Rossini

Sì, spietata, il tuo rigore (Ptolemy) *Giulio Cesare* 2 Handel

Si tu m'aimes, Carmen (Escamillo, Carmen) *Carmen* 4 Bizet

Sì, vendetta (Gilda, Rigoletto) *Rigoletto* 2 Verdi

Sì, vincemmo (Ernesto) *Il pirata* 1 Bellini

Si vous le permettiez, princes . . . Ulysse! (Ulysses, Penelope, ensemble) *Pénélope* 3 Fauré

Sleale! Il segreto fu dunque violato? (Don Alvaro, Don Carlo) *La forza del destino* 3 Verdi

Sleep my beauty, sleep (Levko) *May Night* 3 Rimsky-Korsakov

Sleepwalking Scene: *see* Una macchia è qui tuttora!

Slowly it all comes back (Cressida) *Troilus and Cressida* 1 Walton

Smanie implacabili (Dorabella) *Così fan tutte* 1 Mozart

So anch'io la virtù magica (Norina) *Don Pasquale* 1 Donizetti

Soave sia il vento (Fiordiligi, Dorabella, Don Alfonso) *Così fan tutte* 1 Mozart

So ben che difforme (Nedda, Tonio) *Pagliacci* 1 Leoncavallo

So bin ich nun verlassen (Euryanthe) *Euryanthe* 3 Weber

Soccorso, sostegno accordate . . . Non si pianga (Giulietta, Romeo, ensemble) *I Capuleti e i Montecchi* 1 Bellini

So che per via di trioli (Giacomo) *Giovanna d'Arco* 1 Verdi

Soffriva nel pianto languia (Enrico, Lucia) *Lucia di Lammermoor* 2 Donizetti

Sois immobile (William Tell) *Guillaume Tell* 3 Rossini

Sola, furtiva, al tempio . . . Ah! sì, fa core e abbracciami (Adalgisa, Norma) *Norma* 1 Bellini

Sola, perduta, abbandonata (Manon Lescaut) *Manon Lescaut* 4 Puccini

Sola sola in buio loco (sextet) *Don Giovanni* 2 Mozart

Solche hergelauf'ne Laffen (Osmin) *Die Entführung aus dem Serail* 1 Mozart

Soldiers' chorus: *see* Gloire immortelle de nos aïeux

Solenne in quest'ora (Don Alvaro, Don Carlo) *La forza del destino* 3 Verdi

Soll ich dich, Teurer, nicht mehr sehn (Pamina, Tamino, Sarastro) *Die Zauberflöte* 2 Mozart

Solo un pianto (Neris) *Medea* 2 Cherubini

Sombre forêt (Mathilde) *Guillaume Tell* 2 Rossini

Son geloso del zeffiro errante (Elvino, Amina) *La sonnambula* 1 Bellini

Son giunta! . . . Madre, pietosa vergine (Leonora, Franciscan friars) *La forza del destino* 2 Verdi

Son gobbo, son Demo (Demo, Orestes) *Giasone* 1 Cavalli

Song of the Coat: *see* Vecchia zimarra

Song of the Gnat: *see* Once a gnat was cutting wood

Song of the Hindu Guest (Hindu) *Sadko* iv Rimsky-Korsakov

Song of the Venetian Guest (Venetian) *Sadko* iv Rimsky-Korsakov

Song of the Viking Guest (Viking) *Sadko* iv Rimsky-Korsakov

Song to the moon: *see* O silver moon

Son guerriera che a gloria t'invita (Joan of Arc, Charles VII, Giacomo) *Giovanna d'Arco* prol. Verdi

Son ìo dinanzi al rè? . . . Nell'ispano suol mai l'eresia dominò (Grand Inquisitor, Philip) *Don Carlo* 3/4 Verdi

Son lo spirto che nega sempre (Mefistofele) *Mefistofele* 1 Boito

Son nata a lagrimar (Sextus, Cornelia) *Giulio Cesare* 1 Handel

Sono andati? (Mimì, Rodolfo) *La bohème* 4 Puccini

Son Pereda, son ricco d'onore (Don Carlo) *La forza del destino* 2 Verdi

Son sessant'anni (Gérard) *Andrea Chénier* 1 Giordano

Sonst spielt' ich mit Scepter, mit Krone und Stern (Peter the Great) *Zar und Zimmermann* 3 Lortzing

Son vergin vezzosa (Elvira) *I puritani* 1 Bellini

Sorge infausta una procella (Zoroastro) *Orlando* 3 Handel

Sorgete . . . Lo sognai ferito, esangue . . . Sventurata, anch'io deliro (Imogene) *Il pirata* 1 Bellini

Sortez de l'esclavage (Pollux, Telaira) *Castor et Pollux* 3 Rameau

Sotto al mio piè (Don Carlo, Elisabetta di Valois) *Don Carlo* 1/2 Verdi

Sotto una quercia parvemi . . . Pondo è letal, martiro (Charles VII) *Giovanna d'Arco* prol. Verdi

Vivrà! Contende il giubilo (Leonora, Luna) *Il trovatore* 4 Verdi

Voce di donna o d'angelo (La Cieca) *La Gioconda* 1 Ponchielli

Vo' far guerra, e vincer voglio (Armida) *Rinaldo* 2 Handel

Voi che sapete (Cherubino) *Le nozze di Figaro* 2 Mozart

Voi che sì larghe cure . . . Sleale! Il segreto fu dunque violato? (Don Alvaro, Don Carlo) *La forza del destino* 3 Verdi

Voi che udite il mio lamento (Otho) *Agrippina* 2 Handel

Voici ce qu'il écrit à son frère (Geneviève, Arkel) *Pelléas et Mélisande* 1 Debussy

Voici la vaste plaine . . . En marche (Mireille) *Mireille* 4 Gounod

Voi lo sapete (Santuzza) *Cavalleria rusticana* Mascagni

Vois ma misère, hélas! (Samson) *Samson et Dalila* 3 Saint-Saëns

Volate, amori (Ginevra) *Ariodante* 1 Handel

Vollendet das ewige Werk! (Wotan) *Das Rheingold* Wagner

Volta la terrea (Oscar) *Un ballo in maschera* 1 Verdi

Von den edlen Kavalieren (Nancy, Lady Harriet) *Martha* 1 Flotow

Von Jugend auf in dem Kampfgefild (Huon) *Oberon* 1 Weber

Vor deinem Fenster (Nureddin) *Der Barbier von Bagdad* 1 Cornelius

Vorrei vendicarmi del perfido cor (Bradamante) *Alcina* 2 Handel

Votre toast, je peux vous le rendre . . . Toréador, en garde (Escamillo) *Carmen* 2 Bizet

Vous devez vous animer (Cybele, chorus) *Atys* 1 Lully

Vous êtes mon Prince Charmant (Cendrillon, Prince Charmant) *Cendrillon* 2 Massenet

Vous qui du Dieu vivant (Brogni) *La Juive* 3 Halévy

Vous qui faites l'endormie (Méphistophélès) *Faust* 4 Gounod

Vous voyez de vos fils la mère infortunée (Medea) *Médée* 1 Cherubini

Voyez du haut de ces rivages (Pietro) *La muette de Portici* 5 Auber

Voyons, Manon, plus de chimères (Manon) *Manon* 1 Massenet

W

Wach auf, es nahet gen den Tag (ensemble) *Die Meistersinger* 3 Wagner

Wache, Wala! (Wanderer, Erda) *Siegfried* 3 Wagner

Wahn! Wahn! Überall Wahn (Hans Sachs) *Die Meistersinger* 3 Wagner

Walther's Trial Song: *see* Fanget an! So rief der Lenz in dem Wald

Waltraute's Narration: *see* Seit er von dir geschieden

War es so schmählich (Brünnhilde, Wotan) *Die Walküre* 3 Wagner

Was die Steine glänzen? (Marie) *Wozzeck* 2 Berg

Was duftet doch der Flieder (Hans Sachs) *Die Meistersinger* 2 Wagner

Was gleicht wohl auf Erden (chorus) *Der Freischütz* 3 Weber

Was musst' ich hören, Gott (Erik, Senta) *Der fliegende Holländer* 3 Wagner

Was soll ich dazu sagen (Lady Harriet, Nancy, Lyonel, Plumkett) *Martha* 2 Flotow

Was willst du, fremder Mensch? (Electra, Orestes) *Elektra* Strauss, R.

Wayward sisters (Sorceress) *Dido and Aeneas* 1 Purcell

Wehe, mein Mann! Welchen Weg (Empress) *Die Frau ohne Schatten* 2 Strauss, R.

Wehen mir Lüfte Ruh (Adolar) *Euryanthe* 2 Weber

Wehvolles Erbe (Amfortas) *Parsifal* 1 Wagner

Weia! Waga! Woge, du Welle (Rhinemaidens, Alberich) *Das Rheingold* Wagner

Weiche, Wotan! weiche! (Erda, Wotan) *Das Rheingold* Wagner

Welch ein Geschick! . . . Ha! du solltest für mich sterben (Konstanze, Belmonte) *Die Entführung aus dem Serail* 3 Mozart

Welcher Kummer . . . Traurigkeit (Konstanze) *Die Entführung aus dem Serail* 2 Mozart

Welches Unholds List (Brünnhilde, Hagen, Gunther) *Götterdämmerung* 2 Wagner

Welche Wonne, welche Lust (Blonde) *Die Entführung aus dem Serail* 2 Mozart

Welko! das Bild! (Mandryka, Waldner) *Arabella* 1 Strauss, R.

Wenn der Freude Tränen fliessen (Belmonte) *Die Entführung aus dem Serail* 2 Mozart

Wenn der Himmel hell wird (Jimmy) *Aufstieg und Fall der Stadt Mahagonny* 2 Weill

Wenn sie sich verirrten im Walde dort (Peter, Gertrud) *Hänsel und Gretel* 1 Humperdinck

Wenn zum Gebet (Bostana, Nureddin) *Der Barbier von Bagdad* 1 Cornelius

Wer ein Liebchen hat gefunden (Osmin) *Die Entführung aus dem Serail* 1 Mozart

Westwärts schweift der Blick (Young Sailor) *Tristan und Isolde* 1 Wagner

What is life? (Hermann) *Queen of Spades* 3 Tchaikovsky

When I am laid in earth (Dido) *Dido and Aeneas* 3 Purcell

When monarchs unite (chorus) *Dido and Aeneas* 1 Purcell

When young the Countess used to live in Paris (Tomsky) *Queen of Spades* 1 Tchaikovsky

Where art thou, where? . . . Daylight is fading (Vladimir) *Prince Igor* 2 Borodin

Where'er you walk (Jupiter) *Semele* 2 Handel

Where shall I seek the charming fair (Acis) *Acis and Galatea* 1 Handel

Who hopes to conjure with the world of dreams (Sosostris) *The Midsummer Marriage* 3 Tippett

Index of Operas under Composers